Xtra! for Financial Accounting

Free when bundled with a new text, this CD-ROM provides access to **additional multi-media learning tools** including:

- E-Lectures that review core accounting topics
- Crossword Puzzles to review vocabulary
- Topical and multiple choice quizzes to test understanding of the content
- Spanish Dictionary of Accounting Terms

Personal Trainer® 3.0

Personal Trainer 3.0 helps students complete their homework from the text as well as grade homework for the instructor! Available for sale separately or included in Web-Tutor Advantage, new Personal Trainer 3.0 upgrades include:

1. Enhanced Hints:
   - Up to 3 hints plus an additional hint that the instructor can add
   - Hints can include not only text but PowerPoint® slides as well

2. Enhanced Questions:
   - Now includes all end-of-chapter exercises and problems
   - Students can spell check their answers before submitting

3. Enhanced Instructor Capabilities:
   - Questions can be assigned as "required" or "excluded"
   - Grades can be captured on demand or preset
   - A more flexible gradebook that can display and download any combination of data

4. Enhanced Look-and-Feel:
   - New graphic design
   - Greater ease-of-use

Interactive Study Center for Students

Visit **http://ingram.swlearning.com** to access the following FREE student learning resources:

- Quizzes with feedback
- Hotlinks to the Web sites listed in the text
- PowerPoint presentation slides for review of chapter coverage
- Crossword puzzles for vocabulary study
- Check figures to selected assignments
- Learning objectives from the chapter
- Updates for the latest information about changes in GAAP and any new, important information related to the text

For more information on any of these technology products, including demonstrations, visit:
http://ingram.swlearning.com
or contact your local South-Western Sales Consultant!

3RD EDITION

ACCOUNTING
Information for Decisions

Robert W. Ingram
University of Alabama

Thomas L. Albright
University of Alabama

Bruce A. Baldwin
Arizona State University West

John W. Hill
Indiana University

THOMSON
SOUTH-WESTERN

Australia · Canada · Mexico · Singapore · Spain · United Kingdom · United States

THOMSON

SOUTH-WESTERN

Accounting: Information for Decisions, 3e

Robert W. Ingram, Thomas L. Albright, Bruce A. Baldwin, and John W. Hill

VP/Editorial Director:
Jack W. Calhoun

VP/Editor-in-Chief:
George Werthman

Acquisitions Editor:
Julie Moulton

Senior Developmental Editor:
Sara E. Wilson

Marketing Manager:
Keith Chassé

Production Editor:
Chris Sears

Manufacturing Coordinator:
Doug Wilke

Media Developmental Editor:
Sally Nieman

Media Production Editor:
Robin Browning

Compositor
GGS Information Services, Inc.

Production House:
Litten Editing and Production, Inc.

Sr. Design Project Manager:
Michelle Kunkler

Cover and Internal Designer:
Grannan Graphic Design
Cincinnati, OH

Cover Image:
© Digital Vision

Photo Researcher:
Darren Wright

Printer:
Transcontinental
Beauceville, Quebec

Excerpts from the Krispy Kreme Doughnuts, Inc. 2002 Annual Report reprinted with permission.
The General Mills, Inc. 2002 Annual Report reprinted with permission.

Photo credits: pp. F2, F44, F82, F179, F284, F319, F362, F446, F530—© Getty Images/Jennifer Schefft; p. F224—
© Comstock; p. F255—© Starbucks Coffee Company; p. F479—© Krispy Kreme Doughnut Corp.; p. M2—© Getty
Images/PhotoDisc; p. M29—© Michael Pope/CORBIS; p. M54—© Getty Images/Image Bank; p. M78—© CORBIS;
p. M99—© Tony Freeman/Photo Edit; p. M136—© Getty Images/PhotoDisc; p. M160—© Spencer Grant/Photo
Edit; p. M204—© Getty Images/PhotoDisc; p. M240—© CORBIS; p. M287—© Getty Images/PhotoDisc; p. M330—
Courtesy of BushHog; p. M372—© Getty Images/PhotoDisc; p. M412—© Getty Images/PhotoDisc.

Brief Contents

SECTION M3 Expanded Topics M421

CONTENTS

FINANCIAL ACCOUNTING

STUDENT PREFACE

How to Do Well in this Course

We are going to let you in on some trade secrets instructors seldom tell students. That's why this section is labeled "For Students Only." If instructors find out we have revealed these secrets, we'll probably get a lot of mail.

Getting good grades is not a matter of luck. That's not the secret. Also, it is no secret that doing assignments (on time), going to class (regularly), getting enough sleep and exercise, eating properly, and studying throughout the semester (instead of just at exam time) will improve your grades. But this is hard work. So, what you want is a way to get good grades and not work so hard, right? Well, pay attention—the secret is to work smarter! That's not the same as being smarter, which is a matter of luck. Here's how you work smarter.

Step 1: Determine why this course is important for you. First, figure out why you're taking this class. What are your goals for the class? Do you care about this course? Do you have a strong motivation to learn about accounting? Perhaps being an accountant comes on your list of career options just below sweeping up at McDonalds. Maybe your goal is to make lots of money. Or, maybe you're just in college to have a good time until you inherit the family fortune. In any case, this course is designed for you. One of the surest ways to have a million dollars is to start with ten million and not know anything about accounting and business management. If you don't inherit wealth, you're not likely to get it without speaking the language of business. Accounting is the language! Maybe you just want to get a good job, but you're pretty sure you don't want to be an accountant. Fine! This course isn't going to make an accountant out of you. It will help you understand some of the "mystical rituals" of accounting that non-accountants often find confusing. Whatever type of management position you have in any organization, you can be pretty sure you're going to have to work with accountants and with accounting information. You should know they can have a major effect on your life. Many organizations use accounting information to evaluate their employees for salary and promotion decisions. You should understand how to interpret this information. You may even learn accounting isn't what you think. Whether you grow to love or hate accounting, decide what you can get out of this course that will be useful to you.

Step 2: Find out what your instructors expect of you in this course. Next, check out your instructor. If you're lucky, your instructor is sensitive, warm, caring, has a good sense of humor, is witty, loves teaching, and wants you to do well in the course. If instead your instructor is more normal (and less perfect), remember, the instructor is still the instructor. And as the instructor, she has power over your life. So, find out what she expects from you. What are her goals for the course? What does she want you to know or be able to do once you complete the course? Perhaps she will tell you (good sign), but if not, ask. You should say: "Professor Whatever-Your-Name-Is (it would be wise to use the right name), what's the lowdown on the layout for this course?" This is education jargon for "what are your goals for this course?" This may catch her off guard, so give her a minute or two to think. You may even have to wait until the next class meeting to get your answer. Make sure you and your instructor understand each other's goals

Step 3: Find out how you will be graded. Now, find out how you will be graded. How does the instructor test? Is he one of the picky types: "What is the third word on the fifth line on page 211?" Or, does he go for the broader, thought questions: "Explain how accounting was instrumental in negotiating the third treaty of Versailles in 1623." Does he go for multiple guess, or are short answers his cup of tea? Whatever the method, you need to know what is expected of you and how these expectations translate into grades. Occasionally, you'll find an instructor whose stated expectations don't agree with how he tests and grades. That's why you need to find out about both expectations and grades. If they don't seem to be consistent, you'll have to determine what the instructor really expects.

Step 4: Emphasize learning what's important. Figure out what you need to do to accomplish your goals and meet the instructor's expectations. A major lesson you should learn, if you haven't already, is "what you take from a course (and almost anything else) depends on what you bring to it." Your attitude is important. If you decide something is worth learning, you'll probably find a way to learn it. Not because you're supposed to learn it, but because you want to. "Wanting to" is the biggest part of working smarter. Wanting to learn will go a long way toward helping you get a good grade. Unfortunately, it may not be enough unless what you want to learn is also what your instructor wants you to learn. Therefore, you need to make sure you and your instructor are on the same wavelength. If you're not, talk it over. Find out why the instructor has a different outlook. You may change your opinion about what's important. Determine how to focus your efforts. Not everything in this book or course is equally important. Focus on what's most important to you and to your instructor.

Step 5: Communicate with your instructor. Try to remember your instructor is a person. Even the authors of this book are people. We have wives, children, and pets. Most instructors really want to see you do well, but we need your help. Instructors don't know everything. In particular, we can't read your mind. You need to let your instructor know if you're having problems understanding the material you're expected to learn, figuring out what the instructor expects of you, or figuring out how to prepare for tests and other assignments. Talk with your instructor about problems you're having with the class. Remember, your instructor really is human.

This is your class. You paid for it. OK, maybe it was your parents, or somebody else who put out cold, hard cash for you to take this course. Don't let anybody keep you from getting your money's worth. Working smarter means determining what's important and focusing your attention and efforts on these things. Then, don't be distracted from your goals. If you run into problems, deal with them. If you don't understand something in class or in the book, ask questions. If you're afraid of asking dumb questions in class, remember: looking dumb in class is better than looking dumb on an exam. If you think you may be missing key points, talk with your instructor. If you want to learn, you can.

That's it. Give it try. We think you'll find the course more enjoyable and the experience more rewarding. Of course, you might also try doing assignments, going to class, getting enough sleep and exercise, eating properly, and studying throughout the semester. They usually help, even though they are hard work.

Best wishes to you, not only in this course, but throughout life.

Rob Ingram
Tom Albright
Bruce Baldwin
John Hill

A side note. To aid you in the learning process, the following icons appear throughout the text.

Your instructor may have chosen Personal Trainer® as a supporting product for your course. If so, in the financial chapters, you may see this icon. It identifies those exercises and problems in the financial sections that are recommended for use with this tool. In addition to those, all other exercises and problems throughout the text can be completed online using this product. Personal Trainer is an Internet-based homework tutor designed specifically for students taking an introductory course in accounting. With the help of warm-ups and hints, you can complete assigned or practice by completing unassigned homework online and submit your answers to your instructor.

SPREADSHEET

Excel activities are integrated throughout the text. In the Chapter F1 appendix you will find "A Short Introduction to Excel" that will help you get started. Throughout the text, specific assignments that you may choose to complete using spreadsheet software are identified with this icon. Problems titled "Excel in Action," which contain more assistance with using this very helpful tool, create a continuing financial accounting case and a continuing managerial accounting case that unfold throughout each half of the book. In addition, in Chapters F8 and F9, you will find guidance in "Using Excel" for time value of money problems.

INTERNATIONAL

This icon appears where international financial accounting topics are addressed. You can use this icon to alert you to information that involves the global economy.

http://ingram.
swlearning.com

In addition to providing helpful links to specific resources, as indicated with the icon in the text, this Web site contains many helpful learning aids. You will find Projects on the Web, quiz questions with feedback, PowerPoint® presentation slides for review of chapter coverage, Projects on the Web, check figures to selected assignments, learning objectives from the chapter to help you keep clear focus on the core goals, and updates for the latest information about changes in GAAP and any new, important information related to the text. In addition, this icon lets you know there's a related Internet hotlink connected to the text's Web site.

INSTRUCTOR PREFACE

Enron, Andersen, WorldCom, Tyco, Kmart, FAO Schwarz, the roller-coaster changes in the stock market, the changing interest rates—all these and other companies and topics headline the news and grab our attention. How can investors, creditors, employees, customers, and other stakeholders understand what's going on and how can they minimize their exposure to risk?

Your students may or may not be aware of the concerns of large company investors or creditors. However, they probably do understand there are risks in the business world and that knowing more about the financial information of companies is helpful to controlling those risks. They also may not have much knowledge of the internal accounting concerns of companies that determine pricing, manage costs, communicate data, etc.

For many of your students, this course will be the only accounting course they will have. Thus, it is essential that they take from the course the basic understanding needed to make wise financial choices. Some of your students will choose accounting as their major area. For them, having a strong understanding of accounting and the role of accountants in the global community will serve as a firm foundation upon which they will build the more detailed skills cultivated in their higher-level courses. This third edition of *Accounting: Information for Decisions,* will serve as a carefully crafted tool to assist you in teaching all of your students the language of business as they move forward to be the business decision-makers of tomorrow.

Develop Understanding with Quality Content

NEW! Mom's Cookie Company **and** Young Design, Inc.

These simple, yet realistic cases of small, start-up companies unfold throughout each half of the text and provide students with easy-to-understand examples of the purpose of accounting, its process, and its importance in decision making. As students move from chapter to chapter, they learn how the owners of the companies tackle basic business decisions using accounting information and how their accounting systems develop over time. At the beginning of each chapter, following the opening question, new information about the featured company sets the stage for that chapter's coverage.

What do we need to know to start a business?

In December of 2003, Maria and Stan were very excited about starting a company to sell cookies made using their mother's recipes. To honor their mother, they decided to call the business Mom's Cookie Company. Realizing they did not have much money and had little business experience, the brother and sister made plans to start with a small company. They hope the business will grow as more customers become aware of their products. Maria and Stan know that accountants provide advice to help managers of companies better understand their businesses. Because they had never started a company before, they made an appointment with Ellen Coleman, an accountant who had provided helpful business advice to several of their friends.

From page F2.

NEW! Chapter-Opening Questions

"How much will it cost to borrow money?" "How much do we need to sell to make a profit?" These and other questions are asked by people in the business world everyday. Each chapter begins with its own key question to tell students upfront the overall focus of the chapter's content.

How much will it cost to borrow money?

Maria and Stan have been successful in starting Mom's Cookie Company. The company has been profitable and is growing as more customers demand its products. Maria and Stan are now concerned about meeting the additional demand. They need to expand their operations, and they are considering producing their own products rather than purchasing them from other bakeries. Before they can expand, however, they must obtain additional financing for their company. The time value of money is an important concept that business owners need to understand before they borrow money.

From page F284.

Included with the scenario is "Food for Thought," which asked students to think about what they would do.

FOOD FOR THOUGHT

Suppose you were in Maria and Stan's position. What would you want to know in order to start a business? What goals would you have for the business, and how would you plan to reach those goals? What resources would you need in your business, and how would you finance those resources? How would you organize your company? Who would your customers be? How would you know whether you are reaching your goals or not? These are issues Ellen poses to Maria and Stan.

From page F2.

Each scenario concludes with a discussion among the owners and the company's accountant. For Mom's Cookie Company, the owners are Maria and Stan and the accountant is Ellen. For Young Design, Inc., the owners are Erin and Seth and the accountant is Roberta.

Ellen: *Creating a successful business is not an easy task. You need a good product, and you need a plan to produce and sell that product.*

Maria: *Stan and I think we have an excellent product. We don t have a lot of money for equipment and other resources, but we have identified a bakery that could produce our products using our recipes and according to our specifications.*

Stan: *Also, we have spoken with several local grocery chains that have been impressed with samples and have agreed to sell our products.*

Ellen: *Good. A primary goal of every successful business is to create value for customers. If you focus on delivering a product that customers want at a price they are willing to pay, you are also likely to create value for yourselves as owners of the company. You have to make sure you know what it will cost to run your company and decide how you will obtain the money you need to get*

From page F2.

NEW! Thinking Beyond the Question

The chapter-opening question is revisited in the end-of-chapter section. Students are asked a challenge question that requires them to think beyond what has been presented in the chapter.

Thinking Beyond the Question

What do we need to know to start a business?

The chapter introduction asked you to consider what you would need to know in order to start a company. This chapter identified several important considerations. How would your answer to this question differ if you were starting a service business or a nonprofit service organization as opposed to a retail business?

From page F29.

NEW! Organization and Expansion of Topics

The first seven chapters (F1–F7) of *Accounting: Information for Decisions, 3e,* reflect an *extensive reorganization* of the first six chapters in prior editions. Among other effects, the changes have created a more focused description of the accounting cycle, including more coverage of adjustments and the accrual process. In addition, like-topics have been clustered to increase clarity and continuity for students.

- **Accounting and Organizations.** Chapter F1 provides a *conceptual foundation* for understanding the purpose of accounting in business organizations. The chapter examines the need for information about business activities. Information is linked to a description of business activities and the purpose of businesses. The need for accurate and timely information leads to a brief introduction of the regulatory environment in which accounting and businesses operate. The chapter concludes with a discussion of *the importance of ethics* for accounting.

- **Business Activities—The Source of Accounting Information.** Chapter F2 *links business activities to accounting* through the *accounting equation.* The equation is used to develop a conceptual description of the accounting process for recording business activities. Simple examples are used to introduce accounting for **financing, investing, and operating activities.** The format used for this purpose highlights the relationships between transactions and financial statements. The chapter extends this description to a *brief introduction to financial statements* and the *analysis* of financial statement information. Thus, the chapter explains the purpose of accounting in terms of measuring and recording business activities, reporting information about those activities, and analyzing that information. The book emphasizes the importance of accounting for *decision making.* Accordingly, even procedural issues are linked to the decision focus. Accounting is not just about preparing information. It is about the use of that information to understand organizations and make business decisions.

- **Measuring Revenues and Expenses.** Chapter F3 extends the simple description of accounting for business activities in Chapter F2 to include *timing issues associated with accrual accounting.* The chapter explains accrual accounting concepts, the importance of these concepts, and their relationship to the accounting cycle through adjusting and closing transactions. Students are provided with a solid background in *transaction analysis* developed within a conceptual model of business decision making.

- **Reporting Earnings and Financial Position.** Chapter F4 examines the *income statement, balance sheet, and statement of stockholders' equity*. Examples from both hypothetical and real companies are used to introduce basic financial reporting concepts and to provide a realistic description of variations that exist in practice.
- **Reporting Cash Flows.** Chapter F5 considers the *statement of cash flows*. Both the direct and indirect formats are included. Simple examples are used to describe the indirect format and to re-emphasize the importance of accrual accounting concepts. The chapter also examines the importance of the statement of cash flows for *evaluating business performance*.
- **Full and Fair Reporting.** Chapter F6 examines the broader context of financial reporting, including information in the annual report other than financial statements. It examines the importance of disclosure, accounting regulation, auditing, and internal control. The 3rd edition pulls this material into one primary location to underscore the *importance of accounting as a validative, as well as descriptive, process*.
- **Computerized Accounting Systems.** Chapter F7 examines *accounting systems*, including the flow of data and processing in computerized systems. Similarly, new Chapter M6 examines *computerized manufacturing systems*. A goal of these chapters is to help students see *accounting as a dynamic, technological process*. Students sometimes get the impression that accounting is a clerical process without much technological sophistication. Modern accounting systems require a basic understanding of computer networks and database management systems. The world in which accountants work is not one of traditional journals and ledgers. It is one in which computer systems are essential to processing and analyzing business information. Each of these chapters includes an *illustration of a simple accounting database system*. By working through this project, students learn how basic accounting functions are automated and how computers facilitate the accounting process. The database files that tie to the project are provided on the Student CD-ROM and on the text's Web site (http://ingram.swlearning.com).

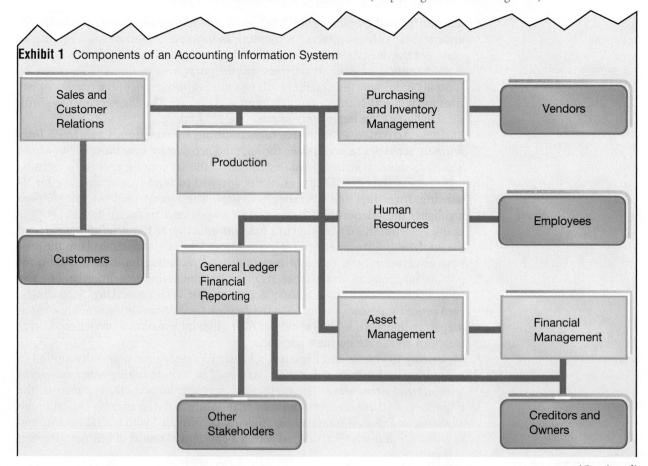

Exhibit 1 Components of an Accounting Information System

(Continued)

All of the components in the system are linked so they share data with each other. Some businesses use one software application that integrates all of these functions. **Systems that integrate most of the business information functions as a basis for management decisions are referred to as** *enterprise resource planning (ERP) systems.* Many large companies have implemented these systems from ERP developers such as SAP®, Peoplesoft®, and Oracle® Financials. Other companies may rely on software from dif

From pages F256–F257.

In the second half of Accounting: Information for Decisions, 3e, several chapters have been revised, reorganized, and enhanced. As with the financial chapters, the changes have created a more focused presentation of job order and process costing, among other important refinements. Here, too, like-topics have been clustered to increase clarity and continuity for students.

- **Accounting and Management Decisions.** Chapter M1 has been simplified and includes an explanation of the scope of managerial accounting in business organizations.
- **Cost Categories and Flows.** Chapter M2 has been streamlined and contains an increased focus on how managerial accounting systems support decision making.
- **Job-Order Costing and Process Costing.** This coverage is significantly revised and covered individually in two separate chapters (Chapters M3 and M4).
- **Cost Allocation and ABC.** Chapter M5 provides all new coverage of this important topic.
- **Analyzing Cost Behavior.** Chapter M7 is a significant revision of cost behavior coverage that had been presented primarily in Ch. M4 of the prior edition.
- **Budgeting.** Now in Chapter M8, this content is substantially revised with more visuals for understanding the relationships of the budgets and where they fit in the business organization.

REVISED! Spreadsheet Presentation
In the financial chapters, the spreadsheet presentation of transactions has been redesigned to more clearly show the effect of income statement accounts on the accounting equation. Through this approach, students see how nominal accounts increase or decrease retained earnings. We have consistently used this format throughout the text to avoid confusion.

Date	Accounts	Cash	Other Assets	= LIABILITIES	+ Contributed Capital	Retained Earnings
Feb. 12	Accounts Receivable Sales Revenue		600			600
Feb. 12	Cost of Goods Sold Merchandise Inventory		−400			−400

From page F84.

NEW! Optional Appendix on Debits and Credits
To provide flexibility in coverage, we have placed content explaining the basics of debits and credits, T accounts, and journal entries in an appendix to Chapter F2. The approach allows instructors ease in including or excluding that material.

ENHANCED! Coverage of Ethics
The emphasis on the importance of ethics begins in Chapter F1 and is revisited and reinforced in many places throughout the text.

The Importance of Ethics

OBJECTIVE 8

Explain why ethics are important for business and accounting.

Ethics are important in business organizations. Ethics involve living by the norms and rules of society. In business, those norms and rules identify appropriate behavior for managers, employees, investors, and other stakeholders. Keeping their investors and other stakeholders fully informed about their business activities is an important ethical norm for managers. Managers who conceal their activities or who misrepresent those activities make it difficult for stakeholders to assess how well a business is performing. Overstating profits, for example, may result in investors allocating more resources to a company than actual results would justify. This misallocation results in a loss of value to society and often leads to financial harm for those who use this information.

From page F22.

P1-19
Obj. 8

Ethics and Moral Hazard

You are the manager of a retail electronics store. Recently, you purchased 200 What-A-Sound portable CD players from a wholesaler in a going-out-of-business sale. These units cost you $80 each, about half of the normal cost of other brands that you sell for $260. You expected to sell these units at the regular price and earn an above-normal profit. After your purchase, you discovered that the units were poorly constructed and would probably last about a third as long as other major brands.

Customers often ask you for a recommendation when considering the purchase of a portable CD player. If you tell them the truth about the What-A-Sound model, you may have difficulty selling these units, even if you offer a steep discount.

Required

A. What will you tell a customer who asks about these units?
B. What are the short-run and long-run implications for your company's profits if (a) you conceal the quality of the units and sell them at their regular price or (b) reveal the quality problem? If you were to choose alternative b, what options might you consider in an effort to minimize the effect of these units on your profits?

From page F40.

REVISED! Case In Point Boxes
The content presented in these boxes provides students with a variety of enrichment information, some featuring the business community in general while others focus on specific examples of company disclosures or practices.

Case In Point

http://ingram.
swlearning.com

Learn more about
target costing.

Target Costing at Hewlett-Packard

The Vancouver Division of **Hewlett-Packard** (HP) uses target costing to work with its suppliers to manage the cost of making the desk jet printer. The facility recently has changed its strategy from producing low-volume, high-margin industrial products to high-volume, low-margin consumer products. HP reports achieving substantial price decreases as a result of their target costing program. In addition, the company uses target costing to support continuous improvement efforts and to identify various activities that cause costs within the value chain.

Source: Anonymous. 2000. Target costing gives HP better control over supply costs. New York: Supplier and Management Report.

From page M40.

ENHANCED! Assignment Material

New exercises and problems have been added. Many problems have been revised as well as updated for real-company information.

NEW! Student CD-ROM

In response to requests from instructors for more assignment material, we have added this new resource, bundled without charge with new texts. It contains alternate exercises, problems, and cases that provide more choices to instructors who may use this as "set B" and a greater opportunity for students who want more practice.

REVISED! Real-World Examples

Real company information usually piques student interest and helps clarify the meaning and relevance of accounting. Throughout the text, examples involving real-world information have been updated in the third edition. Among the companies presented are the following featured companies:

- General Mills, Inc.—Its complete annual report is included at the end of the text and tied to many case assignments in the text.
- Krispy Kreme Doughnuts, Inc.—Its key financial statements and other supporting information is included in several chapters.
- Starbucks Corporation—Its general financial information is presented as a comparison company, with Krispy Kreme, in the analysis chapters.

CASES

C12-1

Objs. 1, 3, 4

Evaluating Investment Decisions

Appendix B of this book contains a copy of the 2002 annual report of **General Mills, Inc.**

Required Review the annual report and write a short report in which you cover each of the following:

A. What major investing decisions did the company make from 2000 to 2002? Include decisions about disposing of as well as acquiring assets. (Hint: See note 2 to the financial statements, as well as the statement of cash flows.)
B. Evaluate the company's growth rate for total assets and net income from 2000 to 2002. (Hint: See the six-year financial summary.)
C. Compute return on assets, asset turnover, and profit margin for the company from 2000 to 2002. Does it appear that the company has made beneficial investing decisions?

From page F476.

INTERNATIONAL

Coverage relating to the international business community is identified by an icon in the margin.

TIMELY! Managerial Topics

Current topics, such as quality management, are featured along with the important traditional ones.

- Strategic Focus: The book's strategic focus demonstrates how businesses and organizations use managerial accounting to achieve operating and organizational objectives.
- Contemporary vs. Traditional Approaches: Contemporary, as well as traditional, management accounting philosophies and methods are covered. The benefits and drawbacks of the different approaches are explained in a simple, straightforward manner.
- Service Industry Coverage: Managerial accounting issues are related to service companies within each managerial chapter and in the end-of-chapter material to provide a broader view of the business environment.

PROVEN! Pedagogical Features

- **Learning Objectives**—serve as on-going reminders to students as to what is key in each part of the chapter and provide a basis for review. These objectives, which are written as measurable goals, are partnered with the assignments so instructors can easily select applicable coverage.
- **Learning Notes**—highlight issues that frequently are troublesome for students or that enrich student understanding.
- **Self-Study Problems**—provide opportunity for students to test themselves as they progress through the chapter.
- **Introducing Students to Excel as a Helpful Tool**—Beginning with A Short Introduction to Excel in the Chapter F1 appendix, continuing throughout the text in the *Excel in Action* problems, and further developed in Chapters F8 and F9 through the *Using Excel* explanations, students learn how to use this very helpful tool in generating financial accounting information.

Appendix | # A SHORT INTRODUCTION TO EXCEL

SPREADSHEET

This introduction summarizes some of the primary operations and functions of a spreadsheet. It is intended to get you started if you have not had previous experience with Excel. There are many operations and functions in addition to those mentioned here.

Identifying and Selecting Cells

A spreadsheet consists of rows and columns. Rows are identified by numbers, and columns are identified by letters. An intersection of a row and column is a cell. A cell is identified by the column letter and row number that intersect at that cell.

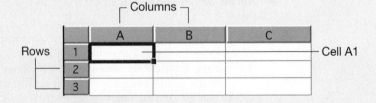

From page F23.

- **Review of Important Concepts**—provides a summary in outline form of each chapter's important concepts.
- **Key Concepts and Terms**—lists, with page references, the concepts and terms that are defined in the chapter.
- **Solutions to Self-Study Problems**—give students the answers to the chapter Self-Study Problems as a way of reinforcing their understanding of the material.
- **Questions**—are specifically designed to stimulate in-class discussion of each chapter's most important concepts.
- **Exercises**—are short assignments that focus on computations and are excellent for in-class demonstration and discussion.
- **Problems**—provide for a more complex learning experience, taking student learning further by focusing on analysis of information. Each chapter contains a problem set of multiple-choice questions, which many instructors like to use as an in-class quiz. A spreadsheet icon identifies assignments that work well with Excel.
- **Cases**—are more challenging than problems and encourage thinking and analytical skills.

SPREADSHEET

Bring Content Alive Through the Technology

ENHANCED! Technology

Personal Trainer® 3.0. (0-324-22251-3) Students can complete textbook end-of-chapter exercises and problems online and receive immediate feedback with Personal Trainer! Additionally, student results instantaneously flow into your gradebook! Each assignment begins with a warm-up, to get students started in the right direction; then hints provide additional assistance, if needed, once students receive the feedback on their work. This new, dynamic version of Personal Trainer offers many other helpful ways to assist both instructors and students.

WebTUTOR Advantage   **WebTutor® Advantage with Personal Trainer.** Available in either WebCT™ (0-324-22252-1) or Blackboard® (0-324-22253-X) platforms, this rich course management product is a specially designed extension of the classroom experience that enlivens the course by leveraging the power of the Internet with comprehensive educational content. WebTutor Advantage on WebCT or Blackboard® includes Personal Trainer to provide both students and instructors an unprecedented real-time, guided, self-correcting study outside the classroom. Instructors or students can use these resources along with those on the Product Web Site to supplement the classroom experience. Use this effective resource as an integrated solution for your distance learning or web-enhanced course! This powerful, turnkey solution provides the following content customized for this edition:

- **E-Lectures**—PowerPoint® slides of the key topical coverage accompanied by audio explanations to provide additional learning support.
- **Interactive Quizzes**—Multiple choice questions to test the knowledge of the chapter content and to provide immediate feedback on the accuracy of the response. These quizzes help students pinpoint areas needing more study.
- **Practice Exercises**—Short exercises with feedback to provide extra practice tied to chapter content.
- **Problem Demonstrations**—Selected Self-Study Problems with an audio step-by-step explanation of the solution to guide student understanding.
- **Video Clips**—Short, high-interest segments that focus on chapter-related topics to provide application of concepts to the real world.
- **Chapter Review**—Comprehensive chapter reviews to reinforce important concepts from each chapter.
- **Flashcards**—A terminology quiz to help students gain a complete understanding of the key terms from the chapter.
- **Spanish Dictionary of Accounting Terminology**—To aid Spanish-speaking students.

- **Crossword Puzzles**—Interactive puzzles that provide an alternative tool for students to test their understanding of terminology.
- **Quiz Bowl Game**—A fun online game, which is similar to Jeopardy!®, to reinforce chapter content.
- **Personal Trainer**—An Internet-based homework tutor for students and instructors. See description in the preceding section.

Access certificates for WebTutor® Advantage with Personal Trainer® can be bundled with the textbook or sold separately. **For more information, including a demo, visit** http://webtutor.swcollege.com. **To adopt the course in either WebCT or Blackboard, contact your sales representative or sign-up at** http://webtutor.thomsonlearning.com.

Xtra! This enrichment resource provides topic reinforcement resources and interactive quizzes so students can test their understanding of the content of the third edition. Free when bundled with a new text, students receive an access code so that they can receive Xtra! reinforcement in accounting.

http://ingram.
swlearning.com

Text Web Site. (http://ingram.swlearning.com) The Web site for the third edition offers you and your student many resources for teaching and learning.

Among the many elements available to *Students* are:

- *Quizzes with feedback*
- *Hotlinks* to many resources on the Web, including all of the Web sites listed in the text; this provides a quick connection to key information
- *PowerPoint® presentation slides* for review of chapter coverage
- *Internet Research and Other Projects* link text content to today's business environment. These assignments challenge students to expand their knowledge, apply what they have learned, and think critically.
- *Projects on the Web* for expanded learning through this helpful resource
- *Check figures* to selected assignments
- *Learning objectives* from the chapter are repeated as a study aid to keep clear focus on the core goals
- *Updates* for the latest information about changes in GAAP and any new, important information related to the text

For Instructors, in addition to full access to the student resources listed above, a password-protected section of the Web site contains a number of resource files, including:

- *Solutions Manual* in Microsoft® Word
- *Cooperative Learning and Instructor's Resource Guide* in Microsoft® Word
- *Solutions to Excel templates* for the *Excel in Action* and other assignments identified by the spreadsheet icon in the text
- *Solution transparency file* in Microsoft® Word
- *Instructor's Manual* for *The Annual Reporting Project*
- Additional *updates* pertinent to instructors

ENHANCED! Additional Support Material

For Students:

- **Student CD-ROM (0-324-22247-5).** Automatically packaged free with new texts, this new set of alternate exercises, problems, and cases has been created by Lydia Schliefer, Clemson University, and Scott Colvin, Naugatuck Valley Community College, to provide instructors an extensive list to choose from and to provide students with more opportunities to practice. Many instructors like to use one version of assignments in class for demonstration and discussion and the other set for homework. Others like to alternate sets from semester to semester. Also included on the CD are the accounting information system database files for Mom's Cookie Company and the Kwiki Oil Company illustrations, which appear in Chapters F7 and M6.

- **Study Guide and Forms (0-324-18528-6 for Chapters F1-F14 and 0-324-22248-3 for Chapters M1-M13).** This guide reinforces and enhances student understanding of the topics covered in the text. It is a thorough, value-adding book, prepared by Stephen Senge (Simmons Graduate School of Management) and George Sanders (Western Washington University). Included are working paper forms for selected text assignments.

- **Annual Report Project and Readings (0-324-18530-8).** This popular project, by Clayton Hock (Miami University) and Bruce Baldwin (Arizona State University West) can be used by either learning teams or individual students. It is tailored to reinforce the concepts presented in the financial accounting chapters of the text. Students work with annual reports of real companies to understand, interpret, and analyze the information. The project guides them through this process. Interesting readings from publications like *The Wall Street Journal* along with supporting Questions for Consideration provide additional enrichment.

For Instructors:

- **Cooperative Learning and Instructor's Resource Guide (0-324-18516-2 for Chapters F1-F14 and 0-324-22235-1 for Chapters M1-M13).** Contained in this supporting item are chapters, prepared by Philip Cottell, Jr. of Miami University, explaining cooperative learning techniques for use in the classroom and matrices that suggest application of techniques to specific end-of-chapter items. In addition, there are outlines of each chapter, teaching notes, and descriptions of the exercises, problems, and cases to assist in class preparation. This guide's content is also available in electronic form on the Instructor's Resource CD-ROM and (restricted) on the product support Web site.

- **Solutions Manual (0-324-18523-5 for Chapters F1-F14 and 0-324-22236-X for Chapters M1-M13).** Author-prepared and carefully verified solutions to all exercises, problems, and cases are presented in this manual.

- **Test Bank (0-324-18525-1 for Chapters F1-F14 and 0-324-22238-6 for Chapters M1-M13).** A complete and plentiful set of newly revised test items in print form; also available in electronic form (using ExamView® software, provided) on the Instructor's Resource CD-ROM.

- **Instructor's Resource CD-ROM with ExamView® (0-324-22239-4 for Chapters F1-F14 and 0-324-22239-4 for Chapters M1-M13).** This IRCD contains the files for key instructor's ancillaries (the Cooperative Learning and Instructor's Resource Guide, the solutions manual, and the PowerPoint® Presentation slides). This gives instructors the ultimate tool for customizing lectures and presentations. The presentation slides reinforce chapter content and provide a rich tool for in-class lectures and out-of-class reviewing. The test bank files on the CD-ROM are provided in ExamView® format. This program is an easy-to-use test creation software compatible with Microsoft® Windows. Instructors can add or edit questions, instructions, and answers, and select questions (randomly or numerically) by previewing them on the screen. Instructors can also create and administer quizzes online, whether over the Internet, a local area network (LAN), or a wide area network (WAN).

- **Solution Transparencies (0-324-18524-3 for Chapters F1-F14 and 0-324-22237-8 for Chapters M1-M13).** Acetate transparencies of the numerical solutions to the exercises, problems, and cases are available to adopters.

- **Annual Report Project and Readings Instructor's Manual (0-324-18529-4).** Prepared by the authors of the Annual Report Project and Readings, this manual provides guidance to assist instructors in maximizing the benefit of the project in their courses. In addition to the printed manual, the files are available in the Instructor Resources section of the text's Web site.

Add Enrichment with Other Accounting Resources

INSIDE LOOK: *Analysis From All Angles.* Accounting is in the news and the classroom with access to this new Web site from Thomson/South-Western. The *Access Card* allows the instructor and the student to utilize information related to the Enron, Andersen, and other "names in the news" that involve accounting-related concerns. Well-known, popular news sources provide the background for the selected current events. Teaching tools are available to the instructor to implement class discussions, while analysis and questions are available to the student to utilize in many accounting discipline areas. This site is intended to help instructors teach and students to learn about critical current issues and understand them in the context of their accounting studies. **For a Demo, go to** http://insidelook.swcollege.com.

Business & Professional Ethics for Directors, Executives, and Accountants, 3e (0-324-20066-8). Leonard J. Brooks, of the University of Toronto, has extensively revised his text to include the latest ethical concerns in today's business environment. Cases, readings and textual material are blended to provide accounting and business students with a concise, practical understanding of how to behave ethically in a post-Enron world. This text includes a complete business and professional ethics guide to working in the age of accounting scandals. Issues and cases in this new edition cover: Enron and Enron-triggered changes in governance for corporations and the accounting profession; increased ethical sensitivity to ethical issues; calls for increased accountability to stakeholders, ethical decision making and behavior; and the development of ethical organization cultures domestically and internationally.

Accounting Ethics in the Post—Enron Age, 1e (0-324-19193-6) (by Iris Stuart and Bruce Stuart, of California State University—Fullerton). With the Enron/Andersen debacle, ethics is becoming an increasingly important (and interesting) part of accounting education. Ethics coverage is also required by the AACSB for accreditation purposes. Most texts include some limited ethics coverage, but many instructors would like to include more. This timely supplement contains ethics cases based on real and hypothetical situations in the business world. Examples include cases tied to Enron, Global Crossing, and Boston Chicken. Identifying ethical dilemmas and projecting their resolution will allow students to develop essential skills for success in their future careers. In each section of the textbook, the problems will be labeled according to subject matter (i.e., bad debt expense, revenue recognition). This allows the instructor to select problems consistent with the needs of the course.

California Car Company: An Active Learning Costing Case, 2e (0-324-18450-6) (by Steven J. Adams and LeRoy J. Pryor, both of California State University, Chico). This award-winning project forms the foundation of much of the management material. Using interlocking-block cars, students learn about the manufacturing process and managerial accounting by creating their own production line. Also, available is a supporting instructor's manual.

An Introduction to Accounting, Business Processes, and ERP (0-324-19161-8) (by Phil Reckers, Julie Smith David, and Harriet Maccracken, all of Arizona State University). Utilizing JD Edwards software demos, an industry leading ERP company, your students will learn an overview of the use of ERP software for accounting and business processes. Unlike any other product on the market, they will not only learn the advantages of technology in accessing business information but will also learn to apply it in three different business models. After each module, student learning is reinforced by quizzing. Equip your students with this class-tested and easy-to-use experience to help them meet the ever-changing challenges of business and technology!

InfoTrac® College Edition. With this resource, your students can receive anytime, anywhere online access to a database of full-text articles from hundreds of popular and scholarly periodicals, such as *Newsweek, Fortune, Entrepreneur, Journal of Accountancy,* and *Nation's Business,* among others. Students can use its fast and easy search tools to find relevant news and analytical information among the tens of thousands of articles in the database—updated daily and going back as far as four years—all at a single Web site. InfoTrac is a great way to expose students to online research techniques, with the security that the content is academically based and reliable. An InfoTrac College Edition subscription card is packaged free with new copies of our financial accounting texts. For more information, visit http://www.swcollege.com/infotrac/infotrac.html.

INTACCT Financial Accounting and INTACCT Managerial Accounting (by D. V. Rama and K. Raghunandan, both of Texas A&M International University). These Internet-based tutorial at http://rama.swcollege.com are designed for use in an introductory accounting course or in any course where a review of the key accounting concepts and terminology is needed. The program offers a visual, user-friendly way to reinforce accounting principles and includes tutorials, demonstration problems, exercises, and an interactive glossary. Users will receive an access certificate that will allow them to do the online tutorial over the full term of a course.

Accounting Career Consultant: Financial Accounting (by Charles Davis and Eric Sandburg). This resource is an online, interactive, tutored simulation. It is designed to complement both the classroom instruction and the text presentations. Each module includes links to review questions with customized feedback (approximately 20 questions), links to resources to further augment learning, and company profiles for the businesses discussed.

The Monopoly Game Practice Set (0-155-04236-X). This fun practice set, by Robert Knechel of the University of Florida, is based on the Monopoly game. This product helps students understand accounting information and transactions as triggered by real business events. Each student's solution is unique but easily graded.

ACKNOWLEDGMENTS

Throughout the writing and development of the three editions of our text, many colleagues have contributed creative, helpful suggestions through reviews, focus groups, surveys, etc. We have considered all of the feedback carefully as each edition has been prepared and will continue to do so in the future. Therefore, in appreciation, we thank the following contributors:

Judy Beebe, Western Oregon University

Scott Colvin, Naugatuck Valley Community College

Elizabeth Davis, Baylor University

Patricia A. Doherty, Boston University

William H. Dresnack, SUNY College at Brockport

Stephen L. Duncan, Navarro College

Rafik Z. Elias, Cameron University

Kel-Ann Eyler, Brenau University

Benjamin Foster, University of Louisville

Roger Gee, San Diego Mesa College

Kathryn Hansen, California State University, Los Angeles

Sheri L. Henson, Western Kentucky University

Clayton Hock, Miami University

Wayne C. Ingalls, University of Maine

David Karmon, Central Michigan University

Laurie Larson, Valencia Community College

Keith Leeseberg, Manatee Community College

Candace Leuck, University of North Carolina—Charlotte

Cathy Lumbattis, Southern Illinois University

J. Russell Madray, Clemson University

Lynn Mazzola, Nassau Community College

Kevin McNelis, New Mexico State University

Duane Milano, Navarro Junior College

Stephen G. Morrissette, University of St. Francis

Carol Nemec, Southern Oregon University

Alfonso R. Oddo, Niagara University

Joseph B. O'Donnell, Canisius College

Joseph Ragan, St. Joseph's University

Pamela Rouse, Butler University

Marc A. Rubin, Miami University

Arline Savage, Oakland University

Lydia Schleifer, Clemson University

David Senteney, Ohio University

Kathleen A. Wilcox, Kennesaw State University

Katherine A. Wilson, Embry-Riddle Aeronautical University

Bert J. Zarb, Embry-Riddle Aeronautical University

In addition, we wish to thank all who worked diligently to provide the carefully crafted content of this edition's supporting materials.

Rob Ingram
Tom Albright
Bruce Baldwin
John Hill

ABOUT THE AUTHORS

Robert W. Ingram

Robert W. Ingram is the Ross-Culverhouse Chair in the Culverhouse School of Accountancy at the University of Alabama. He teaches courses in financial accounting and has been actively involved in course curriculum development. He has served as Director of Education for the American Accounting Association, as a member of the Accounting Education Change Commission, and as editor of *Issues in Accounting Education*, a journal dedicated to accounting education research.

Professor Ingram is a Certified Public Accountant and holds a Ph.D. from Texas Tech University. Prior to joining the faculty at the University of Alabama, he held positions at the University of South Carolina and the University of Iowa, and a visiting appointment at the University of Chicago. His research, which examines financial reporting and accounting education, has been published widely in accounting and business journals. He is the recipient of the National Alumni Association Outstanding Commitment to Teaching Award and the Burlington Northern Foundation Faculty Achievement in Research Award at the University of Alabama. He has also received the Notable Contribution to Literature Award of the Government and Nonprofit Section of the American Accounting Association and the Award for Excellence and Professional Contributions of the Alabama Association for Higher Education in Business.

Professor Ingram is married and has two children. He and his family enjoy sports, travel, reading, music, and art. They live contentedly in Tuscaloosa, Alabama.

Thomas L. Albright

Thomas L. Albright is the J. Reese Phifer Faculty Fellow in the Culverhouse School of Accountancy at the University of Alabama. He teaches courses at the undergraduate and graduate levels in financial and managerial accounting. Professor Albright has received the Professor of the Year award on seven occasions in relation to his work with the MBA and Executive MBA students.

Professor Albright is a Certified Public Accountant (California) and holds a Ph.D. from the University of Tennessee. He has received the Certificate of Merit from the Institute of Management Accountants (IMA) for his work in the area of quality costs. Dr. Albright is actively involved with manufacturing companies in both the United States and Mexico. His work is used to help companies determine more accurate product costs and to develop better performance measures to achieve manufacturing excellence.

Professor Albright lives with his wife, Debby, and their two children, Michael and Jenny. He enjoys scuba diving, underwater photography, and sailing.

Bruce A. Baldwin

Bruce A. Baldwin is Professor of Accounting in the School of Management at Arizona State University West. He has held previous faculty appointments at Arizona State University Main, Portland State University, and Linfield College (Oregon). In addition, he has held visiting appointments at the University of Texas-Austin and the University of Alabama. His primary teaching interests involve financial accounting and reporting issues in courses at both the undergraduate and graduate levels. He is known as a challenging and effective teacher and has won several teaching awards.

Professor Baldwin is well-known for his interest in accounting education issues and has special expertise in testing and measurement. He has served as a consultant to a number of national testing organizations and chaired two AICPA task forces that developed employee assessment materials. Currently he is a member of the Certification Advisory Committee of the Arizona State Board of Accountancy. Dr. Baldwin's research articles on accounting policy standards and accounting education have appeared frequently in journals such as the *Accounting Review, Journal of Accounting Education, Advances in Accounting,* and *Issues in Accounting Education.* He has served as the associate editor of both the *Journal of Accounting Education* and of *Accounting Education: An International Journal.*

Professor Baldwin is married and has two children and four grandchildren. He and his wife Connie live busy and sometimes hectic lives in Phoenix, Arizona. At every possible opportunity they escape to the serenity of the beach at Puerto Penasco, Mexico.

John W. Hill   John W. Hill is Associate Dean, Research and Operations, and Professor of Accounting at the Kelley School of Business, Indiana University where he teaches courses in financial analysis, firm valuation, strategic cost management, and mergers and acquisitions. Professor Hill also serves as Chairman of the Board, Kelley Executive Partners, and is affiliated with the CPA/consulting firm of Clifton Gunderson, LLP as Senior Advisor engaged in business valuation consulting. He has served on several editorial boards and is the recipient of sixteen teaching and research awards including the President's Award for Distinguished Teaching at Indiana University, the Deloitte & Touche/American Accounting Association Wildman Medal, the Silver and Bronze Lybrand Medals, and three Certificates of Merit from the Institute of Management Accountants.

Professor Hill is a member of the Georgia Bar Association and holds a Ph.D. from the University of Iowa. Prior to becoming an academic, he was the chief financial and administrative officer of a bank. Professor Hill has conducted executive education for firms such as Baxter Healthcare, Graco, and John Deere and is engaged in various international executive education and consutling programs. He has has consulted with the Hungarian Telecommunications company, Matav, and taught at the Borsa Italiano (Italian Stock Exchange), the Catholic University of Milan (Italy), University of Lubjyana (Solvenia), and the Ryazan State Pedagogical University (Russia). He is currently beginning a three-year teaching/consulting engagement involving Vietnamese banks.

Professor Hill is a retired Major General, U.S. Marine Corps Reserve, and formerly Vice Commander, Marine Forces Atlantic, Europe, and South. He and his wife alternate living between Bloomington, Indiana, a log cabin in the hills of Brown County, Indiana, and Perdido Key, Florida.

The Accounting Information System

ACCOUNTING AND ORGANIZATIONS

What do we need to know to start a business?

In December of 2003, Maria and Stan were very excited about starting a company to sell cookies made using their mother's recipes. To honor their mother, they decided to call the business Mom's Cookie Company. Realizing they did not have much money and had little business experience, the brother and sister made plans to start with a small company. They hope the business will grow as more customers become aware of their products. Maria and Stan know that accountants provide advice to help managers of companies better understand their businesses. Because they had never started a company before, they made an appointment with Ellen Coleman, an accountant who had provided helpful business advice to several of their friends.

FOOD FOR THOUGHT

Suppose you were in Maria and Stan's position. What would you want to know in order to start a business? What goals would you have for the business, and how would you plan to reach those goals? What resources would you need in your business, and how would you finance those resources? How would you organize your company? Who would your customers be? How would you know whether you are reaching your goals or not? These are issues Ellen poses to Maria and Stan.

Ellen: *Creating a successful business is not an easy task. You need a good product, and you need a plan to produce and sell that product.*

Maria: *Stan and I think we have an excellent product. We don't have a lot of money for equipment and other resources, but we have identified a bakery that could produce our products using our recipes and according to our specifications.*

Stan: *Also, we have spoken with several local grocery chains that have been impressed with samples and have agreed to sell our products.*

Ellen: *Good. A primary goal of every successful business is to create value for customers. If you focus on delivering a product that customers want at a price they are willing to pay, you are also likely to create value for yourselves as owners of the company. You have to make sure you know what it will cost to run your company and decide how you will obtain the money you need to get started.*

Stan: *We have some money in savings, and we plan to obtain a loan from a local bank. Those financial resources should permit us to rent a small office and purchase equipment we need to manage the company. Also, we will need to acquire a truck for picking up the cookies from the bakery and delivering them to the grocery stores.*

Ellen: *You will need a system for measuring your costs and the amounts you sell. That system is critical for helping you determine whether you are accomplishing your goals.*

Maria: *Stan and I don't know much about accounting. Can you help us get started?*

Ellen: *I'll be happy to help you. First, let's explore in more detail some of the issues you need to consider.*

OBJECTIVES

Once you have completed this chapter, you should be able to:

1 Identify how accounting information helps decision makers.

2 Compare major types of organizations and explain their purpose.

3 Describe how businesses create value.

4 Explain how accounting helps investors and other decision makers understand businesses.

5 Identify business ownership structures and their advantages and disadvantages.

6 Identify uses of accounting information for making decisions about corporations.

7 Explain the purpose and importance of accounting regulations.

8 Explain why ethics are important for business and accounting.

INFORMATION FOR DECISIONS

OBJECTIVE 1

Identify how accounting information helps decision makers.

All of us use information to help us make decisions. *Information* **includes facts, ideas, and concepts that help us understand the world.** To use information, we must be able to interpret it and understand its limitations. Poor information or the improper use of information often leads to poor decisions.

As an example, assume you wish to drive from Sevierville to Waynesville. The drive will take several hours and require several turns on unfamiliar secondary roads. Therefore, you use a map, as illustrated in Exhibit 1, to provide information to help guide you along the way.

Exhibit 1
Map from Sevierville to
Waynesville

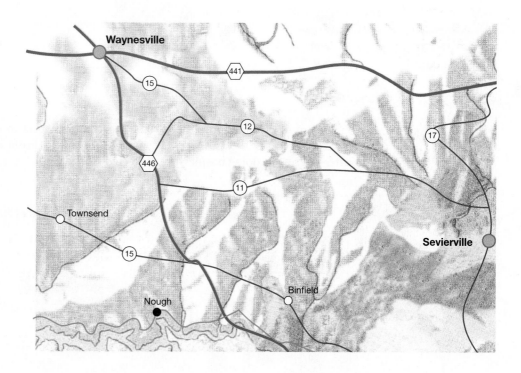

Why is the map useful? The map can help you plan your trip. You have selected a primary goal: arrive at Waynesville. You may have other goals as well, such as getting there as quickly as possible. Or perhaps you wish to stop at various points along the way. The map provides information about alternative routes so that you can select the

INTERNATIONAL

one that is shortest, fastest, or most scenic. Using the map along the way helps you make decisions about where to turn or stop. It helps you determine how far you have traveled and how much farther you have left to go. It helps you decide whether you are on the right road or where you made a wrong turn. It helps you decide where you are, how you got there, and where you are going.

Accounting provides information to help in making decisions about organizations. This information is like a map of an organization. **Accounting information helps decision makers determine where they are, where they have been, and where they are going.** Rather than measuring distances in miles or kilometers, accounting measures an organization's activities by the dollar amounts associated with these activities. The primary measurement unit for accounting information is dollars in the United States or the local currency for other countries.

Maria and Stan have decided to start a business selling cookies. Their company will pay a bakery to produce the cookies and will sell the cookies to local grocery stores. An early decision they have to make is to identify the resources they will need to start and run their business. They will need merchandise (cookies) to sell and will purchase those products from a supplier (the bakery). They will need a place to operate the business and someone to pick up the products and deliver them to sellers (grocery stores). They will need money to pay for the merchandise, rent for their office, wages, equipment, and miscellaneous costs such as supplies and utilities.

As an initial step in deciding whether to start the business, Maria and Stan might consider how much they expect to sell. Suppose that after discussing this issue with grocery store owners, they determine that the company will sell about $12,000 of merchandise each month.

Next, they consider how much money they will need to operate their business. A discussion with the bakery indicates the cost of the merchandise will be $8,000 each month. After consideration of their other needs, they calculate their monthly costs will be:

Merchandise	$ 8,000
Wages	1,000
Rent	600
Supplies	300
Utilities	200
Total	$10,100

From this information, they decide they should expect to earn a profit of $1,900 ($12,000 – $10,100) each month as shown in Exhibit 2. Profit is the amount left over after the cost of doing business is subtracted from sales.

Exhibit 2

Expected Monthly
Earnings for Mom's
Cookie Company

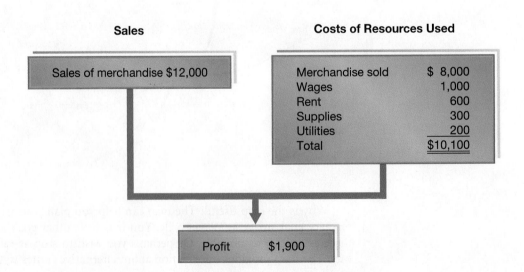

Does this appear to be a good business for Maria and Stan? Suppose they each have $5,000 to invest in the business. They will use this money to purchase merchandise and to pay for rent, wages, and the miscellaneous costs for the first month. Would investing their money in the business be a good idea?

If they don't invest in the business, they could earn interest of about $50 a month on their $10,000 of combined savings. The expected profit of $1,900 is considerably larger. However, they also should consider the wages they could earn if they worked for someone else instead of working in their own company. Additionally, they should consider how certain they are about the amount they can earn from their business and how much risk they are willing to take. Investing in a business is always risky. *Risk* **is uncertainty about an outcome,** such as the amount of profit a business will earn. If the company sells less than Maria and Stan expect, its earnings also will be less than expected. If the company does not do well, they could lose their investments. Are they willing to take that risk? **Accounting can help with these decisions by providing information about the results that owners and other decision makers should expect will occur.** Decision makers then have to evaluate that information and make their decisions.

Accounting is a way of looking at a business. It measures the activities of a business by the dollars it receives and spends. It helps decision makers determine where they started and where they should end up. It helps determine whether expectations are being met. In the case of Mom's Cookie Company, accounting identifies the company's starting point by the $10,000 Maria and Stan invest in their business. It identifies an expected ending point as the amount of profit of $1,900 they expect to earn each month. It provides a means of determining whether expectations are being met by measuring business activities each month to determine whether the company is actually earning $1,900 each month. Like a map, accounting can help decision makers determine that they are not where they want to be. It can help them determine what went wrong and what they might do to get back on the proper route.

Accounting provides a model of a business by measuring the business activities in dollar amounts. Underlying this model is an information system. This system provides a process for obtaining facts that can be converted into useful information. Understanding the system and its processes will help you understand the information provided by accounting.

The purpose of accounting is to help people make decisions about economic activities. Economic activities involve the allocation of scarce resources. People allocate scarce resources any time they exchange money, goods, or services. These activities are so common that almost every person in our society uses the accounting process to assist in decision making.

Accounting provides information for managers, owners, members, and other stakeholders who make decisions about organizations. *Stakeholders* **include those who have an economic interest in an organization and those who are affected by its activities. An** *organization* **is a group of people who work together to develop, produce, and/or distribute goods or services.** The next section of this chapter discusses the purpose of organizations and the role of accounting in organizations.

THE PURPOSE OF ORGANIZATIONS

OBJECTIVE 2

Compare major types of organizations and explain their purpose.

Many types of organizations exist to serve society. Why do these organizations exist? Most exist because people need to work together to accomplish their goals. The goals are too large, too complex, or too expensive to be achieved without cooperation. All organizations provide goods and/or services. By working together, people can produce more and better goods and services.

Organizations differ as to the types of goods or services they offer (Exhibit 3). *Merchandising* **(or** *retail***)** *companies* **sell to consumers goods that are produced by other companies.** Grocery, department, and hardware stores are examples. Mom's Cookie Company is a merchandising company. It purchases merchandise from a bakery and sells the merchandise to grocery stores. *Manufacturing companies* **produce goods that they sell to consumers, to merchandising companies, or to other manufacturing companies.** Examples include automobile manufacturers, petroleum refineries, furniture manufacturers, computer companies, and paper companies. The bakery from which Mom's Cookie Company purchases its cookies is a manufacturing company. *Service companies* **sell services rather than goods.** These companies include banks, insurance companies, hospitals, universities, law firms, and accounting firms. Some companies may be a combination of types. For example, many automobile dealers are both retail and service companies. Restaurants are both manufacturing and service companies.

Exhibit 3
Types of Organizations

Business

Retail

Manufacturing

Service

Nonbusiness

Government

Other Nonprofit

Organizations may be classified by whether or not they attempt to earn a profit. Profits result from selling goods and services to customers at prices greater than the cost of the items sold. **Organizations that sell their goods and services to make a profit are** *business organizations. Governmental and nonprofit organizations,* **sometimes referred to as nonbusiness organizations, provide goods or, more typically, services without the intent of making a profit.** Nonbusiness organizations include civic, social, and religious organizations. Some types of services, such as education and healthcare services, are provided by both business and nonbusiness organizations. Although the products are similar, the goals of the organizations providing these services are different. Nevertheless, all organizations need accounting information for decision making. This book focuses primarily on accounting for business organizations.

Transformation of Resources

A common purpose of organizations is to transform resources from one form to a different, more valuable, form to meet the needs of people. Resources include natural resources (such as minerals and timber), physical resources (such as buildings and equipment), management skills, labor, financial resources, legal rights (such as patents and trademarks), information, and the systems that provide information. The transformation process combines these resources to create goods and services. Transformation may involve making goods or services easier or less expensive for customers to obtain, as in most merchandising and service companies. Or it may involve physically converting resources by processing or combining them, as in manufacturing companies. An easy way to understand the transformation of resources is by thinking about how a bakery takes resources like flour and sugar and transforms them through the mixing and baking process to become cookies. Exhibit 4 illustrates this transformation process.

Organizations are created because many transformations are too difficult or too expensive for individuals to accomplish without working together. By combining their managerial skills, labor, and money, individuals create organizations to provide value that otherwise would be unavailable. Value is added to society when an organization transforms resources from a less desirable form or location to a more desirable form

Exhibit 4
Transformation of Resources into Goods and Services

| Resources | Transformation | Goods and Services |

or location. **The transformation, if it meets a need of society, creates value because people are better off after the transformation than before.** For example, a company that manufactures shirts creates value because the shirts are more useful to those who purchase them than the material from which the shirts are made or the cotton or synthetic fibers used to make the material.

To improve its welfare, a society must encourage organizations to increase the value they create. Because resources are in scarce supply, a society should attempt to use its resources wisely. A major purpose of accounting information is to help decide how to get the most value from scarce resources.

Creating Value

OBJECTIVE 3

Describe how businesses create value.

How can society determine how to use its resources? Decisions about using scarce resources wisely are not easy. Because society is made up of many individuals, disagreement often exists as to how resources should be used. In our society and many others, markets are the means used to promote the wise use of many resources.

Markets exist to allocate scarce resources used and produced by organizations. **A *market* is any location or process that permits resources to be bought and sold.** Competition in a market determines the amount and value of resources available for exchange. The more valuable a resource is in meeting your needs, the more you are willing to pay for it as a buyer, or the more you want for it as a seller.

The price paid for a resource in a competitive market is an indication of the value assigned to it at the particular time the buyer and seller negotiate an exchange. For example, when you buy a box of cookies, you exchange money for it. The amount of money is a measure of the value you place on the product. Thus, the price of goods and services in a market is a basis for measuring value. **Accounting measures the increase in value created by a transformation as the difference between the total price of goods and services sold and the total cost of resources consumed in developing, producing, and selling the goods and services.**

What value results when you purchase cookies? The amount you pay for the cookies is an indication of the value you expect to receive. However, resources were consumed in producing the cookies and making them available to you as illustrated in Exhibit 5.

LEARNING NOTE

Distinguish between prices charged by a business to its customers and prices paid by a business for resources it consumes. A price charged by a business is a **sales price**. A price paid by a business to purchase resources that will be consumed in providing goods and services is a **cost** to the business.

Exhibit 5
Value Created by Transforming Resources

Sales Price of Box of Cookies		Total Cost of Resources Consumed to Produce and Make Box of Cookies Available		Value Added
$3.50	−	$3.00	=	$0.50

If you pay $3.50 for a box of cookies and the total cost of producing the cookies and making them available to you is $3.00, the value added by the transformation is $0.50. The difference between the price you pay and the total cost of the cookies is profit for those who produce and sell the cookies. *Profit* **is the difference between the price a seller receives for goods or services and the total cost to the seller of all resources consumed in developing, producing, and selling these goods or services during a particular period.** Thus, profits are the net resources generated from selling goods and services (resources received from the sales minus resources used in making the sales).

Several types of markets are important in our economy. Markets exist for resources used by organizations. Organizations compete in **financial markets** for financial resources. Investors choose where to put their money to work by selecting among competing organizations. Organizations compete in **supplier markets** for other resources needed to produce goods and services. Competition in these markets determines the costs of materials, labor, equipment, and other resources available to organizations. Organizations compete in **product markets** (markets for goods and services). These markets determine the prices of goods and services available to customers. From the perspective of organizations, financial and supplier markets are input markets; product markets are output markets. All of these markets allocate scarce resources.

Exhibit 6 reports the actual profit earned by Mom's Cookie Company in January, its first month of operations. (Keep in mind, the information presented earlier was the estimated amount of sales, costs, and profit.) The profit of $1,700 represents the difference between the amount of resources created by selling goods to customers and the total cost of resources consumed in providing those goods. Of course, a business venture may not produce a profit. It produces a loss if it consumes more resources than it creates.

Exhibit 6

Profit Earned by Mom's Cookie Company in January

Mom's Cookie Company Profit Earned For January		
Resources created from selling cookies		$11,400
Resources consumed:		
Cost of merchandise sold	$7,600	
Wages	1,000	
Rent	600	
Supplies	300	
Utilities	200	
Total cost of resources consumed		9,700
Profit earned		$ 1,700

This exhibit reports results of activities that occurred during January. These results can be compared with expected results. Mom's Cookie Company had sales of $11,400 compared with expected sales of $12,000. The cost of merchandise sold during January was $7,600 rather than the expected amount of $8,000, and profit earned by the company was $1,700 rather than the expected amount of $1,900. By examining the differences between expected and actual results, Maria and Stan can determine whether they need to make changes in their business. Perhaps they need to find more stores to sell their products, or perhaps they need to advertise their products.

THE ROLE OF ACCOUNTING IN BUSINESS ORGANIZATIONS

Businesses earn profits by providing goods and services demanded by society. Owners invest in a business to receive a return on their investments from profits earned by their business. By investing in a business, owners are forgoing the use of their money for

OBJECTIVE 4

Explain how accounting helps investors and other decision makers understand businesses.

other purposes. In exchange, they expect to share in a business's profits. *Return on investment (ROI)* **is the amount of profit earned by a business that could be paid to owners.** Return on investment often is expressed as a ratio that compares the amount of profit to the amount invested in a business by its owners:

$$\text{Return on Investment} = \frac{\text{Profit}}{\text{Amount Invested}}$$

Profits represent net resources that have been earned through sales transactions. A business may distribute profits to its owners. Alternatively, owners (or managers acting on their behalf) may decide to reinvest profits in a business to acquire additional resources. The business can use the additional resources to earn more profits by expanding its size or by expanding into new locations or product lines. Either way, the owners are usually better off. They receive cash from their investments if profits are withdrawn, or they add value to the business if profits are reinvested.

As shown in Exhibit 6, Mom's Cookie Company earned $1,700 during January. As the owners, Maria and Stan may choose to withdraw some or all of this amount for personal use. It is their return on investment. Alternatively, they might choose to reinvest all or a portion of this profit to enlarge their company by buying a larger amount of merchandise for sale in February.

Return on investment for Mom's Cookie Company for January was $1,700, or 17% ($1,700 ÷ $10,000), relative to the owners' initial investment. If Maria and Stan withdraw more than $1,700 from their business, the additional amount withdrawn is a **return** *of* **investment,** not a return **on** investment. That additional amount is a return of a portion of the amount they originally invested. **For a company to maintain its capital (the amount invested by its owners), it must pay a return to owners from profits the company has earned. Otherwise, the company is reducing its capital by returning a portion of owners' investments to them.**

The amount of return owners receive from a company depends on the company's success in earning a profit. If you are the primary owner of a business, you are actively involved in managing the business, and its success depends largely on your ability and effort. If you are one of many who invest in a company, you probably are not actively involved in the business, and its success depends largely on the abilities and efforts of those who are managing the business. When you invest in a business, you have no guarantee that it will be successful. You are taking a risk that you may not receive a return on your investment, that the return may be smaller than you expected, or even that you might lose your investment.

Why invest in a business if the investment is risky? If a business is successful, its owners can expect to earn a higher rate of return on their investments than they could earn on a safer alternative, such as a savings account. By investing $10,000 in Mom's Cookie Company, Maria and Stan expect to earn $1,900 each month from their investment. If they invested their money in a savings account, they would expect to earn $50 each month. In general, it is necessary to take greater risks in order to earn higher returns. Accounting information helps owners evaluate the risks and returns associated with their investments so they can make good decisions.

To earn profits and pay returns to owners, businesses must operate effectively and efficiently. **An** *effective business* **is one that is successful in providing goods and services demanded by customers.** Effective management involves identifying the right products and putting them in the right locations at the right times. **An** *efficient business* **is one that keeps the costs of resources consumed in providing goods and services low relative to the selling prices of these goods and services.** Managers must control costs by using the proper mix, qualities, and quantities of resources to avoid waste and to reduce costs. The risk of owning a business is lower if the business is effective and efficient than if it is ineffective or inefficient. Efficient and effective businesses are competitive in financial, supplier, and product markets.

Mom's Cookie Company will be effective if it sells products desired by customers and if the products are made available in locations convenient for customers to purchase them. The company will be efficient if it can keep the costs of resources it consumes low relative to the price of the goods it sells. During January, the company was less effective than Maria and Stan had planned because it sold fewer goods than expected. The company was efficient in controlling the cost of resources consumed because its costs were less than the prices of goods sold, thus permitting the company to earn a profit.

Business owners expect to receive a return on their investments. Investors choose among alternative investments by evaluating the amount, timing, and uncertainty of the returns they expect to receive. Businesses that earn high profits and are capable of paying high returns have less difficulty in obtaining investors than other businesses. A business that cannot earn sufficient profits will be forced to become more effective and efficient or to go out of business.

The accounting information system is a major source of the information investors use in making decisions about their investments. Accounting information helps investors assess the effectiveness and efficiency of businesses. It helps them estimate the returns that can be expected from investing in a business and the amount of risk associated with their investments. Financial, supplier, and product markets create incentives for businesses to provide products that society demands. These markets help ensure that scarce resources are used to improve society's welfare. Markets help allocate scarce resources to those organizations that can best transform them to create value.

Accounting **is an information system for the measurement and reporting of the transformation of resources into goods and services and the sale or transfer of these goods and services to customers.** Accounting uses the prices and costs of resources to measure value created by the transformation process and to trace the flow of resources through the transformation process. By tracing the flow of resources, managers and other decision makers can determine how efficiently and effectively resources are being used.

1   SELF-STUDY PROBLEM

John Bach owns a music store in which he sells and repairs musical instruments and sells sheet music. The following transactions occurred for Bach's Music Store during December 2004:

1. Sold $8,000 of musical instruments that cost the company $4,300.
2. Sold $1,400 of sheet music that cost the company $870.
3. The price of repair services provided during the month was $2,200.
4. Rent on the store for the month was $650.
5. The cost of supplies used during the month was $250.
6. The cost of advertising for the month was $300.
7. The cost of utilities for the month was $200.
8. Other miscellaneous costs for December were $180.

Required

A. Determine the profit earned by Bach's Music Store for December.
B. Explain how profit measures the value created by Bach's Music Store.

The solution to Self-Study Problem 1 appears at the end of the chapter.

THE STRUCTURE OF BUSINESS ORGANIZATIONS

OBJECTIVE 5

Identify business ownership structures and their advantages and disadvantages.

Many types of decisions are made in organizations. Accounting provides important information to make these decisions. For example, organizations require financial resources to buy other resources used to produce goods and services. Primary sources of financing for businesses are owners and creditors.

Business Ownership

Businesses may be classified into two categories: those that are distinct legal entities apart from their owners and those that are not distinct legal entities. **A** *corporation* **is** a legal entity with the right to enter into contracts; the right to own, buy, and sell property; and the right to sell stock. Resources are owned by the corporation rather than by individual owners.

Corporations may be very large or fairly small organizations. Small corporations often are managed by their owners. The owners of most large corporations do not manage their companies. Instead, they hire professional managers. These owners have the right to vote on certain major decisions, but they do not control the operations of their corporations on a day-to-day basis. One reason most large businesses are organized as corporations is that corporations typically have greater access to financial markets than other types of organizations.

A corporation may be owned by a large number of investors who purchase shares of stock issued by the corporation. **Each share of** *stock* **is a certificate of ownership that represents an equal share in the ownership of a corporation.** An investor who owns 10% of the shares of a corporation owns 10% of the company and has a right to 10% of the return available to stockholders. *Stockholders,* **or** *shareholders,* **are the owners of a corporation.**

Shares of stock often are traded in stock markets, such as the New York, London, and Tokyo stock exchanges, which are established specifically for this purpose. These markets facilitate the exchange of stock between buyers and sellers. Therefore, unlike other businesses, ownership in many corporations changes frequently as stockholders buy or sell shares of stock. Major corporations, such as **General Motors, Exxon,** or **IBM,** have received billions of dollars from stockholders.

Proprietorships and *partnerships* **are business organizations that do not have legal identities distinct from their owners. Proprietorships have only one owner; partnerships have more than one owner.** For most proprietorships and partnerships, owners also manage the business. Owners have a major stake in the business because often much of their personal wealth is invested in it. The amount of a proprietor's personal wealth and his or her ability to borrow limit the size of a proprietorship. If a proprietorship is profitable, profits earned by the proprietor can be reinvested, and the business can become fairly large.

Partnerships can include several partners; therefore, the money available to finance a partnership depends on the money available from all the partners. New partners can be added, making new money available to the business. While most partnerships are small, large businesses (with as many as a thousand or more owners) sometimes are organized as partnerships. The profit of most proprietorships and partnerships is not taxed. Instead, the profit is income for the owners, who pay income taxes on the profit as part of their personal income taxes.

INTERNATIONAL

Percentage of Companies and Volume of Sales by Type of Organization

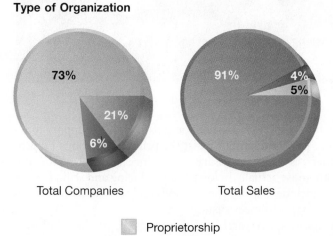

Total Companies	Total Sales
73%	91%
21%	4%
6%	5%

- ☐ Proprietorship
- ■ Partnership
- ☐ Corporation

(Data source: U.S. Census Bureau Web site (http://www.census.gov)

Management of Corporations

Exhibit 7 describes the organizational structure of a typical corporation. A **board of directors** oversees the decisions of management and is responsible for protecting the interests of stockholders. Normally, the board is appointed by management with the approval of stockholders. Top managers often serve on the board along with outside directors who are not part of the corporation's management. The **chairman of the board** often holds the position of **chief executive officer (CEO)** with the ultimate responsibility for the success of the business. The **president,** as **chief operating officer (COO),** is responsible for the day-to-day management of a corporation. In some cases, the president also may be the CEO. The company may appoint any number of **vice presidents,** who are responsible for various functions in the organization. The titles and roles of these managers will vary from corporation to corporation. Along with the CEO and the president, the vice presidents constitute the top management of a corporation. Together, they make planning decisions and develop company goals and policies.

Exhibit 7
Corporate Management Functions

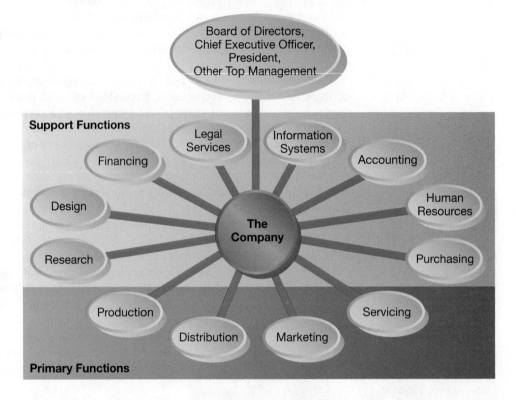

Functions performed within a corporation may be separated into support functions and primary functions. Support functions assist the primary functions by providing information and other resources necessary to produce and sell goods and services. Primary functions are those actually involved in producing and selling goods and services. These functions include distribution of goods and services to customers and servicing the goods and services to meet customer needs.

Among the support functions are research and development, product and production design, finance, legal services, accounting, purchasing, and human resources. The **chief financial officer (CFO)**, who also may be the **treasurer**, is responsible for obtaining financial resources and managing a corporation's cash. The **controller**, as the chief accounting officer, is responsible for accounting and financial reporting, developing and maintaining the accounting information system, and reporting to tax and regulatory authorities.

Primary functions involve production, distribution, sales, and service. **Plant managers** oversee production for specific product lines or geographical locations. These managers often have their own staffs at the divisional or plant level. For example, divisional or plant level controllers exist in many corporations. Research, design, and development staffs also exist at the divisional or plant level in some organizations.

Corporations may be organized by functions such as those described in Exhibit 7. Other corporations are organized primarily by region or product line. For example, multinational companies may be organized into North American, European, and Pacific divisions. Functional areas, such as development and production, report to regional or product managers. Many corporations are finding advantages in changing from a traditional organization structure to teams of managers working together on specific projects. Thus, the idea for a new product may be the responsibility of a team of employees from a company's functional areas, such as engineering, accounting, and marketing. Together, the team decides on a design for the product and on a production process to create efficiency and product quality.

Advantages of Corporations

A corporate form of organization has several advantages over proprietorships or partnerships. Corporations have **continuous lives** apart from those of their owners. If a proprietor or partner sells her or his share of a business or dies, the business ceases to exist as a legal entity. The new owner of the business must reestablish the business as a new legal entity. Most corporations, however, continue unchanged if current owners sell their stock, donate it to charity, give it to relatives, or otherwise dispose of their shares.

Shareholders normally are not liable personally for the debts of a corporation. This is a characteristic known as **limited liability**. If a corporation defaults on debt or enters bankruptcy, its owners may lose a portion or all of their investments in the company, but they are not obligated to use their personal wealth to repay creditors for losses the creditors incurred. In many cases, proprietors and partners are personally liable for the debts of their companies and can be required to use their personal wealth to repay their creditors.

Shareholders of most corporations do not manage the company. They elect members of the board of directors, who then hire **professional managers** to run the corporation. Investors can own part of a corporation or parts of many corporations without having to participate in the day-to-day decisions of running those companies. Many Americans own stock in corporations through personal investments and retirement plans, but they are not required to commit large amounts of their personal time to corporate concerns.

Shareholders cannot enter into contracts or agreements that are binding on a corporation unless they are managers or directors. Therefore, investors in a corporation do not have to be concerned about the abilities of other stockholders to make good business decisions. In contrast, bad decisions by one partner can result in the personal bankruptcy of all partners in a partnership. This problem arises because partners normally are in a mutual agency relationship. *Mutual agency* **permits a partner to enter into contracts and agreements that are binding on all members of a partnership.**

By selling shares to many investors, a corporation can obtain a large amount of financial resources. The **ability to raise large amounts of capital** permits corporations to become very large organizations. Thus, corporations can invest in plant facilities and undertake production activities that would be difficult for proprietorships or partnerships.

LEARNING NOTE

A partnership can be organized as a **limited liability partnership (LLP).** The LLP restricts the personal liability of each partner for obligations created by the company. Many professional service companies, particularly accounting and legal firms, are organized as LLPs. A business also can be organized as a **limited liability company (LLC).** An LLC combines certain advantages of a partnership and a corporation in that it combines the tax treatment of a partnership with the limited liability of corporations. While a corporation can have as few as one shareholder, an LLC usually must have at least two owners. Both LLPs and LLCs are separate legal entities from their owners.

Disadvantages of Corporations

There are several disadvantages to the corporate form of ownership. Most corporations must pay **taxes** on their incomes. Corporate taxes are separate from the taxes paid by shareholders on dividends received from the company. (Some corporations, however, especially smaller ones, are not taxed separately.) Another disadvantage is that corporations are **regulated** by various state and federal government agencies. These regulations require corporations to comply with many state and federal rules concerning business practices and reporting of financial information. Corporations must file many reports with government agencies and make public disclosure of their business activities. Compliance with these regulations is costly. Also, some of the **required disclosures** may be helpful to competitors. Partnerships and proprietorships are regulated also, but the degree of regulation normally is much less than for corporations.

Owners of corporations usually do not have access to information about the day-to-day activities of their companies. They depend on managers to make decisions that will increase the value of their investments. However, managers' personal interests sometimes conflict with the interests of stockholders. This problem produces a condition known as moral hazard. Moral hazard arises when one group, known as **agents** (such as managers), is responsible for serving the needs of another group, known as **principals** (such as investors). *Moral hazard* **is the condition that exists when agents have superior information to principals and are able to make decisions that favor their own interests over those of the principals.**

Without disclosure of reliable information, corporations would have difficulty in selling stock, and investors would be unable to determine whether managers were making decisions that increased stockholder value or were making decisions that took advantage of the stockholders. Accounting reports are major sources of information to help stockholders assess the performance of managers. For example, profit information helps owners evaluate how well managers have used owners' investments to earn returns for the owners. Moral hazard imposes costs on corporations because managers must report to stockholders and, generally, these reports are audited. **An audit verifies the reliability of reported information.**

The size of many corporations makes them **difficult to manage**. An individual manager cannot be involved directly with all the decisions made in operating a large organization. Top-level managers depend on low-level managers to make decisions and to keep them informed about a corporation's operations. This process is costly because coordination among managers may be difficult to achieve. Moral hazard also exists among managers and employees, not just between managers and investors. Corporate goals and policies provide guidance for manager decisions, but communicating goals and policies and providing incentives for managers to implement them often is difficult and expensive. Employees and low-level managers may not report reliable information about their activities to high-level managers if the information is not in their best interests. Multinational corporations, in particular, are complex and difficult to manage. Distant locations for facilities and differences in language and local custom can cause special problems.

The profits of corporations, except for those of small privately-owned ones, referred to as Subchapter S corporations, are taxed separately from taxes paid by the owners of the corporation. The federal government and most state governments impose a corporate income tax on the profits of corporations. This tax is paid by the corporation. In addition, amounts distributed to shareholders are taxed as part of their personal income. Thus, the profits of corporations often are subject to **double taxation**: taxation of the corporation and taxation of the shareholders.

Creditors

In addition to money provided by owners, businesses (and other organizations) may borrow money. Money may be obtained from banks and other financial institutions, or it may be borrowed from individual lenders. **A** *creditor* **is someone who loans financial resources to an organization.**

Most organizations depend on banks and similar institutions to lend them money. Corporations often borrow money from individuals or other companies. Exhibit 8 shows the amount of money several large corporations have received from owners and creditors. The amounts and proportions of financing from owners and creditors vary greatly across companies.

Creditors loan money to organizations to earn a return on their investments. They usually loan money for a specific period and are promised a specific rate of return on their investments. Usually, this is a fixed rate (say 10%). In contrast, owners invest for a nonspecific period (until they decide to sell their investments) and receive a return that depends on the profits earned by the business.

The success of a business determines whether creditors will receive the amount promised by the borrower. When a business fails to generate sufficient cash from selling

Exhibit 8
Sources of Financing for
Selected Corporations

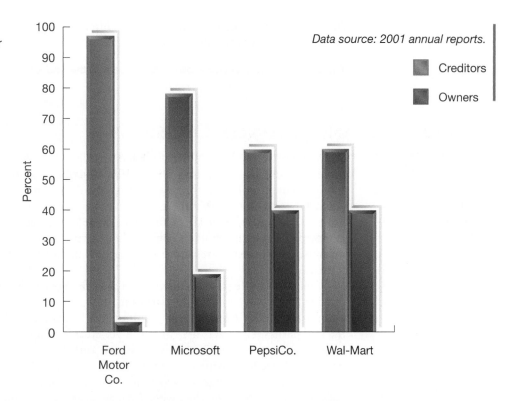

Data source: 2001 annual reports.

goods and services to pay for resources it consumes and to pay its creditors, the creditors may not receive the amount promised. Therefore, creditors estimate the probability that an organization will be able to repay debt and interest. Risk is a concern of both creditors and owners, and accounting information is key in evaluating the risk. Exhibit 9 illustrates the role of owners and creditors in providing financial resources for businesses.

Exhibit 9
Obtaining Financial
Resources

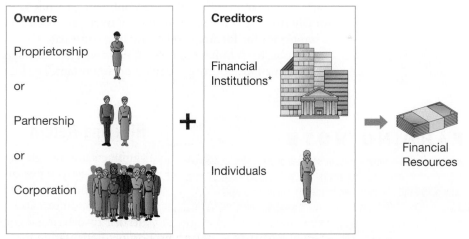

*The term "financial institutions" refers to banks, savings and loans, and similar companies.

2 **SELF-STUDY PROBLEM**   Hammer Hardware Company and **Home Depot** are both retail stores that sell tools, hardware, and household items. Hammer Hardware is owned by Harvey Hammer and is organized as a proprietorship. Home Depot is organized as a corporation and is owned by thousands of investors.

Required Why is the form of ownership different for these companies? What are the advantages and disadvantages of each form?

The solution to Self-Study Problem 2 appears at the end of the chapter.

ACCOUNTING AND BUSINESS DECISIONS

OBJECTIVE 6

Identify uses of accounting information for making decisions about corporations.

The value of accounting information is determined by how well it meets the needs of those who use it. Accounting information describes economic consequences of the transformation process. Information needs of decision makers arise from the many relationships that occur within the transformation process among an organization's stakeholders: managers, investors, suppliers, employees, customers, and government authorities. These stakeholders compete in markets for resources, or they regulate these markets. They exchange resources or services with an organization as part of its transformation process.

Contracts **are legal agreements for the exchange of resources and services.** They provide legal protection for the parties to an agreement if the terms of the agreement are not honored. Contract terms establish the rights and responsibilities of the contracting parties. Contracts are "give and get" relationships. Each party to the contract expects to receive something in exchange for something given. For example, a contract by an employee to provide labor to a company involves the giving of labor services by the employee in exchange for wages and benefits. Contracts with proprietorships and partnerships are between the owners/managers and other contracting parties. In contrast, because corporations are legal entities, contracts can be formed with the corporation as one of the contracting parties. Managers make contracts on behalf of corporations and their owners.

Contracts are enforceable only to the extent that contracting parties can determine whether the terms of the contract are being met. Assume that you sign a contract with a company that calls for you to invest $1,000 in the company and for the company to pay you 10% of the amount the company earns each year. Unless you have reliable information about the company's earnings, you cannot determine whether it is paying you the agreed amount. Therefore, you probably would not agree to the contract. Contracts require information that the contracting parties accept as reliable and sufficient for determining if the terms of the contract have been met. **Accounting information is important for forming and evaluating contracts.**

Exhibit 10 identifies examples of exchanges among stakeholders for which contracts and information about organizations are important. The following sections discuss these exchanges.

LEARNING NOTE

Products can be either goods or services or both. While often we talk about companies that sell goods, you should keep in mind how accounting is important to service companies also.

Risk and Return

Contracts are formed to identify rights and responsibilities. These rights and responsibilities establish how risk and return will be shared among contracting parties. Information about risk and return is needed to determine contract terms. Return is the amount a party to a contract expects as compensation for the exchange outlined in the contract. As noted earlier in this chapter, risk is uncertainty about an outcome; it results from uncertainty about the amount and timing of return. Exhibit 11 describes the returns of two investments (A and B) over several time periods. Which investment is riskier? Returns for investment A are relatively stable and predictable; they are growing at a steady rate. Returns for investment B are less predictable. Investment B is riskier than A, although it may produce higher returns over time than A.

Those who invest in a company expect to earn returns on their investments. At the same time, they must evaluate the risk inherent in investing in the company. What

Exhibit 10

Examples of Exchanges
Requiring Information

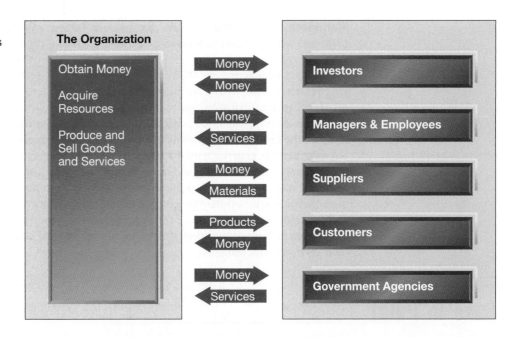

Exhibit 11

An Illustration of Risk
and Return

Time Period	Returns	
	Investment A	Investment B
1	$6	$10
2	6	12
3	7	7
4	7	3
5	8	8
6	8	11

should they earn if the company does well? What might happen if the company does poorly? Risk and return are related in most situations; investors expect to earn higher returns on riskier investments. The higher returns compensate them for accepting higher risk. However, actual returns may differ from expected returns, and so riskier investments may actually result in higher or lower returns than less risky investments. On average, however, higher return should be associated with greater risk; otherwise, investors will not participate in risky investments. Accounting information helps investors predict risk and return associated with investments. The following sections consider the risk and return evaluations made by those who contract with an organization.

Investors and Creditors. Investors and creditors contract with companies to provide financial resources in exchange for future returns. They need information to decide whether to invest in a company and how much to invest. **Accounting information helps investors evaluate the risk and return they can expect from their investments. Also, it helps them determine whether managers of companies they invest in are meeting the terms of their contracts.**

If a company does not earn sufficient profits, it may be unable to repay its creditors, and creditors can force a company to liquidate (sell all its noncash resources) to repay its debts. On the other hand, if a company is profitable, stockholders (investors) normally earn higher returns than creditors because stockholders have a right to share in a company's profits. Creditors receive only the amount of interest agreed to when debt is issued. Consequently, investors and creditors choose between risk and return.

Managers. Owners generally do not manage large corporations. Instead, they hire managers who operate the businesses for them. Managers contract with owners to provide management services in exchange for salaries and other compensation. Owners, or directors who represent them, need information to determine how well managers are performing and to reward managers when they do well. To provide incentives for managers to perform well, owners may offer managers bonuses when a company is profitable. **Accounting information provides a means for owners and managers to determine the amount of compensation managers will receive.**

Compensation arrangements also encourage managers to present their companies' performances in the best light. Often, compensation is linked to profits and other accounting information, giving managers incentives to report numbers that will maximize their compensation. The combination of management control over information and manager incentives to make their companies look good provides an ethical dilemma for managers. Sometimes, they must choose between the company's best interests and their own best interests.

Case In Point

http://ingram.
swlearning.com

Learn more about
Enron.

Moral Hazard—Mismanagement by Managers

In 2001, **Enron Corporation**, the seventh largest U.S. corporation at the time, declared bankruptcy after revealing that its profits had been overstated for several years and that it had failed to report large amounts of debt. The debt was used by the corporation to expand its business operations into new markets and products. Some of these new ventures resulted in losses that were not properly reported by the corporation's management. When revealed, these losses made it difficult for the corporation to obtain additional financing, and it was unable to meet its debt obligations. As a result of these events, the market value of the corporation decreased dramatically, creating losses for many investors. Many employees lost their jobs and retirement savings, and many creditors were unable to collect amounts owed them.

Enron's investors and creditors sued the company's managers, claiming that they had been misled by information reported by the managers. The managers had earned high salaries and other compensation associated with the high profitability and growth they reported for the company. Investors and creditors, and many members of Congress who investigated the collapse of Enron, argued that managers had profited by operating the business for personal gain rather than for the benefit of the company's owners.

Decisions by managers have a direct effect on the risk and return of those who contract with a company. Managers decide which resources to acquire, when to acquire them, and how much to pay for them.

Each investment in a resource involves decisions about the risk and return associated with the investment. An organization is a portfolio (collection) of individual resources. In combination, the risks and returns on the investments in these resources help determine the risk and return of the organization as a whole. One task of management is to select a portfolio of resources that will yield a desired amount of return at a level of risk that managers and owners find acceptable. Investments in proven technology and established products generally are less risky than investments in new technology or products. Investments in resources in some countries are riskier than those in other countries because of those countries' political and economic environments. **Accounting information is useful for identifying the types and locations of an organization's resources.**

A major purpose of accounting is to measure costs associated with the flow of resources through the transformation process. Accounting also measures resources obtained from selling goods and services. The profits earned by a corporation are a major determinant of risk and return. **Information about the results of the operations of a business is used to estimate, compare, and manage companies' risks and returns.**

Employees. Employees have a major effect on a company's risk and return. Wages and quality of work directly affect product quality, sales, costs, and profits. Companies evaluate the cost and productivity of their employees. They compare employee performance with management expectations, examine changes over time, and compare different divisions with each other. **Accounting information helps managers assess employee performance.**

Employees negotiate for wages, benefits, and job security. Compensation is affected by a company's performance and financial condition. Labor unions and other employee groups use accounting information to evaluate a company's ability to compensate its employees. Like other contracting parties, employees evaluate risk and return in an employment relationship. If a company does well, employees expect to be rewarded. If it does poorly, they may face layoffs, wage and benefit cuts, and loss of jobs. **Accounting information helps employees assess the risk and return of their employment contracts.**

Suppliers. An organization purchases materials, merchandise, and other resources from suppliers. These resources are a major cost for most companies. Careful negotiation of prices, credit, and delivery schedules between management and suppliers is required. If a company cannot obtain quality materials when they are needed, it may incur major losses as a result of idle production, waste, lost sales, and dissatisfied customers. If a supplier goes out of business or cannot fulfill its commitments, a company may have difficulty obtaining needed resources. **Accounting information helps companies evaluate the abilities of their suppliers to meet their resource needs.**

Suppliers often sell resources to companies on credit. These suppliers are creditors who are financing the sale of resources to a company in anticipation of future payments. Usually, these loans are for short periods (30 to 60 days), although longer financing sometimes is arranged. When a company is not profitable, its suppliers may have difficulty collecting the amounts owed them. Therefore, suppliers evaluate the risk they are taking in selling on credit to other companies. **Suppliers often use accounting information about their customers to evaluate the risk of a buyer not being able to pay for goods and services acquired.**

Customers. A company is a supplier to its customers. Thus, it evaluates customers in the same way it is evaluated by suppliers. Managers decide the terms of sales by evaluating the risk and return associated with the sales. Riskier customers normally receive less favorable terms. For example, a customer with good credit can purchase a house, car, appliances, and other goods on more favorable terms than can a customer with bad credit.

Customers' decisions to buy products often are affected by their perception of quality and dependability, as well as price. These decisions also may depend on the financial reputation of the seller. Will the company be in business in the future when maintenance, repair, or replacement is needed? Will it be able to honor warranties? Are its profits sufficient to invest in new technology and maintain quality products? **Accounting information is used to assess the risks of buying from specific companies and selling to specific customers.**

Government Agencies. Organizations are required to provide information to government agencies. Governments require businesses to purchase licenses for selling goods and services and to pay fees and taxes for various government services. Often these amounts are determined by the amount of sales or the profitability of an organization. Governments collect information about organizations as a basis for economic forecasts and planning at the local, state, and national levels. Businesses are required to report information to state and federal authorities that regulate business activities to ensure fair trade, fair treatment of employees, and fair disclosure to investors.

Businesses report information to taxing authorities at various levels of government. Reports are required in filing sales, property, payroll, excise, and income taxes. The amount of these taxes is determined by a company's sales, the costs it incurs, and amounts paid to employees. **Government agencies use accounting information to make taxation and regulatory decisions.**

THE REGULATORY ENVIRONMENT OF ACCOUNTING

OBJECTIVE 7

Explain the purpose and importance of accounting regulations.

Accounting information prepared for use by external decision makers is financial accounting information. *Financial accounting* **is the process of preparing, reporting, and interpreting accounting information that is provided to external decision makers.** It is a primary source of information for investors and creditors. Thus, it is very important to the organization when it wants to obtain resources from those external decision makers. It also may affect the decisions of suppliers, customers, and employees. Because of concerns about information reliability and moral hazard, managers of major corporations prepare financial accounting information according to specific rules called *generally accepted accounting principles* (GAAP). *GAAP* **are standards developed by professional accounting organizations to identify appropriate accounting and reporting procedures.** GAAP establish minimum disclosure requirements and increase the comparability of information from one period to the next and among different companies.

This textbook emphasizes financial accounting for corporations. Moral hazard resulting from the separation of owners and managers has led to the creation of a strong regulatory environment for corporations. This environment oversees the development of accounting and reporting requirements for corporations. We will examine this environment and the resulting requirements.

LEARNING NOTE

GAAP apply only to information prepared for use by external decision makers. Because managers control information available inside an organization, accounting standards such as GAAP are not necessary for this information.

Financial accounting usually is distinguished from managerial accounting. *Managerial* **(or** *management***)** *accounting* **is the process of preparing, reporting, and interpreting accounting information that is provided to internal decision makers.** Because managers have control over the information they use internally, this information does not have to be prepared according to GAAP. Accounting information reported by managers to owners and other external decision makers is the subject of financial accounting. It is important to keep in mind, however, that this information also is used by managers. Although managers have access to information that extends beyond that reported to external decision makers, internal and external decisions are related. Therefore, this book will consider internal and external decisions that rely on financial accounting information.

LEARNING NOTE

Managers, as internal decision makers, use financial accounting information to evaluate the performance of their companies. Also, they are concerned about the effect of financial accounting information on the decisions of the other stakeholders because these decisions can affect their companies.

Accounting information reported by corporations to investors must be audited. **An** *audit* **is a detailed examination of an organization's financial reports.** It includes an examination of the information system used to prepare the reports and involves an examination of control procedures organizations use to help ensure the accuracy of accounting information. The purpose of an audit is to evaluate whether information reported to external decision makers is a **fair presentation** of an organization's economic activities. Standards (GAAP) for the preparation and reporting of information help ensure the reliability of accounting information. The auditors, who are independent **certified public accountants (CPAs)**, examine this information to confirm that it is prepared according to GAAP. To be a CPA, a person must pass a qualifying exam and meet education and experience requirements. CPAs are independent of the companies they audit because they are not

http://ingram.
swlearning.com

Learn more about the
CPA exam.

company employees. Rather, they work for an accounting firm that is hired by the company's owners to perform the audit. In the case of a corporation, it is the board of directors, with the approval of stockholders, that hires the auditor. Also, CPAs should have no vested interests in the companies that might bias their audits.

Many corporations must report audited financial accounting information to governmental agencies. Corporations whose stock is traded publicly in the United States report to the **Securities and Exchange Commission (SEC)**. This agency examines corporate financial reports to verify their conformance with GAAP and SEC requirements. If the SEC believes a company's reports have not been prepared in conformance with GAAP, it can refer the company to the Justice Department for criminal and civil charges. In addition, the corporation's auditors can be prosecuted if they fail to meet their responsibilities for ensuring that a corporation's reports are a fair representation of its economic activities.

LEARNING NOTE

GAAP apply to all business organizations. As long as accounting information produced by the business is used for internal purposes only, the company's managers can elect whether or not that information complies with GAAP. Conformity with GAAP is required for information produced for external users, such as creditors. Many privately-owned businesses are audited because they are required to provide accounting information to banks and other financial institutions that lend money to the businesses.

Case In Point

http://ingram.
swlearning.com

Learn more about auditor responsibilities.

Auditor Responsibility

Enron Corporation's audit firm, **Andersen**, was investigated for its role in the misstatement of Enron's financial information. The audit firm admitted that it made mistakes in the audit but argued that Enron's managers had failed to report fully to the auditors about its questionable business activities. Andersen also was charged by the Federal government with destroying information that would have assisted the government in its investigation of Enron's activities. In addition, this industry leader can no longer perform SEC audits. Consequently, Andersen lost a major portion of its business as former clients awarded their audits to other audit firms and as many Andersen employees left the firm.

Critics also questioned Andersen's independence in the audit because the firm earned large consulting fees from Enron. The critics argued that Andersen did not press Enron for proper disclosure of its business activities for fear that it would lose Enron as a client, thereby losing the consulting fees in addition to its audit fees. It is important that audit firms be *perceived* as being independent of their clients, in addition to actually *being* independent. Auditors must continuously assess their independence.

Financial accounting is critical for the operations of a market economy. **Full and fair disclosure** of business activities is necessary for stakeholders to evaluate the returns and risks they anticipate from investing in and contracting with business organizations. **Capital markets**, markets in which corporations obtain financing from investors, in particular, require information that permits investors to assess the risks and returns of their investments. If that information is not available or is unreliable, investors are unable to make good decisions. **Without reliable information about companies' business activities, investors cannot determine which companies are most efficient and effective and are making the best use of resources.** Consequently, resources may be allocated to less efficient and effective companies, resulting in a loss of value for society.

Without good information, contracts cannot be evaluated, and markets cannot function properly. Consequently, accounting plays a critical role in our society. For our society to continue to prosper, it is essential that those who make decisions about resource allocations understand accounting information and how to use that information to evaluate business activities. They need to understand how accounting information is created and the limitations inherent in this information. Failure to understand accounting properly is likely to lead to poor decisions and unsatisfactory economic outcomes.

This book will help you understand why accounting information is important, how this information is produced, and how you can use this information to make good business decisions. It will help you learn to evaluate business activities and to determine which companies are operating most efficiently and effectively. It will help you contribute to improving our society by becoming an informed participant in our market economy.

THE IMPORTANCE OF ETHICS

OBJECTIVE 8

Explain why ethics are important for business and accounting.

Ethics are important in business organizations. Ethics involve living by the norms and rules of society. In business, those norms and rules identify appropriate behavior for managers, employees, investors, and other stakeholders. Keeping their investors and other stakeholders fully informed about their business activities is an important ethical norm for managers. Managers who conceal their activities or who misrepresent those activities make it difficult for stakeholders to assess how well a business is performing. Overstating profits, for example, may result in investors allocating more resources to a company than actual results would justify. This misallocation results in a loss of value to society and often leads to financial harm for those who use this information.

Ethical behavior is particularly important for accounting because the reliability of accounting information depends on the honesty of those who prepare, report, and audit this information. Managers may make decisions that benefit themselves at a cost to investors or other stakeholders. If they then attempt to conceal these decisions by reporting incorrect information, that information is not an accurate description of the economic activities of a business. If employees steal money or other resources from a business and the thefts are not detected, the company's accounting information also will not properly reflect the company's economic situation. If those who audit a company do not ensure that reported information is a fair representation of the company's business activities, those who rely on the information are likely to be disadvantaged.

Those who contract with businesses must consider the ethics of those who manage them. Managers who are willing to bend rules or operate outside of accepted norms are likely to be untrustworthy. An important role of accounting is to evaluate whether appropriate rules are being followed in accounting for reporting business activities. Failure to follow these rules can result in significant economic consequences, as evidenced by the collapse of Enron Corporation. Generally accepted accounting principles and other accounting and auditing rules have been created to help ensure that companies fairly report their business activities. In addition, corporations and other organizations are required to maintain elaborate systems of controls to make it difficult for managers and employees to engage in unethical behavior or misrepresent business activities. We examine ethical issues and controls throughout this book as we consider proper accounting rules and procedures.

3 SELF-STUDY PROBLEM

R. Floorshine is a manufacturer of shoes. The company operates as a corporation and has issued shares of stock to its owners and debt to creditors. It has purchased and leased buildings and equipment. It purchases materials on short-term credit and converts the materials into shoes. The shoes are sold to retail stores, also on a short-term credit arrangement.

Required Identify the primary exchanges and contracts between the company and its stakeholders. Describe the primary information needs associated with these exchanges and contracts.

The solution to Self-Study Problem 3 appears at the end of the chapter.

Appendix | A SHORT INTRODUCTION TO EXCEL

SPREADSHEET

This introduction summarizes some of the primary operations and functions of a spreadsheet. It is intended to get you started if you have not had previous experience with Excel. There are many operations and functions in addition to those mentioned here.

Identifying and Selecting Cells

A spreadsheet consists of rows and columns. Rows are identified by numbers, and columns are identified by letters. An intersection of a row and column is a cell. A cell is identified by the column letter and row number that intersect at that cell.

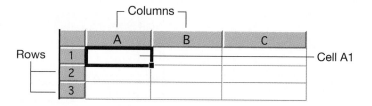

To select a cell, click on the cell using the left mouse button. A cell must be selected before you can enter data or format the cell. Enter data by typing numbers, words, or characters. Enter numbers without commas. Commas can be added using formatting procedures described later. An entire row or column can be selected by clicking on the row or column header. The row header is the leftmost cell in a row that contains the row number. A column header is the topmost cell in a column that contains the cell letter. A group of neighboring cells can be selected by clicking with the left mouse button on the cell in the upper, left corner of the group, then dragging the cursor over all the cells to be selected.

Referencing and Mathematical Operations

The contents of one or more cells can be referenced in another cell. To reference a cell, enter the equal sign followed by the cell being referenced. For example, entering =A1 in cell B1 will copy the contents of cell A1 in cell B1. If the contents of cell A1 are changed, these changes also will appear in cell B1. A common use of cell referencing is to calculate totals from data in a series of cells. For example, the following spreadsheet contains sales data for the first three months of a year. The total appears in cell B5. To calculate the total, you would enter a formula in cell B5. The formula would be =B2+B3+B4.

	A	B
1		Sales
2	January	3,457.38
3	February	3,892.90
4	March	3,204.07
5	Total	10,554.35

Normal mathematical operations can be entered in a cell:

=B2+B3 adds the contents of cells B2 and B3.
=B2−B3 subtracts the contents of cell B3 from cell B2.
=B2*B3 multiplies the contents of cell B2 by the contents of cell B3.
=B2/B3 divides the contents of cell B2 by the contents of cell B3.
=B2^B3 raises the number in cell B2 to the power of the number in cell B3.

Copying Cell Contents

The contents (including a formula) can be copied from one cell or group of cells to another cell or group of cells. To copy the contents, select the cells containing the data to be copied and click on Edit/Copy. Then select the cell you want to copy to (or the upper, left cell of a group of cells) and click Edit/Paste.

The contents of a cell also can be copied to a neighboring cell using a shortcut procedure. In the following example, we want to copy the contents of cell B4 to cell C4. Cell B4 contains the formula =B2+B3. To copy the contents, we select cell B4 and drag the cursor over the box in the lower, right corner of cell B4. The cursor changes shape and appears as crosshairs (+). If we click on the left mouse button while the cursor is in this shape, we can drag the contents of cell B4 to cell C4. The formula =B2+B3 is copied to cell C4, except that the references are automatically adjusted for the new column, and the formula appears as =C2+C3.

	A	B	C
1		Cash	Merchandise
2	Store 1	1,543.02	16,794.23
3	Store 2	4,587.45	24,586.50
4	Total	6,130.47	

Box

When you enter a formula in a cell, such as =B2+B3, the cell addresses are relative addresses. When the formula is copied to another cell, the relative addresses change. Copying the contents of cell B4 above to cell C4 results in an adjustment in the formula so that =B2+B3 is changed to =C2+C3. You can also enter absolute addresses. An absolute address results from entering a dollar sign ($) before a cell address. For example, if you enter =$B2+$B3 in cell B4 and then copy cell B4 to cell C4, the formula in C4 remains =$B2+$B3. You can use absolute addresses for the column (=$B2), the row (=B$2) or both (=$B$2).

Changing Column Widths

You can make a column wider or narrower using the Format/Column/Width menu. A simpler approach is to move the cursor to the right-hand side of the column header of the column you wish to adjust. The cursor changes to appear as ↔. Click and drag the cursor to the right or left to adjust the column width. The same procedure can be used for row height adjustments.

Menus

The top of an Excel spreadsheet contains menus. A brief description of the menu items you are likely to use on a regular basis follows.

File. Use the File menu to open a **New** spreadsheet, to **Open** an existing spreadsheet, to **Save** a spreadsheet, to **Print** a spreadsheet, and to **Close** the Excel program.

Edit. Use the Edit menu to **Delete** a row, column, or cell. Select the row, column, or cell and click Edit/Delete. You can delete the contents of a particular cell by selecting the cell and pressing the Backspace or Delete key.

View. Use the View menu to select which Toolbars appear on the spreadsheet. The Header and Footer command permits you to add titles and comments to spreadsheets that will appear on printed output. The Zoom command allows spreadsheets to be resized as they appear on the monitor to make them easier to see. This command does not affect printed output.

Insert. Use the Insert menu to insert **Rows, Columns,** and **Cells**. To enter a new row, select the row *below* the row you wish to add and click on Insert/Row. To enter a new column, select the column to the *left* of the column you want to add and click on Insert/Column. To enter a new cell, click on the cell where you want to add a new cell and click on Insert/Cell. A dialog box will ask whether you want the existing cell moved to the right or down. When you enter a new cell, all existing cells to the right or below the entered cell will be moved to make room for the new cell.

Format. Use the Format menu to format **Cells**. Select the cells and click on Format/Cells. A dialog box provides options. The **Number** tab provides various formatting options. The **Alignment** tab provides options for how numbers or text will be aligned. The Wrap text box can be checked (click on the box) to allow for more than one line of text to appear in a particular cell.

Tools. Use the Tools menu to check your **Spelling**.

Data. Use the Data menu to **Sort** data. To sort, select all the columns in the spreadsheet and click Data/Sort. A dialog box lets you select the column or columns you want to use to sort the data.

Help. Use the Help menu to get additional directions about using Excel. Click on Help/Contents and Index. Select a topic from the **Contents** tab or click on the **Index** tab. Type the keyword for an item to get additional information and click on the Display button.

Buttons

Several of the buttons under the menu are particularly useful. The identity of each button and its use are described below.

Save. Click to save your spreadsheet. **Save your work often.**

Copy. Copies the contents of a selected cell or group of cells.

Paste. Pastes the contents of a copied cell or group of cells into a selected cell or group.

Format Painter. Copies the format of a selected cell into another cell or group of cells. Select the cell with the format to be copied and click the button. Then click on the cell or click and drag over the cells where the format will be copied.

Σ **AutoSum.** Select a cell to contain the sum of a neighboring set of cells (above or to the left of the selected cell). For example, we want to sum the contents of cells E10 and E11 into cell E12. Select cell E12 and click on the AutoSum button. The =Sum formula appears in cell E12 as shown below. You can change the cells to be included in the sum by clicking on the top cell to be included and dragging the cursor over the cells to be added as part of the sum.

Once the sum formula is correct, click on the checkmark in the selection box at the top of the spreadsheet:

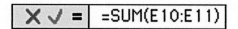

Click on the green checkmark to accept the cell contents. Click on the red X to remove the cell contents.

B *I* <u>U</u> **Format.** Select a cell or group of cells and click on B for bold, I for italics, and U for underline.

Align. Select a cell or group of cells and click on a button to align the cell contents to the left, center, or right of the cell.

Merge and Center. Select two or more neighboring cells in a row and click on the button to merge the cells into a single cell and center the cell contents. For example, the caption (The Book Wermz) in the following example was created by selecting cells B1 and C1 and clicking on the Merge and Center button.

	A	B	C
1		The Book Wermz	
2	Store 1	1,543.0	Merchandise
3	January	4,528.23	145,360.98

Number Formatting. Select a cell or group of cells and click on a button to include a dollar sign in the cell(s), to convert from decimals to percentages, or to add comma separators between thousands' digits in numbers.

Decimal Places. Select a cell or group of cells and click on a button to increase or decrease the number of decimal places showing in the cell(s).

Indent. Select a cell or group of cells and click on a button to indent the cell contents or to remove the indentation.

Borders. Select a cell or group of cells and click on the down arrow. Select the type of border you want for the cell(s) from the options provided. If the option you want is already showing on the button, click on the button to select that option.

REVIEW

SUMMARY of IMPORTANT CONCEPTS

1. The accounting process provides information about business activities to help decision makers allocate scarce resources.
   a. Accounting measures profits created by a business as the dollar amount of resources created from selling goods and services minus the dollar amount of resources consumed in producing and making the goods and services available to customers.
   b. Accounting helps decision makers determine the risk and return they should anticipate from a business investment or activity.

2. Organizations serve the needs of society by providing a means for people to work together to accomplish their goals.
   a. Businesses operate as merchandising, manufacturing, and service companies. Other organizations, like governments and nonprofit organizations, are nonbusiness organizations.
   b. All organizations benefit society by transforming resources from one form to another form that is more valuable in meeting the needs of people.

3. Businesses sell their products and acquire resources in competitive markets.
   a. Markets provide a way for people to express their perceptions of the value of goods and services by the products they purchase and the prices they pay. Markets allocate resources to those companies and activities that market participants believe best meet their needs.
   b. Value created by a business is measured by the difference between the dollar amount of resources created from selling goods and services and the dollar amount of resources consumed in producing and making the goods and services available to customers.

4. Owners invest in a business to receive a return on their investments from business profits. Businesses that operate effectively and efficiently normally will earn higher profits.
   a. Businesses that are not profitable will have difficulty attracting investors and will be forced to change their behavior or to go out of business.

    b.   Markets make financial and other scarce resources available to organizations that can best transform them to maximize their value for society.

5. Businesses operate as corporations, proprietorships, and partnerships.
    a.   Corporations can obtain large amounts of capital by selling stock to many investors.
    b.   Owners of corporations usually hire professional managers to run their businesses. They depend on these managers to run the business for the benefit of owners and to report reliable information about their business activities.

6. Accounting information is used in corporations and other organizations to create and evaluate contracts and other agreements between a company and its stakeholders.
    a.   Accounting information helps investors and creditors assess the return and risk associated with their investments and loans.
    b.   Accounting information is useful for determining management compensation, determining an organization's resources, and evaluating results of its operating activities.
    c.   Accounting information helps managers evaluate employee performance and helps employees evaluate the risk and return of their employment contracts.
    d.   Accounting information helps companies evaluate their suppliers and helps customers evaluate the companies from which they make purchases.
    e.   Accounting information helps government agencies make taxation and regulatory decisions.

7. Because investors and other external stakeholders have limited access to business information, information reported to external parties is regulated.
    a.   Companies must prepare financial accounting information in conformity with generally accepted accounting standards.
    b.   This information is audited by an independent accountant to ensure that it fairly represents a company's business activities.
    c.   Reliable accounting information is essential for the proper operation of markets that depend on the information to determine how to allocate resources.

8. Ethical behavior is important to ensure that businesses are managed properly and that accounting information is reliable. Accounting rules and controls have been created to help monitor and enforce ethical behavior.

DEFINE

TERMS and CONCEPTS DEFINED in this CHAPTER

accounting (F10)
audit (F20)
business organization (F6)
contracts (F16)
corporation (F10)
creditor (F14)
effective business (F9)
efficient business (F9)
financial accounting (F20)
generally accepted accounting principles
  (GAAP) (F20)
governmental and nonprofit organizations
  (F6)
information (F3)
management accounting (F20)
managerial accounting (F20)
manufacturing companies (F6)

market (F7)
merchandising companies (F5)
moral hazard (F14)
mutual agency (F13)
organization (F5)
partnerships (F11)
profit (F8)
proprietorships (F11)
retail companies (F5)
return on investment (ROI) (F9)
risk (F5)
service companies (F6)
shareholders (F11)
stakeholders (F5)
stock (F11)
stockholders (F11)

SELF-STUDY PROBLEM SOLUTIONS

SSP1-1   A.

Bach's Music Store
Profit Earned
For December 2004

Resources created from selling goods and services:		
Musical instruments	$8,000	
Sheet music	1,400	
Repair of instruments	2,200	
Total resources created		$11,600
Resources consumed:		
Cost of instruments sold	4,300	
Cost of sheet music sold	870	
Rent	650	
Supplies used	250	
Advertising	300	
Utilities	200	
Miscellaneous	180	
Total resources consumed		6,750
Profit		$ 4,850

B. The value created by a transformation of resources is the difference between the total price of the goods and services sold and the total cost of the resources consumed in producing these goods and services. This difference is profit for the seller.

SSP1-2   Hammer Hardware is owned and managed by Harvey Hammer. As a small company, Hammer Hardware does not need access to large amounts of capital. Harvey is probably more interested in maintaining control of his company rather than having others invest in it. As a proprietorship, Harvey has total control of the business. All company profits belong to him. A primary disadvantage of the proprietorship is that Harvey is personally liable for all of the company's obligations. He is responsible for paying the company's debts, even if they require use of his personal resources.

Home Depot is a large corporation. To obtain the financial resources the company needs, it sells stock to a large number of investors. These investors expect a return from their investments but have no interest in managing the company. Instead, they hire professional managers to run the company for them. Corporations permit access to large amounts of capital. Also, individual owners are not responsible for the corporation's debt, thus reducing the risk of ownership. A primary disadvantage of corporations is that owners have little access to information about the company. They depend on managers to run the business for the benefit of owners and to provide reliable information about their business activities.

SSP1-3   A. **Exchanges and contracts between managers, owners, and creditors:** Owners and creditors exchange money with Floorshine for the right to receive cash in the future from the company. Contracts exist among managers, owners, and creditors. Managers contract with owners and creditors for money to acquire resources that will generate profits for the company and to employ the resources effectively and efficiently. Managers expect to be rewarded for their effectiveness and efficiency, and owners and creditors expect a fair return on their investments. These contracting parties need information to assess how well managers have performed and to determine how much cash from the company's operations should be distributed to each party. Managers, owners, and creditors decide whether the terms of contracts are being met. Owners hire independent auditors (CPAs) to examine the financial information provided by managers to owners and creditors to ensure its reliability.

B. **Exchanges and contracts between suppliers and managers:** Suppliers exchange goods and services with the company for the right to receive cash. Contracts between suppliers and managers require information to determine that the company receives the correct types and quantities of goods and services at the appropriate times. Also, information is needed to demonstrate that the company has made timely payments for these goods and services.

C. **Exchanges and contracts between employees and managers:** Employees exchange labor services with the company for wages and benefits. Contracts between employees and managers describe the payments, benefits, and rights employees have negotiated with managers. Information is needed to demonstrate that labor services have been provided and employees have been treated fairly. The demands of employees for future wages and benefits depend, in part, on the profitability of the company. Employees and managers need information about the performance of the company to negotiate future contracts.

D. **Exchanges and contracts between customers and managers:** Customers exchange cash for goods and services provided by the company. Customers, such as retail stores, may receive the goods and pay for them later, say within 30 or 60 days. Managers expect to receive the payments when they are due. Contracts between customers and managers call for the delivery of goods to customers and payment to the company. Customers decide whether to continue to purchase the company's goods. The quality and costs of the goods and future prospects for obtaining the goods when needed are relevant pieces of information. Information about the payment history of customers helps managers decide whether to continue to extend credit to customers.

E. **Exchanges and contracts between government agencies and managers:** Government agencies monitor companies to determine if they are engaged in fair trade and labor practices. Managers provide information to demonstrate that the company is conforming to government regulations. Governments provide services to companies in the form of police and fire protection, utilities, sanitation, and streets and roads. Companies pay taxes and fees for these services. Information is required to verify that appropriate amounts of taxes and fees are being paid.

Thinking Beyond the Question

What do we need to know to start a business?

The chapter introduction asked you to consider what you would need to know in order to start a company. This chapter identified several important considerations. How would your answer to this question differ if you were starting a service business or a nonprofit service organization as opposed to a retail business?

QUESTIONS

Q1-1
Obj. 1

What is the purpose of accounting? How does accounting accomplish that purpose?

Q1-2
Obj. 1

How can accounting information help investors understand risk?

Q1-3
Obj. 2

How does the purpose of merchandising, manufacturing, and service companies differ? How do they each create value?

Q1-4
Obj. 2
List an example of each of the following types of organization. Describe how each type of organization differs from each of the others.
  a. Merchandising
  b. Manufacturing
  c. Service
  d. Governmental
  e. Nonprofit

Q1-5
Obj. 3
Sandy Dune overheard some friends from your accounting class discussing the "transformation of resources." She is curious about what this term means and how it applies to organizations and accounting. Explain to Sandy your understanding of the transformation of resources and why it is an important concept in accounting.

Q1-6
Obj. 3
Accounting is an information system that measures and reports the value created when a company transforms resources. Does an accounting system create value? If so, how? If not, why do companies have them?

Q1-7
Obj. 4
Phillip invested $3,000 in a business at the beginning of the year. By the end of the year, the value of this investment had risen to $4,100. Near year-end, the business sent Phillip a check for $2,000. Describe the difference between a return *on* investment and a return *of* investment. What portion of the $2,000 is return on investment and what portion is return of investment?

Q1-8
Obj. 4
How are effectiveness, efficiency, return on investment, and accounting interrelated? Be specific.

Q1-9
Obj. 6
What is a contract, and why are contracts important for business organizations?

Q1-10
Obj. 6
What is meant by risk, and why is it an important concept for decision makers to understand? What is the relationship between risk and accounting?

Q1-11
Obj. 6
Your friend is puzzled that the topic of contracts has come up in your accounting class. Says he, "Contracts are the business of lawyers, not accountants. Why are we studying contracts in an accounting class?" Educate your friend.

Q1-12
Obj. 6
Your uncle tells you that risk is to be avoided when considering potential investments. In fact, he believes the government should ban risky investments to protect the public. Do you agree with your uncle? Why or why not?

Q1-13
Obj. 6
It is often said that there exists a risk-return tradeoff. That is, to obtain a higher return, one must be willing to accept higher risk. If one wishes to incur little risk, one must be willing to accept a smaller return. What evidence of this do you observe in the world around you, either in investments or other aspects of life?

Q1-14
Obj. 6
Why do owners invest in businesses even though such an investment is more risky than investing in U.S. Savings Bonds? If you had $3,000 to invest, how would you decide whether to invest it in businesses or whether to invest it in U.S. Savings Bonds?

Q1-15
Objs. 6, 7
What is the interrelationship among the concepts of risk, moral hazard (when setting executive compensation), and generally accepted accounting principles?

Q1-16
Obj. 7
How does an audit increase the credibility of financial statements?

Q1-17
Obj. 7
An accounting classmate notes that adherence to GAAP is not required for managerial accounting reports. She observes, "If it's so important for financial accounting, it seems reasonable that it would also be useful for managerial reporting." Explain to her why it's more important that financial accounting reports adhere to GAAP than it is for managerial accounting reports to do so. In what ways is managerial accounting different from financial accounting?

EXERCISES

If your instructor is using Personal Trainer in this course, you may complete online the assignments identified by P_T.

E1-1 Write a short definition for each of the terms listed in the *Terms and Concepts Defined in This Chapter* section.

E1-2
Obj. 1

Assume you have a friend, Edwina Polinder, who has no knowledge of accounting. Draft a short memo to Edwina that will help her understand the purpose of accounting.

DATE: (today's date)
TO: Edwina Polinder
FROM: (your name)
SUBJECT: Inquiry about accounting
(your response)

E1-3
Objs. 1, 6

Wilma Borrelli is a stockholder of Essex International, a major supplier of building materials. Wilma received information that Essex sustained a large loss during the most recent quarter and is expecting bigger losses during the coming quarter. How might this information affect those who contract with Essex?

E1-4
Obj. 2
P_T

Match the type of organization with the characteristics and examples provided below:

Type of organization:
1. Merchandising (or retail) companies
2. Manufacturing companies
3. Service companies
4. Governmental and nonprofit organizations

Characteristics and examples:
a. Provide goods or services without the intent of making a profit. Examples include the **IRS** and the **United Way**.
b. Produce goods that are sold to consumers or to merchandising companies. Examples include **Ford Motor Company** and **PepsiCo**.
c. Sell to consumers goods that are produced by other companies. Examples include **Wal-Mart** and **Sears**.
d. Sell services rather than goods. Examples include **H&R Block** and **Delta Air Lines**.

E1-5
Obj. 3
P_T

Leonardo has started a small business making sundials. The following transactions occurred for the business during a recent period. How much profit did the company earn for this period?

Sales to customers	$970
Rent for the period	450
Supplies used during the period	225
Wages for the period	180

E1-6
Obj. 3
P_T

Soft Light Company produces specialty lamps and sells them to retail stores. During the latest year, the company sold 40,000 lamps at an average price of $70 per lamp. The production and distribution costs per lamp were $25, on average. Other costs for the year were $1,200,000 for management salaries and facilities. Total investment in the company is $3,000,000. How much profit did Soft Light earn for the year? Describe the steps you went through to get your answer.

E1-7
Obj. 3
P_T

Fashion Threads Company uses the following four steps to make a particular pair of cotton slacks:

a. Cotton is planted, grown, harvested, and shipped to a textile manufacturer. The cost to produce the cotton associated with the slacks is $5. This amount of cotton is sold to the manufacturer for $5.50.
b. Raw cotton is processed into cotton fabric. The cost of producing the fabric for the slacks, including the cost of the raw cotton, is $13.25. This fabric is sold to a garment manufacturer for $17.
c. Cotton fabric is cut and sewn to produce a pair of slacks. The cost of making the slacks, including the cost of the fabric, is $25. The slacks are sold to a retailer for $30.
d. The cost to the retailer of making the slacks available for sale, including the cost of the slacks, is $34. The retailer sells the slacks for $56.

(Continued)

Use Exhibits 5 and 6 to help you answer the following questions. How much profit is earned at each step in the production and selling process? How much total profit is earned by those involved in making and selling the slacks? Why are customers willing to pay the amounts involved in this process?

E1-8
Obj. 3
P/T

Alexander makes professional baseball gloves by hand. He buys leather for $80 a yard. Padding costs $6 a pound; thread and other materials cost $16 for a month's supply. He pays $500 a month rent for a small shop, and utilities average $150 a month. Shipping costs are about $4.50 per glove. In an average month, Alexander produces and sells 8 gloves. Each glove requires a half yard of leather and a half pound of padding. What is the average cost of a glove made by Alexander? How much profit does Alexander earn on each glove if he sells them for $475 each? How much profit does Alexander earn each month, on average? Exhibits 5 and 6 will help you answer these questions.

E1-9
Obj. 3
P/T

Mario's Restaurant specializes in Italian food. During February, Mario's recorded the following sales to customers and costs of doing business:

Sales to customers	$19,500
Cost of food products used	5,750
Cost of rented building and equipment	4,376
Cost of employee labor services used	3,750
Maintenance and utilities used	2,000

Prepare a schedule that shows the amount of profit (or loss) earned by Mario's Restaurant during February. (Hint: See Exhibit 6.)

E1-10
Obj. 3
P/T

The Quick Stop is a fast-food restaurant. During March, Quick Stop recorded the following sales to customers and costs of doing business:

Sales to customers	$4,400
Cost of food products used	2,100
Cost of rented building and equipment	1,250
Cost of employee labor services used	1,000
Maintenance and utilities used	600

Prepare a schedule that shows the amount of profit (or loss) earned by Quick Stop during March. (Hint: See Exhibit 6.)

E1-11
Obj. 3
P/T

Pam Lucas is a high school student who delivers papers to earn spending money. During May, she received $450 from customers in payment for their subscriptions for the month. She paid $300 for the papers she delivered. In addition, she paid $45 to her parents for use of their car to deliver the papers, and she paid $30 for gas. Prepare a statement to compute the amount of profit Pam earned from her paper route in May. (Hint: See Exhibit 6.)

E1-12
Obj. 4
P/T

On January 1, 2004, Alicia invested $4,000 in a savings account. At the end of January, the account balance had increased to $4,020. The balance at the end of February was $4,040.10. The balance at the end of March was $4,060.30. The increases occurred because of interest earned on the account. What was Alicia's return on investment, in dollars and cents, for each of the three months? What was the total return for the three months taken together?

E1-13
Obj. 4
P/T

Davy Crockett invested $15,000 in Mike Fink Rafting Company. At the end of the year, Crockett's investment was worth $17,250 because of earnings during the year. Fink paid Crockett $3,000 at the end of the year. What was Crockett's return *on* investment (in dollars) for the year? What was his return *of* investment (in dollars) for the year? Did Mike Fink Rafting maintain its capital as a result of these events? Explain.

E1-14
Obj. 4

Flick and Flack are two companies that sell identical products. They are located in different parts of the same city. During September, Flick sold $24,000 of goods, while Flack sold $18,000. Flick's profit was $8,000, and Flack's profit was $2,000. Compare the efficiency and effectiveness of the two companies.

E1-15
Obj. 4

Rogers and Hornsby are two companies that compete in the same market with the same product, a brand of steak sauce. The companies are the same size and sell to the same grocery retailers. Both products are sold by the retailers at the same price. During 2004, Rogers sold 500,000 bottles of its sauce at a profit of 10 cents per bottle. Hornsby sold 425,000 bottles at a profit of 15 cents a bottle. Which company was more effective? Which was more efficient? Which company was more profitable?

E1-16
Obj. 4

You have a choice of investing in either of two companies, Lewis or Clark. Both companies make the same products and compete in the same markets. Over the last five years, the operating results for the two companies have been:

	Lewis	Clark
Sales to customers	$4,500,000	$5,625,000
Profit	$412,500	$675,000
Return on investment per dollar invested	4.5%	7.5%

Which company is more efficient? Which is more effective? In which company would you invest? State the reasons for your answers.

E1-17
Obj. 5

Identify each of the following as describing corporations, proprietorships, and/or partnerships. Some items have more than one answer.

$\frac{P}{T}$

a. Distinct legal entity separate from its owners.
b. More than one owner.
c. Ownership by stockholders.
d. Controlled by a board of directors.
e. Legal identity changes when a company is sold.
f. Limited liability.
g. Mutual agency.
h. Access to large amounts of capital.
i. Direct taxation of profits.
j. Moral hazard usually not a major problem.

E1-18
Obj. 6

Yashiko Takawsa is a loan officer at a major bank. Hendrick Swindler recently applied for a small business loan for his dry cleaning company, Take 'Em to the Cleaners. As part of the application, Swindler was asked to provide financial information about his company. The financial reports revealed that the company had been fabulously profitable. What concerns might Yashiko have about the information provided by Swindler? What actions might she take to relieve these concerns?

E1-19
Obj. 6

Wendy Hu is considering two new products for her office products manufacturing business. One is a laser printer. Wendy has had numerous calls for the product, which will compete with existing well-known brands. The other product is a new computer projection system that permits a presenter to display color computer images without the need of a regular computer or projection system. The product would have little competition. Wendy believes the market will be receptive to this product. What are some of the risks that Wendy must consider in deciding whether to produce the two products?

E1-20
Obj. 7

To encourage its managers to earn a profit for its stockholders, Primrose Mining Company pays a bonus to top managers if the company earns at least a 15% return on investment each year. Management prepares financial reports from which the return on investment is calculated. Should the board and the stockholders be concerned about the reliability of the financial reports? Discuss. What can they do to make sure the reports faithfully represent the company's economic activities?

E1-21
Obj. 8

Andy attends college on a full-time basis and works part-time for Meredith's Garden Center. The owner, Jim Meredith, asked Andy to work late into the night to move merchandise from one warehouse to an empty warehouse located across town. Andy thought his assignment was unusual but was happy to get the extra hours of work.

The next day, Andy overheard the company's auditors discussing their visit to the warehouse where he had moved the merchandise. Apparently, Mr. Meredith was attempting to fool the auditors. They had counted the merchandise on the previous day. On the following day, they had counted the same merchandise a second time but at a different warehouse. Meredith was attempting to acquire a bank loan and wanted to impress the loan officer with a strong financial report. Andy knew Meredith would mislead the auditors and banker but did not know what to do.

What may happen to Andy if he informs the auditors of his activities from the night before? Who may be harmed by Meredith's actions?

PROBLEMS

If your instructor is using Personal Trainer in this course, you may complete online the assignments identified by ⁅T.

P1-1

Obj. 1

Obtaining Funding

Betsy wants to start a business making flags. She has calculated that she will need $62,500 to start the business. The money will be used to rent a building, purchase equipment, hire workers, and begin production and sales. Betsy has $12,500 in savings she can invest in the business.

Required

A. What alternatives might Betsy have for obtaining the additional $50,000 she needs for her business?
B. What information about her business will lenders or investors want to have?

P1-2

Obj. 2

⁅T

Types of Organizations

Provided below are four types of organizations and a list of organizations with which you are probably familiar. Associate each organization with a type of organization.

Types of organizations
Merchandising companies
Manufacturing companies
Service companies
Governmental or nonprofit organizations

Organizations

United Parcel Service (UPS)	Internal Revenue Service (IRS)
Amazon.com	March of Dimes
Dow Chemical Company	JCPenney
United States Postal Service (USPS)	DaimlerChrysler
PepsiCo	Sears
Federal Express (FedEx)	Verizon Communications

P1-3

Obj. 3

⁅T

Determining Profit and Return on Investment

Harry Honda owns a small car dealership. He rents the property he uses, buys cars from a manufacturer, and resells them to customers. During July, Harry sold 14 cars that cost him a total of $189,000. The total amount he received from the sale of these cars was $224,000. Other costs incurred by Harry for the month included rent, $2,550; utilities, $800; insurance, $825; maintenance of property and cars, $500; advertising, $1,000; and property taxes and business license, $200.

Required

A. Prepare a profit report that calculates the amount of profit earned during July.
B. What can Harry do with the profit he earned?
C. Assuming he invested $1,200,000 in the dealership, what was the return on his investment for July expressed as a percentage of his investment?

P1-4

Objs. 3, 4

⁅T

Developing Profit and Return on Investment

Through hard work and careful saving, Hans and his family have $152,000 to start a small specialty foods business. The family estimates sales to customers will be about $4,500 per month during the first year. On the average, expected costs per month are budgeted as follows:

Wages for occasional labor	$ 700	Utilities	$100
Rent on land and buildings	1,200	Advertising	300
Supplies	75	Delivery costs	225

Required

A. What is the projected monthly profit?
B. What is the expected annual return on investment?

P1-5

Obj. 3

P/T

The Relationship between Profit and Value Created

Marty and Judi own and operate Tender Sender Company, a store providing private mail boxes, contract shipping services on commission, and a wide variety of gift and novelty items. The following transactions occurred during the month of February.

1. Sold $6,000 of gift items for which the company had paid $3,100.
2. Advertising, both newspaper and radio, was $1,500.
3. Rent for the month received from mail box customers totaled $1,640.
4. The cost of monthly rent for the store location was $2,200.
5. The cost of utilities for the month was $475.
6. Commissions earned from shipping services for the month totaled $1,588.
7. Sold $3,200 of novelty items that had cost the company $1,450.
8. The cost of supplies used during the month was $384.
9. Other miscellaneous costs for the month of February totaled $250.

Required

A. Prepare a schedule that shows the amount of profit earned by the company during the month of February.
B. Has the company created value? Explain your answer.

P1-6

Objs. 1, 3

P/T

How Businesses Create Value

You are considering opening a shop in a nearby mall that will sell specialty T-shirts. T-shirts, containing designs and words selected by customers, will be produced for customers on order. You will need to borrow $25,000 to begin operations. A local bank has agreed to consider a loan and has asked for a summary plan to demonstrate the performance you expect from your company and your ability to repay the loan. You will pay $5.50 for T-shirts and will sell them for $8. The cost of paint and supplies will be $0.50 per shirt. An examination of similar stores at other malls indicates that you should be able to sell an average of 1,000 shirts per month. Rent for your store will be $300 per month. Utilities will be $150 per month, on average. Wages will be $800 per month.

Required

A. Calculate the expected profit of your company for the first year of operation.
B. Explain how a bank loan officer may use your profit projections to help make the lending decision.

P1-7

Obj. 3

P/T

Measuring Value Created

T. Edison owns her own business and had the following activity during September. She earned $2,600 from royalties on inventions. She consumed resources as follows: $525 for rent, $300 for clerical salaries, $124 for legal services, $100 for office supplies, $90 for utilities, $70 for fuel, and $200 for insurance.

Required

A. Prepare a report in good form, following the example of Exhibit 6, to describe Edison's financial activities for September.
B. How might this information be useful for Edison?
C. Identify some decisions Edison might make using this information.

P1-8

Obj. 3

P/T

The Results of the Transformation Process

Betsy started Betsy's Flag Co. on September 1. During September, Betsy consumed the following resources:

Rent	$ 625	Utilities	250
Supplies	3,000	Repairs	1,500
Fabric	8,750	Wages	2,500
Business license	500		

Betsy created resources by selling flags for $22,000 during the month of September.

Required Determine the profit earned by Betsy during September.

P1-9

Objs. 1, 4

Using Accounting Information for Decisions

The chief financial officer (CFO) of Flash Bulb and Seed Company has prepared the following projections for the month of August.

Expected sales		$480,000
Projected monthly resources consumed:		
Rent	$ 85,000	
Utilities	2,900	
Wages	274,000	
Advertising	115,000	
Repairs	12,000	
Supplies	2,500	
Total cost of resources consumed		491,400
Projected loss		$ (11,400)

Although Flash Bulb and Seed Company predicts a loss for August, the CFO is confident that sales will increase in the future.

Required

A. Why is it important that the CFO prepare a document like this?

B. If the company came to your bank requesting a loan, how would you respond? From the data given, does the firm appear that it is likely to be able to repay a loan? Why?

P1-10

Obj. 4

P/T

Return on Investment and Return of Investment

John invested $250,000 into a business that earned a profit of $2,250 during the past month as shown below. John believes the business will earn an annual profit equal to twelve times the monthly profit. Assume John wants to take $20,000 from the business each year for his personal use.

Resources created from sales		$17,000
Resources consumed:		
Materials	$7,500	
Insurance	1,500	
Rent	2,000	
Utilities	950	
Wages	2,800	
Total cost of resources consumed		14,750
Profit earned		$ 2,250

Required

A. Determine the company's return on investment.

B. Determine John's return of investment.

P1-11

Obj. 5

Choosing a Form of Business Organization

Below are three independent situations.

A. Larry, Ulysses, and Irene are three college student friends planning to set up a summer business at a nearby resort to sell T-shirts, souvenirs, and novelties to tourists. While they have no assets (to speak of) of their own, Larry's uncle has agreed to finance them with upfront capital to acquire merchandise and so on. They plan to operate for only one summer, as all expect to graduate soon and take permanent jobs in a nearby state.

B. Molly and Vicky are twin sisters who have decided to start a computer software consulting firm. Molly is the "techie," and a bit unreliable. Vicky is a highly successful manager gifted with organizational and business skills. Between the two, they believe they can attract and serve a profitable clientele. In fact, they envision rapid expansion of their practice and diversification into a variety of related business activities. Between them, they have only enough liquid capital to start a small operation.

C. Reginald and Ruth Ann are ne'er-do-well offspring of a deceased industrialist who left them each $400 million—most of which they still have. Ever the optimists, they think there is money to be made in the steel business. A friend they met at the country club has persuaded them to provide $10 million to set up a business that would manufacture and distribute a line of lightweight steel kites. Operations would be located in a nearby state.

Required For each of the three independent situations, recommend the form of business organization that you believe would be most appropriate. Explain your reasoning in each case, both in favor of your selection and any reasons against your choice.

P1-12 **Business Ownership Structures**

Obj. 5

Mary Jackson is graduating with a degree in business administration. She has scheduled interviews with a variety of companies. Mary found the following diagram in the packet of information provided by one of the companies:

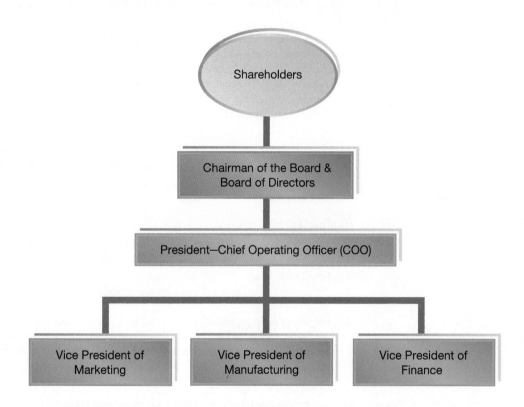

Required

A. Is Mary interviewing with a proprietorship, partnership, or corporation?
B. What are the advantages of this form of organization?
C. In this form of organization, management ultimately is responsible to whom?

P1-13 **Contracts, Risk, and Uses of Accounting Information**

Obj. 6

Sonny Beam established Solar Supply Corporation earlier in the current year. To obtain resources, he contributed $5,000 of his savings to the company, had the company borrow $8,000 from his mother, sold shares of company stock to friends totaling $10,000, and obtained a $25,000 bank loan. The company is obligated to buy out all investors and repay the two loans within 12 months of the business becoming profitable. Sonny located space in a nearby business park and leased it for monthly rent of $1,000 plus 1% of his company's sales. Several competing manufacturers tried to attract him as a distributor of their products. He signed an exclusive agreement with one that offered its products at 52% off their normal sales prices

(Continued)

with 30-day free credit. Sonny hired a sales manager at a salary of $3,000 per month and promised her a profit-sharing plan payable each December 31. Sonny's credit policy is that commercial customers receive 60-day free credit and that retail customers must pay by cash or credit card. All goods carry the manufacturer's warranty and Sonny's secondary warranty of "satisfaction guaranteed or your money back." Because the company is a corporation, it will pay corporate income tax to the city, state, and federal governments. In addition, the state will levy a merchandise tax each July 1.

Required

A. Identify the primary exchanges and contracts between the company and those that interact with it.
B. Which of the parties have taken on risk? For each such party, describe that risk.
C. Which contracts will require the parties to rely on accounting information to verify performance according to the contract? Be specific.

P1-14

Objs. 4, 6

Using Information About Risk to Make Decisions

Nancy and Mauro are reviewing the information given below for different reasons. Nancy is a bank loan officer who has received a 2-year, $50,000 loan application from both firms. Mauro is an independently wealthy investor who is considering investing $50,000 in a company. The information below is just one part of a complete data set about the companies that both persons are reviewing. The data reveal the profit history of the two firms over the last seven years. The companies are very similar except for the way in which their profits vary over the years. (All dollar amounts are in thousands.)

Profits

	2004	2003	2002	2001	2000	1999	1998	Total
Hill Country Enterprises	337	315	303	268	207	225	201	1,856
Low Land Associates	730	(55)	(10)	598	(131)	619	498	2,249

Required

A. Explain the concept of risk and its usual relationship to return on investment.
B. If you were Nancy, would you be more likely to make the loan to Hill Country or to Low Land? Why?
C. If you were Mauro, would you be more likely to invest in Hill Country or Low Land? Why?
D. Suppose the financial information of Low Land Associates (but not that of Hill Country Enterprises) has been audited and verified as being in conformance with generally accepted accounting principles. Would that change your responses to parts (b) and (c) above?

P1-15

Obj. 6

Using Financial Information to Assess Risk

Assume you are the credit manager for a manufacturing company that sells its products to retail businesses. One of your company's sales representatives has been working hard to establish business relationships with two different retailers. Both businesses are interested in marketing your products. Summary earnings information is presented below for each business.

Profits (losses)

	2001	2002	2003	2004
Company A	80,000	20,000	(10,000)	70,000
Company B	30,000	32,000	40,000	43,000

Required

A. Based on the summary financial information, which company is a better credit risk?
B. When a new relationship is established between two businesses, would the customer be interested in information about the supplier's financial condition? Why or why not?

P1-16
Objs. 6, 8
P
T

Accounting Information and Management Compensation

Taylor Grey is the sales manager of an electronics manufacturing company. His annual bonus is based on profits earned by the company. On December 30, Taylor is inquiring about the status of a very large order that he would like to include in the year-end profit figures. Unfortunately, a production machine has broken down. Taylor has been advised the order will not be completed and shipped by the end of the year. The profit figures including and excluding the order appear below.

Profit Including the Order	Profit Excluding the Order
$2,300,000	$1,500,000

Taylor's bonus is 3% of profits.

Required

A. Using the financial information provided, calculate Taylor's bonus under both scenarios.
B. Why do companies use accounting information to evaluate managerial performance?
C. Is there an economic incentive for Taylor to misrepresent the annual sales?

P1-17
Obj. 7

The Value of an Audit

Assume you have inherited a sum of money from a distant relative and are looking for good investment opportunities. You are considering investing in one of two companies, Wonderworks or Hoffstetter's. Both companies are retailing organizations that have earned profits during the month of January as follows:

	Wonderworks		Hoffstetter's	
Resources created		$50,000		$60,000
Resources consumed:				
Cost of merchandise sold	$30,000		$35,000	
Wages	5,000		4,000	
Rent	2,000		2,500	
Supplies	1,500		1,700	
Utilities	700		500	
Total cost of resources consumed		39,200		43,700
Profit earned		$10,800		$16,300

You learn that a CPA examined the financial information provided by Wonderworks and confirmed the information was prepared according to GAAP.

"I don't see any reason to pay a CPA to examine my company's books," Patty Hoffstetter tells you. They add to the cost of conducting business. Hoffstetter's brother-in-law prepared the company's financial information. He has no formal training in accounting but followed the instructions provided in the accounting software package that he purchased from an office supply company.

Required

A. Do you agree that the audit adds no value? Why or why not?
B. GAAP help ensure that users can compare the financial information of two different companies. The two sets of financial information appear identical in format. Are they comparable?

P1-18
Obj. 7

http://
http://ingram.
swlearning.com
Learn more about the SEC.

The Importance of Accounting Regulations

In its 2001 annual report, **Qwest Communications International Inc.** ("Qwest") stated that because of an SEC investigation, it couldn't guarantee that it would not have to restate its earnings (*to make them consistent with GAAP*). A restatement could wipe out more than $500 million of earnings, bringing Qwest close to violating agreements with its creditors. The biggest problem with a restatement is that Qwest faces lawsuits alleging that company executives made misleading statements to prop up the stock price.

Source: www.msnbc.com   *(Continued)*

Required

A. What is the SEC? What is its mission?
B. If a company's management believes they have reported earnings in a meaningful way, why can the SEC force them to restate earnings?
C. If management issued misleading financial information, do the shareholders have a reason to be upset with the company? Explain.

P1-19 **Ethics and Moral Hazard**

Obj. 8

You are the manager of a retail electronics store. Recently, you purchased 200 What-A-Sound portable CD players from a wholesaler in a going-out-of-business sale. These units cost you $80 each, about half of the normal cost of other brands that you sell for $260. You expected to sell these units at the regular price and earn an above-normal profit. After your purchase, you discovered that the units were poorly constructed and would probably last about a third as long as other major brands.

Customers often ask you for a recommendation when considering the purchase of a portable CD player. If you tell them the truth about the What-A-Sound model, you may have difficulty selling these units, even if you offer a steep discount.

Required

A. What will you tell a customer who asks about these units?
B. What are the short-run and long-run implications for your company's profits if (a) you conceal the quality of the units and sell them at their regular price or (b) reveal the quality problem? If you were to choose alternative b, what options might you consider in an effort to minimize the effect of these units on your profits?

P1-20 **Ethics and Moral Hazard**

Obj. 8

You manage an auto service store. One of your major services is brake replacement. You purchase replacement parts at an average cost of $30 per set. Each set contains parts for four wheels and will repair one car. You charge an average of $100 per car for replacing worn brakes, including an average labor cost of $40. Your current volume for brake replacements is about 700 jobs per month. A new vendor has contacted you with an offer to sell you replacement parts at an average cost of $22.50 per set. After checking on the quality of these parts, you find that their average life is about two-thirds that of the parts you are currently using.

Required

A. What are the short-run profit implications of using the $22.50 brakes instead of the $30 brakes?
B. What are the long-run profit implications?
C. What ethical issues should be considered in choosing which brakes to use?

P1-21 **Excel in Action**

$\frac{P}{T}$

SPREADSHEET

Millie and Milo Wermz are the owners and managers of a small bookstore, The Book Wermz, near a college campus. The store specializes in rare and out-of-print books. During September 2004, the company sold $40,000 of books. The books cost the company $28,000. The cost of other resources used during September included:

Wages	$4,200
Supplies	2,000
Rent	1,500
Utilities	300

Required Use a spreadsheet to prepare a report describing profit earned by The Book Wermz for September. The spreadsheet should contain the following heading:

The Book Wermz
Profit Earned
For September 2004

The merge and center button ⊞ can be used to center the heading in the first three rows of the spreadsheet. Select the cells that will contain the heading, and then click the merge button to combine these cells.

The report should list each resource created or consumed during September and should include a formula to automatically calculate the profit earned as the difference between resources created and resources consumed. Use the appropriate format buttons to format the numbers to include commas. Show resources consumed as negative amounts. The first and last numbers in the column should include dollar signs.

The completed worksheet should look like the following example:

	A	B
1	The Book Wermz	
2	Profit Earned	
3	For September 2004	
4		
5	Sales	$ 40,000
6	Cost of goods sold	(28,000)
7	Wages	(4,200)
8	Supplies	(2,000)
9	Rent	(1,500)
10	Utilities	(300)
11	Profit	$ 4,000

Use formula to calculate total

It is important to **save your work on a regular basis**. Save your work before you make any major changes so that mistakes will not require you to redo a lot of work.

P1-22 Multiple-Choice Overview of the Chapter

P/T

1. The basic purpose of accounting is to:
   a. minimize the amount of taxes a company has to pay.
   b. permit an organization to keep track of its economic activities.
   c. report the largest amount of earnings to stockholders.
   d. reduce the amount of risk experienced by investors.

2. A primary purpose of all organizations in our society is to:
   a. make a profit.
   b. minimize the payment of taxes.
   c. provide employment for the largest number of workers possible.
   d. create value by transforming resources from one form to another.

3. Value is created when organizations:
   a. raise capital by borrowing funds from banks, individuals, or other businesses.
   b. pay cash to suppliers, employees, owners, and government.
   c. sell products or services at prices that exceed the value of resources consumed.
   d. invest in machinery.

4. Which of the following are features of the corporate form of business organization?

	Mutual Agency	**Limited Liability**
a.	Yes	Yes
b.	Yes	No
c.	No	Yes
d.	No	No

5. Tammy Faye invested $2,000 in a partnership. One year later, the partnership was sold, and cash from the sale was distributed to the partners. On that date, Tammy received a check for her share of the company in the amount of $2,250. What was Tammy's return on investment?

(Continued)

    a. $0
    b. $250
    c. $2,000
    d. $2,250

6. Sternberg Enterprises developed a new type of roller skate that is very popular because of its high quality and reasonable price. Sternberg is losing money on the product, however, because several key production personnel recently resigned and replacements are not as skilled. Which of the following terms properly describe the firm?

	Effective	Efficient
a.	Yes	Yes
b.	Yes	No
c.	No	Yes
d.	No	No

7. The *transformation of resources* refers to:
    a.   the assessment of employee performance.
    b.   converting resources from one form to a more valuable form.
    c.   procedures designed to reduce a company's risk.
    d.   training methods by which unskilled workers become efficient and effective.

8. An investor is evaluating the potential investments described below. Past financial results of these two companies are judged to be indicative of future returns and risk.

Year	Abercrombie Profits	Fitch Profits
A	$16	$ 6
B	18	48
C	20	3

From the information provided, which investment appears to have the higher return and which the higher risk?

	Highest Return	Highest Risk
a.	Abercrombie	Abercrombie
b.	Abercrombie	Fitch
c.	Fitch	Abercrombie
d.	Fitch	Fitch

9. SEC stands for:
    a.   Securities Excellence Commission
    b.   Securities and Exchange Commission
    c.   Standard Executive Compensation
    d.   Salaried Executive's Council

10. Ethical behavior is particularly important for accounting because:
    a.   companies cannot detect unethical behavior.
    b.   if the reports are wrong, accountants may have to go to jail.
    c.   the SEC cannot carefully audit each company's financial statements.
    d.   the reliability of accounting information depends on the honesty of those who prepare, report, and audit this information.

CASE

C1-1 Understanding the Transformation Process

Obj. 2

Environmental Housing Company designs and builds log homes. It purchases logs and other building materials from other companies. The logs are cut to the dimensions called for in a design and shipped to the customer's building site with other materials for assembly. Environmental Housing employs construction and assembly workers, maintenance personnel, and marketing and service personnel, in addition to its management and office staff. The company is in charge of the construction process until the home is completed and ready for occupancy.

Required Identify the resources, transformation activities, and goods of Environmental Housing's transformation process. Construct a diagram similar to Exhibit 4 that shows the flow of resources through the transformation process.

BUSINESS ACTIVITIES—THE SOURCE OF ACCOUNTING INFORMATION

How do we know how well our business is doing?

After developing an understanding of the purpose of a business and the considerations involved in starting a business, Maria and Stan officially began Mom's Cookie Company in January of 2004. Their first task was to obtain financial resources for the business. Then, they acquired equipment and other resources for the business, and they began to produce and sell their products. In addition, they needed an accounting system to record their business activities and to report how the business was performing.

FOOD FOR THOUGHT

If you were starting a business, what kinds of information would you want to know about your business? How would you keep track of where the company obtained financial resources, how those resources were used, and the amounts of other resources the company has available for use? How would you know how much of your product you were selling and how much it was costing you to acquire and sell the product? For answers to these questions Maria and Stan are meeting with their accountant, Ellen.

Ellen: *Once you start your business, you will need an accounting system for recording business activities and for providing reports to help you understand how your business is performing.*

Maria: *Is this something we can do ourselves?*

Ellen: *Yes, for now, since your business will not be very complicated. You can set up a basic accounting system and keep track of your activities. The system will help you understand your business and events that affect how well you are doing.*

Stan: *How do we get started?*

Ellen: *We will start with a simple set of accounts and look at how these accounts are related. As your company acquires and uses resources, we will record each event. At the end of the month, we will summarize these activities and prepare financial statements.*

Maria: *What will the statements tell us?*

Ellen: *The statements will report the resources available to your company, how you financed those resources, and how the resources were used.*

Stan: *Will we know whether our company is making money?*

Ellen: *Yes, we can prepare a statement that will tell you how much profit the company earns each month. By the time we are finished, you'll have a pretty good idea of whether the company is performing as well as you hope it will.*

OBJECTIVES

Once you have completed this chapter, you should be able to:

1 Identify financing activities and explain why they are important to a business.

2 Demonstrate how accounting measures and records business activities.

3 Identify investing activities and explain why they are important to a business.

4 Identify operating activities and explain how they create profits for a company.

5 Describe how financial reports summarize business activities and provide information for business decisions.

FINANCING ACTIVITIES

OBJECTIVE 1

Identify financing activities and explain why they are important to a business.

A business is an organization that exists for the purpose of making a profit for its owners. A business creates a profit if it can sell goods and services to customers at prices that are greater than the total costs incurred to provide those goods and services. To be successful, a business must be effective in meeting the needs of customers by providing goods and services demanded by customers at prices they are willing to pay. Also, a business must be efficient in controlling costs so that the prices charged to customers exceed the costs to the company of acquiring and selling its products. If a company is successful, it creates value for its owners as well as for other stakeholders. Profit is a measure of the value created by a business for its owners.

Maria and Stan started Mom's Cookie Company in January of 2004. The goods they sell are prepared from their mother's recipes. It is important to keep in mind that a business is a separate entity from its owners. The resources and activities of the business should be kept separate from those of the owners or managers of a business. Throughout this book we will discuss accounting issues related to Mom's Cookie Company. We will be accounting for the company, not for the owners or other stakeholders.

To start their business, Maria and Stan invested $10,000 from their savings. This money enabled the company to acquire resources it would need to operate. **A contribution by owners to a business, along with any profits that are kept in the business, is known as** *owners' equity.* The contribution provides resources to the company and represents a claim by the owners. Owners have a claim to profits earned by a business and to the resources owned by the business.

Because they needed more money to get started, Maria and Stan borrowed $8,000 from a local bank to help finance the business. Borrowing is another source of money for a company and represents a claim by the lender of the money. As noted in Chapter F1, those who lend money to a business are referred to as creditors of the business. Creditors have a claim for repayment of amounts the company borrows and for interest on amounts borrowed. **The amount a company borrows is the** *principal* **of a loan.** *Interest* **is the cost of borrowing and is paid to creditors in addition to the repayment of principal.**

LEARNING NOTE

Keep in mind that the business is an accounting entity separate from its owners. From an accounting perspective, the bank lends the $8,000 to the business, Mom's Cookie Company, not to Maria and Stan.

Contributions by owners and loans from creditors are examples of business activities, as illustrated in Exhibit 1. *Business activities* **are events that occur when a business acquires, uses, or sells resources or claims to those resources.** Exhibit 1 illustrates business activities as the exchange of resources and claims between creditors and owners and the company.

Contributions by owners and loans from creditors are examples of financing activities. *Financing activities* **occur when owners or creditors provide resources to a company or when a company transfers resources to owners or creditors,** as in the repayment of a loan principal. Financing activities provide financial resources for businesses. How

Exhibit 1

Business Activities:
Financing from Owners
and Creditors

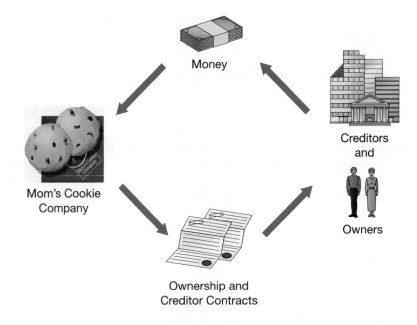

Money

Creditors
and

Owners

Mom's Cookie
Company

Ownership and
Creditor Contracts

businesses use those resources is a topic discussed later in this chapter when we examine investing and operating activities. First, we look at how we account for financing and other business activities.

ACCOUNTING FOR BUSINESS ACTIVITIES

OBJECTIVE 2

Demonstrate how
accounting measures and
records business activities.

Accounting provides a basis for describing business activities. Accounting measures, records, reports, and analyzes business activities using accounts. **An** *account* **is a record of increases and decreases in the dollar amount associated with a specific resource or activity.** Accounting *transactions* **are descriptions of business activities (or events) that are measured in dollar values and recorded in accounts.** In general, the amount recorded for an event is the cash value of resources transferred or used in a business activity.

Financial accounting records transactions by using the accounting equation. The accounting equation shows the fundamental relationship between resources and claims to those resources:

ASSETS = LIABILITIES + OWNERS' EQUITY

Assets **are the resources controlled by a business.** *Liabilities* **are the claims of creditors to a company's resources.** Liabilities are the resources a company would have to transfer to creditors to satisfy those claims. As noted earlier, owners' equity is the claim of owners to a company's resources. Accounts are specific types of assets, liabilities, or owners' equity.

Exhibit 2 illustrates financing activities of Mom's Cookie Company. The company received $10,000 from Maria and Stan. Then, it borrowed $8,000 from a bank. Consequently, the company has assets (cash) valued at $18,000. Creditors have a claim of $8,000, and owners have a claim of $10,000 on the company's assets.

LEARNING NOTE

"Account" is the root of "accounting." The root of "account" is "count." Thus, we can observe that accounting is a process of quantifying ("counting") business activities and recording them in specific information categories as a means of understanding these activities.

Exhibit 2

The Effect of Financing
Activities on the
Accounting Equation

| Assets $18,000 | = | Liabilities $8,000 | + | Owners' Equity $10,000 |

Exhibit 3 provides an accounting representation of financing activities. On January 2, 2004, Mom's Cookie Company received $10,000 from the company's owners. On January 3, 2004, the company received $8,000 from the bank. These events are recorded as increases (or decreases, if needed) in specific accounts.

Exhibit 3

Accounting Representation of Financing Activities

Date	Accounts	ASSETS	=	LIABILITIES	+	OWNERS' EQUITY
	Beginning Amounts	0	=	0	+	0
Jan. 2	Cash	10,000				
	Contributed Capital					10,000
Jan. 3	Cash	8,000				
	Notes Payable			8,000		
	Ending Amounts	18,000	=	8,000	+	10,000

Accounts associated with these transactions include Cash, Contributed Capital, and Notes Payable. *Cash* **refers to financial resources in the form of coins and currency, bank deposits, and short-term investments that can be converted easily into currency and that can be used to pay for resources and obligations of a company.** *Contributed Capital* **is an owners' equity account and identifies amounts contributed to a company by its owners.** *Notes Payable* **is a liability account used to identify amounts a company owes to creditors with whom a formal agreement, or note, has been signed.**

As Exhibit 3 illustrates, accounting measures business activities in terms of dollar values, and records these activities in accounts. Thus, accounting provides a systematic way for a business to keep track of its activities. A review of a company's transactions reveals the events that occurred, when they occurred, the amounts involved, and the resources and claims that were exchanged. Good business decisions depend on accurate and timely information about business activities. Decision makers need to know what the business did and how the business was affected by those activities. Accounting is a primary source of this information. It is important that accounting provide a complete record of a company's business activities. Only then do decision makers have a full and fair description of those activities.

Case In Point

http://ingram.
swlearning.com

Visit the Enron site for the latest news.

Consequences of Unreported Liabilities

One of the primary criticisms of **Enron Corporation**'s accounting was that it failed to report large amounts of debt (liabilities) that the company was responsible for repaying. The company's owners and other stakeholders were not easily able to identify or measure the amount of debt owed by the corporation. Consequently, their investments in Enron were riskier than they thought. When some of Enron's business operations proved to be less profitable than anticipated, the corporation had difficulty meeting its obligations. If owners and other stakeholders had known the true amount of the company's debt, they may have been less willing to purchase the company's stock or lend money to the company, and some owners and creditors may have avoided losses they incurred when the company's actual financial condition became known.

INVESTING ACTIVITIES

Before a company can sell goods and services to customers, it must acquire resources needed to operate the business. The particular resources a business needs depends on what the business is. Maria and Stan do not have sufficient resources to produce their cookies. Instead, they have contracted with a local bakery to make the cookies from

OBJECTIVE 3

Identify investing activities and explain why they are important to a business.

their mother's recipes. The bakery will order containers and package the cookies with the Mom's Cookie Company label. Maria and Stan have arranged to sell the cookies to local grocery stores.

The primary resources Mom's Cookie Company needs are office equipment and delivery equipment. Maria and Stan will use the office equipment to maintain information about the business and to make contacts with the bakery and grocery stores. Delivery equipment will be used to pick up cookies from the bakery and to deliver them to stores. Resources such as office equipment and delivery equipment are long-term resources because they can be used for more than one year. These resources enable a company to acquire and sell its products but are not products themselves. **Activities involving the acquisition or disposal of long-term resources used by a business are** *investing activities.* Exhibit 4 illustrates investing activities for Mom's Cookie Company. Long-term resources (such as office and delivery equipment) are acquired from suppliers. Money, or a promise of future payment, is transferred to suppliers of these resources.

Exhibit 4

Business Activities: Investing in Long-Term Resources

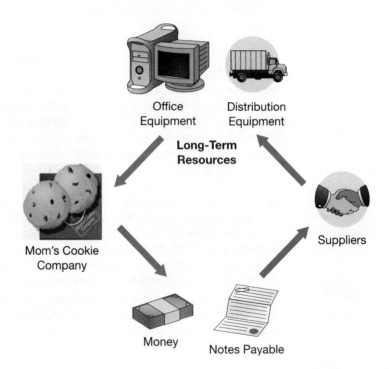

Exhibit 5 provides an accounting representation of investing activities. On January 5, Mom's Cookie Company paid $6,000 for office equipment. On January 6, the company bought a delivery van for $25,000. It paid $3,000 in cash and financed the remaining $22,000 of the purchase price with a note payable.

Exhibit 5

Accounting Representation of Investing Activities

Date	Accounts	ASSETS	=	LIABILITIES	+	OWNERS' EQUITY
	Beginning Amounts	18,000	=	8,000	+	10,000
Jan. 5	Equipment	6,000				
	Cash	−6,000				
Jan. 6	Equipment	25,000				
	Cash	−3,000				
	Notes Payable			22,000		
	Ending Amounts	40,000	=	30,000	+	10,000

The January 6 entry above shows the equipment purchase as a single transaction involving both the borrowing of $22,000 from the bank and the payment of an additional $3,000. An alternative way to record the purchase of the delivery van shows the transaction as a two-step process. First the $22,000 is borrowed from the bank and then the full $25,000 is paid to purchase the van. Recording the transaction in two steps is presented below.

Date	Accounts	ASSETS	=	LIABILITIES	+	OWNERS' EQUITY
	Beginning Amounts	18,000	=	8,000	+	10,000
Jan. 5	Equipment	6,000				
	Cash	−6,000				
Jan. 6	**Cash**	**22,000**				
	Notes Payable			**22,000**		
Jan. 6	**Equipment**	**25,000**				
	Cash	**−25,000**				
	Ending Amounts	40,000	=	30,000	+	10,000

LEARNING NOTE

Account titles vary in practice depending on the needs of a company. Accounts can be divided into as many subcategories as a business needs. For example, Mom's Cookie Company could use separate accounts for Office Equipment and Delivery Equipment if it chose to do so. Although you should not get too concerned about specific account titles, certain titles, such as Notes Payable, are used by most businesses. You should learn the titles that are listed as terms in this book. Remember, what is most important is that the account titles correctly represent the transactions.

Accounts used to record these transactions include Equipment, Cash, and Notes Payable. Observe that the second transaction involves both an investing activity (purchase of equipment) and a financing activity (borrowing to purchase van).

In each transaction, the accounting equation must balance. The January 5th transaction balances because the $6,000 increase in Equipment offsets the amount of the decrease in Cash. The January 6th transaction involves three accounts. Together the net increase in assets of $22,000 ($25,000 − $3,000) equals the increase in liabilities of $22,000.

The ending amounts in Exhibit 5 indicate that the accounting equation is in balance. Each transaction and all transactions taken together must preserve the relationship:

ASSETS = LIABILITIES + OWNERS' EQUITY

Maintaining the accounting equation is an important accounting control. If individual transactions or all transactions as a whole do not preserve the equality, an error has occurred in recording one or more of the business activities.

1 SELF-STUDY PROBLEM

Delphi Co. was started in 2004 when its owners contributed $100,000 to the business and borrowed $120,000 from creditors. These resources were used to purchase equipment at a cost of $160,000. In addition, the company purchased a building at a cost of $400,000, paying $40,000 in cash and signing a note for $360,000 with a local bank.

Required Using the format of Exhibit 5, record these financing and investing activities. Demonstrate that the accounting equation is in balance after the transactions have been recorded.

The solution to Self-Study Problem 1 appears at the end of the chapter.

OPERATING ACTIVITIES

OBJECTIVE 4

Identify operating activities and explain how they create profits for a company.

Financing and investing activities are necessary for a company to obtain the resources it needs to operate, but these activities do not involve operating the business. A business operates by obtaining or creating products or services and selling those products or services to customers. Mom's Cookie Company acquires cookies from a bakery and sells the cookies to grocery stores. *Operating activities* **are those activities necessary to acquire and sell goods and services.** When goods or services are sold to customers, revenue is created. *Revenue* **is the amount a company expects to receive when it sells goods or services.** Revenue can be thought of as the reward earned by serving customers. In addition to goods and services for sale, operating activities use a variety of resources, including employee labor, supplies, and utilities. The consumption of these resources creates expenses. *Expense* **is the amount of resources consumed in the process of acquiring and selling goods and services.** Not all operating activities create revenues or expenses, but most do.

Exhibit 6 illustrates the purchase of goods to sell, which is one aspect of operating activities that does not create a revenue or expense. Cookies are purchased from the bakery in exchange for cash.

Exhibit 6

Operating Activities:
Purchase of Goods for
Sale

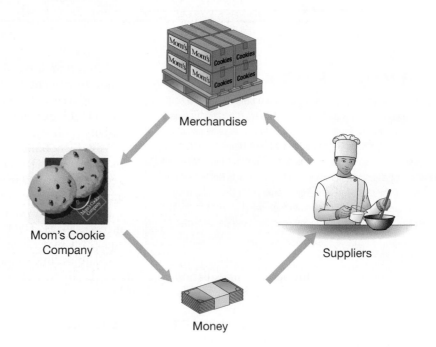

Exhibit 7 describes how this type of transaction might be recorded. Mom's Cookie Company purchased cookies from the bakery at a cost of $9,000 on January 7. *Merchandise Inventory* **is an asset account and identifies the cost of goods a company has purchased that are available for sale to customers.** Observe that in this transaction the company's total assets have not changed. The particular assets controlled by the com-

Exhibit 7

Accounting
Representation of
Purchase of
Merchandise

Date	Accounts	ASSETS	=	LIABILITIES	+	OWNERS' EQUITY
	Beginning Amounts	40,000	=	30,000	+	10,000
Jan. 7	Merchandise Inventory	9,000				
	Cash	−9,000				
	Ending Amounts	40,000	=	30,000	+	10,000

pany have changed. The company now has $9,000 of goods for sale but $9,000 less cash than before. In fact, the company's cash balance is now zero ($18,000 cash raised from financing activities minus $6,000 spent on office equipment, $3,000 for the down payment on a delivery van, and $9,000 spent on merchandise).

Exhibit 8 illustrates a company's sale of goods to a customer. When goods or services are sold to a customer, revenue is earned. The amount of revenue earned is equal to the amount of resources received from the customer in exchange for the goods. In this example, Cash is received from the customer and merchandise is delivered to the customer.

Exhibit 8
Operating Activities:
Selling Goods to
Customers

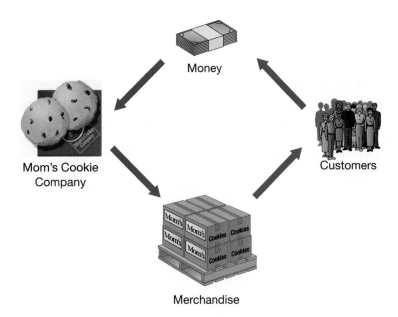

Exhibit 9 describes how this type of transaction can be recorded. Assume Mom's Cookie Company sells 380 boxes of cookies to grocery stores during January in exchange for cash. Each box, which contains several bags of cookies, costs Mom's Cookie Company $20, the amount the company pays the bakery for producing and packaging the cookies. Mom's Cookie Company sells each box to the store for $30. Therefore, 380 boxes cost the company $7,600 (380 boxes × $20) and are sold for $11,400 (380 boxes × $30).

Exhibit 9 Accounting Representation of Operating Activities

Date	Accounts	ASSETS		=	LIABILITIES	+	OWNERS' EQUITY	
		Cash	Other Assets				Contributed Capital	Retained Earnings
	Beginning Amounts	0	+40,000	=	30,000	+	10,000	+0
Jan. 31	Cash	11,400						
	Sales Revenue							11,400
Jan. 31	Cost of Goods Sold							−7,600
	Merchandise Inventory		−7,600					
	Ending Amounts	11,400	+32,400	=	30,000	+	10,000	+3,800

Because revenues and expenses occurred in this transaction, we expand the accounting equation to include them. *Retained Earnings,* **a subcategory of Owners' Equity, are the accumulated profits of a business that have been reinvested in the business.** Revenues increase Retained Earnings and expenses decrease Retained

Earnings. Amounts paid to owners from a company's profits also decrease Retained Earnings. We distinguish Retained Earnings from Contributed Capital because this subcategory identifies the profits earned by a company rather than amounts contributed directly by owners.

Also, notice in Exhibit 9 that Assets have been divided into two categories: Cash (beginning amount is $0) and Other Assets (beginning amount is $40,000). They still total to $40,000, the ending amount in Exhibit 7. Because many transactions involve Cash, separating it from Other Assets makes it easier to keep track of the cash received and paid by a company.

In Exhibit 9, the sale of goods is recorded in two transactions. One records the revenue earned from the sale. The other records the cost of the goods sold. These transactions are central to business operations and should be examined closely.

LEARNING NOTE

The sales transaction in Exhibit 9 is a summary transaction for all sales during January. In reality, sales occur throughout the month, and each sale should be recorded as it occurs. Each transaction would follow the same pattern shown in Exhibit 9. Therefore, to avoid repeating the same transaction several times, we record one summary transaction.

Sales Revenue **identifies the amount a company earns from selling its products.** Revenue ordinarily is measured by the amount of cash received or expected from a customer in exchange for the goods or services transferred. Revenue normally is recorded at the time goods are transferred to customers. A company earns revenue for its owners. Remember that owners have a claim to profits earned by a company. Accordingly, revenue is part of owners' equity. It is an increase in the value of a company for its owners.

Cost of Goods Sold **identifies the cost to the company of the goods transferred to customers.** It is an example of an expense. Expense normally is measured by the cost of resources consumed and is recorded at the time the resources are consumed. Thus, when merchandise is sold to customers, it is consumed from the seller's viewpoint. The seller no longer has control of the resource. Consequently, merchandise has been "used up." An expense reduces owners' equity because it identifies the use of resources for which owners have a claim. It is a decrease in the value of a company for its owners. Thus, **revenues increase owners' equity and expenses decrease owners' equity.**

Revenue minus expense equals profit. Profit results from operating activities and is the difference between revenues earned from selling goods and services and expenses incurred in acquiring and selling those goods and services. Note that in Exhibit 9 the sale resulted in profit of $3,800 ($11,400 − $7,600). The company's assets and owners' equity each increased by $3,800 as a result of the sale.

Remember, Owners' Equity represents the claims of owners to a business. Those claims include contributions made by the owners (Contributed Capital) plus profits earned by the business minus amounts paid by the business to its owners (Retained Earnings).

Other common expenses for a company like Mom's Cookie Company include wages paid to employees, plus the cost of supplies, rent, and utilities. To illustrate, assume the following activities for Mom's Cookie Company during January:

January	6	Paid $300 for supplies used during January
	8	Paid $600 for rent for January
	31	Paid $1,000 for wages for January
	31	Paid $200 for utilities for January

Exhibit 10 illustrates how these activities are recorded. An expense is recorded for the amount of resources used in each transaction. Because these resources were paid for at the time they were consumed, Cash decreases in each transaction.

Exhibit 10 Accounting Representation of Expenses

Date	Accounts	ASSETS Cash	Other Assets	=	LIABILITIES	+	OWNERS' EQUITY Contributed Capital	Retained Earnings
	Beginning Amounts	11,400	+32,400	=	30,000	+	10,000	+3,800
Jan. 6	Supplies Expense							−300
	Cash	−300						
Jan. 8	Rent Expense							−600
	Cash	−600						
Jan. 31	Wages Expense							−1,000
	Cash	−1,000						
Jan. 31	Utilities Expense							−200
	Cash	−200						
	Ending Amounts	9,300	+32,400	=	30,000	+	10,000	+1,700

2 SELF-STUDY PROBLEM

WebTUTOR Advantage

The following events occurred for Mega Co. during January, its first month of business:

Jan.	3	Owners contributed $40,000 to the business.
	5	The company received $25,000 from a bank in exchange for a note payable.
	8	The company paid $35,000 for equipment.
	10	The company paid $20,000 for merchandise.
	11	The company paid $2,000 for supplies used in January.
	15	The company received $12,000 from customers for the sale of merchandise. The merchandise cost Mega Co. $8,000.
	22	The company received $9,000 from customers for the sale of merchandise. The merchandise cost Mega Co. $6,000.
	31	The company paid $3,000 to employees for wages earned in January.
	31	The company paid $800 for utilities used in January.

Required Use the format of Exhibit 10 to record the transactions of Mega Co. for January. The beginning account balances will all be zero.

The solution to Self-Study Problem 2 appears at the end of the chapter.

FINANCIAL REPORTING AND ANALYSIS

OBJECTIVE 5

Describe how financial reports summarize business activities and provide information for business decisions.

The purpose of measuring and recording business activities is to provide useful information to those who need to make decisions. Accounting reports information to decision makers in the form of financial statements. *Financial statements* **are reports that summarize the results of a company's accounting transactions for a fiscal period.** Exhibit 11 lists all of Mom's Cookie Company's transactions for January using the expanded format.

To prepare financial statements, a company needs to identify the balances in its accounts at the end of the fiscal period being reported. Exhibit 12 provides a summary of account balances for Mom's Cookie Company at January 31. Balances for expenses, which reduce owners' equity, are shown in parentheses. All of the summary balances shown in this exhibit are the results of the transactions recorded for the company in Exhibit 11.

Exhibit 11 Transactions for Mom's Cookie Company for January

Date	Accounts	Cash	Other Assets	=	LIABILITIES	+	Contributed Capital	Retained Earnings
	Beginning Amounts	0	+0	=	0	+	0	+0
Jan. 2	Cash	10,000						
	Contributed Capital						10,000	
Jan. 3	Cash	8,000						
	Notes Payable				8,000			
Jan. 5	Equipment		6,000					
	Cash	−6,000						
Jan. 6	Equipment		25,000					
	Cash	−3,000						
	Notes Payable				22,000			
Jan. 6	Supplies Expense							−300
	Cash	−300						
Jan. 7	Merchandise Inventory		9,000					
	Cash	−9,000						
Jan. 8	Rent Expense							−600
	Cash	−600						
Jan. 31	Cash	11,400						
	Sales Revenue							11,400
Jan. 31	Cost of Goods Sold							−7,600
	Merchandise Inventory		−7,600					
Jan. 31	Wages Expense							−1,000
	Cash	−1,000						
Jan. 31	Utilities Expense							−200
	Cash	−200						
	Ending Amounts	9,300	+32,400	=	30,000	+	10,000	+1,700

Exhibit 12

Summary of Account Balances for Mom's Cookie Company at January 31

Account	January 31 Balance	Explanation
Assets:		
Cash	9,300	column total
Merchandise Inventory	1,400	$9,000 − $7,600
Equipment	31,000	$6,000 + $25,000
Liabilities:		
Notes Payable	30,000	$8,000 + $22,000
Owners' Equity:		
Contributed Capital	10,000	
Sales Revenue	11,400	
Cost of Goods Sold	(7,600)	
Wages Expense	(1,000)	
Rent Expense	(600)	
Supplies Expense	(300)	
Utilities Expense	(200)	

The Income Statement

The *income statement* **reports revenues and expenses for a fiscal period as a means of determining how well a company has performed in creating profit for its owners.** An income statement reports revenues, expenses, and profit for a fiscal period.

A *fiscal period* **is any time period for which a company wants to report its financial activities.** Typical periods are months, quarters (three months), and years. Fiscal months usually correspond with calendar months (January, February, etc.). Fiscal years do not have to correspond with calendar years, however. For example, a company may prepare an income statement for the year ended June 30 that would report operating activities for July 1 through June 30 of the following year. Some companies choose months that end on particular days of the week, such as Sunday. Thus, a company might prepare an income statement for the month ended January 29 if the 29th were the last Sunday in the month. For example, **General Mills'** fiscal year always ends on the last Sunday of May. Therefore, fiscal year 2002 ended on May 26, 2002 and included all operating activities since the previous year ended on May 27, 2001. General Mills' 2002 income statement is shown on page 24 of Appendix B at the end of this book.

Exhibit 13 provides an example of an income statement for Mom's Cookie Company for the month ended January 31, 2004. The statement includes all the revenues and expenses recorded for January. *Net income* **is the amount of profit earned by a business during a fiscal period.** It is a measure of the value created for the owners of a business by the operating activities of the business during a fiscal period. Net income (revenue minus expense) increases owners' equity as we observed in the transactions in Exhibit 9. Information in financial statements is summarized from the transactions recorded for a fiscal period. All the sales revenue transactions are added together, for example, to calculate the total sales revenue for January.

Exhibit 13
Income Statement

Mom's Cookie Company
Income Statement
For the Month Ended January 31, 2004

Sales revenue	$11,400
Cost of goods sold	(7,600)
Wages expense	(1,000)
Rent expense	(600)
Supplies expense	(300)
Utilities expense	(200)
Net income	$ 1,700

An income statement provides information about the results of a company's operating activities for a fiscal period. Owners and other decision makers can use the statement to evaluate how well a company has performed.

The Balance Sheet

A *balance sheet* **identifies a company's assets and claims to those assets by creditors and owners at a specific date.** It is a summary of the accounting equation and, like the equation, the total of assets reported on the balance sheet must equal the combined total of liabilities and owners' equity. Exhibit 14 provides a balance sheet for Mom's Cookie Company at January 31, 2004. It reports dollar amounts associated with a company's assets and the sources of financing for those assets. It reports resources and claims at a particular point in time rather than results of activities over a period of time.

A balance sheet usually is prepared at the end of each fiscal period. It reports amounts of assets, liabilities, and owners' equity at that time. We examine the procedure for determining these amounts in more detail in Chapter F3.

Profit is earned by a business for its owners. It may be paid to the owners as a return on their investments, or it may be retained in the business as a means of acquiring additional assets. Thus, retained earnings is the total amount of net income earned

Exhibit 14
Balance Sheet

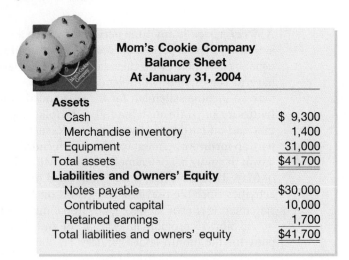

Mom's Cookie Company Balance Sheet At January 31, 2004	
Assets	
Cash	$ 9,300
Merchandise inventory	1,400
Equipment	31,000
Total assets	$41,700
Liabilities and Owners' Equity	
Notes payable	$30,000
Contributed capital	10,000
Retained earnings	1,700
Total liabilities and owners' equity	$41,700

over the life of a company minus the portion of net income paid out to owners. January is the first month of operations of Mom's Cookie Company, so the company has earned net income for only one month. The income statement reported net income for January of $1,700. None of the net income was paid out to owners. Consequently, retained earnings at the end of January is $1,700.

Retained earnings, January 1	$ 0
Net income for January	1,700
Less: Payment to owners in January	0
Retained earnings, January 31	$1,700

Retained earnings is separated from contributed capital in Exhibit 14 to distinguish between the amount paid into the company by Maria and Stan from the amount of profit earned and retained by the company. Amounts paid to owners normally should come from the company's profits. If a company pays its owners more than the company has earned, it is returning a portion of their investment to them. Owners need to know whether amounts paid to them are a return *on* their investments, from profits, or a return *of* their investments, from amounts invested directly by the owners. Thus, Mom's Cookie Company could pay Maria and Stan up to $1,700 from profits earned in January as a return on their investment. Any amount paid in excess of $1,700 would be a return of their investment.

The Statement of Cash Flows

A third financial statement prepared by businesses is the statement of cash flows. **The** *statement of cash flows* **reports events that affected a company's cash account during a fiscal period.** The statement contains three sections corresponding to operating, investing, and financing activities. The operating activities section reports cash from selling goods and services and cash paid for expense-related activities. The investing activities section reports cash paid for equipment and other long-term assets and cash received from selling these assets. The financing activities section reports cash received from creditors and owners, cash paid to creditors as a repayment of amounts borrowed by the company, and cash paid to owners.

Exhibit 15 provides a statement of cash flows for Mom's Cookie Company for January 2004. The source of data for the statement is the cash column for the transactions recorded in Exhibit 11. The results of these transactions are organized into the sections contained in the statement of cash flows.

Exhibit 15
Statement of Cash
Flows

Mom's Cookie Company
Statement of Cash Flows
For the Month Ended January 31, 2004

Operating Activities
Received from customers	$11,400	
Paid for merchandise	(9,000)	
Paid for wages	(1,000)	
Paid for rent	(600)	
Paid for supplies	(300)	
Paid for utilities	(200)	
Net cash flow from operating activities		$ 300
Investing Activities		
Paid for equipment*		(31,000)
Financing Activities		
Received from creditors**	30,000	
Received from owners	10,000	
Net cash flow from financing activities		40,000
Net cash flow for January		9,300
Cash balance, January 1		0
Cash balance, January 31		$ 9,300

*Office Equipment of $6,000 + Delivery Van of $25,000
**Notes Payable of $8,000 + Notes Payable of $22,000

LEARNING NOTE

As noted in the discussion of Exhibit 5, the purchase of the delivery van involved both investing and financing activities. On the statement of cash flows these are treated as two events. The financing transaction is treated as though the company received cash from borrowing money, and the investing transaction is treated as though the company paid cash for the delivery van.

LEARNING NOTE

The statement of cash flows often is prepared using a format different than that described in Exhibit 15. We examine the alternate format in a later chapter.

The statement of cash flows describes the events that affected a company's cash account during a fiscal period. The amount reported as net cash flow for the period is the change in the cash balance. The final line of the statement reports the cash balance at the end of the month and corresponds with the amount reported on the company's balance sheet (see Exhibit 14). Thus, the statement of cash flows is useful for identifying how much cash a company has, where that cash came from, and how the company used its cash during a fiscal period.

The Transformation Process

Businesses transform resources into goods and services for sale to customers. Accounting measures and reports the results of that transformation process. Financing activities describe how a company obtains financial resources from owners and creditors. Investing activities describe how a company uses financial resources to acquire long-term assets to be used by the company. Operating activities describe how a company uses its financial resources and long-term assets to acquire and sell its products.

Exhibit 16 illustrates the relationship among these activities as they are described in the income statement and balance sheet. The balance sheet describes a company's assets. Financial resources to acquire these assets are obtained from (1) financing activities (liabilities and owners' equity) and from (2) revenues earned by the company. When assets are consumed (3), expenses are created that reduce a company's profits. The profits earned during a period (4) increase owners' equity, as reported in retained earnings. The total amount of assets is equal to the total amount of liabilities and owners' equity (5).

Exhibit 16

Reporting the
Transformation Process

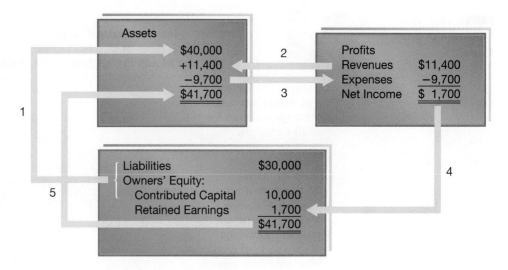

Financial Analysis

Many business decisions rely on accounting information. Decision makers use accounting information to evaluate a company's performance. A variety of analysis tools are available for this purpose. We examine these in later chapters. Financial statement numbers themselves provide useful information. For example, managers need to know how much cash or merchandise inventory a company has available so they can determine whether purchases can or should be made. Creditors need to know about a company's liabilities and profits to determine whether to make additional loans. Analysis often involves a comparison of accounting numbers, such as net income, with other numbers. Sometimes comparisons are made among fiscal periods or among companies. Comparisons are also made among different divisions of a company. For example, a decision maker may be interested in how the East division of a company compares with the West division, or how the U.S. division compares with the European division.

A common analytical tool involves the calculation of ratios. Most ratios compare one financial statement number with another. One example is return on assets. *Return on assets (ROA)* **is the ratio of net income to total assets.** Because total assets are equal to the total investment in a company from creditors and owners, return on assets measures return on total investment in a company. We can calculate return on assets for Mom's Cookie Company at January 31, 2004, as:

$$\text{Return on Assets} = \frac{\text{Net Income}}{\text{Total Assets}} = \frac{\$1,700}{\$41,700} = 4.1\%$$

We can interpret the ratio as the amount a company earned for each dollar of total investment. Thus, Mom's Cookie Company earned 4.1 cents for each dollar of investment in January. It is common to report many ratios, especially those expected to be less than one, as percentages, as shown above. Whether 4.1% is a good return or not can be assessed by comparing the amount with expectations of owners, with returns for similar companies, and with returns for other periods. A good return for one company is not necessarily good for another, particularly if the companies operate in different industries, countries, or geographic regions.

Owners, creditors, and other decision makers can examine return on assets for Mom's Cookie Company to decide whether the company is earning a reasonable profit. If the return is not satisfactory, Maria and Stan can make changes in the business. We examine various means of analyzing a company's performance in this book.

Business analysis relies on accounting and other information to understand how a business is performing and to determine future business activities. Exhibit 17 describes the role of accounting in business organizations. Accounting measures and records business activities. It converts data about business activities into useful information that is reported to decision makers. The information is analyzed to evaluate the performance of a company. Then, decisions are made that affect the company's future business activities. **A primary purpose of accounting is to help people make decisions about business activities. Accounting is the link between business activities and business decisions.**

Exhibit 17
A Model of the
Accounting Process

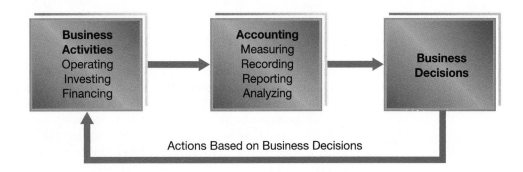

3 SELF-STUDY PROBLEM

Philistine Co. reported the following information for its first month of operations ended August 31, 2004:

WebTUTOR Advantage

Cash	$ 25,000
Merchandise inventory	200,000
Equipment	425,000
Notes payable	350,000
Investment by owners	250,000
Sales revenue	520,000
Cost of goods sold	300,000
Other expenses	140,000
Payments to owners	30,000

Required

A. Prepare an income statement using the format of Exhibit 13.
B. Determine how much retained earnings the company should report at the end of August.
C. Prepare a balance sheet using the format of Exhibit 14.
D. Calculate return on assets for the company for August.

The solution to Self-Study Problem 3 appears at the end of the chapter.

Appendix DEBITS AND CREDITS: ANOTHER WAY TO RECORD TRANSACTIONS

For most of its history, accounting has recorded transactions using debits and credits. They were particularly useful to facilitate the calculation of account balances prior to the advent of computers. Though the accounting process is largely computerized today, debits and credits remain part of the language of accounting. To understand this method, begin with the accounting equation, including revenues and expenses as subcategories of owners' equity, as described in Exhibit 18.

Debits **are increases in elements on the left (assets) side of the accounting equation and decreases in elements on the right (liabilities and owners' equity) side.** *Credits* **are decreases in elements on the left (assets) side of the accounting equation and**

Exhibit 18

Defining Debits and
Credits

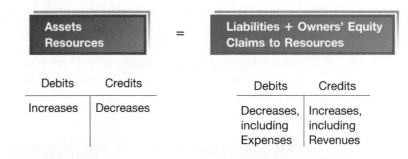

increases in elements on the right (liabilities and owners' equity) side. Because expenses decrease owners' equity, they are recorded as debits (unless expense amounts are being eliminated or offset). Because revenues increase owners' equity, they are recorded as credits (unless revenue amounts are being eliminated or offset).

Each account can be divided into a debit side (on the left) and a credit side (on the right). Transactions are recorded as debits and credits to the appropriate accounts. For example, (a) an owner's contribution of $10,000 to a company could be recorded as in Exhibit 19.

Exhibit 19

Recording a Transaction
with Debits and Credits

Cash is increased, and because it is an asset account, the increase is represented by a debit to the cash account. Contributed Capital is increased, and because it is an owners' equity account, the increase is represented by a credit to the contributed capital account.

For the accounting equation to balance, every transaction must have an equal amount of debits and credits. Therefore, total debits must always equal total credits for a company's transactions or accounts taken as a whole. Consequently, debits and credits provide a useful control to help ensure integrity of the accounting process. If debits do not equal credits, an error has been made.

The T-account format illustrated in Exhibit 19 often is used to describe transactions. This format makes it easy to observe the debit and credit effects of a transaction. If several transactions involve the same account, this format also makes it easy to observe the cumulative effect of the transactions. For example, (b) assume that the company borrowed $8,000 from a bank. Exhibit 20 includes the effect of this transaction, in addition to the transaction shown in Exhibit 19.

Exhibit 20

Recording Additional
Transactions with Debits
and Credits

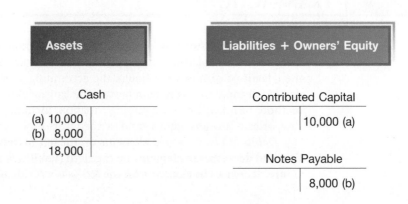

The addition of $8,000 to the cash account is represented by an additional debit entry. The combined effect of the two transactions is apparent after adding the two debit entries.

A third transaction (c), payment of $12,000 for equipment, is illustrated in Exhibit 21. The payment decreases Cash and is recorded as a credit to the cash account. The balance of the account decreases to a debit balance of $6,000. Equipment increases by $12,000, as represented by the debit to that account. Asset accounts normally have debit balances. Liability and owners' equity accounts normally have credit balances. Keep in mind that expenses are decreases in owners' equity and normally have debit balances.

Exhibit 21

Recording a Decrease in an Asset Account

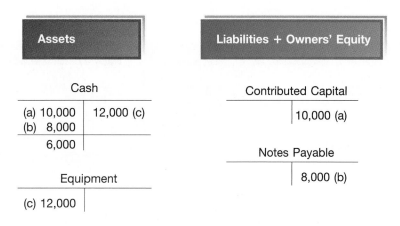

Exhibit 21 illustrates the advantages of a debit and credit system of recording transactions when transactions are recorded manually. Because increases in accounts are separated from decreases, it is simpler to calculate balances than if increases and decreases are recorded in one column. Remember that for most of our history, computers, calculators, and other electronic devices were not available. Account balances had to be determined using basic rules of math. Debits and credits facilitated that process.

Observe from Exhibit 21 that each transaction involves recording debits and credits of equal magnitude. Also note that the accounting equation remains in balance after each transaction. In Exhibit 21, total assets of $18,000 ($6,000 + $12,000) equals total liabilities and owners' equity ($10,000 + $8,000).

An alternative to the T-account approach is the traditional journal format. **The journal is a book (or computer file) in which transactions are recorded individually.** The journal provides for each transaction to be recorded using debits and credits without having to set up T-accounts. T-accounts are useful for simple transactions but become unwieldy when many transactions are being recorded.

Transactions considered in this chapter can be recorded using the traditional journal format as shown in Exhibit 22. The first transaction records cash received by Mom's Cookie Company from the owners. Observe that the total amount of debits equals the total amount of credits. Debits are listed first, and credits are indented to the right. Cash is debited because assets have increased. Contributed Capital is credited because owners' equity has increased. The cells to the right side of the transaction (labeled Effect on Accounting Equation) are not part of the journal entry. We include them as a reminder of the effect the transaction has on the equation. We abbreviate the elements of the accounting equation as follows: A = Assets, L = Liabilities, OE = Owners' Equity, CC = Contributed Capital, and RE = Retained Earnings. Refer to Exhibit 5 for comparison.

The purchase of a delivery van on January 6 by Mom's Cookie Company is shown in Exhibit 23. The purchase increased Equipment, decreased Cash, and increased Notes Payable. Observe that negative signs are not used with debits and credits because the credit to an asset or expense or the debit to a liability, owners' equity, or revenue identifies the amount as a decrease in the account balance.

Exhibit 22 Journal Representation of Financing Transaction

Journal					Effect on Accounting Equation				

Journal			
Date	Accounts	Debits	Credits
Jan. 2	Cash	10,000	
	Contributed Capital		10,000

Effect on Accounting Equation

A	=	L +	OE	
			CC +	RE
+10,000				
			+10,000	

Exhibit 23 Journal Representation of Investing Transaction

Journal			
Date	Accounts	Debits	Credits
Jan. 6	Equipment	25,000	
	Cash		3,000
	Notes Payable		22,000

Effect on Accounting Equation

A	=	L +	OE	
			CC +	RE
+25,000				
−3,000				
		+22,000		

As a final example, Exhibit 24 provides the journal entries for the sale of goods from Exhibit 9. Cash and Sales Revenue increase, thus increasing both assets and owners' equity. Cost of Goods Sold and Merchandise Inventory decrease when goods are sold. Since Cost of Goods Sold is an expense, owners' equity decreases. The decrease in inventory reduces assets.

Exhibit 24 Journal Representation of Sales Transaction

Journal			
Date	Accounts	Debits	Credits
Jan. 31	Cash	11,400	
	Sales Revenue		11,400
Jan. 31	Cost of Goods Sold	7,600	
	Merchandise Inventory		7,600

Effect on Accounting Equation

A	=	L +	OE	
			CC +	RE
+11,400				
				+11,400
				−7,600
−7,600				

REVIEW

SUMMARY of IMPORTANT CONCEPTS

1. Accounting provides information about business activities
   a. Accounting is an information system for measuring, recording, reporting, and analyzing business activities.
   b. Financing activities provide financial resources for a company from creditors and owners. Claims to resources by creditors and owners are recorded in liability and owners' equity accounts.
   c. The accounting equation, Assets = Liabilities + Owners' Equity, provides a basis for recording transactions.
   d. Accounting measures business activities by the cash value of resources transferred or consumed in a transaction.

  e. Investing activities involve acquiring and disposing of long-term assets.

  f. Operating activities involve acquiring and selling goods and services. Revenues identify the amount of goods and services sold to customers. Expenses identify the amount of resources consumed in acquiring and selling goods and services. Profit or net income for a fiscal period is the revenue earned during the period minus expenses incurred during the period.

2. Accounting reports business activities in the form of financial statements.

  a. An income statement reports revenues, expenses, and net income for a fiscal period as a measure of operating results.

  b. A balance sheet reports the assets controlled by a company and the claims to those assets by creditors and owners at a particular time, usually the end of a fiscal period.

  c. A statement of cash flows reports the events that resulted in cash being received or paid by a company during a fiscal period.

  d. Accounting measures and reports the results of the company's transformation of resources into goods and services for sale to customers.

3. Financial analysis involves the interpretation and use of accounting information to make business decisions.

  a. Analysis involves the comparison of accounting numbers with other numbers and comparison among companies or time periods.

  b. Financial ratios compare one financial statement number with another. Return on assets is one ratio used to evaluate a company's performance.

DEFINE

TERMS and CONCEPTS DEFINED in this CHAPTER

account (F46)	investing activities (F48)
assets (F46)	liabilities (F46)
balance sheet (F55)	merchandise inventory (F50)
business activities (F45)	net income (F55)
cash (F47)	notes payable (F47)
contributed capital (F47)	operating activities (F50)
cost of goods sold (F52)	owners' equity (F45)
credits (F59)	principal (F45)
debits (F59)	retained earnings (F51)
expense (F50)	return on assets (ROA) (F58)
financial statements (F53)	revenue (F50)
financing activities (F45)	sales revenue (F52)
fiscal period (F55)	statement of cash flows (F56)
income statement (F54)	transactions (F46)
interest (F45)	

SELF-STUDY PROBLEM SOLUTIONS

SSP2-1

Accounts	ASSETS	=	LIABILITIES	+	OWNERS' EQUITY
Beginning Amounts	0	=	0	+	0
Cash	220,000				
Notes Payable			120,000		
Contributed Capital					100,000
Equipment	160,000				
Cash	−160,000				
Building	400,000				
Cash	−40,000				
Notes Payable			360,000		
Ending Amounts	580,000	=	480,000	+	100,000

SSP2-2

Date	Accounts	ASSETS Cash	Other Assets	=	LIABILITIES	+	Contributed Capital	Retained Earnings
	Beginning Amounts	0	+0	=	0		+0	+0
Jan. 3	Cash	40,000						
	Contributed Capital						40,000	
Jan. 5	Cash	25,000						
	Notes Payable				25,000			
Jan. 8	Equipment		35,000					
	Cash	−35,000						
Jan. 10	Merchandise Inventory		20,000					
	Cash	−20,000						
Jan. 11	Supplies Expense							−2,000
	Cash	−2,000						
Jan. 15	Cash	12,000						
	Sales Revenue							12,000
Jan. 15	Cost of Goods Sold							−8,000
	Merchandise Inventory		−8,000					
Jan. 22	Cash	9,000						
	Sales Revenue							9,000
Jan. 22	Cost of Goods Sold							−6,000
	Merchandise Inventory		−6,000					
Jan. 31	Wages Expense							−3,000
	Cash	−3,000						
Jan. 31	Utilities Expense							−800
	Cash	−800						
	Ending Amounts	25,200	+41,000	=	25,000	+	40,000	+1,200

SSP2-3   A.

Philistine Co.
Income Statement
For the Month Ended August 31, 2004

Sales revenue	$ 520,000
Cost of goods sold	(300,000)
Other expenses	(140,000)
Net income	$ 80,000

B.

Retained earnings, August 1	$ 0
Net income	80,000
Less: Payment to owners	30,000
Retained earnings, August 31	$50,000

C.

Philistine Co.
Balance Sheet
At August 31, 2004

Assets	
Cash	$ 25,000
Merchandise inventory	200,000
Equipment	425,000
Total assets	$650,000
Liabilities and Owners' Equity	
Notes payable	$350,000
Investment by owners	250,000
Retained earnings	50,000
Total liabilities and owners' equity	$650,000

D. Return on Assets = $80,000 ÷ $650,000 = 12.3%

Thinking Beyond the Question

How do we know how well our business is doing?

At the beginning of the chapter we asked how a business can determine how well it is performing. This chapter has described the key elements of a basic accounting system. Accounts are used to record business activities. Account balances are summarized at the end of a fiscal period, and those balances are used to prepare financial statements. Those statements help owners, creditors, and other stakeholders understand the resources available to a company, how the resources were financed, how they were used in the business, how much profit the business earned, and the events that affected the company's cash during the period.

The procedures described in this chapter may appear mechanical. Some of them are. However, sometimes judgments have to be made about when certain events should be recorded. Assuming you are making the accounting decisions for a company, what information do you think would tell you when revenues have been earned and expenses have been incurred? What events would be important for determining when to recognize revenues and expenses?

QUESTIONS

Q2-1
Obj. 1
Joan Hoyt is considering opening a small retail store to sell knives and other kitchen utensils. She has a small amount of money to invest and wants to maintain as much control over the business as she can. She has asked you to help her decide how to finance her business. Describe the primary issues you would suggest Joan to consider.

Q2-2
Obj. 1
Hardly Moving and Storage Corporation needs an additional $1,000,000 in financing to build new facilities. How might Hardly get the money? What issues should company management consider in deciding on the type of financing to use?

Q2-3
Obj. 1
Jerrilyn has invested $5,000 in shares of the stock of Ambitious Enterprises, Inc. From the corporation's perspective, was this a financing activity, an investing activity, or an operating activity? Why?

Q2-4
Obj. 2
Discuss the effect on the accounting equation if a company accurately reports its assets, yet understates its liabilities.

Q2-5
Obj. 2
How are liabilities and owners' equity similar?

Q2-6
Obj. 3
Explain why the accounting equation must balance after each transaction.

Q2-7
Objs. 3, 4
Is purchasing merchandise inventory considered an investing or operating activity? Explain.

Q2-8
Obj. 4
If owners contribute resources to a company, Owners' Equity increases. If a company records Sales Revenue, Owner's Equity also increases. How are Contributed Capital and Sales Revenue dissimilar?

Q2-9
Obj. 4
While reviewing a company's balance sheet, John observed the Retained Earnings account with a balance of $850,000. "Wow," he thought. "That's a lot of cash!" Has John correctly interpreted the company's financial information? Explain.

Q2-10
Obj. 5
Think of a company that operates in the same city as the college you are attending. With that company in mind, identify two examples each of assets, liabilities, owners' equity, revenues, and expenses that the company is likely to report on its financial statements.

Q2-11
Obj. 5
Assume you are reviewing a balance sheet that has assets listed on the left side and liabilities and owners' equity on the right side. What question or questions can you answer by looking at the information on the left side of the balance sheet? What question or questions can you answer by looking at the information on the right side of the balance sheet?

Q2-12
Obj. 5
What types of information are reported, respectively, on the balance sheet, income statement, and the statement of cash flows? Be specific.

Q2-13
Obj. 3
A balance sheet identifies assets and claims to assets. Typically, who has claims on a company's assets?

Q2-14
Obj. 5
Both the income statement and the statement of cash flows provide information about operating activities during a fiscal period. Why are both statements included in a company's financial report? How can decision makers use information in each statement?

Q2-15
Obj. 5
Why are account balances summarized into financial statements? Why don't companies simply distribute a list of year-end account balances?

| **EXERCISES** | *If your instructor is using Personal Trainer in this course, you may complete online the assignments identified by* ᴾᴛ*.* |

E2-1 Write a short definition for each of the terms listed in the *Terms and Concepts Defined in this Chapter* section.

E2-2
Objs. 1, 3, 4
ᴾᴛ

Leonetta Garcetti owns and manages a large construction company. This morning she is faced with the following issues.

1. The office manager just submitted his resignation and the search for a replacement must be organized.
2. A loan officer from the company's bank just phoned saying that the company's application for a $400,000 loan has been approved.
3. Bids from several vendors have been received regarding installation of a new computerized information system. One proposal must be selected.
4. Because the new bank loan has been approved, two short-term loans can be paid off.
5. Old office furniture is awaiting disposal.
6. A long-time customer is unhappy with the firm's latest architectural drawings for a new shopping center complex.
7. A new construction crane is being purchased.
8. An investor has approached Leonetta offering to purchase 20% of her company in exchange for cash.
9. The firm is considering the purchase of exclusive regional rights to a patented construction process.
10. One of the company's customers is behind on scheduled payments. The amounts are large and Leonetta must decide whether to suspend construction on the project involved.

Identify each of the issues above as involving a financing activity, an investing activity, or an operating activity.

E2-3
Objs. 1, 3, 4
ᴾᴛ

For each of the following items, identify which part of the transformation process is involved. Use *F* to indicate a financing activity, *I* to indicate an investing activity, or *O* to indicate an operating activity.

a. _____ New manufacturing equipment was purchased for installation in the factory.
b. _____ Three new salespersons were hired.
c. _____ A loan was obtained from a local bank.
d. _____ A $500 down payment was received from a customer on goods sold.
e. _____ The Human Resources department hired three new employees.
f. _____ The company's worn-out delivery truck was sold to the junk yard for $400.
g. _____ The owner contributed more cash to the business.
h. _____ Refunds totaling $450 were given to several customers.
i. _____ Goods were shipped to a customer in a neighboring state.
j. _____ The remaining balance of a loan was repaid in full.

E2-4
Obj. 2
ᴾᴛ

Popovich Company had the following transactions during June.

June	1	$20,000 of merchandise inventory was purchased with cash.
	15	Sold merchandise for $60,000 cash. The merchandise had cost Popovich $28,000.
	23	Borrowed $200,000 from a bank.
	25	Paid $2,000 for supplies used in June.
	28	June wages of $6,000 were paid.
	30	$100,000 of equipment was purchased using cash.
	30	Paid $4,000 for utilities consumed in June.

Indicate the amount of cash, other assets, liabilities, and/or owners' equity that would result from each transaction by completing the table provided on the next page.

(Continued)

		ASSETS		=	LIABILITIES	+	OWNERS' EQUITY	
Date	Accounts	Cash	Other Assets				Contributed Capital	Retained Earnings
June 1	Beginning Amounts	$40,000	+60,000	=	30,000	+	50,000	+20,000
	Ending Amounts							

E2-5
Obj. 1, 3, 4
P/T

Identify each transaction in E2-4 as financing, investing, or operating.

E2-6
Obj. 2
P/T

Perez Company had the following selected transactions during the month of May. Show how the financial effects of each transaction would be recorded using the following format. The first transaction has been completed as an example.

Juanita Perez invested $10,000 in the company on May 1.

		ASSETS		=	LIABILITIES	+	OWNERS' EQUITY	
Date	Accounts	Cash	Other Assets				Contributed Capital	Retained Earnings
	Beginning Amounts	70,000	+90,000	=	60,000	+	60,000	+40,000
May 1	Cash	10,000						
	Contributed Capital						10,000	

May	5	Sold goods for $30,000 cash. The goods had cost $14,000.
	10	Purchased merchandise inventory for $45,000 cash.
	15	Paid back part of a bank loan, $1,500 (decrease Notes Payable).
	22	Purchased equipment for $4,000 using cash.
	31	Paid the utility company for services consumed, $600.
	31	Paid $7,500 wages for labor services consumed.

E2-7
Objs. 1, 3, 4
P/T

Identify each transaction in E2-6 as financing, investing, or operating.

E2-8
Obj. 2

Rosy Cheeks Company distributes perfumes and cosmetics. The following account changes were made in the company's accounting records during March. For each item, describe the transaction that caused the changes. The first item has been completed as an example.

a. Cash increased $18,000; Contributed Capital increased $18,000.
The owners invested $18,000 in the company.
b. Equipment increased $10,500; Cash decreased $10,500.
c. Cash increased $8,500; Notes Payable increased $8,500.
d. Supplies inventory increased $13,500; Cash decreased $13,500.
e. Merchandise Inventory decreased $9,500; Cost of Goods Sold increased $9,500.
f. Cash increased $23,500; Sales Revenue increased $23,500.
g. Supplies Expense increased $2,250; Supplies inventory decreased $2,250.

E2-9
Obj. 2
P/T

Amelio has operated a one-person law firm for many years. During the first week of February, the following events occurred in his business.

Feb. 2   Collected $1,800 from a client for legal work performed.
3   February's office rent of $1,200 was paid to the landlord.
4   A $300 payment was made on a loan previously obtained from a local bank.
4   The monthly subscription to *Lawyer's Monthly* magazine (a Miscellaneous Expense) was paid: $35.
5   Collected $4,250 for legal services performed.
5   Purchased a computer for $3,200 using cash.
6   Wages were paid to the office staff totaling $525.
6   Office supplies of $128 were purchased for cash and were consumed.

Show how the events above would be recorded using the format demonstrated in the chapter. Beginning account balances were as follows: Cash $5,000, Liabilities $1,500, Contributed Capital $3,000, and Retained Earnings $500. Prepare an income statement for the first week of February.

E2-10
Objs. 1, 3, 4
P̶T

Identify each transaction in E2-9 as financing, investing, or operating.

E2-11
Obj. 2
P̶T

Balance sheet accounts for Dale's Delightful Florist Shoppe at the end of a recent fiscal year are listed below. Prepare a schedule demonstrating that assets = liabilities + owner's equity for the company.

Supplies Inventory	$ 4,150
Buildings	79,500
Cash	1,200
Equipment	12,750
Flowers and Plants	24,780
Notes Payable	58,000
Proprietor's Capital	64,380

E2-12
Obj. 2
P̶T

Harmony Cabot opened a music store in a local mall, selling CDs and tapes. She invested $80,000 in the business and borrowed $140,000 from a local bank. The following additional events occurred during April, the first month of operations:

a. Paid cash for equipment costing $45,150.
b. Purchased an inventory of CDs and tapes for $129,600 in cash.
c. Sold one-third of the CDs and tapes for a cash sales price of $85,000.
d. Paid expenses as follows:

Employee wages	$12,300
Rent	15,500
Utilities	4,800
Postage	650
Insurance	1,290

Record the transactions using the format shown in the chapter.

E2-13
Obj. 4
P̶T

Chang Pottery Works began November with a Retained Earnings balance of $95,000. During November the company earned $15,000 and returned $4,000 to the owners. Prepare a schedule that reports the beginning balance, changes, and ending balance of retained earnings.

E2-14
Obj. 5
P̶T

The following events occurred during December for Christmas Cookie Company:

a. Purchased and consumed $60,000 of flour, sugar, and other ingredients for cookies sold.
b. Paid $97,500 for December wages.
c. Paid $24,000 for utilities consumed in December.
d. Sold $234,000 of cookies and received cash.

Prepare an income statement for Christmas Cookie Company.

E2-15
Obj. 5

P/T

Wheatgerm Healthfoods reported the following information:

Proceeds from issuance of notes payable	$13,057
Additions to plant and equipment	5,379
Proceeds from owners	30,957
Proceeds from sales of plant and equipment	1,986
Payments of debt	80,323

Calculate the net cash flow from (a) financing and (b) investing activities for Wheatgerm.

E2-16
Obj. 5

P/T

Darden Bottling Company has the following information available for the first six months of 2004:

Cash collected from customers	$268,000
Cash paid merchandise inventory	83,500
Cash paid for utilities	20,000
Cash paid for insurance	23,000
Cash paid for equipment	76,500
Cash paid to employees	57,500
Cash paid for postage	7,500
Cash paid to owners	5,000
Cash received from sale of old equipment	18,500

Determine the cash flow from operating activities for the six-month period.

E2-17
Obj. 5

P/T

Listed below are typical accounts or titles that appear on financial statements. For each item, identify the financial statement(s) on which it appears.

Wages expense
Cost of goods sold
Sales revenue
Merchandise inventory
Net income
Retained earnings
Contributed capital
Rent expense
Cash
Notes payable

E2-18
Obj. 5

P/T

After six months of operation, Brother's Lawn Service had the following revenue and expense account balances:

Supplies expense	$ 4,000
Wages expense	6,000
Service revenue	12,300
Utilities expense	500
Rent expense	1,000

Prepare an income statement for Brother's Lawn Service for the first six months of operation that ended June 30, 2004.

E2-19
Obj. 5

P/T

On June 30, 2004, Brothers' Lawn Service had the following account balances:

Cash	$3,000
Notes payable	1,000
Contributed capital	6,700
Retained earnings	800
Supplies inventory	500
Equipment	5,000

Prepare a balance sheet for Brother's Lawn Service.

E2-20

Obj. 2, appendix

P̂T

Record each transaction described in E2-4, using the debit and credit format illustrated in the appendix.

E2-21

Obj. 2, appendix

P̂T

Record each transaction described in E2-6, using the debit and credit format illustrated in the appendix.

PROBLEMS

If your instructor is using Personal Trainer in this course, you may complete online the assignments identified by P̂T.

P2-1

Obj. 2

P̂T

Recording Transactions

Surf-The-Net.com had the following events occur during October:

1. Paid $5,800 for utilities.
2. Made cash sales to customers that totaled $89,460. The merchandise had cost Surf-The-Net.com $60,000
3. Paid $28,600 for new equipment.
4. Repaid a $4,900 bank loan.
5. Borrowed $65,000 from local bank.
6. Paid $59,430 to employees for salaries.
7. Paid $11,900 for maintenance and repair.
8. Received $48,600 from investors.
9. Paid $3,750 for supplies that were used.

Required

A. Record transactions 1–9 using the format illustrated in the chapter.
B. What issues must a manager consider before making a financing decision or investing decision?

P2-2

Objs. 1, 3, 4

P̂T

Classifying Activities as Operating, Investing, or Financing

Refer to the information provided in P2-1.

Required Identify each transaction in P2-1 as a financing, investing, or operating activity.

P2-3

Obj. 2

P̂T

The Accounting Equation

Apollo Corporation reported the following accounts and balances in its financial statements:

Cash	$10,000
Merchandise Inventory	30,000
Equipment	45,000
Notes Payable	20,000
Contributed Capital	35,000
Retained Earnings	30,000

Required Arrange the accounts and balances into the accounting equation as shown below:

Assets = Liabilities + Equity

P2-4

Obj. 2

P̂T

Recording Transactions

Davidson Enterprises had the following transactions during its first month of business, June 2004.

June 1   Lynne Davidson set up a bank account in the business name and deposited $8,000 of her personal funds to it.

     2   June's rent of $525 per month for a store-front location was paid in cash.

     7   Goods for resale costing $3,600 were purchased using cash.

    12   Paid advertising costs of $1,000 for the firm's Gala Grand Opening.

    26   Goods costing $3,000 were sold during June for $7,200 in cash.

    30   Workers were paid $850 and the utility company was paid $228 for June services.

(Continued)

Required

A. Use the format illustrated below to show how these transactions would be recorded.
B. Prepare an income statement that reports the firm's profit during June.
C. Prepare a balance sheet that reports the firm's assets, liabilities, and equity at June 30.

		ASSETS		=	LIABILITIES	+	OWNERS' EQUITY	
Date	Accounts	Cash	Other Assets				Contributed Capital	Retained Earnings
	Beginning Amounts	0	+0 =		0	+	0	+0

P2-5

Objs. 1, 3, 4

$\frac{P}{T}$

Classifying Transactions as Financing, Investing, or Operating

Refer to the information provided in P2-4.

Required Identify each transaction in P2-4 as financing, investing, or operating.

P2-6

Obj. 2

$\frac{P}{T}$

Recording Transactions

Carmen Bay Company sells a variety of souvenirs to tourists on the beach. Teenagers are paid 20 percent of the sales price to hawk the wares up and down the beach and are paid daily. The company was formed only recently and given approval by the local city council to operate. The following events are the first in the company's short history:

1. The company was formed when Carmen Bay contributed $2,150 to the firm.
2. A local bank loaned the firm $4,000 in exchange for the firm's one-year note payable.
3. Merchandise costing $4,100 was purchased with cash.
4. Goods costing $825 were sold to tourists for a total of $2,250 in cash, and the teenagers were paid their commissions.
5. A payment of $1,500 was made to the local bank on the note payable.
6. Carmen Bay withdrew $500 cash for personal use (Hint: reduce retained earnings).

Assume the company uses the following set of accounts:

Cash   Notes Payable
Cost of Sales   Merchandise Inventory
Sales   Contributed Capital
Retained Earnings   Commissions Expense

Required Determine how each event affects the company, and record the events using the format shown below.

		ASSETS		=	LIABILITIES	+	OWNERS' EQUITY	
Date	Accounts	Cash	Other Assets				Contributed Capital	Retained Earnings
	Beginning Amounts	0	+0 =		0	+	0	+0

P2-7

Obj. 2

$\frac{P}{T}$

Recording Transactions

Randi had a hard time finding a summer job when she went home from college, so she decided to go into business for herself mowing lawns. She had the following business activities during the month of June.

June 1 Used $200 of her own money and borrowed $450 from her father to start the business.

2 Rented a used pickup truck from an uncle for $85 per month. Paid for the first month's use.

3 Rented a lawnmower ($75 per month), an edger ($50 per month), and a wheelbarrow ($10 per month) at an equipment rental store. Paid the first month's rental fees in full.

16 During the first two weeks, performed $528 of lawn-mowing services. Customers paid in cash. Paid out $52 for gas, oil, and other supplies.

18 Paid $35 for a newspaper advertisement that had appeared earlier in the month.

30 During the last half of the month, performed $507 of lawn-mowing services and collected the cash.

30 Paid out $107 for gas, oil, and other supplies.

30 Paid back one-half of the amount she had borrowed from her father plus $5 for interest.

Randi knew from taking an accounting class at college that the following accounts would be needed to keep track of her business activities.

Cash	Equipment Rental Expense
Note Payable—Dad	Contributed Capital
Service Revenue	Retained Earnings
Gas and Oil Expense	Advertising Expense

Required

A. Show how each event would be entered into the accounting system.
B. Prepare an income statement for Randi's Lawn-mowing Service for the month of June.
C. Prepare a balance sheet as of June 30.
D. Did Randi make a smart decision when she started her own business? What factors might be considered in making that evaluation?

P2-8
Obj. 2

Reconstructing Events from Information in the Accounting Database

Jill Jones has just established a security alarm maintenance service. She charges $20 per hour per person and is paid by check upon completion of the job. Her expenses are rather low—usually only supplies and transportation. Following are the entries to the accounting system that were made for the first seven transactions of the company.

Date	Accounts	ASSETS Cash	Other Assets	= LIABILITIES	+	OWNERS' EQUITY Contributed Capital	Retained Earnings
1	Cash	5,000					
	Contributed Capital					5,000	
2	Supplies Inventory		300				
	Cash	−300					
3	Cash	4,200					
	Service Revenues						4,200
4	Utilities Expense						−450
	Cash	−450					
5	Transportation Expense						−500
	Cash	−500					
6	Insurance Expense						−700
	Cash	−700					
7	Retained Earnings						−1,300
	Cash	−1,300					
	Ending Amounts	5,950	+300 =			5,000	+1,250

(Continued)

Required

A. For each transaction, describe the event that caused the entry to be made.

B. How much income (or loss) did the company earn?

P2-9 **Understanding Information in the Accounting Information System**

Obj. 2

Jacqueline owns and operates a specialty cosmetics manufacturing firm. Distribution is primarily through boutique shops in regional shopping centers, although some items are sold directly through a network of beauty consultants. Raw materials consist of various lotions, potions, fragrances, oils, and powders. The transactions that occurred during the month of March were entered into the accounting system as follows.

Date	Accounts	Cash	Other Assets	=	LIABILITIES	+	Contributed Capital	Retained Earnings
Mar. 1	Cash	10,000						
	Contributed Capital						10,000	
Mar. 3	Cash	7,000						
	Notes Payable				7,000			
Mar. 5	Merchandise Inventory		8,100					
	Cash	−8,100						
Mar. 18	Cash	15,250						
	Sales Revenue							15,250
	Cost of Goods Sold							−7,500
	Merchandise Inventory		−7,500					
Mar. 18	Wages Expense							−650
	Cash	−650						
Mar. 23	Notes Payable				−2,500			
	Cash	−2,500						
Mar. 31	Retained Earnings							−2,000
	Cash	−2,000						
	Ending Amounts	19,000	+600	=	4,500	+	10,000	+5,100

Required

A. Describe each of the firm's transactions. Specify as much detail about each transaction as you can.

B. Assume an income statement and balance sheet are prepared immediately after the last transaction.
1. What amount of net income would be reported?
2. What total amount of owners' equity would be reported on the balance sheet?

P2-10 **Reconstructing Events from the Financial Statements**

Obj. 2

Costantino Company just started in business. The first seven transactions have been entered into and processed by the company's computerized accounting information system. To be sure the accounting system is operating properly, Jim Costantino, the owner, has printed out the financial statements as produced by the accounting system after seven transactions.

Assets:		Liabilities and Equity:	
Cash	$22,850	Payable to bank	$ 6,285
Equipment	11,000	Payable for equipment	11,000
		Owner investment	15,000
		Retained earnings	1,565
Total assets	$33,850	Total liabilities and equity	$33,850
Revenues	$ 2,250		
Expenses:			
Rent	(400)		
Wages	(250)		
Internet service	(35)		
Net income	$ 1,565		

Required Identify the seven transactions and as much detail about each transaction as you can.

P2-11

Objs. 2, 5

P/T

Recording Transactions and Preparing Financial Statements

Assume that you began a small business in May 2004 by (1) investing $10,000 and (2) borrowing $30,000 from a bank. You (3) purchased equipment for $25,000 cash and (4) purchased merchandise for $12,000 using cash. During the first month of operations, your company (5) sold merchandise for $27,000 in cash. (6) The cost of merchandise sold during the month was $10,000. You (7) repaid $300 of the amount borrowed from the bank. You (8) withdrew $800 from the business for personal use. The name of your business is Sand Dune Trading Company.

Required

A. Record transactions 1–8 using the format illustrated in the chapter.
B. Prepare an income statement for May 2004, the first month of operations.
C. Prepare a balance sheet at the end of the first month.

P2-12

Obj. 5

P/T

Identifying Financial Statements

Refer to the information about financial statements below.

1. The statement provides information about resources consumed during an accounting period.
2. The statement is dated as of a specific point in time.
3. The amounts that are owed to other organizations or individuals are reported.
4. The total amount of capital that has been contributed to the organization is reported.
5. The cash used for investing activities is reported.
6. Information is reported regarding the rewards that have been earned from serving customers during the accounting period just ended.
7. The cash received from financing activities is reported.
8. The statement is not as of a specific date, but covers a period of time.
9. The statement contains information about the financial obligations that were made to acquire resources.
10. The statement reports cash inflows and outflows.

Required For each item above, indicate the financial statement for which the information is true. Use *I* to indicate income statement, *B* to indicate balance sheet, *C* to indicate cash flow statement. If an item is not true for any of the three financial statements, indicate with an *N*.

P2-13

Obj. 5

P/T

Summarizing the Results of Financial Activities

The accounting staff at Moonbeam Enterprises prepares monthly financial statements. At the end of April 2004 the company had the following account balances:

(Continued)

Land	$45,000
Notes payable	33,000
Merchandise inventory	12,480
Buildings	50,000
Cash	10,360
Contributed capital	38,770
Retained earnings, April 30	46,070
Cost of goods sold	15,050
Sales revenue	26,000
Supplies expense	1,300
Income tax expense	1,060
Wage expense	1,500
Insurance expense	550
Interest expense	900

Required Prepare an income statement and balance sheet in good form. For each statement, use a three-line heading on the statement that includes (a) the name of the company, (b) the name of the statement, and (c) the appropriate time period or date.

P2-14   ## Recording Transactions

Objs. 2, 5

P/T

Larrisa Enterprises, Inc., owns and operates a chain of mini-mart stores in a popular summer resort area. Business is highly seasonal with about 80% of annual sales occurring during June, July, and August. Shown below are transactions that occurred during the first week of June.

June 3   Merchandise costing $120,000 was purchased from a supplier using cash.
     4   Dividends of $25,000 were distributed to owners for their own personal use. (Hint: Dividends reduce Retained Earnings.)
     5   Goods costing $112,000 were sold to customers for $140,000 cash.
     5   Advertising was run in local newspapers during the first week. The bill, for $9,000, was paid on June 5.
     6   Electricity, water, natural gas, and Internet charges totaling $450 were paid in cash.
     6   Display equipment was purchased for $15,000 cash.
     7   Employees were paid a total of $12,900 for all work performed through the end of the first week of June.

Required Show how the events above would be entered into the accounting system using the format demonstrated in the chapter. Beginning balances are provided below:

		ASSETS		=	LIABILITIES	+	OWNERS' EQUITY	
Date	**Accounts**	**Cash**	**Other Assets**				**Contributed Capital**	**Retained Earnings**
	Beginning Amounts	90,000	150,000		80,000		60,000	100,000

P2-15   ## Classifying Transactions as Financing, Investing, or Operating Activities

Objs. 1, 3, 4

P/T

Refer to the information provided in P2-14.

Required Identify each transaction in P2-14 as a financing, investing, or operating activity.

P2-16   ## Preparing a Statement of Cash Flows

Obj. 5

P/T

Crimson Florist had the following cash flows for the month of July 2004.

Cash paid for wages	$ 5,000
Cash paid for supplies	2,500
Cash received from sales to customers	15,000
Cash paid for equipment	5,000
Cash received from owners	13,000
Cash paid for utilities	3,500
Cash received from creditors	8,500

The cash balance on July 1 was $3,200.

Required

A. Prepare a statement of cash flows for Crimson Florist.

B. What is the purpose of the statement of cash flows?

P2-17

Obj. 5

P
T

Preparing a Statement of Cash Flows

During January, The College Shop had the following cash flows:

Cash paid for merchandise	$ 4,000
Cash paid for rent	5,300
Cash received from sales to customers	13,000
Cash paid for utilities	200
Cash received from owners	9,000
Cash paid for equipment	7,000
Cash paid for insurance	2,500
Cash received from a bank loan	10,500
Cash paid for wages	1,200

The beginning cash balance was $4,000.

Required Prepare a statement of cash flows for The College Shop.

P2-18

Obj. 5

P
T

Financial Analysis

Holiday Travel Store is a retailer that sells merchandise at a family campground. The company's most recent income statement and balance sheet are presented below:

Holiday Travel Store
Income Statement
For the Year Ended December 31, 2004

Sales revenue	$75,000
Cost of goods sold	(43,000)
Wages expense	(15,000)
Supplies expense	(3,500)
Utilities expense	(2,000)
Rent expense	(8,000)
Net income	$ 3,500

Holiday Travel Store
Balance Sheet
December 31, 2004

Assets	
Cash	$ 900
Merchandise inventory	7,000
Equipment	20,000
Total assets	$27,900
Liabilities and Owners' Equity	
Notes payable	$15,500
Contributed capital	10,000
Retained earnings	2,400
Total liabilities and owners' equity	$27,900

Required

A. Calculate Holiday Travel Store's return on assets.

B. Explain what the ratio means.

C. What kinds of changes might the owners make if the return on assets is not acceptable?

P2-19

Obj. 2, Appendix

Recording Transactions Using the Debit and Credit Format

Refer to the information provided in P2-6.

Required For each transaction described in P2-6, record the transaction using the debit and credit format illustrated in the appendix.

P2-20

Obj. 2, Appendix

Recording Transactions Using the Debit and Credit Format

Refer to the information provided in P2-7.

Required For each transaction described in P2-7, record the transaction using the debit and credit format illustrated in the appendix.

P2-21

SPREADSHEET

Excel in Action

Millie and Milo Wermz are the owners of The Book Wermz. The business is operated as a corporation. The Wermz invested $100,000 in the company when they started it in 1996. This investment represents the company's stockholders' equity. The company's account balances on September 30, 2004—the end of the fiscal year—were: Cash $4,238.72, Inventory of Books $235,892.35, Supplies $2,343.28, Equipment $43,297.00, Notes Payable $123,452.88, Investment by Owners $100,000, and Retained Earnings $62,318.47.

Summary transactions for The Book Wermz for October 2004 included:

Cash sales	$38,246.50
Cost of goods sold	27,318.93

Required Use a spreadsheet to keep track of account balances for The Book Wermz. Enter the titles of accounts in row 1. Use column A for dates. Enter account balances for September 30, 2004 in row 2. A partial spreadsheet is illustrated below as an example:

	A	B	C
1	Date	Cash	Inventory
2	9/30/04	4,238.72	235,892.35

Use the Format menu to adjust cell formats as needed to wrap text for long titles. Use the comma button to format dollar amounts. See instructions from Chapter 1 if you need help with formatting. Include columns for Sales and Cost of Goods Sold. The beginning balances for these two accounts will be $0.

In Row 3, enter the sales transaction for October, and in Row 4 enter the Cost of Goods Sold transaction. Use 10/31/04 as dates for these transactions. Using the illustration of closing the accounts in this chapter, close the revenue and expense accounts for October in Row 5. In Row 6, calculate the account balance for each account at October 31, 2004. Use the Sum function [=Sum(B2:B5)] or button Σ for this purpose. Note that =Sum(B2:B5) performs the same operation as =B2+B3+B4+B5. The ending balances for revenue and expense accounts should be $0 after these accounts have been closed.

Beginning in Row 9, prepare a balance sheet and income statement for The Book Wermz for October 2004. Use the format illustrated in Exhibits 13 and 14 in this chapter. You may need to make some of the columns in the spreadsheet wider to accommodate captions. Format cells with the currency format so that they display $, as shown in Exhibits 13 and 14. You can use the Currency **$** and Comma **,** buttons for this purpose. Cells containing totals should be formatted to contain double underlines. Use the Borders button ⊞ for this purpose.

Use cell references in the financial statements to identify amounts for each account. For example: | **Cash** | =B6 |

Also, use the Sum function or button to calculate totals in the balance sheet and income statement. You should be able to change any of the numbers in the transactions at the top of the spreadsheet and have the financial statements change automatically in response to the new amounts.

P2-22 Multiple Choice Overview of the Chapter

1. Which of the following is a financing activity?
   a. A manufacturing company purchases supplies.
   b. A retail company borrows $40,000 from a bank.
   c. A manufacturing company acquires a new building.
   d. A service organization pays the monthly utility bill.

2. If a company borrows cash from a bank, the effect on the accounting equation is as follows:
   a. Assets increase, Liabilities increase
   b. Assets decrease, Liabilities increase
   c. Assets increase, Liabilities decrease
   d. Assets decrease, Liabilities decrease

3. The balance sheet describes a company's assets. Financial resources to acquire these assets are obtained from
   a. investing activities.
   b. financing activities and revenues earned.
   c. investing activities and expenses paid during a fiscal period.
   d. none of the above.

4. Which of the following is an investing activity?
   a. A manufacturer borrows from creditors.
   b. A service firm pays a return to its stockholders.
   c. A retailer sells goods to a not-for-profit agency at cost.
   d. A government agency purchases a new mainframe computer system.

5. Which of the following is *not* an operating activity?
   a. Merchandise is sold to customers.
   b. Utility bills are paid.
   c. Merchandise is shipped to customers.
   d. Equipment is purchased for use in manufacturing.

6. Return on assets represents
   a. cash that is returned to investors.
   b. merchandise that is returned by customers.
   c. the ratio of income to total assets.
   d. the ratio of merchandise returned by customers to sales.

7. Accounting information is

	Needed by managers for internal decision making	Needed by managers for persons outside the firm
a.	Yes	Yes
b.	Yes	No
c.	No	Yes
d.	No	No

8. Liability and owners' equity accounts usually arise from which type of activities?
   a. Investing activities
   b. Financing activities
   c. Operating activities
   d. Manufacturing activities

9. Expresso Delivery Service purchased a new delivery truck for $21,000 by making a $4,000 cash payment and giving a $17,000 note payable to the seller. How were each of the following affected when this event was recorded in the firm's accounting information system?

	Assets	Liabilities
a.	Increased	Increased
b.	No change	Increased
c.	Increased	Decreased
d.	Decreased	Increased

10. The statement of cash flows for the Halyard Exploration Company reported the following:

Cash paid for equipment	$ 300,000
Cash paid to employees	400,000
Cash paid to owners	150,000
Cash paid to suppliers	560,000
Cash received from customers	1,200,000

What were Halyard's net cash flows from operating, investing, and financing activities?

	Operating	Investing	Financing
a.	$240,000	($300,000)	$(150,000)
b.	$500,000	($860,000)	$200,000
c.	$640,000	($860,000)	$200,000
d.	$240,000	($860,000)	$200,000

11. When an investor contributes cash to a business, the transaction is recorded as follows:

	Debit	Credit
a.	Cash	Retained Earnings
b.	Cash	Contributed Capital
c.	Contributed Capital	Cash
d.	Retained Earnings	Cash

CASE

C2-1

Obj. 6

Designing an Accounting Information System

For about a year, Frank Poppa has been operating a hot dog stand in the parking lot of a major discount retailer in a suburban area. The stand appears to be a pushcart but is actually a small trailer that is towed from home each day. Frank cleverly designed the stand to include storage compartments, napkins, and the like. What started out as a "weekend gig" to pick up a few extra bucks has turned into a full-time occupation. Frank soon found that on a hot summer day, he could easily take in more than $1,000 from sales of a full line of fancy hot dogs and cold sodas.

About four months ago, Frank decided to expand to more locations. He found that large discount retailers were quite happy to provide him adequate space near the front door because customers enjoyed the convenience and the stand helped build traffic for the retailer. Frank formed Poppa's Dogs Company and negotiated contracts with several retailers to provide pushcart operations outside their stores. The contracts generally call for Poppa's Dogs to pay a location fee to the retailer plus 3% of the pushcart's sales.

Frank plans to be very careful when hiring the people necessary to operate the five new pushcart locations. He is confident that he can assess good moral character and avoid hiring anyone who would take advantage of him. Frank will have to spend about $3,000 for each new pushcart and related equipment. In addition, he will have to finance an inventory of hot dogs, condiments, and sodas for each location. A local bank has agreed to provide financing.

Until now, Frank has maintained an informal accounting system consisting of an envelope full of receipts and his personal checking account. The system has served him well enough so far, but he is finding that more and more he is getting his personal financial activities confused with those of his business. Frank is positive that the business is profitable because he seems to have more money left at the end of the month than he did when he was working full time as an auto mechanic. He has decided he needs a better accounting system and has decided to consult with a CPA he knows to see what she might recommend.

Required What information does Frank's current accounting system provide him? What additional information should Frank want from an improved accounting system? Make recommendations to Frank regarding how he can improve his accounting system and identify a chart (list) of accounts that you would expect to find in Frank's new accounting system. For each account, identify whether it is an asset, liability, owner's equity, revenue, or expense.

C2-2

Objs. 1, 3, 4

Financing, Investing, and Operating Activities as Part of the Transformation Process

Environmental Housing Company designs and builds log homes. Financing is provided by owners and creditors, primarily banks. The company owns buildings and equipment it uses in the management, design, transportation, and construction process. It purchases logs and other building materials from other companies. These materials are shipped by the sellers. Homes are designed for customers. Logs are cut to the dimensions called for in a design and shipped to the customer's building site with other materials for assembly. Environmental Housing employs design engineers, construction and assembly workers, maintenance personnel, and marketing and service personnel, in addition to its management and office staff. The company is in charge of the construction process until the home is completed and ready for occupancy. The company gives warranties for one year after completion that state the completed home is free of defects from materials or construction.

Required List decisions involving the acquisition, use, or disposal of resources that Environmental Housing's managers would make at each stage (financing, investing, and operating) of the transformation process.

MEASURING REVENUES AND EXPENSES

How do we know how much profit our business has earned?

With their accountant's help, Maria and Stan set up an accounting system for recording the business activities of Mom's Cookie Company. They prepared financial statements for January from information recorded in their accounting system. However, certain types of transactions were not considered in preparing those statements. A business requires an accounting system that ensures that all revenues and expenses are recorded in the appropriate fiscal period.

FOOD FOR THOUGHT

If you were running a business, how would you know when to record revenues and expenses? It's easy to keep track of cash when your business receives it at the time goods are sold or services are provided. What would you do if your goods are transferred or services are provided to customers in one fiscal period and cash is received in a different period? You might consume resources in one fiscal period but pay for those resources in a different period. When should you recognize the expense? Now that they understand some basic accounting procedures, Maria and Stan discuss the appropriate recognition of revenues and expenses with their accountant, Ellen.

Stan: *We recorded transactions and prepared financial statements for January, but it seems like we haven't included all the business activities that occurred during January. We owe interest on our loan to the bank, and we used equipment we purchased in January without recording any expense.*

Ellen: *You're correct. We created a basic accounting system for recording transactions in January. Now we need to expand that system to include all transactions that should be recorded each month.*

Maria: *Does it really matter that much if we don't include everything in the appropriate month?*

Ellen: *Businesses are required to record revenues and expenses in the fiscal period in which revenues are earned and expenses incurred. Careful identification of the proper amount of revenues and expenses is important to provide accurate and reliable information about your company's performance. If you fail to do so, you may report misleading information. That could cause you to make bad decisions and it may affect decisions by creditors and other stakeholders.*

Stan: *How can we know if we have recorded all the transactions we need to record each month?*

Ellen: *You need to follow the proper accounting rules and procedures. Once you identify the kinds of events that need to be recorded each month, following these rules and procedures will help make sure your financial statements are accurate and reliable. Let's look at these rules and procedures and learn how to apply them to your company.*

OBJECTIVES

Once you have completed this chapter, you should be able to:

1 Explain the concept of accrual accounting and why it is used.

2 Record revenue transactions using accrual accounting.

3 Record expense transactions using accrual accounting.

4 Identify and record adjusting entries at the end of a fiscal period.

5 Prepare closing entries and financial statements at the end of a fiscal period.

6 Identify steps in the accounting cycle.

ACCRUAL ACCOUNTING

OBJECTIVE 1

Explain the concept of accrual accounting and why it is used.

Almost all of the transactions we examined in Chapter F2 involved receipt or payment of cash. Cash often is received from customers at the time goods are sold. Cash often is paid when equipment, merchandise inventory, and supplies are purchased. These transactions involve increasing or decreasing the cash account and recording an offsetting amount to the revenue or expense account that explains the cause of the increase or decrease in cash.

In many cases a company earns revenue or incurs expenses in a fiscal period other than the one in which cash is received or paid. Consider the following examples for Mom's Cookie Company for the first three months of operation:

- Money was borrowed in January, but repayment of principal was not made until later.
- Interest was incurred on debt in January and February, but the interest was not paid until March.
- Goods were sold to customers on credit in February, but cash was not received until March.
- Employees worked in February and earned wages, but the wages were paid in March.
- Customers ordered goods in February and paid cash at the time of the order, but the goods were not delivered to the customers until March.
- Rent was paid on a building in February for use of the building in February, March, and April.

These types of transactions are common for most companies. To accommodate these types of events, businesses use a form of accounting known as accrual accounting. *Accrual accounting* **is a form of accounting in which revenues are recognized when they are earned and expenses are recognized when they are incurred.** To recognize revenues and expenses means to record them as accounting transactions. Normally, revenues are earned when goods are transferred or when services are provided. Expenses are incurred when resources are consumed in the processes of acquiring and selling goods and services. Accrual accounting focuses on business activities to determine when to record revenues and expenses.

A company does not have to receive or pay cash at the time revenues or expenses are recorded. However, the accounting process is more complicated when revenues or expenses are recorded in one period and cash is received or paid in another. Let's consider some examples for Mom's Cookie Company.

REVENUE TRANSACTIONS

OBJECTIVE 2

Record revenue transactions using accrual accounting.

On February 12, 2004, Mom's Cookie Company sold boxes of cookies to a customer for $600 on credit. The boxes cost Mom's Cookie Company $400. The customer paid for the goods on March 10, 2004. Because the revenue was earned in February, Mom's Cookie Company must recognize the revenue in February. The transaction to record the sale would be as follows:

| Date | Accounts | ASSETS | | = LIABILITIES | + OWNERS' EQUITY | |
		Cash	Other Assets		Contributed Capital	Retained Earnings
Feb. 12	Accounts Receivable		600			
	Sales Revenue					600
Feb. 12	Cost of Goods Sold					−400
	Merchandise Inventory		−400			

Neither of these transactions involves cash. Cash was not received from the customer at the time of the sale. Cash was not paid by Mom's Cookie Company for the merchandise at the time of sale, either. The company was selling merchandise that it had already purchased.

Accounts Receivable **is an asset account that increases when goods are sold on credit.** It represents an amount a customer owes to a company. Revenue is recognized because the goods have been transferred to the customer. Mom's Cookie Company has done the work necessary to earn revenue, and accrual accounting requires revenue to be recognized when it is earned.

The sale transaction is linked to a second transaction that occurs on March 10. When the customer pays for the goods, Mom's Cookie Company records the following:

| Date | Accounts | ASSETS | | = LIABILITIES | + OWNERS' EQUITY | |
		Cash	Other Assets		Contributed Capital	Retained Earnings
Mar. 10	Cash	600				
	Accounts Receivable		−600			

Cash increases because it has been received from the customer. Accounts Receivable decreases because the customer has fulfilled the obligation to pay for the goods sold in February. **Revenue is not recognized at the time cash is received because it has already been recognized when goods were sold.** Because the sale occurs at one time and cash is received at a different time, two transactions are needed to record the sale and cash receipt. Accounts Receivable provides a means of linking the two transactions. It records the amount the customer owes the company until the customer pays for the goods. Exhibit 1 describes the effect of the transactions on the Cash, Accounts Receivable, and Sales Revenue accounts.

Accounts Receivable increases at the time of sale in February. The amount the customer owes is decreased when the customer pays cash in March, reducing the Accounts Receivable balance for this sale to zero. The net result of the two transactions is the same as if the customer had paid cash for the goods. However, two transactions are necessary to achieve this result. The first transaction is important because Maria and Stan and other decision makers are interested in when a company sells goods. All of the sales that oc-

Exhibit 1

Linking Revenue and
Cash through Accounts
Receivable

Date	Cash	Accounts Receivable	Sales Revenue
Feb. 12		600	600
Mar. 10	600	−600	
Net result	600	0	600

cur in February should appear on Mom's Cookie Company's income statement for February. The income statement provides information about business activities that occurred during a particular fiscal period. If a company waited until cash was received from customers to record revenues, it would appear that the business sold the goods in the period when cash was received. Instead, accrual accounting ensures that decision makers have information about sales activities for the period in which the sales occurred. In addition, recording accounts receivable provides information about the amount owed by customers that a company expects to collect in a future fiscal period.

Sometimes a company receives cash from a customer before a sale is made. For example, Mom's Cookie Company received an order from a customer on February 24, 2004, for more goods than the company had in its inventory. Maria and Stan agreed to fill the order for the customer but required the customer to pay for the goods at the time of the order. The customer paid $3,000 on February 24, and Mom's Cookie Company ordered the goods from its supplier. The goods were delivered to the customer on March 3.

The payment transaction would be recorded as follows:

		ASSETS		=	LIABILITIES	+	OWNERS' EQUITY	
Date	Accounts	Cash	Other Assets				Contributed Capital	Retained Earnings
Feb. 24	Cash	3,000						
	Unearned Revenue				3,000			

Cash increases by the amount received from the customer. Revenue has not been earned, however, because goods have not been transferred to the customer. Instead, Mom's Cookie Company has incurred a liability as represented by the Unearned Revenue account. *Unearned Revenue* **is a liability account that results when a company receives cash from a customer for goods or services to be provided in the future.** The liability results from the obligation Mom's Cookie Company has to order the goods and provide them to the customer. If the company fails to complete the obligation, it will be required to refund the $3,000 to the customer.

The sales transaction is recorded on March 3 when goods are transferred to the customer.

		ASSETS		=	LIABILITIES	+	OWNERS' EQUITY	
Date	Accounts	Cash	Other Assets				Contributed Capital	Retained Earnings
Mar. 3	Unearned Revenue				−3,000			
	Sales Revenue							3,000
Mar. 3	Cost of Goods Sold							−2,000
	Merchandise Inventory		−2,000					

Once the goods are transferred to the customer on March 3, the obligation has been fulfilled and the liability is eliminated. **In most sales transactions, Sales Revenue is recognized when the goods are transferred to the customer.** The cost of the merchandise to Mom's Cookie Company of $2,000 is also recognized when the goods are transferred to the customer. Again, this process results in revenue being recognized in the period in which it is earned rather than when cash is received. Expenses are recognized when resources are consumed. Exhibit 2 illustrates the effects of these activities on the company's accounts.

Exhibit 2

Linking Cash and Revenue through Unearned Revenue

Date	Cash	Unearned Revenue	Sales Revenue
Feb. 24	3,000	3,000	
Mar. 3		−3,000	3,000
Net result	3,000	0	3,000

Unearned Revenue is an account used to link the receipt of cash in February with the revenue earned in March. This time, cash was received before revenue was recognized. Like Accounts Receivable, amounts are added or subtracted from Unearned Revenue as needed to ensure the proper timing of revenue recognition. The net result of these transactions is the same as if goods were sold for cash.

Transactions in which cash is received before revenue is earned are common for some types of companies. Examples include airlines, magazine publishers, and communications companies. Passengers often purchase airline tickets prior to their flights. At the time of the purchase, the airline records unearned revenue. When the passenger uses the ticket, the airline eliminates the unearned revenue and records passenger revenue. Similarly, subscribers often pay for magazine subscriptions before receiving the issues. At the time of purchase, the magazine records unearned revenue. As issues are published and mailed to subscribers, the amount of unearned revenue is reduced and subscription revenue is recognized. As an example, **AOL Time Warner**, owner of *Time*, *Life*, and other magazines, reported unearned revenues of $1.456 billion for the fiscal year ended December 31, 2001.

LEARNING NOTE

Account titles vary in practice. For example, Unearned Revenue might appear as Customer Deposits, Air Traffic Liability, Prepaid Subscriptions, or Deferred Revenues.

To summarize, companies recognize revenues in the period in which they are earned. Typically, the earnings process is considered complete at the time goods are transferred to customers or services are provided to customers. Exhibit 3 illustrates the relationship between revenue recognition and cash inflow.

Exhibit 3

Revenue Recognition and Cash Flows

Timing Effect	First Period	Second Period	Linking Account
No Accrual or Deferral Needed	Revenue Earned Cash Received		None
Accrued Revenue	Revenue Earned	Cash Received	Accounts Receivable
Deferred Revenue	Cash Received	Revenue Earned	Unearned Revenue

Three possibilities exist concerning the relationship. In all three possibilities, revenue is recognized when it is earned. Cash may be received at the time revenue is earned. In this situation, Revenue and Cash are the only accounts necessary for the transaction. If revenue is earned before cash is received, the revenue is accrued. *Accrued revenue* **is revenue recognized prior to the receipt of cash.** In this situation, Accounts Receivable is used to connect Revenue and Cash. If cash is received before revenue is earned, the revenue is deferred. *Deferred revenue* **is revenue recognized after cash has been received.** Unearned Revenue is used to connect Cash and Revenue.

EXPENSE TRANSACTIONS

OBJECTIVE 3

Record expense transactions using accrual accounting.

In addition to recognizing expenses at the time cash is paid, expenses may also be accrued or deferred. *Accrued expenses* **result when expenses are recognized prior to the payment of cash.** *Deferred expenses* **result when expenses are recognized after the payment of cash.**

For example, assume Mom's Cookie Company purchases $400 of supplies on February 16, 2004. The supplies are not consumed at the time they are purchased. Instead of paying cash for the supplies, the company purchases them on credit, agreeing to pay the supplier by March 16. On March 15, 2004, Mom's Cookie Company sends a check to the supplier. Mom's Cookie Company should record this purchase of supplies as follows:

		ASSETS		=	LIABILITIES	+	OWNERS' EQUITY	
Date	Accounts	Cash	Other Assets				Contributed Capital	Retained Earnings
Feb. 16	Supplies		400					
	Accounts Payable				400			

This transaction records the supplies as an asset and the amount owed the supplier as a liability. *Accounts Payable* **is a liability account that identifies an obligation to pay suppliers in the near future.**

When Mom's Cookie Company uses the supplies, it records an expense. Suppose that the supplies have been consumed by the end of February. The company would record this amount as:

		ASSETS		=	LIABILITIES	+	OWNERS' EQUITY	
Date	Accounts	Cash	Other Assets				Contributed Capital	Retained Earnings
Feb. 28	Supplies Expense							−400
	Supplies		−400					

This transaction records the expense in the fiscal period in which resources were consumed.

Another transaction is necessary to record payment for the supplies. If Mom's Cookie Company sends a check to the supplier on March 15, it would record this:

		ASSETS		=	LIABILITIES	+	OWNERS' EQUITY	
Date	Accounts	Cash	Other Assets				Contributed Capital	Retained Earnings
Mar. 15	Accounts Payable				−400			
	Cash	−400						

LEARNING NOTE

In Chapter F2, we recorded the purchase of supplies as an expense at the time the supplies were acquired because the supplies were used in January. In theory, it is preferable to record the purchase as an asset and then expense the supplies when they are used. Practically, however, it does not matter whether the supplies are recorded as an asset initially if all of the supplies are consumed in the same fiscal period as they were acquired. Either way, the amount will be an expense by the end of the fiscal period.

An expense is not recorded at the time the payment is made because the supplies were consumed in February. Exhibit 4 illustrates the use of the Accounts Payable account to link expenses recognized in one period with cash paid in a subsequent period. The net result of these transactions is the same as if cash had been paid for supplies at the time they were consumed. The transaction was recorded initially to the supplies account. Since the supplies were consumed in February, the transaction could have been recorded initially to supplies expense.

Exhibit 4

Linking Expense and Cash through Accounts Payable

Date	Cash	Supplies	Accounts Payable	Supplies Expense
Feb. 16		400	400	
Feb. 28		−400		−400
Mar. 15	−400		−400	
Net result	−400	0	0	−400

Expenses also may be recognized after cash is paid. For example, assume Mom's Cookie Company pays $600 for rent for use of a building on February 26. However, the rent is for March. The payment would be recorded as follows:

		ASSETS		=	LIABILITIES	+	OWNERS' EQUITY	
Date	Accounts	Cash	Other Assets				Contributed Capital	Retained Earnings
Feb. 26	Prepaid Rent		600					
	Cash	−600						

LEARNING NOTE

Accounts Payable is an example of a general category of liabilities known as accrued liabilities. *Accrued liabilities* record the obligation to make payments for expenses that have been incurred or for assets that have been acquired but for which payment has not been made. Other examples of accrued liabilities include Wages Payable, Interest Payable, and Income Taxes Payable.

The February transaction records the payment for rent. Prepaid Rent is an example of a prepaid expense account. A *Prepaid Expense* **is an asset account that identifies a resource that has been paid for but not used.** The purchase is an asset because a resource has been acquired that will be used in the future. The March transaction records use of the resource. The expense should be recognized in March, when the resource is consumed, rather than in February when cash is paid. The expense has been deferred from the time of the payment to March, when the building is used. By the end of March the rental service has been consumed and the expense would be recorded as follows:

		ASSETS		=	LIABILITIES	+	OWNERS' EQUITY	
Date	Accounts	Cash	Other Assets				Contributed Capital	Retained Earnings
Mar. 31	Rent Expense							−600
	Prepaid Rent		−600					

Exhibit 5 illustrates the use of the prepaid rent account to link cash paid in one period with expense recognized in a subsequent period. Prepaid Rent increases when cash is paid for next month's rent and decreases when the rent is consumed.

Exhibit 5

Linking Expense and Cash through Prepaid Rent

Date	Cash	Prepaid Rent	Rent Expense
Feb. 26	−600	600	
Mar. 31		−600	−600
Net result	−600	0	−600

In summary, accrual accounting records expenses when resources are consumed, not necessarily when cash is paid for those resources. Exhibit 6 illustrates the relationship between expense recognition and cash outflow.

Exhibit 6

Expense Recognition and Cash Flows

Timing Effect	First Period	Second Period	Linking Account
No Accrual or Deferral Needed	Expense Incurred Cash Paid		None
Accrued Expense	Expense Incurred	Cash Paid	Accounts Payable
Deferred Expense	Cash Paid	Expense Incurred	Prepaid Expense

Three possibilities exist concerning the relationship. In all three possibilities, expense is recognized when it is incurred. Cash may be paid at the time expense is incurred. In this situation, Expense and Cash are the only accounts necessary for the transaction. If expense is incurred before cash is paid, the expense is accrued. That is, it is recognized prior to the payment of cash. In this situation, Accounts Payable is used to connect Expense and Cash. If cash is paid before expense is incurred, the expense is deferred. That is, it is recognized after the cash is paid. Prepaid Expense is used to connect Cash and Expense.

By recording revenues when earned and expenses when incurred, a company matches resources consumed by business activities with revenues created by those activities. Consequently, net income (revenues minus expenses) measures business activity for a fiscal period. It is not a measure of how much cash a company received or paid. An important concept in accounting is the *matching principle,* **which requires companies to recognize the expenses used to generate revenue in the same accounting period in which the revenues are recognized.**

An important responsibility of accountants is to make decisions about when revenues and expenses should be recognized. They examine a company's business activities and use appropriate accounting rules to ensure the proper recording of revenue and expense transactions in the fiscal period in which those transactions occur.

1 SELF-STUDY PROBLEM

WebTUTOR Advantage

The following events occurred for Kirkland Co. in January and February:

1. Goods priced at $5,000 were sold on credit on January 15.
2. The cost of the goods sold in transaction 1 was $3,000.

3. Cash of $400 was received on January 23 for goods that will be transferred to customers in February.
4. Cash of $750 was paid on January 25 for supplies that will be used in February.
5. By January 31, employees had earned wages of $2,500 that will be paid in February.
6. On February 3, cash of $2,500 was paid to employees for wages earned in January.
7. On February 6, cash was collected from customers for the sales on January 15.
8. On February 8, goods were transferred to customers that had been paid for on January 23.
9. By February 28, the supplies purchased on January 25 had been consumed.

Required Record all transactions associated with these events in the order in which they occurred.

The solution to Self-Study Problem 1 appears at the end of the chapter.

ADJUSTING ACCOUNT BALANCES

OBJECTIVE 4

Identify and record adjusting entries at the end of a fiscal period.

Some revenues and many expenses are associated with the passage of time. Rent, insurance, and equipment are resources that are purchased in one period and used during future periods. Wages relate to specific periods in which employees work, whether or not they are paid during those periods. Interest on debt accumulates over time. Revenues associated with some services, such as repair and maintenance contracts, also may be earned over time.

These activities often result in an expense or revenue that must be recognized for a fiscal period even though no specific event occurs to create the expense or revenue other than the passage of time. In these situations, a company must adjust its accounts at the end of a fiscal period to record the expenses and revenues that should be recognized for that period.

Let's consider some examples of adjustments for Mom's Cookie Company. Suppose in mid-February, Mom's Cookie Company decided to move to a new building on March 1. The rent for the new offices is $600 a month. On February 24 rent is paid for March and April. The transaction for February would be:

		ASSETS		=	LIABILITIES	+	OWNERS' EQUITY	
Date	Accounts	Cash	Other Assets				Contributed Capital	Retained Earnings
Feb. 24	Prepaid Rent		1,200					
	Cash	−1,200						

The transaction involves payment of rent for two months. The Prepaid Rent account is an asset that identifies the resource available for future use. At the end of March and April, Mom's Cookie Company must record Rent Expense for each month:

		ASSETS		=	LIABILITIES	+	OWNERS' EQUITY	
Date	Accounts	Cash	Other Assets				Contributed Capital	Retained Earnings
Mar. 31	Rent Expense							−600
	Prepaid Rent		−600					
Apr. 30	Rent Expense							−600
	Prepaid Rent		−600					

The accounting entries for March and April are adjusting entries. **An** *adjusting entry* **is a transaction recorded in the accounting system to ensure the correct account balances are reported for a particular fiscal period.** Usually, adjusting entries are made at the end of the fiscal period.

Another example of adjusting entries for Mom's Cookie Company involves interest. As indicated in Chapter F2, the company borrowed $30,000 ($8,000 + $22,000) in January. The bank charges $200 of interest each month but permits the interest to be paid the day after the end of each quarter. Accordingly, Mom's Cookie Company's first interest payment is not due until April 1, 2004. Nevertheless, interest expense accrues each month and should be recognized in the fiscal period in which it is incurred. Mom's Cookie Company would record the following adjusting entries at the end of January, February, and March:

| Date | Accounts | ASSETS | | = | LIABILITIES | + | OWNERS' EQUITY | |
		Cash	Other Assets				Contributed Capital	Retained Earnings
Jan. 31	Interest Expense							−200
	Interest Payable				200			
Feb. 28	Interest Expense							−200
	Interest Payable				200			
Mar. 31	Interest Expense							−200
	Interest Payable				200			

An expense is recorded each month for the interest incurred on the loan. A liability is recorded as well because the interest is not being paid until the end of March. Consequently, an obligation exists for the unpaid interest. **Every adjusting entry, like the three above, includes at least one balance sheet and at least one income statement account.** Adjusting entries always involve recognition of a revenue or expense during a fiscal period.

Another transaction at the beginning of April records payment of the liability that accumulated over the three months. This entry is not an adjusting entry; it is a payment of an obligation when it becomes due. The payment is recorded as follows:

| Date | Accounts | ASSETS | | = | LIABILITIES | + | OWNERS' EQUITY | |
		Cash	Other Assets				Contributed Capital	Retained Earnings
Apr. 1	Interest Payable				−600			
	Cash	−600						

Another example of adjustments involves the use of equipment. Mom's Cookie Company purchased equipment in January for $31,000 ($6,000 + $25,000). The equipment was recorded as an asset at that time. However, equipment and other physical assets usually wear out over time and eventually need to be replaced. Because resources are consumed over a number of fiscal periods, the usage should be recognized as an expense of each of the periods that benefits from that use. *Depreciation* **is the allocation of the cost of assets to the fiscal periods that benefit from the assets' use.** Mom's Cookie Company expenses its equipment at the rate of $520 per month. Consequently, it would record the following adjustments at the end of January and February:

Date	Accounts	ASSETS		= LIABILITIES	+ OWNERS' EQUITY	
		Cash	Other Assets		Contributed Capital	Retained Earnings
Jan. 31	Depreciation Expense					−520
	Accumulated Depreciation		−520			
Feb. 28	Depreciation Expense					−520
	Accumulated Depreciation		−520			

Depreciation Expense identifies the estimated amount of the asset consumed. *Accumulated Depreciation* **is a contra-asset account used to identify the total amount of depreciation recorded for a company's assets.** It is subtracted from the related asset accounts on the company's balance sheet, and therefore is known as a contra account. **A** *contra account* **is an account that offsets another account.**

To understand Accumulated Depreciation, consider the effect the adjusting entries would have on the Accumulated Depreciation account. At the end of January, the account will have a balance of −$520, depreciation for January. At the end of February, the account will have a balance of −$1,040, depreciation for January and February.

Mom's Cookie Company's balance sheet for January and February will report the following:

	January	February
Equipment, at cost	$31,000	$31,000
Less: accumulated depreciation	520	1,040
Equipment, net of depreciation	$30,480	$29,960

The cost of the equipment continues to be reported at its cost of $31,000. The amount of accumulated depreciation increases each month, and the net amount of equipment reported each month decreases at the rate of $520 per month. We examine how depreciation amounts are determined in a later chapter.

The process of recording and reporting depreciation is necessary to make sure a company reports the appropriate expense each fiscal period. The use of Accumulated Depreciation provides useful information to decision makers. Examination of the balance sheet data for Mom's Cookie Company provides Maria and Stan with information about the cost of equipment and about how long the equipment has been used. Creditors and other external users of the company's financial statements might be especially interested in this information. They may want to know if a company's assets are replaced on a regular basis and if plans are being made for replacement as assets age.

Companies record transactions throughout each fiscal period. Accountants determine necessary adjustments for a company and develop and maintain information systems that allow them to determine interest, depreciation, and other expenses and revenues accurately. They adjust accounts at the end of each fiscal period prior to preparing financial statements. The next section considers the final steps in preparing these statements.

2 SELF-STUDY PROBLEM

The following events occurred for Davis Co. during 2004:

WebTUTOR Advantage

1. On September 27, the company paid rent for the following three months of $1,500 per month.
2. The company incurs interest expense of $800 per month. Interest was paid on October 31 for a three-month period, ending with October.
3. The company purchased equipment for $200,000 on January 2, 2004. The equipment is depreciated at the rate of $4,000 per month.

4. The company paid $12,000 for property insurance on January 4, 2004. The insurance is for the 12 months ended December 31, 2004.

Required Record the adjusting entries associated with these events for October.

The solution to Self-Study Problem 2 appears at the end of the chapter.

LEDGER ACCOUNTS

Transactions, like those in this and the preceding chapter, are initially recorded by a company in a journal. A *journal* **is a chronological record of a company's transactions.** The format we have used in this chapter to record transactions is an example of a particular journal format. Each transaction is recorded according to the date the transaction occurred. The accounts affected by the transaction are listed along with the amounts associated with each account. Most companies use a computerized accounting system. Journal entries are recorded on a computer using a format that provides a place for each account to be identified and the amount to be entered. Regardless of the format, journal entries provide for a means of entering transactions in an accounting system.

Once transactions have been entered into a journal, the effects of transactions on particular accounts need to be transferred to those accounts. A *ledger* **is a file in which each of a company's accounts and the balances of those accounts are maintained.** A record is maintained for each account. Each time a transaction is recorded, the effects of that transaction are transferred to the ledger. *Posting* **is the process of transferring transactions to specific accounts in a company's ledger.** Exhibit 7 illustrates this process.

Exhibit 7 Posting Transactions to the Ledger

Journal

Date	Accounts	Cash	Other Assets	=	LIABILITIES	+	Contributed Capital	Retained Earnings
		ASSETS					**OWNERS' EQUITY**	
Jan. 31	Depreciation Expense							−520
	Accumulated Depreciation		−520					
Feb. 28	Depreciation Expense							−520
	Accumulated Depreciation		−520					

Ledger

Accumulated Depreciation

Date	Amount	Balance
Jan. 31	−520	−520
Feb. 28	−520	−1,040

Initially a transaction is recorded using the journal format. The transaction is then posted to the ledger accounts affected by the transaction. The balance of the account is updated to show the effect of the transaction. Thus, after transactions have been posted, the ledger provides a current record of the balance of each of a company's accounts. These balances are the primary source of data for preparing a company's financial statements.

The primary ledger a company uses to record its account balances is referred to as the *general ledger*. Companies often use other special ledgers to maintain information about specific types of account balances. For example, each customer who has purchased goods from a company on credit would be listed in the company's accounts receivable ledger. The accounts in the special ledger are referred to as subsidiary accounts. Subsidiary accounts are accounts of a specific type that are associated with a control account in the general ledger. The total of the balances of all of the subsidiary accounts of a specific type is equal to the balance of the general ledger control account. To illustrate, assume Mom's Cookie Company sells goods on credit to three stores: Hopkins' Grocery, Lori's Market, and Samson's Foods. Mom's Cookie Company maintains a subsidiary accounts receivable account for each store. The amounts owed by each of these stores at the end of February is the subsidiary account balance. The total of these amounts is the balance of accounts receivable for Mom's Cookie Company.

Subsidiary Accounts Receivable:	
Hopkins' Grocery	$1,300
Lori's Market	600
Samson's Foods	900
Accounts Receivable Control	$2,800

The subsidiary accounts are used to keep track of amounts owed by each customer. The control account balance is the amount reported in the company's financial statements.

CLOSING ENTRIES AND FINANCIAL STATEMENTS

OBJECTIVE 5

Prepare closing entries and financial statements at the end of a fiscal period.

At the end of each month, Maria and Stan, with the help of their accountant, prepare financial statements for Mom's Cookie Company. The financial statements report a company's business activities to help managers, creditors, and other stakeholders make decisions.

Summary of Account Balances

To illustrate this process, we begin with a review of all the transactions for Mom's Cookie Company for January. These are presented in Exhibit 8 and include the adjusting entries for interest expense and depreciation expense described in this chapter.

Next we examine a summary of general ledger account balances for Mom's Cookie Company at the end of January. Exhibit 9, on page F96, provides balances for each of the company's general ledger accounts at January 31. The amounts shown are those from Exhibit 12 in Chapter F2, adjusted for interest and depreciation, as described in this chapter.

A purpose of the summary is to make sure that the accounting equation is in balance prior to preparing the financial statements. We can determine that the equation is in balance by reference to Exhibit 9 because:

Assets = Liabilities + Owners' Equity
$41,180 = $30,200 + $10,980

Income Statement

Balances of revenue and expense accounts appear in Mom's Cookie Company's Income Statement for January. Exhibit 10, on page F96, provides this statement. As discussed in Chapter F2, the income statement reports results of operating activities for a particular fiscal period. The statement shows that Mom's Cookie Company earned $980 of profit in January. This amount is less than that reported in Chapter F2 because of the adjusting entries that were considered in this chapter.

Exhibit 8 Transactions for Mom's Cookie Company for January

Date	Accounts	ASSETS Cash	Other Assets	=	LIABILITIES	+	OWNERS' EQUITY Contributed Capital	Retained Earnings
	Beginning Amounts	0	+0	=	0	+	0	+0
Jan. 2	Cash	10,000						
	Contributed Capital						10,000	
Jan. 3	Cash	8,000						
	Notes Payable				8,000			
Jan. 5	Equipment		6,000					
	Cash	−6,000						
Jan. 6	Equipment		25,000					
	Cash	−3,000						
	Notes Payable				22,000			
Jan. 6	Supplies Expense							−300
	Cash	−300						
Jan. 7	Merchandise Inventory		9,000					
	Cash	−9,000						
Jan. 8	Rent Expense							−600
	Cash	−600						
Jan. 31	Cash	11,400						
	Sales Revenue							11,400
Jan. 31	Cost of Goods Sold							−7,600
	Merchandise Inventory		−7,600					
Jan. 31	Wages Expense							−1,000
	Cash	−1,000						
Jan. 31	Utilities Expense							−200
	Cash	−200						
Jan. 31	Interest Expense							−200
	Interest Payable				200			
Jan. 31	Depreciation Expense							−520
	Accumulated Depreciation		−520					
	Ending Amounts	9,300	+31,880	=	30,200	+	10,000	+980

Closing Entries

An intermediate step in preparing financial statements is closing the revenue and expense account balances. Before preparing a balance sheet, the company's accountant closes Mom's Cookie Company's revenue and expense account balances at the end of February. Closing these accounts transfers the balances in these accounts to Retained Earnings. Exhibit 11, on page F97, provides the closing entries for January.

The closing process includes two transactions. In the first, revenue accounts are transferred to Retained Earnings. The closing transaction leaves the revenue account with a zero balance by subtracting the amount of revenue earned during the month from the Sales Revenue account and transferring the balance to Retained Earnings.

In the second transaction in Exhibit 11, expense account balances are transferred to Retained Earnings. The balances of these accounts also are zero after they are transferred to Retained Earnings.

If revenues are greater than expenses for the period, Retained Earnings increases. If revenues are less than expenses, Retained Earnings decreases. Remember that Retained Earnings is an accumulation of a company's profits. If profits are earned during

Exhibit 9

Summary of Account
Balances for Mom's
Cookie Company at
January 31

**Mom's Cookie Company
Account Balances
January 31, 2004**

Account	Balance
Assets:	
Cash	9,300
Merchandise Inventory	1,400
Equipment	31,000
Accumulated Depreciation	(520)
Total Assets	**41,180**
Liabilities:	
Interest Payable	200
Notes Payable	30,000
Total Liabilities	**30,200**
Owners' Equity:	
Contributed Capital	10,000
Sales Revenue	11,400
Cost of Goods Sold	(7,600)
Wages Expense	(1,000)
Rent Expense	(600)
Depreciation Expense	(520)
Supplies Expense	(300)
Utilities Expense	(200)
Interest Expense	(200)
Total Owners' Equity	**10,980**

Exhibit 10

Income Statement for
Mom's Cookie Company

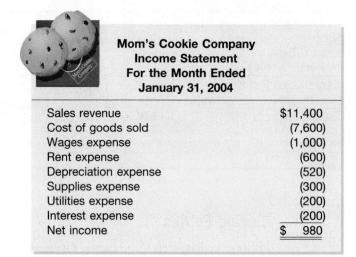

**Mom's Cookie Company
Income Statement
For the Month Ended
January 31, 2004**

Sales revenue	$11,400
Cost of goods sold	(7,600)
Wages expense	(1,000)
Rent expense	(600)
Depreciation expense	(520)
Supplies expense	(300)
Utilities expense	(200)
Interest expense	(200)
Net income	$ 980

a fiscal period, Retained Earnings increases. If losses are incurred during a fiscal period because revenues are less than expenses, Retained Earnings decreases.

Exhibit 12 illustrates the effect of closing entries on ledger account balances. Each account contains the balance of that account prior to the closing entry. *Closing entries* **reset the balances of each revenue and expense account to zero and transfer these balances to Retained Earnings.**

The closing entries zero out the revenue and expense account balances at the end of a fiscal period. Consequently, the next fiscal period begins with zero balances and accumulates revenues and expenses for the new fiscal period. The closing process also transfers the amount of net income for a fiscal period to Retained Earnings. Keep in mind that revenues and expenses are subcategories of owners' equity. The closing process transfers amounts from the income statement accounts to owners' equity on

Exhibit 11 Closing Entries for January for Mom's Cookie Company

Date	Accounts	ASSETS		=	LIABILITIES	+	OWNERS' EQUITY	
		Cash	Other Assets				Contributed Capital	Retained Earnings
Jan. 31	Retained Earnings							11,400
	Sales Revenue							−11,400
Jan. 31	Retained Earnings							−10,420
	Cost of Goods Sold							7,600
	Wages Expense							1,000
	Rent Expense							600
	Depreciation Expense							520
	Supplies Expense							300
	Utilities Expense							200
	Interest Expense							200

Exhibit 12

Effect of Closing Entries on Revenue and Expense Account Balances

Ledger

Retained Earnings

Date	Amount	Balance
		0
Jan. 31	11,400	11,400
Jan. 31	−10,420	980

Sales Revenue

Date	Amount	Balance
		11,400
Jan. 31	−11,400	0

Cost of Goods Sold

Date	Amount	Balance
		−7,600
Jan. 31	7,600	0

Wages Expense

Date	Amount	Balance
		−1,000
Jan. 31	1,000	0

Rent Expense

Date	Amount	Balance
		−600
Jan. 31	600	0

Depreciation Expense

Date	Amount	Balance
		−520
Jan. 31	520	0

Supplies Expense

Date	Amount	Balance
		−300
Jan. 31	300	0

Utilities Expense

Date	Amount	Balance
		−200
Jan. 31	200	0

Interest Expense

Date	Amount	Balance
		−200
Jan. 31	200	0

the balance sheet so that the accounting equation (Assets = Liabilities + Owners' Equity) balances at the end of a fiscal period.

Because revenue and expense accounts are zeroed-out at the end of a fiscal period, they are referred to as temporary accounts. They are used during a fiscal period to collect the results of operating activities. These results are transferred to Retained Earnings at the end of the period. Retained Earnings and other balance sheet accounts are referred to as permanent accounts because their balances continue to accumulate from period to period.

Payments to Owners

Another transaction that affects the balance of Retained Earnings is a payment by a company to its owners. For example, if Maria and Stan decide to withdraw $500 from Mom's Cookie Company at the end of January, the transaction would be recorded like this:

		ASSETS		=	LIABILITIES	+	OWNERS' EQUITY	
Date	Accounts	Cash	Other Assets				Contributed Capital	Retained Earnings
Jan. 31	Retained Earnings							−500
	Cash	−500						

The retained earnings account accumulates profits earned by a company for its owners. The owners may choose to leave the profits in the company or withdraw some of them for personal use. Amounts withdrawn reduce Retained Earnings. The balance of Retained Earnings and Cash for Mom's Cookie Company after the withdrawal would be as follows:

Ledger

Retained Earnings

Date	Amount	Balance
		980
Jan. 31	−500	480

Cash

Date	Amount	Balance
		9,300
Jan. 31	−500	8,800

Post-Closing Account Balances

Let's look at the effects of the closing and withdrawal entries by preparing a summary of account balances after these entries have been posted to ledger accounts. Exhibit 13 provides a post-closing summary for Mom's Cookie Company at the end of February. At this point, the revenue and expense accounts have zero balances.

Balance Sheet

The balance sheet can now be prepared from the post-closing account balances. Exhibit 14 provides the balance sheet for Mom's Cookie Company at January 31, 2004. Observe that the amounts in the balance sheet for January 31 are those in the post-closing summary from Exhibit 13.

Along with the income statement, the balance sheet helps users determine how well the company performed during January. From the income statement, users can

Exhibit 13

Post-Closing Summary
of Account Balances for
Mom's Cookie Company

Mom's Cookie Company
Post-Closing Summary of Account Balances
January 31, 2004

Account	Balance
Assets:	
Cash	8,800
Merchandise Inventory	1,400
Equipment	31,000
Accumulated Depreciation	(520)
Total Assets	**40,680**
Liabilities:	
Interest Payable	200
Notes Payable	30,000
Total Liabilities	**30,200**
Owners' Equity:	
Contributed Capital	10,000
Retained Earnings	480
Sales Revenue	0
Cost of Goods Sold	0
Wages Expense	0
Supplies Expense	0
Rent Expense	0
Depreciation Expense	0
Interest Expense	0
Total Owners' Equity	**10,480**

Exhibit 14

January 31 Balance
Sheet for Mom's Cookie
Company

Mom's Cookie Company
Balance Sheet
At January 31, 2004

Assets	
Cash	$ 8,800
Merchandise inventory	1,400
Equipment	31,000
Accumulated depreciation	(520)
Total assets	$40,680
Liabilities and Owners' Equity	
Interest payable	$ 200
Notes payable	30,000
Total liabilities	30,200
Contribution by owners	10,000
Retained earnings	480
Total liabilities and owners' equity	$40,680

determine the major sources of revenue and expense. From the balance sheet, they can determine the assets controlled by the company and claims to those resources by creditors and owners. When statements for additional months become available, decision makers can compare the statements to determine whether the company is performing better or worse over time. Users can determine how much change there is in assets, liabilities, and owners' equity from one month to the next.

Statement of Cash Flows

A third financial statement, the statement of cash flows, also should be prepared. The adjusting transactions described in this chapter are associated with revenue and expense recognition, not with cash flows. Therefore, the statement of cash flows at the end of January is almost identical to the one in Chapter F2. Exhibit 15 includes the effect of the payment of $500 cash to owners. This payment is a financing activity.

Exhibit 15

A Statement of Cash Flows

Mom's Cookie Company
Statement of Cash Flows
For the Month Ended January 31, 2004

Operating Activities		
Received from customers	$11,400	
Paid for merchandise	(9,000)	
Paid for wages	(1,000)	
Paid for rent	(600)	
Paid for supplies	(300)	
Paid for utilities	(200)	
Net cash flow from operating activities		$ 300
Investing Activities		
Paid for equipment		(31,000)
Financing Activities		
Received from creditors	30,000	
Received from owners	10,000	
Paid to owners	(500)	
Net cash flow from financing activities		39,500
Net cash flow for January		8,800
Cash balance, January 1		0
Cash balance, January 31		$ 8,800

SUMMARY OF ACCOUNTING CYCLE

OBJECTIVE 6

Identify steps in the accounting cycle.

The procedures we have examined in this chapter are often referred to as the accounting cycle. The *accounting cycle* **is the process of recording, summarizing, and reporting accounting information.** As we have discussed in this chapter, the cycle consists of eight steps, as illustrated in Exhibit 16.

Once the accounting cycle is completed for one fiscal period, the accounting records are ready to begin recording transactions for the next fiscal period. As noted in Chapter F2, a fiscal period can be any time period for which managers want accounting information. Most companies prepare financial statements monthly and combine these to prepare statements for quarterly and annual periods.

ACCOUNTING AND ETHICS

The accounting system described in this chapter provides a way for Maria and Stan to monitor their business activities and to make decisions about their company's performance. Also, it provides a means for them to communicate with creditors about the performance of their company. An accounting system with adequate controls to ensure reliable information is expected by stakeholders of most companies and is a legal requirement for companies that sell shares of stock to the public and for many other companies that are regulated by state and local authorities.

These requirements are intended to protect owners, creditors, and other stakeholders from receiving inaccurate or improperly prepared financial information. A good accounting system helps ensure that all transactions are recorded properly and that stakeholders

Exhibit 16 Steps in the Accounting Cycle

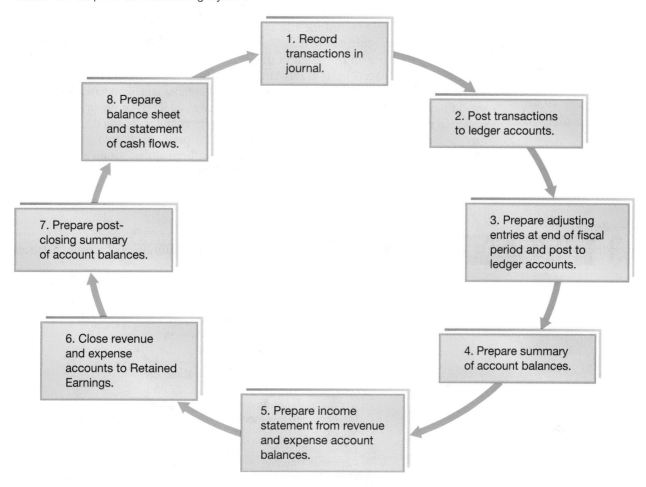

receive information that describes a business's activities on a timely basis. Most businesses are expected to comply with generally accepted accounting principles (GAAP) in preparing financial accounting information. GAAP require the use of the accrual rules and procedures described in this chapter. Making sure that a company's accounting procedures conform with GAAP and creating an accounting system that records and reports all transactions in the appropriate fiscal periods is a major responsibility of a company's management. Failure to understand and implement appropriate accounting procedures is, itself, unethical. Management is responsible for proper use of a company's resources and for proper reporting of its business activities. Managers who fail to take these responsibilities seriously leave a company vulnerable to improper behavior, such as fraud and theft, that reduces the value of the company for its owners and other stakeholders.

Case in Point

http://

http://ingram.
swlearning.com

Learn more about Enron.

Economic Effects of Poor Accounting Practices

The failure of **Enron Corporation's** management to properly account for and report its business activities resulted in an understatement of the company's liabilities and an overstatement of profits. When the company's bad accounting practices became apparent in October 2001, creditors were unwilling to lend additional money to the company and investors tried to dump their stock. The value of Enron's stock dropped rapidly, resulting in losses of millions of dollars for owners. Many of Enron's owners were employees of the company who had invested in the company's stock as part of their retirement plans. Many employees lost their jobs and their retirement savings as a result of these events.

Unethical behavior may occur in businesses because appropriate accounting controls are not in place or are not enforced. For example, an employee sells goods to a customer but does not record the sale and pockets the cash. This behavior leads to incorrect accounting information. Sales Revenue, Cost of Goods Sold, Merchandise Inventory, and Cash are all misstated in this example. In general, unethical behavior by employees and managers leads to misstated accounting information. Protecting a company's accounting records and assets is an important management task. Procedures should be in place to make it difficult for employees at all levels of the organization to engage in unethical behavior. For example, cash registers and scanning devices help ensure that sales made by employees are recorded. Supervisors should compare sales records with cash receipts to make sure cash has not been stolen. **Good accounting is the first line of defense against unethical behavior in business.**

3   SELF-STUDY PROBLEM

Howard Co. provided the following summary of account balances at the end of December 2004.

WebTUTOR Advantage

Howard Co.
Summary of Account Balances
December 31, 2004

Account	Balance
Cash	37,450
Accounts Receivable	2,300
Merchandise Inventory	140,000
Supplies	30,000
Equipment	75,000
Accounts Payable	2,000
Notes Payable	200,000
Investment by Owners	65,000
Retained Earnings	15,000
Sales Revenue	20,000
Cost of Goods Sold	(13,000)
Wages Expense	(2,000)
Depreciation Expense	(750)
Interest Expense	(1,500)

Required Prepare closing entries and a post-closing summary of account balances for Howard Co.

The solution to Self-Study Problem 3 appears at the end of the chapter.

REVIEW

SUMMARY of IMPORTANT CONCEPTS

1. Accrual accounting requires companies to recognize revenues in the fiscal period in which they are earned and to recognize expenses in the period incurred.

2. Accrual accounting requires the use of accounts such as Accounts Receivable and Unearned Revenue to link Cash received in one period with revenues earned in another period.

3. Accrual accounting requires the use of accounts such as Accounts Payable and Prepaid Expenses to link Cash paid in one period with expenses incurred in another period.

4. Adjusting entries record revenues and expenses that occur because of the passage of time to ensure that these revenues and expenses are recognized in the appropriate fiscal period.

5. At the end of a fiscal period, a company closes its revenues and expense accounts to transfer these account balances to retained earnings. The balance sheet reports retained earnings after the accounts have been closed.

6. The accounting cycle is the process of recording transactions, preparing summaries of account balances, closing accounts, and preparing financial statements.

DEFINE

TERMS and CONCEPTS DEFINED in this CHAPTER

accounting cycle (F100)
accounts payable (F87)
accounts receivable (F84)
accrual accounting (F83)
accrued expense (F87)
accrued liabilities (F88)
accrued revenue (F87)
accumulated depreciation (F92)
adjusting entry (F91)
closing entries (F96)
contra account (F92)

deferred expense (F87)
deferred revenue (F87)
depreciation (F91)
general ledger (F94)
journal (F93)
ledger (F93)
matching principle (F89)
posting (F93)
prepaid expense (F88)
unearned revenue (F85)

SELF-STUDY PROBLEM SOLUTIONS

SSP3-1

Date	Accounts	ASSETS Cash	ASSETS Other Assets	=	LIABILITIES	+	OWNERS' EQUITY Contributed Capital	OWNERS' EQUITY Retained Earnings
Jan. 15	Accounts Receivable		5,000					
	Sales Revenue							5,000
Jan. 15	Cost of Goods Sold							−3,000
	Merchandise Inventory		−3,000					
Jan. 23	Cash	400						
	Unearned Revenue				400			
Jan. 25	Supplies		750					
	Cash	−750						
Jan. 31	Wages Expense							−2,500
	Wages Payable				2,500			
Feb. 3	Wages Payable				−2,500			
	Cash	−2,500						
Feb. 6	Cash	5,000						
	Accounts Receivable		−5,000					
Feb. 8	Unearned Revenue				−400			
	Sales Revenue							400
Feb. 28	Supplies Expense							−750
	Supplies		−750					

SSP3-2

		ASSETS		=	LIABILITIES	+	OWNERS' EQUITY	
Date	Accounts	Cash	Other Assets				Contributed Capital	Retained Earnings
Oct. 31	Rent Expense							
	Prepaid Rent		−1,500					−1,500
Oct. 31	Interest Expense							
	Interest Payable				800			−800
Oct. 31	Depreciation Expense							
	Accumulated Depreciation		−4,000					−4,000
Oct. 31	Insurance Expense							
	Prepaid Insurance		−1,000					−1,000

Note: A transaction to record the payment of interest in October for the period August, September, and October also would be recorded. This transaction is not an adjusting entry, however.

SSP3-3

		ASSETS		=	LIABILITIES	+	OWNERS' EQUITY	
Date	Accounts	Cash	Other Assets				Contributed Capital	Retained Earnings
Dec. 31	Retained Earnings							20,000
	Sales Revenue							−20,000
Dec. 31	Retained Earnings							−17,250
	Cost of Goods Sold							13,000
	Wages Expense							2,000
	Depreciation Expense							750
	Interest Expense							1,500

Howard Co.
Post-Closing Summary of Account Balances
December 31, 2004

Account	Balance
Assets:	
Cash	37,450
Accounts Receivable	2,300
Merchandise Inventory	140,000
Supplies	30,000
Equipment	75,000
Total Assets	**284,750**
Liabilities:	
Accounts Payable	2,000
Notes Payable	200,000
Total Liabilities	**202,000**
Owners' Equity:	
Investment by Owners	65,000
Retained Earnings	17,750
Sales Revenue	0
Cost of Goods Sold	0
Wages Expense	0
Depreciation Expense	0
Interest Expense	0
Total Owners' Equity	**82,750**

Thinking Beyond the Question

How do we know how much profit our business has earned?

At the beginning of the chapter we asked how you can know how much profit a company has earned. This chapter described the rules and procedures of accrual accounting. The rules specify when revenues and expenses should be recognized. The procedures help ensure that all revenues and expenses of a fiscal period have been recorded and reported. Understanding accrued and deferred revenues and expenses and adjusting and closing entries help ensure that the proper amount of profit is reported each fiscal period and that other accounting information is correct.

These rules may seem relatively simple. For example, it may be easy to identify when goods are transferred to customers. However, that may not always be the case. Suppose you agree to provide services to a customer over several fiscal periods. You negotiate a price with the customer that covers all of the services to be provided. How much revenue would you recognize each fiscal period while you are providing the services?

QUESTIONS

Q3-1
Obj. 1
Why isn't cash basis accounting the preferred method of reporting on the economic consequences of an organization's activities?

Q3-2
Obj. 1
A friend observes that "in the long run, accrual and cash flow measurements equal out to the same amount. It's only in the short run that they differ." Do you agree or disagree? Explain.

Q3-3
Obj. 1
How is it possible that a company could be very profitable yet be forced to go out of business because it cannot pay its bills?

Q3-4
Obj. 2
How does Accounts Receivable "link" Revenue and Cash?

Q3-5
Obj. 2
Where does the account Unearned Revenue appear in the financial statements? How does Unearned Revenue link Cash with Sales Revenue?

Q3-6
Obj. 2
Accrued revenue and deferred revenue are both accrual concepts. Explain the order in which cash is received and revenue is recognized for each concept.

Q3-7
Obj. 3
On May 31, a company paid $900 rent for June to its landlord. Would you recommend that this expenditure be presented in the end-of-May financial statements as an asset (Prepaid Rent) or as an expense (Rent Expense)? Why?

Q3-8
Obj. 3
Quick Computer Company just spent $35,000 of its cash to purchase merchandise for later resale to customers. Would you agree that since $35,000 of cash has been used up, a $35,000 expense has been incurred in this transaction? Why or why not?

Q3-9
Obj. 4
What is the difference between a subsidiary account and a control account?

Q3-10
Obj. 4
Why are control account balances reported in external financial statements while subsidiary account balances are not? Are subsidiary account balances useful to anyone? Who?

Q3-11
Obj. 4
The textbook lists depreciation as an example of a period cost that often must be updated in the accounting records at the end of a fiscal period. What other examples of period costs that must be updated at period-end can you identify? Why is it necessary to update these items?

Q3-12
Obj. 5
A friend observes that "one of the most useful pieces of information found on a balance sheet is the current market value of assets such as buildings and land." Do you agree or disagree? Why?

Q3-13
Obj. 5
Explain why accountants prepare a summary of general ledger account balances prior to preparing the financial statements.

Q3-14
Obj. 5
Why do accountants close revenue and expense accounts prior to preparing the financial statements?

Q3-15
Obj. 5
Is a payment to owners considered an expense? Explain.

Q3-16
Obj. 6
Why are good accounting practices the first line of defense against unethical behavior in business?

Q3-17
Obj. 6
Why is an accounting system with adequate controls a legal requirement for companies that sell shares of stock to the public?

Q3-18
Obj. 6
Accountants prepare a post-closing summary of account balances as one step of the accounting cycle. Which types of accounts have non-zero balances? Which types of accounts have zero balances?

EXERCISES

If your instructor is using Personal Trainer in this course, you may complete online the assignments identified by $\frac{P}{T}$.

E3-1
Write a short definition for each of the terms listed in the *Terms and Concepts Defined in this Chapter* section.

E3-2
Obj. 1
$\frac{P}{T}$
Jon Harland is a wheat farmer. He owns farm equipment and buildings that cost $600,000 when purchased several years ago. He owes a local bank $425,000 for loans used to purchase these assets. In 2004, Jon sold $650,000 of wheat he raised during the year. He incurred operating costs of $585,000 to produce the wheat. This amount included $33,750 of interest on the bank loans and $52,500 of depreciation on the plant assets. In addition, Jon repaid $40,000 of the outstanding loan balance. The sales and all operating costs, except depreciation, were for cash. How much net income did Jon earn in 2004? What was his net cash flow for the year? Explain the difference.

E3-3
Obj. 1
$\frac{P}{T}$
Jeni Arrington drives for a large moving company. The company contacts Jeni when it has a job for her and furnishes a truck for her use. Jeni picks up the truck, drives to the customer's home, and loads, transports, and delivers the customer's belongings. She returns the truck to the company and receives her pay. Jeni is paid $4.50 per mile for the job. She is responsible for paying for her own gas, food, and lodging. Also, she must hire any helpers she needs to load and unload the truck. Jeni traveled 2,400 miles on a recent job that was completed on June 30. She paid $500 for gas, $116 for food, $204 for lodging, and $100 for helpers. Jeni expects to receive payment on July 5. How much did Jeni earn for the job? How much cash did Jeni spend while providing the service? Why is there a difference in cash flow and net income?

E3-4
Obj. 2
$\frac{P}{T}$
The Hardware Shoppe sold $222,500 of goods during September. It collected $75,000 from these sales plus $165,000 from sales of prior months. Complete the following table:

	Cash Flow for September	Cash Flow in Future	Sales Revenue for September
Cash from prior sales	?		
Cash from September sales	?	?	?
Total cash received in September	?		

E3-5

Objs. 2, 3

P/T

Holes 'R' Us, a blasting services company, has the following information available on December 31, the last day of the company's fiscal year. Each item involves an adjusting entry that must be made before financial statements can be prepared and the books closed for the year. Show how these adjusting entries would be entered into the accounting system.

1. A $35,000 note payable, incurring 9% interest, has been outstanding for the entire year. The note payable was properly recorded when it arose, but no entries regarding this event have been made since.
2. A $12,000 check was received on November 2 from a tenant that subleases part of the company's headquarters building. The amount was in payment of rent for November, December, and January. When the check was received, Cash was increased and Rent Revenue was increased. (Hint: Use a liability account titled Unearned Rent.)
3. On April 1 of the current year, the company purchased a two-year fire insurance policy for $7,200. When the policy was purchased, Cash was decreased and Prepaid Insurance was increased for the entire amount.
4. Wear and tear on the buildings and machinery for the year is estimated to be $42,000.

E3-6

Objs. 2, 3

P/T

Record each transaction of Rose's Flower Shop.

a. Purchased merchandise for sale on October 1 for $3,600, to be paid by October 30.
b. Sold merchandise for $900 cash on October 3. The merchandise cost Rose's $270.
c. Sold merchandise for $1,800 on credit on October 6. The merchandise cost Rose's $590.
d. Ordered $2,150 of merchandise on October 7 from a supplier.
e. $400 of the merchandise purchased on October 1 spoiled on October 9 and had to be trashed, resulting in spoilage expense.
f. Paid $1,800 on October 10 to suppliers for merchandise purchased on October 1.
g. Received $1,200 on October 16 from customers for sales on October 6.

E3-7

Obj. 4

P/T

Complete the following table. Each column represents a different company. All receivables are collected in the year following sale.

	Company A	Company B	Company C
Cash received from customers during 2004	$300,000	$625,000	?
Sales revenue for 2004	$352,500	$580,000	$260,000
Accounts receivable at beginning of 2004	$31,000	?	$35,000
Accounts receivable at end of 2004	?	$85,000	$53,000

E3-8

Objs. 2, 3

P/T

The following information is available at December 31, the end of the fiscal year. It requires that adjusting entries be identified and entered into the accounting system. Unless specifically noted, none of this information has been previously entered into the accounting system. If the information below were ignored, net income for the year would be $72,400.

1. Employees are owed $9,500 for wages they have earned but will not receive until the next regular payroll distribution in five days.
2. A physical count reveals that there is $5,000 of office supplies remaining on hand at the end of the period. The company started the year with $3,500 of office supplies recorded in the Office Supplies Inventory account. During the year, $14,000 of office supplies was purchased, paid for, and charged to Office Supplies Expense.
3. The basement of the building is rented out to another firm and used for storage. At year end, the $2,000 rent for the month of December had not yet been collected.
4. At the end of the year, the company has long-term assets on which $13,600 of depreciation must be recorded.
5. Earlier in the year, a bank loan was obtained and recorded in the accounting system. Since then, interest of $5,200 has been incurred on that loan but it has not yet been recorded or paid.

(Continued)

(a) Using the spreadsheet format, show how this information would be entered into the accounting system. (b) After considering the effects of all five adjusting entries, what is the proper amount of net income that should be reported for the year?

E3-9
Objs. 2, 3
P̧
T

Silberman Company transactions are listed below. Indicate the amount of revenue, expense, and cash flow that results from each. Use the format provided, and place the appropriate amount in each section of the table. Use a separate table for each transaction.

a. $5,000 of supplies were purchased in August for cash. $1,500 of the supplies were consumed in August, and $2,500 were consumed in September.
b. $15,000 of merchandise was sold in September. $6,000 of the sales were on credit.
c. Merchandise that cost Silberman $7,500 was sold in September. Silberman had paid $5,000 for the merchandise in August. The rest was paid for in September.
d. $50,000 was borrowed in August. $2,500 will be repaid each month for 20 months beginning in September. (Ignore interest.)
e. $25,000 of equipment was purchased and paid for in August. $500 of the equipment's revenue-generating ability was consumed in September; the remainder will be consumed in the future.

	Past	September	Future	Total
Revenues				
Expenses				
Cash received				
Cash paid				

E3-10
Obj. 3
P̧
T

The Get Well Medical Clinic paid $50,000 in wages during June. Of this, $5,800 was for wages earned in May. An additional $4,200 of wages was owed to employees for services provided in June. These wages will be paid in July. Complete the following table:

	Cash Flow for June	Cash Flow in July	Wages Expense for June
Cash paid for prior wages	?		
Cash paid for June wages	?	?	?
Total cash paid in June for wages	?		

E3-11
Obj. 3
P̧
T

George Carver borrowed $150,000 on January 1 to open a peanut processing plant. Interest on the loan is $3,750 each quarter. The first interest payment will be made on March 31. Complete the following table:

	January	February	March	Total for Quarter
Cash paid for interest	?	?	?	?
Interest expense	?	?	?	?

E3-12
Obj. 3
$\frac{P}{T}$

Rapid Recovery Chemical Company manufactures prescription drugs. On January 1, 2003, the company purchased new equipment for $450,000 in cash. The company will depreciate the equipment over a 3-year period at $150,000 each year. Complete the following table:

	2003	2004	2005	Total for 3 Years
Cash paid for equipment	?	?	?	?
Depreciation expense	?	?	?	?

Explain the difference between cash flows each year and the amount of depreciation expense recorded.

E3-13
Obj. 3
$\frac{P}{T}$

Tasaka Company manufactures oriental rugs. It pays utility bills at the end of the month in which services are received. The company received the following bills for April, May, and June, respectively: $850, $1,025, $1,150. Complete the following table:

	April	May	June	Total for 3 Months
Cash paid for utilities	?	?	?	?
Utilities expense	?	?	?	?

When are cash and accrual basis measures different? When are they the same?

E3-14
Obj. 4
$\frac{P}{T}$

Each of the following independent situations relates to information available on the last day of the year. Each involves an adjustment that must be made to the accounting system before financial statements can be prepared. Show the effects of each adjusting entry on the accounting system.

a. A $15,000 note payable, incurring 8% interest, has been outstanding the entire year. The note payable was properly recorded when it arose.
b. A $3,000 check was received 2 months ago from a tenant that subleases part of a building. The amount was for 6 months' rent beginning the day the check was received. When received, the entire amount of the check was recorded in a liability account titled Unearned Rent.
c. Exactly halfway through the year just ended, the company purchased a 2-year fire insurance policy for $8,000. When the policy was purchased, the entire amount was recorded in the Prepaid Insurance account.
d. Wear and tear on the buildings and machinery for the year is estimated to be $35,000.

E3-15
Obj. 4
$\frac{P}{T}$

On August 30, 2004, Goya Co. purchased $20,000 of canvas material from a supplier, Ramirez, Inc., on credit. The material is cut into smaller pieces for sale to customers. Prior to the purchase, Goya's merchandise inventory account had a balance of $135,000 and its accounts payable account had a balance of $17,000. Answer each of the following questions: (a) What subsidiary accounts are affected by the purchase and how are they affected? (b) What control accounts are affected and how are they affected? (c) If Goya Co. prepared a balance sheet immediately after recording the purchase, how would the balance sheet report the information associated with the purchase event?

E3-16
Obj. 4
$\frac{P}{T}$

On December 31, 2004, the Washington Music Store reported net income of $1,500 and the following account balances.

(Continued)

Cash	$1,375
Accounts receivable	2,100
Prepaid insurance	900
Equipment & furnishings	3,225
Less: Accumulated depreciation	(500)
Accounts payable	1,100
Wages payable	1,080
Owners' equity	4,920

After this information was prepared, the bookkeeper discovered that he had forgotten to make two necessary adjusting entries for the year and, therefore, they were not reflected in the balances shown. Information concerning the two missing adjusting entries follows:

a. The prepaid insurance involves a 3-year fire insurance policy that was purchased (and went into effect) on January 1, 2004. By the end of the year, a portion of the insurance policy had been used up.
b. The wages payable does not include the wages that were owed at year-end to two workers who had been temporarily assigned to work off the premises. This amount totaled $450.

Using the following schedule, determine the correct year-end amount of (1) total assets, (2) total liabilities, (3) owners' equity, and (4) net income.

	Assets	Liabilities	Equity	Net Income
Year-end amounts before correction				
Adjusting entry (a):				
Adjusting entry (b):				
Year-end corrected amounts	$	$	$	$

E3-17
Obj. 5
On December 31, 2004, Bert's Farm Store had the following account balances in its accounting system. All year-end adjustments had been entered, but the books had not yet been closed.

Bert's Farm Store
Account Balances Before Closing
December 31, 2004

Account	Balance	Account	Balance
Cash	$ 700	Sales Revenue	$2,200
Merchandise	2,800	Cost of Goods Sold	900
Supplies	925	Wages Expense	400
Prepaid Insurance	450	Utilities Expense	150
Equipment	3,550	Depreciation Expense	50
Accumulated Depreciation	1,750	Insurance Expense	100
Interest Payable	150	Supplies Expense	150
Notes Payable	2,000	Interest Expense	100
Owners' Equity	4,175		

a. What is the purpose of closing the books?
b. Prepare all necessary closing entries.
c. After closing, what is the amount of owners' equity that will be reported on the balance sheet?

E3-18
Obj. 5

$\frac{P}{T}$

Constantino Company presented the following general ledger account balances for the month ended December 31, 2005.

Assets:	
Cash	20,600
Accounts Receivable	2,250
Equipment	11,000
Total Assets	**33,850**
Liabilities:	
Wages Payable	250
Payable to Internet Service	35
Notes Payable	17,000
Total Liabilities	**17,285**
Owners' Equity:	
Contributed Capital	13,000
Retained Earnings	1,000
Service Revenue	3,315
Rent Expense	(400)
Wages Expense	(315)
Internet Service Expense	(35)
Total Owners' Equity	**16,565**

    a. Close the books for Constantino Company.
    b. Prepare a post-closing summary of account balances similar to Exhibit 13.

E3-19
Obj. 5

$\frac{P}{T}$

Hydrangea Nurseries had the following general ledger balances at December 31, 2004:

Assets:	
Cash	10,000
Accounts Receivable	25,000
Inventory	50,000
Prepaid Insurance	5,000
Equipment	300,000
Accumulated Depreciation	(80,000)
Total Assets	**310,000**
Liabilities:	
Accounts Payable	35,000
Notes Payable	130,000
Total Liabilities	**165,000**
Owners' Equity:	
Contributed Capital	90,000
Retained Earnings	45,000
Sales Revenue	300,000
Cost of Goods Sold	(140,000)
Insurance Expense	(5,000)
Wages Expense	(75,000)
Utilities Expense	(40,000)
Interest Expense	(10,000)
Depreciation Expense	(20,000)
Total Owners' Equity	**145,000**

    a. Prepare the entry to close the revenue and expense accounts at the end of the year.
    b. Prepare a post-closing summary similar to Exhibit 13.

E3-20 The accounting staff at Taiwan Manufacturing have prepared the following summary of ac-
Obj. 5 count balances at year end. The balances include all transactions for the fiscal year except for
closing entries.

Account	Balance	Account	Balance
Cash	$ 1,850	Sales Revenue	$7,600
Merchandise	8,435	Cost of Goods Sold	2,840
Supplies	2,955	Wages Expense	1,015
Prepaid Insurance	1,375	Utilities Expense	550
Equipment	9,650	Depreciation Expense	660
Accumulated Depreciation	4,100	Insurance Expense	495
Interest Payable	425	Supplies Expense	525
Notes Payable	7,000	Interest Expense	300
Owners' Equity	11,525		

a. What is the purpose of closing the books?
b. Prepare all necessary closing entries.
c. After all closing entries are entered into the accounting system, what will be the
amount of owners' equity reported on the balance sheet?

PROBLEMS

*If your instructor is using Personal Trainer in this course, you may complete online the assign-
ments identified by* P̅T̅ .

P3-1 ### Explaining the Difference between Cash and Accrual Accounting
Obj. 1

The accounting department at Klinger Realty sent the financial reports, as shown below, to
Robin Garrison, general manager. Attached was a note indicating that both sets of data are
based on the same set of events, which occurred during the quarter just completed. Robin was
only recently promoted to this position and is not very knowledgeable about accounting information.

After reviewing this report, Robin was somewhat disturbed because she always had
thought accounting was an exact process. How, she wondered, can there be two different results from the same set of facts? Furthermore, how could they be so different? Which one is
the "true" or "correct" report?

Klinger Realty
Results of Operating Activities
Third Quarter, 2004

	Cash Basis		Accrual Basis	
Cash receipts/revenues:				
Sales commissions	$300,000		$400,000	
Property management	210,000		165,000	
Total		$510,000		$565,000
Cash payments/expenses:				
Office employee wages	(53,000)		(48,000)	
Advertising	(10,000)		(90,000)	
Office supplies	0		(3,400)	
Depreciation—office				
equipment	0		(1,800)	
Rent	(6,000)		(6,000)	
Sales staff commissions	(150,000)		(200,000)	
Property managers' salaries	(116,000)		(90,000)	
Total		(335,000)		(439,200)
Net cash flow		$175,000		
Net income				$125,800

Required Assume that you are called in to advise Ms. Garrison. Write a memo to her explaining why there can be two measures of operating results and why they differ.

P3-2 **Ethics and Accounting Measurement**

Obj. 1

Hardy Rock is proprietor of a jewelry store. In January, he applied for a bank loan and was asked to submit an income statement for the past year, ending in December. Near the end of the prior year, Hardy had purchased merchandise for resale that cost him $60,000. He still owed $45,000 for this merchandise at year end. Half of the merchandise was sold during the Christmas holidays for $75,000. Customers owed Hardy $50,000 for these purchases at year end. Hardy included these transactions as part of his financial statements as follows:

Added to revenues	$75,000
Added to expenses	7,500
Added to net income	$67,500

Hardy reasoned that because he had sold half the merchandise in December, he should report it as revenue, though he had not received all of the cash from customers. Also, he reasoned that because he had paid $15,000 for the merchandise by year end and had sold half of the merchandise, he should report $7,500 of this amount as cost of goods sold.

Required What problems do you see with Hardy's reasoning? Is there an ethical problem with Hardy's treatment of these transactions? What should the effect of these transactions have been on net income?

P3-3 **Revenue Recognition and Accrual Accounting**

Obj. 2

Daisy Political Consultants has been in existence for many years. During the month of November, the following events occurred:

1. The owners contributed an additional $6,500 to the business to finance an expansion of operations.
2. Consulting services totaling $11,000 were performed on credit during November and billed to customers.
3. A loan in the amount of $25,000 was obtained from a wealthy campaign contributor.
4. Expenses in the amount of $6,000 were incurred during the month. One-third had been paid for by month end.
5. Cash of $18,500 was collected from customers for whom services had been performed during September and October.
6. Services totaling $4,500 were performed for customers who had paid in the previous month for the services.

Required Daisy uses accrual basis accounting. For which of the events above should revenue be recorded in November? In each case, how much revenue should be recorded? If an event does not involve revenue, specify why not.

P3-4 **How Unearned Revenue Links Cash and Sales Revenue**

Obj. 2

$\frac{P}{T}$

On March 15, the Spinnaker Company received $4,000 in cash from a customer who ordered a custom sail for her racing yacht. The company completed the sail and delivered it on April 30. The Spinnaker Company incurred costs of $2,500 in making the sail. Assume the company recorded the manufacturing costs in the Merchandise Inventory account.

Required
A. Record the transaction on March 15.
B. Record the transaction on April 30.
C. Prepare a table similar to Exhibit 2 that illustrates how Unearned Revenue links Cash with Sales Revenue.

P3-5

Obj. 3

$\frac{P}{T}$

How Prepaid Insurance Links Cash and Insurance Expense

On January 1, Taylor Manufacturing Company purchased a 12-month insurance policy for $1,200 and recorded it as Prepaid Insurance. On December 31 the bookkeeper observed the prepaid insurance account had a $1,200 balance representing the insurance purchased on January 1.

Required

A. Record the insurance purchase on January 1.
B. Prepare the entry required to record insurance expense for the year appropriately.
C. Prepare a table similar to Exhibit 5 that illustrates how Prepaid Insurance links Insurance Expense and Cash.

P3-6

Obj. 3

$\frac{P}{T}$

Expense Recognition and Accrual Accounting

The local chapter of Helping Hands, a social service organization, had the following economic events occur during the month of May:

1. A luncheon honoring volunteers was held at a cost of $950. By month end the bill hadn't been received or paid.
2. New letterhead and envelopes were printed at a cost of $625 and paid for. The new items will not be used, however, until the old supply is exhausted sometime in June.
3. The executive director was paid her usual salary of $3,800 during May.
4. Prizes, ribbons, and awards for events upcoming in July were delivered by the supplier, who charged $10,175. The amount was paid in cash.
5. The electric bill for April totaled $163 and was paid in full.
6. Radio, TV, and newspaper advertising related to a special fund-raising campaign ran during May. The $7,550 cost had been paid in April.

Required Helping Hands uses accrual basis accounting. For which of the events above should an expense be recorded in May? In each case, how much expense should be recorded? If an event does not involve an expense, specify why not.

P3-7

Objs. 1, 2, 3

$\frac{P}{T}$

Converting Net Income to Cash Flow

Middle East Importers reports the following accrual basis information for a recent month.

Total revenue from sales to customers	$90,000
Total expenses	69,000
Net income	$21,000

In addition, the following account information is known:

	Accounts Receivable	Accounts Payable
Beginning of month balance	$ 9,000	$15,000
End of month balance	21,000	9,000

Required Determine (a) the amount of cash collected from customers during the month, (b) the amount of cash paid out for expenses during the month, and (c) the net cash flow for the month.

P3-8

Objs. 1, 2, 3

$\frac{P}{T}$

Converting Net Cash Flow to Net Income

Khim Lee Company reported the following cash flow information at the end of its first year in business:

Cash received from customers	$235,000
Cash paid out to suppliers of inventory	(55,000)
Cash paid out to employees	(77,500)
Cash paid out for advertising	(12,500)
Cash paid out for taxes	(30,000)
Net cash flow for the year	$ 60,000

Also known at year end was the following:

Amounts not yet collected from customers	$85,000
Amounts owed to suppliers	15,000
Wages owed to employees	22,500
Additional taxes still owed	10,000
Amount remaining in inventory	0

Required Prepare an accrual basis income statement for the company's first year in business.

P3-9

Objs. 1, 2, 3

Ethics and Accounting Measurement

Tinker, Evers, and Chance are partners in a sports equipment megastore. Tinker keeps the accounting records for the partnership because he is skilled in accounting and the other partners are not. The partners have agreed that they will share equally in the company's profits (or losses) at the end of each year. For fiscal 2004, the first year of operations, the company sold $7,600,000 of merchandise. Of this amount, $1,400,000 was still owed to the company by customers at year end. The company purchased and paid for merchandise costing $4,300,000 during 2004; $1,000,000 of this merchandise remained in inventory at year end. The company purchased and paid for $1,400,000 of equipment during the year. The equipment should have a useful life of 7 years. Thus depreciation expenses would be $200,000 each year. Other expenses amounted to $650,000, all paid for in cash. Tinker has prepared the following income statement and distribution of profits for 2004:

Tinker, Evers, and Chance
Income Statement
For Year 2004

Revenues		$6,200,000
Expenses:		
Merchandise	$4,300,000	
Equipment	1,400,000	
Other	650,000	
Total expenses		6,350,000
Net loss		$ 150,000
Distribution of net loss:		
Reduction in owners' capital:		
Tinker		$ 50,000
Evers		50,000
Chance		50,000
Total distribution of net loss		$ 150,000

Evers and Chance are mystified by these results because they thought the company had been performing above their expectations. Tinker assured his partners that his numbers were correct. Tinker has offered to buy out his partners, explaining that "he got 'em into this and should do the right thing." Of course, the other partners will lose half of their original investment if they sell.

Required

A. What problems do you see with Tinker's financial report?
B. Advise the other partners as to whether they should sell out. To support your advice, prepare a revised income statement incorporating any changes you think appropriate to support a prudent decision.

P3-10   Accrual versus Cash Flow

Objs. 2, 3, 4

P/T

The Water Fun Store is a retailer of water sports products for backyard swimming pools. During August, the firm had the following operating activities:

Date	Event
Aug. 1	Bought $5,000 of goods for resale from Pinetree Wholesalers on credit.
5	Paid $450 to the local newspaper for advertising that ran during July.
6	Paid $975 rent for the month of August.
9	Sold goods to customers for $7,350 on credit. These goods had cost the firm $3,600.
10	Paid $3,000 to Pinetree Wholesalers in partial payment for goods purchased August 1.
11	Collected $5,350 from goods sold on August 9.
13	Bought $9,200 of goods for resale from Stanley Company. Paid cash.
16	Paid employees for their work so far in August, $1,050.
19	Sold goods to customers on credit for $6,350. These goods had cost the firm $2,400.
25	Collected $3,700 from the sales made on August 19.
29	Paid $975 rent for the month of September.
31	Employees had earned an additional $1,200 of wages but would not be paid until September 1.

Required

A. Prepare a report of net cash flow from operating activities.
B. Prepare an accrual basis income statement.
C. Which statement documents a more realistic or complete picture of August's activity? Why?

P3-11   Determining Transactions from Changes in Financial Statements

Objs. 2, 3, 4

The Loc-Tite Correctional Facility is a private enterprise prison that contracts services to a midwestern state. At October 1, the beginning of its fiscal year, the organization had the following balance sheet.

Loc-Tite Correctional Facility
Balance Sheet
at October 1

Assets:		Liabilities and Owners' Equity:	
Cash	$ 43,725	Accounts payable	$ 28,350
Supplies	65,700	Bonds payable	450,000
Equipment	350,000	Owners' investment	1,050,000
Building	1,400,000	Retained earnings	883,575
Accumulated			
depreciation	(100,000)		
Land	652,500		
Total	$2,411,925	Total	$2,411,925

During the month of October, a number of economic events occurred and were entered into the accounting system. At the end of October, the company prepared the following financial statements.

Loc-Tite Correctional Facility
Financial Statements

Balance Sheet (at Oct. 31)					Income Statement (for Oct.)	
Assets:			Liabilities and Owners' Equity:		Revenues	$810,000
Cash	$ 58,725		Accounts payable	$ 28,350	Expenses:	
Supplies	28,200		Bonds payable	0	Supplies	37,500
Equipment	350,000		Owners' Investment	1,050,000	Depreciation	8,625
Building	1,400,000		Retained earnings	1,302,450	Wages	345,000
Accumulated						
depreciation	(108,625)					
Land	652,500					
Total	$2,380,800		Total	$2,380,800	Net income	$418,875

Required

A. Identify the transactions that occurred during October.

B. Prepare a schedule that explains the changes in cash balance during October.

P3-12 ## Understanding Going Concern and Accounting Measurement

Objs. 2, 3, 4

P̶T

On March 1, Carl Caldwell started Caldwell Furniture Repair Company. He invested $2,000 of his own money, borrowed $16,000 from his father-in-law at 9% annual interest, and obtained an additional $3,000, 12% loan from Maxibank. He purchased $15,000 of tools and equipment (some new, some used) and bought $5,200 of supplies such as paints, resins, and glue, all for cash. He rented a shop at a local business park by paying $3,600 in advance for the months of March, April, and May. During March he performed repairs totaling $7,600 and used up $2,400 of supplies. Of the repair services performed, 75% were paid for in cash by the end of the month and the balance was expected to be collected in April. Carl estimated that wear and tear on the equipment and tools during March was $250. On March 31, he owed $332 to the electric company and $78 to the water company for services consumed. Also on that date, he paid interest totaling $150 on the two loans.

Required

A. Prepare an income statement for Caldwell Furniture Repair for the month of March.

B. Prepare a separate schedule that explains the changes in cash balance during March.

C. Is the transformation cycle complete or incomplete at the end of March? Explain your answer.

P3-13 ## Accrual versus Cash Flow

Objs. 2, 3, 4

P̶T

Consider each of the five independent situations below.

1. Asia Tea Company purchased a 3-month property insurance policy on March 1 at a cost of $3,600. The insurance became effective immediately although payment was due and paid 45 days later.

2. On February 1, Big Bang Chemical Company signed a contract with a customer. Big Bang agreed to deliver each month, for 3 months, goods priced at $7,500. The first delivery was made on April 1. The customer paid $22,500 for these goods on May 15.

3. Turning Tire Company borrowed $15,000 from a bank on February 1. Terms of repayment are that $1,000 of the principal amount must be repaid on the first day of each following month. In addition, interest at 2% per month on the unpaid balance must accompany each payment.

4. Bureaucrats, Inc. consumes large amounts of office supplies. On February 1, a $10,000 order of supplies was received and paid for. 60% of these supplies were used in March and the rest were used in April. On April 20, a $12,000 order of office supplies was received. The invoice for these goods was paid in May. 30% of these goods were consumed in May and the rest were consumed in June.

(Continued)

5. Sales at the High-Price Furniture Store totaled $45,000 for the month of February. Of this amount, 20% was cash sales, 40% was collected during March, 30% during April, and 10% during May.

Required

A. Determine the proper amount of revenue, expense, and cash flow that should be entered into the accounting system during each month shown. Use the format shown below. The first event is completed as an example.

B. What does this information suggest to you about the pattern in which accrual-based measures are recognized versus cash-based measures?

C. What does this suggest to you about a manager's need for both accrual information and cash flow information?

Event	Revenue, Expense, or Cash Flow?	Month of February	Month of March	Month of April	Month of May	Month of June
1.	Expense	-0-	$1,200	$1,200	$1,200	-0-
	Cash Flow	-0-	-0-	3,600	-0-	-0-
2.						
3.						
4.						
5.						

P3-14   Preparing Financial Statements and Making Decisions

Objs. 2, 3, 4

P/T

The Desert Harbor Inn has been in business for more than 100 years but was recently renovated. On January 1, 2004, the balance sheet of the company was as shown on the next page.

During 2004, the inn earned $165,000 from room rentals and another $35,000 from parking, the gift shop, and other guest services. Of this amount, $187,000 was received in cash by year end; $13,000 was still collectible from credit card companies and one very reliable corporate account. Expenses incurred during the year included staff wages, $49,000; utilities, $10,400; supplies used, $4,300; depreciation on furniture and fixtures, $1,500; depreciation on the building, $3,500; interest on note payable, $4,700; cost of goods sold by gift shop, $11,000; and other miscellaneous expenses of $3,300.

Except for depreciation, supplies consumed, and $890 of wages still owed to employees, all expenses were paid for in cash. Other cash payments included $800 for purchase of supplies and $35,000 paid on the principal of the note payable. Owners withdrew $45,000 from the business for living expenses during the year.

Desert Harbor Inn
Balance Sheet
January 1, 2004

Assets		Liabilities and Owners' Equity	
Cash	$ 4,900	Notes payable	$ 56,500
Supplies on hand	8,800	Investment by owners	60,000
Furniture and equipment	25,000	Retained earnings	19,200
Buildings	95,000		
Accumulated depreciation	(10,000)		
Land	12,000		
Total	$135,700	Total	$135,700

Required

A. Prepare year-end financial statements for the company for 2004. Include an income statement, statement of cash flows, and a balance sheet.

B. From a financial perspective, does this company appear to be one that you would like to own? Why or why not?

P3-15 **Identifying Problems in Financial Reporting**

Objs. 2, 3, 4

Alma Zorditch started an Internet company and has computed the first year's profit as shown below. She is distressed. She thought the business had been going fairly well but does not know how she can live on the meager profit the company has earned. She is considering going out of business. Alma doesn't have any formal training in accounting but once took a 4-hour seminar on the subject. That seminar impressed on her the importance of keeping detailed and accurate records. All the numbers reported below are accurate, but there may be other problems that you can identify.

Zorditch.com
Profits I Made the First Year

Revenue:		
Cash collected from customers	$173,400	
Accounts receivable at year end	18,200	
Total revenue		$191,600
Expenses:		
Money I contributed to start the firm	15,000	
Purchase of office furnishings & equipment	28,500	
Purchase of office supplies	1,560	
Rent on the office space	13,000	
Loan from the bank	50,000	
Wages paid to employees	36,200	
Advertising and promotion	24,280	
Miscellaneous	11,300	
Total expenses		179,840
Profit		$ 11,760

After talking with Alma, you discover the following additional information.

1. When purchased, the office furnishings and equipment have an expected useful life of 5 years. That estimate still appears reasonable.
2. All office supplies have been used up.
3. The rent amount includes $1,000 rent paid in advance for the first month of Year 2.
4. Half of the advertising and promotion amont is for a campaign that will begin 3 months from now. *(Continued)*

Required

A. Study the information given and prepare a new income statement making all changes you believe are appropriate.

B. Wherever your report differs from Alma's, justify the change you have made.

C. Based on your revised income statement, what advice would you have for Alma? List two or three specific suggestions.

P3-16 Adjusting Entries and Closing Entries: Effects on Financial Statements

Objs. 4, 5

The Flash Pan Company manufactures cooking products. On August 1, 2004, the company borrowed $125,000 from creditors. Semiannual interest payments of $7,500 are to be made to creditors beginning January 31, 2005. On July 1, 2004, the company purchased a 1-year insurance policy for $10,000 and recorded it as prepaid insurance. On January 1, 2004, the company purchased equipment for $50,000. The equipment has an expected life of 4 years. On October 1, 2004, the company rented some of its unused warehouse space to another company. The other company agreed to pay $15,000 for the space every 6 months beginning April 1, 2005. Balance sheet and income statement information reported by Flash for the fiscal year ended December 31, 2004 included:

Assets	$625,000
Liabilities	250,000
Owners' equity	337,500
Revenues	150,000
Expenses	112,500
Net income	37,500

The balance sheet did not balance but it was distributed anyway. Later, it was discovered that the company's accounting staff had failed to record any adjusting entries at the end of 2001 for interest, insurance, depreciation, or rent. In addition, no closing entries had been made.

Required

A. Record the adjusting entries that should have been made at year end 2004.

B. Explain why the balance sheet did not balance and whether this was caused by the failure to record adjusting entries or the failure to record closing entries.

C. Identify the corrected amounts for the balance sheet and income statement. Show your work.

P3-17 End-of-Period Adjustments and Closing

Objs. 4, 5

At December 31, 2004, the accountant at Puget Sounds, a recording studio, has entered all the firm's transactions into the accounting system and is beginning the end-of-period process. He asks your help in identifying the necessary adjusting entries. In the first column on page F121, the accountant has listed the company's account balances before considering adjustments. In addition, he has provided other information that may cause you to recommend that certain adjusting entries be made.

1. $4,350 of wages earned by employees during December have not been recorded or paid.

2. The prepaid insurance is for a 3-year policy purchased on the first day of the year just ending.

3. Unearned revenues are for contracts for the use of studio facilities. $12,000 of this amount has been earned by December 31.

4. A count at year-end shows that $10,050 of supplies remain on hand.

5. The note payable was issued on October 1, 2004. Interest accumulates in the amount of $3,000 per month. Interest has not yet been recorded for December.

6. Depreciation on equipment is $1,500 per month. Depreciation on buildings is $600 per month. No depreciation has yet been recorded for the quarter (3 months) just ended.

	Account Balance Before Adjustment	Adjustments	Account Balance After Adjustment
Cash	$ 52,500		
Accounts receivable	35,250		
Supplies	19,200		
Prepaid insurance	4,050		
Equipment	468,000		
Accumulated depreciation—equipment	(129,000)		
Buildings	649,500		
Accumulated depreciation—buildings	(85,500)		
Land	58,500		
Total assets	**$1,072,500**		
Unearned revenues	$ 36,000		
Accounts payable	27,900		
Interest payable	6,000		
Wages payable	0	(1) +4,350	4,350
Notes payable	420,000		
Common stock	300,000		
Retained earnings (a)	224,100		
Total liabilities & stockholders' equity	**$1,014,000**		
Rent revenues	$ 100,500		
Wages expense	(36,000)	(1) −4,350	(40,350)
Supplies expense	0		
Insurance expense	0		
Interest expense	(6,000)		
Depreciation expense	0		
Net income	**$ 58,500**		
(a) Net income has not been added for the current year.			

Required

A. Identify any adjustments you believe necessary and enter their effects in the adjustments column of the table above. Code each adjustment with the number to which it relates. The first item is completed for you as an example.
B. Record the proper ending amount for each account in the final column.
C. On the table you have completed, why doesn't the total of all asset accounts equal the total of all liability and equity accounts?
D. What additional step(s) needs to be performed before financial statements can be prepared? Explain how this will solve the imbalance identified in part (C) above.
E. By what amount (and percentage) would net income have been misstated if no adjusting entries had been recorded by this company?

P3-18 **Types and Treatment of Accounts**

Obj. 5

P/T

Encanto Properties, Inc., uses the accounts listed below.

A. Prepaid Insurance
B. Retained Earnings
C. Accumulated Depreciation
D. Wages Expense
E. Commissions Revenue
F. Interest Payable
G. Supplies
H. Insurance Expense
I. Unearned Rent

J. Prepaid Advertising
K. Notes Payable
L. Cost of Goods Sold
M. Machinery
N. Owners' Capital
O. Accounts Receivable
P. Bonds Payable
Q. Supplies Expense
R. Depreciation Expense

Required (a) For each account above, indicate whether it is an asset, liability, owners' equity, revenue, or expense account. (b) Indicate whether the account is closed at the end of the fiscal year.

P3-19 **Ethical Issues in an Accounting System**

Obj. 6

Ethel Spikes works for Hard Rock Candy Company. She enters customer orders in the company's accounting system. The orders are written on prepared forms by the company's sales representatives (reps). The company employs ten sales reps, who work different territories. The reps are paid on a commission basis for sales made during the preceding month. Sales reports prepared by the accounting department supervisor are used to determine the commissions. Sales reps drop off the forms with the accounting supervisor each week. The supervisor then delivers the forms to Ethel. She enters the orders in a computer and prints out a sales report and sales invoices for each customer. These are picked up by the supervisor, who delivers them to payroll and to shipping. The result of entering the orders in the accounting system is to increase accounts receivable and to increase sales revenue.

Ethel has discovered an interesting regularity in some of the orders. One of the sales reps always reports abnormally high orders from a particular customer. A few days after the end of each month, the rep submits a cancelation form for the customer to eliminate a large portion of the customer's order. The supervisor directs Ethel to record the cancelation by reducing accounts receivable for the customer and recording an increase in an operating expense account. Ethel doesn't know much about accounting. When she asked her supervisor about this procedure, she was told that it was standard for this customer and not to worry about it.

Ethel smells a rat, however, and has considered discussing the matter with the vice president for finance. But she is concerned she may simply be making waves that will alienate her supervisor.

Required Ethel has sought your advice, as a friend, about this matter. What would you recommend to Ethel? What problems do you see in Hard Rock's accounting system? How might these problems be solved?

P3-20 **Describing Processes in an Accounting System**

Obj. 6

Flora Wiser is the daughter of the owner of Wiser Florist Company. She recently completed college with a major in biology and has taken the job of assistant manager. Her primary duties involve purchasing inventory from suppliers. Flora has little understanding of accounting, and you have been asked to help her become familiar with the company's accounting system and how the system processes information.

Required Write a memo to Flora describing the purpose of an accounting system. Describe each of the basic processes that occur within financial accounting systems and how these processes accomplish the purpose of the system.

P3-21 **Excel in Action**

P/T

The problem in Chapter F2 provided account balances for The Book Wermz on September 30, 2004, the end of the company's fiscal year: Cash $4,238.72, Inventory of Books $235,892.35, Supplies $2,343.28, Equipment $43,297.00, Notes Payable $123,452.88, Investment by Owners

SPREADSHEET

$100,000, and Retained Earnings $62,318.47. Chapter F2 also listed summary transactions for October 2004:

Cash sales	$38,246.50
Cost of goods sold	27,318.93

The Equipment account balance of $43,297.00 is net of accumulated depreciation of $12,353.00. Therefore, the Equipment balance before considering the effect of depreciation is $55,650.00.

Other transactions for the month ended October 31, 2004, include:

Cash paid for books purchased	$18,243.27
Cash paid for supplies	1,750.92
Cost of supplies used in October	2,129.48
Employee wages earned and paid in October	3,620.83
Employee wages earned in October but unpaid	527.12
Cash paid for portion of Notes Payable	1,122.77
Cash paid for interest incurred on Notes Payable	823.02
Cash paid for October rent	1,534.86
Depreciation on equipment for October	721.62

In addition, The Book Wermz held classes on book binding for local civic organizations in October. The organizations agreed to a $500 fee for these services but did not make the payment in October.

Required Add the transactions described above to those created in Chapter F2. Additional rows should be added to the spreadsheet for the transactions. Additional columns also will be needed for accounts not included in Chapter F2. The following accounts should be included in the spreadsheet in the order indicated: Cash, Accounts Receivable, Supplies, Inventory, Equipment, Accumulated Depreciation, Wages Payable, Notes Payable, Investment by Owners, Retained Earnings, Sales, Service Revenues, Cost of Goods Sold, Supplies Expense, Wages Expense, Rent Expense, Depreciation Expense, and Interest Expense. The beginning balance of all new accounts except Accumulated Depreciation is $0. The beginning balance of the Accumulated Depreciation account is $12,353 (note this is a negative amount because it is a contra account), and the beginning balance of the Equipment account should be changed to $55,650 (to permit Accumulated Depreciation to be included as a separate account). Column sums should be recalculated to determine totals at October 31. Make sure to close the revenue and expense accounts to Retained Earnings. Use October 31 as the date for all transactions.

Update the balance sheet and income statement by including the effects of the transactions recorded for October. Use cell references in the financial statements to identify amounts for each account. Add captions to identify each statement. The statements should include the name of the company on the top line. The next line should identify the financial statement as a balance sheet or income statement. The third line should identify the date (October 31, 2004 for the balance sheet) or period (for October 2004 for the income statement). List total revenues and total expenses as subtotals on the income statement. Use underlines to separate the subtotals from other numbers. The Borders button ▦ can be used for this purpose.

P3-22 **Multiple-Choice Overview of the Chapter**

P/T

1. The primary difference between control accounts and subsidiary accounts is that
   a. control accounts appear on the balance sheet but subsidiary accounts appear on the income statement.
   b. subsidiary accounts provide detailed information; control accounts provide summary information.
   c. control account balances are reported on the financial statements but subsidiary accounts appear only in the general ledger.
   d. subsidiary accounts are necessary in a manual accounting system but not in a computerized system.

2. At the beginning of the year, Lagos Importers had $750 of office supplies on hand. During the year, an additional $3,250 of supplies were purchased and recorded in

(Continued)

Office Supplies Inventory. At year end, $900 of supplies remained on hand. Just prior to preparing the year-end adjusting entry, the balance in the Office Supplies Inventory account was $1,200. Which of the following is a true statement about the necessary adjusting entry?

a. An asset account must be decreased by $300.
b. An asset account must be decreased by $3,250.
c. An expense account must be increased by $1,200.
d. An expense account must be increased by $900.

3. The balance of the merchandise inventory account increased by $3,000 during February. Which of the following statements can be made as a result of this information?

a. Credit sales for the month were $3,000 greater than cash received from customers.
b. Purchases of inventory for the month were $3,000 less than the cost of merchandise sold for the month.
c. Purchases of inventory for the month were $3,000 greater than the cost of merchandise sold for the month.
d. Merchandise purchased for the month totaled $3,000.

4. Which of the following accounts should always have a zero balance after all closing entries are completed?

a. Interest Expense
b. Interest Payable
c. Prepaid Interest
d. Accounts Payable

5. Tempel Manufacturing uses accrual accounting. Each of the following events occurred during the month of February. Which one of them should be recorded as a revenue or expense for the month of February?

a. Sales of $30,000 were made on credit. They will be collected during March.
b. Collections of $10,000 were made from sales that occurred during January.
c. Materials costing $18,000 were purchased and paid for. It is expected that they will be used during March.
d. A bill in the amount of $8,600 was received from a supplier for goods purchased during January. It was paid immediately.

6. Zinsli Company uses the accrual basis of accounting. Each of the following events occurred during July. Which one of them should be reported as an expense for July?

a. Office supplies costing $800 were used up. They had been purchased and paid for during April.
b. A new delivery truck was purchased on the last day of July. It was not put into use until August.
c. On the third day of the month, $8,000 was paid to employees for hours worked during the month of June.
d. Near the end of the month, August's rent of $1,500 was paid in advance.

7. The following information is available for two companies for the year 2004:

	Handle-Bar Mustache Co. Cash Operating Statement For the Year 2001	Pencil-Thin Mustache Co. Accrual Income Statement For the Year 2004
Receipts/Revenues	$50,000	$55,000
Payments/Expenses	38,000	31,000
Net Cash/Net Income	$12,000	$24,000

Which of the following statements can be determined from the information provided?
a. Pencil-Thin collected more cash from customers during 2004 than did Handle-Bar.
b. Pencil-Thin was profitable during 2004, whereas Handle-Bar may have been profitable.
c. Pencil-Thin was twice as profitable as Handle-Bar.
d. Handle-Bar consumed more total resources during 2004 than did Pencil-Thin.

8. Are the following accounts a liability?

	Depreciation expense	Accounts receivable
a.	Yes	Yes
b.	Yes	No
c.	No	Yes
d.	No	No

9. Using accrual-basis measurement, expenses should be recognized when
a. a business owner recognizes that the firm is generating too much profit.
b. resources are used rather than when they are paid for.
c. cash is paid for resources.
d. sufficient revenue is earned to offset the expenses.

10. Match the account name to the financial statement on which it is reported.

	Accumulated Depreciation	Depreciation Expense
a.	Statement of stockholder's equity	Balance sheet
b.	Balance sheet	Balance sheet
c.	Income statement	Balance sheet
d.	Balance sheet	Income statement

CASES

C3-1   Ethical Issues Involving Revenue Recognition

Obj. 4

Flash Newton is national sales director at Bright & Shiny Toothpaste Company. The firm manufactures and distributes a full line of premium-priced personal care products sold through a carefully selected set of distributors nationwide. The popularity and profit margins of the Bright & Shiny product line make distributorships very profitable and there is intense competition when one becomes available.

Flash, and the regional sales directors working for him, are compensated by a base salary and a significant bonus tied to percentage increases in yearly sales. Because of an impending recession, sales have been mostly flat during the first three quarters of the year. On October 3, Flash convened a national sales meeting with representatives of all distributors. At that meeting, he presented the distributors with Bright & Shiny's newest sales plan. All distributors would be required to buy, during the 4th quarter, up to 2 years' worth of inventory of the firm's products. Further, the prices charged on these special purchases would be 10% greater than usual. Any distributors not agreeing to the proposal would automatically lose their distributorship. Because most distributors are not expected to have cash readily available to pay for these additional purchases under the usual 30-day credit terms, Bright & Shiny will allow up to 12 months to pay.

The new policy has been a huge success and by year end, total orders and shipments to distributors are up by 12% over the previous year. Bright & Shiny recorded all shipments as revenue even though some distributors were told by lower-level managers that they could return unsold products. Because many distributors could not handle the large shipments in their usual storage facilities, many orders have been shipped to third-party warehouses for storage at Bright & Shiny's expense. At Flash's suggestion, and to obtain maximum benefit of this new sales program, the company held the books open for a few days after December 31 to obtain and ship additional orders.

Required Identify and explain any problems you see with the sales plan. If you were Bright & Shiny's CEO, which aspects of the sales plan would you have approved and which would you have denied? Why?

C3-2

Objs. 1, 5

Evaluating the Results of an Organization's Transformation Process

SoftwareSolutions.com has been in business for several years and is publicly traded on a major U.S. stock exchange. It is an Internet wholesaler of a variety of commercial software applications. On January 1, 2004, the company's balance sheet appeared as follows (all amounts are in thousands of dollars):

SoftwareSolutions.com
Balance Sheet
January 1, 2004

Assets		Liabilities & Stockholders' Equity	
Cash	$ 4,240	Wages payable	$ 640
Accounts receivable	6,800	Capital stock (owner's investment)	33,000
Inventory	15,200	Retained earnings	13,600
Buildings & equipment	16,780		
Accumulated depreciation	(4,780)		
Land (for plant expansion)	9,000		
Total assets	$47,240	Total liabilities and stockholders' equity	$47,240

During the first quarter of the current year (January, February, March), the following events occurred.

A. New office furniture costing $500 was purchased on the last day of March. This was to be used in a new sales office that was scheduled to open April 1. The office furniture was paid for in cash.

B. Wages and salaries totaling $3,200 were paid. Of this amount, 20% was to liquidate wages payable that arose in the fourth quarter of the previous year. The company has a policy of not making wage or salary advances to employees.

C. All accounts receivable outstanding at January 1 were collected.

D. The company's advertising agency billed the firm $1,000 for a campaign that had run during the current quarter. The company is planning to pay the bill during April.

E. Sales totaling $18,000 were made to customers. Of these sales, 60% was collected during the first quarter, and the balance is expected to be collected during the next quarter. The goods that were sold had cost the company $13,000 when they were purchased.

F. Dividends were declared and paid to stockholders in the amount of $1,500.

G. Inventory (software programs) costing $10,500 was purchased, of which 10% was paid for by the end of the quarter.

H. A 3-year, $4,000, 12% loan was obtained from a local bank on the last day of the quarter.

I. New shares of stock were sold by the company for $2,000 in cash.

J. A new 3-year lease agreement was signed and executed. The lease required that a $900 monthly rental be paid in advance for the first 2 quarters of the current year. (Total paid is $5,400 = $900 × 6 months.)

K. The accountants calculated that depreciation totaling $350 should be recorded for the quarter for the firm's buildings and equipment.

L. The land that had been held for plant expansion was sold for $9,000.

Required Prepare any summary documents you believe might help management (or interested external parties) better understand the effectiveness or efficiency of the firm's first quarter transformation process. Did the company have a satisfactory first quarter?

COMPREHENSIVE REVIEW

CR3-1 Financial Statement Preparation and Closing Process

Summary account balances for Mom's Cookie Company at the end of February are presented below. The summary includes all transactions for February, not just those described in this chapter. In particular, additional sales transactions have been included.

Mom's Cookie Company
Account Balances
February 28, 2004

Account	Balance
Assets:	
Cash	7,740
Accounts Receivable	1,580
Merchandise Inventories	7,520
Supplies	60
Prepaid Rent	1,200
Equipment	31,000
Accumulated Depreciation	(1,040)
Total Assets	**48,060**
Liabilities:	
Accounts Payable	1,400
Unearned Revenue	3,000
Interest Payable	400
Notes Payable	30,000
Total Liabilities	**34,800**
Owners' Equity:	
Contribution by Owners	10,000
Retained Earnings	480
Sales Revenue	17,160
Cost of Goods Sold	(11,440)
Wages Expense	(1,000)
Rent Expense	(600)
Depreciation Expense	(520)
Supplies Expense	(400)
Utilities Expense	(220)
Interest Expense	(200)
Total Owners' Equity	**13,260**

Required Use the account balances to (a) prepare an income statement for February, (b) close the revenue and expense accounts (show journal transactions and ledger accounts), (c) prepare a post-closing summary of account balances, and (d) prepare a balance sheet.

REPORTING EARNINGS AND FINANCIAL POSITION

How do we report earnings and financial position to stockholders?

Previous chapters described business activities of Mom's Cookie Company and the system the company used to account for those activities. As the business grew during 2004, Maria and Stan needed additional financial resources to take advantage of opportunities to sell more of their product. In October, they decided to issue shares of stock in their company to other individuals. Cash received from issuing the stock was used to acquire additional equipment, particularly delivery vans, and to increase the amount of inventory the company could purchase. Because the company has external investors (stockholders who are not managers of the company), it must report its business activities in conformance with generally accepted accounting principles to ensure these stockholders are properly informed of the company's earnings and financial position.

FOOD FOR THOUGHT

Assume you own shares of stock in Mom's Cookie Company. What information about the company is important to you? As the company prepares to report accounting information to you and its other owners at the end of its 2004 fiscal year, what information must it include in its income statement and balance sheet? What information do corporations report, especially about their earnings and stockholders' equity, that other companies do not? Is there any information about the company that does not have to be disclosed?

Maria and Stan have arranged to meet with their accountant, Ellen, to discuss these issues.

Maria: *We have prepared monthly financial statements for our use in managing the company. I suspect that those statements are not adequate for reporting to our other stockholders.*

Ellen: *That's correct. The statements you have been preparing are fine for internal use and contain correct information. However, formal financial statements for external users need to follow a somewhat different format than those you have been using.*

Stan: *Does this mean we have to redo our accounting system and learn a new way of accounting for our company?*

Ellen: *No. Your accounting system is fine. You just need to modify the format of your statements to organize the information a bit differently, and you need to include more information about earnings and stockholders' equity than you have been reporting.*

Maria: *Will these changes be hard for us to make?*

Ellen: *No. You will need to understand how information is classified in formal financial statements and how corporations report such matters as earnings per share and changes in stockholders' equity. Now that you understand the basic content of financial statements and how business activities are reported in these statements, you shouldn't have much trouble preparing statements for your stockholders.*

THE PURPOSE OF FINANCIAL STATEMENTS

OBJECTIVE 1

Identify the primary financial statements issued by businesses.

Accounting information may serve general and specific purposes. Financial statements are the primary means organizations use to report general-purpose accounting information to external decision makers. Most business organizations prepare three financial statements:

1. An income statement
2. A balance sheet
3. A statement of cash flows

Many corporations also prepare a statement of stockholders' equity because of the variety and complexity of their ownership transactions. This chapter examines the purpose and content of the income statement, the balance sheet, and the statement of stockholders' equity. Chapter F5 examines the statement of cash flows. Information contained in financial statements and in the notes accompanying the statements is the primary focus of financial accounting. Specific-purpose accounting reports and other information used by internal decision makers are subjects of managerial accounting.

The form and content of financial statements evolved throughout the twentieth century and continue to change to meet user needs. Financial statements are used by internal and external decision makers. The format and content of the statements used by managers to make financing, investing, and operating decisions often follow those of statements prepared for external users. Statements for internal use, however, may be prepared in any form and with any content desired by management.

For many years the balance sheet was the primary financial statement reported to external users. It was designed to meet the needs of creditors, who wanted information about resources and claims to these resources. The income statement developed to meet the needs of corporate investors, who wanted information about earnings. Earnings information is useful for evaluating management decisions that affect payments to stockholders and stock values. The statement of stockholders' equity describes transactions affecting stock and the amount and use of retained earnings. The statement of cash flows, which is a more recent addition to external reports, provides information that enables creditors, investors, and other users to assess a company's ability to meet its cash requirements.

Financial statements for general-purpose external reporting normally are prepared according to generally accepted accounting principles (GAAP). As noted previously, GAAP are accounting and reporting standards established by authoritative agencies and monitored and enforced by the federal government. GAAP specify the format and content of the statements, though they permit managers to choose among alternative methods of reporting some transactions. The establishment and enforcement of accounting standards are discussed in Chapter F6.

An income statement (sometimes called an earnings statement, a statement of operations, or a profit and loss (P&L) statement) reports a company's revenues and expenses for a fiscal period. The income statement presents operating results on an accrual basis. It measures the amount of goods and services provided to customers during a fiscal period and resources consumed in providing those goods and services. Revenues and expenses result from the sale and consumption of resources for a fiscal period. Therefore, the income statement reports the results of operating activities for a particular period, such as a month, quarter, or fiscal year.

A balance sheet reports the balances of the asset, liability, and owners' equity accounts at a particular date. Other names for the balance sheet are statement of financial position and statement of financial condition. These names are good descriptions of the statement because it reports the amount of resources available to an organization at a particular date and the sources of financing used to acquire those resources. In combination, the resources and financing are the financial position, or condition, of the organization at the report date.

A *statement of stockholders' equity* **reports changes in a corporation's owners' equity for a fiscal period.** Owners of corporations are known as stockholders or shareholders because they acquire ownership by purchasing shares of stock issued by the corporation. Each share of stock represents an equal share of ownership in a corporation. The primary changes in stockholders' equity result from profits earned during a period, from dividends paid to owners, and from the sale or repurchase of stock by a corporation. *Dividends* **are distributions of cash or stock by a corporation to its stockholders.** The statement of stockholders' equity links the income statement to the balance sheet because it describes how much net income was reinvested as part of retained earnings.

THE INCOME STATEMENT

OBJECTIVE 2

Explain information presented on a company's income statement.

The income statement reports the revenues, expenses, and net income for a fiscal period. Exhibit 1 provides the income statement of Mom's Cookie Company for the year ended December 31, 2004. The income statement reports revenues and expenses that are measured on an accrual basis. Revenues indicate the sales price of goods and services sold during a fiscal period. They do not indicate how much cash was received from the sales during that period. Expenses identify the cost of resources consumed in producing and selling goods and services sold during a fiscal period. They do not identify how much cash was paid for resources during that period. **Net income is not cash.** As a first step in understanding Exhibit 1, observe the general format of the statement. Unlike the statements we described in Chapters 2 and 3 that simply listed revenues and

Exhibit 1

A Corporate Income Statement

Mom's Cookie Company
Income Statement
For the Year Ended December 31, 2004

Sales revenue	$ 686,400
Cost of goods sold	(457,600)
Gross profit	228,800
Selling, general and administrative expenses	(148,300)
Operating income	80,500
Interest expense	(4,800)
Pretax income	75,700
Income taxes	(22,710)
Net income	$ 52,990
Earnings per share	$ 13.25*
Average number of common shares	4,000

*rounded

expenses, the income statements prepared by most companies are divided into several sections. The following paragraphs describe the sections commonly found on income statements.

Gross Profit

The income statement reports *gross profit,* **the difference between the selling price of goods or services sold to customers during a period and the cost of the goods or services sold.** For a merchandising company, the cost of goods sold is the cost of the merchandise inventory sold during a period. For a manufacturing company, cost of goods sold includes the dollar amounts of materials, labor, and other resources that are consumed directly in producing the goods sold during a period. These costs are **product costs**. Product costs are recorded as an asset (Inventory) until goods are sold. Then the costs are matched against the revenues generated from the sale by recording an expense (Cost of Goods Sold) during the same fiscal period as the sale.

Cost of services sold, rather than cost of goods sold, is important for service companies. **The** *cost of services sold* **is the cost of material, labor, and other resources consumed directly in producing services sold during a period.** For example, in a hospital, the cost of nursing is a cost of services. This cost cannot be held as inventory and, therefore, is expensed in the period in which the services are provided.

Gross profit is a measure of how much a company earned directly from the sale of its products during a fiscal period. Every company would like to earn a large gross profit by selling its products at a much higher price than their cost. Competition prevents most companies from being able to do so. Companies must price their products at amounts their customers are willing to pay, which is determined in part by prices of other similar products that customers could buy from other companies. Mom's Cookie Company cannot sell its cookies at a price that is much higher than that of other companies that sell similar cookies. Therefore, Mom's Cookie Company has to purchase the goods it sells at a cost that allows it to earn a reasonable gross profit. The amount of gross profit a company can earn depends on the kinds of products it sells and the markets in which it operates. Some markets are more competitive than others. For example, many competing companies sell computers, but not many sell the operating systems for computers.

Operating Income

The second section of an income statement lists operating expenses other than cost of goods sold or cost of services sold. *Operating expenses* **are costs of resources consumed as part of operating activities during a fiscal period and that are not directly associated with specific goods or services.** Most operating expenses are **period costs** because they are recognized in the fiscal period in which they occur. Operating expenses include selling, general, and administrative expenses incurred during a period.

Corporations usually do not identify specific operating expenses in detail. Salaries for managers and their support staffs who are not involved directly in producing goods and the cost of resources used by managers are operating expenses. These expenses include depreciation, taxes, and insurance on office buildings and equipment, and the costs of supplies and utilities consumed in operating these facilities. Operating expenses also include marketing and product development costs. GAAP require most marketing and selling costs and research and development costs incurred during a fiscal period to be reported as operating expenses of the period in which they occur. Because identifying how much of these costs is associated with benefits of future periods is difficult, GAAP require that these amounts be expensed to avoid an overstatement of profits during the current fiscal period.

The excess of gross profit over operating expenses is *operating income.* If operating expenses are greater than gross profit, a loss from operations results. Operating income is a measure of how much a company earned from its basic business activities.

A company is in the business of acquiring and selling products. Cost of goods sold and other operating expenses include the cost of acquiring and making its products available to customers. Sales revenues, sometimes referred to as operating revenues, are the total prices of the goods sold during a fiscal period. Therefore, operating income is a measure of how much a company made from selling its products, after considering normal and reoccurring expenses of doing business.

Other Revenues and Expenses

Revenues and expenses may occur that are not directly related to a company's primary operating activities. These are considered **non-operating** items and are reported separately on the income statement following operating income. The item listed in this category most often is interest expense. Borrowing money is frequently necessary for an organization's operations; however, except for financial institutions, it is not part of most businesses' primary operating activities. Accordingly, other expenses and revenues are reported on the income statement after operating income. This separate listing distinguishes them from revenues and expenses that result from a business's primary operating activities.

Income Taxes

Most corporations pay income taxes on their earnings. The amount of income tax expense is determined by applying tax rates required by current tax laws and regulations to the income earned by a company during a fiscal period. Exhibit 1 reports that Mom's Cookie Company incurred income taxes of 30% on its pretax income ($22,710 = \$75,700 \times 0.30$).

> **LEARNING NOTE**
>
> Not all U.S. corporations pay income taxes on profits. Certain small corporations, known as Subchapter S corporations in the tax laws, are treated like partnerships for tax purposes. Each stockholder is taxed on his or her share of the corporation's profits.

As noted in Chapter F1, direct taxation of income is one of the disadvantages of corporations. Proprietorships and partnerships do not pay income taxes on their profits directly. Instead, those profits are treated as personal income of the owners. Owners pay income tax on a proprietorship's profits or on their share of the profits of a partnership as part of personal taxes.

Net Income

Net income, or net earnings, is the amount of profit earned by a company during a fiscal period. It represents an increase in owners' or stockholders' equity, and it can be either distributed to owners or reinvested in the company. Distributions to owners, such as dividends, are not an expense. They are a deduction from retained earnings when a transfer is made to owners of a portion of a company's earnings. Undistributed earnings are included in retained earnings on a company's balance sheet.

> **LEARNING NOTE**
>
> It is important to note that cash dividends and cash withdrawals are paid out of cash. Therefore, a company must have sufficient cash available before it can pay dividends or before owners can withdraw money. Remember that net income does not guarantee that a company will have favorable cash flows during a period.

Earnings Per Share

GAAP require that corporate income statements prepared for distribution to stockholders and other external users present earnings per share as part of the statement. *Earnings per share* **is a measure of the earnings performance of each share of common stock during a fiscal period.** *Common stock* **is the stock that conveys primary ownership rights in a corporation.** We examine other types of stock in a later chapter. In general, earnings per share is computed by dividing net income by the average number of shares of common stock outstanding during a fiscal period. By multiplying earnings per share times the number of shares they own, stockholders can identify the amount of profit or loss associated with their individual investments.

The average number of common shares is based on the number of shares a company has outstanding, weighted by the portion of the fiscal period the stock is outstanding. To illustrate, assume Mom's Cookie Company was formed on January 1, 2004, as a corporation by issuing 1,000 shares of stock to Maria and Stan (500 shares each). Then, on September 1, 2004, the company issued an additional 9,000 shares of stock to other stockholders. Consequently, the company had 1,000 shares outstanding for 8 months (January through August) and 10,000 shares outstanding for 4 months (September through December).

The **average number of shares outstanding** was:

$$4,000 \text{ shares} = (1,000 \text{ shares} \times 8/12) + (10,000 \text{ shares} \times 4/12)$$

Earnings per share for Mom's Cookie Company was computed as follows:

$$\$13.25^* \text{ earnings per share} = \frac{\$52,990 \text{ net income}}{4,000 \text{ average common shares}}$$

*rounded

Other Reporting Issues

Income statements of actual companies vary in format and terminology from that presented in Exhibit 1. Though it is not possible to present all the possibilities that you may encounter in practice, certain issues are common for most corporate reports. These are apparent from a review of an actual corporate income statement. Exhibit 2 provides the income statement for **Krispy Kreme Doughnuts, Inc.**, from its 2002 annual report.

Exhibit 2 Income Statement for Krispy Kreme

Krispy Kreme Doughnuts, Inc.
Consolidated Statements of Operations

(In thousands, except per share amounts)

Year ended	Jan. 30, 2000	Jan. 28, 2001	Feb. 3, 2002
Total revenues	$220,243	$300,715	$394,354
Operating expenses	190,003	250,690	316,946
General and administrative expenses	14,856	20,061	27,562
Depreciation and amortization expenses	4,546	6,457	7,959
Income from operations	10,838	23,507	41,887
Interest income	293	2,325	2,980
Interest expense	(1,525)	(607)	(337)
Equity loss in joint ventures	—	(706)	(602)
Minority interest	—	(716)	(1,147)
Loss on sale of property and equipment	—	(20)	(235)
Income before income taxes	9,606	23,783	42,546
Provision for income taxes	3,650	9,058	16,168
Net income	$ 5,956	$ 14,725	$ 26,378
Basic earnings per share	$ 0.16	$ 0.30	$ 0.49
Diluted earnings per share	$ 0.15	$ 0.27	$ 0.45

First note that the title of Krispy Kreme's statement is labeled "consolidated statements of operations." Most large corporations include a number of companies owned by the corporation. **The controlling corporation is referred to as the** *parent* **and the companies owned or controlled by the parent are its** *subsidiaries. Consolidated financial statements* **include the activities of the parent and its subsidiaries as though they were one company.** Thus, Krispy Kreme's income statement reports profits for the entire corporation, including all subsidiaries it owns.

Most corporations, like Krispy Kreme, report income statements for three fiscal years. Krispy Kreme's fiscal year ends with the Sunday closest to the end of January. Three years of data permit readers to evaluate how company performance has changed in recent years. Also observe that amounts, except per share amounts, are in thousands of dollars. Thus, revenues for 2002 were greater than $394 million. *Total revenue* **is the amount earned from selling goods and services.**

The items presented in a company's income statement vary depending on the type of company. Any items that are uncommon and that are important relative to the total income of the company should be reported as a separate income statement item. For example, Krispy Kreme reports store operating expenses and depreciation and amortization as separate operating expenses. *Amortization expense,* like depreciation expense, **is the allocation of the cost of long-term intangible assets to the fiscal periods that benefit from their use.** We consider intangible assets later in this chapter and amortization expense in Chapter F11. Krispy Kreme also lists "equity loss in joint ventures" as a separate item. This loss resulted from a cooperative effort between Krispy Kreme and other companies and represents Krispy Kreme's share of the loss from these ventures.

Krispy Kreme also reports "minority interest" as a separate item. Minority interest on the income statement is that portion of the income of Krispy Kreme's subsidiaries that cannot be claimed by Krispy Kreme. For example, if Krispy Kreme owns 90% of a subsidiary and the subsidiary's net income is $1 million, Krispy Kreme's share of the net income would be $900,000. The remaining $100,000 would be the minority interest in the income. Because the reported revenues and expenses on the consolidated statement include the subsidiary amounts in them, Krispy Kreme subtracts the minority interest on the income statement. This indicates Krispy Kreme does not have a claim to that share of subsidiary income.

Items appearing after income from operations represent revenues and expenses that are not part of a company's primary operating activities. Interest, joint venture income or loss, minority interest, and gain or loss on sale of property and equipment are nonoperating revenues and expenses because they are not part of a company's primary operating activities. Many companies report "net interest" by combining interest revenue and interest expense into one item.

For some corporations, earnings per share is complicated because the company has issued financial instruments, such as long-term liabilities, that can be exchanged for shares of common stock or that might result in the issuance of additional shares if certain conditions are met. If issued, the additional shares of common stock would reduce earnings per share. These companies, like Krispy Kreme, report two sets of earnings per share numbers, **basic and diluted earnings per share**. Basic earnings per share (as described above) is calculated without considering the effect of the additional shares that could be issued. Diluted earnings per share is adjusted for the effects of additional shares that could be issued. Diluted earnings per share is never greater than basic earnings per share. It is a more conservative measure of earnings per share during a period than is basic earnings per share.

LEARNING NOTE

You should become familiar with the variety of terms that are used by companies in their financial statements. "Net earnings" is often substituted for "net income" for example. Real companies do not follow textbook formats in presenting their statements. As you increase your understanding of the basic content of these statements, you will be able to determine the meaning of terms used by most companies.

1 SELF-STUDY PROBLEM

An income statement for **IBM Corporation** for a recent fiscal year is provided below.

WebTUTOR Advantage

IBM Corporation
Income Statement

(Dollars in millions except per share amounts)

FOR THE YEAR ENDED DECEMBER 31:	*2001*
REVENUE:	
Global Services	$34,956
Hardware	33,392
Software	12,939
Global Financing	3,426
Enterprise Investments/Other	1,153
TOTAL REVENUE	85,866
COST OF SALES AND SERVICES:	
Global Services	25,355
Hardware	24,137
Software	2,265
Global Financing	1,693
Enterprise Investments/Other	634
TOTAL COST OF SALES AND SERVICES	54,084
GROSS PROFIT	31,782
OTHER EXPENSE AND INCOME:	
Selling, general and administrative	17,197
Research, development and engineering	5,290
Intellectual property and custom development income	(1,535)
Other (income) and expense	(361)
Interest expense	238
TOTAL OTHER EXPENSE AND INCOME	20,829
INCOME BEFORE INCOME TAXES	10,953
Provision for income taxes	3,230
NET INCOME	$ 7,723
EARNINGS PER SHARE OF COMMON STOCK:	
ASSUMING DILUTION	$4.35
BASIC	$4.45

Required Use this statement to answer the following questions:

1. How much revenue did IBM earn from selling computers?
2. How much revenue did IBM earn from other operating activities?
3. How much gross profit did IBM earn?
4. How much expense did IBM incur for non-operating activities?
5. Approximately how many shares of stock did IBM have outstanding?
6. What were IBM's total product costs?
7. How much net income did IBM earn?
8. How much cash did IBM receive from its operating activities during the year?

The solution to Self-Study Problem 1 appears at the end of the chapter.

The Balance Sheet

A balance sheet reports the asset, liability, and owners' equity account balances for a company at the end of a fiscal period. Exhibit 3 provides a balance sheet for Mom's Cookie Company for the year ended December 31, 2004.

Recall that the total amount of assets reported on the balance sheet at the end of a fiscal period must be equal to the total amount of liabilities and owners' equity. This relationship, assets = liabilities + owners' equity, is the fundamental balance sheet equation.

Exhibit 3 provides a **classified** balance sheet in which assets and liabilities are separated by type. The primary sections of the balance sheet are described in the following paragraphs.

LEARNING NOTE

An organization's **operating cycle** is the period from the time cash is used to acquire or produce goods until these goods are sold and cash is received. The operating cycles of most organizations are less than 12 months. A fiscal year is the primary reporting period for these companies. Occasionally, a company's operating cycle is longer than 12 months. In such cases, which are rare, current assets are defined as those that a company expects to convert to cash or consume during the next operating cycle.

Current Assets

GAAP require companies to report their current assets separately from their long-term assets. *Current assets* **are cash or other resources that management expects to convert to cash or consume during the next fiscal year.** Some current assets are liquid assets. *Liquid assets* **are resources that can be converted to cash in a relatively short period.** Cash equivalents include securities that are easily converted to cash and that have a short maturity, usually less than three

Exhibit 3

A Corporate Balance Sheet

Mom's Cookie Company Balance Sheet At December 31, 2004	
Assets	
Current assets:	
Cash	$ 10,680
Accounts receivable	8,570
Merchandise inventory	23,600
Supplies	690
Prepaid rent	2,000
Total current assets	45,540
Property and equipment, at cost	215,660
Accumulated depreciation	(25,500)
Total assets	$235,700
Liabilities and Stockholders' Equity	
Current liabilities:	
Accounts payable	$ 9,610
Unearned revenue	4,250
Interest payable	650
Notes payable, current portion	5,000
Total current liabilities	19,510
Notes payable, long-term	73,200
Total liabilities	92,710
Stockholders' equity:	
Common stock, 10,000 shares issued	100,000
Retained earnings	42,990
Total stockholders' equity	142,990
Total liabilities and stockholders' equity	$235,700

months. In addition to cash and equivalents, current assets include (1) accounts receivable for which a company expects to receive cash during the next fiscal year, (2) inventory a company expects to sell during the next fiscal year, and (3) resources a company expects to consume during the next fiscal year, such as supplies and prepaid insurance, generally referred to as prepaid expenses.

Property and Equipment

Property and equipment, **often called** *fixed assets* **or** *plant assets,* **are long-term, tangible assets that are used in a company's operations. (***Long-term intangible assets* **are those that provide benefits to the company for more than one fiscal period.)** Unlike inventory, these assets are not intended for resale. U.S. GAAP require fixed assets, other than land, to be depreciated over their estimated useful lives. Depreciation allocates the cost of these assets to the fiscal periods that benefit from their use as a means of matching expenses with revenues. The net value of fixed assets is the cost of the assets minus accumulated depreciation.

Land is not depreciated because it is not used up. Natural resources, such as petroleum, minerals, or timber, are accounted for separately from land and other property assets. The costs of these assets are allocated to expense over the periods that are expected to benefit from the use of the assets. **The process of allocating the cost of natural resources to expenses is known as** *depletion.* We examine depletion in Chapter F11.

Liabilities

GAAP require companies to report their current liabilities separately from their long-term liabilities. *Current liabilities* **are those obligations that management expects to fulfill during the next fiscal year.** *Long-term liabilities* **are those obligations not classified as current liabilities.**

Current liabilities include amounts owed by a company that will be paid during the coming fiscal year. Accounts, wages, interest, and income taxes payable all fit in this category. Unearned revenues that will be earned during the coming fiscal year also are classified as current liabilities.

The portion of long-term debt that will become due and be paid during the next year is a current liability. Exhibit 3 identifies this amount as "Notes payable, current portion." For example, assume Mom's Cookie Co. issued $80,000 in long-term notes payable during 2004. The notes are to be repaid in annual installments of $5,000. Therefore, $5,000 of the notes would be reported as a current liability on a balance sheet prepared at December 31, 2004. The unpaid balance would be reported as a long-term liability. From Exhibit 3 you can determine that $1,800 ($80,000 borrowed less $5,000 current portion and $73,200 long-term portion) of the notes was repaid in 2004, the year of issue.

The difference between current assets and current liabilities is known as *working capital.* Because current assets include those assets that are likely to produce cash inflows for a company and current liabilities include those liabilities that are likely to produce cash outflows, working capital is a measure of a company's liquidity. A company with a large amount of working capital should have little difficulty meeting its short-term obligations. Mom's Cookie Company reports $26,030 ($45,540 of current assets − $19,510 of current liabilities) of working capital in 2004.

Working capital often is reported as a ratio. **The ratio of current assets to current liabilities is the** *working capital ratio* **or** *current ratio.* Mom's Cookie Company's current ratio for 2004 is 2.33 ($45,540 ÷ $19,510).

Stockholders' Equity

Stockholders' equity includes (1) amounts paid by owners to a corporation for the purchase of shares of stock and (2) retained earnings, profits reinvested in the corporation.

Common stock, as noted earlier, conveys basic ownership rights in a corporation. We examine other types of stock in Chapter F9.

OTHER BALANCE SHEET CONTENT

Like the income statement, the balance sheet may appear in a variety of formats. Companies may use reporting rules that differ from those previously described. Some types of companies—many utilities, for example—report fixed assets prior to current assets and report stockholders' equity prior to liabilities. Companies in the United States often use formats that differ from those used in other countries. The items included on a balance sheet depend on the activities of a company.

Exhibit 4 provides the balance sheet from Krispy Kreme's 2002 annual report. Krispy Kreme's balance sheet is **comparative** because it contains information for more than one year. Also, it is consolidated because it includes all the companies owned by the parent corporation.

Other Current Assets

In addition to current assets we considered earlier, Krispy Kreme reports short-term investments and deferred income taxes. **Short-term investments** are stocks or debt of other companies owned by Krispy Kreme that it expects to sell in the near future. **Deferred income taxes** listed as current assets are prepaid taxes. These are taxes that the company has paid but that are associated with income tax expense of the coming fiscal period. The deferred taxes will be written off to income tax expense in a future period.

Krispy Kreme reports its accounts receivable net of allowances. The allowances are **estimated uncollectible accounts**. (These are sometimes referred to as **allowance for doubtful accounts** or **allowance for bad debts**.) When companies sell goods on credit, thus creating accounts receivable, it is likely that some customers will be unable to pay for their purchases. Companies are required by GAAP to estimate the amount of uncollectible receivables each fiscal period and to subtract that amount from their gross accounts receivable. The amount reported on the balance sheet for accounts receivable is the gross amount (total accounts receivable) minus the expected uncollectible amount (allowance). The net amount is the amount the company expects to collect from customers. We examine receivables in more detail in Chapter F13.

Other Long-Term Assets

In addition to property and equipment, long-term assets may include non-current receivables; fixed assets held for sale; prepaid expenses not expected to be consumed in the next fiscal year; long-term legal rights such as patents, trademarks, and copyrights; and long-term investments. These types of assets may be listed on the balance sheet under separate headings if they constitute a significant portion of a company's assets. Otherwise, they often are listed simply as Other Assets.

Accounts and notes receivable that a company does not expect to collect during the next fiscal year are not included among current assets. These items are reported as long-term assets. Fixed assets that a company is not using currently but is holding for future use, disposal, or sale also are included in this category. For example, land held for a future factory site would be listed here.

Long-term legal rights resulting from the ownership of patents, copyrights, trademarks, and similar items are known as *intangible assets,* in contrast to tangible assets such as property and equipment. Goodwill is a special type of intangible asset that can occur when one company acquires another company. *Goodwill* **is the excess of the price paid for a company over the fair market value of the net assets (assets less liabilities) of the acquired company.**

Long-term investments **occur when a company lends money to or purchases stock issued by other organizations and does not intend to sell those investments in the**

Exhibit 4 Balance Sheet for Krispy Kreme

Krispy Kreme Doughnuts, Inc.
Consolidated Balance Sheets

(In thousands)

	Jan. 28, 2001	Feb. 3, 2002
ASSETS		
Current Assets:		
Cash and cash equivalents	$ 7,026	$ 21,904
Short-term investments	18,103	15,292
Accounts receivable, less allowance for doubtful accounts of		
$1,302 (2001) and $1,182 (2002)	19,855	26,894
Inventories	12,031	16,159
Prepaid expenses and other current assets	6,787	16,913
Deferred income taxes	3,809	4,607
Total current assets	67,611	101,769
Property and equipment, net	78,340	112,577
Long-term investments	17,877	12,700
Investment in joint ventures	2,827	3,400
Intangible assets	—	16,621
Other assets	4,838	8,309
Total assets	$171,493	$255,376
LIABILITIES AND SHAREHOLDERS' EQUITY		
Current Liabilities:		
Accounts payable	$ 8,211	$ 12,095
Book overdraft	5,147	9,107
Accrued expenses	21,243	26,729
Revolving line of credit	3,526	3,871
Current maturities of long-term debt	—	731
Income taxes payable	41	—
Total current liabilities	38,168	52,533
Deferred income taxes	579	3,930
Long-term debt, net of current portion	—	3,912
Other long-term obligations	5,950	4,843
Total long-term liabilities	6,529	12,685
Minority interest	1,117	2,491
SHAREHOLDERS' EQUITY:		
Common stock, no par value, 100,000 shares authorized;		
issued and outstanding — 51,832 (2001) and 54,271 (2002)	85,060	121,052
Accumulated other comprehensive income and other items	(1,928)	(2,310)
Retained earnings	42,547	68,925
Total shareholders' equity	125,679	187,667
Total liabilities and shareholders' equity	$171,493	$255,376

coming fiscal year. Companies often invest in other companies to share in their earnings or to obtain access to resources, management skills, technology, and markets available to other companies. If management expects to hold these investments beyond the next fiscal year, they are classified as long-term investments. We examine accounting for each of these assets in later chapters.

Joint ventures reported on the balance sheet is the amount Krispy Kreme has invested in these ventures. **Joint ventures** involve cooperative efforts among two or more companies, with each company providing some of the financing for the venture, and each company sharing in the profits or losses from these ventures.

Other Current Liabilities

The current liabilities listed on Krispy Kreme's balance sheet are similar to those we have discussed for Mom's Cookie Company. The titles used for these liabilities are different, however. Accrued expenses is simply another name for liabilities such as wages payable and rent payable. One of the challenges of reading financial statements is becoming familiar with the wide variety of labels companies use.

The current liability, book overdraft, is a bit unusual. It suggests the company has overdrawn its checking accounts. In actuality it reflects the fact that Krispy Kreme has many bank accounts it uses to pay for business activities in various locations. It moves money from its primary bank accounts to these other accounts daily, as needed to meet operating expenses. At times, checks are written on these local accounts before cash is transferred to the accounts. These amounts are reported in the book overdraft category and indicate timing differences between when checks were written and cash was transferred. The category does not indicate a financial problem for the company. **A careful review of notes to the financial statements sometimes is important to understand the items reported by a company in those statements.**

Other Long-Term Liabilities

In addition to long-term debt, Krispy Kreme reports deferred taxes and minority interest. When **deferred taxes** are reported as a long-term liability, they represent income tax expenses that have not been paid and will not be paid during the coming year. Deferred taxes occur because of timing differences between when corporations recognize revenues and expenses for tax purposes and when those revenues and expenses are recognized for financial reporting purposes. If pretax income on a company's income statement exceeds its taxable income for tax purposes, a portion of the income tax expense a company recognizes will not be paid until some future fiscal period.

Minority interest, also known as **noncontrolling interest** (or **NCI**), represents the portion of a corporation's subsidiaries not owned by the parent corporation. Krispy Kreme reports $2,491,000 of minority interest on its 2002 balance sheet. This is the value of that portion of the subsidiaries not owned by Krispy Kreme. Note that the balance sheet amount refers to the book value of the subsidiary (assets less liabilities) owned rather than to the portion of income associated with noncontrolling owners that is reported on the income statement. Valuation of noncontrolling interest is a topic covered in advanced financial accounting texts.

Stockholders' Equity and Comprehensive Income

Like Mom's Cookie Company, Krispy Kreme reports common stock and retained earnings. The number of shares of common stock authorized is the maximum number of shares the company could issue under its current charter. The number of shares issued (54,271,000 for 2002) is the total number of shares that the company has sold to stockholders.

In addition to net income reported on the income statement, companies must report other comprehensive income. *Comprehensive income* **is the change in a company's owners' equity during a period that is the result of all non-owner transactions and activities.** Comprehensive income includes profits resulting from normal operating activities. It includes any event that changes owners' equity except those arising from dealings with the company's own stockholders. Accordingly, it excludes events such as selling stock or paying dividends. Comprehensive income also includes some activities that are not reported on the income statement.

Three items that are not included in net income are included as part of **other comprehensive income**. These are (a) gains or losses from holding certain marketable securities, (b) certain gains or losses from foreign currency effects on foreign subsidiaries, and (c) certain changes in the minimum liability for employee pensions. These items are reported as part of other comprehensive income that is included in stockholders' equity. Gains and losses from holding marketable securities are discussed in Chapter F11.

INTERNATIONAL

Foreign currency transactions occur when a corporation operates in other countries or owns subsidiaries outside of the U.S. These international activities involve currencies other than U.S. dollars. To prepare financial statements that are stated in U.S. dollars, those activities have to be translated from foreign currency amounts using exchange rates that are appropriate for the transaction. In some cases, U.S. currency must be exchanged for foreign currency or vice versa. Gains or losses can occur from changes in exchange rates. Gains or losses associated with foreign currency translations and exchanges are reported as part of other comprehensive income.

Changes in employee pension liabilities occur when estimates change about the amount a company can earn on assets it has invested to cover these liabilities or when other estimates change that affect the amount employees will receive in pension payments. These changes result in gains or losses that are reported as part of other comprehensive income.

Keep in mind that financial statements of actual companies can be complex because of the many types of business activities in which companies are involved. Understanding basic concepts of assets, liabilities, and owners' equity will help you interpret this information.

2 SELF-STUDY PROBLEM

Listed below are account balances, cash receipts and payments, and other data for Lewy Pasture, Inc., a company that distributes pharmaceutical supplies, for the fiscal year ended October 31, 2004.

webTUTOR Advantage

Accounts payable	$ 22,000
Accounts receivable	11,000
Accumulated depreciation	164,000
Buildings	412,000
Cash	16,000
Common stock	300,000
Cost of goods sold	146,000
Dividends (declared and paid)	17,000
Equipment	245,000
General and administrative expenses	96,000
Goodwill	13,000
Income tax expense	14,000
Income tax payable	6,000
Interest expense	25,000
Interest payable	14,000
Land	35,000
Long-term investments	35,000
Merchandise inventory	62,000
Notes payable, current portion	10,000
Notes payable, long-term	278,000
Prepaid insurance	7,000
Retained earnings, October 31, 2003	25,000
Sales revenue	357,000
Selling expenses	47,000
Supplies	13,000
Wages payable	18,000

The average number of shares of common stock outstanding during the year was 10,000.

Required From the data presented on the previous page, determine the amount of each of the following items for Lewy Pasture's financial statements:

1. Gross profit
2. Income from operations
3. Net income
4. Earnings per share
5. Current assets
6. Land, buildings, and equipment
7. Other assets
8. Total assets
9. Current liabilities
10. Total liabilities
11. Retained earnings, October 31, 2004
12. Total stockholders' equity
13. Total liabilities and stockholders' equity

The solution to Self-Study Problem 2 appears at the end of the chapter.

THE STATEMENT OF STOCKHOLDERS' EQUITY

OBJECTIVE 4

Explain information presented on a company's statement of stockholders' equity.

The statement of stockholders' equity provides information about changes in owners' equity for a corporation during a fiscal period. Exhibit 5 provides an example of this statement for Krispy Kreme. Though Krispy Kreme, like other corporations, presents three years of data for this statement in its annual report, only one year is included in Exhibit 5.

Exhibit 5 reports the number of shares of stock issued by Krispy Kreme at the beginning and end of the 2002 fiscal year, and describes changes in the amount associated with stock options, sale of stock, and other activities. The dollar amount of stock issued increased during 2002, as well. The amount of common stock issued at the end of the 2002 fiscal year ($121,052,000) is equal to the amount reported for common stock on the balance sheet in Exhibit 4.

A primary reason for the increase in common stock was related to **stock options**. Corporations often use stock option plans to provide an opportunity for employees to receive shares of stock for achieving corporate goals. To provide stock to employees and for other purposes, corporations repurchase shares from stockholders.

Retained earnings increased by the amount of net income earned in 2002. Retained earnings would decrease by the amount of dividends paid or promised (declared) during the fiscal year. However, Krispy Kreme did not pay any dividends during its 2002 fiscal year. Dividends are not reported on the income statement because they are not expenses. They are a distribution of net income to owners. **Dividends are a reduction in retained earnings and are reported on the statement of stockholders' equity.**

Accumulated other comprehensive income increases (or decreases) by the amount of other comprehensive income reported during a fiscal period. Krispy Kreme reported a holding loss of $111,000 and foreign currency translation losses of $42,000 during 2002. Remember that these losses are not reported on the income statement in the calculation of net income. The holding loss reported by Krispy Kreme is unrealized because the securities that created the holding loss have not been sold. Their market value decreased during the period, and the amount of the decrease is reported as a holding loss. When Krispy Kreme actually sells the securities, any gain or loss from the sale will be reported on the income statement. Krispy Kreme's other comprehensive income decreased during 2002 and the balance of its accumulated other comprehensive income is negative (a loss). The balance considers the effects of previous years' gains and losses. These gains and losses are added together from year to year to obtain the total reported on the statement of stockholders' equity. The ending balance also is reported on the balance sheet as part of stockholders' equity, see Exhibit 4.

Exhibit 5 Changes in Corporate Equity

Krispy Kreme Doughnuts, Inc.
Consolidated Statement Of Shareholders' Equity

(In thousands)

	Common Shares	Common Stock	Retained Earnings	Accumulated Other Comprehensive Income & Other	Total
Balance at January 28, 2001	51,832	$ 85,060	$42,547	$(1,928)	$125,679
Net income			26,378		26,378
Unrealized holding loss, net				(111)	(111)
Translation adjustment				(42)	(42)
Total comprehensive income					26,225
Proceeds from sale of stock	1,086	17,202			17,202
Exercise of stock options	1,183	13,678			13,678
Other	170	5,112		(229)	4,883
Balance at February 3, 2002	54,271	$121,052	$68,925	$(2,310)	$187,667

The ending balances on the statement of stockholders' equity are the amounts reported on the corporation's balance sheet for the same date. Compare the ending balances in each column of Exhibit 5 with the amounts in Exhibit 4. The statement of stockholders' equity describes the events that changed Krispy Kreme's stockholders' equity during its 2002 fiscal year.

USE OF FINANCIAL STATEMENTS

Financial statements are a primary source of accounting information for external decision makers. External users analyze statements to evaluate the ability of an organization to use its resources effectively and efficiently. By comparing changes in assets, liabilities, earnings, and cash flows over time, users form expectations about return and risk. Comparisons across companies help determine which companies are being managed effectively and provide the best investment opportunities.

Later chapters of this book describe methods of analyzing and interpreting financial statements. The remainder of this chapter considers attributes of financial statements that decision makers should understand when interpreting them.

Interrelationships among Financial Statements

Taken as a whole, financial statements describe business activities that changed the financial condition of a company from the beginning to the end of a fiscal period. Information on the income statement and statement of cash flows explains changes in balance sheet accounts during a period.

The summary information presented in financial statements does not always provide sufficient detail to explain the change in every balance sheet account. Access to individual account balances would be necessary to provide a complete explanation. Nevertheless, the relationships among the financial statements are important. Balance sheets for the beginning and ending of a fiscal period reveal changes in a company's resources and finances. The company's income statement and statement of cash flows reveal major events that caused these changes. **The relationship among financial statements in which the numbers on one statement explain numbers on other statements is called** *articulation.* You should remember that a company's financial statements are not independent of each other. They work together to explain the events that changed the company's financial condition.

Limitations of Financial Statements

OBJECTIVE 5

Identify some of the primary limitations of financial statements.

In spite of the abundant information financial statements provide, their usefulness is limited by certain constraints of the reporting process. Some of these limitations include:

1. Use of estimates and allocations
2. Use of historical costs
3. Omission of transactions
4. Omission of resources and costs
5. Delay in providing information

These constraints result primarily from costs associated with reporting financial information. Information is a resource, and it is costly to provide. Its value is determined by the benefits derived by those who use the information. For information to be valuable, its cost must be less than the benefits it provides to users. Therefore, the amount and type of reported information are constrained by costs and benefits.

The following paragraphs consider these limitations. Users should keep these limitations in mind when interpreting financial statement information.

Use of Estimates and Allocations. Many of the numbers reported in financial statements result from estimates and allocations. For example, depreciation is the allocation of asset costs to expenses over the estimated lives of the assets. These estimates often are not exact because the amount of the asset consumed in a particular fiscal period is difficult to determine. Decisions about when to recognize revenues and expenses frequently require management judgment. These subjective decisions and estimates mean that accounting numbers are not as precise as they might appear.

Use of Historical Costs. Financial statements report primarily the historical cost of assets and liabilities. *Historical cost* **is the purchase or exchange price of an asset or liability at the time it is acquired or incurred.** The recorded values are not adjusted for changes in the purchasing power of money or for changes in the current value of the assets or liabilities. The purchasing power of money changes over time because of inflation; for example, a dollar in 2003 buys less than a dollar bought in 1983. The current value of an asset is the amount at which that asset, in its current condition, could be bought or sold at the present time.

Certain assets and liabilities, particularly financial securities such as investments in stocks, are reported at market value in the United States. We will examine these reporting rules in a later chapter. Some countries, such as the United Kingdom and the Netherlands, permit plant assets and other items to be reported using current values. In these countries, assets and liabilities are restated to approximate their market values at the end of a fiscal period.

INTERNATIONAL

Omission of Transactions. Financial statements include the primary transactions that occur as part of a company's business activities. Nevertheless, **there is no guarantee that all important transactions are fully reported in a company's financial statements.** Some transactions do not result from specific exchanges. They result when revenues or expenses are allocated to fiscal periods. Accountants and managers sometimes disagree about when certain activities should be recognized. Also, they may disagree about the amount that should be reported in the financial statements for these activities. The accounting profession has debated extensively issues such as how to recognize the costs of employee retirement benefits. Today, companies report certain liabilities, assets, and expenses associated with these items that were not reported 10 years ago. Undoubtedly, other issues will arise that will alter information reported in the financial statements.

The importance of information changes over time. Companies develop new financing and compensation arrangements. Reporting rules for these arrangements may not be covered by existing GAAP. If the arrangements become common and new reporting rules would increase the benefits of information for users, GAAP may be created for transactions involving these new arrangements. GAAP are dynamic. They change as the needs of users and economic activities of organizations change.

Omission of Resources and Costs. Certain types of resources and costs are not reported in financial statements. The value of employees is not an asset listed on most balance sheets. Nevertheless, a well-trained and stable workforce and skilled managers may be the resource that adds the most to the value of many companies. Without skilled labor and management, the remaining resources of a company often would have little value. Financial statements do not report these human resources. They are not owned by a company, and their values are difficult and costly to determine. A major portion of the value of many companies derives from their research and development activities, which create new and improved products. The costs of these efforts are expensed when they are incurred each fiscal period even though they may have a major effect on the future earnings of a company. Such costs are expensed because of difficulty in identifying the timing and amount of future benefits a company will receive from these efforts. Nevertheless, the economic value of a company differs from the amount reported on its financial statements because of these measurement limitations.

Delay in Providing Information. Financial statement information is not always timely. Annual financial statements may lag actual events by a year or more; even monthly statements may lag events by several weeks. While such delays may not be a problem for certain types of decisions, they may be critical for others. Users often need more timely sources. Managers, in particular, may need information on an ongoing basis to make effective decisions. Traditional financial statements are only one type of accounting information. Because financial statements are costly to produce and distribute, external reporting is limited to distinct fiscal periods. In addition to annual financial reports, major corporations provide quarterly reports to stockholders. As information technology reduces the cost of reporting, more frequent reporting to external users may become feasible.

Though a variety of problems impair their usefulness, financial statements continue to be a primary source of information for managers and external users about a company's activities. But these problems mean that considerable care is needed to understand accounting information and to use it correctly in making decisions.

3 | **SELF-STUDY PROBLEM** A series of financial statement items is listed below.

Accounts payable	Notes payable
Accounts receivable	Patents
Buildings	Prepaid insurance
Common stock	Retained earnings
Cost of goods sold	Sales revenue
Depreciation expense	Stock issued
Dividends	Stock repurchased
Interest expense	Supplies
Interest payable	Wages expense
Merchandise	Wages payable

Required For each account, indicate the financial statement (income statement, balance sheet, or statement of stockholders' equity) on which the account would appear.

The solution to Self-Study Problem 3 appears at the end of the chapter.

REVIEW

SUMMARY of IMPORTANT CONCEPTS

1. Financial statements report business activities.
   a. Financial statements include the balance sheet, the income statement, the statement of cash flows, and the statement of stockholders' equity.
   b. The income statement reports on the accrual basis the results of a company's operations for a fiscal period. It reports information about the creation and consumption of resources in producing and selling goods and services.
   c. A balance sheet identifies asset, liability, and owners' equity account balances at the end of a fiscal period. Balance sheets classify accounts into current and long-term asset and liability categories. Comparative balance sheets report account balances for more than one fiscal period.
   d. The statement of stockholders' equity describes the results of transactions that have changed the amount of stockholders' equity of a corporation during a fiscal period.

2. The interrelated financial statements, as a set, describe the financial effects of business activities of a company from the beginning to the end of a fiscal period.

3. Consolidated financial statements report the economic activities of a parent and its subsidiaries as though they were one business entity.

4. Financial statements have limitations that affect the usefulness of the information the statements report. These limitations include the need for estimates of financial results, the use of historical costs for representing asset values, and incomplete measures for some resources or transactions that might affect a company's value.

DEFINE

TERMS and CONCEPTS DEFINED in this CHAPTER

amortization expense (F134)
articulation (F144)
common stock (F132)
comprehensive income (F140)
consolidated financial statements (F134)
cost of services sold (F131)
current assets (F136)
current liabilities (F137)
current ratio (F137)
depletion (F137)
dividends (F130)
earnings per share (F132)
fixed assets (F137)
goodwill (F138)
gross profit (F131)
historical cost (F144)

intangible assets (F138)
liquid assets (F136)
long-term intangible assets (F137)
long-term investments (F138)
long-term liabilities (F137)
operating expenses (F131)
operating income (F131)
parent (F134)
plant assets (F137)
property and equipment (F137)
statement of stockholders' equity (F130)
subsidiaries (F134)
total revenue (F134)
working capital (F137)
working capital ratio (F137)

SELF-STUDY PROBLEM SOLUTIONS

SSP-1 (Answers in millions except numbers of shares)

1. Revenue from sale of computers $33,392

2. Other operating revenue:

Services	$34,956
Software	12,939
Financing	3,426
Enterprise investments and other	1,153
Total	$52,474

3. Gross profit $31,782

4. Interest expense* $238

5. Number of shares outstanding ($7,723 net income ÷ $4.45 basic earnings per share) = 1,736 million shares

6. Total product costs $54,084

7. Net income $7,723

8. Net cash from operations cannot be determined from the income statement.

*Other (income) and expense of $(361) may or may not be from non-operating activities. The notes to the income statement would provide more information.

SSP-2

1. Gross profit:

Sales revenue	$357,000
Cost of goods sold	146,000
Gross profit	$211,000

2. Income from operations:

Gross profit	$211,000
General and administrative expenses	96,000
Selling expenses	47,000
Income from operations	$ 68,000

3. Net income:

Income from operations	$ 68,000
Interest expense	25,000
Income tax expense	14,000
Net income	$ 29,000

4. Earnings per share:
Net income ÷ shares of common stock ($29,000 ÷ 10,000) = $2.90

5. Current assets:

Cash	$ 16,000
Accounts receivable	11,000
Merchandise inventory	62,000
Supplies	13,000
Prepaid insurance	7,000
Current assets	$109,000

6. Land, buildings, and equipment:

Land	$ 35,000
Buildings	412,000
Equipment	245,000
Accumulated depreciation	(164,000)
Land, buildings, and equipment	$528,000

7. Other assets:

Long-term investments	$ 35,000
Goodwill	13,000
Other assets	$ 48,000

8. Total assets:

Current assets	$109,000
Land, buildings, and equipment	528,000
Other assets	48,000
Total assets	$685,000

9. Current liabilities:

Accounts payable	$ 22,000
Wages payable	18,000
Interest payable	14,000
Income tax payable	6,000
Notes payable, current portion	10,000
Current liabilities	$ 70,000

10. Total liabilities:

Current liabilities	$ 70,000
Notes payable, long-term	278,000
Total liabilities	$348,000

11. Retained earnings, October 31, 2004:

Retained earnings, October 31, 2003	$ 25,000
Net income	29,000
Dividends	(17,000)
Retained earnings, October 31, 2004	$ 37,000

12. Total stockholders' equity:

Common stock	$300,000
Retained earnings	37,000
Stockholders' equity	$337,000

13. Total liabilities and stockholders' equity:

Total liabilities	$348,000
Stockholders' equity	337,000
Total liabilities and stockholders' equity	$685,000

SSP-3

Item	Financial Statement
Accounts payable	Balance sheet
Accounts receivable	Balance sheet
Buildings	Balance sheet
Common stock	Balance sheet and statement of stockholders' equity
Cost of goods sold	Income statement
Depreciation expense	Income statement
Dividends	Statement of stockholders' equity
Interest expense	Income statement
Interest payable	Balance sheet
Merchandise	Balance sheet
Notes payable	Balance sheet
Patents	Balance sheet
Prepaid insurance	Balance sheet
Retained earnings	Balance sheet and statement of stockholders' equity
Sales revenue	Income statement
Stock issued	Statement of stockholders' equity
Stock repurchased	Statement of stockholders' equity
Supplies	Balance sheet
Wages expense	Income statement
Wages payable	Balance sheet

Thinking Beyond the Question

How do we report earnings and financial position to stockholders?

This chapter describes important rules for corporations and other businesses when they report financial information to external users. We considered the need for separating ordinary revenues and expenses from those, such as interest revenue or expense, that are secondary to a business's primary purpose. Corporations report corporate taxes and earnings per share as part of their income statements. Balance sheets should distinguish between current and long-term assets and liabilities and should report details about common stock issued by a corporation. Changes in stockholders' equity should be described in the statement of stockholders' equity.

Why is it important for businesses to follow specific rules and use common formats in reporting their business activities? What would be the consequences for businesses and the economy if individual companies were permitted to select their own reporting rules?

QUESTIONS

Q4-1
Obj. 1
Are dividends an expense? Sometimes? Always? Never? Explain.

Q4-2
Obj. 1
Identify three questions that can be answered by reviewing a firm's income statement but that cannot be answered by reviewing the firm's balance sheet or statement of stockholders' equity. Be specific.

Q4-3
Obj. 1
Identify three questions that can be answered by reviewing a firm's balance sheet but that cannot be answered by reviewing the firm's income statement or statement of stockholders' equity. Be specific.

Q4-4
Obj. 2
Why are there so many different sections of information on an income statement?

Q4-5
Obj. 2
Why does a parent company prepare consolidated financial statements?

Q4-6
Obj. 2
A friend says, "The income statement doesn't reveal anything about the amount of cash that was received from sales during a fiscal period." Do you agree with this statement? Why or why not?

Q4-7
Obj. 3
Explain the difference between a classified balance sheet and a comparative balance sheet.

Q4-8
Obj. 3
In what way are the depreciation of plant, property, and equipment and the amortization of intangible assets alike? In what way are they different?

Q4-9
Obj. 3
Assume you are reviewing a balance sheet that has assets listed on the left side and liabilities and owners' equity on the right side. What question or questions are answered by looking at the information on the left side of the balance sheet? What question or questions are answered by looking at the information on the right side of the balance sheet?

Q4-10
Obj. 4
If all of the stockholders' equity accounts are reported on the balance sheet, why is the statement of stockholders' equity necessary?

Q4-11
Obj. 4
The statement of stockholders' equity can be thought of as a bridge between the income statement and the balance sheet? Why?

Q4-12
Obj. 4
What does the term *articulation* mean as applied to accounting and financial reporting?

Q4-13 How do the purpose of the income statement, the purpose of the balance sheet, and the pur-
Objs. 3, 4   pose of the statement of stockholders' equity differ?

Q4-14 Why is the use of historical cost information a limitation of financial statements?
Obj. 5

Q4-15 It is often said that measuring performance for a fiscal period requires periodic measurement
Obj. 5   and the use of estimates and approximations. Do you agree that this is true? Why or why not?

EXERCISES

*If your instructor is using Personal Trainer in this course, you may complete online the assign-
ments identified by ᴘ̣т .*

E4-1 Write a short definition for each of the terms listed in the *Terms and Concepts Defined in this
Chapter* section.

E4-2 A list of information contained in financial statements is provided below. For each item, in-
Obj. 1   dicate which financial statement provides the information.
ᴘ̣т
    a. Changes in a corporation's stockholders' equity for a fiscal period
    b. The dollar amount of resources available at a particular date
    c. The amount of credit sales not yet collected
    d. Accrual-based operating results for a fiscal period
    e. The cost of resources consumed in producing revenues for a period
    f. The sources of finances used to acquire resources
    g. The effect of issuing stock on the amount of contributed capital during a period
    h. The amount of profit earned during a period
    i. Revenues generated during a fiscal period

E4-3 For each of the items listed below, indicate the financial statement (or statements) for which
Obj. 1   the information is true. Use *I* to indicate income statement, *B* to indicate balance sheet, and
ᴘ̣т   *SE* to indicate statement of stockholders' equity. If the item below is not true for any of the
three financial statements, indicate with an *N*.

    1. The statement provides information about resources consumed during an accounting
       period.
    2. The portion of profits that were distributed to owners of the firm is disclosed.
    3. The current market value of the firm's resources is reported.
    4. The statement is dated as of a specific point in time.
    5. The amounts that are owed to other organizations or individuals are reported.
    6. The total amount of capital that has been contributed to the organization is reported.
    7. The amount of capital that has been contributed to the organization during the ac-
       counting period just ended is reported.
    8. Information is reported regarding the rewards that have been earned from serving cus-
       tomers during the accounting period just ended.
    9. The statement is not as of a specific date, but covers a period of time.
   10. Reports information that has been developed on the accrual basis.
   11. The statement contains information about the financial sacrifices that were made to ac-
       quire resources.
   12. The statement contains information concerning contributed capital.
   13. The statement contains information concerning the results of operating activities.
   14. The amount of stock sold during the accounting period just ended is disclosed.
   15. The information provided links two other statements.

E4-4 Alex didn't study very hard when he took accounting because he thought he wouldn't ever
Obj. 2   use it on the job at Valentine Company. Yesterday, after preparing all end-of-the-month adjusting entries, both of the company's accounting staff became ill. The company owner, knowing that Alex had taken accounting as part of his college major, asked him to finish the job by
preparing the financial statements. The owner needs the statements tomorrow to present to
her banker. Alex isn't sure that his income statement is prepared properly.

Valentine Company
Income Statement
at September 30, 2004

Sales revenue	$48,500
Wages expense	11,369
Operating income	**37,131**
Operating expenses:	
Advertising	3,133
Cost of goods sold	30,070
Insurance	670
Interest expense	240
Utilities	1,250
Gross profit	**1,768**
Depreciation expense	282
Pretax income	**1,486**
Income tax expense	519
Net income	$ 967

Alex is confident that each revenue account and expense account balance is correct because those were determined by the accounting staff. He is unsure, however, that he has organized them properly on the income statement. Therefore, he is unsure about the summary amounts listed in bold-faced print on the statement.

Rearrange the accounts into proper income statement format. Be sure to date the statement correctly.

E4-5
Obj. 2
P/T

Slotnick Company sells, rents, and services ski equipment. Information about the company's financial performance for a recent fiscal period is provided below.

Average shares outstanding	20,000
Cost of goods sold	$34,000
Debt outstanding	65,000
General and administrative expenses	12,000
Income tax expense	20,000
Interest expense	8,000
Payments to owners	30,000
Rental revenue	45,000
Sales revenue	79,000
Selling expense	27,000
Service revenue	23,000

From the information provided, compute the following amounts for the period:

a. Gross profit
b. Operating expenses
c. Income from operations
d. Pretax income
e. Net income
f. Earnings per share

E4-6
Obj. 2

Flowers by Freddie presented the income statement below for its most recent fiscal year. The items have been numbered for convenience in analysis.

(1) Sales revenue	$371,923
(2) Cost of goods sold	201,668
(3) Gross profit	170,255
(4) Operating expenses	72,853
(5) Operating income	97,402
(6) Other revenues	538
(7) Other expenses	(13,227)
(8) Pretax income	84,713
(9) Income taxes	29,650
(10) Net income	$ 55,063

(Continued)

Answer the following questions. Be specific. Give examples to clarify.

   a. What is the difference between the revenue listed in item 1 and that listed in item 6?

   b. What does item 3 represent, and why is it important?

   c. What do items 2, 4, and 7 have in common?

   d. How are items 2, 4, and 7 different from one another?

   e. How is item 9 similar to items 2, 4, and 7?

   f. Why do you think items 2, 4, 7, and 9 are listed separately on an income statement rather than being lumped together as one item?

E4-7
Obj. 2
$\frac{P}{T}$

An income statement for **Delta Air Lines, Inc.**, for a recent fiscal year is provided below:

Delta Air Lines, Inc.
Consolidated Statements of Operations
For the Year Ended December 31, 2001

(In millions, except per share data)

OPERATING REVENUES:	
Passenger	$12,964
Cargo	506
Other, net	409
Total operating revenues	13,879
OPERATING EXPENSES:	
Salaries and related costs	6,124
Aircraft fuel	1,817
Depreciation and amortization	1,283
Passenger commissions	540
Contracted services	1,016
Landing fees and other rents	780
Aircraft rent	737
Aircraft maintenance materials and outside repairs	801
Passenger service	466
Other	1,917
Total operating expenses	15,481
OPERATING INCOME (LOSS)	(1,602)
OTHER INCOME (EXPENSE):	
Interest expense, net	(410)
Other income	148
LOSS BEFORE INCOME TAXES	(1,864)
INCOME TAX BENEFIT	648
NET LOSS	$ (1,216)
BASIC EARNINGS (LOSS) PER SHARE	$(9.99)
DILUTED EARNINGS (LOSS) PER SHARE	$(9.99)

Note: Modifications have been made to the statement to simplify the presentation.

Use this income statement to answer the following questions:

   a. What was Delta's primary source of revenue?

   b. What percentage of Delta's revenue came from this source?

   c. What were its largest expenses?

   d. How much revenue did Delta earn from transporting passengers?

   e. How much revenue did it earn from operating activities other than transporting passengers?

   f. How much revenue did it earn from nonoperating activities?

   g. How much operating income did Delta earn (or lose)?

   h. How much expense did it incur for nonoperating activities?

   i. Approximately how many shares of stock did Delta have outstanding during the year?

   j. How much profit or loss did Delta report during the fiscal year?

E4-8
Obj. 2

P
T

A recent income statement for **Applebees International** (a restaurant chain) is provided below. It operates both company-owned and franchised restaurants.

Applebees International, Inc.
Income Statement
For the Year Ended December 30, 2001

(Dollars in thousands except per share amounts.)

Revenues:	
Company restaurant sales	$651,119
Franchise income	93,225
Total operating revenues	744,344
Cost of company restaurant sales:	
Food and beverage	175,977
Labor	208,996
Direct and occupancy	164,965
Pre-opening expense	1,701
Total cost of company restaurant sales	551,639
Operating expenses:	
General and administrative expenses	72,935
Amortization of intangible assets	5,851
Loss on disposition of restaurants and equipment	1,492
Operating earnings	112,427
Other income (expense):	
Investment income	1,650
Interest expense	(7,456)
Other expense	(3,993)
Total other expense	(9,799)
Earnings before income taxes	102,628
Income taxes	38,227
Net earnings	$ 64,401
Basic net earnings per common share	$1.74
Diluted net earnings per common share	$1.70

Use this financial statement to answer the following questions:

a. How much revenue did Applebees earn from food and drinks?
b. How much revenue did it earn from other operating activities?
c. How much revenue did it earn from nonoperating activities?
d. What amount of gross profit did Applebees earn? Express your answer both in dollars and as a percentage of total revenues.
e. How much expense did it incur for nonoperating activities?
f. Approximately how many shares of stock did Applebees have outstanding during the year?
g. How much operating income and net income did Applebees earn during the fiscal year? Express your answers both in dollars and as a percentage of total revenues.
h. Can the amount of cash Applebees received from its operating activities during the year be determined from the income statement? If so, what is that amount? If not, why not?

E4-9   SuperQuick Computer Corporation reported the following income statement for a recent
Obj. 2   quarter.

P T

Consolidated Statement of Income **For the Quarter Ended December 31, 2004**	
Sales	$719,150
Cost of sales	549,313
	169,837
Research and development costs	16,900
Selling general and administrative expense	83,771
Other income and expense, net	7,685
	108,356
Income before income taxes	61,481
Provision for income taxes	15,451
Net income	$ 46,030
Earnings per share	$0.93

Assume that Other Income and Expense are nonoperating.

a. What was the company's gross profit for the quarter?
b. What was the amount of the company's product costs expensed during the quarter?
c. What was the amount of its operating expenses?
d. What was the amount of its operating income?
e. What was the amount of its nonoperating income or expense?

E4-10   BioTek's 2005 annual report included the following income statement information.
Obj. 2

P T

(In millions, except earnings per share)			
Year Ended June 30	**2003**	**2004**	**2005**
Revenue	$8,671	$11,358	$14,484
Operating expenses:			
Cost of goods sold	1,188	1,085	1,197
Research and development	1,432	1,925	2,502
Acquired in-process technology	0	0	296
Sales and marketing	2,657	2,856	3,412
General and administrative	316	362	433
Other expenses	19	259	230
Total operating expenses	5,612	6,487	8,070
Operating income	3,059	4,871	6,414
Interest income	320	443	703
Income before income taxes	3,379	5,314	7,117
Provision for income taxes	1,184	1,860	2,627
Net income	$2,195	$ 3,454	$ 4,490
Earnings per share	$0.86	$1.32	$1.67

Ratios often are used to assess changes in financial statement information over time. Use
Bio-Tek's income statements to answer the following questions. Express your answers as percentages.

a. What was the ratio of net income to net revenues each year?
b. What was the ratio of cost of revenues (cost of goods sold) to net revenues each year?
c. What was the ratio of operating expenses to net revenues each year?
d. What was the percentage change in net income between 2003 and 2004 and between
   2004 and 2005? (Hint: Divide the increase in net income from one year to the next by
   the net income for the earlier year.)
e. Did Bio-Tek's operating results improve between 2003 and 2005? Explain your answer.

E4-11
Obj. 3
Ṕ
T

Listed below are selected account balances for Hemmingway Company for June 30, 2004.

Accounts payable	$95,300	Land	$250,000
Accounts receivable	78,100	Merchandise inventory	390,000
Accumulated depreciation	318,000	Notes payable, current portion	50,000
Buildings	750,000	Notes payable, long-term	571,300
Cash	34,500	Prepaid insurance	38,000
Contributed capital	700,000	Retained earnings	279,000
Cost of goods sold	840,000	Supplies on hand	52,000
Equipment	450,000	Trademarks	45,000
Interest payable	38,000	Wages expense	375,000
		Wages payable	36,000

Determine each of the following amounts. (Hint: Not all items will be used.)

a. Current assets
b. Current liabilities
c. Property, plant, and equipment
d. Total assets
e. Long-term liabilities
f. Total liabilities
g. Stockholders' equity
h. Total liabilities and stockholders' equity
i. Working capital

E4-12
Obj. 3
Ṕ
T

Styles Unlimited reported the following information at January 31.

Accounts payable	$ 250
Accounts receivable	1,057
Accrued expenses (current)	348
Cash and equivalents	321
Contributed capital	319
Deferred income taxes (liabilities)	275
Income taxes payable (current)	93
Inventories	734
Long-term debt	650
Other current assets	109
Other current liabilities	16
Other long-term assets	248
Other long-term liabilities	61
Property and equipment, net of depreciation	1,667
Retained earnings, net of adjustments	2,124

Accrued expenses are current liabilities. Deferred income taxes are long-term liabilities.

Use the information provided to prepare a balance sheet for Styles Unlimited in good form.

E4-13
Obj. 3
Ṕ
T

The accounting staff at Marvelous Enterprises prepares monthly financial statements. At the end of April, the company's ledger accounts have the following balances. All adjusting entries have been made and the next step is to prepare the financial statements. The company has 18,200 shares of stock outstanding.

(Continued)

Accounts payable	$17,000	Land	$45,000
Accounts receivable	14,700	Long-term notes payable	33,000
Accumulated depreciation	13,100	Merchandise inventory	12,480
Buildings	50,000	Notes payable, current portion	14,200
Cash	10,360	Patents	3,300
Contributed capital	38,770	Prepaid insurance	1,100
Copyrights and trademarks	5,000	Retained earnings, March 31	8,400
Cost of goods sold	15,050	Sales revenue	26,000
Depreciation expense	1,100	Supplies	3,570
Dividends declared	1,200	Supplies expense	1,300
Income tax expense	1,060	Wage expense	1,500
Insurance expense	550	Wages payable	17,700
Interest expense	900		

Prepare a classified balance sheet in proper format. (Show land separately.) Use a three-line heading on the statement that includes (1) the name of the company, (2) the name of the statement, and (3) the appropriate date. Explain how you determined the April 30 balance in Retained Earnings.

E4-14

Obj. 3

P̸T̸

Jenny didn't study very hard when she took accounting because she thought she would never use it on the job at Tech-Noid Company. Yesterday, after preparing all end-of-the-month adjusting entries, the company's accountant became ill. The company asked Jenny to finish the job by preparing the financial statements. The owner needs the statements tomorrow to present to his banker. Jenny is having trouble getting the balance sheet to balance.

Tech-Noid Company
Balance Sheet
January 31, 2004

Assets		Liabilities and Stockholders' Equity	
Current assets:		**Current liabilities:**	
Inventory	$1,121	Accounts payable	$ 231
Interest payable	100	Accounts receivable	691
Land	2,200	Wages payable	636
Noncurrent assets:		**Long-term liabilities:**	
Buildings and equipment	4,990	7%, 10-year note payable	2,000
Retained earnings	1,398	Accumulated depreciation	531
		Stockholders' equity:	
		Contributed capital	4,230
		Cash	124
Total assets	$9,809	Total liabilities and equity	$8,443

(a) Help Jenny by making a list of the five account categories that are printed in bold-face type on the balance sheet. Leave three lines between each category listed. For each category, write the names of Tech-Noid's accounts that should be reported under it on the balance sheet.
(b) Determine the correct balance sheet amounts for:

1. total current assets
2. total noncurrent assets
3. total assets
4. total current liabilities
5. total long-term liabilities
6. total stockholders' equity
7. total liabilities and equity

E4-15

Objs. 2, 3

$\frac{P}{T}$

Listed below are account balances and other data for Hands & Eyes, Inc., a company that sells crafts and decorative supplies, for the fiscal year ended December 31, 2004.

Accounts payable	$ 41,000	Land	$ 65,000
Accounts receivable	29,000	Long-term investments	46,000
Accumulated depreciation	180,000	Merchandise inventory	79,000
Buildings	430,000	Notes payable, current portion	25,000
Cash	35,000	Notes payable, long-term	307,000
Contributed capital	315,000	Prepaid insurance	22,000
Cost of goods sold	130,000	Retained earnings,	
Dividends (declared and paid)	22,000	Dec. 31, 2003	19,000
Equipment	262,000	Sales revenue	373,000
General and administrative		Selling expenses	34,000
expenses	98,000	Supplies	25,000
Income tax expense	8,000	Trademarks	31,000
Income tax payable	22,000	Wages payable	36,000
Interest expense	33,000	Interest payable	31,000
Shares of common stock			
outstanding:	20,000		

From the data presented above, determine the amount of each of the items that follow. (Hint: Pretax income for the year 2004 = $78,000.)

1. Gross profit
2. Operatintg income
3. Net income
4. Earnings per share
5. Current assets
6. Property, plant, and equipment
7. Other assets
8. Total assets
9. Current liabilities
10. Working capital and working capital ratio
11. Total liabilities
12. Retained earnings, December 31, 2004
13. Total stockholders' equity
14. Total liabilities and stockholders' equity

E4-16

Objs. 2, 3, 4

$\frac{P}{T}$

Listed below are typical accounts or titles that appear on financial statements. For each item, identify the financial statement(s) on which it appears.

a. Loss on sale of equipment
b. Taxes payable
c. Trademark
d. Accumulated other comprehensive income
e. Current assets
f. Investments
g. Rental revenue
h. Gross profit
i. Earnings per share
j. Accumulated depreciation
k. Net income
l. Minority interest
m. Contributed capital
n. Operating income
o. Common stock issued during year

E4-17

Objs. 2, 3, 4

A list of financial statement items is given below.

1. Accounts receivable
2. Rent payable

(Continued)

3. Retained earnings
4. Cost of sales
5. Prepaid rent
6. Supplies expense
7. Equipment
8. Dividends
9. Depreciation expense
10. Copyrights
11. Accrued liabilities
12. Wages payable
13. Land
14. Notes payable
15. Service revenue
16. Inventory
17. Advertising expense
18. Common stock

Use the format shown below. (a) For each account, indicate the financial statement on which the account would appear. (b) Identify the information provided by the account. The first item is completed as an example:

Item	Financial Statement	Information Provided
1. Accounts receivable	Balance sheet	Cash to be received in the future from prior sales

E4-18
Obj. 4

Listed below are financial statements for the Sunflower Company.

Income Statement
For the Year Ended December 31, 2004

Sales revenue	$ 20,000
Cost of sales	(12,000)
Gross profit	8,000
Operating expenses	(4,000)
Selling and administrative expenses	(3,000)
Net income	$ 1,000

Statement of Stockholders' Equity
For the Year Ended December 31, 2004

	Contributed Capital	Retained Earnings	Total
Balance at December 31, 2003	$5,000	$13,000	$18,000
Common stock issued	2,000		2,000
Net income		1,000	1,000
Dividends		(4,000)	(4,000)
Balance at December 31, 2004	$7,000	$10,000	$17,000

Balance Sheet
as of December 31, 2004

Assets:		Liabilities and Stockholders' Equity	
Cash	$ 9,000	Accounts payable	$ 5,000
Accounts receivable	3,000	Notes payable	8,000
Inventory	2,000	Common stock	7,000
Land	16,000	Retained earnings	10,000
Total	$30,000	Total	$30,000

(a) Describe what is meant by the term *articulation*. (b) What evidence of articulation is there in this set of financial statements?

E4-19
Obj. 4
P̶T̶

Crane Pool Corporation reported the following selected information for its 2004 fiscal year.

Contributed capital at June 30, 2003	$ 657
Retained earnings at June 30, 2003	1,536
Dividends	222
Net income	953
Common stock issued	243

Use this information to prepare a statement of stockholders' equity for Crane Pool for the year ended June 30, 2004.

E4-20
Objs. 2, 4
P̶T̶

Use the information provided in Exercise 4-13.

a. Prepare an income statement following the format shown in Exhibit 1. (List expenses separately.)
b. Prepare a statement of stockholders' equity in good form.

(Hint: There was no change in contributed capital during the month.) For each statement, use a three-line heading on the statement that includes (1) the name of the company, (2) the name of the statement, and (3) the appropriate time period or date.

PROBLEMS

If your instructor is using Personal Trainer in this course, you may complete online the assignments identified by P̶T̶ .

P4-1 Identifying the Purpose of Financial Statements

Obj. 1

Assume you are a financial manager with a U.S. corporation. A. Suliman is a recently employed manager in the Middle Eastern division of your corporation and a visitor to the United States. He has little familiarity with financial reporting practices in the United States. Your boss has given you the responsibility of explaining financial reports to Mr. Suliman.

Required Write a short report describing each of the four basic corporate financial statements for Suliman. Make sure you are clear about the purpose of each statement, its contents, and its relationships to the other financial statements.

P4-2 Ethical Issues in Financial Reporting

Obj. 1

Flower Childs is a regional sales manager for Green-Grow, Inc., a producer of garden supplies. The company's fiscal year ends on April 30. In mid-April, Flower is contacted by the president of Green-Grow. He indicates that the company is facing a financial problem. Two years ago, the company borrowed heavily from several banks to buy a competing company and to increase production of its primary products: insecticides and fertilizers. As a part of the loan agreement, Green-Grow must maintain a working capital ratio of 1.5 to 1 and earn a net income of at least $2 per share. If the company fails to meet these requirements, as reflected in its annual financial statements, the banks can restrict future credit for the company or require early payment of its loans, potentially forcing the company into bankruptcy.

The president explains that this fiscal year has been a difficult one for Green-Grow. Sales have slipped because of increased competition, and the rising prices of chemicals have increased the company's production costs. The company is in danger of not meeting the loan requirements. The company could be forced to make drastic cuts or to liquidate its assets. The president informs Flower that her job could be in danger. The president asks her to help with the problem by dating all sales invoices that clear her office during the first half of May as though the sales had been made in April. May is a month of heavy sales volume for the company as retail stores stock up for the coming season. The president believes that the added sales would be sufficient to get the company past the loan problem. He explains that this procedure will be used only this one time. By next year, the company will be in better shape because of new products it is developing. Also, he reminds Flower that her bonus for the year will be higher because of the additional sales that will be recorded for April. He points out that the company is fundamentally in sound financial shape, and that he would hate to see its future jeopardized by a minor bookkeeping problem. He is asking for the cooperation of all of the regional sales managers. He argues that the stockholders, employees, and managers will all be better off if the sales are predated. He wants Flower's assurance that she will co-operate.

Required

A. What effect will predating the sales have on Green-Grow's balance sheet, income statement, and statement of cash flows? Be specific about which accounts will be affected and why.
B. How will this practice solve the company's problem with the banks?
C. What would be the appropriate behavior for the company president under the circumstances the company is facing?
D. What would be the appropriate behavior for Flower?

P4-3 **Identifying and Correcting Errors in an Income Statement**

Obj. 2
P/T

Just after preparing the adjusting entries for the year, the long-time controller at Parrot Company took a leave of absence. Her inexperienced assistant did his best to prepare financial statements from the information the controller had left behind. He had particular difficulty with the income statement.

The item labeled sales expense is the sum of the amounts charged customers during the year for goods and services provided.

Income Statement
December 31, 2004

Sales expense		$260,722
Cost of goods sold		102,690
Net profit		$158,032
Operating expenses:		
Wages	$59,780	
Utilities	9,002	
Interest	14,420	
Depreciation	13,510	
Total operating expense		97,712
Operating income		$ 60,320
Advertising expense		9,968
Pretax income		$ 50,352
Income tax expense		13,150
Net income		$ 63,502
Earnings per share of common stock		
($64,502 ÷ 15,000 shares)		$4.30

Required

A. Identify and list the errors in the income statement above.
B. Prepare a corrected income statement.

P4-4 **Interpreting an Income Statement**

Obj. 2
P/T

Microsoft Corporation's 2002 annual report included the following income statement information.

Microsoft Corporation
Income Statements

(In millions, except earnings per share)

Year Ended June 30	2000	2001	2002
Revenue	$22,956	$25,296	$28,365
Operating expenses:			
Cost of goods sold	3,002	3,455	5,191
Research and development	3,772	4,379	4,307
Sales and marketing	4,126	4,885	5,407
General and administrative	1,050	857	1,550
Total operating expenses	11,950	13,576	16,455
Operating income	11,006	11,720	11,910
Losses on equity investees and other	(57)	(159)	(92)
Investment income (loss)	3,326	(36)	(305)
Income before income taxes	14,275	11,525	11,513
Provision for income taxes	4,854	3,804	3,684
Income before accounting change	9,421	7,721	7,829
Cumulative effect of accounting change			
(net of income taxes of $185)		(375)	
Net income	$ 9,421	$ 7,346	$ 7,829
Basic earnings per share:			
Before accounting change	$ 1.81	$ 1.45	$ 1.45
Cumulative effect of accounting change		(0.07)	
	$ 1.81	$ 1.38	$ 1.45
Diluted earnings per share:			
Before accounting change	$ 1.70	$ 1.38	$ 1.41
Cumulative effect of accounting change		(0.06)	
	$ 1.70	$ 1.32	$ 1.41
Weighted average shares outstanding:			
Basic	5,189	5,341	5,406
Diluted	5,536	5,574	5,553

Required Ratios often are used to assess changes in financial statement information over time. Use Microsoft's income statements to answer the following questions. Express your answers as percentages.

A. What was the ratio of net income to net revenues each year?
B. What was the ratio of cost of revenues (cost of goods sold) to net revenues each year?
C. What was the ratio of operating expenses to net revenues each year?
D. What was the percentage change in net income between 2000 and 2001, and between 2001 and 2002? (Hint: Divide the increase in net income from 2000 and 2001 by the net income for 2000.)
E. Did Microsoft's operating results improve between 2000 and 2001? Between 2001 and 2002? Explain your answers.

P4-5

Objs. 2, 3, 4

P̸T

Comprehensive Income

The Lo Company imports and sells Chinese furniture in the United States. Its new accountant has been assigned the task of preparing the income statement. She knows that the FASB is now requiring that certain unrealized gains and losses be reported as part of comprehensive income. She has the following information available for the year just ended.

1. Loss on cumulative effect of change of depreciation method, net of tax	$	840
2. Gain from disposal of discontinued operations, net of tax		3,500
3. Cost of goods sold		180,000
4. Revenue received in advance		2,500
5. Work in process inventory		135,000
6. Interest expense		4,000

(Continued)

7. Provision for income tax	11,700
8. Sale of treasury stock at a price greater than cost	5,050
9. Sales revenue	250,000
10. Unrealized gain on increase of market value of investment	1,240
11. Sale of stock to investors	60,300
12. General and administrative expense	27,000
13. Gain on retirement of debt	4,200
14. Unrealized loss on foreign currency translation (regarding foreign subsidiary)	3,600
15. Cash received from customers	75,000
16. Dividends paid to shareholders	8,000

Required

A. From the information given above, decide which items should appear in the income statement, which would appear on a separate statement of comprehensive income, and which would not appear on either. If an item does not appear on either statement, indicate where it would be found. Also indicate which are transactions with owners.

B. Using the information above, prepare an income statement and a separate statement of comprehensive income.

P4-6

Obj. 3

P
T

Reading and Interpreting a Balance Sheet

A recent balance sheet for **Walt Disney Company** is provided below.

Walt Disney Company
Consolidated Balance Sheets

(In millions, except per share data)

September 30	2001	2000
ASSETS		
Current Assets		
Cash and cash equivalents	$ 618	$ 842
Receivables	3,343	3,599
Inventories	671	702
Television costs (current)	1,175	1,162
Other assets	1,222	1,258
Total current assets	7,029	7,563
Film and television costs	5,235	5,339
Investments	2,061	2,270
Parks, resorts and other property, at cost		
Attractions, buildings and equipment	20,635	19,202
Accumulated depreciation	(7,728)	(6,892)
	12,907	12,310
Intangible assets, net	14,540	16,117
Other assets	1,927	1,428
Total assets	$43,699	$45,027

(Continued)

September 30	2001	2000
LIABILITIES AND STOCKHOLDERS' EQUITY		
Current Liabilities		
Accounts payable and other accrued liabilities	$ 4,603	$ 5,161
Current portion of borrowings	829	2,502
Unearned royalties and other advances	787	739
Total current liabilities	6,219	8,402
Borrowings	8,940	6,959
Other noncurrent liabilities	5,486	5,210
Minority interests	382	356
Stockholders' Equity		
Common stock	12,096	12,101
Retained earnings	12,171	12,767
Adjustments	(1,595)	(768)
Total stockholders' equity	22,672	24,100
Total liabilities and stockholders' equity	$43,699	$45,027

Note: Slight modifications have been made to the format of the statement to simplify the presentation.

Required Respond to the following questions.

A. Do you agree that Disney's balance sheet is both classified and comparative? Explain why or why not.
B. At year-end 2001, what percentage of total assets was composed of current assets? Had this percentage increased or decreased since year-end 2000?
C. What was Disney's amount of working capital at year-end 2001? Did it change significantly from year-end 2000?
D. Compute the working capital ratio at year-end 2001 and year-end 2000. Did it improve or deteriorate between 2000 and 2001?
E. Film and television costs is the amount paid to produce movies or television shows. Explain why it appears in two places on the balance sheet.
F. What were the amounts of total assets, total liabilities, and stockholders' equity at year-end 2001 and year-end 2000?
G. Did Disney's overall financial position improve between 2000 and 2001? Explain.

P4-7 **Identifying and Correcting Errors in a Balance Sheet**

Obj. 3
P
T

Ceramics, Inc. reported the following balance sheet for the year 2004.

Balance Sheet
For the year ending December 31, 2004

Assets:	
Cash	$ 2,000
Accounts payable	500
Inventory	900
Equipment	1,000
Land	1,500
Total assets	$ 6,000
Liabilities:	
Accounts receivable	$ 3,000
Accrued liabilities	1,000
Total liabilities	4,000
Stockholders' equity:	
Common stock	1,800
Retained earnings	5,100
Total stockholders' equity	6,900
Total liabilities and stockholders' equity	$10,900

(Continued)

Required

A. Identify and list the errors in the balance sheet above.
B. Prepare a corrected balance sheet.

P4-8 Interpreting an Income Statement

Obj. 2
P
T

A recent Consolidated Statement of Income for the **Coca-Cola Company** and Subsidiaries is presented below.

Consolidated Statements of Income
The Coca-Cola Company and Subsidiaries

Year Ended December 31	2001	2000	1999
(In millions except per share data)			
NET OPERATING REVENUES	$20,092	$19,889	$19,284
Cost of goods sold	6,044	6,204	6,009
GROSS PROFIT	14,048	13,685	13,275
Selling, administrative and general expenses	8,696	8,551	8,480
Other operating charges	0	1,443	813
OPERATING INCOME	5,352	3,691	3,982
Interest income	325	345	260
Interest expense	(289)	(447)	(337)
Other income (loss)	282	(190)	(86)
INCOME BEFORE INCOME TAXES AND CUMULATIVE EFFECT OF ACCOUNTING CHANGE	5,670	3,399	3,819
Income taxes	1,691	1,222	1,388
INCOME BEFORE CUMULATIVE EFFECT OF ACCOUNTING CHANGE	3,979	2,177	2,431
Cumulative effect of accounting change, net of income taxes	(10)	0	0
NET INCOME	$ 3,969	$ 2,177	$ 2,431
BASIC NET INCOME PER SHARE			
Before accounting change	$1.60	$0.88	$0.98
Cumulative effect of accounting change	0.00	0.00	0.00
	$1.60	$0.88	$0.98
DILUTED NET INCOME PER SHARE			
Before accounting change	$1.60	$0.88	$0.98
Cumulative effect of accounting change	0.00	0.00	0.00
	$1.60	$0.88	$0.98
AVERAGE SHARES OUTSTANDING	2,487	2,477	2,469
Dilutive effect of stock options	0	10	18
AVERAGE SHARES OUTSTANDING ASSUMING DILUTION	2,487	2,487	2,487

Note: Slight modifications have been made to the statement to simplify the presentation.

Required

A. What is the amount of cost of goods sold for 1999, 2000, and 2001? What kinds of costs are included in cost of goods sold?
B. What does gross profit represent? Calculate gross profit as a percentage of net operating revenues for each year. What do you observe?
C. How does gross profit differ from operating income?
D. Is Coca-Cola more profitable in 2001 than in 1999? Explain.

P4-9 Understanding Working Capital and Long-Term Debt

Obj. 3
P
T

A recent Consolidated Balance Sheet for the Coca-Cola Company and Subsidiaries is presented on the following page.

Required

A. Is Coca-Cola a larger or smaller company in 2001 than in 2000? Explain.
B. What is the total amount of long-term debt? Explain why Coca-Cola classifies long-term debt into two categories.
C. What is working capital?
D. How much working capital does Coca-Cola report in 2001 and 2000? What conclusions can you make as a result of your calculations? (Note: This problem takes an interesting twist. Think about the implication of your calculations.)

Consolidated Balance Sheets
The Coca-Cola Company and Subsidiaries

December 31	2001	2000
ASSETS		
CURRENT		
Cash and cash equivalents	$ 1,866	$ 1,819
Marketable securities	68	73
	1,934	1,892
Trade accounts receivable, less allowances of		
$59 in 2001 and $62 in 2000	1,882	1,757
Inventories	1,055	1,066
Prepaid expenses and other assets	2,300	1,905
TOTAL CURRENT ASSETS	7,171	6,620
INVESTMENTS AND OTHER ASSETS		
Investments	5,422	5,765
Other assets	2,792	2,364
	8,214	8,129
PROPERTY, PLANT AND EQUIPMENT		
Land	217	225
Buildings and improvements	1,812	1,642
Machinery and equipment	4,881	4,547
Containers	195	200
	7,105	6,614
Less allowances for depreciation	2,652	2,446
	4,453	4,168
TRADEMARKS AND OTHER INTANGIBLE ASSETS	2,579	1,917
	$22,417	$20,834

(Continued)

December 31	2001	2000
LIABILITIES AND SHARE-OWNERS' EQUITY		
CURRENT		
Accounts payable and accrued expenses	$ 3,679	$ 3,905
Loans and notes payable	3,743	4,795
Current maturities of long-term debt	156	21
Accrued income taxes	851	600
TOTAL CURRENT LIABILITIES	8,429	9,321
LONG-TERM DEBT	1,219	835
OTHER LIABILITIES	961	1,004
DEFERRED INCOME TAXES	442	358
SHARE-OWNERS' EQUITY		
Common stock, $.25 par value; Authorized: 5,600,000,000 shares; Issued: 3,491,465,016 shares in 2001; 3,481,882,834 shares in 2000	873	870
Capital surplus	3,520	3,196
Reinvested earnings	23,443	21,265
Accumulated other comprehensive income and unearned compensation on restricted stock	(2,788)	(2,722)
	25,048	22,609
Less treasury stock, at cost (1,005,237,693 shares in 2001; 997,121,427 shares in 2000)	13,682	13,293
	11,366	9,316
	$22,417	$20,834

Note: Slight modifications have been made to the statement for purposes of simplifying the presentation.

P4-10 Using the Balance Sheet to Determine Asset Composition

Obj. 3

P
T

Recent Balance Sheets for **Microsoft Corporation** are presented below.

Microsoft Corporation
Balance Sheets
(In millions)

June 30	2001	2002
Assets		
Current assets:		
Cash and equivalents	$ 3,922	$ 3,016
Short-term investments	27,678	35,636
Total cash and short-term investments	31,600	38,652
Accounts receivable, net	3,671	5,129
Inventories	83	673
Deferred income taxes	1,522	2,112
Other	2,334	2,010
Total current assets	39,210	48,576
Property and equipment, net	2,309	2,268
Equity and other investments	14,361	14,191
Goodwill	1,511	1,426
Intangible assets, net	401	243
Other long-term assets	1,038	942
Total assets	$58,830	$67,646

(Continued)

June 30	2001	2002
Liabilities and stockholders' equity		
Current liabilities:		
Accounts payable	$ 1,188	$ 1,208
Accrued compensation	742	1,145
Income taxes	1,468	2,022
Short-term unearned revenue	4,395	5,920
Other	1,461	2,449
Total current liabilities	9,254	12,744
Long-term unearned revenue	1,219	1,823
Deferred income taxes	409	398
Other long-term liabilities	659	501
Commitments and contingencies		
Stockholders' equity:		
Common stock and paid-in capital-shares authorized 12,000; shares issued and outstanding 5,383 and 5,359	28,390	31,647
Retained earnings, including accumulated other comprehensive income of $587 and $583	18,899	20,533
Total stockholders' equity	47,289	52,180
Total liabilities and stockholders' equity	$58,830	$67,646

Required

A. Microsoft reports property and equipment, net on the balance sheet. Calculate property and equipment as a percentage of total assets for 2001 and 2002.

B. Microsoft reports cash and short-term investments as a current asset. Calculate cash and short-term investments as a percentage of total assets.

C. Comment on your analysis from Requirements A and B.

D. Calculate the working capital ratio for 2001 and 2002. Discuss your results.

P4-11 **Preparing Financial Statements**

Objs. 2, 3

P/T

Argyle Company has the following account balances at December 31, 2004. During the year, Argyle had 10,000 shares of stock outstanding.

Argyle Company
Account Balances
at December 31, 2004

Account	Balance
Cash	$ 4,650
Accounts receivable	16,350
Inventory	30,500
Supplies	7,700
Prepaid insurance	3,550
Equipment	42,500
Accumulated depreciation—equipment	17,500
Buildings	170,000
Accumulated depreciation—buildings	105,000
Land	10,000
Patents	3,000
Accounts payable	18,250
Wages payable	3,450
Interest payable	1,700
Income taxes payable	4,050
Notes payable, current portion	2,500

(Continued)

Account	Balance
Notes payable, long-term	37,500
Owners' investment	25,000
Retained earnings, December 31, 2003	60,150
Dividends	15,000
Sales revenue	130,000
Cost of goods sold	62,500
Wages expense	16,000
Utilities expense	2,000
Depreciation expense	1,050
Insurance expense	1,500
Supplies expense	2,300
Interest expense	3,650
Advertising expense	1,450
Patent expense	400
Income tax expense	11,000

Required

A. Prepare an income statement in good form based on Argyle Company's account balances.

B. Prepare a classified balance sheet as of December 31, 2004. Include appropriate headings and subheadings.

P4-12 Preparing Financial Statements

Objs. 2, 3
P
T

The following account balances are provided for Rustic Company at December 31, 2004. Revenues and expense accounts cover the fiscal year ending on that date. All numbers are dollars except shares outstanding.

Account	Amount
Accounts payable	$ 14,000
Accounts receivable	18,000
Accumulated depreciation	30,000
Cash	6,000
Common stock, par value	20,000
Cost of goods sold	35,000
Current portion of long-term debt	2,000
Income taxes	6,000
Interest expense	4,000
Interest payable	500
Inventory	34,000
Long-term debt	40,000
Net income	12,000
Paid-in capital in excess of par	30,000
Patents and trademarks	4,000
Prepaid insurance	2,500
Property, plant and equipment, cost	150,000
Retained earnings	78,000
Sales revenues	110,000
Selling, general, and administrative expenses	65,000
Service revenues	12,000
Supplies	3,000
Wages payable	3,000
Shares outstanding	20,000

Required

A. Prepare an income statement in good form for Rustic Company.

B. Prepare a classified balance sheet.

P4-13 **Information in the Statement of Stockholders' Equity**

Obj. 4
P
T

A recent annual report for **Wal-Mart Stores, Inc.** and its subsidiaries is provided below.

Required From the information provided, answer the following questions:

A. What is the total amount of contributed capital as of January 31, 1999?
B. Did total contributed capital increase or decrease between January 31, 1999 and January 31, 2001? By what amount?
C. How much profit has been distributed to owners in cash during the three years covered by this statement?
D. Has stockholders' equity increased or decreased over the three years and what is the main reason?
E. Compute the ratio of cash dividends to net income for each year. Did the portion of profits paid out in dividends each year increase, decrease, or stay about the same?
F. Compute the percentage change in net income between 2000 and 2001, and between 2001 and 2002. (Hint: Divide the increase in net income from 2000 to 2001 by the net income for 2000.) Do you believe this is an encouraging sign or a discouraging sign?
G. Compute the percentage change in dividends between 2000 and 2001, and between 2001 and 2002. Is the rate of dividend increase greater or smaller than the rate of profit increase?

Wal-Mart Stores, Inc.
Consolidated Statements of Shareholders' Equity

(Amounts in millions)	Number of shares	Common stock	Capital in excess of par value	Retained earnings	Other accumulated comprehensive income	Total
Balance January 31, 1999	4,448	$445	$ 435	$20,741	($509)	$21,112
Comprehensive Income						
Net income				5,377		5,377
Other accumulated comprehensive income					54	54
Total Comprehensive Income						**5,431**
Cash dividends ($.20 per share)				(890)		(890)
Purchase of Company stock	(2)		(2)	(99)		(101)
Stock options exercised and other	11	1	281			282
Balance January 31, 2000	4,457	446	714	25,129	(455)	25,834
Comprehensive Income						
Net income				6,295		6,295
Other accumulated comprehensive income					(229)	(229)
Total Comprehensive Income						**6,066**
Cash dividends ($.24 per share)				(1,070)		(1,070)
Purchase of Company stock	(4)		(8)	(185)		(193)
Issuance of Company stock	11	1	580			581
Stock options exercised and other	6		125			125
Balance January 31, 2001	4,470	447	1,411	30,169	(684)	31,343
Comprehensive Income						
Net income				6,671		6,671
Other accumulated comprehensive income					(584)	(584)
Total Comprehensive Income						**6,087**
Cash dividends ($.28 per share)				(1,249)		(1,249)
Purchase of Company stock	(24)	(2)	(62)	(1,150)		(1,214)
Stock options exercised and other	7		135			135
Balance January 31, 2002	4,453	$445	$1,484	$34,441	($1,268)	$35,102

Note: Slight modifications have been made to the statement for purposes of simplifying the presentation.

P4-14   Understanding Stockholders' Equity

Obj. 4

Recent stockholders' equity statements for Microsoft are presented below.

Required

A. What was the amount of common stock and paid-in capital at June 30, 2000, 2001, and 2002?
B. Does Microsoft pay dividends on common stock?
C. How can you explain the increase in Common stock and paid-in capital over the three-year period?
D. Without consulting Microsoft's Statement of Income, can we determine net income reported in 2000, 2001, and 2002? Why or why not?
E. Microsoft's Stockholders' Equity Statements report Common stock repurchased. Why do you think a company would repurchase its own shares? If the shares are later reissued at a higher price, do you think Microsoft should report a gain on shares reissued?

Microsoft Corporation
Stockholders' Equity Statements

(In millions)

Year Ended June 30	2000	2001	2002
Convertible preferred stock			
Balance, beginning of year	$ 980	$ 0	$ 0
Conversion of preferred to common stock	(980)		
Balance, end of year	0	0	0
Common stock and paid-in capital			
Balance, beginning of year	13,844	23,195	28,390
Common stock issued	3,554	5,154	1,801
Common stock repurchased	(210)	(394)	(676)
Other, net	6,007	435	2,132
Balance, end of year	23,195	28,390	31,647
Retained earnings			
Balance, beginning of year	13,614	18,173	18,899
Net income	9,421	7,346	7,829
Other comprehensive income:			
Cumulative effect of accounting change		(75)	
Other, net	(283)	(826)	(86)
Translation adjustments and other	23	(39)	82
Comprehensive income	9,161	6,406	7,825
Preferred stock dividends	(13)		
Common stock repurchased	(4,589)	(5,680)	(6,191)
Balance, end of year	18,173	18,899	20,533
Total stockholders' equity	$41,368	$47,289	$52,180

Note: Slight modifications have been made to the statement to simplify the presentation.

P4-15   Using Interrelationships among Financial Statements

Objs. 2, 3, 4

$\frac{P}{T}$

Corey Issacson is an investor in Stone Cold Enterprises. Last week he received the company's most recent financial statements but some of the numbers were smudged and unreadable. Each of the unreadable numbers is represented with a letter on the following page.

Stone Cold Enterprises
Comparative Balance Sheet
December 31, 2004 and 2005

(In thousands)	December 31, 2005	December 31, 2004
Assets		
Cash	$ 2,940	$ 1,020
Accounts receivable	1,850	1,225
Merchandise	2,855	1,000
Prepaid insurance	(a)	3,000
Property, plant and equipment	25,000	(b)
Accumulated depreciation	(c)	(6,250)
Other assets	8,400	3,000
Total assets	$35,545	$ (d)
Liabilities and equity:		
Accounts payable	$ 1,580	$ 950
Wages payable	125	700
Rent payable	500	500
Long-term notes payable (8%)	12,000	12,000
Common stock	(e)	(f)
Retained earnings	(g)	10,845
Total liabilities and equity	$ (h)	$ (i)

Stone Cold Enterprises
Statement of Stockholders' Equity
Year Ended December 31, 2005

	Common Stock	Retained Earnings	Total
Balance, December 31, 2004	$3,000	$ (j)	$ (k)
Issued common stock	(l)		(m)
Net income		14,495	14,495
Dividends paid		(9,000)	(9,000)
Balance, December 31, 2005	$5,000	$ (n)	$21,340

Stone Cold Enterprises
Income Statement
Year Ended December 31, 2005

Sales revenue		$103,000
Cost of goods sold		66,000
Gross profit		37,000
Operating expenses:		
Wages	$5,490	
Interest	(o)	
Rent	(p)	
Insurance	1,000	
Depreciation	1,250	
Total operating expenses		(q)
Pretax income		(r)
Income taxes (35%)		(s)
Net income		$ (t)

(Continued)

Additional information:

1. No items of plant, property and equipment were purchased or sold during the year.
2. The prepaid insurance account represents the remaining portion of a four-year policy purchased on January 1, 2004.
3. The rent payable account at year end (both years) represents December's rent that had not yet been paid.

Required Use your knowledge regarding the interrelationships among financial statements to determine each of the missing amounts.

P4-16   **Preparing Financial Statements**

Objs. 2, 3, 4
P
T

ABC, Inc. has the following account balances at December 31, 2004.

Accounts payable	$17,080	Income tax expense	$ 1,300
Accounts receivable	9,400	Land	50,000
Accumulated depreciation	26,100	Notes payable	30,000
Buildings	60,000	Retained earnings,	
Cash	20,880	December 31, 2003	17,000
Contributed capital	31,000	Sales revenue	26,000
Cost of goods sold	15,600	Supplies	7,500
Depreciation expense	2,200	Wages expense	3,000
Dividends paid	1,200	Wages payable	23,900

During the year 2004, the company issued $6,000 of new common stock.

Required From this information, prepare (A) an income statement, (B) a statement of stockholders' equity, and (C) a classified balance sheet. (D) Show how the three financial statements articulate. (Note: In parts (A), (B), and (C), include appropriate headings and subheadings in the financial statements that you prepare.)

P4-17   **Understanding the Information in Financial Statements**

Objs. 2, 3, 4

Today is April 1 and Dale has just received the annual report of Clam Chowder Company, in which he owns stock. Displayed below are the comparative balance sheet and income statement that have drawn his attention.

Balance Sheet	Dec. 31, 2005	Dec. 31, 2004	Income Statement	For Year 2005
Cash	$ 1,244	$ 1,512	Sales revenue	$485,000
Accounts receivable	6,914	5,886	Cost of goods sold	300,700
Inventory	11,211	9,099	Gross profit	184,300
Buildings and equipment	49,900	46,500	Operating expenses:	
Accumulated depreciation	(5,319)	(2,497)	Advertising	31,330
Land	22,000	22,000	Depreciation	2,822
			Utilities	19,200
Total assets	$85,950	$82,500	Wages	113,698
			Operating income	17,250
Accounts payable	$ 2,313	$ 1,988		
Interest payable	-0-	2,563	Interest expense	2,400
Wages payable	7,364	6,327	Pretax income	14,850
7%, 10-year note payable	20,000	20,000	Income tax expense	5,200
Contributed capital	42,300	42,300		
Retained capital	13,973	9,322	Net income	$ 9,650
Total liabilities and equity	$85,950	$82,500	Earnings per share	$ 3.86

After reviewing this information, Dale makes the following comments.

1. I'm surprised that the value of the company's land has not increased. Prices have been increasing rapidly in the area the company is located.

2. I'm sure that I received a dividend from this company, but they don't report that they paid any.
3. I don't see how the company's cash balance could have declined when it took in $485,000 in cash from sales to customers.
4. I see that the value of the buildings and equipment declined by $2,822. That seems about right.
5. I don't understand why the company's highly trained workforce is not listed as an asset. It is one of the most important resources that the company has.
6. One thing I really like about this company is the up-to-the-minute financial reports it provides.
7. It's good to see that the value of the inventory has increased since last year.

Required

A. Help Dale better understand these financial statements by responding to each of his comments. Explain whether you agree or disagree with each comment and why.
B. Did the company declare and pay cash dividends during the year just ended? If so, what total amount was distributed?
C. Approximately how many shares of stock does the company have outstanding?

P4-18

Objs. 2, 3, 4

The Transformation Process as Reported in Financial Statements

Far East Specialties is an import company, financed primarily by stockholders and bank loans. It imports handmade goods from Central and East Asia to the United States, where they are sold to retail stores. The company's buyers contract with small companies for goods, which the buyers ship to a central location in the United States. The goods are inventoried and then redistributed as orders are received from retailers. The company receives a bill from the manufacturers along with the goods it receives. Payment is made each month. Bills are sent to retailers along with orders. Most retailers pay their bills each month, as well. It can be several months from the time goods are shipped to the United States until cash is received from retailers.

Required

A. Explain how the various aspects of Far East Specialties' transformation process are reported in its financial statements. That is, consider the events just described and identify where information about each event is reported in the financial statements. In particular, consider the relationship the company has with its investors, suppliers, and customers.
B. Why is it important that time, and the timing of events, be considered in reporting accounting information?

P4-19

Obj. 5

Limitations on Financial Statements

Markus O'Realius is considering the purchase of Caesar Company. The potential seller has provided Markus with a copy of the business's financial statements for the last three years. The financial statements reveal total assets of $350,000 and total liabilities of $150,000. The seller is asking $300,000 for the business. Markus believes that the business is worth only about $200,000, the amount of owners' equity reported on the balance sheet. He has asked your assistance in determining a price to offer for the business.

Required Write a memo to Markus explaining why he should not interpret the balance sheet as an accurate measure of the value of the business. Describe limitations of financial statements that might mean that the market value of the business was higher (or lower) than the financial statement amounts.

P4-20

Obj. 5

Limitations of Financial Statements

Limits, Ltd. had the following financial statements for the fiscal year ending December 31, 2004 (the statement of stockholders' equity and the statement of cash flows are not shown).

(Continued)

Limits, Ltd.
Income Statement
For the Year Ending December 31, 2004

Sales revenue		$20,000
Operating expenses:		
Cost of sales	$1,000	
Wages expense	800	
Advertising expense	100	
Depreciation expense	300	
Research and development expense	300	
Total operating expense		2,500
Operating income		17,500
Other expenses:		
Interest expense		500
Income before taxes		17,000
Income tax		5,100
Net income		$11,900

Limits, Ltd.
Balance Sheet
as of December 31, 2004

Assets		Liabilities and stockholders' equity	
Current assets:		Current liabilities:	
Cash	$ 2,300	Accounts payable	$ 3,000
Accounts receivable	8,000	Wages payable	7,600
Inventory	15,000	Interest payable	900
Total current assets	25,300	Total current liabilities	11,500
Property, plant and equipment:		Notes payable, long-term	9,000
Equipment	21,000	Total liabilities	20,500
Accumulated depreciation	(8,000)	Stockholders' equity:	
Buildings	90,000	Owners' investment	9,700
Accumulated depreciation	(85,000)	Retained earnings	13,100
PP&E	18,000	Total stockholders' equity	22,800
		Total liabilities and	
Total assets	$43,300	stockholders' equity	$43,300

Required The text lists several limitations of financial statements. Using the financial statements given here, identify as many examples of limitations or items that relate to limitations of financial statements as you can.

P4-21 Excel in Action

Listed below are account balances and other data for The Book Wermz at the close of November 30, 2004. Revenue and expense account balances are for the month of November. All amounts are dollars except shares of common stock. The Book Wermz operates as a corporation.

SPREADSHEET

Accounts payable	$ 6,131.77
Accounts receivable	375.00
Accumulated depreciation	13,891.82
Cash	12,307.99
Contributed capital	100,000.00
Cost of goods sold	30,937.32
Depreciation expense	817.20
Dividends paid	1,500.00

Equipment	57,650.00
Income tax expense	897.45
Interest expense	932.03
Inventory	235,255.06
Notes payable, current portion	1,122.77
Notes payable, long-term	120,084.57
Rent expense	1,738.15
Sales	43,312.25
Service revenues	1,566.23
Shares of common stock	1,000
Supplies	2,130.12
Supplies expense	2,411.53
Wages expense	4,697.35
Wages payable	1,150.68

Required Use the account balances to produce an income statement, a statement of stockholders' equity, and a balance sheet for The Book Wermz in a spreadsheet. The financial statements should follow the examples illustrated in Chapter F4. The balance sheet should contain columns for November and October. October 31 balances should be obtained from data provided in the Chapter F3 spreadsheet problem.

Enter account titles in column A. Use columns B, C, and D as necessary for amounts. Use the Borders button ⊞ ▾ to produce single and double lines by selecting the cell to be formatted, using the button down arrow to select the proper line type, and clicking on the button. Use the Indent button ⊯ to indent titles and captions as needed by selecting the cell and clicking on the button. Use the Comma ＇ and Currency ＄ buttons to format amounts by selecting the cell and clicking on the appropriate buttons. The Comma button also formats numbers so that negative amounts appear in parentheses. The first and last amounts in a column of numbers should include dollar signs as illustrated in the chapter. Set column widths by placing the cursor at the right edge of a column header so the Change Width cursor ↔ appears. Then click and drag the column to the right or left as needed. Use functions to sum subtotals and totals, =SUM(B5:B8) for example, so the spreadsheet will automatically recalculate any changes in account numbers. To merge adjacent cells for titles, select the cells to be merged and click on the Merge Cells button. Put titles in bold type by selecting the cell containing the title and clicking on the Bold Type button **B**.

Suppose sales for November had been $45,000 and the cash balance at November 30 had been $13,995.74. How much net income would the company report for November? How much total assets and stockholders' equity would it report at November 30?

P4-22 **Multiple-Choice Overview of the Chapter**

1. Which of the following is *not* a statement you would expect to find in a corporate annual report?
   a. Statement of financial position
   b. Statement of earnings
   c. Statement of stockholders' equity
   d. Statement of accounts receivable

2. The following information was reported on the income statement of Wagon Wheel Company.

Sales revenues	$450,000
Cost of goods sold	200,000
Selling, general, and administrative expenses	150,000
Interest expense	30,000

Wagon Wheel's gross profit and operating income would be

	Gross profit	Operating income
a.	$300,000	$70,000
b.	$250,000	$70,000
c.	$250,000	$100,000
d.	$100,000	$70,000

(Continued)

3. Which of the following is a *false* statement regarding the statement of stockholders' equity?
   a. It lists changes in contributed capital and retained earnings for a fiscal period.
   b. It contains information about net income and dividends for a fiscal period.
   c. It reports the net change in stockholders' equity for a fiscal period.
   d. It reports increases or decreases in stocks and bonds for a fiscal period.

4. The following assets appear on the balance sheet for Astroid Company:

Accounts receivable	$ 50,000
Accumulated depreciation	160,000
Cash	20,000
Intangible assets	60,000
Inventory	100,000
Plant assets	400,000

   The amount of current assets reported by Astroid is
   a. $170,000.
   b. $150,000.
   c. $230,000.
   d. $470,000.

5. A balance sheet that provides information for more than one fiscal period is:
   a. a classified balance sheet.
   b. a comparative balance sheet.
   c. a consolidated balance sheet.
   d. a combined balance sheet.

6. Working capital is the amount of
   a. cash and cash equivalents available to a company at the end of a fiscal period.
   b. long-term investments available at the end of a fiscal period less long-term debt at the end of the period.
   c. current assets available at the end of a fiscal period less current liabilities at the end of the period.
   d. total assets available at the end of a period that can be converted to cash.

7. Orange Bowl Company reported plant assets for the latest fiscal year of $5 million, net of accumulated depreciation. From this information, which of the following is an accurate statement about the company?
   a. The book value of the company's plant assets at the end of the fiscal year was $5 million.
   b. The company would have to pay $5 million to replace its assets if they were replaced at the end of the fiscal year.
   c. The amount the company would receive if it sold its plant assets at the end of the fiscal year would be $5 million.
   d. The amount the company paid for the plant assets it controlled at the end of the fiscal year was $5 million.

8. A consolidated financial statement is one in which
   a. more than one year's financial data is included.
   b. the personal financial activities of the owner are combined with those of the company.
   c. the income statement and the balance sheet are combined into a single statement.
   d. the financial information of multiple corporations is reported as if they were a single firm.

9. Which of the following is *false*?
   a. Financial statement information is not always presented in a timely manner.
   b. The purpose of a balance sheet is to report the market value of assets and liabilities.
   c. Certain types of resources and costs are not reported in financial statements.
   d. Many of the numbers reported in financial statements result from estimates and allocations.

10. Where on an income statement would you expect to fin
pense?
   a. just after cost of goods sold
   b. grouped with other operating expenses
   c. as part of cost of goods sold
   d. following income taxes

CASES

C4-1 Evaluating the Transformation Process

Objs. 1, 5

Italiano Pizza Company has just completed its first month in business. The owners, Charla and Maria, had previously worked for a major pizza chain but were convinced that they could offer a better product in a better atmosphere. They knew the importance of accurate financial records and hired a bookkeeper. Yesterday, the bookkeeper hand-delivered financial statements to the owners and announced her resignation. You have been retained by Charla and Maria to interpret the following financial information and explain its significance.

Italiano Pizza Company
Financial Statements
After One Month in Business

Balance sheet accounts				Income statement accounts	
Assets:		Liabilities + Owners' Equity:		Revenues	$ 4,000
Cash	$ 2,240	Wages payable	$ 180	Expenses:	
Food products	980	Advertising payable	400	Store rent	800
Supplies	1,000	Loan from bank	6,800	Food products	1,475
Prepaid rent	2,400	Owners' investment	4,340	Wages	990
Equipment	5,150			Advertising	1,430
Accumulated				Interest	40
depreciation	(50)			Supplies	375
Total	$11,720	Total	$11,720	Depreciation	50
				Net income	$(1,160)

Required

A. Discuss whether the information provided could be helpful to the owners and, if so, describe how. If not, describe why not.

B. Identify at least 10 events that occurred as part of the transformation process during the firm's first month in business. For each event, identify the amount of cash involved.

C. Did Charla and Maria make a good judgment when they decided to get into this business? Would you recommend that they continue with the pizza business or discontinue it? What additional information would be helpful to you in making such a recommendation?

C4-2 The Financial Statements of General Mills, Inc.

Objs. 2, 3, 4

The **General Mills** 2002 Annual Report is reproduced in Appendix B at the end of the text.

Required

A. Answer the following questions about the General Mills Consolidated Statements of Earnings:

   1. General Mills recorded sales of almost $8 billion. Is this the amount of cash collected? Explain.

   2. Sales increased each year from 2000 to 2002. Compute the percentage increase for each year.

(Continued)

3. What is the largest expense for General Mills? Compute this expense as a percentage of sales for each of the three years. Is there a trend?
4. Compare the net income figures for three years. What do you observe?
5. Explain why a company's stock price generally is influenced by the amount of net income.
6. General Mills paid dividends in 2002, 2001, and in 2000, yet the corresponding total dividend payments do not appear as expenses on the income statement. Why not?

B. Answer the following questions about the General Mills Consolidated Balance Sheets:
1. Why does a company have assets?
2. What is the total amount of assets at the end of 2002?
3. For 2002, compare the assets at the beginning of the year to the assets at the end of the year.
   a. Compute the percentage increase in assets during the year.
   b. Which type of assets account for most of the increase?
4. What two groups have contributed assets to General Mills and have claims on the company's assets?

C. Answer the following questions about the General Mills Consolidated Statement of Stockholders' Equity:
1. General Mill's total stockholders' equity has increased significantly from May 27, 2001 to May 26, 2002. What is the major cause of the increase in stockholders' equity?
2. The consolidated statement of stockholders' equity identifies comprehensive income. Briefly explain the concept of comprehensive income. What kinds of activities are included in comprehensive income?

REPORTING CASH FLOWS

How is cash flow information determined and reported to external users?

Chapter F4 examined the reporting of operating results and financial position to stockholders and other external users. Corporations and other companies also report information about their cash flows for a fiscal period to external users. The statement of cash flows identifies the cash created by and used for operating, investing, and financing activities. Stan and Maria realize it is important for their company to provide information about how much cash is generated from business activities and how this cash was used. In addition to helping them, as managing owners of the firm, this information helps external stockholders and other decision makers determine whether a company is likely to grow and to meet its financial obligations.

FOOD FOR THOUGHT

As a stockholder of Mom's Cookie Company, what information about cash flows do you need to make decisions about your investment? How do companies determine how much cash they received and paid during a fiscal period? Knowing they need to provide key cash flow information to stockholders and others, Maria and Stan have arranged to meet with their accountant, Ellen, to discuss these issues.

Stan: We prepared an income statement, balance sheet, and statement of stockholders' equity for our stockholders. I understand we also need to report cash flow information.

Ellen: Yes, the statement of cash flows is an important part of your total financial report. This statement requires you to look carefully at your business activities to identify activities that created cash and those that used it.

Maria: We know how much cash the company had at the end of the year. Many of our transactions during the year involved cash. Do we have to look at all of these transactions to prepare the statement of cash flows?

Ellen: No. You can summarize your cash flows without looking at individual transactions. Most of the information for the statement can be obtained from the income statement and balance sheets you have already prepared.

Stan: Those statements don't include much cash information. How can they tell us anything about cash flows?

Ellen: The income statement contains information about the results of operating activities measured using the accrual basis. Timing differences between when revenues and expenses were recognized and when cash was received and paid are reported on the balance sheets for this fiscal year end and the prior one. Preparing the statement of cash flows is largely a matter of adjusting income statement numbers for these timing differences and looking at other activities that increased or decreased balance sheet amounts during the year.

Maria: That sounds complicated.

Ellen: It requires a good understanding of accrual accounting and working systematically with the income statement and balance sheet numbers. Once you learn how the statement is prepared, you'll have a good understanding of how accrual and cash flow information is related. Also, you will see how valuable cash flow information can be for understanding your company.

OBJECTIVES

Once you have completed this chapter, you should be able to:

1 Explain information reported on a statement of cash flows using the direct format.

2 Explain information reported on a statement of cash flows using the indirect format.

3 Interpret cash flow information as a basis for analyzing financial performance.

THE STATEMENT OF CASH FLOWS

The purpose of the statement of cash flows is to identify the primary activities of a fiscal period that resulted in cash inflows and outflows for a company. The statement describes the cash flow results of financing, investing, and operating activities for a company for a fiscal period, and it explains the change in a company's cash balance during the period. GAAP permit the statement of cash flows to be presented in either of two formats: direct or indirect. The two formats differ only with respect to the presentation of operating activities.

THE DIRECT FORMAT

OBJECTIVE 1

Explain information reported on a statement of cash flows using the direct format.

Some companies, especially smaller companies, use the direct format to present the statement of cash flows. Most large corporations use the indirect format. Exhibit 1 provides an example of the cash flow statement for Mom's Cookie Company using the direct format.

The direct format of the statement of cash flows presents each major source and use of cash. The statement of cash flows is divided into three sections corresponding to the three primary types of business activities: operating, investing, and financing.

The source of data for the direct format of the statement of cash flows is the transactions that affect the cash account. The operating cash flow section of the statement includes those transactions that affected cash and were associated with operating activities: sales to customers, purchases of merchandise, wages, and other operating activities. GAAP require that interest payments be included in the operating activities section of the statement of cash flows because interest expense is reported on the income statement. Thus, **operating cash flows are the cash equivalent of the accrual results reported on the income statement**. That is, they represent a cash-basis income statement for the fiscal period.

The investing activities section includes cash transactions associated with the purchase or sale of long-term assets. The financing activities section includes cash transactions associated with debt (short- or long-term) and owners' equity, including payments to owners.

The direct format of the statement of cash flows lists the direct effects of transactions that affect the cash account during a period. It answers the question, "Where did cash come from and where did cash go?" Therefore, it is an explanation of business activities that resulted in an increase or decrease in cash. In total, these activities explain the change in a company's cash account balance for a fiscal period. Because 2004 was Mom's Cookie Company's first year of operations, the beginning cash balance was $0.

The company's ending cash balance was equal to the net increase in cash for 2004, $10,680. The net increase (or decrease) in cash for a fiscal period is the sum of net cash flow from operating, investing, and financing activities.

Exhibit 1

Statement of Cash Flows, Direct Format

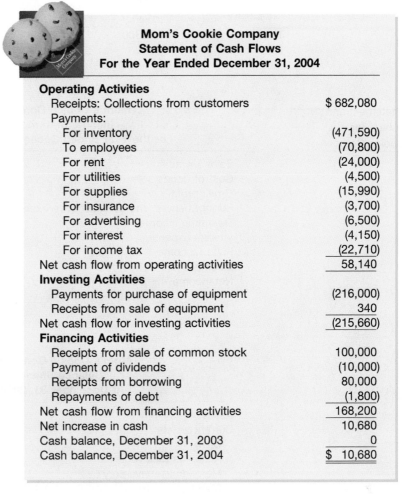

Mom's Cookie Company
Statement of Cash Flows
For the Year Ended December 31, 2004

Operating Activities	
Receipts: Collections from customers	$ 682,080
Payments:	
For inventory	(471,590)
To employees	(70,800)
For rent	(24,000)
For utilities	(4,500)
For supplies	(15,990)
For insurance	(3,700)
For advertising	(6,500)
For interest	(4,150)
For income tax	(22,710)
Net cash flow from operating activities	58,140
Investing Activities	
Payments for purchase of equipment	(216,000)
Receipts from sale of equipment	340
Net cash flow for investing activities	(215,660)
Financing Activities	
Receipts from sale of common stock	100,000
Payment of dividends	(10,000)
Receipts from borrowing	80,000
Repayments of debt	(1,800)
Net cash flow from financing activities	168,200
Net increase in cash	10,680
Cash balance, December 31, 2003	0
Cash balance, December 31, 2004	$ 10,680

Operating Activities

Operating activities are transactions involving the acquisition or production of goods and services and the sale and distribution of these goods and services to customers. Cash flow from operating activities identifies cash received from the sale of goods and services. Also, it identifies cash paid for resources used to provide goods and services. An important relationship exists between the income statement and the operating activities section of the statement of cash flows—both are based on the same set of activities. On the income statement, operating activities are measured on an accrual basis. On the cash flow statement, these activities are measured on a cash basis. These amounts can be compared to determine timing differences between accrual basis recognition of revenues and expenses and cash flows for the period.

To understand how the cash flow numbers in Exhibit 1 were computed, we need to refer to the income statement and balance sheet from Chapter F3. These are reproduced in Exhibit 2.

Selling, general and administrative expenses are as follows:

Wages	$ 70,800
Utilities	4,500
Insurance	3,700
Advertising	6,500
Depreciation	25,500
Rent	22,000
Supplies	15,300
Total	$148,300

Exhibit 2

Income Statement and
Balance Sheet for
Mom's Cookie Company

Mom's Cookie Company
Income Statement
For the Year Ended December 31, 2004

Sales revenue	$ 686,400
Cost of goods sold	(457,600)
Gross profit	228,800
Selling, general and administrative expenses	(148,300)
Operating income	80,500
Interest expense	(4,800)
Pretax income	75,700
Income taxes	(22,710)
Net income	$ 52,990

Mom's Cookie Company
Balance Sheet
At December 31, 2004

Assets	
Current assets:	
Cash	$ 10,680
Accounts receivable	8,570
Merchandise inventory	23,600
Supplies	690
Prepaid rent	2,000
Total current assets	45,540
Property and equipment, at cost	215,660
Accumulated depreciation	(25,500)
Total assets	$235,700
Liabilities and Stockholders' Equity	
Current liabilities:	
Accounts payable	$ 9,610
Unearned revenue	4,250
Interest payable	650
Notes payable, current portion	5,000
Total current liabilities	19,510
Notes payable, long-term	73,200
Total liabilities	92,710
Stockholders' equity:	
Common stock, 10,000 shares issued	100,000
Retained earnings	42,990
Total stockholders' equity	142,990
Total liabilities and stockholders' equity	$235,700

INUOME
STATEMENT
+INC

-Exp

Of these items, wages, utilities, insurance, and advertising were paid in cash. Observe that there are no noncash assets or liabilities (prepaid insurance or wages payable, for example) on the balance sheet associated with these items. **Depreciation expense does not require the payment of cash.** Rent and supplies expenses were not completely paid in cash because prepaid rent and supplies are reported on the balance sheet. Income tax also was paid in cash. Again, observe that there are no noncash assets or liabilities associated with income taxes, such as income taxes payable. There are noncash assets and liabilities associated with sales revenue, cost of goods sold, and interest expense. These assets and liabilities result from timing differences between when revenues and expenses are recognized and when cash is received or paid. Therefore, they must be adjusted to determine cash flows. Exhibit 3 explains the calculation of operating cash flows from the data in Exhibit 2.

Exhibit 3 Calculation of Operating Cash Flows for Direct Method

Accounts	Accrual	Adjustment	Cash Flow	Explanation
a. Sales Revenue	$ 686,400			Accrual
Less: Accounts Receivable		$ (8,570)		Sales for which cash not received
Add: Unearned Revenue		4,250		Cash received but not yet earned
Cash Collected from Customers			$ 682,080	Cash flow
b. Cost of Goods Sold	(457,600)			Accrual
Add: Merchandise Inventory		(23,600)		Cash paid but goods not sold
Less: Accounts Payable		9,610		Goods purchased but cash not paid
Cash Paid for Merchandise			(471,590)	Cash flow
c. Wages	(70,800)			Cash paid equals accrual amount
Utilities	(4,500)			Cash paid equals accrual amount
Insurance	(3,700)			Cash paid equals accrual amount
Advertising	(6,500)			Cash paid equals accrual amount
Income Taxes	(22,710)			Cash paid equals accrual amount
Cash Paid for Other Operating Items			(108,210)	Cash paid equals accrual amount
d. Rent Expense	(22,000)			Accrual
Prepaid Rent		(2,000)		Cash paid but not expensed
Cash Paid for Rent			(24,000)	Cash flow
e. Supplies Expense	(15,300)			Accrual
Supplies		(690)		Cash paid but not expensed
Cash Paid for Supplies			(15,990)	Cash flow
f. Interest Expense	(4,800)			Accrual
Interest Payable		650		Cash not paid in 2004
Cash Paid for Interest			(4,150)	Cash flow
g. Depreciation Expense	(25,500)		0	Accrual
		25,500		Cash not paid
			0	Cash flow
Net Income	$ 52,990			
Net Cash Flow from Operating			$ 58,140	

To determine cash collected from customers (a), revenue is adjusted for cash not received (because it is still owed) and for cash received that has not been earned. To determine cash paid for merchandise (b), cost of goods sold is adjusted for cash paid for merchandise that has not been sold and for amounts owed suppliers. It is important in these computations that expenses and cash outflows are shown as negative amounts.

Other operating cash flows are either accrued expenses that were paid in cash, as those in (c), or expenses that require adjustment, as with rent, supplies, and interest.

To determine cash paid for rent (d), rent expense is adjusted for cash paid for rent of future periods. To determine cash paid for supplies (e), supplies expense is adjusted for supplies that have been purchased but that have not been used. To determine cash paid for interest (f), interest expense is adjusted for interest that has not been paid.

Depreciation and amortization expenses (g) are tied to operating activities but are not cash flow items. When the direct format is used, these expenses are not listed in the statement of cash flows.

Investing Activities

Investing activities involve acquisition or sale of long-term assets and financial investments during a fiscal period. As noted above, depreciation and amortization expenses are not part of investing activities. Cash flow for investing activities occurs when fixed assets are purchased or sold, not when these assets are depreciated.

Calculation of investing cash flow in Exhibit 1 is straightforward. Mom's Cookie Company purchased $216,000 of equipment for cash in 2004. It sold equipment for $340 in cash. Investing cash flow is simply the amount paid for long-term assets minus the amount received from selling these assets.

Some transactions affect investing and financing activities without affecting cash directly. For example, suppose a company borrows $300,000 from a bank to purchase a building. The transaction increases Buildings and Notes Payable but does not have a direct effect on Cash. GAAP require that such transactions be reported. Most of these events are reported as though they were cash transactions: cash received from borrowing and then paid for property and equipment.

Financing Activities

Financing activities are transactions between a company and its owners or creditors. The financing activities section reports only the cash flow effects of transactions associated with borrowing or repaying debt and investments by owners. Cash flows result when debt is issued or repaid and when stock is issued or repurchased. Payment of dividends or other cash distributions to owners also are financing activities.

The calculation of financing cash flow for Mom's Cookie Company is straightforward. The company received $100,000 from issuing common stock and paid $10,000 of dividends to stockholders. It received $80,000 of cash from borrowing and paid back $1,800 of the amount borrowed. (It is important to remember the repayment of debt is the repayment of the amount actually borrowed, not the payment of interest on the borrowed money. As noted above, the payment of interest is an operating activity.)

GAAP require a schedule to reconcile cash flows from operating activities with net income when the direct format is used. This schedule is similar to the presentation of the statement of cash flows using the indirect format described in the next section of this chapter.

1   **SELF-STUDY PROBLEM**   Listed below are cash activities for Jerome, Inc. for a recent fiscal period. Jerome's cash balance at the beginning of the period was $16,350.

WebTUTOR Advantage

Paid for dividends	$ 2,500
Paid to employees	4,000

Listed below are cash activities for Jerome, Inc. for a recent fiscal period. Jerome's cash balance at the beginning of the period was $16,350.

Paid for dividends	$ 2,500
Paid to employees	4,000
Paid for utilities	2,200
Paid for equipment	13,500
Received from sale of stock	100,000
Paid for supplies	1,800
Paid for inventory	8,400
Received from customers	14,750
Paid for debt repayment	35,000

Received from sale of land	20,000
Paid for building	75,000

OBJECTIVE 2

Explain information reported on a statement of cash flows using the indirect format.

Required Use these activities to prepare a statement of cash flows for Jerome, Inc., using the direct format. What were Jerome's primary sources and uses of cash for the period?

The solution to Self-Study Problem 1 appears at the end of the chapter.

THE INDIRECT FORMAT

The direct format of the statement of cash flows identifies the sources of cash received and the purposes for which cash is paid during a period. Thus, operating activities identify cash received from customers and paid to suppliers, employees, and so on. In practice, however, this format is rarely used by major corporations.

Instead, nearly all major corporations use the indirect format for reporting the statement of cash flows. **The differences between the direct and indirect formats are in the operating activities section only.** The indirect format reconciles net income on an accrual basis with cash flow from operating activities on a cash basis. It answers the question, "Why was cash flow from operations different from net income?" Consequently, operating cash flows are presented as the indirect result of changes in current assets, current liabilities, and other accounts.

Exhibit 4 provides the statement of cash flows for Mom's Cookie Company using the indirect method. In this method, the operating activities section begins with net income. This is the amount reported on the company's income statement (see Exhibit 2). The indirect format begins with the results of operating activities reported on an accrual basis (net income) and adjusts this amount to arrive at the amount that explains the results of operating activities on a cash basis (net cash flow from operating activities). Adjustments are made for activities that had a different effect on net income than they had on cash flow. Observe that **the net cash flows in each section (operating, investing, and financing) are the same as those reported using the direct method** in Exhibit 1. In fact, the investing and financing sections are identical in the two methods.

The operating activities section looks quite different, however. To understand this method, refer to Exhibit 3. The adjustments column of the exhibit identifies the differences between the accrual amounts from the income statement and the cash flow amounts. Starting with net income, we can simply list these adjustments to compute cash flow from operating activities. The indirect method does just that. It starts with the accrual amount (net income) and lists the adjustments necessary to determine cash flow from operating activities.

Though the determination of the adjustments may seem somewhat complicated,

Exhibit 4

Indirect Format of
Statement of Cash
Flows

Mom's Cookie Company
Statement of Cash Flows
For the Year Ended December 31, 2004

Operating Activities	
Net income	$ 52,990
Depreciation expense	25,500
Increase in accounts receivable	(8,570)
Increase in merchandise inventory	(23,600)
Increase in supplies	(690)
Increase in prepaid rent	(2,000)
Increase in accounts payable	9,610
Increase in unearned revenue	4,250
Increase in interest payable	650
Net cash flow from operating activities	58,140
Investing Activities	
Payments for purchase of equipment	(216,000)
Receipts from sale of equipment	340
Net cash flow for investing activities	(215,660)
Financing Activities	
Receipts from sale of common stock	100,000
Payment of dividends	(1,800)
Receipts from borrowing	80,000
Repayment of debt	(10,000)
Net cash flow from financing activities	168,200
Net increase in cash	10,680
Cash balance, December 31, 2003	0
Cash balance, December 31, 2004	$ 10,680

they are actually fairly simple. They consist of subtracting any revenues that did not result in cash inflow or adding any expenses that did not require cash outflow. Most adjustments are associated with current assets and current liabilities, with the exclusion of financial resources such as cash and investments.

When current assets increase during a fiscal period, one of two things has occurred:

- Revenue was earned but cash was not received—increase in accounts receivable, or
- Cash was paid for resources that have not been expensed—increase in inventory or prepaid expenses.

In either case, cash flow is less than net income. Therefore, **increases in current assets are subtracted from net income to calculate operating cash flow.**

When current assets decrease, the opposite has occurred, either:

- Cash has been received from customers that was not earned this period—decrease in accounts receivable, or
- Resources have been used that were not paid for this period—decrease in inventory or prepaid expenses.

In either case, cash flow is greater than net income. Therefore, **decreases in current assets are added to net income to calculate operating cash flow.**

When current liabilities increase, either:

- Cash has been received from customers but has not been earned—increase in unearned revenue, or
- Resources have been used but payment has not been made—increase in accounts

In either case, cash flow is less than net income. Therefore, **decreases in current liabilities are subtracted from net income to calculate operating cash flow.**

Exhibit 5 summarizes these rules. The rules apply to changes in current asset and current liability accounts during a fiscal period. Because 2004 was the first year of operations for Mom's Cookie Company, the beginning balances of all current asset and current liability accounts was zero. Consequently, the changes in these accounts were equal to the ending balances. When working with a company that has beginning and ending balances, it is necessary to compute the change in current asset and current liability balances and use these in the calculations in Exhibit 2. Also keep in mind that some current asset and current liability accounts, such as short-term investments and short-term debt (including the current portion of notes payable), are not associated with operating activities. These accounts are associated with financial resources and involve investing activities (for assets) or financing activities (for liabilities). Finally, some revenue and expense items, depreciation and amortization expenses in particular, do not require cash payments. Therefore, they are always added to net income to calculate operating cash flow.

Exhibit 5

Rules for Adjusting Net Income to Calculate Operating Cash Flow

Event	Rule
Increase in Current Assets	Subtract from Net Income
Decrease in Current Assets	Add to Net Income
Increase in Current Liabilities	Add to Net Income
Decrease in Current Liabilities	Subtract from Net Income

Exhibit 6 provides the statement of cash flows for Krispy Kreme Doughnuts, Inc., from the company's 2002 annual report. Though the statement contains more items than that for Mom's Cookie Company, the interpretation is similar. For each operating cash flow adjustment, a note identifies why the amount was added (or subtracted). All of these items identify either revenues for which cash was not received, cash received that was not earned, expenses for which cash was not paid, or cash paid for which expenses were not incurred. In short, all are timing differences between when revenue or expense was recognized and when cash was received or paid.

We can determine from Exhibit 6 that, usually, all of Krispy Kreme's current assets and current liabilities increased. Observe that receivables, inventories, and prepaid expenses were all subtracted, and accounts payable and other current liabilities were added.

It is not uncommon for a company to report a noncash revenue (or gain) or a noncash expense (or loss). Gains are always subtracted because they increase net income but do not provide cash inflow, and losses are always added because they decrease net income but do not require cash outflow. Gains and losses from sales of long-term assets (plant assets or investments) are subtracted (for gains) or added (for losses) because these gains and losses do not provide or use cash as part of operating activities. Cash received or paid from these transactions is correctly reported in the investing activities section.

The investing activities section of Krispy Kreme's cash flow statement is similar to that for Mom's Cookie Company. Purchases of property and equipment and other long-term assets decrease cash flow. Sale of these items increases cash flow. The financing activities section also is similar. Borrowing and issuing stock increase cash flow, and repayment of debt and payments to owners decrease cash flow.

The net increase in cash of $14,878,000 in 2002 explains the change in Krispy Kreme's cash account reported on its balance sheet. (See Exhibit 4 in Chapter F4.)

Exhibit 6 Indirect Format of Statement of Cash Flows

Krispy Kreme Doughnuts, Inc.
Consolidated Statements of Cash Flows

In thousands

Year ended	Jan. 30, 2000	Jan. 28, 2001	Feb. 3, 2002
CASH FLOW FROM OPERATING ACTIVITIES:			
Net income	$ 5,956	$ 14,725	$ 26,378
Items not requiring (providing) cash:			
Depreciation and amortization	4,546	6,457	7,959
Deferred income taxes	258	1,668	2,553
Loss on disposal of property and equipment, net	—	20	235
Other	1,012	2,357	11,573
Change in assets and liabilities:			
Receivables	(4,760)	(3,434)	(13,317)
Inventories	(93)	(2,052)	(3,977)
Prepaid expenses	(1,619)	1,239	(682)
Income taxes, net	(2,016)	902	(2,575)
Accounts payable	540	2,279	3,884
Accrued expenses	4,329	7,966	4,096
Deferred compensation	345	(15)	83
Net cash provided by operating activities	8,498	32,112	36,210
CASH FLOW FROM INVESTING ACTIVITIES:			
Purchase of property and equipment	(11,335)	(25,655)	(37,310)
Proceeds from disposal of property and equipment	—	1,419	3,196
Acquisitions	—	—	(20,571)
Investments in joint ventures	—	(4,465)	(1,218)
(Increase) decrease in other assets	1,309	(3,216)	(4,237)
(Purchase) sale of investments, net	—	(35,371)	7,877
Net cash used for investing activities:	(10,026)	(67,288)	(52,263)
CASH FLOW FROM FINANCING ACTIVITIES:			
Repayment of long-term debt	(2,400)	(3,600)	—
Net short-term (repayments) borrowings	—	(15,775)	345
Borrowings of long-term debt	4,282	—	4,643
Proceeds from stock offering	—	65,637	17,202
Proceeds from exercise of stock options	—	104	3,906
Cash dividends paid	(1,518)	(7,005)	—
Other	934	(144)	5,483
Net cash provided by financing activities:	398	39,019	30,931
Net increase (decrease) in cash and cash equivalents	(1,130)	3,843	14,878
Cash and cash equivalents at beginning of year	4,313	3,183	7,026
Cash and cash equivalents at end of year	$ 3,183	$ 7,026	$ 21,904

Note: Modifications have been made to the original format to simplify the presentation.

2 SELF-STUDY PROBLEM   The following information appears on the income statement and balance sheet of Bryson Co. for a recent fiscal period.

WebTUTOR Advantage

Net income	$16,540
Depreciation and amortization expense	3,560
Increase in accounts receivable	2,500
Decrease in merchandise	3,200
Increase in supplies	430
Increase in accounts payable	660
Decrease in wages payable	375
Increase in interest payable	280
Decrease in income tax payable	700

Required Use the information provided to prepare the operating activities section of the statement of cash flows for Bryson Co. using the indirect format.

The solution to Self-Study Problem 2 appears at the end of the chapter.

INTERPRETING CASH FLOWS

OBJECTIVE 3

Interpret cash flow information as a basis for analyzing financial performance.

Understanding a company's cash flows and the reasons for the cash flows is critical to investors, managers, and other decision makers. To survive and prosper, a company must create sufficient cash flows to pay its bills, repay its debt, and provide a reasonable return to its owners. The statement of cash flows provides important information for evaluating past decisions and future prospects.

A company's net income and operating cash flow are seldom equal. A major difference between the two amounts is Depreciation and Amortization Expense. This expense reduces net income but does not require the use of cash. As shown in Exhibit 6, much of the difference between Krispy Kreme's net income and its operating cash flows is due to its depreciation and amortization expense. Other differences are explained by changes in current asset and current liability accounts. Changes in these accounts can provide useful information about a company's operations. Increases in current assets (Accounts Receivable and Inventory) and increases in Accounts Payable are common for companies that exhibit increases in net income. Higher sales lead to more receivables and require larger amounts of inventories. Payables also increase because of the increased demand for inventories. Increases in operating cash flows over time and large operating cash flows relative to net income (as seen in Exhibit 6) usually indicate good financial performance.

The amount of cash flow from operating activities normally is approximately equal to the amount of cash flow from (for) investing activities plus the amount of cash flow from (for) financing activities. A company depends on its operating activities to meet most of its cash flow needs. In the long run, operating cash flows must be sufficient to meet the cash needs of a company. If net operating cash flows are negative, a company is normally facing serious financial problems. In the short run, the company may be able to borrow cash or sell long-term assets to generate cash. But in the long run, it will be unable to stay in business using these methods. Creditors will refuse to lend money to a company that cannot create operating cash flows to ensure repayment of the debt. Also, the company will run out of assets that it can sell and still stay in business. Accordingly, negative operating cash flows combined with cash inflows from investing activities (from selling assets) and cash inflows from financing activities (from borrowing) is clearly a negative sign.

A company that is performing well normally creates net cash flow from operating activities. This excess cash can be used for expansion (to buy additional assets) or for financing purposes (to repay debt, repurchase stock, or pay dividends to stockholders). Accordingly, a combination of positive net cash flows from operating activities and negative cash flows for investing activities normally is a sign of good performance **and growth**. A growing company usually is increasing in value. As the company expands by purchasing more assets, it has the ability to produce and sell more products, which may result in additional profitability and increased operating cash flows. Observe that Krispy Kreme is using most of its operating cash flows for investing purposes. The company is acquiring additional assets each year.

If a company creates more cash from operating activities than it can use for investing purposes, it normally will use the cash to repay debt or to make payments to stockholders. If these payments are large, they may be an indication that the company is performing well but does not have a lot of good investing opportunities. Krispy Kreme was not able to generate sufficient cash flows from operating activities to meet its investing needs. Additional cash was obtained from financing activities.

A company with a lot of good investing opportunities may borrow money or sell stock to provide additional cash to take advantage of these opportunities. Thus, cash inflow from financing activities is a positive sign if a company is using this cash to purchase additional assets (for investing activities). Cash inflow from financing activities is a bad sign if the cash is used for operating activities. This may indicate that the company cannot create enough cash from its operations to meet ongoing needs.

The cash flow information presented in Exhibit 6 suggests that Krispy Kreme was performing well during the three years reported. Operating cash flows were large and generally increasing, and cash was being invested in additional assets. The company was not experiencing any difficulty in repaying debt or in meeting any of its cash flow needs.

Exhibit 7 summarizes the types of information provided by a cash flow statement. Other cash flow combinations are possible, but these are the most common and the most likely to provide a clear indication of how well a company is performing.

Exhibit 7

Cash Flow Patterns and the Financial Health of a Company

Operating Cash Flows	Investing Cash Flows	Financing Cash Flows	Normal Interpretation
+	−	+	The company is prosperous and growing. Financing cash flow is used to take advantage of growth opportunities.
−	+	+	The company is facing serious financial problems. It is selling assets and using financing activities to meet current cash needs.
+	+ or −	−	The company is prosperous but may not have a lot of good growth opportunities. It is using operating cash to pay off debt and pay stockholders.
+ or −	+	−	The company may be facing a current cash flow problem. It is selling assets to supplement current cash flows to cover its financing needs. This is especially a problem if the company is short of cash to repay debt.

The amount of change in a company's cash balance usually is not of major importance. This change usually is small, and a small increase or decrease does not signal financial problems or strengths. In particular, you should not assume that a net decrease in cash is an indication of a major financial problem for a company. You should **focus instead on changes in operating, investing, and financing cash flows.**

Case in Point

http://ingram.swlearning.
com

Find out more about
United Airlines.

Cash Flow Problems

The airlines industry faced financial problems in 2001 because of the declining economy. As economic activity decreases, fewer people travel and airline revenues decrease. The tragic events of September 11 were catastrophic for the industry. Many flights were cancelled, and passenger mileage dropped dramatically. The result of these events was a sharp decrease in profits and operating cash flows, leaving many airlines struggling for survival.

The following information was reported by United Airlines in its 2001 annual report:

(In millions) Year Ended December 31	2001	2000	1999
Net earnings (loss)	$(2,145)	$ 50	$ 1,235
Cash flows from (for) operating activities	(160)	2,472	2,421
Cash flows from investing activities	(1,969)	(2,521)	(1,624)
Cash flows from (for) financing activities	2,138	1,418	(877)

Profits decreased steadily from 1999 to 2001. Operating cash flow became negative in 2001. To meet its investing cash flow needs, the company increased its borrowing in 2001. The company's assets did not increase much from 2000 to 2001. Most of its investing activities were to replace existing assets. Most of United's assets were airplanes that it could not sell, since there was a surplus among all airlines. Some of the airplanes were mothballed pending an increase in demand.

Borrowing to meet operating and investing needs is a short-term solution. A company cannot stay in business long if it does not generate sufficient cash from operating activities to cover ordinary operating costs, replace assets, and repay creditors.

---

3 **SELF-STUDY PROBLEM** A statement of cash flows is provided below for Sound Bytes Company.

WebTUTOR Advantage

Sound Bytes Company Statement of Cash Flows For the Year Ended December 31, 2004	
Operating Activities	
Net income	$ 40,698
Adjusted for:	
Increase in accounts receivable	(23,034)
Increase in merchandise	(36,780)
Increase in accounts payable	22,479
Increase in prepaid expenses	(12,340)
Decrease in other payables	(3,982)
Depreciation and amortization	35,612
Net cash flow from operating activities	22,653
Investing Activities	
Sale of plant assets	86,511
Financing Activities	
Repayment of debt	(115,240)
Net decrease in cash	(6,076)
Cash balance, December 31, 2003	15,495
Cash balance, December 31, 2004	$ 9,419

Required Use the statement to answer the following questions.

A. How much cash flow did the company create from its operating activities?
B. What are the primary explanations for the difference between the company's net income and operating cash flow?
C. How did the company use its cash flows?
D. How well does the company appear to be performing based on its cash flow information?

The solution to Self-Study Problem 3 appears at the end of the chapter.

REVIEW

SUMMARY of IMPORTANT CONCEPTS

1. The statement of cash flows reports the cash inflows and outflows associated with the operating, investing, and financing activities of a company for a fiscal period. The statement may be presented in a direct or indirect format.
   a. The direct format lists cash activities associated with operating activities for a fiscal period.
   b. The indirect format reports cash flow from operating activities by adjusting net income for operating activities that did not generate or use cash during a fiscal period. These adjustments consist of revenues or expenses (such as depreciation) that did not have a cash effect and changes in current asset and current liability accounts.

2. Cash flow information is important to decision makers.
   a. Information about the sources and uses of cash indicates a company's ability to meet its payment obligations now and in the future.
   b. Cash flow information, along with information on the income statement and balance sheet, provides insight into a company's operating, investing, and financing activities.

SELF-STUDY PROBLEM SOLUTIONS

SSP5-1

Jerome, Inc.
Statement of Cash Flows

Operating Activities	
Received from customers	$ 14,750
Paid for merchandise	(8,400)
Paid to employees	(4,000)
Paid for utilities	(2,200)
Paid for supplies	(1,800)
Net cash flow for operating activities	(1,650)
Investing Activities	
Received from sale of land	$ 20,000
Paid for building	(75,000)
Paid for equipment	(13,500)
Net cash flow for investing activities	(68,500)
Financing Activities	
Received from sale of stock	$100,000
Paid for debt repayment	(35,000)
Paid for dividends	(2,500)
Net cash flow from financing activities	62,500
Net decrease in cash	(7,650)
Cash balance at beginning of period	16,350
Cash balance at end of period	$ 8,700

The company's primary sources of cash were from selling stock, selling land, and from sales of goods to customers. Its primary uses of cash were the purchase of a building and equipment and the repayment of debt.

SSP5-2

Bryson Co.
Statement of Cash Flows

Operating Activities	
Net income	$16,540
Adjustments to reconcile net income to cash flows:	
Depreciation and amortization expense	3,560
Increase in accounts receivable	(2,500)
Decrease in merchandise	3,200
Increase in supplies	(430)
Increase in accounts payable	660
Decrease in wages payable	(375)
Increase in interest payable	280
Decrease in income tax payable	(700)
Net increase in operating cash flows	$20,235

SSP5-3 A. Net cash flow from operating activities was $22,653.
B. Primary explanations of the differences are increases in current assets (merchandise and receivables), an increase in accounts payable, and depreciation and amortization expense.
C. Cash flows from operating and investing activities were used to repay debt.
D. The company does not appear to be performing very well. Its operating cash flows were much less than its net income. The increase in merchandise and receivables and the increase in payables suggest that the company was not selling the inventory it was acquiring, was having difficulty collecting from its customers, and was having difficulty paying its suppliers. Selling plant assets to meet current cash needs is also a sign of poor financial performance. The company apparently needed more cash than it could create from its operating activities to meet its obligations. It was forced to sell assets to raise cash. In the long run, a company cannot survive by selling assets to repay debt.

Thinking Beyond the Question

How is cash flow information determined and reported to external users?

This chapter examined the opening question by describing two methods of preparing the statement of cash flows. Both methods use income statement and balance sheet amounts to determine cash flows. It is important to understand the relationships among the statements to obtain a complete picture of a business.

Is it possible for a profitable business to fail? What do you think are the primary causes of business failure? How are a company's financial statements useful for identifying financial problems that may lead to failure? What role does the statement of cash flows play in decision making by investors and creditors?

QUESTIONS

Q5-1
Obj. 1

What question is the direct format of the statement of cash flows designed to answer?

Q5-2
Objs. 1, 2

If a company acquires machinery in exchange for a long-term note payable, both a financing activity and an investing activity have taken place. Explain how this is true.

Q5-3
Objs. 1, 2

If long-term assets are acquired in exchange for shares of stock, no cash is involved. Will this transaction be reported on the statement of cash flows? If not, why not? If so, how?

Q5-4
Objs. 1, 2

The direct format and indirect format relate only to the operating activities section of the statement of cash flows. Regarding the investing and financing activities sections, are they presented in a direct-type format or an indirect-type format?

Q5-5
Objs. 1, 2

Why does the cash effect of interest appear as an operating activity, rather than a financing or investing activity?

Q5-6
Obj. 2

Explain why depreciation expense and amortization expense are added back to net income in the determination of cash flows from operations when the indirect format is used.

Q5-7
Obj. 2

In indirect format, why is an increase in accounts receivable subtracted from net income in computing cash flow from operations?

Q5-8
Obj. 2

What question is the indirect format of the statement of cash flows designed to answer? Explain.

Q5-9
Obj. 1

Why would one usually expect a growing company to have negative cash flow from investing activities?

Q5-10
Obj. 3

Why is it a bad sign if cash flow from operations is consistently negative?

Q5-11
Obj. 3

Why is it a bad sign if cash flow from investing activities is consistently positive?

Q5-12
Obj. 3

Assume a company consistently produces net cash inflow from operations. To what uses might this cash inflow be applied?

Q5-13
Obj. 3

Assume a company consistently reports a net cash outflow from financing activities. What does this suggest about the company?

Q5-14
Obj. 3

Upon studying its statement of cash flows, you note that over the last three years a firm has consistently reported negative cash flow from operating activities, positive cash flow from investing activities, and negative cash flow from financing activities. What does this combination of cash flows suggest to you about the firm?

Q5-15
Obj. 3

Explain how a company can have a net loss for a fiscal period but have a net increase in cash from operating activities.

Q5-16
Obj. 1

A company operating in a mature industry with few opportunities for growth or expansion will generally report negative cash flow from financing activities. Why? Where might this cash be going?

EXERCISES

If your instructor is using Personal Trainer in this course, you may complete online the assignments identified by ᵽ꜓.

E5-1
Obj. 1
ᵽ꜓

The following information reflects cash flow and other activities of Better Vision Eyeglass Company for three months ended March 31, 2004.

Paid for equipment	$42,000	Paid to owners	$12,000
Paid for income taxes	3,000	Paid to suppliers	39,000
Paid for insurance	200	Depreciation expense + Don't include 13,000	
Paid for interest	450	Received from customers	87,500
Paid for utilities	790	Received from issuing long-term debt	23,000
Paid for advertising	300	Received from sale of land	19,500
		Paid to employees	18,000

Use this information to answer the following questions:

a. What was net cash flow from operating activities for the period?
b. What was net cash flow from financing activities for the period?
c. What was the net cash flow from investing activities for the period?
d. What was the net change in cash for the period?

E5-2
Obj. 1
ᵽ꜓

For each of the items listed below, identify whether the item would appear on the statement of cash flows (direct format) as part of the computation of cash flow from operating activities, investing activities, financing activities, or would not appear at all. Also, indicate whether the item is added or subtracted in computing cash flow using the direct method of preparing the statement of cash flows.

a. Purchase of plant assets
b. Cash paid to suppliers
c. Cash collected from customers
d. Payment of long-term debt
e. Net income
f. Depreciation expense
g. Payment of dividends
h. Issuing stock
i. Cash paid to employees
j. Cash paid for income taxes
k. Disposal of plant assets

E5-3
Obj. 1
ᵽ꜓

Northport Bottling Company has the following information available for the first six months of 2004.

Cash collected from customers	$268,000
Cash paid to suppliers	82,500
Cash paid for utilities	20,000
Cash paid for insurance	23,000
Cash paid for equipment	75,000
Cash paid to employees	57,500
Cash paid for interest	9,000
Cash paid for dividends	5,000
Cash received from disposal of equipment	18,500

Determine the cash flow from operating activities for the six-month period.

E5-4
Obj. 1
ᵽ꜓

Bay View Company reported the following information at the end of its most recent fiscal year.

Cash paid for fire insurance	$ 5,000
Cash paid for dividends	22,600
Cash paid to suppliers of inventory	119,850
Cash paid for interest	3,750
Cash collected from customers	187,200
Cash received from disposal of equipment	38,000
Cash paid for utilities	9,400
Cash paid to employees	31,500
Cash paid for equipment	65,100

(Continued)

Determine each of the following amounts. Show your work neatly and clearly.

a. Net cash flow from operating activities (direct format)
b. Net cash flow from financing activities
c. Net cash flow from investing activities

E5-5
Obj. 1
P/T

Eden Healthfoods reported the following information.

Proceeds from issuance of long-term debt	$13,057
Additions to plant and equipment	5,500
Proceeds from sales of businesses	30,957
Proceeds from sales of plant and equipment	1,986
Payments of debt	83,000

Calculate the net cash flow from (a) financing and (b) investing activities for Eden.

E5-6
Objs. 1, 2
P/T

All of the following statements apply to the statement of cash flows covering a given period. If a statement applies only to the direct format, write *D* in the space allowed. If a statement applies only to the indirect format, write *I* in the space allowed. If a statement applies to both formats, write *B* in the space allowed.

_____ a. The amount of cash received from customers is listed.
_____ b. A purpose of the statement is to reconcile the amount of cash generated by operating activities to the amount of net income generated by operating activities.
_____ c. The amount by which cash receipts from customers differed from sales is reported.
_____ d. Certain revenues and expenses that did not generate or consume cash are listed.
_____ e. The amount of net income is listed on the face of the statement.
_____ f. The amount of cash paid to suppliers of inventory is included.
_____ g. The amount of cash paid for taxes is reported.
_____ h. The amount of cash raised from selling bonds to investors is listed on the face of the statement.
_____ i. The purpose of the statement is to reveal the amount of cash received from or paid out for specific operating activities.
_____ j. The amount of cash paid to acquire land and buildings is included.

E5-7
Objs. 1, 2
P/T

Each of the items found below might appear on a statement of cash flows.

	Statement Section	Statement Format	Added or Subtracted?
1. Decrease in taxes payable			
2. Cash paid to suppliers of inventory			
3. Dividends declared and paid			
4. Depreciation expense			
5. Sale of stock			
6. Increase in accounts receivable			
7. Cash collected from customers			
8. Purchase of plant assets			
9. Payments on long-term debt			
10. Cash paid for taxes			
11. Increase in wages payable			
12. Purchase of treasury stock			

For each item, indicate answers as shown.

a. Would it appear on the statement of cash flows under the operating activities (*O*), investing activities (*I*), or financing activities (*F*) section?
b. Would it appear in the direct format (*D*), indirect format (*I*), or in both formats (*B*)?
c. Would it be added (*1*) or subtracted (*2*) in computing cash flow?

E5-8

Obj. 2

P T

For each item in the following list, identify whether it would appear on the statement of cash flows (indirect format) as part of the computation of cash flow from operating activities, cash flow from investing activities, or cash flow from financing activities. Also, indicate whether the item is added or subtracted in computing cash flow using the indirect method of preparing the statement of cash flows.

    a. Purchase of plant assets
    b. Increase in accounts payable
    c. Decrease in accounts receivable
    d. Payment of long-term debt
    e. Net income
    f. Depreciation expense
    g. Payment of dividends
    h. Issuing stock
    i. Increase in inventory
    j. Decrease in taxes payable
    k. Disposal of plant assets

E5-9

Obj. 2

P T

The following information is available for Guardian Company for the first month of 2004.

Revenues	$15,000
Expenses	8,000
Increase in accounts receivable	700
Decrease in inventory	1,200
Decrease in supplies	400
Increase in accounts payable	1,100
Decrease in wages payable	900
Depreciation expense	800
Patent expense	300

Determine the cash flow from operating activities for the month.

E5-10

Obj. 2

P T

Use the information provided in each of the following independent situations to answer the questions. For each situation, briefly explain the reasoning behind each of your calculations.

    a. Cash paid to suppliers for merchandise during a period was $37,500. Accounts payable decreased during the period by $3,000. Inventory increased during the period by $3,500. What was the cost of goods sold for the period?
    b. Interest paid during a period was $4,000. Interest payable decreased during the period by $1,200. What was the interest expense for the period?
    c. Cash flow from operations for a period was $28,000. Current assets decreased during the period by $6,000. Current liabilities decreased during the period by $2,000. What was net income for the period?
    d. Cash collected from customers for a fiscal period was $27,000. Accounts receivable increased during the period by $3,000. What was sales revenue for the period?

E5-11

Obj. 2

P T

Use the information provided in each of the following independent situations to answer the questions. For each situation, briefly explain the reasoning behind each of your calculations.

    a. Net cash flow from operations for a period was $30,000. Noncash revenues for the period were $11,000. Noncash expenses for the period were $13,200. What was net income for the period?
    b. Wages expense for a period was $69,000. Wages payable increased during the period by $10,500. How much cash was paid to employees during the period?
    c. Cash collected from customers for a fiscal period was $224,500. Sales revenue for the period was $241,000. Accounts receivable at the beginning of the period was $36,000. What was the balance in accounts receivable at the end of the period?
    d. Net income for a period was $45,000. Current assets increased during the period by $7,500. Current liabilities increased during the period by $10,000. How much was cash flow from operations for the period?

E5-12

Obj. 2

Changes in account balances are shown in the following chart. For each item, where appropriate, indicate the adjustment that would be made to net income in the operating cash flow

(Continued)

section of a cash flow statement using the indirect method and the reason for the adjustment. Item *a* is provided as an example.

Account Balance	Adjustment and Reason
a. Accounts receivable increased $10,000	Subtract $10,000 from net income because cash collected from customers was $10,000 less than sales for the period.
b. Accounts payable increased $7,500	
c. Inventory decreased $50,000	
d. Notes payable increased $100,000	
e. Equipment decreased $80,000	
f. Prepaid insurance decreased $22,000	
g. Wages payable decreased $8,000	
h. Unearned revenue increased $13,000	

E5-13
Obj. 2
P
T

The following information was reported by **The Boeing Company** in its 2000 annual report (in millions of dollars).

Decrease in inventories	$1,097
Decrease in short-term investments	100
Depreciation and amortization	1,479
Decrease in accounts payable	311
Increase in accounts receivable	768
Increase in income taxes payable	421
Net earnings	2,128
Other additions to net income	1,796

What was Boeing's cash flow from operating activities for the fiscal year?

E5-14
Obj. 2

Martha Rosenbloom holds stock in several major corporations. Each year she receives a copy of the companies' annual reports. She looks at the pictures, reads the discussion by management, and examines some of the primary financial statement numbers. She has a pretty good understanding of some of the financial statement information. She tells her friends that she doesn't know how to make heads or tails of the statement of cash flows, however. She doesn't understand how depreciation and changes in current assets and liabilities have anything to do with cash. A mutual friend, Arthur Doyle, has found out that you are taking accounting and asks you to help Martha. Write Martha a letter explaining the cash flow from operating activities section of the statement of cash flows found in most annual reports. Martha's address is 945 Oak Lane, Anytown, USA.

E5-15
Obj. 2

Great Adventure Travel Company had the following adjustments to net income when computing its cash flow from operations for the year just ended.

Net income		$326,000
Add: Adjustments		
(1) Depreciation	$13,000	
(2) Decrease in accounts receivable	2,000	
(3) Increase in inventory	(4,500)	
(4) Decrease in accounts payable	(3,000)	7,500
Cash flow from operations		$333,500

a. Explain why it is generally necessary to make additions to and subtractions from net income when computing cash flow from operations in the indirect format.
b. For each adjustment (labeled 1 through 4), explain why that specific adjustment was necessary to determine cash flow from operations.

E5-16
Obj. 3

Bingle, Bangle, and Bungle all manufacture toys. At year end 2004, they reported the following information.

	Bingle	Bangle	Bungle
Cash flow from operating activities	$ 6,862	$ 14,656	$ 3,052
Cash flow from (for) investing activities	(4,409)	457	938
Cash flow from (for) financing activities	(834)	(12,476)	(2,307)

Respond to each of the following questions.

a. Which company had the largest amount of cash flow from operating activities? Which had the smallest?

b. Would you generally expect cash flow associated with investing activities to be negative? Why or why not?

c. In what ways does Bingle appear to be different from the other two companies? What do these differences suggest about the companies?

E5-17
Obj. 3

Consider the pattern in following selected year-end data for Landsdowne Company.

Year	1	2	3	4	5	6
Cash flow from						
operating activities	$20,000	$25,000	$18,000	$12,000	$ 6,000	$ 2,000
Receivables	35,000	37,000	42,000	45,000	50,000	53,000
Inventory	70,000	76,000	80,000	84,000	86,000	90,000
Payables	24,000	28,000	32,000	46,000	57,000	66,000
Net income	50,000	53,000	55,000	59,000	63,000	55,000

Provide an explanation for the changes over the six-year period. Year 6 is the most recent year. What difficulties do you believe the company is facing?

E5-18
Obj. 3

Sommer Company has experienced the following results over the past three years.

Year	1	2	3
(In thousands)			
Net income (loss)	$ 2,000	$(10,000)	$ (8,000)
Depreciation and amortization	(9,000)	(11,000)	(14,000)
Net cash flow from operating activities	13,000	15,000	18,000
Net expenditures for plant assets	9,000	6,000	5,000

The price of Sommer's common stock has declined steadily over the three-year period. At the end of year 3, it is trading at $10 per share. Early in year 4, Bottom Fischer, who specializes in taking over poorly performing businesses, has offered shareholders of Sommer $18 per share for their stock. Why would Fischer be willing to pay such an amount? What does he see in the company that suggests value?

E5-19
Obj. 3

Rockman Associates has reported the following selected account balances on its most recent balance sheet.

Account and balance	Anticipated future event and cash flow
a. Accounts receivable, $12,000	$12,000 of cash should be received from customers during the next fiscal year. This will appear in the operating activities section.
b. Prepaid insurance, $22,000	
c. Merchandise, $50,000	
d. Treasury stock, $33,000	
e. Accounts payable, $6,500	
f. Machinery, $92,000	
g. Notes payable, long-term, $88,000	
h. Unearned revenue, $10,000	
i. Taxes payable, $7,800	
j. Retained earnings, $56,000	

For each item, describe the anticipated future event and cash flow (if any) that is expected to occur and in which section of a future statement of cash flows it will appear. The first item is completed as an example.

PROBLEMS

If your instructor is using Personal Trainer in this course, you may complete online the assignments identified by ₚₜ.

P5-1 **Preparing a Statement of Cash Flows (Direct Format)**

Obj. 1

ₚₜ San Garza Properties has been in business for many years. On December 31, 2003, the firm's cash balance was $9,121. During January of 2004, the 14 events below were recorded in the company's accounting system.

Date	Accounts	Cash	Other Assets (ASSETS)	= LIABILITIES	+ Contributed Capital (OWNERS' EQUITY)	Retained Earnings (OWNERS' EQUITY)
1	Cash	18,000				
	Bank Loan Payable			18,000		
2	Rent Expense					−3,000
	Cash	−3,000				
3	Office Furniture		5,500			
	Cash	−5,500				
4	Merchandise		9,000			
	Accounts Payable			9,000		
5	Cash	10,000				
	Common Stock				10,000	
6	Advertising Expense					−2,200
	Cash	−2,200				
7	Accounts Receivable		18,000			
	Sales Revenue					18,000
8	Merchandise		−7,500			
	Cost of Goods Sold					−7,500
9	Cash	8,100				
	Accounts Receivable		−8,100			
10	Accounts Payable			−7,000		
	Cash	−7,000				
11	Computer Equipment		4,800			
	Cash	−4,800				
12	Wages Expense					−1,400
	Wages Payable			1,400		
13	Dividends					−2,000
	Cash	−2,000				
14	Bank Loan Payable			−5,000		
	Interest Expense					−135
	Cash	−5,135				

Required Prepare a statement of cash flows for the month of January 2004. Use good form and the direct format.

P5-2 **Preparing the Statement of Cash Flows (Direct Format)**

Obj. 1

ₚₜ Planet Accessories Company reported the following balance sheet and income statement at year-end 2004. In addition, dividends totaling $1,000 were paid.

Required

A. Assume the company uses the direct format to prepare its statement of cash flows. What amounts would be reported on the 2004 statement of cash flows for each of the following?

1. Cash collections from customers (Hint: Inspect Sales Revenue and the change in Accounts Receivable.)
2. Cash paid to suppliers of inventory (Hint: Assume all purchases were made for cash.)
3. Cash paid for insurance (Hint: Inspect the insurance expense account and the change in the prepaid insurance account.)
4. Cash paid for rent (Hint: Inspect Rent Expense and the change in Rent Payable.)
5. Cash paid for depreciation
6. Cash paid for wages

B. What items and amounts would be reported under cash flow from investing activities? (Hint: Inspect the changes in long-term asset accounts.)
C. What items and amounts would be reported under cash flow from financing activities? (Hint: Inspect the changes in long-term liability and stockholders' equity accounts.)
D. Prepare a statement of cash flows using the direct format.

Balance Sheets at December 31	2004	2003	Income Statement for 2004	
Cash	$ 826	$ 553	Sales revenue	$135,800
Accounts receivable	8,950	8,000	Cost of goods sold	54,300
Inventories	11,600	10,100	Gross profit	81,500
Prepaid insurance	400	300	Operating expenses:	
Property, plant and equipment	8,750	3,735	Advertising	17,029
Less: Accumulated depreciation	(2,900)	(1,900)	Depreciation	1,000
Land	5,850	4,850	Insurance	4,800
			Rent	14,255
Total assets	$33,476	$25,638	Wages	33,400
			Operating income	11,016
Rent payable	$ 3,750	$ 4,000	Interest expense	650
Wages payable	1,750	1,400	Income before taxes	10,366
Loan payable, long-term	9,200	5,200	Taxes	3,628
Common stock, $1 par value	5,400	4,400	Net income	$ 6,738
Retained earnings	17,950	12,212		
Treasury stock	(4,574)	(1,574)		
Total liabilities and shareholders' equity	$33,476	$25,638		

P5-3
Obj. 2
P/T

Reconciling Net Income and Cash Flow from Operations

For the fiscal year just completed, Dollar Sine Enterprises had the following summary information available concerning operating activities. The company had no investing or financing activities this year.

Sales of merchandise to customers on credit	$307,400
Sales of merchandise to customers for cash	88,250
Cost of merchandise sold on credit	200,000
Cost of merchandise sold for cash	57,400
Purchases of merchandise from suppliers on credit	233,700
Purchases of merchandise from suppliers for cash	48,100
Collections from customers on accounts receivable	321,000
Cash payments to suppliers on accounts payable	293,600
Operating expenses (all paid in cash)	93,500

Required

A. Determine the amount of:
1. net income for the year.
2. cash flow from operations for the year (direct format).
B. Indicate the direction and amounts by which each of these accounts changed during the year.
1. Accounts receivable
2. Merchandise inventory
3. Accounts payable
C. Using your results above, prepare the operating activities section of the statement of cash flows (indirect format).

P5-4 Preparing a Statement of Cash Flow (Indirect Format)

Obj. 2

P T

Reuben Corporation has completed its comparative balance sheet and income statement at year-end 2004.

December 31,

Comparative Balance Sheet	2004	2003	Income Statement for 2004	
Cash	$ 4,400	$ 3,550	Sales revenue	$355,000
Accounts receivable	4,100	5,300	Cost of goods sold	241,400
Inventory	5,700	4,100	Gross profit	$113,600
Prepaid advertising	900	1,200	Operating expenses:	
Buildings and furnishings	20,000	20,000	Advertising	8,300
Accumulated depreciation	(6,000)	(5,000)	Depreciation	1,000
Land	14,000	10,000	Insurance	3,500
Total assets	$43,100	$39,150	Rent	31,200
			Wages	57,380
Rent payable	$ 2,800	$ 2,600	Operating income	12,220
Taxes payable	1,600	2,000	Interest expense	1,450
Wages payable	2,000	900	Income before tax	10,770
Loan payable, long-term	14,000	22,250	Taxes	3,770
Common stock	16,000	10,000	Net income	$ 7,000
Retained earnings	6,700	1,400		
Total liabilities and equity	$43,100	$39,150		

Additional information:

1. A payment of $8,250 was made on the loan principal during the year.
2. Just before year-end, a dividend was distributed to stockholders.
3. A parcel of land was acquired early in the year.
4. New shares of common stock were sold during the year.

Required Prepare a statement of cash flows in good form using the indirect format.

P5-5 Preparing the Statement of Cash Flows (Indirect Format)

Obj. 2

P T

Refer to the financial statement information in Problem P5-2 and use it to complete the requirements below.

Required

A. Assume the company uses the indirect format to prepare its statement of cash flows. What amounts would be reported on the 2004 statement of cash flows for each of the following?
   1. Net income
   2. Adjustment for depreciation expense
   3. Adjustment for accounts receivable
   4. Adjustment for inventories
   5. Adjustment for prepaid insurance
   6. Adjustment for rent payable
   7. Adjustment for wages payable
B. What items and amounts would be reported under cash flow from investing activities? (Hint: Inspect the changes in long-term asset accounts.)
C. What items and amounts would be reported under cash flow from financing activities? (Hint: Inspect the changes in long-term liability and stockholders' equity accounts.)
D. Prepare a statement of cash flows using the indirect format.

P5-6 **Interpreting Cash Flows**

Obj. 3

The statement of cash flows for **Rowe Furniture Corporation** is shown below. Based in Salem, Virginia, the firm manufactures upholstered household furniture including sofas, sofa beds, and chairs.

Required Use the statement of cash flows to answer the following questions.

A. What were Rowe's primary sources of cash in 2001? Were these different than in the prior two years?

B. What were Rowe's primary uses of cash in 2001? Were these different than in the prior two years?

C. What were the primary reasons for the decrease in cash flow from operating activities between 2000 and 2001?

D. Evaluate Rowe's cash flows over the period shown. Has the company been able to finance its growth, dividends, and acquisition of treasury stock out of cash flow from operations? Explain.

E. Over the past three years, what were the primary reasons that cash flows from operations differed so much from net income?

F. The portion of the statement titled "Reconciliation of net earnings to net cash provided by operating activities" is a required disclosure. Of what does this section and presentation remind you? Might this disclosure requirement help explain why so few companies use the direct method? Explain.

The Rowe Companies Annual Report 2001
Consolidated Statements of Cash Flows

	Year Ended		
	12/2/01 (52 weeks)	12/3/00 (53 weeks)	11/28/99 (52 weeks)
		(in thousands)	
Increase (Decrease) In Cash			
Cash flows from Operating Activities			
Cash received from customers	$ 329,683	$ 379,400	$ 295,563
Cash paid to suppliers and employees	(328,948)	(354,570)	(274,870)
Income taxes paid, net of refunds	585	(6,183)	(7,726)
Interest paid	(4,642)	(5,693)	(2,686)
Interest received	480	288	159
Other receipts—net	1,109	1,156	1,684
Net cash and cash equivalents provided by (used in) operating activities	(1,733)	14,398	12,124
Cash flows from Investing Activities			
Proceeds from sale of property and equipment	1,056	21	19
Capital expenditures	(3,317)	(9,155)	(8,830)
Payments to acquire businesses	—	(5,160)	(8,892)
Net cash used in investing activities	(2,261)	(14,294)	(17,703)
Cash flows from Financing Activities			
Net borrowings (payments) under line of credit	5,368	(164)	2,071
Proceeds from issuance of long-term debt	6,865	13,020	25,132
Payments to reduce long-term debt	(3,821)	(11,922)	(14,522)
Proceeds from loans against life insurance policies	3,014	—	—
Proceeds from issuance of common stock	27	51	460
Dividends paid	(1,379)	(1,849)	(1,714)
Purchase of treasury stock	(16)	(951)	(3,224)
Net cash provided by (used in) financing activities	10,058	(1,815)	8,203
Net increase (decrease) in cash and cash equivalents	6,064	(1,711)	2,624
Cash at beginning of year	3,393	5,104	2,480
Cash at end of year	$ 9,457	$ 3,393	$ 5,104

(Continued)

The Rowe Companies Annual Report 2001
Reconciliation of Net Earnings (Loss) to Net Cash
Provided by (Used In) Operating Activities:

	Year Ended		
	12/2/01 (52 weeks)	12/3/00 (53 weeks) (in thousands)	11/28/99 (52 weeks)
Net earnings (loss)	$ (6,189)	$ 3,544	$13,901
Adjustments to reconcile net earnings (loss) to net cash provided by (used in) operating activities, net of acquisition and disposition of businesses			
Loss on disposition of Wexford	—	5,455	—
Depreciation and amortization	8,569	8,581	6,165
Provision for deferred compensation	173	816	1,083
Payments made for deferred compensation	(813)	(160)	(319)
Deferred income taxes	1,001	(2,099)	(472)
Provision for losses on accounts receivable	4,421	1,485	413
Loss (gain) on disposition of assets	15	29	4
Change in operating assets and liabilities net of effects of acquisition and disposition of businesses			
Decrease (increase) in accounts receivable	4,649	5,564	(9,379)
Decrease (increase) in inventories	227	(832)	(5,692)
Decrease (increase) in prepaid expenses and other	1,679	(887)	(795)
Decrease (increase) in other assets	(352)	472	(1,210)
Increase (decrease) in accounts payable	(10,277)	(4,750)	3,830
Increase (decrease) in accrued expenses	(4,433)	(1,715)	2,170
Increase (decrease) in customer deposits	(403)	(1,105)	2,425
Total adjustments	4,456	10,854	(1,777)
Net cash provided by (used in) operating activities	$ (1,733)	$14,398	$12,124

Note: Slight modifications have been made to the format of the statement to simplify the presentation.

P5-7 Errors in Reporting Cash Flow from Operating Activities

Obj. 3

Starkovich Architects, Inc. uses the direct format to prepare the statement of cash flows. At year-end 2004, the following comparative balance sheet and abbreviated income statement were available as shown.

December 31

Comparative Balance Sheet	2004	2003	Income Statement for 2004	
Cash	$ 3,400	$ 2,750	Service revenue	$ 73,000
Accounts receivable	5,800	4,300	Commission revenue	42,100
Inventory	4,700	5,100	Advertising expense	(13,400)
Land	10,000	10,000	Rent expense	(24,000)
Total assets	$23,900	$22,150	Wages expense	(42,600)
			Taxes expense	(12,000)
Rent payable	$ 2,500	$ 2,900	Net income	$ 23,100
Taxes payable	1,600	1,600		
Wages payable	3,200	1,050		
Common stock	15,000	15,000		
Retained earnings	1,600	1,600		
Total liabilities and equity	$23,900	$22,150		

From this information, the accounting staff prepared the operating activities section of the statement of cash flows shown on the following page using the direct format.

Starkovich Architects, Inc.
Operating Activities (Direct Format)
Year Ending December 31, 2004

Operating Activities	
Cash received from customers	$115,100
Cash paid for advertising	(13,400)
Cash paid for rent	(23,600)
Cash paid for wages	(40,450)
Cash paid for taxes	(11,000)
Cash provided by operating activities	$ 26,650

Required

A. What evidence can you identify to suggest that certain items are misstated in the computation of cash flow from operating activities? For each item that you believe is misstated, specify why you know this. (You may assume that the income statement and balance sheets are correct as presented.)
B. Prepare a revised computation of cash flow from operating activities incorporating the necessary changes.

P5-8 Depreciation and Cash Flow

Obj. 3

A colleague is about to make a presentation to the management group regarding a $2 million capital investment proposal. She is quite sure that the management group will press her to identify a new source of financing to support the proposed investment. She shows you the operating activities section of the company's most recent statement of cash flows. (Amounts are in thousands of dollars.)

Your colleague is aware that there are a variety of methods acceptable under GAAP by which depreciation expense can be computed. Further, she knows that the company currently uses a very conservative method that results in low depreciation expense, especially in the early years of an asset's life. Your colleague is going to suggest that the firm use a more aggressive depreciation policy that will result in higher depreciation expense for the next several years. Says she, "The higher depreciation expense will generate more cash from operating activities. According to the cash flow statement here, adding back greater depreciation expense will result in more cash provided by operating activities. See?" Assume it's quite reasonable that the firm use a more aggressive depreciation method.

Required

A. What format is this company using to prepare the statement of cash flows?
B. Do you agree with your colleague's thinking? Why or why not?
C. Construct a numerical example to prove your argument.

P5-9 Interrelationships among Financial Statements

Objs. 2, 3
P/T

Avnet, Inc. is a manufacturer of electronic instruments and controls with corporate headquarters in Phoenix, Arizona. Following are comparative income statements and comparative statements of cash flow from a recent annual report.

(Continued)

Avnet, Inc. and Subsidiaries
Consolidated Statements of Operations

(In thousands, except per share amounts)	Years Ended		
	June 28, 2002	June 29, 2001	June 30, 2000
Sales	$8,920,248	$12,814,010	$9,915,042
Cost of sales	7,697,434	10,948,484	8,470,257
Gross profit	1,222,814	1,865,526	1,444,785
Selling, general and administrative expenses	1,225,799	1,611,874	1,076,793
Operating income (loss)	(2,985)	253,652	367,992
Other income, net	6,755	25,495	10,452
Interest expense	(124,583)	(191,895)	(94,798)
Income (loss) from continuing operations before income taxes	(120,813)	87,252	283,646
Income tax (provision) benefit	36,377	(87,155)	(121,082)
Income (loss) from continuing operations	(84,436)	97	162,564
Income from discontinued operations, net of income taxes of $0, $1,611 and $100, respectively	—	2,416	828
Gain on disposal of discontinued operations, net of income taxes of $0, $8,611 and $0, respectively	—	12,889	—
Income (loss) before cumulative effect of change in accounting principle	(84,436)	15,402	163,392
Cumulative effect of change in accounting principle	(580,495)	—	—
Net income (loss)	$ (664,931)	$ 15,402	$ 163,392
Earnings (loss) per share from continuing operations:			
Basic	$ (0.71)	$ —	$ 1.52
Diluted	$ (0.71)	$ —	$ 1.50
Earnings (loss) per share before cumulative effect of change in accounting principle:			
Basic	$ (0.71)	$ 0.13	$ 1.53
Diluted	$ (0.71)	$ 0.13	$ 1.51
Net earnings (loss) per share:			
Basic	$ (5.61)	$ 0.13	$ 1.53
Diluted	$ (5.61)	$ 0.13	$ 1.51
Shares used to compute earnings (loss) per share:			
Basic	118,561	117,263	106,627
Diluted	118,561	118,815	108,257

Note: Slight modifications have been made to the format of the statement to simplify the presentation.

Avnet, Inc. and Subsidiaries
Consolidated Statements of Cash Flows

(In thousands)	Years Ended		
	June 28, 2002	June 29, 2001	June 30, 2000
Cash flows from operating activities:			
Net income (loss)	$ (664,931)	$ 15,402	$ 163,392
Income from discontinued operations, net of income taxes	—	(2,416)	(828)
Gain on disposal of discontinued operations, net of income taxes	—	(12,889)	—
Cumulative effect of change in accounting principle	580,495	—	—
Net income (loss) from continuing operations	(84,436)	97	162,564
Non-cash and other reconciling items:			
Depreciation and amortization	103,879	119,398	83,516
Deferred taxes	10,828	(79,659)	(40,159)
Other, net	121,240	296,450	43,339
	151,511	336,286	249,260
Changes in (net of effects from businesses acquisitions and dispositions):			
Receivables	433,863	315,669	(453,330)
Inventories	552,621	248,978	(535,844)
Payables, accruals and other, net	(161,690)	(714,733)	245,532
Net cash flows provided from (used for) operating activities	976,305	186,200	(494,382)
Cash flows from financing activities:			
Sales (repayments) of accounts receivable	(150,000)	350,000	—
Issuance of notes in public offerings, net	394,328	572,389	358,326
(Repayment) issuance of debt, net	(1,051,375)	(453,210)	695,966
Cash dividends	(26,546)	(27,387)	(18,180)
Other, net	24,225	10,834	29,157
Net cash flows (used for) provided from financing activities	(809,368)	452,626	1,065,269

(Continued)

(In thousands)	Years Ended		
	June 28, 2002	June 29, 2001	June 30, 2000
Cash flows from investing activities:			
Purchases of property, plant and equipment	(83,750)	(125,421)	(92,488)
Acquisitions of operations, net	(31,547)	(858,851)	(675,030)
Investments in non-consolidated entities, net	(2,544)	(2,955)	(42,972)
Proceeds from sale of discontinued operations	—	226,390	—
Net cash flows used for investing activities	(117,841)	(760,837)	(810,490)
Effect of exchange rate changes on cash and cash equivalents	12,859	(7,468)	(995)
Net decrease in cash from discontinued operations	—	(25,073)	(11,082)
Cash and cash equivalents:			
-(decrease) increase	61,955	(154,552)	(251,680)
-at beginning of year	97,279	251,831	519,924
-at end of year	$ 159,234	$ 97,279	$ 268,244

Note: Slight modifications have been made to the format of the statement to simplify the presentation.

Required Answer the following questions.

A. Which reporting format does Avnet use for the statement of cash flows?
B. Compare the three-year trends of sales and net income. Do they exhibit an encouraging pattern? Why or why not? Discuss.
C. How does the pattern of cash flow from operations match up with the trends of net income and sales for the most recent three years?
D. During the most recent year shown, determine whether the following balance sheet accounts increased or decreased.
   1. Cash
   2. Receivables
   3. Inventory
   4. Payables
E. Study the overall pattern and components of financing cash flows. What have been the major sources and uses of cash during the three years shown? What do you conclude from this information?
F. Study the overall pattern and components of investing cash flows. What have been the major sources and uses of cash during the three years shown? What do you conclude from this information?

P5-10 Evaluating Information from a Statement of Cash Flows

Obj. 3

Circuit City is the nation's largest retailer of brand-name consumer electronics and major appliances. Its headquarters are in Richmond, Virginia. The company's comparative statements of cash flows from a recent annual report are shown on the next page.

Required Answer the following questions.

A. For the three years shown, compare the trend in net income to the trend in cash provided by operations.
B. What were the three most significant reasons that cash provided by operations was positive for fiscal 2002?
C. Inspect the information shown under investing activities. Also note the amount of depreciation and amortization reported under operating activities. Does this company's long-term asset base appear to be expanding, shrinking, or staying about the same size? Explain your answer.

Circuit City Stores, Inc.
Consolidated Statements of Cash Flows

(In thousands)	Years Ended February 28 or 29		
	2002	2001	2000
OPERATING ACTIVITIES:			
Net earnings	$ 218,795	$ 160,802	$ 197,590
Adjustments to reconcile net earnings to net cash provided			
by operating activities of continuing operations:			
Loss from discontinued operations	—	—	16,215
Loss on disposal of discontinued operations	—	—	114,025
Depreciation and amortization	150,711	153,090	148,164
Unearned compensation amortization of restricted stock	15,678	11,365	12,096
Loss on disposition of property and equipment	13,735	4,674	17
Provision for deferred income taxes	31,166	19,765	43,053
Changes in operating assets and liabilities, net of effects			
from business acquisitions:			
(Increase) decrease in net accounts receivable and retained			
interests in securitized receivables	(140,766)	7,541	(18,922)
Decrease (increase) in inventory	124,337	(67,655)	(184,507)
Decrease (increase) in prepaid expenses and other current assets	16,312	(41,426)	81,316
(Increase) decrease in other assets	(720)	1,012	240
Increase (decrease) in accounts payable, accrued expenses and			
other current liabilities and accrued income taxes	336,774	(64,193)	244,559
Increase (decrease) in deferred revenue and other liabilities	71,186	(17,855)	(15,565)
NET CASH PROVIDED BY OPERATING ACTIVITIES			
OF CONTINUING OPERATIONS	837,208	167,120	638,281
INVESTING ACTIVITIES:			
Cash used in business acquisitions	—	(1,325)	(34,849)
Purchases of property and equipment	(213,997)	(285,556)	(222,268)
Proceeds from sales of property and equipment, net	187,426	115,695	100,151
NET CASH USED IN INVESTING ACTIVITIES			
OF CONTINUING OPERATIONS	(26,571)	(171,186)	(156,966)
FINANCING ACTIVITIES:			
Proceeds from (payments on) short-term debt, net	9,037	(1,805)	(5,011)
Principal payments on long-term debt	(132,388)	(178,060)	(2,707)
Issuances of Circuit City Group Common Stock, net	17,920	26,912	6,942
Issuances of CarMax Group Common Stock, net	(1,958)	(263)	1,914
Proceeds from CarMax Group Common Stock offering, net	139,546	—	—
Dividends paid on Circuit City Group Common Stock	(14,556)	(14,346)	(14,207)
NET CASH PROVIDED BY (USED IN) FINANCING ACTIVITIES			
OF CONTINUING OPERATIONS	17,601	(167,562)	(13,069)
CASH USED IN DISCONTINUED OPERATIONS [NOTE 15]	(22,837)	(26,174)	(90,193)
Increase (decrease) in cash and cash equivalents	805,401	(197,802)	378,053
Cash and cash equivalents at beginning of year	446,131	643,933	265,880
Cash and cash equivalents at end of year	$1,251,532	$ 446,131	$ 643,933

Note: Slight modifications have been made to the format of the statement to simplify the presentation.

P5-11 **Evaluating Income and Cash Flows**

Objs. 2, 3

$\frac{P}{T}$

Selected financial statement information is reported below for Office Decor Company. All amounts are in thousands.

For the Year Ended December 31, 2004

Sales revenue	$11,200
Cost of goods sold	6,400
Operating expenses	2,800
Net income	2,000
Dividends paid	1,000

(Continued)

December 31	2004	2003
Cash	$ 1,340	$1,940
Accounts receivable	4,600	2,200
Inventories	9,400	5,000
Accounts payable	3,800	2,600
Notes payable	10,000	6,000

Required Prepare a statement of cash flows (indirect format) for Office Decor, assuming that all important cash flow activities are reflected in the information provided above. Examine the financial information presented for Office Decor Company. What financial problems do you see? What are some potential causes of these problems?

P5-12   Interpreting a Cash Flow Statement

Obj. 3

P/T

Sara Lee Corporation, a food products company headquartered in Chicago, Illinois, recently reported the following cash flow statement.

Consolidated Statements of Cash Flows

Dollars in millions	Years Ended	June 29 2002	June 30, 2001	July 1, 2000
Operating Activities				
Income from continuing operations		$ 1,010	$ 1,603	$ 1,158
Adjustments for non-cash charges included in income from continuing operations				
Depreciation		471	392	402
Amortization of intangibles		111	207	200
Unusual items				
Gain on disposal of Coach business		—	(967)	—
Charges for exit activities and business dispositions		101	500	—
Increase in deferred taxes		21	88	48
Other non-cash credits, net		7	(62)	(38)
Changes in current assets and liabilities, net of businesses acquired and sold				
Decrease (increase) in trade accounts receivable		93	42	(116)
Decrease (increase) in inventories		304	25	(152)
Decrease (increase) in other current assets		7	(11)	(47)
(Decrease) in accounts payable		(417)	(133)	(56)
Increase (decrease) in accrued liabilities		27	(164)	57
Net cash from operating activities—continuing operations		1,735	1,520	1,456
Operating cash flows (used by) from discontinued operations		—	(24)	84
Net cash from operating activities		1,735	1,496	1,540
Investment Activities				
Purchases of property and equipment		(669)	(532)	(647)
Acquisitions of businesses and investments		(1,930)	(300)	(743)
Dispositions of businesses and investments		23	1,819	21
Sales of assets		113	65	64
Other		(12)	13	9
Net cash (used in) from investment activities		(2,475)	1,065	(1,296)
Financing Activities				
Issuances of common stock		109	104	84
Purchases of common stock		(138)	(643)	(1,032)
Borrowings of long-term debt		1,362	1,023	725
Repayments of long-term debt		(503)	(390)	(502)
Short-term borrowings (repayments), net		124	(1,914)	1,022
Payments of dividends		(484)	(486)	(485)
Net cash from (used in) financing activities		470	(2,306)	(188)
Effect of changes in foreign exchange rates on cash		20	(21)	(21)
(Decrease) increase in cash and equivalents		(250)	234	35
Cash and equivalents at beginning of year		548	314	279
Cash and equivalents at end of year		$ 298	$ 548	$ 314

Required Use the information from the statement of cash flows for Sara Lee Corporation to answer the following questions.

A. What was the amount of change in Sara Lee's cash account for 2002?
B. What were the primary sources of cash for the company?
C. What were the primary uses of cash?
D. Why were depreciation and amortization added to net income in computing cash flow from operating activities?
E. Why were the decreases in inventories and trade accounts receivable added to net income in computing cash flow from operating activities?
F. Why were the purchase of property and equipment, sales of assets and acquisitions of businesses listed as investing activities?
G. Did short-term debt increase or decrease during the year?
H. How much new long-term debt was issued during the year? How much old long-term debt was paid off?
I. Does the company appear to be facing a cash flow problem? Explain your answer.

P5-13 Interpreting Cash Flows

Obj. 3

The operating activities section of Bernstein Company's cash flow statement is reported below.

(In millions)	2004	2003	2002
Net income	$ 391	$ 455	$467
Depreciation and amortization	258	247	223
Special and nonrecurring items	(3)	0	0
Changes in current assets and liabilities:			
Accounts receivable	(220)	(102)	(66)
Inventories	(112)	(73)	(45)
Accounts payable	15	(22)	19
Income taxes	6	(7)	30
Other accrued expenses	(17)	26	11
Cash flow provided by operations	$ 318	$ 524	$639

Required What does this information reveal about why cash flow from operations has decreased by 50% over the three-year period? Be specific and explain the basis for your conclusions.

P5-14 Interpreting the Cash Flow Statement

Obj. 3
P̶T̶

Best Buy Company, Inc., a retailer of consumer electronics headquartered in Minnesota, recently reported the following partial cash flow statement and income statement.

	(Dollars in millions) Year Ended March 2, 2002
Cash flows from operating activities	
Net income	$ 570
Adjustments to reconcile net income to net cash:	
Depreciation and amortization	309
Increase in accounts receivable	(18)
Decrease in inventories	(330)
Increase in other assets	(39)
Increase in accounts payable	529
Increase in accrued expenses and other	557
Net cash provided by operating activities	$1,578

	(Dollars in millions) Year Ended March 2, 2002
Revenues	$19,597
Cost of goods sold	15,167
Gross profit	4,430
Selling, general, and administrative expenses	3,493
Interest expense, net	1
Income before provision for income taxes	936
Provision for income taxes	366
Net income	$ 570

Required Use the information from the financial statements to answer each of the following questions.

A. How much cash did Best Buy collect from customers in the fiscal year ended March 2, 2002?

B. How much cash did Best Buy pay out for inventory in the fiscal year ended March 2, 2002? The increase in Accounts Payable arose from purchases of inventory that had not yet been paid for.

C. How much cash did Best Buy pay out for selling, general, and administrative expenses in the fiscal year ended March 2, 2002? The changes in other assets and in accrued expenses and other are related to selling, general, and administrative expenses.

P5-15 Comparing Cash Flows

Obj. 3

Summarized cash flow statements for 2001 are shown below for two computer industry firms: **Intel Corporation**, based in Santa Clara, California, and **Apple Computer**, headquartered in Cupertino, California.

(In millions)	Intel Corporation	Apple Computer
Net income	$ 1,291	$ (25)
Adjustments:		
Depreciation and amortization	6,469	102
(Increase) decrease in accounts receivable	1,561	487
(Increase) decrease in inventories	24	22
(Increase) decrease in other assets	898	118
Increase (decrease) in payables	(2,484)	(416)
Changes in taxes	(84)	(36)
Other adjustments	979	(67)
Net cash provided by operating activities	8,654	185
Net cash provided by (used in) investing activities	(195)	892
Net cash provided by (used in) financing activities	(3,465)	42
Net change in cash	4,994	1,119

Required Write a short report comparing the financial performance of the two companies. In what important ways were the results for both companies similar? In what important ways were the results different?

P5-16 Interpreting Cash Flows

Obj. 3

$\frac{P}{T}$ **Required** Identify whether each of the following statements is true or false. Explain your answers. Write in complete sentences. Computations may be used as part of your explanation.

A. When a company prepares a cash flow statement using the indirect method, it adds depreciation expense to net income because depreciation is a source of cash during a fiscal period.

B. Alpha Company reported an increase in Accounts Receivable of $2 million during 2004. As a result, Alpha's cash flow from operating activities was $2 million less than its operating revenues.

C. Beta Company purchased $40 million of merchandise inventory during 2004. Beta's accounts payable increased from $5 million to $8 million during the year. Beta's cash flow statement (indirect method) would report an adjustment to net income of −$3 million.

D. Delta Company reported cost of goods sold of $27 million for 2004. Its merchandise inventory increased by $8 million during the year. If all inventory purchased was paid for in cash, then Delta's cash payments to suppliers of inventory during the year were $35 million.

E. Gamma Company reported the following:

Net cash flow for operating activities	$80
Net cash flow from investing activities	35
Net cash flow from financing activities	50
Net change in cash	$ 5

From this information, it appears that Gamma is facing financial problems.

P5-17 The Differential Effect of Transactions on Net Income and Cash Flow
Obj. 3

During March, each of the following events occurred at Frolic Park, Inc.

Event	Type of Activity	Effect on March's Net Income	Effect on March's Cash Flow
1. Sold $18,000 of goods on credit to customers. Received a 25% down payment with the balance on account.			
2. Paid $500 cash for office supplies that will be used during April.			
3. Received $3,000 from a customer in full payment of her account balance.			
4. Borrowed $80,000 from a local bank to be repaid in monthly installments plus interest starting in April.			
5. Paid rent on the office space ($1,200 per month) for the months of February, March, and April.			
6. Distributed monthly paychecks to employees totaling $13,300. 30% was for work performed in February and the balance for work performed in March.			
7. Purchased new Internet server equipment at a cost of $50,000.			
8. Purchased a 3-year fire insurance policy at a total cost of $10,800. Its coverage began on March 1.			
9. Purchased merchandise from suppliers on credit at a cost of $70,000.			
10. Collected $22,000 from customers in payment of their accounts. 80% of this amount was from sales recorded in February and the balance was from March sales.			
11. Collected four months' rent in advance (at $700 per month) from a tenant who will move in on April 1.			
12. Paid $45,000 to suppliers in partial payment for goods purchased in #9 above.			
13. Sold $33,000 of merchandise to customers on credit.			
14. Sold an investment in stocks and bonds for $28,000; the same amount that had been paid for it. A 3-year, 9% note receivable was accepted in full payment.			
Totals for March			

(Continued)

Required

A. Identify whether each transaction is an operating, investing, or financing activity.
B. For each event, identify the effect it had on March's net income and on March's cash flow from operations.
C. What does this problem suggest to you about the hazards of trying to manage an organization with accrual-basis accounting information only? Discuss.

P5-18 **Comparing Cash Flow Statements Among Firms**

Obj. 3

Sheik, Speer, and Love are three companies in similar industries. Five years of summarized cash flow data are available for each firm. Year 5 is the most recent.

	Year 5	Year 4	Year 3	Year 2	Year 1
Sheik Company:					
Operating activities	$ 30	$ 31	$ 28	$ 26	$ 28
Investing activities	3	1	6	5	4
Financing activities	(31)	(28)	(33)	(30)	(32)
Speer Company:					
Operating activities	(15)	(3)	7	14	26
Investing activities	8	4	(9)	(17)	(35)
Financing activities	6	0	3	4	11
Love Company:					
Operating activities	9	6	3	2	(1)
Investing activities	(13)	(12)	(11)	(10)	(10)
Financing activities	8	7	8	10	9

Study the information carefully. What clues can you find in the information concerning what is (or has been) going on with each firm? Do their business histories appear similar or dissimilar? Does the situation of one or more firms appear more favorable than one or more of the others?

Required For each firm, describe and discuss what you have learned from reviewing its summarized cash flow information.

P5-19 **Interpreting the Cash Flow Statement**

Obj. 3

$\frac{P}{T}$

Embarcadero Company's most recent statement of cash flows is shown on the next page.

Required Use Embarcadero's statement of cash flows to answer the following questions.

A. What was the primary source of cash inflow for the company?
B. Why was the company able to report a net cash inflow from operations when it incurred a net loss for the period?
C. What were the primary uses of cash during the period?
D. Did Receivables, Inventories, and Accounts Payable increase or decrease during the year?
E. If revenues (as reported on the income statement) were $3,960 for the year, how much cash was collected from customers during the year?

Embarcadero Company
Consolidated Statement of Cash Flows
For the Year Ended December 31, 2004

Operating activities	
Net loss	$ (682)
Adjustments to reconcile NI to cash flows:	
Depreciation and amortization	592
Noncash gains and losses, net	(136)
Changes in:	
Accounts receivable	172
Inventories	110
Other current assets	(24)
Accounts payable	98
Other current liabilities	148
Cash provided by operations	278
Investing activities	
Investments and acquisitions	(424)
Capital expenditures	(42)
Sales of investments	206
Cash used by investing activities	(260)
Financing activities	
Increase in long-term debt	1,014
Repurchase of common stock	(740)
Dividends paid	(402)
Cash provided by financing activities	(128)
Decrease in cash	$ (110)

P5-20 **Interrelationships among the Income Statement, Balance Sheet, and**
Objs. 2, 3 **Statement of Cash Flow**

P
T

Frontera Corporation reported the following income statement and comparative balance sheet for the year ended December 31, 2004.

Income Statement (for the Year Ended December 31, 2004) (In thousands)	
Sales revenue	$6,930
Cost of goods sold	3,660
Gross profit on sales	3,270
Operating expenses:	
Wages	855
Depreciation	102
Rent	546
Advertising	1,224
Operating income	543
Other revenues and expenses:	
Interest revenue	84
Interest expense	(24)
Income before taxes	603
Income tax expense	210
Net income	$ 393

(Continued)

Balance Sheet (at December 31)	2004	2003
Assets:		
Cash	$ 482	$ 318
Accounts receivable	246	189
Inventory	471	483
Prepaid advertising	54	21
Total current assets	1,253	1,011
Buildings and equipment	2,811	1,974
Accumulated depreciation	(922)	(820)
Land	350	300
Investments, long-term	250	400
Total assets	$3,742	$2,865
Liabilities and stockholders' equity:		
Rent payable	$ 450	$ 478
Wages payable	32	24
Total current liabilities	482	502
Notes payable, long-term	1,150	750
Common stock	1,400	1,100
Retained earnings	710	513
Total liabilities and equity	$3,742	$2,865

Frontera Corporation used the indirect format to prepare the statement of cash flows, but it has been misplaced and is not available.

Required Use your knowledge of financial statements to answer each of the questions that follow. For each item you list as part of your answer, describe fully why the item appears on the statement of cash flows.

A. Which line items from the income statement will also be found in the operating activities section of the statement of cash flows?
B. Which line items from the balance sheet contain information that will be reflected in the operating activities section?
C. Which line items from the income statement will also be found in the investing activities section?
D. Which line items from the balance sheet contain information that will be reflected in the investing activities section?
E. Which line items from the income statement will also be found in the financing activities section?
F. Which line items from the balance sheet contain information that will be reflected in the financing activities section?

P5-21 Evaluating Income and Cash Flows

Obj. 3
$\frac{P}{T}$

Selected financial statement information is reported on the next page for Beltway Distributors, Inc.

Required
A. Prepare a statement of cash flows (indirect format) for Beltway Distributors, assuming that all important cash flow activities are reflected in the information provided.
B. Assume this has been the pattern of cash flows for several years. What does this imply about the firm's business situation?

For the Fiscal Year Ended January 30, 2004 (In thousands)		
Sales revenue		$35,400
Cost of goods sold		22,700
Operating expenses (except depreciation)		4,500
Depreciation expense		2,900
Net income		5,300
Dividends declared and paid		5,000
For January 30	**2004**	**2003**
Cash	$ 2,050	$ 1,950
Accounts receivable	8,600	13,400
Inventories	23,500	27,100
Accounts payable	8,600	8,800
Bank loan payable	18,700	30,000

P5-22 Excel in Action

P/T

SPREADSHEET

The following information is available for The Book Wermz for November, 2004. All numbers are dollar amounts.

Cash balance, November 30	$12,307.99
Cash balance, October 31	15,389.55
Cash paid for debt repayment	1,122.77
Cash paid for dividends	1,500.00
Cash paid for equipment	2,000.00
Cash paid for interest	932.03
Cash paid for merchandise	33,243.92
Cash paid for rent	1,738.15
Cash paid for supplies	2,576.93
Cash paid for taxes	897.45
Cash paid for wages	4,073.79
Cash received from customers	45,003.48
Decrease in accounts receivable	125.00
Depreciation expense	817.20
Increase in accounts payable	6,131.77
Increase in inventory	8,438.37
Increase in supplies	165.40
Increase in wages payable	623.56
Net income	2,447.45

Required Use the data provided to prepare a statement of cash flows for The Book Wermz for November using a spreadsheet. Prepare the statement using both the direct and indirect formats. Show cash outflows as negative amounts. Use the appropriate formatting buttons to include commas and dollar signs as needed. Use the Merge Cells and Bold buttons to position and format titles. The captions for the direct format statement should appear in column A and the amounts should appear in column B. The captions for the indirect format should appear in column D and the amounts should appear in column E. Use functions to sum subtotals and totals, such as =SUM(B5:B8), so that changes to any of the amounts being totaled will be automatically recalculated.

Suppose net income had been $2,600 and the amount of cash received from customers had been $45,156.03. What would operating cash flow have been?

P5-23 Multiple-Choice Overview of the Chapter

P/T

1. The primary difference between a statement of cash flows prepared in direct format and one prepared in indirect format is
   a. in how net cash flow from operations is computed.
   b. that the indirect approach always results in higher net cash flow.
   c. in how net cash flow from investing activities is reported.
   d. that the beginning-of-the-year cash balance is included in direct format but not in indirect.

2. The statement of cash flows for the Halyard Exploration Company reported the following:

Cash paid for equipment	$ 300,000
Cash paid to employees	400,000
Cash paid to owners	150,000
Cash paid to suppliers	560,000
Cash received from creditors	200,000
Cash received from customers	1,200,000

   What were Halyard's net cash flows from operating, investing, and financing activities?

	Operating	Investing	Financing
a.	$240,000	($300,000)	$ 50,000
b.	$500,000	($860,000)	$200,000
c.	$640,000	($860,000)	$200,000
d.	$240,000	($860,000)	$200,000

3. Haddad Company is a well-established, growing company. Which categories of activities would you generally expect to generate positive cash flows?
   a. Operating activities only
   b. Financing activities only
   c. Investing activities only
   d. Both operating activities and financing activities
   e. Both financing activities and investing activities

4. A statement of cash flows has been prepared in the indirect format. Depreciation expense has been added back to net income because depreciation is
   a. not really an expense and to list it as such understates profitability.
   b. an investing activity and should be reported in that section.
   c. a source of cash for the company.
   d. a noncash expense.

5. Zeff Company reports positive operating cash flows, near zero investing cash flows, and negative financing cash flows. This may indicate that the company
   a. is raising new capital to purchase long-term assets for expansion.
   b. does not have many good growth opportunities.
   c. has severe cash flow problems caused by too-rapid growth.
   d. is unable to provide goods and services that customers want.

6. A statement of cash flows prepared using the indirect format would report an increase in Accounts Receivable as
   a. an addition to cash flow from financing activities.
   b. a subtraction from cash flow from financing activities.
   c. an addition to net income in computing cash flow from operating activities.
   d. a subtraction from net income in computing cash flow from operating activities.

7. Flag Ship Company reported depreciation and amortization expense of $300,000 for the latest fiscal year. The depreciation and amortization expense
   a. increased cash flow for the year $300,000.
   b. decreased cash flow for the year $300,000.
   c. had no effect on cash flow for the year.
   d. had an effect on cash flow if assets were purchased during the year.

8. Rust Iron Company purchased a three-month insurance policy on March 1, 2004. The company paid $3,000 for the policy. The amount of insurance expense and cash outflow the company should report for March would be

	Insurance Expense	Cash Outflow
a.	$3,000	$3,000
b.	3,000	1,000
c.	1,000	3,000
d.	1,000	1,000

9. Micro Fish Company recognized $10,000 of interest expense in 2002. The balance of the company's interest payable account decreased $2,000. The amount of cash paid by the company for interest in 2002 was
   a. $10,000.
   b. $12,000.
   c. $2,000.
   d. $8,000.

10. Operating activities are reflected on a company's balance sheet primarily in
    a. plant assets.
    b. current assets and liabilities.
    c. income from operations.
    d. cash flow from operating activities.

CASES

C5-1 General Mills, Inc., Statement of Cash Flows

Objs. 2, 3

The General Mills 2002 Annual Report is reproduced in Appendix B at the end of the text.

Required Answer the following questions about the General Mills Consolidated Statement of Cash Flows.

A. What are the three categories of cash flows shown on the company's cash flow statement?
B. Compare the net income figure to the amount of net cash provided by operating activities for each of the three years. What do you observe?
C. Has the net cash provided by operating activities been large enough to meet the net investing cash outflow? Explain where the difference came from (or went).
D. Compare the dividend payments to the income amounts for the current year. (Note: You may find it helpful to calculate the dividend payout ratio, which is the total dividends for the period ÷ net income for the period. This ratio is explained further in Ch. F10.)

C5-2 Analysis of Corporate Financial Statements

Obj. 3

The 2002 financial statements for **General Mills, Inc.** are provided in Appendix B near the end of this text. Examine these statements and answer the following questions.

Required

A. What were General Mills' major operating activities during 2002? What were the major differences between the accrual and cash flow effects of these activities?
B. What were the company's returns on total assets (net income ÷ total assets) for 2002 and 2001? Did the return improve or deteriorate from 2001?
C. If you owned 10,000 of the company's common stock, what would be your claim on the company's earnings for 2002? Was this a larger or smaller claim than you would have had for 2001?
D. What were the company's major sources of cash for 2002? In general, what did the company do with the cash it received?
E. What were the major financing activities during 2002? In general, how would you describe the company's financing activities overall during the last three years?
F. What major investing activities occurred in 2002?
G. As of the end of 2002, what were the company's most important reported assets? What other resources may be important to the company that are not reported on its balance sheet?

C5-3 Interpreting Cash Flows

Obj. 3 Review the financial report of General Mills, Inc., in Appendix B.

Required Prepare a short report analyzing each of the following issues.

A. What were the accrual and cash basis results of operating activities for 2002? Explain any major differences between the two results.

B. Inspect the balance sheet to identify which current assets and liabilities increased and decreased during 2002. What was the amount of cash collected from customers during 2002?

C. What have been the relative amounts and trends in net income and cash flow from operating activities over the 2000–2002 period? What accounts for the differences you observe?

D. How would you assess the company's financial performance for 2002?

C5-4 Comparing Direct Format and Indirect Format Statements of

Objs. 1, 2, 3 **Cash Flow**

ABM Industries, headquartered in San Francisco, sells a wide variety of industrial and commercial services. Its 2001 statement of cash flows (**direct format**) is shown below exactly as it appeared in the firm's annual report. If ABM Industries had chosen to use the **indirect format**, it would have appeared as shown on page F221. All amounts are in thousands of dollars.

ABM Industries Incorporated and Subsidiaries
Consolidated Statements of Cash Flows

YEARS ENDED OCTOBER 31 (in thousands)	2001	2000	1999
CASH FLOWS FROM OPERATING ACTIVITIES:			
Cash received from customers	$ 1,918,558	$ 1,739,297	$ 1,589,775
Other operating cash receipts	5,523	2,347	1,491
Interest received	859	580	870
Cash paid to suppliers and employees	(1,822,629)	(1,686,988)	(1,522,495)
Interest paid	(2,991)	(3,209)	(2,025)
Income taxes paid	(33,524)	(33,102)	(32,311)
Net cash provided by operating activities	65,796	18,925	35,305
CASH FLOWS FROM INVESTING ACTIVITIES:			
Additions to property, plant and equipment	(16,922)	(18,717)	(19,451)
Proceeds from sale of assets	1,253	1,164	922
Decrease (increase) in investments and long-term receivables	49	370	(1,885)
Purchase of businesses	(23,401)	(14,191)	(10,980)
Proceeds from sale of business	12,000	—	—
Net cash used in investing activities	(27,021)	(31,374)	(31,394)
CASH FLOWS FROM FINANCING ACTIVITIES:			
Common stock issued, including tax benefit	26,688	16,381	17,178
Common stock purchases	—	(8,390)	(5,448)
Preferred stock redemption	(6,400)	—	—
Dividends paid	(16,202)	(14,539)	(13,055)
(Decrease) increase in bank overdraft	(15,952)	10,985	2,492
Long-term borrowings	108,000	126,000	57,064
Repayments of long-term borrowings	(133,857)	(118,127)	(61,847)
Net cash (used in) provided by financing activities	(37,723)	12,310	(3,616)
Net increase (decrease) in cash and cash equivalents	1,052	(139)	295
Cash and cash equivalents beginning of year	2,000	2,139	1,844
CASH AND CASH EQUIVALENTS END OF YEAR	$ 3,052	$ 2,000	$ 2,139

**Reconciliation of Net Income to Net Cash
Provided by Operating Activities:**

Net income	$ 32,826	$ 44,343	$ 39,667
ADJUSTMENTS:			
Depreciation	13,710	12,265	10,815
Amortization	12,618	11,259	9,883
Provision for bad debts	6,134	2,971	2,257
Gain on sale of assets	(41)	(265)	(160)
Gain on sale of business	(718)	—	—
Increase in deferred income taxes	(12,138)	(5,517)	(6,537)
Increase in trade accounts receivable	(24,340)	(65,555)	(39,304)
Increase in inventories	(3,223)	(2,217)	(331)
Increase in prepaid expenses and other current assets	(3,045)	(1,200)	(1,950)
(Increase) decrease in other assets	40	2,475	(3,295)
(Decrease) increase in income taxes payable	(1,267)	765	1,791
(Decrease) increase in retirement plans accrual	(903)	3,092	3,320
Increase in insurance claims liability	18,872	7,155	4,500
Increase in trade accounts payable and other accrued liabilities	27,271	9,354	14,649
Total adjustments to net income	32,970	(25,418)	(4,362)
NET CASH PROVIDED BY OPERATING ACTIVITIES	$ 65,796	$ 18,925	$ 35,305
SUPPLEMENTAL DATA:			
Non-cash investing activities:			
Common stock issued for net assets of business acquired	$ 1,666	$ 1,581	$ 1,710

Required Study the two statements of cash flow and answer the following questions.

A. Describe how the statements are similar. Be specific.
B. Describe how the statements are dissimilar. Be specific.
C. Note the reconciliation of net income to net cash provided by operating activities that appears at the bottom of the direct format statement. Of what does this disclosure remind you? What information does it provide?
D. What questions can be answered by reading one of the statements that cannot be answered by reading the other?
E. Which statement format do you believe presents more understandable information? Describe and discuss your beliefs.
F. If you had the power to dictate that one format should be used in financial reporting instead of the other, which would you recommend? Why?

If the indirect format had been used:

Years Ended October 31 (In thousands)	2001	2000	1999
Cash flows from operating activities:			
Net income	$ 32,826	$ 44,343	$ 39,667
Adjustments to reconcile net income to cash flow from operating activities:			
Depreciation and amortization	26,328	23,524	20,698
Provision for bad debts	6,134	2,971	2,257
Gain on sale of assets	(41)	(265)	(160)
Gain on sale of business	(718)	—	—
Increase (decrease) in deferred income taxes	(12,138)	(5,517)	(6,537)
Increase in accounts receivable	(24,340)	(65,555)	(39,304)
Increase in inventories	(3,223)	(2,217)	(331)
Increase in prepaid expenses and other current assets	(3,045)	(1,200)	(1,950)
Decrease (increase) in other assets	40	2,475	(3,295)
Increase (decrease) in income taxes payable	(1,267)	765	1,791
(Decrease) increase in retirement plans accrual	(903)	3,092	3,320
Increase (decrease) in insurance claims liability	18,872	7,155	4,500
Increase in accounts payable and other accrued liabilities	27,271	9,354	14,649
Net cash provided by operating activities	65,796	18,925	35,305

(Continued)

Years Ended October 31 (In thousands)	2001	2000	1999
Cash flows from investing activities:			
Additions to property, plant and equipment	(16,922)	(18,717)	(19,451)
Proceeds from sale of assets	1,253	1,164	922
Increase (decrease) in investments and long-term receivables	49	370	(1,885)
Purchase of businesses	(23,401)	(14,191)	(10,980)
Proceeds from sale of business	12,000	—	—
Net cash used in investing activities	(27,021)	(31,374)	(31,394)
Cash flows from financing activities:			
Common stock issued	26,688	16,381	17,178
Common stock purchases	—	(8,390)	(5,448)
Preferred stock redemption	(6,400)	—	—
Dividends paid	(16,202)	(14,539)	(13,055)
Increase (decrease) in bank overdraft	(15,952)	10,985	2,492
Long-term borrowings	108,000	126,000	57,064
Repayments of long-term borrowings	(133,857)	(118,127)	(61,847)
Net cash (used in) provided by financing activities	(37,723)	12,310	(3,616)
Net (decrease) increase in cash and cash equivalents	$ 1,052	$ (139)	$ 295
Cash and cash equivalents beginning of year	2,000	2,139	1,844
Cash and cash equivalents end of year	$ 3,052	$ 2,000	$ 2,139

COMPREHENSIVE REVIEW

CR5-1 Preparing Financial Statements

Alice Springs Merchandise is a retail company that sells general household products. Account balances for the company's fiscal years ended January 31, 2004, and 2005 are provided on the next page. Changes in balance sheet account balances also are provided. Additional information for the 2005 fiscal year includes the following:

- The company paid $38,802 for additional property and equipment and received cash from the sale of equipment of $1,967.
- Amounts borrowed or repaid are equal to changes in Notes Payable, Current and changes in Notes Payable, Long-Term.
- The change in Common Stock is the amount of stock issued or repurchased during the year.
- The balance of Retained Earnings includes the effects of net income and dividends.

Required From the information provided, prepare the following in good form.

A. An income statement containing separate columns for 2005 and 2004.
B. A balance sheet containing separate columns for 2005 and 2004.
C. A schedule like Exhibit 3 in this chapter (page F183) that includes the adjustments necessary to calculate operating cash flow. The adjustments should be the changes in the appropriate account balances.
D. A statement of cash flows for 2005 using the direct method.
E. A statement of cash flows for 2005 using the indirect method.

	2005	2004	Change
Sales Revenue	$ 589,351	$ 530,666	
Cost of Goods Sold	(359,504)	(328,343)	
Wages Expense	(123,764)	(117,136)	
Rent Expense	(30,116)	(28,052)	
Depreciation Expense	(24,871)	(22,628)	
Supplies Expense	(13,555)	(10,751)	
Cash	63,168	57,845	5,323
Accounts Receivable	48,386	43,106	5,280
Merchandise Inventory	130,247	117,202	13,045
Prepaid Rent	2,530	2,314	216
Supplies	1,129	952	177
Property and Equipment	365,398	328,563	36,835
Accumulated Depreciation	(43,848)	(18,977)	(24,871)
Accounts Payable	25,953	23,674	2,279
Wages Payable	10,272	9,500	772
Unearned Revenue	12,966	11,675	1,291
Notes Payable, Current	47,249	44,249	3,000
Notes Payable, Long-Term	214,838	222,467	(7,629)
Common Stock	102,629	95,581	7,048
Retained Earnings	153,103	123,859	29,244
Dividends Paid	8,297	5,250	

General Mills, Inc., Statement of Cash Flows

The General Mills 2002 Annual Report is reproduced in Appendix B at the end of the text.

Required Answer the following questions about the General Mills Consolidated Statement of Cash Flows.

A. What are the three categories of cash flows shown on the company's cash flow statement?
B. Compare the net income figure to the amount of net cash provided by operating activities for each of the three years. What do you observe?
C. Has the net cash provided by operating activities been large enough to meet the net investing cash outflow? Explain where the difference came from (or went).
D. Compare the dividend payments to the income amounts for the current year. (Note: You may find it helpful to calculate the dividend payout ratio, which is the total dividends for the period ÷ net income for the period. This ratio is explained further in Ch. F10.)

Analysis of Corporate Financial Statements

The 2002 financial statements for **General Mills, Inc.** are provided in Appendix B near the end of this text. Examine these statements and answer the following questions.

Required

A. What were General Mills' major operating activities during 2002? What were the major differences between the accrual and cash flow effects of these activities?
B. What were the company's returns on total assets (net income ÷ total assets) for 2002 and 2001? Did the return improve or deteriorate from 2001?
C. If you owned 10,000 of the company's common stock, what would be your claim on the company's earnings for 2002? Was this a larger or smaller claim than you would have had for 2001?
D. What were the company's major sources of cash for 2002? In general, what did the company do with the cash it received?

FULL AND FAIR REPORTING

How do we ensure that reports to external users fairly present business activities?

Previous chapters examined how businesses collect and record information about their activities and report this information in the form of financial statements. Maintaining a reliable accounting system and reporting information that fairly presents a company's business activities is an important task. Because stockholders and other external users rely on a corporation's managers to provide this information, the financial reporting process is regulated. Corporations and other businesses must conform with regulations and standards that describe accounting procedures, the content and format of financial statements, and other information that must accompany those statements.

Maria and Stan, like other managers, must ensure that their corporation conforms with these requirements. Maintaining an accounting system and producing financial statements is not sufficient. Maria and Stan must be aware of the requirements that ensure that businesses fairly present their activities and make sure they conform with those requirements.

FOOD FOR THOUGHT

As a stockholder, what information, in addition to financial statements, do you and other external users need to understand the business activities of Mom's Cookie Company? How can you be sure information provided by the business is accurate and reliable? Maria and Stan are discussing these issues with Ellen, their accountant.

Maria: *I've noticed that many corporations produce elaborate annual reports for their stockholders. Is this something we need to do for Mom's Cookie Company?*

Ellen: *Providing financial statements is not all you have to do to report to your stockholders. An annual report that contains those statements is necessary. It does not have to be elaborate, but it does have to contain certain information.*

Stan: *Our financial statements describe our business activities. Why aren't these adequate?*

Ellen: *You need to help your stockholders understand the information in your statements. You must discuss and analyze the financial statement information to identify activities that are key to understanding the performance of your company. And, you must provide disclosures about assumptions you made and methods you used in preparing the statements. In some cases, the statements may not fully inform users about your activities. You may need to provide details about some of your business activities.*

Maria: *Once we prepare all this information, do we simply have it printed and mail it to our stockholders?*

Ellen: *Before you send any financial information to external users for your fiscal year, you must have that information audited.*

Stan: *Who do we get to do the audit?*

Ellen: *The audit must be performed by an independent Certified Public Accountant. The CPA must be someone who is not employed by your company and who has no financial ties to your company. I'll help you identify someone for the job. First, let's examine the broader picture of corporate financial reporting and the regulations that govern that activity.*

OBJECTIVES

Once you have completed this chapter, you should be able to:

1 Explain the purpose of accounting regulation.

2 Describe how accounting standards are established in the United States.

3 Explain the purpose of the Financial Accounting Standards Board's conceptual framework.

4 Identify supplementary information to the financial statements in a corporate annual report.

5 Describe the purpose of internal controls and types of controls that should be evident in business organizations.

THE PURPOSE OF ACCOUNTING REGULATION

OBJECTIVE 1

Explain the purpose of accounting regulation.

Decision makers who are not managers of a business have limited access to information about the business. These external users rely on financial reports for much of the information they need to make decisions. Stockholders and creditors use accounting information to decide whether to purchase or sell stock and whether to make loans to a company. Suppliers also make decisions about whether to sell goods and provide services to a business on credit. Government authorities use accounting information to determine taxes owed by businesses and whether companies have met legal requirements and regulations. Even customers and employees may use accounting information to determine the financial viability of a company from which they purchase goods and services or for which they work.

Accounting regulations protect the interests of external decision makers by ensuring that information for evaluating the performance and financial condition of a business is available and that the information is prepared according to specific guidelines. These guidelines provide assurance that the information is reliable and comparable over time and across companies.

Though many accounting regulations apply to any business that provides financial reports to external users, they are particularly applicable to publicly traded corporations. These are businesses whose stock can be bought and sold in stock markets. Because owners of these businesses are not involved in their day-to-day operations, they have special information needs. Shareholders of most corporations do not manage the companies in which they invest. They elect members of a corporation's board of directors, who then hire professional managers to run the corporation. Investors can own part of a corporation or parts of many corporations without having to participate in the day-to-day decisions of running those companies. Many Americans own stock in corporations through personal investments and retirement plans, but they are not required to commit large amounts of their individual time to these businesses.

Corporations have continuous lives apart from those of their owners. If a proprietor or partner dies or sells her or his share of a business, the business ceases to exist as a legal entity. The new owner of the business must reestablish the business as a new legal entity. Most corporations, however, continue unchanged if current owners sell their stock. Thus, while proprietorships and partnerships are separate accounting entities from their owners, most are not separate legal entities. They have no legal identity apart from their owners. Most corporations *are* separate accounting and legal entities.

The purchaser of a corporation's stock needs assurance that the shares are reasonably priced and represent a legitimate business. To ensure access to capital markets, corporations prepare accounting information in conformity with generally accepted accounting principles (GAAP). Accounting regulations assure investors of the financial integrity of a corporation. Compliance with these regulations is costly. Large corporations maintain large staffs to handle financial reporting requirements and pay large fees to independent auditors who report on the reliability of financial information reported to external users.

Sources of Accounting Regulation

http://ingram.
swlearning.com

Learn more about the
NYSE.

Accounting regulation involves both government and private organizations. The first significant regulation of accounting and financial reporting in the United States was provided by the New York Stock Exchange (NYSE). The NYSE was formed in 1792 to facilitate the growing trade in corporate stocks. By the early 1900s the exchange required listed companies to provide accounting information to their stockholders. Listing requirements have changed over time. Today, corporations listed on exchanges must conform with GAAP and government regulations for the sale of securities.

Adoption of the 16th Amendment to the U.S. Constitution in 1913 permitted federal taxation of individual and corporate income. Taxation of income is not possible without rules and reporting requirements that determine how income will be computed. Consequently, the U.S. government and state governments have an interest in ensuring that businesses comply with accounting standards.

The early 1900s was a period of intense corporate activity. Many corporations were created, and many individuals invested in stock. During the 1920s the average price of corporate shares increased dramatically for many companies. That growth ended abruptly in late 1929, when stock prices plummeted to levels below those of the early 1920s. Many stockholders lost their life savings, and many companies were forced out of business. The collapse of the stock market in 1929 resulted in a demand for increased regulation of corporate financial reporting. Many people believed a cause of the collapse was a lack of sufficient information about corporate activities and a lack of government oversight of the stock markets.

http://ingram.
swlearning.com

Learn more about the
SEC.

In response to these concerns, the U.S. Congress passed the *Securities Act of 1933*. This legislation **required most corporations to file registration statements before selling stock to investors.** As a part of these statements, corporations were required to provide financial reports containing balance sheets and income statements. Additional legislation, the *Securities Exchange Act of 1934,* **required corporations to provide annual financial reports to stockholders.** The legislation also required that these reports be audited by independent accountants. The 1934 act also created the *Securities and Exchange Commission (SEC)*, a federal agency that reports to Congress. The SEC **was given responsibility for overseeing external financial reporting by publicly traded corporations.**

Currently, the SEC requires publicly traded corporations to publish annual and quarterly financial reports. In addition, annual and quarterly registration statements must be filed by corporations with the SEC. Annual registration statements filed by corporations with the SEC are known as Form 10-K reports. They are required by Section 10-K of the 1934 act. Quarterly statements are known as 10-Q reports.

During the twentieth century, financial accounting has become a highly regulated and formalized process. Publicly traded corporations must provide audited financial reports to stockholders. The managers and auditors of companies who fail to provide this information, or who do so fraudulently, are subject to civil and criminal prosecution. The SEC reviews corporate reports to ensure they conform with GAAP. The SEC can require corporations that do not conform with GAAP to restate their financial statements. Under extreme circumstances, the SEC can halt the trading of a company's stock. If it believes a corporation's managers have attempted to mislead stockholders by their reports, the SEC can refer the matter to the Justice Department for criminal and civil proceedings. An announcement that the SEC is opening an investigation of a company's accounting practices often has a major impact on the company's stock price. Evidence of improper accounting practices is a major cause of lawsuits by investors against corporate managers and their auditors.

Case in Point

http://ingram.
swlearning.com

....

**Learn more about
Enron.**

The Effect of an SEC Investigation

In October 2001, Enron Corporation announced that it was being investigated by the SEC for its accounting and reporting practices. On the day of the announcement, its stock price dropped 20%.

USA Today reported that, on October 22, Enron's stock closed at $20.65 per share, a drop of $5.40 or 21%. That effectively decreased the company's market capitalization by $4.1 billion, which was the NYSE's largest percentage loser that day. The stock price actually fell below $20 per share at one point during the day. Enron's stock had not traded that low for almost four years.

Enron's stock had experienced very heavy losses throughout the prior week. The closing price on October 22 reflected a 75% drop for the year to date. This was very different from the same time during 2000 when the stock price rose by 87%.*

The Rise and Fall of Enron's Stock Price

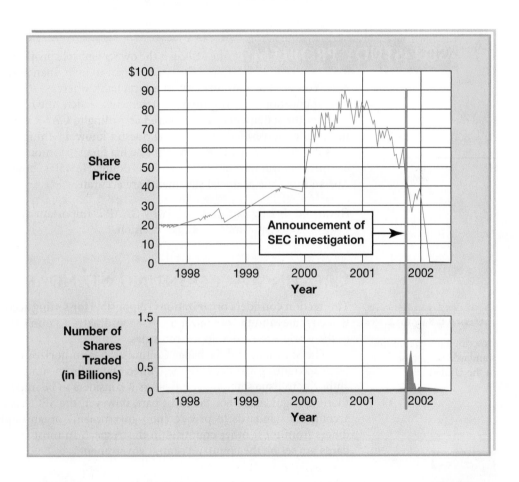

The decline in stock price was one of the major causes of Enron's bankruptcy and the primary cause of lawsuits against the company by its stockholders. The restatement resulted in a reduction in Enron's stockholders' equity of approximately $1.2 billion resulting from a write-down of earnings from 1997 through 2000. In addition, the company's reported debt increased by over $600 million.†

*Source: *USA Today*, 10/22/01, www.usatoday.com/money/energy/2001-10-22-enron.htm.
†Source: www.enron.com/corp/pressroom/releases/2001/ene/78-SECReleaseLtr.html.

The failure of corporations to report fairly their activities to stockholders is a major concern in a capitalistic economy. The stock markets are a primary mechanism for the allocation of financial resources. Society benefits when resources are allocated to the most efficient and effective companies. Misleading information can result in markets allocating resources to companies that are not efficient or effective. When investors become aware that information is misleading, they may suffer losses as many investors attempt to sell their shares.

These problems can lead to a crisis of confidence in the markets if investors are unsure of whom they can trust and whether they are being treated fairly. Improper and inadequate reporting affect everyone. The economy suffers because resources are not being properly allocated. The decrease in economic activity has a ripple effect that leads to decreased sales and profits for other companies, loss of jobs for employees, and loss of taxes for government organizations.

Accounting regulations are important because they provide standards for determining whether corporations are reporting their activities fairly to stockholders. The next section examines the processes and organizations associated with establishing accounting standards.

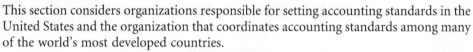

SELF-STUDY PROBLEM Abe Milton is the owner and sole proprietor of Honest Abe's Used Cars. Abe needs a loan to help finance an expansion of his business. You are the loan manager of a local bank where Abe has applied for a loan. The loan application requires financial statements, which Abe has supplied. You asked Abe whether the statements were prepared according to GAAP and whether they have been independently verified. Abe says he doesn't know anything about GAAP and that he does not permit anyone else to examine his financial information because he is afraid competitors will find out how well he is doing. He notes, however, that he is "Honest" Abe and that the financial statements are accurate.

Required Briefly explain to Abe why GAAP is important and why moral hazard is an issue of concern in making a loan decision.

CREATING ACCOUNTING STANDARDS

OBJECTIVE 2

Describe how accounting standards are established in the United States.

This section considers organizations responsible for setting accounting standards in the United States and the organization that coordinates accounting standards among many of the world's most developed countries.

The Securities and Exchange Commission is authorized by law to establish and enforce accounting standards in the United States. From time to time, the SEC uses that authority to issue standards on matters it considers to be important and in need of authoritative guidance. For the most part, however, the SEC has delegated the setting of accounting standards to private (non-government) organizations. The United States differs from most other countries in this respect. In most countries, accounting standards are set by the country's central government.

INTERNATIONAL

Standard-Setting Organizations

Several organizations are responsible for establishing accounting standards in the United States. Different organizations set standards for businesses and other non-governmental organizations than the ones that establish standards for governments. In addition, an international organization exists for coordinating standards across countries and for establishing standards that are used in some countries.

LEARNING NOTE

Accounting standards are established by the government in most countries. These standards are part of the nation's laws and are the responsibility of government agencies.

http://ingram.
swlearning.com

Learn more about the FASB.

http://ingram.
swlearning.com

Learn more about the GASB and the GAO.

http://ingram.
swlearning.com

Learn more about the IASB.

INTERNATIONAL

The *Financial Accounting Standards Board (FASB)* **has been the primary organization for setting accounting standards for businesses in the United States since 1973.** The FASB has seven full-time members and is privately funded. It is not a government organization. The FASB also sets accounting and financial reporting standards for nonprofit organizations other than governmental units. It is headquartered in Norwalk, Connecticut. The FASB employs a research staff to study accounting problems. It periodically issues *Statements of Financial Accounting Standards*, which are authoritative guidelines for accounting and financial reporting in the United States.

The *Governmental Accounting Standards Board (GASB)* **sets accounting standards for state and local governmental units.** Like the FASB, the GASB is a private rather than a governmental organization. The GASB also is headquartered in Norwalk, Connecticut, and shares staff and facilities with the FASB. The federal government is not subject to FASB or GASB standards but establishes its own accounting rules. The *General Accounting Office (GAO)* **is the primary federal government agency that oversees accounting in the federal government.**

The regulation of financial accounting and reporting is an international activity. Considerable diversity exists in accounting standards among nations. The International Accounting Standards Committee (IASC) was created in 1973 as an international effort to study accounting issues and to reduce the diversity of standards. The IASC was reconstituted as the *International Accounting Standards Board (IASB)* in 2001. The IASB **recommends accounting standards that it believes are appropriate for a broad range of global activities involving companies in many nations.** The IASB describes itself on its website (http://www.iasb.org.uk) as follows:

> ... [A]n independent, privately-funded accounting standard setter based in London, UK. Board Members come from nine countries and have a variety of functional backgrounds. The Board is committed to developing, in the public interest, a single set of high quality, understandable and enforceable global accounting standards that require transparent and comparable information in general purpose financial statements. In addition, the Board cooperates with national accounting standard setters to achieve convergence in accounting standards around the world.

Accounting standards are important to protect the interests of investors, managers, and the general public. Therefore, the standards must be perceived as being reasonable and responsive to the needs of different constituents. Arbitrary and unnecessary standards do not serve the needs of society. For these reasons, accounting standards are established through a political process. This process gives interested parties an opportunity to express their opinions and to provide information that may have a bearing on prospective standards. The fact that accounting standards are referred to as generally accepted accounting principles is not accidental. To serve the needs of society, accounting standards must be accepted by those who are affected by them.

LEARNING NOTE

The IASB has issued accounting standards that identify preferred accounting methods. Many countries have adopted these standards for accounting and financial reporting.

The Standard-Setting Process

The process used by the FASB to create accounting standards is typical of that used by other organizations, such as the GASB and the IASB. The process consists of the following steps:

1. Accounting issues are identified and evaluated for consideration.
2. A discussion memorandum is issued and responses are solicited.
3. Public hearings are held.
4. An exposure draft is issued and responses are solicited.
5. Additional public hearings are held as needed.

6. A standard is issued.
7. Existing standards are reviewed and modified as needed.

Accounting issues may be identified by accounting professionals, managers, investors, or the FASB staff. The staff evaluates the issues, and the board determines those issues that appear to be important enough to address.

A *discussion memorandum* **is a document that identifies accounting issues and alternative approaches to resolving the issues.** All interested parties are encouraged to respond to a discussion memorandum. The board develops a proposed standard after reviewing responses to a discussion memorandum and issues its proposal in the form of an exposure draft. **An** *exposure draft* **is a document that describes a proposed accounting standard.** It identifies requirements that may be contained in an actual standard. Responses again are solicited, and public hearings sometimes are held.

Once the board reviews responses to an exposure draft, it may modify and reissue the exposure draft or issue a standard. **An accounting standard is an official pronouncement establishing acceptable accounting procedures or financial report content. FASB standards are known as** *Statements of Financial Accounting Standards.* To issue a standard, at least five of the seven members of the board must agree to it. Once a standard has been issued, it becomes part of GAAP. Standards can be reviewed at any time to determine if they are serving their intended purposes and can be modified or replaced if they are found to be ineffective.

The FASB's Conceptual Framework

OBJECTIVE 3

Explain the purpose of the Financial Accounting Standards Board's conceptual framework.

The conceptual framework was developed by the FASB in the late 1970s and early 1980s to provide guidance in the development of accounting standards. **The** *FASB conceptual framework* **is a set of objectives, principles, and definitions to guide the development of new accounting standards.**

The FASB conceptual framework includes four major components:

1. Objectives of financial reporting
2. Qualitative characteristics of accounting information
3. Elements of financial statements
4. Recognition and measurement in financial statements

Objectives of financial reporting provide an overall purpose for financial reports. The purpose of financial reports is to provide information useful to current and potential investors, creditors, and other users. Financial reports should help these decision makers assess the amounts, timing, and uncertainty of prospective cash flows. Financial reports should also provide information about resources, claims to resources, and changes in resources for business organizations.

Qualitative characteristics are attributes that make accounting information useful. **Understandability** and **usefulness** for decision making are the most important characteristics. **Relevance** and **reliability** are considered to be the two primary qualities that result in accounting information being useful. **To be relevant, information should be timely and have predictive or feedback value. To be reliable, information should faithfully represent economic events and should be verifiable and neutral.** Information about an organization is more valuable when it can be compared with information from other organizations and when it is prepared using consistent methods over time.

Elements of financial statements provide definitions of the primary classes of items contained in financial statements. Elements include assets, liabilities, equity, investments by owners, distributions to owners, revenues, expenses, gains, and losses.

Recognition and measurement criteria identify information that should be contained in financial statements. The primary financial statements are described in the conceptual framework, along with the items that should be contained in each statement.

LEARNING NOTE

The accounting systems of most organizations report periodically the estimated results of financing, investing, and operating activities. Such **periodic measurement** is needed to ensure the timely reporting of financial information that is needed for effective decision making.

DISCLOSURE AND FAIR REPRESENTATION

OBJECTIVE 4

Identify supplementary information to the financial statements in a corporate annual report.

In addition to establishing acceptable accounting procedures and methods and guidelines for the format and content of financial statements, GAAP require companies to include information in addition to their financial statements in annual reports to stockholders. This information includes management's discussion and analysis of the company's business activities and disclosures about methods used in determining accounting information and details about those activities that are not evident in the financial statements.

Corporate annual reports usually include the following:

- a letter from the president or chief executive officer of the company
- a description of the company's products and business activities
- a summary of selected business data
- a discussion by management of the company's performance
- financial statements
- notes to the financial statements
- a statement of management responsibility for the financial statements
- an audit report

The president's letter and the description of a company's products and business are not part of the financial section of a company's annual report. Management has a fair amount of discretion in what to include in these sections. The president's letter often summarizes the company's financial performance for the year. As long as information contained in the letter is consistent with that reported in the financial section, it is not subject to accounting regulation.

The following paragraphs describe the financial section items contained in an annual report, with the exception of financial statements that were examined in Chapters 4 and 5. Appendix B of this book contains the financial section of General Mills' 2002 annual report. You may wish to refer to the appendix for a better idea of the contents of each item in the financial section.

Summary Business Data

Financial and non-financial data often are included for various periods beyond those covered by the primary financial statements. For example, Exhibit 1 provides a five-year summary reported in Krispy Kreme's annual report.

Krispy Kreme, like Mom's Cookie Company, sells products through stores. The amount the company sells depends on the number of stores selling its products. Some of these stores are stand-alone businesses that specialize in Krispy Kreme's products. Others are small shops that are part of another business. These shops are located in service stations, grocery stores, and similar locations.

The summary data reported in Exhibit 1 is useful for determining trends in Krispy Kreme's business activities. The data indicate a steady growth in sales, income, assets, and stores over the five years. The company has grown substantially over this period in most categories.

Management's Discussion and Analysis

Corporate annual reports should include discussion and analysis of the company's financial performance. This section, known as *management's discussion and analysis (MD&A),* **explains important events and changes in performance during the years presented in the financial statements.**

Typical issues considered in the MD&A include the following:

- a comparison of operating results among the data provided in the company's income statement

Exhibit 1 Summary Business Data from a Corporate Report

	In Thousands, Except Per Share Data and Store Numbers				
YEAR ENDED	Feb. 1 1998	Jan. 31 1999	Jan. 30 2000	Jan. 28 2001	Feb. 3 2002
Statement of Operations Data:					
Total revenues	$158,743	$180,880	$220,243	$300,715	$394,354
Operating expenses	140,207	159,941	190,003	250,690	316,946
General and administrative expenses	9,530	10,897	14,856	20,061	27,562
Depreciation and amortization expenses	3,586	4,278	4,546	6,457	7,959
Provision for restructuring	—	9,466	—	—	—
Income (loss) from operations	5,420	(3,702)	10,838	23,507	41,887
Interest expense (income), net, and other	895	1,577	1,232	(1,698)	(2,408)
Equity loss in joint ventures	—	—	—	706	602
Minority interest	—	—	—	716	1,147
Income (loss) before income taxes	4,525	(5,279)	9,606	23,783	42,546
Provision (benefit) for income taxes	1,811	(2,112)	3,650	9,058	16,168
Net income (loss)	$ 2,714	$ (3,167)	$ 5,956	$ 14,725	$ 26,378
Net income (loss) per share:					
Basic	$ .09	$ (.09)	$ .16	$ .30	.49
Diluted	.09	(.09)	.15	.27	.45
Shares used in calculation of net income (loss) per share:					
Basic	29,136	32,996	37,360	49,184	53,703
Diluted	29,136	32,996	39,280	53,656	58,443
Cash dividends declared per common share	$ .04	$ .04	$ —	$ —	$ —
Operating Data (Unaudited):					
Systemwide sales	$203,439	$240,316	$318,854	$448,129	$621,665
Number of stores at end of period:					
Company	58	61	58	63	75
Franchised	62	70	86	111	143
Systemwide	120	131	144	174	218
Average weekly sales per store:					
Company	$ 42	$ 47	$ 54	$ 69	$ 72
Franchised	23	28	38	43	53
Balance Sheet Data (at end of period):					
Working capital	$ 9,151	$ 8,387	$ 11,452	$ 29,443	$ 49,236
Total assets	81,463	93,312	104,958	171,493	255,376
Long-term debt, including current maturities	20,870	21,020	22,902	—	4,643
Total shareholders' equity	38,265	42,247	47,755	125,679	187,667

Source: Krispy Kreme 2002 annual report.

- liquidity and cash flows as indicated by cash and short-term investments and the statement of cash flows
- major business risks
- financial risks such as foreign currency exchange rates, equity security prices, and interest rate changes on debt securities
- changes in accounting methods used by the company
- subsequent events

Exhibit 2 provides excerpts from the MD&A section of Krispy Kreme's 2002 annual report. The items in this section of the annual report describe the company's performance for the last year compared with previous years. Business risk issues, such as Krispy Kreme's exposure to changes in interest rates, are identified. The section also identifies new accounting standards the company has adopted and the effects of these standards.

Exhibit 2

Management's Discussion and Analysis from a Corporate Report

MANAGEMENT'S DISCUSSION AND ANALYSIS OF FINANCIAL CONDITION AND RESULTS OF OPERATIONS

OVERVIEW

As noted above, we operate on a 52 or 53-week fiscal year. Our operations for fiscal 2002 contained 53 weeks while fiscal 2001 contained 52 weeks.

Systemwide sales for the fiscal year increased 38.7% to $621.7 million compared to $448.1 million in the prior year. The increase was comprised of an increase of 24.6% in Company Store sales, to $266.2 million, and an increase of 51.6% in Franchise Store sales, to $355.5 million. The increase was the result of sales from new stores opened during the fiscal year and an increase in systemwide comparable sales. . . . The total number of stores at the end of the fiscal year was 218. Of those, 52 are Associate franchise stores, 91 are Area Developer franchise stores and 75 are Company stores. Systemwide comparable store sales increased 12.8% in the fiscal year. We believe continued increased brand awareness and growth in off-premises sales contributed significantly to this increase in our systemwide comparable store sales. Adjusting for the number of weeks in fiscal 2002, the increase in systemwide sales was 35.8%.

LIQUIDITY AND CAPITAL RESOURCES

We funded our capital requirements for fiscal 2000, 2001 and 2002 primarily through cash flow generated from operations, as well as proceeds from the initial public offering completed in April 2000 and follow on public offering completed in early February 2001. Over the past three years, we have greatly improved the amount of cash we generate from operations. We believe our cash flow generation ability is becoming a financial strength and will aid in the expansion of our business.

CASH FLOW FROM OPERATIONS

Net cash flow from operations was $8.5 million in fiscal 2000, $32.1 million in fiscal 2001 and $36.2 million in fiscal 2002. Operating cash flow in each year has benefited from an improvement in our net income and was offset by additional investments in working capital, primarily accounts receivable and inventories.

QUANTITATIVE AND QUALITATIVE DISCLOSURE ABOUT MARKET RISKS

We are exposed to market risk from changes in interest rates on our outstanding bank debt. Our revolving line of credit bears interest at either our lender's prime rate minus 110 basis points or a rate equal to LIBOR [London InterBank Offered Rate] plus 100 basis points. We can elect the rate on a monthly basis.

RECENT ACCOUNTING PRONOUNCEMENTS

In July 2001, the Financial Accounting Standards Board (the "FASB") issued SFAS No. 141, "Business Combinations". SFAS No. 141 addresses financial accounting and reporting for business combinations and supersedes APB Opinion No. 16, "Business Combinations", and SFAS No. 38 "Accounting for Preacquisition Contingencies of Purchased Enterprises". All business combinations in the scope of this Statement are to be accounted for using one method, the purchase method. The Company adopted the provisions of this pronouncement for all business combinations subsequent to June 30, 2001. Its adoption did not have a significant impact on the consolidated financial statements.

Notes to the Financial Statements

Notes to the financial statements are important for helping readers interpret the statements. They describe how some of the numbers were computed and provide additional information about items reported in the statements. Exhibit 3 contains example notes

Exhibit 3

Notes to the Financial
Statements from a
Corporate Report

NATURE OF BUSINESS AND SIGNIFICANT ACCOUNTING POLICIES

NATURE OF BUSINESS. Krispy Kreme Doughnuts Inc. and its subsidiaries (the "Company") are engaged principally in the sale of doughnuts and related items through Company-owned stores. The Company also derives revenue from franchise and development fees and the collection of royalties from franchisees. Additionally, the Company sells doughnutmaking equipment and mix and other ingredients and supplies used in operating a doughnut store to Company-owned and franchised stores.

BASIS OF CONSOLIDATION. The consolidated financial statements include the accounts of the Company and its wholly-owned subsidiaries. All significant intercompany accounts and transactions are eliminated in consolidation.

FISCAL YEAR. The Company's fiscal year is based on a fifty-two/fifty-three week year. The fiscal year ends on the Sunday closest to the last day in January. The years ended January 30, 2000 and January 28, 2001 contained 52 weeks. The year ended February 3, 2002 contained 53 weeks.

PROPERTY AND EQUIPMENT. Property and equipment are stated at cost less accumulated depreciation. Major renewals and betterments are charged to the property accounts while replacements, maintenance, and repairs which do not improve or extend the lives of the respective assets are expensed currently. Interest is capitalized on major capital expenditures during the period of construction.

USE OF ESTIMATES IN PREPARATION OF FINANCIAL STATEMENTS. The preparation of financial statements in conformity with generally accepted accounting principles requires management to make estimates and assumptions that affect the reported amounts of assets and liabilities and disclosure of contingent assets and liabilities at the date of the financial statements and the reported amounts of revenues and expenses during the reporting period. Actual results could differ from those estimates.

ADVERTISING COSTS. All costs associated with advertising and promoting products are expensed in the period incurred.

REVENUE RECOGNITION. A summary of the revenue recognition policies for each segment of the Company is as follows:

- Company Store Operations revenue is derived from the sale of doughnuts and related items to on-premises and off-premises customers. Revenue is recognized at the time of sale for on-premises sales and at the time of delivery for off-premises sales.
- Franchise Operations revenue is derived from: (1) development and franchise fees from the opening of new stores; and (2) royalties charged to franchisees based on sales. Development and franchise fees are charged for certain new stores and are deferred until the store is opened. The royalties recognized in each period are based on the sales in that period.

from the 2002 annual report of Krispy Kreme. These notes identify when certain revenues and expenses were recognized and the amounts of certain expenses that were not reported individually in the financial statements. We will examine other notes in future chapters as we examine specific accounting and reporting issues.

Notes to the financial statements provide information about how amounts reported in the financial statements were determined and provide more detailed information about some income statement items. Exhibit 3 contains only a few of these notes. They describe such matters as when revenue is recognized, how the company's fiscal year is defined, and how advertising expenses are determined and reported. Other notes provide similar information about other financial statement items. These notes are intended to assist readers in understanding and interpreting the information reported in the financial statements. They are an important part of the financial statement presentation and should be included when audited financial statements are presented.

The Auditors' Report

The auditors' report is an important item accompanying a company's financial statements. Auditors issue an audit report upon completion of their audit work. **An** *audit* **involves a detailed, systematic investigation of a company's accounting records and procedures for the purpose of determining the reliability of financial reports.** The auditor attempts to verify that the numbers and disclosures made by management in its financial reports are consistent with the company's actual financial position, operating results, and cash flows. Records, operating procedures, contracts, resources, and management policies and decisions are examined to provide evidence of the fairness of financial report information. Auditors determine if control procedures to ensure the integrity of accounting information exist and are being used. They compare the information in financial reports with information from prior years and other sources to confirm the fairness of the reports.

Attestation **occurs when an auditor affirms the fairness of financial statements and other information.** The audit report, or audit opinion, provides public notice of the auditors' belief about the fairness of the accompanying financial information. Exhibit 4 provides the auditors' report from Krispy Kreme's annual report.

Exhibit 4
Independent Auditors' Report

KRISPY KREME DOUGHNUTS, INC.
REPORT OF INDEPENDENT ACCOUNTANTS

To the Board of Directors and Shareholders of Krispy Kreme Doughnuts, Inc.

In our opinion, the accompanying consolidated balance sheets and the related consolidated statements of operations, of shareholders' equity and of cash flows present fairly, in all material respects, the financial position of Krispy Kreme Doughnuts, Inc. and its subsidiaries (the Company) at January 28, 2001 and February 3, 2002, and the results of their operations and their cash flows for each of the three years in the period ended February 3, 2002, in conformity with accounting principles generally accepted in the United States of America. These financial statements are the responsibility of the Company's management; our responsibility is to express an opinion on these financial statements based on our audits. We conducted our audits of these statements in accordance with auditing standards generally accepted in the United States of America, which require that we plan and perform the audit to obtain reasonable assurance about whether the financial statements are free of material misstatement. An audit includes examining, on a test basis, evidence supporting the amounts and disclosures in the financial statements, assessing the accounting principles used and significant estimates made by management, and evaluating the overall financial statement presentation. We believe that our audits provide a reasonable basis for the opinion expressed above.

PricewaterhouseCoopers LLP

Greensboro, North Carolina
March 8, 2002, except Note 21 for
which the date is March 27, 2002

The auditors' report is addressed to the board of directors and shareholders of the company. Normally, an audit is performed on behalf of the shareholders and other external parties. Audits may be requested for special purposes also—for example, to secure a bank loan or as part of merger negotiations. In such a case, the auditors' report would be addressed to the intended users.

The audit report states the auditor's opinion. Most audit reports provide an **unqualified opinion**. Such an opinion states that the auditor believes that the financial statements fairly present the company's actual economic events for the period covered by the audited statements. Fair presentation means that the financial statements are prepared in conformity with GAAP and are free from material omissions and misstatements. An unqualified opinion means that the auditor has not stated any qualifying (limiting) conditions or exceptions in the opinion. If the financial statements do not fully conform to GAAP or if serious concerns exist as to the ability of a company to continue as a going concern, the auditor lists qualifications to the opinion that the reader should consider in interpreting the financial information.

The auditors' report identifies the statements and fiscal periods covered by the audit. A typical audit will cover all the primary financial statements: income statement, balance sheet, and statement of cash flows. The audit normally covers the most recent three years of operations. For most large corporations, the audited financial statements are the consolidated statements of the parent and its subsidiaries.

The auditors' report describes the responsibilities of auditors and management. Management is responsible for preparing the statements. Auditors are responsible for competently using the technology available to them to confirm (or disconfirm) the assertions of management made in its financial statements and related disclosures.

The report summarizes the audit process. *Generally accepted auditing standards (GAAS)* **include procedures used in conducting an audit to help auditors form an opinion about the fairness of the audited statements.** GAAS are developed in the United States by the Auditing Standards Board (ASB). The ASB is a division of the American Institute of Certified Public Accountants (AICPA). Auditing standards are published and updated periodically by the AICPA. Failure to conform to GAAS in an independent audit is a major violation of a CPA's responsibilities.

From evidence collected from applying GAAS, auditors assert that the financial statements are free of material misstatement. Materiality is a criterion for establishing the importance of a potential misstatement in audited financial statements. Financial statements contain estimates and allocations that depend on management judgment. In addition to finding errors in accounting records, auditors may disagree with managers about their estimates and allocations. Unless these errors and disagreements are material (important) to the overall amounts reported on the financial statements, however, auditors are not required to take action on these issues.

Auditors examine accounting records on a "test basis." Auditors do not examine 100% of a company's transactions. Instead, they use sampling techniques to select representative transactions. By verifying these transactions, auditors form an opinion about the financial statements as a whole. Sampling is necessary because the cost of auditing all of a company's records would be prohibitive.

LEARNING NOTE

Unless information is found that raises doubts about a company's ability to continue operating in the future, it is assumed to be a *going concern*. This means the company is **an organization with an indefinite life that is sufficiently long that, over time, all currently incomplete transactions will be completed.**

The content of the auditors' report is standard for most corporations. Some audit firms issue an audit report that contains several paragraphs. The paragraphs contain the same type of information as that included in the paragraph in Exhibit 4.

Auditors' reports must be signed by the public accounting firm that performed the audit, thus indicating its responsibility. The date of the auditors' report is the date on which all audit work was completed for the periods covered by the report. The auditor is responsible for disclosing any material information that might affect a decision maker's interpretation of the financial statements through the date of the audit report.

LEARNING NOTE

Auditors' reports for foreign corporations differ from those for U.S. corporations. Different countries establish their own auditing and accounting standards. The format of the auditors' report depends on the auditing standards of the country in which a company has its principal operations.

INTERNATIONAL

The auditor certifies that financial statements present fairly a company's business activities. The audit is not a guarantee that a company will be successful. If a company is not performing well, the financial statements should reveal the company's problems. It is up to stockholders to interpret the statements and assess the company's performance. Good information should lead to informed decisions about whether to invest in a company or not. Good information does not mean a company is doing well or that investors are likely to earn high returns. The audit certifies the quality of financial information, not the quality of management or the ability of management to make good business decisions.

Report of Management Responsibilities

In addition to the auditors' report, the annual report usually contains a statement of management responsibilities. Exhibit 5 contains a typical statement of management responsibilities.

Management is responsible for preparing financial statements and related information that fairly reports the business activities of a corporation. This information should be prepared in conformity with GAAP. Management is also responsible for developing and implementing a system of internal controls. *Internal controls* **are procedures a company uses to protect its assets and ensure the accuracy of its accounting information.** The next section of this chapter describes internal controls in more detail.

Exhibit 5

Report of Management Responsibilities

The management of Mom's Cookie Company is responsible for the preparation and integrity of the financial statements included in this Annual Report to Shareholders. The financial statements have been prepared in conformity with accounting principles generally accepted in the United States of America and include amounts based on management's best judgment where necessary. Financial information included elsewhere in this Annual Report is consistent with these financial statements.

Management maintains a system of internal controls and procedures designed to provide reasonable assurance that transactions are executed in accordance with proper authorization, that transactions are properly recorded in the Company's records, that assets are safeguarded and that accountability for assets is maintained. The concept of reasonable assurance is based on the recognition that the cost of maintaining our system of internal accounting controls should not exceed benefits expected to be derived from the system. Internal controls and procedures are periodically reviewed and revised, when appropriate, due to changing circumstances and requirements.

Independent auditors are appointed by the Company's Board of Directors and ratified by the Company's shareholders to audit the financial statements in accordance with auditing standards generally accepted in the United States of America and to independently assess the fair presentation of the Company's financial position, results of operations and cash flows. Their report appears in this Annual Report.

The Audit Committee, all of whose members are outside directors, is responsible for monitoring the Company's accounting and reporting practices. The Audit Committee meets periodically with management and the independent auditors to ensure that each is properly discharging its responsibilities. The independent auditors have full and free access to the Committee without the presence of management to discuss the results of their audits, the adequacy of internal accounting controls and the quality of financial reporting.

A corporation's board of directors should establish an audit committee. The committee should be made up of members of the board who are not part of the corporation's management. The audit committee is responsible for receiving information from the independent auditors and from those in the corporation who implement and evaluate internal controls. Accounting and auditing problems should be reported to the audit committee. The committee can discuss problems with management and can take steps to correct the problems if necessary.

2 SELF-STUDY PROBLEM

Listed below are statements about auditing:

A. An independent audit guarantees the accuracy of financial information.
B. An auditor does not have to examine all of an audited company's transactions to certify the reliability of the company's financial statements.
C. An auditor must follow generally accepted auditing standards in performing an audit.
D. An auditor is responsible only for the period covered by the financial statements audited when preparing an audit report.

Required Identify each statement as true or false and explain your reasoning.

INTERNAL CONTROLS

OBJECTIVE 5

Describe the purpose of internal controls and types of controls that should be evident in business organizations.

An essential requirement of any accounting system is that it provide accurate data. Incorrect data are not useful and can lead to poor decisions. Consequently, controls are important in a company to help ensure that data are accurate. Incorrect data can result from errors in recording data or from events that affect a company's assets. For example, if Mom's Cookie Company purchased inventory at a cost of $1,200, it would be incorrect to record the amount owed the supplier as $1,150. It is correct to record an increase in Accounts Payable and Merchandise Inventory of $1,200. However, if the merchandise is stolen from the company, the accounting data are in error because they are not consistent with the amount of the asset actually available to the company. Accordingly, a company uses a system of internal controls both to protect assets and to ensure accuracy of accounting information.

Management Philosophy

A strong system of internal controls begins with a management philosophy that encourages appropriate security and behavior in a company. If top management takes a lax attitude about these matters, it is unlikely that it will develop and enforce an effective system. Accordingly, top management should develop policies and ensure that these are communicated throughout the company. It should also ensure that procedures are developed to monitor and enforce control policies. If Maria and Stan want their company's employees to act with integrity, they must establish a tone of ethical conduct by acting with integrity themselves and by creating and enforcing policies and procedures that require ethical behavior in conducting business activities.

Part of management philosophy should involve developing rewards and incentives that encourage employees to take appropriate actions. For example, a bonus system that places too much emphasis on sales quotas could encourage employees to create false sales, to predate sales orders, and to make credit sales to risky customers. A good system of rewards will encourage employees to focus on the value and ongoing success of a company.

Business Ethics

Management should create a code of ethics and other documents that establish company policy and inform employees of acceptable and expected behavior. These policies

http://ingram.
swlearning.com

**Learn more about the
Foreign Corrupt Prac-
tices Act.**

should consider the relationship between a company and its customers, employees, suppliers, stockholders, and community. As an example, Exhibit 6 identifies the contents of **United Technologies Corporation's** Code of Ethics.

A major purpose of internal controls is to ensure compliance with laws and regulations. If a company fails to comply with laws, it can be subject to civil and criminal penalties resulting in significant losses. Antitrust laws prohibit collaboration among competitor companies that leads to unfair pricing or trade practices. Companies that sell similar products in the same markets cannot collude to set prices or limit competition. The Foreign Corrupt Practices Act prohibits companies from offering or accepting bribes or other payments to obtain business or influence the behavior of customers or government authorities.

Ethical behavior involves treating individuals and companies fairly and providing full disclosure of information that might affect their decisions. Moral hazard is a potential problem in dealing with customers, suppliers, employees, and others who interact with a company. The company often has access to information that is not available to external stakeholders. Full disclosure is often a remedy for moral hazard. In the long run, fair treatment and disclosure will create a reputation for a company that will lead to financial benefits.

Exhibit 6

Ethical Issues
Associated with
Corporate Conduct

Relationships between the Company and:	Important Issues:
Customers	• Quality and safety of products • Honesty in dealings • Avoid conflicts of interest • Protection of confidential information • Comply with Foreign Corrupt Practices Act
Employees	• Equal opportunity in hiring, compensation, and treatment • Privacy of information about employees • Treatment with dignity and respect • Provide a safe and healthy work environment • Provide opportunity for development
Suppliers	• Fair competition
Stockholders	• Provide superior returns • Protect and improve investment value • Protect assets • Accurate accounting information and disclosure of business activities
Competitors	• Fairness • Comply with antitrust laws
Communities	• Responsible corporate citizenship • Abide by laws • Participate in civic affairs • Support through corporate philanthropy • Comply with laws concerning political donations • Comply with export laws • Protect environment

Source: www.utc.com/profile/ethics.

Computer System Controls

Many internal controls should be built into computer information systems. These **controls protect a company's information resources from unauthorized access, improper use, and destruction.** System controls determine who can gain access to various parts of a company's database. Users should have **appropriate identification and passwords** to log onto networks or to use network resources. Users typically are assigned to groups based on the type of work they perform. For example, data entry personnel in the sales division are permitted access to those files in the database that need to be updated when customers submit orders. They should not have access to other data in the system that they do not need in the course of their work.

System controls also manage databases to prevent several users from trying to update particular records at the same time. While one user is accessing a record or file, other users are locked out so that conflicting or incomplete changes cannot be made.

Other controls **check data for errors** to make sure that data entered in a system are reasonable and appropriate. For example, a system may refuse to prepare a check for an amount larger than $1,000. This control prevents a clerk from accidentally writing large checks by mistyping data or omitting a decimal. **Automatic numbering** should be used to identify transactions and source documents such as sales orders, invoices, and purchase orders. Each transaction or document is assigned a number that follows a preset sequence. Consequently, each item can be tracked and missing items can be identified. Using automatic numbering makes it more difficult for employees to create fictitious transactions or falsify data by recording transactions and then deleting them from the system. Missing numbers are easily identified, and those responsible for deleting the numbered items can be held responsible.

Many other controls can be built into computer systems. Examples include the use of software and hardware to make it difficult for unauthorized users to break into computer networks and databases. The software and hardware also can monitor systems to detect attempts to gain unauthorized access.

Duplicate copies of databases often are maintained so that if one database system fails, the other is available for use. **Backup systems and data** are necessary to prevent data from being lost if database system fails and to permit a company to continue to operate even if it has computer problems. Databases are backed up on a regular basis. Data are copied to tape or other permanent storage devices so they can be retrieved in case of a major problem with the active database. These backup data are stored in locations away from where the working database is maintained.

Complete computer systems must be protected. Many companies maintain centralized computer information system facilities. These facilities must be protected from destruction by natural disasters (fire, flood, earthquake) and from those who might attempt to destroy a company's systems (terrorists, disgruntled employees, competitors). An important control is a **disaster recovery plan** that a company can rely on to get its computer systems back into working order in case of a major disaster. Such a plan usually requires access to facilities, hardware, and software at locations other than those normally used.

Human Resources Controls

Many internal controls focus on a company's human resources. Important controls involve **hiring qualified employees** who have the appropriate skills for a particular job. **Background checks** can identify employees who have a history of improper behavior. A **good training program** can ensure that employees develop and maintain the skills needed for their jobs.

An important control involves **segregation of duties** so that an employee does not have access to resources and information that would make it easy for the employee to misuse those resources. For example, an employee should not have access both to a resource and to the accounting for that resource. If an employee has control over merchandise, supplies, or cash, that employee should not have control over records showing the amount of the resources received or transferred. Computer programmers and systems developers should not have access to actual operations of computer systems. Developers create the systems and can use them to create improper transactions that can transfer cash or other resources to improper persons. Developers can also destroy systems by creating programs to erase data or corrupt program logic. Disgruntled employees can be a major risk to an organization, especially if they understand and have access to a company's computer system.

Employees should understand their responsibilities and authority. They should know what they are permitted to do in their jobs and what they are not permitted to do. They should clearly understand lines of authority in a company. **Employees should be supervised** and inappropriate behavior should be reported and addressed.

Physical Controls

Safeguarding assets often involves controlling physical access. Merchandise and materials can be secured in warehouses or display cases. Merchandise can be tagged electronically to make shoplifting or theft difficult. Surveillance equipment can monitor important resources. Cash registers, vaults, and safety deposit boxes secure financial resources.

Conclusion

A strong system of internal controls is essential for protecting any information system. Though not all controls relate directly to how information is processed, the integrity of accounting information depends on controls that protect data and the systems used to process those data. An internal control system is an important part of an accounting information system. Without internal controls, users could not rely on accounting information as an accurate description of a company's economic activities.

THE RESPONSIBILITIES OF ACCOUNTANTS

Throughout this chapter we have considered various regulatory functions associated with accounting. Accountants and the accounting profession have primary responsibility for these functions. Accountants work to prepare **financial information** contained in companies' annual reports. They **manage the information systems** used to record and report this information. They help other managers **interpret information** reported by the accounting system and make sure the information is reliable and conforms with GAAP and legal requirements.

Accountants serve on organizations like the FASB and SEC that **establish and monitor accounting standards**. They research accounting issues, prepare standards, and research company financial reporting practices. Independent CPAs **audit business financial reports** to ensure that they fairly present the companies' business activities. The audit is an important tool in maintaining strong capital markets. If managers fail in their responsibilities to report fairly to external users, independent audits are a major line of defense to prevent misleading information from reaching investors. Consequently, auditors are held to a high standard of professional responsibility and integrity. Audit failure is a major source of concern for the SEC and society in general. CPAs and the audit firms in which they work are required to maintain current professional knowledge and are reviewed on a regular basis to make sure their practices are consistent with current standards.

Case in Point

http://ingram.
swlearning.com

Learn more about the largest public accounting firms.

The Consequences of Audit Failure

Concerns about Enron Corporation's accounting practices led to close scrutiny of the company's audit firm, Arthur Andersen. Congressional hearings raised concerns that the auditor failed to protect the public interest and was involved in business activities with Enron that reduced the audit firm's independence. The Justice Department indicted Andersen for obstruction of justice because its employees destroyed documents that the Justice Department believed were important for its investigation of Enron's and Andersen's activities. In addition, Andersen was sued for billions of dollars by Enron stockholders and creditors. Because of these events, many of Andersen's other audit clients replaced the firm as their independent auditors. Andersen was forced to lay off many of its employees, and many others resigned to take positions with other audit firms or companies.

Prior to these events, Andersen was one of the "Big Five" accounting firms, along with Deloitte & Touche, Ernst & Young, KPMG, and PricewaterhouseCoopers. The events associated with Enron removed Andersen from the ranks of the "Big Five" and seriously jeopardized its ability to continue as an audit firm.

In addition to working as external auditors, accountants also work as **internal auditors**. Internal auditors work for businesses and are responsible for developing and monitoring internal control systems and for auditing a company's divisions for compliance with accounting rules, company policies, and legal requirements. They also may evaluate the performance of a division or company to improve efficiency and effectiveness.

3 SELF-STUDY PROBLEM

Deborah Stinger works in the systems development department of a major company. She helped develop the company's computerized accounting system. Occasionally, she fills in for one of the operators in the accounts payable department. This operator is responsible for processing checks to suppliers for purchases made by the company. While filling in, Deborah created an account of a fictitious company, just to see if the system could be tricked into writing checks for nonexistent purchases. She added data to the company's file and entered some phony purchases. The computer wrote the checks, and they were mailed to a post office box Deborah opened. Over the last few years, Deborah has written over $80,000 in checks to her fictitious company.

Required Identify some internal control deficiencies in the accounting system that have allowed Deborah to embezzle money from her company.

REVIEW

SUMMARY of IMPORTANT CONCEPTS

1. Accounting regulations are important to protect the interests of external users of accounting information who have limited access to business information. GAAP help ensure that reliable information is available to control moral hazard on the part of corporate managers.

2. Several events and organizations are important for the development of accounting regulations in the United States.
   a. The first regulations were established by the New York Stock Exchange.
   b. The Securities Act of 1933 and the Securities and Exchange Act of 1934 are major laws that affect accounting and financial reporting in the United States.

3. Several organizations play a role in setting and enforcing accounting standards.
   a. The SEC has the authority to establish and enforce accounting standards in the United States.
   b. The FASB is a private-sector organization that is largely responsible for setting accounting standards in the United States.
   c. The GASB is a private-sector organization that establishes accounting standards for state and local governments in the United States.
   d. The IASB is a private-sector organization that helps develop global accounting standards.

4. Accounting standards are set through a process of public discussion that permits those affected by standards to have input into the standard-setting process.

5. The FASB's conceptual framework provides guidance for the development of financial accounting standards for business organizations.

6. Annual reports contain information supplemental to financial statements that is important for understanding and interpreting those statements.
   a. Supplemental financial disclosures provide information about business activities and for periods other than those covered by the primary financial statements.
   b. Notes to the financial statements provide additional information about business activities and explain methods used in preparing financial statements.
   c. The auditors' report describes the audit and expresses an opinion as to whether the financial statements are a fair presentation of a company's business activities in conformity with GAAP.
   d. The report of management's responsibilities identifies responsibilities of managers for financial statements and internal controls and describes a company's audit committee.

7. Internal controls are designed to protect a company's assets and ensure the reliability of its accounting information.
   a. Management is responsible for establishing an environment of integrity in which internal controls are important.
   b. Management should establish a code of ethics and inform employees of expected and appropriate behavior.
   c. Computer controls are important for protecting a company's data and computer systems.
   d. Human resource controls are designed to control the behavior of employees and managers and to provide expectations about appropriate behavior.
   e. Physical controls are designed to protect assets and to limit access to important resources.

8. Accountants and the accounting profession are responsible for development and enforcement of accounting regulations.

DEFINE

TERMS and CONCEPTS DEFINED in this CHAPTER

attestation (F235)
audit (F235)
discussion memorandum (F230)
exposure draft (F230)
FASB conceptual framework (F230)
Financial Accounting Standards Board (FASB) (F229)
General Accounting Office (GAO) (F229)
generally accepted auditing standards (GAAS) (F236)
going concern (F236)
Governmental Accounting Standards Board (GASB) (F229)

internal controls (F237)
International Accounting Standards Board (IASB) (F229)
management's discussion and analysis (MD&A) (F231)
Securities Act of 1933 (F226)
Securities and Exchange Commission (SEC) (F226)
Securities Exchange Act of 1934 (F226)
Statements of Financial Accounting Standards (F230)

SELF-STUDY PROBLEM SOLUTIONS

SSP6-1 GAAP are guidelines for the preparation of financial statements and other accounting information. They are important because they provide standards for the content and format of financial reports. How earnings and other accounting information are measured is important for determining the reliability and usefulness of the information. If each company chose its own accounting rules, it could select those rules that made the company appear successful.

Moral hazard results when a person, like Abe, has incentives to behave in ways that can be harmful to others, such as creditors, who have a financial stake in the person's activities. To get a loan, Abe has an incentive to make his company appear financially strong. If he fails to repay the loan, the bank will lose money. Reliable financial information is a means of controlling moral hazard so that the bank can make a decision based on an accurate view of the company's business activities. GAAP help ensure that financial information is reliable.

SSP6-2 A. False. An independent audit provides reasonable assurance about the reliability of audited financial information. Auditors rely on information provided by management and on evidence collected from a sample of a company's transactions.

B. True. The cost of examining all of a company's transactions is usually too high. Auditors examine a representative sample of transactions.

C. True. GAAS are procedures that auditors must follow in performing an audit to help ensure the audit has been performed properly.

D. False. The auditor is responsible for making sure a company notifies readers of its financial reports of any events occurring between the end of the period covered by the financial statements and the date of the audit report that would have a material affect on interpretation of the financial statements.

SSP6-3 Internal control deficiencies include access to the accounting system by an employee who should not have access. Limitations on physical access, passwords, and employee identification numbers should have prevented Deborah from gaining access to the system. Deborah should not have authority to use the system. Another deficiency was the failure to separate systems development from computer operations personnel. Deborah was able to embezzle funds because she understood the computer programs that created accounting files. Computer operators normally do not have sufficient knowledge of the system to manipulate it in this manner. An additional deficiency was the failure of the system to verify transactions or compare amounts from one part of the system to another. For example, use of sequentially numbered purchase orders should make it difficult for an employee to create fictitious data without the system identifying a problem.

Thinking Beyond the Question

How do we ensure that reports to external users fairly present business activities?

Full and fair reporting involves reliable financial statements that accurately report a company's business activities. Information to describe, interpret, and extend that information also is important. Audits and internal controls also help ensure full and fair reporting. To what extent should full and fair reporting protect external users from poor management decisions? Does full and fair reporting guarantee that stakeholders will not suffer losses from their contractual relations with a business? Why or why not?

QUESTIONS

Q6-1
Obj. 1
Other than business managers, who relies on financial reports to make decisions?

Q6-2
Obj. 1
Compliance with regulations is costly. Why are public companies required to comply with GAAP?

Q6-3
Obj. 2
Why does the FASB issue a discussion memorandum prior to releasing an exposure draft of a new pronouncement?

Q6-4
Obj. 2
The SEC is authorized by law to establish and enforce accounting standards in the United States. Why are most accounting standards used by businesses issued by the FASB?

Q6-5
Obj. 3
What are the elements of financial statements, according to the FASB's conceptual framework? Where would an investor find these elements?

Q6-6
Obj. 3
One of the major components of the FASB conceptual framework is the objectives of financial reporting. What are the objectives of financial reporting?

Q6-7
Obj. 4
A friend has been reviewing the annual report of a firm in which he has invested. He says, "I'm worried because the auditors gave an unqualified opinion on the financial statements. You'd think a big company like this would have auditors that were qualified." Clear up your friend's misunderstanding.

Q6-8
Obj. 4
What is the purpose of notes to financial statements? If a firm does a good job presenting its financial statements, why are notes necessary?

Q6-9
Obj. 4
What is an audit and why is it important?

Q6-10
Obj. 5
Why is it necessary for managers and other decision makers to understand how accounting information is developed and reported? Shouldn't it just be management's job to manage and the accountant's job to account? Explain.

Q6-11
Obj. 5
What are the two primary purposes of internal controls?

Q6-12
Obj. 5
Explain why internal controls are important to a computerized management information system and identify several such controls that are commonly used.

Q6-13
Obj. 5
Why is management philosophy an important internal control issue?

Q6-14
Obj. 5
Identify some human resource controls that can be used in a company and explain why they are important.

Q6-15
Obj. 5
Identify some physical controls that can be used in a company and explain why they are important.

EXERCISES

If your instructor is using Personal Trainer in this course, you may complete online the assignments identified by ᵖ⁄ₜ.

E6-1
Objs. 1–5
Write a short definition for each of the terms listed in the *Terms and Concepts Defined in this Chapter* section.

E6-2
Obj. 1
Three major developments in the history of accounting involved the development of the New York Stock Exchange, the 16th Amendment to the U.S. Constitution, and the events subsequent to the stock market crash of 1929. Explain briefly the significance of each of these events for contemporary accounting.

E6-3
Obj. 1

Identify the major reporting requirements associated with each of the following:

    a. Securities Act of 1933
    b. Securities and Exchange Act of 1934
    c. 10-K report
    d. 10-Q report

E6-4
Obj. 2
P/T

Identify each of the following:

    a. The private sector organization currently responsible for setting financial accounting standards in the United States.
    b. The private sector organization currently responsible for setting state and local governmental accounting standards in the United States.
    c. The organization that exists to influence the development of international accounting standards.
    d. The federal agency that oversees accounting at the federal government.
    e. The organization responsible for the enforcement of financial accounting standards in the United States.

E6-5
Obj. 2

How would you react to the following statement? "Accounting standards impose costs on corporations and their managers to protect the interests of investors."

E6-6
Obj. 2

What is meant by the term "generally accepted accounting principles?" What is the significance of the phrase "generally accepted?"

E6-7
Obj. 3

What is the purpose of the qualitative characteristics of financial reports? What are the primary qualitative characteristics as defined by the FASB?

E6-8
Obj. 3

What is the FASB's conceptual framework?

E6-9
Obj. 4

Identify each of the sections of an auditors' report and explain its purpose.

E6-10
Obj. 4

Corporate annual reports include a discussion and analysis of the company's financial performance. What is the purpose of this discussion?

E6-11
Obj. 4

General Mills Corporation had sales of almost $8 billion in fiscal year 2002 from Betty Crocker, Pillsbury, Wheaties, Cheerios, Pop Secret popcorn, and other products. The company reported total assets of more than $16.5 billion. Inspect the General Mills' balance sheet found in Appendix B at the back of this book. (a) Does it seem strange to you that such a big company is able to report all of its assets using only nine different accounts? How is this possible? (b) Why is this done? (c) Would this level of detail meet the needs of the general manager of the Pillsbury division, or the managers in other divisions of the company? Discuss.

E6-12
Obj. 4

Quick Transport Company owns a large fleet of trucks that move freight throughout the country. Some of these trucks cost hundreds of thousands of dollars and are operated for 15 years or more before being replaced. The company issues long-term debt to pay for most of its equipment. The company's fiscal year ends on June 30. For each fiscal year, the company prepares financial reports that include estimates of its results of operations for the year. How do the operations of Quick illustrate the periodic measurement and going concern principles of accounting?

E6-13
Obj. 4

Bill's grandparents have been buying shares of stock for his college education fund since the day he was born. Yesterday, Bill received the annual report of Thompson Consolidated Shoulderpads, Inc., and is telling you about it. Bill says:

> "I feel really good about the company because its financial statements were prepared and audited by a well-known national accounting firm. Not only that, but the firm received an unqualified audit report. This means that the auditor checked out all the company's transactions and that the company is healthy. Since the auditors think the company is doing well, I think I'll invest some of my summer job savings in it."

How would you respond to your friend? Do you believe he has a good understanding of what information is conveyed by an auditors' report? Discuss.

E6-14
Obj. 5

What is the role of an accountant who works for a business organization?

E6-15
Obj. 5

P/T

Selma Fromm is a recent graduate in accounting. She has taken a position with Hand Writer Company. The company has three divisions that manufacture three products: pencils, pens, and colored markers. Financial information for the most recent fiscal period for each division includes the following:

	Pencils	Pens	Markers
Division revenues	$200,000	$ 300,000	$100,000
Division expenses	140,000	160,000	60,000
Division assets	600,000	1,000,000	200,000

One of Selma's regular duties is to prepare an analysis of the performance of each division. Prepare an analysis of division performance from the information provided. Which of the divisions appears to be most profitable? Is this responsibility typical of the tasks often performed by accountants who work for business organizations? Explain.

E6-16
Obj. 5

What is the purpose of internal auditing? Why is it important to an organization?

E6-17
Obj. 5

List and briefly describe the primary internal control procedures discussed in the chapter.

E6-18
Obj. 5

What is the role of an independent CPA?

E6-19
Obj. 5

Mag's Pie Shop is a rapidly growing baker and distributor of specialty pies for festive occasions. Mag's CPA adviser keeps recommending that Mag install better internal controls over the business. Specifically, the CPA recommends that Mag separate the company's record-keeping function from the physical control of cash and other assets. The CPA also recommends that Mag use only preprinted and prenumbered forms for all business transactions.

a. What is the purpose of internal controls? Be specific.
b. For each internal control suggested by the CPA, give one example of an unsatisfactory situation or event that the control would prevent.

E6-20
Obj. 5

Ima Crook is a sales clerk for Free Cash Company. Ima runs a cash register. Each day she obtains $200 from a supervisor and places the money in the cash register to make change. Customers bring goods to the sales counter, where Ima takes their money and writes out a sales slip using a form provided for this purpose. If requested by the customer, she writes out a separate slip for the customer. Ima works from 9 A.M. to 5 P.M. except for breaks and lunch when she is replaced by a coworker who runs the cash register for her. At 5 P.M. Ima takes all the cash from her cash register and puts it in an envelope along with the sales receipts and hands the envelope to a supervisor. Ima just bought a new $50,000 car and paid cash. What internal control problems exist in this situation? What can be done to solve the problems?

PROBLEMS

If your instructor is using Personal Trainer in the course you may complete online the assignments identified by P/T.

P6-1
Obj. 1

The Importance of Financial Accounting Standards

Accounting and financial reporting is highly regulated in the United States. Standards specify the types of information to be reported and how accounting numbers are to be calculated. Listed below are groups who benefit from these standards.

A. managers
B. stockholders
C. creditors
D. governmental authorities
E. employees

Required Explain why financial accounting standards are important to each of these groups.

P6-2   **The Role of Accounting Regulation**

Obj. 1

On Wednesday, July 10, 2002, the *Wall Street Journal* reported the following headlines:

> *Securities Threat*[1]
> *Bush Crackdown on Business Fraud Signals New Era*
> *Stream of Corporate Scandals Causes Bipartisan Outrage; Return of Big Government?*
> *Fiery Rhetoric on Wall Street*

President Bush's tongue-lashing of big business marks a swing of the American political pendulum away from a quarter-century of bipartisan deference to capitalists. "We will use the full weight of the law to expose and root out corruption."

"Book-cooking" has eroded "the trust and the confidence that is absolutely vital to the function of our capital markets," Rep. Patrick Toomey, a Republican from Pennsylvania, said.

Required   Discuss the role of accounting regulation. Why is trust vital to the function of our capital markets?

P6-3   **Setting Accounting Standards**

Obj. 2

Accounting standards are set in the United States in the private sector. Public hearings and written documents provide feedback during development of the standards. Opportunity is provided to those affected by standards to contribute information to standard-setting organizations such as the FASB.

Required   List the major steps in the standard-setting process. Explain the purpose of each of the primary documents that results from the process.

P6-4   **Obtaining the Most Recent Information about FASB Activities**

Obj. 2

Visit the FASB's website at http://www.fasb.org and prepare a report that summarizes the various types of information available on the site.

P6-5   **Obtaining the Most Recent Information about IASB Activities**

Obj. 2

Visit the International Accounting Standards Board's website at http://www.iasb.org.uk and prepare a report that summarizes the various types of information available on the site. Are there similarities between the processes of developing standards used by the IASB and the FASB? Explain.

P6-6   **The Purpose of the Conceptual Framework**

Obj. 3

The Financial Accounting Standards Board developed a conceptual framework to provide guidance in the development of financial accounting standards.

Required   Identify the primary components of the conceptual framework for business organizations and explain the purpose of each component.

P6-7   **The Conceptual Framework—Qualitative Characteristics**

Obj. 3

Draw a diagram that describes the relationships among the qualitative characteristics as defined in the FASB conceptual framework. Explain your diagram.

P6-8   **Ethical Issues in Auditing**

Objs. 3, 4

Larry Clint is the president of Hometown Bank. The bank has several thousand depositors and makes loans to many local businesses and homeowners. Blanche Granite is a partner with a CPA firm hired to audit Hometown Bank. The financial statements the bank proposes to issue for the 2004 fiscal year include the following information.

http://ingram.
swlearning.com
....
Access the FASB and IASB sites through the text's Website.

---

[1]   *The Wall Street Journal*, Wednesday, July 10, 2002, Eastern Edition, p. A1.

Loans receivable	$4,000,000
Total assets	5,000,000
Net income	1,000,000

During the audit, Blanche discovers that many of the loans were made for real estate development. Because of economic problems in the region, much of this real estate remains unsold or vacant. The current market value of the property is considerably less than its cost. Several of the developers are experiencing financial problems, and it appears unlikely that the bank will recover its loans if they default. Blanche described this problem to Larry and proposed a write-down of the receivables to $2,800,000. The $1,200,000 write-down would be written off against earnings for 2004.

Larry is extremely upset by the proposal. He notes the write-off would result in a reported loss for the bank for 2004. Also, the bank would be in jeopardy of falling below the equity requirements imposed by the bank regulatory board to which the bank is accountable. He fears the board would impose major constraints on the bank's operations. Also, he fears depositors would lose confidence in the bank and withdraw their money, further compounding the bank's financial problems. He cites several economic forecasts indicating an impending improvement in the region's economy. Further, he notes the bank's demise would be a major economic blow to the local economy and could precipitate the bankruptcy of some of the bank's major customers.

Blanche acknowledges that Larry is correct in his perceptions of the possible outcomes of the write-off. Larry proposes an alternative to Blanche. The bank will write down the receivables by $300,000 for 2004. The remaining losses will be recognized over the next three years, assuming property values have not improved. Larry also tells Blanche that if she is unwilling to accept his proposal, he will fire her firm and hire new auditors. The bank has been a long-time client of Blanche's firm and is one of its major revenue producers. Blanche also recognizes Larry's proposal is not consistent with accounting principles.

Required What are the ethical problems Blanche faces? What action would you recommend she take?

P6-9 Evaluating the Quality of Financial Reports

Obj. 4

The following statements describe the annual report issued by Short Sheet Company for the fiscal year ended December 31, 2004.

A. The report was issued on October 1, 2005.
B. The balance sheet included management's estimates of the increased value of certain fixed assets during 2004.
C. Procedures used to calculate revenues and expenses were different for 2004 than for 2003 and earlier years.
D. Short's financial statements were audited by an accounting firm owned by the president's brother.
E. Some of the company's major liabilities were not included in the annual report.

Required For each statement, identify the qualitative characteristic that has been compromised.

P6-10 Understanding the Auditors' Report

Obj. 4

A standard auditors' report contains reference to each of the following:

A. Responsibility
B. Generally accepted auditing standards
C. Material misstatement and material respects
D. A test basis
E. Present fairly . . . in conformity with generally accepted accounting principles

Required Explain why each of these terms is important for understanding the auditors' report and the audit process.

P6-11 Distinguishing Among Types of Accounts

Obj. 4

Bonner Systems uses the following accounts when preparing its financial reports.

	Type of Account					Financial Statement	
	Asset	Liability	Equity	Revenue	Expense	Income Statement	Balance Sheet
1. Wages Payable							
2. Accounts Receivable							
3. Retained Earnings							
4. Buildings							
5. Supplies Used							
6. Inventory							
7. Sales (for cash)							
8. Accumulated Depreciation							
9. Loan from Bank							
10. Land							
11. Owners' Investment							
12. Supplies							
13. Sales (on credit)							
14. Bonds Payable							
15. Unearned Revenue							
16. Wages Earned by Employees							
17. Utilities Consumed							

Required

A. Place a mark in the appropriate column to indicate the type of account.
B. Place a mark in the appropriate column to indicate on which financial statement that account is reported.

P6-12 Interpreting Information Reported on Financial Statements

Obj. 4

The two most recent monthly balance sheets of Strauss Instrument Company are shown below. Also shown is the most recent monthly income statement.

Balance Sheet	May 31	June 30		May 31	June 30
Assets:			Liabilities and Owners' Equity:		
Cash	$ 3,200	$ 1,375	Accounts payable	$ 2,300	$ 2,300
Accounts receivable	5,700	5,900	Wages payable	1,900	1,400
Equipment	26,300	26,300	Notes payable	48,600	40,100
Building	115,000	115,000	Owners' investment	43,000	47,000
Accumulated depreciation	(28,000)	(28,500)	Retained earnings	26,400	29,275
Total	$122,200	$120,075		$122,200	$120,075

Income Statement for June

Service revenues	$ 7,300
Rent expense	(1,300)
Wages expense	(1,900)
Supplies expense	(400)
Depreciation expense	(500)
Interest expense	(325)
Net income	$2,875

Required From the financial statements presented, identify and record the transactions that occurred during June. Use the spreadsheet format shown on the next page to record the transactions. One transaction is shown as an example.

		ASSETS		=	LIABILITIES	+	OWNERS' EQUITY	
Accounts		Cash	Other Assets				Contributed Capital	Retained Earnings
Beginning Amounts		3,200	+119,000	=	52,800	+	43,000	+26,400
1	Cash	+7,100						
	Accounts Receivable		+200					
	Service Revenues							+7,300

P6-13 Management Discussion and Analysis

Obj. 4

The letter to the shareholders from Douglas N. Daft, Chairman, Board of Directors, and Chief Executive Officer of Coca-Cola is provided on the text's Web site and on the student CD that accompanies this text. This letter appeared in the company's 2001 annual report.

Required Read Chairman Daft's letter and comment on the following:

A. To whom is the letter addressed?
B. What is the overall tone of the letter?
C. What time periods are addressed in the letter? (past, present, future)
D. What are the accomplishments mentioned in the letter?

P6-14 Management Discussion and Analysis

Obj. 4

The letter to the shareholders from Douglas N. Daft, Chairman, Board of Directors, and Chief Executive Officer of Coca-Cola is provided on the text's Web site and on the student CD that accompanies this text. This letter appeared in the company's 2001 annual report.

Required Read Chairman Daft's letter and comment on the following:

A. Which segments of the market represent the largest growth for Coca-Cola?
B. Comment on the level of detail contained in the letter. For example, are the bulleted points shown on the last page of the letter detailed, or general in nature?
C. The second paragraph of the chairman's letter makes reference to the nature of the competitive environment. What is the tone of the second paragraph? What is Chairman Daft telling the reader?

P6-15 Earnings Restatement and Stock Prices

Objs. 4, 5

In April, 2001, the management of U.S. Aggregates, Inc., a producer of aggregates made of a combination of crushed stone, sand, and gravel, announced that the company would be restating its earnings for the first three quarters of 2000. After the announcement, the company's stock price per share dropped more than 75% from its high for the period affected by the company's restatement of earnings.

Financial irregularities of other companies have been announced in recent years. In late May, 2001, trading of the stock of U.S. Wireless Corporation was halted on the Nasdaq Stock Exchange when its share price dropped significantly. This sudden drop occurred when the company announced irregularities had been uncovered and it had replaced its chairman and chief executive. The price went from a high of $24.50 in March, 2000 to a low of $2.91.

Required

A. Did these companies practice full and fair disclosure? Why did the stock price of U.S. Aggregates and U.S. Wireless Corporation fall when investors learned that the company had produced financial information that was incorrect?
B. Do you believe "financial shenanigans" by management is an ethical issue? Explain.

P6-16   Evaluating Internal Control Procedures

Obj. 5

Consider each of the following situations.

A. Sales clerks in a retail store are assigned to a specific cash register. They are given a cash drawer containing $100 in change at the beginning of their shifts. They are required to record the amount of each purchase in the cash register. The cash register records an identification and price for each item purchased. Cash payments are collected from customers and placed in the cash drawer. A copy of the cash register sales slip is given to the customer. At the end of each shift, the employee takes the cash drawer and cash register tape to a supervisor who counts the cash, verifies the sales, and signs an approval form. The sales clerk also signs the form that identifies the amount of cash and amount of sales for the day.

B. A ticket seller at a movie theater is issued a cash drawer with $100 in change and a roll of prenumbered tickets when the theater opens each day. The seller collects cash from customers and issues the tickets. Each customer hands a ticket to a ticket taker who tears the ticket in half and gives half back to the customer. At the end of the day, the ticket seller returns the cash drawer and tickets to a supervisor.

Required For each situation, discuss why the procedures are used and how they provide effective internal control.

P6-17   Evaluating Internal Control

Obj. 5

The Spring Valley Church is a small congregation with about 50 members. The church is financed by member donations. Most of these donations are collected during the Sunday morning service. Many of the donations are in cash. Other donations are by checks made payable to the church. Harvey Plump has served as treasurer for the church since becoming a member a few years ago. The church accepted Harvey's offer to serve as treasurer as an indication of his interest in being active in the church. Harvey listed several previous experiences with financial matters on his resume as qualifying him for the position.

Once donations are collected each week, Harvey takes the money to the church office where he counts it. He makes out a deposit slip and deposits the money in the church's account at a local bank. He records the deposit in the church's check register. He writes checks to pay the church's expenses. In some cases, he writes small checks to himself as reimbursement for incidental expenses he pays for the church. He opens bank statements received by the church each month and reconciles them with the church's check register. Harvey prepares a monthly statement of cash received and disbursed that is distributed to members of the congregation.

The church always seems to be lacking sufficient financial resources. A recent meeting was held to discuss expansion of the church's building, but current finances seem to make expansion impossible. Some members don't understand why the church's financial condition appears to be so bleak, since they believe they are making large donations.

The church has asked you to help them evaluate their financial situation.

Required Evaluate the internal control problems of the Spring Valley Church. What explanation can be provided for the church's financial problems?

P6-18   Internal Controls for Cash Sales

Obj. 5

You and a friend have finished your Christmas shopping at the mall and have decided to relax and have lunch in a small restaurant in the food court. After selecting your entrees, you notice a sign on the cash register that reads "If you do not receive a receipt, your meal is free." Your friend is puzzled by the sign and asks you the purpose of giving away a free meal if a cashier forgets to give you a receipt.

Required Is the policy of providing a free meal if a receipt is not given a form of internal control? Why or why not?

P6-19 Multiple-Choice Overview of the Chapter

P/T

1. To protect its assets and accounting information, a company should
   a. give one person sole responsibility for the accounting system.
   b. control access to its networks and databases.
   c. permit access to accounting records only by top managers.
   d. hire only employees with college degrees.

2. The purpose of an auditors' report is to show that
   a. a CPA has prepared the company's financial statements.
   b. all of the company's transactions have been inspected for accuracy.
   c. an independent party believes that the financial statements do not contain any significant errors.
   d. the company is healthy, profitable, and likely to remain that way into the foreseeable future.

3. An organization's plan and the procedures used to safeguard assets, ensure accurate information, promote efficiency, and encourage adherence to policies is its
   a. internal control system.
   b. cost accounting system.
   c. financial accounting system.
   d. management information system.

4. An auditors' report made by an independent accounting firm
   a. is addressed to a company's managers.
   b. must contain only three paragraphs.
   c. is dated at the balance sheet date of the audited financial statements.
   d. identifies the responsibilities of the auditor.

5. The Securities and Exchange Act of 1934 established the
   a. FTC.
   b. SEC.
   c. FASB.
   d. GAO.

6. A 10-K report is
   a. a quarterly financial report for the SEC.
   b. a registration for a new stock issue with the SEC.
   c. an annual financial report for the SEC.
   d. a report of change in auditors for the SEC.

7. Financial accounting standards for businesses currently are established in the United States primarily by the
   a. Federal Accounting Standards Board.
   b. Financial Accounting Standards Board.
   c. Securities and Exchange Commission.
   d. Accounting Principles Board.

8. All of the following are qualitative characteristics of financial reporting except
   a. relevance.
   b. reliability.
   c. representational faithfulness.
   d. conservatism.

9. The Governmental Accounting Standards Board (GASB) sets standards for
   a. not-for-profit organizations.
   b. state and local governments.
   c. state and federal governments.
   d. the federal government.

10. The FASB releases the following document(s) as part of creating new standards.
    a. discussion memorandum
    b. exposure draft
    c. b only
    d. a and b

CASES

C6-1   Examining an Audit Report

Obj. 4

Examine the auditors' report provided as part of the 2002 annual report of **Nike, Inc.**, and answer the following questions.

REPORT OF INDEPENDENT ACCOUNTANTS

To the Board of Directors and Shareholders of Nike, Inc.

In our opinion, the consolidated financial statements listed in the index appearing under Item 14(A)(1) on page 55 present fairly, in all material respects, the financial position of Nike, Inc. and its subsidiaries at May 31, 2002 and 2001, and the results of their operations and their cash flows for each of the three years in the period ended May 31, 2002 in conformity with accounting principles generally accepted in the United States of America. In addition, in our opinion, the financial statement schedule listed in the index appearing under Item 14(A)(2) on page 55 presents fairly, in all material respects, the information set forth therein when read in conjunction with the related consolidated financial statements. These financial statements and financial statement schedule are the responsibility of the Company's management; our responsibility is to express an opinion on these financial statements and financial statement schedule based on our audits. We conducted our audits of these statements in accordance with auditing standards generally accepted in the United States of America, which require that we plan and perform the audit to obtain reasonable assurance about whether the financial statements are free of material misstatement. An audit includes examining, on a test basis, evidence supporting the amounts and disclosures in the financial statements, assessing the accounting principles used and significant estimates made by management, and evaluating the overall financial statement presentation. We believe that our audits provide a reasonable basis for our opinion.

As discussed in Note 1 to the consolidated financial statements, effective June 1, 2001, the Company changed its method of accounting for derivative instruments in accordance with Statement of Financial Accounting Standards No. 133 Accounting for Derivative Instruments and Hedging Activities and Statement of Financial Accounting Standards No. 138, Accounting for Certain Derivative Instruments and Certain Hedging Activities.

PRICEWATERHOUSECOOPERS LLP
Portland, Oregon
June 27, 2002

Required

A. Who was Nike's external auditor? What date did the auditor complete its audit work?
B. What was the auditor's responsibility with respect to the company's financial statements? What was the responsibility of management?
C. What kind of opinion did Nike's auditors issue? Why is this opinion important to the company?
D. How does PricewaterhouseCoopers' audit opinion differ from the Krispy Kreme's opinion shown in this chapter?

C6-2   General Mills, Inc., Management Responsibilities and Audit Opinion

Objs. 4, 5

The General Mills 2002 Annual Report is reproduced in Appendix B at the end of the text.

Required Answer the following questions about the General Mills Report of Management Responsibilities and the Report of the Independent Public Accountants.

A. Who is responsible for the accounting numbers in the annual report?
B. What safeguards are in place to ensure the accuracy of the reported numbers?
C. Does the independent accountant state that the reported amounts are correct? What does the CPA assure?
D. Why does General Mills hire a CPA to audit the financial statements?

COMPUTERIZED ACCOUNTING SYSTEMS

How do we implement a computerized accounting system?

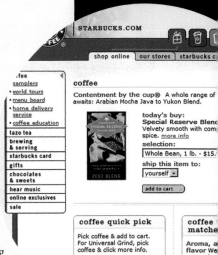

As Mom's Cookie Company has grown and become more complex, a simple accounting system kept with pencil and paper has become increasingly inadequate. Large numbers of transactions, more customers and products, and more complex business activities mean that the company is likely to benefit from a computerized accounting system. Maria and Stan are now realizing that their manual system needs to be replaced by a computerized one.

FOOD FOR THOUGHT

How does a computerized accounting system differ from a manual system? What issues must a company consider with regard to a computerized system? Maria and Stan discuss these questions with Ellen, their accountant.

Maria: *Recording transactions and preparing financial reports with our current accounting system is labor intensive and a bit slow. It takes us several hours a week to record transactions and prepare reports. Sometimes we are several days or even weeks behind in updating our accounts. Should we be looking at a computerized accounting system?*

Ellen: *Yes, there are a number of good systems on the market that are not expensive and that will meet your needs.*

Stan: *How different are these systems from what we have been using? Will a computerized system be difficult for us to learn?*

Ellen: *No, computerized systems use similar concepts to the manual approach you have been using. The computer will provide a means for you to record data. The main advantage of a computer system is that the system can do much of the work for you. Once data are recorded, the system automatically updates account balances and prepares financial statements.*

Maria: *That sounds easy. Are there problems with computer systems that we will need to avoid?*

Ellen: *You need to make sure the system is secure and that you have good backup procedures to protect your data in case the system fails. Let's look at some key issues that are important for understanding these systems.*

OBJECTIVES

Once you have completed this chapter, you should be able to:

1 Identify the primary components of a computerized accounting system.

2 Describe the components of a computerized accounting system used to process data and produce useful information.

3 Describe how data are processed in various modules of an accounting system.

4 Explain the use of relational databases to perform accounting functions.

5 Describe how a database system can be used to create a simple accounting system.

COMPONENTS OF A COMPUTERIZED ACCOUNTING SYSTEM

OBJECTIVE 1

Identify the primary components of a computerized accounting system.

http://ingram.
swlearning.com

Learn more about these ERP developers and other computerized accounting systems.

Many of the mechanical functions of an accounting system—posting to ledger accounts, updating account balances, and preparing schedules and reports from account balances—can be automated. Computers are capable of processing data through a series of steps to produce standard outputs such as reports. Consequently, certain accounting functions are automated in most companies.

Computerized accounting systems, even those for small companies like Mom's Cookie Company, are composed of modules. Each module provides a mechanism for recording and reporting specific types of business activities. Common modules are those associated with the most common business activities: sales and customer relations, purchasing and inventory management, production (for manufacturing companies), human resources, asset management, and financial management. A separate module is usually responsible for the general ledger and external financial reporting (GAAP-based financial statements) functions. Exhibit 1 illustrates an accounting system as a set of component modules.

All of the components in the system are linked so they share data with each other. Some businesses use one software application that integrates all of these functions. **Systems that integrate most of the business information functions as a basis for management decisions are referred to as** *enterprise resource planning (ERP) systems.* Many large companies have implemented these systems from ERP developers such as SAP®, Peoplesoft®, and Oracle® Financials. Other companies may rely on software from different vendors for different components of their systems. Many smaller companies rely on software that handles most of the company's accounting functions. These systems lack the capabilities of larger systems but provide for most of the common accounting and financial reporting functions small businesses need. Thus, computerized accounting systems can be small basic systems such as QuickBooks®, MAS, Peachtree®, or Simply Accounting®; middle market systems such as Microsoft® Great Plains or ACCPAC®; or large-scale systems such as SAP and Oracle Financials. Regardless of size, each of these systems is made up of component modules.

Each component in the information system has a particular role. This role depends on the stakeholders who interact with the component.

- The **sales module** receives sales order data from customers and maintains accounts receivable information.
- The **purchases and inventory management module** provides purchase order data to vendors. Vendors are those who supply specific products to a company. This module maintains accounts payable and inventory information.
- The **human resources module** maintains data about employees, including hours worked and wage rates. It is used for preparing payroll and payroll tax information.

Exhibit 1 Components of an Accounting Information System

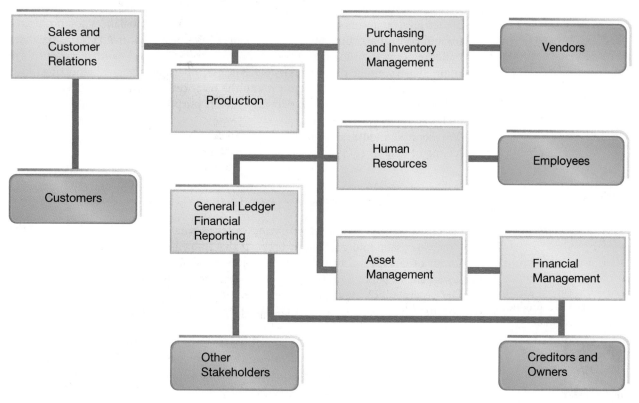

- The **production module** tracks the flow of costs through the manufacturing process.
- The **asset management module** identifies long-term asset costs, their expected useful lives, and where these assets are located in a company.
- The **financial management module** keeps track of debt, repayment schedules, interest rates, and shareholder information.
- The **general ledger/financial reporting module** provides information for use by external stakeholders, including shareholders and government regulators.

The accounting process in a computerized system involves all modules. Each module maintains data for specific entities and activities. **The computerized system records financial data about individual items of importance to a company in** *subsidiary accounts.* These accounts include transactions for individual customers, suppliers, or products. Thus, when Mom's Cookie Company sells goods to a customer on credit, it uses the system to record customer and product identification data so that it can determine what was sold and to whom it was sold. A separate subsidiary account is maintained for each customer to keep track of that customer's sales and payments. **Records for all subsidiary accounts of a particular type are maintained in a subsidiary ledger.** A subsidiary accounts receivable ledger, for example, would consist of all the individual customer accounts, with data about purchases and payments for each customer. In a computerized accounting system, a subsidiary ledger is a file that provides records for a particular type of entity or activity. Thus, a customer file would contain data for the amount owed by that customer and when payment was due.

Control accounts **are summary accounts that maintain totals for all subsidiary accounts of a particular type.** For example, the balance of the accounts receivable control account is the sum of the balances of all accounts receivable subsidiary accounts for the company's customers. The same is true for inventory accounts for products a company sells and for accounts payable accounts for amounts owed to vendors.

A company maintains subsidiary accounts for management purposes. For example, Mom's Cookie Company must be able to respond when a specific customer inquires about his current account balance or wishes to dispute a billing statement. A company reports control account balances in financial statements to external users and in reports for higher level management decisions. Accordingly, account balances for both subsidiary and control accounts are updated on a regular basis. Control account balances are maintained in a company's general ledger. **Records for each control account are maintained in a company's** *general ledger.* The general ledger/financial reporting module keeps track of each control account and the balances in each account. The general ledger module uses these data to prepare general purpose financial statements for a company.

We examine modules in greater detail later in the chapter. First, we consider the processing of data in computerized systems.

DATA PROCESSING IN A COMPUTERIZED SYSTEM

OBJECTIVE 2

Describe the components of a computerized accounting system used to process data and produce useful information.

http://ingram.
swlearning.com
....
Visit the online shopping sites of Amazon.com, Southwest Airlines, and Banana Republic.

Each component of an information system receives data, stores the data, processes the data to create useful information, and reports that information, as indicated in Exhibit 2.

Input originates in business activities and can come from a variety of sources. It may originate as paper documents, such as **sales orders** prepared by or for customers or **sales receipts** indicating the sale of goods to customers. Data must be entered into the computer system. Data entry may take place when clerical personnel transfer data by typing, or keying, information from paper documents to computer files. Increasingly, data are entered directly into computer systems. For example, many retail stores use scanners to read bar code data from products. The bar codes are linked to the company's inventory data so that sales prices, costs, and inventory amounts are recorded without data having to be keyed.

Many companies provide web-based input systems that permit customers to place orders directly using the Internet. Companies like **Amazon.com**, **Southwest Airlines**, and **Banana Republic** provide for online shopping, reservations, and sales. Data entered by customers updates company order and inventory files. Customers also can retrieve information about their orders from these systems.

Exhibit 2 Data Processing in a Computerized Information System

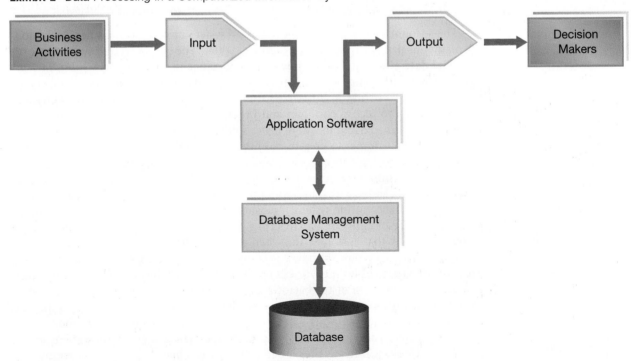

Exhibit 3 provides a web page from **Starbucks'** web site. It provides options for on-line shopping such as selection of products and shipping information. Other web pages provide for payment using a credit card. These pages are connected to Starbucks' accounting system so that sales, inventory, and customer information can be updated automatically.

Exhibit 3

Example of Web-Based Input

Reprinted with permission of Starbucks Coffee Company © 2002. All rights reserved

Using computer networks, such as the Internet, to make customer sales is referred to as *E-business.* Some E-business systems, like Starbucks', provide a means for a company to receive sales orders from customers. These systems are referred to as business-to-customer, or b2c, systems. Other systems permit companies to order goods from vendors and to track order information. These systems are referred to as business-to-business, or b2b, systems. In either system, customers do most of their own data entry. These data become the basis for recording sales, accounts receivable, cost of goods sold, and related transactions. Thus, many routine transactions are recorded and processed automatically without the seller having to take special steps.

Application software **includes the computer programs that permit data to be recorded and processed.** If a customer enters an order using a web browser, application software is needed to collect that data, to record it in the company's files, and to process the data to ensure that the appropriate actions occur. For example, a customer order must be recorded, the shipping department must be notified of the order so the goods can be shipped, a bill may need to be prepared and sent to the customer, and sales and accounts receivable accounts need to be updated. Application software automates these functions.

Databases store data used by various components of a system. Data are transferred by application software to databases. **A** *database* **is a set of computerized files in which company data are stored in a form that facilitates retrieval and updating of the data. A** *database management system* **controls database functions to ensure data are recorded properly and are accessed only by authorized users.**

Computerized information systems have many internal controls. These controls are important for protecting data and for helping to prevent errors. Controls, such as passwords, ensure that data are not accessed or modified by unauthorized personnel. Controls built into database management systems prevent more than one user from updating a particular record at the same time and make sure that all appropriate parts of a database are updated when a transaction is recorded.

Other controls require management action. For example, databases must be backed up on a regular basis so data will not be lost if a computer system fails or is destroyed. A company also must have a plan in case its computer system is destroyed because of natural disaster, sabotage, or terrorism. Failure to provide backup systems can result in a company being unable to do business if its primary system is unusable.

Output from information systems often is in the form of reports. These reports may contain prescribed information and may be prepared automatically by a system. They may be print reports or electronic documents that are sent to users. Many output reports can be modified and retrieved as needed by users. For example, managers at Mom's Cookie Company need to know which customer accounts are overdue by more than 30 days. They need a report that gives them an up-to-date listing of grocery stores that are late in paying their accounts. Other managers need to know how much of each type of cookie the company sold in the last month. Database systems are useful because they allow users to query the database to obtain current information.

Regardless of which of the modules in a company's accounting system is involved, data flow through the system from inputs to outputs. How the data are processed depends on the module. Data flows are initiated by business activities, but they also stimulate these activities. For example, a customer order creates data that are processed by the system. Also, data about the order result in goods being shipped to the customer. Thus, business activities create data that are processed to create additional business activities.

Computerized systems rely on networks for processing data. **A** *computer network* **is a set of hardware devices that are linked so they can exchange data among themselves using software.** Exhibit 4 illustrates a computer network. Input devices, such as scanners, and client workstations allow data input as well as data access. A **client** is a computer or other network device that uses software to request services from other software.

Exhibit 4
A Computer Network

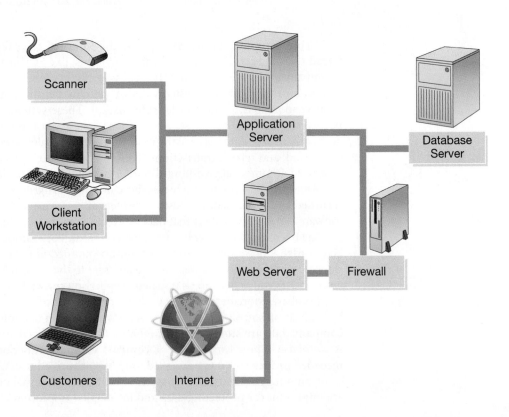

The services are provided by server software that resides on another computer, referred to as a **server**. Networks involve the cables that connect the clients and servers and the hardware and software needed to make the networks function properly. Most networks are client-server networks because they provide for the exchange of data between clients and servers.

Application software usually resides on one or more **application servers** on the network. Application servers are connected to **database servers**, which store and manage data. Companies engaged in E-business or that permit their employees to connect to their network from locations outside of the business, often use web servers to provide the software needed to interact across the Internet. The Internet provides a network so that almost any computer can connect to a company to do business.

Networks pose security problems, especially when they are connected to the Internet. A **firewall** usually is special software running on a computer that makes it difficult for unauthorized users to gain access to a company's internal network. Data must pass through the firewall, where they are examined and filtered to determine whether they should be passed to the internal network. Firewalls can be placed at many locations in a network. Typically they are placed between devices that provide services to external users and the internal network to prevent unauthorized access to data and devices inside the firewall.

The next section examines various modules in a company's accounting system.

1 SELF-STUDY PROBLEM

Lavender's is a plant nursery that supplies specialty plants to other nurseries around the country. It also sells plants to customers from a retail store.

Required Describe the components of a computer network that Lavender's might use to run its business. Explain the purpose of each component.

ACCOUNTING SYSTEM MODULES

OBJECTIVE 3

Describe how data are processed in various modules of an accounting system.

The following section examines each of several primary modules in an accounting system. Each module obtains, processes, and reports information for a particular type of business activity.

The Sales Module

Accounting systems are designed to meet information needs associated with business activities. These needs vary from company to company. For example, a retail company that sells goods directly to customers for cash relies primarily on point-of-sales systems that provide for collecting data about the goods that are sold and the amount received from customers. A company like **McDonalds** does not need to maintain data about its customers, for example. However, a company that sells goods using an order system, like Amazon.com, General Mills, or Southwest Airlines, must maintain customer data that identifies customers, addresses, billing information, and, perhaps, shipping information.

Exhibit 5 illustrates a sales and customer relations module for a company that receives orders from customers and sells goods on credit. To illustrate, Mom's Cookie Company permits its commercial customers, such as grocery stores, to submit orders by phone or by mail. When Fair-Price Foods submits a sales order, that order is received by the sales division at Mom's Cookie Company. The sales division checks to make sure the product is available. Also, the sales division checks with the credit department to make sure Fair-Price Foods has not exceeded its credit limit and that its payments are not overdue. If the sale is approved, the sales division notifies the shipping division at

Exhibit 5
A Sales Processing
Module

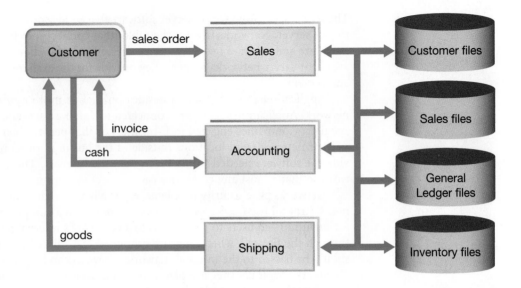

Mom's Cookie Company, which ships the cookies to the customer. The sales division also notifies the accounting department of the order. Accounting updates the customer file for the amount the customer owes. The transaction is recorded to sales revenue and accounts receivable. The general ledger accounts are posted either at the time the transaction is recorded or on a periodic basis. Inventory files are updated for the goods shipped to the customer. Accounting sends an **invoice** to the customer for the amount of the sale. The invoice notifies Fair-Price Foods of the amount owed and requests payment. When Fair-Price Foods pays for the order, the accounting department updates the customer's account and accounts receivable in the general ledger. The cash is transferred to a bank.

Good internal control requires that the personnel who account for the cash should not also have physical access to the cash. Therefore, these functions should be separated within the accounting department.

How much human intervention is needed in the processing of these data depends on the company and the sophistication of its computer systems. In many companies, the computer system handles most of these activities.

Sales, accounting, and shipping functions all are sources of data in the sales module. In addition, these functions also receive information from the system. An important part of this system is its ability to provide information to decision makers. The database files provide up-to-date data about sales activities. The sales department retrieve data about particular customers, such as what they purchased and how much they have purchased. These data guide decisions about advertising and promotion campaigns and about sales bonuses and commissions. Purchasing and production use this information to determine which products to purchase or produce and the amounts needed. The profitability of products and profits earned from sales to certain customers may help a company determine its strategy for which products or types of customers to emphasize. Customers who do not pay their accounts on a timely basis may be flagged to prevent future sales. A company can also use these data to evaluate performance. For example, a company may monitor how long it takes to process orders and ship goods. Unnecessary delays may help explain decreased sales or dissatisfied customers.

Accounting for transactions is an important part of each systems module. The sales department notifies accounting of a customer order. Shipping notifies accounting of goods shipped to customers. Accounting compares data from sales and shipping and bills the customer. **Accounts receivable and sales revenue transactions are recorded at the time goods are shipped to customers. Cash and accounts receivable transactions are recorded when cash is received.** These transactions update the general ledger account balances in the General Ledger files. However, they are a relatively small part of the overall data processing that occurs in the sales module. A considerable amount of data are collected and processed to keep track of customers, sales, shipments, inventory, receivables, and cash flow.

The Purchasing and Inventory Management Module

The purchasing and inventory management functions are responsible for the acquisition of merchandise and supplies. In a manufacturing company, these functions indicate when to acquire materials that are used in the products the company manufactures. Inventory management involves keeping track of the amounts and locations of inventories and making sure these inventories are available when needed.

Exhibit 6 illustrates the purchasing and inventory management module. Purchasing is responsible for placing orders with vendors when additional merchandise or materials are needed. Vendor files identify approved vendors for each type of merchandise or material. Mom's Cookie Company purchases cookies from several bakeries. As additional cookies are needed to sell to grocery stores, orders are placed with the bakeries. Vendor files identify the names, locations, and contacts for each vendor. Also, they keep track of amounts owed to each vendor and when payments are due. Inventory files identify each type of cookie and the number of cases Mom's Cookie Company has available for sale. When inventory levels fall below a predetermined minimum, the purchasing department contacts a vendor and orders additional cookies. The receiving department receives cookies from the bakeries. The vendor sends a bill to the accounting department. Accounting compares the bill with information from the receiving department to verify that the goods were received. Once the billing information is verified, the vendor records are updated. Accounting also uses information from the receiving department to update inventory records to show the number of cases of each type of cookie available for sale.

Exhibit 6

A Purchases and Inventory Management Module

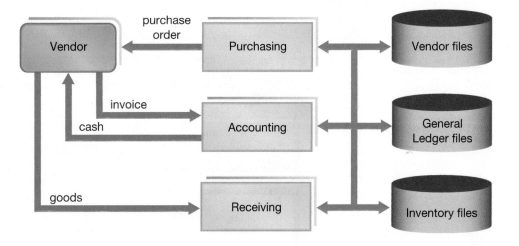

When accounts payable become due to vendors, cash is transferred to the vendors in the form of checks or electronic transfers to the vendor bank accounts. Accounts payable and cash accounts are updated for these transfers.

The system permits appropriate personnel to determine the amount of each inventory item available, the cost of these items, and amounts owed to each vendor. In addition, the efficiency of vendors in responding to orders can be determined. Thus, the purchasing department may be interested in which vendors respond promptly and provide the best service in response to a company's orders.

Many vendors now permit their customers to place orders online. The purchaser can identify the items to be purchased and the cost of these items and submit an order directly to the vendor's computer system. The customer may also be able to connect to the vendor's system to determine product availability and when goods are expected to be shipped.

The interaction of a company and its suppliers is known as *supply-chain management.* Companies reduce purchasing and inventory costs by developing relationships with vendors to supply needed products promptly and efficiently. Many companies rely on close relationships with suppliers to make sure materials and merchandise are available when they are needed. If suppliers are reliable, the purchasing company can place orders and receive goods as they are needed rather than having to maintain large amounts of inventory. In addition, companies depend on their suppliers to provide inventory of the type and quality they need. Companies also work with suppliers to make sure they are getting the best deal possible on the goods they need.

If Mom's Cookie Company cannot get the cookies it needs from bakeries, if the quality of the cookies is not satisfactory, or if the costs are too high, it will not meet the needs of its customers.

The Human Resources Module

The human resources function in a business is responsible for hiring and training employees. The data needed to account for employee activities involve employees' hours and their wages or salaries. How these data are obtained and processed depends on the type of company and the type of work employees perform.

Exhibit 7 illustrates the processing of employee wages for a manufacturing company, such as Parma's Bakery, one of Mom's Cookie Company's suppliers. Employees' hours are collected from time sheets or are entered automatically as employees log into computer systems to obtain data and perform tasks. The wage rate data are maintained by the personnel department. Accounting receives time data from the production division and wage rate information from personnel to determine how much each employee has earned each pay period.

Exhibit 7

A Human Resources Module

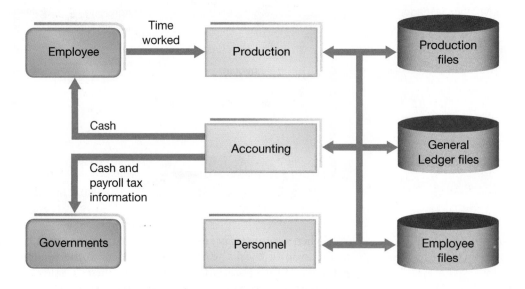

Wage data are important for several activities. Amounts earned by and owed to each employee are in employee files. These data are used to process payroll information and to prepare paychecks or to transfer cash to employee bank accounts. Payroll taxes, such as income taxes, and benefits, such as retirement and health insurance, also usually are tied to amounts earned by employees. A company must keep track of taxes and other amounts associated with wages and provide information about these amounts to governments and other organizations. Payments also must be made to these organizations for payroll taxes and benefits.

Wage information also is important for determining production costs. Labor costs become part of the cost of manufacturing, as examined in the discussion of the production module in the next section. Amounts paid to employees and governments affect wages and taxes payable accounts and cash in a company's general ledger accounts.

The Production Module

Manufacturing companies carry out many complex activities and transactions. These companies may produce many different products, and each product may require numerous types of materials and processing activities. Many costs have to be recorded and many events have to be tracked by a manufacturing company's information system.

Exhibit 8 illustrates basic components of a production module. The manufacturing process usually responds to the actual or expected demand for a company's products. Sales orders or forecasts are inputs for the production planning and scheduling process. Planning and scheduling functions determine which products, how much of each, and when various products will be produced.

Exhibit 8

A Production Module

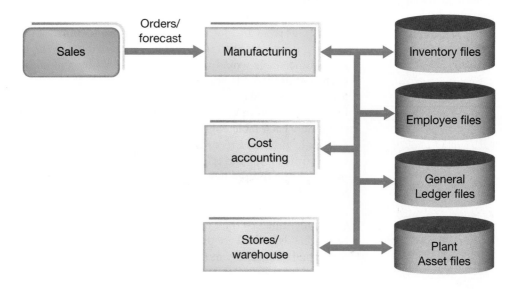

A special accounting function, known as **cost accounting**, keeps track of the costs of resources used in the manufacturing process. Materials, labor, and the costs of other resources used in producing goods must be identified and tracked throughout the manufacturing process. Materials and supplies are obtained from stores (or the manufacturers' storage facilities) and placed into production. The costs of these materials must be identified in association with particular jobs or goods that are being produced. The wages earned by employees who work on these jobs or goods also must be identified. Other costs are associated with plant assets used in the production process, including utilities, insurance, and other resources used during a production period. Once goods are completed, they are shipped to customers or transferred to warehouses for storage until they are shipped.

Cost accounting identifies and records these costs. They are used to determine the costs of goods produced during a period or the cost of completing a particular order. These data become cost of goods sold once goods are completed and sold to customers. For example, Parma's Bakery keeps track of all the ingredients used in preparing an order for Mom's Cookie Company. Also, it keeps track of the labor costs associated with producing the cookies. These costs, along with other production costs, are used to identify Parma's cost for the goods prepared for Mom's Cookie Company. These costs are important for Parma to make sure it has earned a profit from the order.

Each module in an accounting system is responsible for data associated with certain business activities. As noted earlier, each module collects, records, and processes data and provides information to decision makers. The next section considers how a database system functions to provide these information services.

2 SELF-STUDY PROBLEM

Suppose you were in charge of production at Parma's Bakery.

Required What actions would you perform that would require you to interact with the company's computer system?

THE STRUCTURE OF ACCOUNTING SYSTEMS

OBJECTIVE 4

Explain the use of relational databases to perform accounting functions.

Most computerized accounting systems are constructed as relational databases. A *relational database* **is a set of related files that are linked so that files can be updated and information can be retrieved from the files efficiently.**

A relational database stores data in tables. A *table* **is a file that contains data represented as rows and columns.** Each column identifies a particular attribute of the entity or process described in the table. Each attribute in the table is referred to as a **field**. A customer table would include customer name and address attributes, for example. Each row in the table contains a record of data for a particular entity. Rows in a customer table would contain data for each customer, for example. Separate tables are used for specific types of entities (customers and products) and processes (sales orders and shipping). Each table contains one or more **primary keys** that uniquely identifies the entities or processes recorded in the rows of the table. These primary keys are used to connect the tables into relationships. The primary key in one table connects to the primary key or a **foreign key** in another table. A foreign key is a field that is a primary key in a different table.

Exhibit 9 illustrates the tables and relationships in a database. The boxes represent tables, identified by their captions at the top. Fields stored in each table are listed in the boxes. Fields in bold are primary keys. Lines connect the primary and foreign keys that form the relationships in the database.

Exhibit 9 Tables in a Relational Database

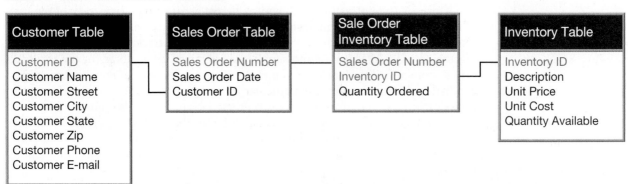

The relationships permit a change to a field to affect each table containing that field. For example, when a sales order number is entered into the system, the Sales Order Number field is updated in the Sales Order and Sales Order Inventory tables. The relationships also permit a user to obtain data from more than one table. For instance, by using a particular sales order number, a user can obtain data from the Sales Order and Sales Order Inventory tables because these tables are linked by the sales order number. The sales order number can then be used to identify the customer and the items the customer has ordered.

Thus, a relational database is a network of information objects that permits efficient storage and retrieval of data. Knowing the relationships in the database, a user can retrieve any combination of fields to serve a particular decision need.

Individual tables in the database store data about a particular entity or activity. Exhibit 10 provides an example of a simple table. The top row identifies the attributes stored in the table. The remaining rows are records. The first column of each record identifies the sales order number that identifies that record. Records are listed sequentially by sales order number, which is the primary key for the table. Other fields identify other attributes associated with each sales order, such as the date and an identifier for the customer who placed the order.

Exhibit 10

A Table in a Database

Sales Order Number	Sales Order Date	Customer ID
SO12473	04/12/04	CU3452
SO12474	04/12/04	CU2490
SO12745	04/13/04	CU2873

Data are entered into a database using **forms**. Forms are computer screens that provide templates for entering data. Exhibit 11 provides an illustration of a simple form. The form provides input areas where data are keyed into the system. Form fields are linked to attributes in tables in the database. Thus, when a new sales order number is entered in the form in Exhibit 11, data are added to the sales order table in the company's database.

Exhibit 11

A Form for Data Entry

Sales Order Number	SN001
Sales Order Date	9/2/04
Customer ID	CID001
Name	Moore Clothing Co.

Product ID	Type	Style	Quantity On Hand	Quantity Ordered
PID01010	Blanket	Blue	44	10

Record: of 1

As noted earlier, most data needed by a computerized system may be entered automatically through scanning devices. Customers enter data in forms when they place orders using web-based systems. However, most data needed in database systems are entered by company employees who are responsible for various data entry functions.

Each module of a computerized accounting system consists of tables and forms that collect and store data for the activities associated with that module. Individual tables often are part of more than one module. For example, an inventory table may be accessed by the sales module to determine product availability and price. It may be accessed by the purchasing module to update it for goods received from vendors.

The following section illustrates a database accounting system that is typical of real accounting systems, though it uses simple examples with limited transactions and examines only a small part of a total accounting system. The illustration is designed to help you see how accounting data are processed in a real system from data entry to storage and financial reporting.

An Illustration of an Accounting System

OBJECTIVE 5

Describe how a database system can be used to create a simple accounting system.

This section illustrates various components of a computerized accounting system. The illustration examines the sales module of Mom's Cookie Company's accounting system. Example transactions are provided for September 2004 to illustrate sales activities: receiving sales orders, shipping goods to customers, updating inventory files, invoicing customers, receiving cash, updating accounting records, and producing summary reports.

The electronic file used in this module is a Microsoft® Access database, which can be found in the CD that accompanies this text or which can be downloaded from http://ingram.swlearning.com. Directions for use of the software are provided as part of the description that follows. To use the database, you must have a computer with a Microsoft® Windows® operating system and Access 2000 or a more recent version.

Access is application software built around a database system. It is inadequate for large-scale accounting applications but is useful for illustrating database systems. Unlike most business systems, all of the software runs on a workstation. Though it can be configured to run on a network with separate client and server components, it is easier to use and easier to understand when it is operated from a single computer.

Copying and Opening the Database

It is highly recommended that the database be copied to a hard disk before it is used. To copy the database, open Windows® Explorer and select the drive where the database is located. Click on MomsCookies.mdb and drag it to a folder. Release the mouse button, and the database will be copied. It is a good idea to make several copies of the database under different names (MomsCookies1.mdb, MomsCookies2.mdb, and so on). If the database is modified or accidentally corrupted, you still have an unmodified version for use.

Use one of the following options to open the database.

Option 1. Open Access by clicking Start, Programs, Microsoft Access. Once Access has opened, click File, Open Database. Double-click MomsCookies.mdb in the folder to which it was copied.
Option 2. Open Windows Explorer. Select the folder in which the database was copied. Double-click on MomsCookies.mdb.

Database files can become large when they are modified through use. It is a good idea to compact the database periodically. To compact the database, open it in Access, click Tools, Database Utilities, Compact Database. The database will be compacted automatically. Compacting removes unused space in the database. Running a database from a floppy disk requires frequent compacting.

Database Contents

A database consists of objects. Once you open MomsCookies.mdb database, these objects appear in various categories: tables, queries, forms, reports, macros, and modules. Examine these categories. **Tables** contain the data stored in the system. **Queries** are short programs that permit a user to obtain data from one or more tables. **Forms** provide a means for entering or reading data stored in the database. **Reports** provide summary information intended primarily to be printed. **Macros** are sequences of steps a user performs to complete a particular task. A macro runs a task without the user having to enter each keystroke separately. **Pages** provide a means of creating web documents for accessing a database. **Modules** are computer programs (written in Visual Basic) to provide higher level functions in the database. The Mom's Cookie Company database contains no macros or modules. Also, pages are not included in this illustration.

Tables

Tables are the key to understanding a database. Tables contain the data in the database. Other objects manipulate these data by adding new data, modifying existing data, deleting data, or retrieving data.

Begin by examining the tblProduct table. Click on the Tables tab in the Database window. Double-click on tblProduct or click on tblProduct and then click the Open button. Columns in the table identify categories (also known as fields or attributes) of data. The Product ID is a code that uniquely identifies each product. Name and Size describe the products. Unit Price and Unit Cost indicate the selling price and cost per unit. Quantity on Hand indicates the number of units available for sale. Units for Mom's Cookie Company are cases. Each case contains 20 bags of cookies that the grocery store sells individually. The stores must purchase the cookies in cases rather than as individual bags of cookies, however. Additional products could be added to the table by entering data in the bottom row. Existing data can be modified by entering the data in the appropriate cell. For example, if the unit price for PID0201 increased to $35.00, the new price could be entered in the Unit Price column for this product. Close the table by clicking the **X** box in the upper right corner of the table window. Do not click the **X** box in the Access window (top right of screen) or you will close the Access program. If you close Access by mistake, reopen it and the MomsCookies.mdb database.

Next examine the tblCustomer table. This table identifies Mom's Cookie Company's existing customers. Each customer is identified by a Customer ID. The table includes name and address data to identify where to ship goods and mail invoices. Close the table.

The tblProduct and tblCustomer tables are examples of master files. Master files contain data that are relatively stable and that may be updated periodically.

You can examine the relationships among all the tables in the database by clicking on the relationships button ▣ in the top row (toolbar) of buttons in the Database window. (This looks similar to Exhibit 9.) The relationship diagram that appears contains the tables and identifies the fields in each table. Lines in the diagram link the primary and foreign keys. Close the relationship window by clicking on the bottom X in the upper right corner of the screen.

Entering Transactions

You will have a chance to examine other database objects as you work through the process of entering transactions and producing information.

Sales Orders

Begin with a sales order. Open the tblSalesOrder table. Each order is identified by a Sales Order Number. The Order Date and Customer ID also are listed for each order. (This is similar to Exhibit 10.) The Customer ID connects each sales order to a specific customer. Close this table and open the tblSOProduct table. This table identifies the Sales Order Number, Product ID, and Quantity Ordered. This table connects to both the tblSalesOrder and tblProduct tables. Scroll down the table to the final row. Note the data for the last sales order. Once a new sales order is entered, new rows will appear in the tblSalesOrder and tblSOProduct tables. Close the table.

Personnel in the sales department would normally enter sales orders. To enter a transaction, click on the Forms tab of the Database window. Then open the frmSales-Order form. Notice that the form identifies the Sales Order Number, Date, and Customer ID. (This is similar to Exhibit 11.) It also identifies customer name and address information and information about the products ordered. You can click on the Record selector arrow ▶ at the bottom of the form window to view existing orders. To enter a new order, click on the New Record selector arrow ▶* at the bottom of the form window. Two sets of arrows appear near the bottom of the form. Use the bottom set of arrows to move among the sales orders. Enter a new Sales Order Number, *SN010*, at the top of the form. You may wish to press the Caps Lock key when entering transaction data. Press the Tab key to go to the Sales Order Date box. Type *09/30/04* in the box. Click on the Customer ID selector arrow ▾ to see a list of customers. Click on CID003. The name of the customer appears on the form as confirmation of the customer's identity. Click on the Product ID selector arrow, and click on PID0201. The product Type, Style, and Quantity on Hand appear on the form. Tab to the Quantity Ordered box and enter *12*. Click on the second Product ID selector arrow, click on PID0202, tab to the Quantity Ordered box, and enter *9*. To save the order, you can click the new record selector arrow ▶* at the bottom of the form or close the form window.

To view the data entered for the order, open the tblSalesOrder and tblSOProduct tables, scroll to the last row, and observe the new data. Close each table after you view it.

You can view a summary of sales orders, including the one just entered, by selecting the Reports tab on the Database window and double-clicking on rptSalesOrders. A report appears listing the orders for September. To see the entire report you may need to enlarge the window and set the zoom control on the menu bar to 75% [75% ▾]. Sales orders are listed in the report by date. The order you just entered is listed at the bottom of the report. If you wish, print a copy of the report. Only transactions occurring in September 2004 are included in reports in this tutorial. Close the report when you have finished examining it.

Reports in the Mom's Cookie Company database are derived from queries. Queries obtain data from tables, manipulate these data in some cases to produce new data items, and store them temporarily. Click on the Queries tab to view the queries. Double-click on qrySalesOrders and view the data that appear in the rptSalesOrders report. Queries can be used to present data in table form when a formal report is not needed. Each of the reports described in this tutorial is associated with a query. Close the query.

Shipping Information

Once an order is received, personnel in the shipping department can review the order information. Review can take place on screen or from a printed copy of the sales order report. The shipping department then selects the goods and prepares them for shipment. Also, they update shipping records and prepare a shipping report.

To view shipping data, click on the Tables tab in the Database window and double-click on the tblShipping table. The table contains the Sales Order Number, Product ID, Date Shipped, and Quantity Shipped for each order shipped. The table also contains an Inventory Updated field. When a shipment is entered in this table, the Updated field is set to No, indicating that inventory records have not been updated. Observe that all the fields contain Yes in the tblShipping table, indicating that inventory records have been updated for all shipments. Close the table.

To enter a shipment, click on the Forms tab in the database window and double-click on the frmShipping form. This form indicates the Sales Order Number, customer information, and product information for each shipment. You can review previous entries by clicking on the selection arrow at the very bottom of the Form window ▶. To enter data for the sales order you just completed, click on the Last Record arrow at the bottom of the form window ▶|. The form will display the Sales Order Number of the order you just entered, SN010. The customer information also is displayed for this order. Click on the Product ID selection arrow and click on the product being shipped,

PID0201. Press the Tab key and enter 09/30/04 for the shipping date. Press the Tab key again and enter 12 for quantity shipped. Click on the second Product ID selection arrow and repeat the process for the second item ordered (PID0202, 09/30/04, 9). Close the form to save the data.

You can view a report of shipments by clicking on the Reports tab of the Database window and double-clicking on rptShipping. You may need to expand the Report window and set the zoom to 75% to see the entire report. Use the Record selection arrows at the bottom of the Report window to view each page of the report. To see the most recent shipment, click on the Last Record selection arrow ⏭. A copy of the shipping report can be printed and enclosed with the goods shipped to the customer. A copy also may be sent to the billing department, or the shipping data may be viewed electronically by that department. Close the report.

Open the tblShipping table and scroll to the bottom of the table to view the data. Observe that the Inventory Updated field contains No for the items just shipped. It is important for the shipping personnel to update the inventory records so that the quantity of each product available is correct. Quantity available data are contained in the tblProducts table. Close the tblShipping table and open the tblProducts table. Note the Quantity on Hand for the products associated with the sales order you entered, PID0201 (29 units) and PID0202 (47 units). Close the table.

To update the inventory records, click on the Queries tab of the Database window and double-click on the qryUpdateShipments query. If you are asked if you want to run an update query, click the YES button. A dialog box appears asking for the sales order number associated with the records to be updated. Enter the number for the shipment, SN010, and click the OK and Yes buttons. The inventory records have now been updated. Verify the update by opening the tblProducts table and viewing the Quantity on Hand for PID0201 (29 − 12 = 17 units) and PID0202 (47 − 9 = 38 units). Also, if you examine the tblShipping table, you will find that the Inventory Updated field has been changed to Yes for the last shipment. The change to this field is an important control. Once inventory quantity has been updated for a particular Sales Order Number, it cannot be updated again. Close any tables you have open.

Receiving Goods

As goods are shipped, the quantity of goods available for sale decreases. The supply of goods must be increased periodically. In the case of Mom's Cookie Company, the increase occurs when goods are received at the warehouse from the supplier's manufacturing division. When goods are received, the receiving department places the goods in the appropriate location to be retrieved by shipping personnel. In addition, they update inventory records by completing the frmProductReceipt form. Click on the Forms tab of the Database window and double-click on frmProductReceipt to open this form. Review the form contents, then click on the New Record arrow ▶* at the bottom of the form window. Enter the following data in the form: Product Receipt Number, 10906; Product ID, PID0201; Receipt Date, 9/30/04; and Quantity Received, 25. Close the form.

The data entered in the form update the tblProductReceipt table. Open this table to see the items received. The Inventory Updated field is set to No for the most recent acquisition to indicate that the inventory records have not been updated for this receipt. Close the table.

To update the inventory records, click on the Queries tab of the Database window and double-click on the qryUpdateReceipts query. If you are asked if you want to run an update query, click the YES button. Enter the Product Receipt Number for the inventory item you entered in frmProductReceipt, 10906. Click the OK and Yes buttons and the inventory records are updated. To verify the update, open the tblProduct table and examine the Quantity On Hand value for PID0201 (17 + 25 = 42 units). Close the table. Open the tblProductReceipt table and confirm that the Inventory Updated field has changed to Yes. Close the table.

A report of available inventory is provided by rptInventory. Click on the Reports tab and double-click rptInventory. Each product is listed with quantity and cost data. The balance of the inventory account is the total cost for all products. Close the report.

Billing Customers

Once a shipment is made, the accounting department prepares a sales invoice to mail to the customer. The accounting department also creates the accounting transactions associated with the sale of goods to the customer. These transactions involve recording Sales and Accounts Receivable for the sales price of the goods shipped. In addition, Cost of Goods Sold and Inventory are adjusted for the cost of the goods shipped.

To view sales invoice data, click on the Tables tab of the Database window and double-click on the tblSalesInvoice table. This table contains Sales Invoice Number, Date, Sales Order Number, and Amount Billed associated with each invoice. Close the table.

Before preparing an invoice, the accounting department needs to determine the amount a customer owes. This information is found on the sales order and shipping reports. The Mom's Cookie Company database allows users to calculate the amount associated with each sales order. Click on the Queries tab and double-click on qrySales-Amount. Each sales order is listed with the amount owed. Close the query.

To prepare a sales invoice, click on the Forms tab of the Database window and double-click on frmSalesInvoice. You can review previously entered invoice data by clicking on the selection arrow at the bottom of the form. To enter a new sales invoice, click on the New Record arrow ▶* at the bottom of the form. Enter 10910 for the sales invoice number, 9/30/04 for the sales invoice date, and SN010 for the sales order number. Click the Tab key. Customer information appears on the form. Enter Amount Billed, 765. Do not enter the dollar sign. Close the form to save the data. You can verify that the data have been saved by clicking on the Tables tab of the Database window and double-clicking on the tblSalesInvoice table. Scroll down to view the last record in the table. Close the table.

View or print sales invoices from the rptSalesInvoice report on the Reports tab. Double-click on the report and scroll through the records to view each sales invoice. The last entry is the sales invoice you just prepared. Close the report.

Reporting Sales and Income

Once goods are shipped to customers, the accounting system updates Sales and Cost of Goods Sold. Obtain a list of sales from the rptSalesbyCustomer report. Double-click on the report. All sales for September are listed for each customer, including the most recent sale to customer CID003. Close the report.

A simple income statement is provided by rptIncomeStatement. The only income statement accounts included in this tutorial are Sales and Cost of Goods Sold. The simplified income statement lists these accounts, which have been updated for all transactions in September. Close the report.

Cash Receipts and Accounts Receivable

The last step in the revenue cycle is recording cash received from customers. The rptAccountsReceivable report lists the amounts sold to each customer, the cash received from these sales, and the amount the customer owes. Double-click on the report to view this information. Note the amount owed by customer CID001, $3,180. Close the report.

To record a cash receipt, open the frmCashReceipts form in the Forms tab. Use the Record selection arrow at the bottom of the form to scroll through the cash receipts. Go to record number 4. Observe that the sales order number and customer information appear on the form. Sales invoice number and cash receipts data do not appear because the cash has not been received. When a customer pays an invoice, a check is mailed to Mom's Cookie Company along with a copy of the sales invoice (the copy is known as a remittance advice). The accounting department receives the remittance advice and records the sales invoice number and amount of cash received. The check is deposited in a bank account.

To record a cash receipt for SN004, enter the sales invoice number associated with this sales order, 10904. Enter the cash receipt date, 9/30/04, and enter the cash receipt amount, 2280. Do not enter a dollar sign or comma. Close the form to update the records.

The tblCashReceipts table contains data on the amounts paid for each invoice. The rptAccountsReceivable report has been updated for the amount paid by customer CID001. Review the table and report to confirm that the cash receipt has been recorded. Close the table and report. Close the Access program.

Summary

Most companies use computerized accounting systems. These systems contain modules to handle the business activities that are accounted for in the system. Network components and database systems in accounting modules capture, store, and process data.

3 SELF-STUDY PROBLEM

The accounting system described in the last section of this chapter did not provide separate accounts for sales revenue and accounts receivable. Suppose you wanted to determine the accounts receivable for Mom's Cookie Company at the end of September.

Required Describe the steps you would go through to obtain the data necessary to determine accounts receivable for the company as reported in an accounts receivable report.

REVIEW

SUMMARY of IMPORTANT CONCEPTS

1. Accounting systems contain modules. Each module handles data collection, processing, and reporting for a particular type of business activity, such as sales or purchasing.

2. Computer systems receives input from data entry sources, use application software to process the data, and store the data in databases. Database management systems control database operations as well as access to the database. Application software obtains data from the database and provides information as output to decision makers.

3. Accounting systems are implemented on computer networks. Client workstations and input devices, such as scanners, provide input to the system. Application servers, web servers, and database servers respond to client requests by processing and storing data, and by making information available to users.

4. The sales module receives customer orders, processes shipments, bills customers, and maintains data about customer purchases and receivables.

5. The purchasing and inventory management module is responsible for the acquisition of merchandise, materials, and supplies. It tracks available inventories, processes orders, and identifies goods received and on hand. It also determines amounts owed to vendors.

6. The human resources module maintains employee information, processes payroll, and monitors amounts owed to employees and to government agencies for payroll taxes.

7. The production module tracks the flow of costs from materials, labor, and other sources into the production process. It tracks these costs until goods are completed and shipped to customers. It may also assist managers with scheduling production jobs and monitoring the availability of materials for use in the production process.

8. Accounting systems usually are implemented as relational database systems. These systems contain tables that are linked through primary and foreign keys to facilitate the processing of data. Data are input in electronic forms. Queries allow users to access data and produce reports for decision makers.

DEFINE

TERMS and CONCEPTS DEFINED in this CHAPTER

application software   (F259)
computer network   (F260)
control accounts   (F257)
database   (F259)
database management system
  (F259)
E-business   (F259)

enterprise resource planning (ERP) systems
  (F256)
general ledger   (F258)
relational database   (F266)
subsidiary accounts   (F257)
supply-chain management   (F264)
table   (F266)

SELF-STUDY PROBLEM SOLUTIONS

SSP7-1   A client workstation and scanning device might be used to input data from local customers. A web server would be needed to provide access for web orders. An application server would provide the software needed to collect and process the data and convert data into reports. A database server would store data for customer orders, plant inventories, and shipments. A network would connect the servers and the client workstation and scanning device. An Internet connection would be needed to connect the web server to the Internet.

SSP7-2   To produce a product, such as cookies, you would need data about the materials needed to produce the product, availability of these materials, and production processes. You would need to schedule the production to make sure materials, labor, and equipment, such as mixers and ovens, are available. You would need information about sales orders so you know how much of each product to produce. Also, you would need to transfer goods from process to process as they are manufactured, and eventually you would need to transfer completed goods to shipping or to retail outlets. As you engage in these activities, you would need to update the company's information system so that the cost of goods produced could be determined.

SSP7-3   To determine accounts receivable, you would need to compare the amount shipped to each customer with the amount paid by the customer at a particular date. This comparison would require a query that retrieved data from several tables. The fields involved in this query are underlined in the following diagram.

The Customer ID would be needed to identify each customer. All sales orders for each customer would need to be examined, using the Sales Order Number. Each sales order would be used to identify the product ordered, based on the Product ID, the cost per unit of each product (Unit Cost), and the Quantity Shipped. The total of unit cost times quantity shipped would determine the amount of each order for each customer. The Date Shipped field or the Sales Invoice Date would be used to establish the date of each receivable. The Cash Receipt Date and Cash Receipt Amount would determine when the customer made a payment. Comparing the total of the sales to each customer minus the total of cash received at a particular date would determine how much the customer owes at that date. A total of amounts owed for all customers would determine total accounts receivable.

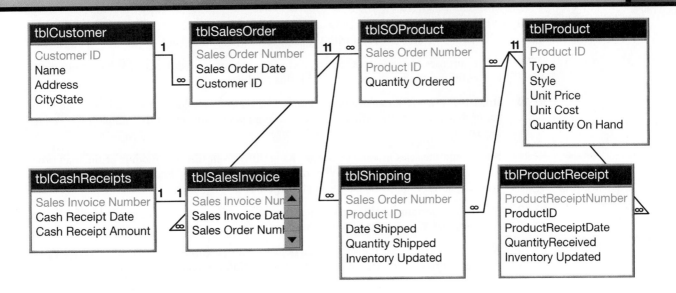

Thinking Beyond the Question

How do we implement a computerized accounting system?

Computerized accounting systems reduce the labor needed to record accounting information and prepare accounting reports. How can computerized systems also help managers, investors, and other stakeholders with their analysis and decision making tasks?

QUESTIONS

Q7-1
Obj. 1
Why are integrated business systems more efficient than using individual systems for different functions in a business?

Q7-2
Obj. 3
Suppose a company sells to customers on-line. Customers are required to pay for their orders with credit cards at the time of the order. What primary activities would be required of the sales module to process and account for these orders?

Q7-3
Obj. 3
The human resources module described in Exhibit 7 is for a manufacturing company. How would the module differ for a retail or service company?

Q7-4
Obj. 2
What is a computer network? Why are they used by businesses to maintain accounting systems?

Q7-5
Obj. 2
What is the purpose of a database management system?

Q7-6
Obj. 3
Irmo Company's asset management module lists each piece of equipment the company has purchased, when it was purchased, its cost, its expected life, and its location in the company. Why would the company want this information?

Q7-7
Obj. 3
Kreel Company's financial management module lists each loan the company has outstanding, when the money was borrowed, the amount borrowed, the interest rate, the dates payments were made, and the amounts of these payments. Why is this information important to the company?

Q7-8
Obj. 3
What purposes does a retail company's purchasing module serve? What accounts and types of transactions are associated with this module?

Q7-9
Obj. 3
What purposes does a service company's human resources module serve? What accounts and types of transactions are associated with this module?

Q7-10
Obj. 3
Street Inc.'s financial management module lists each stockholder's name, address, the number of shares owned, and when the stock was purchased. How might the company use this information?

Q7-11
Obj. 3
Why would the sales module of **Burger King** differ from the sales module of the mail order clothing company, **Lands' End**? What transactions would Lands' End record as part of its sales process that would differ from those of Burger King?

Q7-12
Obj. 3
Why is it important for the accounting department of a company to receive data from sales and shipping? What internal control function is served by this process?

Q7-13
Obj. 3
Why is it important for the accounting department of a company to receive data from purchasing and receiving? What internal control function is served by this process?

EXERCISES

If your instructor is using Personal Trainer in this course, you may complete online the assignments identified by ᴾT.

E7-1
Write a short definition for each of the terms listed in the *Terms and Concepts Defined in this Chapter* section.

E7-2
Objs. 1, 2, 3, 4, 5
ᴾT
Complete each sentence with the appropriate term.

1. Systems that integrate most of the business information functions are referred to as
_____.

2. Financial data about individual items of importance to a company are recorded in
_____.

3. Summary accounts that maintain totals for all subsidiary accounts of a particular type are called _____.

4. A _____ is an accounting record of each (control) account and the balance of each such account.

5. The use of computer networks, such as the Internet, to provide for customer sales is referred to as _____.

6. A computer program that permits data to be recorded and processed is one kind of
_____.

7. A _____ is a set of computerized files in which company data are stored in a form that facilitates retrieval and updating of the data.

8. A _____ controls database functions to ensure data are recorded properly and can be accessed only by those authorized to record, update, or retrieve the data.

9. The interaction of a company and its suppliers is known as_____.

10. A _____ is a set of related files that are linked so the files can be updated and information can be retrieved from the files efficiently.

E7-3
Objs. 1, 2, 3, 4, 5
ᴾT
Match each term with the appropriate definition.

a. application software
b. control accounts
c. database management system
d. database
e. E-business
f. enterprise resource planning (ERP) systems

g. general ledger
h. relational database
i. subsidiary accounts
j. supply-chain management

____ 1. A set of computerized files in which company data are stored in a form that facilitates retrieval and updating of the data

____ 2. A set of related files that are linked so the files can be updated and information can be retrieved from the files efficiently

____ 3. An accounting record of each (control) account and the balance of each such account

____ 4. Controls database functions to ensure data are recorded properly and can be accessed only by those authorized to record, update, or retrieve the data

____ 5. Includes the computer programs that permit data to be recorded and processed

____ 6. Type of account in which financial data about individual items of importance to a company are recorded

____ 7. Summary accounts that maintain totals for all subsidiary accounts of a particular type

____ 8. Systems that integrate most of the business information functions

____ 9. The interaction of a company and its suppliers

____ 10. Term that refers to the use of computer networks, such as the Internet, to provide for customer sales

E7-4
Obj. 1

A friend is confused about entries to computerized accounting systems. She says, "I understand that there are both subsidiary accounts and control accounts, but why are the effects of individual transactions entered only into the subsidiary accounts? Doesn't this cause the subsidiary accounts and the control to report different information?" Explain the difference between a general ledger and a subsidiary ledger and the difference in how the information contained in each is used.

E7-5
Obj. 2

Lands' End, Inc., is a large, well-known mail-order retailer. Assume you logged onto its web site, ordered three pairs of shorts, and paid for them by credit card. Describe the business activities that would occur at Lands' End, including linkages to the accounting system, in handling your order.

E7-6
Objs. 2, 3

Great Plains Manufacturing recently ordered 100 tons of raw materials including steel, aluminum, glass, and various plastics. Today, the goods were received via rail at the company's warehouse. Identify the documents that will be handled today (either by hand or electronically) and identify the specific and/or control accounts affected by this event.

E7-7
Obj. 4

Modern accounting information systems often are maintained as relational databases. What is a relational database and what are the advantages of these database systems? Identify parts of a relational database and explain the purpose of each part.

E7-8
Obj. 2

Computerized accounting systems create special control problems for an organization. Common control procedures used by organizations include the following:

a. Use of passwords to access terminals and programs
b. Limits placed on amounts that the computer will accept for various transactions
c. Backing up of data and programs regularly
d. Separation of design from operation of systems

Explain the purpose of each control procedure.

E7-9
Obj. 4
P̧T

Howard Company sells woolen goods and maintains its accounting system using a relational database. To prepare information about sales transactions, the company uses the following tables in its database. The fields that appear in each table are in brackets following the table.

- customers [customer ID, name, shipping address, phone number]
- sales orders [sales order number, customer ID, order date, product ID, order quantity]
- inventory [product ID, product name, quantity on hand, unit price]
- customer shipments [sales order number, shipping date]
- sales invoice [sales invoice number, sales order number, invoice date]
- cash receipts [sales invoice number, cash receipt amount, receipt date]

For each of the following events, identify the tables that would be needed to record the event.

1. Received an order from Jones & Sons for 12 blankets on November 3.
2. Shipped the blankets to Jones & Sons and billed the customer on November 6.
3. Received cash from Jones & Sons for the purchase on December 5.

E7-10
Obj. 4

Refer to information provided in E7-9 as you answer the following questions.

1. If a manager for Howard Company wanted to query the company's database to obtain information about customer sales during November, which tables should she use to obtain the information? Explain why.
2. If the same manager wanted to query the database to obtain information about amounts owed by customers at the end of November, which tables should she use to obtain the information? Explain why.

E7-11 Computer networks in many organizations include client software, business management pro-
Obj. 2   grams and databases on servers, and connections among the computers running these programs. For each of the following activities, identify the portions of the computer system that
would be affected. Explain how the portions are affected.

1. Access to company data is requested
2. Records are updated
3. Data are transferred between a client and a server
4. New data for processing are entered
5. Data being used by another user are required
6. Data to print a report are obtained

E7-12 One Star Co. recently lost all of its customer and accounts receivable records. An irate cus-
Obj. 2   tomer walked into the company's sales office and took a sledge hammer to the company's
computer. The company now has no basis for determining which customers owe it money or
how much they owe. Identify control problems that permitted the loss to occur and controls
that should have been in place to prevent the loss. Why is this an accounting problem?

PROBLEMS

*If your instructor is using Personal Trainer in this course, you may complete online the assign-
ments identified by $\frac{P}{T}$.*

P7-1 ### Purpose of Relational Databases
Obj. 4

Barbury Company sells machine parts to manufacturing companies. Parts usually are purchased to replace worn or broken parts. Most of Barbury's customers order goods by phone
or through Internet connections from regional sales offices throughout North America. Sales
are made on credit and are shipped immediately to avoid manufacturing delays at customer
plants. Barbury uses a relational database for its accounting system.

Required Explain the purpose of a relational database and why it is useful to a company.
Describe the parts of a relational database and identify specific examples of how these parts
would be used by Barbury to obtain and fill customer orders.

P7-2 ### Tables and Forms in Relational Databases
Obj. 4

Exhibit 9 in this chapter provides examples of tables that might appear in a company's relational database. Exhibit 11 provides an example of a sales order form.

Required Using these exhibits as examples, explain the purpose of tables and forms in a relational database. Be specific about what the rows and columns in a table represent and how
individual entities are identified in tables. Explain how forms are related to tables.

P7-3 ### Computer Networks
Obj. 2

You have just been hired as an account representative for a large financial institution. Your
supervisor shows you to your desk that contains a workstation. She explains that the workstation is part of a wide-area network connecting all of the bank's offices through a client-
server system. All of the bank's data are maintained in databases on servers and are accessed
through a database management system. To obtain account information, you must log on to
the network and use the bank's account service program on your workstation to retrieve data
from the database.

Required What is the supervisor talking about? Explain the function of each part of the
bank's computer network. Why do most companies use computer networks for their accounting systems?

P7-4 ### Controlling Networks
Obj. 2

Dora Company uses a client-server network for its accounting system. The company's database servers are kept at a central computer center. Users of the system access the company's

database through workstations on their desks. Data are updated continuously throughout the day based on sales, production, billing, and other transactions recorded by users. Dora is a large company and its network connects offices in several states.

Required Identify four threats to the accounting system and accounting data that exist in Dora's network system that should be managed through internal controls. Identify an internal control that would be useful for dealing with each threat.

P7-5
Obj. 4

Web Interfaces to Relational Databases

Connect to http://www.amazon.com on a web browser.

Required Identify the data items that are collected and processed by Amazon's web interface as part of selecting and placing an order for a book. How might these items be stored in a relational database? Identify potential tables and fields in the tables associated with these items.

P7-6
Obj. 3

Tables in Relational Databases

You have been assigned the responsibility of developing a purchasing module for a retail company.

Required Identify the tables that you think would be necessary as part of a relational database that will store data for the module. Identify the fields that will be important in each table and the primary and foreign keys that will link the tables together.

P7-7
Obj. 2

Application Software

An Excel spreadsheet provides an example of an application program that can be used as a simple database.

Required Describe the applications that a spreadsheet can provide and how a spreadsheet could be used as a database. How do the application functions in the software differ from the database functions?

P7-8
Obj. 2

Database Management Systems

Open an Access database like the Mom's Cookie Company database described in this chapter. Examine the Tools menu in the database window.

Required What database management functions are provided by the Tools menu options? Based on your examination, what are some of the primary purposes of a database management system?

P7-9
Obj. 2

Network Components

Trainor Company has decided to market its pet supplies on the Internet. It has developed a web site so that customers can identify products and order them online.

Required Describe a network configuration that Trainor might use to support its E-business activities.

P7-10
Obj. 4

Fields in a Relational Database

Linden Company sells more than 100 different types of nuts, bolts, and screws. Each product has an identification number and is described by its type, size, and material composition. Each product is purchased from one vendor.

Required Linden Company is developing a database system for its inventory. What fields would be important to include in the database for the inventory items? Why would these fields be important?

P7-11
Obj. 4

Relational Database Design

Niven Company manufactures and sells ornamental flamingoes. The flamingoes come in one color, pink, but come in three sizes, small, medium, and large. Customers order the products through the web by specifying the quantity of each product, and by providing a shipping address and credit card number. The credit card is verified and the customer's account is charged when the order is placed. Orders are rejected if the card cannot be charged.

Required Design a relational database system that Niven might use for its products and orders. Identify the tables, fields, and primary and foreign keys that would be part of the database.

P7-12
Obj. 4

Diagramming a Relational Database

Plaxa Company developed a design for its order system that consisted of three tables. Tables and associated fields are listed below. The primary keys for each table are underlined.

> Product Table [Product ID, Size, Price, Quantity Available]
> Customer Table [Customer ID, Name, Address, City, State, Zip, email]
> Order Table [Customer ID, Product ID, Order Date, Quantity Ordered]

Required Provide a relational diagram for the order system like that illustrated in Exhibit 9.

P7-13
Obj. 4

Determining Revenue in a Relational Database System

Refer to P7-12. Plaxa ships its products on the same day orders are received.

Required Describe the process that Plaxa would use to determine the amount of sales it made during a particular period.

P7-14

Multiple-Choice Overview of the Chapter

1. Which of the following statements does NOT describe an advantage of a computerized accounting system?
   a. Many accounting cycle steps are performed by the computer.
   b. It is easier to control than a manual system.
   c. It is faster than a manual system.
   d. Fewer opportunities for error exist than in a manual system.

2. Which of the following is NOT part of a computer network?
   a. transmitters
   b. clients
   c. servers
   d. databases

3. Data needed by a computerized accounting system may be entered
   a. automatically through scanning devices.
   b. by customers who enter data in forms when they place orders using web-based systems.
   c. by a company's employees.
   d. by all of the above.

4. An information system that integrates most of the business information functions of a company is known as an
   a. enterprise resource planning system.
   b. enterprise manufacturing relations system.
   c. enterprise resource module system.
   d. enterprise business planning system.

5. The part of a computer system that controls access to data and ensures reliability of processing in the system is the
   a. relational database.
   b. application software.
   c. database management system.
   d. control module.

6. The part of a client-server system that requests services from the system is the
   a. database server.
   b. application server.
   c. web server.
   d. client.

7. The Internet is an example of a
   a. client.
   b. network.
   c. server.
   d. database.

8. The module in an accounting system that is most concerned with vendors is the
   a. sales module.
   b. purchases module.
   c. human resources module.
   d. financial management module.

9. The field in a table that uniquely identifies records in the table is the
   a. primary key.
   b. foreign key.
   c. relation key.
   d. access key.

10. The part of a relational database system that permits users to define the information provided as output from the system is a
    a. form.
    b. table.
    c. query.
    d. report.

CASE

C7-1 | **Working with a Relational Database System**

Obj. 5

Mom's Cookie Company received an order from Fair-Price Foods on September 30, 2004 for seven boxes of Terrific Cookies, 24 oz. size.

Required Use the Mom's Cookie Company database to record the sale. Begin with the Sales Order form. Use 09/30/04 for all dates. Follow the example in the chapter for processing the order. Once the order has been recorded, complete the Shipping form, and then the Sales Invoice form. Print the Sales Invoice for this sale.

Analysis and Interpretation of Financial Accounting Information

THE TIME VALUE OF MONEY

How much will it cost to borrow money?

Maria and Stan have been successful in starting Mom's Cookie Company. The company has been profitable and is growing as more customers demand its products. Maria and Stan are now concerned about meeting the additional demand. They need to expand their operations, and they are considering producing their own products rather than purchasing them from other bakeries. Before they can expand, however, they must obtain additional financing for their company. The time value of money is an important concept that business owners need to understand before they borrow money.

FOOD FOR THOUGHT

If you were going to borrow money, how much would you have to pay back over the life of the loan? How much would you have to pay each period? How much interest expense would you incur? Borrowing money always involves an investment by one entity, a bank for example, in another entity, such as Mom's Cookie Company. The amount repaid by the borrower includes interest in addition to the amount borrowed. Maria and Stan are considering borrowing from a local bank but have decided to discuss the loan with their accountant, Ellen, to determine how much the loan will cost.

Stan: *Ellen, Maria and I are considering expanding our business. To finance the expansion, we will need a loan. We are concerned about how much the debt will cost us and how much cash we will need to repay the principal and interest.*

Ellen: *You should be concerned about these issues. You should never borrow money without a clear idea of how much you will have to repay.*

Maria: *We know we'll have to repay the principal of the loan plus interest. We're not sure, however, how much the bank will require us to repay each period.*

Ellen: *To understand loan payments, you need to understand time value of money concepts. Interest computations can be complex, depending on when payments are made and whether you repay the loan in a single payment or in a series of payments. Let's review these concepts.*

OBJECTIVES

Once you have completed this chapter, you should be able to:

1 Define future and present value.

2 Determine the future value of a single amount invested at the present time.

3 Determine the future value of an annuity.

4 Determine the present value of a single amount to be received in the future.

5 Determine the present value of an annuity.

6 Determine investment values and interest expense or revenue for various periods.

FUTURE VALUE

OBJECTIVE 1

Define future and present value.

Suppose a wealthy relative gives you $1,000 on January 1, 2004. You may use it as you like. What could you do with this money? One option is to spend it. You probably would have no difficulty identifying things you would like to buy. The total amount of goods you could purchase in January 2004 would be $1,000, the amount of money you have.

Suppose, however, that instead of spending the money immediately, you decide to invest it in a savings account at a local bank. The bank agrees to pay 5% interest on your savings account. Consequently, if you invest your money with the bank for a year, you will earn $50 interest ($1,000 principal invested × 5% interest rate).

The value of your investment in the future, at December 31, 2004, for example, is the future value of the investment. **The *future value* of an amount is the value of that amount at a particular time in the future.** The future value of $1,000 invested on January 1, 2004, at 5% interest is $1,050 on December 31, 2004. The amount invested is the present value of the investment. **The *present value* of an amount is the value of that amount on a particular date prior to the time the amount is paid or received.** The present value of $1,050 received on December 31, 2004, is $1,000 on January 1, 2004, assuming 5% interest is earned.

The future value of an investment is expected to be larger than its present value. The difference between future and present value of a single investment is the amount of interest earned by the investor. If you choose to invest in savings for a year, you are forgoing the option to buy goods you might like to have. The interest you earn on your savings is compensation for delaying your purchases to some time in the future.

In many situations, the relationship between future and present value is easily determined. The future value (FV) is the present value (PV) plus the interest earned (or expected) for the period of the investment. The interest earned is determined by the interest rate (R) paid on the investment. Therefore, we can express the relationship between future and present value as follows:

$$FV = PV(1 + R)^t$$

For example:

$$\$1,050 = \$1,000(1.05)$$

where 0.05 (5%) is the interest rate on the investment.

LEARNING NOTE

Interest rates are stated as annual rates unless you are told otherwise. The amount of interest financial institutions pay on savings and for other investments usually is stated as an annual percentage rate.

OBJECTIVE 2

Determine the future value of a single amount invested at the present time.

Compound Interest

Suppose you decide to leave your money in the savings account for a second year, until December 31, 2005. How much would your investment be worth at that time? Assuming that you do not withdraw the interest earned for the first year ($50) and the bank continues to pay 5% interest, the value of your investment at the end of the second year would be as follows:

$1,102.50 = $1,050(1.05)

This amount is the future value on December 31, 2005, of the amount invested at the beginning of 2004. The earnings for the second year are higher than those for the first year because in the second year you earn interest both on the amount originally invested ($1,000) and on the amount earned in the first year ($50). Earning interest in one period on interest earned in an earlier period is known as **compound interest**. An investor earns compound interest any time an investment extends beyond one period and interest earned in prior periods is not withdrawn.

When compound interest is earned, computing the future value of an investment is more complicated. The simple equation previously described cannot be used. For example, the future value on December 31, 2005, of a $1,000 investment made on January 1, 2004, would be as follows:

$1,102.50 = $1,000(1.05)(1.05)

or:

$1,102.50 = $1,000(1.05)^2$

We express the equation for computing the future value of an investment when interest is compounded like this:

$FV = PV(1 + R)^t$

where t is an exponent representing the number of periods of investment.

To illustrate, assume that you invest $500 for three years at 8% interest. How much would your investment be worth at the end of three years? This is another way of saying, What would be the future value of your investment at the end of three years? Compute the answer as follows:

$629.86 = $500(1.08)^3 = $500(1.08)(1.08)(1.08)$

Future value calculations of this type are relatively simple with a calculator that has an exponential function.

USING EXCEL

For Future Value of a Single Amount

SPREADSHEET

Spreadsheet programs also are commonly used for future value calculations. The future value of $500 that earns interest at 8% compounded for three years can be calculated by entering the following formula in a cell: =500*(1.08^3). The caret symbol (^) is used in Excel for exponents. The amount appearing in the cell is the future value ($629.86 in this example).

Tables also are available to assist with these calculations. Table 1 at the back of this text can be used for this purpose. This table contains the interest factors for computing future values for various interest rates and time periods. Remember, the interest factor is represented by $(1 + R)^t$ in the future value equation.

Excerpt from Table 1   Future Value of a Single Amount

	Interest Rate								
Period	0.01	0.02	0.03	0.04	0.05	0.06	0.07	**0.08**	0.09
1	1.01000	1.02000	1.03000	1.04000	1.05000	1.06000	1.07000	1.08000	1.09000
2	1.02010	1.04040	1.06090	1.08160	1.10250	1.12360	1.14490	1.16640	1.18810
3	1.03030	1.06121	1.09273	1.12486	1.15763	1.19102	1.22504	**1.25971**	1.29503

For example, the interest factor for 8% and three years in Table 1 is 1.25971. This number is equivalent to $(1.08)^3 = (1.08)(1.08)(1.08) = 1.25971$. The table provides the interest factor to simplify future value calculations. Thus, if you want to calculate the future value of $500 invested for three years at 8%, use the interest factor from Table 1:

$629.86 = $500 × 1.25971

Using Table 1, compute the future value of a single amount as follows:

FV = PV × IF (Table 1)

where *FV* is the future value of the amount invested, *PV* is the present value (the amount invested), and IF is the interest factor from Table 1.

LEARNING NOTE

Future and present value calculations often contain rounding errors that depend on the number of decimal places included in computing interest factors. In this book, we round computations to the nearest cent or, for large amounts, to the nearest dollar.

The future value equation $[FV = PV(1 + R)^t]$ is useful for determining the future value of an investment. In addition to this information, you might want to determine the amount earned on an investment each period. For example, if you invested $500 for three years at 8% interest, how much interest would you earn each year? A table like the one shown in Exhibit 1 is useful for this purpose.

Exhibit 1   Interest Table for an Investment of $500 for Three Years at 8%

A Year	B Value at Beginning of Year	C Interest Earned (Column B × Interest Rate)	D Future Value at End of Year (Column B + Column C)
1	500.00	40.00	540.00
2	540.00	43.20	583.20
3	583.20	46.66	629.86
Total		129.86	

Column B shows the amount the investment is worth at the beginning of each year. Column C shows the amount of interest earned each year, and column D reports the amount the investment is worth at the end of each year. The total in column C is the total interest earned for three years. This table illustrates how the value of an investment grows over time as interest is earned and reinvested. A bank could use the same type of table to calculate the amount of interest expense incurred and the amount owed the investor in a savings account each period.

OBJECTIVE 3

Determine the future value of an annuity.

Future Value of an Annuity

The future value calculations so far have been limited to determining the future value of a single investment, such as the future value of $1,000 invested on January 1, 2004. Now, consider a situation in which a series of investments is made. For example, suppose you invest $500 at the end of each year for three years. How much will your investments be worth at the end of three years if you earn 8% interest each year? This type of investment situation is known as an annuity. **An *annuity* is a series of equal amounts received or paid over a specified number of equal time periods.**

Calculate the future value of these investments by computing the future value of the amount invested each year and adding all the amounts together.

LEARNING NOTE

It is important to know *when* amounts are paid or received when working with annuities. An annuity in which amounts are paid or received at the *end* of each fiscal period is known as an ordinary annuity. An annuity in which amounts are paid or received at the *beginning* of each fiscal period is known as an annuity due. We limit our discussion to ordinary annuities, which are typical for most accounting transactions.

End of Year 1	End of Year 2	End of Year 3	Future Value at End of Year 3
Invested for 2 years $500 ————————————————————————→			$ 583.20 = $500 × 1.08²
	Invested for 1 year $500 ————————————————→		540.00 = 500 × 1.08¹
		Invested for 0 years —→	500.00 = 500 × 1.08⁰

Future value of total investment	$1,623.20
Total amount invested over 2 years*	1,500.00
Interest earned over 2 years	$ 123.20

Though three payments are made, the period covered is only two years because the first payment is made at the end of year 1.

LEARNING NOTE

Any amount raised to the zero power is 1. Therefore, $(1.08)^0 = 1$. Also, $(1.0)^0 = 1$, $(1.1)^0 = 1$, and $(200)^0 = 1$. Using an expression such as $\$500 \times (1.08)^0$ is the same as saying that $500 invested at any point in time is worth $500 at that point in time because no interest has been earned. Another way of saying the same thing is to say that the future value of any amount at zero periods in the future is that amount. The interest factor for any interest rate at zero periods in the future is 1.0.

The $500 invested at the end of the first year is worth $583.20 at the end of the third year. The $500 invested at the end of the second year is worth $540.00 at the end of the third year, and the $500 invested at the end of the third year is worth $500.00 at the end of the third year. Thus, the future value of the total investment is the sum of these amounts, $1,623.20.

This calculation is the same as:

$$\$1,623.20 = \$500[(1.08)^0 + (1.08)^1 + (1.08)^2]$$

Therefore, we could use Table 1 to identify the interest factors for 8% and one and two periods.

Excerpt from Table 1   Future Value of a Single Amount

	Interest Rate								
Period	0.01	0.02	0.03	0.04	0.05	0.06	0.07	**0.08**	0.09
1	1.01000	1.02000	1.03000	1.04000	1.05000	1.06000	1.07000	**1.08000**	1.09000
2	1.02010	1.04040	1.06090	1.08160	1.10250	1.12360	1.14490	**1.16640**	1.18810
3	1.03030	1.06121	1.09273	1.12486	1.15763	1.19102	1.22504	1.25971	1.29503

The interest factor for zero periods is 1. Thus, the interest factor for the annuity is the sum of interest factors for zero, one, and two periods (3.2464 = 1.00 + 1.08 + 1.1664). Then, we multiply this interest factor times the amount invested each period to compute the future value of the annuity:

$$\$1{,}623.20 = \$500 \times 3.2464$$

Alternatively, tables are available that contain the interest factors for computing the future value of an annuity. Table 2 at the back of this book is this type of table. Using the table simplifies the calculation by providing the interest factor.

Excerpt from Table 2   Future Value of an Annuity

	Interest Rate								
Period	0.01	0.02	0.03	0.04	0.05	0.06	0.07	**0.08**	0.09
1	1.00000	1.00000	1.00000	1.00000	1.00000	1.00000	1.00000	1.00000	1.00000
2	2.01000	2.02000	2.03000	2.04000	2.05000	2.06000	2.07000	2.08000	2.09000
3	3.03010	3.06040	3.09090	3.12160	3.15250	3.18360	3.21490	**3.24640**	3.27810

USING EXCEL

For Future Value of an Annuity

SPREADSHEET

We could use a spreadsheet and enter the amounts invested in a cell to calculate their future value: =(500*(1.08^2))+(500*1.08)+500. The first term in parentheses is the future value of $500 at the end of two periods. The second term in parentheses is the future value of $500 at the end of one period, and the last term is the final investment of $500. The amount appearing in the cell is the future value of the annuity ($1,623.20 in this example).

Spreadsheets also contain built-in functions for calculating the future value of an annuity. Locate these functions by clicking on the Function f_x button.

From the pop-up menu, select the type of function you want. The future value of an annuity (FV) function is in the Financial category.

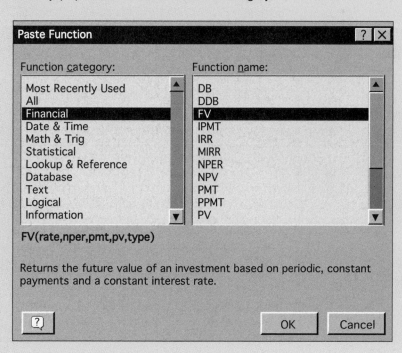

Click the OK button and the following box appears. Complete the box by entering the interest rate (Rate), number of periods for which investments will be made (Nper), and the amount invested (Pmt). The Pv and Type boxes can be left blank. Note that the amount invested is entered as a negative number because it is a cash outflow to the investor.

FV

Rate	0.08	= 0.08
Nper	3	= 3
Pmt	-500	= -500
Pv		= number
Type		= number

= 1623.2

Returns the future value of an investment based on periodic, constant payments and a constant interest rate.
Type is a value representing the timing of payment; payment at the beginning of the period = 1; payment at the end of the period = 0 or omitted.

[?]   Formula result = $1,623.20   OK   Cancel

The amount appearing in the cell used to reference the FV function is the future value of the investment ($1,623.20 in this example). The function can be entered in the worksheet's cell directly by typing =FV(.08,3,−500). It is important that the values (known as arguments to a function) be entered in the cell in the correct order. The function for the future value of an annuity is =FV(Interest Rate, Number of Periods, Amount Invested).

Annuities are common in business activities. For example, suppose Mom's Cookie Company agrees to invest $5,000 for each of its employees in a retirement plan at the end of each year. If the investment earns 7% and an employee works 20 years before retiring, how much will be available when the employee retires? Using Table 2, we can calculate the future value of an annuity of $5,000 per year for 20 years.

Excerpt from Table 2   Future Value of an Annuity

	Interest Rate								
Period	0.01	0.02	0.03	0.04	0.05	0.06	**0.07**	0.08	0.09
1	1.00000	1.00000	1.00000	1.00000	1.00000	1.00000	1.00000	1.00000	1.00000
2	2.01000	2.02000	2.03000	2.04000	2.05000	2.06000	2.07000	2.08000	2.09000
3	3.03010	3.06040	3.09090	3.12160	3.15250	3.18360	3.21490	3.24640	3.27810
⋮	⋮	⋮	⋮	⋮	⋮	⋮	⋮	⋮	⋮
19	20.81090	22.84056	25.11687	27.67123	30.53900	33.75999	37.37896	41.44626	46.01846
20	22.01900	24.29737	26.87037	29.77808	33.06595	36.78559	**40.99549**	45.76196	51.16012

$204,977 = $5,000 × 40.99549

where 40.99549 is the interest factor for 7% and 20 periods. The table is simply a labor-saving device to reduce the number of calculations for this type of problem. Alternatively, we could use a financial calculator or computer program that has future value functions.

USING EXCEL

For Future Value

SPREADSHEET

The future value of the investment can be calculated in Excel by entering =FV(.07,20,−5000) in a cell.

Using Table 2, we compute the future value of an annuity as follows:

FVA = A × IF (Table 2)

where *FVA* is the future value of the annuity, *A* is the amount invested at the end of each period, and *IF* is the interest factor from Table 2.

In addition to determining the future value of an annuity, you might want to determine the amount earned each period. For example, if you invested $500 at the end of each year for three years at 8% interest, how much interest would you earn each year? A table like the one shown in Exhibit 2 is useful for this purpose.

Exhibit 2 Interest Table for an Annuity of $500 at End of Each Year for Three Years at 8%

A	B	C	D	E
Year	Value at Beginning of Year	Interest Earned (Column B × Interest Rate)	Amount Invested at End of Year	Future Value at End of Year (Columns B + C + D)
1	0.00	0.00	500.00	500.00
2	500.00	40.00	500.00	1,040.00
3	1,040.00	83.20	500.00	1,623.20
Total		123.20	1,500.00	

Column B shows the amount the investment is worth at the beginning of each year before the contribution is made for that year. Column C contains the amount of interest earned for the year, and column D contains the amount invested at the end of each year. Column E reports the amount the investment is worth at the end of each year. The total in column C is the total interest earned for three years. Interest earned on the annuity is greater than that earned on a single investment of the same amount because the investment is growing each period by the additional amount invested as well as by the amount of interest earned.

Another question you might want to answer is, How much would you need to invest each period to accumulate a certain amount? For example, suppose you want to accumulate $1,000 over the next three years to take a trip to Mexico after you graduate from college. How much would you need to invest at the end of each year to accumulate $1,000 at the end of three years, assuming that you invest the same amount each year and can earn 6% on your investment?

We can answer this question using the future value of an annuity equation and Table 2.

$$FVA = A \times IF \text{ (Table 2)}$$
$$\$1,000 = A \times 3.18360$$
$$A = \$1,000 \div 3.18360$$
$$A = \$314.11$$

By investing $314.11 at the end of each year for three years, you can accumulate $1,000.

USING EXCEL

For Calculating a Payment

SPREADSHEET

> We can calculate the amount of the payment in Excel using the payment function (PMT). To determine the amount, enter =PMT(0.06,3,,1000) in a cell. The arguments of the function are PMT(Interest Rate, Number of Periods,, Future Value of the Annuity). Note that there are two commas following the number of periods because an argument has been omitted. We will use that argument in a future computation. The amount appearing in the cell where the function is entered is the amount of the annuity payment. It appears as a negative amount because it is a cash outflow to the investor.

1 SELF-STUDY PROBLEM

WebTUTOR Advantage

Harry Morgan recently graduated from college and started his first full-time job. He wants to accumulate enough money in the next five years to make a down payment on a house. He has $3,000 that he can invest at the beginning of the five-year period. His investment will earn 8% interest.

Required

A. How much would Harry's $3,000 investment be worth at the end of the five-year period? How much interest would he earn for the five years?

B. Independent of part (A), suppose the amount Harry needs for a down payment at the end of five years is $10,000. He wants to invest equal amounts at the end of each year for the next five years to accumulate the $10,000 he needs. How much would he need to invest each year, assuming that he earns 8% interest? How much would his investment be worth at the end of each year for the five-year period? How much would Harry invest over the five years? How much interest would he earn over the five years?

The solution to Self-Study Problem 1 appears at the end of the chapter.

PRESENT VALUE

OBJECTIVE 4

Determine the present value of a single amount to be received in the future.

In many business activities, it is important to calculate the present value of an investment rather than the future value. In this section, you will learn how to calculate the present value of an investment from information about the future value. To illustrate, suppose a company offered to sell you an investment that pays $3,000 at the end of three years. You want to earn 8% return on your investment. How much would you be willing to pay for the investment?

To solve this problem, you should recognize that the $3,000 to be received at the end of three years is the future value of the investment. The amount you would pay for the investment at the beginning of the three-year period is the present value of the investment. Use the future value equation described earlier to solve the problem.

$$FV = PV(1 + R)^t$$
$$\$3,000 = PV(1.08)^3$$
$$PV = \$3,000 \times \frac{1}{(1.08)^3} = \$3,000 \div 1.08^3$$
$$PV = \$2,381.50$$

Thus, the present value of the investment—the amount you would be willing to pay at the beginning of the three-year period—is $2,381.50.

We can also use Table 1 to solve the problem.

$$FV = PV \times IF \text{ (Table 1)}$$
$$\$3,000 = PV \times 1.25971$$
$$PV = \$3,000 \div 1.25971$$
$$PV = \$2,381.50$$

We can rewrite the future value equation as a present value equation.

$$PV = FV \times \frac{1}{(1 + R)^t}$$

USING EXCEL

For the Present Value of a Single Amount

SPREADSHEET

The present value of the investment can be calculated in Excel by entering =3000*(1/(1.08^3)) in a cell. The amount appearing in the cell ($2,381.50 in this example) is the present value of the investment.

Tables are available that provide interest factors for computing the present value of an investment. Table 3 at the back of this book is an example of such a table. To illustrate, the interest factor for computing the present value of an investment of three periods at 8% is 0.79383 from Table 3.

Excerpt from Table 3   Present Value of a Single Amount

	Interest Rate								
Period	0.01	0.02	0.03	0.04	0.05	0.06	0.07	**0.08**	0.09
1	0.99010	0.98039	0.97087	0.96154	0.95238	0.94340	0.93458	0.92593	0.91743
2	0.98030	0.96117	0.94260	0.92456	0.90703	0.89000	0.87344	0.85734	0.84168
3	0.97059	0.94232	0.91514	0.88900	0.86384	0.83962	0.81630	**0.79383**	0.77218

The present value of an investment that pays $3,000 at the end of three years at 8%, then, is as follows:

$$\$2,381.49 = \$3,000 \times 0.79383$$

This is the same amount computed above, except for the effect of a rounding error. The interest factor for computing the present value of an investment is 1 divided by the interest factor for computing the future value of the same investment (same period and interest rate). Thus, 0.79383 in Table 3 for three periods at 8% equals $1 \div 1.25971$ from Table 1 for three periods at 8%.

Using Table 3, we can compute the present value of a single payment as follows:

$$PV = FV \times IF \text{ (Table 3)}$$

where PV is the present value, FV is the future value (the payment made in the future), and IF is the interest factor from Table 3.

In addition to determining the present value of an investment, you might want to determine the amount earned each period. For example, if your investment paid $3,000 at the end of three years and earned 8% interest, how much interest would you earn each year? A table like the one shown in Exhibit 3 is helpful.

Exhibit 3 Interest Table for a Present Value of $2,381.49 for Three Years at 8%

A Year	B Present Value at Beginning of Year	C Interest Earned (Column B × Interest Rate)	D Value at End of Year (Column B + Column C)
1	2,381.49	190.52	2,572.01
2	2,572.01	205.76	2,777.77
3	2,777.77	222.23	3,000.00
Total		618.51	

Column B shows the amount the investment is worth at the beginning of each year. Column C shows the amount of interest earned each year, and column D reports the amount the investment is worth at the end of each year. The total in column C is the total interest earned for three years. Values in Exhibit 3 are calculated the same way as in Exhibit 1. The present value of the investment must be calculated before the table can be prepared. The amount computed for the future value at the end of the investment period should be the future value of the investment (see $3,000 in Exhibit 3).

Present Value of an Annuity

OBJECTIVE 5

Determine the present value of an annuity.

The investment situation in the previous section assumed that a single amount was received at the end of an investment period. It is common for investments to pay an equal amount each period over an investment period. For example, assume that you could purchase an investment that would pay $1,000 at the end of each year for three years, and that you expect to earn a return of 8%. How much would you be willing to pay for the investment?

Calculate the present value of this annuity by calculating the present value of each payment and adding them together.

Present Value at Beginning of Year 1	Amount Received		
	End of Year 1	End of Year 2	End of Year 3
$ \ 925.93 = \$1{,}000 \div (1.08)^1$ ◀————	$1,000		
$857.34 = \$1{,}000 \div (1.08)^2$ ◀————————		$1,000	
$793.83 = \$1{,}000 \div (1.08)^3$ ◀————————————————			$1,000
$2,577.10 Present value of total investment			

$3,000.00 Total amount received over 3 years
2,577.10 Present value of total investment
$ 422.90 Interest earned over 3 years

The first row in this calculation is the present value of $1,000 received at the end of the first year, the second row is the present value of $1,000 received at the end of the second year, and the third row is the present value of $1,000 received at the end of the third year.

Alternatively, we could use the interest factors from Table 3 for one, two, and three periods at 8% and add them together to determine the interest factor.

Excerpt from Table 3   Present Value of a Single Amount

	Interest Rate								
Period	0.01	0.02	0.03	0.04	0.05	0.06	0.07	**0.08**	0.09
1	0.99010	0.98039	0.97087	0.96154	0.95238	0.94340	0.93458	**0.92593**	0.91743
2	0.98030	0.96117	0.94260	0.92456	0.90703	0.89000	0.87344	**0.85734**	0.84168
3	0.97059	0.94232	0.91514	0.88900	0.86384	0.83962	0.81630	**0.79383**	0.77218

$2,577.10 = $1.000 \times (0.92593 + 0.85734 + 0.79383)$
$2,577.10 = 1.000×2.57710

USING EXCEL

For the Present Value of an Annuity

SPREADSHEET

Use the PV function in Excel to calculate the present value of an annuity. The function can be accessed by using the function button and completing the pop-up box or by entering the function directly in a cell. The present value of an annuity function is PV(Interest Rate, Number of Periods, Amount Invested each Period). Accordingly, we can enter =PV(0.08,3,−1000) in a cell. The amount appearing in the cell is the present value of the annuity ($2,577.10 in this example). Remember that the amount invested is entered as a negative value.

To avoid the need to add interest factors together, tables are available that provide this addition. Table 4 inside the back cover of this book is an example of this type of table. Notice that the interest factor in this table for an annuity of three periods at 8% is 2.57710, the sum of the interest factors for one, two, and three years from Table 3. Using this table, we can calculate the present value of an annuity as follows:

PVA = A × IF (Table 4)

where *PVA* is the present value of an annuity, *A* is the amount of the periodic payment of the annuity, and *IF* is the interest factor from Table 4.

Excerpt from Table 4   Present Value of an Annuity

	Interest Rate								
Period	0.01	0.02	0.03	0.04	0.05	0.06	0.07	**0.08**	0.09
1	0.99010	0.98039	0.97087	0.96154	0.95238	0.94340	0.93458	0.92593	0.91743
2	1.97040	1.94156	1.91347	1.88609	1.85941	1.83339	1.80802	1.78326	1.75911
3	2.94099	2.88388	2.82861	2.77509	2.72325	2.67301	2.62432	**2.57710**	2.53129

Again, in addition to determining the present value of an annuity, you might want to determine the amount earned each period. For example, if you purchased an investment that paid $1,000 each year for three years at 8% interest, how much interest would you earn each year? A table like the one shown in Exhibit 4 is useful for this purpose.

Exhibit 4 Interest Table for an Annuity of $1,000 Each Year for Three Years at 8%

A Year	B Present Value at Beginning of Year	C Interest Earned (Column B × Interest Rate)	D Total Amount Invested (Column B + Column C)	E Amount Paid at End of Year	F Value at End of Year (Column D − Column E)
1	2,577.10	206.17	2,783.27	1,000.00	1,783.27
2	1,783.27	142.66	1,925.93	1,000.00	925.93
3	925.93	74.07	1,000.00	1,000.00	0.00
Total		422.90		3,000.00	

This table is a bit more complicated than those presented earlier. The first step in preparing this table is to calculate the present value of the annuity. This amount ($2,577.10) is the present value at the beginning of the first year. Interest for the first year is earned on this amount, as shown in column C by multiplying the present value in column B by the interest rate (8%). Column D shows the amount of the investment after interest is earned for the period. It is the sum of columns B and C. However, an amount ($1,000) is paid out of the investment each year. The amount left in the investment at the end of the year (column F) then is the amount in column D minus the amount paid in column E. The amount in column F is what is available at the beginning of the next year before interest is earned for the year (column B).

Observe that the value of the investment decreases over time because the amount of the annuity ($1,000) is paid out each year. Once the final payment is made at the end of the life of the investment, the value of the investment is zero (year 3, column F).

Exhibit 4 describes the amount of interest earned, the amount paid, and the value for each period of an annuity. Note that the amount earned from the annuity over the three years is equal to the difference between the amount received over the life of the annuity and the present value of the annuity (the amount paid for the investment): $422.90 = $3,000 − $2,577.10.

2 SELF-STUDY PROBLEM

WebTUTOR Advantage

H. Greely has the option of buying either of two investments. One investment pays $5,000 at the end of four years. The other investment pays $1,000 at the end of each year for four years. Both investments earn 8% interest.

Required Which investment is worth more at the beginning of the four-year period? How much interest will Greely earn from each investment over the four-year period?

The solution to Self-Study Problem 2 appears at the end of the chapter.

LOAN PAYMENTS AND AMORTIZATION

OBJECTIVE 6

Determine investment values and interest expense or revenue for various periods.

Economic decisions frequently require the use of present value calculations. These calculations are used in a variety of transactions recorded in accounting systems. For example, assume that you want to buy a used car. You negotiate with a dealer to purchase a car for $5,000, which you arrange to borrow from a local bank. The bank charges 12% interest on the loan, which is to be repaid in two years in equal monthly payments. How much will your payments be each month? How much interest will you pay over the two years?

To answer these questions, you should recognize that this problem involves the present value of an annuity. The amount you borrow ($5,000) is the present value of the amount you will repay in equal installments. Because the repayment is in equal monthly installments, this investment is an annuity. In effect, the bank is investing $5,000 in you at the beginning of the two-year period in exchange for monthly payments that will earn 12% (annual) return for the bank.

When amounts are paid or received on less than an annual basis, the interest rate and number of periods must be adjusted for the shorter period. An annual rate of 12% is equivalent to a monthly rate of 1% (12% ÷ 12 months). Two years of monthly payments result in 24 monthly payments (12 × 2). Therefore, instead of an interest factor of 12% for 2 years, we should use an interest factor of 1% for 24 months. Interest is compounded monthly, and a portion of the loan principal is being repaid each month along with the interest.

We can use Table 4 to solve this problem:

http://ingram.
swlearning.com

Calculate a loan schedule online.

$$PVA = A \times IF \text{ (Table 4)}$$
$$\$5,000 = A \times 21.24339$$
$$A = \$5,000 \div 21.24339$$
$$A = \$235.37$$

Excerpt from Table 4   Present Value of an Annuity

	Interest Rate								
Period	0.01	0.02	0.03	0.04	0.05	0.06	0.07	0.08	0.09
1	0.99010	0.98039	0.97087	0.96154	0.95238	0.94340	0.93458	0.92593	0.91743
2	1.97040	1.94156	1.91347	1.88609	1.85941	1.83339	1.80802	1.78326	1.75911
3	2.94099	2.88388	2.82861	2.77509	2.72325	2.67301	2.62432	2.57710	2.53129
⋮	⋮	⋮	⋮	⋮	⋮	⋮	⋮	⋮	⋮
23	20.45582	18.29220	16.44361	14.85684	13.48857	12.30338	11.27219	10.37106	9.58021
24	**21.24339**	18.91393	16.93554	15.24696	13.79864	12.55036	11.46933	10.52876	9.70661

Thus, the answer to the first question (How much would you pay each month?) is $235.37. Remember that the interest rate used in this computation is 1% per month and the number of periods is 24 months. The interest rate must be adjusted for the period of the annuity. An annual rate of 12% is equivalent to a monthly rate of 1%.

USING EXCEL

For Calculating a Payment

SPREADSHEET

Solve the problem using the payment function in Excel. Enter =PMT (.01,24,5000). The amount appearing in the cell is the amount of the annuity payment ($235.37 in this example). The arguments of the function are PMT(Interest Rate, Number of Periods, Present Value of the Annuity). Observe that this is the same function that we used to calculate the amount of payments for the future value of an annuity. The payment function is PMT(Interest Rate, Number of Periods, Present Value of Annuity, Future Value of Annuity). Either the third or fourth argument should be skipped depending on which value is being calculated. The third argument (Present Value of Annuity) is skipped if the last argument is included. In this case, an extra comma is needed after the second argument to indicate that the third argument has been omitted.

To determine how much interest you would incur on the loan, we need to prepare a table similar to the one in Exhibit 4. Exhibit 5 provides this information. This table usually is referred to as a loan amortization (or loan payment) table. It is a little different from Exhibit 4. A column has been added in Exhibit 5 to calculate the principal repaid each period, and the total investment column in Exhibit 4 has been omitted. Exhibits 4 and 5 contain essentially the same information. Formats of these tables vary in practice, but they all provide the same basic information.

Exhibit 5   Amortization Table for Automobile Loan of $5,000 for 24 Months at 1% per Month

A	B	C	D	E	F
Month	Present Value at Beginning of Month	Interest Incurred (Column B × Interest Rate)	Amount Paid	Principal Paid (Column D − Column C)	Value at End of Month (Column B − Column E)
1	5,000.00	50.00	235.37	185.37	4,814.63
2	4,814.63	48.15	235.37	187.22	4,627.41
3	4,627.41	46.27	235.37	189.10	4,438.31
⋮	⋮	⋮	⋮	⋮	⋮
23	463.70	4.64	235.37	230.73	232.97
24	232.97	2.33	235.30	232.97	0.00
Total		648.81	5,648.81		

This exhibit provides useful information about the loan. The total interest incurred over the life of the loan is $648.81. This amount equals the difference between the amount paid over the life of the loan ($5,648.81) and the amount borrowed ($5,000). The amount of interest incurred decreases each month (column C) because a portion of the loan principal is repaid each month (column E). Notice that the payment made each month ($235.37) repays a portion of the amount borrowed and pays the interest expense for the month. The amount of the loan repaid each month (column E) is the amount of the payment (column D) minus the interest expense for the month (column C). The amount owed decreases to zero over the 24 months. The final payment in month 24 (column D) is adjusted slightly because of rounding error. These characteristics are typical of many loan arrangements, especially consumer loans used to purchase autos, appliances and similar goods, and homes.

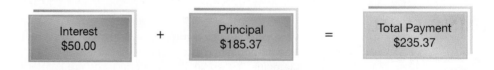

| Interest $50.00 | + | Principal $185.37 | = | Total Payment $235.37 |

The information in Exhibit 5 can be used to determine the transactions that the bank would record each month. It also can be used to determine transactions for the borrower (for example, if the borrower were a company concerned with this information).

Consider first the transactions that would be recorded by the bank for the first month of the loan, assuming the loan was made on April 1, 2004:

		ASSETS		=	LIABILITIES	+	OWNERS' EQUITY	
Date	Accounts	Cash	Other Assets				Contributed Capital	Retained Earnings
Apr. 1, 2004	Notes Receivable		5,000.00					
	Cash	−5,000.00						
Apr. 30, 2004	Cash	235.37						
	Notes Receivable		−185.37					
	Interest Revenue							50.00

The first transaction, at the beginning of the month (April 1), records the amount of the loan as a decrease in Cash and an increase in Notes Receivable. The second transaction, at the end of the month (April 30), records the amount received from the customer ($235.37) and the amount earned for the first month ($50.00). The balance in Notes Receivable ($4,814.63 = $5,000 − $185.37) is the amount owed to the bank by the customer at the end of the first month.

Similar transactions could be recorded by the customer:

		ASSETS		=	LIABILITIES	+	OWNERS' EQUITY	
Date	Accounts	Cash	Other Assets				Contributed Capital	Retained Earnings
Apr. 1, 2004	Cash	5,000.00						
	Notes Payable				5,000.00			
Apr. 30, 2004	Notes Payable				−185.37			
	Interest Expense							−50.00
	Cash	−235.37						

The first transaction records the amount received from the bank and the liability to the bank. The second transaction records the payment at the end of the first month. The amount paid reduces the liability to the bank and pays interest expense for the first month.

The bank records transactions for payments received each month over the life of the loan. The amount of principal paid and the amount of interest earned change each month. In the last month of the loan (March 2006), the bank would record the following:

		ASSETS		=	LIABILITIES	+	OWNERS' EQUITY	
Date	Accounts	Cash	Other Assets				Contributed Capital	Retained Earnings
Mar. 31, 2006	Cash	235.30						
	Notes Receivable		−232.97					
	Interest Revenue							2.33

After this transaction is recorded, the balance of Notes Receivable will be zero. The loan will have been paid off.

The customer also could record transactions each month. The amount of principal repaid and the interest expense incurred would change each month. The final payment would reduce the Notes Payable balance to zero.

UNEQUAL PAYMENTS

Investments do not always involve single amounts or annuities. For example, suppose Jill Johnson invested a portion of her salary at the end of each of four years. The amounts she invested in those years were $700, $800, $900, and $1,000, respectively. How much would her investments be worth at the end of the fourth year of investing if she earned 6% each year?

In this type of situation, each investment must be considered separately because the amounts invested are not the same each period.

Amount Invested at End of Year 1	End of Year 2	End of Year 3	End of Year 4	Future Value at End of Year 4
$700 ————————————————————————→				$ 833.71
	$800 ——————————————————→			898.88
		$900 ——————————→		954.00
			$1,000 ——→	1,000.00
			Total	$3,686.59

The future value of the amounts can be determined using interest factors from Table 1.

$$FV = PV \times IF \text{ (Table 1)}$$
$$\$833.71 = \$700 \times 1.19102 \text{ (6\%, 3 periods)}$$
$$898.88 = \$800 \times 1.12360 \text{ (6\%, 2 periods)}$$
$$954.00 = \$900 \times 1.06000 \text{ (6\%, 1 period)}$$
$$\underline{1,000.00} = \$1,000 \times 1.00000 \text{ (6\%, 0 period)}$$
$$\underline{\$3,686.59}$$

Observe that the amount invested at the end of the first year ($700) will be invested for four years, the amount invested at the end of the second year will be invested for three years, and so forth. Accordingly, the interest factor for the first investment is for four years, and the number of periods decreases by one for each successive investment.

LEARNING NOTE

A common mistake is to match investments with the incorrect period of investment. Consider how long an amount will be invested until the end of the investment period when computing future value, or until the beginning of the investment period when computing present value.

To continue the illustration, suppose you can purchase an investment that is expected to pay $200, $300, and $400 at the end of the next three years. You expect the investment to earn 7% interest. How much should you pay for the investment?

You want to determine the present value of the amounts you expect to receive. The relevant period is from the time when the amount will be received to the beginning of the investment period. For example, the first amount ($200) will be received at the end of one year; therefore, the relevant period is one year. The present value of the investment would be as follows:

Present Value at Beginning of Year 1	Amount Received		
	End of Year 1	End of Year 2	End of Year 3
$186.92 ←————————	$200		
262.03 ←———————————————————		$300	
326.52 ←———————————————————————————————			$400
$775.47 Total			

The present value of the investment would be as follows:

$$PV = FV \times IF \text{ (Table 3)}$$
$$\$186.92 = \$200 \times 0.93458 \text{ (7\%, 1 period)}$$
$$262.03 = \$300 \times 0.87344 \text{ (7\%, 2 periods)}$$
$$\underline{326.52} = \$400 \times 0.81630 \text{ (7\%, 3 periods)}$$
$$\underline{\$775.47}$$

COMBINING SINGLE AMOUNTS AND ANNUITIES

In some cases an investment involves both a single amount and an annuity. For example, suppose you could purchase an investment that offered to pay $100 at the end of each year for 10 years and $1,000 at the end of the 10-year period. If you expect the investment to earn 8% interest, how much would you pay for the investment at the beginning of the 10-year period? To answer this question, compute the present value of the annuity and add the present value of the single amount.

$$PVA = A \times IF \text{ (Table 4)}$$
$$\$671.01 = \$100 \times 6.71008$$
$$PV = FV \times IF \text{ (Table 3)}$$
$$\$463.19 = \$1,000 \times 0.46319$$

Therefore, the amount you should pay is $1,134.20 = $671.01 + $463.19.

Any investment problem can be thought of as a single amount, a series of single amounts, an annuity, or a combination of these arrangements.

SUMMARY OF FUTURE AND PRESENT VALUE CONCEPTS

Future and present value consider timing differences between when cash is received or paid and the present period. They are based on the simple concept that a dollar received in the future is worth less than a dollar received at the present time. The difference between the two amounts depends on the rate of interest and the time period. Amounts invested today must increase in value to compensate the investor for forgoing the use of the amount invested. The higher the interest rate required from an investment, the greater the future value must be relative to the present value. The longer an investor must wait before receiving the future value, the larger the future value must be relative to the present value. Exhibit 6 illustrates the basic concepts of future and present value.

Exhibit 6
Future and Present
Value Concepts

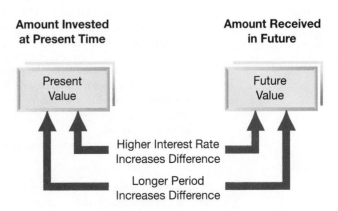

The interest rate an investment is expected to earn depends on the risk associated with the investment. The greater the uncertainty about the amount to be received from an investment, the higher the interest rate investors require before they will invest. Therefore, relatively safe investments, such as savings accounts, pay lower interest than relatively risky investments, such as corporate debt, where the chance of bankruptcy affects the amount an investor may receive. Similarly, the rate of interest a bank charges a customer for a loan depends on the customer's credit history as an indication of the probability that the customer will repay the amount borrowed, plus interest, when due.

3 | SELF-STUDY PROBLEM

Required Calculate each of the following at the beginning of year one.

WebTUTOR Advantage

A. The present value of $100 received at the end of two years at 10%.
B. The present value of $100 received at the end of three years at 10%.
C. The present value of $100 received at the end of three years at 8%.
D. The present value of $100 received at the end of each year for three years at 10%.
E. The present value of $50 received at the end of one year, $100 received at the end of two years, and $150 received at the end of three years at 10%.

Use your answers to demonstrate the effect of time periods and interest rates on the difference between the future and present values of investments by comparing A and B, B and C, B and D, and D and E.

The solution to Self-Study Problem 3 appears at the end of the chapter.

REVIEW

SUMMARY of IMPORTANT CONCEPTS

1. The future value of an investment is the amount the investment will be worth at some particular time in the future.
   a. The future value of an investment equals the present value times an interest factor that depends on the rate of interest earned on the investment and the number of periods it is invested.
   b. The future value of an annuity is the future value of a series of equal amounts paid at equal intervals.

2. The present value of an investment is the amount the investment is worth at the beginning of an investment period.
   a. The present value of an investment equals the future value times an interest factor. The interest factor for the present value is the reciprocal of the interest factor for the future value: interest factor for PV = 1 ÷ interest factor for FV.
   b. The present value of an annuity is the present value of a series of equal amounts paid at equal intervals.

3. Loan payments are determined from the present value of the loan (the amount borrowed) and the interest factor (interest rate and time period).
   a. A loan amortization table is useful for determining the amount of interest incurred, the amount of principal repaid each period on the loan, and the amount owed at the end of each period.
   b. A loan amortization table provides a basis for transactions recorded by the borrower and lender.

4. Future and present value calculations may involve a series of unequal payments or a combination of an annuity and a single amount.

5. Three factors important for calculating any future or present value are the amount of the payments, the interest rate, and the time periods when payments are made.

TERMS and CONCEPTS DEFINED in this CHAPTER

annuity (F288)   present value (F285)
future value (F285)

SELF-STUDY PROBLEM SOLUTIONS

SSP8-1   A. FV = PV × IF (Table 1)
               FV = $3,000 × 1.46933
               FV = $4,407.99
               The amount of interest earned would be $1,407.99 = $4,407.99 − $3,000.

   B.   FVA = A × IF (Table 2)
         $10,000 = A × 5.86660
              A = $1,704.56

Column E in the following interest table identifies the amount the investment is worth at the end of each year. The total of column D is the amount Harry invested over the five years. The total of column C is the amount of interest earned over the five years.

A	B	C	D	E
			Amount	
	Value	Interest Earned	Invested	Future Value at
	at Beginning	(Column B ×	at End of	End of Year
Year	of Year	Interest Rate)	Year	(Columns B + C + D)
1	0.00	0.00	1,704.56	1,704.56
2	1,704.56	136.36	1,704.56	3,545.48
3	3,545.48	283.64	1,704.56	5,533.68
4	5,533.68	442.69	1,704.56	7,680.93
5	7,680.93	614.48	1,704.56	9,999.97
Total		1,477.17	8,522.80	

SSP8-2   Option 1:

$$PV = FV \times IF \text{ (Table 3)}$$
$$\$3,675.15 = \$5,000 \times 0.73503$$
$$\text{Interest earned} = \$1,324.85 = \$5,000 - \$3,675.15$$

Option 2:

$$PVA = A \times IF \text{ (Table 4)}$$
$$\$3,312.13 = \$1,000 \times 3.31213$$
$$\text{Interest earned} = \$687.87 = \$4,000 \text{ (\$1,000 per year} \times 4 \text{ years)} - \$3,312.13$$

Option 1 is worth more, even though he will receive payments sooner from option 2.

SSP8-3   PV = FV × IF
   A. $82.65 = $100 × 0.82645 (Table 3)
   B. $75.13 = $100 × 0.75131 (Table 3)
   C. $79.38 = $100 × 0.79383 (Table 3)
   D. $248.69 = $100 × 2.48685 (Table 4)
   E. $45.45 = $50 × 0.90909
        $82.65 = $100 × 0.82645
       $112.70 = $150 × 0.75131
       $240.80

Comparison of A and B: The present value of an investment decreases relative to the future value as the time until the investment is received increases.

Comparison of B and C: The present value of an investment decreases relative to the future value as the interest rate increases. A higher interest rate results in a higher amount of interest being earned for investment B ($24.87 = $100 − $75.13) than for investment C ($20.62 = $100 − $79.38).

Comparison of B and D: The present value of an investment increases as the number of payments received increases. Thus, an annuity is more valuable than a single payment when each annuity payment is as large as the single payment.

Comparison of D and E: Both D and E pay $300 over three years. Investment D is worth more than investment E, however, because a larger amount is received sooner from D than from E.

Thinking Beyond the Question

How much will it cost to borrow money?

Most debt requires periodic payments of principal and interest. Consequently, debt often involves computations of annuities, particularly the present value of annuities. Determining the payment amount and the total cost of borrowing depends on the interest rate and the number of periods over which the debt is repaid.

As a borrower, you may be able to negotiate the number of periods over which debt is repaid. For example, you may be able to repay a loan over five or ten years. Often, agreeing to a shorter borrowing period means getting a loan with a lower interest rate. Why would that be true? What factors would encourage a lender to require a higher or lower rate of interest from a borrower? What kinds of information would a lender look for in the financial statements of a borrower like Mom's Cookie Company? Why? What financial information could help a borrower bargain for a lower rate or more money?

QUESTIONS

Q8-1
Obj. 1
A friend remarks, "I just got out of an accounting lecture about future value and present value. Frankly, I don't have a clue what the professor was talking about. And we have a quiz on Wednesday. Help!" Come to your friend's rescue. Clearly and concisely explain what is meant by the terms *future value* and *present value*.

Q8-2
Obj. 1
What does this statement mean? "The future value of $1,000 is an amount greater than $1,000."

Q8-3
Obj. 1
Why is the present value of $10,000 less than $10,000?

Q8-4
Obj. 2
You are inspecting Table 1 at the back of this book. At the intersection of the 10% column and the 18-period row you find the following number: 5.55992. Interpret that number. What does it mean?

Q8-5
Obj. 2
Freida invested $3,000 in an investment plan that guarantees 7% compound interest annually. The interest is deposited into the account at the end of each year. The account has now been open 30 years. As the years went by, were the earnings from interest in any given year larger than the year before, smaller than the year before, or the same as the year before? Explain the reason for your answer.

Q8-6
Obj. 2
Why do the interest factors in Table 1 (at the back of this book) get larger and larger as you move from the upper left corner of the table to the lower right corner?

Q8-7
Obj. 2
Your boss has asked you what the ending balance will be if he puts $8,000 into an investment earning 9% interest compounded annually. He plans to leave the money untouched for 29 years. Unfortunately, you only have your accounting textbook available to help you and you find that Table 1 (inside the front cover) only goes up through 25 periods. How can you solve this problem using only Table 1? What will be the ending amount in the account?

Q8-8
Obj. 3
Kelly Walker places 5% of her salary each year into a company-sponsored 401k retirement plan. Assume her annual salary is $100,000 and deposits are made to the retirement plan at the end of each year. What will be the balance in her 401k account at the end of 25 years if she never receives a pay raise and the plan earns 11% per year?

Q8-9
Obj. 3
You are inspecting Table 2 at the back of this book. At the intersection of the 6% column and the 13-period row you find the following number: 18.88214. Interpret that number. What does it mean?

Q8-10
Obj. 4
Why do the interest factors in Table 3 (inside the back cover of this book) get smaller and smaller as you move from the upper left corner of the table to the lower right corner?

Q8-11
Obj. 4
Your boss has asked you what amount she must invest today at 8% interest so that she will have $350,000 available to pay off a lump-sum debt that comes due in 32 years. In other words, what is the present value of $350,000 that must be paid in 32 years assuming an 8% rate? Unfortunately, you only have your accounting textbook available to help you and you find that Table 3 (inside the back cover) only goes up through 25 periods. How can you solve this problem using only Table 3? What is the present value?

Q8-12
Obj. 5
Why do the interest factors in Table 4 (inside the back cover of this book) get smaller as you move from left to right, but larger as you move from top to bottom?

Q8-13
Obj. 5
Jeraldo invested $4,100 into a financial instrument that promised to pay him $1,000 at the end of each year for the next five years. The salesperson explained that this would earn for him a 5% rate of return. At the end of five years, Jeraldo noticed that the dollar amount of his interest earnings had been smaller and smaller as the years went by. Explain why this happened.

Q8-14
Obj. 6
Determine whether the rows in Tables 1 through 4 (at the back of your textbook) are labeled in years or in periods. Does it make a difference whether they are labeled in years or periods? Why?

Q8-15
Obj. 6
Imelda is making equal-sized monthly payments of $288 on her car loan. She has only 18 payments left. Each month, the portion of her payment that goes to pay interest and the portion that goes to repay principal is different. Why? Is there any pattern to this change in portions? Explain why or why not.

EXERCISES

If your instructor is using Personal Trainer in this course, you may complete online the assignments identified by $\frac{P}{T}$ *.*

E8-1
Write a short definition for each of the terms listed in the *Terms and Concepts Defined in this Chapter* section.

E8-2
Obj. 2
$\frac{P}{T}$
Assume that you borrow $25,000 on April 1, 2004, at an annual rate of 7%. How much will you owe on March 31, 2005 if you make no payments until that date? How much will you owe on March 31, 2006 if you make no payments until that date? If you pay the interest incurred for the first year on March 31, 2005, how much will you owe on March 31, 2006 if you make no other payments until that date?

E8-3
Obj. 2
$\frac{P}{T}$
Today is Dave's 40th birthday. He is experiencing a midlife crisis and is thinking about retirement for the first time. To supplement his expected retirement pension, he deposits $8,000 in an investment account guaranteed to return him 6% interest annually.

a. What balance will he have in this account on his 65th birthday?
b. How much interest will he earn between now and then?

SPREADSHEET

E8-4
Obj. 2
P T

You just won last night's lotto drawing for the $1,000,000 prize. It will be paid to you in 20 installments of $50,000 each. You will receive the first payment today and receive an additional $50,000 payment at the end of each of the next 19 years. What is the present value of your winnings if 7 1/2% is the appropriate rate? Use an Excel spreadsheet and the PV function to determine the solution. (Hint: What is the present value of the amount you received today? How many periods long is the remaining annuity?)

E8-5
Obj. 3
P T

Renalda is saving for a once-in-a-lifetime trip, to begin seven years from today. She plans to visit the South Pacific and Far East. Today she starts her savings plan; she will deposit $1,500 at the end of each of the next seven years into a 5% savings account.

    a. What amount will she have in her account when she begins her trip?
    b. What amount of the total will be from her own deposits and what amount will she have earned in interest?

E8-6
Obj. 3
P T

Optimism, Inc. anticipates the need for factory expansion four years from today. The firm has determined that it will have the necessary funds for expansion if it puts $400,000 per year into a stock portfolio expected to earn 9% per year. Deposits will be made at the end of each year.

    a. How much is the company planning to raise toward factory expansion with this plan?
    b. What amount would the company expect to raise if it could invest $400,000 per year for seven years?
    c. Why is the answer to part b more than twice as large as the answer to part a even though the length of the annuity is less than twice as long?

E8-7
Obj. 3
P T

Use an Excel spreadsheet and the FV function to determine the following:

    a. The future value of a $2,000 annuity for 30 years at 8% compounded annually.
    b. The future value of a $2,000 annuity for 30 years at 8% compounded semiannually.
    c. The future value of a $2,000 annuity for 30 years at 8% compounded quarterly.
    d. How much extra interest is earned on the annuity above simply by changing the compounding period from annually to quarterly?
    e. How much extra interest would be earned by changing from annual compounding to daily compounding?
    f. Louisa set up an individual retirement account (IRA account) on her 35th birthday. She contributed $2,000 to the account on each subsequent birthday through her 65th. The account earned 8% compounded annually. What amount of interest (in dollars) will she have earned on this investment?
    g. Suppose she had started the IRA account 10 years earlier when she was 25 years old. How much additional interest would she have earned on this investment by age 65? (Hint: Her first payment into the account was on which birthday?)

SPREADSHEET

E8-8
Obj. 4
P T

Assume you will receive $1,000 at the end of year 1. What is its present value at the beginning of year 1 if you expect an 8% rate of return? What is the present value if you expect a 9% return? 10%? What can you conclude about the effect of the rate of return on the present value of cash to be received in the future?

E8-9
Obj. 4
P T

What is the present value of $800 to be received at the end of one year if it must provide a return of 8%? What is the present value of $900 to be received at the end of one year? $1,500? What can you conclude about the effect of the amount expected to be received on its present value?

E8-10
Obj. 4
P T

What is the present value of $1,000 to be received at the end of one year if it must provide a return of 5%? What is the present value of $1,000 to be received at the end of two years? Three years? What can you conclude about the effect of time until receipt on the present value of future cash inflows?

E8-11
Obj. 4
P T

Assume that you received a loan on July 1, 2004. The lender charges annual interest at 5%. On June 30, 2009, you owe the lender $510.52. Assuming that you made no payments for principal or interest on the loan during the five years, how much did you borrow?

E8-12
Obj. 5
P T

What is the present value of an annuity of $200 per year for five years if the required rate of return is 8%? What is the present value of the annuity if the required rate of return is 10%?

E8-13 A wealthy uncle has offered to give you either of two assets:
Obj. 5 end of three years or (b) an asset that pays $100 at the end o
$\frac{P}{T}$ that both assets earn a 7% annual rate of return. Which ass

E8-14 Lincoln Corporation expanded recently by investing $100,000 i
Obj. 5 creased annual operating cash inflows by $50,500 and annual o
These increases are expected for a total of six years. At that ti
lete and worthless. (Assume that operating cash inflows and out

    a. If the corporation requires a return of 8% on its investi
       ment decision? Show calculations to prove your answer.
    b. If you decide that the company has not met its investme
       nual net cash inflow over the six-year period would give the desired rate of return?
    c. Assuming that operating cash outflows do not change, what is the necessary increase in
       operating cash inflows that is needed to earn an 8% return?

E8-15 Katina Washington is currently employed as a computer programmer by Megatel Company.
Objs. 2, 5 Her dream, however, is to start her own computer software firm. To provide cash to start her
$\frac{P}{T}$ own business in six years she will invest $10,000 today. She thinks the investment will earn a
12% annual return.

SPREADSHEET

    a. How much would Katina have in her account at the end of six years if she earns 12%
       on the investment? How much of this would be interest earned during the six years?
    b. Assume, instead, that Katina has decided she needs $20,000 to begin business. She
       wants to invest equal amounts at the end of each year for the next six years to accumu-
       late the $20,000 needed at that time.
       i. How much must be invested each year, assuming that it earns 12% interest?
       ii. How much will the investment be worth at the end of each of the next six years?
       iii. How much will Katina have put into the account over the six years?
       iv. How much interest will be earned over the six years?

E8-16 I. M. Cansado is about to retire. He has a retirement account that allows two payment op-
Objs. 4, 5 tions. Under Option 1, he can choose to receive $140,000 at the end of six years. Under Op-
$\frac{P}{T}$ tion 2, he can choose to receive $20,000 at the end of each year for six years. An interest rate
of 10% is applicable to both plans. (a) Which retirement plan has the highest present value at
the beginning of the six-year period? (b) Which option would you recommend?

E8-17 Complete the tables and answer the questions.
Objs. 2, 3, 4, 5
$\frac{P}{T}$ a.

Single Sum	Rate	Time	Compounding Frequency	Interest Factor	Future Value
$1,000	12%	2 years	Annual	_____	_____
$1,000	12%	2 years	Semiannual	_____	_____
$1,000	12%	2 years	Quarterly	_____	_____
$1,000	12%	2 years	Monthly	_____	_____

    b. Summarize the effect of changing the compounding period on the future value of a
       single sum. Explain why this effect appears reasonable.
    c. What effect do you think that changing the compounding period of an annuity would
       have on its future value? Explain why you think this.
    d.

Single Sum	Rate	Time	Compounding Frequency	Interest Factor	Present Value
$1,000	12%	2 years	Annual	_____	_____
$1,000	12%	2 years	Semiannual	_____	_____
$1,000	12%	2 years	Quarterly	_____	_____
$1,000	12%	2 years	Monthly	_____	_____

    e. Summarize the effect of changing the compounding period on the present value of a
       single sum. Explain why this effect appears reasonable.
    f. What effect do you think that changing the compounding period of an annuity would
       have on its present value? Explain why you think this.

E8-18
Obj. 6
$\frac{P}{T}$
An investment is expected to pay a return of $100 per year. The interest rate for the investment is 6%. What will the price of the investment be if it has a life of 5 years? 10 years? 20 years?

E8-19
Obj. 6
$\frac{P}{T}$
What is the present value of an investment that pays $80 at the end of each year for 10 years and pays an additional $1,000 at the end of the tenth year if the required rate of return is 7%? 8%? 9%?

E8-20
Obj. 6
$\frac{P}{T}$
An investment has a life of 10 years. The rate of return for the investment is 6%. What will the price of the investment be if it is expected to pay a return of $10 per year? $100 per year?

E8-21
Obj. 6
$\frac{P}{T}$
What is the maximum amount a company should pay for equipment that it expects will increase its net income and cash flow by $250,000 per year for five years? The company requires a 12% return on its investment.

E8-22
Obj. 6
$\frac{P}{T}$
Old Money Company borrowed $1 million from a bank on January 1, 2004. The loan is to be repaid in annual installments over a three-year period. The bank requires a 9% return.

a. What is the amount of Old Money's required payment to the bank each year?
b. How much interest expense will Old Money incur each year?
c. Show how this loan would be entered into Old Money's books on January 1, 2004.
d. Show how Old Money's first annual installment payment would be entered into its books. Use the format below for parts C and D.

		ASSETS		=	LIABILITIES	+	OWNERS' EQUITY	
Date	Accounts	Cash	Other Assets				Contributed Capital	Retained Earnings

E8-23
Obj. 6
$\frac{P}{T}$
Lily Pewshun negotiated a three-year, 9%, $46,000 loan from her bank. It called for three equal-sized year-end payments.

a. Determine the amount of her payment each year (round to the nearest dollar).
b. Show how the loan, and each of the three payments, would be entered into her accounting system (round each amount to the nearest dollar). Use the format shown below.

		ASSETS		=	LIABILITIES	+	OWNERS' EQUITY	
Date	Accounts	Cash	Other Assets				Contributed Capital	Retained Earnings

E8-24
Objs. 4, 5, 6
$\frac{P}{T}$
a. Calculate each of the following:
   i. The present value of $300 to be received at the end of three years if invested at 6%.
   ii. The present value of $300 to be received at the end of four years if invested at 6%.
   iii. The present value of $300 to be received at the end of four years if invested at 5%.
   iv. The present value of $300 to be received at the end of each year for four years if invested at 6%.

     v. The present value of $100 to be received at the end of one year, $200 to be received at the end of two years, $300 to be received at the end of three years, and $600 to be received at the end of four years at 6%.
  b. Inspect your results. What do they suggest to you about the effect of time periods and interest rates on the present value of amounts to be received in the future?

E8-25

Objs. 3, 5, 6

SPREADSHEET

Use an Excel spreadsheet and the FV, PV, and PMT functions to determine the amount of each of the following. R = the annual interest rate and t = number of years. When there are multiple cash flows per year, the amount of the annuity shown below is the amount of each individual cash flow (not the total cash flow for the year). Round all answers to the nearest dollar.

  a. Present value of a $500 annuity when R = 11% compounded annually and t = 18
  b. Future value of a $2,400 annuity when R = 5% compounded annually and t = 25
  c. Future value of a $950 annuity when R = 12.8% compounded semiannually and t = 15
  d. The annual annuity payment that will provide $13,400 in eight years when R = 9% compounded annually
  e. Present value of a $10,000 annuity when R = 8% compounded quarterly and t = 10
  f. Future value of a $238 annuity when R = 7% compounded annually and t = 16
  g. Present value of a $1,000 annuity when R = $6\frac{3}{8}$% compounded annually and t = 3
  h. Present value of a $700 annuity when R = 10% compounded semiannually and t = 11
  i. The semiannual annuity payment that will pay off, over six years, a $9,860 debt owed today if R = 13%
  j. Future value of a $1 annuity when R = 8% compounded annually and t = 200

PROBLEMS

If your instructor is using Personal Trainer in this course, you may complete online the assignments identified by ᴾ𝓣.

P8-1

Objs. 2, 3

ᴾ𝓣

Computing Future Value

Arthur has just graduated from college and has his first job. His salary is that of an entry-level employee, so he has to budget his money carefully. However, he does understand the need to save money for the future.

Required

  A. Assume that he deposits $500 at the end of each year for 10 years into an investment account earning 7%. He then stops making deposits and uses the money instead for house and car payments. How much will be in the investment account at the end of the 10-year period?
  B. Assume Arthur decides to keep the investment but does not make any additional contributions. How much will be in the account when he retires, after working for another 25 years?
  C. Assume that Arthur does not begin saving until he has worked for 20 years. If he plans to retire in 15 years from that time, how much would he have to invest at the end of each year, in an account earning 7%, to equal the balance in the account in part B?
  D. Calculate the total amount of cash that Arthur would pay in under parts A and B combined and the amount he would pay in under part C. Why is there a difference?

P8-2

Obj. 3

ᴾ𝓣

Computing Future Value

Stevie Gordon, age 40, is evaluating several supplemental retirement annuity plans offered by her employer. In general, all the plans call for Stevie to make annual contributions, some of which will be partially matched by the employer. The two plans drawing most of her attention are as follows. Plan 1 requires $3,000 annual end-of-year contributions by Stevie; the employer will match 20% of Stevie's contribution each year; and the plan guarantees an 8% overall return. Plan 2 requires $2,500 annual end-of-year contributions by Stevie; the employer will match 85% of Stevie's contribution; and the plan guarantees a 6% overall return.

Required Which option has the higher expected future value when Stevie reaches age 65? Which option would you recommend to Stevie? Why?

P8-3
Obj. 3
P/T

The Power of Compound Interest

Prudence and Margo are identical twins. Early on, it became clear that Prudence was a bit of a plodder whereas Margo was the fun-loving, carefree type. At age 15, both started working regularly after school. Prudence became a saver while Margo specialized in stimulating the economy with immediate purchases. Following her grumpy old grandfather's advice, Prudence began making annual contributions of $2,000 to an IRA (individual retirement account) on her 16th birthday. Margo's response to her grandfather's suggestion was "gimme a break."

Two strange events occurred, however, on their 23rd birthday. First, Prudence made her annual $2,000 IRA contribution, bringing her balance to $21,273.26. She never contributed again. Second, Margo promised to begin making $2,000 annual contributions to an IRA on her 26th birthday. She kept her promise and continued through her 65th birthday, which is today. Tomorrow, each will begin making withdrawals from their IRAs, which have been earning an 8% return.

Required

A. How much cash did Prudence contribute to her IRA over the years? How much cash did Margo contribute?
B. What is the balance in Prudence's IRA account today? (Hint: The interest factor for the future value of a single sum for 42 periods at 8% is 25.33948.)
C. What is the balance in Margo's IRA account today? (Hint: The interest factor for the future value of an ordinary annuity for 40 periods at 8% is 259.05652.)
D. Suppose Prudence had never stopped making contributions to her IRA. What would be her account balance today? (Hint: The interest factor for the future value of an ordinary annuity for 50 periods at 8% is 573.77016.)
E. What lesson does this suggest about the power of compound interest?

P8-4
Objs. 3, 4

Using Time Value Techniques in Retirement Planning

Starla has decided to retire in 12 years. She has $44,400 available today and wants to invest the money to supplement her pension plan.

Required

A. Assume Starla wants to accumulate $100,000 by her retirement date. Will she achieve her goal if she invests $44,400 today and earns 7%?
B. If Starla invests, a total of $44,400 through a series of 12 equal annual installments instead of a single amount, would Starla accumulate the desired $100,000? The first investment would be made one year from today. Show calculations and explain what you find.
C. If the amount accumulated in part A does not equal $100,000, approximately how many years would be required, assuming the same interest rate and equal annual deposits as above.

P8-5
Objs. 4, 5

Computing Present Value

Tyrone Flower plans to choose one of three investments. Investment A pays $500 at the end of each year for four years. Investment B pays $2,250 at the end of four years. Investment C pays $300 at the end of each year for three years and pays $1,200 at the end of the fourth year. Tyrone requires a return of 8% on each of these investments.

Required Provide information to help Tyrone decide how much he should pay for each of these investments.

P8-6
Objs. 2, 3, 5
P/T

Annuity Deposits at the Beginning of Periods Versus Deposits at the End

Laura has decided to set up an IRA (Individual Retirement Account) in which she will make a deposit to her plan at the end of each year, beginning one year from today. She expects to earn 9% on her investment, over a period of 10 years.

SPREADSHEET

Required

A. If she invests the maximum amount of $3,000 at the end of each of the 10 years, how much will she have accumulated after 10 years? How much of this will be interest?

B. Assume the same facts as stated previously, except that Laura plans to make her deposit for each of the 10 years beginning today. How much will she have accumulated 10 years from today? (Hint: You do not have a table in the text for this type of annuity. But you can compute the future value of each deposit separately and add the totals together.) How much of the ending account balance will be composed of interest?

C. Refer to the answers for parts A and B. Which one is larger? Why? Explain.

P8-7

Objs. 4, 5

$\frac{P}{T}$

Using Time Value to Determine a Company's Pension Liability

Cellex Manufacturing is a family-owned company preparing its year-end 2004 financial statements. The firm will follow generally accepted accounting principles for the first time. Therefore, it is required to record, for the first time, a long-term liability for its employee pension plan. Employees who retire from the company will be paid $10,000 at the end of each year following retirement for five years. Below is the number of employees expected to receive benefits and their projected retirement dates:

1. Ten employees retiring at the end of 2008
2. Twenty employees retiring at the end of 2013
3. Thirty employees retiring at the end of 2018

Required

A. If all employees retire when scheduled and receive their full expected retirement benefits, what total amount of cash will this require?

B. If the applicable interest rate is 7%, what is the amount of the liability that should be recorded for 2004? (Hint: Calculate the solution in two steps. First, calculate the present value of a five-year annuity for each of the three employee groups. Second, calculate the present value of those three amounts based on the number of years until each annuity begins.)

C. Using the format presented in the chapter, show how the liability would be recorded in the accounting system.

P8-8

Objs. 4, 5

$\frac{P}{T}$

SPREADSHEET

Using Spreadsheet Functions in a Car Buying Decision

Ricardo recently received a major promotion at work and a significant raise. He is shopping for a new car. He really likes large sport utility vehicles and has his eye on one priced at $35,000. He is not sure how to finance the vehicle, however. He has three choices.

1. The dealer has offered to finance the vehicle with zero down on a six-year, 14% loan.
2. A local bank will finance the vehicle for five years at 10% if he makes a 15% down payment.
3. His credit union will finance the vehicle for four years at 8% if he makes a 25% down payment.

Under all three options, equal-sized end-of-the-month payments are required. Ricardo has the cash available for a down payment but was hoping to use it for other purposes.

Required Use the Excel PMT function to help you answer the following questions.

A. For each financing alternative, identify the rate, number of periods, and amount that you must enter into the PMT function.

B. What is the size of the monthly payment under each alternative?

C. Based only on your answers to parts A and B, which option looks best to you?

D. What is the sum of the payments required under each financing option?

E. What total amount of interest will be paid under each financing option?

F. Based on the information available, which financing option would you recommend to Ricardo?

P8-9

Obj. 6

$\frac{P}{T}$

Refinancing Decisions

The Taylors are considering refinancing the loan on their home. Currently, they have a 30-year loan with an 8% annual interest rate. The original loan was for $250,000, but over three years the Taylors have reduced the loan balance to $243,200. A local bank has offered them a 15-year loan with a 6.5% annual interest rate. The bank will charge a 1% fee of

$2,432 (0.01 × $243,200 = $2,432) to prepare the paperwork associated with the new loan. The fee will be added to the existing loan balance if the Taylors refinance.

SPREADSHEET

Required

A. Using a spreadsheet program such as Excel, determine the Taylors existing monthly payment. Next, multiply their payment times the number of months remaining on the loan to determine the total amount of payments remaining.
B. Determine the monthly payment if the Taylors refinance their loan.
C. What will be the total amount the Taylors will pay the bank over the life of the loan if they refinance?
D. What advice would you give the Taylors?

P8-10 Repaying a Note

Obj. 6

P/T

Georgia Company borrowed $600,000 from a bank on May 1, 2004. The bank required a return of 12% on the loan. The loan is to be repaid over 12 months in equal installments. Georgia Company's fiscal year ends on December 31.

SPREADSHEET

Required

A. Prepare an amortization table for the loan for the 12-month period.
B. How much interest expense would Georgia report on the loan for its 2004 fiscal year?
C. How much interest expense would it report for 2005?
D. What amount of liability would Georgia report for the loan at the end of 2004?
E. What amount would it report at the end of 2005?

P8-11 Understanding an Amortization Table

Obj. 6

P/T

On January 1, 2004, Waldman Enterprises purchased machinery on credit by signing a note payable for the full purchase price. The note payable called for interest to be paid on the unpaid balance and required three equal end-of-year payments. Waldman's accounting staff prepared the following amortization table related to the note:

Year	Balance at Beginning of Year	Interest Expense	End-of-Year Payment	Balance at End of Year
1	$2,577.10	$206.17	1,000.00	?
2	1,783.27	142.66	1,000.00	?
3	925.93	74.07	1,000.00	?

Required

A. What was the purchase price of the machinery?
B. What was the interest rate called for by the note?
C. By what amount was the principal balance of the note reduced during the first year?
D. What amount will be reported on Waldman's year 2 income statement regarding this note? What will it be labeled?
E. What amount will be reported on Waldman's year 3 statement of cash flows regarding this note?
F. What amount will be reported on Waldman's year 1 balance sheet regarding this note? In what section and under what title will it be reported?

P8-12 Preparation of an Amortization Table

Obj. 6

P/T

Rebecca is the owner of Sunnybrook Farm. On January 1, 2004, the beginning of the company's fiscal year, Rebecca borrowed $750,000 at 10% annual interest to purchase equipment. The loan is to be repaid over five years in equal annual installments. (Round each amount to the nearest dollar.)

SPREADSHEET

Required

A. What is the amount of Rebecca's loan payment each year?
B. Prepare an amortization table for the loan.
C. What will be the amount of interest expense reported by Sunnybrook Farm for the loan in 2004 and in 2005?

P8-13 Entering Loan Data into the Accounting System

Obj. 6

P̸T

Turn Buckle Company financed new equipment costing $50,000 with a five-year loan from a local bank. The bank charged 11% interest on the note. (Round each amount to the nearest dollar.)

Required

A. What would Turn Buckle's annual payments be to the bank each year, assuming that the note and interest are paid in equal annual installments?
B. How much interest expense would the company record for the first year of the note and for the second year?
C. Using the format presented in the chapter, show how the first and second year-end loan payments would be recorded in the accounting system.

P8-14 Calculation of Notes Payable

Obj. 6

P̸T

You have decided to purchase a car. You have found a clean used car that will cost you $8,500. You can finance your purchase through the dealer at an annual rate of 12% for 24 months. The dealer requires a down payment of $2,000.

SPREADSHEET

Required

A. What will be the amount of your monthly payments?
B. How much will you pay the dealer over the life of the loan?
C. How much of this amount will be interest?
D. If you decide to pay off the loan at the end of the first year, how much will you owe the dealer?

P8-15 Reconstructing Facts from Partial Information

Obj. 6

P̸T

Mezzelano Company was involved in a transaction in which a three-year note was exchanged. The note requires equal year-end payments. The accounting department prepared the following amortization table and sent you a copy. All amounts were rounded to the nearest dollar. Unfortunately, the copy machine malfunctioned, and none of the column headings are readable on your copy.

(i)	(ii)	(iii)	(iv)	(v)	(vi)
1	130,000	10,400	50,444	40,044	89,956
2	89,956	7,196	50,444	43,248	46,708
3	46,708	3,737	50,444	46,708	-0-

Required

A. Identify each of the missing column headings. Explain why each one must be as you identified it.
B. What is the principal amount of the note?
C. What is the interest rate of the note?
D. Is this an amortization table for a note receivable or a note payable? How can you tell? Discuss.
E. At the end of year 2, what amount from this table will be reported on the income statement?
F. At the end of year 2, what amount from this table will be reported on the balance sheet?
G. At the end of year 2, what total amount from this table will be reported on the statement of cash flows (direct approach)?

P8-16 Combining Two Annuities of Different Size

Obj. 6

P̸T

The Faithful Servants Church has started a building fund. Annual end-of-year deposits of $4,000 will begin at the end of the current calendar year. The accumulating balance will earn 6% compound interest per year. The $4,000 deposits are expected to be made for eight years and then increased to $7,000 for four additional years.

(Continued)

Required

A. What balance will be in the fund immediately after the 12th deposit is made?
B. If no further deposits are made, and the balance is left to earn interest for 10 more years, what amount will be in the account?
C. What amount of interest revenue will be earned by the building fund up to the date of the 12th deposit?

P8-17 Computing Withdrawals from an Annuity
Objs. 5, 6

$\frac{P}{T}$

Kwana Lovejoy received a cash gift of $30,000 from his grandfather exactly one year before he planned to start college. The gift was to be used to help pay Kwana's tuition and so it was deposited into an investment account earning 7% per year. The plan is for Kwana to withdraw equal annual amounts for each of four years so that at the end of that time, there will be a zero balance in the account and he will have completed his undergraduate degree.

Required

A. Given the above conditions, how much should Kwana withdraw at the beginning of each of his four college years?
B. What total amount of interest will the investment earn over the four years?
C. Assume that Kwana's grandfather agrees to allow him to withdraw a total of $12,000 at the beginning of his first year of college. (This will allow Kwana to pay his tuition and to buy a cheap used car.) What equal annual withdrawals can Kwana then make for the remaining three years of college?

P8-18 The Effect of Interest Rate on Cost of an Investment
Objs. 5, 6

$\frac{P}{T}$

Milo Moneybags is considering an investment that will pay him $1,050 at the end of each year for seven years and then will pay a lump sum of $15,000 at the end of that time.

Required

A. If Milo requires his investments to earn 9% interest, what is the maximum amount he should pay for the investment at the beginning of the seven-year period?
B. Assume Milo requires his investment to earn 5% interest. What is the maximum amount he should pay for the investment described in part A?
C. Which investment will cost Milo the greater amount? Why is there a difference in the costs?

P8-19 Using Spreadsheet Functions in a Home-Buying Decision
Objs. 5, 6

$\frac{P}{T}$

SPREADSHEET

Prosperous Pauline is about to make an offer to buy a home. The list price is $235,000 but Pauline will make an offer of $209,500. She plans to make a $21,500 down payment with the balance financed with a 30-year mortgage at 8.4% annual interest. Pauline wonders what her monthly "principal and interest" payment would be under these circumstances. Use an Excel spreadsheet (and the PMT function) to help you answer the questions below.

Required

A. What is the interest rate that should be entered into the PMT function?
B. What is the number of periods that should be entered into the PMT function?
C. What is the amount that should be entered into the PMT function?
D. What is the amount of Pauline's monthly "principal and interest" payment?
E. When Pauline makes her first payment, what amount will go to pay interest and what amount will be repayment of principal? (Hint: What amount did she owe during the first month and what rate of interest did she incur during the month?)
F. Suppose Pauline decides to obtain a 15-year mortgage instead and that the annual rate is 8%. What will be the amount of her monthly payment?
G. How much interest will Pauline avoid paying if she takes the 15-year mortgage instead of the 30-year mortgage?

P8-20 Excel in Action

$\frac{P}{T}$

In December 2004, Millie and Milo Wermz decided to purchase the property they had been renting for The Book Wermz. The cost of the building was $120,000 and the cost of the land was $60,000. A local bank agreed to lend $160,000 toward the purchase price in exchange for

SPREADSHEET

a mortgage on the property. The loan is to be repaid in equal monthly installments over 30 years beginning in January 2005. Interest on the loan is 8% and is fixed over the term of the loan.

Required

A. Determine the monthly payments on the loan using a spreadsheet. Enter the following captions in cells A1 to A4: Principal, Period, Interest Rate, Payment. In cell B1, enter "160000", the amount borrowed. In cell B2, calculate the number of months over which the loan will be repaid (=30*12). In cell B3, calculate the monthly interest rate on the loan (=0.08/12). In cell B4, use a function to calculate the payment amount. Click on the Function f_x button, select Financial from the Category list, and select PMT from the list of functions. Click the OK button. In the dialog box, enter B3 for Rate, B2 for Nper, and B1 for Pv. (You can move the box by clicking and dragging it so that the data you entered in the spreadsheet are visible.) Nper is the number of periods and Pv is the present value of the loan (the amount borrowed). Leave the Fv and Type boxes blank, and click on the OK button. Cell B4 contains the monthly payment amount as a negative number, because it is a cash outflow. Make this number positive by clicking on cell B4 and changing the formula to read =PMT(B3,B2,B1)*(−1). You can make this change in the formula bar just above the column headers and then click the green checkmark.

Beginning in cell A6, prepare an amortization table for the first year of the loan. Enter captions in row 6 like those in Exhibit 5 of this chapter. Center the captions, use text wrapping, and make the captions bold.

Enter 1 through 12 in column A, beginning with cell A7.

In cell B7, reference the principal amount (=B1).

In cell C7, calculate the interest expense for the first month, the principal times the monthly interest rate (=B7*$B$3). Note that an absolute address should be provided for the interest rate ($B$3) because you will always reference this cell to determine the rate.

In cell D7, reference the amount paid (=$B$4). Again, use an absolute address.

In cell E7, calculate the principal paid (=C7–D7).

In cell F7, calculate the amount owed at the end of the month (=B7–E7).

In cell B8, reference the amount owed at the beginning of the second month (=F7).

Copy the contents of cells C7 through F7 to cells C8 through F8. Then copy the contents of cells B8 through F8 to the remaining rows to complete the monthly calculations.

In cell A19, enter "Total."

In cell C19, calculate the total interest expense for 2005 using the sum function.

In cell D19, calculate the total amount paid on the loan for 2005 using the sum function.

Format the numbers in the spreadsheet using the Comma button. Use single lines to separate captions from calculations in the amortization table. Use single lines before totals and double lines after totals.

B. How much does The Book Wermz owe the bank on December 31, 2005? What amount of interest expense is incurred the first year?

C. Suppose the Wermz's decided to repay the loan over 15 years instead of 30 years. What would be the monthly payment? Change the number of periods in cell B2 to 15 years (=15*12). What amount would be owed on December 31, 2005? What is the total interest incurred in the first year?

D. Suppose the interest rate charged by the bank was 9% over a 30-year repayment period. What effect would this rate have on the monthly payments and total interest for the first year?

P8-21 Multiple-Choice Overview of the Chapter

1. For a given amount, interest rate, and number of years, which of the following will yield the highest number?
   a. Future value of a single sum
   b. Future value of an annuity
   c. Present value of a single sum
   d. Present value of an annuity

(Continued)

2. You have purchased an investment at a price of $1,500. It guarantees a 7% return, compounded annually, over its 10-year life. At the end of 10 years, your $1,500 will be returned to you plus all investment profit. Your investment revenue will be
   a. larger each year than the year before.
   b. smaller each year than the year before.
   c. equal each year to the year before.
   d. larger than the year before for the first five years and then smaller for the next five years.

3. The present value of an investment is $600. The investment earns a 7% annual rate of return. The investment consists of one payment made at the end of two years. The amount an investor should receive from the investment at the end of the second year would be
   a. $600 \div (1.07)^2$.
   b. $600 \times (1.07)^2$.
   c. 600×1.07.
   d. $600 \div 1.07$.

4. The present value of an investment that paid $500 at the end of three years and earned a 6% return would be
   a. $419.81.
   b. $471.70.
   c. $30.00.
   d. $470.00.

5. The present value of an investment that paid $100 at the end of each year for five years and earned a 6% return would be
   a. $470.00.
   b. $471.70.
   c. $373.63.
   d. $421.24.

6. A company borrowed $100,000 from a bank on July 1, 2004. The company made monthly payments of $5,235 on the note at the end of each month from July through December. Total interest expense on the note for this six-month period was $4,410. If this is the company's only note, what amount should the company report on its December 31, 2004 balance sheet for notes payable?
   a. $100,000
   b. $95,590
   c. $73,000
   d. $68,590

7. You are inspecting a present value table. As the interest rate increases, you should expect the table value to:
   a. increase.
   b. decrease.
   c. increase if it is a present value of a single sum table, but decrease if it is a present value of an annuity table.
   d. decrease if it is a present value of a single sum table, but increase if it is a present value of an annuity table.

8. A friend obtained a $7,500 car loan from a local bank at 9% interest. The loan requires 36 equal-sized monthly payments. The portion of the payment that goes to pay interest will
   a. increase each month.
   b. decrease each month.
   c. stay the same each month.
   d. decrease for the first 18 months and then increase during the last 18 months.

9. Clementine is part owner of a mining venture. A saver by nature, she puts part of her profits into a 6% savings account every other month. The first month she deposited $50. She has increased each of three subsequent deposits by $10. If she wants to fore-

cast what the account balance will be after 10 months, she should use which of the following tables?
a. Future value of a single sum
b. Future value of an annuity
c. Present value of a single sum
d. Present value of an annuity

10. Assume that you borrowed $1,000 from a bank. The bank charges 12% interest and requires that the loan be repaid in 24 monthly installments. The interest expense you would incur for the first year would be:
a. $120.
b. more than $120.
c. less than $120.
d. less than interest expense for the second year.

CASES

C8-1 Borrowing Costs
Obj. 6

Darren Driver is in the market for a new car. He has found a model he likes and has received prices from two dealers. The first dealer will charge $20,500 for the car. Darren will receive a rebate of $1,400 from the manufacturer, for a net price of $19,100. The dealer also will allow Darren $3,600 for his old car as a trade-in. The dealer will finance the purchase for four years at 12% per year. Interest and principal will be paid in four annual installments. The second dealer will charge $19,000 for the car after a $1,000 rebate. This dealer will allow $3,000 for the old car and will finance the purchase for four years at 10% per year, also payable in four annual installments.

Required Which is the better deal? Provide evidence to support your answer. (You are not required to prepare an amortization table.)

C8-2 Principal and Interest Payments
Obj. 6

Homer has decided to purchase a house. The price of the house is $80,000 after a down payment of $20,000. The bank will finance the purchase for 25 years at 9%. Alternatively, it will finance the house for 15 years at 8%. Under either option, the bank wants Homer to retire the loan by making a series of equal-sized year-end payments.

Required Evaluate the options for Homer. Write a memo to Homer (in good form) that explains how much total interest he will pay under each option and how much his total payments will be each year and over the life of the loan. Advise Homer about which choice he should take and the factors that are important in making the decision. (You do not have to prepare an amortization table.)

C8-3 Evaluating Contract Proposals
Obj. 6

Fleet LaMont, a running back, was selected #1 in the recent draft of the National Football League. Fleet's agent and the team's general manager are locked in arduous negotiations. Each side has presented several proposals, but no agreement is in sight. All proposed contracts, except #6 on the next page, are guaranteed. This means the contractual payments must be made even if Fleet is injured or cut from the team. Under contract proposal #6, all payments to Fleet may be cancelled by the team if Fleet is injured or cut. The average career in the NFL is less than four years. A brief summary of each proposal follows:

(Continued)

Contract Proposal	Sum of Cash Payments in Contract	Summary of Terms
1	$3,000,000	A three-year contract at $1 million per year payable quarterly starting on the date of signing the contract.
2	$4,000,000	A four-year contract at $1 million per year payable at the end of each completed year of the contract.
3	$2,900,000	A four-year contract with signing bonus of $900,000 (payable at signing) plus end-of-quarter salary payments of $125,000. The salary payments would begin three months after signing the contract.
4	$26,200,000	A three-year contract at $400,000 per year paid at each year-end plus a single $25 million payment to be paid 25 years after signing.
5	$2,500,000	A three-year contract with 2.5 million signing bonus and no salary payments.
6	$9,000,000	A six-year contract at $1,500,000 per year. Payable quarterly, cancelable if Fleet is injured or cut from the team.

Required Carefully evaluate each contract proposal. Fleet believes a 4% interest rate is appropriate for determining the present value of his contract offers. If you were Fleet, which contract would you accept? Write a memorandum to your agent explaining which contract you have chosen and the financial and non-financial reasons that support your decision. Be sure to include a discussion of why your choice is superior to each of the other alternatives.

FINANCING ACTIVITIES

What are the fundamental accounting issues associated with financing activities?

As companies grow, they often need additional financial resources to pay for new assets. Successful companies frequently borrow from various sources and issue stock as a means of acquiring necessary financial resources. Maria and Stan have decided that it's time for Mom's Cookie Company to increase the size of its operations. Consequently, they need to understand various types of financing activities and how to account for these activities.

FOOD FOR THOUGHT

What are the primary characteristics of debt and equity? How do these characteristics affect how we account for financing activities? Maria and Stan are considering these questions. The company has hired Ellen as a full-time accountant, and Maria and Stan are seeking her advice.

Stan: *To become a larger company, we need additional financing.*

Ellen: *Yes, and you need to understand how the financing will affect the company.*

Maria: *Financing provides additional money for us to use in the company.*

Ellen: *That's correct, but different types of financing involve different types of commitments and can affect your ability to control the company and make decisions in the future.*

Stan: *So, we need to understand how financing activities will affect our company.*

Ellen: *Yes, but first you need to understand some fundamental accounting issues associated with these activities.*

Maria: *We hired you to do that for us.*

Ellen: *True, but you need to understand these issues as well. They affect the company's cash flows and will affect your ability to raise additional funds in the future. To make decisions about how much debt and equity you want to issue, you need to understand how financing activities affect your company's balance sheet, income statement, and statement of cash flows.*

OBJECTIVES

Once you have completed this chapter, you should be able to:

1 Identify information that companies report about obligations to lenders and explain the transactions affecting long-term debt.

2 Describe appropriate accounting procedures for contingencies and commitments, including capital leases.

3 Identify information reported in the stockholders' equity section of a corporate balance sheet and distinguish contributed capital from retained earnings.

4 Explain transactions affecting stockholders' equity and describe how these transactions are reported in a company's financial statements.

5 Distinguish between preferred stock and common stock, and discuss why corporations may issue more than one type of stock.

TYPES OF OBLIGATIONS

Organizations engage in activities that obligate them to make future payments of cash or to provide goods or services. Most obligations are reported as liabilities on a company's balance sheet. Liabilities result from transactions with creditors, suppliers, customers, employees, and others.

An organization incurs debt when it borrows from creditors. For example, a company may borrow from a bank, another company, or an individual. The lender agrees to provide resources to the borrower. In exchange, the borrower signs a note (a contract), promising to repay the amount borrowed (the principal) plus interest.

In addition to contracting with creditors, organizations contract with suppliers, employees, and other providers of goods and services. Retail stores, for example, often acquire merchandise on credit from manufacturers and agree to pay for the goods in the near future. Companies also contract with their employees, exchanging wages for labor. Some compensation, such as retirement benefits, may be deferred to the future. Obligations to creditors, suppliers, and employees are all part of an organization's liabilities.

The term *liabilities* refers to an organization's obligations to deliver payments, goods, or services in the future. A liability links a past event (receiving something of value) and a future event (giving value back for what was received). **So, three attributes define a liability for an organization: (1) a present responsibility exists to transfer resources to another entity at some future time, (2) the organization cannot choose to avoid the transfer, and (3) the event creating the responsibility has already occurred.**[1]

Exhibit 1 presents the liabilities reported on the balance sheet of Mom's Cookie Company. The liabilities are like those of most companies. They include obligations to lenders (Notes Payable and Interest Payable), suppliers (Accounts Payable), employees (Wages Payable), and customers (Unearned Revenue).

Many of the liabilities reported by a company are associated with its operating activities. These liabilities result from transactions with suppliers, employees, and customers and involve resources used to produce and sell products. These obligations will be considered in a future chapter that examines operating activities. This chapter focuses on liabilities resulting from borrowing money from creditors.

---

[1] "Elements of Financial Statements," *FASB Statement of Financial Accounting Concepts*, no. 6 (1985).

Exhibit 1

Balance Sheet
Presentation of
Liabilities for Mom's
Cookie Company

December 31,	2005	2004
Liabilities:		
Current liabilities:		
Accounts payable	$ 16,260	$ 9,610
Wages payable	3,590	
Unearned revenue	2,770	4,250
Interest payable	810	650
Notes payable, current portion	6,000	5,000
Total current liabilities	29,430	19,510
Notes payable, long-term	80,200	73,200
Total liabilities	$109,630	$92,710

DEBT OBLIGATIONS

OBJECTIVE 1

Identify information that
companies report about
obligations to lenders and
explain the transactions
affecting long-term debt.

An organization's short-term and long-term borrowings are obligations to creditors. Typically, those obligations are a major portion of a company's liabilities. Debt is separated on a balance sheet into current- and long-term amounts (as in Exhibit 1).

Short-Term Debt

An organization has an obligation to repay short-term debt during the coming fiscal period. That debt consists of all obligations that mature during that time, including installments of long-term debt. For example, notes that will come due in 2004 are classified as current liabilities on the December 31, 2003 balance sheet.

Long-Term Debt

Long-term debt includes **notes** and **bonds payable**. Notes and bonds payable are contracts between borrowers and creditors. In the contract, the borrower agrees to repay the amount borrowed at specified dates and agrees to pay specified amounts of interest.

A note usually is an agreement between a company and a financial institution that lends money to the company. A bond is debt in the form of a certificate in which the issuer (borrower) agrees to pay the maturity value of the bond at a predetermined date. Bonds often are marketable and are sold through brokers, like stock. Individuals, companies, and institutions can buy and sell bonds. Most corporate bonds have maturity values of $1,000 per bond. They can be sold to many individuals or organizations, permitting an issuer to borrow large amounts of money.

Some companies issue debt that is secured by specific assets, such as land, buildings, or equipment. These obligations are referred to as **secured debt** or **secured loans**. If a company does not have the cash to pay back secured debt when it comes due, the company must sell those assets pledged as security to pay the debt or transfer ownership of the assets to the creditor. Other types of debt are unsecured. For example, major corporations often issue **debentures**, which are unsecured bonds. If a company cannot repay this type of debt, it can be forced to liquidate (sell some or all of its noncash assets). In this situation, debentures and other unsecured debts are repaid from the sale of assets that are not pledged as security for secured debt. Therefore, secured debt typically is less risky than unsecured debt.

Debt can be issued with any maturity date. Most bonds mature in 10, 20, or 30 years from the date on which they are issued. In the notes of their financial reports, companies must disclose the maturity dates of their long-term debt and other relevant information.

http://ingram.swlearning.
com

....

**Learn more about
bonds.**

Case In Point

http://ingram.swlearning.
com
....
**Find out more about
Krispy Kreme.**

Disclosure of Long-Term Debt

The disclosure of long-term debt information communicates information that may be significant to a company's investors and creditors. Information about the expected debt payments for the next several years helps external entities determine the risk they may face if they lend the company money or buy its stock.

For example, **Krispy Kreme Doughnuts** reported the following information about its long-term debt in its 2002 annual report:

BANK FINANCING. On December 29, 1999, the Company entered into an unsecured Loan Agreement (the "Agreement") with a bank to increase borrowing availability and extend the maturity of its revolving credit facility. The Agreement provides a $40 million revolving line of credit which replaced a $28 million line of credit and $12 million term loan. The Agreement, as amended, expires on June 30, 2004.

Summaries of our contractual obligations and other commercial commitments as of February 3, 2002 are as follows:

(Dollars in Thousands)

Contractual Cash Obligations	Total Amount	Payments Due In Fiscal 2003	Payments Due In Fiscal 2004	Payments Due In Fiscal 2005	Payments Due Beyond Fiscal 2005
Long-term debt	$ 4,643	$ 731	$ 523	$ 540	$ 2,849
Operating leases	$58,001	$ 9,845	$7,478	$5,640	$35,038
Total	$62,644	$10,576	$8,001	$6,180	$37,887

Debt obligations have many different characteristics. Some require periodic interest and principal payments until the debt is repaid; others require principal repayment at the end of the debt's life. For example, most corporate bonds are repaid at the end of a fixed period, such as 10 years. But other bonds repay a portion of the principal each year over the life of the bond issue. Bond issues that require a portion of the bonds to be repaid each year are called **serial bonds**. They commonly are issued by governments.

A company can repurchase its own debt if it has enough cash and wants to reduce its liabilities. Or a company can repurchase its existing debt and replace (refinance) it with new debt. Refinancing becomes attractive when the general level of interest rates in the economy goes down. A company then can issue new debt at a lower rate of interest than its existing debt.

Some bonds require bondholders to resell the bonds to the issuing company at specific dates and prices if the issuer chooses to repurchase the bonds. **Callable bonds** are bonds that a company can reacquire after the bonds have been outstanding for a specific period. For example, a company might issue 30-year bonds that are callable after five years at 102% of maturity value. The 2% premium is compensation for calling the bonds.

LEARNING NOTE

A gain increases net income, and a loss decreases it. The terms *gain* and *loss* are commonly used instead of *revenue* and *expense* for items that are not a primary part of a company's operating activities.

When a company repurchases its debt, it may realize a gain or loss. For example, if debt is recorded on a company's books at $2,000,000, and the company repurchases the debt for $2,050,000, the company records a loss of $50,000. If, on the other hand, the repurchase price is less than the issuing price (book value) of the debt, the issuer would record a gain.

Debt Transactions

As an illustration of transactions involving issuing and repaying debt, assume that Mom's Cookie Company issued $20,000 of five-year bonds on January 1, 2005. The bonds pay $1,600 of interest (8% of $20,000) annually at the end of each year. The $20,000 is the amount the company will pay creditors at the end of the five-year period and is known as the **maturity value** or **face value** of the bonds. The annual interest paid on the debt (8%) is the **stated rate** of interest. Bonds often are sold to yield a return to creditors that is greater or less than the stated rate. For example, Mom's Cookie Company's bonds might be sold to give creditors a return of 9%. The actual rate of return earned by creditors is the **effective rate** of interest.

The effective rate of interest is determined by the amount creditors are willing to pay for the bonds and affects the amount of cash the company receives from its bonds when they are sold. A company may set the stated interest rate paid on debt it issues at any level it wishes. Suppose a company wants to borrow $100 for one year and agrees to pay $5 interest (5%) on the debt. A creditor agrees to loan $100 to the company but demands 8% interest. As shown in Exhibit 2, if the company agrees to this rate, the creditor can obtain an 8% return by lending the borrower $97.22 at the beginning of the year and receive $105 (the amount the borrower wants to pay) at the end of the year. The interest rate earned by the creditor is still 8% ($105 ÷ $97.22 = 1.08). In this alternative, the creditor **discounts** the amount of the loan (reduces the amount of the loan) by an amount sufficient to provide an 8% return.

Exhibit 2
Effective and Stated Rates of Interest

Rate borrower pays (stated rate)	5%
Rate lender demands (effective rate)	8%
Interest paid by borrower ($100 × 0.05)	$5.00
Amount lender pays borrower at beginning of year	$97.22
Amount borrower pays lender at end of year	$105.00
Interest earned by borrower ($105.00 − $97.22)	$7.78
Interest rate earned by borrower $7.78 ÷ $97.22	8%

This method is common for bonds and certain other types of debt issued by companies. The borrower determines the amount of interest paid, and creditors set the price of the bonds to earn the interest rate they require. If a deal cannot be struck between the borrower and creditors, the borrower can look for other financing arrangements and the creditors can look for other investments.

To determine the amount received, we need to calculate the present value of the bonds, the amount they are worth at the time they are issued. The present value of a bond is the present value of the amounts the purchasers of the bonds (creditors) will receive over the life of the bonds. As illustrated in Exhibit 3, the purchasers of Mom's Cookie Company's bonds will receive five annual interest payments of $1,600 ($20,000 × 8%) plus $20,000 when the bonds mature. (See Chapter F8 for coverage of present value calculations.)

Therefore, the present value of the bonds is the present value of an annuity plus the present value of a single amount. We can use the present value tables (Table 3 and Table 4) to determine the present value of the bonds.

Let's assume the bonds will be sold to yield a 9% return to creditors. Therefore, we need to determine the present value of the interest that will be received by creditors plus the present value of the principal:

PV of bonds = PV of annuity + PV of single amount
PV of bonds = $1,600 × 3.88965 (5 periods, 9%) + $20,000 × 0.64993 (5 periods, 9%)
PV of bonds = $6,223 + $12,999
PV of bonds = $19,222

Exhibit 3

Example of the Relationship of Bond Cash Flows to Present Value

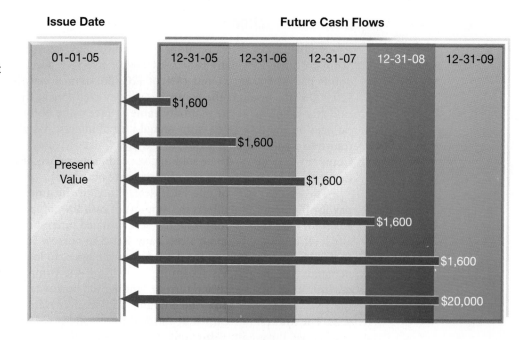

Thus, the amount Mom's Cookie Company will receive from selling the bonds is $19,222. Observe that the effective rate of interest (9%) is used to determine the interest factor for the present value calculation. Mom's Cookie Company receives *less than* maturity value for the bonds because the effective rate of interest (9%) on the bonds is higher than the stated rate (8%). When the effective rate is higher than the stated rate, bonds sell at a **discount**. Mom's Cookie Company's bonds sold at a discount of $778 ($20,000 − $19,222), or approximately 96% of maturity ($19,222 ÷ $20,000). When bonds sell at maturity value, they are said to sell at **par**. If they sell at less than maturity value, they are said to sell at a discount. The issue price often is stated as a percentage of par, such as 96% of par. If bonds sell at more than maturity value, they sell at a **premium**. We will consider a premium later in this section.

To determine transactions recorded for the bonds, we need to prepare an amortization table similar to that described in the previous chapter. Exhibit 4 provides an amortization table for Mom's Cookie Company's bonds.

USING EXCEL

For Present Value of Bonds

SPREADSHEET

Alternatively, we can use a spreadsheet to calculate the present value of the bonds. The annuity portion can be calculated using the PV function. In Excel, the function entered in a cell would be: =PV(0.09,5,−1600), where 0.09 is the effective interest rate, 5 is the number of periods, and −1600 is the amount of payment each period. Remember that the function uses a negative value for payments in computing the present value. This function returns a value of $6,223 (rounded to the nearest dollar) and is equivalent to the amount determined by using Table 4. The present value of the maturity value of $20,000 can be calculated in Excel by entering =20000/(1.09) ^5, where 20000 is the maturity value, 1.09 is one plus the actual rate of interest, and 5 is the number of periods. This equation returns $12,999 (rounded to the nearest dollar) the same value as that calculated from Table 3. Adding the two values together ($6,223 + $12,999) results in the total present value of $19,222.

To prepare the table, we first determine the present value of the bonds. This amount is entered in column B for year 1. The interest expense on the bonds is the present value

Exhibit 4 Bond Amortization Table*

A Year	B Present Value at Beginning of Year	C Interest Incurred (Column B × Real Interest Rate)	D Amount Paid	E Amortization of Principal (Column C − Column D)	F Value at End of Year (Column B + Column E)
2005	19,222	1,730	1,600	130	19,352
2006	19,352	1,742	1,600	142	19,494
2007	19,494	1,754	1,600	154	19,648
2008	19,648	1,768	1,600	168	19,816
2009	19,816	1,783	1,600	183	20,000
Total		8,778	8,000	778	

*Slight adjustments have been made for rounding errors.

from column B times the real interest rate (9%). Consequently, the interest expense incurred by Mom's Cookie Company for the first year is $1,730 ($19,222 × 9%), shown in column C. The amount of interest Mom's Cookie Company pays each year is $1,600 (column D). The difference between the amount of interest expense (column C) and the amount of interest paid (column D) is the amortization of bond principal (column E). When bonds are issued at a discount, the amortization is added to the beginning-of-period present value to calculate the end-of-period value (column F). These calculations continue for each period. Observe that the value of the bonds at the end of the five-year period is their maturity value, the amount Mom's Cookie Company will repay in the fifth year.

The transactions associated with the bonds begin with their sale on January 1, 2005:

Date	Accounts	ASSETS Cash	ASSETS Other Assets	=	LIABILITIES	+	OWNERS' EQUITY Contributed Capital	OWNERS' EQUITY Retained Earnings
Jan. 1, 2005	Cash Bonds Payable	19,222			19,222			

The amount of liability owed by Mom's Cookie Company when the bonds are issued is the amount received for the bonds.

At the end of the first year, Mom's Cookie Company records the interest paid and interest expense:

Date	Accounts	ASSETS Cash	ASSETS Other Assets	=	LIABILITIES	+	OWNERS' EQUITY Contributed Capital	OWNERS' EQUITY Retained Earnings
Dec. 31, 2005	Interest Expense Bonds Payable Cash	−1,600			130			−1,730

The difference between the cash paid and the interest expense is added to Bonds Payable when bonds are issued at a discount. The amount Mom's Cookie Company owes its creditors at the end of the first year is $19,352 ($19,222 + $130), as shown in Exhibit 4.

Mom's Cookie Company continues to record the interest payments and interest expense each year. In the fifth year, it records the final interest payment:

Date	Accounts	ASSETS		=	LIABILITIES	+	OWNERS' EQUITY	
		Cash	Other Assets				Contributed Capital	Retained Earnings
Dec. 31, 2009	Interest Expense							−1,783
	Bonds Payable				183			
	Cash	−1,600						

This transaction increases Bonds Payable to its maturity value of $20,000.

Then, Mom's Cookie Company pays creditors the maturity value of the bonds:

Date	Accounts	ASSETS		=	LIABILITIES	+	OWNERS' EQUITY	
		Cash	Other Assets				Contributed Capital	Retained Earnings
Dec. 31, 2009	Bonds Payable				−20,000			
	Cash	−20,000						

Over the life of the bonds, Mom's Cookie Company pays its creditors $28,000 ($20,000 maturity value + $8,000 interest payments). The amount the company received for the bonds was $19,222. Therefore, its total interest expense for the bonds was $8,778 ($28,000 − $19,222). This amount provided creditors with a 9% effective rate of return over the life of the bonds.

The information used in this example as a basis for transactions recorded by the issuer of debt also can be used for transactions involving the purchasers of the debt. If several creditors bought Mom's Cookie Company's bonds, the amounts recorded by each creditor would be a portion of the total. The totals for all the creditors would be the same as the amounts recorded by Mom's Cookie Company. Instead of recording interest expense and interest paid, the creditors would record interest revenue and interest received. Their cash outflow at the time of purchase would be $19,222, and the cash received at the end of the five-year period would be $20,000.

When the effective rate of interest on debt is less than the stated rate, the debt is said to be issued at a **premium**. The borrower receives *more* for the bonds when they are sold than the maturity value of the bonds: The bonds sell at more than 100% of par. A premium *reduces* the interest expense on the debt each period. A portion of the amount paid by the borrower each period is a repayment of the amount borrowed, in addition to the payment of interest. The amount of principal amortized each period is *subtracted* from the beginning-of-period present value to calculate the end-of-period value in the amortization table. Self-Study Problem 1 illustrates transactions involving the sale of bonds at a premium.

If the effective and stated rates of interest are the same, bonds are sold at their maturity value (100% of par) and no premium or discount is recorded. Interest expense will equal interest paid each period. Exhibit 5 summarizes the relationships between effective and stated interest rates.

http://ingram.swlearning.com

Find out about getting online bond quote information.

Exhibit 5 The Relationship between Effective and Stated Interest Rates

Interest Rate Comparison	Bonds Sell At	Relation between Interest and Amount Paid	Effect on Principal Each Period
Effective Rate > Stated Rate	Discount	Interest Expense > Amount Paid	Increase
Effective Rate = Stated Rate	Par	Interest Expense = Amount Paid	No Change
Effective Rate < Stated Rate	Premium	Interest Expense < Amount Paid	Decrease

1 SELF-STUDY PROBLEM

WebTUTOR Advantage

Assume that instead of issuing its debt to yield an effective rate of 9%, Mom's Cookie Company issued the debt to yield an effective rate of 7%.

Required Using the information provided in the previous example as a guide:

A. Calculate the present value of the bonds at the time they are issued.
B. Prepare an amortization table.
C. Record transactions for Mom's Cookie Company for the first and fifth years.

The solution to Self-Study Problem 1 appears at the end of the chapter.

FINANCIAL REPORTING OF DEBT

A corporation's financial statements and accompanying notes provide much useful information. They help readers calculate the amount of debt a company has outstanding, and they also indicate changes in debt, the interest rates on debt, the interest expense during a given fiscal period, and current and future cash flows associated with existing debt and interest payments.

Exhibit 6 shows the items that would be reported on Mom's Cookie Company's financial statements at the end of each fiscal year during the life of the bonds described in the previous section. Amounts are from the amortization table in Exhibit 4.

The amount owed by Mom's Cookie Company to its creditors at the end of each year is reported on the balance sheet. At the end of the first three years, these amounts are reported as long-term debt. At the end of the fourth year, the amount owed is reported as a current liability because it will be repaid in the following fiscal year. At the

Exhibit 6 Financial Statement Presentation of Debt Activities for Mom's Cookie Company

December 31,	2009	2008	2007	2006	2005
Balance sheet					
Liabilities:					
Current maturities of long-term debt	—	$19,816	—	—	—
Long-term debt	—	—	$19,648	$19,494	$ 19,352
Income statement					
Nonoperating expenses:					
Interest expense	$ 1,783	1,768	1,754	1,742	1,730
Statement of cash flows					
Cash flow from operating activities:					
Interest paid	(1,600)	(1,600)	(1,600)	(1,600)	(1,600)
Cash flow from financing activities:					
Long-term debt issued	—	—	—	—	192,222
Debt repaid	(20,000)	—	—	—	—

end of the fifth year, the company reports no liability for these bonds because they have been repaid.

Interest expense, based on the effective rate of interest, is reported each year on the income statement. For most companies, interest expense is a nonoperating expense and is reported on the income statement after operating income.

The amount of interest paid is reported each year on the statement of cash flows as part of operating activities. If the indirect format of the statement is used, interest paid may not appear as a separate item on the statement of cash flows. In that case, the amount of interest paid usually is listed either at the bottom of the statement of cash flows (as supplemental data) or in the notes to the financial statements.

When debt is issued, the amount of cash received is reported on the statement of cash flows as cash from financing activities. When debt is repaid, the amount of cash paid is listed there as cash paid for financing activities.

OTHER OBLIGATIONS

OBJECTIVE 2

Describe appropriate accounting procedures for contingencies and commitments, including capital leases.

Other types of obligations that involve financing activities also are reported on the balance sheet or in notes to the financial statements. Among those obligations are contingencies and commitments.

Contingencies

A *contingency* **is an existing condition that may result in an economic effect if a future event occurs.** GAAP require companies to report contingencies that could result in future obligations.

For most contingencies, a current obligation does not exist. If some future event occurs, however, an obligation might result. For example, suppose Mom's Cookie Company guarantees debt of one of its customers, Fair Price Foods. If Fair Price Foods is unable to make the loan payments, Mom's Cookie Company becomes liable for the payments. Mom's Cookie Company does not have a liability, however, unless Fair Price Foods is unable to pay.

Other common contingencies involve environmental costs and litigation. Government regulations in recent years have made companies contingently liable for costs associated with environmental cleanup and restoration if the companies are found not to have met regulatory requirements. Companies often face lawsuits associated with problems such as product defects and unfair treatment of employees. Until these suits are settled, a company is contingently liable for losses associated with the litigation.

Under certain circumstances, contingencies are reported as liabilities. **If a contingency probably will result in a loss, and the amount of the loss can be reasonably estimated, it should be included as a liability on a company's balance sheet.** Also, the amount of the expected loss is recognized on the income statement in computing net income.

Case In Point

Disclosure of Contingencies

In its 2002 annual report, Krispy Kreme reported the following contingency:

> In order to assist certain associate and franchise operators in obtaining third-party financing, the Company has entered into collateral repurchase agreements involving both Company stock and doughnut-making equipment. The Company's contingent liability related to these agreements is approximately $1,266,000 at January 28, 2001 and $70,000 at February 3, 2002.

Commitments

A *commitment* **is a promise to engage in some future activity that will have an economic effect.** Commitments usually involve agreements to purchase or sell something in the future. For instance, airlines place orders with airplane manufacturers several years prior to completion of the planes. These commitments will require the airlines to finance their purchases at some time in the future, but they are not liabilities until the airplanes have been manufactured and ownership is transferred to the airlines.

Leased assets are a common form of commitment. Certain leases, called **capital leases**, are financing arrangements and are examined in the next section. In addition to capital leases, companies use **operating leases** to obtain machinery, equipment, and other resources. Costs of operating leases are recorded as expenses in the period in which the leased assets are used. Liabilities are not recorded for operating leases. Some operating leases cannot be canceled, however, resulting in a commitment for future payments. The amount of future payments is reported in the notes to the financial statements. Companies typically report the amount they are committed to paying for operating leases in each of the next five years and the total amount of commitments that extend beyond five years. Disclosures like these help investors and other decision makers forecast future cash flows and profits.

Case In Point

Disclosure of Lease Agreements

Krispy Kreme reported the following lease arrangements in its 2002 annual report:

The Company conducts some of its operations from leased facilities and, additionally, leases certain equipment under operating leases. Generally, these have initial lease terms of 5 to 18 years and contain provisions for renewal options of 5 to 10 years.

At February 3, 2002, future minimum annual rental commitments, gross, under noncancelable operating leases, including lease commitments on consolidated joint ventures, are as follows:

	In Thousands
Fiscal Year Ending In	**Amount**
2003	$ 9,845
2004	7,478
2005	5,640
2006	4,074
2007	3,562
Thereafter	27,402
	$58,001

Rental expense, net of rental income, totaled $6,220,000 in fiscal 2000, $8,540,000 in fiscal 2001, and $10,576,000 in fiscal 2002.

Capital Leases

Leases often provide a means of financing asset acquisitions. When a company leases a resource, usually buildings or equipment, for most of the useful life of the resource and controls the resource as though it had been purchased, the lease is treated as a capital lease. **Capital leases are recorded as liabilities, and the related leased resources are recorded as assets.**

http://ingram.swlearning.
com
....
**Find out more about
leasing.**

For example, suppose Mom's Cookie Company signs a lease on January 1, 2005 to acquire computer equipment. The lease is for three years, the assumed useful life of the equipment. The company agrees to pay $10,000 a year, including 8% interest. In effect, Mom's Cookie Company is purchasing the equipment and borrowing money from the lessor (the company that owns the equipment and leases it to Mom's Cookie Company) to finance the purchase.

To determine the amount of the lease obligation, we have to calculate the present value of the lease payments. We can make this calculation using the interest factor in Table 4 because the lease payments are an annuity. We use the interest factor for three periods at 8%:

$$\text{PVA} = A \times \text{IF (Table 4)}$$
$$\$25{,}771 = \$10{,}000 \times 2.57710$$

USING EXCEL

For Present Value of
Leases

SPREADSHEET

Alternatively, we can use the present value function in a spreadsheet. In Excel, we would enter the function $=PV(0.08,3,-10000)$ to make this calculation. The amount returned is $25,771, rounded to the nearest dollar.

Mom's Cookie Company records the present value of lease payments as an asset and a liability:

Date	Accounts	ASSETS		=	LIABILITIES	+	OWNERS' EQUITY	
		Cash	Other Assets				Contributed Capital	Retained Earnings
Jan. 1, 2005	Leased Assets		25,771					
	Capital Lease Obligation				25,771			

Other transactions associated with the lease payments are like those for repayment of a loan. The amortization table in Exhibit 7 provides the necessary information.

This table is like that for a note that is repaid in equal installments, as described in Chapter F8. Observe that a portion of the principal is repaid each period, along with the interest.

Mom's Cookie Company records the payments and interest expense each period. For example, the transaction for the first year is:

Date	Accounts	ASSETS		=	LIABILITIES	+	OWNERS' EQUITY	
		Cash	Other Assets				Contributed Capital	Retained Earnings
Dec. 31, 2005	Capital Lease Obligation				−7,938			
	Interest Expense							−2,062
	Cash	−10,000						

Exhibit 7 Amortization Table for a Capital Lease

A Year	B Present Value at Beginning of Year	C Interest Incurred (Column B × Real Interest Rate)	D Amount Paid	E Amortization of Principal (Column C − Column D)	F Value at End of Year (Column B + Column E)
Dec. 31, 2005	25,771	2,062	10,000	(7,938)	17,833
Dec. 31, 2006	17,833	1,427	10,000	(8,573)	9,260
Dec. 31, 2007	9,260	740	10,000	(9,260)	0
Total		4,229	30,000	(25,771)	

This transaction reduces the capital lease liability by the amount of principal paid. Over the course of the three years, the entire principal will be repaid. The amount of lease liability remaining at the end of the first year ($17,833 from Exhibit 7) is reported as a liability on Mom's Cookie Company's balance sheet at December 31, 2005.

From the perspective of the lessor, the $25,771 present value of the lease is the amount received for the equipment and is treated as sales revenue. Amounts received in excess of the present value are interest revenue. Therefore, the lessor would record $2,062 of interest revenue in the first year (see Exhibit 7).

STOCKHOLDERS' EQUITY

OBJECTIVE 3

Identify information reported in the stockholders' equity section of a corporate balance sheet and distinguish contributed capital from retained earnings.

Liabilities are obligations that a company has a legal responsibility to meet. Creditors' claims against a company are enforceable by law. Stockholders' equity also represents claims against a company, claims by investors who own a corporation's stock. As long as a company is a going concern (is expected to continue to exist), those claims are met by the company's profits. Ordinarily, a company is not obligated to make payments to its stockholders or to repay them the amounts they have invested.

Profit is the value created from selling goods and services during a period in excess of the costs of resources consumed during that period. That excess value increases the value of stockholders' claims. When a company distributes its profit in the form of dividends or incurs a loss, the amount of stockholders' claims decreases.

The claims of creditors are honored before those of owners. In general, creditors' claims are met before cash or other assets are distributed to owners (stockholders). As a result, there is an important difference between liabilities and owners' equity, and liabilities and equity are separated on a company's balance sheet.

Exhibit 8 provides the owners' equity section of Mom's Cookie Company's balance sheet. Corporate owners' equity is referred to as **stockholders'** or **shareholders' equity** because owners hold shares of stock as an indication of their ownership.

Exhibit 8

Stockholders' Equity for Mom's Cookie Company

December 31,	2006	2005
Stockholders' equity:		
Common stock, $1 par value, 50,000 shares authorized, 20,000 and 10,000 shares issued	$ 20,000	$ 10,000
Paid-in capital in excess of par value	190,000	90,000
Retained earnings	130,417	42,990
Treasury stock, 1,000 shares at cost	(12,000)	0
Total stockholders' equity	$328,417	$142,990

http://ingram.swlearning. com

Find answers to frequently asked questions about the stock market.

The exhibit shows information about two main types of stockholders' equity: contributed capital and retained earnings. *Contributed capital* **is the direct investment made by stockholders in a corporation.** Contributed capital for Mom's Cookie Company consists of common stock and paid-in capital in excess of par value. **Retained earnings** is the accumulation of profits reinvested in a corporation. A third type of equity reported by many companies, including Mom's Cookie Company, is treasury stock. *Treasury stock* **is stock repurchased by a company from its stockholders.** The cost of treasury stock is deducted from stockholders' equity because it is an amount that a company has repaid to stockholders.

Companies often repurchase their stock to distribute it to employees as part of employee stock ownership plans and to provide bonuses and other compensation for managers and employees. Some companies repurchase stock to reduce the number of shares available in the market. Usually, fewer shares results in a higher stock price. Also, a company may repurchase its own shares to prevent another company from buying them. One company can take control of another company by buying its shares. Fewer shares outstanding makes it more difficult for another company to obtain a controlling interest.

Some corporations do not have treasury stock. All corporations have contributed capital and retained earnings. Retained earnings may be a negative amount, referred to as a deficit.

Contributed Capital

Corporations issue shares of stock in exchange for cash (and sometimes other resources, such as property). *Common stock* **or** *capital stock,* **represents the ownership rights of investors in a corporation.** Each share of common stock represents an equal share in the ownership of a corporation. Owners of the shares have the right to vote on the activities of the corporation and to share in its earnings. For example, suppose a corporation has 100,000 shares of common stock outstanding. Someone who owns 10,000 shares controls 10% of the votes that can be cast on issues voted on by stockholders. That investor also has the right to 10% of the dividends paid to common stockholders.

U.S. corporations must be chartered by a state. **A** *charter* **is the legal right granted by a state that permits a corporation to exist.** The charter establishes a corporation as a legal entity. It also sets limits on the corporation's activities to protect owners and others who contract with the corporation. Among other things, a corporation's charter specifies the maximum number of shares of stock the corporation is authorized to issue. Mom's Cookie Company is authorized to issue up to 50,000 shares of common stock. At the end of 2006 it had issued 20,000 shares, and at the end of 2005 it had issued 10,000 shares (Exhibit 8).

Most shares of common stock are issued with a par value because states often require that corporate stock have a par value. **The** *par value* **of stock is the value assigned to each share by a corporation in its corporate charter.** A state may require that a corporation maintain an amount of equity equal to or greater than the par value of its stock. That equity cannot be transferred back to the owners unless the corporation liquidates its assets and goes out of business.

Originally, par value was designed to protect a corporation's creditors by making owners keep a certain level of investment in the corporation. This protection was important when the sale of stock and financial reporting were largely unregulated. With increased regulation and requirements for financial reporting, par value has lost much of its importance. In some states, charters do not require a par value. Stock issued without a par value is known as **no-par stock**. In states where charters do require a par value, that value often is set very low. A dollar per share, or less, is common.

Stock usually is sold at a price greater than par value. For example, the 20,000 shares of Mom's Cookie Company's common

Percentage of Major Corporations with Par, No-Par, and Stated Value Stock

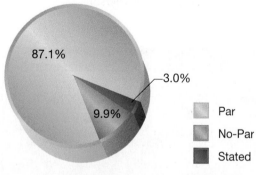

(Data source: Accounting Trends & Techniques, 2001)

**Percentage of Major Corporations
Reporting Treasury Stock**

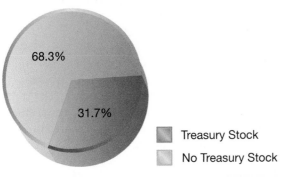

Treasury Stock

No Treasury Stock

(Data source: Accounting Trends & Techniques, 2001)

stock that had been issued by the end of 2006 were sold for $210,000 ($20,000 + $190,000 in Exhibit 8). Of this amount, $20,000 is reported as par value (20,000 shares × $1 par). The remainder of the amount the company received from selling its stock is reported as paid-in capital in excess of par value ($190,000).

Paid-in capital in excess of par value **is the amount in excess of the stock's par value received by a corporation from the sale of its stock.** Corporate financial reports refer to this amount by many names: among them are paid-in capital, contributed capital in excess of par, proceeds in excess of par value, additional paid-in capital, surplus, and premium on capital stock.

Occasionally, a corporation establishes its own **stated value** for no-par stock. That value appears on the balance sheet in place of par value.

In addition to the number of shares authorized, a corporation reports the number of shares of stock issued (sold) to investors. **Issued shares** are shares that have been sold by a corporation to investors. **Outstanding shares** are shares currently held by investors. The difference (if any) between the number of shares issued and the number outstanding is the number of shares of treasury stock. Thus, at the end of 2006, Mom's Cookie Company had issued 20,000 shares, but only 19,000 shares were outstanding. The remaining 1,000 shares were owned by Mom's Cookie Company (Exhibit 8).

A company repurchases its own shares for various purposes. Many companies give these shares to managers or employees as additional compensation for their work for the company, especially if they or the company have performed well.

Retained Earnings

Retained earnings is profit reinvested in a corporation. Retained earnings also is referred to by a variety of names, such as reinvested earnings, profit retained in the business, or earnings reinvested in the business. The amount of retained earnings is the accumulated net income invested in corporate resources.

For example, assume the following information for Mom's Cookie Company for 2005 and 2006:

Year	Net Income	Dividends	Increase in Retained Earnings	Balance of Retained Earnings
2004				$ 0
2005	$ 52,990	$10,000	$42,990	42,990
2006	107,427	20,000	87,427	130,417

At the end of 2005, Mom's Cookie Company had retained earnings of $42,990. During 2005, the company earned net income of $52,990 and paid dividends of $10,000. Therefore, its retained earnings increased by $42,990 ($52,990 − $10,000). Each year, net income is added to retained earnings, and dividends are subtracted. A net loss would be subtracted from retained earnings.

There is an important difference between contributed capital and retained earnings. Retained earnings results from profits that could be used to pay dividends to stockholders. Dividends paid from retained earnings are a return to stockholders from a company's earnings. If dividends in excess of retained earnings are paid, this is a return of contributed capital. The company is repaying investors a portion of the amount they contributed to the company when they purchased the company's stock. Therefore, it is important to distinguish between contributed capital and retained earnings.

2   SELF-STUDY PROBLEM

Bovine Company, a dairy, began operations in January 2004. It issued 100,000 shares of $1 par value common stock. The stock sold for $5 per share. The company's charter permits it to issue 250,000 shares of stock. In 2005, the company repurchased 8,000 shares of stock at a cost of $7 per share. Bovine's net income and cash dividend payments have been as follows:

Year	Net Income	Dividends
2004	$ (60,000)	$ 0
2005	140,000	50,000
2006	220,000	100,000

Required Draft the stockholders' equity section of Bovine's balance sheet for the years ended December 31, 2006 and 2005.

The solution to Self-Study Problem 2 appears at the end of the chapter.

CHANGES IN STOCKHOLDERS' EQUITY

OBJECTIVE 4

Explain transactions affecting stockholders' equity and describe how these transactions are reported in a company's financial statements.

The statement of stockholders' (or shareholders') equity describes events that changed the amount of stockholders' equity during a fiscal period. Exhibit 9 provides the statement of stockholders' equity for Mom's Cookie Company. Beginning and ending balances are the same as those reported in the company's balance sheet (Exhibit 8).

The format of the statement of stockholders' equity varies from corporation to corporation, but all statements list the events that changed stockholders' equity during the past fiscal year. Most corporations report this information for the most recent three fiscal years. Some companies report this information as a schedule in the notes section of their financial reports, rather than as a separate statement.

Exhibit 10 illustrates transactions that affect stockholders' equity for most companies.

Exhibit 9 Statement of Stockholders' Equity for Mom's Cookie Company

	Common Stock	Paid-In Capital	Retained Earnings	Treasury Stock	Total
December 31, 2005	$10,000	$ 90,000	$ 42,990	$ 0	$142,990
Net income			107,427		107,427
Dividends			(20,000)		(20,000)
Stock purchased				(12,000)	(12,000)
Stock issued	10,000	100,000			110,000
December 31, 2006	$20,000	$190,000	$130,417	$(12,000)	$328,417

Equity Transactions

The statement of stockholders' equity summarizes equity transactions for a fiscal period. From the information in Exhibit 9, we can reconstruct the transactions for 2005 for Mom's Cookie Company.

Exhibit 10 Examples of Transactions That Affect Common Stockholders' Equity

Transaction	Common Stock	Paid–In Capital	Retained Earnings	Treasury Stock
Issue New Shares	Increase	Increase		
Earn Net Income Incur Net Loss			Increase or Decrease	
Pay Dividends			Decrease	
Repurchase Stock				Decrease*

*An increase in treasury stock decreases stockholders' equity.

		ASSETS		=	LIABILITIES	+	OWNERS' EQUITY	
Date	Accounts	Cash	Other Assets				Contributed Capital	Retained Earnings
Dec. 31, 2005	Net Income* Retained Earnings							−87,427 87,427
Dec. 31, 2005	Retained Earnings Cash	−20,000						−20,000
Dec. 31, 2005	Treasury Stock Cash	−12,000					−12,000	
Dec. 31, 2005	Cash Common Stock Paid-In Capital	110,000					10,000 100,000	

*Individual revenue and expense accounts would be closed and the balances transferred to retained earnings. In total, these amounts are equal to net income. Transactions are assumed to have occurred on December 31.

The first transaction transfers net income earned during 2005 to retained earnings. The second transaction deducts the amount of dividends paid during 2005 from retained earnings. The third transaction records the purchase of treasury stock, and the final transaction records the amount received from the sale of common stock. Note that, other than closing revenue and expense accounts to retained earnings, equity transactions normally do not involve revenues or expenses. **A company cannot earn profit from equity transactions.** When treasury stock is sold at a price higher than its cost, the incremental amount is added to Paid-In Capital. When treasury stock is sold at a price less than its cost, the amount is deducted from Paid-In Capital.

Equity transactions affect a company's balance sheet, statement of stockholders' equity, and statement of cash flows. Exhibits 8 and 9 contain the balance sheet and statement of stockholders' equity effects. Exhibit 11 shows the statement of cash flow effects for Mom's Cookie Company for 2005.

The cash flow effects result from transactions affecting cash during the fiscal period. All of these effects result from financing activities and either increase (stock issued)

Exhibit 11

Equity Transaction
Effects on Statement of
Cash Flows for Mom's
Cookie Company

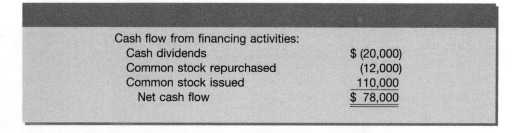

Cash flow from financing activities:	
Cash dividends	$ (20,000)
Common stock repurchased	(12,000)
Common stock issued	110,000
Net cash flow	$ 78,000

http://ingram.swlearning.
com

....

Find out what compa-
nies have declared div-
idends recently.

or decrease (payment of dividends and repurchase of stock) cash. Cash flows associated with net income, which increases Retained Earnings, are reported as part of operating activities on the statement of cash flows.

Cash Dividends

Several issues are important in recording cash dividend transactions. Cash dividends are paid only on shares outstanding. They are not paid on shares held in treasury; a company does not pay dividends to itself.

Three dates are important for dividend transactions. The *date of declaration* **for dividends is the date on which a corporation's board of directors announces that a dividend will be paid. The** *date of record* **for a dividend is the date used to determine those owners who will receive the dividend.** All registered owners on the date of record receive the dividend. The *date of payment* **for a dividend is the date on which the dividends are mailed to those receiving dividends.**

Dividends declared during a fiscal period are reported on the statement of stockholders' equity as a reduction in retained earnings. Dividends paid are reported on the corporation's statement of cash flows for that period. Those amounts are not always the same. For example, a company may declare a dividend near the end of its fiscal year but not pay the dividend until the following fiscal year. Dividends declared but not paid are reported as a current liability, Dividends Payable.

Issuing New Stock

When a company issues new shares of stock, each current stockholder normally has a right to purchase a portion of the new shares equal to the percentage of shares he or she owned prior to the sale. **The right to maintain the same percentage of ownership when new shares are issued is known as the** *preemptive right* **of stockholders.** This right prevents management from diluting the control (and wealth) of current owners by selling new shares to someone other than the current owners. Of course, current owners may choose not to purchase those shares.

When a company prepares to issue new shares, it normally issues stock rights to existing owners. *Stock rights* **authorize the recipient to purchase new shares.** The number of rights a stockholder receives depends on the number of shares the stockholder owns. Stock rights may be sold to others if the original recipient does not want to purchase the new shares.

Stock Dividends

Corporations sometimes issue stock dividends. *Stock dividends* **are shares of stock distributed by a company to its current stockholders without charge to the stockholders.** The effect of a stock dividend is to increase the number of shares of stock a company has outstanding and the number held by each stockholder. The increase in the number of shares held by each stockholder is in proportion to the number that stockholder owned before the distribution.

For example, assume that you owned 1,000 shares of Druid Company's stock on June 1, 2004, the date the company distributed a 5% stock dividend. You would receive 50 additional shares (1,000 shares × 5%). The total number of shares of common stock outstanding increased by 5% as a result of this distribution.

Unlike cash dividends, stock dividends do not decrease a company's cash. No cash is paid out. The amount of the stock dividend is subtracted from retained earnings and added to contributed capital. Therefore, the total amount of stockholders' equity does not change. The amount transferred is the market price of the stock at the time the dividend is declared.

Total Shares Outstanding	Stock Dividend	New Shares Issued	Market Value per Share	Effect on Balance Sheet
100,000	5%	5,000	$10	Contributed Capital* + $50,000 Retained Earnings − $50,000

*This amount would be allocated to Common Stock for 5,000 shares × par value and to Paid-In Capital In Excess of Par for the remainder of the $50,000. If the stock is no-par, all $50,000 is applied to Common Stock.

Sometimes corporations issue large stock dividends known as stock splits. **When a corporation declares a** *stock split,* **it issues a multiple of the number of shares of stock outstanding before the split.** For example, a company might issue two new shares for every one of its old shares.

A split does not change a company's total stockholders' equity. Usually, a company will reduce the par value of its common stock in proportion to the size of a stock split. Thus, if the par value is $1 per share before a 2-for-1 split, the par value will be $0.50 per share after the split. By changing the par value, the company keeps the same amount of contributed capital on its books after the split, and no account balances are altered.

2-for-1 Split	Total Shares Outstanding	Par Value per Share	Total Par Value
Before split	100,000	$1.00	$100,000
After split	200,000	$0.50	$100,000

If a company does not reduce its par value, an amount equal to the par value of the additional stock is transferred from retained earnings to contributed capital. The market value of a company's stock also adjusts to a stock split. For example, if stock was selling at $10 per share before a 2-for-1 split, it should sell at about $5 per share after the split. Companies often use stock splits to reduce the price of their stock to make it more attractive to investors who have to pay less to purchase the stock than prior to the split.

PREFERRED STOCK

OBJECTIVE 5

Distinguish between preferred stock and common stock, and discuss why corporations may issue more than one type of stock.

Some corporations issue more than one class of stock. The classes usually have different voting and dividend rights. A corporation's annual report describes the different classes of stock issued by the company. In addition to common stock, many companies issue preferred stock.

Preferred stock **is stock with a higher claim on dividends and assets than common stock.** Cash dividends must be paid to preferred stockholders before they can be paid to common stockholders. Also, preferred stockholders generally have a liquidation preference over common stockholders. That is, if a corporation has to liquidate its assets, preferred stockholders are repaid for their investments before common stockholders but after creditors. Preferred stock, therefore, is less risky as an investment than common stock but is more risky than bonds or other debt investments.

Preferred stockholders normally do not have voting rights in a corporation. They share in the profits of a corporation but not in decisions about the company's operations.

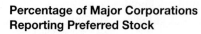

Percentage of Major Corporations Reporting Preferred Stock

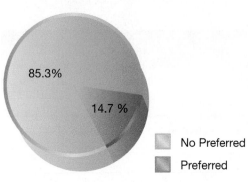

85.3%

14.7 %

☐ No Preferred

☐ Preferred

(Data source: Accounting Trends & Techniques, 2001)

Preferred stock attracts investors who want to take less risk than that taken by common stockholders. If a company does well, holders of preferred stock receive a reasonable return on their investments and may be able to exchange their preferred shares for shares of common stock. If a company does poorly, preferred stockholders are likely to receive higher returns than common stockholders. Again, they have more protection against loss in case of liquidation.

Usually, a paid-in capital in excess of par value account is not reported for preferred stock. The stock often is issued at par value or has no par value. In some cases, a **liquidation value** or **dividend rate** is reported for preferred stock. A liquidation value is the amount stockholders would receive for each share if the company were to liquidate, assuming that sufficient cash were available after creditors had been paid to pay the full liquidation value. The dividend rate identifies the annual dividend paid on the stock as a percentage of the par value or liquidation value of the stock. For example, if preferred stock has a stated or par value of $10 per share and a dividend rate of 5%, the company would pay a cash dividend of $0.50 per share ($10 × 5%) each year to preferred stockholders.

Preferred stockholders receive cash dividends in the same way that common stockholders do. However, the amount of the dividend payment for the two types of stock often differs. Usually, preferred stockholders receive the stated dividend rate, while dividends to common stockholders depend on a company's profitability. When a company is highly profitable, it normally pays larger dividends to common stockholders than it does when it is less profitable. If it is unprofitable, it may skip dividends for the year.

Preferred stock often is **cumulative**. This means that any dividends not paid to preferred stockholders in prior years must be paid in the current year before any dividends can be paid to common stockholders. Most often, cash dividends are paid quarterly on both common and preferred stock, resulting in a cash outflow and reduction of retained earnings.

Dividends, whether on common or on preferred stock, are not an expense. They are a distribution of profits. Because preferred dividends are paid before common dividends, they reduce the amount of net income available for common stock dividends. **Net income available for common stockholders** is net income minus dividends on preferred stock.

Some companies issue **redeemable preferred stock**. This stock is repurchased by the issuing company at a particular time, usually within a few years after it is issued. Because it has a fixed life and does not have voting rights, redeemable preferred stock is not included as part of stockholders' equity. It is reported as a separate item between liabilities and equity on the balance sheet.

Companies may issue bonds or preferred stock that can be converted into shares of common stock. These securities are referred to as **convertible securities**. The number of shares of stock received in exchange for each bond or share of preferred stock is set at the time the convertible securities are sold.

Convertible bonds and preferred stock attract investors who want the greater protection of bonds or preferred stock but who also want the chance to share in a company's earnings if it is successful. Investors can convert their bonds or preferred stock into common stock if a company performs well. Because of this conversion feature, convertible bonds often pay a lower rate of interest and convertible preferred stock pays a lower dividend than do similar nonconvertible securities.

Case In Point

http://ingram.swlearning.
com
....
Learn more about
PepsiCo.

Disclosure of Preferred Stock Information

PepsiCo, Inc., reported stockholders' equity in its 2001 annual report as follows:

	(In millions)
Preferred Stock, no par value	$ 26
Common Shareholders' Equity	
Common stock, par value 1⅔¢ per share (issued 1,782 and 2,029 shares, respectively)	$ 30
Capital in excess of par value	13
Retained earnings	11,519
Accumulated other comprehensive loss	(1,646)
Less: repurchased common stock, at cost (26 and 280 shares, respectively)	(1,268)
Total Common Shareholders' Equity	**$ 8,648**

A note provides the following information about PepsiCo's stock:

> As of December 29, 2001, there were 3.6 billion shares of common stock and 3 million shares of convertible preferred stock authorized, which are designated as $5.46 cumulative preferred convertible stock. Of the authorized convertible preferred shares, 803,953 shares were issued and 736,153 shares were outstanding. Each share is convertible at the option of the holder into 4.9625 shares of common stock. The convertible preferred shares may be called for redemption at $78 per share plus accrued and unpaid dividends upon written notice.

INTERNATIONAL REPORTING OF FINANCING ACTIVITIES

INTERNATIONAL

Foreign corporations report debt and stockholders' equity much as U.S. corporations do. Most industrialized nations use similar reporting rules, though some big differences exist. Each nation sets its own accounting and reporting rules. Therefore, it is not always safe to assume that the amounts in a foreign company's statements mean the same as those in a U.S. company's statements.

LEARNING NOTE

If a foreign corporation has stock listed on U.S. stock exchanges, it normally issues annual financial reports that conform with U.S. GAAP. These companies may issue different annual reports to stockholders in their own countries, using different accounting rules.

Financial terms vary from country to country. For example, common stock may be known as share capital. Share premium may refer to paid-in capital in excess of par value. Earned surplus or profit and loss may be used instead of retained earnings. Reserve accounts also are common in many foreign countries. Such accounts identify portions of stockholders' equity that are restricted for a particular purpose and cannot be used to pay dividends.

OTHER RELATED TOPICS

This section describes other related topics that may be observed for some companies.

Stock Options

Stock options are rights to purchase shares of a company's stock at a specified price. Options often are granted to employees and managers of a company as part of compensation. For example, assume that employees receive options to purchase 10,000 shares of their company's stock on January 2, 2004. The options permit employees to purchase shares at $50 per share on January 2, 2005. If the company does well in 2004 and the stock price rises above $50, employees will profit from using (exercising) their options. Options provide an incentive for employees to be productive and help a company's stock price to increase.

A company sometimes may sponsor an employee stock ownership plan (ESOP). The company makes shares of its stock available to the plan. The shares are distributed when employees earn them through service to the company. These shares are like treasury stock until they are earned by employees. A company's stockholders' equity, therefore, may include an item for employee compensation related to an ESOP that reduces its stockholders' equity.

Stock option plans can be complex. Many types of plans exist, and accounting for them varies according to plan type and terms. Stock option plans often bring tax benefits to corporations. The terms of stock option plans, therefore, often are determined by tax regulations.

Noncontrolling Interest

Noncontrolling interest, sometimes called minority interest, is the portion of a subsidiary company's equity owned by shareholders other than the parent corporation. For example, assume that Parent Company owns 80% of Subsidiary Company's stock. Subsidiary Company reports total stockholders' equity of $2 million for fiscal 2004. Therefore, the noncontrolling interest (20% $\times$ $2,000,000) is $400,000. Parent Company reports this amount as noncontrolling interest on its balance sheet.

Corporations report noncontrolling interest in different ways. Some report it as part of stockholders' equity, a portion of the corporation's total equity held by outside interests. Others report noncontrolling interest as a liability, a claim by outside interests against a portion of the corporation's resources. Most companies include noncontrolling interest as a separate category between liabilities and equity.

Appropriation of Retained Earnings

An appropriation of retained earnings transfers part of the retained earnings balance to a restricted retained earnings account. The restricted amount cannot be distributed as dividends. The new account title might be Retained Earnings—Appropriation for Plant Expansion, or something similar. Appropriations are rare among U.S. companies but sometimes are found in the financial statements of foreign companies.

Foreign Currency Adjustments

These adjustments to stockholders' equity are commonly made by multinational corporations. Multinationals are companies that operate in both foreign and domestic (U.S.) markets. Some of their operations are conducted in foreign currency—British pounds or Japanese yen, for example. When preparing financial statements in the United States, multinationals translate their foreign operations into U.S. dollars. Foreign currency translation is the process of converting the financial results of operations in a foreign currency into U.S. dollars for financial-reporting purposes.

A translation adjustment is the gain or loss that results when the operations of a company's foreign subsidiaries are translated from foreign to U.S. currency for reporting consolidated financial statements. These adjustments may result in gains or losses depending on whether the dollar has gained or lost value relative to other currencies. Translation adjustments are reported in the stockholders' equity section of the balance sheet as part of other comprehensive income. Gains are added in computing total stockholders' equity and losses are deducted.

3 SELF-STUDY PROBLEM

Required Use information from the accompanying financial statements of Lesco, Inc. to answer the following questions:

webTUTOR Advantage

A. What was Lesco's total contributed capital for 2004?
B. How many shares of common stock were outstanding at the end of 2004?
C. What dollar amount of treasury stock did Lesco hold at the end of 2004?
D. What dollar amount of stock did Lesco repurchase during 2004? How much did it issue?
E. What was the amount of dividends paid in 2004?
F. How much net cash flow came from financing activities associated with stockholders' equity during 2004, excluding the effect of net income? What were the sources of that cash flow?
G. How much net income came from financing activities associated with stockholders' equity during the current year?

Lesco, Inc.
Balance Sheet (Excerpt)
December 31, 2004

Stockholders' Equity

Common stock, $0.10 par value,	
1,000,000 shares authorized,	
700,000 shares issued	$ 70,000
Paid-in capital in excess of par value	810,240
Retained earnings	356,812
Treasury stock (30,000 shares at cost)	(42,296)
Total stockholders' equity	$1,194,756

Lesco, Inc.
Statement of Stockholders' Equity
December 31, 2004

	Common Stock	Paid-In Capital	Retained Earnings	Treasury Stock	Total
December 31, 2003	$65,000	$747,196	$306,201	$(33,941)	$1,084,456
Net income			92,611		92,611
Dividends			(42,000)		(42,000)
Stock purchased				(8,355)	(8,355)
Stock issued	5,000	63,044			68,044
December 31, 2004	$70,000	$810,240	$356,812	$(42,296)	$1,194,756

The solution to Self-Study Problem 3 appears at the end of the chapter.

REVIEW

SUMMARY of IMPORTANT CONCEPTS

1. Liabilities result from contractual relationships with lenders, suppliers, customers, employees, governments, and other parties.

2. Three attributes of a liability are (1) a present responsibility to repay (transfer resources) at some future time, (2) the binding nature of the agreement (to return resources), and (3) the occurrence of the original transfer of value at some time in the past.

3. Debt obligations include notes and bonds payable.
   a. Debt is recorded at its present value.
   b. Principal repaid and interest are recorded over the life of the debt.
   c. An amortization table is useful for determining amounts recorded and reported for debt obligations.

4. Other obligations include contingencies and commitments, including leases.
   a. Contingencies are possible future events that may result in obligations.
   b. Commitments are agreements to use or acquire resources in the future.
   c. Capital leases are financing arrangements that result in a company recording assets and liabilities for the present value of future lease payments.

5. Stockholders' equity includes contributed capital and retained earnings.
   a. Contributed capital includes the par (or stated) value of stock plus paid-in capital in excess of par (or stated) value. If stock has no par or stated value, the entire amount of contributed capital is reported as common or capital stock.
   b. Stock repurchased by a corporation from its stockholders is reported on the balance sheet as treasury stock.

6. Transactions affecting stockholders' equity include paying cash dividends, issuing stock, repurchasing stock, and those transactions that result in net income.
   a. The effects of these transactions are summarized in the statement of stockholders' equity.
   b. A company cannot create income through transactions involving its own stock.
   c. The main stockholders' equity transactions that affect cash flow are the issuance or repurchase of stock and the payment of cash dividends.
   d. Stock dividends increase the number of shares outstanding but do not change the total equity balance and do not affect cash.

7. Corporations may issue preferred stock in addition to common stock. Preferred stock has a higher claim to dividends and assets than common stock. Some preferred stock and some bonds that are issued are convertible; this feature permits the purchaser to exchange the securities for common stock.

8. Amounts reported in the financial statements of foreign corporations often are determined using rules that are different from those used in the United States. Terms used in these reports also may differ from those used in the United States.

9. Some companies engage in special financing arrangements or activities that affect their financial statements.
   a. A company sometimes grants employees or managers stock options that permit them to purchase the company's stock at a specified price.
   b. Noncontrolling interest is the portion of a parent company's subsidiary that is not owned by the parent.
   c. An appropriation of retained earnings separates a portion of retained earnings so that it cannot be used to pay dividends.
   d. A foreign currency adjustment is a gain or loss that results when a company translates foreign operations into U.S. dollars for financial reporting purposes.

DEFINE

TERMS and CONCEPTS DEFINED in this CHAPTER

capital stock (F332)	paid-in capital in excess of par value (F333)
charter (F332)	par value (F332)
commitment (F329)	preemptive right (F336)
common stock (F332)	preferred stock (F337)
contingency (F328)	stock dividends (F336)
contributed capital (F332)	stock rights (F336)
date of declaration (F336)	stock split (F337)
date of payment (F336)	treasury stock (F332)
date of record (F336)	

SELF-STUDY PROBLEM SOLUTIONS

SSP9-1   A. Present value of bonds = PV of annuity (interest) + PV of maturity value

PV = $1,600 × 4.10020 (Table 4, 5 periods, 7%) + $20,000 × 0.71299 (Table 3, 5 periods, 7%)
PV = $6,560 + $14,260 = $20,820

B.

A Year	B Present Value at Beginning of Year	C Interest Incurred (Column B × Real Interest Rate)	D Amount Paid	E Amortization of Principal (Column C − Column D)	F Value at End of Year (Column B + Column E)
2005	20,820	1,457	1,600	(143)	20,677
2006	20,677	1,447	1,600	(153)	20,525
2007	20,525	1,437	1,600	(163)	20,362
2008	20,362	1,425	1,600	(175)	20,187
2009	20,187	1,413	1,600	(187)	20,000
Total		7,180	8,000	(820)	

C. First year:

Date	Accounts	ASSETS Cash	Other Assets	=	LIABILITIES	+	OWNERS' EQUITY Contributed Capital	Retained Earnings
Jan. 1, 2005	Cash	20,820						
	Bonds Payable				20,820			
Dec. 31, 2005	Interest Expense							−1,457
	Bonds Payable				−143			
	Cash	−1,600						

Date	Accounts	ASSETS Cash	Other Assets	=	LIABILITIES	+	OWNERS' EQUITY Contributed Capital	Retained Earnings
Dec. 31, 2009	Interest Expense							−1,413
	Bonds Payable				−187			
	Cash	−1,600						
Dec. 31, 2009	Bonds Payable				−20,000			
	Cash	−20,000						

SSP9-2   Fifth year:

Bovine Company Stockholders' Equity		
December 31,	2006	2005
Common stock, $1 par value, 250,000 shares authorized, 100,000 shares issued	$100,000	$100,000
Paid-in capital in excess of par value	400,000	400,000
Retained earnings	150,000	30,000
Treasury stock, 8,000 shares at cost	(56,000)	0
Total stockholders' equity	$594,000	$530,000

SSP9-3
A. Contributed capital = $880,240 = $70,000 common stock + $810,240 paid-in capital in excess of par value
B. Shares outstanding = 670,000 = 700,000 issued − 30,000 treasury shares
C. Treasury stock = $42,296
D. Stock repurchased = $8,355; stock issued = $68,044
E. Dividends paid = $42,000
F. Cash flow:

Paid for dividends	$(42,000)
Purchase of stock	(8,355)
Sale of stock	68,044
Net cash flow	$ 17,689

G. Net income from financing activities = $0. Financing activities do not create net income.

Thinking Beyond the Question

What are the fundamental accounting issues associated with financing activities?

Financing activities for corporations involve issuing debt and stock. These activities provide financial resources for the corporation to grow. Debt has to be repaid along with interest. Stockholders expect dividends or increases in stock prices resulting from profits earned by the corporation. How do managers decide how much of their financing should come from debt and how much from equity? What effect does the mix of debt and equity have for a corporation's profits and risk?

QUESTIONS

Q9-1   Why is it useful to report short-term liabilities separately from long-term liabilities when
Obj. 1   preparing the balance sheet?

Q9-2   What are the differences among debentures, serial bonds, and callable bonds?
Obj. 1

Q9-3   Distinguish between the stated rate and the effective rate. Under what circumstances are these
Obj. 1   rates the same? Under what circumstances are these rates different?

Q9-4
Obj. 2
While studying for an accounting exam, a friend observes that a capital lease is merely a means of financing the acquisition of assets. Do you agree? Explain the basis for your answer. If you agree, describe the ways in which a capital lease is similar to other financing activities. If you disagree, describe the ways in which it is different.

Q9-5
Obj. 2
What is a contingency, and how does it differ from a liability? Under what conditions should a contingency be reported as if it were a liability?

Q9-6
Obj. 2
How is a commitment different from a contingency?

Q9-7
Obj. 3
You and Bob are studying for an upcoming accounting exam. Bob says, "Contributed capital is basically the stockholders' equity of the company. It includes things like common stock, paid-in capital in excess of par, preferred stock, and retained earnings." Do you agree? Discuss.

Q9-8
Obj. 1
A friend remarks that, as he understands it, most current liabilities appearing on the balance sheet arise from transactions involving operating activities. Do you agree? List three current liabilities that might appear on the balance sheet. For each one, explain the underlying transaction that must have occurred for that specific liability to arise. Indicate, for each liability, whether it is the result of an operating activity, a financing activity, or an investing activity.

Q9-9
Obj. 3
Jane has just purchased, from Beach Club Inc., 5,000 shares of Beach Club's $10 par value common stock at a price of $40 per share. Explain how this event should be accounted for by Beach Club. Indicate which accounts will be involved and the amounts.

Q9-10
Obj. 4
GAAP require that a firm disclose the details of changes to all stockholders' equity accounts. What are the two primary techniques that companies use to meet this obligation?

Q9-11
Obj. 4
The text states that "a company cannot earn profit from equity transactions." Why might this be? If a company buys widgets at $10 and resells them at $13, there is a $3 profit. What's the difference if a company buys back some of its own stock for $25 per share and resells it at $28 per share? Why do you think that GAAP do not allow a profit (or loss) to be recorded on equity transactions?

Q9-12
Obj. 4
Clearly distinguish among the following terms: date of declaration, date of record, and date of payment. Construct a realistic example in which you use these terms.

Q9-13
Obj. 5
Preferred stock generally does not have voting rights and its holders, therefore, do not have a formal voice in company affairs. Why, then, is it said that preferred stock is a less risky investment than common stock?

Q9-14
Obj. 5
If preferred stock generally has a dividend preference over common stock anyway, what is gained by holding preferred stock that is cumulative?

Q9-15
Obj. 5
Preferred stock generally pays a larger return to investors than do bonds but a lesser return than earned by common stockholders. Why?

Q9-16
Obj. 5
Clarify the differences among the following terms: contributed capital, common stock, capital stock, preferred stock, and treasury stock.

EXERCISES

If your instructor is using Personal Trainer in this course, you may complete online the assignments identified by ᴾᴛ.

E9-1
Write a short definition for each of the terms listed in the *Terms and Concepts Defined in this Chapter* section.

E9-2
Obj. 1
ᴾᴛ
Oxford Company issued $1 million of five-year, 8% bonds on January 1, 2004. The bonds pay interest semiannually. How much did the bonds sell for under each of the following situations?

    a. The bonds sold to yield a real rate of 10%.
    b. The bonds sold to yield a real rate of 6%.
    c. The bonds sold to yield a real rate of 8%.

E9-3

Obj. 1

P̸T̸

For each of the following independent situations, determine: (a) whether the bonds sold at face (maturity) value, at a premium (more than face value), or at a discount (less than face value), and (b) whether interest expense recognized each year for the bonds was less than, equal to, or greater than the amount of interest paid on the bonds.

     a. Bonds with a stated rate of 7% were sold to yield an effective rate of 9%.
     b. Bonds with a stated rate of 10% were sold to yield an effective rate of 8%.
     c. Bonds with a stated rate of 6% were sold to yield an effective rate of 6%.

E9-4

Obj. 1

P̸T̸

Herbal Enterprises issued 10-year bonds with a face value of $10 million on October 1, 2005. The bonds pay interest at 7% annually. The bonds sold at 93.29% of face value to yield an effective rate of 8%.

     a. How much interest expense should Herbal recognize on the bonds for the fiscal year ended September 30, 2006?
     b. What amount of net liability would the company report for the bonds on its 2006 balance sheet?
     c. How much total expense would the company recognize for the bonds over the 10 years they are outstanding?

E9-5

Obj. 1

Today is the fiscal year end for the Benson Boat Company. The regular year-end interest payment on its 9% bonds payable was made earlier today. All necessary entries were recorded. Bonds Payable now has a balance of $186,400. The chief financial officer (CFO) has proposed buying back this debt in the open market later today for $175,000. The debt is not due for repayment for another seven years. Explain how this proposed action would affect this year's (a) income statement, (b) balance sheet, and (c) statement of cash flows. Be specific.

E9-6

Obj. 1

P̸T̸

Linfield Company sold 20-year bonds having a face value of $200,000 at a price of $180,364. The bonds pay annual interest at 7% and were priced to yield an effective return of 8%. Using the format presented in this chapter, record the following:

     a. The issuance of the bonds.
     b. The first payment of interest.
     c. The repayment of principal at maturity. Assume that the last payment of interest has already been made and recorded.

E9-7

Obj. 1

P̸T̸

SPREADSHEET

The Digital Manufacturing Company issued $600,000 of six-year bonds on January 1, 2004. The bonds pay interest of 7% on the face value (0.07 × $600,000 = $42,000). The bonds were sold to give creditors a return of 6%.

     a. Calculate the present value of the bonds at the time they are issued.
     b. Prepare an amortization table for the bonds.
     c. Record Digital Manufacturing's bond transactions at January 1, 2004, December 31, 2004, and December 31, 2009.

E9-8

Obj. 1

P̸T̸

The Calvert Corporation plans to expand its operations. To obtain the necessary cash, $5 million of 6%, five-year bonds were issued on January 1, 2005. The bonds pay interest annually.

     a. Assume Calvert Corporation issued the bonds to yield an effective rate of 7%. Calculate the selling price of the bonds and describe the interest rate conditions under which the bonds were sold.
     b. Now, assume Calvert Corporation issued the bonds to yield an effective rate of 5%. Calculate the selling price of the bonds and describe the conditions under which the bonds were sold.
     c. Without setting up an amortization table, calculate the total amount of interest expense over the life of the bonds in parts a and b above. How do they compare? Why?

E9-9

Obj. 1

P̸T̸

The Medical Lake Clinic acquired diagnostic equipment via a five-year capital lease. Medical Lake Clinic promised to make five end-of-year lease payments of $5,200. Each payment is to include 9% interest. Using the format presented in this chapter, record:

     a. The entry necessary at the beginning of the lease.
     b. The entry necessary at the date of the first lease payment.

E9-10

Obj. 2

For each of the situations that follow, determine whether a liability should be reported on the balance sheet. If a liability should be reported, suggest an account name and indicate whether it should be reported as a current liability or as a long-term liability. If no liability should be reported, indicate why.

a. The last installment payment on a three-year note payable is due next month.
b. Specialized production machinery has been acquired under a capital lease.
c. A $14 million lawsuit has been filed by a customer who claims injury from one of the company's products.
d. The labor services of employees have been consumed but not paid for yet. Payment is not anticipated until the next regular payday in two weeks.
e. A 20-year issue of bonds has been outstanding for 19 years and is expected to be repaid in cash at its maturity date.
f. The company has signed a contract promising to buy $600,000 worth of merchandise during the coming year.

E9-11

Objs. 1, 2

P/T

Below are listed key word clues and descriptions. The key word clues relate to different features or aspects of debt. Match the letter of each clue to the most relevant description provided. Use each clue only once.

a. bond
b. callable
c. capital
d. commitment
e. contingency
f. current
g. debenture
h. effective
i. liability
j. maturity value
k. nominal
l. operating
m. secured
n. serial

_____ 1. Obligations expected to be discharged within one year
_____ 2. A financial instrument that promises to repay principal at maturity and to pay interest each period until then
_____ 3. An obligation to convey resources to another entity in the future
_____ 4. Debt that is backed up by specific assets of the debtor company
_____ 5. A bond backed only by the general creditworthiness of the issuing company
_____ 6. Bonds that can be reacquired at the request of the issuing company
_____ 7. The amount repaid to bondholders at the end of the bond's life
_____ 8. The rate of interest that determines the amount of cash sent to bondholders each period
_____ 9. Bonds that mature a portion at a time over the life of the issue
_____ 10. The actual (or real) rate of return earned by the holder of a bond
_____ 11. A type of lease that results in a liability being reported on the balance sheet
_____ 12. An existing condition that may result in an economic effect later
_____ 13. A promise to engage in some future economic activity
_____ 14. A lease that does not result in a liability being reported on the balance sheet

E9-12

Obj. 3

P/T

Bohannan Company's charter allows it to sell 400,000 shares of $4 par value common stock. So far, the firm has sold 80,000 shares for a total of $780,000. Just yesterday, the company reacquired 1,000 shares from a disgruntled shareholder at a price of $10 per share.

a. What is a charter and by whom is it issued?
b. What total amount of contributed capital should this company report in the stockholders' equity section of its balance sheet?
c. What was the average selling price of each share of common stock?
d. How many shares of stock are outstanding?
e. What balance should be reported in stockholders' equity for Common Stock?

E9-13

Obj. 3

P/T

The charter of Pelenova, Inc. states that it may issue up to one million shares of common stock. Over the life of the company, 255,000 shares have been sold to investors. Total profits over the life of the company have been $876,000, and exactly one-half of that amount has been paid out in dividends. As of today's balance sheet date, the company holds 13,000 shares that have been bought back from shareholders.

a. What is the number of authorized shares?
b. What is the number of issued shares?
c. What is the number of outstanding shares?

E9-14
Obj. 3

The Quick Chips Company, a fast-food manufacturer, began operations in January 2004. It issued 500,000 shares of $0.25 par value common stock. The stock sold for $20 per share. There are 600,000 shares authorized. In 2006, the company repurchased 15,000 shares of stock at a cost of $26 per share. Quick Chips's net income and cash dividend payments have been as follows:

Year	Net Income	Dividends
2004	$(100,000)	$ 0
2005	250,000	75,000
2006	400,000	150,000

Draft the stockholders' equity section of Quick Chips's balance sheet for the years ended December 31, 2005 and 2006.

E9-15
Obj. 4
P̶T̶

Harbor Company reported net income of $1.7 million for the year ending December 31, 2004. On January 27, 2005, the board of directors met and decided that each of the firm's 400,000 outstanding common shares should receive a dividend of $0.65. The board voted to distribute the dividend on March 15 to those stockholders who owned the shares as of February 10.

a. Identify the date of declaration, the date of record, and the date of payment.
b. What percentage of net income was distributed in dividends?
c. Why do you suppose the company did not distribute 100% of net income as dividends? What else can companies do with profits?

E9-16
Obj. 4

On March 1, Tubac Company distributed a $3.00 cash dividend to each of its 54,000 outstanding shares of $4 par value common stock. On June 12, the company declared and issued a 5% stock dividend when the market price of the stock was $7 per share. On September 20, the company declared a 2-for-1 stock split and changed the par value accordingly. Describe how the company's year-end income statement, balance sheet, statement of cash flows, and statement of stockholders' equity will be affected by the

a. cash dividend,
b. stock dividend, and
c. stock split.

E9-17
Obj. 4
P̶T̶

Fast Start Corporation manufactures automobile ignitions. Selected portions of the company's recent financial statements are given below.

Fast Start Corporation
Balance Sheet (Excerpt)
December 31, 2004

Stockholders' equity:	
Common stock, $0.50 par value, 2,000,000 shares authorized, 1,400,000 shares issued	$ 700,000
Paid-In capital in excess of par value	8,200,000
Retained earnings	4,600,000
Treasury stock (60,000 shares at cost)	(480,000)
Total stockholders' equity	$13,020,000

Fast Start Corporation
Statement of Stockholders' Equity
December 31, 2004
(in thousands)

	Common Stock	Paid-In Capital	Retained Earnings	Treasury Stock	Total
December 31, 2003	$650	$7,450	$4,035	$(260)	$11,875
Net income			900		900
Dividends			(335)		(335)
Stock purchased				(220)	(220)
Stock issued	50	750			800
December 31, 2004	$700	$8,200	$4,600	$(480)	$13,020

a. What was Fast Start's total contributed capital at year end?

b. How many shares of common stock were outstanding at year end?

c. What dollar amount of treasury stock did Fast Start hold at year end?

d. What dollar amount of treasury stock did Fast Start repurchase during the year? How much common stock did the company issue?

e. What was the amount of dividends paid during the year?

f. How much cash flow came from financing activities associated with shareholders' equity during the current year, excluding the effect of net income? What were the sources of that cash flow?

g. How much net income came from financing activities associated with stockholders' equity during the current year?

E9-18
Objs. 4, 5

Study the partial statement of stockholders' equity below. The left-most column, which usually contains the explanations of events affecting stockholders' equity, is missing. You may assume that the first number in a column is the beginning balance and the last number is the ending balance.

Preferred Stock	Common Stock	Paid-In Capital	Retained Earnings	Treasury Stock	Total
$55,000	$20,000	$315,000	$182,183	$(7,212)	$564,971
			23,488[a]		23,488
			(8,500)[b]		(8,500)
				1,906[c]	1,906
	5,000[d]	85,000[e]			90,000
$55,000	$25,000	$400,000	$197,171	$(5,306)	$671,865

Using your knowledge of the statement of stockholders' equity, explain what underlying event caused each of the five items on the statement that are marked by a letter.

E9-19
Obj. 5
P/T

San Diego Company has 4,000 shares of $100 par value, 7% cumulative preferred stock outstanding. In addition, the company has 10,000 shares of common stock outstanding. The company began operations and issued both classes of stock on January 1, 2004. The total amount of cash dividends declared and paid during each of the first four years of the company's life is shown below. Complete the table by indicating the dollars of dividends that should be paid each year to each class of stock.

Year	Total Dividends Paid	Dividends to Preferred	Dividends to Common	Unpaid Dividends to Preferred
2004	$50,000			
2005	10,000			
2006	45,000			
2007	70,000			

E9-20
Objs. 3, 4, 5
P/T

Below are listed key word clues and descriptions. The key word clues relate to different features or aspects of equity. Match the letter of each key word clue to the most relevant description provided. Use each clue only once.

a. authorized	f. declaration	k. preemptive	p. split
b. charter	g. issued	l. preferred	q. stock
c. common	h. outstanding	m. record	r. treasury
d. contributed	i. par	n. redeemable	
e. cumulative	j. payment	o. retained	

(Continued)

_____ 1. Shares of a company's own stock that have been reacquired by the company
_____ 2. Capital resulting from direct investments made by stockholders in the company
_____ 3. Earnings that have not been distributed to owners as dividends
_____ 4. The voting stock in a corporation
_____ 5. The actual number of shares that have been sold or given to stockholders
_____ 6. The document granted by a state that gives a corporation the legal right to exist
_____ 7. An arbitrary value assigned to a share of stock (not a very meaningful value)
_____ 8. The maximum number of shares that a corporation is permitted to issue
_____ 9. Stock that receives a fixed dividend amount
_____ 10. The number of shares that are currently in the hands of stockholders
_____ 11. The date on which a corporation announces that a dividend will be paid
_____ 12. Preferred stock that will be repurchased by the issuing company at a fixed future date
_____ 13. A type of dividend in which new shares are distributed to existing stockholders
_____ 14. The privilege of existing stockholders to buy a prorata share of any new stock that is offered for sale
_____ 15. The date on which a dividend is distributed to stockholders
_____ 16. A very large stock dividend
_____ 17. A feature that encourages corporations to make up any previously omitted dividends on preferred stock
_____ 18. The date that determines who will receive a dividend that has been declared

E9-21

Objs. 4, 5

$\frac{P}{T}$

Sweetwater Company reports the following stockholders' equity section of the balance sheet.

Preferred stock, $50 par value, 8% cumulative	$ 2,500,000
Common stock, $2 par value	800,000
Paid-in capital in excess of par value, common stock	11,000,000
Retained earnings	4,894,000
Total	$19,194,000

a. How many preferred shares are outstanding?
b. How many common shares are outstanding?
c. At what average price was the common stock sold?
d. If the firm declares dividends totaling $376,000, what amount per share will be paid to the preferred stockholders and what amount per share will be paid to common stockholders? (Assume that there are no unpaid prior dividends on the preferred stock.)

PROBLEMS

If your instructor is using Personal Trainer in this course, you may complete online the assignments identified by $\frac{P}{T}$.

P9-1

Obj. 1

$\frac{P}{T}$

Bond Amortization Table

On January 1, 2004, Holstein Enterprises issued bonds. Its accounting department prepared the amortization table below.

Year	Present Value at Beginning of Year	Interest Incurred	Amount Paid	Amortization of Principal	Value at End of Year
1	384,440	34,600	32,000	2,600	387,040
2	387,040	34,834	32,000	2,834	389,874
3	389,874	35,089	32,000	3,089	392,963
4	392,963	35,367	32,000	3,367	396,330
5	396,330	35,670	32,000	3,670	400,000
Total		175,560	160,000	15,560	

Required

A. What was the total face value of the bonds issued?
B. At what price were the bonds sold?
C. What is the stated rate, or nominal rate, of interest for these bonds?
D. What is the real, or effective, rate of interest for these bonds?
E. What amount will appear on the year 3 income statement related to these bonds?
F. What amount will appear on the year 4 balance sheet related to these bonds?
G. Explain the interrelationship among the three items reported in the last row of the table (the row labeled Total).

P9-2
Obj. 1

P/T

Bonds and the Accounting System

Pattison Associates issued 4-year bonds with a face value of $300,000 to yield an effective rate of 6%. The bonds pay interest annually and were sold at a price of $310,394.

SPREADSHEET

Required

A. What was the stated rate for these bonds?
B. Show what information would be entered into the accounting system regarding these bonds on the date of issue. Using the format presented in this chapter, record the entry necessary at issuance and at the first interest payment date, and the entry at the final interest payment date. (Hint: It may be helpful to prepare an amortization table.)

P9-3
Obj. 1

P/T

Issuance and Amortization of Bonds

Sky King Company sold $9 million of four-year, 8% debentures on July 1, 2004. The bonds sold to yield a real rate of 7%. Interest is paid annually on June 30.

SPREADSHEET

Required

A. Determine the price of the bonds.
B. Prepare an amortization schedule for the bonds.
C. Using the format presented in this chapter, record the entry to the accounting system that is necessary to recognize interest on the bonds at June 30, 2005.
D. Assume the bonds had been sold to yield a real rate of 9%. At what price would they have sold?

P9-4
Obj. 1

P/T

Issuance and Amortization of Bonds

Plum Grove Company sold $10 million of four-year, 9% debentures on July 1, 2004. The bonds sold to yield an effective rate of 10%. Interest is paid annually on June 30.

SPREADSHEET

Required

A. Determine the price of the bonds.
B. Prepare an amortization schedule for the bonds.
C. Using the format presented in this chapter, record the entry to the accounting system that is necessary to recognize interest on the bonds at June 30, 2005.
D. Assume the bonds had been sold to yield 8%. At what price would they have sold?

P9-5
Obj. 1

Ethical Issues Related to Debt

Slick Tawker is an investment broker. Recently he contacted potential investors and offered to sell them bonds that were paying a 10% annual rate of interest. He noted that the bonds were paying a much higher return than other investments and that similar bonds were selling at a real rate of 6% interest. The bonds had a 10-year maturity and paid interest semiannually. Several investors purchased the bonds because of the high rate of interest but later were concerned to learn that the maturity value of $1,000 per bond was considerably less than the $1,350 they had paid for each bond.

Required Compare the price of the bonds sold by Slick to bonds yielding a real rate of 6%. What was the approximate real rate of return earned by the investors? Did they have a right to be concerned about their investments? Do you see any ethical problems with Slick's sales pitch?

P9-6

Obj. 1

$\overset{P}{T}$

Choosing between Financing Options

The management of Poliwog Financial plans to borrow $50,000 to carry out current operations. Two repayment options are available. The appropriate interest rate is 8%.

> Option 1: The company may repay the amount borrowed by making four equal annual payments, the first one due in one year.
>
> Option 2: The company may pay just the interest annually, and then pay the entire amount of $50,000 at the end of four years.

Required

A. Identify the amount of the annual payment required under Option 1 and the amount of the required annual interest payment under Option 2.
B. Identify the total cash outflows and the total interest expense incurred for the four years under each option.
C. Explain why there is a difference in the total cash outflow and total interest expense between the two plans.
D. Which plan would you recommend to the company?

P9-7

Obj. 2

$\overset{P}{T}$

SPREADSHEET

Acquiring Assets via Capital Lease

Jessica Johnson Logging Company is considering the acquisition of a new bulldozer. Big Dig, Inc. has offered to lease the equipment to Johnson Company for all 12 years of its useful life at annual year-end lease payments of $24,500. Each payment will include 9% interest. At the end of 12 years of lease payments, Big Dig, Inc. will allow Johnson to keep the bulldozer.

Required

A. At what amount should the bulldozer and lease obligation be recorded on Johnson's books at the date of acquisition?
B. Prepare an amortization table covering only the first four years of the lease.
C. Explain why a $24,500 lease payment doesn't cause the amount owed to decrease by $24,500.
D. Explain why Johnson's interest expense gets smaller for each successive year of the lease.
E. Using the format presented in this chapter, record the entry to capitalize the bulldozer and lease obligation on Johnson's books.
F. Using the format presented in this chapter, record the entry to recognize the first year-end lease payment.

P9-8

Obj. 2

$\overset{P}{T}$

Determining Lease Payments

Garcia Orchards & Processing Company has been taking bids for three new tractors. Goldbaum Equipment has made an offer to sell a qualifying model for $41,000 each. In addition, Goldbaum has offered to finance the transaction through a capital lease over the expected 15-year life of the tractors with no money down. No mention of the size of the required year-end lease payments has been made yet, but Garcia knows that Goldbaum will expect a 9% return on the lease arrangement.

Required If Garcia accepts this option:

A. What will be the size of each annual year-end lease payment?
B. What amount will Garcia capitalize on its balance sheet for the tractors and for the lease obligation? What does this amount represent?
C. Using the format presented in this chapter, record the entry to set up the lease on Garcia's books.
D. What total amount will Garcia pay over the life of the lease for financing? (Hint: You do not need to prepare an amortization table.)
E. Using the format presented in this chapter, record the entry necessary when Garcia makes the first lease payment.
F. When the second year's lease payment is recorded, will the amount of interest expense be larger or smaller than that for the first year? Explain.

P9-9
Obj. 2

P
T

Choosing between Financing Options

Careful Electric Company is planning to purchase equipment for one of its generating plants. Dealer A has offered to sell the equipment at a total cost of $2 million, including installation. This dealer requires a 6% return and is willing to spread the payments over a 10-year period. Payments are to be made at the end of each year in equal installments.

Dealer B is asking $1.8 million for the same equipment and will charge an additional $50,000 for installation, to be paid when the equipment is delivered. Payments can be spread over 10 years, made at the end of each year. This dealer requires an 8% return.

Required

A. Calculate the amount of the annual payments required by each dealer. Round to nearest whole dollar.
B. Determine the projected total cash outflow under each option.
C. If Careful could pay cash for the new equipment, how much money (interest) would it save under each option?
D. Which option should be chosen?
E. Assume the equipment is acquired using the financing offered by Dealer A. How will the financing activities section of the statement of cash flows be affected by these transactions in the first year?

P9-10
Obj. 2

P
T

SPREADSHEET

Using Spreadsheet Functions to Evaluate a Lease Proposal

FencePost.com needs additional equipment to expand production capacity. A vendor has suggested a lease plan in which FencePost would make end-of-the-month payments for five years of $3,250. At that point the equipment would be worthless and discarded. The vendor expects to earn a return on this financing arrangement of 9.75% compounded annually. The chief financial officer at FencePost recognizes this arrangement would be accounted for as a capital lease.

Required

A. Use the PV function in an Excel spreadsheet to determine the amount at which the lease would be recorded in the accounting system. List the arguments you inserted into the formula.
B. Show how this transaction would be entered into the accounting system at inception of the lease.
C. Prepare an amortization table for the lease (first four months only).
D. Show the entry that must be made on the date of the first lease payment.
E. Explain how you can tell that the vendor earns a 9.75% rate of return on this transaction.

P9-11
Obj. 2

P
T

SPREADSHEET

Using Spreadsheet Functions to Evaluate a Lease Proposal

Rampaging Technology, Inc. is growing rapidly and is expanding its production capacity. An equipment supplier has suggested a lease plan based on a selling price of $350,000. Rampaging would make five equal-size end-of-the-year payments and then own the machine. The supplier expects to earn a return on this financing arrangement of 11.35% compounded annually. Such a lease would be accounted for as a capital lease.

Required

A. Use the PMT function in an Excel spreadsheet to determine the amount of the annual payment that would be required. List the arguments you inserted into the formula.
B. Show how this transaction would be entered into the accounting system at inception of the lease.
C. Prepare an amortization table for the lease.
D. Explain why the annual interest expense decreases during each of the five years.
E. Show the entry that must be made on the date of the first lease payment.
F. Explain how you can tell that the vendor earns an 11.35% rate of return on this transaction.

P9-12
Obj. 4

Reporting Changes in Stockholders' Equity

On the next page is shown the stockholders' equity section of Tulip Company's balance sheet at December 31, 2004:

(Continued)

Common stock, $2 par value, 5,400,000 shares	
authorized, 2,200,000 shares issued and outstanding	$ 4,400,000
Paid-in capital in excess of par value	30,800,000
Retained earnings	46,000,000
Total stockholders' equity	$81,200,000

All of the following occurred in year 2005 and were properly recorded.

1. The company purchased 30,000 shares of its own stock at $21 per share on January 2.
2. The company purchased 20,000 shares of the Sumo Corporation at $6 per share on February 14.
3. The company declared and issued a 10% stock dividend on March 2. The fair market value of the stock at that time was $25 per share.
4. The company declared and paid a cash dividend of $0.40 on its common stock on July 21.
5. The company reported a net loss of $5,200,000 on December 31.

Required

A. Prepare the stockholders' equity section as of December 31, 2005 after all the events described above have been properly accounted for.
B. Describe the effects on the financing section of the year 2005 statement of cash flows.

P9-13   **Stock Splits and Stock Dividends**

Obj. 4

The Carpelli Corporation manufactures solar panels that provide electricity for businesses and homes. The company has been doing well for several years and so the board of directors has decided to declare a stock split in the amount of two shares for every share of stock held by shareholders. The split will be effective as of February 15, 2005.

Below is the stockholders' equity section of the Carpelli Corporation's balance sheet at December 31, 2004.

Common stock, $4 par, 250,000 shares authorized,	
100,000 shares issued and outstanding	$ 400,000
Additional paid-in capital in excess of par	1,200,000
Retained earnings	3,600,000
Total	$5,200,000

Required

A. Prepare the stockholders' equity section for the Carpelli Corporation's balance sheet after the stock split. How many shares of stock will be issued to the shareholders? Assume the market value of the stock is $18 per share on February 15, 2005.
B. Assume that the Carpelli Corporation's board of directors decided to declare a 100% stock dividend instead of the split. Prepare the stockholders' equity section after the stock dividend. How many shares of stock will be issued to the shareholders? (Note that for a large stock dividend—100% in this case—the dollar amount transferred from retained earnings to contributed capital will be the par value of the stock, instead of the market price.)
C. Compare the stockholders' equity sections after the split and after the dividend. How do they differ?
D. What should be the selling price of the stock after the split? After the dividend?

P9-14   **The Statement of Stockholders' Equity and Other Financial Statements**

Objs. 3, 4

Olafson Electronics reported the following statement of stockholders' equity at the end of its 10th year in business.

Required For each of the five lettered items in the statement on the next page, indicate where that same information will be found on one or more other financial statements. Be specific as to the statement(s) and the specific section of the statement(s).

	Preferred Stock	Common Stock	Paid-In Capital	Retained Earnings	Treasury Stock	Total
December 31, year 9	$21,000	$10,000	$188,000	$77,831	$(10,094)	$286,737
Net income				26,182[a]		26,182
Dividends				(14,300)[b]		(14,300)
Stock purchased					(1,263)[c]	(1,263)
Stock issued		4,000	75,000			79,000[d]
December 31, year 10	$21,000	$14,000[e]	$263,000	$89,713	$(11,357)	$376,356

P9-15 Convertible Preferred Stock

Obj. 5

The Bedford Bicycle Company has 3,000 shares of $10 par preferred stock outstanding. The stock originally had been issued for $16 per share. It is convertible into shares of common stock at the rate of five shares of $1 par common for every share of preferred. No cash would be paid by the converting shareholders. This convertible preferred stock pays a dividend of $1 per share per year.

Required

A. Assume there are 40,000 shares of common stock outstanding, originally issued at $30 per share, but having a current market value of $32 per share. The retained earnings account balance is $3,200,000. Prepare the stockholders' equity section of the balance sheet before conversion of any preferred stock.

B. Now, assume that all of the preferred stock is converted to common stock. Prepare the stockholders' equity section of the balance sheet. Compare and explain the totals in stockholders' equity before and after the conversion of the preferred stock.

C. Explain how the conversion of preferred stock into common stock will be reported in the financing section of the cash flow statement.

D. Assume that the Velasquez Corporation is similar to the Bedford Bicycle Company in many respects including the fact that it has $10 par value preferred stock outstanding. Velasquez pays a dividend of $1.60 per share per year on its preferred stock; the stock is not convertible to common. What do you think is the main reason for the difference in dividend rates between the two companies?

P9-16 Understanding the Stockholders' Equity Section of the Balance Sheet

Objs. 3, 4, 5

P/T

Saigon Building Supply was organized and began operations on January 1, 2004. At December 31, 2005, it reported the following stockholders' equity section on its comparative balance sheet.

December 31,	2005	2004
Stockholders' equity		
8.5% preferred stock, $10 par value,		
10,000 shares authorized and issued	b	a
Common stock, $2 par value,		
300,000 shares authorized,		
110,000 and 90,000 shares issued	d	c
Paid-in capital in excess of par value	f	e
Retained earnings	h	g
Treasury stock (4,500 and 3,100 shares at cost)	j	i
Total stockholders' equity	$1,411,750	$1,037,800

(Continued)

The company reported net income of $75,000 for calendar year 2004 and $125,000 for 2005. The firm's dividend policy is to pay out 10% of its profits each year in dividends. The date of payment is always April 1 of the following year. Treasury stock was acquired at a cost of $12 per share in 2004. At December 31, 2005, the average cost of treasury stock was $13.50 per share. The common shares sold during 2005 were sold at $14 each.

Required Replace each of the italicized letters with the correct numerical value.

P9-17

Objs. 3, 4, 5

P
T

Interpreting the Stockholders' Equity Section of the Balance Sheet

Hampton, Inc. began operations on January 1, 2005. On December 31, 2006, it reported the following stockholders' equity section of its balance sheet.

December 31,	2006	2005
Stockholders' equity		
7% cumulative preferred stock, $100 par value	$ 300,000	$ 300,000
Common stock, $2 par value	150,000	120,000
Paid-in capital in excess of par value	830,000	620,000
Retained earnings	362,500	157,500
Treasury stock	(16,800)	(25,725)
Total stockholders' equity	$1,625,700	$1,171,775

The company has a policy of paying out 10% of its net income as cash dividends. The date of declaration is always 30 days after the end of the year, and the date of payment occurs 60 days after the end of the year. At year-end 2005, the average price of treasury stock was $10.50. At year-end 2006, the average price of treasury stock was $12.

Required

A. How many preferred shares have been issued as of year-end 2005 and 2006?
B. How many common shares have been issued as of year-end 2005? As of year-end 2006?
C. How many treasury shares are there at year-end 2005? At year-end 2006?
D. How many common shares are outstanding at year-end 2005? At year-end 2006?
E. What was the average price (at original issuance) of common stock as of year-end 2005?
F. What was the average selling price of the shares issued during 2006?
G. What was net income for 2005? For 2006?
H. What was the dividend per share paid to preferred stock on March 1, 2006?
I. What was the dividend per share paid to common stock on March 1, 2006?
J. What is the dividend per share that is scheduled to be paid to common stock on March 1, 2007? Why?

P9-18

Objs. 3, 4, 5

P
T

Interpreting the Stockholders' Equity Section of the Balance Sheet

Nakishima Industries reported the following stockholders' equity section of its balance sheet at December 31, 2005.

December 31,	2005	2004
Stockholders' equity		
8.5% cumulative preferred stock, $25 par value	$ 450,000	$ 375,000
Common stock, $5 par value	680,000	575,000
Paid-in capital in excess of par value, common	4,050,000	2,500,000
Retained earnings	9,400,300	7,300,800
Treasury stock	(1,970,050)	(1,510,000)
Total stockholders' equity	$12,610,250	$ 9,240,800

The company has paid cash dividends annually for 24 years. There are no dividends in arrears. The date of declaration is always March 1 and the amount of dividends declared is always 25% of prior year net income. Year 2004 net income was $2.0 million. At year-end 2005, the average cost of treasury stock was $31 per share. At year-end 2004, the average price of treasury stock was $25.

Required

A. How many preferred shares have been issued as of the end of 2005 and 2004?
B. How many common shares have been issued as of the end of 2005? As of year-end 2004?
C. How many treasury shares are there at year-end 2005 and at year-end 2004?
D. How many common shares are outstanding at year-end 2005 and at year-end 2004?
E. As of year-end 2005, what was the average price (at original issuance) of common stock?
F. What was the average selling price of the common shares issued during 2005?
G. What was net income for 2005?
H. What was the amount of the dividend per share paid to preferred stock during 2005?
I. What was the amount of the dividend per share paid to common stock during 2005? (Assume there were 54,600 common shares outstanding at the date of the 2005 dividend distribution.)
J. What is the dividend per share that is scheduled to be paid to common stock in 2006? (Assume there will be no change in the number of shares outstanding between December 31, 2005 and the distribution of dividends in 2006.)

P9-19

Objs. 1, 2, 3, 4, 5

Determining Whether a Liability Exists

Determine if a liability should be recorded in each of the following cases involving the Soft-Wear Manufacturing Company. If there is no liability, explain how the item should be recorded.

A. The company guarantees to repair or replace any of its products that are defective.
B. The company estimates that some customers will not pay for merchandise purchased on credit.
C. The company obtains an asset and signs a lease that extends for one-third of the useful life of the asset.
D. The company is being investigated for potential pollution problems by the Environmental Protection Agency. The company's engineers believe it is likely that the company will be held responsible for an expensive cleanup activity.
E. The company has issued bonds that are maturing at the end of the current month.
F. The company is being sued by an unhappy customer. The case has not yet come to court.
G. The company has declared a 20% stock dividend.
H. The company has declared a $0.25 cash dividend to be paid on all outstanding shares.
I. The preferred stock is cumulative and dividends have not been paid for three years.
J. The company has a noncontrolling interest of 3%.
K. The company has bonds outstanding that are convertible into common stock. The company's accountants believe that bond holders are likely to convert their bonds because the company has performed exceptionally well this year.
L. Stock options have been issued to the company's executives. The options have not yet been exercised.

P9-20

SPREADSHEET

Excel in Action

In March 2005, the Wermz's decided to expand their business. They purchased an existing chain of bookstores for a price of $5 million. They financed their purchase by issuing $3 million of common stock and by issuing $2 million of 20-year bonds payable. Interest will be paid monthly beginning in April 2005. The stated rate of interest on the bonds is 9% (annual interest payments are 9% of $2 million). The bonds were sold to earn a 9.25% interest rate (the actual annual rate of interest is 9.25%).

Required Use a spreadsheet to determine the present value of the bonds. Enter the captions (as shown in the example on the next page) in cells A1 to A7.
　　In cell B1, enter the maturity value of the bonds.
　　In cell B2, calculate the amount of interest paid each month.
　　In cell B3, calculate the actual monthly interest rate.

(Continued)

In cell B4, calculate the number of months during which interest will be paid.

In cell B5, calculate the present value of the interest payments. Use the PV function (click on the Function button and select Financial and PV). Enter the rate (B3), number of periods (B4), and monthly payments (B2). The resulting value is negative because it is a cash outflow. Change the amount to a positive value by multiplying by (-1).

In cell B6, calculate the present value of the maturity value of the bonds. The calculation is based on the equation $PV = MV/(1+R)^t$, where PV is present value, MV is maturity value (B1), R is the actual interest rate (B3), and t is the number of periods until maturity (B4).

In cell B7, calculate the total maturity value of the bonds.

	A	B
1	Maturity	
2	Interest Payments	
3	Actual Interest Rate	
4	Periods	
5	Present Value of Interest	
6	Present Value of Principal	
7	Total Present Value	

Beginning in cell A9, prepare an amortization table for April through December 2005 for the bonds. Use Exhibit 3 in this chapter as an example. Use formulas for all spreadsheet calculations. (See the Continuous Problem in Chapter F8 if you need help.) How much interest expense will The Book Wermz incur on the bonds in 2005? How much interest will the company pay? How much liability will the company report for the bonds at the end of 2005?

Suppose the effective interest rate was 8.75%. What would be the present value of the bonds? How much interest expense would the company incur in 2005?

Suppose the effective interest rate was 9.0%. What would be the present value of the bonds? How much interest expense would the company incur in 2005?

P9-21 Multiple-Choice Overview of the Chapter

$\frac{P}{T}$ 1. Which of the following are attributes of a liability?

	Result from a Prior Transaction	Involve a Promise to Convey Resources in the Future
a.	Yes	Yes
b.	Yes	No
c.	No	Yes
d.	No	No

2. Which of the following should be reported on a year-end balance sheet under the heading of short-term debt?

	Wages Already Earned by Employees but Not Yet Paid	30-Year Debentures That Have Been Outstanding for 29 Years
a.	Yes	Yes
b.	Yes	No
c.	No	Yes
d.	No	No

3. A contingency is reported on the balance sheet as a liability if
   a. it arises from a potential claim regarding damage to the environment.
   b. a loss is probable and it can be reasonably estimated.
   c. a lawsuit has been filed.
   d. it involves a potential loss of a large amount of money.

4. The stockholders' equity section of Tarro Company's balance sheet includes the following selected information.

Common stock, $1 par, 15,000 shares authorized,
   9,000 shares issued, 7,000 shares outstanding $ 27,000
Additional paid-in capital in excess of par value   14,000
Retained earnings   (20,000)
Treasury stock

What is the correct balance of the common stock account?
  a. $15,000
  b. $11,000
  c. $9,000
  d. $7,000

5. A stockholder who owns 5% of the common stock of a corporation has a right to each
   of the following except
   a. 5% of any dividends paid to common stockholders.
   b. to cast votes on matters brought to stockholders for a vote.
   c. to receive a dividend of 5% of net income for the current period.
   d. to purchase 5% of any additional common stock issued by the company.

6. A corporation had retained earnings of $400,000 at December 31, 2004. Net income for
   2005 was $175,000, and the company paid a cash dividend of $75,000. Also, the company repurchased shares of its stock during the year at a total cost of $50,000. The bal-
   ance of retained earnings at December 31, 2005, would be
   a. $450,000.
   b. $550,000.
   c. $575,000.
   d. $500,000.

7. A corporation issued a 10% stock dividend during its 2005 fiscal year. The market
   value of the stock was $20 per share at the time the dividend was issued. One million
   shares of stock were outstanding. The par value of the stock was $1 per share. Which
   of the following correctly identifies the effect on the financial statements of this transaction?

	Assets	Equity	Net Income
a.	Increase	Decrease	No effect
b.	No effect	Decrease	No effect
c.	No effect	No effect	No effect
d.	No effect	Decrease	Decrease

8. Which of the following is *not* a true statement about preferred stock?
   a. Preferred stockholders receive a current cash dividend before common stockhold-
      ers do.
   b. Preferred stockholders receive a stated dividend each year.
   c. Preferred stock generally does not have voting privileges.
   d. The cumulative feature serves to protect preferred stockholder interests.

9. The statement that "dividends are not an expense" is
   a. always true.
   b. never true.
   c. sometimes true.
   d. frequently true.

10. The presence of a foreign currency adjustment on the balance sheet means that
    a. the company owns at least one foreign subsidiary.
    b. the company's primary operations are located in a foreign country.
    c. shares of the company's stock have been sold to foreign investors.
    d. retained earnings of a foreign subsidiary have been appropriated.

CASES

C9-1 Making Credit Decisions

Objs. 1, 2, 3, 4

Suppose that you are an employee of the loan department of Metropolitan Bank, and one of your primary tasks is analyzing information provided by organizations applying for commercial loans. Most applicants are small businesses seeking additional capital to acquire long-term assets. Other applicants are seeking financing to acquire existing businesses. A typical applicant is Cleopatra Jones, who owns Cleopatra's, a women's clothing store. Ms. Jones has applied for a loan of $50,000 to finance an expansion of her business.

Required Identify the types of information you would need from Ms. Jones to help you make a loan decision. Explain why each type of information would be useful.

C9-2 Interpreting Stockholders' Equity

Objs. 3, 4, 5

Selected disclosures from a consolidated balance sheet are shown below.

December 31,	2004	2003
(in millions)		
Total assets	**$3,759.7**	**$3,774.4**
Total liabilities	**$2,411.9**	**$2,652.3**
Stockholders' equity:		
Preferred stock	785.1	789.0
Common stock, shares issued:		
2004 = 171.2; 2003 = 162.6	0.9	0.8
Retained earnings (accumulated deficit)	79.9	(114.0)
Other capital	481.9	446.3
Total stockholders' equity	$1,347.8	$1,122.1
Total liabilities and stockholders' equity	**$3,759.7**	**$3,774.4**

A note to the financial statements reveals:

The Company has 180,000,000 authorized shares of common stock. In February of 2002, the Certificate of Incorporation of the Company was amended to change the par value of the common stock from $4 per share to $0.01 per share.

In 2003, the Company resumed payment of dividends on preferred stock, which had been suspended in February 2002. Preferred dividends of $53.9 million and $61.4 million were in arrears at December 31, 2004 and December 31, 2003, respectively.

Required Prepare a report that explains the following:

A. Of what economic significance is the par value of a company's stock? What is the significance of the decision to restate the par value of the stock? What is the advantage for the company?

B. What are the primary attributes of preferred stock? In what ways is preferred stock equity? In what ways is it debt? Why do companies issue preferred stock?

C. What effect does the suspension of dividends on the preferred stock have on the financial statements? What economic effect does it have on the company? If the preferred stock and dividends in arrears were reported as liabilities, what would be the effect on the company's balance sheet?

D. Assess the position of the company's common stockholders at the end of 2004.

C9-3
Objs. 1, 2, 3, 4, 5

Analyzing Liabilities and Stockholders' Equity

Review the financial statements of **General Mills, Inc.**, provided in Appendix B of this book.

Required Write a report that covers the following:

A. How important were liabilities as a source of financing for assets as of the end of fiscal 2002? What are some of the implications of this? Discuss.

B. What were the company's most significant liabilities at year-end 2002? Did the relative significance of certain liabilities change from the prior year? Describe any material changes.

C. Did financing activities concerning liabilities affect cash flows during 2002? Did financing activities concerning liabilities affect its net income in 2002? Identify any such affects.

D. Describe any significant changes in the stockholders' equity section of the balance sheet that occurred between year-end 2001 and year-end 2002. For any significant changes, indicate what caused them to change.

ANALYSIS OF FINANCING ACTIVITIES

How do we finance our business?

Chapter 9 discussed financing activities, including accounting for debt and equity. Accounting involves more than determining amounts to report in financial statements. It involves the analysis of information about business activities to understand those activities and how they affect the performance and value of a business.

If Maria and Stan are going to increase the size of their business, they will need additional financing. They need to be aware of the effect that debt and equity have on a business's profitability and value. And they need to make financing decisions that increase company value and permit it to survive for the long run.

Maria, the company president, Stan, the vice president of operations, and Ellen, the vice president of finance of Mom's Cookie Company, sat in Maria's office discussing financial plans for their company. Maria and Stan formed the company to sell cookies produced from their mom's recipes. Initially, the company purchased its products from bakeries because it did not have sufficient financial resources to buy the equipment and facilities it would need to manufacture its own products. As the company's products have become more popular, Maria and Stan have decided to expand their company. The volume of sales is sufficient to warrant acquiring production facilities. Ellen was hired recently as vice president of finance to help the company with its growth potential. They have met to discuss how to finance their company's expansion.

FOOD FOR THOUGHT

What issues should managers consider when deciding on the amounts of debt and equity financing to use in a company? How should investors analyze a company's financial statements to assess managers' financing decisions and the effects of these decisions on profits and company value?

Maria: I've noticed that different companies use different amounts of debt and equity financing. How can we determine the right amounts for our company?

Ellen: One issue we can look at is the effect that different forms of financing can have on the risk and return of owners and other stakeholders.

Stan: Can it really make that much of a difference?

Ellen: Yes. Many companies have a hard time surviving because they made financing decisions that were not right for the companies. There are good reasons that some companies use more debt than others. Let's take a look at some of these reasons.

OBJECTIVES

Once you have completed this chapter, you should be able to:

1 Define capital structure, and explain why it is important to a company.

2 Explain when it is beneficial for a company to use financial leverage.

3 Explain why cash flows are important for a company's financing decisions.

4 Use financial statements to evaluate the financing activities of different companies.

5 Determine and explain the effect of financial leverage on a company's risk and return.

6 Use cash flow and liquidity measures to evaluate financing decisions.

7 Explain why financing activities are important for determining company value.

FINANCING DECISIONS

Maria, Stan, and Ellen know that if the company is properly managed, it will have a good chance of making a lot of money. They also knew of several companies like theirs, with promising futures, that failed within a few years because of poor financial management. They are determined not to make the same mistakes. Let's follow their conversation as they discuss their financing alternatives.

Stan continued the conversation. "The potential for our product is good. At our current growth rate, we should sell $3 million of product next year, and I believe sales will grow at a rate of 20% per year for the foreseeable future. We need $5 million to fund production facilities and to expand production and marketing activities. Of this amount, $4 million will go into plant assets."

Capital Structure Decisions

OBJECTIVE 1

Define capital structure, and explain why it is important to a company.

Maria spoke next, "OK, we know we have great potential. We have a quality product that meets the needs of a large market. Our current concern is how do we finance our production costs? I think we might want to use as much debt as possible. A friend of mine from college is a manager with a company that uses well over 50% debt in its capital structure, and the company has been very successful. What do you think?"

Stan interrupted, "What do you mean by capital structure?"

"*Capital structure* **is the relative amounts of debt and equity used by a company to finance its assets,**" Ellen answered. "Those are our basic choices. Either we can borrow money, or we can issue stock. Some companies are successful using a lot of debt, but our situation is different. I think we should rely primarily on equity."

"I don't understand," Stan replied. "What difference does it make? We need $5 million. As long as we get it from someone, why should we care where it comes from? A dollar of debt will pay for just as many assets as a dollar of equity."

"Yes," answered Ellen, "but that's not the complete story. Let's look at some numbers. Exhibit 1 contains projected sales and operating income figures for the next three

Exhibit 1

Projected Sales and Income for Mom's Cookie Company

(In thousands)	Year 1	Year 2	Year 3
Sales	$ 3,000	$ 3,600	$ 4,320
Cost of goods sold	(1,800)	(2,160)	(2,592)
Operating expenses	(1,000)	(1,000)	(1,000)
Operating income	200	440	728
Income taxes	(60)	(132)	(218)
Net income	$ 140	$ 308	$ 510

years based on Stan's estimates. Operating costs will be high relative to sales next year because of initial training and development costs and special marketing efforts to increase customer awareness of our product. Also, we will not be producing at full capacity until we get more of our product into customers' hands and they see how good it is."

"I still don't see the point," Stan observed.

Ellen responded, "Well, let's see what happens to our profits and stockholder returns depending on how we finance our operations. Exhibit 2 provides a simplified balance sheet for Mom's Cookie Company, assuming that we finance our company without any long-term debt. These numbers assume that we invest $4 million in plant assets and start with $1 million in current assets. Further, I assume that current assets will increase at the same rate as sales, 20% per year. Plant assets will be replaced each year as they wear out to maintain a constant investment, at least for the first few years. Also, I assume that we issue $4.2 million of stock and use current liabilities to fund the remainder of our assets. Some of our current assets, such as inventories, can be purchased on short-term credit from suppliers. Therefore, Accounts Payable and other current liabilities will provide a source of funding for a portion of current assets."

Exhibit 2

Projected Summary
Balance Sheet for
Mom's Cookie Company

(In thousands)	Year 1	Year 2	Year 3
Assets:			
Current assets	$1,000	$1,200	$1,440
Plant assets	4,000	4,000	4,000
Total assets	$5,000	$5,200	$5,440
Liabilities:			
Current liabilities	$ 800	$ 960	$1,152
Long-term debt	0	0	0
Total liabilities	800	960	1,152
Stockholders' equity	4,200	4,240	4,288
Total liabilities and equity	$5,000	$5,200	$5,440

"Using this financing arrangement," Ellen continued, "our income statement will look like Exhibit 1, which does not include any interest expense. A useful measure of performance, in addition to net income, is return on equity. *Return on equity (ROE)* **is net income divided by stockholders' equity.** It measures net income relative to the amount invested by stockholders in a company, including retained earnings. Investors and financial analysts use return on equity to compare the performances of companies, either to compare one company with another or to compare a company's performance in one period with its performance in another period. From the data in Exhibits 1 and 2, we can compute Mom's Cookie Company's return on equity as shown in Exhibit 3.

Exhibit 3

Return on Equity (Net
Income ÷ Stockholders'
Equity) for Mom's
Cookie Company

(In thousands)	Year 1	Year 2	Year 3
Net income	$ 140	$ 308	$ 510
Stockholders' equity	$4,200	$4,240	$4,288
Return on equity	3.3%	7.3%	11.9%

"Exhibit 3 indicates that stockholders will earn 3.3 cents next year for each dollar they invest in Mom's Cookie Company," Ellen observed. "Three years from now, they will earn 11.9 cents for each dollar invested. Now let's see what happens if we include long-term debt in our capital structure."

The Effect of Financial Leverage

OBJECTIVE 2

Explain when it is beneficial for a company to use financial leverage.

"Let's look at the numbers," Ellen continued. "Exhibit 4 describes the results if we use $2.5 million of liabilities and $2.5 million of equity next year. This would give us an initial **debt-to-equity ratio** of 1.0 ($2.5 million of liabilities ÷ $2.5 million of equity) and a **debt-to-assets ratio** of 0.5 or 50% ($2.5 million of liabilities ÷ $5 million of assets). These ratios are used frequently as measures of capital structure; the higher the ratios, the more debt in a company's capital structure. It's not uncommon for some companies to have a debt-to-assets ratio of 70% or more, as you noted earlier, Maria. But in our case I think it is unwise.

"As you can see in Exhibit 4," Ellen continued, "net income would be lower each year because of interest expense on the long-term debt. I have assumed a 10% interest rate, which is about what debt would cost us. Our rate would be higher than that for established companies because of the risk associated with an unproven company like ours. Also, I have assumed that we will maintain a debt-to-equity ratio of 1.0 each year.

Exhibit 4

Projected Financial Results for Mom's Cookie Company Based on a 1.0 Debt-to-Equity Ratio

(In thousands)	Year 1	Year 2	Year 3
Sales	$ 3,000	$ 3,600	$ 4,320
Cost of goods sold	(1,800)	(2,160)	(2,592)
Operating expenses	(1,000)	(1,000)	(1,000)
Operating income	200	440	728
Interest expense	(170)	(164)	(157)
Pretax income	30	276	571
Income taxes	(9)	(83)	(171)
Net income	$ 21	$ 193	$ 400
Assets:			
Current assets	$ 1,000	$ 1,200	$ 1,440
Plant assets	4,000	4,000	4,000
Total assets	$ 5,000	$ 5,200	$ 5,440
Liabilities:			
Current liabilities	$ 800	$ 960	$ 1,152
Long-term debt	1,700	1,640	1,568
Total liabilities	2,500	2,600	2,720
Stockholders' equity	2,500	2,600	2,720
Total liabilities and equity	$ 5,000	$ 5,200	$ 5,440
Return on equity	0.8%	7.4%	14.7%

"While net income is lower each year, stockholders' equity also is lower, primarily because we will not need to issue as much stock to finance the company. Observe from Exhibit 4, however, that return on equity is lower in the first year if we use debt. In the second year, return on equity is about the same whether we use debt or not (compare with Exhibit 3). In the third year, as profits increase, return on equity is higher if we use debt than if we use only equity.

"Exhibit 5 provides a graph that helps explain the effect of using debt. The graph shows the amount of return on equity Mom's Cookie Company would report at various levels of sales revenues. Return on equity varies more when larger amounts of debt are used."

"This effect is known as financial leverage," Maria remarked. *Financial leverage (FL)* **is the use of debt to increase a company's return on equity.** The more debt there is in a company's capital structure, the greater the financial leverage. As you can see from the graph, financial leverage magnifies return on equity. When return on equity is low, financial leverage makes it lower. When return on equity is high, financial leverage makes it higher.

Exhibit 5

The Effect of Financial
Leverage on Return on
Equity

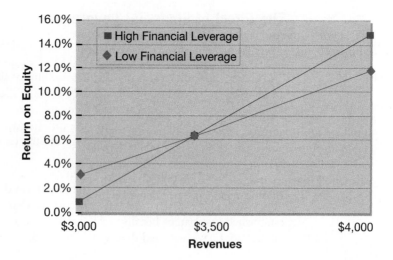

"The magnification effect of financial leverage can be thought of as a simple formula:

Return on Equity (ROE) = Return on Assets (ROA) × Financial Leverage (FL)

$$\frac{Net\ Income}{Stockholders'\ Equity} = \frac{Net\ Income}{Total\ Assets} \times \frac{Total\ Assets}{Stockholders'\ Equity}$$

As explained earlier in this chapter, net income divided by stockholders' equity is return on equity. Recall from Chapter 2 that net income divided by total assets is known as **return on assets (ROA)**. The formula for calculating **financial leverage (FL)** is **total assets divided by stockholders' equity**. If a company has a lot of debt, the ratio of total assets to stockholders' equity will be large.

"You can see the effect of leverage by looking at Mom's Cookie Company's numbers. In the first year, if we don't use any long-term debt, the formula would look like this:

$$\frac{ROE}{\$4,200} = \frac{ROA}{\$5,000} \times \frac{FL}{\$4,200}$$
$$3.3\% = 2.8\% \times 1.19$$

The only leverage we would have would come from current liabilities.

"If we use $2.5 million of liabilities, the formula would show this:

$$\frac{ROE}{\$2,500} = \frac{ROA}{\$5,000} \times \frac{FL}{\$2,500}$$
$$0.8\% = 0.4\% \times 2.0$$

"If we don't use any long-term debt, the magnification factor is about 1.2. If we use long-term debt, the magnification factor is 2.0. Though higher financial leverage works against us when our profits are low, it works for us in later years when we start making more profit."

"That's why I thought we should use a relatively large amount of debt," Maria continued. "We expect Mom's Cookie Company to earn a lot of money in the next few years. If we use a lot of debt, we can leverage those earnings to generate a high return on equity. This will make our company more valuable and probably will make us rich. Ellen's graph in Exhibit 5 demonstrates what will happen. In the third year, return on equity will be about 15% if we use long-term debt, but it will be only about 12% if we don't. I don't see why you want to avoid debt, Ellen."

Ellen replied, "If we could be sure of the numbers in Stan's estimates, I would agree that financial leverage would make Mom's Cookie Company more valuable. However, you have to remember that these numbers are only estimates, and that we are dealing with a relatively unknown product in a highly competitive market. Suppose we don't start out with sales of $3 million, and suppose sales don't grow at 20% per year. That financial leverage magnification factor will continue to work against us as long as our profits are low. We need to examine some other factors, as well. Let's take a break and continue our discussion later."

1 SELF-STUDY PROBLEM

WebTUTOR Advantage

Financial statement information is presented below for Andromeda Corporation, which manufactures airline-tracking equipment. Andromeda is considering a change in its capital structure. Management has proposed issuing $200 million of additional long-term debt. The long-term debt would be used to repurchase a portion of the company's common stock. This purchase would reduce the company's stockholders' equity by $200 million. The interest expense on the additional debt would be $14 million. The company's tax rate is 35% of pretax income.

(In millions)	2004
Sales	$982
Cost of goods sold	607
Operating expenses	294
Operating income	81
Interest expense	(6)
Pretax income	75
Income taxes	(26)
Net income	$ 49
Assets:	
Current assets	$277
Plant assets	555
Total assets	$832
Liabilities:	
Current liabilities	$212
Long-term debt	75
Total liabilities	287
Stockholders' equity	545
Total liabilities and equity	$832

Required

A. Compute Andromeda's return on equity for 2004 as reported.
B. Compute what Andromeda's return on equity would have been in 2004 if the company had issued the additional debt and had repurchased common stock. You will need to recompute net income beginning with operating income. Also, recompute liabilities and equity on the balance sheet. Round to the nearest million dollars.
C. Based on these computations, would the change in capital structure be good for Andromeda's stockholders?

The solution to Self-Study Problem 1 appears at the end of the chapter.

EFFECTS OF FINANCING DECISIONS ON CASH FLOW AND LIQUIDITY

OBJECTIVE 3

Explain why cash flows are important for a company's financing decisions.

Ellen continued the discussion after the break. "Also, consider our cash flows. We will have a lot of cash outflows next year to increase the size of the business. We will have to extend credit to some of our customers just to compete in this market. Consequently, some of our sales may not be collected for several months. At the same time, we will be paying for materials and labor to create our products.

"If we add interest payments to our cash demands, we could face cash flow problems, especially if sales are less than expected. If sales are lower than we anticipate, we can cut back on materials purchases and reduce labor costs, but we can't skip interest payments. If we can't make those payments and still have enough money to meet our normal operating needs, we'll be in serious trouble before we give our company time to prove itself. If we get into cash flow problems because of too much debt, we'll have trouble staying in business. We will have difficulty borrowing additional money because creditors already will be concerned about getting repaid for the original loan. We won't be in a good position to sell additional stock, either. Who will want to buy stock in a company that can't pay its debts?

"No, Maria, I really think our situation is too risky to use much debt. Our sales may be lower than expected, and our profits may be more volatile than we anticipate. Until we get the business on solid ground and know more about our market, I think we should stick with equity financing. At some time in the future, once we are more established and can be pretty sure of our profits and cash flows, we might consider using more financial leverage."

Dividend Decisions

Maria and Stan still were not completely satisfied. "What about dividends?" Stan asked. "I understand what you are saying about interest, but won't we have to pay dividends on the stock we sell? Investors aren't going to give us their money without expecting something in return. If we pay dividends, we'll be facing the same cash flow problems we would if we use debt."

"I don't think so," Ellen responded. "People who invest in new companies like ours know the risk they are taking. They invest for long-run profits and stock value, not for short-run dividends. If we convince the market of our growth potential and demonstrate good growth in the first few years, we will create good value for our stockholders.

"Dividend policy is an important financing decision for a company. Managers must decide how much cash dividend to pay each fiscal period. Dividend policies vary considerably among companies. Some companies, especially new ones like ours with good growth potential, do not pay dividends.

"Stockholders benefit from their investments in two ways. One way is by receiving dividends. The other way is by having the value of their stock increase over time. Mom's Cookie Company has great growth potential. If we invest the cash from our operating activities back in the company to create greater production and sales capacity and earn higher profits, our investors will be better off than if we pay dividends. If we can increase sales by 20% each year, the value of our stock is likely to climb at a much higher rate than if we pay cash dividends and grow more slowly because we don't have enough cash to invest. Exhibit 6 illustrates the dividends relative to investment of cash.

"Stockholders realize the value of growth. Many growth companies don't pay dividends or pay only low dividends. Companies like **Microsoft** and **Intel** have paid very few dividends, but they have made millions for their investors because of higher stock values. Of course, we have to deliver growth, not just promise it. If we don't pay dividends because we aren't creating enough profits and cash flows to make these payments, we'll be in trouble. But we would be in more trouble if we had a lot of interest to pay. Interest would decrease our profits and cash flows, compounding our problems. If we can't become profitable and grow at a reasonable rate, we won't be in business long, regardless of how we finance Mom's Cookie Company.

Exhibit 6

Stockholders Benefit from Dividends and from Investment of Cash in Productive Assets

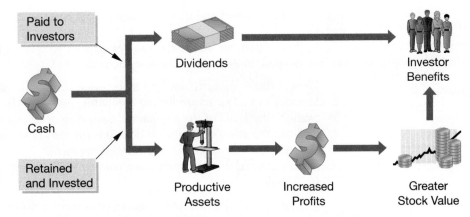

"Thus, dividends are not a concern. Stockholders won't expect them initially and will be satisfied as long as the price of their stock increases each year consistent with their expectations. Mom's Cookie Company will be a less risky company if we avoid much debt. Keep in mind that investors expect a higher return from a high-risk company than from a low-risk company. We are already a high-risk company because we are new and we are operating in a highly competitive market. Financial leverage would increase this risk even more and might scare away many investors. At a minimum, it would reduce the amount we will receive from selling stock. If we increase our risk, investors will bid the price of our stock down because they will be more uncertain about our ability to survive and generate future profits."

Other Financing Alternatives

"What about other alternatives?" Stan queried. "We could lease some of our plant assets. Wouldn't that be an alternative to equity financing?"

"Yes," Maria added, "and what about preferred stock? Could we use that rather than common stock for some of our financing needs?"

Ellen responded, "Leases wouldn't improve our situation very much. We would still have to make payments each period. Most of the leases would be long-term capital leases that are equivalent to debt. We would be making interest and principal payments just the way we would be paying other creditors. Leases would add to our risk and liquidity problems just like other forms of debt.

"We would also need to be careful with preferred stock. If we sell preferred, we probably will have to make dividend payments to the preferred stockholders. Also, our common stock will be a bit riskier because of the dividend and liquidation preferences of the preferred stock. If we are not as successful as we hope to be in the first few years, common stockholders stand to lose more money if we issue preferred stock than if we don't. If we can sell enough common stock to meet our financing needs and can get a reasonable price for our stock, I would not issue preferred stock. Let's use preferred stock as an alternative only if we can't meet all of our needs by issuing common."

Maria and Stan left the meeting feeling comfortable with Ellen's explanations. They had high expectations for their product, and they had faith in Ellen's understanding of financing activities.

INTERPRETATION OF FINANCING ACTIVITIES

The first part of this chapter examined the financing decisions of managers and the effects of these decisions on a company's financial statements. This section examines financial statement information provided by actual corporations. We use this information to demonstrate how investors and other decision makers can interpret the financing activities of companies and make decisions about companies' risk, return, and value attributes.

In this section, we will use a five-step process to analyze accounting information for the purpose of evaluating financing activities.

1. Identify financing activities for one or more companies and fiscal periods.
2. Measure capital structure for the companies and periods.
3. Evaluate the effect of the companies' financing decisions on risk and return.
4. Evaluate the effect of financing decisions on cash flows and determine the ability of companies to make debt and interest payments.
5. Examine the relationship between a company's financing decisions and its value to stockholders.

Exhibit 7 provides selected financial statement information for **Krispy Kreme Doughnuts, Inc.** and **Starbucks Corporation**. Both companies produce and sell food products. Therefore, they are comparable with respect to many activities.

A General Overview

Our analysis begins with a general overview of the two companies. In Exhibit 7, it appears that Starbucks is more profitable than Krispy Kreme. Net income for both companies is positive in both years. However, Starbucks' net income is considerably higher than Krispy Kreme's.

When comparing different companies, one must keep in mind that the sizes of the companies usually are different. For that reason, ratios are used to make the financial statement numbers comparable. For example, observe that Starbucks was more than 10 times larger than Krispy Kreme, based on the assets reported by each company. Accordingly, we should expect Starbucks' net income to be larger than Krispy Kreme's.

Exhibit 7 Selected Income Statement and Balance Sheet Information for Krispy Kreme and Starbucks

	Krispy Kreme		Starbucks	
(In thousands)	2001	2000	2001	2000
Total revenues	$ 300,715	$ 220,243	$ 2,648,980	$ 2,177,614
Operating expenses	(250,690)	(190,003)	(2,052,969)	(1,745,228)
General and administrative expenses	(20,061)	(14,856)	(151,416)	(89,902)
Depreciation and amortization expenses	(6,457)	(4,546)	(163,501)	(130,232)
Income from operations	23,507	10,838	281,094	212,252
Interest income (expense)	276	(1,232)	7,828	(51,682)
Income before income taxes	23,783	9,606	288,922	160,570
Provision for income taxes	(9,058)	(3,650)	(107,712)	(66,006)
Net income	$ 14,725	$ 5,956	$ 181,210	$ 94,564
Assets:				
Total current assets	$ 67,611	$ 41,038	$ 593,925	$ 458,234
Long-term assets	103,882	63,920	1,257,114	1,033,312
Total assets	$ 171,493	$ 104,958	$ 1,851,039	$ 1,491,546
Liabilities and Equity:				
Total current liabilities	$ 38,168	$ 29,586	$ 445,264	$ 311,666
Total long-term liabilities	7,646	27,617	29,848	31,481
Total liabilities	45,814	57,203	475,112	343,147
Shareholders' Equity:				
Common stock	85,060	15,475	791,622	750,872
Retained earnings	42,547	34,827	589,713	408,503
Other	(1,928)	(2,547)	(5,408)	(10,976)
Total shareholders' equity	125,679	47,755	1,375,927	1,148,399
Total liabilities and shareholders' equity	$ 171,493	$ 104,958	$ 1,851,039	$ 1,491,546

A common method for comparing the income of different companies is to compute **return on assets**, the ratio of net income to total assets. In 2001, Krispy Kreme's return on assets was 8.6% ($14,725 ÷ $171,493), compared with Starbucks' return on assets of 9.8% ($181,210 ÷ $1,851,039). In 2000, Krispy Kreme's return on assets was 5.7% ($5,956 ÷ $104,958), compared with Starbucks' 6.3% ($94,564 ÷ $1,491,546). Both companies were more profitable in 2001 than in 2000. However, Starbucks was more profitable in both years than Krispy Kreme.

Comparing Capital Structures

As a second step in our analysis of financing activities, we compare the capital structures of the two companies. We use ratios such as **debt to assets** and **assets to equity** for this purpose. These measures compare the amount of debt (debt to assets) or equity (assets to equity) a company uses to finance its assets with the company's total investment in assets. **A high debt-to-assets ratio or a high assets-to-equity ratio indicates that a company is using a lot of debt in its capital structure.**

LEARNING NOTE

Many ratios do not have standard definitions. Various decision makers and companies compute ratios differently. For example, debt to assets may include all liabilities in the numerator, or it may include only long-term debt. The denominator may use assets from the beginning of the year, from the end of the year, or an average for the year. Therefore, be careful in comparing companies. Make sure you understand how ratios were computed and make sure the ratios were computed the same way for each company.

We include all liabilities as part of debt. For 2001, Krispy Kreme's debt-to-assets ratio was 26.7% ($45,814 ÷ $171,493), approximately equal to Starbucks' debt-to-assets ratio of 25.7% ($475,112 ÷ $1,851,039). In 2000, Krispy Kreme's debt-to-assets ratio was much larger at 54.5% ($57,203 ÷ $104,958).

Another measure of capital structure useful for comparing the effects of financing activities is **financial leverage**: the ratio of assets to stockholders' equity. For 2001, this ratio was 1.36 ($171,493 ÷ $125,679) for Krispy Kreme and 1.35 ($1,851,039 ÷ $1,375,927) for Starbucks. Though this ratio uses a different scale from the one used for the debt-to-assets ratio, it provides the same type of information. These ratios indicate that Krispy Kreme and Starbucks used about the same amount of debt in their capital structures in 2001. In 2000, Krispy Kreme's financial leverage of 2.20 ($104,958 ÷ $47,755) was much larger than Starbucks' financial leverage of 1.30 ($1,491,546 ÷ $1,148,399). Note that a company that uses more debt in its capital structure has a higher debt-to-assets or assets-to-equity ratio than one that uses less debt.

THE EFFECT OF FINANCIAL LEVERAGE ON RISK AND RETURN

OBJECTIVE 5

Determine and explain the effect of financial leverage on a company's risk and return.

A third step in our analysis is to determine the effect of financial leverage on the risk and return of our companies. A ratio commonly used for this purpose is **return on equity**: net income divided by stockholders' equity. This ratio is affected by a company's capital structure. The use of financial leverage (higher amounts of debt) magnifies a company's return on assets.

Return on Equity = Return on Assets × Financial Leverage

$$\frac{\text{Net Income}}{\text{Stockholders' Equity}} = \frac{\text{Net Income}}{\text{Total Assets}} \times \frac{\text{Total Assets}}{\text{Stockholders' Equity}}$$

For example, Krispy Kreme's return on equity in 2001 was 11.7% ($14,725 ÷ $125,679). This amount is equal to Krispy Kreme's return on assets times its asset to equity ratio: 11.7% = 8.6% × 1.36. Krispy Kreme's financial leverage resulted in a return on equity that was larger than its return on assets. What do these numbers mean in practical terms? Think of them this way: If Krispy Kreme had financed its assets using equity without any liabilities, its stockholders would have made 8.6 cents for each dollar they invested in Krispy Kreme, including reinvested profits, in 2001. But, because Krispy

Kreme used debt in its capital structure, its stockholders made 11.7 cents for each dollar invested.

In 2000, Krispy Kreme's return on equity was 12.5% ($5,956 ÷ $47,755) and was higher than return on assets (5.7%) because of financial leverage: 12.5% = 5.7% × 2.20. Again, you can think of these numbers in practical terms by saying that stockholders earned 12.5 cents in 2000 for each dollar invested. If Krispy Kreme had not used debt in its capital structure, its stockholders would have earned 5.7 cents for each dollar invested. Thus, **financial leverage works for stockholders when a company performs well.**

Financial leverage also worked for Starbucks' stockholders because the company was profitable in both years. Return on equity was 13.2% ($181,210 ÷ $1,375,927) in 2001 and 8.2% ($94,564 ÷ $1,148,399) in 2000. In each year, return on equity was greater than return on assets because of financial leverage.

Observe that Krispy Kreme's return on equity went down from 2000 to 2001, even though its net income more than doubled. The decrease in return on equity was the result of the change in financial leverage, which decreased from 2.20 to 1.36. Because it used less debt and more equity in its capital structure in 2001 than in 2000, Krispy Kreme earned a lower return for its stockholders.

So, why did Krispy Kreme reduce its financial leverage from 2000 to 2001? If financial leverage increases return on equity, why not use a lot of financial leverage? There is a cost to using a lot of debt in a company's capital structure. That cost is higher risk. Financial risk increases when a company uses a lot of debt because debt and interest must be paid whether or not a company is profitable and creates operating cash flows. Exhibit 8 illustrates the relationship between financial leverage and return on equity.

Exhibit 8

The Effect of Financial Leverage on Risk and Return

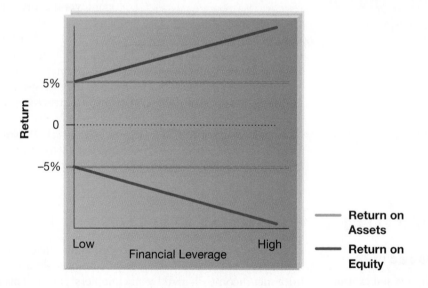

The return on assets lines identify positive and negative returns of 5%. As a company's financial leverage increases, its return on equity increases relative to its return on assets when return on assets is positive. But when return on assets is negative, return on equity decreases relative to return on assets as financial leverage increases. Accordingly, financial leverage increases uncertainty about the returns that stockholders will earn at a particular level of return on assets or for a particular amount of net income. Uncertainty increases as the volatility of return increases. Return on equity varies more (is more volatile) for higher amounts of financial leverage.

Therefore, companies trade off return for risk. Higher risk, in the form of higher financial leverage, has the potential to create higher returns. But it also has the potential to create lower returns if a company is not profitable. As an example, if Krispy Kreme had reported a net loss of $5,956,000 in 2000 rather than a net income, its return on assets would have been −5.7% and its return on equity would have been −12.5%. **When a company's earnings are negative, the use of debt in the capital structure results in a lower return for stockholders than when debt is not used.**

---

2 SELF-STUDY PROBLEM

Examine the information for Andromeda Company provided in Self-Study Problem 1. Suppose Andromeda's operating income in 2004 is $70 million, as summarized below:

WebTUTOR Advantage

(In millions)	2004
Operating income	$ 70
Interest expense	(6)
Pretax income	64
Income taxes	(22)
Net income	$ 42
Assets:	
Total assets	$832
Liabilities:	
Current liabilities	$212
Long-term debt	75
Total liabilities	287
Stockholders' equity	545
Total liabilities and equity	$832

Required

A. Compute return on equity for Andromeda as reported above.
B. Compute the return on equity as it would be if the company issued $100 million of long-term debt to repurchase stock. Additional interest expense would be $8 million, and the tax rate is 35%.
C. What effect would the additional debt have on Andromeda's risk and return?

The solution to Self-Study Problem 2 appears at the end of the chapter.

OTHER RISK CONSIDERATIONS

OBJECTIVE 6

Use cash flow and liquidity measures to evaluate financing decisions.

The fourth step in the analysis of financing activities involves evaluating the ability of each company to make debt and interest payments. Creditors and stockholders are concerned about a company's ability to meet its obligations, including the payment of interest, as they become due. Debt ratios, such as the ratio of debt to total assets, provide information that is helpful in evaluating default risk. **Default risk** is the likelihood that a company will not be able to make debt or interest payments when they come due. As the amount of debt in a company's capital structure increases, the likelihood of default increases because principal and interest payments become larger.

Therefore, though financial leverage can increase a company's return on equity, the amount of financial leverage a company can use is limited by the amount of principal and interest the company can pay and still have enough cash to cover expenses, purchase new assets, and pay dividends. Also, as financial leverage increases, the interest rate demanded by creditors is likely to increase. Creditors demand higher returns as compensation for the higher default risk of a company's debt. Creditors may impose limitations on a company's ability to borrow additional money, require it to maintain a certain debt ratio, or limit its ability to pay dividends unless certain ratios are maintained. These limitations are called **debt covenants**, and they protect the interests of creditors against a company becoming too risky or paying cash to stockholders when it has too much debt.

Case in Point

Disclosure of Debt Covenants

A note in Krispy Kreme's 2001 annual report describes its debt covenants:

> The loan agreement entered into on December 29, 1999, requires us to maintain a consolidated tangible net worth [stockholders' equity] of $41 million through January 28, 2001. For each fiscal year thereafter, the agreement requires us to maintain a consolidated tangible net worth of $41 million plus (1) an amount equal to 75% of the net proceeds from our April 2000 initial public offering, and (2) 50% of our net income for each fiscal year. Capital expenditures for each fiscal year are limited to $35 million. The loan agreement also contains covenants which place various restrictions on sales of properties, . . . , the payment of dividends and other customary financial and nonfinancial covenants.

In addition to debt ratios, creditors consider cash flow and liquidity measures. **A commonly used liquidity measure is the** *current ratio:* **current assets divided by current liabilities. If this ratio is low, especially if it is less than one, or if it decreases substantially over time, the risk that a company may not be able to pay its current obligations increases.**

The current ratio for Krispy Kreme in 2001 was 1.77 ($67,611 ÷ $38,168). In 2000, this ratio was 1.39 ($41,038 ÷ $29,586). Thus, Krispy Kreme substantially increased its current assets in 2001 and increased its current ratio. Starbucks' current ratio decreased to 1.33 ($593,925 ÷ $445,264) in 2001 from 1.47 ($458,234 ÷ $311,666) in 2000. Note, Starbucks' current ratio was lower than Krispy Kreme's in 2001. That means Krispy Kreme was in a better position to meet its current liability obligations than was Starbucks.

Exhibit 9 provides selected cash flow information for Krispy Kreme and Starbucks. Both companies reported positive operating cash flows and negative investing cash flows. This pattern is common for many companies. Operating activities should provide a primary source of cash for a company. Cash created from selling goods and services can be used to expand a company's activities by investing the cash in additional long-term assets. Thus, both Krispy Kreme and Starbucks were growing as a result of reinvestment of cash flows into long-term assets.

Exhibit 9
Selected Cash Flow Information for Krispy Kreme and Starbucks

(In thousands)	Krispy Kreme 2001	Krispy Kreme 2000	Starbucks 2001	Starbucks 2000
Net operating cash flow	$ 30,576	$ 8,980	$ 460,826	$ 321,796
Net investing cash flow	(67,288)	(10,026)	(433,053)	(376,454)
Financing cash flow:				
From issuing debt	3,526	4,282		
From issuing stock	65,637		59,639	68,721
For purchase of stock			(49,788)	
For payment of dividends	(7,005)	(1,518)		
For payment of long-term debt	(22,901)	(2,400)	(685)	(1,889)
Other financing activities	1,298	(448)	5,481	(7,776)
Net financing cash flow	40,555	(84)	14,647	59,056
Net change in cash	$ 3,843	$ (1,130)	$ 42,420	$ 4,398

Both Krispy Kreme and Starbucks generated large cash flows from their operating activities in 2001. In 2001, Krispy Kreme's **operating cash flows to total assets** was 17.8% ($30,576 ÷ $171,493). Starbucks' ratio was 24.9% ($460,826 ÷ $1,851,039). Thus, both companies had large amounts of cash to invest. The ratio of **investing cash flow to total assets** was 39.2% ($67,288 ÷ $171,493) for Krispy Kreme and 23.4% ($433,053 ÷ $1,851,039) for Starbucks. Both companies were investing their cash in additional assets, indicating that the companies were growing.

Krispy Kreme invested more cash than it created from operating activities during 2001. As indicated in Exhibit 9, the company financed these acquisitions by issuing additional stock. A portion of the cash from the stock issue was used to repay long-term debt. Starbucks also issued stock in 2001 (and in 2000). The shares were issued in conjunction with stock option and employee stock purchase plans. To obtain shares needed for these plans, Starbucks repurchased shares of its stock (Exhibit 9). Krispy Kreme reduced its financial leverage in 2001. Both companies were growing, using operating and financing cash flows to pay for the growth.

Krispy Kreme paid dividends in 2001 and 2000. Starbucks did not make dividend payments in either year. A measure of the relative size of dividend payments is the **dividend payout ratio**, the ratio of dividends to net income. Krispy Kreme's dividend payout ratio for 2001 was 47.8% ($7,005 ÷ $14,725) up from 25.5% ($1,518 ÷ $5,956) in 2000.

Krispy Kreme's payment of large amounts of dividends was inconsistent with a high growth strategy. Normally, growth companies retain most of their profits, reinvesting them in additional assets. The dividends paid by the company in 2000 and 2001 were part of a commitment to owners prior to the initial public sale of stock by the company in 2000. It was not the intent of the company to continue making dividend payments. A note in Krispy Kreme's 2001 annual report states:

> Krispy Kreme presently intends to retain its earnings to finance the expansion of its business and does not anticipate paying cash dividends in the foreseeable future.

Krispy Kreme's operations and financial position were better in 2001 than they had been in previous years. Its net income, operating cash flow, and investing cash flow (outflow) were much larger in 2001 than in 2000.

Both Krispy Kreme and Starbucks reduced their financial risks in 2001 by reducing their long-term debt. Consequently, in 2001, both companies were growing rapidly and had relatively low financial risk.

FINANCING ACTIVITIES AND COMPANY VALUE

OBJECTIVE 7

Explain why financing activities are important for determining company value.

The final step in the evaluation of financing activities is assessing the relationship between financing decisions and company value. As we have seen from examining the financing activities of Krispy Kreme and Starbucks, financing activities affect a company's risk and return. Financial leverage can work for or against a company and its stockholders. When a company does well, financial leverage can be useful. Stockholders earn higher returns than they would if a company had no financial leverage. **When a company is not doing well, financial leverage is detrimental.** Stockholders earn lower returns. In addition, creditors face higher default risk, and a company has less cash to meet its other needs because it is forced to make interest and principal payments.

A measure of a company's value to investors is the **market-to-book-value** ratio. **Market value** is the price of a company's stock times the number of shares of stock outstanding. It is a measure of the total value placed on a company by the securities market. **Book value** is the amount of stockholders' equity reported by a company on its balance sheet.

Krispy Kreme's market value in 2001 was $442 million and its book value was $125.679 million (Exhibit 7). Therefore, its market-to-book-value ratio was 3.52. In practical terms, this ratio says that every dollar invested in Krispy Kreme by stockholders, including retained earnings, was worth $3.52 at the end of the 2001 fiscal year. In 2000, Krispy Kreme's market-to-book-value ratio was 0.98. Consequently, Krispy Kreme's favorable operating results and lower financial risk resulted in much higher value in 2001 than in 2000.

Starbucks' market-to-book-value ratio was 6.08 in 2001. Starbucks was worth $6.08 at the end of the 2001 fiscal year for each dollar invested by stockholders. The company's market-to-book-value ratio was 3.93 in 2000. Therefore, Starbucks, like Krispy Kreme, gained value from 2000 to 2001.

Financing activities affect company value. A company that is performing well can increase return to its stockholders by including debt in its capital structure. How much debt a company uses depends on several factors. In particular, a company with stable earnings and operating cash flows can afford more debt than one with unstable earnings and cash flows. If a company runs the risk of not performing well (because of volatile product markets or poor sales, for example), debt can increase the likelihood that the company will earn lower returns and be unable to pay its creditors. A company that is growing rapidly already has a large amount of risk associated with its growth activities. It is investing with the expectation that it will be able to earn high returns on its investment in the future. Maintaining low financial risk can be advantageous, at least until the company determines whether its investment strategy is working.

Company value also is affected by the purpose of financing activities. A company's value is likely to increase if it is using financing activities to acquire additional assets. These assets help the company grow because it can use them to produce and sell more products and earn additional income from these sales. If debt or stock is issued because of operating cash flow problems, however, a company's value is likely to decrease.

Exhibit 10 provides a summary of the ratios for Krispy Kreme and Starbucks that have been presented in this chapter.

Exhibit 10

Summary of Ratios for Krispy Kreme and Starbucks

Ratios	Krispy Kreme		Starbucks	
	2001	2000	2001	2000
Return on Assets	8.6%	5.7%	9.8%	6.3%
Debt to Assets	26.7%	54.5%	25.7%	23.0%
Financial Leverage (Assets to Equity)	1.36	2.20	1.35	1.30
Return on Equity	11.7%	12.5%	13.2%	8.2%
Current Ratio	1.77	1.39	1.33	1.47
Operating Cash to Assets	17.8%	8.6%	24.9%	21.6%
Investing Cash to Assets	39.2%	9.6%	23.4%	25.2%
Dividend Payout	47.8%	25.5%	0.0%	0.0%
Market to Book Value	3.52	0.98	6.08	3.93

3 **SELF-STUDY PROBLEM**   Data are provided on the next page for Alzona Company, a large trucking company.

WebTUTOR Advantage

Required

A. Compute the following ratios for each year: debt (long-term) to assets, assets to stockholders' equity, return on assets, return on equity, current, dividend payout, and market to book value.

B. Describe the company's financing activities for 2004 and evaluate the effect they had on the company's stockholders.

The solution to Self-Study Problem 3 appears at the end of the chapter.

(In millions)	2004	2003
Current assets	$ 433	$ 378
Total assets	1,237	1,065
Current liabilities	389	343
Long-term debt	422	404
Stockholders' equity	426	318
Operating income	151	127
Interest expense	(34)	(31)
Income taxes	(40)	(33)
Net income	77	63
Operating cash flows	113	102
Investing cash flows	(154)	(112)
Financing cash flows	60	8
Debt issued	30	20
Debt repurchased	(12)	(10)
Stock issued	50	25
Dividends paid	(20)	(16)
Market value	643	512

REVIEW

SUMMARY of IMPORTANT CONCEPTS

1. Capital structure refers to the relative amounts of debt and equity used by a company to finance its assets.
   a. The use of larger amounts of debt reduces net income because of additional interest expense.
   b. The use of larger amounts of debt also reduces the amount of equity a company needs to finance its assets.
   c. Therefore, additional debt increases return on equity when a company is performing well, but decreases return on equity when the company is performing poorly.
   d. The amount of debt a company uses depends on its expectations about performance, the potential volatility of its performance, and the amount of risk it is prepared to take.

2. Debt increases a company's risk.
   a. Financial leverage magnifies a company's returns, making them potentially more volatile.
   b. Debt increases risk because of the potentially negative effect on stockholder return and the potential for default on debt and interest payments.
   c. Debt also affects liquidity and cash flow. Interest and debt payments require the use of cash. If a company does not have sufficient cash to meet these and other needs, it may be unable to make payments when they are due.

3. Dividend policy is another financing decision.
   a. The amount of cash dividends a company pays depends on the alternatives the company has for using its cash.
   b. If a company has good investment opportunities, stockholders may be better off leaving cash in the company and letting management invest it in additional assets.
   c. Stockholders benefit both from receiving dividends and from increases in stock value because of company profitability and growth.

4. Investors can use accounting information to understand a company's financing activities.
   a. Analysis begins with identifying financing activities and profitability for one or more periods or companies.
   b. The second step is measuring capital structure.
   c. The third step is evaluating the effect of financing decisions on risk and return.

   d. The fourth step is evaluating the effect of financing decisions on cash flows and determining the ability of a company to make debt and interest payments.

   e. The fifth step involves examining the relationship between a company's financing decisions and its market value.

5. Important ratios for analysis of financing activities of a company and for comparing the results of those activities between different companies:

   a. Return on equity (ROE): Net income divided by stockholders' equity (which is also equal to ROA times FL)—measures net income relative to the amount invested by the owners of the company. The owners' investment in the company includes not only contributed capital but also retained earnings.

   b. Debt-to-equity ratio: Total debt divided by total stockholders' equity—measures the company's capital structure in terms of the relationship between the company's obligations to its creditors and the investment by the owners.

   c. Debt-to-assets ratio: Total debt divided by total assets—measures the company's capital structures in terms of the proportion of total assets that are financed by debt.

   d. Return on assets (ROA): Net income divided by total assets—measures the amount of return the company has earned from its assets.

   e. Financial leverage (FL): Total assets divided by total stockholders' equity—measures how well the company has used debt to increase its return on equity.

   f. Current ratio: Current assets divided by current liabilities—a liquidity measure of a company's ability to cover its current debts with its current assets.

   g. Operating cash flow to total assets: Net operating cash flow divided by total assets—measures the portion of net cash inflow (outflow) that contributed to (depleted) total assets.

   h. Investing cash flow to total assets: Net investing cash flow divided by total assets—measure the portion of net cash outflow (inflow) that was provided by (contributed to) total assets.

   i. Dividend payout ratio: Total dividends divided by net income—measures the portion of net income that is paid to stockholders as dividends.

   j. Market value: Total shares outstanding times the market value per share—measures the total value placed on the company by the securities market.

   k. Book value: Total assets minus total liabilities—measures the amount of stockholders' equity on the balance sheet.

   l. Market-to-book-value ratio: Market value of the entire company divided by the book value of the entire company.

DEFINE   TERMS and CONCEPTS DEFINED in this CHAPTER

capital structure   (F363)

current ratio   (F374)

financial leverage (FL)   (F365)

return on equity (ROE)   (F364)

SELF-STUDY PROBLEM SOLUTIONS

SSP10-1   A. Return on equity = $49 ÷ $545 = 9.0%
B. Revised financial statement numbers:

(In millions)	2004	
Sales	$982	
Cost of goods sold	607	
Operating expenses	294	
Operating income	81	
Interest expense	(20)	$6 from old debt + $14 from new
Pretax income	61	
Income taxes	(21)	$61 × 0.35
Net income	$ 40	
Assets:		
Current assets	$277	
Plant assets	555	
Total assets	$832	
Liabilities:		
Current liabilities	$212	
Long-term debt	275	
Total liabilities	487	
Stockholders' equity	345	
Total liabilities and equity	$832	
Return on equity = $40 ÷ $345 = 11.6%		

C. Issuing additional debt reduces net income because of the additional interest expense. However, stockholder's equity is reduced as well because the additional debt was used to repurchase stock. Therefore, return on equity would be higher if the debt were issued (increasing from 9% to 11.6%). Based on this information, increasing financial leverage is a good decision for this company. Whether it will continue to be a good decision in the future depends on whether the company continues to be profitable.

SSP10-2   A. Return on equity (as reported) = $42 ÷ $545 = 7.7%
B. Financial statement effects of issuing $100 million of debt:

(In millions)	2004	
Operating income	$ 70	
Interest expense	(14)	$6 from old debt + $8 from new
Pretax income	56	
Income taxes	(20)	$56 × 0.35
Net income	$ 36	
Assets:		
Total assets	$832	
Liabilities:		
Current liabilities	$212	
Long-term debt	175	
Total liabilities	387	
Stockholders' equity	445	
Total liabilities and equity	$832	
Return on equity = $36 ÷ $445 = 8.1%		

C. Higher financial leverage increases risk. If net income and return on assets are low, financial leverage reduces return on equity. If net income and return on assets are high, financial leverage increases return on equity. Consequently, financial leverage may increase or decrease return. It increases risk.

Andromeda's return on equity in 2004 increases from 7.7% to 8.1% when the additional debt is issued. However, uncertainty about future net income and return on equity increases because of the increase in financial leverage. If Andromeda can continue to earn a profit, the additional debt should result in a higher return on equity in the future than if the debt were not issued.

SSP10-3   A.

	2004	**2003**
Debt to assets	0.34 = $422 ÷ $1,237	0.38 = $404 ÷ $1,065
Assets to stockholders' equity	2.90 = $1,237 ÷ $426	3.35 = $1,065 ÷ $318
Return on assets	0.062 = $77 ÷ $1,237	0.059 = $63 ÷ $1,065
Return on equity	0.181 = $77 ÷ $426	0.198 = $63 ÷ $318
Current ratio	1.11 = $433 ÷ $389	1.10 = $378 ÷ $343
Dividend payout	0.260 = $20 ÷ $77	0.254 = $16 ÷ $63
Market to book value	1.51 = $643 ÷ $426	1.61 = $512 ÷ $318

B. Alzona's primary financing activities in 2004 consisted of issuing additional debt ($18 million more than it repaid), issuing $50 million of stock, and paying $20 million of dividends. The company's performance was strong. Its net income and operating cash flows were positive and increased from 2003 to 2004. Additional financing activities were used to support investing activities. Additional assets were acquired in 2003 and 2004, indicating growth.

Alzona's financial leverage decreased during 2004. Therefore, though its return on assets increased from 2003 to 2004, its return on equity decreased. Thus, because the company was performing well, stockholders would have benefited from an increase in financial leverage. The decrease in financial leverage reduced stockholder return (return on equity). The lower return on equity was accompanied by a decrease in company value (market to book value). Both profitability and capital structure affect company value.

Thinking Beyond the Question

How do we finance our business?

Financial decisions are critical for a company. It is important for a company to create value for its owners by earning a high return and by controlling its risk. Higher financial leverage can result in both high returns and high risk. Consequently, managers must examine the tradeoff and choose an amount of financial leverage that is appropriate for their company. That amount will be different for different companies. When is it appropriate for a company to have a large amount of financial leverage? What kinds of companies are likely to have high financial leverage? Why?

QUESTIONS

Q10-1
Obj. 1

What is capital structure? Why do the capital structures of companies vary?

Q10-2
Obj. 1

Why is return on equity such a valuable measure to investors?

Q10-3
Obj. 2

Company X and Company Y are both managed successfully by teams of highly respected executives. The firms operate in different industries. After careful analysis, you observe that Company X employs a very high level of financial leverage while Company Y employs almost none. How can both sets of executives be highly respected when their firms employ such different levels of financial leverage?

Q10-4
Obj. 2

Why would stockholders tend to believe that return on equity is a more important measure of a company's performance than is return on assets?

Q10-5
Obj. 3

Why does the use of financial leverage cause the current ratio to be lower than if no financial leverage was used?

Q10-6
Obj. 3

Some companies, such as Microsoft, have never paid a dividend and are unlikely to do so anytime soon. If an investment is never going to yield a dividend, why would anyone buy stock in such a company?

Q10-7
Obj. 4

You are reviewing the balance sheets of Alpha Company and Beta Company. You observe that Alpha has $800,000 of long-term debt and that Beta has $4,000,000. Which company is more highly leveraged? If you need additional information to answer this question, identify what information you could use.

Q10-8
Obj. 4

Beaumont Company has no current liabilities. Its only long-term debt is $20 million of bonds payable. The company's debt-to-assets ratio is 0.20 and its assets-to-equity ratio is 1.25. What is the company's debt-to-equity ratio?

Q10-9
Obj. 5

Does the use of financial leverage always have a favorable impact on the firm and its owners? If not, explain the circumstances under which it would not be desirable to employ financial leverage.

Q10-10
Obj. 5

How does the use of financial leverage affect the risk and return of a company?

Q10-11
Obj. 6

When a company issues long-term debt, creditors often require the company to agree to certain restrictions on future activities. For example, a restriction may limit a company's debt-to-assets ratio and its dividend payout ratio. What is the purpose of these restrictions? How do they benefit creditors?

Q10-12
Obj. 6

Evaluate the following statement: Companies that issue a lot of new debt and equity to create cash are usually in a bad financial condition.

Q10-13
Obj. 6

Ernesto wants some advice. He heard that some companies pay out a large portion of their earnings as dividends to stockholders. Other companies pay few or no dividends. A friend told him that dividends affect the value of stock and that he should invest in stocks that pay high dividend rates. What advice would you give Ernesto about this matter?

Q10-14
Obj. 7

Applause Company has a market to book ratio of 0.75 to 1. Bravo Company has a market-to-book-value ratio of 3.4 to 1. What information does the market-to-book-value ratio capture and what does this ratio tell you about the companies mentioned?

Q10-15
Obj. 7

What relationship would you expect between financial leverage and the market-to-book-value ratio? Does a high value in one lead to a high value in the other? Or a low value in the other? Or do you think there is not necessarily a relationship? Explain your reasoning.

EXERCISES   *If your instructor is using Personal Trainer in this course, you may complete online the assignments identified by* ℙ.

E10-1   Write a short definition of each of the terms listed in the *Terms and Concepts Defined in this Chapter* section.

E10-2   Describe how each of the following transactions affects the capital structure of a company. Is
Obj. 1   there an effect on the short-term liability portion, the long-term liability portion, the equity
ℙ   portion, or is there no effect at all?

    a. The issuance of common stock
    b. The sale of bonds
    c. The purchase of equipment for cash
    d. The purchase of inventory on credit
    e. The purchase of treasury stock
    f. The borrowing of cash, with a two-year note, from a bank
    g. The declaration of dividends to stockholders
    h. The payment of dividends

E10-3   Given below is the most recent balance sheet of Carousel Company.
Obj. 1

Carousel Company
Balance Sheet
at December 31, 2004

Assets		Liabilities and equity	
Cash	$ 6,000	Accounts payable	$ 3,100
Accounts receivable	13,200	Wages payable	3,000
Prepaid rent	2,800	Bonds payable (due 2008)	33,000
Inventory	10,000	Common stock	17,000
Machinery	14,000	Retained earnings	17,400
Land	13,500	Treasury stock	(14,000)
Total assets	$59,500	Total liabilities and equity	$59,500

    a. Describe the firm's capital structure.
    b. How would the capital structure be different if the company had raised the needed capital by issuing additional stock instead of the bonds that are due in 2008?

E10-4   Why is return on equity commonly used along with net income to evaluate a company's per-
Obj. 2   formance? Assume that a company issued long-term bonds during a fiscal period, increasing its interest expense. The bonds were used to finance new plant assets. What effect would the financing and asset acquisition have on the company's financial leverage? What effect should the additional financing have on the company's risk and return?

E10-5   The following summary information is available regarding Robinson Sports Gear. The income
Obj. 2   statements are for the respective fiscal years, and the balance sheets are as of the end of each fiscal year.

Income Statements	2005	2004	2003	Balance Sheets	2005	2004	2003
Net sales	$53	$48	$45	Total current assets	$26	$13	$ 5
Cost of sales	31	28	27	Total long-term assets	41	22	9
Other expenses	15	15	15	Total liabilities	12	8	2
Net income	$ 7	$ 5	$ 3	Total stockholders' equity	$55	$27	$12

    a. What does this income statement information suggest to you about this firm and its attractiveness as a potential investment?
    b. Compute the return on equity for each of the three years.
    c. How does the return on equity information change your initial conclusion about the attractiveness of this company as an investment?

d. What do your responses to parts a and c suggest to you about evaluating a company?

E10-6
Obj. 2
A friend is studying for an accounting exam and exclaims, "I'm really confused by all this leverage stuff. What is leverage, anyway? How does it affect a company? And what has it got to do with the debt-to-equity ratio or debt-to-assets ratio? The professor keeps saying that a company with a low debt-to-equity ratio might want to increase its leverage. What's she talking about, anyway?" Write an explanation of these issues that your friend can use to study for his exam.

E10-7
Obj. 2
P̲
T
At year end 2004, Istanbul Company had stockholders' equity of $18 million. Stockholders' equity at year end 2004 consisted of one million shares of common stock. For 2004, the company reported net income of $4 million. The company paid common dividends of $2 per share in 2004. Compute Istanbul's return on equity for 2004. What would this amount have been if the company had issued bonds at the beginning of 2004 and had used the proceeds to repurchase common stock, reducing stockholders' equity at the end of 2004 to $14,540,000? Assume net income decreased to $3.79 million as a result of additional interest expense, and dividends per share remained at $2 per share for common stock.

E10-8
Obj. 2
P̲
T
Boswell Company expects net income of $5 million for 2005. Pretax earnings are projected to be $7 million. The company's average total assets during 2005 were $25 million. It had no liabilities or preferred stock. It had 1 million shares of common stock outstanding. Boswell is considering issuing $10 million of debentures to repurchase 300,000 shares of its common stock. If the debt had been outstanding in 2005, the company would have paid $900,000 in interest expense. Calculate the company's net income and return on equity for 2005 as reported and as they would have been if the debt had been issued. Assume average stockholders' equity of $15 million for computing return on equity with debt financing and that the tax rate is 28.6%.

E10-9
Obj. 2
Kandahar Company had stockholders' equity of $100 million in 2004 and long-term debt of $10 million. It had 10 million shares of common stock outstanding. Its interest expense was $800,000, and its income tax rate was 30%. The company expects that its annual income before interest and taxes will run between $5 million and $15 million for the foreseeable future. The average is expected to be about $8 million. The company is considering issuing $25 million of additional debt to replace three million shares of its common stock. The additional debt would cost the company $3 million a year in interest. If you were asked by the company for advice on whether to issue the debt, what advice would you give?

E10-10
Obj. 2
Linfield Company has assets of $200 million and long-term debt of $110 million. The debt consists primarily of callable debentures having interest rates ranging from 10% to 12%. (Callable debentures are bonds that a company can recall and pay off at any time it chooses.) Over the last couple of years, the general level of interest rates has decreased by about 2.5%. Linfield could issue new debt today at a rate of approximately 8%. Also, over the last two years, Linfield's stock price has increased about 30%. How might this information affect Linfield's management when it considers financing decisions for the future?

E10-11
Objs. 2, 3
P̲
T
Selected information is provided below for **Georgia-Pacific Corporation** from its 2001 annual report:

(In millions)	2001	2000	1999
Interest expense	$1,080	$ 595	$ 426
Income tax expense	181	210	448
Net income (loss)	(407)	505	1,116
Cash from operations	1,482	1,556	1,272
Total assets	26,364	29,418	15,505
Stockholders' equity	4,905	5,722	3,875

Evaluate the effect of the company's capital structure on its profitability, cash flow from operations, and risk for the three years presented.

E10-12
Objs. 2, 3
P/T

Metro Flight Service reported net income of $8 million in 2005. Its average stockholders' equity of $22 million included preferred stock of $5 million that was outstanding throughout the year. The company paid dividends of $2 million on common stock and $400,000 on preferred stock. (a) Calculate the company's return on equity for 2005. (Note: When a company has preferred stock outstanding, the preferred dividends must be deducted from the numerator and preferred stock must be deducted from the denominator when computing returns on equity.) (b) Management is thinking of issuing $5 million of additional common stock to repurchase all of its preferred stock. Is the replacement of preferred stock with common stock a good idea in this case?

E10-13
Obj. 3

Selected information from the year-end financial statements of Arabia Company is presented below. All amounts are in millions of dollars.

	2005	2004	2003	2002
Net income	$ 36	$ 38	$ 42	$ 44
Interest expense	6	8	6	8
Current assets	64	66	64	60
Current liabilities	56	48	36	30
Total liabilities	122	116	118	102
Stockholders' equity	400	382	376	340
Cash from operations	34	40	38	46

Management is considering the issuance of $200 million of new bonds that would pay 9% interest. Based on the information presented here, how do you believe the financial markets will respond to the proposed bond offering? Why or why not?

E10-14
Objs. 2, 4
P/T

For each of the events or transactions below, indicate the effect on each ratio listed. Use *I* to indicate increase, *D* to indicate decrease, and *NE* to indicate no effect.

	Debt to Equity	Debt to Assets	Financial Leverage	Current Ratio
a. Sold common stock to investors	___	___	___	___
b. Borrowed cash from a bank on long-term note	___	___	___	___
c. Paid cash dividends on stock	___	___	___	___
d. Sold inventory for cash (at a small profit)	___	___	___	___
e. Paid off loan in part b	___	___	___	___
f. Bought stock of another company	___	___	___	___
g. Purchased treasury stock	___	___	___	___

E10-15
Obj. 4

Intel Corporation reported the following information in its 2001 annual report:

(In millions)	2001
Current Liabilities:	
Short-term debt	$ 409
Long-term debt, current portion	0
Total current liabilities	6,570
Long-Term Liabilities:	
Long-term debt	1,050
Deferred income taxes	945
Stockholders' Equity:	
Common stock	8,833
Other	(153)
Retained earnings	27,150
Total stockholders' equity	38,830

Evaluate Intel's capital structure. Explain which amounts you would include in a computation of the company's debt-to-equity ratio and why.

E10-16
Obj. 4
P̶T̶

Selected information from the 2001 annual reports of **Eastman Chemical Company** and **Microsoft** is given below. All amounts are in millions.

	Eastman Chemical	Microsoft
Current assets	$1,458	$39,637
Total assets	6,086	59,257
Current liabilities	958	11,132
Long-term debt	2,143	0
Other long-term items	1,607	836
Total stockholders' equity	1,378	47,289
Net income	(179)	7,346

a. For each of the companies, compute the following values: (i) return on assets, (ii) total assets to total equity, (iii) return on equity, (iv) long-term debt-to-equity ratio, and (v) long-term debt-to-assets ratio.
b. Inspect the values you have computed for the items in a. What do these indicators tell you about financing strategy and financing decisions that have been made by the management of these two firms? Have the decisions been similar or different? How have these financing decisions affected returns to stockholders? Discuss.

E10-17
Obj. 4

Given below are selected data for **Wal-Mart** for the years ended January 31, 2002 and 2001:

	2002	2001
Long-term debt to equity	0.45	0.40
Long-term debt to assets	0.19	0.16
Return on equity	20.1%	22.0%
Return on assets	8.5%	8.7%
Financial leverage	2.36	2.49
Current ratio	1.0	0.90

Study the information above and discuss what the changes from 2001 to 2002 mean. What conclusion can you make about Wal-Mart's financing activities?

E10-18
Obj. 4

Assume the following summarized balance sheet information at December 31, 2004:

	Giffin Co.	Good Co.
Current assets	$35,000	$45,000
Long-term assets	65,000	55,000
Current liabilities	10,000	20,000
Long-term liabilities	60,000	10,000
Common stock, $10 par	25,000	60,000
Retained earnings	5,000	10,000
Operating income	40,000	40,000
Interest rate for long-term liabilities	10%	10%
Income tax rate	40%	40%

(Continued)

a. Describe how these two firms compare regarding the use of leverage.

b. Is the firm with the higher degree of leverage using it effectively? Discuss. Show any supporting computations clearly and neatly.

E10-19
Obj. 5

Given below is the most recent set of financial statements for BeanSprout Farms.

Balance Sheet at December 31, 2004		Income Statement for Year 2004		
Assets:		Sales revenue	$82,000	
Cash	$ 6,000	Cost of sales	51,000	
Marketable securities	2,800	Gross margin		$31,000
Accounts receivable	5,200	**Expenses:**		
Inventory	5,000	Wages	14,000	
Machinery, net	21,000	Depreciation	2,000	
Land	10,500	Interest	1,000	
		Bad debts	3,000	20,000
Total assets	$50,500	Pretax income		11,000
		Taxes (30%)		3,300
Liabilities and Equity:		Net income		$ 7,700
Accounts payable	$ 3,100			
Notes payable (due 2008)	12,000			
Common stock ($1 par)	4,000			
Paid-in capital	16,000			
Retained earnings	15,400			
Total liabilities and equity	$50,500			

a. Calculate return on assets and return on equity.

b. Assume the company had $18,000 less of contributed capital and $18,000 more of long-term debt. Recalculate return on assets and return on equity.

c. Assume the company replaced all its long-term debt with equity capital. Recalculate return on assets and return on equity.

d. Discuss how financial leverage affects return on assets and return on equity as shown in the results above.

E10-20
Objs. 3, 6

Information from the annual reports of two companies is provided below:

(In millions)	2002	2001	2000
General Mills			
Net income	458	665	614
Dividends	358	312	329
Wal-Mart			
Net income	6,671	6,295	5,377
Dividends	1,249	1,070	890

What do the dividend policies indicate about future prospects for the two companies?

E10-21
Obj. 7

Data from the 2001 annual reports of **J.C. Penney** and **Home Depot** are shown below. The objective of this assignment is to determine which company is more highly regarded by the financial markets.

	J.C. Penney	Home Depot
Common stockholders' equity (millions)	$6,129	$18,082
Common shares (millions)	264	2,346
Market price per common share	$23.70	$49.40

a. In general, what information is revealed by computation of the market-to-book-value ratio?

b. Compute the market-to-book-value ratio for J.C. Penney and Home Depot.

c. What do you conclude from the results of the market-to-book-value ratios of the two companies?

E10-22
Obj. 7
℉

Data are provided below for Register Company, a large security company. All amounts are in millions of dollars.

	Year 2005	Year 2004
Current assets	$ 736	$ 643
Total assets	2,103	1,810
Current liabilities	541	475
Long-term debt	862	815
Stockholders' equity	700	520
Operating income	241	200
Interest expense	(58)	(53)
Income taxes	(68)	(56)
Net income	115	91
Operating cash flows	192	173
Investing cash flows	(262)	(190)
Financing cash flows	102	14
Debt issued	51	34
Debt repurchased	(20)	(17)
Stock issued	85	43
Dividends paid	(34)	(27)
Market value	1,093	870

a. Compute the following ratios for each year: debt (long-term) to assets, assets to stockholders' equity, return on assets, return on equity, current ratio, dividend payout, and market to book value.

b. Identify and describe the company's financing activities for 2005. Be specific.

c. Evaluate the effects the firm's financing activities had on the company's stockholders.

PROBLEMS

If your instructor is using Personal Trainer in this course, you may complete online the assignments identified by ℉.

P10-1
Obj. 2
℉

Capital Structure and Return on Equity

Financial statement information is presented on the next page for Platform Corporation, a manufacturer. Platform is considering a change in its capital structure. Management has proposed issuing $150 million of additional long-term debt. The long-term debt would be used to repurchase a portion of the company's common stock. This purchase would reduce the company's stockholders' equity by $150 million. The interest expense on the additional debt would be $9 million. The company's tax rate is 30% of pre-tax income.

Required

A. Compute Platform's return on equity for 2004 as reported.

B. Compute what Platform's return on equity would have been in 2004 if the company had issued the additional debt and had repurchased common stock before the year began. You will need to recompute net income beginning with operating income. Also, recompute liabilities and equity on the balance sheet. Round to the nearest million dollars.

C. Based on these computations, would the change in capital structure be good for Platform's stockholders? Explain your reasoning.

(Continued)

Income Statement		Balance Sheet	
Fiscal Year 2004 (In millions)		**At Year-end (In millions)**	
Sales	$ 893	**Assets:**	
Cost of goods sold	(552)	Current assets	$252
Operating expenses	(267)	Plant assets	505
Operating income	74	Total assets	$757
Interest expense	(8)	**Liabilities and Equity:**	
Pretax income	66	Current liabilities	$197
Income taxes	(20)	Long-term debt	100
Net income	$ 46	Total liabilities	297
		Stockholders' equity	460
		Total liabilities and stockholders' equity	$757

P10-2

Objs. 1, 2, 4

P/T

Observing Changes in Capital Structure from Comparative Balance Sheets

Shown below are comparative balance sheets for Claudia Company at December 31.

	2005	2004
Assets:		
Cash	$ 12,000	$ 7,400
Accounts receivable	16,200	8,100
Inventory	10,000	8,000
Prepaid rent	5,600	5,100
Machinery, net	28,000	30,000
Land	27,000	27,000
Total assets	$ 98,800	$85,600
Liabilities and Equity:		
Accounts payable	$ 6,200	$ 5,800
Wages payable	5,800	6,100
Bonds payable (long-term)	46,000	16,400
Common stock	34,000	34,000
Retained earnings	34,800	26,400
Treasury stock	(28,000)	(3,100)
Total liabilities and equity	$ 98,800	$85,600

Net income for 2005 was $8,400. In 2004, it was $7,300.

Required

A. Identify the changes in capital structure that occurred during fiscal 2005.
B. Compute the (long-term) debt-to-equity ratio and (long-term) debt-to-assets ratio for both 2004 and 2005.
C. What were the return on assets and return on equity in 2004?
D. What were the return on assets and return on equity in 2005?
E. What role did the changes in capital structure have on return on assets and return on equity in 2005?

P10-3

Obj. 4

P/T

Comparing Capital Structures

Financial information from the 2001 annual reports of two companies is provided on the next page. **Intel Corporation** is a manufacturer of semiconductors (primarily computer microprocessors). **Pacific Gas & Electric** is a privately owned utility.

(In millions) Intel Corporation	2001	(In millions) Pacific Gas & Electric	2001
Current assets	$17,633	Current assets	$ 9,773
Plant assets, net	18,121	Plant assets, net	19,167
Other noncurrent assets	8,641	Other noncurrent assets	6,922
Total assets	44,395	Total assets	35,862
Current liabilities	6,570	Current liabilities	2,544
Long-term debt	1,050	Long-term debt	3,019
Other noncurrent liabilities	945	Other noncurrent liabilities	5,355
Preferred stock	0	Preferred stock	437
Stockholders' equity	35,830	Common stock equity	2,398

Required

A. Identify at least three measures that can be used to assess capital structure. Compute their values for these two companies. (Hint: Treat preferred stock as a liability.)

B. Compare and contrast the capital structures of the two companies.

C. Why might these differences in capital structure exist between the two companies?

P10-4   **Evaluating Financing Alternatives**

Obj. 4

P/T

Information is provided below for the Baker Mountain Company.

(In thousands, except per share amounts)	2004
Operating income	$ 306,679
Interest expense	(55,528)
Income taxes (40%)	122,517
Net income	176,350
Earnings per share (144.6 million shares)	1.23
Total assets	3,297,390
Short-term borrowing	1,612
Current portion of long-term debt	247
Total current liabilities	635,320
Long-term debt	673,588
Deferred income taxes	150,460
Other long-term liabilities	51,178
Total stockholders' equity	1,689,209

Assume that during 2004, Baker Mountain Company had the opportunity to acquire additional assets at a price of $500 million. The additional assets were expected to increase the company's operating income by $80 million annually (to $386,679,000) for the foreseeable future. They could be financed either by selling stock or issuing debt.

Required Prepare a pro forma (projected) income statement for each financing alternative. Start with operating income. Compute pro forma return on assets and pro forma return on equity under each alternative. Discuss whether Baker Mountain should finance the acquisition with debt or stock. Assume that debt could be issued at a 7% interest rate.

P10-5   **Evaluating Financing Alternatives**

Obj. 4

P/T

Given on the next page are the balance sheet and income statement for fiscal 2004 for the Crossroads Company.

(Continued)

Balance Sheet

Assets:

Cash	$ 14,000
Inventory	42,000
Investments	11,000
Buildings (net)	47,000
Land	37,000
Total assets	$151,000

Liabilities and Equity:

Accounts payable	$ 17,000
Notes payable	32,000
Common stock	61,000
Retained earnings	41,000
Total liabilities and equity	$151,000

Income Statement

Sales revenue	$358,000
Cost of sales	227,000
Gross margin	131,000
Interest expense	(5,000)
Other fixed expenses	(70,000)
Taxes (40%)	(22,400)
Net income	$ 33,600

Crossroads Company plans to purchase new productive equipment, for $200,000, that will increase the company's revenues by 20% during 2005. Management would like to maintain the company's current return on equity if at all possible. Crossroads can finance the purchase by selling stock or issuing long-term debt at 6% interest.

Required

A. Prepare a pro forma (projected) income statement for 2005 assuming the new equipment is financed through the issuance of new equity.
B. Prepare a pro forma (projected) income statement for 2005 assuming the new equipment is financed through the issuance of new long-term debt.
C. Assess the company's two options and make a recommendation for financing the new equipment that best matches management's objective. Can you think of any other alternatives that management might consider?

P10-6   Analyzing Financing Activities and Capital Structure

Obj. 4

Presented below is condensed and summary information from the financial statements of **Tommy Hilfiger Corporation**.

Consolidated Balance Sheets (In thousands, except share data)	March 31, 2002	March 31, 2001
Assets:		
Current assets	$ 893,888	$ 851,644
Property and equipment, net	302,937	281,682
Intangible assets	1,390,092	1,206,358
Other assets	7,534	2,872
Total Assets	$ 2,594,451	$ 2,342,556
Liabilities and shareholders' equity:		
Current liabilities	$ 302,697	$ 260,268
Long-term debt	575,287	529,495
Other noncurrent liabilities	219,005	204,200
Shareholders' equity*	1,497,462	1,348,593
Total liabilities and shareholders' equity	$ 2,594,451	$ 2,342,556
*Common shares outstanding	96,031,167	95,169,402

Required

A. Analyze the capital structure of Tommy Hilfiger Corporation and discuss your findings.
B. Analyze Tommy Hilfiger's liquidity and discuss your findings. (Hint: Assume the average current ratio of companies in this industry is 1.84.)

P10-7 Evaluating the Effects of Financial Leverage

Objs. 4, 5

Information is provided below from the 2001 annual report of Pacific Gas & Electric.

(In millions)	2001	2000
Operating income (loss)	$ 2,478	$(5,201)
Interest expense	974	619
Pretax income (loss)	1,611	(5,637)
Income taxes (benefit)	596	(2,154)
Net income (loss)	1,015	(3,483)
Total assets	35,832	36,152
Total stockholders' equity	2,398	1,410
Long-term debt	3,019	3,342

The interest expense relates primarily to the long-term debt.

Required

A. Calculate the company's return on equity for 2001 and 2000.
B. How much did the company's financial leverage help or hurt the stockholders each year?
C. What would have happened to return on equity in these two years if, prior to 2000, the company had sold more common stock and used the proceeds to pay off debt?

P10-8 Identifying Capital Structure Choices

Objs. 3, 5

You are a financial manager with a medium-sized company, Kangaroo Express. The company is owned and managed by the Marsupial family. Currently, 60% of the company's financing is composed of long-term notes, 20% is current liabilities, and the remainder consists of stock held by members of the Marsupial family. You have been asked to meet with the company's top management to discuss the company's capital structure and plans to raise capital for expansion.

Required Write a short report describing alternative types of financing Kangaroo Express might consider. Explain the risk and return implications of each alternative for the Marsupials.

P10-9 Comparing Capital Structures and the Effect of Leverage

Objs. 4, 5

Given below are summary financial statements for two companies.

	2005	2004	2003
Clipper Company:			
Total assets	$6,000	$5,500	$5,000
Total liabilities	3,273	4,014	3,750
Net income	300	200	100
Dividends	75	50	25
Battle Company:			
Total assets	$7,000	$6,000	$5,000
Total liabilities	5,333	4,286	3,333
Net income	300	200	100
Dividends	150	100	50

Required

A. Compute the debt-to-equity ratios for, and compare the capital structures of, the two companies.

(Continued)

B. Compute and compare the return on equity, return on assets, and financial leverage factors of the two companies.

C. Compute and compare the dividend payout ratios of the two companies.

D. After this analysis, which company would you prefer to invest in and why?

P10-10   **Evaluating the Effect of Financial Leverage on Risk**

Obj. 5

P
T

Information is provided below for two companies, describing likely outcomes for the companies in various economic circumstances.

	Halyard Company			Spinnaker Company		
	Bad Year	Normal Year	Good Year	Bad Year	Normal Year	Good Year
Assets	$800	$800	$800	$800	$800	$800
Debt	200	200	200	600	600	600
Equity	600	600	600	200	200	200
Net income	(25)	75	175	(25)	75	175

Required

A. Calculate the following ratios for each company. Interpret the results of your calculations and explain what you conclude from the ratios.
  i. Debt-to-equity ratio
  ii. Debt-to-assets ratio

B. Calculate the following for each company under each economic circumstance.
  i.   Return on assets
  ii. Financial leverage
  iii. Return on equity

C. Evaluate the effect of financial leverage on the risks of the two companies.

P10-11   **Evaluating the Effect of Financial Leverage**

Obj. 5

Information is provided below for two companies that have the same capital structure but different amounts of net income for the three years presented:

James Company:	2005	2004	2003
Assets	$3,000	$2,000	$1,000
Debt	1,800	1,200	600
Equity	1,200	800	400
Net income (loss)	1,000	500	250

Joyce Company:	2005	2004	2003
Assets	$3,000	$2,000	$1,000
Debt	1,800	1,200	600
Equity	1,200	800	400
Net income (loss)	(400)	(200)	300

Required

A. Calculate the following ratios for each company for each of the three years given:
  1. Debt-to-equity ratio
  2. Debt-to-assets ratio
  3. Return on assets
  4. Financial leverage
  5. Return on equity

B. Graph the results of the return on assets and return on equity calculations, putting the three years along the X (horizontal) axis and the percentages along the Y (vertical) axis. Discuss your conclusions.

C. For each company, reverse the amounts shown for debt and equity on the previous page. (For example, in 2005 both companies would have $1,200 of debt and $1,800 of equity.) Repeat the requirements for parts A and B. Discuss your conclusions and how they differ from the results you obtained in part B.

P10-12 Additional Debt, Capital Structure, and Return on Equity

Obj. 5

Louisiana Company's fiscal year 2004 operating results and year-end balance sheet are as shown below.

Partial 2004 Income Statement (in millions)

Operating income	$122
Interest expense	(16)
Pretax income	106
Income taxes (30%)	(32)
Net income	$ 74

Year-end 2004 Balance Sheet

Total assets	$1,514
Liabilities:	
Current liabilities	$ 394
Long-term debt	200
Total liabilities	594
Stockholders' equity	920
Total liabilities and stockholders' equity	$1,514

Required

A. Compute return on equity for the company based on the information reported above.

B. Determine what the company's return on equity would have been in 2004 if, before the year began, the company had issued $225 million of additional long-term debt (at 8% interest) and had repurchased common stock. (Hint: You will need to recompute net income, liabilities, and stockholders' equity. Round financial statement amounts to the nearest million dollars.)

C. What effect would the additional debt have on the company's risk and return?

P10-13 Analyzing Performance and the Effect of Financial Leverage

Obj. 5

The following financial statement information is from the annual report of **Best Buy, Inc.**, a large retailer of electronics.

Consolidated Statements of Operations (In millions, except per share amounts)

For the fiscal years	2002	2001	2000
Net revenue	$19,597	$15,327	$12,494
Cost of goods sold	15,167	12,268	10,101
Gross profit	4,430	3,059	2,393
Selling, general, and administrative expense	3,493	2,455	1,854
Operating income	937	604	539
Net interest revenue	(1)	37	24
Earnings before income taxes	936	641	563
Income tax expense	366	245	216
Net income	$ 570	$ 396	$ 347
Total assets	$ 7,375	$ 4,840	$ 2,995
Stockholders' equity	2,521	1,822	1,096

Required

A. Analyze the profit performance of Best Buy, Inc., and discuss your findings.

B. Analyze the effect of financial leverage on Best Buy, Inc., and discuss your findings.

P10-14   ## Evaluating Financing Cash Flows

Objs. 3, 4, 6   Information is provided below from the 2001 annual report of **Johnson & Johnson**:

(In millions)	2001	2000
Cash flows from financing activities:		
Dividends to stockholders	$(2,047)	$(1,724)
Repurchase of common stock	(2,570)	(973)
Proceeds from short-term debt	338	814
Retirement of short-term debt	(1,109)	(1,485)
Proceeds from long-term debt	14	591
Retirement from long-term debt	(391)	(35)
Proceeds from the exercise of stock options	514	387
Net cash used by financing activities	$(5,251)	$(2,425)

Required Evaluate Johnson & Johnson's financial condition from the information provided. Do the financing activities indicate that the company is facing financial problems? Explain your thinking. What effect have these activities had on the company's capital structure?

P10-15   ## Analyzing Credit-Paying Ability

Objs. 3, 4, 6   Sunny Meadow Enterprises disclosed the following information in its 2004 annual report:

(In millions)	2004	2003
Net income (loss)	$ (31.0)	$ 58.6
Net cash flow from operating activities	6.8	144.2
Net cash flow from financing activities	135.8	(339.6)
Interest payments	65.9	81.4
Current portion of long-term debt	27.7	31.6
Total current liabilities	357.2	344.0
Total liabilities	1,384.3	1,210.9
Total current assets	695.9	626.3
Total assets	2,160.5	2,073.5

You are a financial analyst with a large investment company. Several clients are creditors and stockholders of the company. One client in particular, Wellington Smythe, has expressed concern about the company's recent net loss. He is concerned about the company's ability to meet its principal and interest payments and the effect of this on the company's stockholders.

Required Write a memo to Wellington explaining whether you think he should be concerned about the company's ability to meet its obligations and whether stockholders should be concerned about the company's performance. Use relevant information from the data presented above to support your explanations.

P10-16   ## Analyzing Capital Structure Decisions

Objs. 4, 5, 6   Companies are sometimes acquired by investors using a technique called a leveraged buyout (LBO). Selected information for a company both before and after such a transaction is given on the next page. The information is typical of an LBO.

Required

A. From the information for the years before and after the LBO, how would you define an LBO?

B. In the year after the LBO, how could Interest Expense exceed Interest Paid?

C. Is the company more risky or less risky after the LBO? Discuss.

D. After the LBO, net income was drastically reduced. Do you think the firm is in immediate danger? Discuss.

(In millions)	Year After the LBO	Year Before the LBO
Net income (loss)	$ (747)	$ 786
Operating income	1,334	1,498
Interest expense	1,909	318
Interest paid in cash	1,293	318
Cash provided by operations	1,687	1,901
Current maturities of long-term debt	1,711	105
Total current liabilities	3,269	2,680
Long-term debt	14,266	2,525
Stockholders' equity	804	3,925

P10-17

Objs. 6, 7

Evaluating Financing Cash Flows

Add the following excerpts from the statement of cash flows from Tommy Hilfiger Corporation to the information provided in Problem 10-6.

Consolidated Statements of Cash Flows
For the Fiscal Year Ended March 31

(In thousands)	2002	2001	2000
Cash flows from operating activities	$ 353,300	$ 190,968	$ 231,209
Cash flows from investing activities	$(301,984)	$ (73,890)	$(151,984)
Cash flows from financing activities			
Proceeds of long-term debt	$ 144,921	—	$ 20,000
Payments on long-term debt	(155,538)	(50,000)	(40,000)
Proceeds from the exercise of stock options	7,997	3,710	8,933
Purchase of treasury shares	—	(61,231)	—
Short-term bank borrowings (repayments), net	20,120	(523)	(711)
Net cash provided by (used in) financing activities	$ 17,500	$(108,044)	$ (11,778)

In addition, Tommy Hilfiger Corporation provided the following information and quotation in the section of its annual report entitled "Market for Registrant's Common Equity And Related Matters."

	High	Low
Fiscal year ended March 31, 2002		
Fourth quarter	16.06	11.20
Fiscal year ended March 31, 2001		
Fourth quarter	17.25	9.06

"Tommy Hilfiger Corporation has not paid any cash dividends since its IPO in 1992, and has no current plans to pay cash dividends."

Required

A. Describe and summarize the company's financing cash flows for the fiscal periods covered by the information provided.

(Continued)

B. Besides the quotation from the annual report, how else do you know that the company has not been paying dividends?

C. Compute the market to book value at the points in time for which you have the necessary information available in the problem. Describe any changes over that period that you observe.

P10-18   **Ethical Issues in Financing Decisions**

Objs. 6, 7

Randy Slowpush is chief financial officer (CFO) for Endrun Financial Corp. Because the rapidly growing company wishes to maximize financial leverage, the company is in constant need of new debt capital. As CFO, Randy is famous for creative financing techniques by which the firm is able to raise money without reporting the debt on its own balance sheet. A common technique is to establish a partnership, partially owned by Randy, that borrows money to finance certain business ventures on behalf of Endrun Corp. Endrun secretly guarantees the loans by pledging to issue its own stock, if necessary, to repay the partnership loans.

Randy then negotiates contracts with Endrun, on behalf of the partnerships, to manage specified business activities for Endrun. Often he negotiates with Endrun employees who report to the CFO. In 2002, Randy earned $30 million from operating about 15 of these partnerships. Endrun benefits from this arrangement by keeping the debt off its books, which keeps its leverage ratios in an acceptable range, which keeps its interest rates low on the debt it does report. Stockholders and creditors are not aware of these arrangements.

Required Are these activities unethical? Why or why not?

P10-19   **Evaluating Financing Choices**

Obj. 6

P/T

Aitken Company needs cash. The company has several hot new products and sales are growing rapidly. The controller has just presented CEO Jim Aitken the following balance sheet updated through today, saying, "we've got to raise $90,000 cash immediately."

Assets		Liabilities	
Cash	$ 11,200	Accounts payable	$ 18,550
Accounts receivable	15,000	Other short-term liabilities	39,550
Inventory	10,000	Long-term debt	100,000
Machinery, net	107,500	**Stockholders' equity**	
Buildings, net	253,600	Contributed capital	200,000
Land	80,000	Retained earnings	119,200
Total assets	$477,300	Total liabilities and equity	$477,300

The controller proposed three options to raise the $90,000: (1) obtain a short-term bank loan, (2) sell new shares of common stock, or (3) issue long-term bonds payable. She also presented the CEO with the following information about financial ratio benchmarks for companies in their industry.

Ratio	High	Average	Low
Current ratio	2.5	1.5	1.0
Long-term debt to equity	0.28	0.40	0.53
Long-term debt to assets	0.19	0.26	0.35
Assets to equity	1.3	1.7	2.0

Required

A. Compute today's value of the four ratios for which benchmarks are given.

B. Evaluate each value computed in part A with its industry benchmark. Which ratio values are strong? Which are weak?

C. Compute pro-forma (projected) ratio values under each of the three financing options. That is, for each option, what would be the new ratio values immediately after that option was implemented?

D. Evaluate your results from part C. Which financing option would best strengthen the company's financial position as measured by the four ratios considered? Explain.

P10-20   Excel in Action

SPREADSHEET

The Book Wermz issued common stock and bonds in March 2005. Following that, the company created projected income statement and balance sheet account balances for the fiscal year ended December 31, 2005 that appear below. Only selected balances are presented.

Operating income	$ 647,585
Total assets	5,623,107
Long-term debt	2,097,416
Stockholders' equity	3,370,241

Assume that interest expense is 9% of long-term debt and the company's income tax rate is 35%.

Required Enter the data shown above for The Book Wermz in columns A and B of a spreadsheet. Calculate interest expense, pretax income, income taxes, and net income for the company for 2005 using the assumptions provided. Then, calculate return on assets, financial leverage (Assets ÷ Stockholders' Equity), and return on equity. Place captions in column A and amounts in column B.

Copy the data from column B to column C. Assume that the company's long-term debt decreased by $1 million and its stockholders' equity increased by $1 million. Adjust these amounts in the spreadsheet. What effect would this change have on the company's return?

Copy the data from column C to column D. Assume that the company's long-term debt increased by $1 million and its stockholders' equity decreased by $1 million relative to the amounts in column B. Adjust these amounts in the spreadsheet. What effect would this change have on the company's return?

Suppose that the company's operating income for 2005 was $200,000. What effect would this change have on the company's return under each of the scenarios described above? Copy columns B, C, and D to columns E, F, and G and change the operating income in columns E, F, and G to $200,000.

Graph the relation between financial leverage and return on equity. Select the rows in which these two calculations appear on your spreadsheet. Click on the Chart Wizard 📊 button. Select XY (Scatter) as the chart type and click the Next button. Make sure the Rows button is checked in the Series field. Click the Next button. In the Titles tab, enter "Effect of Financial Leverage on Return" for the chart title. Enter "Financial Leverage" for the Value (X) axis, and "Return on Equity" for the Value (Y) axis. In the Legend tab, click the Show Legend box so the checkmark is removed. Click the Next button. Click on the As object in button and then the Finish button. You can resize the chart by clicking on it, clicking any of the small boxes around the edge of the chart and dragging the chart to the size and shape you want. You can move the entire chart by clicking on the chart (not one of the boxes) and dragging it to a new location. Various parts of the graph can be reformatted by clicking on the graph item with the right mouse button and selecting Format from the dialog box. For example, if you want to remove the shading from the plot area, click on the shaded area with the right mouse button, select Format Plot Area, and click on the None button in the Area category. You can change colors, fonts, axes, numbers of decimals, and other properties using this method.

What can you conclude about the relation between financial leverage and return on equity?

P10-21   Multiple-Choice Overview of the Chapter

1. The way a company finances its assets and operating activities is its
   a. capital structure.
   b. financial leverage.
   c. return on equity.
   d. present value.

2. Honey Farms Company reported the following information.

Net sales	$ 85
Net income	10
Total assets	103
Total liabilities	41
Stockholders' equity	62

(Continued)

Return on equity is
a. 6.2%.
b. 9.7%.
c. 11.8%.
d. 16.1%.

3. Financial leverage always
   a. increases profits.
   b. decreases profits.
   c. increases risk.
   d. decreases risk.

4. Which of the following ratios is an indicator of liquidity?
   a. Debt to assets
   b. Current assets to current liabilities
   c. Assets to equity
   d. Net income to equity

5. Financing with capital leases and financing with preferred stock are similar in that both
   a. require the payout of fixed amounts each period.
   b. increase the amount of net income available to common stockholders.
   c. increase the riskiness of the firm's common stock.
   d. cause cash flow from operations to be smaller than it otherwise would be.

6. At year end, J. J. Walker Company had total assets of $90,000 and total stockholders' equity of $50,000. The firm's return on assets was 12% for the year. What were net income and return on equity?

	Net Income	Return on Equity
a.	$4,800	9.6%
b.	$6,000	12.0%
c.	$10,800	21.6%
d.	$16,800	33.6%

7. Crispy Chips, Inc. earned net income this past year of $100,000 on assets of $1.9 million and stockholders' equity of $1.2 million. To raise $500,000 of additional capital, Crispy can either issue long-term debt paying 9% interest or issue additional common stock. Use of the new capital should raise net income, before considering any new interest cost, by $68,000. To maximize return on equity, Crispy should
   a. not issue any new debt or equity.
   b. issue new equity only.
   c. issue new debt only.
   d. issue half in new equity and half in new debt.

8. High amounts of financial leverage are most common for companies with
   a. small proportions of plant assets and stable earnings.
   b. large proportions of plant assets and stable earnings.
   c. small proportions of plant assets and unstable earnings.
   d. large proportions of plant assets and unstable earnings.

9. Low dividend payout ratios are common for companies
   a. with low growth potential.
   b. in stable industries.
   c. with high growth potential.
   d. with stable earnings.

10. If a company is having difficulty paying interest and principal on its debt, creditors should be particularly concerned with
    a. its return on assets.
    b. its return on equity.
    c. its debt to equity ratio.
    d. its cash flows.

CASES

C10-1

Obj. 4

Evaluating Capital Structure

Selected information for Terabyte Technology, Inc. is provided below:

(In millions except per share amounts)	2005	2004
Earnings before interest and taxes	$ 742	$ 799
Interest expense	129	133
Earnings before income taxes	613	666
Income taxes	159	167
Net income	454	499
Net income per share	3.44	3.80
Average shares outstanding	131.9	131.3
Total current assets	4,487	4,452
Total assets	9,375	8,742
Total current liabilities	3,063	3,048
Long-term debt	954	792
Deferred income taxes	196	203
Other liabilities	532	442
Total stockholders' equity	4,630	4,257
Net cash provided by operations	1,358	1,307
Net cash used for investing activities	(1,232)	(1,443)
Net cash provided by financing activities:		
Increase (decrease) in notes payable and current portion of long-term debt	(143)	208
Increase in long-term debt	135	7
Issuance of common stock	19	55
Payment of dividends	(100)	(100)
Net cash provided by (used for) financing activities	(89)	170

Required Write a short report describing Terabyte's capital structure. Consider changes in the company's capital structure in 2005, and identify the causes of these changes. Identify Terabyte's primary source of financing in 2005, and evaluate the company's financial condition at the end of 2005.

C10-2

Objs. 4, 5

Evaluating Capital Structure Decisions

At year end 2004, the capital structure of Hard Luck Casino, Inc. was as follows:

Current liabilities	$ 2,400,000
Long-term debt (9% bonds)	5,000,000
Preferred stock, $100 par	1,000,000
Common stock, no par value	15,000,000
Retained earnings	2,600,000
Total liabilities and equity	$26,000,000

During 2004, the company earned net income of $3 million. It paid the required preferred dividends of $80,000 and paid dividends to common stockholders of $750,000.

Required For each of the following independent scenarios, assume it occurred or was true during year 2004. Explain the effect the scenario would have had on the company's net income, return on assets, and return on equity for year 2004. What effect would you expect the event to have had on the riskiness of each type of security issued by Hard Luck Casino?

A. On January 2, 2004, the company issued $5 million of new common stock and used the proceeds to repurchase its bonds.

(Continued)

B. Because of new competition during 2004, the company's profits had been $1 million less than reported on the previous page.

C. On January 2, 2004, the company issued $8 million of new bonds to finance the purchase of additional plant assets. The bonds were issued at a market rate of 10%. The new assets produced $1.6 million of additional profits before considering the added interest cost.

C10-3 **Analyzing Financing Decisions**

Objs. 4, 5, 6, 7

Sporty Footware, Inc. reported the following financial information at year-end 2004:

Consolidated Statements of Operations
For the Year Ended December 31,

(In thousands, except per share amounts)	2004	2003	2002
Net revenue	$847,110	$661,688	$478,131
Cost of goods sold	447,524	344,884	258,419
Gross profit	399,586	316,804	219,712
Selling, general, and administrative expenses	236,571	190,976	132,270
Income from operations	163,015	125,828	87,442
Interest expense	(1,258)	(761)	(754)
Interest income	7,013	6,181	5,712
Income before income taxes	168,770	131,248	92,400
Provision for income taxes	55,590	44,866	30,900
Net income	$113,180	$ 86,382	$ 61,500

Consolidated Balance Sheets (In thousands, except share data)	December 31, 2004	December 31, 2003
Assets:		
Current assets	$438,284	$332,353
Property and equipment, net	160,089	121,540
Other assets	19,637	9,192
Total Assets	$618,010	$463,085
Liabilities and shareholders' equity:		
Current liabilities	$ 92,398	$ 61,686
Other liabilities	6,550	2,425
Long-term debt	—	1,510
Shareholders' equity*	519,062	397,464
Total liabilities and shareholders' equity	$618,010	$463,085
*Common shares outstanding	37,557,934	37,249,529

Consolidated Statements of Cash Flows
For the Year Ended December 31

(In thousands)	2004	2003	2002
Cash flows from operating activities	$108,049	$ 62,635	$34,227
Cash flows from investing activities	$ (67,814)	$(83,960)	$21,520
Cash flows from financing activities			
Proceeds from the exercise of employee stock options	$ 5,685	$ 3,929	$13,027
Tax benefit from exercise of stock options	2,703	5,812	17,715
Short-term bank borrowings, net	—	(5,975)	5,700
Payments on long-term debt	(1,510)	(279)	(275)
Other	30	3	12
Net cash provided by financing activities	$ 6,908	$ 3,490	$36,179

Other information:

1. The company has a policy of not paying dividends.
2. Year-end stock prices were as follows:

   2004 = $61.50

   2003 = $59.13

Required Would you lend money to this firm? Would you buy its common stock? Why or why not? Conduct whatever analysis and evaluation you believe would be helpful to answer these questions. Support your answer by referencing your analysis.

INVESTING ACTIVITIES

How do we account for investing activities?

Long-term assets are necessary to support a company's operating activities. Facilities are needed to produce and sell products. Other long-term assets recognize the cost of intellectual property and other legal rights controlled by a company, as well as investments and other financial resources. As a company becomes larger, it invests in more assets and often requires more types of assets to support its business activities.

Maria, Stan, and Ellen are considering expanding Mom's Cookie Company. They are aware that they will need additional property and equipment for the company to produce and sell its products to a larger market.

FOOD FOR THOUGHT

If you were advising the owners of Mom's Cookie Company what kinds of long-term assets would you recommend they invest in and how should they account for those various assets? Are there any tax issues that might have an impact on the way they account for the new investments?

Stan has called a meeting with Maria and Ellen to talk about expansion plans. They begin their discussion of the assets the company will need by considering different types of assets and how to account for them.

Stan: *If we are going to produce and sell more of our products, we will need to acquire additional plant and equipment.*

Maria: *Are there other long-term assets that we will require?*

Ellen: *Other long-term assets may be useful. For example, we may want to protect some of our recipes and our brand name with patents and trademarks. We may need to make some financial investments to provide financial resources when we need them in the future.*

Stan: *Acquiring long-term assets is really just a matter of buying them and putting them to work, isn't it? These activities really don't have much effect on our profits, do they?*

Ellen: *How we depreciate our property and equipment will have an effect on profitability and the timing of our income tax payments. Other revenues and expenses can result from other activities, such as income earned from investments in marketable securities.*

Maria: *Perhaps we should examine these investing activities and how they can affect our financial statements before we make any more decisions.*

OBJECTIVES

Once you have completed this chapter, you should be able to:

1 Identify types of long-term assets, their purposes, and the measurement basis companies use to record their assets.

2 Apply appropriate measurement rules to the purchase, depreciation, and disposal of plant assets.

3 Apply appropriate measurement rules to the purchase and use of natural resources.

4 Apply appropriate measurement rules to the purchase, valuation, and sale of long-term and short-term investments.

5 Explain accounting issues associated with intangible and other long-term assets.

6 Summarize the effects of investing activities on a company's financial statements.

TYPES OF ASSETS

OBJECTIVE 1

Identify types of long-term assets, their purposes, and the measurement basis companies use to record their assets.

Investing activities supply the resources that an organization needs to operate. Most of those resources are reported as assets, although some—for example, the value of management and employee skills—are not. On its balance sheet, a company reports those assets for which it can reasonably identify costs and that are important to its operations. Exhibit 1 provides the asset section of the balance sheet Mom's Cookie Company reported in its 2005 annual report. This exhibit is used as a basis for discussing the types of assets most corporations report.

Exhibit 1

Balance Sheet Presentation of Assets for Mom's Cookie Company

December 31,	2005	2004
Assets		
Current assets:		
Cash	$ 17,510	$ 10,680
Accounts receivable	15,400	8,570
Merchandise inventory	75,920	23,600
Supplies	2,480	690
Prepaid rent	3,500	2,000
Total current assets	114,810	45,540
Long-term investments	4,000	0
Property and equipment, at cost	572,467	215,660
Accumulated depreciation	(53,630)	(25,500)
Property and equipment, net	518,837	190,160
Intangible assets	1,600	0
Other long-term assets	850	0
Total assets	$640,097	$235,700

Most companies divide their assets into two major categories: current and long-term. **Current assets are those that management expects to convert to cash or consume during the coming fiscal year.** Most current assets are created or used as part of a company's operating activities. The company uses those assets to produce and sell goods and services. Accounts receivable and inventories are examined in Chapter F13 when we consider operating activities. (Prepaid expenses were discussed in an earlier chapter.) Cash is created and

LEARNING NOTE

In rare cases, a company's cycle of conversion, or operating cycle, is longer than a year. An **operating cycle** is the period from the time cash is paid for inventory until the inventory is sold and converted back to cash. In these cases, the company uses the longer operating cycle, rather than the fiscal year, as a basis for determining its current assets.

used in all types of activities. We consider the effects of investing activities on cash in this chapter.

Long-term assets include assets a company uses to produce and sell its products. These assets **provide benefits to a company that extend beyond the coming fiscal year** or operating cycle. Long-term assets usually are divided into four categories, though some companies choose not to invest in all four categories.

Long-term investments are investments in financial securities. These securities are debt or equity issued by other companies or organizations.

Property, plant, and equipment includes investments in tangible assets, such as equipment, buildings, and land, that a company intends to use in the future to produce or sell its products. The amount paid for these assets, their cost, is reported on the balance sheet or in a note to the balance sheet. In addition, the amount of depreciation recorded on the assets since they were acquired is reported as accumulated depreciation, either on the balance sheet or in a note. The difference between the cost of these assets and accumulated depreciation is the amount actually used to compute total assets on the balance sheet. This amount generally is referred to as **net** property, plant, and equipment or net fixed assets. The cost of these assets sometimes is referred to as **gross** property, plant, and equipment.

The source of financing for plant assets does not affect the way the assets are reported on the balance sheet. Whether a company pays for the assets from cash it has accumulated, borrows money from creditors, or issues stock, the assets are still reported as plant assets. Plant assets acquired by capital leases also are included as part of property, plant, and equipment and are depreciated along with other assets.

Intangible assets are those that provide legal rights or benefits to a company. These assets include patents, copyrights, trademarks, and goodwill. A company benefits from these assets because it controls rights to certain property, processes, brands, or markets that give the company an advantage relative to its competitors.

Other assets include miscellaneous resources that are important to a particular company. These may include long-term receivables, long-term prepaid assets, buildings and equipment that a company is attempting to sell, and natural resources, such as timber, oil, or minerals.

The total amount reported by a company for its assets is the sum of current and long-term assets.

We will consider accounting for each of these types of assets in the sections that follow. We begin the discussion with plant assets, because these are the most common type of long-term assets and the most important for most companies.

PROPERTY, PLANT, AND EQUIPMENT

OBJECTIVE 2

Apply appropriate measurement rules to the purchase, depreciation, and disposal of plant assets.

Plant assets include the land, buildings, and equipment a company uses in its operating activities. Mom's Cookie Company reported plant assets of $518,837 in 2005 (see Exhibit 1). That amount was net (after subtraction) of accumulated depreciation.

The transactions associated with plant assets include their purchase and disposal and their valuation on the balance sheet at the end of each fiscal period. The purchase and disposal of plant assets are recorded at cost, the amount paid for the assets or received when the assets are sold. The disposal of plant assets usually results in cash inflow and recognition of a gain or loss. Plant assets are reported on the balance sheet at cost less accumulated depreciation. Companies provide information about primary categories of plant assets in their balance sheets or in notes to their financial statements.

Land does not depreciate because it is not consumed. Companies generally buy land for office, manufacturing, and other facilities. Land used for these purposes is reported as part of property, plant, and equipment. The cost of consuming natural resources—oil or timber, for example—is described later in this chapter.

Plant Asset Cost

The cost of plant assets includes the amount paid for the assets plus the cost of transportation, site preparation, installation, and any construction necessary to make the assets usable for their intended purpose. The cost of land includes the cost of preparing the land for construction and use. Improvements to the land (such as paving and lighting) are treated as separate assets and are depreciated along with other plant assets.

Case In Point

Reporting Long-Term Assets

Krispy Kreme Doughnuts provided the following information about its property and equipment in its 2002 annual report.

In thousands

	Jan. 28, 2001	Feb. 3, 2002
Land	$11,144	$ 14,823
Buildings	29,637	39,566
Machinery and equipment	65,119	86,683
Leasehold improvements	10,440	13,463
Construction in progress	556	1,949
	116,896	156,484
Less: accumulated depreciation	38,556	43,907
Property, and equipment, net	$78,340	$112,577

LEARNING NOTE

If a capital lease is used to acquire plant assets, the present value of the future lease payments at the time the property is acquired is used as the cost of the assets.

To illustrate, assume that on Sept. 12, 2005, Mom's Cookie Company purchased a small parcel of property. The company paid $40,000 for the property, which included a building and office equipment. In addition, the company spent $10,000 in October to renovate the building.

To account for this acquisition, Mom's Cookie Company must separate the $400,000 cost of the property into its components: land, building, and equipment. This separation is necessary because the building and equipment will be depreciated, whereas the land will not be depreciated. The cost of the property is assigned to components on the basis of the relative fair market values of the various assets acquired. For example, assume that Mom's Cookie Company has the property appraised and determines that 70% should be allocated to the building, 20% to the land, and 10% to the equipment. It would record the $400,000 purchase as follows:

		ASSETS		=	LIABILITIES	+	OWNERS' EQUITY	
Date	Accounts	Cash	Other Assets				Contributed Capital	Retained Earnings
Sept. 12, 2005	Land		80,000					
	Buildings		280,000					
	Equipment		40,000					
	Cash	−400,000						

Assume that the $10,000 renovation cost included $7,500 for replacement of the building's roof and $2,500 for painting. Both of these costs relate to the building. However, the costs fall into two categories: those that extend the life or enhance the value of the property ($7,500 for roof replacement) and those that are ordinary repairs or maintenance ($2,500 for painting). **Expenditures made to acquire new plant assets or to extend the life or enhance the value of existing plant assets are known as** *capital expenditures.* Capital expenditures are recorded as assets because they create future benefits. **Expenditures to repair or maintain plant assets that do not extend the life or enhance the value of the assets are known as** *operating expenditures.* Operating expenditures are recorded as expenses because they are costs associated with the use or consumption of a resource.

Accordingly, the $10,000 renovation cost is recorded as follows:

		ASSETS		=	LIABILITIES	+	OWNERS' EQUITY	
Date	Accounts	Cash	Other Assets				Contributed Capital	Retained Earnings
Oct. 31, 2005	Buildings		7,500					
	Maintenance Expense							-2,500
	Cash	-10,000						

In addition to purchase and renovation costs, interest on debt used to finance the construction of assets is included as part of the cost of these assets. For example, if Mom's Cookie Company borrowed $100,000 at 8% for one year to finance construction of a building, the $8,000 interest paid on the loan would be assigned to the buildings account. This interest is capitalized (recorded as an asset) because it is part of the cost of constructing the asset. The total cost of the building, including interest, is depreciated over its useful life.

Depreciation

Buildings, equipment, and other plant assets that are consumed are depreciated over their estimated useful lives. **Depreciation** is the process of allocating the cost of plant assets to expense over the fiscal periods that benefit from their use. Because the actual consumption of a plant asset usually is impossible to determine, depreciation involves arbitrary allocations of costs. These allocations attempt to match the cost of consuming plant assets with the periods that benefit from using the assets. However, assumptions normally must be made about how much of the asset has been consumed. A variety of depreciation methods exist, but most fall into three general categories:

- *Straight-line depreciation* **allocates an equal amount of the cost of a plant asset to expense during each fiscal period of the asset's expected useful life.**
- *Accelerated depreciation* **allocates a larger portion of the cost of a plant asset to expense early in the asset's life.**
- *Units-of-production depreciation* **produces a level amount of depreciation expense per unit of output (rather than per fiscal period).**

Straight-Line Depreciation. Suppose that Mom's Cookie Company purchased equipment on January 1, 2004 at a cost of $50,000. Management expects the equipment to have a useful life of four years. At the end of four years, it expects to sell the equipment for $2,000 (called its residual value) and replace it with new equipment. The amount of depreciation the company should record over the life of the equipment is $48,000: cost minus residual value ($50,000 − $2,000). **Residual** or **salvage value** is the amount management expects to receive for an asset at the end of the asset's useful life. This amount may result from selling or trading in the asset. The residual value is zero for many assets.

Straight-line depreciation allocates $12,000 ($48,000 ÷ 4) of the cost to depreciation expense each year over the life of the asset:

Straight-line depreciation expense = (cost − residual value) ÷ expected life of asset

During 2004, Mom's Cookie Company would record depreciation expense on the equipment as follows:

		ASSETS		=	LIABILITIES	+	OWNERS' EQUITY	
Date	Accounts	Cash	Other Assets				Contributed Capital	Retained Earnings
Dec. 31, 2004	Depreciation Expense Accumulated Depreciation		−12,000					−12,000

Accumulated Depreciation is a contra-asset account that offsets Equipment. The **net** or **book value** of a plant asset is the net cost of the asset after accumulated depreciation has been subtracted. A depreciation schedule describes the depreciation and book value of an asset over the asset's useful life. Exhibit 2 provides a depreciation schedule for the equipment purchased by Mom's Cookie Company in 2004.

Exhibit 2
Straight-Line
Depreciation Schedule

Year	Beginning Book Value	Depreciation Expense	Accumulated Depreciation	Ending Book Value
2004	$50,000	$12,000	$12,000	$38,000
2005	38,000	12,000	24,000	26,000
2006	26,000	12,000	36,000	14,000
2007	14,000	12,000	48,000	2,000

An equal amount of depreciation is recorded each fiscal period. At the end of four years, the book value of the asset is $2,000, the amount that management expects to receive for the asset. The total amount of depreciation a company records each fiscal period is the sum of the amounts recorded for all of its individual plant assets. Therefore, a company prepares a depreciation schedule for each major type of plant asset.

Because depreciation is an estimation process, the amounts may change over time. For example, at the end of 2005, Mom's Cookie Company's managers may decide that they will be able to use the equipment for three more years (for a total life of five years), at which time the equipment will have a residual value of $2,000. As a result of this change in estimate, the equipment depreciation schedule would be revised as shown in Exhibit 3.

Depreciation expense for 2006 through 2008 is determined as follows:

Revised depreciation expense = (book value − residual value) ÷ estimated useful life
$8,000 = ($26,000 − $2,000) ÷ 3 years

A change in estimate affects depreciation in periods after the change is made. Amounts recorded in previous periods are not revised.

Exhibit 3
Revised Straight-Line
Depreciation Schedule

Year	Beginning Book Value	Depreciation Expense	Accumulated Depreciation	Ending Book Value
2004	$50,000	$12,000	$12,000	$38,000
2005	38,000	12,000	24,000	26,000
*2006	26,000	8,000	32,000	18,000
*2007	18,000	8,000	40,000	10,000
*2008	10,000	8,000	48,000	2,000

*Changed from Exhibit 2.

Straight-line depreciation is easy to compute and provides a reasonable estimate of the consumption of most plant assets. Consequently, it is the most commonly used method for determining depreciation in financial reports of major corporations.

Depreciation Methods Used by Major U.S. Corporations for Financial Reporting

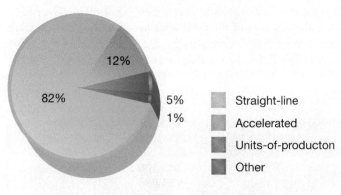

12%
82%
5%
1%

▢ Straight-line
▢ Accelerated
▢ Units-of-producton
▢ Other

(Data source: AICPA, Accounting Trends and Techniques, 2001)

Accelerated Depreciation. Accelerated depreciation allocates more depreciation expense to the earlier years of an asset's estimated life than to the later years. Several methods of computing accelerated depreciation are commonly used. One frequently used method is referred to as double-declining-balance. Double-declining-balance depreciation allocates to depreciation expense twice the straight-line rate times the book value of an asset. The straight-line rate is 1 divided by the estimated useful life of the asset. Thus, an asset with a life of four years has a straight-line rate of 1/4, or 25%. Double this rate would be 2/4, or 50%.

To illustrate, if Mom's Cookie Company used double-declining-balance depreciation for the equipment purchased at the beginning of 2004, it would compute depreciation for each year of the life of the asset as shown below.

Double-declining-balance depreciation expense = book value × (2 ÷ expected useful life)

The asset cannot be depreciated below its residual value, which is $2,000. Thus, the amount of depreciation expense recorded in 2007, the last year of the equipment's life, is $4,250 ($6,250 − $2,000), the amount needed to fully depreciate the asset, leaving a book value equal to the residual value.

Year	Depreciation Expense	=	Book Value	×	Depreciation Rate
2004	$25,000		$50,000		2/4
2005	12,500		25,000		2/4
2006	6,250		12,500		2/4
2007	4,250				

Note that book value, not cost, is used and the residual value is not subtracted in the calculation. For example, at the beginning of 2004, the original cost of $50,000 equals the book value. At the beginning of 2005, the book value is now $25,000 ($50,000 cost minus $25,000 accumulated depreciation).

Mom's Cookie Company should record $48,000 of depreciation over the life of the asset, just as when straight-line depreciation is used. The depreciation method does not change the total amount of depreciation recorded. It changes the amount allocated to each fiscal year.

Exhibit 4 provides a depreciation schedule for the equipment, assuming double-declining-balance depreciation.

Exhibit 4
Double-Declining-Balance Depreciation Schedule

Year	Beginning Book Value	Depreciation Expense	Accumulated Depreciation	Ending Book Value
2004	$50,000	$25,000	$25,000	$25,000
2005	25,000	12,500	37,500	12,500
2006	12,500	6,250	43,750	6,250
2007	6,250	4,250	48,000	2,000*

*The residual value

USING EXCEL

For Calculating Depreciation

SPREADSHEET

A spreadsheet contains functions for calculating depreciation. In Excel, the functions can be selected by clicking on the Function f_x button and selecting the Financial category. The SLN function calculates straight-line depreciation, and the DDB function calculates double-declining-balance depreciation. Double-clicking on the function name brings up a dialog box. Enter the cost, salvage value, and life of the asset. The life should be expressed in the appropriate time units (years or months for example), depending on the period for which depreciation expense is being calculated. For double-declining-balance depreciation, the period for which the depreciation is being calculated must also be entered. The period is a number relative to the beginning of the asset's life. For example, if depreciation is being calculated on an annual basis, the first year of an asset's life would be 1, the second year 2, and so forth. A dialog box appears below showing the data for an asset with a cost of $10,000, a salvage value of $1,000, and a life of five years. The calculation is for the first year of the asset's useful life (Period = 1). If the function were selected from cell A1, the cell would report the amount calculated by the function of $4,000.

DDB	▼ ✕ ✓ =	= DDB(10000,1000,5,1)

DDB

Cost	10000	▦	= 10000
Salvage	1000	▦	= 1000
Life	5	▦	= 5
Period	1	▦	= 1
Factor		▦	= number

= 4000

Returns the depreciation of an asset for a specified period using the double-declining balance method or some other method you specify.

Period is the period for which you want to calculate the depreciation. Period must use the same units as Life.

[?]   Formula result = 4000   OK   Cancel

Reasons for Using Accelerated Depreciation. Accelerated depreciation methods are used for two primary reasons. In some cases, an asset is more useful earlier in its life than later, and the useful life may be difficult to estimate. For example, computer equipment becomes obsolete quickly. Accordingly, a company may accelerate the depreciation of computer equipment to ensure that most of the cost has been depreciated when the equipment is replaced.

A second, and more common, reason for using accelerated depreciation is for tax purposes. Depreciation expense is deductible in computing taxable income and income taxes. For example, assume that in 2004, Mom's Cookie Company reported $100,000 of income before depreciation and taxes. Exhibit 5 describes the effects on Mom's Cookie Company's income taxes of using straight-line and accelerated depreciation.

Exhibit 5

Comparison of Straight-Line and Accelerated Depreciation Methods in 2004

	Straight-Line	Accelerated
Income before depreciation and taxes	$100,000	$100,000
Depreciation expense	12,000	25,000
Pretax income	88,000	75,000
Income taxes (35%)	30,800	26,250
Net income	$ 57,200	$ 48,750

In 2004, straight-line depreciation expense (from Exhibit 2) results in higher pretax income, income taxes, and net income. Because double-declining-balance depreciation expense (from Exhibit 4) is higher in the earlier years, the taxable (pretax) income, income taxes, and net income are lower than under the straight-line method. For tax purposes, a company prefers to report lower pretax income and pay lower income taxes. Therefore, companies commonly use accelerated depreciation methods for tax purposes as a way of postponing the tax obligation. The specific method used depends on income tax regulations. Companies typically report the maximum amount of depreciation permitted by law for tax purposes. Larger amounts of depreciation expense reduce tax payments in the current fiscal period, thereby reducing cash outflows for tax purposes. By reducing its cash outflows, a company preserves more of its cash for other purposes.

For financial reporting purposes, companies prefer to report higher amounts of net income in the earlier years. Therefore, they generally use straight-line depreciation in preparing their financial statements. Companies may use straight-line depreciation when preparing their financial statements and accelerated depreciation when preparing their tax returns. Small companies often use accelerated depreciation methods for both purposes to avoid the need for two sets of accounting records. Note that *over the life of the asset*, the same total amount of depreciation expense is recognized under the straight-line method as under the accelerated methods. Thus, the same amount of total income tax is paid under those methods.

Companies disclose the accounting methods they use for recording and depreciating their plant assets in notes to their financial statements. These notes identify the depreciation method used and provide other relevant information.

Case In Point

Disclosure of Depreciation Policy

In its 2002 annual report, Krispy Kreme provided the following description of its depreciation policy:

Property and equipment are stated at cost less accumulated depreciation. Major renewals and betterments are charged to the property accounts while replacements, maintenance, and repairs which do not improve or extend the lives of the respective assets are expensed currently. Interest is capitalized on major capital expenditures during the period of construction.

Depreciation of property and equipment is provided on the straight-line method over the estimated useful lives: Buildings—15 to 35 years; Machinery and equipment—3 to 15 years; Leasehold improvements—lesser of useful lives of assets or lease term.

The difference between straight-line and accelerated depreciation is a major source of deferred taxes. **Deferred taxes** are taxes that a company would owe if it used the same methods for preparing its tax return that it used for preparing its financial statements. For example, using the Exhibit 5 information, Mom's Cookie Company would record its taxes for 2004 as:

| | | ASSETS | | = | LIABILITIES | + | OWNERS' EQUITY | |
| | | Cash | Other Assets | | | | Contributed Capital | Retained Earnings |
Date	Accounts							
Dec. 31, 2004	Income Tax Expense							−30,800
	Income Tax Payable				26,250			
	Deferred Tax Liability				4,550			

Income tax payable is the amount Mom's Cookie Company owes based on its tax return. Income tax expense is the amount of tax it would owe if straight-line depreciation had been used for tax purposes. The difference between the payable and the expense is recorded as Deferred Taxes. Deferred taxes are the taxes Mom's Cookie Company has deferred (postponed) to some future period by using accelerated depreciation for tax purposes. Because the company expects to pay these taxes in the future, they are recorded as a long-term liability. Companies frequently report deferred taxes as long-term liabilities on their balance sheets.

LEARNING NOTE

Occasionally, a company will record a deferred tax charge. This charge appears on the balance sheet as a long-term asset. It represents a prepayment of taxes that the company will owe in the future.

Units-of-Production Depreciation. Some companies use the units-of-production method to depreciate production equipment and facilities across units of output. For example, suppose that at the beginning of 2005, Mom's Cookie Company purchased a truck to deliver goods to customers. The truck cost $30,000. Management expects the useful life of the truck to be 100,000 miles, at which time it will be sold for $10,000, and a new truck will be acquired. Rather than depreciating the truck over time, it will be depreciated based on mileage. A depreciation rate per mile for the truck can be computed as follows:

Units-of-production depreciation rate = (cost − residual value) ÷ estimated units
$0.20 per mile = ($30,000 − $10,000) ÷ 100,000 miles

If the truck were driven 12,000 miles in 2005, Mom's Cookie Company would record depreciation expense of $2,400 (12,000 miles × $0.20 per mile).

Companies often use the units-of-production method for production equipment. Also, it often is used by transportation and airline companies for depreciating trucks, automobiles, and airplanes.

Book and Market Value of Plant Assets. The book value of plant assets is the cost of the assets less accumulated depreciation. This amount is not an indication of the market value of the assets, which may be much higher than the book value in some cases. For example, land and buildings purchased by a company often increase in value over time because of inflation, increased demand for property, and increased construction costs. This difference between the market and book value of assets is an unrecorded asset. The market value of a company's stock is likely to include investors' estimates of the value of this unrecorded asset.

Disposing of Plant Assets

To dispose of plant assets—by retiring or selling them—a company must eliminate their cost and accumulated depreciation from its accounting records. For example, suppose that Mom's Cookie Company sells equipment on February 10, 2005. The equipment cost the company $20,000 when purchased. Accumulated depreciation on the equipment at the time it is sold is $14,000, and the company receives $8,000 for the equipment. It would record the sale as follows:

		ASSETS		=	LIABILITIES	+	OWNERS' EQUITY	
Date	**Accounts**	**Cash**	**Other Assets**				**Contributed Capital**	**Retained Earnings**
Feb. 10, 2005	Cash	8,000						
	Accumulated Depreciation		14,000					
	Equipment		−20,000					
	Gain on Asset Sale							2,000

This transaction eliminates the cost of the asset ($20,000) from Mom's Cookie Company's accounts. Also, it eliminates the accumulated depreciation taken on the asset ($14,000). The difference between the amount received ($8,000) and the book value of the asset at the time of the sale ($6,000 = $20,000 − $14,000) is recorded as a gain. This gain is reported as nonoperating income on the company's 2005 income statement. If the book value at the time of the sale had been greater than the amount received, Mom's Cookie Company would have recorded a Loss on Asset Sale.

1 SELF-STUDY PROBLEM

WebTUTOR Advantage

Banana Boat Company purchased equipment on January 1, 2004 at a cost of $400,000. The equipment had an expected life of three years and could be used to produce one million units of product. Its estimated residual value was $40,000. Income before depreciation and taxes in 2004 was $2 million. The company's tax rate was 35%.

Required

A. Prepare a depreciation schedule for the equipment for its three-year life, using straight-line and double-declining-balance depreciation methods.
B. Determine the amount of depreciation expense the company would record in 2004 if the units-of-production method were used and 300,000 units were produced.
C. Which of the three methods would result in the lowest tax liability for 2004?

The solution to Self-Study Problem 1 appears at the end of the chapter.

NATURAL RESOURCES

OBJECTIVE 3

Apply appropriate measurement rules to the purchase and use of natural resources.

Paper, petroleum, and mining companies, among others, invest in natural resources. They purchase or lease land that contains timber, oil, or minerals. The cost of the land primarily reflects those natural resources.

The amount a company reports for natural resources on its balance sheet is the cost of the asset less depletion. *Depletion* **is the systematic allocation of the cost of natural resources to the periods that benefit from their use.** Assume that Silicon Company bought land containing minerals on April 1, 2004, for $8 million. The company would record the transaction as follows:

		ASSETS		=	LIABILITIES	+	OWNERS' EQUITY	
Date	Accounts	Cash	Other Assets				Contributed Capital	Retained Earnings
Apr. 1, 2004	Mineral Rights Cash	−8,000,000	8,000,000					

Assume that the company estimated that the land contained 80,000 tons of minerals when it was purchased. The estimated cost per ton was $100 ($8,000,000 ÷ 80,000 tons). In 2004, Silicon mined the land and removed 16,000 tons of the minerals. These minerals then were sold to customers. The value of the asset consumed during 2004, $1.6 million ($100 × 16,000 tons), would be recorded in this way:

		ASSETS		=	LIABILITIES	+	OWNERS' EQUITY	
Date	Accounts	Cash	Other Assets				Contributed Capital	Retained Earnings
Dec. 31, 2004	Cost of Goods Sold Mineral Rights	−1,600,000						−1,600,000

The amount reported by Silicon on its 2004 balance sheet for Mineral Rights would be $6,400,000 ($8,000,000 cost − $1,600,000 accumulated depletion). The amount of the asset reported would decrease each year as additional minerals are mined and accumulated depletion increases.

This example assumes that the land has no real value apart from the value of the mineral deposits. If the land does have other value, that value would be recorded as a separate asset. Only the value of the minerals would be depleted.

GAAP require that companies report natural resources at their book value (cost − accumulated depletion). The market value of natural resources is not reported on the financial statements, although some companies disclose information about the current value of those assets in notes to their financial statements. Remember that market value can be much higher than book value. Companies that own oil and timber reserves, for example, have experienced dramatic increases in the market value of those resources in recent years because of rising demand. The market value of a company's stock reflects the unrecorded value of those assets.

LONG-TERM AND SHORT-TERM INVESTMENTS

OBJECTIVE 4

Apply appropriate measurement rules to the purchase, valuation, and sale of long-term and short-term investments.

This section examines accounting for investments in debt and equity securities. It considers transactions and reporting issues for both short-term and long-term investments.

Types of Securities

Companies often invest in securities issued by other organizations. Securities include common and preferred stocks, bonds, certificates of deposit, and notes. Stocks are referred to as equity securities. Other securities are debt securities. If securities are readily exchangeable for cash (can be sold easily) they are **marketable securities**. A company never reports its own debt or equity securities as assets. Instead, those securities are reported as liabilities (debt) and stockholders' equity (equity securities).

Companies invest in marketable securities for many reasons. When there is a temporary surplus of cash, the cash is invested on a short-term basis to earn a return until cash is needed. Long-term investments meet different needs. Some are used to fund the future repurchase or repayment of a company's own debt or to provide for future retirement and other employee benefits. Often, investments in other companies are made to gain access to markets, resources, and technology controlled by these companies.

GAAP differentiate between two types of investments:

(1) investments that give the investor significant influence or control over the company issuing the securities, and
(2) investments that do not.

Investments That Yield Significant Influence or Control. These investments are always reported as a long-term asset. A company acquires significant influence over another company when it holds a large block of the second company's voting securities. Generally, this means 20% to 50% of the outstanding shares of common stock. When significant influence occurs, the equity method is used. A company acquires control over another firm by holding a very large block (usually a majority) of its voting securities. In this situation, the consolidation method is used. The equity and consolidation methods are discussed in the final section of this chapter.

Investments That Do Not Yield Significant Influence or Control. GAAP identify three categories of investments that do not yield significant influence or control. Each is treated differently in the financial statements. The three categories are as follows:

1. **Held-to-maturity securities** are investments in debt securities that the investor has the intent and ability to hold until the debt's maturity date. They are reported on the balance sheet as a long-term asset except during the year just prior to maturity when they should be reported as a current asset.
2. **Trading securities** are investments in either debt or equity securities that a company buys and sells on a regular basis. They are reported on the balance sheet under current assets.
3. **Available-for-sale securities** are investments in securities that a company could sell but that it does not trade regularly. These investments are reported as a current asset or noncurrent asset, depending on management's expectation regarding when the investments will be sold.

All investments in securities are recorded initially at cost. Cost includes brokerage commissions, fees, and taxes. (For illustrative purposes in this chapter, these additional costs are assumed to be zero.) Held-to-maturity securities (always debt securities) are reported on the balance sheet at **amortized cost**: original cost adjusted for amortization of premium or discount. **Trading securities and available-for-sale securities are reported on the balance sheet at current market value.** This is referred to as *mark-to-market accounting*.

Held-To-Maturity Securities

Only debt securities may fall into this category. To illustrate, assume that Big Foods Corporation bought Mom's Cookie Company bonds on January 1, 2005. Big Foods paid $208,201 for the bonds which mature in 2009 at their face value of $200,000. The bonds pay annual interest of 8%. Interest payments are made on December 31. Big Foods intends to hold these bonds long-term and records the purchase of this investment as follows:

Date	Accounts	ASSETS		=	LIABILITIES	+	OWNERS' EQUITY	
		Cash	Other Assets				Contributed Capital	Retained Earnings
Jan. 1, 2005	Long-Term Investment		208,201					
	Cash	−208,201						

On December 31, 2005, Big Foods receives its first interest payment. The amount received is $16,000 (8% × $200,000 face value). Recall from our discussion in Chapter F9 that when bonds are issued at a price different from par, the premium or discount must be amortized. The interest earned each period is adjusted as the premium or discount is amortized over the life of the bonds. Because Big Foods paid $208,201 for Mom's Cookie Company's bonds, it would amortize the $8,201 premium over the life of the bonds. Big Foods has determined that $1,426 of premium should be amortized upon receipt of the first interest payment. It would record the amortization along with the interest earned as follows:

Date	Accounts	ASSETS		=	LIABILITIES	+	OWNERS' EQUITY	
		Cash	Other Assets				Contributed Capital	Retained Earnings
Dec. 31, 2005	Cash	16,000						
	Long-Term Investment		−1,426					
	Interest Income							14,574

Cash received ($16,000) less the amortization ($1,426) during the period is reported as interest income for the period ($14,574). Assume Big Foods plans to hold the bonds until they mature in 2009. The bonds would be classified as held-to-maturity securities. At the end of its 2005 fiscal year, Big Foods must report its investment on the balance sheet at amortized cost of $206,775 ($208,201 cost − $1,426 amortization).

Trading Securities and Available-for-Sale Securities—Investments in Debt

If, instead, the bonds are held as trading securities or available-for-sale securities, they will be reported on the balance sheet at current market value. When the investment's amortized cost is different from its current market value, an unrealized holding gain or loss is recognized. The holding gain or holding loss is unrealized because actual sale of the investment has not yet occurred. Unrealized holding gains or losses are an indication of the gain or loss that would occur if the investment were sold at the balance sheet date.

To illustrate, assume the December 31, 2005 market price of Mom's Cookie Company bonds owned by Big Foods is $205,000. An adjusting entry is needed to update the balance in the long-term investment account from amortized cost of $206,775 ($208,201 − $1,426) to current market value of $205,000. That entry would appear as follows:

| Date | Accounts | ASSETS | | = | LIABILITIES | + | OWNERS' EQUITY | |
		Cash	Other Assets				Contributed Capital	Retained Earnings
Dec. 31, 2005	Unrealized Holding Loss* Long-Term Investment		−1,775				−1,775*	

*Amortized cost ($206,775) − current market value ($205,000) = $1,775 unrealized holding loss. This is included as part of Other Comprehensive Income in the stockholders' equity section of the balance sheet.

The only difference in accounting for trading securities and available-for-sale securities is in how the Unrealized Holding Loss (or Gain) is reported in the financial statements. Trading securities are expected to be sold in the near future. Therefore, **for trading securities, the unrealized holding gain or loss is reported on the income statement as part of net income.** This gives an early signal to readers as to the likely outcome when the securities are sold. **Available-for-sale securities** are not expected to be sold in the near future. Therefore, **the unrealized holding gain or loss is reported as part of Other Comprehensive Income in the stockholders' equity section of the balance sheet.**

Trading Securities and Available-for-Sale Securities—Investments in Equity

The accounting for trading securities and available-for-sale securities is very similar. Both are recorded initially at cost and reported on the balance sheet at current market value. Assume that Big Foods Corporation purchased 10,000 shares of Mom's Cookie Company common stock for $12 per share on October 1, 2005. Assume these are available-for-sale securities that are not expected to be sold anytime soon. Big Foods would record the purchase as follows:

| Date | Accounts | ASSETS | | = | LIABILITIES | + | OWNERS' EQUITY | |
		Cash	Other Assets				Contributed Capital	Retained Earnings
Oct. 1, 2005	Long-Term Investment Cash	−120,000	120,000					

On December 31, 2005, the closing market price of Mom's Cookie Company stock was $14 per share. Thus, the value of Big Foods' investment has increased by $20,000 [($14 − $12) × 10,000 shares)]. Big Foods would record the increase in market value as follows:

| Date | Accounts | ASSETS | | = | LIABILITIES | + | OWNERS' EQUITY | |
		Cash	Other Assets				Contributed Capital	Retained Earnings
Dec. 31, 2005	Long-Term Investment Unrealized Holding Gain*		20,000				20,000*	

*This is included as part of Other Comprehensive Income in the stockholders' equity section of the balance sheet.

Because these are available-for-sale securities, the Unrealized Holding Gain is reported on the balance sheet as a component of stockholders' equity. It is not part of net income. If the securities had been trading securities, the Unrealized Holding Gain would be reported on the income statement as part of net income. Either way, the Long-Term Investment will be reported on the balance sheet at current market value.

Big Foods' December 31, 2005 financial statements will combine the long-term investments and unrealized holding gain (or loss) accounts for both of its long-term investments. Big Foods owns bonds with a market value of $205,000 and stock with a market value of $140,000. Therefore, assuming both securities are available-for-sale, Big Foods will report its investments as shown in Exhibit 6.

Exhibit 6

Balance Sheet Excerpts and Supporting Computations for Big Foods Corporation for Long-Term Investments

Balance Sheet
December 31, 2005

Assets		Stockholders' equity	
Long-term investments	$345,000	Other comprehensive income	$18,225

Computations

Cost of bonds	$208,201	Unrealized holding loss on	
Amortization of premium	(1,426)	bonds	$ (1,775)
Unrealized holding loss	(1,775)	Unrealized holding gain on	
Cost of stock	120,000	stock	20,000
Unrealized holding gain	20,000	Net unrealized holding gain	$18,225
Long-term investments	$345,000		

If the investments were trading securities, the only difference would be that the $18,225 unrealized holding gain ($20,000 − $1,775) would be reported on the income statement rather than as part of other comprehensive income. In either case, Big Foods also would disclose the cost of its long-term investments ($328,201 = $208,201 for bonds + $120,000 for stock) on the balance sheet or in a note.

When Big Foods sells an investment, it records a realized gain or loss that is reported in computing net income on its income statement. For example, assume Big Foods' management changes its mind and sells Mom's Cookie Company stock on April 20, 2006, at a price of $17 per share. Big Foods has earned $50,000 on its investment [($17 − $12) × 10,000 shares]. It records the transaction as follows:

		ASSETS		=	LIABILITIES	+	OWNERS' EQUITY	
Date	Accounts	Cash	Other Assets				Contributed Capital	Retained Earnings
Apr. 20, 2006	Cash	170,000						
	Unrealized Holding Gain*						−20,000*	
	Long-Term Investment		−140,000					
	Investment Income							50,000

*This is included as part of Other Comprehensive Income in the stockholders' equity section of the balance sheet.

This transaction records the realized gain ($50,000) and eliminates the long-term investment in stock and unrealized holding gain amounts that were recorded during 2005. The long-term investment amount of $140,000 is the cost ($120,000) plus the increase in market value that was added to the account on December 31, 2005 ($20,000). The realized gain ($50,000) would be reported by Big Foods as nonoperating income on its income statement for 2006. This is the amount Big Foods actually earned from its investment in Mom's Cookie Company stock.

As noted previously, the rules described above do not apply when a company owns a significant or controlling interest in another company. A company is considered by GAAP to have significant influence over another company when it owns 20% to 50% of the other company's common stock. This level of ownership suggests that the investor can influence management decisions of the issuing company. Therefore, special accounting rules, known as the **equity method**, are used to account for these investments. These rules are summarized in the appendix to this chapter.

If a company owns more than 50% of the common stock of another corporation, it controls the other corporation. In this situation, the investor is the parent corporation and the issuer of the stock is a subsidiary of the parent. The parent includes the subsidiary as part of its consolidated financial statements. That is, the financial statements of the parent treat the parent and subsidiary corporations as though they were one company. A summary of accounting for consolidations appears at the end of this chapter.

LEARNING NOTE

Occasionally a firm will acquire nonmarketable securities. This means there is no active market for the security and it cannot readily be converted to cash. GAAP require the cost method be used to account for these investments. Under the cost method, the investment is recorded at cost and no further adjustments are made to the investment account. Dividends or interest received on such an investment are recorded as Investment Income.

Short-Term Investments

Investments in short-term marketable securities are accounted for at market value. Investments are classified as short-term if management expects to sell the investments during the coming fiscal year. Short-term investments are reported as current assets. Therefore, they are separated from long-term investments on the balance sheet. The accounting procedures to record the purchase price and end-of-period adjustment for current market price are identical to those for long-term investments.

Exhibit 7 summarizes the appropriate treatment for investments in securities.

Exhibit 7
Investments in Marketable Securities

Type of Investment	Recorded	Accounting Method	Treatment of Unrealized Holding Gain (Loss)
Acquires significant influence	At cost	Equity	none
Acquires control	At cost	Consolidation	none
Held-to-maturity	At cost	Amortized cost	none
Trading	At cost	Mark to market	Reported on income statement as Other Income
Available-for-sale	At cost	Mark to market	Report on balance sheet in Other Comprehensive Income

2 SELF-STUDY PROBLEM

WebTUTOR Advantage

Delta Can Company purchased 10,000 shares of Flatland Aluminum Company's common stock on June 1, 2004. Delta paid $230,000 for the stock. On December 1, 2004, Delta received a dividend check from Flatland for $25,000. The market value of Flatland's stock on December 31, 2004, the end of Delta's fiscal year, was $27 per share. On December 1, 2005, Delta received a dividend check from Flatland for $30,000. The market value of Flatland's stock on December 31, 2005, was $26 per share. Delta sold its investment in Flatland on March 5, 2006, for $245,000. Delta owned 5% of Flatland's common stock and had planned to keep its investment long term.

Required

A. Using the format presented in this chapter, record all transactions for Delta involving its investment in Flatland and explain the purpose of each transaction.
B. Calculate the amounts Delta would report on its 2004 and 2005 balance sheets for its investment in Flatland.

The solution to Self-Study Problem 2 appears at the end of the chapter.

INTANGIBLE ASSETS

OBJECTIVE 5

Explain accounting issues associated with intangible and other long-term assets.

INTERNATIONAL

Intangible assets include legal rights, such as copyrights, patents, brand names, and trademarks that a company owns. The purchase price and/or legal fees associated with acquiring those rights are recorded as assets and, with the exception of goodwill, are amortized over the life of the assets, usually on a straight-line basis.

GAAP require that intangibles other than goodwill be amortized over a period of 40 years or less. (The longer the amortization period, the lower the expense recognized each year.) A company that purchases intangible assets for $1 million and amortizes those assets over 40 years would recognize $25,000 of amortization expense each year.

U.S. GAAP do not allow companies to report the estimated market value of their brand names, trademarks, and other intangibles as part of their assets. Only the costs associated with those items can be reported as assets on the balance sheet. Nevertheless, brand names and trademarks can be among a corporation's most valuable resources. For example, the **Coca-Cola** brand name has been estimated at a value of more than $25 billion. Many companies would report much higher asset and stockholders' equity amounts if they could include the market value of intangible assets. Great Britain and certain other countries allow corporations to report the estimated market value of intangible assets, which is why some British companies report higher asset and equity values than their U.S. counterparts.

An intangible asset reported by many companies is goodwill. *Goodwill* **is the excess of the purchase price of a company over the fair market value of its net assets** (assets − liabilities). To illustrate, assume that Big Foods Corporation purchased Value-Right Company on January 1, 2005, for $5 million. As part of the purchase negotiation, Value-Right Company's assets and liabilities were appraised and were determined to have current market values of $8 million and $3.5 million, respectively. Accordingly, the purchase resulted in Big Foods' recognizing $500,000 of goodwill:

Market value of Value-Right Company assets	$8,000,000
Market value of Value-Right Company liabilities	3,500,000
Market value of Value-Right Company net assets	$4,500,000
Amount paid by Big Foods Corporation	$5,000,000
Market value of Value-Right Company net assets	4,500,000
Goodwill (excess of amount paid over market value)	$ 500,000

Goodwill is common when one company purchases another company. Often the amount paid is greater than the value of identifiable assets. The purchaser is buying a company, not individual assets. The company as a whole may have more value than the sum of its assets because it is an established business. Its managers, employees, customers, suppliers, brand recognition, and other components add value that is not recognized on the balance sheet. Accordingly, goodwill is recorded as an indication of this value.

Goodwill remains on a company's balance sheet at cost unless the value of the goodwill is impaired. Goodwill is impaired when it becomes apparent the investment is less valuable than the purchaser originally expected. The balance of the goodwill account should be written down, and a loss should be recognized for the amount of the impairment.

OTHER LONG-TERM ASSETS

Long-term assets that are not included in one of the other primary categories (plant assets, long-term investments, or intangible assets) are considered other long-term assets.

An example of this type of asset is deferred charges. *Deferred charges* **are the assets that result when a company prepays expenses that produce long-term benefits.** Deferred charges typically are amortized over future periods. Start-up costs—the costs of the legal fees, support services, and advertising necessary to start a new business, division, or project—often are capitalized and reported as deferred charges. These costs are recorded as Organizational Costs or a similar asset account.

Certain other assets do not fit into standard asset categories. For example, plant assets that a company has removed from service and is trying to sell are listed as other assets, not as plant assets.

Some assets are specific to an industry or company—for example, software development costs in the computer industry. A description of those assets often is provided in the notes to the financial statements.

Most assets are recorded at cost when they are purchased. This cost is expensed over the life of the asset as the asset is consumed or as its value declines. When an asset is sold, a gain or loss equal to the difference between the book value of the asset and its selling price is recognized.

FINANCIAL REPORTING OF INVESTING ACTIVITIES

OBJECTIVE 6

Summarize the effects of investing activities on a company's financial statements.

Investing activities affect the balance sheet, income statement, and statement of cash flows as described in Exhibit 8. Long-term assets (items a through d) appear on the balance sheet. The accumulated amount of holding gains and losses (item e) appears as an adjustment to stockholders' equity.

The income statement is affected by depreciation and amortization expense (item f), interest income (item g), and gains and losses from the sale of plant assets, long-term investments, and other long-term assets (item h).

Both the operating activities and the investing activities sections of the statement of cash flows are affected by investing activities. Depreciation and amortization expense (item i) is added to net income in computing operating cash flow using the indirect method. These are noncash expenses. Also, in computing operating cash flows, gains from the sale of long-term assets are subtracted and losses are added (item j). All cash flows associated with the sale of long-term assets are included in investing activities (items k, l, and m). Therefore, in terms of the operating activities section, the gain or loss is treated as a noncash item so that it is not included twice. Gains do not increase operating cash flows and losses do not reduce operating cash flows.

Cash received from the sale of long-term assets (items k, l, and m) and cash paid for long-term assets (items n, o, and p) are reported as investing activities. The total of these cash outflows and inflows is net cash from (for) investing activities (item q).

Exhibit 9 contains the investing activities section of Mom's Cookie Company's statement of cash flows for 2005. These amounts help explain changes in the company's long-term assets as presented on its balance sheet (Exhibit 1). Though the numbers on the cash flow statement do not always explain all changes in long-term assets, they should explain most of these changes. Some balance sheet changes are associated with noncash transactions. However, most changes in long-term assets involve the receipt or payment of cash and are reported in the investing activities section of the statement of cash flows.

Exhibit 8 Financial Statement Presentation of Investing Activities

Balance Sheet		**Income Statement**
	Assets			Operating revenues
	Current assets			Operating expenses, except depreciation
(a)	**Long-term investments**			and amortization expense
(b)	**Property, plant, and equipment**		(f)	**Depreciation and amortization expense**
(c)	**Intangible assets**			Operating income
(d)	**Other assets**			Interest expense
	Liabilities		(g)	**Interest income**
	Stockholders' Equity		(h)	**Gains or (losses) from sale**
	Common stock			**of long-term assets**
	Retained earnings			Pretax income
(e)	**Net holding gains (losses)**			Income taxes
				Net income

Statement of Cash Flows
  Cash flow from operating activities:
  Net income
(i) **Add depreciation and amortization expense**
(j) **(Subtract gains) add losses from sale of long-term assets**
  Other adjustments
  Net cash flow from operating activities
  Cash flow from (for) investing activities:
(k) **Sale of property, plant, and equipment**
(l) **Sale of investments**
(m) **Other (purchases) or sales of long-term assets**
(n) **(Capital expenditures)**
(o) **(Purchase of investments)**
(p) **(Acquisitions)**
(q) **Net cash flow from (for) investing activities**

Exhibit 9

Investing Activities from Mom's Cookie Company's Statement of Cash Flows

Cash flow from (for) investing activities:	
Purchase of property and equipment	$(365,000)
Sale of property and equipment	8,000
Purchase of investments	(6,000)
Sale of investments	2,000
Net cash flow for investing activities	$(361,000)

3 SELF-STUDY PROBLEM

Silicon Company reported the following transactions for the year ended December 31, 2004:

WebTUTOR Advantage

- Sale of plant assets with a book value of $22,000 for $16,000, reporting a loss of $6,000
- Sale of securities with a book value of $10,000 for $14,000, reporting a gain of $4,000
- Depreciation and amortization expense of $8,000
- Interest and dividends from investments of $2,000
- Acquisitions of plant assets for $35,000
- Acquisitions of long-term investments for $10,000
- Net income of $50,000

Required Prepare the operating and investing sections of Silicon's cash flow statement, assuming that no other activities affected those sections. You can assume that Silicon received cash for the interest and dividend income in 2004.

The solution to Self-Study Problem 3 appears at the end of the chapter.

OTHER INVESTMENT ISSUES

Companies, especially large corporations, often own significant interests in other companies. As a general rule, if a company owns 20% to 50% of the common stock of another company, it is considered by GAAP to have *significant influence* over that company. If a company owns more than 50% of another company, it owns a *controlling interest* in the company. The following sections summarize accounting rules for these situations.

Equity Method

When one company owns 20% to 50% of the common stock of another company, it normally uses the equity method to account for its investment. The investment is recorded at cost. For example, assume that Big Foods Corporation purchased 30,000 shares of Little Market Corporation's 100,000 shares of common stock at a price of $20 per share on January 1, 2004. Big Foods Corporation would record the purchase as follows:

| Date | Accounts | ASSETS | | = | LIABILITIES | + | OWNERS' EQUITY | |
		Cash	Other Assets				Contributed Capital	Retained Earnings
Jan. 1, 2004	Long-Term Investment		600,000					
	Cash	−600,000						

At the end of the 2004 fiscal year, Little Market reported a net income of $500,000 and paid dividends of $200,000. Under the equity method, Big Foods records 30% (the percentage of stock it owns) of Little Market's net income as investment income:

| Date | Accounts | ASSETS | | = | LIABILITIES | + | OWNERS' EQUITY | |
		Cash	Other Assets				Contributed Capital	Retained Earnings
Dec. 31, 2004	Long-Term Investment		150,000					
	Investment Income							150,000

Little Market's net income increases its retained earnings. Therefore, the book value of Little Market increases by $500,000. Big Foods recognizes 30% of this increase as an increase in the value of its investment.

Dividends paid by Little Market reduce Little Market's retained earnings and book value. Therefore, Big Foods recognizes 30% of this decrease as a decrease in the value of its investment:

		ASSETS		=	LIABILITIES	+	OWNERS' EQUITY	
Date	Accounts	Cash	Other Assets				Contributed Capital	Retained Earnings
Dec. 31, 2004	Cash	60,000						
	Long-Term Investment		−60,000					

In this transaction, Big Foods receives cash from Little Market, but the value of Big Foods' investment decreases in proportion to the decrease in Little Market's retained earnings.

The equity method is appropriately named because it adjusts the investment account of the investor in proportion to changes in the book value of the investee's stockholders' equity. It ignores changes in market value. Investments that use the equity method often are listed separately from other investments on a company's balance sheet or are described in a note to the financial statements. Also, income from equity method investments often is separated from other income on a company's income statement. It is labeled *equity income* or a similar title. Investment income is a nonoperating-income item for most companies.

Consolidations

If a corporation owns more than 50% of the common stock of another company, it normally reports consolidated financial statements. These statements are issued by the parent corporation and include the financial activities of the parent and its subsidiaries. The process of consolidating a parent and its subsidiaries can be complex. Account balances for the parent and all of its subsidiaries are combined. Any intercompany transactions, such as sales by a subsidiary to the parent or a loan from the parent to the subsidiary, are eliminated. Only transactions of the parent and its subsidiaries with external parties are reported in the consolidated statements.

If the parent corporation does not own 100% of the common stock of a subsidiary, the portion that the parent does not own is known as **minority interest** or **noncontrolling interest**. The portion of a subsidiary's stockholders' equity that belongs to noncontrolling stockholders (owners other than the parent) is reported on the consolidated balance sheet as noncontrolling interest. This amount often appears after liabilities and before stockholders' equity. The portion of a subsidiary's net income that belongs to noncontrolling stockholders is reported on the consolidated income statement as noncontrolling interest in income. This amount is subtracted in determining the parent's consolidated net income because it is the portion of the subsidiary's net income not earned by the parent.

REVIEW

SUMMARY of IMPORTANT CONCEPTS

1. Investing activities involve the acquisition, use, and disposal of long-term assets.
    a. Long-term investments are investments in stocks and bonds of other companies that managers expect to hold for longer than the coming fiscal year.
    b. Property, plant, and equipment are tangible assets used in a company's production and selling activities.
    c. Intangible assets are legal rights that a company has exclusive use of to create future profits.
    d. Other long-term assets are miscellaneous items that are not included in another category (e.g., property held for disposal).

2. Investments in plant assets are the most important long-term assets for most companies.
   a. Plant assets are recorded at cost when they are acquired.
   b. Plant assets are depreciated over their estimated useful lives.
      (1) Straight-line depreciation is used for financial reporting by most companies.
      (2) Accelerated depreciation methods often are used for computing taxable income.
      (3) Units-of-production depreciation may be used for machinery and equipment that has an estimated life in terms of units of activity rather than time.
   c. Plant assets are reported on the balance sheet at their book value (cost minus accumulated depreciation).
   d. When plant assets are sold, a gain or loss equal to the difference between the book value and the sale price of the assets is recognized.

3. Natural resources are recorded at cost, and depletion expense is recorded as the resources are consumed.

4. Long-term and short-term investments involve investments in debt or equity securities of other companies.
   a. Investments in securities are recorded at cost.
   b. Interest income is recorded in the period earned and usually is reported as nonoperating income.
   c. Investments in debt securities are reported on the balance sheet at cost if the debt is to be held to maturity or at market value if it is not to be held to maturity.
   d. Investments in equity securities are reported at market value on the balance sheets of most companies.
   e. Holding gains or losses generally are reported as adjustments to stockholders' equity.
   f. Special accounting methods (the equity method and consolidation) are used when one company owns a significant interest (20% or more) in another company.

5. Intangible assets include legal rights, such as patents and copyrights, and goodwill.
   a. Intangible assets are recorded at cost and, except for goodwill, are amortized over their useful lives, not to exceed 40 years.
   b. Goodwill is the excess of the purchase price of a company over the market value of that company's net assets (assets minus liabilities).
   c. Goodwill is not amortized but is written down in value, and a loss is recognized, if its value is impaired.

6. Other long-term assets include deferred charges, plant assets held for sale, organization costs, and specialized assets that are not classified in one of the other asset categories.

7. Investing activities affect a company's balance sheet (particularly assets), income statement (depreciation and amortization expense, investment income, and gains and losses from sale of assets), and statement of cash flows (particularly the investing activities section).

8. As a general rule, special accounting methods are used when a company owns 20% or more of the common stock of another corporation.
   a. The equity method is used for investments of 20% to 50%.
   b. Consolidation is used when a company owns more than 50% of another company's common stock.

DEFINE   *TERMS and CONCEPTS DEFINED in this CHAPTER*

accelerated depreciation (F406)	mark-to-market accounting (F414)
capital expenditures (F406)	operating expenditures (F406)
deferred charges (F420)	straight-line depreciation (F406)
depletion (F412)	units-of-production depreciation (F406)
goodwill (F419)	

SELF-STUDY PROBLEM SOLUTIONS

SSP11-1 A. Straight-line depreciation schedule ($400,000 − $40,000) ÷ 3 years = $120,000 per year

Year	Beginning Book Value	Depreciation Expense	Accumulated Depreciation	Ending Book Value
2004	$400,000	$120,000	$120,000	$280,000
2005	280,000	120,000	240,000	160,000
2006	160,000	120,000	360,000	40,000

Double-declining-balance depreciation schedule ($400,000 × 2/3 = $266,667)
($133,333 × 2/3 = $88,889)

Year	Beginning Book Value	Depreciation Expense	Accumulated Depreciation	Ending Book Value
2004	$400,000	$266,667	$266,667	$133,333
2005	133,333	88,889	355,556	44,444
2006	44,444	4,444	360,000	40,000

B. Units-of-production depreciation rate = ($400,000 − $40,000) ÷ 1,000,000 units = $0.36 per unit. Depreciation expense for 2004 = 300,000 units × $0.36 = $108,000.

C.

	Straight-Line	Double-Declining-Balance	Units-of-Production
Income before depreciation and taxes	$2,000,000	$2,000,000	$2,000,000
Depreciation expense	120,000	266,667	108,000
Income before taxes	1,880,000	1,733,333	1,892,000
Income taxes (35%)	658,000	606,667	662,200
Net income	$1,222,000	$1,126,666	$1,229,800

Double-declining-balance results in the lowest income tax liability for 2004.

SSP11-2   A.

Date	Accounts	Cash	Other Assets	=	LIABILITIES	+	Contributed Capital	Retained Earnings
June 1, 2004	Long-Term Investment		230,000					
	Cash	−230,000						
Dec. 1, 2004	Cash	25,000						
	Investment Income							25,000
Dec. 31, 2004	Long-Term Investment		40,000					
	Unrealized Holding							
	Gain (Loss)*						40,000*	
Dec. 1, 2005	Cash	30,000						
	Investment Income							30,000
Dec. 31, 2005	Unrealized Holding							
	Gain (Loss)*						−10,000*	
	Long-Term Investment		−10,000					
Mar. 5, 2006	Cash	245,000						
	Unrealized Holding							
	Gain (Loss)*						−30,000*	
	Long-Term Investment		−260,000					
	Investment Income							15,000

*This is included as part of Other Comprehensive Income in the stockholders' equity section of the balance sheet.

The transaction of 6/1/04 records the investment at cost. The transactions of 12/1/04 and 12/1/05 recognize dividends received as realized investment income. This income is reported on the income statement in computing net income for each fiscal year. The transaction of 12/31/04 records the increase in market value of the investment. This increase is an unrealized holding gain; it is not included as part of net income because an actual sale of the investment has not occurred. The transaction of 12/31/05 records a decrease in market value that is an unrealized holding loss. The loss is not included in computing net income because a sale has not occurred. The transaction of 3/5/06 recognizes a gain on the sale of the investment. This gain is reported as part of net income because the investment has been sold. Realized income and gains (or losses) are recorded when resources are received or investments are sold. Holding gains and losses are recorded when the market value of investments changes during a fiscal period, but the investments have not been sold.

B.

	2004	2005
Cost of investment	$230,000	$230,000
Holding gain	40,000	40,000
Holding loss		(10,000)
Market value of investment	$270,000	$260,000

SSP11-3

Silicon Company
Statement of Cash Flows
For the Year Ended December 31, 2004

Cash flow from operating activities

Net income	$ 50,000
Adjustments for noncash items:	
Depreciation and amortization expense	8,000
Loss from sale of plant assets	6,000
Gain from sale of investments	(4,000)
Net cash flow from operating activities	$ 60,000
Cash flow for investing activities	
Capital expenditures	$(35,000)
Sale of plant assets	16,000
Purchase of investments	(10,000)
Sales of investments	14,000
Net cash flow for investing activities	$(15,000)

Interest and dividend income is part of net income. Assuming that cash was received for the interest and dividends, no adjustment would be made for this amount.

Thinking Beyond the Question

How do we account for investing activities?

This chapter described various types of long-term assets and how companies account for the acquisition, use, and disposal of these assets. Which assets a company invests in can be important decisions that affect the performance of the company. How do investing decisions affect a company's profitability and value?

QUESTIONS

Q11-1
Obj. 1
Archer Company produces sporting goods equipment. Identify and describe briefly the types of assets Archer is likely to own and report on its financial statements. (Hint: You may find it helpful to review Exhibit 1 in this chapter.)

Q11-2
Obj. 1
The gross amount of property, plant, and equipment is usually different from the net amount of property, plant, and equipment. Explain the difference between the two terms and what they represent. In what way is one or the other of these terms related to book value?

Q11-3
Obj. 1
Old Treetrunk is an exotic brand of whiskey. It is aged for 13 years in old tree trunks to give it the smooth taste for which it is well known. The manufacturer of this product makes nothing else. The company's office equipment typically lasts for about eight years before replacement. Under what asset category should the office equipment be reported on a classified balance sheet?

Q11-4
Obj. 2
Does it make sense to you that the cost of interest incurred to finance the construction of assets is included as part of the cost of the asset? Why or why not?

Q11-5
Obj. 2
Do you agree that the units-of-production method always results in more rapid depreciation of an asset than does the straight-line method? Explain.

Q11-6
Obj. 2
What is the difference between a capital expenditure and an operating expenditure? Explain how each is accounted for and why the treatment is different.

Q11-7
Obj. 3
A friend says, "The accounting terms *depletion* and *depreciation* describe basically the same thing." Do you agree or disagree? Why?

Q11-8
Obj. 3
The term *depletion expense* seldom appears on income statements, even if the company is a timber grower, mine owner, or owner of oil wells. If the cost of natural resources "harvested" never shows up on the income statement under depletion expense, how is this cost accounted for? Explain your answer.

Q11-9
Obj. 4
Generally, under GAAP, market value is not used as the valuation basis for assets. Cost is used instead. For marketable securities, however, market value is frequently used. What's different about marketable securities that makes it reasonable for this class of asset to be reported at market value when most other assets are reported at cost?

Q11-10
Obj. 4
Barbara is studying the annual reports of three different companies that her accounting group will use for its term project. She sees that two of the companies have made investments in the common stock of Microsoft, Inc. What bothers her is that one company has reported the investment as a current asset, while the other company has reported its investment as a long-term asset. Explain to Barbara why it is permissible, and preferable in certain circumstances, for the exact same type of asset to be reported differently.

Q11-11
Obj. 4
Sometimes unrealized holding gains and losses are reported on the income statement. At other times they are reported on the balance sheet under stockholders' equity. What causes this difference in treatment? Does this different treatment make sense to you? Why or why not?

Q11-12
Obj. 5
If market value is such a good basis for reporting certain marketable securities on the balance sheet, why not use market value as the basis for reporting intangible assets?

Q11-13
Obj. 5
How does goodwill arise and come to be reported on a balance sheet? How is the amount calculated? What does goodwill represent?

Q11-14
Obj. 6
Five years ago, Reeco Company paid $40,000 to acquire a building site. Since then the company has abandoned its expansion plans and yesterday sold the site for $65,800 in cash. How will this transaction be reported on the company's next cash flow statement? (Assume the indirect format is used.)

Q11-15
Obj. 6
Explain how a manager can use accounting information as a means of controlling assets and ensuring their security.

EXERCISES

If your instructor is using Personal Trainer in this course, you may complete online the assignments identified by ᴾT.

E11-1
Write a short definition for each of the terms listed in the *Terms and Concepts Defined in this Chapter* section.

E11-2
Obj. 1
ᴾT
Below is a list of accounts and year-end balances taken from the general ledger of Deep Drillers, Inc.

Treasury stock	$ 3,000	Accumulated depreciation	$ 40,000
Building	160,000	Goodwill	10,000
Land	120,000	Storage tanks	90,000
Drilling equipment	230,000	Trademark	4,000
Accounts receivable	25,000	Oil wells	500,500
Dividend income	6,600	Investment in Susanna Co.*	195,600
Accounts payable	5,400	Construction in process	56,300
Common stock	250,000	Inventory of tools	36,000
Accumulated depletion	15,000		

*Deep Drillers owns 42% of Susanna's common stock.

Prepare the long-term asset section of the balance sheet in good form. (Hint: Not all of the accounts need to be used.)

E11-3
Obj. 1
You are reviewing the balance sheet of Worldwide Technology, a manufacturer of assorted electronic components. You observe the following account classifications.

a. Intangible assets
b. Inventories
c. Investment in marketable securities
d. Property, plant, and equipment
e. Accounts receivable

For each of the classifications listed above, indicate whether it probably involves current assets or long-term assets. For each classification, give two examples of assets that might be reported there. Also indicate what attribute is being reported for each example you give (e.g., original cost, depreciated cost, market value, and so on).

E11-4
Obj. 1
P/T
The poorly trained bookkeeper at Flowing Water Company has shown you the long-term asset section of the company's balance sheet that he will soon distribute to stockholders. For your convenience, each item is identified with a letter. These letters will not appear in the finished document.

Long-term investments:
(a) Machinery, net $181,600
(b) Office supplies 8,710
(c) Land 78,000
Property, plant, and equipment:
(d) Patents 27,000
(e) Processing plant, net 206,960
(f) Obsolete equipment awaiting sale, net 16,800
Intangible assets:
(g) Prepaid insurance (for next three years) 21,000
(h) Common stock of Flower Corporation 83,000
Other long-term assets:
(i) Cash 4,722
(j) Standby equipment, net (used only during peak production) . 21,000
(k) Goodwill 14,000
(l) Investment in bonds of Beech Brothers, Inc. 46,000

Write down each of the four category headings above. After each heading, list the letters of the items you believe should be reported under that heading.

E11-5
Obj. 2
Camey Corporation purchased delivery equipment on January 1 at a cost of $300,000. The equipment is expected to have a useful life of seven years or 250,000 miles, and to have no salvage value. How much depreciation expense should be recorded during the first year using the straight-line, double-declining-balance, and units-of-production methods? During the year, the equipment was used for 80,000 miles. The company's fiscal year-end is December 31. Assume that revenue for the year is $376,300 and that all expenses, other than for depreciation, total $225,492. Would the use of one depreciation method instead of another have a material effect on the income statement? Discuss. (Ignore taxes.)

E11-6
Obj. 2
P/T
Asia Company purchased a building on March 1, 1985 at a cost of $4 million. For financial reporting purposes, the building was being depreciated over 372 months at $10,000 per month. The remaining $28,000 of the cost was the estimated salvage value. The building was sold on October 31, 2004 for $7.2 million. An accelerated depreciation method allowed by the tax code was used to record depreciation for the tax return. As of October 31, 2004, the company had recorded $3.3 million of depreciation for tax purposes using an accelerated basis. Determine (a) the amount of gain or loss that should be reported on the income statement regarding the sale of the building, (b) the amount of gain or loss that should be reported on the tax return regarding the sale of the building, and (c) why a company would use straight-line depreciation for financial reporting purposes and accelerated depreciation for tax purposes.

E11-7   Lincoln Hospital, Inc., acquired new specialized diagnostic equipment at a cost of $430,000.
Obj. 2   The equipment had an estimated useful life of eight years and an estimated residual value of
 P̲ $30,000. Lincoln uses the straight-line depreciation method. After five years, management de-
 T   termined that the equipment was in danger of becoming obsolete. During year 6, the estimated useful life of the equipment was revised to a total of seven years with a new estimated
residual value of $20,000. Determine (a) the book value of the equipment that would be re-
ported on the balance sheet at the end of year 5, and (b) the new amount of depreciation expense that would be reported on the year 6 and year 7 income statements. (c) Does the need
for revision of the depreciation estimates indicate that a poor job of estimating was originally
done? Discuss.

E11-8   Franchesca Company recorded the following transactions during its 2004 fiscal year:
Obj. 2

   a. Costs incurred for buildings under construction but not completed by year-end:

Labor	$350,000
Materials	675,000
Utilities	87,000
Special tools and equipment	22,000
Interest on construction loan	94,000

   b. The cost of an addition to an existing building was $840,000.
   c. The cost of repairs to equipment was $90,000. These repairs are required on a regular
      basis and do not affect the estimated useful life of the equipment.

How would each of these transactions affect Franchesca's financial statements for 2004? Assume cash had been paid for all costs by the end of the fiscal year.

E11-9   Leslie Company sells business stationery, imprinted with a customer's business name and ad-
Obj. 2   dress. To do this, it purchased a printing machine costing $48,000 on January 1, 2001. The
 P̲   machine has an expected useful life of five years and an estimated salvage value of $3,000.
 T   Leslie Company uses straight-line depreciation for all of its depreciable assets.
      On August 1, 2004, the manager of the print shop was persuaded to purchase a new ma-
chine that operated more efficiently. The old machine was sold at that time for $5,000.

   a. Calculate the depreciation expense recorded on the old machine for each year of use.
   b. Calculate any gain or loss on disposal of the old machine.
   c. Show how information about the printing machine transactions would be reported on
      the statement of cash flows for years 2001 through 2004. Assume the indirect format is
      used.
   d. How would the information about the printing machine affect the income statement
      for years 2001 through 2004?

E11-10   Energy Company owns rights to coal reserves in several states. The rights cost the company
Obj. 3 $140 million. The reserves were expected to produce a total of 50 billion tons of coal. During
 P̲   the company's 2004 fiscal year, five billion tons of coal were mined from the reserves. Prior
 T   to 2004, 30 billion tons of coal had been mined. How much depletion expense should the
company record in 2004? At what amount should the company report the coal reserves on its
balance sheet at the end of 2004? What effect would the depletion expense have on the company's cash flows in 2004?

E11-11   In 1975, the Big Tree Timber Company purchased 1,000 acres of recently cut forest land for
Obj. 3 $4,500,000. It planted new seedling trees at a cost of $1,200,000. Over the years, an additional
 P̲ $450,000 was spent thinning and monitoring the rapidly growing forest. Commercial harvest
 T   operations began on this property in 2004. During the year, 10% of the harvestable timber
was cut and sold. Near year-end, a rival firm offered to purchase the remaining uncut timber
(but not the land it is on) for a price of $30 million. Big Tree Timber turned down the offer
and will harvest the remaining trees over the next four years. At that time, the acreage will be
replanted with new seedlings. (a) What total amount of cost should be subject to depletion
expense in this problem? Why? (b) What amount of depletion expense should be reported on
the 2004 income statement? (c) What information discussed above should be reported on the
year-end 2004 balance sheet? (d) What important information about Big Tree Timber Company will not be reported on the income statement or balance sheet? If it is not reported on
the financial statements, how might this important information be communicated to interested parties?

E11-12
Obj. 4

P
T

Hot Water Company purchased 1,000 shares of Big Pipe Company's common stock for $24 each. It was a small investment, but Hot Water intended to hold the investment for the long term. At year-end, the total market value of the shares had increased to $27,500. Six months into the following year, Hot Water decided to sell the investment at its then-current market price of $30 per share. (a) Show how the initial purchase of the shares would be recorded in Hot Water's accounting system. (b) Show any entry to the accounting system that should be made at the end of the first year. (c) Show how the sale of the investment would be recorded in the accounting system.

E11-13
Obj. 4

P
T

Julie McBeth Company made two short-term investments in marketable securities during the current fiscal year. At year-end, the following summary information was available.

a. Purchased 5% of the outstanding common shares of Duncan Company for $300,000 plus brokerage fees of $30,000.
b. Purchased 2% of the outstanding common shares of Macduff Company for $400,000 plus brokerage fees of $40,000.
c. At year-end, the Duncan shares had a market value of $350,000. The Macduff shares had a market value of $360,000. McBeth owned no other investments in common stock.

Show how the two purchases of stock and the year-end information would be entered into McBeth's accounting system. What information regarding these investments will you expect to see reported on the year-end balance sheet? Be specific as to account names, their location on the balance sheet, and dollar amounts.

E11-14
Obj. 4

P
T

Isabella Company made small investments in the common stock of two companies during the current year. Isabella wishes to establish a long-term business relationship with each firm and purchased the shares as a good faith gesture. Each of the firms had millions of shares outstanding at the time.

a. Purchased 20,000 shares of Othello Company at $15 per share and paid a brokerage fee of $14,000.
b. Purchased 25,000 of the outstanding shares of Ferdinand Company for $16 per share and paid a brokerage fee of $18,000.
c. At year-end, the Othello shares had a market value of $350,000. The Ferdinand shares had a market value of $395,000.

At year-end, Isabella owned no other investments in common stock. Show how the two purchases of stock and the year-end information would be entered into Isabella's accounting system. What information regarding these investments will you expect to see reported on the year-end balance sheet? Be specific as to account names, their location on the balance sheet, and dollar amounts.

E11-15
Obj. 4

P
T

Manatee Company purchased $800,000 of long-term bonds on January 1, 2004 at face value. The bonds pay interest at an 8% annual rate on each June 30 and December 31. Semiannual payments were received, as promised, on June 30, 2004, and December 31, 2004. Manatee's fiscal year ends December 31. At December 31, 2004, the market value of the bonds was $786,000. The bonds were sold on July 1, 2005 for $820,000. (a) Show how the purchase of the bonds and the receipt of the first interest payment would be entered into the accounting system. Indicate how information about this bond investment will be reported on Manatee's December 31, 2004, balance sheet if (b) management intends (and is able) to hold the bonds until maturity, or (c) management intends to hold the bonds for a few years and then sell them. Be sure to include the dollar amounts of any information that you suggest should be reported.

E11-16
Obj. 4

P
T

Arkansas Company purchased 20,000 shares of Mena Company's common stock on May 15, 2002. Arkansas paid $380,000 for the stock. On September 12, 2002, Arkansas received a dividend check from Mena for $12,000. The market value of Mena's stock on December 31, 2002 was $24 per share. On September 12, 2003, Arkansas received a dividend check from Mena for $14,400. The market value of Mena's stock on December 31, 2003 was $22 per share. Arkansas sold its investment in Mena's stock on April 6, 2004, for $400,000. Throughout this period, Arkansas Company owned 8% of Mena's stock and intended for it to be a long-term investment.

(Continued)

1. Using the format presented in this chapter, record all transactions for Arkansas Company involving its investment in Mena and explain the purpose of each transaction.
2. Determine the amounts Arkansas Company would report on its 2002 and 2003 balance sheets (or notes) for its investment in Mena.

E11-17
Obj. 5

Dundee Enterprises purchased 100% of Newberg Company's common stock for $200 million in cash. At the time of the purchase, the fair market value of Newberg's assets was $350 million. The fair market value of its liabilities was $180 million. (a) Explain the meaning of goodwill. (b) Why might a rational decision maker pay more than the fair market value of the assets acquired? (c) How does goodwill affect a company's financial reports? (d) What amount of goodwill should be recorded by Dundee? (e) What reason other than goodwill can you think of that might explain why a company would pay more than fair value when acquiring the assets of another firm?

E11-18
Obj. 5
P
T

Joyful Sound Music Company purchased the net assets (i.e., assets minus liabilities) of Metrodome Company for $845,000. Metrodome is a retailer of music, instruments, and related items. Its net assets have been carried on its own books at a total of $530,000. An appraisal of all of Metrodome's assets and liabilities revealed a net fair market value of $783,000. Joyful is willing to pay extra because of Metrodome's very loyal retail customers, most of whom have dealt exclusively with the company for more than 30 years. (a) What is the amount of goodwill that Joyful should record at acquisition of Metrodome? (b) What might cause the purchased goodwill in this situation to become impaired?

E11-19
Objs. 2, 5
P
T

SPREADSHEET

Use the straight-line (SLN) and double-declining-balance (DDB) functions in Excel or another spreadsheet program to calculate the required amounts in the following situations.

a. Machinery was purchased at its invoice price of $296,016. This amount did not include sales tax of 6.15%. The estimated useful life was 13 years and residual value was estimated at $15,000. Use the straight-line depreciation method. (1) Determine the amount of depreciation for the first year of the machinery's use. (2) Determine the amount of depreciation for the eighth year of the machinery's use. (3) Determine the book value of the machinery at the end of the 12th year of use.

b. Computer equipment having an expected life of five years was purchased at a cost of $112,316. Because the new equipment differed from the old, minor remodeling of the office space was necessary at a cost of $6,152 before installation could occur. The computer equipment is expected to have a $5,000 residual value. Use the double-declining-balance method. (1) Determine the amount of depreciation for the first year of the equipment's life. (2) Determine the amount of depreciation for the fourth year of the equipment's life.

c. A patent was acquired at a cost of $1.3 million. The patent has a remaining legal life of 13 years, but technology is changing so rapidly in this industry that management believes the patent rights will be worthless at the end of six years. Straight-line amortization is used. (1) Determine the amount of amortization for the fourth year of the patent's life. (2) Determine the book value of the patent at the end of six years.

E11-20
Obj. 6

You are reviewing the balance sheet, income statement, and statement of cash flows of a large, well-known company. It has operations in several different lines of business and in several countries. As you inspect these financial statements, you are searching for information about the company's investing activities. First, define the term *investing activities.* Second, make a list, one for each of the three financial statements, of the information about investing activities that might be found on that statement. Carefully specify the information you might expect to see reported and indicate exactly where it would be found on the statement.

E11-21
Obj. 6
P
T

Zirconium Graphics Company reported the following information for the year ended December 31:

a. Sale of plant assets having a book value of $30,000 for $22,000 cash
b. Sale of securities with a book value of $26,000 for $28,000 cash
c. Depreciation and amortization expense of $7,500
d. Interest and dividends received from investments totaling $4,000 in cash
e. Acquisitions of plant assets for $50,000 in cash
f. Acquisitions of long-term investments for $16,000 in cash
g. Net income of $60,000

Prepare the operating and investing sections of Zirconium's cash flow statement, assuming that no other activities affected those sections.

E11-22 *(Based on the Other Investment Issues section)* On January 1, Baruti Company acquired 4,000 shares of Biltmore Company's common stock at a price of $9 per share. Baruti did so to establish a long-term working relationship with Biltmore Company. At December 31, Biltmore reported net income of $30,000 and paid a $0.50 cash dividend on each of its 16,000 common shares. On that same date, the market value of Biltmore common stock was $11 per share. (a) Which accounting method should be used to account for this investment? Why? (b) Record all entries that should be made to the accounting system during the year as a result of this investment. (c) At what amount should the investment be reported on Baruti's end-of-year balance sheet? Show how you arrived at your solution.

PROBLEMS

If your instructor is using Personal Trainer in this course, you may complete online the assignments identified by $\frac{P}{T}$.

P11-1
Obj. 2

Comparing Depreciation Methods

Clary Jensen Farms purchased power equipment with an expected useful life of four years or 1,000 hours of usage. The equipment was purchased on January 1, 2004, for $125,000. It is expected to have a salvage value of $5,000 at the end of four years. During 2004, the equipment was used for 260 hours. Assume that usage for the next three years will be 220 hours, 313 hours, and 207 hours, respectively.

Required

A. Prepare a depreciation schedule for the asset showing the book value and depreciation expense on the asset each year using the straight-line, double-declining-balance, and units-of-production methods.
B. Which method would you prefer to use for financial reporting purposes if you were general manager of the company? Which method would you prefer to use for tax purposes? Explain.
C. Which method has the greatest effect on cash flow each year? Why?

P11-2
Obj. 2

Comparing Depreciation Methods and Cash Flow

U.S. income tax law permits some assets to be depreciated using an accelerated method during the early years of an asset's life. In later years, a switch to the straight-line depreciation method is allowed if it produces more favorable tax results. (More favorable tax results occur when application of the straight-line method to the remaining book value of the asset produces a depreciation amount greater than that scheduled to be taken under the usual double-declining-balance method.) Pandora Company purchased equipment on March 1, 2004, at a cost of $2,100,000. The equipment was depreciated for a full year in 2004. It was expected to have a useful life of six years and no residual value.

Required

A. Prepare a schedule that shows the amount of depreciation that Pandora Company would take on the asset each year for tax purposes if it applied the usual double-declining-balance method over the asset's six-year life.
B. Prepare a similar schedule using the modified double-declining-balance method described above.
C. Show how the cash flow for taxes paid would differ under the straight-line method and the modified double-declining-balance method over the six-year period. The tax rate is 35%.
D. Summarize how the choice of a depreciation method affects cash flows for taxes.

P11-3
Obj. 2

Determining Acquisition Cost and First-Year Depreciation

Matta Company has just acquired two assets:

1. New diagnostic equipment for the medical services division was acquired at an invoice price of $93,000. This did not include the 8.7% sales tax. Transportation cost of $2,650 was incurred to ship the equipment from the factory to Matta's medical

(Continued)

center. During transit, the driver "forgot" to acquire a special required permit, and Matta was fined $425. When the equipment was unloaded at the medical center, eight feet of wall on the right side of the entry door had to be dismantled (and then rebuilt) to provide a larger opening to get the equipment into the building. The cost of labor and materials was $750. In addition, while the equipment was being moved through the opening, the left side of the doorway was inadvertently damaged. Fortunately, this cost only an additional $300 because workers were already on site. Setup and testing costs to calibrate the equipment properly before it could be used on patients cost another $2,700.

2. Manufacturing equipment was acquired by the semiconductor electronics division. The supplier of the equipment agreed to deliver the equipment, install it, and calibrate it to Matta's specifications, all as part of the negotiated selling price. Sales tax of 7.5% was not included in the selling price and was paid separately. Matta and the supplier agreed on the following terms: a $77,000 down payment, followed by three equal annual installment payments of $85,000 that include 8% interest on the unpaid balance. (Hint: Calculate the present value of the installment payments.)

Required

A. Matta's accounting staff has requested your advice and counsel as to the cost at which each of these assets should be entered into Matta's accounting records. Provide that advice, carefully specifying exactly how you came to each judgment you made.

B. Determine the amount by which net income would differ in the first year if Matta chose to use the straight-line depreciation method instead of double-declining-balance. Both assets have estimated useful lives of six years and zero estimated residual value.

P11-4 ## Purchase versus Self-Construction of an Asset

Obj. 2

P/T

Texas Company has outgrown its current office building and is considering a replacement. There are two options available.

1. An existing building and its land can be purchased for $6,000,000. The market value of the land alone is $100,000. The building can be renovated for $500,000. The estimated life of the building would be 20 years with no salvage value. Texas can borrow the money needed for the purchase at an interest rate of 8%. The loan will be repaid in 14 equal annual payments, made at the end of each year.

2. A new building can be constructed by the company for its own use. The following costs would be incurred:

Architect's plans	$ 100,000
Materials	1,750,000
Labor costs	3,675,000
Other fees and permits	200,000

The company already owns and has paid for the land, which cost $100,000. To help finance construction of the building, Texas can obtain a one-year loan for $4,500,000 at an interest rate of 7%. The loan would be repaid in one year just as construction of the building was completed. The estimated life of the new building would be 25 years.

Required

A. Determine the equal annual payments to be made under the first option. What would be the interest expense incurred during the first year of the loan?

B. Calculate the projected yearly depreciation expense for the building under each option. Use the straight-line method.

C. What effects, arising from either of the two options, would appear on the statement of cash flows?

D. Mr. L. Horn, the controller, points out that the company can save money if it constructs its own building. He compared the cost of the existing building and land of $6,500,000 to the cost of the constructed building and land of $6,140,000. He wants to show the difference in the two amounts on the income statement as Gain on Construction. Do you support this idea? Why or why not?

P11-5
Obj. 2

P̶T̶

SPREADSHEET

Depreciation and Disposal of Assets

Diamondback Mfg. is buying a new grinding machine. The machine costs $124,000 and is assumed to have a salvage value of $4,000 in five years. The manufacturer's description of the machine indicates that it should operate for 30,000 hours. The company's accountant is trying to decide whether to depreciate the machine by the straight-line method, the double-declining-balance method, or the units-of-production method. The machine will be purchased on January 1 of the coming year.

Required

A. Set up depreciation schedules for the straight-line and double-declining-balance methods. (Hint: You may wish to use the SLN and DDB functions in an Excel spreadsheet.)

B. Using the units-of-production method, calculate the hourly rate and yearly depreciation, assuming the machine is used evenly throughout its life. Comment on the reasonableness of this assumption.

C. Assume that after using the machine for three-and-a-half years, a new and improved machine is purchased. The old machine is then sold for $25,000. Calculate any gain or loss on the sale of the machine under each of the three depreciation methods. (Note: When calculating the gain or loss for the units-of-production method, assume that the machine was not used equally each year. Instead, assume the actual hours used each year were 6,000, 7,000, 8,000, and 4,000. Discuss any differences found in the gain or loss.)

D. With regard to the year of disposal of the machine, indicate what would appear on the income statement and the statement of cash flows for each method. Assume the indirect method is used for the statement of cash flows.

P11-6
Obj. 2

P̶T̶

SPREADSHEET

Using Spreadsheet Functions in Depreciation Calculations

Rodriguez Company acquired sophisticated production equipment at a cost of $450,000. In addition, the firm paid $7,540 to have the equipment delivered and another $11,435 was spent on installation and testing. The annual cost paid to insure the equipment while used in production is $3,000. The expected life of the new equipment is six years, and the estimated salvage value is $40,000. Management, however, is concerned about changing technology in the industry. With each year that passes, it will become more and more likely that new production technology will render this equipment obsolete. Management needs to choose between use of straight-line depreciation and double-declining-balance. The company expects that income before depreciation expense and income taxes will be approximately $160,000 per year. The firm's corporate tax rate is 35%.

Required

A. Determine the cost of the equipment that should be recorded in the accounting system.

B. Use the straight-line (SLN) and double-declining-balance (DDB) functions from Excel or another spreadsheet program as an aid to constructing a schedule that shows (1) depreciation expense each year under each alternative, and (2) ending book value each year under each alternative.

C. Prepare a projected income statement for the six years assuming straight-line depreciation is used. (You need to prepare only one projected income statement because all years yield exactly the same result.) Start with Income Before Depreciation and Taxes and conclude with Net Income.

D. Prepare projected income statements for all six years assuming double-declining-balance depreciation is used. Start with Income Before Depreciation and Taxes and conclude with Net Income.

E. Compare your results from parts C and D. Why is it important that a reader of financial statements consult the notes to the financial statements to determine the depreciation method in use?

P11-7
Obj. 2

P̶T̶

Depreciation Policy and Moral Hazard

Clemson Manufacturing Company produces specialty textiles. On January 1, it purchased a new weaving machine at a cost of $600,000. The machine has an expected life of five years

(Continued)

SPREADSHEET

and an estimated salvage value of $40,000. The company manager thinks the machine can be used to weave 4.0 million yards of fabric. The net income before depreciation and taxes in the first year was $3,600,000. The company's tax rate is 30%.

Required

A. Prepare a five-year depreciation schedule for the machinery under both straight-line and double-declining-balance methods. (Hint: You may wish to use the SLN and DDB functions in an Excel spreadsheet.)

B. Determine the amount of depreciation expense the company would incur during the first year if the units-of-production method were used and 1.2 million yards of fabric were produced.

C. Which of the three methods would result in the lowest income tax expense for the first year?

D. Which of the three methods would result in the highest net income for the first year?

E. Assume the income tax must be paid immediately at year-end. Assume also you are the chief executive officer (CEO) of the corporation and are paid a significant bonus based on reported profit for the year. Which accounting method would you recommend be used regarding this new equipment? Why?

P11-8 The Effect of Depreciation on Net Income and Taxes

Obj. 2

P/T

SPREADSHEET

McGuire Batt Company produces a wide line of insulation materials. On January 1, it acquired new production equipment at a cost of $1,200,000. The machine has an expected life of four years and an estimated salvage value of $80,000. The engineering specifications of this new equipment state that it will produce two million units of product over its useful life. For the first year, the company's net income before considering depreciation and taxes was $7.2 million. The company's tax rate was 35%.

Required

A. Prepare a four-year depreciation schedule for the machinery under both straight-line and double-declining-balance methods. (Hint: You may wish to use the SLN and DDB functions in an Excel spreadsheet.)

B. Determine the amount of depreciation expense the company would record on its income statement for the first year if the units-of-production method were used and 400,000 units were produced.

C. Which of the three methods would result in the lowest income tax expense for the first year?

D. Which of the three methods would result in the highest net income for the first year?

P11-9 Choices in Depletion and Depreciation Methods

Objs. 2, 3

P/T

Sioux City Minerals acquired a copper mine, paying $40,000,000. The mine is expected to be productive for 10 years and yield 500,000 tons of copper ore. At the end of that time, the property will be donated to the state. To produce the ore, the company purchased mining equipment at a cost of $4,800,000, which is expected to have a useful life of 12 years with no salvage.

Required

A. Assuming that 30,000 tons of ore were produced and sold in the first year of operations, calculate the depletion for the mine and the depreciation of the machinery.

B. Assume the same facts as in part A above, except that the machinery can be used only for this copper mine and will not be moved once the mine is abandoned. How do you believe the equipment should be depreciated in this case? Explain why. What would be the depletion and depreciation for the first year under your approach?

C. If the ore is sold for $120 per ton, calculate the profit under parts A and B above. If there is a difference in the two amounts, explain why.

D. Assume that after the first year, when 30,000 tons were produced, a mining engineer estimates that a total of 570,000 additional tons of ore can still be recovered from the mine. What would be the depletion of the mine and the depreciation of the machinery if 25,000 tons of copper were produced in the second year? (Assume straight-line depreciation.)

E. What would be the book values of the mine and the machinery at the end of the second year?

P11-10 Reporting Investments

Obj. 4

Portia Enterprises manufactures automobiles and occasionally makes small investments in other corporations for long-term purposes. During its 2003 fiscal year, Portia purchased 100,000 common shares (10%) of Leonardo Company for $3,470,000. Also, it purchased 5% of the common stock of Shylock Company for $2,690,000. During 2003, Portia received $500,000 of dividends from Leonardo. At the end of the fiscal year, the investment in Leonardo had a market value of $3,100,000. The investment in Shylock had a market value of $2,800,000. Portia owned no other stock investments during 2003. During its 2004 fiscal year, Portia sold the Shylock investment for $2,900,000 and made a small investment in Balthasar Company for $1,930,000. During 2004, Portia received $500,000 of dividends from Leonardo. At the end of 2004, the Leonardo investment had a market value of $3,350,000 and the Balthasar investment had a market value of $1,940,000. Portia owned no other stock investments during 2004. All of Portia's investments were properly accounted for as long-term investments.

Required

A. At year-end 2004, should these investments be classified as held-to-maturity, trading, or available-for-sale? Why?
B. Prepare a schedule calculating the amount Portia would report for long-term investments on its balance sheet at the end of 2003 and 2004.
C. Prepare a schedule calculating the effect of Portia's investment activities on its income for 2003 and 2004.

P11-11 Accounting for Investments in Securities

Obj. 4

P/T

At December 31, 2004, Optimax Medical Company owned small investments in the common stock of other firms as follows:

Company	Number of Shares Owned	Purchase Price per Share
1. Fleet Company	1,000	$37.50
2. Regency, Inc.	2,200	$10.40
3. Demetri Products	700	$52.00
4. Paxton Technology	1,500	$22.50

Optimax management expects to sell its investments in Fleet and Paxton during the 2005 fiscal year. It does not, however, expect to sell its investments in Regency or Demetri at any time in the foreseeable future. The market value of each investment at the end of the 2004 fiscal year was as follows:

Fleet	$39,000
Regency	24,000
Demetri	34,940
Paxton	33,020

During 2004, Optimax received $3,900 of dividends from Fleet and $1,700 of dividends from Demetri. Optimax Company owned no other stock investments during 2004.

Required

A. Determine the amounts that should be reported on the December 31, 2004 balance sheet under the following classifications. Show how you determined each amount.
1. Short-term investments
2. Long-term investments
3. Stockholders' equity
B. What information about these investments should appear on 2004's income statement? Be specific.

(Continued)

C. How is it helpful to readers of the financial statements to see information about the market value of common stock investments when Optimax didn't pay those amounts to obtain the shares? Explain.

P11-12

Obj. 4

P/T

SPREADSHEET

Accounting for Investments in Bonds

Nilani Company purchased 100 Arapaho Company bonds on April 1, 2004. The bonds pay interest semiannually on March 31 and September 30 at an annual coupon rate of 9%. The bonds sold at an effective yield of 8%. The effect of brokerage fees is included in computing the effective yield. The bonds mature on March 31, 2006, at their face value of $1,000 per bond. Nilani's fiscal year ends on September 30.

Required

A. Compute the price Nilani paid for Arapaho's bonds. (Hint: Determine the present value of the interest payments and principal repayment as demonstrated in Chapter F8.)
B. Prepare an amortization schedule for Nilani's investment.
C. Assume that the bonds are classified as held-to-maturity securities. Use the format presented in this chapter to show how the bond transactions would be entered into Nilani's accounting system in 2004, 2005, and 2006.
D. What is the total interest revenue from these bonds that Nilani will report on its 2004, 2005, and 2006 income statements? How does total interest revenue compare to Nilani's net cash flow from this bond investment during those same three years? Show your computations.
E. What does the result in part D suggest to you regarding the similarities and differences between accrual and cash-based measures?

P11-13

Obj. 4

P/T

Accounting for Investments in Bonds

On January 1, the Cheng Corporation purchased $10,000 of 5%, five-year bonds as a long-term investment. Interest is paid annually. The company is not involved in active trading of securities.

Required Using the format presented in the chapter, record each of the following transactions.

A. Record the purchase of the bonds for $10,000.
B. Record the receipt of the first interest payment on the bonds in part A.
C. Assuming the company intends to hold the bonds to maturity, what entry is necessary at the end of the first year if the market value of the bonds is $10,400 at that time?
D. Show how the answer to part C would differ if the company does not intend to hold the bonds to maturity.
E. Assume that the company purchased these bonds at a cost of $10,445. This price yields an effective rate of 4%.
F. Record the receipt of the first interest payment on the bonds purchased in part E.
G. Assuming the company intends to hold the bonds to maturity, prepare the necessary entry at the end of the first year to reflect the $10,400 market value of the bonds.
H. Show how the answer to part G would differ if the company does not intend to hold the bonds to maturity.
I. Report the carrying value (book value) of the bonds at the end of the first year in parts C, D, G, and H. Explain how the amounts have been calculated.
J. Prepare an amortization table for the bonds purchased in E, assuming the company holds the bonds to maturity. What is the total amount of cash received? What is the total amount of interest revenue? What is the difference between the two?

P11-14

Obj. 4

P/T

Investments in Debt Securities

On January 1, Gandini Company purchased $300,000 face value of Battaglia's 8.4% bonds at a price of $283,439. At this price, the bonds yielded 9% annually. At December 31, Gandini received an interest check on these bonds of $25,200. The market price of these bonds that day was $282,000.

Required

A. Using the format presented in this chapter, show the entries that would be made to the accounting system to record the purchase of this investment and receipt of the interest check. Assume this is a long-term investment.

B. Show how this investment should be reported in the year-end financial statements by completing the table of information that follows.

	If the bonds are . . .		
	Held-to-maturity securities	Trading securities	Available-for-sale securities
Accounting method to be used			
Amount of unrealized holding gain (loss) to be reported on income statement			
Amount of unrealized holding gain (loss) to be reported on balance sheet			
Amount of discount amortized during first year			
Balance of investment account on balance sheet at end of the first year			

P11-15

Obj. 4

P̅T̅

Investments in Equity Securities

On August 22, 2004, Burgess Company purchased 20,000 common shares of Radius Measurement, Inc. at a price of $8 per share. Brokerage commissions, taxes, and transfer fees totaled an additional $800. At December 31, 2004, Burgess still owned the securities but the aggregate market value had declined to $148,000. This is a long-term investment.

Required

A. Using the format presented in this chapter, show the entries that would be made to the accounting system to record the purchase of these securities.

B. Show how this investment should be reported in the year-end 2004 financial statements by completing the table of information below.

	If the total number of Radius common shares outstanding totals		
	1 million	80,000	30,000
Accounting method to be used			
Amount of unrealized holding gain (loss) to be reported on income statement			
Amount of unrealized holding gain (loss) to be reported on balance sheet			
Balance of investment account on balance sheet			

C. Assume the investment in common stock was sold on January 23, 2005 at a price of $171,400. Use the format presented in this chapter to show the entry to record this event. Assume the investment has always been on the books as available-for-sale securities.

P11-16

Objs. 2, 3, 5

P̅T̅

Depreciation, Amortization, and Depletion

The accounting staff at Golden Mining Company will soon prepare year-end entries to the accounting system to record the partial consumption of certain long-term assets. Your advice is sought regarding each of the following situations.

1. A mining site was acquired 10 years ago at a cost of $4,900,000. This included $700,000 to prepare an environmental impact statement, conduct a required survey, and build

(Continued)

road access. The mine was expected to produce approximately 20 million tons of high-grade ore, after which the site could be sold for $500,000. This past year, 3.0 million tons were produced, processed, and sold.

2. Trucks and machinery having an estimated useful life of five years are being depreciated by the double-declining-balance method. These assets were purchased for $152,000 and have an estimated residual value of $22,000. This is the end of their third year in use.

3. A patent relating to the ore-refining process was purchased three years ago at a cost of $57,000. At the time of purchase, the patent had a remaining legal life of eight years. Management wants the required write-off of the patent's cost to have the minimum effect on net income that is allowed under the circumstances.

Required

A. Assist the accounting staff by suggesting the year-end entries that should be made to the accounting system for each of the situations above.
B. Assume the trucks and machinery have always been depreciated using the straight-line method. Assume further that it was determined during the current year that the estimated useful life would actually be a total of 10 years with a residual value of $2,000. What amount of depreciation expense would have been reported during each of the first two years under the straight-line method? What amount of depreciation expense will be reported for the current year and the years that follow under the straight-line method?

P11-17   ## Accounting for Fixed, Natural, and Intangible Assets

Objs. 2, 3, 5

P/T

On the last day of the fiscal year, the chief financial officer of MultiPlex Industries is reviewing several accounting matters. They are as follows:

1. Equipment purchased seven years ago at a cost of $450,000 was sold yesterday as scrap metal at a price of $3,000. It had originally been estimated to have a 10-year life with a $50,000 residual value. The straight-line method has been used.

2. Early in the current year, the mineral rights to a bauxite mine were acquired at a cost of $5.5 million. Mining consultants have estimated there are about 350,000 tons of recoverable ore that can be removed and processed.

3. Just yesterday, the company purchased a subsidiary company by paying the $2.8 million purchase price. Investigation prior to the acquisition reveals the market value of the subsidiary's identifiable assets totals $1.9 million.

Required Use the format presented in this chapter for parts A, B, C, and E.

A. Prepare the entry to record the current year's depreciation expense.
B. Prepare the entry to record yesterday's sale of old machinery. Also show how you arrived at the amounts you entered.
C. During the year just ended, 77,000 tons of bauxite ore was removed, processed, and sold from the mine. Prepare the appropriate entry to record the expense.
D. Explain what goodwill represents.
E. Prepare the entry to record the purchase of the subsidiary.

P11-18   ## Accounting for Plant Assets

Objs. 2, 6

P/T

Garland Company purchased construction equipment on July 1, 2001, for $800,000. The equipment was expected to have a useful life of five years and a residual value of $50,000. On June 30, 2004, Garland no longer needed the equipment and sold it for $311,000. Garland's accounting year ends on December 31. The company uses the straight-line depreciation method.

Required

A. Information about this equipment must be entered into the accounting system on July 1, 2001; December 31, 2001; December 31, 2002; December 31, 2003; and June 30, 2004. Show how that information should be entered, using the format shown in this chapter. (Hint: On June 30, 2004, be sure to record depreciation expense for the six months immediately preceding sale of the equipment.)

B. Why was a gain (or loss) recorded at the date of disposal? What caused this to occur? Does a loss mean that the company has been negligent in selling the asset? Does a gain on sale mean that the company has been skillful in selling the asset? Explain.

C. Calculate the cumulative net effect that all transactions involving the equipment had on Garland's pretax income from 2001 through 2004. Also, calculate the cumulative net effect that all transactions involving the equipment had on cash flows for this period. Explain the relationship between (1) the effect on pretax income and (2) the effect on cash flows.

P11-19   ## Ethics in Financial Reporting

Obj. 6

Show-Me-the-Money, Inc. is a medium-sized bank. The bank's stock is owned primarily by residents in the city where the bank operates. During the last decade, the bank lent money for numerous real estate developments. Most of the loans went to developers who constructed office space and expected to repay the loans from office rent. Aggressive lending and building practices resulted in overbuilding. A downturn in the local economy drastically reduced demand for office space. As a result, many of the buildings are now largely empty. Rent from the facilities is insufficient to pay interest on several of the bank's larger loans. The bank has permitted several borrowers to restructure their loans, providing a longer period of repayment and lower interest rates. The market value of the property backing these loans has decreased approximately 40% since its construction. The bank's proposed year-end balance sheet reports loans in the bank's long-term investment portfolio at $43 million. This amount is net of a loan loss reserve of $5 million. The balance sheet also includes $18 million of property among the bank's assets. This property was acquired through foreclosures on several loans. The property is valued at the present value of the original loan payments, including interest the bank expected from the original borrowers. The bank is collecting rent from tenants and expects to sell the property when real estate values return to higher levels. The bank's total assets are $80 million, and total stockholders' equity is $10 million. The bank's proposed income statement for the year reports profits of $6 million. The year-end audit is now underway, and the bank's auditors are reviewing the proposed financial statements. They have questioned management about its loans and property values. The auditors believe that the current market value of the loan portfolio is about $35 million. They are less sure about the value of the property. The bank's managers are arguing that the current market value of the loans is not relevant because they do not expect to sell the loans. Instead, they expect to hold the loans until they mature. Also, they do not plan to sell the property until they can recover the amount the bank invested.

Required Do you believe the investors and creditors of the bank will be well served by the financial statements that the bank's management proposes to report? Explain. Do you see any ethical problems with the way the bank's managers want to report its assets? Why? What problems may arise for the bank if it reports its loans at current market value?

P11-20   ## The Equity Method

(Based on the Other Investment Issues section) On January 1, Schuster Company bought 2,400 of Helio Corporation's 10,000 outstanding shares of common stock as a long-term investment. The stock was acquired at a cost of $24,000. On December 31, Helio reported net income of $38,000 and paid dividends totaling $6,000. On the same date, the market value of Helio's common stock was $15 per share.

Required

A. Use the format presented in this chapter to show how the events described above would be entered into Schuster's accounting system.

B. Describe how this would be reported on Schuster's year-end financial statements by completing the table that follows.

Question	Solution
1. In which section of the balance sheet will this investment be reported? Be specific.	
2. What amount will be reported on the balance sheet for this investment? Show your work.	

(Continued)

Question	Solution
3. What amount of income will be reported on the income statement related to this investment? Explain.	
4. What information will be reported about any unrealized holding gain or loss? Explain.	

P11-21   Excel in Action

P/T

SPREADSHEET

The Book Wermz expanded its operations in March 2005 by purchasing an existing chain of bookstores. The total cost of the purchase was $5 million. Of this amount, $2.2 million was allocated to the cost of buildings, $1.0 million to the cost of store equipment, and $275,000 to the cost of transportation equipment. The buildings have an estimated useful life of 30 years (360 months) and a salvage value of $100,000. The store equipment has an estimated useful life of five years (60 months) and a salvage value of $50,000. The transportation equipment has an estimated useful life of three years (36 months) or 90,000 miles and a salvage value of $75,000. The Book Wermz uses straight-line depreciation for financial reporting purposes. For income tax purposes, it uses double-declining-balance depreciation for buildings and store equipment and units-of-production depreciation for transportation equipment.

Required Use a spreadsheet to prepare a depreciation schedule for The Book Wermz for the assets described. The depreciation schedule will contain data for April through December 2005. Rows 1 through 3 should contain "The Book Wermz", "Depreciation Schedule", and "April-December 2005". Beginning in cell A5, list the following captions in column A: Asset, Cost, Salvage, Life (months), and Method. In column B, provide the data for Buildings that correspond to the captions in column A. Repeat the process for Store Equipment in column D and for Transportation Equipment in column F.

In cell A10 enter "Month", followed by the numbers 1 through 9 (corresponding to April through December) in cells A11 through A19. In cell B9, enter "Straight-Line". In cell C9, enter "Declining-Balance".

In cell B11, enter a function to calculate the straight-line depreciation for April for Buildings. Click on the Function button, select the Financial category, and select SLN from the Function name list. In the dialog box, enter the appropriate cell addresses for each of the values requested to complete the function. For example, enter $B$6 for cost. Make sure you include the $ sign in front of the cell references for cost, salvage, and life because the references are to fixed locations (cells B6 to B8). Once the calculation is completed for April, copy cell B11 to cells B12 to B19 to provide calculations for May through December. The amount of depreciation in each cell should be the same. In cell B20, calculate the total depreciation for 2002 using the Summation button.

In cell C11, enter a function to calculate the double-declining-balance depreciation for April for Buildings. Repeat the process used for straight-line depreciation, except use the DDB function in the Financial category. The references in the dialog box will be the same as those for straight-line depreciation. You will need to include a reference for Period. The reference is A11 for April. Do not enter $ signs for this reference because the reference will change for months May through December. You may leave the Factor reference blank. The factor is 2 for double-declining-balance, and 2 is the default for the DDB method. Once the calculation is made for April, copy cell C11 to cells C12 to C19. The amount of depreciation should be less each month than the preceding month (declining balance). Total the column of depreciation amounts in cell C20.

In columns D and E, repeat the processes described above for Store Equipment.

In column F, enter data for Transportation Equipment and calculate straight-line depreciation. In column G enter data for the units-of-production method. In cell G10, enter the caption "Miles". In cells G11 through G19 enter the miles the equipment was used each month, as follows: 1500, 1800, 2000, 2800, 3000, 2500, 2700, 2600, and 2200. In cell H10, enter the caption "Expense". In cell H11, calculate the amount of depreciation for April using the equation =$F$6*(G11/90000). Copy cell H11 to cells H12 through H19. Calculate totals for each column in row 20.

In columns I and J, calculate the total straight-line and accelerated depreciation amounts for each month. Total each column in row 20.

Calculate the tax savings to The Book Wermz of using accelerated depreciation for tax purposes. In column A, enter captions for "Total Accelerated", "Total Straight-line", "Difference", "Tax rate", and "Tax savings", beginning in cell A22. In column B, enter the amounts (cell references) that correspond with the total amounts. Use an equation to calculate the difference and assume a tax rate of 35%.

Format cells to provide a business appearance to the spreadsheet.

Suppose the life of the buildings was 380 months and the life of the store equipment was 72 months. How much depreciation would the company report and how much tax would it save?

P11-22   **Multiple-Choice Overview of the Chapter**

$\frac{P}{T}$ 1. Which of the following is (are) used to determine how a given asset will be reported on the balance sheet?

	The Expected Period of Time Until the Asset Will be Converted to Cash or Used Up	The Source of Financing That Was Used to Acquire the Asset
a.	Yes	Yes
b.	Yes	No
c.	No	Yes
d.	No	No

2. Belly-Acres Land Company made capital expenditures during the current year. At year-end, these expenditures should be reported on the
   a. income statement as expenses.
   b. balance sheet under current assets.
   c. balance sheet under long-term assets.
   d. statement of cash flows under operating activities.

3. The Song-in-My-Heart Record Store reported $20,000 of depreciation expense on assets acquired at the beginning of the current year. The assets' original cost was $50,000 with an estimated useful life of five years. The method used by Song-in-My-Heart for depreciating the assets was the
   a. straight-line method.
   b. cost recovery method.
   c. units-of-production method.
   d. double-declining-balance method.

4. The Shiny Metal Mining Company acquired mineral rights for $3,100,000. Geological studies indicate that two million tons of economically recoverable ore are likely to be present on the site. Subsequently, the rights to remaining minerals can be sold for approximately $300,000. The firm estimates that it will take about five years to mine the ore. In the first year, 600,000 tons of ore were recovered, processed, and sold. What is the amount of depletion for the first year?
   a. $930,000
   b. $840,000
   c. $620,000
   d. $560,000

5. Assuming an estimated useful life of three years and zero residual value, which of the following depreciation methods will always result in the least depreciation expense in the first year?
   a. Straight-line
   b. Double-declining-balance
   c. Units-of-production
   d. Cannot be determined from the information given

6. Boswell Company purchased its first investment in available-for-sale securities during the current year. At year-end, the current market value of the marketable securities is greater than the price paid to acquire them. As a result of this information, the company should report an unrealized holding
   a. loss on its income statement.
   b. gain on its income statement.
   c. loss on the balance sheet.
   d. gain on the balance sheet.

(Continued)

7. Hwan Manufacturing Company owns held-to-maturity bonds that were acquired at a premium. Each period that Hwan holds the investment, amortization of the premium will have which one of the following effects?
   a. The amount of interest revenue reported on the income statement will increase.
   b. The amount of cash received will decrease.
   c. The book value of the investment will decrease.
   d. The rate of return earned on the investment will decrease.

8. The excess of cost over the market value of identifiable net assets acquired in a purchase of another company should be reported in the financial statements as
   a. a current asset.
   b. an intangible asset.
   c. an expense of the period in which the acquisition occurs.
   d. a revenue of the period in which the acquisition occurs.

9. Which of the following is a *false* statement about intangible assets, other than goodwill?
   a. They have no physical substance.
   b. They have no real economic value.
   c. They can often be purchased or sold.
   d. They are amortized over their useful lives.

10. Khim Singer Company sold obsolete machinery that was no longer used in its factory. The transaction resulted in a loss being recorded in the company's accounting system. Information about this event will appear on which of the company's year-end financial statements?

	Income Statement	Statement of Cash Flows (Indirect Format)
a.	Yes	Yes
b.	Yes	No
c.	No	Yes
d.	No	No

11. *(Based on the Other Investment Issues section)* Farma Pharmaceutical Company has invested in the common stock of Bailey Biotech. The primary factor that will determine whether the equity method or the consolidation method is used to account for this is size of the
    a. investment.
    b. industry.
    c. parent company.
    d. total assets.

12. *(Based on the Other Investment Issues section)* On January 1 of the current year, Nancy Enterprises acquired 14,000 shares of the 40,000 outstanding shares of Tang Toys for $100,000. During the year, Tang Toys had net income of $50,000 and paid $10,000 in dividends. At December 31 of the current year, Nancy Enterprises should report what amount as its investment in Tang Toys?
    a. $96,500
    b. $103,500
    c. $114,000
    d. $117,500

CASES

C11-1   **Comparison of Purchase and Leasing of Plant Assets**

Objs. 2, 6

Swenson Company plans to acquire new chemical processing equipment on January 1, the beginning of the company's fiscal year. The equipment costs $2 million. Swenson can either borrow $2 million from a bank or lease the equipment. Both the bank and the leasing company believe that a 10% interest rate is appropriate, given Swenson's credit history. A lease would be accounted for as a capital lease (as discussed in Chapter F8). The equipment is expected to have a useful life of four years, which would be the same as the lease period. The equipment is expected to have zero residual value. Swenson normally uses the straight-line method to depreciate its equipment. The lease alternative would require year-end payments of $635,000 each year. If money is borrowed from a bank, four year-end payments would be required. Each payment would include one-fourth of the principal amount borrowed plus all of the interest expense that had been incurred on the unpaid balance during the year.

Required As the Chemical Division manager, you have been asked to evaluate the alternatives and to recommend the best choice for acquiring the equipment. Determine the comparative effects of purchasing versus leasing the equipment on Swenson's income statement, balance sheet, and statement of cash flows over the four-year period. Evaluate the alternatives and make a recommendation to top management.

C11-2 Analysis of Investment Activities

Objs. 2, 4, 6

Appendix B of this book contains a copy of the 2002 annual report of **General Mills, Inc.**

Required Review the annual report and write a short report in which you respond to each of the issues raised below.

A. Identify the accounting methods used by the company to account for plant assets, intangible assets, research and development costs, and advertising costs. (Hint: This information is disclosed in the notes to the financial statements.)

B. Identify the cost of each of the company's types of plant assets and the total amount of accumulated depreciation on these assets at the end of the most recent period reported.

C. Explain how the company reports its holdings of marketable securities in the financial statements. What percentage of its marketable securities (based on market value) are expected to be liquidated within one year? What percentage over more than one year and up to seven years? What amount over more than seven years? (Hint: This information is in the notes.)

D. Explain the change in the company's plant asset accounts during the most recent year reported by an analysis of its investment activities and depreciation. (Hint: Because of certain accounting complexities, you won't be able to prove the change exactly. But see how much of the change you can explain.)

F12

ANALYSIS OF INVESTING ACTIVITIES

How do assets create value for our business?

Chapter F11 discussed investing activities, including accounting for the acquisition, use, and disposal of long-term assets. Decisions about long-term assets affect the profitability and value of a company. Property and equipment are necessary to support operating activities. Manufacturing companies require equipment and facilities to produce goods, and all companies require equipment and facilities to support administrative and sales functions. The amounts and types of assets a company acquires affect a company's expenses and cash flows. Good asset investments support additional sales and profits. Poor investments lead to higher expenses and reduced profits.

Maria and Stan have decided that, for Mom's Cookie Company to grow and become more valuable, it will need to produce its own goods. The company will need to invest in production equipment and facilities. They have to make decisions about the types and amounts of assets to acquire.

FOOD FOR THOUGHT

If you are managing Mom's Cookie Company, what issues should you consider when deciding on the amounts and types of assets to use in the company? How should investors analyze the company's financial statements to assess management's investing decisions and the effects of these decisions on profits and company value?

Maria, president, Stan, vice president of operations, and Ellen, vice president of finance of Mom's Cookie Company, met to discuss investing plans for their company.

Maria: *We need to identify the equipment and facilities required for Mom's Cookie Company to become a manufacturing company. Is there anything special we need to consider?*

Ellen: *First, make sure the assets we acquire will permit us to produce the amount of goods we need and keep our production costs low enough so that we can make a profit.*

Stan: *Also, it's important for us to make sure the facilities and processes we use permit us to produce high-quality goods.*

Maria: *Do we have to trade off quality for cost? Are there other issues that affect our decision?*

Ellen: *We should consider how the assets we acquire will affect our cost structure. Some costs don't increase as sales increase, and other costs do. Cost structure can have an important effect on the profitability of Mom's Cookie Company.*

OBJECTIVES

Once you have completed this chapter, you should be able to:

1 Explain why investing decisions are important to a company and how they can affect its profits.

2 Explain how operating leverage affects a company's risk and profits.

3 Use financial statements to evaluate investing activities for various companies.

4 Explain how investing activities affect company value, and use accounting information to measure value-increasing activities.

5 Identify ways in which a company can use its assets to improve effectiveness and efficiency.

6 Explain why accounting information about long-term assets is useful for creditors.

INVESTING DECISIONS

OBJECTIVE 1

Explain why investing decisions are important to a company and how they can affect its profits.

Maria, Stan, and Ellen continue to discuss investing activities for their new company. The three managers had decided earlier to finance their company primarily by issuing common stock. Their decisions now involve the types of long-term assets the company needs.

Maria observed: "We decided last week that we probably will need $5 million to fund production facilities and production and marketing costs. We assumed that we will require $4 million for plant assets. Now we should decide on the specific types of assets we'll need. We want to be sure that $5 million will be adequate."

"I have looked at various alternatives," Stan remarked, "and I have some estimates for us to consider. Our production process involves mixing ingredients to make cookie dough, shaping or forming the cookies, baking the cookies, examining the finished product for quality, and packaging the cookies for sale. Exhibit 1 illustrates the production process.

Exhibit 1 The Production Process for Mom's Cookie Company

"Obviously," continued Stan, "we need equipment such as mixers and ovens. Also, we need equipment to move the materials between processes. We need enough building space to produce the product and provide storage for materials and finished goods."

"That seems fairly simple," Maria interrupted. "Can't we just buy what we need?"

"Well, it's not quite that simple," Stan responded. "We have to make some choices. For example, we have to decide how much of each type of equipment we need. We can start small and add more equipment as demand increases, but because the equipment has to be special-ordered, this will be a relatively expensive approach in the long run, assuming that our demand increases as we expect. If we start with smaller mixers and ovens, we will not be able to increase capacity very much once demand picks up.

"Perhaps the biggest decision we have to make," Stan continued, "is how much automation we want in the production process. We can use rather simple equipment that requires a lot of manual labor. For example, we can use pushcarts to move materials from one process to the next. Materials can be loaded into mixers and ovens by hand. And, we can use workers to inspect and package the finished products. These processes will require relatively large amounts of labor but will allow us to invest less in equipment.

"As an alternative, we can purchase more sophisticated equipment. Exhibit 2 shows this alternative. This equipment completes most of the processes with little human involvement. Conveyors can move materials to locations where ingredients are automatically loaded. The equipment prepares the dough, forms the cookies, and transfers them to ovens. Workers would have to make sure the equipment is functioning properly and make changes in settings for different types of cookies. This option calls for fewer employees. However, the employees would require more skills, so we would have to pay them more. Also, if we use automated equipment, we must acquire sufficient machinery to meet expected demand for the foreseeable future. It is expensive to increase the size of an automated production process, and therefore our initial investment will be larger than if we start with manual equipment.

Exhibit 2 An Alternative Production Process for Mom's Cookie Company

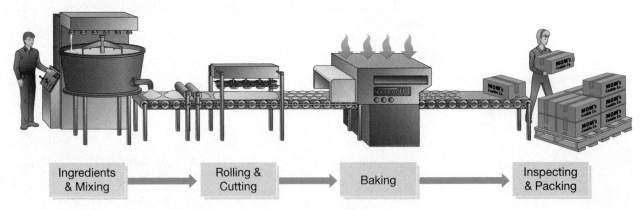

| Ingredients & Mixing | → | Rolling & Cutting | → | Baking | → | Inspecting & Packing |

"Thus, our basic choice is manual or automated equipment. If we select manual equipment, we can start with less investment and add equipment as demand increases. If we select automated equipment, we must invest more initially, but we will have the capacity we expect to need. Also, we will be able to produce a higher quality product. An automated production process is more reliable."

Maria observed, "This decision is more complicated than I had realized. What effect do the choices have on our expected profits?"

Investment Decisions and Profit

"The potential effects are quite large," Ellen responded. "Exhibit 3 provides some summary information.

"We expect sales of $3 million next year. That is the amount I assume in Exhibit 3," Ellen noted. "The amount we will need to invest initially in equipment differs between alternatives."

Exhibit 3

Expected Effects of Mom's Cookie Company's Investing Decisions with Sales of $3 Million

(In thousands)	Manual	Automated
Assets:		
Current assets	$ 1,000	$ 1,000
Plant assets	3,500	4,000
Total assets	$ 4,500	$ 5,000
Sales	$ 3,000	$ 3,000
Cost of ingredients	(800)	(800)
Depreciation	(250)	(300)
Wages and benefits	(780)	(700)
Other operating expenses	(1,000)	(1,000)
Operating income	170	200
Interest expense	(170)	(170)
Pretax income	—	30
Income taxes	—	(9)
Net income	$ —	$ 21

"If we use manual equipment, our initial equipment investment would be $3.5 million. The automated equipment alternative requires an initial investment of $4 million. Consequently, the amount of capital required to finance the company will be larger if we use automated equipment.

"The choice of equipment affects our projected income statement in two ways. The amount of depreciation differs because of the amounts invested in equipment. Annual depreciation expense will be lower for manual equipment. The choice also affects the amount of labor cost we can expect. The automated equipment alternative results in lower wages and benefits, saving us $80,000 next year. Other income statement amounts, except taxes, do not vary between the alternatives.

"The bottom line is, we should expect profit to be zero in the first year if we choose the manual equipment alternative. We earn a $21,000 profit if we choose automated equipment. Keep in mind, however, that we have to invest more money if we go with automated equipment."

"Okay," Stan remarked, "but what happens in the future? We expect sales to increase each year. Can we produce enough product to meet higher demand in the future?"

"The answer depends on which alternative we choose," Ellen answered. "Exhibit 4 provides similar information to Exhibit 3, assuming sales of $3.6 million, the amount we expect in the second year of operations.

"If we select the manual equipment, we will have to purchase an additional $250,000 of equipment to meet the higher demand. The advantage of using manual equipment is that we can start with less equipment and add more equipment as demand increases. For example, we can start with five mixers and add a sixth when we need it. If we use automated equipment, we must purchase large automated mixers and ovens to meet our expected sales of $3 million. However, we can increase production to $3.6 million without adding equipment. Another advantage of the automated equipment is that we can increase production without increasing labor costs. If we use manual machines, we will need additional employees to operate the new machinery.

"The result of these changes is that at $3.6 million of sales, depreciation and labor costs increase for the manual equipment alternative. Also, we will use more ingredients regardless of the type of equipment we use. Other costs do not increase, however. Therefore, our net income is positive for each alternative. The automated equipment alternative provides much higher income, however, as you can see in Exhibit 4."

Exhibit 4

Expected Effects of Mom's Cookie Company's Investing Decisions with Sales of $3.6 Million

(In thousands)	Manual	Automated
Assets:		
Current assets	$ 1,200	$ 1,440
Plant assets	3,750	4,000
Total assets	$ 4,950	$ 5,440
Sales	$ 3,600	$ 3,600
Cost of ingredients	(960)	(960)
Depreciation	(275)	(300)
Wages and benefits	(936)	(700)
Other operating expenses	(1,000)	(1,000)
Operating income	429	640
Interest expense	(170)	(170)
Pretax income	259	470
Income taxes	(78)	(141)
Net income	$ 181	$ 329

"So it looks like the choice is clear," Maria concluded. "The automated equipment appears to be the best choice. It results in higher net income at the $3 and $3.6 million sales levels. Shouldn't we select that alternative?"

Investment Decisions and Risk

"Probably," Ellen agreed. "But we need to consider the risk associated with each alternative. The automated equipment requires a larger investment. Also, we cannot reduce our costs very much if our sales don't meet expectations. Look at Exhibit 5, for example."

"In this exhibit, sales for next year are assumed to be $2.8 million, less than we expect but still a possibility. A real advantage of using manual equipment is apparent at this level. We can buy less equipment and still produce enough cookies to meet demand. Also, we can hire fewer employees and save some labor costs. Therefore, though we incur a loss, it is less than the loss incurred with the automated alternative. Also, the cash we save from buying less equipment will help us stay in business until demand increases.

"A disadvantage of the automated equipment is that we cannot reduce labor costs. We will need the same number of employees to operate and maintain the equipment whether we sell $2.8 million of product or $3.6 million. Once we have the automated equipment, our costs would remain fairly constant regardless of how much we produce. And, we can't downsize our operations and still stay in business. All of the equipment will be needed to manufacture any reasonable amount of product.

Exhibit 5

Expected Effects of Mom's Cookie Company's Investing Decisions with Sales of $2.8 Million

(In thousands)	Manual	Automated
Assets:		
Current assets	$ 900	$ 900
Plant assets	3,400	4,000
Total assets	$ 4,300	$ 4,900
Sales	$ 2,800	$ 2,800
Cost of ingredients	(747)	(747)
Depreciation	(233)	(300)
Wages and benefits	(728)	(700)
Other operating expenses	(1,000)	(1,000)
Operating income	92	53
Interest expense	(170)	(170)
Pretax income	(78)	(117)
Income taxes	23	35
Net income	$ (55)	$ (82)

"Exhibit 6 illustrates the relation between sales and net inc[...] tive. Manual equipment is the safer choice. If sales are lower than[...] likely to survive if we invest in this equipment. On the other h[...] more money if we go with automated equipment."

Exhibit 6 A Comparison of the Effects of Investment Decisions on Profits of Mom's C[...]

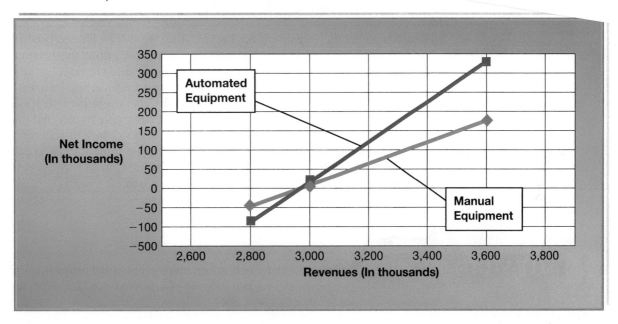

"The trade-off we are considering is typical of many companies," Ellen noted. "One alternative results in higher fixed costs than the other. **Fixed costs** are costs that do not increase in proportion to increases in sales. **Variable costs** are those that do increase in proportion to increases in sales. In our situation, if we go with automated equipment, most of our costs will be fixed. We can't cut costs much if sales are lower than expected, but we don't increase costs much if sales increase. Consequently, we lose more money if sales are low and make more money if sales are high than we would with an alternative that has fewer fixed costs. If we use manual equipment, our costs increase more rapidly as sales increase, but they also decrease more rapidly as sales decrease."

Ellen continued, "**The use of fixed costs to increase net income as sales increase is known as** *operating leverage.* Automation often results in higher operating leverage because a larger portion of total operating expenses is fixed. Other common causes of high operating leverage are large investments in plant assets and labor costs that don't change much in proportion to sales. High operating leverage increases risk, but it also increases the potential for high profits."

Case in Point

The Effect of High Operating Leverage

Airlines are an example of companies with high operating leverage. It costs an airline about the same amount to fly an airplane whether it is full or empty. The cost of the airplane, the flight crew, maintenance, and fuel are largely fixed when a plane flies between two cities. The amount of revenue the airline earns depends on the number of tickets it sells. If the plane is full, the airline earns a good profit. If it is empty, the airline loses a lot of money. Other industries with high operating leverage are utilities, because they require a large investment in equipment regardless of how much they sell, and publishing companies. It costs almost as much to publish a book or magazine if one copy is sold as it does if a thousand copies are sold.

"We'll have to be sure our sales projections are accurate if we decide on automated equipment," Stan remarked. "But, I think it's the best choice for us."

"We know we have a good product," Maria added. "I think the advantages of automation are worth the risk. We'll have the production capacity we expect to need in the future."

"More importantly," Stan observed, "we will have a higher quality product. Once the equipment is working properly, it doesn't make many mistakes. We will save on waste from defective products, and we won't run as much risk of losing customers because of poor quality."

Ellen completed the conversation. "I agree. Also, we will be able to produce our product faster and deliver it to customers in a shorter period. I think the advantages of the automated equipment outweigh the risks of higher operating leverage. In addition, the company's financial leverage will be low because we are financing primarily with equity. Because our financial risk is low, we can afford higher operating risk. If sales are lower than expected, we won't run a major risk of not being able to pay creditors. Investors will expect high growth in profits. We have a better chance of achieving high growth with automated equipment because profits increase more rapidly as sales increase. If our revenues are much less than we expect or if we can't increase revenues each year, we probably won't be in business very long anyway."

1 SELF-STUDY PROBLEM

Financial statement information is presented below for Alchemy Corporation, a producer of pharmaceuticals. The company expects sales to increase by about 10% in 2004.

WebTUTOR Advantage

(In millions)	2003 Actual	2004 Expected
Sales	$988	$1,087
Cost of goods sold	(660)	(726)
Operating expenses	(294)	(300)
Operating income	34	61
Interest expense	(6)	(6)
Pretax income	28	55
Income taxes	(10)	(19)
Net income	$ 18	$ 36

Alchemy's management is considering automating much of the company's production process. The automation would result in about half of the company's cost of goods sold being fixed. Currently, most of these costs vary in proportion to sales, as shown in the financial numbers presented above.

Required

A. Assume that half ($330 million) of Alchemy's cost of goods sold in 2003 is fixed and that the other half increases in proportion to sales, an increase of 10%. Compute the company's expected cost of goods sold and net income in 2004. Assume that income taxes are 35% of pretax income. Round to the nearest million.

B. Compare your results with those presented above, which assume that cost of goods sold varies in proportion to sales. What effect would the automation have on Alchemy's profitability? What effect would it have on the company's risk? Explain your answer.

The solution to Self-Study Problem 1 appears at the end of the chapter.

INTERPRETATION OF INVESTING ACTIVITIES

OBJECTIVE 3

Use financial statements to evaluate investing activities for various companies.

The first part of this chapter examined the investing decisions of managers and the effects of these decisions on a company's financial statements. This section examines financial statement information provided by actual corporations. We use this information to demonstrate how decision makers interpret the investing activities of companies and make decisions about companies' risk, return, and value attributes.

In the remaining sections of this chapter, we will consider the following issues as we look at the analysis of accounting information for the purpose of evaluating investing activities:

1. Identification of investing activities for one or more companies and fiscal periods
2. Consideration of asset growth for company profits and value
3. Measurement of the effects of asset growth
4. Examination of the effects of investing activities and growth on risk
5. Examination of creditors' use of accounting information about investing activities

Identifying Investing Activities

Exhibit 7 provides selected financial statement information for **Krispy Kreme Doughnuts, Inc.**, and **Starbucks Corporation**. Because the companies are in similar businesses, their assets and investment activities are similar. As a first step in our analysis, we want to identify the companies' long-term assets and the changes in these assets resulting from investing activities.

Exhibit 7 Selected Financial Statement Information for Krispy Kreme and Starbucks

(In thousands)	Krispy Kreme 2001	Krispy Kreme 2000	Starbucks 2001	Starbucks 2000
Balance Sheet				
Current assets	$ 67,611	$ 41,038	$ 593,925	$ 458,234
Long-term assets:				
Property and equipment, cost	116,896	93,243	1,741,031	1,377,162
Accumulated depreciation	(38,556)	(32,659)	(605,247)	(446,403)
Plant and equipment, net	78,340	60,584	1,135,784	930,759
Long-term investments	22,572	—	63,097	55,839
Other assets	2,970	3,336	58,233	46,714
Total assets	$171,493	$104,958	$1,851,039	$1,491,546
Income Statement				
Total revenues	$300,715	$220,243	$2,648,980	$2,177,614
Depreciation and amortization expenses	6,457	4,546	163,501	130,232
Net income	14,725	5,956	181,210	94,564
Statement of Cash Flows				
Cash flow from (for) investing activities:				
Purchase of property and equipment	$ (25,655)	$ (11,335)	$ (384,215)	$ (316,450)
Proceeds from disposal of property and equipment	1,419	830	—	—
(Increase) decrease in other assets	(1,348)	479	(9,071)	(6,318)
Purchase of investments, net	(41,704)	—	(39,767)	(53,686)
Net cash used for investing activities:	$ (67,288)	$ (10,026)	$ (433,053)	$ (376,454)

It is apparent from Exhibit 7 that Starbucks is larger than Krispy Kreme in terms of total assets. In 2001, Starbucks was more than 10 times as large as Krispy Kreme. The size difference also is apparent from a comparison of long-term assets. For example, Starbucks' net property and equipment was more than 14 times greater than that of Krispy Kreme in 2001.

Plant assets account for most of the long-term assets of both companies. Long-term investments and other assets are not especially important for either company. Neither company has been active in acquiring other companies, which would result in long-term investments or other assets such as goodwill.

Though Krispy Kreme was smaller than Starbucks, it grew at a faster rate from 2000 to 2001. Krispy Kreme's total assets increased 63% [($171,493 − $104,958) ÷ $104,958] during this period while Starbucks' total assets increased 24% [($1,851,039 − $1,491,546) ÷ $1,491,546]. Krispy Kreme's property and equipment grew by 29% [($78,340 − $60,584) ÷ $60,584] relative to Starbucks' growth of 22% [($1,135,784 − $930,759) ÷ $930,759]. The more rapid growth was associated with a larger increase in revenues for Krispy Kreme relative to Starbucks. Krispy Kreme's revenues grew 37% [($300,715 − $220,243) ÷ $220,243], and Starbucks' revenues grew 22% [($2,648,980 − $2,177,614) ÷ $2,177,614].

Other information about changes in long-term assets is provided by the investing activities section of the statement of cash flows. During 2001, Krispy Kreme paid $25.7 million for additional property and equipment. Krispy Kreme reported depreciation and amortization expenses for 2001 of $6.5 million. Therefore, Krispy Kreme's new purchases of plant assets were $19.2 million ($25.7 − $6.5) more than the amount of long-term assets allocated to expenses during 2001. For a company to grow, it must acquire assets in addition to those necessary to replace assets that are being consumed during a period.

Starbucks' capital expenditures for new plant assets amounted to $384 million in 2001. This amount was much larger than the amount of depreciation and amortization expense Starbucks recorded in 2001 ($163.5 million).

The Importance of Asset Growth

OBJECTIVE 4

Explain how investing activities affect company value, and use accounting information to measure value-increasing activities.

Growth in assets is important to the value of a company and the wealth of its stockholders. For most companies, the ability to produce and sell products depends on having the necessary assets to support these activities. A manufacturing company must have equipment and facilities to produce goods. A merchandising company must have equipment and facilities to store, transport, display, and sell its goods. The amount a company can sell depends on how much it can produce or on how much it can make available to customers.

Both Krispy Kreme and Starbucks sell merchandise to customers through stores. The number and size of the stores limits the amounts that can be sold. When Krispy Kreme opens new stores, asset growth results. The investment in these stores adds to the company's total assets. It also provides the basis for additional sales and profits. As we noted in the previous section, revenues grew for both Krispy Kreme and Starbucks from 2000 to 2001. In addition, Krispy Kreme reported an increase in net income of 147% [($14,725 − $5,956) ÷ $5,956] and Starbucks reported an increase of 92% [($181,210 − $94,564) ÷ $94,564]. Starbucks opened 1,208 new stores during its 2001 fiscal year, ending the year with 4,709 stores. Krispy Kreme opened 26 new stores, ending the year with 174 stores.

Measuring the Effects of Growth

Additional investment and asset growth are valuable when a company uses these assets to generate higher profits. Additional investment is not valuable for its own sake. For example, if a company pays $1 million for an additional store, but it is not able to make a profit from the store, the investment is not a good decision.

A common measure of the outcome of a company's investment decisions is return on assets (ROA).

$$\text{Return on Assets} = \text{Net Income} \div \text{Total Assets}$$

Return on assets compares profits from producing and selling goods and services with the total amount invested in assets.

From Exhibit 7, we see that Krispy Kreme's return on assets for 2001 was 8.5%.

$$0.085 = \$14,725 \div \$171,493$$

Starbucks' return on assets for 2001 was 9.8%.

$$0.098 = \$181,210 \div \$1,851,039$$

Thus, compared with Krispy Kreme, Starbucks was creating a higher return on its investment in assets. For every dollar invested in assets by Starbucks, the company earned 9.8¢ of profit. For every dollar invested in assets by Krispy Kreme, it earned 8.5¢.

One way to examine events that affect a company's return on assets is to separate return on assets into components. Two primary components of return on assets are asset turnover and profit margin. *Asset turnover* **is the ratio of revenues to total assets:.**

Asset Turnover = Revenues ÷ Total Assets

It is a measure of the ability of a company to use its assets to sell its products. Revenues include sales and service revenues that result from a business's primary operations. A company with a high asset turnover is more effective in using its assets than one with a low asset turnover.

Profit margin (**or** *return on sales*) **is the ratio of net income to revenues.**

Profit Margin (or Return on Sales) = Net Income ÷ Revenues

It is a measure of the ability of a company to produce profits from its sales. A company with a high profit margin is more efficient in controlling costs than one with a low profit margin.

Return on assets is the product of asset turnover and profit margin.

Return on Assets = Asset Turnover × Profit Margin

We can determine Krispy Kreme's and Starbucks' asset turnover and profit margin from information in Exhibit 7. These amounts are provided in Exhibit 8.

Exhibit 8

Asset Turnover and Profit Margin for Krispy Kreme and Starbucks

	Krispy Kreme		Starbucks	
	2001	2000	2001	2000
Asset Turnover	1.754	2.098	1.431	1.460
Profit Margin	4.90%	2.70%	6.84%	4.34%
Return on Assets	8.59%	5.67%	9.79%	6.34%

A practical way to interpret asset turnover is to translate the ratio into dollars. Krispy Kreme's asset turnover of 1.75 in 2001 means that the company was able to generate $1.75 of sales for every $1 it had invested in assets. In 2001, Starbucks was able to generate $1.43 of sales for each dollar of investment. Therefore, Krispy Kreme was more effective than Starbucks in using its assets in 2001. Krispy Kreme also had a higher asset turnover ratio than Starbucks in 2000. Both companies, particularly Krispy Kreme, were less effective in 2001 than in 2000, as measured by the decrease in their asset turnover ratios.

Similarly, we can translate profit margin into dollars. Krispy Kreme's profit margin of 4.9% in 2001 means that the company was able to generate 4.9¢ of net income for every $1 of sales. This ratio was an increase from 2.7¢ for every $1 of sales in 2000. Starbucks' profit margin in 2001 was 6.8%, an increase from 4.3% the prior year.

A small change in profit margin can have a major effect on a company's performance. Though Krispy Kreme's and Starbucks' asset turnover ratios decreased, their profit margins increased from 2000 to 2001. The increase in profit margins resulted in higher return on assets for both companies because they were doing a better job of controlling costs in 2001 than in 2000.

Comparing asset turnover with profit margin provides information about why Starbucks was earning a higher return on assets than Krispy Kreme. Starbucks earned a higher profit margin, which more than offset the effect of its lower asset turnover. Profitability depends on the ability of a company to use its assets to sell products and on the ability of a company to earn a profit from those sales. Krispy Kreme was doing a relatively good job of selling its products but was not earning as much profit on those sales as Starbucks.

2 SELF-STUDY PROBLEM

Accounting information is provided below for two hardware companies that compete for customers.

WebTUTOR Advantage

(In millions)	Moreco		DealRight	
	2004	2003	2004	2003
Total assets	$48.3	$44.7	$120.6	$118.4
Revenues	67.9	61.0	159.1	143.2
Net income	5.3	4.2	9.5	10.0

Required

A. Compute asset turnover, profit margin, and return on assets for each year and company. Also, compute asset, revenue, and net income growth rates for each company from 2003 to 2004.

B. Evaluate the performance of each company with respect to the other and also in terms of changes from 2003 to 2004. Identify reasons for the differences in performance.

The solution to Self-Study Problem 2 appears at the end of the chapter.

THE EFFECT OF INVESTMENT ON EFFECTIVENESS AND EFFICIENCY

OBJECTIVE 5

Identify ways in which a company can use its assets to improve effectiveness and efficiency.

Investment is important for a company. As a company acquires additional assets, it should be able to produce and sell more products and earn higher profits. Asset growth can increase a company's profits and return on assets if the additional assets improve the company's effectiveness and/or efficiency. Effectiveness increases when the dollar amount of sales increases more rapidly than the dollar amount of additional investment. As discussed in the previous section, we can observe this increase in effectiveness by examining the asset turnover ratio. Increases in asset turnover result when a company invests in new locations that produce large increases in sales. Asset turnover also increases when a company sells products in high demand. If Starbucks has products in its stores that customers are not willing to buy, its sales will be low relative to the amount it has invested in assets. If it replaces these products with others that customers are interested in buying, its asset turnover will increase. Also, it can increase asset turnover by closing locations that do not create high sales and moving its assets to locations that produce higher sales.

Efficiency increases when a company is able to earn greater profit for each additional dollar of product it sells. Efficiency depends on reducing costs relative to the amount sold.

Effectiveness and efficiency often go together. For example, assume that Mom's Cookie Company invests $5 million in assets. It pays employees $700,000 in wages and benefits each year. Utilities and other costs amount to $300,000 per year. Average cost of goods sold for its products is 60% of sales revenues, and income taxes are 30% of pretax income. In 2004, the store sold $3.0 million of goods. Therefore, its net income would be as follows:

Sales	$ 3,000,000	
Cost of goods sold	(1,800,000)	60% of sales
Other operating expenses	(1,000,000)	
Pretax income	200,000	
Income taxes	(60,000)	
Net income	$ 140,000	

Suppose that by changing some of its product line, the company can increase sales to $3.3 million without any additional asset investment and without hiring additional employees or increasing utilities or other costs. Its net income would then be as follows:

Sales	$ 3,300,000	
Cost of goods sold	(1,980,000)	60% of sales
Other operating expenses	(1,000,000)	
Pretax income	320,000	
Income taxes	(96,000)	
Net income	$ 224,000	

Observe that an increase in sales of 10% (from $3 million to $3.3 million) results in an increase in net income of 60% (from $140,000 to $224,000). Exhibit 9 describes the effects of the increase in sales on the company's asset turnover, profit margin, and return on assets.

Exhibit 9

The Effect of a Sales Increase on Return on Assets

	Before	After
Sales Revenues (in millions)	$3	$3.3
Asset Turnover	0.600	0.660
Profit Margin	4.67%	6.79%
Return on Assets	2.80%	4.48%

The increase in sales improves the company's asset turnover. It is using its assets more effectively to generate more sales. No additional investment was made to create the additional sales. Company management found a better way to use the company's assets. Profit margin increased 60% (from 2.8% to 4.48%) as a result of the sales increase. This increase in profit margin resulted because many of the company's costs did not change in proportion to the increase in sales. Only cost of goods sold increased as sales increased. Therefore, the company's profits grew much more rapidly than its sales as a result of operating leverage. The more effective use of assets produced a dramatic increase in profits. Thus, a primary management decision involves finding the best locations and assets in which to invest and then using those assets effectively and efficiently to generate profits.

If a company's sales decrease, its profits often decrease more rapidly than its sales. Each dollar of lost sales is not matched by a dollar's decrease in expenses. For example, a company must employ sufficient workers to conduct its business, and so a decrease in sales often does not result in a proportional decrease in wages and benefits. Equipment and building costs often cannot be reduced in the short run. Therefore, profits decrease more rapidly than sales.

If sales decrease for any length of time, a company must find ways to reduce its investment so that it can eliminate unnecessary costs. Companies sell buildings, equipment, and other assets that are not being used effectively. Often these assets must be sold at less than their book values (cost minus accumulated depreciation), resulting in losses that reduce the company's already low net income. Also, a company may have to incur separation or relocation costs for employees who are terminated or moved to other locations. Thus, in the short run, downsizing a company usually results in extra costs and low net income or a net loss. If a company can close stores that are not profitable or get rid of assets it does not need, it may be able to become profitable and earn a return on assets that is competitive with those of other companies in its industry. If a company is not successful in these efforts, it is likely to be purchased by another company or to go out of business.

Thus, although asset growth is important to creating company value, growth must be accompanied by increases in sales and profits that compensate the company and its owners for the additional investment. If a company's growth is not effective, its additional investments reduce its return on assets. Eventually, the company is forced to sell assets that are not productive in an effort to return to a satisfactory level of profitability. This process often is costly and difficult. Investment in assets is essential. Effective asset growth increases company value. Growth also is risky. Investment in the wrong assets, investment in too many assets, or improper management of assets generally leads to poor profitability and can jeopardize a company's existence.

INVESTING ACTIVITIES AND CREDITOR DECISIONS

OBJECTIVE 6

Explain why accounting information about long-term assets is useful for creditors.

A company's investing activities may be particularly important to its creditors. Companies often borrow money to acquire long-term assets. Accordingly, the ability of a company to repay creditors and pay interest usually is connected to its ability to use its long-term assets to generate profits and cash flows. If a company is unsuccessful in creating profits from its assets, it usually must sell a portion of its assets to create cash to repay its creditors. If the company is very unsuccessful and goes out of business, it sells its assets and uses the cash to pay off its debts. In some cases, specific debts are connected to particular assets that are used as security for the debts. If a company cannot repay these debts, the assets securing the debts must be transferred to creditors or sold to repay creditors.

Because of these relationships, the value of a company's long-term assets is particularly important to creditors. When a company's assets decrease in value, its debt becomes riskier. Consequently, accounting measurement rules traditionally are very conservative in the measurement of the value of assets, particularly tangible assets such as property, plant, and equipment. These rules attempt to ensure that a company does not overvalue assets on its balance sheet. Assets are recorded at cost and, except for certain financial assets that can be sold at market value, are not written up to a higher value, even if their market value increases. Thus, a building that is purchased for $1 million in 2003 is recorded at cost and is depreciated over its useful life. The amount reported on the balance sheet for the building will always be less than $1 million, regardless of how much the owner could receive if the building were sold.

Accounting standard setters in the United States have been reluctant to permit companies to write up their assets to market value for fear the amounts recorded would be highly subjective and might overstate asset value. In many cases, it is difficult to determine the market value of an asset. Further, the market value of an asset that is being used productively may be much higher than the market value of the same asset if it must be sold to repay debts.

Accounting measurement rules require companies to write down their assets, however, if the market values of the assets decrease below their book values. For example, assume that a company owns a building that it purchased for $1 million. Accumulated depreciation on the building at the end of 2004 was $600,000. Therefore, the book value at the end of 2004 was $400,000. At this time, the company determined that the market value of the building was $250,000. Accounting rules require the company to write down the asset by $150,000 ($400,000 − $250,000), recognizing a loss for this amount.

This measurement rule, known as **lower of cost or market**, is intended to protect investors, particularly creditors, by ensuring that assets are not overstated.

Accounting rules in the United States differ from those of certain other countries with respect to the amount reported for long-term assets. Some countries—Great Britain, for example—permit companies to recognize increases in the market values of many assets. These increases in values also increase the stockholders' equities of these companies.

3 SELF-STUDY PROBLEM

Information is provided below for two paper products companies.

(In millions)	Tenix Company		Beson Company	
	2004	2003	2004	2003
Property and equipment	$471	$523	$214	$203
Total assets	654	708	323	308
Current liabilities	112	124	86	79
Long-term debt	435	440	125	130
Stockholders' equity	107	144	112	99
Asset impairment charge	(30)	—	—	—
Operating income	8	12	30	24
Interest expense	(38)	(39)	(10)	(9)

Required If you were a creditor of these companies, would you be concerned about the ability of either company to repay its debts? Explain your answer.

The solution to Self-Study Problem 3 appears at the end of the chapter.

REVIEW

SUMMARY of IMPORTANT CONCEPTS

1. The assets in which a company invests affect its profitability.
    a. Assets are necessary for a company to produce products and sell them to customers.
    b. Managers must determine the particular assets a company needs and how much of each type of asset it needs.
    c. Managers may have to choose among different assets that provide the same function.
    d. Choices concerning the amount and type of asset affect the capacity of a company to produce and sell products and the costs of those products.

2. Investing decisions often affect the proportion of a company's costs that are fixed or variable.
    a. High operating leverage results when a company has a lot of fixed costs.
    b. Costs that may be fixed are depreciation costs on assets and labor costs for workers who use those assets.
    c. A company with high fixed costs is riskier than one with low fixed costs because its profits change more rapidly as sales change.
    d. High operating leverage is an advantage when a company's sales are relatively high and when they increase. It is a disadvantage when sales are low or when they decrease.

3. A company's balance sheet and cash flow statement provide information about its investing activities.
    a. The balance sheet identifies the types and amounts of long-term assets that a company controls. Also, it provides a basis for determining increases and decreases in these amounts.

b. The cash flow statement identifies amounts invested in long-term assets during a period and amounts received from the sale of these assets.
c. Financial statement information is useful for measuring growth and change in a company's assets and, therefore, change in its ability to produce and sell products.

4. Asset growth increases a company's value by permitting it to increase sales and profits.
   a. Return on assets is a commonly used measure of a company's success in using its assets.
   b. Return on assets is affected by a company's effectiveness and efficiency.
   c. Asset turnover is a measure of effectiveness that considers the ability of a company to use its assets to create sales.
   d. Profit margin is a measure of efficiency that considers the ability of a company to create profits from its sales.
   e. Return on assets is the product of asset turnover times profit margin.

5. How a company uses its assets affects its effectiveness and efficiency.
   a. A company uses its assets effectively when it acquires the amounts of assets it needs to produce products it can sell and when it places these assets in locations that permit it to sell large quantities of products.
   b. If a company acquires too many assets, it can attempt to sell some assets to increase its profits and return on assets. In the short run, downsizing by selling unproductive assets usually is costly. In the long run, it may permit a company to survive and become competitive.
   c. A company uses its assets efficiently when it uses these assets to increase sales so that revenues increase faster than expenses.

6. Accounting information uses conservative values for most long-term assets.
   a. Conservatism results when increases in asset values above their cost or book value are not recorded but decreases in value are recorded.
   b. Conservatism protects the interests of creditors by ensuring that asset values are not overstated.
   c. If a company is unable to repay its debts, it may have to sell its assets to make these payments.

DEFINE

TERMS and CONCEPTS DEFINED in this CHAPTER

asset turnover (F455)   profit margin (F455)
operating leverage (F451)   return on sales (F455)

SELF-STUDY PROBLEM SOLUTIONS

SSP12-1   A. Expected cost of goods sold for 2004 = $693

$660 ÷ 2 =	$330	(half is fixed)
($660 ÷ 2) × 1.10 =	363	(half varies with sales, increasing by 10%)
Total cost of goods sold	$693	

(In millions)	2003 Actual	2004 Expected
Sales	$988	$1,087
Cost of goods sold	660	693
Operating expenses	294	300
Operating income	34	94
Interest expense	(6)	(6)
Pretax income	28	88
Income taxes (35%)	(10)	(31)
Net income	$ 18	$ 57

B. Because a portion of the cost of goods sold is fixed, these costs do not increase with sales. Therefore, the cost of goods sold is lower if the production process is automated and sales increase. Lower cost of goods sold results in higher net income.

Higher fixed costs increase operating leverage and increase the company's risk. Though profits are higher if sales increase, if sales decrease they will be lower than they would be with the nonautomated option. Fixed costs do not decrease in proportion to sales when sales decrease. Therefore, profits decrease more rapidly for companies with high operating leverage when sales decrease. Expenses that vary in proportion to sales decrease as sales decrease and, consequently, do not affect net income as much as fixed expenses do.

SSP12-2   A.

	Moreco		DealRight	
	2004	**2003**	**2004**	**2003**
Asset turnover	67.9 ÷ 48.3 = 1.406	61.0 ÷ 44.7 = 1.365	159.1 ÷ 120.6 = 1.319	143.2 ÷ 118.4 = 1.209
Profit margin	5.3 ÷ 67.9 = 0.078	4.2 ÷ 61.0 = 0.069	9.5 ÷ 159.1 = 0.060	10.0 ÷ 143.2 = 0.070
Return on assets	1.406 × 0.078 = 0.110	1.365 × 0.069 = 0.094	1.319 × 0.060 = 0.079	1.209 × 0.070 = 0.085
Asset growth	(48.3 − 44.7) ÷ 44.7 = 0.081		(120.6 − 118.4) ÷ 118.4 = 0.019	
Revenue growth	(67.9 − 61.0) ÷ 61.0 = 0.113		(159.1 − 143.2) ÷ 143.2 = 0.111	
Net income growth	(5.3 − 4.2) ÷ 4.2 = 0.262		(1.319 − 1.209) ÷ 1.209 = 0.091	

B. Moreco's return on assets increased from 2003 to 2004, while DealRight's return on assets decreased. Moreco's return on assets is higher in both years than DealRight's. Accordingly, Moreco is making better use of its assets to create profits.

Moreco's asset turnover increased from 2003 to 2004, as did DealRight's asset turnover. Therefore, both companies became more effective in using their assets to produce sales. Moreco's asset growth was higher than DealRight's, however. Therefore, Moreco was more successful in investing in productive assets, leading to higher sales and profits.

DealRight's major problem was a decrease in profit margin. DealRight became less efficient than Moreco. Moreco's profit margin increased. The greater increase in Moreco's profit margin could result from higher operating leverage. Moreco has more fixed costs that did not increase in proportion to sales. Another reason could be greater cost control. Some of DealRight's costs increased more rapidly than its sales, thus reducing profits.

SSP12-3   Creditors should be more concerned about Tenix Company than about Beson Company. Tenix reported a sizable decrease in plant assets. Much of this decrease was due to a writedown of assets because their market value was below their book value. Total plant assets are not much higher than long-term debt. Accordingly, the ability of Tenix to repay its debts in the event it went out of business is questionable. In addition, Tenix's profits are negative after deducting interest expense. The company is not earning sufficient profits to meet interest requirements. Tenix's performance is poor. Therefore, the likelihood that it could go out of business is relatively high, in which case it may have difficulty paying off all of its creditors.

Beson, in contrast, appears to be in relatively good shape. Its performance is strong, and its plant assets are large in proportion to long-term debt.

Thinking Beyond the Question

How do assets create value for our business?

Investing decisions affect a company's profits, risk, and value. Investment decisions that result in fixed costs increase risk and the ability of a company to create higher profits and sales. Managing risk involves selecting the amounts and types of long-term assets a company uses. Those decisions also affect performance measures such as return on assets. Asset costs affect net income as assets are consumed and total assets increase as more assets are acquired. A low return on assets is an indicator of poor investing decisions. If a company is not satisfied with its investing decisions and the performance of its assets, what can it do to improve that performance?

QUESTIONS

Q12-1
Obj. 1
Why are investing activities critical to the success of a company?

Q12-2
Obj. 1
How do investing activities affect a company's growth?

Q12-3
Obj. 1
How do investing choices affect the choices available to a company in the future? Explain.

Q12-4
Obj. 2
A friend who is approaching retirement is discussing her investment plan. She tells you that she wants to find a mutual fund that invests in stock of companies with high fixed costs, such as airlines, software developers, and publishers. "The higher fixed costs should make expenses more predictable, and earnings should be more reliable." What is your analysis of your friend's strategy?

Q12-5
Obj. 3
The balance sheet and statement of cash flows provide information about a company's access to and use of cash. What differences would you expect to see in the information related to cash on these statements for a company reporting strong financial performance and a company reporting weak financial performance?

Q12-6
Obj. 3
In reviewing a company's financial statements you observe that the company is consistently profitable and has consistent positive cash flows from operations and investing activities. Its cash flow from financing activities is consistently negative. What does this suggest to you about the company?

Q12-7
Obj. 3
Why do some companies have a very large portion of total assets invested in property, plant, and equipment while other companies have just a small portion of assets invested in this manner?

Q12-8
Obj. 3
What useful information can be obtained by comparing a firm's cost of plant, property, and equipment to the amount of its accumulated depreciation?

Q12-9
Obj. 4
Why might a company wishing to increase its asset turnover acquire new assets? Wouldn't the greater amount of assets merely decrease asset turnover?

Q12-10
Obj. 4
How do investing activities affect company value?

Q12-11
Obj. 4
How is return on assets related to investing decisions?

Q12-12
Obj. 5
Asset turnover is a measure of effectiveness. How can a firm increase its effectiveness?

Q12-13
Obj. 5
How is it possible that profits can increase by 40% when sales increase by a much smaller amount?

Q12-14
Obj. 6

Why is information about investing activities of interest to creditors?

Q12-15
Obj. 6

Malcolm Greenlees is a friend who is planning to be a business manager. In a recent discussion about financial matters, Malcolm made the following statement. "A company's balance sheet measures the value of a company's resources. Investors can use this value for pricing the company's stock and for comparing the values of different companies. Creditors can use it for evaluating loan risk." How would you respond to Malcolm?

EXERCISES

If your instructor is using Personal Trainer in this course, you may complete online the assignments identified by $\frac{P}{T}$.

Note: *Financial measurements have been presented in their simplest form in this chapter in order to place emphasis on thinking about the measurement and its connection with accounting, rather than on the complexities of calculation. Simplified calculations are also used in these end-of-chapter materials. In other texts, for example, return on assets may be calculated based on average total assets for the year, rather than on ending assets, and the income figure used may have the effects of interest and taxes removed.*

E12-1

Write a short definition for each of the terms listed in the *Terms and Concepts Defined in this Chapter* section.

E12-2
Obj. 2
$\frac{P}{T}$

Sanders Company recorded sales revenues of $10 million for the year just ended. It recorded expenses totaling $9 million. Of these expenses, $4 million were expenses that would not have been different if sales revenue had been different. They were fixed expenses.

a. Prepare a table showing how much net income Sanders would have earned on sales of $8 million, $10 million, and $12 million.
b. Suppose the company's total expenses had been $9 million, and of that amount, the fixed expenses had been $6 million. The remaining expenses would have varied proportionately with sales revenue. Prepare a table showing how much net income Sanders would have earned on sales of $8 million, $10 million, and $12 million.
c. What conclusions about the effect of operating leverage on net income can you draw from this analysis?

E12-3
Obj. 2

The Kolby and Kent companies both increased sales by 30% this year when compared with last year's results. Kolby's net income increased 40% as a result of the increased sales. Kent's net income increased 20%. Explain why differences in operating leverage may have resulted in a higher increase in net income for Kolby than for Kent. Provide a diagram to illustrate your explanation.

E12-4
Obj. 2
$\frac{P}{T}$

Given below is selected information about two companies.

	Company A	Company B
Sales	$10,000	$10,000
Fixed costs	4,000	7,000
Variable costs	5,000	2,000

a. Calculate net income for each company.
b. What is operating leverage? Is it present in the operations of these two companies? If so, which company uses the greater amount of operating leverage?
c. If sales decrease by 10%, which company will report the higher net income?
d. If sales increase by 10%, which company will report the higher net income?

E12-5
Obj. 3
$\frac{P}{T}$

Selected accounting information is provided below for two companies.

(In millions)	2001	2000	1999	1998
Total assets:				
Sara Lee	$10,167	$11,611	$10,292	$10,989
Merck & Co.	44,007	40,155	35,934	31,853
Depreciation and amortization:				
Sara Lee	599	602	533	618
Merck & Co.	1,464	1,277	1,145	1,015
Capital expenditures:				
Sara Lee	532	647	535	474
Merck & Co.	2,725	2,728	2,561	1,973

(Continued)

What trends in asset investments are apparent from the data presented? (Hint: Compare total assets, capital expenditures to total assets, and capital expenditures to depreciation and amortization for each year.)

E12-6
Obj. 3

At the end of its most recent fiscal year, Shangri-La Company owned the following investments.

Investment	Historical Cost	Fair Market Value
A	$650,000	$765,000
B	840,000	730,000

Other assets had a book value of $2.4 million and liabilities had a book value of $2.8 million. Shangri-La's net income for 2004 was $280,000. If the company sold investment A at the end of the year for cash, what effect would the sale have on its financial statements and return on assets (ignoring the effect of income taxes)? Assume that assets are reported on the financial statements at historical cost. What effect would the sale of investment B have on the company's financial statements and return on assets? Compare these amounts to those that would be reported if no investments were sold. Does this example help explain why mark-to-market accounting is often required by GAAP? Discuss.

E12-7
Obj. 3
P/T

Selected financial information is reported below for two companies in the computer manufacturing business. The information was taken from the firms' 2001 annual reports.

(In millions)	Compaq	IBM
Plant assets, at cost	$7,098	$38,395
Depreciation expense	1,036	4,195
Net cash outflow for plant assets	927	4,495

a. Compute the ratio of depreciation expense to plant assets at cost for both firms. What do your results suggest?
b. Compute the ratio of cash invested for plant assets to plant assets at cost for both firms. What do your results suggest?

E12-8
Objs. 3, 4
P/T

Following is selected information from Dell Computer Corporation.

Fiscal Year Ended (In millions)	February 1, 2002	February 2, 2001	January 28, 2000
Net revenue	$31,168	$31,888	$25,265
Net income	1,246	2,177	1,666
Cash from operations	3,797	4,195	3,926
Cash used in investing	(2,260)	(757)	(1,183)
Cash used in financing	(2,702)	(2,305)	(695)
Capital expenditures	(303)	(482)	(401)

With the information provided, calculate whatever ratios you can and describe the trends you observe.

E12-9
Obj. 4

The following information is for **McDonald's Corporation** from its 2001 annual report.

(In millions)	2001	2000	1999
Revenues	$14,870	$14,253	$13,259
Net income	1,637	1,977	1,948
Total assets	22,535	21,684	20,983

Evaluate McDonald's Corporation's investing decisions by computing and analyzing its asset turnover, profit margin, and return on assets for 1999 through 2001.

E12-10
Obj. 4

The following information was reported by McDonald's Corporation in its 2001 annual report.

(In millions)	2001	2000	1999
Cash flow from operating activities	$ 2,688	$ 2,752	$ 3,009
Total assets	22,535	21,684	20,983

Evaluate McDonald's Corporation's investing decisions by computing the ratio of cash flow from operating activities to total assets for 1999 through 2001. Compare the cash flow ratio with return on assets from E12-9. What do you conclude, given this information?

E12-11
Obj. 4
$\overset{P}{T}$

Information is provided below for two companies that produce similar jewelry items for the same market.

(In thousands)	Lucy's Lockets		Desi's Delights	
	2005	**2004**	**2005**	**2004**
Sales	$630	$550	$650	$675
Net income	59	50	59	64
Total assets	500	450	875	880

Compute the asset turnover, profit margin, and return on assets for each company for each of the two years. Compare the performances of the two companies. Look at changes within each company and consider differences between the two companies.

E12-12
Obj. 4
$\overset{P}{T}$

Given below is information about four companies.

	Able Co.	Baker Co.	Charlie Ltd.	Dilbert Inc.
Sales	$1,000	$2,000	$2,000	$600
Profit margin	0.18	0.06	0.11	0.24
Asset turnover	1.30	1.60	1.20	1.15

a. Which company generated the greatest profit?
b. Which company is the most efficient? Why?
c. Which company is the most effective? Why?
d. Which company has the greatest total assets?

E12-13
Obj. 4
$\overset{P}{T}$

Following is information about current and projected sales and expenses for Squiggy Company. The company's total assets are also given.

	Current Sales	Decrease of 20%	Increase of 20%
Sales	$ 50,000	$ 40,000	$ 60,000
Less: Fixed costs	(10,000)	(10,000)	(10,000)
Variable costs	(10,000)	(8,000)	(12,000)
Net income	$ 30,000	$ 22,000	$ 38,000
Total assets	$ 25,000	$ 25,000	$ 25,000

a. Calculate the percentage changes in net income that would occur under each projection.
b. Calculate the percentage changes in return on assets, profit margin, and asset turnover that would occur under each projection.

E12-14
Obj. 4

At a meeting of the top managers in your company, President Anne Thompson points out that stockholders have been pressuring the organization to increase return on assets. She asks for suggestions. Four of your colleagues respond in the following manner:

- "Sales, sales, sales. You've got to have more revenue to increase return."
- "Cut the expenses. How can you get a higher return if you don't keep more of your sales dollar?"
- "Expansion! More productive assets! Growth is the way to go."
- "No, no! Cut the assets! Sell those that will bring the best price!"

Evaluate your coworkers' comments. Will these strategies produce a definite increase in return on assets? What are the risks and rewards of each strategy?

E12-15
Obj. 5

In a continuation of E12-14, another member of the group comments that to maximize return on assets, both efficiency and effectiveness are necessary. Explain what is meant by "efficiency" and "effectiveness," how they relate to return on assets, and whether you agree with your colleague's comment.

E12-16

Obj. 5

P/T

Bumblebee Enterprises is considering adding another product line. Below are results from last year and pro forma (expected) results with the addition of the new line. Little change in sales from the current product lines is expected.

(In millions)	Last Year	Pro Forma
Sales	$260	$322
Net income	24	32
Total assets	300	372

Analyze the changes in effectiveness, efficiency, and return on assets that would be expected if the product line were added. Would you recommend addition of the product line?

E12-17

Obj. 5

P/T

The following information is available for Cello Company:

	2005	2004	2003
Sales	$15,000	$ 8,000	$ 4,000
Net income	5,250	2,800	1,200
Average assets	30,000	20,000	10,000

Calculate the return on assets, profit margin, and asset turnover for each year and discuss the reasons for the change in return on assets over the three years.

E12-18

Obj. 6

Winger, Inc. is in the business of renting medical equipment for home health care. New government standards for lifts for disabled patients have rendered some equipment obsolete. Winger owns 10 four-year-old machines, each with a cost of $6,000. They have been depreciated using the straight-line method over an estimated life of 10 years. Since some parts can be used, they still have a resale value of approximately $1,000 each. Explain what accounting measure is required, what the effects on the financial statements will be (including amounts), and why this measure is important to creditors of Winger.

E12-19

Obj. 6

Yarrow Company increased its investment in long-term assets by 20% in the past three years. This investment was financed by rapid increases in cash generated from operating activities. Cash from operating activities also was used to repay about 30% of Yarrow's long-term debt and to repurchase 10% of its common stock. What effect would you expect these events to have on the company's return on assets and return on equity? Does the company appear to be a good prospect for additional debt financing?

E12-20

Objs. 3, 6

P/T

Abdullah Company reported the following information on its statement of cash flows.

(In millions)	2005	2004	2003
Net cash provided by operating activities	$ 3,195	$ 2,869	$ 2,688
Net cash from (used by) investing activities:			
Capital expenditures	(2,661)	(1,358)	(523)
Sales of equipment and property	293	305	257
Investments in other companies	(272)	0	0
Other	392	(627)	(924)
Total investing activities	$(2,248)	$(1,680)	$(1,190)
Net cash from (used by) financing activities:			
Payments on long-term debt	(547)	(648)	(2,130)
Repurchase of common stock	(994)	(740)	0
Other	627	200	614
Total financing activities	$ (914)	$(1,188)	$(1,516)

Interest expense for the past three years has been $372, $420, and $514. The company does not pay dividends. What information about the company's future prospects is communicated by its investing and financing activities during this period? Does the company appear to be a good prospect for new debt financing to be spent on additional capital assets?

PROBLEMS

If your instructor is using Personal Trainer in this course, you may complete online the assignments identified by ᵖ₇.

P12-1

Objs. 1, 2

Determining Investment Strategy for a New Company

You have graduated with a business degree, and you have worked for three years for a small management consulting firm. Ivan Steeger (1352 Bull Run Road, Milltown, OR 97111) is a client who has been involved with several businesses in the past. He expects to be the major provider of equity capital for a new mail-order low-fat cookie business. His co-owners, who have baking expertise and a talent for developing recipes, will run the business.

The owners are about to meet to determine what equipment they will purchase for the business. Ivan gives you the following information about the business and their plans:

- Ivan will be providing about 25% of the financing; the remainder will be debt. Ivan will probably have to give his personal guarantee for much of the debt. The exact amount of debt will depend on the price of the equipment they decide to purchase.
- They expect business growth of about 20% for each of the first five years.
- All of the equipment has an expected life of at least five years. They will definitely purchase mixing and baking equipment. They must decide whether to add equipment that will shape cookies automatically, or hire employees to do the shaping.
- They also must decide what capacity they prefer in their initial equipment purchase. Smaller-capacity equipment would handle their expected demand for the first two years, operating eight hours a day. Equipment with twice the capacity would cost approximately 50% more.

Ivan asks for recommendations about discussion items for the meeting.

Required Write Ivan a letter in which you suggest major issues the owners should consider in making decisions about investments in equipment. You can assume that Ivan has some understanding of business terminology.

P12-2

Objs. 1, 2

The Effect of Investment Strategy and Operating Leverage on Risk and Profits

Following is a set of pro forma (or projected) income statements for a company. The columns labeled *A* are projected results for the company if it follows Strategy A. The columns labeled *B* are projected results for the company if it follows Strategy B.

	Low sales		Medium sales		High sales	
	A	**B**	**A**	**B**	**A**	**B**
Sales	$3,000	$3,000	$4,000	$4,000	$5,000	$5,000
Cost of sales	(180)	(180)	(240)	(240)	(300)	(300)
Depreciation	(315)	(450)	(355)	(450)	(395)	(450)
Wages expense	(1,300)	(1,500)	(1,600)	(1,500)	(1,800)	(1,500)
Other operating expenses	(1,000)	(1,000)	(1,000)	(1,000)	(1,000)	(1,000)
Operating income	205	(130)	805	810	1,505	1,750
Income tax (expense) or savings	(72)	46	(282)	(284)	(527)	(613)
Net income	$ 133	$ (84)	$ 523	$ 526	$ 978	$1,137

Required Study the information given and discuss each of the following.

A. The comparative risk of Strategy A versus Strategy B, as shown in the projected net income results
B. The company's operating leverage
C. The company's investment strategy

P12-3

Obj. 2

ᵖ₇

Evaluating the Effects of Operating Leverage on Profits

Yamhill County currently provides garbage removal services for two of the four small towns within its boundaries. In addition, it provides garbage removal services for residents who live in outlying rural areas. Each town has the option of contracting for garbage removal service from the county or providing service itself. Garbage volume and the resulting revenue from each town served is approximately the same; garbage volume for those who live in outlying rural areas is approximately that of two towns. Under the current situation, the following revenues and costs are incurred.

Revenue from garbage removal services	$2,000,000
Fixed expenses (don't change when revenues change)	600,000
Variable expenses (change proportionately when sales change):	
Wages	1,100,000
Truck maintenance	100,000

The Yamhill County commissioners are considering purchase of new garbage trucks that lift and crush the garbage more efficiently. This would double the fixed expenses and cut the existing variable expenses in half.

Required

A. Prepare a three-column pro forma income statement for the Yamhill County garbage service assuming the existing equipment continues in use. Show (1) the amount of projected net income if only outlying rural areas are served, (2) income if outlying rural areas plus those of two towns are served, and (3) income if outlying rural areas and four towns are served. Use the following format.

	Outlying rural areas only	Outlying rural areas plus two towns	Outlying rural areas plus four towns
Revenues			
Fixed expenses			
Variable expenses	_____	_____	_____
Net income	_____	_____	_____

B. Using the same format, prepare another three-column pro forma income statement showing garbage service with the new equipment under each of the three income situations listed in the first requirement.

C. Explain the effects that changing to new trucks could have on Yamhill County's profits and risks from the garbage service.

P12-4 Comparing Operating Leverage

Obj. 2

Information is provided below from the annual reports of two manufacturing companies operating in different industries.

	Solution Software, Inc.		Fashion Clothing Co.	
(In millions)	Sales	Earnings	Sales	Earnings
2001	$ 4,600	$1,150	$3,800	$300
2002	6,000	1,500	4,800	400
2003	8,700	2,200	6,500	550
2004	11,400	3,500	9,200	800
2005	14,500	4,500	9,500	850

Required Prepare a graph to illustrate the relationship between each company's earnings and its sales over the five years. Which company has the higher operating leverage? What effect does operating leverage have on the companies' operating income?

P12-5

Obj. 2

P/T

Comparing Operating Leverage

Information is provided below from the 2002 annual reports of **Dell Computer Corporation** and **Tommy Hilfiger Corporation**.

(In millions)	Dell	Hilfiger
Net revenue	$ 31,168	$ 1,877
Cost of goods sold	(25,661)	(1,073)
Gross margin	5,507	804
Operating expenses	(3,236)	(618)
Operating income	$ 2,271	$ 186

Assume the cost of goods sold is variable and the operating expenses are half fixed and half variable.

Required

A. Compute Dell's projected operating income if sales decreased to 80% of current sales or increased to 120% of current sales.
B. Compute Hilfiger's projected operating income if sales decreased to 80% of current sales or increased to 120% of current sales.
C. Compare and discuss the results of your projections. Identify the company that has the higher operating leverage.

P12-6

Obj. 2

P/T

Operating Leverage and Risk

Financial statement information is presented below for Hillary Corporation, a producer of mountain climbing gear. The company expects sales to increase by about 20% in 2004.

(In millions)	2003 Actual	2004 Expected
Sales	$692	$830
Cost of good sold	462	554
Operating expenses	206	247
Operating income	24	29
Interest expense	(5)	(5)
Pretax income	19	24
Income taxes	(7)	(8)
Net income	$ 12	$ 16

Hillary's management is considering automating much of the company's production process. The automation would result in about half of the company's cost of goods sold being fixed. Currently, most of these costs vary in proportion to sales, as shown in the financial numbers presented above.

Required

A. Assume that half ($231 million) of Hillary's cost of goods sold in 2003 is fixed and that the other half increases in proportion to sales, an increase of 20%. Compute the company's expected cost of goods sold.
B. Using the same assumptions as part A, compute expected net income for 2004. Assume that income taxes are 35% of pretax income. Round to the nearest million.
C. Compare your results with those presented above, which assume that cost of goods sold varies in proportion to sales. What effect would the automation have on Hillary's profitability? What effect would it have on the company's risk? Explain your answer.

P12-7 **Assessing the Effects of Operating Leverage**

Objs. 2, 3

P/T

Information is provided below from the financial statements of two companies for 2004.

2004	Jekle	Hyde
Total assets	$30,000	$80,000
Total debt	10,000	50,000
Total equity	20,000	30,000
Sales	28,000	75,000
Operating expense	20,000	60,000
Operating income	8,000	15,000
Interest expense	800	5,000
Pretax income	7,200	10,000
Income taxes (30%)	2,160	3,000
Net income	5,040	7,000

Jekle's operating expenses include fixed costs of $5,000. Hyde's operating expenses include fixed costs of $50,000. All other operating expenses vary in proportion to sales for both companies. Assume that during 2005 sales for both companies increased by 20% from the amount reported, to $33,600 for Jekle and to $90,000 for Hyde.

Required

A. Compute the net income Jekle and Hyde would report for 2005 if sales increased by 20%.
B. Compute return on assets for Jekle and Hyde in 2004 and 2005, assuming the increase in sales and no change in total assets.
C. Explain why the increase in sales would affect Jekle and Hyde differently and explain which company is riskier.

P12-8 **Comparing Cash Flows**

Obj. 3

Cash flow information is provided below for two companies in the health-care products industry. Cash outflows are shown in parentheses.

(In millions)	2001	2000	1999	Total
Johnson & Johnson				
Operating activities	$ 8,864	$ 6,903	$ 5,920	$ 21,687
Investing activities	(4,093)	(2,665)	(3,093)	(9,851)
Financing activities	(5,251)	(2,425)	(2,347)	(10,023)
Warner-Lambert				
Operating activities	$ 9,080	$ 7,687	$ 6,131	$ 22,898
Investing activities	(4,312)	(3,641)	(2,817)	(10,770)
Financing activities	(5,071)	(3,447)	(3,869)	(12,387)

Required Analyze the companies' cash flows for 1999 to 2001 and for the three years in total. Explain how the two companies compare in terms of their cash flow trends.

P12-9 **Assessing Asset and Investment Strategy**

Obj. 3

Widgets, Inc. and Gizmos, Inc. both manufacture accessories for computer users. The table below shows their investment policies and operating results for the past two years.

	Widgets, Inc.		Gizmos, Inc.	
(In thousands)	2004	2003	2004	2003
Plant and equipment	$2,400	$2,200	$4,300	$4,400
Accumulated depreciation	600	580	2,200	1,900
Total assets	5,000	4,300	8,000	8,100
Net income	432	320	(615)	(140)
Depreciation	320	290	520	541
Cash flow from operations	710	644	(105)	376
Cash flow from investing activities	(305)	(274)	205	56
New investment in plant and equipment	316	280	180	220

Required Explain what the preceding numbers tell you about the two companies' assets and investment policies. Include any information you find that would indicate financial problems within either company.

P12-10 Comparing Cash Flows

Obj. 3

Cash flow information is provided below for two companies in the food products industry. Cash outflows are shown in parentheses.

(In millions)	2001	2000	1999	Total
Earthgrains Co.				
Operating activities	$ 165	$ 107	$ 130	$ 402
Investing activities	(123)	(742)	(216)	(1,081)
Financing activities	(39)	608	93	662
Campbell Soup Co.				
Operating activities	$ 1,106	$1,165	$ 954	$ 3,225
Investing activities	(1,122)	(204)	(322)	(1,648)
Financing activities	15	(943)	(636)	(1,564)

Required Analyze the companies' cash flows for 1999 through 2001 and for the three years in total. Explain how the two companies compare in terms of their cash flow trends.

P12-11 Comparing Investment Activities

Objs. 3, 4

Information is provided below from the 2001 annual reports of **PepsiCo, Inc.** and **The Coca-Cola Company**.

(In millions except per share amounts)	PepsiCo	Coca-Cola
Current assets	$ 5,853	$ 7,171
Investments and other assets	4,125	8,214
Plant assets, at cost	12,180	7,105
Plant assets, net	6,876	4,453
Intangibles, net	4,841	2,579
Total assets	21,695	22,417
Current liabilities	4,998	8,429
Long-term debt	2,651	1,219
Shareholders' equity	8,648	11,366
Net income	2,662	3,969
Net sales	26,935	20,092
Interest expense	219	289
Depreciation and amortization	1,082	803
Net cash provided by operating activities	4,201	4,110
Net cash from (used) in investing activities	(2,637)	(1,188)
Net cash from (used) in financing activities	(1,919)	(2,830)
Earnings per share	1.51	1.60
Market value of equity	86,475	117,226

Required Use appropriate accounting ratios discussed in this chapter and any other ratios you think are helpful to compare the investing activities and performances of the two companies for 2001. What important differences exist in the investing and financing activities of the companies? How do these differences affect the risk and return of the companies? How would you expect these differences to affect the market-to-book value and book value-to-cash flow from operating activities ratios of the two companies?

P12-12 Measuring the Results of Investing Activities

Obj. 4

Accounting information is provided below for two companies in the hair care products industry.

	Faucett Company		Danson Industries	
(In millions)	2004	2003	2004	2003
Total assets	$33.8	$26.8	$84.4	$71.0
Sales	40.7	30.5	95.5	71.6
Net income	3.7	2.5	6.7	6.0

Required

A. Compute asset turnover, profit margin, and return on assets for each year and company. Also, compute asset growth for each company from 2003 to 2004.

B. Evaluate the performance of each company with respect to the other and also in terms of changes from 2003 to 2004. Identify reasons for the differences in performance.

P12-13 Evaluating Investment Decisions

Objs. 4, 5

The information below was reported by PepsiCo, Inc. in its 2001 annual report.

(In millions)	2001	2000	1999
Net sales	$26,935	$25,479	$25,093
Net income	2,662	2,543	2,505
Cash flow from operating activities	4,201	3,330	3,605
Cash invested in other companies	(432)	(98)	(430)
Cash purchases of plant assets	(1,324)	(1,352)	(1,341)
Cash flow from financing activities	(1,919)	(2,648)	(1,828)
Cash dividends paid	(994)	(949)	(935)
Total assets	21,695	20,757	19,948

Required Identify and evaluate PepsiCo's investment decisions over the three years shown. Include in your analysis an examination of changes in efficiency and effectiveness.

P12-14 Comparing Investment Performance

Objs. 4, 5

The information below is for two companies in the same industry.

	Griffith, Inc.		Johnson, Inc.	
(In millions)	2005	2004	2005	2004
Sales	$8,223	$7,338	$9,430	$9,400
Net income	817	701	822	840
Total assets	7,250	6,490	8,347	8,350
Total liabilities	3,200	3,030	5,230	4,960
Market value	9,200	7,650	5,220	5,790

Required

A. Compute the asset turnover, profit margin, return on assets, and market to book value for each year and company. Also compute asset growth for each company from 2004 to 2005.

B. Compare the performances of the two companies over the two-year period with respect to effectiveness and efficiency.

C. Explain what reasons you find for the differences in the market value of the two companies. Could there be additional explanatory factors that do not appear in these numbers?

P12-15 Investing Decisions Regarding Product Lines

Objs. 4, 5

The company for which you work has a significant investment in the stock of Star-Beasts, Inc. (SBI), which currently manufactures one kind of toy, a large and lovable stuffed monster. SBI is considering expansion of its production facilities and would finance the expansion with long-term borrowing at an expected interest rate of 10%. The market would seem to support the manufacture and sale of 20% more monsters at the current profit margin. The added facilities would cost approximately $3.4 million. Alternatively, SBI could add one of two new lines: a mechanical dragon or a game called Starship Troopers.

The numbers below indicate current operating results and projections for the effects of added facilities for manufacturing the new lines. The numbers do not include interest on the new facilities or the company's 35% income tax rate.

(In thousands)	Current Operations	Addition of Dragons	Addition of Games
Sales	$9,860	$3,300	$2,900
Operating expenses	7,240	2,450	2,300
Interest expense	1,100	?	?
Total assets	8,422	?	?
Capital expenditures	?	3,450	1,800

Required

A. In addition to showing the current income statement, prepare pro forma income statements for SBI under each of the three strategies: expanding manufacturing of the current product and adding each of the new lines.
B. Determine the return on assets for the current situation and for each of the three strategies.
C. Indicate under which strategy you would feel most confident about the value of your company's investment, and explain why.

P12-16 Evaluating Investment Decisions

Objs. 3, 4, 5

Creative Technology, Inc. reported the following information in its 2004 annual report.

(In millions except EPS)	Total Assets	Long-Term Debt	Additions to Plant Assets	Net Income	Earnings per Share
2004	$31,471	$702	$4,032	$6,068	1.73
2003	28,880	448	4,501	6,945	1.93
2002	23,735	728	3,024	5,157	1.45
2001	17,504	400	3,550	3,566	1.01
2000	13,816	392	2,441	2,288	0.65

Required Using appropriate accounting ratios discussed in this chapter and any other ratios you think are helpful, evaluate the firm's investment decisions for the period from 2000 to 2004.

P12-17 Comparing Investment Performance

Objs. 4, 5

$\frac{P}{T}$

Information is provided below for Tommy Hilfiger Corporation and **Nike, Inc.**

(In millions)	Hilfiger 2002	Hilfiger 2001	Nike 2002	Nike 2001
Total assets	$2,594	$2,343	$6,443	$5,820
Total liabilities	1,097	994	2,604	2,325
Revenues	1,877	1,881	9,893	9,489
Operating income	186	197	1,068	1,014
Net income	135	131	663	590
Depreciation and amortization	114	107	277	214
Cash from operations	353	191	1,082	657
Cash from investing	(302)	(74)	(303)	(342)
Cash from financing	18	(108)	(478)	(350)
Additions to plant assets	(97)	(74)	(283)	(318)

Required

A. Compute the asset turnover, profit margin, and return on assets for each year and company.
B. Compare the effectiveness and efficiency of the two companies.
C. Compare the investing activities of the two companies over the two years and discuss your findings.

P12-18 **Analyzing Ability to Meet Debt Payments**

Obj. 6

Sporting Life, Inc., is a large retail chain of sporting goods stores. In a recent annual report, the following information was presented.

(In millions)	2004	2003	2002
Sales	$15,833	$15,668	$15,229
Operating income	1,455	1,341	893
Net income	662	536	266
Interest expense	304	418	499
Total assets	13,464	13,738	14,264
Long-term debt	3,057	3,919	4,606
Shareholders' equity	5,709	5,256	4,669
Cash provided by operating activities	1,690	1,573	1,220
Cash (used) by investing activities	(445)	(318)	(650)
Cash provided (used) by financing activities	(1,080)	(1,262)	(594)

Cash for investing activities was used primarily for property and equipment purchases. Cash used by financing activities was primarily to pay off long-term debt and acquire treasury stock.

Required

A. Assume that you work for an investment firm that has an opportunity to invest in notes that are part of Sporting Life's long-term debt. Write a short report in which you analyze the firm's ability to meet its debt payments, based on the information given.

B. Prepare a list of the most important additional pieces of information you would want before making a final decision about the investment. This list should include some accounting information; it might also include nonaccounting and nonquantitative items.

P12-19 **Assessing Credit-Worthiness**

Obj. 6

Year-end financial information is provided below for two companies that make baseball caps.

	Cobb Industries		Speaker, Inc.	
(In millions)	2004	2003	2004	2003
Property, plant, and equipment	$283	$314	$171	$162
Total assets	392	424	259	246
Current liabilities	67	74	69	63
Long-term debt	261	264	100	104
Stockholders' equity	64	86	90	79
Asset impairment charge	(18)	—	—	—
Operating income	5	7	24	19
Interest expense	(23)	(24)	(8)	(7)

Required Study the information provided. If you were a creditor of these companies, would you be concerned about the ability of either company to repay its debts? Explain your answer.

P12-20 **Excel in Action**

P/T

SPREADSHEET

The Book Wermz reported sales for 2005 of $6,230,000. Cost of goods sold was 55% of sales, and operating expenses were $2,155,000. Interest expense was $190,000. Income taxes were 35% of pretax income. Total assets at the end of 2005 were $5,623,000.

Required Use the information provided to produce an income statement for The Book Wermz for the year ended December 31, 2005. Enter appropriate captions for the statement at the top of the spreadsheet and appropriate captions in column A. Enter amounts in column B. Use equations to calculate subtotals and totals. Calculate cost of goods sold as sales × 0.55 and income taxes as pretax income × 0.35.

Following the income statement, enter the total assets data and calculate asset turnover, profit margin, and return on assets. Enter captions in column A and calculations in column B. Use cell references to the income statement and total assets in these calculations.

Suppose that the company's management believes that it can increase sales by reducing product prices. Cutting the prices relative to the costs of the goods sold would increase the ratio to 60%, but is expected to increase total sales to $7 million. Operating expenses and interest expense are relatively fixed and would not be affected by these changes. Total assets also would not be affected. In column C calculate the effects of the changes on the company's income statement and financial ratios. Copy the data from column B to column C and make changes as needed. Would the pricing change be advantageous to the company?

Another alternative for the company is to raise prices relative to cost of goods sold and significantly increase advertising. The increase in prices would reduce cost of goods sold to 50% of sales. The additional advertising expenses would increase operating expenses to $3 million. Total sales are expected to increase to $7.5 million. Interest expense and total assets would not be affected by these changes. In column D calculate the effects of the changes on income and the financial ratios. Would the company benefit from these changes?

P12-21 **Multiple-Choice Overview of the Chapter**

P/T

1. As defined in this text, return on assets involves a comparison of total assets with
   a. net income.
   b. net income adjusted for dividends.
   c. net income adjusted for income taxes.
   d. net income adjusted for interest expense.

2. A high asset turnover indicates that a company
   a. buys and sells its long-term assets more frequently than most companies, so that it tends to operate with state-of-the-art equipment.
   b. generates a large amount of profit compared to its total assets.
   c. generates a large amount of sales compared to its total assets.
   d. uses fixed costs to increase net income as sales increase.

3. The substitution of fixed costs for variable costs affects which of the following most directly?
   a. Stockholders' equity
   b. Financial leverage
   c. Gross profit margin
   d. Operating leverage

4. A company with good investment opportunities normally can increase its stockholders' wealth by
   a. increasing the portion of net income paid out in dividends
   b. investing in new assets.
   c. reducing the amount invested in new assets.
   d. reducing its rate of return on new assets.

5. Company A has a higher proportion of fixed to variable costs than Company B. Both have a positive net income. The sales revenues of both companies increased by 10%. You would expect
   a. Company A's expenses to increase more rapidly than Company B's.
   b. Company A's expenses to decrease while Company B's increase.
   c. Company A's net income to decrease while Company B's increases.
   d. Company A's net income to increase more rapidly than Company B's.

6. Company A and Company B are similar in size and in many other respects. The companies reported the following net cash flow from (used for) investing activities in their 2005 annual reports.

(In millions)	2005	2004	2003
Company A	$(460)	$(350)	$(265)
Company B	200	35	(80)

(Continued)

From this information, you would expect
a. Company A to be growing more rapidly than Company B.
b. Company B to be growing more rapidly than Company A.
c. Company B to have better investment alternatives than Company A.
d. Company A to pay higher dividends than Company B.

7. Relative to Company A, Company B is more capital-intensive, has a higher debt to asset ratio, and pays out a smaller portion of its net income as dividends. Company A's asset growth rate has been larger than Company B's. From this information, it is likely that
a. Company A is riskier than Company B.
b. Company B is riskier than Company A.
c. Company A has a higher market value than Company B.
d. Company B has a higher market value than Company A.

8. Which of the following net cash flow patterns is typical of a company with high growth potential and strong financial performance?

	Cash Flow from Operating Activities	Cash Flow from Investing Activities
a.	Outflow	Outflow
b.	Outflow	Inflow
c.	Inflow	Inflow
d.	Inflow	Outflow

9. Which of the following is evidence of effective use of assets?
a. Earning higher amounts of profit for each dollar of sales
b. Selling long-term assets promptly when sales drop
c. Increasing sales more rapidly than the dollar amount of additional investment
d. Planning for assets that have high fixed cost and low variable cost, in order to make use of operating leverage

10. Under generally accepted accounting principles in the United States, most assets are valued on the balance sheet at
a. cost.
b. cost, or a lower value if they are impaired.
c. cost, or a higher value if evidence of increase is verifiable.
d. fair market value.

CASES

C12-1   Evaluating Investment Decisions

Objs. 1, 3, 4

Appendix B of this book contains a copy of the 2002 annual report of **General Mills, Inc.**

Required Review the annual report and write a short report in which you cover each of the following:

A. What major investing decisions did the company make from 2000 to 2002? Include decisions about disposing of as well as acquiring assets. (Hint: See note 2 to the financial statements, as well as the statement of cash flows.)
B. Evaluate the company's growth rate for total assets and net income from 2000 to 2002. (Hint: See the six-year financial summary.)
C. Compute return on assets, asset turnover, and profit margin for the company from 2000 to 2002. Does it appear that the company has made beneficial investing decisions?

C12-2   Analysis of an Acquisition

Obj. 3

You are a financial analyst with a major corporation, High Hopes Company. You have been assigned the task of evaluating a potential acquisition candidate, Roll-the-Dice, Inc. Selected accounting information for the two companies is presented on the next page. Information for 2003 and 2004 reports actual company results. Results for 2005 are projected from information available at the beginning of the year.

(In millions)	2005	2004	2003
High Hopes Company			
Depreciation and amortization expense	$ 13.4	$ 13.1	$ 11.6
Operating income	46.3	42.7	37.5
Interest expense	4.9	5.1	5.5
Provision for income taxes	14.1	11.8	11.0
Net income	27.3	25.8	21.0
Total assets	305.7	292.1	274.8
Total liabilities	125.9	128.0	135.2
Total stockholders' equity	179.8	164.1	139.6
Net cash flow from operating activities	40.4	38.5	32.8
Net cash flow used for investing activities	(14.1)	(12.8)	(9.8)
Net cash flow used for financing activities	(25.3)	(25.7)	(23.0)
Roll-the-Dice, Inc.			
Depreciation and amortization expense	$ 5.4	$ 5.2	$ 4.5
Operating income	22.8	19.3	12.9
Interest expense	3.7	3.5	3.0
Provision for income taxes	6.5	4.7	4.2
Net income	12.6	11.1	5.7
Total assets	114.3	111.0	93.4
Total liabilities	35.8	33.2	31.8
Total stockholders' equity	78.5	77.8	73.5
Net cash flow from operating activities	18.7	16.4	14.6
Net cash flow used for investing activities	(13.7)	(7.9)	(18.3)
Net cash flow from (used for) financing activities	(4.5)	(8.6)	3.8

The acquisition, if it were to occur, would result in High Hopes purchasing all of the common stock of Roll-the-Dice at a price of $130 million. To finance the acquisition, High Hopes plans to issue $130 million of long-term debt at 10.7% annual interest. The debt principal would be repaid in equal installments over 10 years. The interest would be paid annually on the unpaid principal. The fair market value of Roll-the-Dice's identifiable assets is $107 million. The fair market value of its liabilities is $35.8 million. Goodwill from the acquisition will not be amortized. There are no intercompany transactions between High Hopes and Roll-the-Dice. Assume that High Hopes' income tax rate is 34%.

Required Prepare a summary pro forma income statement and statement of cash flows for High Hopes for 2005, assuming it acquires Roll-the-Dice at the beginning of 2005. What recommendation would you make to High Hopes' management concerning the acquisition?

C12-3 **Return-based Bonus, Ethics, and Accounting Standards**

Objs. 4, 6

Employees of the divisions of JX Controls, Inc. receive a bonus of 4% of their salary in any year in which the divisional return on assets is above 10%. Toward the end of 2004, accountants for the fire alarm division projected the following year-end numbers:

Sales	$1,230,000
Cost of goods sold*	758,000
Other expenses†	322,000
Total divisional assets	1,590,000

*All products have the same gross margin.
†All are fixed expenses.

At a meeting of divisional managers, Susan Torres, divisional vice president, told the group, "We've never received the bonus, although several other divisions have. Our employees work just as hard, and many of them really need the extra money for their families; I'd like us to get the bonus for them, as well as for ourselves. What ideas do you have for pulling it off?"

A variety of ideas were raised:

- "Let's do what we can about sales. We have an order for $40,000 in goods to be shipped in early January; could we get those out the door in December, and add that gross margin to this year's numbers?"

(Continued)

- "Sure—good idea. We might even accidentally overship by 20% and record the extra in this year's sales."
- "Could we slow down a bit on paying our bills? Wouldn't a few suppliers be willing to wait until January—maybe for about $50,000?"
- "We've got that old forming machine that hasn't been used for a year; it's really useless. It's on the books at $60,000 and is 70% depreciated, but it's worth only about $3,000 as scrap. Have we written it down?"
- "The projection includes that new $90,000 bending machine that just came in. We should have delayed ordering it—but we haven't booked it. Could we forget to record the machine and the payable until January?"

Required Write a short report reacting to the meeting. Determine which proposals would both be in accordance with accounting standards and actually raise return on assets. Calculate return on assets for the current projection, and with the inclusion of those measures that meet these two tests. Also include your thoughts about the advantages and disadvantages of such a bonus system.

OPERATING ACTIVITIES

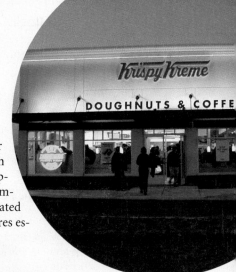

How do we account for operating activities?

Operating activities involve selling goods and services, using assets, and using other resources, such as labor. Often these activities include transactions that occur in different fiscal periods. Accounting for these activities requires determining the appropriate period in which to recognize revenues and expenses and accounting for timing differences between when revenues and expenses are recognized and when related events occur. Determining revenues and expenses for a fiscal period sometimes requires estimates.

FOOD FOR THOUGHT

Why is it necessary for a company to estimate revenues and expenses for a fiscal period? What factors should be considered when making the estimates? How do the estimates affect the reported financial information?

Maria, Stan, and Ellen discuss revenue and expense recognition for Mom's Cookie Company. Ellen, the vice president of finance, is aware that some of their activities will require estimates. She discusses these activities with Maria and Stan.

Ellen: *We have to make some decisions about how we will estimate some of our revenue and expense amounts.*

Stan: *Estimates? I thought accounting was all about identifying precise amounts.*

Ellen: *Actually, quite a few activities require estimation. For example, because we sell goods on credit, we will have to estimate the amount of doubtful accounts we expect each fiscal period.*

Maria: *Why can't we just write off accounts after we determine they cannot be collected?*

Ellen: *Accounting principles require that estimated amounts of doubtful accounts be recognized as expenses in the same fiscal period in which the goods were sold that created those accounts. Matching expenses with related revenues is important for proper measurement of operating results during a fiscal period.*

Stan: *Are there a lot of estimation issues we need to consider?*

Ellen: *There aren't too many for our company. A major consideration is the method we use for estimating inventory costs. Unit costs change over time, and we have to decide which costs to associate with goods sold during a period. It isn't reasonable for us to identify the exact cost of each unit we sell. Instead, we will need a systematic method of estimating that cost.*

Maria: *Does it really matter which method we use? Will it affect our income or cash flows?*

Ellen: *These decisions can affect our income statement and our cash flows, particularly as a result of their effect on tax payments. Let's examine some of these issues.*

OBJECTIVES

Once you have completed this chapter, you should be able to:

1 Identify the purpose and major components of an income statement.

2 Explain and apply rules for measuring revenues and receivables and reporting revenue transactions.

3 Describe reporting rules for inventories and cost of goods sold and compare

reporting of inventories for merchandising and manufacturing companies.

4 Explain and apply rules for measuring cost of goods sold and inventories and describe the effects of income taxes on the choice of inventory estimation method.

5 Identify routine and nonroutine events that affect a company's income statement.

BASIC OPERATING ACTIVITIES

OBJECTIVE 1

Identify the purpose and major components of an income statement.

The income statement reports the results of operating activities for a fiscal period on an accrual basis. Exhibit 1 provides the income statement for Mom's Cookie Company for 2004 and 2005. Early in 2005, the company expanded its operations by issuing common stock and some long-term debt. The financing was used to acquire property and plant to permit the company to produce its own cookies.

Exhibit 1

Income Statement for Mom's Cookie Company

For the Year Ended December 31,	2005	2004
Net sales revenue	$ 3,235,600	$ 686,400
Cost of goods sold	(1,954,300)	(457,600)
Gross profit	1,281,300	228,800
Selling, general and administrative expenses	(1,094,700)	(148,300)
Operating income	186,600	80,500
Interest expense	(20,400)	(4,800)
Pretax income	166,200	75,700
Income taxes	(49,860)	(22,710)
Net income	$ 116,340	$ 52,990
Earnings per share	$ 0.29	$ 0.13

The first item on the income statement is net sales revenues. Companies with large amounts of service revenues report these in addition to sales revenues. Recall from Chapter F4, the term "operating revenues" is sometimes used to refer to sales and service revenues. Net revenues result from subtracting discounts and returns from gross revenues, as discussed in a later section. Cost of goods sold is subtracted from net sales revenue to compute gross profit. The expenses for marketing and distributing a company's products and managing its operations are subtracted from gross profit to calculate operating income. Non-operating expenses or losses, such as interest expense, are subtracted and non-operating income or gains are added, to compute income before taxes. Income tax expense is subtracted from income before taxes to calculate net income. Finally, earnings per share is reported on a corporate income statement.

REVENUES AND RECEIVABLES

OBJECTIVE 2

Explain and apply rules for measuring revenues and receivables and reporting revenue transactions.

Operating revenues result from the sale of goods and services to customers. Operating revenues are the first items on the income statement and affect both cash and accounts receivable on the balance sheet, as illustrated in Exhibit 2. Cash received from customers is reported on the statement of cash flows, either directly, or indirectly as net income adjusted for the change in accounts receivable. Most companies recognize operating revenues at the time they transfer ownership of goods or services to customers. Ownership of most goods passes to the buyer at the time the goods are delivered or shipped to the buyer. Retail companies usually recognize revenues at the time a sale is made, when the customer takes possession of the goods. Most service companies recognize revenues at the time services are performed.

Exhibit 2 The Effect of Sales and Services on the Financial Statements

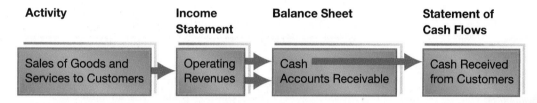

Manufacturing companies and some merchandising companies ship goods to customers. Ownership of these goods is transferred to the buyer at the location named in the sales terms. For example: When goods are shipped **FOB** (free on board) **destination**, ownership of goods is transferred to the customer when the goods are delivered (and the seller usually pays the shipping costs). When goods are shipped **FOB shipping point**, ownership passes to the customer when the goods are picked up by the shipper (and the buyer usually pays the shipping costs).

As a general rule, **revenue should be recognized when four criteria have been met:**

1. The selling company has completed most of the activities necessary to produce and sell the goods or services.
2. The selling company has incurred the costs associated with producing and selling the goods or services or can reasonably measure those costs.
3. The selling company can measure objectively the amount of revenue it has earned.
4. The selling company is reasonably sure that it is going to collect cash from the purchaser.

LEARNING NOTE

If the buyer pays for goods or services before the criteria for revenue recognition have been met, the seller recognizes **unearned revenue** (a liability). When the criteria are met, the seller recognizes the revenue and reduces the unearned revenue account.

For most companies, these criteria have been met when goods are transferred or when services are provided to customers who pay for them or who are obligated to pay for them.

Special measurement and recognition issues arise when revenues are earned over an extended period, as from a long-term construction or service contract; when some customers can be expected to return a portion of goods purchased; when some customers are likely not to pay for their purchases; and when the seller provides a warranty for the goods or services sold.

Recognizing Revenue for Long-Term Contracts

Certain types of revenues create recognition problems because the activities that produce the revenues occur over more than one fiscal period. Revenues earned from long-term contracts often are recognized in proportion to the passage of time or in proportion to the amount of the contract that has been completed. For example, if a company contracts to provide maintenance services over a three-year period for $75,000, it might recognize $25,000 of revenue each year. In this case, the company assumes that it is going to provide approximately the same amount of service each year.

In the case of construction contracts—to construct an airplane or a building, for example—the seller usually estimates the portion of the contract that has been completed during a fiscal period. A corresponding portion of revenues then is recognized for that period. To illustrate, assume that Constructo Company contracts to construct a building for $20 million. The project will take three years to complete. At the end of 2004, the first year of the project, Constructo estimates that approximately 20% of the work has been completed. Therefore, it recognizes $4 million ($20 million × 20%) of revenue on the project for 2004. Also, it recognizes its costs associated with the project in computing net income for 2004.

Case in Point

http://ingram.
swlearning.com

....

**Learn more about The
Walt Disney Company.**

Revenue Recognition Policies

Companies in the entertainment industry often earn revenues over an extended period as customers purchase tickets. **Walt Disney Company** is an example of this type of company. Disney's revenue recognition policy states:

Revenue Recognition

Revenues from the theatrical distribution of motion pictures are recognized when motion pictures are exhibited. Revenues from video sales are recognized on the date that video units are made widely available for sale by retailers. Revenues from the licensing of feature films and television programming are recorded when the material is available for telecasting by the licensee and when certain other conditions are met.

Broadcast advertising revenues are recognized when commercials are aired. Revenues from television subscription services related to the Company's primary cable programming services are recognized as services are provided.

Merchandise licensing advance and guarantee payments are recognized when the underlying royalties are earned.

Revenues from advance theme park ticket sales are recognized when the tickets are used. Revenues from participants at the theme parks are generally recorded over the period of the applicable agreements commencing with the opening of the related attraction.

Internet advertising revenues are recognized on the basis of impression views in the period the advertising is displayed, provided that no significant obligations remain and collection of the resulting receivable is probable. Direct marketing and Internet-based merchandise revenues are recognized upon shipment to customers.

(2002 Annual Report)

Sales Discounts and Returns

Revenues are reported on the income statement net of discounts and expected returns. A **discount** is a reduction in the normal sales price. Companies usually offer discounts from the normal price to encourage customers to buy large quantities of goods (a quantity discount) or to pay their accounts early (a **sales discount**). Discounts reduce revenues. Consequently, a company should record as revenue only the amount it actually expects to receive from a sale.

Suppose that Mom's Cookie Company sells goods priced at $5,000 to a customer on November 4, 2004, and offers a 2% discount if the customer pays in full within 10 days of the purchase. If the customer pays within the discount period (within the 10 days), Mom's Cookie Company earns revenue of $4,900 after subtracting the discount of $100 ($5,000 × 2%). If the customer does not pay within the discount period, Mom's Cookie Company earns $5,000.

Many companies record the sale at the full price ($5,000) and then deduct the discount if the customer pays within the discount period. For example, Mom's Cookie Company would record the sale as follows:

| Date | Accounts | ASSETS | | = | LIABILITIES | + | OWNERS' EQUITY | |
		Cash	Other Assets				Contributed Capital	Retained Earnings
Nov. 4, 2004	Accounts Receivable		5,000					
	Sales Revenue							5,000

Then, if the customer pays within the discount period, the company would record this:

| Date | Accounts | ASSETS | | = | LIABILITIES | + | OWNERS' EQUITY | |
		Cash	Other Assets				Contributed Capital	Retained Earnings
Nov. 10, 2004	Cash	4,900						
	Sales Discount							−100
	Accounts Receivable		−5,000					

The sales discount reduces the gross sales revenue of $5,000 to the net sales revenue of $4,900, the amount actually earned. The company reports net sales revenue on its income statement (see Exhibit 1).

Like sales discounts, **sales returns** are subtracted from sales revenues in reporting net operating revenues on the income statement. In certain industries, companies sell merchandise with the expectation that buyers will return some of that merchandise. Publishing companies, for example, often allow retailers to return unsold books and magazines for credit against the amount they owe.

Let's assume that Textbook Publishing Company sells $5 million of books during fiscal year 2004. It records sales revenues and accounts receivable in the amount of $5 million. From past experience, the company estimates that $500,000 of its 2004 sales will be returned in 2005. So Textbook Publishing should record an adjustment to its revenues and receivables at the end of 2004:

| Date | Accounts | ASSETS | | = | LIABILITIES | + | OWNERS' EQUITY | |
		Cash	Other Assets				Contributed Capital	Retained Earnings
Dec. 31, 2004	Sales Returns							−500,000
	Allowance for Returns		−500,000					

Allowance for Returns reduces the amount of Accounts Receivable reported on the balance sheet, and Sales Returns reduces the amount of Sales Revenue on the income statement.

Future returns are estimated so that revenues for the fiscal period in which the sales were made can be measured more accurately. If Textbook Publishing waits until returns are received in 2005, its sales revenues for 2004 will be overstated on the 2004 income statement. A major principle of accounting is the **matching principle:** An effort is made to match revenues and expenses in the period in which they occur so that revenues, expenses, and net income are not misstated. Sales returns should be matched with the sales that result in the returns. The matching principle often requires that future events be estimated, such as the amount of future returns. These estimates are not completely accurate, but reported revenues and expenses usually are more correct when adjusted using these estimates than when no adjustment is made.

The amount of operating revenue a company reports on its income statement ($3,235,600 for Mom's Cookie Company in 2005 from Exhibit 1, for example) is the net amount of revenue earned after discounts and returns have been subtracted. Operating revenues usually are labeled "net operating revenues" or "net sales" as an indication that returns and discounts have been subtracted.

When actual goods are returned to a company, the amount of the return is written off against the allowance for returns account. Accounts Receivable is reduced by the amount of the return if the customer purchased on credit. Otherwise, a cash refund may be paid. In addition, Cost of Goods Sold and Merchandise are adjusted, assuming that the goods are put back into inventory to be resold. To illustrate, assume that Textbook Publishing received a return of $100,000 (sales price) on January 12, 2005, from a credit customer. The goods cost the company $75,000. Textbook Publishing would recognize the return in its accounts as follows:

Date	Accounts	Cash	Other Assets	=	LIABILITIES	+	Contributed Capital	Retained Earnings
			ASSETS				**OWNERS' EQUITY**	
Jan. 12, 2005	Allowance for Returns Accounts Receivable		100,000 −100,000					
Jan. 12, 2005	Merchandise Inventory Cost of Goods Sold		75,000					75,000

Observe that the balance of the cost of goods sold account is reduced by the cost of the goods returned.

Case in Point

http://ingram. swlearning.com

Learn more about AOL Time Warner, Inc.

Merchandise Return Policy

AOL Time Warner produces magazines, books, CDs, and other products. Its revenue recognition policy notes the following:

In accordance with industry practice, certain products (such as magazines, books, home videocassettes, compact discs, DVDs, and cassettes) are sold to customers with the right to return unsold items. Revenues from such sales are recognized when the products are shipped based on gross sales less a provision for future estimated returns.

(2001 Annual Report) In 2003, the company changed its name to Time Warner.

Uncollectible Accounts

Companies that sell goods and services on credit are likely to incur some bad debts. Some customers will be unable to pay for the goods and services they receive. Companies estimate the amount of receivables that are likely to be uncollectible and report this amount as a contra-asset such as **Allowance for Doubtful Accounts** or a similar title. This allowance is deducted from Accounts Receivable and the net amount of Accounts Receivable is reported on the balance sheet. The amount of the allowance is estimated at the end of fiscal periods, at least at the end of the fiscal year. For example, assume Mom's Cookie Company has a balance in Allowance for Doubtful Accounts of $1,000 at the end of its 2004 fiscal year before adjustments are made for the year. Management evaluates the company's credit sales and outstanding receivables and determines that the amount of the allowance account at the end of the year should be $5,000. Thus, the account would need to be increased by $4,000 ($5,000 balance needed − $1,000 current balance). As shown here, an expense of $4,000 would also be recognized.

		ASSETS		=	LIABILITIES	+	OWNERS' EQUITY	
Date	Accounts	Cash	Other Assets				Contributed Capital	Retained Earnings
Dec. 31, 2004	Doubtful Accounts Expense Allowance for Doubtful Accounts		−4,000					−4,000

Companies base their estimates of the amount of doubtful accounts they expect on experience and on analysis of customer accounts. Some companies know from experience with their customers that a certain percentage of their credit sales is likely to become uncollectible. In other cases, the amount of uncollectible accounts changes in response to changes in general economic conditions. For example, during economic recessions, more people are out of work and many people earn less money than when the economy is strong. During these periods, the portion of uncollectible accounts associated with automobiles, houses, major appliances, and other goods purchased on long-term contracts increases, and sellers of these goods should increase their expected uncollectible accounts.

Many companies inspect their accounts receivable at year end to determine which accounts are at risk. Accounts that remain unpaid over a long period are more likely to be uncollectible. Consequently, companies often estimate that a higher percentage of older accounts will become uncollectible and use this information in estimating Doubtful Accounts Expense.

When a company identifies receivables as being uncollectible, those receivables are written off and the Allowance for Doubtful Accounts is adjusted. For example, assume that on February 12, 2005, Mom's Cookie Company determines that $800 owed by Home Goods Company cannot be collected because the company has gone out of business. Mom's Cookie Company would record the write off of the account as follows:

		ASSETS		=	LIABILITIES	+	OWNERS' EQUITY	
Date	Accounts	Cash	Other Assets				Contributed Capital	Retained Earnings
Feb. 12, 2005	Accounts Receivable Allowance for Doubtful Accounts		−800 800					

The balance of the Allowance for Doubtful Accounts is reduced by the amount written off. Accounts Receivable are reduced. The specific account for Home Goods Company is written down to zero by this transaction. Note that an expense is not associated with this transaction. The expense was recorded at the end of 2004 when doubtful account expense was recorded based on estimates for the year. The sale to Home Goods Company occurred in 2004. Accordingly, the expense associated with not collecting the account was also recorded (as an estimate) in 2004.

Doubtful accounts expense is a selling expense. It results from a decision to sell goods to a customer on credit. The cost associated with this decision is the cost of a bad sales decision. Companies attempt to set credit policies so that they can avoid these costs. However, they must balance these costs with lost sales that would result if the company refused to sell goods on credit.

Warranty Costs

Companies, especially manufacturing companies, often offer warranties on goods they produce. A defective product can be returned to the seller for replacement or can be returned to the manufacturer for repair or replacement. The manufacturer incurs costs when goods are replaced or repaired, and these costs should be matched with the revenues resulting from the sale of the defective products. Therefore, companies estimate expected warranty costs each fiscal period and record these as expenses of the period in which goods were sold.

For example, when **Ford Motor Company** ships cars and trucks to dealers, it estimates the warranty costs it expects on these vehicles. These costs are recorded as expenses in the period in which revenues are recognized. Liabilities also are recognized for these expected obligations. Generally, warranty costs are combined with other financial statement items and are not reported separately in a company's financial statements. Most companies are not eager for customers or competitors to have information about their warranty costs.

As an illustration, assume Harris Company, a retailer, sells appliances with a 90-day warranty. From sales in March 2004, it estimates expected warranty costs of $12,000 will be incurred in April, May, and June to repair and replace defective parts. To match the expense with the sales, the expected costs are recorded at the end of March as follows:

		ASSETS		=	LIABILITIES	+	OWNERS' EQUITY	
Date	Accounts	Cash	Other Assets				Contributed Capital	Retained Earnings
Mar. 31, 2004	Warranty Expense							−12,000
	Warranty Obligations				12,000			

When actual warranty claims are received in April, May, and June, costs of these claims are written off through the liability account. No new expense is recognized. For example, assume that on May 15, Harris replaces a faulty motor on an appliance. The cost of the motor ($300) and labor to install the motor ($100) are recorded as follows:

		ASSETS		=	LIABILITIES	+	OWNERS' EQUITY	
Date	Accounts	Cash	Other Assets				Contributed Capital	Retained Earnings
May 15, 2004	Warranty Obligations				−400			
	Parts Inventory		−300					
	Wages Payable				100			

Revenues and expenses associated with selling goods and services should be recognized in the fiscal period in which the revenues are earned. Because the outcomes of some of the events associated with these revenues and expenses are not known until a later fiscal period, it is often necessary to estimate these effects. The estimates are recorded in the fiscal period in which the revenues are earned, and these amounts are adjusted in later periods when actual amounts are known. Doubtful accounts expense, sales returns, and warranty expense are all examples of these required estimates.

---

1 SELF-STUDY PROBLEM

Bonsai Company, a wholesaler of Asian foods, reported the following transactions for 2004:

webTUTOR Advantage

1. Purchased $400,000 of merchandise inventory on credit.
2. Sold goods priced at $750,000 on credit.
3. The cost of merchandise sold to customers was $388,000.
4. Paid $384,000 to suppliers of merchandise.
5. Received $720,000 in cash from customers.
6. Granted $17,000 of sales discounts to customers for payment within the discount period.
7. Estimated that $10,000 of the year's credit sales would be uncollectible.
8. Wrote off $8,000 of accounts as uncollectible.

Required Using the format shown in this chapter, record each of the transactions and determine the amount of net income and net operating cash flow associated with these transactions.

The solution to Self-Study Problem 1 appears at the end of the chapter.

INVENTORIES AND COST OF GOODS SOLD

OBJECTIVE 3

Describe reporting rules for inventories and cost of goods sold and compare reporting of inventories for merchandising and manufacturing companies.

To generate revenues, merchandising and manufacturing companies have to acquire or produce goods for sale. These activities increase Inventories on the balance sheet and reduce Cash and/or increase Accounts Payable, as illustrated in Exhibit 3. Once goods are sold, Inventories are reduced and Cost of Goods Sold is recognized. Therefore, the amount reported for inventories on the balance sheet is related to the amount reported for Cost of Goods Sold on the income statement and to Net Operating Cash Flow on the cash flow statement.

Accounting for Inventories and Cost of Goods Sold involves measurement and reporting rules. Measurement rules determine how costs are computed; reporting rules identify how these costs are reported on the income statement and the balance sheet.

Exhibit 3
The Effect of Inventory Transactions on the Financial Statements

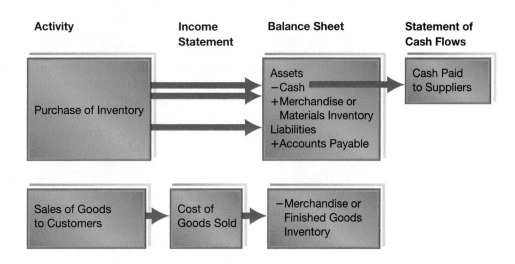

Reporting Inventories and Cost of Goods Sold

Inventories and Cost of Goods Sold are reported by both merchandising and manufacturing companies. Inventory transactions of manufacturing companies are more complex than those of merchandising companies because manufacturing companies must account for the production of goods. We will begin with merchandising companies and then examine manufacturing companies.

Merchandising Companies. Accounting for Merchandise Inventory is fairly simple. When it buys inventory, a company increases the balance of Merchandise Inventory. When it sells inventory, a company decreases the inventory account balance. Suppose that Mom's Cookie Company purchases $10,000 of inventory on May 4, 2004 on credit, and sells $4,000 of that inventory on May 6. Mom's Cookie Company would record these transactions as follows:

Date	Accounts	ASSETS		=	LIABILITIES	+	OWNERS' EQUITY	
		Cash	Other Assets				Contributed Capital	Retained Earnings
May 4, 2004	Merchandise Inventory		10,000					
	Accounts Payable				10,000			
May 6, 2004	Cost of Goods Sold							−4,000
	Merchandise Inventory		−4,000					

The second transaction considers only the cost of the sale, not the amount of revenue earned.

A payment by Mom's Cookie Company on May 12 for half of the inventory purchased on May 4 would result in the following:

Date	Accounts	ASSETS		=	LIABILITIES	+	OWNERS' EQUITY	
		Cash	Other Assets				Contributed Capital	Retained Earnings
May 12, 2004	Accounts Payable				−5,000			
	Cash	−5,000						

This transaction reduces the payable and results in a cash payment to suppliers, which would be reported on the statement of cash flows.

In addition to recording the purchase and sales transactions that affect the financial statements, companies maintain detailed records that describe each item of inventory and the quantity purchased and sold. Those records help a company determine the number of units on hand, the demand for each item, and when to reorder. Also, these records are used for control purposes. Periodically, companies verify their inventory records by taking a physical count of inventory to make sure their records are consistent with the amount of inventory actually on hand.

Like sales discounts, **purchase discounts**, for paying for goods or services within the discount period, should be subtracted in computing amounts reported in the financial statements. For example, if Mom's Cookie Company receives a $200 discount on its $10,000 purchase for paying the account payable within a discount period, it should record the inventory at $9,800, reducing Inventory and Accounts Payable by $200.

LEARNING NOTE

The cost of inventory includes the amount paid for the goods plus any shipping costs paid by the buyer. Goods in transit between the seller and the buyer should be included as part of the buyer's inventory at year end if ownership of the goods has been transferred to the buyer at that time.

Manufacturing Companies. Accounting for the inventory transactions of a manufacturing company is more complex than that for a merchandising company because a manufacturing company produces inventory rather than purchasing it from a supplier. Most manufacturing companies separate their inventories into three categories: raw materials inventory, work-in-process inventory, and finished goods inventory. Exhibit 4 illustrates the relationships among these categories.

Exhibit 4

Components of
Manufacturing Inventory

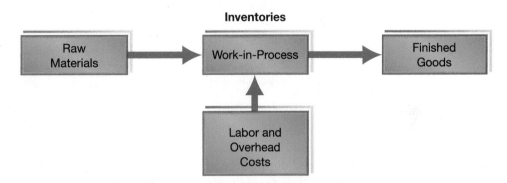

Inventories

Raw materials inventory **includes the costs of component parts or ingredients that become part of the product being manufactured.** Raw materials are reported on the balance sheet as the cost of the components or ingredients a company has purchased that have not yet been placed into production. For example, the raw materials for Mom's Cookie Company would consist primarily of the flour, sugar, and other ingredients.

Work-in-process inventory **includes the costs of materials, labor, and overhead that have been applied to products that are in the process of being manufactured.** Materials costs are determined from the amounts paid for raw materials. As raw materials are used in the production process, the costs of these materials are transferred from Raw Materials Inventory to Work-in-Process Inventory. Labor costs, often referred to as direct labor, are added to Work-in-Process Inventory based on the amount earned by factory workers. Overhead costs include the costs of supplies, utilities, depreciation, maintenance, and similar items that are necessary for the manufacturing process.

Finished goods inventory **includes the costs of products that have been completed in the manufacturing process and are available for sale to customers.** These costs include the costs of the materials, labor, and overhead necessary to produce completed products.

For example, assume that Mom's Cookie Company begins producing its own cookies early in January 2005. Exhibit 5 describes production activities for January and February.

At the beginning of January, Mom's Cookie Company has no manufacturing inventories. During January, the company purchases $65,000 of materials and uses $62,000 of materials. At the end of January, the company would report raw materials inventory of $3,000. That amount becomes the beginning materials inventory for February. If the company purchases $66,000 of materials in February and uses $67,000 of materials in production in February, it would report raw materials inventory of $2,000 at the end of February.

Work-in-process for January includes the costs of materials, labor, and overhead that went into production during January. The cost of goods that are completed during the month is transferred to finished goods inventory, leaving a balance of $4,000 for work-in-process inventory at the end of January. February's production begins with the $4,000 of inventory. Additional production costs of materials, labor, and overhead

Exhibit 5

Computation of
Manufacturing Inventory
Costs

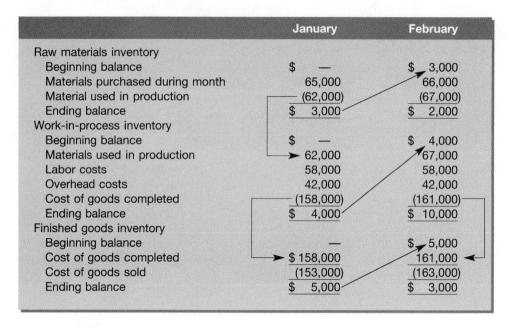

	January	February
Raw materials inventory		
Beginning balance	$ —	$ 3,000
Materials purchased during month	65,000	66,000
Material used in production	(62,000)	(67,000)
Ending balance	$ 3,000	$ 2,000
Work-in-process inventory		
Beginning balance	$ —	$ 4,000
Materials used in production	62,000	67,000
Labor costs	58,000	58,000
Overhead costs	42,000	42,000
Cost of goods completed	(158,000)	(161,000)
Ending balance	$ 4,000	$ 10,000
Finished goods inventory		
Beginning balance	—	$ 5,000
Cost of goods completed	$ 158,000	161,000
Cost of goods sold	(153,000)	(163,000)
Ending balance	$ 5,000	$ 3,000

are added during February. The cost of completed goods is subtracted, leaving a balance of $10,000 at the end of February.

Finished goods inventory for January is the cost of goods completed during January less the cost of goods sold for the month. The ending balance of $5,000 is carried over as the beginning balance for February. The cost of goods completed during February is added and the cost of goods sold during February is subtracted, leaving a balance of $3,000 for finished goods inventory at the end of February.

Manufacturing companies do not recognize expenses for the materials, labor, and overhead used in the production process until goods are sold. Those expenses are part of the company's inventories until finished goods are sold. At that time, production costs are transferred to expense as Cost of Goods Sold. This accrual accounting procedure matches expenses with revenues in the period in which the revenues are recognized. The costs of goods that have not been sold at the end of the fiscal period are reported on the balance sheet as part of a company's inventories. Each inventory category (Raw Materials, Work-In-Process, and Finished Goods) may be reported on the balance sheet. In some cases, manufacturing companies report the amount of total inventories on the balance sheet and report the amounts of the various categories in a note.

Case in Point

Manufacturing Inventories

Krispy Kreme reported the following total manufacturing inventories in its 2002 annual report.

(In thousands)	2002	2001
Inventories		
Raw materials	$5,674	$3,809
Work-in-process	28	248
Finished goods	4,280	2,328
Total manufacturing inventories	$9,982	$6,385

MEASURING INVENTORY

OBJECTIVE 4

Explain and apply rules for measuring cost of goods sold and inventories and describe the effects of income taxes on the choice of inventory estimation method.

The examples presented in the previous sections are relatively straightforward because we assume that we know the cost of each inventory item. If a company sells 10 inventory items and each item costs $50, cost of goods sold is $500. A problem arises, however, when a company does not know the precise cost of an inventory item and the cost must be estimated. A major reason inventory costs are estimated is that the costs of merchandise, raw materials, labor, utilities, supplies, and other resources change over time.

Hydro Company sells and services agricultural irrigation equipment. On March 20, 2004, Hydro purchased 20 pump motors at $200 each. Hydro already had 8 identical motors on hand, for which it had paid $175 each. On March 22, 2004, a customer purchased one motor. Should the company record the cost of goods sold for the motor as $175 or as $200?

The decision about which cost to record ($175 or $200) affects both the income statement and the balance sheet. If $175 is used, this amount is subtracted from Merchandise Inventory and transferred to Cost of Goods Sold. All of the motors that cost $200 are left in Merchandise Inventory.

Most companies that sell products for which one unit of inventory is like other units of inventory estimate their cost of goods sold rather than trying to keep track of the cost of each individual unit. Exceptions to this practice are made when the cost of individual inventory items is large and one item is easily distinguished from another. For example, a car dealer keeps track of each car or truck in its inventory. For companies that estimate inventory costs, common methods are first-in, first-out (FIFO); last-in, first-out (LIFO); and weighted-average.

The *first-in, first-out method* **assumes that the units of inventory acquired first are sold first.** If Hydro used FIFO, it would record the cost of the motor sold on March 22 as $175 because this is the cost of the oldest items in Hydro's inventory.

The *last-in, first-out method* **assumes that the last units of inventory acquired are the first sold.** If Hydro used LIFO, it would record the cost of the motor sold on March 22 as $200 because this is the cost of the most recent items in Hydro's inventory.

The *weighted-average method* **uses the average cost of units of inventory available during a period as the cost of units sold.** Hydro's average inventory cost for pump motors on March 22 would be as follows:

	Units	Cost per Unit	Total Cost
Beginning	8	$175	$1,400
Purchased	20	200	4,000
Total	28		$5,400
Average cost per unit ($5,400 ÷ 28 units)			$192.86

Accordingly, Hydro would record cost of goods sold of $192.86 for the motor it sold on March 22.

Inventory estimation methods often are used even when a company knows which items of inventory are being sold. For example, Hydro could use LIFO for its motor sales even if the salesperson is sure that the motor delivered to the customer is one left over from last year. Most companies sell their oldest goods first, to avoid spoilage and obsolescence. But they may use LIFO to account for those goods anyway. LIFO often is used by companies because of its beneficial income tax effects.

Perpetual and Periodic Inventory Methods

The determination of inventory costs differs depending on whether a company uses perpetual or periodic inventory systems. *Perpetual inventory system* **refers to a system of recording cost of goods sold and updating inventory balances at the time goods** are sold. *Periodic inventory system* **refers to a system of recording cost of goods sold and updating inventory balances at the end of a fiscal period.** Because technology makes it feasible to identify costs at the time sales occur, the perpetual system is used by many companies.

Let's examine the effects of these inventory systems for Mom's Cookie Company. Suppose that the company has finished goods inventory of $3,000 at the end of February 2005. The inventory includes 150 cases of cookies at a cost of $20 per case. During March, the company completes a batch of 3,000 cases at a cost of $20.30 per case on March 8, a second batch of 3,000 cases at $20.60 on March 18, and a third batch of 3,000 cases at $20.90 on March 28. It shipped orders for 5,200 cases on March 20 and 3,600 cases on March 31. Exhibit 6 summarizes these events.

Exhibit 6
Unit Costs and Sales for Mom's Cookie Company for March

	Units (Cases)	Unit Cost	Total Cost
March 1 Inventory	150	$20.00	$ 3,000
March 8 Batch	3,000	20.30	60,900
March 18 Batch	3,000	20.60	61,800
March 20 Sales	5,200		
March 28 Batch	3,000	20.90	62,700
March 31 Sales	3,600		
Total Cost of Goods Available for Sale			$188,400

Perpetual System. To determine cost of goods sold using the perpetual system, calculate the cost at the time of each sale. On March 20, the company sold 5,200 cases. Using FIFO, the cost of these units would be $106,130, as shown in Exhibit 7. Using FIFO, the earliest inventory batches are sold first. Consequently, the March 1, March 8, and a portion of the March 18 batches are used in the calculation of Cost of Goods Sold.

Exhibit 7   Calculation of Perpetual Inventory Cost for March 20 Sales

	Units (Cases) Available	Units Sold March 20	Units Left	Unit Cost	Total Cost
FIFO Inventory Cost					
Beginning Inventory	150	150	0	$20.00	$ 3,000
March 8 Batch	3,000	3,000	0	20.30	60,900
March 18 Batch	3,000	2,050	950	20.60	42,230
Cost of Goods Sold		5,200			$106,130
Ending Inventory on March 20					
(cost from March 18)			950	20.60	$ 19,570
LIFO Inventory Cost					
Beginning Inventory	150	0	150	$20.00	$ 0
March 8 Batch	3,000	2,200	800	20.30	44,660
March 18 Batch	3,000	3,000	0	20.60	61,800
Cost of Goods Sold		5,200			$106,460
Ending Inventory on March 20					
(cost from March 1)			150	20.00	$ 3,000
(cost from March 8)			800	20.30	16,240
Total			950		$ 19,240

The cost of goods sold using LIFO would be $106,460, as shown in Exhibit 7. Using LIFO, the most recent inventory layers are assumed to be sold first. Thus, for the March 20 sale, the cost of inventory from March 18 and a portion of cost of inventory from March 8 are included in cost of goods sold.

After the March 20 sale, Mom's Cookie Company would have 950 cases left in inventory. Using FIFO, the cost of these units is $20.60 per case, as shown in Exhibit 7. On March 20, a batch of 3,000 cases was produced. The company sold an additional 3,600 cases on March 31. The cost of these units using FIFO would be $74,955, as shown in Exhibit 8. The FIFO calculation assumes the units that cost $20.60 were sold along with a portion of the units from the March 28 batch.

Using LIFO, the inventory available on March 20, after the sales, included 150 cases that cost $20.00 per case and 800 cases that cost $20.30 per case. When goods are sold on March 31, the most recent goods available, those from March 28, are assumed to be sold first. Exhibit 8 shows the cost of goods sold for March 31 as $74,880, using LIFO.

Exhibit 8 Calculation of Perpetual Inventory Cost for March 31 Sales

	Units (Cases) Available	Units Sold March 31	Units Left	Unit Cost	Total Cost
FIFO Inventory Cost					
Beginning Inventory	950	950	0	$20.60	$19,570
March 28 Batch	3,000	2,650	350	20.90	55,385
Cost of Goods Sold		3,600			$74,955
Ending Inventory on March 31					
(cost from March 28)			350	20.90	$ 7,315
LIFO Inventory Cost					
Beginning Inventory	150	0	150	$20.00	$ 0
March 8 Inventory	800	600	200	20.30	12,180
March 28 Batch	3,000	3,000	0	20.90	62,700
Cost of Goods Sold		3,600			$74,880
Ending Inventory on March 31					
(cost from March 1)			150	20.00	$ 3,000
(cost from March 8)			200	20.30	4,060
Total			350		$ 7,060

Thus, for the month of March:

	FIFO	LIFO
Total cost of goods sold	$181,085[1]	$181,340[2]
Ending inventory on March 31	7,315	7,060
Total goods available for sale during March	$188,400	$188,400

[1]($106,130 + $74,955)
[2]($106,460 + $74,880)

The weighted average method would calculate cost of goods sold based on the average cost of inventory available at the time of each sale. Exhibit 9 provides calculations for Mom's Cookie Company for March.

The company's inventory on March 20 includes 6,150 units at a combined cost of $125,700. Therefore, the average cost per unit is $20.439 ($125,700 ÷ 6,150 units). Cost of goods sold for the March 20 sale is $106,283 (5,200 units × $20.439), leaving an inventory of 950 units at a cost of $19,417 (950 units × $20.439).

Exhibit 9

Calculation of Perpetual Average Inventory Cost for March Sales

	Units (Cases)	Unit Cost	Total Cost	Cost of Goods Sold
Beginning Inventory	150	$20.00	$ 3,000	
March 8 Batch	3,000	20.30	60,900	
March 18 Batch	3,000	20.60	61,800	
March 20 Average Cost	6,150	20.439	125,700	
March 20 Sales	5,200	20.439	106,283	$106,283
March 20 Inventory	950	20.439	19,417	
March 28 Batch	3,000	20.90	62,700	
March 31 Average Cost	3,950	20.789	82,117	
March 31 Sales	3,600	20.789	74,841	74,841
Ending Inventory	350	20.789	$ 7,276	$181,124

When goods are sold on March 31, the average inventory cost is recalculated. March 31 inventory includes 3,950 units at a combined cost of $82,117. Therefore, the average cost per unit is $20.789 ($82,117 ÷ 3,950 units). Cost of goods sold for the March 31 sale is $74,841 (3,600 units × $20.789). Ending inventory for March is $7,276 (350 units × $20.789). Therefore, total cost of goods available for sale in March is $188,400 ($106,283 + $74,841 + $7,276), which agrees with the total under FIFO and under LIFO.

The average method is sometimes referred to as the **moving average method** when the perpetual system is used because the average unit cost is recalculated each time a sale is made based on units available at that date.

Periodic System. Using the periodic system, a company records inventory costs at the end of a fiscal period. Thus, Mom's Cookie Company would record the cost of all the goods it sold during March at the end of the month. The cost of goods sold for March would be $181,085 using FIFO and $181,340 using LIFO, as shown in Exhibit 10.

Exhibit 10 Calculation of Periodic Inventory Cost for March

Cost of Goods Sold for March	Units (Cases) Available	Units Sold	Units Left	Unit Cost	Total Cost
FIFO Inventory Cost					
Beginning Inventory	150	150	—	$20.00	$ 3,000
March 8 Batch	3,000	3,000	—	20.30	60,900
March 18 Batch	3,000	3,000	—	20.60	61,800
March 28 Batch	3,000	2,650	350	20.90	55,385
Cost of Goods Sold for March		8,800			$181,085[1]
Ending Inventory (from March 28)			350	20.90	$ 7,315[1]
LIFO Inventory Cost					
Beginning Inventory	150	—	150	$20.00	$ —
March 8 Batch	3,000	2,800	200	20.30	56,840
March 18 Batch	3,000	3,000	—	20.60	61,800
March 28 Batch	3,000	3,000	—	20.90	62,700
Cost of Goods Sold for March		8,800			$181,340[2]
Ending Inventory (from March 1)			150	20.00	$ 3,000
(from March 8)			200	20.30	4,060
Total			350		$ 7,060[2]

[1]Total goods available for sale for March = $181,085 + $7,315 = $188,400.
[2]Total goods available for sale for March = $181,340 + $7,060 = $188,400.

If the weighted average method is used, the cost of goods sold for a period is calculated from the total units available during the period and the combined cost of these units, as described in Exhibit 11. Mom's Cookie Company had 9,150 units available during March at a combined cost of $188,400. Therefore, the average cost per unit was $20.59 ($188,400 ÷ 9,150 units). Cost of goods sold for March is $181,193 (8,800 units × $20.59). Ending inventory for March is $7,207 (350 units × $20.59).

Exhibit 11

Calculation of Periodic Average Inventory Cost for March Sales

	Units (Cases)	Unit Cost	Total Cost
Beginning Inventory	150	$20.00	$ 3,000
March 8 Batch	3,000	20.30	60,900
March 18 Batch	3,000	20.60	61,800
March 28 Batch	3,000	20.90	62,700
Average Cost	9,150	20.59	188,400*
Cost of Goods Sold	8,800	20.59	181,193
Ending Inventory	350	20.59	$ 7,207

*Total goods available for sale in March

Under the periodic inventory system, as under the perpetual inventory system, all methods have the same total goods available for sale for March, $188,400.

Companies that use the periodic system may not keep track of units sold during each fiscal period. Instead, they may count the number of units available at the end of a period to determine how many units were sold. Generally, this approach is only used when it is not feasible or cost effective to keep track of units sold.

This method is frequently used for supplies or similar prepaid items for which it is not feasible to maintain detailed inventory records. For example, assume Mom's Cookie Company had 4 cases of copier paper at the beginning of March at a cost of $50 per case. During March, the company purchased 10 cases at a cost of $52 per case. A count at the end of March revealed that 2 cases remained on hand. Supplies expense and supplies on hand at the end of March could be calculated using FIFO as follows:

Beginning inventory	$ 200	4 cases × $50
Purchases	520	10 cases × $52
Supplies available	720	
Ending inventory	(104)	2 cases × $52
Supplies expense	$ 616	

Inventory Estimation and Income Taxes

The primary reason for the use of LIFO is the tax advantage LIFO provides to many companies. LIFO results in the most recent inventory costs being subtracted when computing net income. FIFO results in the oldest inventory costs being subtracted. In inflationary periods, the LIFO method usually produces a higher cost of goods sold and a lower pretax income than does the FIFO method. Accordingly, income taxes also are lower.

Exhibit 12 compares income statements for Mom's Cookie Company assuming the use of FIFO and LIFO. The LIFO column is identical to the income statement in Exhibit 1, which assumed the company used the LIFO method. If the company had used FIFO instead of LIFO, its cost of goods sold for 2005 would have been $1,946,800. The cost is lower because the company would have used the cost of its oldest inventory items when recording cost of goods sold, and the cost of most of the items it sells has increased during the year. The lower cost of goods sold results in higher gross profit, operating income, and pretax income. Selling, general, and administrative expenses and nonoperating items are not affected by the choice of inventory estimation method.

Exhibit 12

Income Statement for Mom's Cookie Company Using FIFO and LIFO Inventory Estimation

For the Year Ended December 31, 2005	FIFO	LIFO
Sales revenue	$ 3,235,600	$ 3,235,600
Cost of goods sold	(1,946,800)	(1,954,300)
Gross profit	1,288,800	1,281,300
Selling, general, and administrative expenses	(1,094,700)	(1,094,700)
Operating income	194,100	186,600
Interest expense	(20,400)	(20,400)
Pretax income	173,700	166,200
Income taxes	(52,110)	(49,860)
Net income	$ 121,590	$ 116,340

Income tax expense is higher if FIFO is used because the income tax rate Mom's Cookie Company pays on its pretax income is the same (about 30%) whether FIFO or LIFO is used. Therefore, if FIFO is used, income tax expense is $52,110. If LIFO is used, income tax expense is $49,860. Consequently, if Mom's Cookie Company used FIFO, it would incur $2,250 in additional taxes compared with using LIFO. FIFO results in higher net income for Mom's Cookie Company, but it also results in higher income taxes.

Income tax regulations require that, in most cases, a company that uses LIFO to estimate cost of goods sold in computing its income taxes also must use LIFO to estimate cost of goods sold on its income statement. This rule, called a tax conformity rule, is unusual. Tax regulations normally permit companies to use different accounting measurement rules for estimating revenues and expenses for tax and income statement purposes. For example, a company can use accelerated depreciation for computing income taxes and straight-line depreciation for computing net income. As a result of this tax rule, a company often has to choose between reporting higher net income by using FIFO and paying lower taxes by using LIFO. Once a company chooses an inventory estimation method, it is required by GAAP to use the method consistently from year to year. A change from one method to another (from LIFO to FIFO, for example) is permitted only in infrequent circumstances when management can justify the change because of important changes in the company's business.

INTERNATIONAL

LEARNING NOTE

Most countries do not allow the use of LIFO. Therefore, multinational firms, including large U.S. corporations, normally use FIFO for inventories held in foreign countries even if they use LIFO for similar inventories held in the United States. Companies can use LIFO for some inventories and FIFO or the weighted-average method for others.

It is important to understand why many companies use LIFO even though it results in lower net income. To understand the reasoning, consider Mom's Cookie Company's operating cash flows. Although the choice of inventory method affects Cost of Goods Sold on the income statement, it has no effect on the amount of cash paid to suppliers. Assume the company paid $2 million for the inventory it purchased in 2005. Regardless of whether the company uses FIFO or LIFO, it still pays the same amount for this inventory. Also, the amounts of cash collected from customers and paid for other resources consumed in 2005 are the same, regardless of which inventory method the company uses. The only effect the company's inventory method has on its cash flows is the amount of income taxes it pays. Therefore, using LIFO reduces cash payments for taxes and leaves the company with more net cash flow from operating activities.

Remember that net income is an accrual-basis estimate of the net amount of cash a company will receive once it has collected cash from customers and paid for all resources consumed in operating activities. If Mom's Cookie Company uses FIFO, its net income is higher than if it uses LIFO, but its net operating cash flow is lower. Therefore, the higher income results from accounting estimation, not from real economic activity that creates additional resources for the company. Thus, if the company used FIFO, it might look as if it were performing better than if it used LIFO, but the appearance is deceiving. Actually, the company is performing better if it uses LIFO because of the lower tax payments. To understand and interpret net income, it is important to understand accounting measurement rules.

Companies that use FIFO normally do so for sound economic reasons. For example, if the cost of inventory decreases over time because of improvements in technology or increased competition, FIFO produces a tax advantage over LIFO. The oldest items in inventory cost more than the newest items. Including the cost of the oldest items in cost of goods sold reduces taxable income and income taxes. Accordingly, computer and other high-technology companies that experience decreases in inventory costs normally use FIFO.

Lower of Cost or Market Inventory Valuation. GAAP require companies to compare the costs determined through inventory estimation methods with the current market cost of the inventories on hand at the end of a fiscal year. **If current market costs are below the costs resulting from the use of an estimation method such as FIFO or LIFO, the inventories must be written down to the current market costs. This requirement is referred to as the** *lower of cost or market inventory* **rule.** Such writedowns are more common when FIFO is used because FIFO normally results in a higher estimated inventory value at year end. Therefore, FIFO inventory costs are more likely than LIFO costs to be higher than market.

A problem with reporting inventory at the lower of cost or market is that the market value of inventories is not always easy to determine. GAAP specify a procedure for computing market value that considers the current replacement cost and the amount a company expects to receive from selling the inventory less the profit it expects to earn from the inventory. Once a market value has been determined, it is compared with the cost of inventory. If the market value is less than cost, the inventory is written down to market.

LEARNING NOTE

An excess of market value over cost is not recognized through a valuation adjustment. This is another example of the conservatism of accounting measurement.

A writedown results in a loss that is recognized in the period in which the inventory decreases in value. To illustrate, assume that Tucker Company, which sells electronic equipment through its retail stores, acquired $500,000 of merchandise on August 18, 2004. By December 31, 2004, the end of the company's fiscal year, it had sold $300,000 of the merchandise. It was having difficulty selling the remaining $200,000 of merchandise because a competitor was marketing newer products at lower prices. Tucker estimated that the market value of its remaining inventory was $140,000 on December 31. Accordingly, it would recognize the decline in market value as follows:

| | | ASSETS | | = | LIABILITIES | + | OWNERS' EQUITY | |
| | | Cash | Other Assets | | | | Contributed Capital | Retained Earnings |
Date	Accounts							
Dec. 31, 2004	Loss on Inventory							−60,000
	Merchandise Inventory		−60,000					

Comparing Inventory Costs among Companies

GAAP require companies to disclose the methods they use to measure inventories and cost of goods sold. GAAP also require companies that use LIFO to disclose the effect of the method on the reported value of inventory. For example, **Sears, Roebuck & Co.** reported in its annual report for the fiscal year ended in 2001 that it used LIFO to determine most of its inventory costs. It also reported that these inventory costs were $590 million lower in 2001 than if FIFO had been used. Sears' cost of goods sold was higher using LIFO. Sears used LIFO because of its tax advantages. Furthermore, managers are aware that investors, creditors, and other users of accounting information who understand accounting methods recognize that higher net income is not beneficial unless it results from real economic improvement in a company's performance. Managers who use accounting methods to dress up their earnings to make them look better than they really are often lose the trust of investors and other users of financial statements when they learn of this type of behavior.

Case in Point

http://ingram.
swcollege.com

Learn more about WorldCom.

The Importance of Reliable Accounting Information

WorldCom, Inc., revealed in June 2002 that it had understated expenses by approximately $4 billion during 2001 and 2002 and that the company would have reported net losses during this period if the expenses had been stated correctly. The company's stock price dropped to around 9¢ per share after the information was released. At the beginning of 2002, the stock was trading at approximately $14 per share.

The FIFO, LIFO, and weighted-average methods are used by both merchandising and manufacturing companies. In recent years, however, many manufacturing companies have tried to reduce their inventories. Those companies buy materials as they are needed, "just in time" to be used in the manufacturing process. Materials are acquired at a rate sufficient to meet orders without accumulating large amounts of inventories. Companies that use just-in-time manufacturing procedures report relatively small amounts of inventory, and they expense almost all of their manufacturing costs each period as part of the cost of goods sold. For these companies, the method used to estimate inventory is less important than it is for companies with large inventories.

2 SELF-STUDY PROBLEM

WebTUTOR Advantage

Fashion Mart is a clothing retailer. During 2004, the company recorded $28 million of cost of goods sold. If it had used LIFO, it would have reported $30 million of cost of goods sold. The company's income tax rate was 35%. Sales revenue for the year was $45 million, and other expenses were $8 million.

Required

A. What would the difference in Fashion Mart's net income and cash flow from operating activities have been if it had used LIFO instead of FIFO in 2004?
B. What factors should the company consider in deciding which inventory estimation method to use?

The solution to Self-Study Problem 2 appears at the end of the chapter.

OTHER OPERATING ACTIVITIES AND INCOME STATEMENT ITEMS

In addition to operating revenues and cost of goods sold, operating expenses, other revenues and expenses, income taxes, and special items affect a company's income statement. The next two sections describe items that are reported in each of these categories.

Operating Expenses

OBJECTIVE 5

Identify routine and nonroutine events that affect a company's income statement.

Most operating expenses other than cost of goods sold are period costs. Period costs are expensed in the fiscal period in which they occur. These costs usually reduce cash or other current assets or increase current liabilities on the balance sheet. The use of cash is a cash outflow on the statement of cash flows. Exhibit 13 illustrates these relationships.

Exhibit 13

The Effect of Period Costs on the Financial Statements

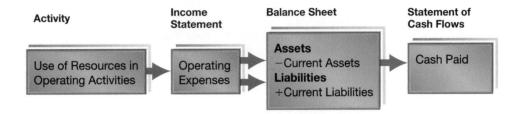

For most companies, period expenses result from marketing, research and development, and general administrative activities. Marketing costs include the costs of advertising, direct selling and distributing, depreciation of assets used primarily in selling activities, and the salaries and commissions of the sales force. Research and development costs are the costs of creating new products and production processes. Administrative costs include the depreciation of plant assets used in administrative activities (office buildings and equipment) and the salaries of managers and office workers.

The costs of certain operating activities are always expensed in the period in which the activities occur and resources are consumed. For example, GAAP require that research and development costs be expensed when they occur because of uncertainty about the future benefits to a company of these activities. In most cases, cash is paid for resources used in operating activities at about the time they are consumed. Accordingly, companies seldom use long-term debt (bonds or notes payable) to finance these activities.

The costs of other operating activities are expensed when certain events occur, which may be long before cash payments are made. As a result, long-term liabilities are associated with these items. A primary example is deferred compensation. Deferred compensation results when a company agrees to pay employee retirement benefits. These benefits are earned by employees as they work for the company. Therefore, the company recognizes expenses each period as the benefits are earned. Payments may be deferred for years, however, until benefits are paid to employees after they retire. Consequently, companies often record long-term liabilities associated with these future payments. The last section of this chapter describes deferred compensation expenses and liabilities in more detail.

Corporations often report operating expenses on one line on their income statements (see Exhibit 1). Exceptions are made for some items, however. For example, GAAP require companies to report separately any unusual revenues or expenses that are material in amount. Separate reporting of these items calls attention to them. Among these types of items are expenses associated with restructuring a company's operations. Restructuring occurs when a company eliminates certain products, closes facilities, reduces its labor force, or sells off nonproductive assets. **Sears**, for example, reported "special charges" of $542 million for its fiscal year ended in 2001. These charges were associated with workforce reductions and facilities consolidations. These items are reported separately because they are not ordinary operating activities. Certain other expenses that are important to a company's operating activities—research and development expenses and depreciation expenses, for instance—also must be disclosed, either separately on the income statement or in notes to the financial statements. The last section of this chapter considers other income and expense items that often appear in corporate financial statements or notes to the statements.

Other Revenues and Expenses

Other revenues include interest and other investment income, such as dividends or gains from the sale of stocks and bonds. Other expenses include interest on short-term and long-term debt, including interest on capital lease obligations. These amounts are accrued. The amount of revenue reported is the amount earned, regardless of whether cash has been received. The amount of expense reported is the amount of obligation incurred during the current fiscal year, regardless of whether cash has been paid.

As shown in Exhibit 1, Mom's Cookie Company reported interest expense of $20,400. Items of this type are not part of the company's normal operating activities. Accordingly, they are reported after "operating income" to distinguish them from operating revenues and expenses. These activities are reported as part of the operating activities section of the statement of cash flows, however, because they are reported on the income statement.

Income Taxes

The income statement reports the amount of income taxes that a company would incur if its pretax income were all taxable in the current fiscal year. To determine the income tax expense reported on the income statement, most companies simply multiply their pretax income times the corporate tax rate. This rate includes federal and state income taxes and is adjusted for foreign taxes for multinational corporations. Consequently, the rate is not the same for all companies. The federal corporate tax rate in the United States was 35% in 2002. State and foreign tax rates vary.

For many companies, net income is the amount left after income taxes are deducted from pretax income. For other companies, special items (discussed in the next section) that affect net income are reported after income taxes.

Non-recurring Gains and Losses

Certain gains and losses are reported separately on a company's income statement after the calculation of income associated with normal business activities. These items are reported separately because they are not expected to recur. The three types of non-recurring items reported separately are discontinued operations, extraordinary items, and the cumulative effect of a change in accounting methods.

Discontinued operations **are product lines or major parts of a company from which the company will no longer derive income because it has sold or closed the facilities that produced the product line or that included that part of the company.** Two types of gains or losses associated with discontinued operations are reported. One is the gain or loss associated with operations that are being discontinued. Another is the gain or loss associated with the sale of the discontinued facilities.

For example, assume Beverly Company manufactures boats and sporting equipment. It decides to dispose of its boating division in 2004. On September 30, 2004, the company sells the division at a loss of $3 million, after taxes. From January 1 to September 30, 2004, the division earned a profit of $1.2 million, after taxes. The company would report these items separately on its income statement for the fiscal year ended December 31, 2004, as follows:

Income before taxes	$10,000,000
Provision for income taxes	(2,600,000)
Income before discontinued operations	7,400,000
Loss on sale of discontinued operations, net of tax effect of $850,000	(3,000,000)
Operating profit of discontinued operations, net of tax effect of $420,000	1,200,000
Net income	$ 5,600,000

Non-recurring items are reported net of the tax effect associated with that item because if the non-recurring item had not occurred, the associated tax effect would not have occurred either. Income taxes associated with normal business activities are reported separately as provision for income taxes or income tax expense. The tax effect usually offsets a reported gain or loss. A gain results in additional taxes. A loss results in tax savings because the loss can be deducted from other taxable income.

Extraordinary items **are gains or losses that are both unusual and infrequent for a particular company.** Losses associated with natural disasters often are reported as extraordinary items. The key to identifying those that are extraordinary is whether or not the event rarely occurs. For example, damage caused by an earthquake in California would not be considered an extraordinary loss since earthquakes are not rare in that area. However, damage caused by an earthquake in Nebraska would be considered extraordinary since that would be a rare event. Like discontinued operations, extraordinary items are reported net of taxes.

A *cumulative effect of a change in accounting method* **is a gain or loss associated with changing accounting methods or adopting new accounting standards.** For example, when a company adopts a new standard, it may be required to report expenses that it was not required to report in the past. When the standard is adopted, the company estimates the amount of expense that it would have reported in years prior to the adoption if the new standard had been followed and reports this amount as a cumulative effect of a change in accounting method. Companies are expected to apply accounting methods consistently from one fiscal period to another. Consequently, companies usually do not change accounting methods once they have adopted them. Thus, it is relatively uncommon for a company to switch from FIFO to LIFO, for example. If a switch is made, the company estimates the difference in expenses it would have reported in prior years if the alternate method had been used and reports that amount as a cumulative effect of a change in accounting method.

Net income is the amount earned by a company's stockholders (both preferred and common stockholders) during a fiscal period. **The amount earned by common stockholders is known as** *net income available for common stockholders* and is equal to net income minus any dividends paid to preferred stockholders. For example, if Harris Company reported net income of $156,000 and paid $13,000 in preferred dividends in 2004, its net income available for common stockholders would be $143,000 ($156,000 of net income − $13,000 of preferred dividends).

When a company reports non-recurring items on its income statement, it also reports earnings per share separately for these items. In addition, earnings per share is based on income available for common stockholders. If Harris reported an extraordinary loss of $7,000 and had 20,000 shares of common stock outstanding throughout 2004, it would report earnings per share as follows:

Income before extraordinary items	$7.50 ($163,000 − $13,000) ÷ 20,000
Extraordinary loss (net of tax effect of $3,000)	(0.35) $7,000 ÷ 20,000
Net income	$7.15 ($156,000 − $13,000) ÷ 20,000

3 SELF-STUDY PROBLEM

King Company, a manufacturer of mattresses, reported the following items on its income statement for 2004.

WebTUTOR Advantage

A. Net operating revenues, $845,000
B. Cost of goods sold, $320,000
C. Selling and administrative expenses, $280,000
D. Research and development expenses, $78,000
E. Net interest expense, $4,000
F. Provision for income taxes, $50,000
G. Current year loss from discontinued operations of $30,000, net of tax benefit of $10,000

H. Loss from sale of discontinued operations of $100,000, net of tax benefit of $30,000
I. Cumulative effect (gain) of change in accounting principle of $120,000, net of tax of $40,000
J. Preferred stock dividends, $60,000

The company had 10,000 shares of common stock outstanding throughout the fiscal year.

Required Compute each of the following:

A. Operating income
B. Income (loss) from continuing operations, before taxes
C. Income (loss) before discontinued operations and the cumulative effect of the accounting change
D. Net income (loss)
E. Net income (loss) available for common shareholders
F. Earnings per share for continuing operations
G. Earnings per share for discontinued operations
H. Earnings per share for the cumulative effect of the accounting change
I. Earnings per share for net income (loss)

The solution to Self-Study Problem 3 appears at the end of the chapter.

Other Topics

This section describes three types of items that may appear on companies' income statements.

Equity Income

Equity income is income that a company earns using the equity method of accounting for investments in other companies (see Chapter F11). For example, assume that Alpha Company owns 40% of Beta Company's common stock and Beta reports net income of $10 million in 2004. Alpha would report $4 million ($10 million × 40%) of Beta's income as equity income on its 2004 income statement.

Noncontrolling Interest in Income

As discussed in Chapter F4, consolidated financial statements report the combined activities of a parent corporation and its subsidiaries as the operations of one company. When the parent owns less than 100% of a subsidiary's common stock, the portion it does not own is known as noncontrolling (or minority) interest. If Alpha Company owns 80% (the controlling interest) of Delta Company, the remaining 20% is noncontrolling interest. The portion of the subsidiary's net income attributable to noncontrolling interest is reported on the income statement as minority interest in income of consolidated subsidiaries. This amount is subtracted (assuming positive income) or added (assuming a loss) in computing net income because it is a portion of subsidiary income that has not been earned by the parent.

As an example, Krispy Kreme reported the following information on its 2002 income statement (in thousands):

Minority interest	$ (1,147)
Income before income taxes	42,546
Provision for income taxes	(16,168)
Net income	$26,378

Deferred Compensation

Some operating expenses are not disclosed separately on the income statement but are described in detail in notes to the statement. For example, deferred employee compensation expenses are a subject of considerable disclosure by some companies. Deferred compensation involves retirement benefits, such as pensions and health-care benefits, provided to employees once they retire. If companies agree to provide these benefits, employees earn the benefits over the course of their working careers. The amount of benefits earned is determined by the wages employees earn and the length of time they work for a company. Consequently, companies incur expenses for these future benefits during the working careers of their employees.

To illustrate, assume that Alpha Company determines that the amount of benefits earned by employees at the end of 2004 is $60 million. This amount is referred to as the company's projected benefit obligation. If the fair market value of the assets Alpha has set aside to meet this obligation is $50 million, the company would report a pension liability of $10 million.

Projected benefit obligation	$60
Fair value of plan assets	50
Pension liability	$10

In addition to the liability, Alpha will report an expense associated with benefits earned by employees during 2004. Assume that benefits earned amounted to $8 million and earnings on pension plan assets amounted to $6 million. Alpha would report a net pension expense of $2 million.

Service cost (benefits earned)	$8
Return on plan assets	6
Net pension expense	$2

The calculation of deferred compensation costs is complex because it requires estimation of future benefits that will be earned by employees after they retire. Thus, a company must estimate how long employees will work, what amounts they will earn in the future, and how long they will receive benefits once they retire. The present values of these amounts then are estimated as a basis for determining the amount of funding currently required.

REVIEW

SUMMARY of IMPORTANT CONCEPTS

1. The income statement reports the results of operating activities on an accrual basis.

2. Revenues result from the sale of goods and services to customers and increase cash and/or accounts receivable.
   a. Revenues should be recognized when all of the following events have occurred:
      (1) The seller has completed most activities necessary to produce and sell its products.
      (2) The seller has incurred the costs necessary to produce and sell its products or can reasonably estimate those costs.
      (3) The seller can measure objectively the amount of revenue it has earned.
      (4) The seller is reasonably sure of collecting cash from the buyer.
   b. Revenues from long-term contracts are recognized each fiscal period in proportion to the passage of time or the amount of work covered by the contract that has been completed.
   c. Sales discounts and returns are deducted from gross revenues in computing the amount of net revenue reported on the income statement.

    d. Uncollectible accounts expense is estimated each fiscal year to match the cost of expected doubtful accounts of customers with the revenues that resulted in the doubtful accounts.

    e. Warranty expenses are estimated each fiscal year to match these costs with revenues that resulted in the costs.

3. Companies purchase inventories, which are recorded as assets and are expensed as cost of goods sold when the inventory is sold to customers.

    a. Merchandise companies account for the purchase and sale of merchandise.

    b. Manufacturing companies account for raw materials inventories and for work-in-process and finished goods inventories, which include the costs of materials, direct labor, and manufacturing overhead.

4. Most companies estimate inventory and cost of goods sold amounts using one of three methods.

    a. First-in, first-out (FIFO) assumes that the units of inventory acquired first are sold first.

    b. Last-in, first-out (LIFO) assumes that the units of inventory acquired most recently are sold first.

    c. Weighted-average uses the average cost of inventory available to determine the cost of units sold.

    d. Perpetual inventory systems, which recognize cost of goods sold as inventory is sold, are used by most companies. Periodic inventory systems, which determine cost of goods sold from a count of inventory on hand at the end of a period, are used when the costs of perpetual systems exceed the benefits of timely inventory information.

    e. LIFO is used by many companies that experience increases in inventory costs over time because it results in lower income taxes and, therefore, higher net operating cash flow.

    f. Companies that use LIFO for determining their income taxes also must use LIFO in preparing their financial statements.

    g. If the market value of inventory at the end of a fiscal period is lower than the cost of the inventory, the inventory should be written down to market value, regardless of which inventory estimation method is used.

5. The income statement reports the effects of other operating activities.

    a. Operating expenses usually are period costs that reduce cash and/or increase liabilities.

    b. Some costs, such as research and development, are always expensed in the period in which they occur.

    c. Some activities, such as deferred compensation, are expensed as benefits are earned, though costs associated with providing the benefits are not incurred until years after the expenses are recognized.

    d. Income taxes are recorded by corporations based on federal, state, and foreign tax rates.

6. Non-recurring items are reported after ordinary income and income taxes on the income statement and are reported net of tax effects.

7. Certain activities often are reported on the income statement or in notes to the financial statements.

    a. Equity income is income a company earns using the equity method of accounting for investments in other companies.

    b. Noncontrolling interest income is the portion of a subsidiary's net income that is allocated to noncontrolling interests (owners of the subsidiary other than the parent corporation).

    c. Deferred compensation arrangements often require a company to recognize a liability and expense for benefits earned by employees.

DEFINE

TERMS and CONCEPTS DEFINED in this CHAPTER

cumulative effect of a change in accounting method (F501)
discontinued operations   (F500)
extraordinary items   (F501)
finished goods inventory   (F489)
first-in, first-out (FIFO) method   (F491)
last-in, first-out (LIFO) method   (F491)
lower of cost or market inventory   (F497)

net income available for common stock-holders   (F501)
periodic inventory system   (F492)
perpetual inventory system   (F491)
raw materials inventory   (F489)
weighted-average method   (F491)
work-in-process inventory   (F489)

SELF-STUDY PROBLEM SOLUTIONS

SSP13-1

Item	Accounts	ASSETS — Cash	ASSETS — Other Assets	=	LIABILITIES	+	OWNERS' EQUITY — Contributed Capital	OWNERS' EQUITY — Retained Earnings
1.	Merchandise Inventory		400,000					
	Accounts Payable				400,000			
2.	Accounts Receivable		750,000					
	Sales Revenue							750,000
3.	Cost of Goods Sold							−388,000
	Merchandise Inventory		−388,000					
4.	Accounts Payable				−384,000			
	Cash	−384,000						
5.	Cash	720,000						
	Accounts Receivable		−720,000					
6.	Sales Discounts							−17,000
	Accounts Receivable		−17,000					
7.	Doubtful Accounts Expense							−10,000
	Allowance for Doubtful Accounts		−10,000					
8.	Allowance for Doubtful Accounts		8,000					
	Accounts Receivable		−8,000					

Income

Gross sales revenue	$750,000
Sales discounts	−17,000
Net sales revenue	$733,000
Cost of goods sold	−388,000
Doubtful accounts expense	−10,000
Net income	$335,000

Cash Flow (Direct Method)

Cash received from customers	$720,000
Cash paid to suppliers	384,000
Net operating cash flow	$336,000

Cash Flow (Indirect Method)

Net income	$335,000
Increase in net receivables	−3,000
Increase in merchandise	−12,000
Increase in accounts payable	16,000
Net operating cash flow	$336,000

SSP13-2 A.

(In millions)	FIFO	LIFO
Sales revenue	$ 45.00	$ 45.00
Cost of goods sold	(28.00)	(30.00)
Other expenses	(8.00)	(8.00)
Pretax income	$ 9.00	$ 7.00
Income tax expense (35%)	(3.15)	(2.45)
Net income	$ 5.85	$ 4.55

Fashion Mart's cost of goods sold would have been $2 million larger using LIFO rather than FIFO. As a result, its net income would have been $1.3 million ($5.85 − $4.55) less if it had used LIFO. However, it would have incurred $0.7 million ($3.15 − $2.45) less in income taxes if it had used LIFO. Therefore, its net cash flow from operating activities would have been $0.7 million greater if it had used LIFO.

B. If Fashion Mart expects the costs of its inventory items to increase over time, LIFO will result in lower income taxes than FIFO. Therefore, the company will have higher net operating cash flow using LIFO. On the other hand, if the costs of inventory items are likely to decrease over time (perhaps because of improved production processes or greater competition among suppliers), FIFO will result in lower income taxes and higher net operating cash flow.

SSP13-3

	Net operating revenues	$845,000
	Cost of goods sold	(320,000)
	Selling and administrative expenses	(280,000)
	Research and development expenses	(78,000)
A.	Operating income	$167,000
	Net interest expense	(4,000)
B.	Income from continuing operations, before taxes	$163,000
	Provision for income taxes	(50,000)
C.	Income before discontinued operations and cumulative effect of accounting change	$113,000
	Discontinued operations:	
	Current period loss, net of tax of $10,000	(30,000)
	Loss from sale of discontinued operations, net of tax of $30,000	(100,000)
	Cumulative effect of change in accounting principle, net of tax of $40,000	120,000
D.	Net income	$103,000
	Preferred dividends	(60,000)
E.	Net income available for common shareholders	$ 43,000
	Earnings per share:	
F.	Continuing operations [($113,000 − 60,000) ÷ 10,000 shares]	$ 5.30
G.	Discontinued operations ($130,000 ÷ 10,000 shares)	(13.00)
H.	Cumulative effect of accounting change ($120,000 ÷ 10,000 shares)	12.00
I.	Net income available for common shareholders [($103,000 − $60,000) ÷ 10,000 shares]	$ 4.30

Thinking Beyond the Question

How do we account for operating activities?

This chapter considered the estimation and reporting of revenues and expenses. A company's income statement is affected by estimates of sales returns, doubtful accounts, warranty costs, inventory costs, and similar items. Also, it is affected by whether revenues and expenses require separate reporting and whether they are associated with recurring or non-recurring activities. Why should stockholders and other decision makers care about estimation methods and in which part of the income statement a company reports its business activities?

QUESTIONS

Q13-1
Obj. 1
If the purpose of the income statement is to report the results of operating activities, why is there a section on the statement of cash flows that reports the results of operating activities?

Q13-2
Obj. 1
Why is an income statement divided into so many different categories? Couldn't all the revenues and all the expenses each be totaled and then subtracted from each other to determine net income? Wouldn't this make accounting easier to learn?

Q13-3
Obj. 1
A friend tells you, "I just ignore the income statement when I'm making an investment decision. All I care about is the cash, so that the company can pay me dividends. The balance sheet tells me about the cash the company's got; the cash flows statement tells me about its changes in cash. Who cares about the income statement? It's just a bunch of inaccurate stuff loaded with estimates." Do you agree with your friend's statements about the nature of the income statement and about its lack of importance? Explain why or why not.

Q13-4
Obj. 2
When goods are sold FOB shipping point, the buyer usually pays the freight cost. Does this make sense? Why or why not?

Q13-5
Obj. 2
Sales discounts and sales returns are accounted for as reductions of revenue. If they were accounted for as expenses, wouldn't the effect on net income be the same? Why not just treat sales discounts and sales returns as expenses?

Q13-6
Obj. 3
Gross profit results from a company's transactions with its customers and suppliers. What types of transactions affect gross profit? How does the accounting for timing differences between cash flow and accrual measurements of these transactions affect financial statements?

Q13-7
Obj. 3
At a meeting of your manufacturing team, a coworker groans: "We were working so hard to get the income for our bonus this year. Then they got all that raw material inventory in—and even paid for it. We don't need it yet. Why didn't they wait until January?" Will the raw materials inventory affect this year's income? Does it matter whether it was paid for this year or in January? Explain your answers.

Q13-8
Obj. 3
On December 28, Hadley Company purchased goods FOB destination at a cost of $38,000. The goods arrived at Hadley's warehouse and were unloaded on January 5. Hadley's bookkeeper is unsure whether these goods should be included in merchandise inventory on the December 31 balance sheet. Should they? Why or why not?

Q13-9
Obj. 4
A friend notes that when a company uses an accounting method such as LIFO, FIFO, or weighted-average, it is merely estimating (guessing) about the amount of inventory on hand. Is this true?

Q13-10
Obj. 4
Some corporations use FIFO to estimate their inventory costs. Others use LIFO. What issues are important to this decision? What effect can the choice have on a company's net income and cash flow from operating activities?

Q13-11
Obj. 4
When inventory prices are rising, the LIFO method yields lower net income and lower values for ending inventory than does FIFO. The opposite is true when prices are declining. Why is this the case?

Q13-12
Obj. 4
GAAP require companies to report inventories on a lower of cost or market basis. What is the purpose of this measurement rule? What effect does it have on a company's financial statements?

Q13-13
Obj. 5
You are aware that GAAP require expenditures for research and development to be charged to expense when incurred. This implies that such expenditures do not provide any benefit to future accounting periods. Do research and development expenditures have future economic benefit? If not, why not? If so, why might GAAP require companies to account for them as if they did not?

Q13-14
Obj. 5
You are an investor in the common stock of Malapoosa Company. You notice in the firm's most recent annual report that net income was $3.75 million but that the net income available for common stockholders was only $3.0 million. Explain the difference between the two amounts.

Q13-15
Obj. 5
An acquaintance with an interest in investing says, "Earnings per share is so complicated! I really only want one number—how much the company earned on my investment. But this company has earnings per share on income from continuing operations, on a discontinued segment, and on an extraordinary item, and then, finally, on net income. Which number is most important to me, as an investor?" Answer your acquaintance.

EXERCISES

If your instructor is using Personal Trainer in this course, you may complete online the assignments identified by ᵖ𝓣 .

E13-1
Write a short definition of each of the terms listed in the *Terms and Concepts Defined in this Chapter* section.

E13-2
Obj. 1
ᵖ𝓣
At December 31, 2004, the general ledger of Hoffman Electric had the following account balances. All adjusting entries (except for income taxes at 35%) have been made. The company had 10,400 shares of common stock outstanding during the year.

Accounts payable	$ 8,950	Equipment	$ 80,300
Accounts receivable	14,970	Gain on sale of land	4,800
Accrued liabilities	21,000	Interest expense	1,420
Accumulated depreciation	15,300	Merchandise	18,465
Advertising expense	9,968	Land	30,000
Cash	9,530	Retained earnings*	57,984
Common stock	36,000	Sales revenue	260,772
Cost of goods sold	102,690	Utilities expense	9,002
Depreciation expense	13,510	Wages expense	59,780

*Balance at January 1, 2004

Prepare an income statement in good form. (Hint: See Exhibit 1.)

E13-3
Obj. 1
An excerpt from the income statement from the 2001 annual report of **Alcoa, Inc.** is provided below.

For the year ended December 31,	2001
(In millions except share amounts)	
Revenues	
Sales	$22,859
Other income, net	308
	23,167

Costs and expenses

Cost of goods sold	17,857
Selling, general, administrative, and other expenses	1,276
Research and development expenses	203
Provision for depreciation, depletion, and amortization	1,253
Interest expenses	371
Other expenses	566
	21,526

Earnings

Income before taxes on income	1,641
Provision for taxes on income	525
Income from operations	$ 1,116
Minority interests' share	(208)
Net income	$ 908
Earnings per common share	$ 1.06

Briefly explain each item presented on the income statement. (Minority interest may be ignored if you are not studying the Other Topics section at the end of the chapter.) How much gross profit and operating income did Alcoa report for 2001?

E13-4
Obj. 2

San Miguel Company manufactures specialized industrial equipment. The equipment often is sold under credit terms that provide for payment over a two- or three-year period. A substantial prepayment is required before equipment is manufactured. The purchaser accepts title to the equipment at the time it is received. San Miguel also sells service contracts on the equipment it sells. These multiyear contracts stipulate that San Miguel will provide periodic maintenance on the equipment and will repair the equipment if it breaks down. Explain (a) when San Miguel should recognize revenue from its equipment sales and (b) when it should recognize service contract revenue. In each case, explain why this revenue timing is proper.

E13-5
Obj. 2
P/T

Goodman Company sold merchandise during its 2004 fiscal year. The total sales price of the merchandise was $30 million. Because of quantity sales discounts, the company billed its customers $29.1 million for the merchandise. Goodman sells goods to retailers who have a right to return the merchandise within 90 days if it does not sell. Goodman expects a return rate of 6% of the amount sold. How much revenue should Goodman recognize for 2004? Justify your answer.

E13-6
Obj. 2
P/T

At year-end 2004, Fenton Company reported gross accounts receivable of $3,650,000 and an allowance for doubtful accounts of $450,000. During its fiscal 2005 year, it recorded sales of $18,600,000 on credit, and collected $18,750,000 from customers. It wrote off $165,000 of bad debts and estimated that it required an allowance for doubtful accounts at the end of 2005 equal to 3% of its 2005 sales. (a) Use the format presented in this chapter to identify how each of the year 2005 events would be entered into the accounting system. (b) What was the net amount of accounts receivable reported by Fenton on its 2005 balance sheet?

E13-7
Obj. 2

For each of the following transactions of Yeats Machinery, indicate in which month or months the related revenue or expense should appear in the monthly income statement, and why.

a. In January, the firm receives an order for a $200,000 machine, along with a 30% cash deposit. The machine is manufactured in March and April, and is delivered to the customer on April 16. The remainder of the price is collected in May.

b. Components to be used in manufacturing the above machine are received in February and paid for in March.

c. Workers are paid for the work on the machine in April and May. Quarterly payments for their health insurance are made in June. Workers also will receive pension benefits at some point because of the work they did during this period. (Hint: Health insurance and pension benefits are part of the cost of labor.)

d. The company estimates there is a 5% chance that it will have to replace parts of the machine during the two-year warranty period.

E13-8
Obj. 2
P/T

Geyser Company began operations in 2004. It had credit sales of $4 million and cash sales of $1 million. The chief accountant decided to estimate doubtful accounts expense at 5% of total credit sales. During the year, $3.5 million of the credit sales were collected from customers and by the end of the year, $150,000 had been written off as uncollectible.

At the end of the second year of operations, credit sales were $6 million and cash sales were $1.5 million. The accountant decided that it would be more accurate to base doubtful accounts expense on ending Accounts Receivable. Accordingly, it was estimated that the ending balance of Allowance for Doubtful Accounts should have a balance equal to 8% of Accounts Receivable. During the year, $5.4 million was collected from customers and $180,000 was written off as uncollectible.

For each of the two years, determine the following amounts:

a. The ending balance of Accounts Receivable
b. The estimated Doubtful Accounts Expense
c. The ending balance in the Allowance for Doubtful Accounts

E13-9
Obj. 2
P/T

During 2004, Abdulla Construction Company started a two-year construction project having a total contract price of $1,800,000. At December 31, 2004, the firm's construction engineers estimated that the project was 35% completed. To date, 35% of the budgeted $1,250,000 in costs had been incurred.

What amounts of (a) revenue, (b) expense, and (c) gross profit should be reported by this company at the end of 2004?

E13-10
Obj. 2
P/T

Sandoval, Inc. signed a $40 million contract to build a new office building. The company expected that the project would take about two and one-half years. During the first year, the company incurred the following costs:

Raw materials	$4 million
Direct labor	6 million
Overhead (insurance, equipment rental, etc.)	2 million

At the end of the first year, management is very pleased with its construction to date. The costs incurred are consistent with the estimate that the project is 40% completed.

Determine the amount of (a) revenue and (b) expense that the builder should report on its income statement at the end of the first year.

E13-11
Objs. 2, 3
P/T

Boris, Inc. purchased an inventory item for $400 on February 27, 2004, and paid the bill on March 12. On April 4, Boris sold the item for $625; the customer paid in full on May 15. Use the format presented in the chapter to identify how each of these events would affect Boris's account balances. What is the net effect of these transactions on Boris's 2004 income statement? What is the net effect on total assets?

E13-12
Objs. 2, 3
P/T

The Nifty Threads Company, a popular clothing store, had the following transactions for 2004.

1. Nifty Threads purchased $600,000 of clothing from several manufacturers, on credit.
2. The company sold clothing on credit at prices totaling $855,000.
3. The cost of clothing sold to customers was $491,000.
4. The company received a discount of $35,000 on its purchases.
5. The company received $788,000 in cash from customers.
6. The company paid $565,000 to the clothing manufacturers.
7. The company granted $22,000 of sales discounts to customers for payment within the discount period.
8. The company estimated that $16,000 of the year's credit sales would be uncollectible.
9. The company wrote off $12,000 as uncollectible.

a. Using the format shown in this chapter, record each of the transactions.
b. Determine the amount of net income and net operating cash flow associated with these transactions.

E13-13
Objs. 2, 3
P/T

Yeltsin Company purchased a truckload of 1,000 small motors for an invoice price of $50 each on January 28. Since the company paid the bill within 10 days, on February 6, it received a 2% discount. It then sold the parts to Hi-Lo Manufacturing for $65 each on March 27; since Hi-Lo paid within 10 days, on April 5, it was granted a 1% discount. Calculate the full effect of these transactions on Yeltsin's monthly income statements for January, February, March, and April.

E13-14
Objs. 1, 3
P/T

Think carefully about each of the following statements. For each one, indicate whether you believe it to be always true, generally true, generally false, or always false. For any item you judge to fall into the last three categories, describe your reasoning.

a. Sales discounts are reported on the income statement as an operating expense.
b. When a company writes off an uncollectible account against Allowance for Doubtful Accounts, the net amount of Accounts Receivables reported on the balance sheet does not change.
c. Jabba Company purchased inventory for its retail store. Jabba should include in the cost of this inventory the amount charged by the freight company to deliver the goods to Jabba's store.
d. Most retail stores will report three categories of inventory: raw materials, work-in-process, and finished goods.
e. When merchandise is sold to customers, the entries to Sales Revenue and Accounts Receivable will be for different amounts than the entries to Merchandise and Cost of Goods Sold.
f. A purchase of merchandise for later resale to customers has no effect on the income statement.
g. Purchase discounts received from vendors should be deducted when determining and reporting the cost of merchandise.
h. **Ford Motor Company** just received 1,000 steering wheels for a particular line of cars it manufactures. The cost of these items should be recorded initially in Work-in-Process Inventory.
i. The cost of wages earned by factory employees should be reported on the income statement as Wages Expense during the accounting period in which employees earned them.
j. Diggin Deep Company, a gold mining firm, sold gold bars to Lookin' Good, Inc. The second firm is a manufacturer of jewelry. Diggin Deep sold finished goods but Lookin' Good bought raw materials.

E13-15
Obj. 4
P/T

Dickinson Company is a wholesaler of garden supplies. At the beginning of the year, the company owned 100 bags of Power-Gro lawn fertilizer at a cost of $8 per bag. Before the spring gardening season, it purchased its entire supply of Power-Gro for the year, 500 bags at $8.30 each and 400 bags at $8.50 each. During the year, it sold 880 bags for $12 each. (a) Calculate ending inventory, cost of goods sold, and gross profit under three cost estimating procedures: periodic FIFO, periodic LIFO, and weighted-average. (b) Which results in the highest gross profit? The lowest? Why?

E13-16
Obj. 4
P/T

InterMetals, Inc. reported ending inventories of $1,687 million at year-end 2004 and $1,911 million at year-end 2005. It used periodic LIFO for most of its inventories. If it had used periodic FIFO, it would have reported inventories of $1,948 for 2004 and $2,405 for 2005. Assuming an income tax rate of 35%, what effect did the use of periodic LIFO instead of periodic FIFO have on the company's reported net income and income taxes?

E13-17
Obj. 4
P/T

Domestic Company sells kitchen appliances. During the year just ended, the company sold 210,000 units and recorded cost of goods sold totaling $42 million. If periodic LIFO had been used, the company would have reported $44 million of cost of goods sold. Inventory to replace the units sold was purchased during the year for $45 million. The year-end Accounts Receivable balance did not differ from the prior year-end. The company's income tax rate was 30%. Sales revenue for the year was $60 million and other expenses (all paid in cash) were $12 million.

a. What would net income have been if Domestic had used periodic LIFO instead of periodic FIFO?
b. What would the company's cash flow from operating activities have been if it had used periodic LIFO instead of periodic FIFO?
c. Does the inventory method that results in increased net income also produce increased operating cash flow? Explain why or why not.

E13-18
Objs. 2, 4

Ten transactions are shown on the next page as they were entered into the accounting system. For each, explain the event that caused the entry to be made.

(Continued)

		ASSETS		=	LIABILITIES	+	OWNERS' EQUITY	
Event	Accounts	Cash	Other Assets				Contributed Capital	Retained Earnings
a.	Accounts Receivable		50,000					
	Sales Revenue							50,000
b.	Inventory		−8,000					
	Cost of Goods Sold							−8,000
c.	Cash	2,000						
	Accounts Receivable		−2,000					
d.	Inventory		35,000					
	Accounts Payable				35,000			
e.	Inventory		−5,000					
	Accounts Payable				−5,000			
f.	Doubtful Accounts							
	Expense							−800
	Allowance for							
	Doubtful Accounts		−800					
g.	Accounts Receivable		−400					
	Allowance for							
	Doubtful Accounts		400					
h.	Cash	980						
	Accounts Receivable		−1,000					
	Sales Discounts							−20
i.	Allowance for Returns		−300					
	Sales Returns							−300
j.	Warranty Expense							−250
	Warranty Obligations				250			
Totals		2,980	67,900		30,250			−40,630

E13-19
Obj. 4
P/T

The following information regarding inventory transactions is available for the month of May.

Date	Type of Event	Number of Units	Unit Cost	Total Cost
May 1	Beginning inventory	100	$12	$1,200
3	Purchase	50	14	700
12	Sale	70		
15	Sale	60		
20	Purchase	100	15	1,500
28	Sale	60		

Determine the correct balances at May 31 for Merchandise Inventory and Cost of Goods Sold under each of the following inventory methods: (a) periodic FIFO, (b) periodic LIFO, and (c) weighted-average.

E13-20
Obj. 4
P/T

Small Part Company had the following information regarding inventory transactions available at the end of October. Year-to-date Cost of Goods Sold at October 1 was $236,700.

Date	Type of Event	Number of Units	Unit Cost	Total Cost
October 1	Beginning inventory	9,000	$10	$ 90,000
4	Purchase	3,000	12	36,000
11	Sale	8,000		
15	Sale	2,000		
22	Purchase	10,000	14	140,000
29	Sale	5,000		

Determine the correct year-to-date balances at October 31 for Merchandise Inventory and Cost of Goods Sold under each of the following inventory methods: (a) periodic FIFO, (b) periodic LIFO, and (c) weighted-average.

E13-21
Obj. 4
P / T

Randolph Company is a retailer that sells appliances to institutions such as schools, universities, and state governments. During the month of January, Randolph Company recorded the following information:

	Units	Unit Cost	Total Cost
January 1 inventory	550	$300	$165,000
Purchases January 5	100	305	30,500
Sales January 7	300		
Purchases January 10	600	310	186,000
Sales January 31	500		

Assuming Randolph Company uses a perpetual FIFO inventory system, determine the cost of goods sold and value of the ending inventory.

E13-22
P / T *Obj. 4*

Using the data provided in E13-21, calculate the cost of goods sold and value of the ending inventory if Randolph Company uses a perpetual LIFO inventory system.

E13-23
Obj. 5

A partial income statement is shown below for Mavis Company.

(In thousands)	2004
Income before extraordinary items and taxes	$4,523
Provision for income taxes	1,036
Income before extraordinary items	$3,487
Extraordinary loss from condemnation of land for a freeway (net of tax benefits of $322)	644
Net income	$2,843

Earnings per share	Basic	Diluted
Income before extraordinary items	$1.16	$1.00
Extraordinary items	0.21	0.19
Net income	$0.95	$0.81

(a) Why are earnings per share presented for both before and after the extraordinary items?
(b) On how many shares was Mavis computing basic earnings per share? Diluted earnings per share? (c) What kinds of items might account for the additional shares used for the calculation of diluted earnings per share?

E13-24
Obj. 5
P / T

The Hot Aire Company reported the following items on its income statement for 2004.

a. Net operating revenues, $956,000
b. Cost of goods sold, $312,000
c. Selling and administrative expense, $245,000
d. Research and development expenses, $122,000
e. Net interest expense, $8,500
f. Provision for income taxes, $85,920
g. Current year loss from discontinued operations of $24,000, net of tax benefit of $7,680
h. Loss from sale of discontinued operations of $89,000, net of tax benefit of $24,480
i. Cumulative effect (gain) of change in accounting principle of $11,050, net of tax benefit of $3,536
j. Preferred stock dividends, $48,000

The company had 25,000 shares of common stock outstanding throughout the fiscal year.

Compute each of the following:

A. Operating income
B. Income (loss) from continuing operations, before taxes
C. Income (loss) before discontinued operations and the cumulative effect of the accounting change
D. Net income (loss)
E. Net income (loss) available for common shareholders
F. Earnings per share from continuing operations
G. Earnings per share from discontinued operations
H. Earnings per share from the cumulative effect of the accounting change
I. Earnings per share from net income (loss)

E13-25   The Oregon Ironworks Company had the following income statement items for the year 2004.

Obj. 5

Income from continuing operations, before taxes	$228,000
Current year loss from discontinued operations	(10,750)
Gain from sale of discontinued operations	2,750
Extraordinary loss from hurricane	(22,500)
Cumulative effect from change of depreciation method	6,000
Tax rate, applicable to all income statement items	30%
Number of shares of common stock outstanding during 2004	79,800

a. Beginning with "Income from continuing operations, before taxes," prepare the remaining sections of the income statement.
b. Calculate earnings per common share for all sections of the income statement. The company has no preferred stock outstanding. (Note: The information about special items should be listed in the following order: discontinued operations, extraordinary items, changes in accounting method.)

E13-26   Explain whether each of the following would be expensed on the income statement in 2004 or in some later year, and why.

Objs. 2, 3, 5

a. Inventory purchased in 2004 but sold in 2005.
b. Estimated warranty costs for goods sold in 2004; the warranty servicing will take place in 2005 and 2006.
c. Bad debts caused by 2004 sales; the actual bad receivables will not be identified until a later year.
d. Research and development costs incurred in 2004 but aimed at producing a better product in later years.

PROBLEMS

If your instructor is using Personal Trainer in this course, you may complete online the assignments identified by ᴾT.

P13-1   **Income Statement Preparation**

Obj. 1

On January 1, 2004, Pete Rabbit began Leafy Green Corporation, a salad bar supply business, by investing $5,000 cash and a delivery van worth $7,200 in exchange for 1,000 shares of $2 par common stock. Pete expects the van to have a remaining life of three years with no salvage value; he plans to use straight-line depreciation. Two friends invested $2,000 each, receiving 150 shares of stock each.

The next day, Leafy Green borrowed $8,400 at 8% annual interest for operating funds. The loan is to be repaid or refinanced in three months.

Salad ingredients for the month of January cost $8,000; Leafy Green has paid for 75% of this. The company has delivered prepared salad bar materials to three customers, each of whom has been billed $5,000; two of the three have paid. No ingredients were on hand at the end of the month.

Other operating expenses, paid in cash, were $4,500.

Required Prepare an income statement for Leafy Green Corporation, for the month of January 2004. Include earnings per share.

P13-2   **Revenue Recognition**

Obj. 2

Several situations in which the timing of revenue is in doubt are listed below.

a. An appliance manufacturer sent out a truckload of dishwashers FOB destination in late January; they arrived February 2 and were paid for in March. Monthly income statements are prepared.
b. A magazine publisher sold two-year subscriptions for a monthly publication.
c. An auto dealer sold five-year service contracts for cash at the time of the auto sale.
d. A home decorating center sold wallpaper with a 60-day right to return of up to 25% of an order. For the past several years, returns have been fairly consistent, with one in 10 customers returning some paper; the average return is 1.2 rolls.

e. A bridge construction firm is involved in only one project at a time; the average project takes three years. The contract price is firm and definitely collectible; total costs of the project can be estimated.

Required First, explain what events generally must occur before any revenue is recognized. Then discuss when each of the above situations should result in revenue recognition, and why.

P13-3 **Revenue Recognition**

Obj. 2

The following excerpt is from **Unisys Corporation's** 2001 annual report.

> **Revenue Recognition.** Revenue from hardware sales is recognized upon shipment and the passage of title....Revenue from software licenses is recognized at the inception of the initial license term and upon execution of an extension to the license term....Revenue from equipment and software maintenance is recognized on a straight-line basis as earned over the lives of the respective contracts....For contracts accounted for on the percentage-of-completion basis, revenue and profit recognized in any given accounting period is based on estimates of total projected contract costs, the estimates are continually reevaluated and revised, when necessary, throughout the life of a contract.

Required What is meant by revenue recognition? Why does Unisys use different revenue recognition principles for different types of revenue? What are the critical events for each of these types of revenue? Why is estimation involved in revenue recognition for the multiyear, fixed-price contracts?

P13-4 **Computing Accounts Receivable**

Obj. 2

P/T

Georgia Company reported accounts receivable of $16.5 million at the end of its 2004 fiscal year. This amount was net of an allowance for doubtful accounts of $1,800,000. During 2005, Georgia sold $56.5 million of merchandise on credit. It collected $57.9 million from customers. Accounts valued at $1,980,000 were written off as uncollectible during 2005. Georgia's management estimates that 10% of the year-end Accounts Receivable balance will be uncollectible.

Required Answer each of the following questions:

A. What amount will Georgia report for accounts receivable and the allowance for doubtful accounts at the end of 2005?
B. What is the Doubtful Accounts Expense for 2005?
C. How will the accounts receivable and allowance accounts be presented on the balance sheet? Show the balance sheet.
D. Why do companies record expenses for doubtful accounts based on estimates from receivables or sales during the prior year rather than recording the expenses when accounts are written off in a future period?
E. If estimated uncollectibles as a percentage of sales or receivables were to increase over several years, what information might this provide to decision makers?

P13-5 **Inventory Transactions of Manufacturing Companies**

Obj. 3

P/T

O'Neill Company began the year with $870,000 of raw materials inventory, $1,390,000 of work-in-process inventory, and $620,000 of finished goods inventory. During the year, the company purchased $3,550,000 of raw material and used $3,720,000 of raw materials in production. Labor used in production for the year was $2,490,000. Overhead was $1,380,000. Cost of goods sold for the year was $7,500,000. The ending balance of Finished Goods Inventory was $530,000.

Required Use Exhibit 5 in the chapter as a format for developing a schedule to show the effect of these events on O'Neill's inventory accounts for the year.

P13-6 **Classification of Manufacturing Costs**

Obj. 3

P/T

The following information is taken from the records of the Carolby Company, a manufacturer of lawn furniture. Indicate whether the cost of each item should be included as part of the finished goods cost or should be treated as an expense. For the items that become part of the cost of finished goods, indicate whether each should be designated as materials, labor, or factory overhead.

a. Salaries of sales office staff
b. Electric utilities for the factory area
c. Office supplies
d. Paint and miscellaneous plastic parts
e. Depreciation on factory equipment
f. Depreciation on delivery vans
g. Salaries of factory foremen
h. Miscellaneous factory supplies
i. Steel rods used for chair frames
j. Plastic sheets used for table tops
k. Salaries of furniture assemblers
l. Insurance on the factory
m. Insurance on the administrative offices
n. Advertising in trade magazines
o. Lawn furniture sold to retailers
p. Rental of storage facilities for materials
q. Rental of storage facilities for finished goods

Required Briefly explain your reasoning for classifying the various items as part of the cost of goods manufactured or as an expense.

P13-7 Inventories

Objs. 3, 4

Modern Industries manufactures a variety of computer parts and accessories in a rapidly changing technological environment. At year-end 2004, it reported the following comparative information regarding inventories.

(In millions)	2004	2003
Raw materials and parts	$14	$16
Work in process	28	31
Finished goods	25	28
Total inventories	$67	$75

The 2004 income statement reflected cost of sales of $3,165 million. In the operating activities section of the statement of cash flows, the $8 million decrease in inventories was added to net income. Notes to the financial statements included the following:

- Inventories are reported at the lower of cost (first-in, first-out) or market. If the cost of the inventories exceeds their market (replacement) value, a writedown to market value is taken currently.
- The company participates in a highly competitive industry that is characterized by rapid changes in technology, frequent introductions of new products, short product life cycles, and downward pressures on prices and margins.

Required Answer the following questions related to Modern Industries' inventories.

A. Describe the nature of each of the three inventories listed on the balance sheet. When does each become an expense?
B. Why is the inventory decrease added to net income on the statement of cash flows?
C. Many U.S. corporations use the LIFO inventory method to save income taxes. Why might a computer industry manufacturer like this firm decide to use FIFO instead? Explain.

P13-8 Inventory Transactions and Periodic Inventory Costing Methods

Objs. 3, 4

P_T

Culture Music Store had the following selected account balances on October 1.

Merchandise inventory (1,000 units)	$ 7,000
Accounts receivable	15,000
Allowance for doubtful accounts	(1,200)
Warranty obligations	500

Goods are sold with a 60-day money-back guarantee against defects. During October, the following transactions occurred.

1. The store purchased 4,000 units of inventory on credit at a total invoice cost of $32,000. The goods, which were received in October, were purchased FOB destination and the seller paid freight costs of $250.
2. During the first week of the month, 700 units were sold on credit at prices averaging $12 each.
3. A clerk noticed that 50 recordings purchased in part 1 were mislabeled. These units were returned to the vendor for full credit.
4. During the second week, a cash-only sale was held and 1,200 units sold at an average price of $10 each.
5. Customers returned a total of 53 units that had been sold in part 2. The goods were in salable condition and returned to the shelf.
6. The vendor was paid in full for the goods purchased in part 1.
7. Checks were received from customers who purchased goods in part 2. All took the 2% discount that was offered for paying within 10 days.
8. A total of 1,600 units were sold during the rest of the month at prices averaging $13. Three-quarters of the sales were on credit.
9. At month-end, management estimated that 10% of the goods sold in parts 4 and 8 would be returned as defective.
10. Also at month-end, management estimated that $344 of this period's credit sales would be uncollectible.

Required

A. Show how each of the transactions would be entered into the accounting system assuming the firm uses the periodic FIFO inventory method.
B. Prepare an income statement for the month of October assuming that operating expenses (other than warranty expense and doubtful accounts expense) totaled $2,500 and the company's tax rate is 35%.
C. By what amount would net income have been different if the periodic LIFO method had been used? Prepare a schedule that proves your solution.
D. By what amount would net cash flow from operating activities have been different if the periodic LIFO method has been used? Explain your solution.

P13-9
Objs. 3, 4
P/T

Accounting Errors Regarding Operating Activities

At year-end, the accounting department at Bell-Jones Industries had prepared the following balance sheet and income statement.

Balance sheet		Income statement	
Cash	$ 58,000	Net sales	$ 1,855,000
Accounts receivable	215,000	Service contracts	792,000
Less: Allowance for returns	9,000	Cost of goods sold	(1,298,500)
Allowance for doubtful accounts	(3,000)	Operating expenses:	
Merchandise	136,000	Wages	(537,300)
Buildings and equipment	413,000	Rent	(60,000)
Less: Accumulated depreciation	(107,800)	Advertising	(282,000)
Land	79,000	Doubtful accounts	0
Total assets	$ 799,200	Depreciation	(26,800)
		Warranties	(55,000)
Accounts payable	$ 108,200	Operating income	$ 387,400
Wages payable	25,000	Interest revenue	1,350
Warranty obligations	61,000	Income before taxes	388,750
Common stock	300,000	Provision for taxes	136,063
Retained earnings	305,000	Net income	$ 252,687
Total liabilities and stockholders' equity	$ 799,200		

Just prior to the arrival of the outside auditors, one of the accounting staff brought a list of items to the chief financial officer. The staff member was concerned that these items had not been properly accounted for in the financial statements.

1. A source document showing a customer's return of goods had been missing until just now and had not been processed through the accounting system. The goods had been sold on account to the customer for $9,000 during the current year and were returned to the warehouse for sale to others. The company's normal gross profit on sales is 30%.
2. Just before year-end, inventory had been purchased on credit at a cost of $60,000, FOB destination. By year-end, it had not yet arrived but it had been included in the ending inventory anyway.
3. At the end of the prior year, there was $80,000 of inventory in transit from a supplier. The goods had been purchased FOB shipping point but had not yet arrived. The goods had been included in last year's ending inventory anyway.
4. An error had been made in computing the warranty costs for goods sold during the current year. A total of $55,000 had been charged to Warranty Expense, but the correct amount was $75,000.
5. Near year-end, a $100,000 service contract was obtained from a major customer. It was a renewal of an existing contract that would otherwise have expired during the coming year. Because this type of work had been performed many times before for this customer, the contract was entered into the accounting system as a credit sale during the year just ended. Collection of the cash will occur as the services are performed.
6. The adjusting entry to allowance for returns had not yet been recorded at year-end. Using the firm's usual approach, an additional $10,300 should be recorded.
7. No adjusting entry had been made at year-end to account for doubtful accounts. Using the firm's usual approach, $5,960 should be charged to expense.

Required

A. Show any entries to the accounting system that you believe should be made as a result of this information. If an item does not require an entry, explain why.
B. What is the proper amount of operating income that should be reported for the period? Prepare a schedule to show how you determined this amount.

P13-10
Objs. 3, 4
Ⓟ
Ⓣ

Identifying Perpetual Inventory Costing Methods

At the end of the first quarter, yesterday, a staff accountant prepared the information below. It is a schedule of merchandise inventory and cost of goods sold under each of the three most common costing methods: perpetual LIFO, perpetual FIFO, and perpetual weighted-average. Unfortunately, she forgot to label which one was which and today is her day off.

Schedule of merchandise inventory and cost of goods sold

Summary of inventory transactions:
  Beginning inventory: March 1 = 9,000 units at $10 each
  Purchases: March 3 = 3,000 units at $12 each
        March 24 = 10,000 units at $14 each
Sales: March 11 = 7,000 units at $15
    March 15 = 2,000 units at $15
    March 30 = 4,000 units at $17

Costing results using method A:	Merchandise Inventory	Cost of Goods Sold
March 1 beginning balances	$ 90,000	$236,700
March 3 purchase	36,000	—
March 11 sale	−73,500	73,500
March 15 sale	−21,000	21,000
March 24 purchase	140,000	—
March 30 sale	−52,760	52,760
March 31 ending balances	$118,740	$383,960

(Continued)

Costing results using method B:	Merchandise Inventory	Cost of Goods Sold
March 1 beginning balances	$ 90,000	$236,700
March 3 purchase	36,000	—
March 11 sale	−70,000	70,000
March 15 sale	−20,000	20,000
March 24 purchase	140,000	—
March 30 sale	−50,000	50,000
March 31 ending balances	$126,000	$376,700

Costing results using method C:	Merchandise Inventory	Cost of Goods Sold
March 1 beginning balances	$ 90,000	$236,700
March 3 purchase	36,000	—
March 11 sale	−76,000	76,000
March 15 sale	−20,000	20,000
March 24 purchase	140,000	—
March 30 sale	−56,000	56,000
March 31 ending balances	$114,000	$388,700

Required

A. Match each set of cost results above with the inventory costing method used to generate it. (Hint: In which direction are prices moving?)

B. Prove your results by showing how the amount for the first sale was computed under each method.

P13-11 Periodic Inventory Estimation and Income Control

Obj. 4

P/T

Rousseau Company uses the periodic LIFO inventory estimation method. At the beginning of the current fiscal year, the company's inventory consisted of the following:

Units	Unit Cost	Total Cost
8,000	$22	$176,000
4,000	23	92,000
2,000	32	64,000
2,000	34	68,000
16,000		$400,000

These units were produced over several years, during which inventory costs had increased rapidly. During the current year, Rousseau produced 20,000 additional units of inventory at an average cost of $36 per unit. The average sales price of units sold during the year was $55.

Required Answer the following questions.

A. What would be Rousseau's gross profit and average gross profit per unit if it sold 20,000, 24,000, 28,000, or 36,000 units during the year?

B. Assume that Rousseau sold 36,000 units during the year. How many units would it need to produce to minimize the tax effect of its gross profit? How many units would it need to produce to maximize its gross profit?

C. If you were a manager of Rousseau and you wanted to control the amount of gross profit reported by the company, what could you do? If you wanted to develop an accounting standard that could prevent this type of management manipulation of income, what kind of standard might you propose?

P13-12 Accounting Choice Decisions

Obj. 4

P/T

Shim Company reported sales revenue of $10 million for the year. The company uses FIFO for inventory estimation purposes. Cost of goods sold was $3.8 million. If the company had used LIFO, its cost of goods sold would have been $4.5 million. The company reported depreciation expense of $1.2 million on a straight-line basis. If the company had used accelerated depreciation, it would have reported depreciation expense of $1.7 million. Other expenses, excluding income tax, were $3 million. The company's income tax rate was 30%.

Required

A. Compute Shim's net income as reported and as it would have been reported if LIFO and accelerated depreciation had been used.
B. What effect would the choice of accounting methods have on the company's cash flows from operating activities during the year if the same methods were used for both financial reporting and tax purposes?

P13-13 **Perpetual and Periodic Inventory Systems**

Obj. 4

$\frac{P}{T}$

Records of the Genesis Corporation reveal the following information about inventory during the year.

January 1	Beginning inventory	1,000 units	@ $10
March 15	Purchase of inventory	3,500 units	@ $12
July 21	Sale of inventory	4,000 units	
September 12	Purchase of inventory	1,600 units	@ $14
October 31	Sale of inventory	1,200 units	

The company's accountant is trying to decide whether to determine Cost of Goods Sold using the perpetual inventory system (calculating Cost of Goods Sold after every sale) or the periodic inventory system (calculating Cost of Goods Sold at the end of the year only). Assume the company uses the LIFO method for inventory costing.

Required Using the information given above, answer each of the following questions.

A. How many units have been sold? How many units remain in ending inventory?
B. What is Cost of Goods Sold using the perpetual method? The periodic method? What is the cost of ending inventory for each method?
C. Is there a difference in net income for each method? Why? (Assume for purposes of this question that Sales Revenue is $85,000 and all other expenses are $5,600.)
D. What are the advantages of using perpetual? Using periodic?

P13-14 **Preparing an Income Statement**

Objs. 1, 5

$\frac{P}{T}$

Shriver Company's accounting system listed the following information for the company's 2004 fiscal year (in millions):

Average common shares outstanding	2.4
Cost of goods sold	$170.3
Extraordinary gain	18.2
Gain on sale of securities	8.6
General and administrative expenses	75.5
Income taxes (35% of pretax income)	
Interest expense	12.0
Interest income	5.9
Loss associated with cumulative effect of accounting change	4.0
Loss from discontinued operations	13.1
Sales of merchandise	320.8
Selling expenses	30.2

Required Prepare an income statement for Shriver Company for the year ended December 31, 2004. Assume that the tax rate of 35% applies to special items as well as ordinary income. (Hint: Discontinued operations are listed before extraordinary items, which are listed before accounting changes.)

P13-15

Objs. 1, 5

Interpreting an Income Statement

Worldwide Corporation reported the following income statement for 2005.

(In millions)	2005	2004	2003
Product sales	$ 3,355	$ 3,298	$ 3,236
Service sales	2,941	2,591	2,543
Sales of products and services	6,296	5,889	5,779
Cost of products sold	(2,549)	(2,523)	(2,508)
Cost of services sold	(1,931)	(1,754)	(1,743)
Costs of products and services sold	(4,480)	(4,277)	(4,251)
Provision for restructuring	(86)	(23)	(249)
Marketing, administration, and general expenses	(1,686)	(1,184)	(1,313)
Other income and expenses, net	149	(288)	(154)
Interest expense	(233)	(134)	(165)
Loss from continuing operations before income taxes and minority interest in income of consolidated subsidiaries	(40)	(17)	(353)
Income taxes	7	13	116
Minority interest in income of consolidated subsidiaries	(11)	(9)	(9)
Loss from continuing operations	(44)	(13)	(246)
Discontinued operations, net of income taxes:			
Income from operations	135	90	71
Estimated loss on disposal of discontinued operations	(76)		(95)
Income (loss) from discontinued operations	59	90	(24)
Income (loss) before cumulative effect of change in accounting principle	15	77	(270)
Cumulative effect of change in accounting principle Postemployment benefits			(56)
Net income (loss)	$ 15	$ 77	$ (326)

Required Answer each of the following questions.

A. For 2005, calculate the gross profit on product sales and on service sales. Why are these shown separately?

B. What is a "provision for restructuring"? What is a "discontinued segment"? Why is it that the restructuring provision is part of operating income, but the discontinued segment is not?

C. Some businesses show interest expense in a separate section with a title like "Other Revenues and Expenses," below Income from Operations. Would Worldwide's operating income have been positive in the years presented if it did not include interest expense?

D. Why is "income taxes" a positive number, not an expense?

E. What is a "cumulative effect of change in accounting principle"?

F. Which would be of more use in attempting to predict the financial future of the company: income from continuing operations or the final net income numbers, including the discontinued operations and the effect of the change in accounting principle?

G. Why are the effects of the discontinued segment and the change in accounting principle presented net of any tax effect?

P13-16

Objs. 1, 5

P T

Presentation of the Income Statement

Pelican Enterprises had the following account balances in its general ledger at June 30, 2004, the end of the company's fiscal year. All adjusting entries (except for the accrual of income taxes at 30%) had been entered. The company had an average of 900,000 shares of common stock outstanding during the year.

(Continued)

General ledger account balances (in thousands)

Accounts receivable	$ 349	Land	$1,980
Accumulated depreciation	922	Loss on sale of old machinery	255
Advertising expense	1,224	Merchandise inventory	471
Buildings and equipment	4,811	Notes payable, long-term	150
Cash	482	Preferred stock, 7%	300
Common stock	2,400	Prepaid advertising	54
Cost of goods sold	3,660	Rent expense	546
Depreciation expense	102	Rent payable	450
Extraordinary gain on		Retained earnings	513
extinguishment of debt	40	Sales revenue	6,930
Investments, long-term	250	Service revenue	3,382
Interest revenue	44	Wages expense	855
Interest expense	124	Wages payable	32

Required

A. Prepare an income statement in good form, including earnings per share information.
B. Have the closing entries been made to the accounting system? How can you tell? (Hint: You might want to review the accounting cycle in Chapter F3.)
C. What is the amount of net income available to common stockholders? Why is this important information?
D. Why do you think that GAAP require that gross profit, operating income, pretax income, and net income be separately disclosed?

P13-17   The Effect of Accounting Choices

Objs. 2, 4, 5

P/T

Ginsberg Company is a recently formed, publicly traded company. At the end of its most recent fiscal year, the company reported the following information.

a. Sales revenues were $13,680,000, and 360,000 units were sold. Credit sales were $10,000,000. Uncollectible accounts associated with credit sales are estimated to be between 3% and 4%.
b. At the beginning of the year, 140,000 units of inventory were on hand at a unit cost of $10 per unit; during the year, 250,000 units were purchased at $10.50, and, later, 150,000 units were purchased at $11.50 per unit.
c. Plant assets included equipment with a book value of $3,375,000 and buildings with a book value of $8,260,000. The equipment has an estimated remaining useful life of between four and seven years. The buildings have an estimated remaining useful life of between 25 and 35 years.
d. Intangible assets (excluding goodwill) cost $1,200,000 and have a remaining useful life of no less than 10 years.
e. The company has the option of adopting a new accounting standard for the fiscal year. If the standard is adopted, the cumulative effect of the accounting change, before the tax effect, will be a loss of $1,100,000.
f. The company's tax rate is 34%. Other operating expenses were $6,245,000. Interest expense was $460,000. There were 500,000 shares of common stock outstanding throughout the year.

Management has not yet made decisions about how to treat items a through e. A choice is necessary in each instance. The chief financial officer has asked you to determine the range of net income that might be reported depending on the choices that are made.

Required Prepare two different pro forma (projected) income statements for the year.

A. With the first income statement, show the minimum net income the company could report under GAAP.
B. With the second income statement, show the maximum net income that could be reported under GAAP.
C. What does this suggest to you about comparing the reported net income of one firm versus the others?

P13-18 **Identifying Operating Activities from Entries to the Accounting**
Objs. 2, 3, 4, 5 **System**

Goose Hollow Company had the following entries to its account system during a recent week.

Event	Accounts	Cash	Other Assets	=	LIABILITIES	+	Contributed Capital	Retained Earnings
a.	Accounts Receivable		18,000					
	Sales Revenue							18,000
	Merchandise Inventory		−14,600					
	Cost of Goods Sold							−14,600
b.	Merchandise Inventory		−33,000					
	Accounts Payable				−33,000			
c.	Cash	4,365						
	Accounts Receivable		−4,500					
	Sales Discount							−135
d.	Allowance for Doubtful Accounts		1,100					
	Accounts Receivable		−1,100					
e.	Cash	−2,500						
	Accounts Payable				−2,500			
f.	Accounts Receivable		−6,000					
	Allowance for Returns		6,000					
	Merchandise Inventory		4,200					
	Cost of Goods Sold							4,200
g.	Finished Goods Inventory		13,000					
	Work-in-Process Inventory		−13,000					
h.	Warranty Expense							−15,750
	Warranty Obligations				15,750			
i.	Allowance for Returns		−8,300					
	Sales Returns							−8,300
j.	Doubtful Accounts Expense							−3,740
	Allowance for Doubtful Accounts		−3,740					
k.	Merchandise Inventory		−800					
	Loss on Inventory							−800

Required Study each entry and write a short description of the event that occurred to cause the entry.

P13-19   Reporting Equity Income, Noncontrolling Interest, and Pension Information

(Based on the Other Topics section.) A partial income statement for Half Moon, Inc. is reported below.

Half Moon, Inc. Partial Income Statement For Year Ending December 31, 2004	
Sales revenue	$3,504,600
•	
•	
•	
Operating income	$ 587,300
Equity income in related company (Able Co.)	40,000
Income before income taxes	$ 627,300
Provision for income taxes	219,500
Income before noncontrolling interests	$ 407,800
Noncontrolling interest in net income of subsidiary (Baker Co.)	(2,466)
Net income	$ 405,334

In addition, the following disclosure was found in the notes to the financial statements.

Note 7:	Projected benefit obligation	$1,500,000
	Fair value of plan assets	1,300,000
	Pension liability	$ 200,000
	Service cost	$ 103,400
	Return on plan assets	100,100
	Net pension expense	$ 3,300

Required Explain each of the following.

A. What information is conveyed by the line labeled "Equity income in related company"? Describe the situation that must prevail for this line to appear on an income statement.

B. What information is conveyed by the line labeled "Noncontrolling interest in net income of subsidiary"? Describe the situation that must prevail for this line to appear on an income statement. Why is this amount subtracted in this case?

C. What information is conveyed by each of the first three lines of Note 7?

D. What information is conveyed by each of the second set of three lines of Note 7?

P13-20   Excel in Action

The Book Wermz purchases books for all of its stores through a central purchasing department. Books are then shipped to different stores for sale. One of the company's largest selling items is an edition of Webster's dictionary. A large volume of sales occurs in August and September each year to students returning to school. At the beginning of August 2004, the company's inventory of dictionaries included 245 units purchased on April 12, 2004 at $27.00 per unit, 360 units purchased on May 3, 2004 at $29.00 per unit, and 1,000 units purchased on July 24, 2004 at $32.00 per unit. No purchases were made in August. The Book Wermz sold 1,447 units of the dictionary during August.

Required Use a spreadsheet to prepare a schedule of Cost of Goods Sold and Ending Inventory for the dictionary for August. Show both FIFO and LIFO inventory numbers.

Enter the captions illustrated on the next page at the top of the spreadsheet.

	A	B	C	D	E	F	G
1	The Book Wermz						
2	Inventory of Webster's Dictionary						
3	August 31, 2004						
4							
5	FIFO Basis						
6				Cost of Goods Sold		Ending Inventory	
7	Date Purchased	Units Available	Cost per Unit	Units	Cost	Units	Cost

Beginning in row 8, enter data in each column for each of the purchase dates. In the Cost of Goods Sold columns, enter the number of units sold and the cost of these units (units sold × cost per unit) from each inventory layer[1] using the FIFO method. In the Ending Inventory columns, provide the same data for units remaining in inventory at the end of August. Use formulas for all calculations so that if the units available or cost per unit numbers changed, these changes would automatically be updated in columns D–G.

In row 11, sum columns B and D–G, using the Summation button.

Beginning in row 13, repeat the captions, data, and calculations using the LIFO method. You can copy the data from the FIFO section, select cell A13, and paste the data. Then make any needed changes for the LIFO calculations.

Beginning in row 21, provide a calculation of the amount of income taxes the company would save if it used the LIFO method in August. The company's income tax rate was 35%. Place captions in column A and calculations in column B. The calculations should report the amount of LIFO cost, FIFO cost, the excess of LIFO over FIFO costs, the company's income tax rate, and the tax savings.

Format the schedule using underlines, commas, and appropriate alignment so that it is easy to read and has a formal appearance.

Suppose the number of units available from the April purchase was 545 and the cost of the May purchase was $31.00 per unit. What would cost of goods sold be for August for the dictionaries? What would the ending inventory be at the end of August?

P13-21   Multiple-Choice Overview of the Chapter

P
T

1. The excess of sales revenues over cost of goods sold for a fiscal period is
   a. net income.
   b. income before taxes.
   c. operating income.
   d. gross profit.

2. Timing differences between sales revenues recognized during a fiscal period and cash collected from customers during the period affects the change in the balance of
   a. accounts receivable.
   b. unearned revenue.
   c. gross profit.
   d. allowance for doubtful accounts.

3. A transaction to estimate the amount of doubtful accounts expense for a fiscal period would affect the
   a. accounts receivable and doubtful accounts expense accounts.
   b. allowance for doubtful accounts and doubtful accounts expense accounts.
   c. allowance for doubtful accounts and accounts receivable accounts.
   d. allowance for doubtful accounts and sales revenue accounts.

4. Universal Joint Company publishes a monthly periodical, *Grease Today*. At the beginning of March, the company's unearned revenues included 1,200 one-year subscrip-

---

[1] Each purchase represents an inventory layer. For example, Book Wermz has a beginning inventory layer of 245 units at $27.00 per unit. The company acquired additional inventory layers at $29.00 and $32.00 per unit.

(Continued)

tions at $36 each. During March, the company received 200 new subscriptions. The March issue was shipped to all subscribers on March 25. The amount of subscription revenue the company should recognize in March is

a. $7,200.
b. $4,200.
c. $3,600.
d. $600.

5. Inventory prices on the balance sheet are closest to current costs for a company that estimates its inventories using

a. FIFO.
b. LIFO.
c. weighted-average.
d. a method that cannot be determined from the information given.

6. A company will report the highest net income if

a. it uses LIFO inventory, with rising prices and increasing inventory levels.
b. it uses LIFO inventory estimating, under all conditions.
c. it uses FIFO inventory, with rising prices and increasing inventory levels.
d. it uses FIFO inventory estimating, under all conditions.

7. Warranty expense should appear in the income statement in the period when

a. the product is manufactured.
b. the product is sold.
c. a defective item is repaired or replaced.
d. the warranty period ends and all expense is known.

8. Merchandise in transit at the end of the accounting period that has been shipped FOB shipping point should be included in the ending inventory of

a. the buyer.
b. the seller.
c. both the buyer and the seller.
d. the freight company.

9. Redford Company reported net income of $40 million for its most recent fiscal year. The company recorded interest expense of $10 million for the year. Also, it paid preferred dividends of $2 million and common dividends of $5 million. The average number of common shares outstanding for the year was 10 million. The company would report earnings per share of common stock for the year of

a. $4.00.
b. $3.80.
c. $3.30.
d. $2.30.

10. Given the following information, determine Cost of Goods Sold for the month using the perpetual LIFO method.

Date	Event	Units	Unit Cost
May 1	Beginning inventory	100	$5
5	Purchase of inventory	10	6
12	Sale of inventory	20	
18	Purchase of inventory	10	7
23	Purchase of inventory	10	8
28	Sale of inventory	25	

a. $225
b. $285
c. $325
d. $425

11. When a periodic inventory system is used, cost of goods sold is calculated as

a. beginning inventory + purchases − ending inventory.
b. beginning inventory + purchases + ending inventory.
c. ending inventory + purchases − beginning inventory.
d. beginning inventory + ending inventory − purchases.

12. A major disadvantage of a periodic inventory system is
    a. the added expense of applying it.
    b. the required technology for applying it.
    c. the lesser degree of control and information it provides.
    d. the requirement for an inventory count, which is never necessary with a perpetual system.

13. *(Based on the Other Topics section.)* Deferred compensation, such as pension benefits and health care for retirees, should be expensed
    a. when a plan is adopted.
    b. while employees are working.
    c. when employees retire.
    d. when paid to retirees.

CASES

C13-1
Objs. 2, 4, 5

Examining Operating Activities

Appendix B of this book contains a copy of the 2002 annual report of **General Mills, Inc.**

Required Review the annual report and answer each of the following questions.

A. What was the primary inventory estimation method used by General Mills? What is the effect on the company's cost of goods sold and operating income of using this primary method as compared to other methods? (Hint: Look at Notes 1c and 6. The "Reserve for LIFO" is an estimate of the difference between FIFO and LIFO values.)
B. What was the amount of General Mills' allowance for doubtful accounts for 2002? Did the relationship between estimated doubtful accounts and net sales change from 2000 to 2002?
C. How much income tax expense did General Mills recognize as expense for 2002? How much income tax did the company owe for 2002? What were the primary causes of the difference between income tax expense and income tax payable? How much income tax did General Mills pay in 2002? (Hint: See Note 16 as well as the statement of earnings. The total to be paid for 2002 is "Total Current.")
D. How much did General Mills report for depreciation and amortization and for interest expense in 2002? How much cash did General Mills pay for depreciation, amortization, and interest in 2002? (Hint: See the income statement and Note 13.)

C13-2
Objs. 2, 3, 4

The Effect of Accounting Choices on Reported Results

Sunlight Incorporated and Moonbeam Enterprises both began operations on the first day of 2004. Both operate in the same industry, sell the same products, and have many of the same customers. Both companies have just reported financial results at the end of 2004. By a remarkable coincidence, the sales revenue reported by both companies was exactly the same. Overall, however, Moonbeam's net income was approximately 75% greater than Sunlight's. You are a little surprised by this because it was generally thought by those in the industry that Sunbeam had been the better managed and more successful firm.

(Continued)

Income Statements for Year 2004	Sunlight Incorporated	Moonbeam Enterprises
Sales revenue	$31,000	$31,000
Cost of goods sold	20,000	18,600
Gross profit	$11,000	$12,400
Operating expenses:		
Depreciation	1,100	1,100
Insurance	550	610
Supplies	1,300	1,300
Uncollectible accounts	1,240	310
Warranties	620	0
Wages	1,500	1,570
Total operating expenses	6,310	4,890
Operating income	4,690	7,510
Interest expense	900	900
Pretax income	3,790	6,610
Income tax expense	1,298	2,314
Net income	$ 2,492	$ 4,296
Earnings per share	$ 1.25	$ 2.15

Upon reviewing the notes that accompany the financial statements, however, you observe the following.

1. At year-end, Sunlight recorded allowances in its accounting system for expected sales discounts (of $113) and expected sales returns ($1,345). Moonbeam, while having the same types of products and customers, did not believe it had enough information to record estimates after only one year in business.
2. Both companies reported sales totaling 1,200 units. Sunlight recognizes revenue when goods are shipped to customers. Moonbeam recognizes revenue when the order is received. As of year-end, the last 100 units that Moonbeam has reported as sales have not yet been shipped to customers because Moonbeam is temporarily out of stock. An employee forgot to re-order the item on time and now the manufacturer's plant is down for annual maintenance at year-end. Production is scheduled to resume on January 15. As soon as these units are received at Moonbeam's warehouse, they will be shipped to the customers who ordered them.
3. Moonbeam used the perpetual FIFO method of inventory estimation, but Sunlight used perpetual LIFO. Both companies had the same inventory costs and reported inventory transactions as follows.

Event	Units	Cost per Unit	Total Cost
Beginning inventory	0	$ 0	$ 0
Purchase	200	12	2,400
Purchase	500	15	7,500
Sales	300		
Purchase	400	17	6,800
Sales	500		
Purchase	300	19	5,700
Sales	300		
Sales*	100		

*As the wholesale cost of goods increased during the year, both firms increased selling prices, too. This last batch of sales (as reported by each firm) was sold at $30 per unit. Unlike other sales, this batch of goods was sold for cash and no returns were allowed.

4. At year-end, both companies were concerned about uncollectible accounts. Being new in the business, neither firm had much history upon which to base an estimate. Nevertheless, Sunlight estimated that approximately 4% of sales would be uncollectible. Moonbeam was more optimistic and estimated the rate at only 1%.
5. The companies differ in how they account for warranty expenses. Sunlight's management estimated the cost of future warranty claims (for goods sold during the year just

ended) and recorded an expense for that amount. Moonbeam decided that the amount would be immaterial and it would just charge these claims to expense in the later years when they were paid.

Required Which firm had the better financial results for its first year of operation? Why? Prepare any tables or schedules that you think would support your conclusion or be helpful to illustrate the basis for your conclusion.

ANALYSIS OF OPERATING ACTIVITIES

How do operations create value for our business?

A goal of operating activities is to create value for customers who purchase a company's products. By creating value for customers, a company also can create value for its owners. To do this, a company must produce and sell its products efficiently and effectively. The opportunities, challenges, and uncertainties that arise from operating activities require managers to make operating decisions. Accounting information describes the results of operating activities. It can be used to identify and evaluate management decisions. Also, it can help decision makers form expectations about a company's economic future and make decisions that will affect that future.

Company managers like Stan, Maria, and Ellen make strategic decisions that determine how a company will compete in its product markets. The managers, investors, creditors, and other stakeholders must then evaluate how successful the strategy has been.

FOOD FOR THOUGHT

As an advisor to the managers of Mom's Cookie Company, what issues do you think they should consider when deciding on the strategy the company will use to compete? How can managers and other decision makers evaluate how well the strategy is working?

Maria, Stan, and Ellen are meeting to decide on an operating strategy for Mom's Cookie Company.

Maria: *Our company operates in a very competitive industry. We need to determine how we are going to price our products and what competitive strategy we will use to create sales and profits.*

Stan: *We have to sell our products at a relatively high price to make a profit. I realize that our sales volume will decrease if our prices are too high, but I was hoping we could depend on the high quality of our products to create sales.*

Ellen: *I think we should focus on the quality of our products. Our cookies appeal to customers who are willing to pay for the added flavor and consistent quality. Our operating strategy should focus on what makes our products special.*

Maria: *Okay, let's figure out how we can make that strategy work and the effect the strategy should have on the performance of the company.*

OBJECTIVES

Once you have completed this chapter, you should be able to:

1 Explain the relationship between product pricing and sales volume in creating revenues and profits.

2 Explain how operating strategy affects a company's return on assets.

3 Define cost leadership and product differentiation, and explain how companies use these strategies to create profits.

4 Evaluate operating performance by using accrual and cash flow measures.

5 Examine return on equity and explain how operating, investing, and financing activities are interconnected.

6 Describe the primary components of an accounting system and how they are useful for understanding business activities.

OPERATING DECISIONS

OBJECTIVE 1

Explain the relationship between product pricing and sales volume in creating revenues and profits.

After their discussions of financing and investing activities described in previous chapters, Maria, president, Stan, vice president of operations, and Ellen, chief financial officer of Mom's Cookie Company, met to discuss operating activities of their company. "In our previous discussions, we decided to finance our company primarily with common stock and to invest in automated equipment for our production process," Maria began. "Now, we need to make some operating decisions. In particular, we need to determine how to price our products so that they continue to be competitive and profitable. First, let's think about the basic factors that affect profitability. Net income is revenues minus expenses. Return on assets is net income divided by total assets.

Net income = revenues − expenses
Return on assets = net income ÷ total assets

"Return on assets provides a simple measure for evaluating how well we use our assets to create profits. We need to determine how to create a return on assets that will satisfy our stockholders. We have already decided on an automated production process that will require an initial investment in assets of $5 million. Also, expenses created by this process are mostly fixed. Exhibit 1 summarizes, from our prior discussions, our expected initial investment and expected operating results for the next two years.

Exhibit 1

Summary of Expected Assets and Expected Operating Results for Mom's Cookie Company

(In thousands) Assets	Initial Investment	Operating Results	Year 1	Year 2
Current assets	$1,000	Sales revenues	$ 3,000	$ 3,600
Plant assets	4,000	Cost of ingredients	(800)	(960)
Total assets	$5,000	Depreciation	(300)	(300)
		Wages and benefits	(700)	(700)
		Other operating expenses	(1,000)	(1,000)
		Operating income	200	640
		Interest expense	(20)	(20)
		Pretax income	180	620
		Income taxes	(54)	(186)
		Net income	$ 126	$ 434

Maria continued: "We expect our return on assets to be only 2.5% ($126 ÷ $5,000) in the first year. By the second year, we expect to be earning a higher profit, and we believe our future profitability will be much higher. If our investment in assets remains at approximately $5 million, our return on assets should increase to 8.7% in year two. What we can see from Exhibit 1 is that assets and expenses are pretty well determined by our production process and will not increase much until we can sell more of our product than we can produce. The real issue, then, is how to generate as much revenue as possible from our product."

Stan observed, "What I hear you saying is this: The major purpose of our company is to earn a satisfactory return for our stockholders by creating value for our customers. We have a valuable product, and we can produce it efficiently. Though these are necessary attributes of a successful business, they do not guarantee our success. We have to develop a strategy for creating profits by competing with other producers."

"Right," Maria said. "And, again, the basics are pretty straightforward. Revenue depends on two factors, number of units sold (generally referred to as sales volume) and price per unit.

Sales revenues = sales volume × price per unit

The more units we sell at a given price, the more revenue we earn. More revenue means higher net income and higher return on assets."

"Also, we know that sales volume and price are indirectly related," Ellen noted. "As price goes up, sales volume goes down. Therefore, we need to determine a price that will allow us to maximize our revenues. What we can charge is affected by the prices charged by our competitors and what our customers are willing to pay. You've looked at the competition, Stan. What are your thoughts on this matter?"

"The industry is dominated by a few major producers," Stan replied. "All of these companies produce very similar products. Consequently, competition is based largely on price. Each company attempts to sell its products at as low a price as possible. All of the companies charge about the same amount. One company cannot raise its prices without losing customers. If a company's prices get much higher than those of other companies, customers simply will buy from a competitor who sells at a lower price. Producers, then, must set prices that are close to their competitors' and that allow them to earn a reasonable profit. The most efficient producers earn the most money because they keep their production and marketing costs low. To keep these costs low, it is usually necessary to produce in high volume because so many of the costs are fixed, as we have seen for our company. Companies have to invest a lot in plant assets to get into this business. Therefore, they have to sell a lot of product to cover the costs of their investment and earn a reasonable return on assets."

DEVELOPING AN OPERATING STRATEGY

OBJECTIVE 2

Explain how operating strategy affects a company's return on assets.

"Companies in our industry don't earn a huge profit on each item sold," Ellen continued. "A commonly used measure of profitability relative to amount of sales is profit margin, or return on sales. **Profit margin** is the ratio of net income to sales, or operating, revenues and is a measure of a company's ability to create profit from its sales.

Profit margin = net income ÷ sales revenues

Average profit margin in our industry is about 7%. A practical way of thinking about this measure is that companies earn 7¢ for each $1 of revenue they earn.

"Because profit margin is fairly low," Ellen went on, "companies must sell a lot of product to earn a reasonable profit. A commonly used measure of sales volume relative to total investment is asset turnover. **Asset turnover** is the ratio of sales, or operating, revenues, to total assets and is a measure of a company's ability to generate sales from its investment in assets.

$$\text{Asset turnover} = \text{sales revenues} \div \text{total assets}$$

"Average asset turnover in our industry is 1.2. A practical way of thinking about this measure is that companies generate $1.20 of sales revenue for each $1 invested in assets.

"You can see that **return on assets** is a combination of profit margin and asset turnover.

$$\text{Return on assets} = \text{profit margin} \times \text{asset turnover}$$
$$\frac{\text{Net income}}{\text{Total assets}} = \frac{\text{net income}}{\text{sales revenues}} \times \frac{\text{sales revenues}}{\text{total assets}}$$

Therefore, average return on assets in our industry is 8.4% = 7% profit margin × 1.2 asset turnover. This should be our target for the second year of operations."

"Our products are different from most competing products, however," Maria interjected. "We can compete by offering quality and taste that are not available from our competitors. Our marketing research has demonstrated that our customers are willing to pay more for our products than for those of our competitors."

"That's what we're counting on," Stan replied. "We can't price our products too much above those of our competitors, but we can command a premium because of the distinct quality and taste we offer. Thus, we can expect customers to pay a bit more for our products than for those of our competitors.

"Exhibit 2 contains some estimated sales figures for years 1 and 2. Scenario 1 estimates revenues using average industry prices and expected unit sales for Mom's Cookie Company. Scenario 2 estimates revenues using a 10% premium over the average industry price. Expected unit sales will be lower in scenario 2 than in scenario 1 because of the higher price. I don't expect the decrease in sales volume to be very large, however, because of the added value of our products. I think most customers will pay a higher price if we can make them aware of the higher quality.

Exhibit 2

Estimated Sales Volume at Different Price Levels for Mom's Cookie Company

	Units		Revenues	
Unit Price	Year 1	Year 2	Year 1	Year 2
Scenario 1: Sell at average industry price				
$27	108,000	130,000	$2,916,000	$3,510,000
Scenario 2: Sell at premium price (10% above industry average)				
$30	100,000	120,000	$3,000,000	$3,600,000

"As you can see from the first scenario, if we charge average industry prices, we will fall below our expected total sales revenues of $3 million in year 1 and $3.6 million in year 2. The 10% premium gets us to our target sales revenue levels each year."

Maria asked, "If the higher price produces more revenue, why not use a higher premium, say 20%? Why should we be content with a 10% premium? Surely our quality justifies the higher price."

"We have to be careful," Stan answered. "We are marketing a new product, and customers will have to determine for themselves that it is a better product than they can get from our competitors. We expect sales to increase each year as more customers discover our product. If we start out with too high a price, however, customers will be discouraged from trying our product. Our marketing people have done some market tests, and they believe a premium of much above 10% will slow sales considerably over the first few years. Our primary challenge in the first couple of years is to get the product into the hands of customers. Once they are sold on its value, we can consider higher prices.

"Also, a 10% premium earns us a competitive return in the second year. Exhibit 3 computes our expected profit margin, asset turnover, and return on assets in year 2. At estimated sales of $3.6 million, we expect to earn a profit of $434,000 (from Exhibit 1). Assuming that we maintain a total investment in assets of $5 million, we will earn a return on assets of 8.68% in year 2, which is slightly above the industry average of 8.4%."

Exhibit 3

Expected Return on Assets for Mom's Cookie Company in Year 2

Estimated sales revenues	$3,600,000	
Estimated net income	434,000	
Estimated assets	5,000,000	
Profit margin	12.06%	$434,000 ÷ $3,600,000
Asset turnover	0.720	$3,600,000 ÷ $5,000,000
Return on assets	8.68%	12.06% × 0.720

"Is it reasonable to expect our total assets to stay at $5 million, Ellen?" Maria asked.

"I think so," Ellen responded. "We won't need much additional plant investment, and I think we can keep current assets fairly constant. I don't see anything wrong with Stan's estimates."

Stan continued, "You can see that our asset turnover is lower than average—0.72 (Exhibit 3), compared with 1.2 for the industry. We are not going to sell enough product, even if we sell at the industry average price, to generate a high asset turnover. Our product is too new. It will take several years for us to build sales volume. Our asset turnover should increase over time.

"We make up for the low asset turnover with a high profit margin, however. Our expected profit margin is a little over 12% (Exhibit 3), compared with 7% for the industry. As asset turnover increases, a high profit margin will earn us a much higher return than the industry average. A key to our success is sales volume. If we can increase sales each year without incurring a lot of additional expenses, we should make a lot of money."

Maria and Ellen nodded in agreement. "Now let's see if we can make our plans work," Maria said, closing the meeting.

1 SELF-STUDY PROBLEM   Information is presented below for two appliance companies.

WebTUTOR Advantage

(In thousands)	Ardmore	Bellwood
Sales revenues	$ 800	$800
Net income	100	80
Total assets	1,000	800

Required

A. Compute profit margin, asset turnover, and return on assets for each company.
B. Compare the operating strategies of the two companies and explain which company is doing the better job with its strategy.
C. Using the information presented, discuss how each company could improve its profits and return on assets.

The solution to Self-Study Problem 1 appears at the end of the chapter.

INTERPRETATION OF OPERATING ACTIVITIES

OBJECTIVE 3

Define cost leadership and product differentiation, and explain how companies use these strategies to create profits.

To create profits and value for stockholders, a company must use its assets effectively to create and sell products demanded by customers. Also, it must operate efficiently so that revenues exceed expenses. Companies that are more effective and efficient earn higher profits and are more valuable than less effective and less efficient companies. Asset turnover is a measure of effectiveness. A company that sells more of its products will have a higher asset turnover than a company with the same amount of assets that sells less of its product. Profit margin is a measure of efficiency. A company that is efficient in controlling costs and converting resources into products will have a higher profit margin than a company with the same amount of sales that is less efficient.

Asset turnover and profit margin are not the same for all companies, even those that are highly profitable and create high value. Among highly profitable companies, asset turnover is higher for some and profit margin is higher for others. These components of return on assets provide useful information about companies' operating activities. To illustrate, consider the information in Exhibit 4.

Exhibit 4 Profit Margin, Asset Turnover, and Return on Assets for Krispy Kreme and Starbucks

(In thousands)	Krispy Kreme		Starbucks	
	2001	2000	2001	2000
Net income	$ 14,725	$ 5,956	$ 181,210	$ 94,564
Sales revenues	300,715	220,243	2,648,980	2,177,614
Total assets	171,493	104,958	1,851,039	1,491,546
Profit margin (net income ÷ sales revenues)	4.9%	2.7%	6.8%	4.3%
Asset turnover (sales revenues ÷ assets)	1.75	2.10	1.43	1.46
Return on assets (margin × turnover)	8.6%	5.7%	9.8%	6.3%

This exhibit provides information for **Krispy Kreme Doughnuts, Inc.** and **Starbucks Corporation**. It compares profit margin, asset turnover, and return on assets for the companies. Starbucks is a much larger company than Krispy Kreme. Though the numbers vary a bit from 2000 to 2001, Krispy Kreme has a smaller profit margin but a higher asset turnover than Starbucks in both years.

Cost Leadership and Product Differentiation Strategies

Differences in profit margin and asset turnover among companies are not accidents. The strategies companies use to create profits differ. To generate high returns, companies with lower asset turnovers, like Starbucks, must generate high profit margins. Thus, they must carefully control production and selling costs to make sure they earn a reasonable profit on each dollar of product sold. Observe from Exhibit 4 that Starbucks earned 6.8¢ on each dollar of sales in 2001, compared with 4.9¢ for Krispy Kreme.

Companies like Starbucks can earn higher profit margins because they sell products that are differentiated from their competitors' products. These products offer certain qualities or features that build a customer following. Starbucks is known world wide as a premium coffee company. It offers a variety of coffee products that customers demand because of their taste. These customers are willing to pay more for Starbucks' products than for more ordinary or generic coffee products offered by many restaurants and fast food companies.

Krispy Kreme also has a specialized product, but its products are less distinct from competitors than Starbucks' products. Its products command less of a premium. Consequently, Krispy Kreme depends more on asset turnover to generate a return than does

Starbucks. Low profit margin companies must sell in high volumes to make a profit. Therefore, high asset turnover is essential to their success.

Because they must keep their prices low to generate high sales volume, low profit margin companies must keep their operating expenses low so they can earn a profit. These companies use a **cost leadership strategy** to generate profits. They lead their competitors in selling high quantities of products by keeping the prices of these products low. High profit margin companies use a **product differentiation strategy**. They compete by offering products with special features or qualities that customers are willing to buy.

Exhibit 5 illustrates these operating strategies. **Cost leadership and product differentiation are two ends of a competitive spectrum.** Krispy Kreme and Starbucks are not at either end of the spectrum. However, Starbucks falls closer toward the product differentiation end than Krispy Kreme does. Most companies fall somewhere between the two ends of the spectrum. In fact, many companies offer several products or product lines of the same type to compete across the spectrum. For example, manufacturers of TVs and other electronic equipment offer products in various sizes and with various features to appeal to customers who want a low-cost product and to those who want special features. Most automobile companies offer brands and models of various sizes and with various features. Some of these brands or models are targeted toward customers who are looking primarily for economical transportation. Others are targeted toward customers who are looking primarily for style or comfort.

Exhibit 5

Cost Leadership and Product Differentiation as Alternative Operating Strategies

Operating Strategy	Profit Margin	Asset Turnover
Cost Leadership	Low	High
Product Differentiation	High	Low

Both asset turnover and profit margin are important for all companies. A company using a cost leadership strategy relies on high sales volume. It cannot ignore profit margin, however. Because this type of company earns a relatively low profit margin, a small drop in this margin can make a big difference in the company's profitability. As we can see in Exhibit 4, Krispy Kreme's return on assets was lower in 2000 than in 2001 because of its lower profit margin. Similarly, asset turnover is important for a product differentiation company. If Starbucks permits its asset turnover to drop, it will earn a lower return on assets.

Cost leadership and product differentiation describe different ways in which companies compete to earn a profit. Both Krispy Kreme and Starbucks have gained success by effectively selling products and efficiently controlling costs. The companies use different strategies to create success, however. A company's operating strategy determines the types of decisions that are important for the company's success.

Cost leadership companies typically buy and sell in high volume. They keep their operations streamlined to keep costs low. Usually, few specialized customer services are offered. Sales facilities typically are not elaborate. Advertising often emphasizes low prices and convenient "one-stop" shopping. Little research and development activity takes place.

Product differentiation companies produce and sell specialized products. They emphasize service quality and often use elaborate selling facilities—compare the facilities of brand-name stores in a typical mall with those of discount stores like **Wal-Mart**, for example. Advertising emphasizes the high quality or special features of their products and how these products are better than products offered by competitors. An attempt is made to build brand loyalty. Research and development activities often are critical for these companies. For example, **Microsoft** has become one of the most profitable software companies by continuing to develop products that are not available from other producers.

Comparing Accrual and Cash Flow Measures of Operating Performance

OBJECTIVE 4

Evaluate operating performance by using accrual and cash flow measures.

Return on assets measures performance using accrual-based net income. Operating cash flow is also an important measure of operating activities. If a company does not convert its profits into cash, the profits are a misleading performance indicator. The ratio of **operating cash flow to total assets** is useful for comparing the operating cash flows of different companies. It is a measure of cash flow generated during a period through the use of assets to produce and sell goods and services.

Exhibit 6 provides operating cash flow to total assets information for Krispy Kreme and Starbucks. Consistent with its return on assets, Krispy Kreme's operating cash flows were lower than those of Starbucks in both years. Starbucks was converting a larger portion of its earnings into cash than was Krispy Kreme in these years.

Exhibit 6

A Comparison of Operating Cash Flows for Krispy Kreme and Starbucks

(In thousands)	Krispy Kreme		Starbucks	
	2001	2000	2001	2000
Net income (loss)	$14,725	$5,956	$181,210	$94,564
Depreciation and amortization	6,457	4,546	177,087	142,171
Receivables	(3,434)	(4,760)	(17,177)	(25,013)
Inventories	(2,052)	(93)	(19,704)	(19,495)
Prepaid expenses	1,239	(1,619)	(10,919)	(700)
Income taxes, net	902	(2,016)	34,548	5,026
Accounts payable	1,591	1,570	54,117	15,561
Other current liabilities	8,956	4,966	38,622	38,849
Other	2,192	430	23,042	70,833
Net cash provided by operating activities	$30,576	$8,980	$460,826	$321,796
Operating cash flows to total assets	17.83%	8.56%	24.90%	21.57%

The operating activities sections of the statements of cash flows shown in Exhibit 6 provides information about the changes in cash flows from 2000 to 2001. Both companies show increases in operating cash flows. Part of the increase was associated with higher net income. Net cash flow was substantially higher than net income because of depreciation and amortization expenses that did not require cash payments and increases in accounts payable and other current liabilities. Both companies were incurring higher costs that were not paid for in 2001. These higher costs were associated with growth; receivables and inventories increased.

The statement of cash flows is useful for identifying the amount of cash a company is generating from its operating activities. It provides a means of determining why this cash flow is greater or less than a company's net income.

Further Evaluation of Operating Strategy

As we have discussed, profit margin and asset turnover are useful measures for understanding and evaluating a company's operating strategy. Each of these ratios can be separated into other ratios for more detailed analysis of a company's operating activities. For example, assets can be divided into individual asset categories for a more detailed examination of turnover. The categories that are most often examined are inventory and receivables. Inventory turnover and receivables turnover compare income statement numbers with balance sheet numbers.

Inventory turnover **is the ratio of cost of goods sold (from the income statement) to inventory (from the balance sheet); it measures the success of a company in converting its investment in inventory into sales.** Though inventory is necessary for many companies, it is expensive for a company to maintain large amounts of inventory. If the amount of inventory increases relative to selling activities, as measured by cost of goods sold, a company is less effective in using its resources. A major decrease in inventory turnover or a ratio that is lower than that of similar companies indicates that a company is investing too heavily in inventory for the amount of product it is selling.

Exhibit 7 provides selected financial statement information for Krispy Kreme and Starbucks. The exhibit provides several financial ratios for the two companies. Inventory turnover was higher for Krispy Kreme than for Starbucks in both years. The higher ratio indicates that Krispy Kreme was selling its inventory faster than Starbucks, consistent with the companies' overall asset turnover ratios.

Exhibit 7 Selected Financial Statement Information and Ratios for Krispy Kreme and Starbucks

(In thousands)	Krispy Kreme 2001	Krispy Kreme 2000	Starbucks 2001	Starbucks 2000
Sales revenues	$300,715	$220,243	$2,648,980	$2,177,614
Cost of goods sold	150,414	114,000	1,175,787	1,047,138
Gross profit	150,301	106,243	1,473,193	1,130,476
Income from operations	23,507	10,838	281,094	212,252
Interest expense	607	1,525	2,087	2,104
Net income	14,725	5,956	181,210	94,564
Accounts receivable	19,855	17,965	90,425	76,385
Inventories	12,031	9,979	221,253	201,656
Property and equipment	78,340	60,584	1,135,784	930,759
Total assets	171,493	104,958	1,851,039	1,491,546
Total liabilities	45,814	57,203	480,041	346,735
Total shareholders' equity	125,679	47,755	1,375,927	1,148,399
Total liabilities and shareholders' equity	171,493	104,958	1,851,039	1,491,546
Market value	482,430	173,605	3,209,064	2,686,807
Inventory turnover (cost of sales ÷ inventory)	12.50	11.42	5.31	5.19
Days' sales in inventories (inventory ÷ (cost of sales ÷ 365))	29.19	31.95	68.68	70.29
Accounts receivable turnover (sales ÷ receivables)	15.15	12.26	29.29	28.51
Average collection period (receivables ÷ (sales ÷ 365))	24.10	29.77	12.46	12.80
Fixed asset turnover (sales ÷ fixed assets)	3.84	3.64	2.33	2.34
Gross profit margin (gross profit ÷ sales)	50.0%	48.2%	55.6%	51.9%
Operating profit margin (operating income ÷ sales)	7.8%	4.9%	10.6%	9.7%
Financial leverage	1.36	2.20	1.35	1.30
Times interest earned	38.73	7.11	134.71	100.87
Return on equity (ROA × financial leverage)	12%	12%	13%	8%
Market to book value (market value ÷ equity)	3.52	0.98	6.08	3.93

A ratio related to inventory turnover is *day's sales in inventories,* **the ratio of inventory to average daily cost of goods sold.** Average daily cost of goods sold is computed by dividing cost of goods sold by 365. This ratio measures the average number of days for a company to sell its total inventory, or how many days' supply of inventory it keeps on hand. Inventories for both Krispy Kreme and Starbucks consist primarily of ingredients, not finished goods. Starbucks maintains higher inventory levels than Krispy Kreme. These ratios did not change much for either company from 2000 to 2001. An increase in day's sales in inventories signals that a company is not selling its products as quickly and often is a sign that the company is likely to become less profitable.

Accounts receivable turnover **is the ratio of sales revenues (from the income statement) to accounts receivable (from the balance sheet); it measures a company's ability to convert revenues into cash.** A higher ratio indicates that a greater portion of sales is being collected in cash during a period. Krispy Kreme had higher amounts of receivables relative to sales in both years. Therefore, its accounts receivable turnover was lower in both years.

A ratio related to accounts receivable turnover is *average collection period,* **the ratio of accounts receivable to average daily sales.** Average daily sales are computed by dividing sales revenue by 365. This ratio measures how long it takes a company, on average, to collect its receivables. The ratio was higher in both years for Krispy Kreme. An increase in the ratio may signal that a company is having difficulty collecting cash from its customers.

Another turnover ratio is *fixed asset turnover,* **the ratio of sales revenues to fixed assets (property and equipment).** The ratio measures the effectiveness of a company in using its investment in fixed assets to create sales. The ratio was higher for Krispy Kreme than Starbucks in both years. Krispy Kreme generates higher sales relative to its investment in fixed assets than Starbucks. This higher ratio is associated with a cost leadership strategy that requires less elaborate stores than companies using the product differentiation strategy. Starbucks' stores are often located in high-cost facilities such as in airports and urban areas. Starbucks' operating strategy involves selling to high-income customers who are willing to pay for premium products. Krispy Kreme sells to average-income consumers, particularly to families with children. Many of its stores are in smaller cities and towns.

Asset turnover, inventory turnover, day's sales in inventories, accounts receivable turnover, average collection period, and fixed asset turnover are primarily effectiveness measures. They indicate how well a company is using its assets to sell its products and collect cash from its customers. These ratios improved slightly for Krispy Kreme and Starbucks from 2000 to 2001.

In addition to examining turnover ratios to evaluate effectiveness, we can examine changes in the components of profit margin to provide additional information about a company's efficiency. Two commonly used components are gross profit margin and operating profit margin. Both ratios compare income statement numbers with other income statement numbers.

Gross profit margin **is the ratio of gross profit (sales revenues minus cost of goods sold) to sales revenues; it measures efficiency in the production or purchase of goods for sale.** A high gross profit margin indicates that a company is controlling its product costs. Product costs are the costs of merchandise for merchandising companies and production costs for manufacturing companies. A decrease in gross profit margin or a margin lower than that of similar companies indicates that a company is not efficient in producing or purchasing goods for sale. Exhibit 7 indicates that Krispy Kreme's gross profit margins were lower than those of Starbucks. Starbucks' gross profit margin increased from 2000 to 2001, explaining much of the increase in the company's return on assets during this period (see Exhibit 4).

Operating profit margin **is the ratio of operating income (sales revenues minus operating expenses) to sales revenues.** When compared with gross profit margin, operating profit margin is an indicator of a company's efficiency in controlling operating costs other than product costs. These costs are primarily period expenses associated with selling and administrative activities. Consequently, operating profit margin can be used to evaluate a company's efficiency in controlling its selling and administrative costs.

Krispy Kreme's operating profit margin increased from 4.9% in 2000 to 7.8% in 2001 (Exhibit 7). However, Krsipy Kreme's operating profit margin was much lower in both years than was Starbucks'. Krispy Kreme's overall lower profit margin is associated with its lower operating profit margin. The low operating profit margin had a major effect on Krispy Kreme's return on assets. When a company's profit margin is low, consistent with a cost leadership strategy, a small increase in profit margin usually has a significant effect on net income and return on assets. Cost control is especially important for these companies. Accordingly, Krispy Kreme's increase in operating profit margin results in an increase in return on assets from 2000 to 2001 (see Exhibit 4).

Linking Operating and Investing Activities with Financing Activities

Return on assets (and operating cash flow to assets) links a company's operating activities (profits or operating cash flows) with its investing activities (total assets). Thus, return on assets measures the ability of a company to use its investments to generate operating results. Completing the link among operating, investing, and financing activities requires that we examine financial leverage and return on equity.

Recall from Chapter F10 that return on equity is return on assets times financial leverage as measured by the assets to equity ratio. Thus, return on equity is a summary measure of the success of a company's financing, investing, and operating activities. We can separate return on equity into three components.

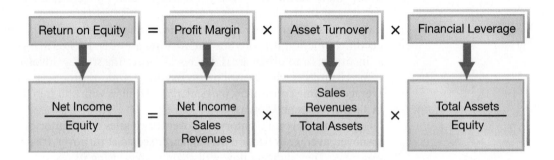

Profit margin measures the ability of a company to operate efficiently to produce profits (operating activities). Asset turnover measures the ability of a company to create sales (operating activities) from investments in assets (investing activities). Assets to equity measures the capital structure (financing activities) used by a company to pay for its assets (investing activities). Companies can use each of these components to improve their returns to stockholders and their company value.

Exhibit 7 includes return on equity and market to book value ratios for Krispy Kreme and Starbucks. Krispy Kreme had higher financial leverage than Starbucks did in 2001. This leverage worked in favor of Krispy Kreme. Financial leverage resulted in higher return on equity than in return on assets. Krispy Kreme and Starbucks had similar amounts of financial leverage in 2001. Because Starbucks' return on assets was a little higher than Krispy Kreme's, its return on equity also was a bit higher.

Financial leverage can result in higher return for a company's stockholders. However, the higher return is associated with greater financial risk because debt and interest must be paid. Another ratio that is used to measure financial risk is *times interest earned,* **the ratio of operating income (income before interest and taxes) to interest expense.** The ratio is larger when a company incurs relatively small amounts of interest. From Exhibit 7, we can see that Krispy Kreme was incurring much higher interest expense and a lower times interest earned than Starbucks. Krispy Kreme's ratio improved from 2000 to 2001 but was still lower than Starbucks' ratio. Though the companies' financial leverages were similar in 2001, Krispy Kreme was using more debt that required interest payments than Starbucks. Much of Starbucks' liabilities were payables that did not incur interest.

Krispy Kreme's low market to book value in 2000 was attributable to its poor performance. As that performance improved in 2001, the market value increased. Starbucks' market to book value was higher in both years. The company was growing rapidly and had relatively low amounts of debt. The times interest earned ratio is particularly informative because it indicates the higher level of financial risk associated with Krispy Kreme that is evident in the company's lower market to book value.

Thus, a company's value depends on its operating activities in relation to its investing and financing activities. All of these activities are interrelated and must be considered together to understand a company's performance. Financial statements are a

LEARNING NOTE

In this book, we have discussed some major issues that are important for understanding financial accounting information and using this information to evaluate performance. We have focused on those issues that we believe are most important. Our discussion has not included many other issues that are relevant for understanding and using accounting information because space prohibits coverage of all relevant topics. Other topics are covered in more advanced accounting and business courses.

major source of information for measuring and evaluating these activities. They provide information about both the results of activities for a period and changes in results from one period to the next. Thus, both return on assets and equity and the amount of change in return on assets and equity from one period to the next are important for evaluating performance. Companies with high and increasing returns usually are more valuable than companies with low and decreasing returns.

2 SELF-STUDY PROBLEM

Information is provided below for two companies that produce and sell plastic containers.

WebTUTOR Advantage

(In thousands)	Caseopia 2004	Caseopia 2003	Dragoon 2004	Dragoon 2003
Sales revenues	$750	$700	$320	$300
Cost of goods sold	450	420	208	180
Gross profit	300	280	112	120
Operating expenses	120	135	50	43
Operating income	180	145	62	77
Net income	100	87	37	46
Accounts receivable	46	43	23	20
Inventories	82	80	50	42
Total assets	960	900	500	450

Required

A. Compute profit margin, gross profit margin, operating profit margin, asset turnover, accounts receivable turnover, inventory turnover, and return on assets for each company.
B. Use these ratios to evaluate the operating activities of each company and to compare the companies' performance.

The solution to Self-Study Problem 2 appears at the end of the chapter.

THE BIG PICTURE

OBJECTIVE 6

Describe the primary components of an accounting system and how they are useful for understanding business activities.

In this final section, we summarize the primary topics covered in this book. It is important to see how each topic fits into the overall story in order to understand the importance of accounting as a business tool.

Exhibit 8 illustrates the role of accounting in the business decision process. A business is a transformation process in which (1) financial resources are obtained through financing activities, (2) financial resources are used to acquire other resources through investing activities, and (3) resources are used to produce and sell goods and services through operating activities. Accounting is an information system for measuring and reporting the transformation of resources into goods and services and the sale or transfer of these goods and services to customers. Thus, the accounting system provides information about activities that have occurred in the transformation process. This information is used by decision makers both to evaluate past activities and to plan for future activities that are part of the transformation process. Accordingly, the accounting system links past events to future events.

Accounting information plays a crucial role in business decisions. Accounting information, like any other information, tells only a partial story. Certain aspects of a company's activities are measured, summarized, and reported. Other aspects are ignored. Assumptions and estimations are necessary to measure certain activities for

Exhibit 8
Accounting and
Business Decisions

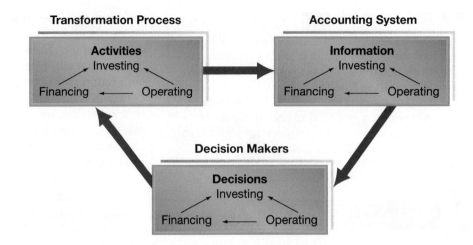

which more specific, timely information is not available. Thus, the picture of a company provided by accounting information is incomplete and does not fully represent the actual company. The picture that is presented depends on the particular set of rules used to measure and report the company's activities. Organizations that set accounting standards, like the FASB, influence the type of picture that is presented.

Accounting information provides a representation of a company. The company is too complex to be represented completely. An information system identifies certain attributes of the company and summarizes a large amount of complex data to make them useful to decision makers. As a result, the representation of the company is only an approximation of the company. Rules used by the system affect how the company is represented. A different set of rules would result in a different representation. Accordingly, if decision makers are to use the representation provided by the system, they need to understand the system so that they are not misled by differences between the representation and the actual company. Consequently, it is essential for those who use accounting information to make business decisions to understand major components of the accounting system.

Exhibit 9 provides a more detailed description of the accounting system. The primary components of the system include measurement rules, processing and storage procedures, reporting rules, and reports.

Exhibit 9
The Accounting
Information System

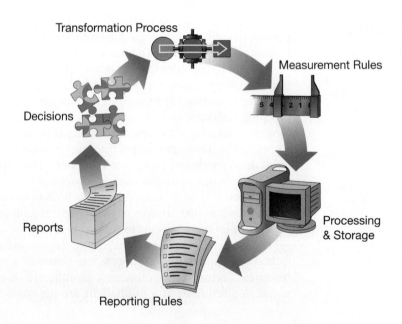

Measurement rules determine which attributes of the transformation process enter the accounting system. Measurement units used to measure activities in the transformation process are primarily dollar values, based on the historical costs of resources acquired or used in the transformation process. Transactions (primarily exchanges of resources) are measured on an accrual basis. This basis recognizes events in the transformation process when they cause resources to increase or decrease, rather than when cash is received or paid. These events are recognized in specific fiscal periods so that activities in the transformation process can be determined and evaluated on a timely basis. Expenses are matched with revenues in the period in which resources are consumed. The matching of expenses with revenues in particular fiscal periods requires estimation of the financial effects of some events. For example, depreciation and inventory estimation are used to allocate asset costs to specific periods. Accounting measurement rules often are conservative. These rules recognize expenses or losses in the period in which an asset is likely to have been consumed or impaired or in which a liability is likely to have been incurred. Revenues or gains often are deferred, however, until all events that created the revenue or gain have been completed. Conservatism recognizes that the financial effects of events often are estimates and attempts to ensure that revenues and profits are not overstated by optimistic managers. The values of certain resources that are difficult to measure objectively, such as management or employee skills and brand names, are excluded from accounting measurement.

Processing and storage procedures determine how information from the transformation process enters the accounting system and how this information is summarized and stored so that it can be provided to decision makers. Double-entry bookkeeping has been the traditional method of recording transactions in an accounting system. Each transaction is recorded in two or more accounts, which are information categories that can be classified into five types: assets, liabilities, owners' equity, revenues, and expenses. The accounting cycle is a process for entering, processing, and summarizing accounting information. The process involves (1) examining business activities, (2) recording transactions, (3) updating account balances, (4) making end-of-period adjustments, (5) preparing financial statements, and (6) closing revenue and expense accounts. In most businesses, many of these steps are performed by computer programs. Internal control procedures ensure the accuracy of information in the accounting system.

Reporting rules determine the type and format of information reported by an accounting system. Reporting rules govern the separation of accounting information into individual financial statements. The rules specify the order of accounts or activities and the amount of detail reported in financial statements and accompanying notes. Direct and indirect formats for reporting the statement of cash flows are examples of reporting rules. Other examples include requirements that companies report their accounting policies and certain measurement rules in notes to financial statements. In general, reporting rules require companies to provide sufficient information in their financial statements or accompanying notes so that users are fully informed about the companies' financial activities. Reporting rules also specify the timing of reports. For example, most corporations are required to provide annual reports and quarterly updates to their stockholders. In addition to general reports such as financial statements, specific reporting rules may be used to design reports for special uses, such as those for managers and taxing authorities.

Accounting reports are the summary documents provided to decision makers. Financial statements (income statement, balance sheet, statement of cash flows, and statement of stockholders' equity) are the primary financial accounting reports. These statements usually are accompanied by notes that explain numbers or activities in the statements. Financial statements reported to external decision makers usually are accompanied by an audit report that expresses the auditor's opinion about whether the statements fairly present the company's financial position and results of operations. Accounting reports also may contain explanations by company management about events reported in the financial statements.

Decisions of managers, owners, creditors, and others depend, in part, on their understanding of the information reported by a company's accounting system. Managers make financing, investing, and operating decisions that determine the future of a company. These decisions rely on information about past financing, investing, and operating activities, and on estimation of the effects of decisions on future activities. Owners, creditors, and other users evaluate managers' financing, investing, and operating activities. They use accounting information to assess how well a company has performed and how well it is likely to perform in the future.

Information about financing activities identifies a company's capital structure and the particular types of debt and equity a company uses to finance its assets. Financial statements help users determine the effects of financial leverage on profitability and the ability of a company to meet its debt obligations. They provide information about when obligations will become due and about changes in financing, such as new borrowing, repaying debt, and selling and repurchasing stock.

Information about investing activities identifies both the types of assets a company has acquired and the changes in these assets over time. Financial statement users can assess whether a company is growing (by acquiring additional assets) and whether those assets are being used productively to generate additional sales and profits. Information about assets also is useful for evaluating uncertainty about future profits if a company's sales are lower than expected. Companies with high operating leverage (high fixed to total costs) are sensitive to sales volatility because they cannot reduce many of their costs—for example, those associated with production facilities—in the short run.

Information about operating activities identifies how well a company is able to use its assets to create sales and to control production and selling costs so that it earns a profit. This information also is useful for assessing a company's ability to convert profits to cash and its ability to pay dividends or invest in growth opportunities. Separate reporting of unusual or nonrecurring events helps users distinguish ordinary events from those requiring special analysis.

Exhibit 10 summarizes information derived from financial statements for evaluating a company's performance and assessing its value. Company value is depicted on the

Exhibit 10 Using Accounting Information to Make Decisions About Company Value

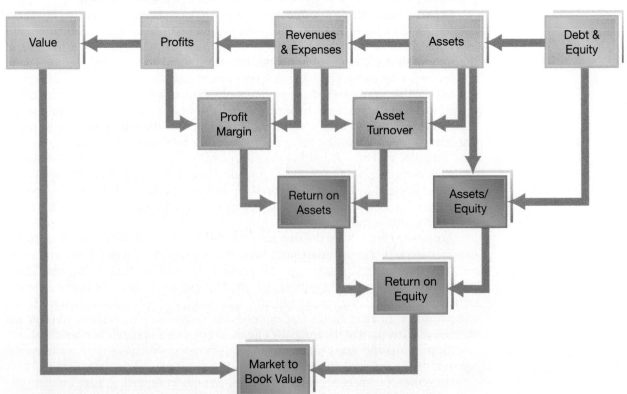

top line of the illustration as being derived primarily from a company's ability to earn profits. Profits, in turn, depend on a company's ability to sell goods and services (revenues) and its ability to use resources efficiently in producing and selling those products (expenses). Revenues and expenses depend on a company's investment in assets that can be used to produce and sell its products. A larger investment in assets should permit a company to generate higher revenues, but it also results in higher expenses. The ability of a company to invest in assets depends on financing available from debt and equity. The amounts of debt and equity and the mix of debt relative to equity affect investment decisions and operating results. Profits from operating results also are a source of equity through retained earnings.

Accounting measures such as profit margin and asset turnover summarize relationships among the various activities that create company value. Profit margin links profits to revenues. Asset turnover links revenues to assets. Return on assets links profits to assets. Return on equity links revenues to equity and encompasses all of the accounting relationships from profits through revenues and expenses, assets, debt, and equity. Therefore, it incorporates all of the activities in a company's transformation process: financing, investing, and operating. Finally, market to book value links company value (market value of stockholders' equity) to accounting numbers. When the accounting performance measures depicted in the exhibit are high, company value typically is high.

Consequently, understanding accounting information is important for understanding company value. Understanding the accounting system, including the rules used to measure and report information and the procedures used to capture and summarize this information, is critical to understanding accounting information. The primary goal of this book has been to help you understand the components of the accounting system, how they work, and how they can be used to understand business activities.

3 SELF-STUDY PROBLEM

To understand a company's operating activities, it is important to understand the relationships among operating, investing, and financing activities and to understand the accounting system that provides information about these activities.

Required Explain why.

The solution to Self-Study Problem 3 appears at the end of the chapter.

REVIEW

SUMMARY of IMPORTANT CONCEPTS

1. Operating decisions involve choices about how a company will produce and sell products to earn revenues and make a profit.
   a. Sales revenue depends on sales volume and price per unit, which are indirectly related. An increase in price usually results in a decrease in volume.
   b. The prices a company can charge for its products depend on what customers are willing to pay based on the value of the products to them and the prices charged by competitors.
   c. If a market is highly competitive and companies in the market produce very similar products, the companies usually will compete on the basis of price. They will keep their prices low to attract customers and will depend on high sales volume to earn a profit.
   d. If a company can distinguish its products from competitors' products by special features or qualities, it can charge a higher price and earn more per unit from customers who are willing to pay for these features or qualities.
   e. Asset turnover measures the volume of sales (in dollars) relative to a company's investment in assets. Companies that compete using low prices require high asset turnover to earn a high profit and return on assets.

f. Profit margin measures the amount of income a company can earn on its sales. Companies that compete using special product features use high profit margin to earn a high profit and return on assets.

2. The operating strategies that companies select depend on the types of products they produce and sell.
   a. Companies that rely on low costs use a cost leadership strategy and require high asset turnover.
   b. Companies that rely on product features use a product differentiation strategy and require high profit margin.
   c. Product differentiation companies normally rely on brand-name identification, advertising of product features, and research and development activities to a greater extent than cost leadership companies.
   d. Many companies provide different products and product lines to compete in both cost leadership and product differentiation markets.

3. Various measures can be used to evaluate the success of a company's operating strategy.
   a. Profit margin, asset turnover, and return on assets are commonly used measures.
   b. The ratio of operating cash flow to assets measures a company's ability to convert its profits into cash.
   c. Inventory turnover measures a company's ability to convert its investment in inventory into sales.
   d. Day's sales in inventories measures the average number of days for a company to sell its total inventory, or how many days' supply of inventory it keeps on hand.
   e. Accounts receivable turnover measures a company's ability to convert its credit sales into cash.
   f. Average collection period measures how long it takes a company to collect its receivables.
   g. Fixed asset turnover measures the effectiveness of a company in using its investment in fixed assets to create sales.
   h. Gross profit margin measures a company's efficiency in the production or purchase of goods for sale.
   i. Operating profit margin measures a company's efficiency in controlling selling and administrative expenses in addition to its efficiency in controlling product costs.
   j. Return on equity includes the effect of financing in evaluating overall company performance and links operating, investing, and financing activities.
   k. Times interest earned measures the ability of a company to meet its interest requirements.

4. Accounting provides information about a company's transformation process to help decision makers identify and evaluate past activities and plan for and form expectations about future activities.
   a. To use accounting information effectively, decision makers must understand the accounting system that provides the information.
   b. The system consists of measurement rules, processing and storage procedures, reporting rules, and reports that provide particular types of information about a company's activities.
   c. Decision makers who understand how information is produced by the accounting system can use this information to assess performance and company value.

DEFINE

TERMS and CONCEPTS DEFINED in this CHAPTER

accounts receivable turnover (F538)	gross profit margin (F539)
average collection period (F539)	inventory turnover (F537)
day's sales in inventories (F538)	operating profit margin (F539)
fixed asset turnover (F539)	times interest earned (F540)

SELF-STUDY PROBLEM SOLUTIONS

SSP14-1   A. Profit margin = net income ÷ sales revenues

Ardmore: $100 = $800 ÷ 12.5%
Bellwood: $80 = $800 ÷ 10%

Asset turnover = sales revenues ÷ total assets

Ardmore: $800 = $1,000 ÷ 0.8
Bellwood: $800 = $800 ÷ 1.0

Return on assets = profit margin × asset turnover

Ardmore: 12.5% = 0.8 × 10%
Bellwood: 10.0% = 1.0 × 10%

B. Ardmore appears to charge higher prices for its products than Bellwood. It earns more for each dollar of sales (12.5¢ for Ardmore versus 10¢ for Bellwood). Bellwood sells more of its product than Ardmore, however. It sells $1 of product for each $1 invested in assets, whereas Ardmore sells 80¢ for each $1 invested. By charging lower prices, Bellwood is able to sell more product.

Ardmore earns a higher net income than Bellwood, but each company earns the same return on assets. Therefore, neither company is more profitable than the other relative to their investments in assets. We can conclude that each company is profitable, but the companies use different strategies to create their profits. Ardmore apparently sells products with features or quality that are more desirable than those of Bellwood. Customers are willing to pay more for these products, though they purchase fewer of them. Bellwood competes by selling lower-price products and by selling a higher volume than Ardmore.

C. The primary factors involved in creating a high return on assets are revenues, expenses, and assets. Revenues depend on sales price and volume. Companies are more effective if they can sell more of their products to earn higher revenues without increasing expenses. Companies increase revenues by increasing sales prices if they sell the same number of units. Also, they increase revenues by increasing sales volume if they sell at the same price. They earn higher net income if they reduce expenses without decreasing sales revenues. Finally, companies increase return on assets by reducing the amount of assets they need to earn a given amount of net income. Companies are more efficient if they reduce assets or expenses without reducing revenues. Thus, companies become more profitable by becoming more effective or efficient.

SSP14-2   A.

	Caseopia		Dragoon	
	2004	**2003**	**2004**	**2003**
Profit margin	$100 ÷ $750 = 13.3%	$87 ÷ $700 = 12.4%	$37 ÷ $320 = 11.6%	$46 ÷ $300 = 15.3%
Gross profit margin	$300 ÷ $750 = 40.0%	$280 ÷ $700 = 40.0%	$112 ÷ $320 = 35.0%	$120 ÷ $300 = 40.0%
Operating profit margin	$180 ÷ $750 = 24.0%	$145 ÷ $700 = 20.7%	$62 ÷ $320 = 19.4%	$77 ÷ $300 = 25.7%
Asset turnover	$750 ÷ $960 = 0.781	$700 ÷ $900 = 0.778	$320 ÷ $500 = 0.640	$300 ÷ $450 = 0.667
Accounts receivable turnover	$750 ÷ $46 = 16.304	$700 ÷ $43 = 16.279	$320 ÷ $23 = 13.913	$300 ÷ $20 = 15.000
Inventory turnover	$450 ÷ $82 = 5.488	$420 ÷ $80 = 5.250	$208 ÷ $50 = 4.160	$180 ÷ $42 = 4.286
Return on assets	$100 ÷ $960 = 10.4%	$87 ÷ $900 = 9.7%	$37 ÷ $500 = 7.4%	$46 ÷ $450 = 10.2%

B. Dragoon's return on assets was higher than Caseopia's in 2000. During 2001, Caseopia's return on assets increased while Dragoon's decreased, so that Caseopia's return was higher in 2001. Several factors account for these changes. Dragoon's profit margin decreased while Caseopia's increased. This change was due to a decrease in Dragoon's gross profit margin and an increase in Caseopia's operating profit margin. Dragoon was less efficient in 2001 than in 2000 in controlling production costs, and Caseopia was more efficient in controlling selling and administrative costs. Asset turnover increased slightly for Caseopia and decreased slightly for Dragoon. Accounts receivable turnover was lower in 2001 than in 2000 for Dragoon. Dragoon's performance was worse in 2001 than in 2000, primarily due to its lower profit margin. Caseopia's performance was better in 2001, primarily due to its higher profit margin. Caseopia's profit margin and asset turnover ratios were higher in 2001 than Dragoon's, indicating that it was the better-performing company.

SSP14-3 Operating activities involve the production and sale of goods and services. Producing and selling products requires investment in assets that are used in the production and selling processes. As a company increases in size by investing in additional assets, it should be able to produce and sell more products. Thus, revenues, expenses, and operating cash flows are affected by a company's assets. Assets are financed by debt and equity, including retained earnings. Consequently, the more assets a company has, the more debt and equity it requires. The types of financing a company uses affect its financial leverage. The types of assets it uses affect its operating leverage. Increases in financial and operating leverage increase uncertainty about a company's future profitability. Therefore, operating, investing, and financing activities are linked; one type of activity has a major effect on the other types of activities. Operating activities cannot be evaluated separately from investing and financing activities. Relationships among these activities are important for understanding a company's past performance and potential future performance.

A company's accounting system provides information for understanding the company's financing, investing, and operating activities. This information has to be interpreted by decision makers. Interpretation depends on understanding how the information was created. For example, accounting systems use measurement and reporting rules to determine what information will be reported to decision makers and how activities will be measured. These rules result in a particular presentation of a company's activities; the presentation would be different if other rules were used. Users should understand that accounting information, like any information, provides only an approximation of the underlying company. Not all aspects of a company are reported. Those that are reported are determined by the system. Therefore, understanding the information and being able to use it effectively to make decisions requires the decision maker to understand the biases and limitations of the information system.

Thinking Beyond the Question

How do operations create value for our business?

Companies use different strategies to earn profits. Successful use of these strategies results in high return on the company's investment and a high return for its stockholders. A careful review of a company's financial statements can provide useful information for evaluating the company's performance. Why is accounting essential for good business decisions?

QUESTIONS

Q14-1
Obj. 1
Sales at Tulip Manufacturing Company are expected to double during the coming year. The company has unused capacity available and should be able to handle the new business. If a large portion of the company's costs are fixed, what would you expect to happen to profits during the coming year?

Q14-2
Obj. 1
Sales at Borderline Insurance Agency are expected to double during the coming year. The company has been growing in recent years but generally has no trouble hiring more agents or leasing additional equipment when needed. If a large portion of the company's costs are variable, what would you expect to happen to profits during the coming year?

Q14-3
Obj. 2
The sales manager at Buff & Tuff Health Machines has just completed a sales presentation to staff indicating that the firm will, from now on, pursue a product differentiation strategy. He notes that this should have the effect of increasing the company's asset turnover ratio with only a minor decrease in its profit margin. Does the sales manager's presentation make sense? Why or why not?

Q14-4
Obj. 2
Generic Chemical, Inc. produces standardized products that become raw materials for other companies. One competitor's goods are chemically identical to those of any other company. In general, would you expect this firm to have a high profit margin, high asset turnover, both, or neither? Why?

Q14-5
Obj. 2
Mystic Communications leads its industry in product innovation. Its financial success has been the result of creating innovative products, getting them to market quickly, and building consumer acceptance. By the time competitors develop effective alternative products, Mystic has moved on to other new products and markets. The cost of maintaining facilities to invent and produce these products is high. Would you expect this company to have a high profit margin, high asset turnover, both, or neither? Why?

Q14-6
Obj. 3
What are the primary differences between cost leadership and product differentiation?

Q14-7
Obj. 3
How are the cost leadership and product differentiation strategies used to improve return on assets and profitability? In particular, how would you expect the choice of strategy to affect the components of return on assets reported by companies using these strategies?

Q14-8
Obj. 3
A marketing manager in your company tells you, "We've got this great product—it's really special, much better than the competition's. But we just can't sell very much because our prices are so high. We'd make much more money if we lowered the prices." Do you agree? Why or why not? What other information would you want to have before making a final pricing decision?

Q14-9
Obj. 4
Under normal operating conditions, what relationship do you expect to find between net income and net cash flow from operations? Which will be higher? Why? What will the major reconciling items be between the two?

Q14-10
Obj. 4
Concerning net income and net cash flow from operations, will trends in one tend to be followed by changes in the other? Explain. What trends might appear in a company with financial problems?

Q14-11
Obj. 4
The company you work for has a good return on assets, but inventory turnover and receivables turnover are low for your industry. You also have ongoing cash flow problems. Is there a connection? Explain the connection between inventory turnover, receivables turnover, and the generation of cash flow from operations.

Q14-12
Obj. 5
Why should the growth and variability of earnings affect the value of a company's common stock? Explain.

Q14-13
Obj. 5
Return on assets and return on equity are measures of performance. What is the difference between the two measures? Be specific.

Q14-14
Obj. 5
Think about how the nature of financing, investing, and operating activities differ. What is meant by "operating strategy"? How might one decide what strategy is most appropriate for a particular company?

EXERCISES

If your instructor is using Personal Trainer in this course, you may complete online the assignments identified by ⁀.

E14-1   Write a short definition of each of the terms listed in the *Terms and Concepts Defined in this Chapter* section.

E14-2
Obj. 1
⁀
You are preparing for a meeting at which your company will discuss its selling price for a new product. You have already made the decision to invest $2.3 million in production facilities with a capacity to produce 350,000 units per year. Fixed expenses, including depreciation and minimal advertising, will be $300,000 per year. Variable expenses will be $4 per unit. Your marketing people have developed three sales scenarios:

a. At a price of $7 per unit, below much of the competition, you sell 200,000 units per year.

b. At a price of $9 per unit, the average among the competition, you sell 135,000 units per year.

c. At a price of $7 per unit, with an additional $400,000 per year spent to advertise your low price, you sell 300,000 units per year.

Prepare a schedule (according to the following format) that shows the pro forma (or expected) profit from each scenario.

	Strategy A	Strategy B	Strategy C
Unit price			
Estimated sales in units			
Sales revenue			
Variable expenses			
Fixed expenses			
Additional advertising			
Total expenses			
Pro forma operating profit	=====	=====	=====

Which scenario would you recommend? Why?

E14-3
Obj. 1
The Lakeside Symphony Association is a not-for-profit organization. The primary function of the association is to operate the Lakeside Symphony Orchestra for the benefit of local citizens. The board of directors of the organization is discussing ticket prices for the upcoming season. Ticket receipts do not cover all costs of a concert; donations must be solicited for the remainder, but finding enough donors is difficult, and funds are always scarce.

Each concert has fixed orchestra costs of approximately $28,000, primarily for paying the musicians. The only variable costs are programs, tickets, and refreshments served at a reception following the concert; these total about $2 per attendee. Orchestra managers estimate that they can sell 1,300 tickets for the average concert at $12, 1,100 tickets at $15, or 800 tickets at $20.

Which option do you recommend? Why? Are the financial measurements used in this chapter appropriate for a not-for-profit situation like this? Why or why not? What nonfinancial considerations should enter into the decision?

E14-4
Obj. 1
Garden Company has the capacity to produce 200,000 tillers. Variable costs are $30 per tiller. Fixed costs are $1,500,000. Should the company aim to sell 200,000 at $100 each, 160,000 at $125 each, or 125,000 at $160 each? Explain your recommendation. What will the company have to do to carry out the strategy you recommend?

E14-5
Obj. 2
Three companies have the following financial results:

	Company A	Company B	Company C
Profit margin	0.05	0.40	0.25
Asset turnover	6.00	0.75	1.20
Return on assets	30%	30%	30%

What can you conclude about the financial results and the operating strategy of each company?

E14-6
Objs. 2, 3
$\dfrac{P}{T}$

Selected information from the annual report of **Home Depot, Inc.** is provided below. The report is for the fiscal year ended February 3, 2002.

(In millions)	
Net sales	$53,553
Net income	3,044
Total assets	26,394

Calculate Home Depot's profit margin, asset turnover, and return on assets. In comparison with the companies shown in Exhibit 4 in this chapter, what strategy does Home Depot appear to be using to generate profits?

E14-7
Objs. 2, 3
$\dfrac{P}{T}$

Selected information from the 2001 annual reports of **Hershey Foods Corp.** and **William Wrigley Jr. Co.** is provided below. Both companies are prominent in the sugar and confectionary products industry.

(In millions)	Hershey Foods	Wrigley
Net sales	$4,557	$2,430
Net income	207	363
Total assets	3,247	1,766

Compare the operating strategies of the two companies by calculating profit margin, asset turnover, and return on assets. Which company appears to be doing the better job with its strategy?

E14-8
Objs. 2, 3

The numbers below are from the records of two small local restaurants.

	Pat's Place	Henry's Hangout
Sales	$220,000	$190,000
Net income	80,000	30,000
Total assets	530,000	210,000

What do these numbers tell you about the operating strategy for each restaurant? What could each do to improve its return on assets?

E14-9
Objs. 2, 3
$\dfrac{P}{T}$

The numbers below are from the 2001 annual reports of two major airlines.

	Southwest Airlines		Delta Air Lines	
(In millions)	2001	2000	2001	2000
Sales	$5,555	$5,650	$13,879	$16,741
Net income (loss)	511	603	(1,216)	828
Total assets	8,997	6,670	23,605	21,931

Calculate return on assets, asset turnover, and profit margin. Which airline appears to be more successful? Do you find evidence of differences in operating strategies, or do both appear to compete on the same basis? What could the less successful line do to improve profits?

E14-10
Obj. 3
$\dfrac{P}{T}$

Styles, Inc., a clothing manufacturer, reported the information given below over a three-year period.

	2005	2004	2003
Sales	$ 9,000	$ 6,000	$3,000
Net income	1,683	852	288
Total assets	20,036	10,650	3,692
Inventory	1,500	960	500
Cost of goods sold	5,500	3,500	1,800
Fixed assets	4,000	2,500	1,500

(a) Compute the firm's profit margin, asset turnover, days' sales in inventory, fixed asset turnover, and return on assets for each year shown. (b) Discuss the company's operating strategy over this time period.

E14-11
Obj. 4
P̯T

Selected summary information is presented below for two companies.

(In millions)	Fasani Enterprises 2005	Fasani Enterprises 2004	Thunderbird Corporation 2005	Thunderbird Corporation 2004
Total assets	$7,446	$6,512	$8,452	$7,786
Net sales	6,812	5,746	8,910	7,388
Net income	414	366	312	816
Depreciation and amortization	366	314	268	244
Decrease (increase) in receivables	12	(8)	(326)	(262)
Decrease (increase) in inventories	174	116	84	(32)
Increases (decrease) in payables	264	124	(114)	(62)
Cash flow from operations	$1,230	$ 912	$ 224	$ 704

a. Calculate the ratios of cash flow from operations to net income and to total assets.
b. Evaluate the success of each company at using assets to generate cash flow from operations.
c. What are the major causes of the difference between net income and cash flow for the two companies?

E14-12
Obj. 4

Information is provided below from the 2002 annual report of the **Walt Disney Company**.

(In millions)	2002	2001	2000
Net earnings (loss)	$ 1,236	$ (158)	$ 920
Net cash from operating activities	2,286	3,048	3,755
Net cash from (for) investing activities	(3,176)	(2,015)	(1,091)
Net cash from (for) financing activities	1,511	(1,257)	(2,236)

(a) Evaluate Disney's performance over the three years presented. Would you characterize the company as growing, stable, or declining? (b) Is it surprising that the change in net earnings differs from the change in net cash from operating activities over the period? Which measure of operating activities is more stable? Why?

E14-13
Obj. 4
P̯T

Information is provided below for **Federated Department Stores**, owner of several department store chains, including Bloomingdale's, Macy's, and The Broadway. The amounts given are from Federated's annual report for the year ended February 2, 2002.

(In millions)	Fiscal 2001	Fiscal 2000
Sales	$15,651	$16,638
Cost of goods sold	9,584	9,955
Operating income	1,104	1,691
Net income (loss)	(276)	(184)
Accounts receivable	2,379	2,435
Merchandise inventories	3,376	3,626
Total assets	15,044	15,574
Cash provided by operating activities	1,372	1,332

Calculate inventory turnover, accounts receivable turnover, gross profit margin, and operating profit margin. Compare your results with those for Wal-Mart shown below. To what extent are the differences explained by the differing operating strategies of the two retailers?

(In millions)	Wal-Mart 2002	Wal-Mart 2001
Inventory turnover	7.6	7.0
Accounts receivable turnover	108.9	108.2
Gross profit margin	21.2%	21.4%
Operating profit margin	4.6%	5.0%

E14-14
Obj. 4
P̸T

Following is an income statement for Crystal Corporation.
Calculate three ratios that indicate efficiency and interpret the results.

Crystal Corporation
Income Statement
For the Year Ending December 31, 2004

Sales revenue		$50,000
Less: Cost of goods sold		25,000
Gross profit		$25,000
Other operating expenses:		
Advertising	$3,000	
Utilities	3,500	
Wages	2,500	9,000
Operating income		$16,000
Less: Income taxes		5,600
Net income		$10,400

E14-15
Obj. 4

Footpedal Enterprises has been in business for five years. This past year was the best year yet, as demonstrated by several indicators shown below.

	2005	2004	2003	2002	2001
Inventory turnover	5.2	4.7	4.3	4.5	4.1
Accounts receivable turnover	6.0	5.7	5.4	5.4	5.3
Gross profit margin	23.2	22.8	22.9	22.6	21.8
Operating profit margin	12.1	12.0	11.9	11.8	11.9

Your new assistant wonders why upper management is so happy that the inventory turnover, the accounts receivable turnover, the gross profit margin, and the operating profit margin all increased this year. Explain why an increase in each of these items is a positive indicator.

E14-16
Obj. 4
P̸T

The selected information below has been taken from the last two annual reports of Rasheed Company.

	2005	2004
Accounts receivable	$ 1,466	$ 1,330
Merchandise inventory	2,093	1,947
Total assets	13,707	12,829
Total stockholders' equity	4,386	4,180
Sales revenue	14,472	13,971
Cost of goods sold	11,481	11,606
Operating income	1,636	1,509
Net income	1,170	1,020
Interest expense	1,000	900
Fixed assets	8,000	7,500

a. Compute each of the following ratios for both years.
  1. Inventory turnover
  2. Accounts receivable turnover
  3. Gross profit margin
  4. Operating profit margin
  5. Profit margin
  6. Asset turnover
  7. Return on assets
  8. Return on equity
  9. Times interest earned
  10. Day's sales in inventory
  11. Average accounts receivable collection period
  12. Fixed asset turnover

(Continued)

b. Has the company's financial performance improved or deteriorated during the most recent year? Was the firm more effective, more efficient, both, or neither? Which factors contributed to the improvement? Did any factors hurt overall performance? Explain.

E14-17
Obj. 4

Your assistant has just provided you with your company's latest financial results. Unfortunately, several of the numbers are smudged and unreadable. They are each represented below by a letter.

Balance sheet (as of month-end)		Income statement (as of month-end)		
Cash	$ 482	Sales revenue		$10,377
Accounts receivable	(a)	Cost of goods sold		6,226
Merchandise inventory	(b)	Gross profit		(f)
Buildings and equipment	$3,411	Operating expenses:		
Accumulated depreciation	(922)	Advertising	$350	
Investments, long-term	250	Depreciation	500	
Land	980	Rent	(g)	
Total assets	$ (c)	Wages	376	(h)
		Income before taxes		$ 1,945
Accounts payable	$ 977	Income taxes (35%)		(i)
Notes payable, long-term	(d)	Net income		$ (j)
Common stock	3,400			
Retained earnings	1,491			
Total liabilities and equity	$ (e)			
Summary ratio values				
1. Accounts receivable turnover	5.62			
2. Inventory turnover	7.15			
3. Return on assets	18.27			
4. Return on equity	(k)			

Determine the missing amounts above. (Round amounts to the nearest dollar.)

E14-18
Obj. 5

The following information was taken from the 2001 annual report of **General Electric Company** (in billions).

Net income	$ 13.7
Interest expense	11.1
Total assets	495.0
Total stockholders' equity	54.8

Calculate return on assets and return on equity. What conclusions can you draw about the effect of financial leverage on return to stockholders? Will financial leverage benefit stockholders under all conditions?

E14-19
Obj. 5

Bootstrap Computer Company reported the following summary information in its annual report.

	2004
Sales	$27,000
Net income	5,049
Total assets	60,108
Stockholders' equity	40,070
Fixed assets	25,000
Income before interest & taxes	10,278
Interest expense	2,500

a. Compute each of the following ratios:
   i. Profit margin
   ii. Asset turnover
   iii. Return on assets
   iv. Return on equity
   v. Fixed asset turnover
   vi. Times interest earned

b. Explain how the return on equity measure includes information about all three activities in the transformation process.

E14-20
Obj. 5
P/T

The following summary information is taken from the annual reports of **McDonald's Corporation** and **Wendy's International**. All amounts are in millions.

	McDonald's		Wendy's	
	2001	**2000**	**2001**	**2000**
Sales revenue	$14,870	$14,243	$2,391	$2,237
Operating income	2,697	3,330	307	271
Net income	1,637	1,977	194	170
Total assets	22,535	21,684	2,076	1,958
Stockholders' equity	9,488	9,204	1,030	1,126

a. Compute profit margin, asset turnover, return on assets, financial leverage, and return on equity for both firms for both years.

b. Which company is more profitable? What similarities or differences do you observe in how these two companies earned their profits during the periods shown?

E14-21
Objs. 5, 6
P/T

Market to book value links company value to accounting numbers. It is related to a variety of attributes. Complete the table below by indicating whether the value of each attribute indicates a high market to book value company or a low one. The first item is completed as an example.

Attribute	Magnitude of Attribute	Expected Company Value
Asset growth	High	High
Debt to assets	Low	
Dividend payout	Low	
Equity growth	Low	
Investing cash outflow	High	
Operating cash inflow	Low	
Research and development expenditure	High	
Return on assets	Low	
Return on equity	High	
Sales growth	High	

E14-22
Obj. 6
P/T

Accounting reports provide a variety of information for evaluating a company. For each accounting number in the following list, write the letter from the description in the right-hand column that indicates the type of information provided by the number.

Accounting Information

_____ Asset turnover
_____ Financial leverage
_____ Growth in assets
_____ Growth in equity
_____ Growth in sales
_____ Growth in return on equity
_____ Investing cash flow
_____ Operating cash flow
_____ Profit margin
_____ Research and development
_____ Return on assets
_____ Return on equity
_____ Fixed asset turnover
_____ Times interest earned
_____ Day's sales in inventory
_____ Average accounts receivable collection period

Description

a. Ability to create value for stockholders from operating activities
b. Measures the effectiveness of a company in using its investment in fixed assets to create sales
c. Ability to generate sales from total investment
d. Ability to generate profit from sales
e. Use of debt to increase return to stockholders
f. The ratio of operating income to interest expense
g. Direction and amount of change in future return on equity
h. Potential for higher return
i. The ratio of accounts receivable to average daily sales
j. Reinvestment of earnings to increase value of company for stockholders
k. Reinvestment of operating cash to increase value of company for stockholders
l. Growth potential through innovation
m. Ability to create value from total investment
n. Source of cash for new investment and payments to stockholders
o. Ratio of inventory to average daily cost of goods sold
p. Potential for additional sales from increased investment

E14-23 Following is the income statement and balance sheet of a company that just sold stock to the
Obj. 6 public for the first time.

Balance sheet at July 31, 2004	
Cash	$ 3,500
Accounts receivable	2,000
Inventory	1,700
Buildings, net	18,000
Total assets	$25,200
Accounts payable	$ 1,500
Wages payable	500
Common stock	10,000
Retained earnings	13,200
Total liabilities and equity	$25,200

Income statement for July 2004	
Sales revenue	$5,000
Cost of sales	1,000
Gross profit	$4,000
Operating expenses:	
Wages	$ 500
Depreciation	400
Interest	200
Operating income	$2,900
Income taxes	1,015
Net income	$1,885

The following terms are described under Objective 6 in this chapter. Find and list examples
of each of these concepts in the financial statements above.

a. Measurement units
b. Historical costs
c. Accrual basis
d. Fiscal periods
e. Matched
f. Estimation

PROBLEMS

*If your instructor is using Personal Trainer in this course, you may complete online the assign-
ments identified by $\frac{P}{T}$.*

P14-1 **Return Analysis**
Obj. 2
$\frac{P}{T}$

Information is provided below for three manufacturers from their 2001 annual reports.

(In millions)	Caterpillar, Inc. (agricultural machinery)	Kellogg Co. (foods)	Eli Lilly & Co. (pharmaceuticals)
Net sales	$20,450	$ 8,853	$11,543
Net income (loss)	805	474	2,780
Total assets	30,657	10,369	16,434
Total stockholders' equity	5,611	872	7,104

Required

A. Calculate asset turnover, profit margin, return on assets, and return on equity for each
company.
B. Evaluate the relationship between asset turnover and profit margin and between return
on assets and return on equity for the companies.

P14-2

Obj. 2

P/T

Evaluating Operating Strategies

Information is presented below for two furniture companies.

(In thousands)	Colony	Vernon
Operating revenues	$1,360	$1,440
Net income	180	130
Total assets	1,900	1,370
Fixed assets	1,400	1,000

Required

A. Compute profit margin, asset turnover, fixed asset turnover, and return on assets for each company.
B. Compare the operating strategies of the two companies and explain which company is doing the better job with its strategy.
C. Using the information presented, discuss how each company could improve its profits and return on assets.

P14-3

Objs. 1, 2, 3

P/T

Operating Strategy Decisions and Product Pricing

You are working as an assistant to the vice president for marketing at Long Life Incorporated, a startup manufacturer of a healthy, minimally refined breakfast cereal. Since little processing will be done, much of the cost of the product will be in the premium ingredients. The company will be investing $3 million in processing and packaging facilities to produce a maximum of 15,000 cases of cereal per month. It will advertise and market only in a restricted regional area in the foreseeable future, although expansion is possible in the long run. Fixed costs for operating the facility will be approximately $85,000 per month. Variable costs, primarily for ingredients and labor, are expected to be approximately $17 per case.

In the past, most cereals of this sort have been sold at specialty stores for high prices. However, in recent years, some have moved into supermarkets at prices that are competitive with those of traditional cereals. A marketing research study has given you estimated results after the first year for three possible scenarios:

1. Sell to supermarkets for $29 per case, spend $25,000 per month on advertising, and sell approximately 11,000 cases per month. The average price grocery stores pay competitors for a case of this size is $30, and $25,000 is a minimal monthly budget for advertising in the local area.
2. Sell to supermarkets for $31 per case, spend $40,000 per month on advertising, and sell approximately 12,000 cases per month.
3. Sell to specialty stores for $34 per case, spend only $7,000 per month advertising in health food periodicals, and sell approximately 7,500 cases per month.

Required

A. Prepare a schedule (using the format on the next page) that shows the pro forma (or expected) profit from each scenario.
B. Write a report for your company president and vice presidents in which you analyze each of the above strategies and make a recommendation concerning which one to choose.
C. Also include discussion of any long-term trends and other outside factors that you feel should be considered in making this strategic decision.

(Continued)

	Strategy 1	Strategy 2	Strategy 3
Selling price per case			
Estimated monthly sales (cases)			
Sales revenue			
Expenses:			
Fixed, per month			
Advertising, per month			
Variable per case			
Total monthly expenses			
Pro forma monthly profit			
Pro forma annual profit			
% return on $3 million investment			

P14-4 Product Pricing Decisions

Objs. 1, 3

You have been hired as a marketing manager for NuTech Appliance Company. The company manufactures major home appliances, such as refrigerators, stoves, and dishwashers. NuTech is about to add a new dishwasher to its lineup. The new appliance will have standard features, appearance, and quality, except that it will be considerably quieter than similar models from the competition.

The president of the company, Marta Feliz, has asked you to prepare a memo describing the factors you believe the company should consider in pricing the new product.

Required Write a memo to Feliz. Describe the measurement or measurements you would hope to maximize through a pricing decision. Then explain what factors should be considered, including information from within and outside of the company. Describe estimates that you would want to develop before making a final pricing decision.

P14-5 Assessing Operating Strategies

Objs. 2, 3

Discount Shoes and Elegant Footwear are both retail shoe companies. Both have outlets in major cities throughout the United States. Discount Shoes uses a cost leadership strategy, and Elegant Footwear uses a product differentiation strategy.

Required Answer each of the following questions.

A. What differences would you expect to observe between the two companies with respect to the location and design of their stores, the types of products they sell, and the types of service they provide?
B. Compare the companies' expected sales revenues, cost of goods sold, operating expenses, merchandise inventory, and plant assets based on the strategies they use to generate profits.

P14-6 Comparing Operating Strategies

Objs. 2, 3

Companies' operating strategies often result in differences in the following attributes: (a) types of products, (b) sales price per unit, (c) profit margin, (d) asset turnover, and (e) amount invested in assets.

Required Discuss the types of competitive strategies a company might use and how each strategy would affect each of the attributes listed above. What factors are likely to affect the strategy selected by a company?

P14-7 Accrual- and Cash-Based Measurement of Success

Objs. 2, 3, 4

The information below is extracted from the 2001 annual reports of three personal computer companies.

(In millions)	Compaq 2001	Compaq 2000	Apple 2001	Apple 2000	Dell 2001	Dell 2000
Sales	$33,554	$42,222	$5,363	$7,983	$31,168	$31,888
Net income (loss)	(785)	569	(25)	786	1,246	2,177
Total assets	23,689	24,856	6,021	6,803	13,535	13,670
Operating cash flow	1,482	565	185	868	3,797	4,195

Required Use appropriate analytical tools, including ratios, to answer the following questions.

A. Which company is most successful at generating net income from its assets?
B. Does this greater success result from the company using its assets more effectively to generate sales or from its generating greater profit from its sales? How do the profit margins compare?
C. Which company is most successful at generating cash flow from its assets?

P14-8 **Analyzing Cash Flow from Operations**

Obj. 4

$\frac{P}{T}$

Selected information is presented below for two companies that compete in the same industry.

	Park Enterprises		Schleifer, Inc.	
	2005	2004	2005	2004
Sales revenue	$1,811	$1,476	$1,967	$2,212
Cost of goods sold	1,391	1,137	1,773	1,641
Ending accounts receivable	317	314	299	386
Ending inventory	115	216	132	355
From the statement of cash flows:				
Net income	$ 131	$ 79	$ (163)	$ 85
Depreciation and amortization	29	21	31	25
(Increase) decrease in accounts receivable	(21)	(86)	87	(70)
(Increase) decease in inventory	100	(14)	223	(137)
Increase (decrease) in accounts payable and other current liabilities	121	62	(32)	55
Other items	(19)	26	(41)	(5)
Cash flow from operations	$ 341	$ 88	$ 105	$ (47)

Required Using this information, examine the details of how each company generates cash from operations.

A. Determine which company requires less time to convert inventory to sales. Consider this in relation to gross profit margins.
B. Determine which company requires less time to collect its receivables from its customers.
C. For each company and each year, examine and comment on the differences between net income and cash flow from operations. What does this show you about the operating strengths or weaknesses of the companies?

P14-9   Evaluating Operating Performance

Obj. 4

P/T

The following information was taken from the 2005 annual report of Hogar Products, Inc. The company manufactures a wide variety of household products.

Year ended December 31	2005	2004	2003
(In millions, except per share data)			
Net sales	$3,720	$3,336	$2,973
Cost of products sold	2,548	2,260	2,020
Gross income	$1,172	$1,076	$ 953
Selling, general, and administrative expenses	583	498	462
Trade names and goodwill amortization	55	32	24
Operating income	$ 534	$ 546	$ 467
Nonoperating (income) expenses:			
Interest expense	60	76	59
Other, net	(211)	(15)	(18)
Income before taxes	$ 685	$ 485	$ 426
Income taxes	289	192	169
Net income	$ 396	$ 293	$ 257
Earnings per share:			
Basic	$2.44	$1.81	$1.60
Diluted	$2.38	$1.80	$1.60

Required

A. How much did sales grow from 2003 to 2004 and from 2004 to 2005?
B. Restate each item on the income statement (except earnings per share) as a percent of net sales. [Hint: Sales always = 100%; 2005 cost of product sold = 68.5% ($2,548 ÷ $3,720).]
C. What have the changes in relative revenues and expenses had on operating income and net income over the three-year period?
D. What conclusions can you draw about the company's operating leverage? Are most of its costs fixed or variable?

P14-10   Evaluating Operating Performance and Efficiency

Obj. 4

P/T

Information is provided below for **Coca-Cola Company** and **PepsiCo, Inc.,** for the years 1999–2001.

	Coca-Cola			PepsiCo		
(In millions)	2001	2000	1999	2001	2000	1999
Net sales	$20,092	$19,889	$19,284	$26,935	$25,479	$25,093
Gross profit	14,048	13,685	13,275	16,181	15,253	14,767
Operating profit	5,352	3,691	3,982	4,021	3,818	3,483
Net income	3,969	2,177	2,431	2,662	2,543	2,505

Required

A. Compute the three ratios that reflect operating efficiency.
B. Discuss the operating performance of Coca-Cola and PepsiCo using the information you obtained in part A.

P14-11   Evaluating Operating Performance and Effectiveness

Obj. 4

P/T

Information is provided below for Coca-Cola Company and PepsiCo, Inc. for 2001 and 2000.

	Coca-Cola		PepsiCo	
(In millions)	2001	2000	2001	2000
Net sales	$20,092	$19,889	$26,935	$25,479
Cost of sales	6,044	6,204	10,754	10,226
Net income	3,969	2,177	2,662	2,543
Total assets	22,417	20,834	21,695	20,757
Accounts receivable, net	1,882	1,757	2,142	2,129
Inventories	1,055	1,066	1,310	1,192
Cash from operations	4,110	3,585	4,201	4,440

Required

A. Prepare a schedule showing the values of three turnover ratios for each company for the two years shown.

B. Discuss the effectiveness of Coca-Cola and PepsiCo using the results of these turnover ratios.

C. Using this information, discuss the cash operating performance of Coca-Cola and PepsiCo.

P14-12   Analyzing Cash Flow from Operations

Obj. 4

Information is provided below for **Hasbro, Inc.** and PepsiCo, Inc.

	Hasbro		PepsiCo	
(In millions)	**2001**	**2000**	**2001**	**2000**
Net income	$ 60	$ (145)	$ 2,662	$ 2,543
Depreciation and amortization	226	264	1,082	1,093
Increase (decrease) from changes in current assets and liabilities:				
Accounts and notes receivable	99	396	7	(52)
Inventories	109	70	(75)	(51)
Prepaid expenses and other current assets	46	(84)	(6)	(35)
Accounts payable, accrued liabilities, and income taxes payable	(195)	(292)	158	554
Other adjustments	27	(46)	373	388
Cashflows from operations	$ 372	$ 163	$ 4,201	$ 4,440
Total assets	$3,369	$3,828	$21,695	$20,757
Accounts receivable and notes receivable, net	572	686	2,142	2,129
Inventories	217	335	1,310	1,192
Net sales	2,856	3,787	26,935	25,479
Cost of goods sold	1,223	1,674	10,754	10,226

Required

A. Compare the two companies as to their ratios of operating cash flow to total assets and their ratios of operating cash flow to net income.

B. Compare the two companies as to their ability to convert revenues to cash.

P14-13   Linking Operating, Investing, and Financing Activities

Objs. 3, 4, 5

Information is provided below for **Minnesota Mining and Manufacturing Corporation** (known as 3M) and **Eastman Chemical Co.** for 2001 and 2000.

	3M Corp.		Eastman Chemical	
(In millions)	**2001**	**2000**	**2001**	**2000**
Net sales	$16,079	$16,724	$5,390	$5,292
Net income (loss)	1,430	1,782	(175)	303
Total assets	14,606	14,522	6,092	6,550
Total stockholders' equity	6,086	6,531	1,382	1,812

Required

A. Calculate profit margin, asset turnover, return on assets, financial leverage, and return on equity.

B. Discuss the results and compare the companies' effectiveness, efficiency, operating strategy, use of investments in assets, and financing activity.

P14-14   Comparing Results from Different Operating Strategies

Objs. 3, 5

Big Bend, Inc. and Longbow, Ltd. have both been in the chemical business for several decades. Each has developed a strong reputation in the industry and both are known for strong management. Big Bend tends to sell specialty products in small batches that are custom made.

(Continued)

Longbow operates more in large-scale sales of commodity-type products that become raw material for a wide variety of plastics and polymers. Selected information is presented below for two recent fiscal periods.

(In millions)	Big Bend		Longbow	
	2005	2004	2005	2004
Total assets	$34.2	30.2	$ 38.2	36.1
Total stockholders' equity	9.96	8.82	17.3	16.3
Sales revenue	40.3	35.9	206.5	193.3
Net income	3.68	3.13	6.4	5.8

Required

A. Considering only the brief written descriptions of the two firms, would you expect one or the other to use a product differentiation strategy? Or cost leadership strategy? Explain.
B. Compute the profit margin, asset turnover, and return on assets for 2005 for both firms. Are your expectations from part A borne out by the data for 2005?
C. What changes in profit margin, asset turnover, and return on assets have occurred between 2004 and 2005?
D. Compute the return on equity for both firms for both years.
E. Which is a more successful strategy, product differentiation or cost leadership? Explain.

P14-15   **Evaluating Growth and Value**

Obj. 5

$\frac{P}{T}$

Information is provided below from the 2002 annual reports of **Sara Lee Corporation** and **Dell Computer**.

(In millions)	2002	2001	2000	1999	1998
Sara Lee					
Total assets	$13,753	$10,167	$11,611	$10,292	$10,784
Common stockholders' equity	1,742	1,122	1,234	1,266	1,816
Sales	17,628	16,632	16,454	16,277	16,526
Dell					
Total assets	$13,535	$13,670	$11,471	$ 6,877	$ 4,268
Common stockholders' equity	4,694	5,622	5,308	2,321	1,293
Sales	31,168	31,888	25,265	18,243	12,327

Required

A. Calculate the annual growth in assets, common equity, and sales for each company from 1998 through 2002. (Hint: To compute the growth rate from year to year, use the following formula—[(later year amount − earlier year amount) ÷ earlier year amount].)
B. Evaluate and compare the two companies' growth rates. As an investor, would the difference in growth rates make one firm more attractive as an investment than the other? Explain.

P14-16 **Connecting Operating Activities, Financing Activities, and Value**

Obj. 5
P
T

Billboards–R–Us and Outdoor SignCorp have the following selected information available.

	2005	2004	2003	2002
Billboards–R–Us:				
Total assets	$12,431	$11,665	$10,862	$ 9,989
Stockholders' equity	3,939	3,326	3,551	3,382
Net income (millions)	804	199	704	761
Diluted earnings per share	1.62	0.37	1.40	1.54
Market value per share	28.50	20.63	24.25	24.81
Total market value	13,680	9,902	11,761	11,810
Outdoor SignCorp:				
Total assets	$ 6,101	$ 5,533	$ 4,828	$ 4,077
Stockholders' equity	2,246	1,816	1,390	1,528
Net income (millions)	740	694	331	644
Diluted earnings per share	5.48	5.17	2.45	4.78
Market value per share	97.13	77.00	67.50	69.13
Total market value	13,112	10,326	9,113	9,311

Required

A. Calculate the return on assets, return on equity, and market to book value for each year.
B. Evaluate the effects that operating activities and financing activities appear to have had on the value of each company to its stockholders.
C. Has the stock price responded as you would expect? Explain.

P14-17 **Evaluating Operating Performance**

Obj. 5
P
T

Information is provided below for two companies that produce and sell audio-magnification devices for the hearing impaired.

	John, Inc.		Roberta Company	
	2005	2004	2005	2004
Sales revenue	825	770	352	330
Cost of goods sold	540	504	250	216
Gross profit	285	266	102	114
Operating expenses	168	189	70	60
Operating income	117	77	32	54
Interest expense	30	20	10	8
Income before tax	87	57	22	46
Tax	30	20	8	16
Net income	57	37	14	30
Accounts receivable	78	73	39	34
Inventories	139	136	85	71
Fixed assets	900	850	600	550
Total assets	1,630	1,530	850	765

Required

A. For each company and each year, compute the following measures:
   1. Profit margin
   2. Gross profit margin
   3. Operating profit margin
   4. Asset turnover
   5. Accounts receivable turnover
   6. Inventory turnover
   7. Return on assets
   8. Fixed asset turnover
   9. Times interest earned
   10. Day's sales in inventory
   11. Average collection period for accounts receivable

(Continued)

B. For each year, prepare a schedule summarizing which company had the better value of each ratio.

C. Prepare a schedule that shows, for each company, whether the value of each ratio improved or declined.

D. Which firm had the stronger operating performance during the periods studied? Briefly summarize why.

P14-18 Usefulness and Limitations of Financial Statement Information

Obj. 6

You work as part of a team that selects parts suppliers for a large manufacturer. Your company is highly dependent on your suppliers, and you want long-term relationships. You want suppliers who are financially stable, without cash flow problems. If they need more capacity in order to grow with you, you want them to be able to attract additional investors.

One of your team members claims that financial statements tell you everything you need to know to determine the future stability and growth potential of a supplier. Another claims that financial statements are useless in the process, and that talking with the people in the company is the only route to judging its future.

Required Discuss the strengths and weaknesses of financial statements in assisting you as you try to determine the stability and growth potential of possible suppliers. What can you learn about a company from a standard set of financial statements? What are the limitations of financial statements? What would you look at in the statements to judge a supplier's ability to remain in business and avoid cash flow problems? What relationships in the statements would help you judge whether the company could attract additional capital for growth?

P14-19 Value of Accounting and Auditing Standards

Obj. 6

In the United States, the Financial Accounting Standards Board sets measurement and reporting standards for financial statements. For large companies, the Securities and Exchange Commission imposes some additional standards. The Auditing Standards Board of the American Institute of CPAs determines standards for conducting an audit. Similar bodies perform these functions in other countries. A major effort is being made to set worldwide standards.

Required Describe and evaluate these standards, answering the following questions.

A. What are measurement and reporting standards?

B. Why are measurement and reporting standards important to users of financial statements?

C. What is an audit?

D. Why are auditing standards important to financial statement users?

E. What advantages and disadvantages do you see to having separate accounting and auditing standards for each country?

P14-20 Excel in Action

P/T

Accounting information is provided below for The Book Wermz and two of its competitors for the fiscal year ending December 31, 2005.

SPREADSHEET

	The Book Wermz	Book Farm	Special Editions
Sales	$6,230,000	$20,584,000	$4,896,200
Cost of goods sold	3,426,500	13,390,200	2,153,100
Operating expense	2,155,000	5,212,600	1,852,000
Interest expense	190,000	670,500	106,000
Inventory	1,987,600	5,845,000	2,246,000
Total assets	5,623,000	13,254,000	6,895,000
Stockholders' equity	3,370,000	6,687,000	4,826,000

Required Enter the data in a spreadsheet. Use the data to prepare an income statement for each company to include gross profit, operating income, pretax income, and net income. The income tax rate for each company is 35% of pretax income. Use formulas for computed values so that changes in any of the numbers shown above will be recomputed automatically in the spreadsheet. Format the income statement appropriately.

Following the income statement, enter the balance sheet data for each company.

Use the income statement and balance sheet data to calculate the following ratios, which should follow the balance sheet data: gross profit margin, operating profit margin, profit margin, inventory turnover, asset turnover, return on assets, financial leverage (assets/equity), and return on equity. The calculations should use cell references to the income statement and balance sheet data. Each ratio should include four digits to the right of the decimal.

Following the ratios, provide a brief response to the following questions.

1. Which company appears to be using a cost leadership strategy most effectively?
2. Which company appears to be using a product differentiation strategy most effectively?
3. What strategy does The Book Wermz appear to be following and how effective has this strategy been?
4. What effect has financial leverage had on the companies' ratios?

Format each response so that it appears as wrapped text in a cell that is the width of the columns used to enter data in the spreadsheet.

Include the following captions at the top of the spreadsheet: "Financial Analysis Comparison", followed by "December 31, 2005". Captions should be centered over the spreadsheet columns in which accounting information appears.

P14-21   Multiple-Choice Overview of the Chapter

1. If a company sets its product price too high, the primary danger is that
   a. asset turnover will be too low.
   b. gross profit margin will be too low.
   c. inventory turnover will be too high.
   d. accounts receivable turnover will be reduced.

2. A company's profit margin is the ratio of its earnings to its
   a. total assets.
   b. total liabilities.
   c. operating income.
   d. operating revenues.

3. A company that follows a product differentiation strategy tends to have
   a. high profit margin and asset turnover.
   b. low profit margin and asset turnover.
   c. high profit margin and low asset turnover.
   d. low profit margin and high asset turnover.

4. Chrysanthemum Company reported a profit margin of 5% and an asset turnover of 2.0 for the fiscal year. The company's return on assets for the year was
   a. 10%.
   b. 3%.
   c. 2.5%.
   d. 2%.

5. Which company is likely to have the lowest ratio of cash flow from operations to net income?
   a. A shrinking company that is reducing inventory and receivables
   b. A growing company with increasing inventory and receivables
   c. A company with new, expensive assets and high depreciation charges
   d. A company with a growing deferred tax liability

6. High receivables turnover is evidence of
   a. extension of credit to customers who are poor credit risks.
   b. high sales volume.
   c. low efficiency.
   d. rapid collection of cash from customers.

(Continued)

7. A tendency to sell products rapidly is evidenced by
   a. low asset turnover.
   b. high inventory turnover.
   c. high operating leverage.
   d. a cost leadership operating strategy.

8. Which of the following is the strongest indicator of a high-value company?
   a. High market to book value
   b. High gross profit margin
   c. High financial leverage
   d. High ratio of operating cash flow to net income

9. The difference between a company's return on assets and its return on equity can be explained by the company's
   a. operating leverage.
   b. asset turnover.
   c. financial leverage.
   d. profit margin.

10. Accounting can best be defined as
    a. a precise reporting system for giving decision makers a total picture of all events occurring in a business entity.
    b. an information system for measuring the transformation process in a business entity and reporting results to decision makers.
    c. a procedure for recording the transactions of a business entity, usually using a system of debits and credits.
    d. a set of rules, developed by standard-setting bodies, for measuring and reporting.

CASES

C14-1   **Analysis of Operating Activities**

Objs. 3, 4, 5   Appendix B of this book contains a copy of the 2002 annual report of **General Mills, Inc.**

Required Review the annual report and answer each question or follow the directions given.

A. Compute profit margin, asset turnover, and return on assets for the company for 2000 to 2002. Evaluate the changes you see in these measures over the three years. (Hint: See also the six-year financial summary shown in the annual report for the data necessary to make some of your calculations.)

B. Compare your ratio calculations with those in Exhibit 4. Based on this and any other evidence contained in the annual report, does it appear that General Mills is using a cost leadership strategy or a product differentiation strategy?

C. Compute receivables turnover, inventory turnover, and gross profit margin for 2002 and 2001. Evaluate any changes you find.

D. Compute the return on equity for each of the three years and compare it with the return on assets. Do the changes in return on equity result more from changes in net income or from changes in the amount of stockholders' equity?

E. Financial statements present only a partial, highly summarized view of a company. Assume that you are considering investing in General Mills' common stock. List several items that are contained in the statements but are based on estimates. Also list several items you would like to know about the company that are not revealed in this annual report.

C14-2   **Analysis of an Investment**

Objs. 4, 5   You are an investment analyst. Some of your clients have talked with you about an investment they are considering in a new company, Beach Front Resorts. This company will construct condominiums and rent them to tourists. The total investment required for the project is $5.5 million. Individual investors are expected to invest not less than $100,000 each. They could borrow up to this amount at 10% annual interest. The development will contain 50 units that will cost $80,000 per unit to construct. Land for the development will cost $250,000, and $300,000 will be held in reserve for first-year operating costs for the year beginning January 1, 2004. The remaining investment capital will be used for furnishings, streets, parking lots, sidewalks, and landscaping. Buildings will be depreciated over a 20-year period. Other depreciable assets will be depreciated over five years. Straight-line depreciation will be used.

Based on an analysis of similar developments in the area, units should rent for an average of $1,300 per week. Each unit should rent for at least 25 weeks per year. On the average, each unit is expected to rent for 30 weeks per year. Maintenance and operating costs are expected to average $200 per unit-week for 52 weeks. Management costs will be $250,000 per year. A reserve fund will be established with annual reinvestments of profits of $200,000 for future repair and replacement of property. The remaining profits will be distributed to investors in proportion to their investments. The company is not subject to income tax.

Required

A. Calculate the net income and cash flow to investors from operating activities expected from the project in 2004, assuming average rentals of 25 and 30 weeks. Assume that cash flows are equivalent to revenues and expenses except for depreciation. Which is more relevant to the investment decision, net income or cash flow? Why?

B. Assume that investors could expect to receive net cash flows from their investments for 10 years at the amounts expected for 2004. At the end of 10 years, they expect to be able to sell their investments for $1.2 million. What is the present value of the cash flows, assuming 25-week and 30-week average rentals each year? The expected rate of return is 10%.

C. What effect does the company's operating leverage have on its expected operating results?

D. Would you recommend that your clients invest in Beach Front Resorts? What factors are important to this decision other than those considered above?

C14-3 ## Making an Investment Decision

Objs. 4, 5

A friend has given you a hot tip on an investment opportunity in a business venture. You would have to invest $20,000 in the business for a 10% ownership share. The business would import goods from South America and sell them in several large cities in the United States.

The total investment in the company will be $500,000, including debt of $300,000 at 12% interest. The investment will be used to acquire merchandise, equipment, and facilities, and to cover initial operating costs. Expected sales each year will be $1,000,000, though sales could be as low as $700,000. Annual expenses include wages of $100,000 plus sales commissions of 15% of sales, transportation costs of 8% of sales, cost of goods sold of 30% of sales, depreciation of $80,000, insurance and miscellaneous costs of $30,000, and interest. The debt will be repaid along with interest in equal annual installments over a five-year period. The business will operate for five years and then be liquidated. The expected liquidation value is $200,000, after repayment of debt. Each year $100,000 will be reinvested for asset replacement and upkeep. The remaining cash flows will be distributed to the owners.

Required

A. Prepare an income statement for the company for the first year assuming (1) expected sales and (2) minimum sales.

B. Calculate return on assets, return on equity, profit margin, and asset turnover for results based on (1) and (2) above.

C. Determine the annual debt payment and prepare an amortization schedule for the first two years.

D. Prepare a cash flow statement for the company for year 1 based on (1) and (2) in part A above, assuming that all cash flows are approximately equal to revenues and expenses except depreciation. Also, calculate the cash distribution to owners.

E. Assuming that you require a 12% return on your investment, would you invest in this business if annual sales are $1,000,000? If annual sales are $700,000? (Hint: Compare the present value of expected cash distributions to the cost of the investment.)

F. Should you invest in this company? Support your opinion with material from parts A through E and any other factors that you feel are relevant. Evaluate any risks involved, including those related to high financial or operating leverage.

SECTION
M1

Systems for Product Costing and Decision Making

ACCOUNTING AND MANAGEMENT DECISIONS

What basic financial information do we need to run a business?

Erin Stein and Seth Phillips have been friends for many years. Both share a common hobby of designing and making furniture. Recently, Erin and Seth decided to launch a new business, Young Designs, Inc., making children's furniture such as bunk beds. They hope to use their carpentry talents to create a new line of furniture that will be unique and distinctive and to sell the furniture to retail firms such as furniture and department stores. Erin and Seth have begun their business planning. One issue that has arisen is what type of information they will need to properly manage the business. Neither Erin nor Seth has a background in accounting. They decide to visit a local CPA and ask for her advice on how to set up an accounting information system that can provide the right information for management decision making.

FOOD FOR THOUGHT

Imagine yourself in the role of a business adviser. How might you advise Erin and Seth? First, consider what basic activities will be required to establish and run the business. Second, identify what types of business decisions Erin and Seth will need to make that will require the use of financial information. Third, think about what basic types of financial information will be needed to make these decisions. Now, let's join the conversation Erin and Seth are having with their accountant, Roberta Hernandez.

Roberta: *First, to establish the business, you will need to decide what pieces of furniture you intend to produce and project how much of each piece you will sell. Then, you will need to decide what types of equipment and how many employees will be needed to manufacture the furniture.*

Erin: *Seth and I have already discussed our planned sales by product and the equipment we will need. Our projections allow for substantial growth in both types of products and sales for the first few years of the business. We will also need information about the cost of operating and maintaining this equipment, the cost of raw materials used to make the furniture, and the cost of the labor to produce it.*

Roberta: *Excellent. You will likely need information about the cost of making the furniture to determine how to price your products and whether your profit margins are acceptable. Also, have you thought about how much cash you will need?*

Seth: *I assumed we could collect enough cash from our customers to meet our needs.*

Roberta: *You will have to purchase raw materials and labor to make the furniture and then pay for these resources before you collect from the customers. Consequently, you need enough cash to take care of obligations for materials and labor until you are paid by customers. Also, your cash requirements will likely grow as the business grows, so you will need to plan on growth in cash along with growth in sales.*

Erin: *That's fine for starting up the business, but what about once it is up and running?*

Roberta: *Periodically, perhaps once a month, you will need to have information about how well the business is doing in terms of sales, cost of manufacturing, costs of selling and administration, and profitability. This will enable you to better manage sales and costs. You will also want to know the financial condition of your business in terms of assets and liabilities and cash flows. I suggest both monthly and annual budgets. That way, each period you can compare how well your business is actually performing to how well you expected it to perform when you created the budget.*

OBJECTIVES

Once you have completed this chapter, you should be able to:

1 Explain the purpose of managerial accounting and why it is important.

2 Explain the role of managerial accounting in planning and control decisions.

3 Discuss ways in which managerial accounting interacts with marketing and operations.

4 Explain the scope of managerial accounting.

INTRODUCTION TO MANAGERIAL ACCOUNTING

OBJECTIVE 1

Explain the purpose of managerial accounting and why it is important.

Managerial accounting **is the process of preparing, reporting, and interpreting accounting information for use by an organization's internal decision makers.** Different management functions within a company, such as marketing and operations, require types of accounting information for decision making that differ from the needs of external decision makers and from those of other managers. For example, marketing managers consider the cost per unit of a product when they determine a price for that product. On the other hand, operations managers may be interested in the cost of the labor, materials, and overhead required to make the product. Thus, the needs for managerial accounting information differ depending on the types of decisions being made.

Also, new demands for information arise as the business environment changes. For instance, as the profit earned on a line of products begins to shrink, accurate information about the cost of manufacturing the product becomes critical if the product is to remain profitable. A shrinking profit may indicate a shift in consumer preferences and a need to change the way a company competes. In that instance, the company may need to become a low-cost producer rather than competing on the basis of product features or quality.

Changes in companies' strategies have taken place in recent years because of intense foreign competition and the growing complexity of business. These changes have increased demand for accurate, high-quality managerial accounting information. However, systems that produce high-quality information often are expensive. The more detailed and accurate the information, the more it costs to produce. This cost includes the cost of the accounting systems that produce information and the cost of the services of the employees who design and manage these systems. Therefore, companies must balance the level of detail and accuracy they demand from their accounting systems in order to make good business decisions with what is affordable.

Corporate Structure and Accounting Information Needs

As companies grow, they divide managerial responsibilities among a larger number of people. Businesses frequently are organized according to functions to assist in decision making and control. For example, a company might be structured around the functions of accounting, finance, information systems, marketing, and production. Middle managers report to the company's top managers. Top managers develop company goals and the plans to achieve these goals. Top management also is responsible for reporting to stockholders, creditors, and other external decision makers. As illustrated in Exhibit 1, the types of information that different decision makers need depend on their positions in an organization's structure. Those at the top of the structure require less detailed and timely information about the ongoing operations of a company than those at the bottom of the structure.

Each function in a business usually has subdivisions, resulting in an organization with several layers of management. Typically, the higher managers are in the structure,

Exhibit 1

Types of Users and Information Needs

Users	Accounting Information Needs
External Users	
Stockholders, creditors	Summary information about performance for a period of time (financial accounting)
Top Management	
Board of directors	Information for evaluating performance,
Chief executive officer	for establishing goals, and for devising plans to meet goals (financial and managerial accounting)
Functional and Division Managers	
Accounting	Timely and detailed information for
Finance	evaluating performance and implementing
Information systems	plans (primarily managerial accounting)
Marketing	
Operations	
Product and territory sales managers	
Plant managers	
Middle Managers	
Sales representatives	Very timely and detailed information for
Production managers	day-to-day decisions to achieve
Purchasing managers	company goals (managerial accounting)
Service managers	

the more responsibility they have for results and the more authority they have to make decisions. These decisions often require information that is more timely and detailed than the information required by external decision makers. Therefore, in markets where the prices and costs of products change frequently, marketing managers may need continuous information about product costs to make profitable sales.

Some of the accounting information used for internal decision making is the same as that reported to external decision makers. For example, the product cost information used for internal decisions also may be used in valuing inventories for a company's financial statements. Top managers often examine financial accounting information to evaluate a company's overall performance. However, the managerial accounting information provided to decision makers within the organization differs in many respects from the information reported externally. These differences will be considered in this and future chapters.

Financial accounting provides information that conforms with generally accepted accounting principles (GAAP). GAAP help to ensure that information is consistent from period to period and is comparable across companies. This information is valuable particularly to stakeholders, such as stockholders and creditors, who have limited access to information about companies.

An accountant who produces managerial accounting information for a specific company is referred to as a *management accountant.* Because managerial accounting information is used only within a company, it does not have to conform to GAAP. Rather, it is produced in a variety of formats that meet the particular information needs of a company's managers. Thus, the type, format, amount of detail, and timeliness of the information differ between financial and managerial accounting.

The Changing Needs of Business

Prior to World War II, the United States produced about one-fourth of the world's total goods and services. After World War II, all of the world's major economies except the United States had been severely damaged by the war. In contrast, the United States emerged with a huge productive capacity, greatly increased by the war effort, and a labor force swollen by returning veterans. As a result, following the war, the United States produced about one-half of the world's total goods and services. Most products consumed in the United States were produced in this country. In this type of environment, U.S. businesses could survive using less than optimal business practices. The situation began to change, however, with the growth of economies in Western Europe and Asia during the 1960s and 1970s. Foreign competitors seriously challenged U.S. companies with high-quality, technologically sophisticated products. U.S. companies had to change if they were to remain competitive in a global economy.

In recent years, changes in the ways companies market and produce their goods and services have led to changes in managers' needs for accounting information. For example, increased foreign competition has led U.S. firms to place more emphasis on the quality of the goods and services they produce. This emphasis on quality and the increasing complexity of business have increased the demand for timely and accurate information, thereby changing the role of managerial accounting.

Competition is driving many manufacturing and service companies to redesign their marketing and operations to meet the demands of a changing marketplace. Examples of such changes are just-in-time manufacturing, time-based competition, and total quality management, which are described later in this chapter. Managerial accounting systems are being redesigned to meet the changing information needs caused by these changes in the way products and services are created and delivered.

Today, many U.S. businesses are changing their management philosophies to become more competitive. These changes frequently involve:

- New marketing strategies directed at global markets
- Emphasis on customer satisfaction, including a focus on product quality and variety
- Large investments in new production technologies, including increased reliance on robotics and computerized manufacturing
- New relationships between management and labor that emphasize a greater role for labor in many decisions
- Creation of management teams to make key business decisions with representatives from the various functional areas of business, including accounting
- Development of real-time (immediate) business information systems, including use of the Internet to facilitate communication within a company and between a company and its stakeholders

These changes have created a new business environment, which has brought a high degree of product and service complexity, a greater number of parts that go into products, and new types of business transactions.

Managerial accounting must change in two ways if businesses are to compete successfully in this new competitive environment. First, management accountants must become involved in making decisions about a company's products and the processes used to create, market, and deliver these products. Through this involvement, management accountants can identify the critical accounting information needs of other decision makers. Second, decision makers throughout a company must be able to use accounting information properly. This means that decision makers must have a knowledge of managerial accounting concepts and techniques. It also means that they must be aware of the potential inaccuracies in accounting information. Companies that fail to make these changes in their managerial accounting systems are likely to receive inadequate information that leads to poor decisions.

The Quality of Accounting Information

The quality of information must be weighed against its cost. To be useful, information must have the potential to affect decisions and influence behavior. If a company is to perform well, information must be accurate enough to lead to the right decisions and behaviors. Accounting information often is not as accurate as many decision makers believe, however.

Accountants and managers select the methods used to produce accounting information. GAAP permit choices among methods of measuring certain business activities and reporting them to external decision makers, such as the choice of inventory and depreciation methods. Estimation also is used in preparing accounting information, such as estimation of the expected useful lives of depreciable assets. When accounting information is prepared for *internal purposes*, a company is not restricted to any particular accounting method. Nevertheless, companies often use the same accounting methods for internal purposes that they use for external purposes. Unfortunately, accounting systems and methods designed for external reporting are not always well suited for internal use. For example, GAAP require the use of historical costs in accounting for plant assets. Using historical costs in plant replacement decisions, however, may lead to poor decisions.

The decision about using financial accounting systems for internal purposes usually involves weighing the increased accuracy that comes from a separate management accounting system against the costs of maintaining two systems. Greater accuracy in accounting information is costly, because greater accuracy frequently involves more extensive data collection. Thus, a company must decide how much accuracy it needs and how much it is willing to pay for this accuracy. Further, **a particular accounting system that is adequate for one company may be inadequate for another because of differences in strategies, markets, production and delivery systems, and controls.**

All accounting systems rely on assumptions and choices, such as the choice of LIFO or FIFO to estimate inventory and cost of goods sold. The usefulness of an accounting system depends largely on how well these assumptions fit the intended purpose of the information. For example, if products are sold separately, accurate costs for each individual product are needed, but the accuracy of individual product costs may not be as important if products are sold only as a bundle. Therefore, the following are important questions when assessing the adequacy of managerial accounting systems:

- What is the intended use of the information produced by a system?
- How accurate does the information need to be?
- Is greater accuracy worth the additional cost?

1 SELF-STUDY PROBLEM

Miko Song is chief executive officer of a manufacturing company that produces paper products. Lars Dalton is head of one of the company's manufacturing plants. Deborah Styles is in charge of scheduling production in one of the plant's production processes that converts paperboard into containers.

Required Explain why the accounting information needs of the three managers are different and briefly describe the type of information needed by each.

The solution to Self-Study Problem 1 appears at the end of the chapter.

THE ROLE OF MANAGERIAL ACCOUNTING IN PLANNING AND CONTROL

OBJECTIVE 2

Explain the role of managerial accounting in planning and control decisions.

Managerial accounting traditionally has been viewed as providing information needed for two management functions, planning and control. Planning and control are important for business success. Managerial accounting information is very important to planning and control.

Recall the issues faced by Erin and Seth in the scenario at the beginning of the chapter. They were deciding what types of financial information are needed for their new business. This decision really revolves around planning and control. Exhibit 2 illustrates the planning and control process. Managers **(a) develop goals,** such as a target return on assets, which are major outcomes desired by top management. Next, managers **(b) set specific objectives,** such as target income for each division of the company, and **(c) develop plans** for achieving these objectives. Then management **(d) implements**

Exhibit 2

The Planning and
Control Process

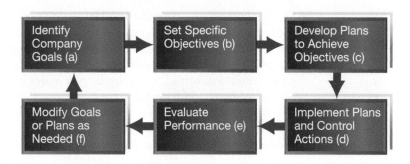

the plans and controls the actions of employees to ensure proper execution of the plans. Managers **(e) evaluate the performance of products, services, activities, and people** who are responsible for them. As feedback about how well plans are being met is received, adjustments are made. This means that management **(f) modifies its goals** or changes its plans or procedures for meeting these goals. The process then is repeated. Managerial accounting provides financial numbers used in making these planning and control decisions.

As an illustration, consider the process of purchasing various types of synthetic fiber used to make carpet at Charles Robert Carpets (CRC), a manufacturer of carpet for automobiles, recreational vehicles, and boats. Before the beginning of the year, management sets a goal to maintain production costs at a specific level (a). It establishes a specific objective by identifying a planned cost for each type of synthetic fiber used in its products (b). The purchasing department, which is responsible for purchasing all raw materials used in production, is held accountable for meeting this objective. It creates a plan to meet the objective by identifying sources of materials and negotiating costs with suppliers (c). The purchasing department buys the materials at the agreed-upon costs (d). After the year begins, the vice president of operations, who is responsible for the purchasing department, receives periodic reports identifying the actual cost of various types of fiber and comparing these costs to planned costs (e). If the actual costs exceed the planned costs, the differences are investigated to determine their cause. The production cost goal may have to be adjusted, or a new source of materials may be sought in order to achieve the existing goal (f).

Planning

Planning involves creating a map for achieving corporate goals and objectives. Planning can be strategic or operational. **Strategic planning involves identifying a company's long-run goals and developing plans for achieving these goals.** Strategic plans often involve large investments. Strategic decisions include starting a new line of products, building a new plant, or entering a foreign market for the first time. In Erin and Seth's case, they have to decide what types of furniture Young Designs, Inc., will make. This illustrates a strategic decision since it will impact the long-term activities and success of the business.

An example of strategic planning at CRC is a long-term plan for financing a new line of boat carpets. Strategic planning almost always involves top management because of its importance to a company's long-run success. CRC's chief executive, marketing, operations, and financial officers probably would participate in a decision to expand into a new product line.

Operational planning **involves identifying objectives for day-to-day activities.** For example, CRC will need to plan the types and amounts of carpet to be produced each day to meet sales requirements for the boat line. Except in small companies, operational plans often are made by middle management with input from top management. In planning CRC's daily production requirements, the production manager will work with managers in marketing, purchasing, and accounting to plan production and to ensure that sufficient materials are available to meet production goals.

Operational planning also involves setting performance objectives, **which are standards for the desired performance of various divisions of a company.** Every department is expected to meet specific performance objectives. The marketing department has sales quotas, and the production department has production quantity and quality expectations. Performance standards are a major part of operational planning and are used to evaluate performance.

Managerial accounting is important in strategic and operational planning. An important part of strategic planning is long-range financial planning. Companies often develop strategic, long-range financial plans that set target financial results several years into the future. These plans are supported by operational plans that forecast the monthly or quarterly financial results necessary to achieve the company's long-range financial plans. **The master budget is a one-year financial plan for a company.** As shown in Exhibit 3, the master budget ties together long-range financial plans and day-to-day financial objectives for the company's divisions and departments. It is developed from other operational plans for specific activities, such as sales, production costs, and operating expenses. The master budget identifies required investment in new plant assets and expected cash flows. It also describes expected profits for a company's product lines and major divisions.

Exhibit 3 Levels of Planning

Type of Plan	Planning Time Horizon	Nature of Planning
Strategic financial plan	Several years in the future	Sets major financial goals, such as long-range profitability, targeted stock price, and market share.
Master budget	Annual	Provides a one-year financial master plan linking long-range planning with operational planning. Developed from operational budgets such as projected sales, production, operating expenses, and cash flows.
Operational budgets	Monthly to quarterly	Provide specific inputs to the master budget. Often developed at the divisional and departmental levels as well as for the company as a whole.

Operational planning often involves departmental budgeting, analysis of budgeted versus actual revenues and costs, and evaluation of departmental performance. Inadequate and inaccurate data can result in budgets that provide poor plans. Imagine what would happen if CRC's budget greatly overstated the profits that could be generated by a new product line. CRC would invest in new plant assets and market its new line, only to discover that its profits were much lower than expected.

Decision making during the planning process often involves choosing among alternatives. For example, management may need to decide whether to use available cash (1) to offer a new line of products or (2) to invest in new equipment that will improve the quality of existing products. Once a plan is adopted, however, management must continue to make decisions in order to implement the plan. Management accountants become involved in several types of ongoing decisions. Examples include decisions:

- to continue producing a product or to drop it from a product line,
- to retain or close a branch or plant facility,
- to accept or reject a special product order from a customer,
- to complete a product or sell it partially completed at a lower price,
- to produce more of one product or more of another, and
- to keep, reduce, or eliminate certain costs.

Control

Once a plan is in place, it is necessary to monitor the performance of a company and its members. In all but the smallest companies, monitoring usually means assigning the responsibility for achieving certain objectives to specific managers and evaluating their success. Control involves identifying and rewarding behavior that encourages desired outcomes and detecting and correcting behavior that does not. It is concerned with controlling people's behavior so that desired outcomes are achieved. A company identifies performance characteristics useful for evaluating results. Measurement of these characteristics can be objective or subjective, formal or informal, but in any case it is tied to some form of incentive system. Identification and detection can be accomplished using three methods:

- Directly observing behavior to assess the quantity and quality of effort
- Measuring the outcomes of behavior
- Establishing informal work environment habits (corporate culture) that guide behavior

Many businesses use some combination of all three methods of control. For example, **Schofield Electronic Instruments, Inc.,** uses direct **observation of behavior** by office managers to control the quality and efficiency of clerical personnel in the telephone sales department. These employees perform tasks such as answering incoming calls, returning customers' calls, taking orders, and processing order forms. Their work is observable by the department manager, who can control behavior and take corrective action. For example, if telephones are unanswered after several rings, an office manager can temporarily reassign people to telephone duty to correct the situation. In this environment, performance measurement tends to be subjective and is based on effort.

Control of outside sales personnel is a different matter. Because outside sales representatives frequently travel alone, their behavior is not directly observable. Therefore, Schofield **measures** sales **outcomes** to control behavior. Representatives are assigned sales dollar quotas and are evaluated on whether they meet these quotas. A large portion of a sales representative's compensation is determined by sales outcomes.

Laboratory workers responsible for the research and development (R&D) of new products are governed in the short run mainly by yet another form of control. Because of the highly creative nature of their work, and their tendency to work in informal teams, R&D workers' behavior is not easy to observe directly. Schofield does not use short-term outcome measures, such as the number of new products developed, to evaluate R&D personnel because it is better to develop one outstanding new product than several poor ones. Instead, Schofield uses **cultural controls** for R&D personnel. Its culture emphasizes using R&D time and funds carefully to improve upon competitors' products and to develop ways to manufacture similar products at a lower cost than competitors. Researchers are guided by Schofield's culture, which defines the type and extent of risks the company is willing to take in the R&D area.

Incentives are important to the control process. **Incentives** are the rewards, monetary and nonmonetary, used to encourage employees to make decisions that are consistent with company goals. Examples of incentives are salaries, bonuses, special benefits, such as the use of a company car, and awards, such as recognition for outstanding performance.

Exhibit 4 shows the role of incentives in the corporate planning and control process. Planning influences measurement because plans establish measurable performance targets.

Exhibit 4
Role of Incentives, Evaluation, and Rewards in Corporate Planning and Control

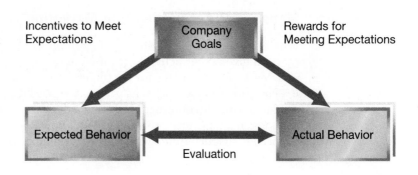

Measurement aids in controlling performance. Measures provide a means of comparing planned performance results (expected behavior) with actual results. Measurement, in turn, is linked to financial and nonfinancial incentives. These incentives are based on achievement of planned results (meeting goals) and motivate the company's members to accomplish corporate objectives.

Accounting usually is important when outcomes are measured and evaluated. Some accounting measures are collected specifically for the purpose of measuring performance. Such was the case suggested in the scenario at the beginning of the chapter. Erin and Seth were advised by Roberta to develop a monthly budget that could be compared with each month's actual results. In this way, budgets are used expressly to help measure and control performance. Other measures are collected for other reasons and are used to measure performance as a matter of convenience. Incentives and measurement do not always lead to the desired behavior or outcomes, however, as explained in the following section.

Ethics and Control

Ethics involves standards of conduct for members of organizations. Well-designed managerial accounting systems encourage ethical behavior on the part of employees. Management should try to eliminate features of managerial accounting systems that inadvertently encourage unethical behavior. For example, many companies consider it improper for an employee to record transactions associated with one period in another period in order to make performance appear better than it really is. Senior management should make it clear that this type of behavior is considered unethical. Senior management should also be careful to design managerial accounting systems with safeguards that limit employees' ability to engage in this kind of behavior.

The Institute of Management Accountants (IMA) has created ethical standards for management accounting. Certified Management Accountants (CMAs) are accountants who have received professional certification by the IMA. CMAs are expected to adhere to the ethical standards set forth by the IMA. Throughout this text you are challenged to think about ethics.

http://ingram.
swlearning.com

Learn more about the
IMA and the CMA
certification.

LEARNING NOTE

People who are evaluated on the basis of managerial accounting reports sometimes will try to make their performance look better by manipulating the numbers in the reports. If in doing this they take actions that are not in the company's best interests, the company will suffer in the long run. Managers responsible for designing managerial accounting systems need to consider the possibility of this kind of behavior when creating these systems.

INTERACTIONS AMONG ACCOUNTING, MARKETING, AND OPERATIONS

OBJECTIVE 3

Discuss ways in which managerial accounting interacts with marketing and operations.

Marketing and operations managers use accounting information extensively in day-to-day decisions. Pricing and production activities depend heavily on accounting measurement. Consequently, as shown in Exhibit 5, a close relationship among accounting, marketing, and operations managers is needed in most companies, both to facilitate day-to-day decisions and to formulate marketing and production strategy.

Managerial Accounting and Marketing

Why is accounting information so important in marketing decisions? The marketing function involves the activities required in order to advertise, promote, and sell products. Marketing is essential for the success of a company because it drives sales revenue. If a company cannot market its products, it has little need for other functions such as production and accounting. Marketing strategy also affects a company's plant investment and manufacturing strategies. Recall how Roberta informed Erin and Seth about the need to first determine what products would be sold and in what quantities to help

Exhibit 5 Examples of Ways Accounting, Marketing, and Operations Work Together

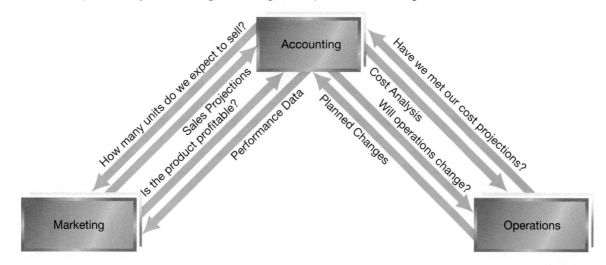

determine their needs for plant assets and cash. Without knowing the firm's marketing decisions, it is virtually impossible to determine the types and quantities of products to produce. This information, in turn, is necessary to make decisions about the type and amount of labor, materials, and equipment necessary for production.

For companies to be competitive in the new business environment, they require accurate and timely information to support their marketing efforts. As customers have demanded faster response times, companies have given their sales forces more authority to make decisions. The sales forces, in turn, rely on up-to-date accounting information to monitor and control sales activity. A company must price its products competitively and meet profit objectives. Manufacturing cost per unit of product frequently affects the product price. For example, a manufacturer may set the price of a product at some percentage above cost to achieve a target profit. Using inaccurate unit costs to set prices can have serious adverse consequences. Further, many companies allocate resources to divisions based on their profitability. If profit data are inaccurate, poor resource allocation decisions can result. These decisions, in turn, can lead to reduced profits and lower company value.

As noted earlier, sales representatives are often compensated on the basis of sales results. The commissions they are paid may be based on profits rather than on unit or dollar sales. Accounting information can help representatives negotiate prices with customers. Also, it can help them to identify products that produce high profits so that they can encourage sales of these products.

Organizations usually compete as either (1) low-cost producers of products and services or (2) providers of products and services that are differentiated in terms of quality and performance, or both. A company's accounting system should provide information that is consistent with the company's marketing strategy. For example, detailed and timely reporting of production costs to marketing is likely to be more important for success with a low-cost strategy than with a product-differentiation strategy. Thus, accounting information should meet the needs of a company's marketing managers.

Managerial Accounting and Operations

Operations refers to the actions necessary to create and deliver products or services. Operations decisions also rely on accounting information. For example, production is concerned with manufacturing or acquiring the products that a company sells, including obtaining the raw materials necessary for the production process. This means that production managers need information about the costs of production, such as labor and materials. Production managers often compare the actual cost of production to costs that were forecast during the company's budgeting process to determine whether production costs are being properly controlled.

Traditional production methods sometimes have failed to produce quality products that can compete in a global market. As a result, production managers in many companies have changed to new manufacturing methods, such as just-in-time and flexible manufacturing. Just-in-time manufacturing improves product quality and speeds up delivery times. Flexible manufacturing helps meet customer demands for a wider variety of products. At the same time, production managers have reduced inventory costs and reduced the time required to manufacture products by using automated processes. This need for faster production has led to efforts to compress product-development and production cycles. These changes affect production managers' information needs and require adjustments in managerial accounting systems.

Other Effects on Marketing and Operations

Developing a marketing plan is one area in which marketing and accounting interact at the strategic level. In addition to being concerned about unit costs, marketing personnel are concerned about such strategic issues as competitors' costs and marketing strategies, and the cost and profit implications of changes in product mix. At the operational planning level, accounting and marketing managers work together to make decisions about pricing individual products and monitoring competitors' responses to this pricing, tracking sales force time and costs, accounting for advertising and promotion costs for individual products, and monitoring marketing and distribution expenditures. For example, at the operational level, financial measures of quality, such as warranty cost, can be linked to nonfinancial measures of quality, such as defective parts per thousand. This linkage provides information about which parts generate the most warranty costs and helps focus management's attention on those areas where quality improvement can be most effective in reducing costs.

At the strategic planning level of operations, accounting can play an important role in providing information about the costs and benefits of alternative strategies to improve quality, delivery, and service. For example, information about a company's share of the market for a product line and about the profitability of that product line can be combined. This allows the company to weigh lowering prices to increase sales against maintaining prices in order to make a higher profit on each unit of product sold.

Though manufacturing companies have been the focus of much of this discussion, service companies face similar issues. In these companies, pricing and resource allocation decisions are sometimes more troublesome than in manufacturing companies because measuring service costs and profits is more difficult. Consider the difficulties a bank faces in determining the cost of checking accounts. Transactions involving checking accounts are performed by many different departments within the bank. Examples are check cashing, check processing, electronic funds transfers, and new customer services. Because these departments handle many other types of transactions as well as checking, it is difficult to determine the portion of each department's costs that is associated with checking accounts. In some service businesses, a lack of accurate cost data has led to poor decisions because managers have little guidance as to which services are profitable and which are not.

Because of the role that product cost data play in strategic marketing and production decisions, it is difficult to overestimate the importance of accounting to business strategy. Companies often focus on the operational aspects of accounting information and forget the strategic aspects. However, they ignore the strategic implications of managerial accounting information at their peril. There are numerous examples of businesses that made poor strategic decisions, or even failed, because of inaccurate accounting data.

Case in Point

The Importance of Accounting Information for Operating Decisions

Managerial accounting information showed a division of a major manufacturer to be losing money. The company decided to put the division up for sale. A group of employees in the division purchased it. Under the new ownership, the division immediately became profitable. A major reason was that when the division was part of the major manufacturer, it was charged for costs incurred by the manufacturer's other divisions. When it became a separate company, it was no longer charged for these costs. Errors in the managerial accounting system led the manufacturer's management to believe that the division was unprofitable when, in fact, it was profitable. The result was a bad business decision.

2 SELF-STUDY PROBLEM

An automobile parts manufacturer was concerned about the company's poor financial performance and complaints from customers about late deliveries and low product quality. The company was plagued by overproduction of some products and underproduction of others. The company's marketing department often promoted products on which it earned a small profit instead of products on which it earned a higher profit.

Required How could the company's problems be reduced by better communication among accounting, marketing, and operations?

The solution to Self-Study Problem 2 appears at the end of the chapter.

THE SCOPE OF MANAGERIAL ACCOUNTING

OBJECTIVE 4

Explain the scope of managerial accounting.

Managerial accounting relates to your course in financial accounting, but is different in many important aspects. Exhibit 6 illustrates the role of managerial accounting in business organizations. Managerial accounting systems capture the results of business activities and report these results to decision makers using financial and operational reporting systems. You are already familiar with financial reporting systems from your financial accounting course. Based on a general ledger, these systems capture information used to prepare a company's financial statements. Both external and internal decision makers use this information. Later chapters demonstrate how management accountants trace manufacturing costs through the general ledger to determine ending balances of various inventory accounts and cost of goods sold.

Exhibit 6 The Role of Managerial Accounting in Business Organizations

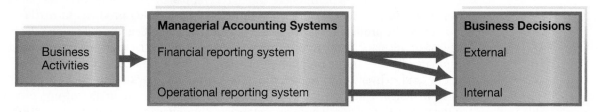

Managerial accounting systems capture the dynamics of a manufacturing process. Some accounting systems are designed to capture costs associated with a variety of unique products, such as custom-built homes. Other accounting systems capture manufacturing costs associated with producing homogeneous products, such as gasoline or synthetic fiber. Managers need accurate cost information to support a variety of cost-related decisions. For example, managers often make pricing decisions to ensure their products are competitive in the market.

Managers rely on operational reporting systems to understand certain dynamics of their processes. Operational reporting systems capture nonfinancial information such as the number of units produced, time required for production, and defect rates. Managers use information from both systems to justify capital investments in new property, plant, and equipment and other innovations to help their companies remain competitive. Thus, managerial accounting extends the financial reporting view of traditional accounting.

Much of the traditional accounting system involves measuring and reporting business activities in terms of the dollar values associated with these activities. Financial statements express business activities in terms of the dollar amounts of assets, liabilities, owners' equity, revenues, expenses, and cash flows associated with a company's activities for a fiscal period or at the end of a fiscal period. Accounting, especially managerial accounting, does not focus exclusively on financial data, however. Accounting measurement, especially in the contemporary business environment, includes quantitative and qualitative data about the effectiveness and efficiency of business activities. These measures are necessary to meet information needs of managers who are concerned with creating value in their organizations.

Nonfinancial Performance Measures

Financial results are affected by how effectively and efficiently an organization runs. Understanding the factors that affect effectiveness and efficiency, measuring these factors, and evaluating the measures are important management tasks. Nonfinancial measures often are needed for many of these factors.

Operations managers can reduce product costs by eliminating waste, scrap, and spoilage in the production process; product defects; and activities that do not add value to a company's products. Activity measures, such as the amount of materials used to produce each unit of product, are useful for determining efficiency in the manufacturing process. Quality measures also are important. The number of defects and customer satisfaction measures, for example, can help a company determine how well its production process is working. These measures help managers evaluate their processes so that costs associated with warranties, product returns, and reworking defective products, as well as lost revenues, can be reduced.

Many companies have attempted to reduce inventory costs by only producing those goods that are needed to meet customer orders and by placing materials into production as soon as they are received. These processes reduce storage costs and the amount of cash necessary to acquire materials and maintain inventory. For this type of production process to work, receiving, production, and delivery schedules must be carefully coordinated. Information about the time required to complete products, materials required to complete orders, and constraints that limit the ability of a company to meet its production demands are critical for the success of this type of operation.

Highly competitive markets often require companies to develop, produce, and deliver products quickly. Measuring the time required to bring products to market and structuring the production process to create flexible and efficient production schedules are critical to many companies. Companies operating in these environments need to eliminate idle time in the production process, eliminate unnecessary operations or activities, and deliver completed products to customers quickly. Production processes must be designed that can be converted quickly from the production of one product to the production of another. Investments in technology and computer-controlled machinery often are needed to support these activities. Benefits of acquiring this type of equipment and modifying production processes are important to measure, along with the costs of these acquisitions and changes. Benefits may be intangible, such as improved customer relations and larger sales potential, as well as tangible, such as short-run sales dollars.

Costs are clearly important for management decisions. However, cost data often are not sufficient for making informed decisions. Managers need information about *cost drivers*—**those activities that create costs.** Attempting to reduce costs without changing the activities that create the costs can be dysfunctional. For example, managers may reduce repair and maintenance costs by postponing these activities. The result, however, is likely to be inefficient operations and higher costs to replace and repair equipment in the future. Focusing strictly on costs can lead to short-run improvements in profits that are detrimental to long-term success. Incentive and reward systems should be developed that lead to long-run profits as a result of continuously improving product quality.

Quality is a major factor in determining the success of most business organizations. Short-term cost reductions that jeopardize the quality of a company's goods and services or the interaction between the company and its customers or suppliers can lead to lower company value. Consequently, costs must be considered in the context of the broader scope of a company's goals. A broad set of measures for evaluating company performance generally leads to better results than a narrow focus on current-period costs.

Because of the additional information needs of managers in modern business organizations, management accountants have become essential players in upper- and middle-level management decisions. Accountants work with other managers in teams to make strategic and operating decisions. By working together, these management teams can examine short-run and long-run implications of decisions and consider financial and nonfinancial consequences of decisions.

Service Companies

As the United States economy has matured, it has changed from being principally a manufacturing economy to being a service economy. This means that more companies are providing services than goods. This change has implications for the use of managerial accounting. The production of tangible products makes tracing costs to products somewhat different in manufacturing companies than in service companies. For example, manufacturing companies have inventories of materials and finished goods, whereas service companies do not.

Like manufacturing companies, service companies require relevant, timely, and accurate accounting information in order to make sound decisions. However, service companies have often been slower to use managerial accounting than manufacturing companies, perhaps partly because many service companies, such as airlines, railroads, and banks, have been regulated. Regulation may have made service companies less cost conscious than manufacturing companies because it often limited the services that companies could provide and fixed the prices that they could charge.

In recent years, many service industries have been deregulated. Examples are the airline and banking industries. Deregulation means that these companies will be operating in a more competitive environment. As competition increases, so does the need for better accounting information. Companies need to know the costs of their services with more accuracy. They need to be able to predict the financial results of changes in marketing and operations. Without relevant, timely, and accurate managerial accounting information, it is unlikely that service companies can prosper.

3 **SELF-STUDY PROBLEM** A division of a major corporation that manufactures transmissions for trucks and other heavy vehicles installed a new manufacturing system. Parts made by many departments must be assembled to form the transmission. Under the new manufacturing system, the parts should arrive at the point in production where they are ready at the time they are needed. The division spent a great deal of time training its production personnel in the new system. Despite these efforts, however, the results were disappointing. Departments continued to manufacture more parts than were needed, and quality did not improve as much as had been expected.

Management was disappointed. The firm had spent a great deal of time and effort implementing the new manufacturing system, with poor results. They began to look at the managerial accounting system that was used to measure departmental performance and discovered some problems. The division had long used an accounting system that emphasized producing as many parts as possible as fast as possible. Because labor was paid by the hour, the more component parts a department could make in a day, the lower its labor cost per unit. Consequently, department managers pressed for higher production volume despite the change in production philosophy.

Required Why did the information provided by the accounting system lead to the wrong results? What types of information might the accounting system provide that would be useful for achieving management's objectives?

The solution to Self-Study Problem 3 appears at the end of the chapter.

REVIEW

SUMMARY of IMPORTANT CONCEPTS

1. Managerial accounting refers to accounting information developed for use by decision makers inside the company.
   a. Managerial accounting is different from financial accounting.
   b. Managerial accounting is not governed by GAAP.
   c. The information produced by managerial accounting systems is important to many business decisions, especially marketing and operations decisions.

2. Managerial accounting interacts with decisions by other functions, notably marketing and operations.
   a. Marketing decisions often are based on the cost of manufacturing a product.
   b. Operations decisions frequently require cost and other accounting data for purposes of cost control and quality assurance.

3. Businesses' needs for accounting information are changing.
   a. Global competition and the need for higher quality are driving U.S. businesses to control costs and produce higher-quality products, creating new accounting information needs.
   b. Management accountants need to be involved in business functions like marketing and operations to ensure that the information they produce is timely and accurate enough and appropriate to the decisions being made.

4. The traditional view of managerial accounting needs to be changed to fit the new business environment.
   a. Managerial accounting has been traditionally viewed in the context of planning and control at the operational level.
   b. This view has been expanded to include a more strategic focus and the demands made by the new business environment.

5. Managerial accounting involves nonfinancial as well as financial measures of business activities.
   a. Measures of activity, such as material usage and defect rates, are useful for understanding and reducing production costs.
   b. Measures of time required for production and delivery are important for reducing inventory requirements and increasing efficiency.
   c. Global competition requires many companies to produce products quickly. Determining the benefits of investments in modern technology are important for operating in this environment.
   d. Managers need to understand cost drivers, the activities that create costs, in order to control costs. Focusing on cost reduction in the short run may not lead to long-term success.
   e. Companies often need to focus their efforts on improving the quality of their products and activities. A broad set of measures for evaluating company performance is needed for these efforts.

   f. Accountants work in teams with other managers to make strategic and operating decisions.
   g. Managerial accounting is important for service companies as well as manufacturing and retail companies.

DEFINE
TERMS and CONCEPTS DEFINED in this CHAPTER

cost drivers (M15)   managerial accounting (M3)
management accountant (M4)   operational planning (M7)

SELF-STUDY PROBLEM SOLUTIONS

SSP1-1   The kinds of decisions made by the three managers differ; therefore, the information they need differs. Miko needs information for making and evaluating strategic decisions. Lars needs information for planning and controlling the ongoing operations of the plant. Deborah needs information for efficient planning of production in the process she runs.

   As chief executive officer, Miko needs summary information about the company's performance. She needs to know general operating information, such as the amount of sales and net income for a period, and company-wide performance measures, such as return on assets. Comparative information about the company's plants and products would be used to evaluate performance and to make strategic decisions about whether to retain the plants or products.

   A plant manager needs information specific to the plant. This information can be used to evaluate plant efficiency and effectiveness. Information about production costs, plant profitability, and production delays can help Lars assess whether the plant is meeting expected performance objectives. If objectives are not being met, Lars needs information to help determine causes for the failures.

   Deborah needs specific information about production needs on a day-to-day basis. She needs to know which products need to be produced and the quantities demanded. She needs to be able to evaluate costs associated with the production process to eliminate unnecessary costs and to provide production cost information to other decision makers.

SSP1-2   Poor financial performance often is a symptom of poor communication within an organization. If accounting and marketing communicated about product costs and profits, the marketing department could focus on the products that are the most profitable. Without good cost information, the marketing department can only guess about which products should be promoted. If it had this information, it could focus its advertising and sales efforts on more profitable products. It could offer discounts and other incentives on these products if doing so would increase sales volume and create higher overall profits.

   If accounting and operations communicated, the operations department would have better information about which products were being sold and when the orders were needed. Information about operating costs could help operations schedule production more efficiently to meet demand and avoid costly delays or hurried production. Hurried production often results in poor quality of output.

SSP1-3   The basic problem in this situation was that division management failed to take its management accounting system into consideration when it implemented a new manufacturing system. The division wanted to minimize the costs associated with the inventory of component parts used to manufacture the transmissions, in the belief that this would lower the overall costs of production. Parts were not to arrive at the place where they were needed until just before they were actually used in production. Only the exact number of parts that were needed at the time were to be manufactured.

   Problems arose when the division attempted to operate the new manufacturing system in conjunction with the old managerial accounting system. The old accounting system was ill suited to the new manufacturing system because the way in which it measured departmental performance was not aligned with the desired performance under the new manufacturing system.

   The old accounting system had measured the efficiency of each individual department in making the individual parts of the transmissions, not the overall cost of making the transmissions. Efficiency was defined as the number of parts made per labor hour used. Under the old system, departments were evaluated in terms of cost per component manufactured, with lower being considered better. Each department therefore had an incentive to make as many parts as possible during a given period of time. The result was that some departments made parts faster than they could be used in manufacturing. Thus, excess parts often accumulated at various stages in the production process. This resulted in a costly buildup of inventory awaiting further processing.

Despite the training on the goals of the new manufacturing system, the department managers continued to act as they had under the old system, making as many parts as possible. This meant that the expected savings in inventory costs were not realized. Only after management recognized the problem and changed the managerial accounting system to one that recognized the reduction in inventory cost achieved by making only what was needed at the time did the managers' behavior become aligned with the division's goals. Perhaps the most important lesson to learn from this situation is that human beings respond to the way they are measured. Even though the department managers knew that they were supposed to reduce production to the level required for current needs, they continued to produce as much as possible to make their accounting reports look better. It is important to ensure that accounting systems used to measure human performance are aligned with corporate goals and objectives.

Thinking Beyond the Question

What basic financial information do we need to run a business?

In the opening scenario, you learned about some of the information needs identified by Erin and Seth. What role could a management accounting information system play in changing management's behavior? How can changing the way a business activity is measured also change decisions about that activity? Refer back to the scenario at the beginning of the chapter. For example, what are the implications of Erin and Seth measuring production efficiency versus the quality of their products? Is there a tradeoff in this decision?

QUESTIONS

Q1-1
Obj. 1
Managerial accounting is useful only to profit-oriented manufacturing companies. Do you agree? Why or why not?

Q1-2
Obj. 1
Rita Patterson went into the marketing field because she "hated accounting." Rita has been working for a large multinational company and is being promoted to assistant product manager. In her new job, Rita will prepare sales quotes for various large clients. Should Rita expect to use managerial accounting techniques in her new job? Why or why not?

Q1-3
Obj. 1
James and Hanna are senior accounting students at the state university. James plans to find a job in financial accounting, whereas Hanna wants to work in managerial accounting. What is the difference between these two types of accounting?

Q1-4
Obj. 1
If managerial accounting is primarily concerned with costs of business activities, why are both financial and nonfinancial measures of business activities important?

Q1-5
Obj. 1
Managerial accounting is important for all forms of business. How is managerial accounting different for retail, manufacturing, and service companies?

Q1-6
Obj. 1
It is important for middle- and upper-level managers throughout an organization to understand accounting information. Do you agree or disagree? Why?

Q1-7
Obj. 1
An accounting classmate notes that adherence to GAAP is not required for managerial accounting reports. She observes, "If it's so darned important for financial accounting, it seems reasonable that it would also be useful for managerial reporting." Do you agree or disagree? Why? Explain to her why it's more important that financial accounting reports adhere to GAAP than it is for managerial accounting reports to do so.

Q1-8
Objs. 1, 2
Why does the accounting system used for financial statement preparation not always provide the information that managers need for decision-making purposes?

Q1-9
Obj. 2
Tri-States Manufacturing produces a line of electric fans. Over the past several years, the company has seen its profit margin on fans decline from 12% to 8%. How has the decrease in profit margin affected the company's need for managerial accounting information?

Q1-10
Obj. 2
In order to meet increasing demand for its product, Hathaway Industries is considering an expansion of its manufacturing facilities. What sort of planning does this decision represent, strategic or operational? Explain your answer.

Q1-11
Obj. 2
Webco Products manufactures a line of small ice chests. The production department has experienced problems working with some of the raw materials used in the production process. The company is considering a change in materials that would increase the cost of an ice chest by 5%. What sort of planning does this decision represent, strategic or operational? Explain your answer.

Q1-12
Obj. 2
Advent Technologies, Inc., has developed a detailed planning and budgeting program that involves almost every layer of management. Tina Riser, plant manager, made this comment: "I don't know why we put so much effort into these budgets; after we complete them, we never see them again until the end of the year." If it is true that managers are not held accountable to budgets, does this represent a weakness in planning or in control? Explain your answer.

Q1-13
Obj. 2
Why is accounting important for planning and control decisions?

Q1-14
Obj. 3
Why must marketing and production managers have accounting information to make decisions? Are there any other managers needing accounting information?

Q1-15
Obj. 3
If marketing and operations managers need information for decision making, why don't they collect and keep the information themselves instead of relying on the accounting department to provide the needed information?

Q1-16
Obj. 4
Virgil Cartwright is a medical doctor with a small family practice. Each time a patient visits the doctor, certain medical and administrative costs are incurred. Would you agree that patients are a cost driver for the doctor? Explain your answer.

EXERCISES

If your instructor is using Personal Trainer® in this course, you may complete your assignments online.

E1-1
Write a short definition for each of the terms listed in the *Terms and Concepts Defined in this Chapter* section.

E1-2
Complete each of the following sentences with the proper term or terms.

1. Managerial accounting information is used primarily by __internal__ decision makers.
2. An accountant who produces information for use within a specific company is referred to as a(n) __management accountant__
3. __Strategic__ involves the identification of long-run goals and plans to achieve these goals.
4. __Operational__ involves the identification of objectives for day-to-day activities.
5. A financial plan that summarizes operational activities for the coming year is known as the __master budget__
6. Managerial accounting exists primarily to assist in the management functions of __planning__ and __control__.

E1-3
Obj. 1

Alberta Enterprises is being audited by a local public accounting firm. The management of Alberta hired an independent accountant to prepare financial statements in good form for presentation to the board of directors. The financial statements will contain an auditor's report stating that the financial statements have been prepared in accordance with generally accepted accounting principles.

Brent Haskill, production manager at Alberta, reviewed the financial statements prepared by the independent accountant and noted that the reported inventory value was higher than that contained in the company's monthly operating report. Brent asked the company's accountant to explain the difference. The accountant explained that the auditors adjusted inventory to a LIFO basis in accordance with GAAP, whereas the company does not reflect LIFO calculations in the monthly operating report.

a. Does managerial accounting prescribe specific methods that must be followed? Since the inventory value was adjusted by the independent accountant, would the company's inventory valuation be worthless to its managers? Why or why not?

b. Must accounting information be calculated in accordance with generally accepted accounting principles to be useful to managers? Why or why not?

E1-4
Obj. 1

Dream Easy, a manufacturer of mattresses, sells 10 different models of mattresses. Each model generates $4,000,000 in sales each year. Dream Easy currently does not have the resources to be able to determine the profitability of each product line. Steve, the company president, has a hunch that one of the models is not profitable, and estimates a loss of $400,000 each year. He suggests installing a new managerial accounting information system at a cost of $120,000 per year. This system would determine the profitability of each product line, so Dream Easy could stop manufacturing unprofitable models.

Assuming Steve's assumption is correct, should Dream Easy install the new system? Explain.

E1-5
Obj. 1

An advertising firm has 100 clients, each generating $500,000 in sales. It currently generates profitability reports only by office. One office president suggests that the firm produce profitability reports for each individual client. He estimates that 30 clients are running at a net loss of 20% on their sales. A new client reporting system could be installed for $1,000,000. This system would identify the clients that are losing money, so the advertising firm could drop those clients or develop a plan to make them profitable.

Assuming the office president's assumptions are correct, should the advertising firm install the new system? Explain.

E1-6
Obj. 2

During the planning process, a company identifies its goals, its objectives, and its plans for reaching those goals. To ensure these plans are implemented, managers must control employees' behavior. One method of control is measuring the outcomes of behavior. Managerial accountants develop accurate and timely measurements of these outcomes.

Match the measurements with the decisions that managers must make.

Measurements:
  i. Data that show how reduction in costs will impact revenues
  ii. Data that show how a product's elimination will affect the company's total profitability
  iii. Data that show the profitability per unit for each product line and the investments needed to increase production and sales
  iv. Data that show the costs and revenues of a custom ordered product
  v. Data that show the costs and revenues for completing a partially completed product

Decisions:
  a. To continue producing a product or to drop it from a product line
  b. To accept or reject a special product order from a customer
  c. To complete a product or sell it partially completed at a lower price
  d. To produce more of one product or more of another
  e. To keep, reduce, or eliminate certain costs

E1-7
Obj. 2

Identify each of the following as a planning or control decision:

a. Decision to buy new production machinery. planning

b. Decision to change the mix in a chemical compound used to produce a synthetic fiber to reduce the cost of the product. control

    c. Decision to replace a factory that is no longer efficient. *Control*

    d. Decision to retrain workers to enhance long-run productivity. *planning*

    e. Decision to open retail stores in a foreign country. *planning*

    f. Decision to count goods for sale to verify inventory records. *Control*

    g. Decision to sell a production plant that is no longer profitable. *planning*

    h. Decision to survey customers to determine their satisfaction with a company's products. *Control*

E1-8
Objs. 2, 3

Ally's Bowling produces bowling balls. The company focuses on making high-end, custom balls. Ally's decides to enter a new highly competitive market, in which it will focus on a low-cost strategy. Describe Ally's changes in information needs with the new product line.

E1-9
Objs. 2, 3

Unisco Products manufactures a line of children's toys that are painted in bright, colorful tones. One of the most popular toy colors is yellow oxide. The company has become aware, however, that the yellow oxide paint it is using is possibly toxic. Accordingly, the company has sought a replacement paint of the same color that is guaranteed safe. The only feasible replacement it has found will cost three times as much as the paint currently being used. Switching to this paint would require a substantial increase in the toy's sales price to cover the added cost.

    Rosemary Terry, marketing manager, insists that sales of this toy will decline significantly if the price is increased to cover the additional paint cost.

    a. Does paint add value to the product? Why or why not?

    b. How does managerial accounting create an ethical concern for managers at Unisco? Explain your answer.

E1-10
Obj. 3

A manufacturer of printers is considering making a new high-end laser printer. Market research estimates your company could sell 2,000 of these printers per year at $3,000 each, without reducing the sales of any other product. The marketing manager asks you, a managerial accountant, to determine if the company should make this printer. What information would you need to make this decision?

E1-11
Obj. 3

The vice president of marketing is struggling at determining the selling price of a new toaster oven. He estimates that the company could sell 20,000 units if the price is set at $30 each, but if the price is dropped to $25 each, he estimates sales would rise to 23,500 units. What managerial accounting information could you provide him to assist in the pricing decision?

PROBLEMS

If your instructor is using Personal Trainer® in this course, you may complete your assignments online.

P1-1
Obj. 1

http://ingram.
swlearning.com

Learn more about
UTC's ethics code.

Ethics and Managerial Accounting

Many business organizations have adopted codes of ethics that describe expected behavior for managers with respect to other stakeholders. For example, **United Technologies Corporation** publishes an extensive Code of Ethics that describes the relationships between the company and other parties. Excerpts from the code follow:

Our Customers
We are committed to providing high quality and value, fair prices and honest transactions to those who use our products and services. We will deal both lawfully and ethically with all our customers.

Our Employees
We are committed to treating one another fairly and to maintaining employment practices based on equal opportunity for all employees. We will respect each other's privacy and treat each other with dignity and respect irrespective of age, race, color, sex, religion, or nationality. We are committed to providing safe and healthy working conditions and an atmosphere of open communication for all our employees.

Our Suppliers
We are committed to dealing fairly with our suppliers. We will emphasize fair competition, without discrimination or deception, in a manner consistent with long-lasting business relationships.

(Continued)

Required Why is ethical behavior important for managerial accounting? How does ethical behavior in accounting affect the relationship between a company and its customers, employees, and suppliers?

P1-2 Managerial Accounting and Performance Measures

Objs. 1, 2

An-Hour Foto provides film processing at a single store location. The store has a policy that film will be developed in 24 hours, or the processing is free. It also has a policy that it will refund customers' money for any pictures that were poorly developed.

In order to improve income without raising prices, the company must find ways to reduce costs. To this end, the company has experimented with a new chemical used in its film processing. Management has determined that the new chemical takes longer to process film and is more sensitive to improper handling than the old chemical. While the new chemical is less expensive than the old chemical, the amount of free processing and photo returns have increased since the company switched to this chemical. Accordingly, management must decide whether to continue using the new chemical or return to the old chemical.

Required

A. How can managerial accounting be used to assist the company in determining whether to continue using the new chemical?
B. What are some of the nonfinancial measures provided by managerial accounting to assist managers in the decision-making process?

P1-3 Accounting Information and Business Decisions

Objs. 1–3

Ned Bonapart is purchasing manager for a clothing store. On April 12, Ned received the following weekly report for men's suits purchased from one of the company's suppliers. Ned immediately ordered another 12 wool suits and another 20 cotton suits from the manufacturer.

Merchandise Report
April 12

Fabric Type	Usual Order Quantity	Unit Cost	Last Order Date	Actual Number on Hand	Desired Number on Hand
Wool	12	$120	Feb. 15	5	10
Cotton	20	80	Mar. 2	8	15
Synthetic	25	75	Mar. 10	20	15

Required

A. What information did Ned consider in making his decision?
B. How does the merchandise report assist him with the decision? Does this report appear to meet his information needs for the decision he made?
C. What effect does the information in the report and Ned's decision have on the future of the company?

P1-4 Strategic and Operational Planning

Obj. 2

Rebecca owns several successful coffeehouses. Each one has its own manager and is operated independently of the others. Rebecca meets with the manager of each location each month to review operating results. During this meeting, the manager must present a projection of operations for the coming month. Rebecca reviews the sales projections and any promotional campaigns and entertainment that the manager is planning to use.

Based on the success of her current coffeehouses, Rebecca is considering opening three new facilities. She has found three locations where long-term leases can be obtained. All locations are in high traffic areas near a mall or shopping center. Rebecca has determined the cost to furnish the shops with equipment and has obtained approval from a bank that will assist in the required financing.

Required

A. In what ways do the coffeehouses utilize managerial accounting in the operational planning process?
B. Explain how Rebecca utilizes strategic planning.

P1-5 Strategic and Operational Planning

Obj. 2

Workout Enterprises owns a chain of successful fitness centers. The founder and CEO, Sally, sets a company-wide return on assets goal of 30%. In order to meet this objective Sally determines that she will need to open three new fitness centers in the next year. Sally looks at 30 potential sites for her new stores and determines the three that will maximize her return. In setting the master budget, Sally meets with the general manager of each store to predict the sales for their store and to review their performance from the previous year.

Required

A. How does Sally utilize managerial accounting information in the strategic planning process?
B. How does Sally utilize managerial accounting information in the operational planning process?
C. Why does Sally review the previous year's performance with each manager?

P1-6 Accounting and Planning Decisions

Obj. 2

Myrla Rhyman is planning to start a new business as a systems consultant. She has saved $7,000 to invest in the business. She expects to receive $3,800 each month, on average, from sales to customers. She expects that she will need cash to pay the following items each month, on average: rent, $900; supplies, $500; utilities, $100; other, $250. She will need to purchase $13,000 of equipment to start the business; in addition, she will need $3,000 to cover initial operating costs. A local bank has agreed to consider a loan to help Myrla start her business and has asked her to develop a plan that describes her expected cash receipts and payments for the first year. The plan should show how much cash she will need for the business, how much she will need to borrow, and how she expects to pay back the loan. Monthly payments will be required to pay off the loan and interest. The bank will charge $10 per year in interest for each $100 borrowed until the loan is repaid at the end of the year. Myrla has asked you to prepare a plan for her to submit to the bank.

Required Prepare a plan for Myrla. Describe any assumptions you make.

P1-7 Planning and Control Decisions

Obj. 2

Joyce Mercer is manager of the Long-Term Care Division of the Olin County Health Department. The division has a $100 million budget and is responsible for providing long-term care services (often in nursing homes) to the elderly and physically disabled. The division contracts with providers for nursing home care, adult day care, in-home visiting nurses, and a variety of other long-term care services. As manager, Joyce makes a variety of planning and control decisions on a daily basis. On a recent Tuesday morning, Joyce sat at her desk with the following issues and decisions needing attention:

1. Two months ago, the family of a nursing home patient filed a complaint alleging mistreatment of the patient. An investigation revealed substance to the complaint, and several remedial actions have been developed. Joyce must decide which actions to require of the nursing home.
2. For nearly a year, a task force in Joyce's department has been developing an experimental alternative to nursing home care. It will require a waiver of the federal Medicaid rules, but it has the potential to provide better-quality care at a lower cost to taxpayers. Joyce must decide whether to proceed with this initiative via a formal request to Washington, DC.
3. Budget problems caused the state legislature to reduce funding for a certain program. A citizens committee has recommended priorities to Joyce for trimming the program. Joyce must make and announce the final decision today.
4. Joyce is contemplating engagement of a consultant to conduct an evaluation of her division. Such an evaluation would judge whether the goals and objectives of her unit are being carried out in an effective and efficient manner.
5. Joyce's immediate superior has proposed moving a service unit currently located in another division to the Long-Term Care Division. The unit is not operating effectively because of a variety of problems within the unit. Joyce must provide a written recommendation to her supervisor by tomorrow about how this new unit could be integrated into the work of her division.

(Continued)

Required

A. Describe the differences between a planning decision and a control decision.
B. Specify whether each issue described previously is primarily a planning decision or primarily a control decision. Briefly justify your answer. If an issue involves elements of both planning and control, indicate why you believe this is true.

P1-8   Planning and Business Decisions

Obj. 2   (All of the knowledge required to solve this problem is not contained in this chapter. The problem is based on material covered in financial accounting and is included here to prompt thinking about accounting problems, accounting processes, and decisions.) Van Gogh is considering a business opportunity selling artificial flowers, especially irises and lilies. He needs $25,000 in financing to begin operations. He has $15,000 in savings that he can invest. He has spoken with a local bank about borrowing the additional $10,000 he needs. The bank has indicated that it will consider the loan but has asked for a set of financial statements that describes what Van believes the company's financial condition will look like at the end of the first three months of operations. Van has asked for your assistance in preparing the financial statements. He has provided you with the following expectations:

1. Plant assets costing $22,500 will be needed.
2. Inventory of $5,000 will be purchased for the first month. The inventory will be paid for in the month following purchase. The amount of inventory purchased each month will equal the amount sold in the prior month.
3. Average monthly sales should be about $7,500. Two-thirds of the sales will be for cash each month, and one-third will be for credit. Credit sales will be collected in the month following sale.
4. The cost of the inventory sold will be $4,000 each month.
5. The interest on the loan will require a payment of $125 at the end of each month. An additional $100 will be paid to the bank each month to repay the loan.
6. Operating expenses, other than depreciation, each month should be $1,000. These will be paid in cash. Depreciation should be $200 each month.
7. Van expects to withdraw $1,000 from the business each month for living expenses.

In addition, he has provided the following work sheet, completed for the first month of operations:

	First Month	Second Month	Third Month
Sales revenues	$ 7,500		
Cost of goods sold	(4,000)		
Gross profit	3,500		
Depreciation	(200)		
Other operating expenses	(1,000)		
Income from operations	2,300		
Interest expense	(125)		
Net income	$ 2,175		
Cash	$ 5,275		
Accounts receivable	2,500		
Inventory	1,000		
Plant assets, net of depreciation	22,300		
Total assets	$31,075		
Accounts payable	$ 5,000		
Notes payable	9,900		
Investment by owner	15,000		
Retained earnings	1,175		
Total liabilities & owners' equity	$31,075		

Required Complete the work sheet for the second and third months.

P1-9   **Cost Management**

Objs. 2, 3

UniversEd employs faculty from various universities on a part-time basis for specific education and consulting jobs. These professors come from many disciplines including accounting, economics, finance, information systems, marketing, operations, and strategic planning.

UniversEd has two different lines of business, providing customized financial education to corporate executives from large firms and providing financial consulting services to small firms. In its executive education line of business, UniversEd educates international executives from various firms in the United States, Europe, and the Far East in such financial topics as analyzing firm performance and controlling financial risks. In its consulting line of business, UniversEd uses cost management concepts to work with businesses to improve their financial performance and provide economic value added through better utilization of assets and cost control. In both lines, client satisfaction is very important to firm performance but can be measured in different ways.

Recently, UniversEd undertook a consulting job for a small parts manufacturer, AAA, that sells alternators to large automobile manufacturers and auto parts companies. AAA makes over 600 different types of alternators, some of which management suspects are not profitable to make in the small quantities demanded by AAA's customers. AAA's current management accounting system does not permit AAA's management to tell which products are profitable and which are not. UniversEd's task is to help management develop a management accounting system that will improve the manufacturer's performance and add economic value for its investors.

Required

A. Why does UniversEd sometimes employ faculty with expertise in disciplines such as marketing and operations when delivering financial executive education and consulting services?

B. Why might UniversEd's two lines of business require different performance measures to evaluate success? What measures might be good indicators of whether or not UniversEd is performing well in each of its two lines of business?

C. What things should AAA's new management accounting do to help AAA's management create value for its shareholders? Give an example of possible performance measures for AAA's delivery and accounting departments.

P1-10   **Planning for Marketing Decisions**

Objs. 2, 3

(All of the knowledge required to solve this problem is not contained in this chapter. The problem is based on material covered in financial accounting and is included here to prompt thinking about accounting problems, accounting processes, and decisions.) You are working as an assistant to the vice president for marketing at Long Life Incorporated, a startup manufacturer of a healthy, minimally refined breakfast cereal. Since little processing will be done, much of the cost of the product will be in the premium ingredients. The company will be investing $3 million in processing and packaging facilities to produce a maximum of 15,000 cases of cereal per month. It will advertise and market only in a restricted regional area in the foreseeable future, although expansion is possible in the long run. Fixed costs for operating the facility will be approximately $85,000 per month. Variable costs, primarily for ingredients and labor, are expected to be approximately $17 per case.

In the past, most cereals of this sort have been sold at specialty stores for high prices. However, in recent years, some have moved into supermarkets at prices that are competitive with those of traditional cereals. A marketing research study has given you estimated results after the first year for three possible scenarios:

1. Sell to supermarkets for $29 per case, spend $25,000 per month on advertising, and sell approximately 11,000 cases per month. The average price grocery stores pay competitors for a case of this size is $30, and $25,000 is a minimal monthly budget for advertising in the local area.

2. Sell to supermarkets for $31 per case, spend $40,000 per month on advertising, and sell approximately 12,000 cases per month.

3. Sell to specialty stores for $34 per case, spend only $7,000 per month advertising in health food periodicals, and sell approximately 7,500 cases per month.

(Continued)

Required

A. Prepare a schedule that shows the expected profit from each scenario.
B. Write a report for your company president and vice presidents in which you analyze each of the strategies and make a recommendation concerning which one to choose.
C. Include discussion of any long-term trends and other outside factors that you feel should be considered in making this strategic decision.

P1-11 **Excel in Action**

SPREADSHEET

Music Makers produces compact disks for various software and music companies. Music Makers receives a master version of the software or music from a customer in computer form. The company copies the master version of the data to blank CDs, packages the CDs, and ships the completed product to the customer.

Because its product is generic, Music Makers relies on being a low-cost producer of CDs in order to remain competitive. It also relies on a quality production process to ensure customer satisfaction. The company is considering upgrading some of its production equipment to include faster copying capability and to automate some parts of the packing process that are now done manually.

Currently, the cost of producing a CD for Music Makers, including materials and labor, is $1.10 per CD. In addition, depreciation on equipment, utilities, and other period costs are $324,000 per month. The company currently is producing 500,000 CDs each month. If it upgrades its equipment, Music Makers' production costs will decrease to $1.06 per unit, but its period costs will increase to $340,000 per month.

Required Use a spreadsheet to prepare a cost comparison for Music Makers. Your spreadsheet should appear similar to the following example. Use the formatting instructions that follow the example for this purpose.

	A	B	C
		Current	**Upgraded**
1			
2	Production cost per unit		
3	Monthly volume		
4			
5	Production cost		
6	Period cost		
7	Total cost		

The spreadsheet should automatically calculate the total production and total cost for each option. Enter =B2*B3 in cell B4 to calculate the balance that appears in this cell, for example. The contents of cell B3 can be copied to cell C4. Use the Comma button **ɟ** to format columns B and C beginning with row 2 to display two decimal places and include commas to separate thousands from hundreds. Draw a line to separate totals from other amounts. Also, use a double line beneath the amounts in the Total cost rows to indicate totals. Select the appropriate cells and click on the borders button. ▦ ▾ Use the drop-down arrow to select the line style from the options provided. Align text on the left-hand side of each column and align numbers on the right-hand side by selecting the appropriate cells and clicking on the alignment buttons. ▤ ▤ ▤ You may use dollar signs for dollar amounts in your spreadsheet by selecting on the appropriate cell and clicking on the dollar button. **$** Captions in row 1 should be centered and in bold type.

Your spreadsheet can be modified as needed by inserting or deleting rows, columns, or cells. To insert a row, column, or cell, select the row above the row to be added, the column to the left of the column to be added, or the cell(s) where you want the new cell(s) to appear. Click on the Insert menu and select the appropriate item. To delete a row, column, or cell, select that row, column, or cell(s) and click on the Edit menu. Then click on Delete.

It is important to **save your work on a regular basis.** Save your work before you make any major changes so that mistakes will not require you to redo a lot of work.

Which options provide the lower cost for Music Makers? Assume that production volume decreased to 300,000 units per month. Which option would produce the lower cost?

P1-12   Multiple-Choice Overview of the Chapter

1. Management accounting is concerned primarily with providing:
   a. information in accordance with generally accepted accounting principles.
   b. information to stockholders, creditors, and others outside the organization.
   c. information to managers inside the organization.
   d. information to regulatory agencies.

2. The managerial functions of planning, control, and decision making typically are:
   a. approached in precisely the same way in every organization.
   b. carried out simultaneously, with decision making being an inseparable part of the other functions.
   c. carried out independently of one another, so that a function may be omitted without negative effects.
   d. conducted only by the managers of manufacturing entities.

3. In decision making, a manager uses:
   a. financial accounting information exclusively.
   b. information from his or her department only, ignoring other departments' costs and activities.
   c. information that must conform to generally accepted accounting principles.
   d. information that is relevant to the decision even if the information does not conform to generally accepted accounting principles.

4. Daley is a stockholder of Public Company, Inc. In his role as a stockholder, Daley would most likely use:
   a. managerial accounting information developed by the organization.
   b. financial information contained in Public's annual report.
   c. accounting information obtained directly from Public's computer system.
   d. no accounting information about Public, since it is not available to outsiders.

5. Budgets are:
   a. a form of planning for an organization's operating and financial matters.
   b. concerned only with the company's cash position.
   c. typically not prepared on an annual basis.
   d. usually prepared for an organization as a whole, not for individual departments.

6. Management accounting in the beginning of the 21st century would be most accurately described as a:
   a. branch of financial accounting.
   b. form of accounting that is concerned mainly with production-related managerial decisions.
   c. form of accounting that is necessary if a business is to successfully compete in a global business environment.
   d. branch of industrial technology.

7. The primary difference between a planning decision and a control decision is that:
   a. investors make planning decisions, while management makes control decisions.
   b. planning decisions involve dollars, while control decisions involve qualitative factors.
   c. planning decisions involve revenues, while control decisions involve expenses.
   d. planning decisions are developmental, while control decisions are corrective.

8. A difference between the information needs of top management and those of middle managers of a business is that:
   a. top managers make planning decisions, while middle managers make control decisions.
   b. top managers are concerned with profits, while middle managers are concerned with costs.
   c. middle managers require more timely and detailed information than top managers.
   d. middle managers require less accurate information than top managers.

9. Which of the following is a control decision?
   a. Developing goals
   b. Determining strategic objectives
   c. Determining operational objectives
   d. Measuring outcomes

10. The use of managerial accounting in service organizations:
    a. is pointless, since service organizations produce no tangible product.
    b. provides timely, relevant, and accurate information to managers.
    c. occurs more than the use of managerial accounting in manufacturing companies.
    d. is required by regulatory agencies.

CASE

C1-1   Cost Management in a University

Objs. 1–4

Most states now require five years of education for accounting graduates to sit for the Certified Public Accountant (CPA) examination. Many accounting jobs, however, do not require a CPA license, so some students still seek only four-year degrees. The Business School at Cassidy University offers three degrees in accounting: (1) Bachelor of Science (BS) in Accounting, (2) Master of Professional Accountancy (MPA), and (3) Master of Business Administration in Accounting (MBA). Tuition for a semester of graduate study costs approximately twice as much as a semester of undergraduate study. Undergraduate students who meet certain academic requirements are normally admitted to the BS program at the end of their sophomore year after taking a series of prerequisite courses. The school operates undergraduate and graduate placement services to assist students in finding employment. The school also operates an Accounting Graduate Programs office with a staff to administer the accounting graduate programs. The programs office has an annual budget that sets targets for tuition revenues, teaching costs, administrative costs, and merit-based financial aid provided to students. The school is adding a new building to accommodate its graduate programs.

The BS degree is a four-year degree with a curriculum similar to other four-year accounting programs. Each year the school graduates about 275 students with this degree. Some graduates of the BS program are employed as management accountants by corporations or governments. Others are employed by CPA firms and expect to complete a fifth year of education later. Undergraduate tuition costs are similar to those at other universities.

The MBA is a two-year degree in which high-performing students can convert to graduate student status at the end of their junior year in the BS program and continue their education for two more years. Upon graduation, these students receive both BS and MBA degrees. In the first year of the MBA program, students take graduate courses in a broad variety of disciplines such as accounting, economics, finance, information systems, marketing, and quantitative methods. Using a series of intensive business simulations the students learn how to integrate six basic business processes to achieve business success. In the second year of the MBA, accounting students take one of four accounting tracks: consulting, assurance, taxation, or information systems. In addition to an accounting track, the students also take a complementary, nonaccounting concentration of advanced graduate courses in areas such as finance, marketing, operations, or tax law. Finally, the students receive instruction in leadership, cognitive development, oral and written communications, and self-assessment skills throughout the two years of graduate study. The school expects to graduate about 60–120 students each year from the MBA program. Recently, graduates of the MBA program received starting salaries approximately 33% higher than graduates of the BS program.

The MPA is a one-year degree with a BS degree as a prerequisite for entry. Admitted students have grade point averages and standardized test scores similar to students admitted to the MBA program. The curriculum in the one year of graduate study is similar to that of the second year of the MBA program. The school expects to graduate about 80 students each year from the MPA program. Most students entering the MPA program come from undergraduate programs at other schools. Recently, graduates of the MPA program received starting salaries approximately 20% higher than graduates of the BS program.

Required

A. Describe how the Business School adds value and who receives this value.
B. How must the school manage the economic and quality aspects of its activities to be successful?
C. What are the major cost drivers involved in the school's educational process? How do you think the school might attempt to control costs?

COST CATEGORIES AND FLOWS

How can accounting classifications help us understand costs?

Erin and Seth believe they have designed a product that customers will want to buy. Seth understands how to make the product, and Erin has developed a marketing plan. In order to make a profit, Erin and Seth must control their costs so the revenue they receive from selling their products is greater than the costs of producing and selling them. Therefore, the next problem Erin and Seth must address involves understanding costs.

FOOD FOR THOUGHT

Put yourself in the role of Seth and Erin. What would you like to know about costs? Would you want to understand how the cost of making the product differs from the cost of selling the product and administering the business? Let's join Erin and Seth as they discuss the accounting information they will need to make pricing decisions.

Seth: *I've been thinking about how to distinguish between costs incurred to make products and those incurred to generate sales. I think we should classify all costs that result from production activities as product costs.*

Erin: *That makes sense because all of these costs can be traced to the products we make. For example, we can identify materials such as lumber and hardware used in making each product. Also, we can trace the labor of production employees to the products.*

Seth: *You're right. But I haven't figured out what to do with the costs of a lot of miscellaneous items such as factory insurance, glue, sandpaper, and varnish. The managers where I worked previously talked about overhead costs. These must be the kinds of costs they were talking about.*

Erin: *What about the other costs of administering our business and selling products? For example, we will have consulting charges from Roberta and travel expenses as I visit potential customers. These costs shouldn't be part of the product cost.*

Seth: *I think you're right. But, after we have classified our costs, what then? Isn't the purpose of an accounting system to help us make better decisions? How do we use all of this information?*

OBJECTIVES

Once you have completed this chapter, you should be able to:

1   Differentiate between product costs and period expenses.

2   Explain how direct material, direct labor, and manufacturing overhead costs flow through an accounting system.

3   Discuss methods for proactively managing inventory levels and manufacturing costs.

PINE BELT FURNITURE COMPANY: MARKETS AND MANUFACTURING PROCESSES

OBJECTIVE 1

Differentiate between product costs and period expenses.

Pine Belt Furniture Company manufactures and sells mid-priced pine furniture to retailers. The company's product line consists primarily of bedroom sets. Pine Belt markets its products to cost-conscious buyers who want quality products but cannot afford furniture constructed of expensive wood, such as maple, oak, or mahogany. Marketing studies indicate the company's typical customer is under 30 years old, recently married, and has an annual family income of less than $50,000. Pine Belt recognizes the needs of cost-conscious buyers and has developed marketing and manufacturing strategies to meet those needs.

The designs for new products at Pine Belt begin with the engineering department. There the product and the manufacturing process are designed at the same time, minimizing manufacturing costs. Once product design and manufacturing processes are complete, raw materials (lumber and hardware) are ordered from suppliers and placed into raw materials inventory. Pine Belt works closely with its suppliers to minimize variation in the quality of the materials it buys. In addition, as materials are delivered and placed into inventory, quality control engineers select random samples for inspection and testing. Working with customers' orders, production schedulers at Pine Belt try to group similar products so that they can be manufactured at the same time. The manufacturing process involves cutting the lumber into components, assembling the components, and finishing the assembled product.

When an order is received on the manufacturing floor, an equipment operator removes raw materials from the storage area and places them into production. Processing steps involve cutting lumber to meet specifications, cutting square edges of the lumber at appropriate points to produce curves or other geometric designs, cutting dovetail joints where two pieces of lumber will be attached, and drilling holes to accommodate hardware. In the assembly department, the wooden components are assembled and hardware is attached. Here the pieces of lumber are glued, clamped, and screwed together. In the finishing stage, the assembled products are sanded and stained to darken the wood and to accent the grain. Next a polyurethane finish is applied to the surface to protect against scratching and other damage during use. Pine Belt applies five coats of polyurethane to each product. Workers lightly buff the surface with steel wool between each coat. When the last coat of polyurethane has dried, the product is boxed and shipped to retail furniture stores. Exhibit 1 illustrates Pine Belt's production process.

Many of Pine Belt's activities involve selling and administration. For example, the company employs salespersons who visit furniture retailers to promote the product line. In addition, the company employs a variety of people who serve in an administrative capacity. For example, Pine Belt Furniture has accounting, marketing, and human resources departments. Individuals employed in these functions support the manufacturing efforts of the company, but are not directly involved in making the company's products. Pine Belt incurs expenses for other types of selling and administrative activities. For example, the company contracts with a trucking company

Exhibit 1 Production Process at Pine Belt

A. Cutting

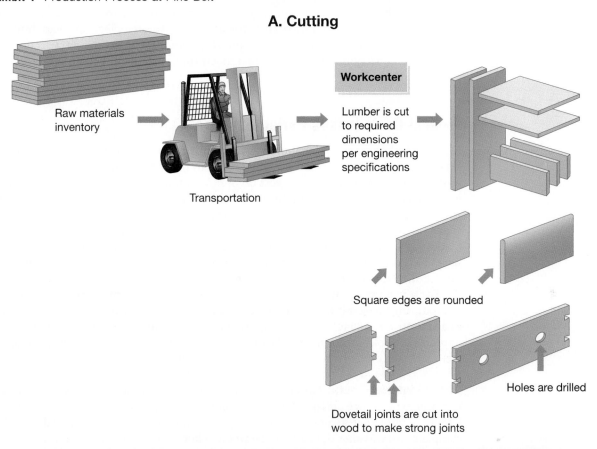

Raw materials inventory

Transportation

Workcenter

Lumber is cut to required dimensions per engineering specifications

Square edges are rounded

Holes are drilled

Dovetail joints are cut into wood to make strong joints

B. Assembly

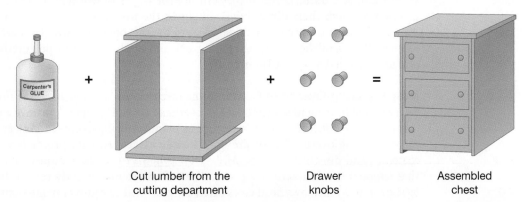

Carpenter's GLUE + Cut lumber from the cutting department + Drawer knobs = Assembled chest

C. Finishing

Sand Paper + Stain + Polyurethane + Steel wool between coats = Finished chest

to transport its finished products to retail stores. Pine Belt incurs many of the costs that are familiar to you from studying retail organizations in your financial accounting course. The company incurs costs for utilities, insurance, legal services, building rent, office supplies, and depreciation on office equipment. In the next section, we consider why accountants separate manufacturing costs from selling and administrative expenses.

Product Costs versus Period Expense

Erin and Seth, who own a manufacturing company, discussed the importance of understanding their production and selling costs in order to control them and to earn a profit. Before managers can use cost accounting information to make decisions, they must understand how that information is gathered. In your study of financial accounting you learned that most expenses are classified as either operating expenses or cost of goods (or services) sold. Period expenses are the costs of selling and administrative activities. Examples of period expenses include rent, interest, taxes, losses on equipment sales, and administrative salaries. These expenses are recognized on the income statement during the fiscal period in which they are incurred.

For a manufacturing company, cost of goods sold represents resources consumed in producing the goods that were sold during a fiscal period. Unsold goods are reported as assets on the balance sheet. Thus, product costs do not become expenses until the products are sold. Accountants classify resources consumed during production as direct materials, direct labor, and manufacturing overhead.

Direct Material Costs. The costs of significant raw materials from which a product is manufactured are classified as *direct material costs*. For example, Pine Belt uses lumber to construct its product line. The cost of lumber is a direct material cost. The company also classifies the costs of the wooden knobs or brass drawer pulls that workers attach to furniture as direct material costs.

Direct Labor Costs. *Direct labor costs* **are the wages of workers who add value to a product through their direct involvement in the production process.** For example, Pine Belt's direct labor costs include wages of the saw operators who cut parts from the lumber. Wages of those who assemble parts and apply stain and polyurethane finish also are classified as direct labor costs.

Manufacturing Overhead Costs. In the discussion at the beginning of this chapter, Seth recalled hearing managers speak of overhead costs. He seemed to have a vague idea about the kinds of costs that are classified as manufacturing overhead. As a general rule, manufacturing overhead costs are not as easily associated with products as are direct materials and direct labor costs. *Manufacturing overhead costs* **result from activities that support a manufacturing process but often are not directly related to any specific product.** Thus, overhead costs often are classified as indirect manufacturing costs. While examples of direct materials and direct labor at Pine Belt have been identified, certain types of materials and labor are classified as indirect. For instance, the salary of the quality inspector and wages of workers who maintain equipment and clean the manufacturing area are considered indirect labor costs.

The cost of indirect materials is a manufacturing overhead cost. At Pine Belt, those costs include the costs of saw blades in the cutting department, glue and screws in the assembly department, and steel wool in the finishing department. How do accountants decide whether to treat glue and screws as direct materials or indirect materials? Generally they use a cost/benefit rule. If the cost of tracking an item exceeds the benefit or value of that information, the cost of the item should be assigned to an overhead category and later allocated to products in a logical manner. For example, the cost of glue (about $0.03 per unit) is not worth measuring separately as a direct material cost. We consider overhead allocation in Chapter M3.

In addition to indirect labor and indirect materials, Pine Belt incurs other overhead costs in the production process as follows:

- Electricity for the manufacturing equipment
- Fire insurance on factory assets
- Supplies (cleaning rags, solvents, brooms, safety glasses, ear plugs, and dust masks) for equipment operators
- Depreciation on factory buildings and manufacturing equipment

Associating overhead costs with individual products is one of the most challenging and interesting aspects of management accounting. We further explore these issues in Chapter M5.

---

1 SELF-STUDY PROBLEM

WebTUTOR Advantage

Greencut Manufacturing produces energy-efficient lawn mowers for homeowners. Workers at Greencut manufacture the mower bodies from steel sheets and then attach a gasoline-powered engine, a blade, a handle, and four wheels to each unit.

The following events took place during the month of January:

1. Greencut bought steel sheets (cost, $5,000) for constructing mower bodies.
2. Steel sheets (cost, $2,000) were removed from raw materials inventory and delivered by forklift operators (total January wages, $5,000) to a metal-press machine operator (total January wages, $3,000), who pressed the flat sheets of steel into mower housings. Forklift operators delivered the mower housings to an automated painting booth. There, workers (total January wages, $2,000) placed the housings onto overhead conveyor hooks that moved through a booth containing robotic paint sprayers. All surfaces of the mower housing were sprayed with paint (total paint cost, $1,000). The painted housings moved along the conveyor belt into a dryer that was heated with propane gas (total January gas cost, $1,000).
3. After drying, forklift operators transported the painted housings to the assembly area. At the same time, engines, blades, handles, and wheels were removed from the inventory of "purchased parts" (total cost of parts removed from inventory, $20,000) and delivered by forklift to the assembly area. Finally, workers installed a motor, a blade, a handle, and four wheels to each housing (total January wages of assemblers, $6,000).
4. Greencut estimates depreciation costs on plant equipment to be $24,000 for the month of January.
5. Following assembly, the completed mowers were crated and shipped to retail stores throughout the world.

Required Classify each of Greencut's costs in January as direct material, direct labor, or overhead.

The solution to Self-Study Problem 1 appears at the end of the chapter.

HOW MANUFACTURING COSTS FLOW THROUGH AN ACCOUNTING SYSTEM

OBJECTIVE 2

Explain how direct material, direct labor, and manufacturing overhead costs flow through an accounting system.

Your financial accounting course addressed inventory reporting issues for retail and manufacturing organizations. Recall that retail organizations purchase completed goods from suppliers, add a markup, and sell the finished goods to their customers. Thus, a retail organization typically reports one type of inventory (finished goods) on its balance sheet. On the other hand, manufacturing organizations purchase raw materials from suppliers and convert them into finished goods during the manufacturing process.

Most manufacturing companies report three types of inventory on their balance sheets, raw materials, partially completed goods known as work-in-process (WIP), and finished goods. When retail and manufacturing organizations sell finished goods, the unit cost is reported on the income statement as cost of goods sold.

Companies use accounting systems to help them keep track of the various types of inventory and cost of goods sold. Exhibit 2 illustrates the flow of product costs through an accounting system. When materials are removed from raw materials inventory and placed into production, the work-in-process inventory account is increased. Accordingly, the raw materials inventory balance is reduced by the same amount, representing the cost of raw materials placed into production. As direct labor is used to convert the direct materials in the production area, these costs also are added to work-in-process inventory. Finally, various types of overhead costs are incurred during production and are added to the work-in-process inventory.

Exhibit 2 Cost Flows Through the Accounting System of a Manufacturing Company

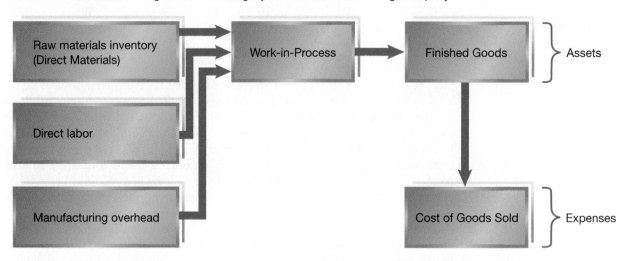

When goods are completed and moved from the production facility to the completed goods warehouse, accountants must adjust the work-in-process and finished goods inventory values. The cost of the completed products is added to the finished goods inventory account and removed from the work-in-process account. As shown in Exhibit 2, the final step involves transferring costs from the finished goods inventory to cost of goods sold. The accounting system records this transfer when the products are sold. Raw materials, work-in-process, and finished goods inventory appear on the balance sheet as assets. Their production costs appear as cost of goods sold on the income statement when the products are sold.

Exhibit 2 provides a general model of cost flows through an accounting system. Let's look at some actual transactions and see how the system keeps track of manufacturing costs. Assume the following activities took place at Pine Belt during January:

(a) Purchased raw materials (lumber, knobs, hardware) costing $50,000.
(b) Placed raw materials costing $20,000 into production.
(c) Incurred labor costs of $8,000 for cutting, assembling, and finishing activities.
(d) Purchased and consumed manufacturing supplies, such as sandpaper, stain, varnish, glue, and screws, costing $300.
(e) Incurred depreciation in the amount of $1,000 on manufacturing equipment.
(f) Incurred other overhead costs (including fire insurance, supervisors' salaries, and various utilities) in the amount of $5,000.
(g) Completed furniture costing $40,200.
(h) Sold furniture that cost $45,000 to produce.
(i) Paid 10% sales commissions on the furniture sold in transaction (h).

In addition to transactions (a)–(i), Pine Belt reported the following inventory balances at January 1:

Raw materials inventory	$10,000
Work-in-process inventory	40,000
Finished goods inventory	15,000

We use Exhibit 3 to illustrate cost flows through Pine Belt's accounting system. The columns in Exhibit 3 represent raw materials inventory, work-in-process inventory, finished goods inventory, and cost of goods sold. Without preparing journal entries, we may trace costs through our simple accounting system using plusses and minuses to indicate increases and decreases as resources flow through Pine Belt's accounting system.

Exhibit 3 Cost Flows Through Pine Belt's Accounting System

	Raw Materials	Work-in-Process	Finished Goods	Cost of Goods Sold
	Inventory			
Beginning balance	$10,000	$40,000	$15,000	
	+50,000 (a)			
	−20,000 (b)	+20,000 (b)		
Ending balance	$40,000	+8,000 (c)		
		+300 (d)		
		+1,000 (e)		
		+5,000 (f)		
		−40,200 (g)	+40,200 (g)	
	Ending balance	$34,100	−45,000 (h)	+45,000 (h)
			Ending balance $10,200	Ending balance $45,000

As shown in Exhibit 3, the beginning balances of raw materials inventory, work-in-process inventory, and finished goods inventory are $10,000, $40,000, and $15,000, respectively. We add or subtract transaction values from these balances as resources are placed into production, converted, completed, and sold. For example, a raw materials purchase of $50,000 increases the raw materials inventory account as shown by transaction (a). When raw materials costing $20,000 are placed in production, work-in-process inventory increases by $20,000 and raw materials inventory decreases by $20,000, as shown by transaction (b). Transaction (c) indicates Pine Belt incurred direct labor costs of $8,000 while manufacturing its products. These costs also are added to the work-in-process account in Exhibit 3.

In Chapter M3 we learn more about applying overhead to products. For now, let's put all overhead costs directly into work-in-process inventory as these costs are incurred. Transactions (d), (e), and (f) represent various types of overhead costs consumed during the production process. Each of these costs is added to work-in-process inventory.

Transaction (g) tells us Pine Belt completed furniture costing $40,200. As these goods are moved from the production area to the finished goods warehouse, the accounting system increases the finished goods inventory account by $40,200 and reduces the work-in-process inventory account by $40,200.

Transaction (h) indicates goods costing $45,000 were sold. The transaction to record cost of goods sold and reduce finished goods inventory is identical for a retail store and a manufacturing company. In each case, finished goods inventory is reduced and cost of goods sold is increased.

Transaction (i) is not shown in Exhibit 3. Sales commissions are period expenses rather than product costs. Thus, we omit the transaction from our product cost model.

Having recorded transactions (a)–(h), we may sum the columns to calculate the ending balances for each account. Exhibit 3 reports ending balances for raw materials, work-in-process, and finished goods inventory of $40,000, $34,100, and $10,200, respectively. In addition, cost of goods sold for the period is $45,000.

Here are several key points to remember about the way costs flow through the accounting system of a manufacturing company. First, when materials are placed into production, their costs become part of work-in-process inventory. In addition, direct labor and overhead costs become part of work-in-process inventory as labor and overhead are used to convert raw materials to products. Accountants often refer to direct labor and overhead costs as conversion costs. *Conversion costs* **are the costs of activities required to convert materials into products.** Imagine a product with hooks on it. As it moves through the factory, direct labor and overhead costs are attached to the hooks. When the product is finished, all of the costs that have "hooked on" to the product during manufacturing become part of finished goods inventory and, ultimately, the cost of goods sold.

Companies typically provide details of their inventory values in the notes to the financial statements. Exhibit 4 is from the **Vulcan Materials Company** 2002 annual report and illustrates the financial statement disclosure of various types of inventory. Included are finished products, raw materials, products (work) in process, and operating supplies and other inventories.

Exhibit 4

Excerpt from the Vulcan Materials Company 2002 Annual Report—Inventory Note Disclosure

Note 2 Inventories Inventories at December 31 were as follows (in thousands of dollars):			
	2002	2001	2000
Finished products	$189,378	$176,940	$155,258
Raw materials	10,191	13,284	15,578
Products in process	486	564	1,020
Operating supplies and other	39,531	37,627	27,188
Total inventories	$239,586	$228,415	$199,044

2 SELF-STUDY PROBLEM

WebTUTOR Advantage

To solve this problem, use the information in Self-Study Problem 1. In addition, assume Greencut does not carry work-in-process or finished goods inventory. All units are completed and sold during the month. Salespersons earned commissions of $10,000 in January.

Required

A. Prepare an exhibit similar to Exhibit 3 that shows the effects of January's activities on the company's raw materials inventory, purchased parts inventory, work-in-process inventory, finished goods inventory, and cost of goods sold. Assume that all beginning balances on January 1 were zero, except for purchased parts inventory, which had a beginning balance of $25,000.
B. What was the company's cost of goods sold for January?
C. What was the value of Greencut's raw materials and purchased parts inventories at the end of January?

The solution to Self-Study Problem 2 appears at the end of the chapter.

MANAGERIAL ACCOUNTING SYSTEMS TO SUPPORT DECISION MAKING

Previous sections of this chapter considered how to classify production costs and administrative expenses. We also addressed production cost flows through an accounting

Discuss methods for proactively managing inventory levels and manufacturing costs.

system to determine values for inventory and cost of goods sold. However, the purpose of understanding these costs, and the activities that drive them, is to help managers make better decisions. Thus, recording, summarizing, and reporting inventory costs are just part of the inventory picture. Management uses accounting information to coordinate activities with suppliers and customers. Suppliers that provide raw materials or components used in assembling a product are an integral part of a company's ability to profitably deliver goods to its customers. Reliable delivery of quality material and components from suppliers is necessary for a business to meet obligations to its customers. These interrelationships are known as a value chain. **The *value chain* is the set of value-creating activities that extends from the production of raw materials, to the sale of finished goods, to servicing customers after the sale.** The value chain includes activities both inside and outside a company. Managing the value chain requires a company to look beyond its own operations to those of its customers and suppliers. For example, to eliminate or reduce cost-creating activities, companies develop close relationships with customers and suppliers to reduce costs of excess inventories of raw materials and finished products.

Value chain analysis permits management to identify when a company has a competitive advantage by understanding the value added at each stage in the chain. When value chain analysis is applied at an operational level, non-value-adding activities within a company's production and delivery processes are eliminated or reduced. Identifying product costs helps managers identify and reduce the costs of making and handling inventory. Many companies use an inventory system called just in time (JIT) to make their manufacturing operations more efficient.

Just-in-time manufacturing (JIT) **is a manufacturing philosophy that attempts to improve efficiency by reducing inventory levels.** Under JIT, no product or component is manufactured until it is needed. JIT seeks to reduce the amount of time spent creating products, minimize inventories, improve quality, and reduce costs. Inventories of raw materials, component parts, and finished products held just in case they might be needed are eliminated. Managerial accounting can support JIT by supplying information that identifies sources of delay, error, and waste in the manufacturing system.

A goal of JIT systems is to reduce the length of time it takes to manufacture and deliver a product. JIT concepts require processing small batches that match demand, and to maximize time spent adding value to products. Examples include:

- Reducing the time required to respond to customer demands such as cashing checks at banks,
- Moving finished products faster to reduce inventory, and
- Reducing distribution time once products leave the factory.

Thus, value chain and JIT concepts permit managers to examine relationships among themselves, their suppliers, and customers. These concepts are important to managers when proactively controlling costs.

Proactively Controlling Costs Using Target Costing

Target costing begins by understanding customer expectations for product cost, quality, and functionality. Managers then design a product that meets their customers' expectations. Targets are established for product costs that permit the company to meet specific profits levels. Suppliers are involved to ensure raw materials meet cost and quality targets. In addition, delivery terms often are consistent with JIT concepts. We illustrate the integrative nature of target costing using Pine Belt Furniture Company.

Assume that the managers at Pine Belt have made the strategic decision to expand the product line to offer a product that can compete with those offered by high-quality furniture manufacturers. The first piece in the new line is a bedroom chest of drawers constructed from clear (knot-free) pine and solid brass drawer pulls.

Pine Belt's managers have invested resources in engineering drawings, product prototypes, and studies of manufacturing processes before implementing full-scale production of the chest. Naturally they want to recover their investment and earn a profit on the sale of the new product. To determine the price of the chest, managers first estimated the per-unit costs of producing it.

Pine Belt's management offered the following explanation of the unit costs:

Direct materials. The chest differs from other products in the line because expensive, knot-free wood and solid brass are used in its construction.

Direct labor. Managers predict the direct labor costs of the chest in the cutting department will be identical to that of other products in the line. However, they expect direct labor costs to go up in the assembly and finishing departments because the process of assembling and finishing the chest is more complex and time-consuming than for other products in the line.

Manufacturing overhead. Management expects an increase in the manufacturing costs per unit due to additional engineering time and new equipment purchased solely to assemble and finish the product.

The total estimated materials, labor, and overhead cost per unit is $475. Pine Belt generally adds a 30 percent markup to the unit cost when it quotes prices to customers. The markup is calculated as follows:

Unit manufacturing cost × Markup percentage = Markup
$475.00   ×   0.30   = $142.50

The managers at Pine Belt calculate the selling price to a furniture store as follows:

Unit manufacturing cost + Markup = Selling price
$475.00   + $142.50 = $617.50

Using costs to help them determine a selling price, Pine Belt's managers set the wholesale price of the chest at $618. After applying their own markup, retailers must sell the chest for approximately $1,000. Unfortunately, after producing a new catalog and price list, as well as floor models of the chest for display in retailers' showrooms, the managers at Pine Belt hear some disappointing news. Retailers are not interested in carrying the line because consumers are not willing to pay $1,000 retail for pine furniture, even when that furniture is constructed of knot-free lumber and solid brass pulls. How could this happen? The management of Pine Belt carefully studied the components of product cost, yet found the flagship of its product line sank! What went wrong?

This situation illustrates a traditional cost-based pricing policy in which the following steps occur:

1. A product and manufacturing process are designed.
2. The product is manufactured.
3. Manufacturing costs are accumulated.
4. The unit cost plus markup determines the selling price.
5. The company tries to sell the product.

Pine Belt failed to analyze the market before developing its new product. Although the new chest seemed to meet consumers' demands for quality and functionality, it did not meet their price demands. By adding a markup to its manufacturing costs, Pine Belt's managers overpriced the chest.

Target costing changes the focus of product pricing. Instead of production costs determining the selling price, the selling price determines the production costs. The purpose of a target costing system is to provide quality and functionality at a cost that achieves long-term profit objectives. The process of calculating a target cost is as follows:

1. Determine the quality and functionality consumers want in a new product and the price they are willing to pay for that product.

2. Subtract the manufacturer's required profit margin from the price to determine what the manufacturer can spend to produce the product.
3. Study the feasibility of the new product. Can the company produce a product consumers want at a price the market will accept?

The target cost calculation involves an understanding of the relationships among three variables: the selling price, the targeted manufacturing cost (cost), and the required profit margin. The relationship among the variables is defined as follows:

Selling price − Required profit margin = Target cost

Suppose market research sets the wholesale price of the chest at $400. Management has determined a margin of 23 percent on sales is required for long-term profitability. The company's required margin and target cost are calculated as follows:

$$
\begin{aligned}
\text{Margin} &= \text{Selling price} \times 0.23 \\
&= \$400 \qquad \times 0.23 \\
&= \$92
\end{aligned}
$$

The target cost information for Pine Belt can be summarized as follows:

Selling price	$400
Less required margin	−92
Target cost	$308

Determining the cost at which Pine Belt must deliver the chest is the first step in using target costing for strategic purposes. Clearly the managers at Pine Belt have a problem: To market the new chest successfully, they must reduce the unit cost of producing the chest from $475 to $308.

One way companies begin to address a cost problem is by forming a multidisciplinary team, a team whose members are drawn from different functions such as marketing, accounting, finance, production, purchasing, and engineering. The team looks for ways to save costs and to eliminate inefficiencies.

Pine Belt's team would evaluate major production costs. Managers would discuss redesigning the manufacturing process and reconsidering the types of materials used. Using value chain concepts, they would examine ways to reduce suppliers' costs. They would study the sources of overhead costs and methods of reducing those costs. However, if the team determines that they cannot produce the chest for $308, Pine Belt should not produce the product. Exhibit 5 compares the cost-plus philosophy with the target costing philosophy.

Exhibit 5

Cost-Plus and Target Costing Philosophies

Cost-plus philosophy

Cost + Markup = Selling price

Implications:
- Cost is the starting point (given)
- Markup is added (given)
- The firm puts the product on the market and hopes the selling price is accepted

Target costing philosophy

Selling price − Required margin = Target cost

Implications:
- Markets determine prices (given)
- Required margins must be sustained for survival (given)
- Target cost is the residual, the variable to be managed

Case In Point

http://ingram.
swlearning.com

Learn more about
target costing.

Target Costing at Hewlett-Packard

The Vancouver Division of **Hewlett-Packard** (HP) uses target costing to work with its suppliers to manage the cost of making the desk jet printer. The facility recently has changed its strategy from producing low-volume, high-margin industrial products to high-volume, low-margin consumer products. HP reports achieving substantial price decreases as a result of their target costing program. In addition, the company uses target costing to support continuous improvement efforts and to identify various activities that cause costs within the value chain.

Source: Anonymous. 2000. Target costing gives HP better control over supply costs. New York: Supplier and Management Report.

Cost Information for Service Organizations

In service organizations, costs attach to services in much the same way as they do in manufacturing organizations; only the nature of the product is different. For example, a hospital doesn't produce a tangible product, such as furniture. Its product is an intangible service, patient health care. When a patient leaves the health-care system, the costs of providing care become part of the cost of services provided, the service organization's equivalent to cost of goods sold. This section describes cost categories and cost control in a service environment. As you will see, many similarities exist between a service and manufacturing organization.

Cost Categories

Hospitals, like manufacturers, classify costs as direct and indirect. The costs of nurses' salaries, drugs, and X-rays are all direct costs of delivering care to patients. Like direct costs in manufacturing, direct costs in a hospital are easily associated with a patient. Hospitals and most other service organizations generally have a large proportion of indirect costs that must be assigned to individual patients or customer services in some manner. Among a hospital's indirect costs are salaries of administrators, admission and discharge personnel, and insurance specialists.

Cost Control

In today's economy, all businesses are taking steps to control production costs. Health-care providers face a special challenge. At one time, hospitals were reimbursed by insurance companies (or the federal government in the case of Medicare) based on their costs of treating patients. Today, insurance companies are applying pressure by limiting the fees they pay for each type of treatment. Because their revenue largely is determined by insurance providers, hospitals can operate profitably only if they manage costs effectively.

Manufacturing companies use target costing to help provide products desired by customers at costs that ensure profitability. Hospitals use a similar technique called critical path. They identify the steps necessary for each procedure from pre-admission to discharge. By standardizing procedures, health-care providers often find ways to reduce inefficiency and costs. The critical path helps service organizations control costs in a similar way that target costing helps manufacturing companies control costs.

3 **SELF-STUDY PROBLEM** Greencut is considering adding a mulching lawn mower to its product line. The new mower cuts grass clippings into fine particles, eliminating raking, bagging, and disposing of lawn wastes. The new product is intended to meet the needs of urban and environmentally conscious homeowners.

WebTUTOR Advantage

Greencut wants to conduct a target costing exercise to determine the cost at which the new product must be produced. Market surveys indicate that retailers typically pay $300 and sell for $500 products with similar features. Thus, the company expects the wholesale price for the new mower to be $300. Greencut's required margin on sales is 26 percent.

Required Calculate the target cost of the new mower and Greencut's required markup.

The solution to Self-Study Problem 3 appears at the end of the chapter.

REVIEW *SUMMARY of IMPORTANT CONCEPTS*

1. Costs may be classified according to a number of categories including:
   a. Product cost versus period expense.
   b. Direct materials, direct labor, or overhead.

2. Manufacturing costs flow through an accounting system as products physically move through the factory.
   a. When raw materials are acquired, their value is added to raw materials inventory.
   b. When raw materials are placed into production, their costs, along with the costs of labor and overhead, are added to work-in-process inventory.
   c. The cost of completed goods is transferred to finished goods inventory.
   d. The costs in finished goods inventory are transferred to cost of goods sold when the units are sold.

3. Managers use cost information to help them make better decisions.
   a. Understanding the value chain enables managers to work with their customers and suppliers to minimize costs and to provide high-quality products or services.
   b. Just-in-time inventory practices help companies reduce inventory levels and the time required to produce and deliver a product.
   c. Target costing helps managers in the introduction of new products.

4. Organizations that produce services instead of tangible products also incur production costs.
   a. The costs of services are classified as direct or indirect.
   b. Service organizations often implement cost control procedures to identify and eliminate waste.

DEFINE *TERMS and CONCEPTS DEFINED in this CHAPTER*

conversion costs (M36)
direct labor costs (M32)
direct material costs (M32)

just-in-time manufacturing (JIT) (M37)
manufacturing overhead costs (M32)
value chain (M37)

SELF-STUDY PROBLEM SOLUTIONS

SSP2-1 The costs identified by Greencut included the following:

Direct material
Steel
Paint
Wheels, motors, handles, and blades

Direct labor
Metal-press machine operator
Spray-booth workers
Assembly area workers

Overhead
Indirect materials:
    Propane gas
Indirect labor:
    Forklift operators' wages
Other manufacturing overhead costs:
    Depreciation on the plant equipment

SSP2-2   A.

Inventory

	Raw Materials	Purchased Parts	Work-in-Process	Finished Goods	Cost of Goods Sold
Beg. bal.	$ 0	$ 25,000	$ 0	$ 0	$ 0
	+5,000 (a)	−20,000 (h)	+2,000 (b)	+64,000 (k)	+64,000 (l)
	−2,000 (b)	End. $ 5,000	+5,000 (c)	−64,000 (l)	End. $ 64,000
	End. $ 3,000		+3,000 (d)	End. $ 0	
			+2,000 (e)		
			+1,000 (f)		
			+1,000 (g)		
			+20,000 (h)		
			+6,000 (i)		
			+24,000 (j)		
			−64,000 (k)		
			End. $ 0		

Key to cost flows:
(a) Greencut purchased steel sheets that were placed into raw materials inventory.
(b) Steel was removed from inventory and placed into production as work-in-process inventory.
(c) Overhead for the forklift operators' wages was incurred.
(d) Direct labor costs of $3,000 for the metal-press operator were incurred.
(e) Direct labor wages for paint booth/conveyor operators were incurred.
(f) Direct materials cost of $1,000 for paint was incurred.
(g) Overhead cost (indirect materials) for the propane gas was consumed.
(h) Purchased parts (direct materials) were transferred from inventory to production.
(i) Direct labor costs ($6,000) for workers in the assembly area were incurred.
(j) Depreciation on manufacturing assets was estimated to be $24,000 during the month.
(k) Completed mowers were transferred to the finished goods inventory.
(l) Finished mowers costing $64,000 were sold.

Note: Sales commissions are not part of product costs or the cost of goods sold. Sales commissions are a period expense and are reported on the income statement below gross profit.

B. Cost of goods sold in January was $64,000.

C. The balance in raw materials inventory was $3,000, and the balance in purchased parts inventory was $5,000.

SSP2-3   Required margin = Required percentage × Sales price
                 = 0.26 × $300
                 = $78

The target cost information for Greencut may be summarized as follows:

Selling price (wholesale)	$300
Less required margin	−78
Target cost	$222

Thinking Beyond the Question

How can accounting classifications help us understand costs?

In the opening scenario, Erin and Seth were considering ways to classify costs and to use their accounting reports. Can managers use cost reports based on past activities to help control future costs?

QUESTIONS

Q2-1
Obj. 1
Your textbook is manufactured from a number of materials including paper, ink, and glue. Typically, publishing company accountants consider paper and ink direct materials; however, they consider glue an indirect material. How do accountants make these distinctions?

Q2-2
Obj. 1
Wendell Fromm Company manufactures hand tools that are used in many factory applications. The company manufactures tools from metal alloys and incurs labor and overhead costs during the manufacturing process. What costs should Wendell Fromm include in the cost of goods sold section of its income statement? Why?

Q2-3
Obj. 1
Carlton Industries manufactures orthopedic devices, such as hips and joints, from specialty metals. Each device is produced individually based on the dimensions of a specific patient. The company ships the devices to surgeons as soon as production is completed. Define and explain the different types of inventory accounts that Carlton would use in its manufacturing environment. What costs are associated with each of these accounts?

Q2-4
Obj. 1
The nurses on the fourth floor of Western Medical Center care for and administer drugs to patients who have undergone orthopedic surgery. Also located on the fourth floor is a mobile X-ray station that Western recently purchased for $250,000. How would you classify the costs of nursing care and drugs? How would you classify the depreciation costs associated with the X-ray machine? Explain your answer.

Q2-5
Obj. 1
If product costs eventually become expenses when a product is sold, why are accountants so careful when making product cost and period expense classifications?

Q2-6
Obj. 1
Can service organizations, such as legal and accounting firms, report work-in-process and finished goods inventories on their balance sheets?

Q2-7
Obj. 1
How are direct labor costs different from indirect labor costs?

Q2-8
Obj. 2
Why do manufacturing companies typically report three kinds of inventory on the balance sheet, while merchandising companies typically report only one kind of inventory?

Q2-9
Obj. 2
What is meant by the term "conversion costs"? What kinds of costs would you classify as a conversion cost?

Q2-10
Obj. 3
How does the target costing approach to new product introduction differ from the traditional cost-plus approach? Are these differences important? Why or why not?

Q2-11
Obj. 3
Discuss how JIT and supply chain concepts are related.

Q2-12
Obj. 3
What steps are required to develop a target cost? How are these steps different from the cost-plus approach?

| **EXERCISES** | *If your instructor is using Personal Trainer® in this course, you may complete your assignments online.* |

E2-1   Write a short definition for each of the terms listed in the *Terms and Concepts Defined in this Chapter* section.

E2-2   Westco, Inc., has the following costs and expenses. Complete the schedule provided. Indicate
Obj. 1   the classification of each item listed. The first one is done for you.

	Period Expense	Product Cost Direct	Product Cost Indirect
a. Factory depreciation IC			X
b. Packaging materials DC			
c. President's salary PE			
d. Sales commissions PE			
e. Machine lubricants ID			
? f. Magazine subscriptions, factory break room IC, PE			
g. Insurance on finished goods PE,			
h. Workers' wages in assembly department DC			
i. Salary of payroll clerk PE			
? j. Grounds upkeep ? PE			
? k. Shop rags ?			
? l. Training program, factory workers PE, DC			
m. Ink used in textbook production DC			
n. Health insurance, factory workers PE			
o. Glue used in production of wooden chairs IC			
p. Life insurance on executives PE			
? q. Raw steel, toolbox production ?			
r. Gas for salesperson's car PE			
s. Sales travel expenses IC			
t. Disposal of machine coolants IC			

E2-3   a.   The costs of significant raw materials from which a product is manufactured are classi-
Objs. 1–3   fied as _____.

      b.   _____ are the costs of activities required to convert materials into products.

      c.   _____ result from activities that support a process but often are not directly related to any specific product.

      d.   The _____ is the set of value-creating activities that extends from the production of raw materials, to the sale of finished goods, to servicing customers after the sale.

      e.   _____ are the wages of workers who add value to a product through their direct involvement in the production process.

      f.   _____ is a manufacturing philosophy that attempts to improve efficiency by reducing inventory levels.

E2-4   Classify each of the following costs as either a product cost or a period expense. Briefly jus-
Obj. 1   tify your answers.

      a.   Wages for factory maintenance workers
      b.   Direct materials
      c.   Sales salaries and commissions
      d.   Depreciation expense, office equipment
      e.   Machinery repairs and maintenance
      f.   Advertising
      g.   Property taxes, factory building
      h.   Indirect materials
      i.   Accounting fees
      j.   Warehousing costs for finished goods
      k.   Production supervisor's salary
      l.   Utilities for plant
      m.   Rent on factory buildings

E2-5
Obj. 1

Matt Holgren is the marketing manager for a small manufacturing firm. The salespersons in his division are paid commissions of 29% of the gross margin of each product sold. Because a salesperson complained that gross margin was calculated improperly when preparing a commission check, Matt is auditing the commission report that follows:

Item #531

Sales price:		$1,300
Costs:		
Raw materials	$375	
Raw material transportation	110	
Direct labor	90	
Manufacturing overhead	200	
Finished goods transportation	150	
Administrative costs	60	
Total		985
Gross margin		$ 315

Commission: $315 × 0.29 = $91.35

   a. If gross margin is computed according to GAAP, does the salesperson have a valid complaint? Explain.

   b. What type of behavior is management attempting to promote by basing commissions on gross margin rather than on total sales dollars? Explain.

E2-6
Obj. 1

For all costs you identified as product costs in E2-4, indicate whether each should be classified as a direct material, direct labor, or manufacturing overhead cost. Justify your answer.

E2-7
Obj. 1

Exercise 2-5 identifies two forms of transportation cost: raw material transportation and finished goods transportation. Explain why GAAP require two different accounting treatments for transportation costs.

E2-8
Obj. 2

The partial information that follows pertains to the operations of Good Time Clock Company for 2004:

Raw materials inventory, January 1, 2004	$ 5,000
Raw materials inventory, December 31, 2004	2,000
Direct labor charged to production during 2004	18,000
Factory overhead costs incurred during 2004	15,000
Cost of goods manufactured for the year 2004	45,000
Work-in-process inventory, January 1, 2004	5,000
Work-in-process inventory, December 31, 2004	15,000
Finished goods inventory, January 1, 2004	15,000
Cost of goods sold	40,000

Determine (a) the cost of materials purchased, (b) the cost of raw materials used during the year, and (c) the balance in the finished goods inventory account on December 31, 2004.

E2-9
Obj. 2

Wendy Minor is the plant controller at Medical Supply Company. She is reviewing year-end balances of raw materials, work in process, and finished goods. In attempting to control inventory carrying costs, management has established programs designed to minimize inventory levels throughout the organization. Relevant data are presented as follows:

	Raw Materials	Work in Process	Finished Goods
January 1, 2004	$550,000	$900,000	$650,000

Data for year ended December 31, 2004

Raw material purchases	$1,350,000
Raw material issued to production	1,150,000
Direct labor costs incurred	2,250,000
Manufacturing overhead costs incurred	3,000,000
Goods completed and transferred to finished goods inventory	6,050,000
Cost of goods sold	6,550,000

(Continued)

a. Compute the ending balances of each inventory account.

b. Has the company been successful in reducing inventory balances? Explain.

c. What types of costs may be associated with high levels of inventory?

E2-10
Obj. 3

Rowflex manufactures exercise equipment that is sold through major retail chain stores. The company has developed a new exercise bench. Based on the company's market research, the selling price should not exceed $450. If Rowflex requires a margin of $75, determine the target cost and explain why the cost is important to the company's planning process.

E2-11
Obj. 3

Calico has the following products. Complete the schedule below. The first one has been done for you.

Item Description	Target Unit Cost	Target Margin	Target Margin %	Selling Price
Item A	$15	$ 5	25% *14.29%*	$20
Item B	$72	? *12*	?	$84
Item C	? *$59.50*	? *10.50*	15%	$70
Item D	$42	$ 6	? *12.5%*	? *$48*
Item E	? *$84*	$12	? *12.5%*	$96

Note: Target margin is expressed as a percentage of selling price.

E2-12
Obj. 3

April Incorporated is developing a product that will sell for $160 per unit. The unit cost of the product is expected to include direct materials ($70), direct labor ($35), and manufacturing overhead ($15). What is the margin as a percentage of sales?

E2-13
Obj. 3

Refer to the information in E2-12. If April requires a margin on sales of 30%, how much cost must be eliminated from the product to reach this margin if there is no change in the sales price?

PROBLEMS

If your instructor is using Personal Trainer® in this course, you may complete your assignments online.

P2-1
Obj. 1

Ethics—Product versus Period Classification

Assume management intentionally misclassified a period expense as a product cost in order to meet analysts' earnings expectations. The fraud later was discovered during the annual audit.

Required Explain how the misclassification enabled management to boost the company's earnings.

P2-2
Obj. 1

Accounting Irregularities at WorldCom

In a widely publicized accounting scandal, management at **WorldCom** was accused of recording $11 billion of operating expenses as long-term assets on its balance sheet. The action significantly increased the company's reported earnings.

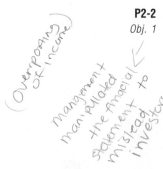

(Overstating or income) management manipulated the financial statement to mislead investors

Required

A. Explain how misclassifying expenses allowed the company's management to overstate earnings.

B. Does the WorldCom case represent an ethical issue?

P2-3
Obj. 1

Cost Classification

Tim Ricker lives in Atlanta. He is a toolmaker for Georgia Industries, a manufacturer of heavy equipment such as backhoes, graders, and earthmoving equipment. Tim makes specialty tools and jigs that are used on different machines in the plant. His annual salary is $35,000. Ann Thompson also works for Georgia Industries. She is an independent sales representative who lives in El Paso, Texas. She is paid a straight salary of $25,000 but also earns a 5% commission on sales. Ann is responsible for accounts in the west Texas area, works out of an office in her home, and is reimbursed by Georgia Industries for her travel expenses. The company provides Ann with a leased vehicle and a gasoline credit card.

Required

A. Is Tim's salary a manufacturing or nonmanufacturing expense? If manufacturing, would it be classified as direct labor? Explain your answer.

B. Is Ann's salary a manufacturing or nonmanufacturing expense? Are the commissions she earns manufacturing or nonmanufacturing? Explain your answer.

P2-4 Cost Flows in an Accounting System

Obj. 2

Bama Company showed the following balances in its inventory accounts as of January 1, 2004:

Raw materials inventory	$10,000
Work-in-process inventory	20,000
Finished goods inventory	10,000

The following transactions took place during 2004:

1. Manufacturing overhead costs of $96,000 were incurred and placed into work-in-process.
2. Raw material purchases totaled $34,000.
3. Direct labor charges in the amount of $119,000 were paid.
4. The cost of goods sold was determined to be $225,000.
5. Raw materials in the amount of $34,000 were placed into production.
6. The ending finished goods inventory balance was $14,000.

Required

A. Prepare a schedule that shows the raw materials, work-in-process, finished goods, and cost of goods sold accounts. Determine the year-end balance for each account.

B. A variety of individuals may find these balances useful. For example, bank loan officers, production managers, and sales managers may make decisions using comparative account balances. Describe how each of these individuals might use the data.

C. What trends do you observe in the raw materials, work-in-process, and finished goods inventory accounts?

D. If the marketing department forecasts flat or slightly declining sales for the coming year, what recommendations might you make to the company about managing inventory levels?

P2-5 Cost Flows through an Accounting System

Obj. 2

Clearview Glass Company purchases sand and various chemicals to be melted in the company's glass furnace. The molten glass flows along a conveyor system that defines sheet thickness and width and cools the molten glass. At the end of the process, workers cut the sheets of glass to a variety of dimensions and package them for delivery to their customers. During the month, Clearview purchased sand and chemicals totaling $190,000 and placed $175,000 of the amount purchased into production. Natural gas consumed in the melting process equaled $200,000. The manufacturing process is machine-intensive, thus depreciation on the furnace and conveyor systems totaled $300,000. Direct labor totaled $80,000. Supplies purchased and consumed in cutting and packaging equaled $65,000. The company's beginning sand and chemical inventory was valued at $18,000, while the beginning work-in-process inventory was valued at $75,000. Ending work-in-process inventory was valued at $60,000. During the month Clearview sold goods costing $795,000 for $1,330,000. The beginning inventory of finished goods was reported on the company's balance sheet at $90,000. General, selling, and administrative costs were recorded at $400,000.

Required

A. Prepare a schedule similar to Exhibit 3 to illustrate how costs flow through Clearview's accounting system.

B. Calculate the cost of goods manufactured.

C. Determine the balance in the raw materials and finished goods inventory accounts.

D. Having determined production costs, a manager might use this information to support decision making in a variety of ways. How might a production manager use cost and profitability information? How might a marketing manager use cost and profitability information?

P2-6 **Decision Making—Inventory and Cost of Goods Sold**

Obj. 2

SPREADSHEET

The accounting firm of Lawton and Smith provides tax preparation services for its clients. Secretaries typically contact the client to schedule an appointment. When a client arrives at the firm's office, a partner conducts an interview and collects documentation supporting the information for the tax return. A staff accountant is given the interview notes and supporting documents, such as Form W-2 and cancelled checks, and enters the data into a computer program. The partner is responsible for reviewing the accuracy of the return before a secretary duplicates and packages it.

During the month of March, Lawton and Smith incurred revenue and costs as follows:

Revenues	$95,000
Product costs	
Secretarial salaries	$ 4,000
Partner salaries	15,000
Various overhead accounts	5,000
Professional accountant salaries	30,000
Computer supplies purchased and consumed	2,000
Period expenses	
Building rent (administrative portion)	3,000
Utilities (administrative portion)	700
Depreciation on furniture (administrative portion)	7,000

The company maintained insignificant balances of supplies that can be ignored, but reported work-in-process and finished services inventories on March 1 as $20,000 and $5,000, respectively. On March 31, the company reported work-in-process and finished services inventories as $15,000, and $7,000, respectively.

Required

A. Identify each product cost as direct materials, direct labor, or overhead.
B. Calculate the cost of services provided (cost of goods sold) during March.
C. Calculate cost of services sold percentage and the gross margin percentage as a percentage of revenues.
D. How might your analysis support partners in decisions concerning the firm?

P2-7 **Accounting for Inventory at Ford Motor Company**

Obj. 2

Ford Motor Company reported the following information in the notes of its 2002 annual report:

Note 5. INVENTORIES—AUTOMOTIVE SECTOR
Inventories at December 31 were as follows (in millions):

	2002	2001
Raw materials, work-in-process and supplies	$3,174	$2,430
Finished products	4,763	4,602
Total inventories	7,937	7,032
Less adjustment	(957)	(905)
Total inventories	$6,980	$6,127

Required

A. Speculate on the types of raw materials Ford Motor Company reported in its annual report.
B. What is an example of work-in-process for Ford Motor Company? Have inventories increased or decreased during the reporting period? What might explain the increase or decrease?

P2-8 **Manufacturing Cost Flows**

Objs. 2, 3

O'Neill Company began the year with $870,000 of raw materials inventory, $1,390,000 of work-in-process inventory, and $620,000 of finished goods inventory. During the year, the company purchased $3,550,000 of raw material and used $3,720,000 of raw materials in production. Labor used in production for the year was $2,490,000. Overhead was $1,380,000. Work-in-process completed and transferred to finished goods inventory was $7,410,000. Cost of goods sold for the year was $7,500,000.

Required

A. Determine the ending balance in the raw materials, work in process, and finished goods inventory accounts.
B. Assume O'Neill practices JIT inventory management. Its goal is to reduce inventory levels, improve quality, and reduce costs. Comment on O'Neill's success in reducing inventory levels. *JIT is working*

P2-9
Obj. 3
Target Cost Calculation and Use

Go-yo is a company that designs, manufactures, and markets the world's best competition yo-yos. The company's engineers have designed a new product to be manufactured using a titanium bearing. Such a design will permit the user to accomplish more sophisticated tricks resulting from the yo-yo's ability to "sleep" for longer periods of time. Market research has determined that customers will pay $225 for such a product. A margin of 30% (based on the selling price) is required.

Required

A. Calculate the target cost for Go-yo's new yo-yo.
B. If the estimated cost to produce the product exceeds the target cost, what options are available to Go-yo's management?

P2-10
Obj. 3
Target Costing and Managerial Action

SPREADSHEET

Surgery Corporation has developed a surgical instrument that permits less invasive surgical procedures, resulting in less scarring and quicker rehabilitation. Management believes demand for the instrument will come primarily from sports medicine clinics that specialize in athletic-related injuries. Because health-care providers are under intense pressure from insurance companies to control costs, Surgery understands the new instrument must be priced to permit clinics to earn a reasonable return from surgical procedures.

Surgery's marketing department conducted numerous interviews and surveys with potential customers to determine a price that would be attractive to buyers. In addition, the interviews revealed numerous ideas for product enhancement. Based on these efforts, the marketing vice president recommended a target price of $270,000. Surgery intends to finance the development of the new instrument by issuing bonds. The vice president of finance estimates the margin on sales must be approximately 15% to provide an adequate rate of return to investors.

Required

A. Determine the target cost for the new surgical instrument.
B. Explain why understanding cost behavior is crucial for estimating cost reductions associated with the target costing process.
C. What actions might managers consider if a cost study results in an estimated cost of $240,000 to produce the new surgical instrument? Elaborate.
D. Identify the functional areas of those who would be selected to evaluate the problem. Explain your reasoning.

P2-11
Obj. 3
Just-in-Time Manufacturing

Happy PC makes personal computers for home consumers. The company decides to switch to a just-in-time manufacturing system. Since Happy PC's manufacturing processes have changed, the managerial accounting information measured must change.

Required

A. What accounting information is needed to evaluate the just-in-time manufacturing process?
B. How detailed should the information be?

P2-12
Obj. 3

Managerial Accounting and Value Chain Analysis

Jenny Smith, the owner of Blasto Walkmans, analyzed the high warranty costs the company was incurring. She determined one of the major defects was the result of a low-priced battery device provided by a supplier.

Required

A. How can managerial accounting be used to assist Jenny in determining whether she should install a more expensive, higher-quality battery device?
B. How could Jenny use value chain analysis to provide better information in making this decision?

P2-13

Excel in Action

SPREADSHEET

Music Makers copies software and music to CDs and packages these products for customers. The company's production process includes two departments. The first department copies the software to blank CDs. The second department places the CDs in plastic containers, places printed title pages in the CDs, wraps the containers in cellophane, and transfers the boxes to shipping.

During March, Music Makers started and completed 500,000 units. There were no beginning work-in-process or finished goods inventories. Material costs per unit were:

Blank CDs	$0.70
Plastic containers	0.09
Printed material	0.06
Cellophane	0.01

Labor costs were $40,000 in the copying department and $60,000 in the packaging department. Manufacturing overhead was $20,000 in the copying department and $6,000 in the packaging department.

The company's inventory at the beginning of March included $8,000 of blank CDs, $1,800 of plastic containers, and $2,500 of cellophane. Printed materials are not inventoried. They are received from printers as needed for the products. During March, Music Makers purchased blank CDs costing $355,000, plastic containers costing $60,000, and cellophane costing $3,000. By the end of the month, the company had shipped goods costing $520,000 to customers. The remaining goods were in the finished goods inventory.

Required Use a spreadsheet to calculate inventory balances and manufacturing costs for Music Makers for March. The following partial spreadsheet is illustrated as an example:

	A	B	C	D	E	F	G	H	I
1		CD Inventory	Container Inventory	Cellophane Inventory		Copying WIP	Packaging WIP	Finished Goods	Cost of Goods Sold
2	Beginning	8,000	1,800	2,500	Beginning	–	–	–	–
3	Purchases				Materials				
4	To production				Labor				
5	Ending				Overhead				
6					Transferred in				
7					Transferred out				
8					Ending				

Use the Format menu to adjust cell formats as needed to wrap text for long titles. Use the comma button to format dollar amounts. See instructions from the appendix, *A Short Introduction to Excel*, if you need help with formatting.

Materials costs include the costs of materials used in the department during March. These should be calculated by multiplying unit costs times the number of units produced. Use references to other cells in your calculations where possible. For example, the material costs in the copying department (column F) are equal to the CD inventory costs transferred out of raw materials (column B). Transferred-in costs are those from a preceding process. Consequently, the costs transferred in to packaging are those transferred out (total costs) from copying, and the costs transferred in to finished goods are those transferred out from packaging. Transferred-in costs should be positive and transferred-out costs should be negative. Multiply the amount in a cell by (21) to make it negative. For example, 5100*(21) will result in 2100.

Format cells so that totals are separated from other cells by single underlines and cells containing totals contain double underlines. Use the Borders button ⊞ ▾ for this purpose.

P2-14 Multiple-Choice Overview of the Chapter

1. During May 2003, Bennett Manufacturing Company purchased $43,000 of raw materials. The company's manufacturing overhead for the month totaled $27,000 and the total manufacturing costs were $106,000. Assuming a beginning inventory of raw materials of $8,000 and an ending inventory of raw materials of $6,000, direct labor must have totaled:
   a. $34,000.
   b. $38,000.
   c. $36,000.
   d. $45,000.

2. The wages of the maintenance personnel in a manufacturing plant are an example of:

	Indirect Labor Costs	Manufacturing Overhead Costs
a.	No	Yes
b.	Yes	No
c.	Yes	Yes
d.	No	No

3. The distinction between indirect and direct costs depends on:
   a. whether the costs are product costs or period expenses.
   b. whether the company has paid for the resource consumed.
   c. whether the costs can be easily traced to specific units of production.
   d. the manager responsible for controlling the cost.

4. The Rockin Roller Company manufactures rocking chairs. The following costs have been identified with rocking chairs produced during the current month:

   • $100,000 of springs were purchased and used. Each chair requires 2 springs at a cost of $10 per spring.
   • $1,700 of glue was used from one-gallon containers.
   • $500 of stain was used to touch up spots on the chairs.

   The total amount of indirect materials for the month would be:
   a. $102,200.
   b. $500.
   c. $2,200.
   d. $1,700.

5. Product costs appear on the balance sheet only:
   a. if goods are partially complete at the end of the period.
   b. if goods are unsold at the end of the period.
   c. if raw materials used to make the goods have been paid for.
   d. Both a and b are correct.

6. The value chain for a given product or service:
   a. reflects all activities associated with providing the particular product or service.
   b. identifies non-value-adding activities that should be eliminated or reduced.
   c. includes activities both inside and outside the company.
   d. All of the above are correct.

7. Costs flow through an accounting system as follows:
   a. raw materials, work in process, cost of goods sold, finished goods.
   b. finished goods, cost of goods sold, work in process, raw materials.
   c. raw materials, work in process, finished goods, cost of goods sold.
   d. raw materials, finished goods, cost of goods sold.

8. Target costing begins with a:
   a. target cost to which a markup is added.
   b. selling price from which a required margin is subtracted.
   c. required margin that is added to a target cost.
   d. selling price to which a markup is added.

9. The target cost calculation involves understanding the relationship among three variables:
   a. target cost, required profit margin, and selling price.
   b. selling price, target cost, and gross profit.
   c. gross profit, selling price, and cost of goods sold.
   d. target cost, selling price, and dividends.

10. Service organizations are different from manufacturing companies.
   a. Thus, product costing techniques are not relevant to them.
   b. Service costs are reported as a cost of services provided.
   c. Service organizations classify their costs as direct and indirect.
   d. Both b and c are correct.

CASE

C2-1 The Supply Chain at General Mills

Obj. 3

The 2002 **General Mills** annual report disclosed the following information:

Part A.

TO OUR SHAREHOLDERS:

For General Mills, fiscal 2002 was a year of significant change. On Oct. 31, 2001, we completed our long-anticipated acquisition of Pillsbury. Overnight our annualized revenues nearly doubled, our workforce more than doubled, and our portfolio of leading brands expanded to include the *Pillsbury Doughboy, Progresso, Totino's, Green Giant, Old El Paso*, and more. Over the next seven months, we rapidly integrated work teams and activities. By year-end, much of the hard work to create one sales force, one supply chain organization and one unified marketing plan for our businesses was completed. As a result, we entered 2003 more confident than ever that the combination of General Mills and Pillsbury creates a powerful consumer foods company with excellent prospects for delivering superior long-term growth and returns.

The strategies that will drive our growth in 2003—and beyond—are the same ones that have guided General Mills in the past:

The first key is product innovation...

Our second growth strategy is channel expansion. Today's consumers are picking up groceries in lots of new places, from general merchandise chains to convenience stores. In addition, sales for food eaten away from home are expected to grow faster than at-home food sales over the long term. Our Bakeries and Foodservice business is focused on expanding sales of our products with foodservice distributors and operators, bakeries, convenience stores and vending companies. Adding Pillsbury quadrupled the size of this business for General Mills, and we are already generating new volume by selling General Mills product lines to established Pillsbury customers and vice versa.

Our final key strategy is margin expansion... And beyond (efficiencies resulting by combining Pillsbury and General Mills) we expect our larger supply chain to create opportunities for ongoing productivity savings as we (realize cost savings resulting from our larger size after the acquisition).

Part B.

The following information appears in the notes to consolidated financial statements.

6. INVENTORIES

The components of inventories are as follows:

In Millions

	May 26, 2002	May 27, 2001
Raw materials, work in process and supplies	$ 234	$129
Finished goods	753	326
Grain	99	94
Other	(31)	(30)
Total inventories	$1,055	$519

Required

A. In general, describe General Mills' supply chain.
B. Discuss how the acquisition of Pillsbury radically altered General Mills' supply chain.
C. Evaluate the various types of inventory reported at May 26, 2002, and May 27, 2001. What kinds of products are included in the first three categories shown in note 6?

PRODUCING GOODS AND SERVICES: BATCH PROCESSING

How do we assign overhead costs to our products?

Erin and Seth now understand the importance of product costs and realize they need the monthly financial reports to show the costs of manufacturing each type of product their company manufactures. Erin and Seth manufacture products when they are ordered, and frequently the job requires specific modifications to meet customer needs. Seth is particularly concerned about accurately assigning manufacturing costs to products. There is still confusion about how to assign overhead to each product. Erin has suggested tracking the direct costs, such as the cost of wood and labor to make the furniture, to each order. Next, a portion of overhead costs, such as insurance, electricity, and glue, would be assigned to each job.

FOOD FOR THOUGHT

If you were advising Seth and Erin, what would be your recommendation for assigning overhead costs to the furniture they manufacture? Let's join Erin, Seth, and Roberta again as they discuss the situation.

Erin: *We've been trying to decide how to assign overhead costs to our products. If we divide the month's total overhead costs by the month's total direct labor hours, we'll have an average overhead cost for each labor hour. Then, we can assign overhead to our products by multiplying the overhead cost per hour by the number of labor hours worked on a particular job.*

Seth: *But I see a problem with assigning costs. Unlike materials and labor, we do not receive the bill for some overhead costs until weeks later. We probably won't know our actual total overhead costs when we complete a job or even at the end of the month. I guess we would have to assign some amount of estimated overhead.*

Roberta: *You are correct; we need a way to estimate overhead and assign it to units of product. Let's discuss the details of how we go about this.*

OBJECTIVES

Once you have completed this chapter, you should be able to:

1 Explain the importance of unit costs to managerial decision making.

2 Apply overhead costs to products using a predetermined overhead rate.

3 Determine unit cost using job-order costing.

THE IMPORTANCE OF UNIT COSTS

OBJECTIVE 1

Explain the importance of unit costs to managerial decision making.

Retail organizations purchase completed goods from suppliers, add a markup, and sell the finished goods to their customers. Thus, a retail organization typically reports one type of inventory (finished goods) on its balance sheet. On the other hand, manufacturing organizations purchase raw materials from suppliers and convert them into finished goods during the manufacturing process. **The *unit cost* of an individual product is the total manufacturing cost for a period divided by the number of units produced in that period.** As we saw in Chapter M2, most manufacturing companies report three types of inventory on their balance sheets, raw materials, work-in-process (partially completed goods), and finished goods. When retail and manufacturing organizations sell finished goods, the product's unit cost is reported on the income statement as cost of goods sold.

Unit costs also play an important role in the strategic and operational decisions of marketing and operations managers. For example, unit costs assist in determining whether to market a product as a high-priced specialty product or a low-priced commodity. Unit costs also help managers determine whether to discontinue a product if profit margins are too small (or even negative). Managers also use unit costs to help determine the selling price of a product. Production managers use unit cost information to control costs. Service organizations use unit costs to determine the cost of services and to analyze whether costs are in line with strategic plans. Because unit costs are used extensively in managerial decisions in both manufacturing and service organizations, it is important to know how to develop those costs and how to assess their accuracy.

Managers are concerned about determining the most accurate unit costs and using that information effectively. To develop unit costs, a company must measure total production costs and then assign these costs to individual units. Typically, labor and materials costs are easily traced to products. However, overhead costs must be allocated in some manner. This chapter describes two methods, actual costing and normal costing, for assigning overhead costs to products. Most companies use one of these methods. The chapter also describes job-order costing systems used to keep track of materials, labor, and overhead costs incurred by individual jobs, or batches, of product. In choosing methods for measuring and assigning costs, unit cost not only is a basis for managerial decision making, it also is an outcome of the decision-making process.

Unit costs play an essential role in establishing the value of a company's inventories, and they also are a key element in the decisions managers make about products. For example, managers use product cost information to answer questions such as:

- How should we price a particular product? (Product pricing)
- Should we continue to offer a particular product? (Marketing strategy and Product life cycle)
- What is the best way to allocate our limited production resources? (Allocating resources)
- On which products should marketing focus its efforts to maximize profits? (Unit profit margin)

Product Pricing

Choosing the right selling price for its products is extremely important to the success of a company. A company that does not make an adequate profit on its products cannot survive over the long term. Pricing decisions often are based on unit cost, the prices competitors charge for similar products, and market research on how customers will respond to different prices. Knowing the cost to make a product is important when there is no competitive market for a product. In this case, the unit cost of the product may be the only information available to guide management in setting the price. Managers must set selling prices above product costs in order to earn a profit. The importance of unit cost to a pricing decision often depends on the company's marketing strategy.

Marketing Strategy

Some companies choose to compete by marketing their products at low prices. For example, **Hyundai** offers cars priced far below those offered by **Mercedes**. Likewise, **Timex** offers watches at prices far below those of **Rolex**. On the other hand, Mercedes and Rolex differentiate their products on a quality dimension that Hyundai and Timex do not attempt to match. A company's need for accounting information depends on its marketing strategy. Companies that use a low-price strategy have a greater need for accurate cost information than those that differentiate their products and sell them at higher prices. Profit margins (price minus total manufacturing cost) usually are lower on low-priced products; therefore, controlling costs is very important to these companies. Accurate information about manufacturing costs is required for careful cost control. Companies that differentiate their products tend to have higher profit margins. Thus, tight cost controls generally are less critical to the profitability of their products than are product quality and brand image.

Product Life Cycle

Product life cycle also plays an important role in determining the need for accurate unit costs. As shown in Exhibit 1, products tend to have finite lives characterized by growth, followed by stability, and then decline. Although the lengths of various products' life cycles may vary, a product's life cycle generally is characterized as follows:

(a) A company introduces a new product (growth stage).
(b) The company builds market share in anticipation of future profits (growth stage).
(c) The company focuses on holding the market share of the mature product (hold stage).
(d) The company maximizes the available return as sales of the product decline (harvest stage).
(e) When profits are no longer adequate, the company eliminates the product (divest stage).

Exhibit 1

A Product Life Cycle

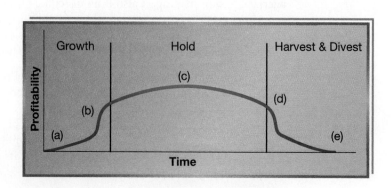

In the growth stage after a product has been introduced (a), the producer normally is interested in building market share. *Market share* **is the portion of sales captured by a particular product relative to total sales of all similar products.** For example, assume total sales of all brands of soft drinks are $45 billion per year. If **Coca-Cola Company's** sales are $20 billion, the company has a 44 percent ($20/$45) market share. During the growth phase, a company often is willing to sacrifice profits to encourage new customers to buy its product. For example, when cellular phone companies give away phones, they are trying to encourage prospective customers to subscribe to their services. In the building phase (b), a company may not be concerned about maintaining tight cost control. It is willing to spend money on product improvements and marketing to build market share. As products mature (c), a company is less willing to spend money on further product and market development. Instead, it concentrates on maintaining market share and profits. As the emphasis shifts to profits, cost control and accuracy of unit costs become more important because of greater emphasis on profitability. In the harvest stage (d), the company's focus is on earning as much profit as possible from the product until, finally, the product is eliminated (e).

Allocating Resources

Unit costs help managers decide how to allocate limited production and marketing resources. When a company's production resources prevent the company from making enough products to meet the demand for those products, managers must decide how much of each product to make. The question here is "What mix of products will provide the greatest profit for the company?" Similarly, when a company's marketing budget does not allow advertising to emphasize all of its products, managers must decide which products to promote. Unit costs help managers make these kinds of decisions by allowing managers to compare profit margins across their product line. Generally, they decide to produce a mix of products that maximizes net income.

Unit Profit Margin

Unit costs also play a role in the decision to continue to offer a product. *Unit profit margin* **is the difference between the selling price per unit of a product and the unit cost.** If the unit profit margin is too low to meet the company's profit goals for that product, the company may discontinue it. A company estimates its profit margin on a particular product by multiplying the unit profit margin times the number of units it expects to sell.

---

1 | SELF-STUDY PROBLEM | Jeff Arnold recently graduated from a business school and joined the family business as a production manager. At his first management meeting with marketing, production, accounting and administrative personnel, a great deal of attention was focused on the unit cost of products.

Required What are four kinds of decisions managers make that draw on unit cost information? Why is the unit cost information an important factor in these decisions?

The solution to Self-Study Problem 1 appears at the end of the chapter.

MEASURING COSTS

The first step in calculating product costs is determining which costs should be included. As we saw in Chapter M2, direct materials, direct labor, and manufacturing overhead traditionally have been included in product cost calculations. This is because generally

OBJECTIVE 2

Apply overhead costs to products using a predetermined overhead rate.

accepted accounting principles (GAAP) require companies to include the full costs of production in inventory costs reported in their financial statements. Many companies use their financial accounting systems to provide internal information for management decisions. However, management accounting information is not required to conform to GAAP. Accountants may accumulate product costs differently from those reported in the financial statements. We further explore different ways to calculate unit costs for internal purposes in Chapter M7.

Two basic methods, actual costing and normal costing, are used to measure product costs. *Actual costing* **measures product costs based on the actual costs of direct materials, direct labor, and overhead incurred in producing the products.** *Normal costing* **measures product costs by adding the actual costs of direct materials and direct labor to an estimated overhead cost incurred in producing the products.** The difference between the two methods is whether actual or estimated overhead costs are used in determining a product's cost.

When a company uses actual costing, it assigns direct materials, direct labor, and manufacturing overhead costs to work-in-process inventory as those costs are incurred. Chapter M2 illustrated the use of an actual cost system. Measuring the costs of direct materials and direct labor usually is not difficult. Measuring manufacturing overhead, however, can be a problem. The company often does not know the actual cost of overhead until after a product is produced or even sold. The total actual overhead cost is not known with certainty until the bills arrive. Thus, many companies rely on estimates of overhead to measure unit costs.

As in actual costing, normal costing measures actual direct materials and direct labor costs incurred in producing a product. However, normal costing uses estimates of manufacturing overhead to assign overhead to products. These overhead cost estimates are applied to products using a predetermined overhead rate.

A *predetermined overhead rate* **is an estimate of the amount of overhead assigned to a product for each unit of activity.** To establish a predetermined rate, a company first must choose an activity base. **An** *activity base* **is a production activity (such as direct labor hours or machine hours) or a measure of the cost of production activity (such as direct labor cost).** A company selects a particular activity base because management believes overhead costs increase in proportion to the activity base. For example, if accountants think overhead cost varies according to the number of machine hours, they would select machine hours as the activity base. If more machine hours are used, we might expect to consume greater amounts of electricity, water, chemicals, natural gas, and supplies. If fewer machines hours are used, fewer resources should be consumed. Thus, accountants look for a relationship between overhead costs and an activity base. At the beginning of its fiscal year, a company divides the total overhead it expects to incur during that year by the amount of the activity base expected for that period. Then, as products are manufactured, the company multiplies the amount of the activity base used during the period by the predetermined overhead rate. The result is the estimated overhead cost for the products manufactured.

Any cost allocation method relies on the use of estimates. The use of estimates in accounting is not uncommon. As you saw in your financial accounting course, accountants often rely on estimates when preparing financial statements. For example, they estimate depreciation expense for fixed assets and an allowance for uncollectible accounts. Accountants also use estimates to prepare a company's internal reports.

Iron Mountain Gear: The Product and Manufacturing Process

Examples in this chapter are based on the manufacturing operations of Iron Mountain Gear (IMG), a company that makes backpacks for outdoor enthusiasts. The manufacturing process begins after purchasing fabric, aluminum, and a variety of other materials from suppliers. Using computer-controlled machinery, fabric is cut into various components whose dimensions are determined from engineering specifications. Next, the fabric components and zippers and various closures are sewn together by operators using industrial-grade sewing machines. Aluminum tubing, purchased from suppliers, is used to construct the backpack frame that is joined to the fabric backpack. Finally, shoulder straps provided by suppliers are attached to complete the backpack.

IMG uses normal costing to measure its product costs. The company's accountant expects to incur manufacturing overhead costs totaling $250,000 in the coming year. Direct labor hours is used as the activity base to allocate these overhead costs to products. Based on expected sales and production levels, the company should use 5,000 hours of direct labor in the coming year. Using direct labor hours as an allocation base, the predetermined overhead rate for the coming year is calculated at $50 per hour as follows:

$$\text{Predetermined overhead rate} = \text{Estimated overhead costs} \div \text{Estimated activity base}$$
$$= \$250,000 \div 5,000 \text{ direct labor hours}$$
$$= \$50$$

Thus, for each direct labor hour actually worked, the company will add $50 of overhead to the work-in-process inventory. Overhead is traced to individual products in a similar manner. For example, assume IMG produces a backpack that requires 6/10 of a machine hour for the cutting and sewing operations. Overhead cost applied to the backpack would be $30 ($50 × 6/10 = $30). Materials and labor costs would be added to overhead to determine the total unit cost of a backpack. Later in this chapter we explore systems that allow managers to record the amount of materials, labor, and overhead costs associated with each batch of product.

Exhibit 2 illustrates transactions that affect IMG's various inventory and cost of goods sold accounts during an accounting period. The cost flows do not illustrate all accounts affected by a transaction. For example, when raw materials are purchased on credit, Accounts Payable and Raw Materials Inventory are both increased. However, Exhibit 2 illustrates only the flow of product costs and the effect on inventory and cost of goods sold.

Exhibit 2 Cost Flows Through Iron Mountain Gear's Accounting System

	Raw Materials	Work-in-Process	Finished Goods	Cost of Goods Sold
		Inventory		
Beginning balance	$10,000	$40,000	$15,000	
	+50,000 (a)			
	−28,000 (b)	+28,000 (b)		
Ending balance	$32,000	+15,000 (c)		
		+18,000 (e)		
		−63,000 (f)	+63,000 (f)	
	Ending balance	$38,000	−65,000 (g)	+65,000 (g)
			Ending balance $13,000	−1,000 (h)
				Ending balance −64,000

Manufacturing Overhead				
	+17,000 (d)			
	−18,000 (e)			
Overapplied overhead	1,000			
	−1,000 (h)			
Ending balance	0			

The beginning balances of the raw materials, work-in-process, and finished goods inventories are $10,000, $40,000, and $15,000, respectively. Transaction (a) records the purchase of $50,000 of raw materials. When raw materials costing $28,000 are removed from inventory and placed into production in transaction (b), the raw materials inventory and work-in-process inventory accounts are decreased and increased, respectively. IMG incurred direct labor costs of $15,000 in transaction (c). Recall from Chapter M2 that direct materials and direct labor are placed into the work-in-process inventory as materials and labor are added to the manufacturing process.

Exhibit 2 introduces a new account, known as Manufacturing Overhead. Actual overhead costs increase the manufacturing overhead account balance, while the application of manufacturing overhead to work-in-process reduces the manufacturing overhead account balance. Actual overhead costs of $17,000 are accumulated in the manufacturing overhead account as shown in transaction (d). However, overhead is applied using a predetermined overhead rate of $50 per direct labor hour. In January, assume the company used 360 direct labor hours in manufacturing operations. In transaction (e), the estimated cost of overhead of $18,000 (360 hours × $50) is recorded in the work-in-process inventory account.

Transaction (f) records the transfer of completed goods costing $63,000 to manufacture. Thus, work-in-process inventory is reduced and finished goods inventory is increased by $63,000. Goods costing $65,000 were sold. Transaction (g) records the effect on the finished goods inventory and cost of goods sold accounts.

Because normal costing uses estimates of overhead costs, the amount of overhead costs allocated to work-in-process inventory often differs from actual overhead incurred. In comparing transactions (d) and (e) in Exhibit 2, we see the company overapplied its overhead costs. The amount of overhead costs applied to inventory ($18,000) was $1,000 more than the actual overhead costs ($17,000) incurred during the period. Transaction (h) transfers the underapplied overhead to the cost of goods sold account. At the end of an accounting period, the manufacturing overhead account always is adjusted to a zero balance. Any overapplied or underapplied overhead is transferred to the cost of goods sold account. If the actual overhead costs had been more than the amount of overhead recorded in the work-in-process inventory account, the company would have underapplied its overhead costs. Often companies investigate the underapplied or overapplied overhead, known as a variance, to learn why it occurred. We further explore overhead variances in Chapter M9. Exhibit 3 summarizes the steps for applying overhead in a normal costing system.

Exhibit 3

Application of Overhead Costs in a Normal Costing System

Establishing the predetermined overhead rate
At the beginning of the fiscal year:
1. Estimate total manufacturing overhead costs for the period.
2. Choose a relevant activity base and estimate the activity level for the year.
3. Calculate the predetermined overhead rate by dividing the estimate of total manufacturing overhead costs by the estimated activity base.

Assigning (or applying) overhead costs using the predetermined overhead rate
At the end of each accounting period:
1. Determine the actual activity level during the period.
2. Multiply the actual activity level by the predetermined overhead rate.
3. Transfer any remaining balance in the manufacturing overhead account to the cost of goods sold account.

2 SELF-STUDY PROBLEM

Russell Lumber Company uses an actual costing system. The company's controller has been wondering what would be the effect of using a normal costing system to assign overhead. She has determined that under the normal costing approach the predetermined overhead rate would be calculated based on machine hours. Russell Lumber Co. expects to use 50,000 machine hours during the year. Overhead is expected to be approximately $750,000 for the year. The company used 4,500 machine hours during March. Russell Lumber reported the following events:

(a) Raw lumber was purchased for $110,000.
(b) $100,000 in raw lumber was used in production.
(c) $40,000 in direct labor was incurred.
(d) $60,000 in overhead was incurred.

Required Compute the work-in-process inventory using both actual and normal costing for the month of March. Explain why the numbers are different. Assume all of the products produced in March were sold in that month. What would be the amount of the adjustment to the cost of goods sold account for the overapplied or underapplied overhead? Would cost of goods sold increase or decrease as a result of this adjustment? Why?

The solution to Self-Study Problem 2 appears at the end of the chapter.

JOB-ORDER COSTING

OBJECTIVE 3

Determine unit cost using job-order costing.

Companies that produce a variety of products or services typically use job-order costing. *Job-order costing* **identifies and assigns production costs to a particular job.** Accounting systems help managers keep track of production costs. For example, a *job cost sheet* **is used to identify each job and to accumulate the costs of manufacturing associated with that job.** Job cost sheets can be either a sheet of paper or a record in a computer file. Both forms allow space to record all the costs of direct materials, direct labor, and manufacturing overhead associated with a job. The job cost sheet functions like a work-in-process inventory account. If a company uses only job-order costing, the total of all of its job cost sheets should equal the total work-in-process inventory account. Exhibit 4 provides an example of a job cost sheet used by IMG for a production run, or batch, of backpacks.

Exhibit 4 A Job Cost Sheet

Job Number	225P		Date	6-12-04
Product	High Forest Backpack		By	Linda Smith
Units	40		Ship	6-30-04

Materials		Direct Labor				Overhead		
Requistion Number	Amount	Employee Number	Hours	Rate	Amount	Hours	Rate	Amount
X2134	$100.00	59	6	$9.35	$56.10	24	$50.00	$1,200.00
X2147	$420.00	107	18	$13.55	$243.90			
Total Materials	$520.00	Total Direct Labor			$300.00	Total Overhead		$1,200.00
Total Job Cost								$2,020.00

In the job cost sheet illustrated in Exhibit 4, job 225P was completed on June 12, 2004, resulting in forty backpacks produced. Materials were issued twice in the amounts of $100 and $420, respectively, as shown by requisitions X2134 and X2147. Thus, total material costs for the job were $520.

Two employees worked on the job. Employee 59 worked 6 hours and was paid $9.35 an hour, and employee 107 worked 18 hours at a rate of $13.55 per hour. Total direct labor cost for the job was $300.00 [(6 × $9.35) + (18 × $13.55)]. The job sheet also shows the amount of overhead that has been applied to the job. In this example, the activity base is direct labor hours and the predetermined overhead rate is $50 per hour. Because 24 (6 + 18) labor hours were charged to job 225P, a total of $1,200 (24 × $50) of overhead was applied.

The total cost of job 225P was $2,020, the sum of direct materials, direct labor, and overhead applied ($520 + $300 + $1,200). The cost per product for the 40 products produced in this job was $50.50 ($2,020 ÷ 40 products). Once the job was completed, the costs of the 40 products were transferred to finished goods inventory at $50.50 per product. When the products are sold, the $50.50 product cost will be used to determine the amount that appears on the income statement as cost of goods sold.

Materials are ordered for individual jobs using a materials requisition form as shown in Exhibit 5. According to the materials requisition form, 100 pounds of aluminum tubing were used in job 225P. Each pound of material cost $1. The total materials cost assigned to job 225P was $100. The document identifies the specific type and quantity of materials that have been drawn from the storeroom and the job to which the materials should be charged. The form is a means of controlling raw materials inventories because each requisition must be signed by the employee issuing and the employee receiving the materials. The form also is used as a source document for recording the actual materials used on a particular job.

Exhibit 5
A Materials Requisition Form

Materials Requisition Number	X2134	Date	June 11, 2004	
Job Number	225P			
Item Description	Quantity		Unit Cost	Total Cost
Aluminum tubing	100 lbs.		$1.00	$100.00
Issued by Murry Roberts				
Received by Frank Jones				

Case In Point

Job Order Costing at Ki-Tek

Ki-Tek manufactures kites. The company uses a job system to record the cost of producing its products. Ki-Tek replaced its error-prone manual data entry system with hand-held data collection terminals that read bar coding. Management estimates the new system has reduced product costing errors by 50 percent.

Source: Automatic I.D. News. Cleveland, May 1997. Vol. 13, Issue 6, page 33.

Costs in the Service Sector

Companies in the service sector also use unit costs to set prices and manage costs. Those companies can use job-order or process costing systems. For example, **MCI** provides telephone services. MCI can use a process costing system to account for costs because the unit of product (one minute of telephone connect time) is like all of the other units; each unit of product consumes a similar amount of costs. The average cost of a minute of connect time gives MCI's managers information they need to decide how much they must charge to make a profit. MCI must set its price low enough to be competitive with other phone companies such as **AT&T**. If the unit cost of telephone connect time at MCI is too high for the company to earn a reasonable profit, the company must look for ways to lower its costs. It cannot simply raise prices to earn higher profits without losing customers to competitors.

Service organizations also can use job-order costing. For example, public accounting firms audit their clients' financial statements. The primary cost to those firms in providing this service is employee wages. Auditors track the time each individual spends on each task they perform in the audit. The times of all employees who work on the audit of a particular client are multiplied by a price per hour to assign costs to each audit.

3 SELF-STUDY PROBLEM

WebTUTOR Advantage

Robotool Corporation is a machine shop that manufactures replacement parts for industrial machinery. Production at Robotool is characterized by small lot sizes and precision manufacturing. A recent production run of five gears, Job 2B38, required the following activities and costs:

Raw materials requisitioned:
10 pounds of brass at $11.65 a pound

Labor	Hours	Rate
Cutting and forming	3	$ 9.75
Lathe and milling	4	11.50
Finishing	1	10.00

Robotool applies overhead to jobs on the basis of direct labor hours using a predetermined rate of $25 an hour.

Required Calculate the total cost of Job 2B38 and the average cost per unit produced.

The solution to Self-Study Problem 3 appears at the end of the chapter.

REVIEW

SUMMARY of IMPORTANT CONCEPTS

1. Unit costs have two primary functions.
   a. Accountants use unit costs to determine the value of ending inventory and cost of goods sold.
   b. Managers use unit costs as the basis of decisions about pricing products, continuing a product line, allocating limited resources, and establishing marketing strategies.

2. According to GAAP, unit costs must reflect the costs of direct materials, direct labor, and manufacturing overhead.

3. Most companies use one of two methods for measuring costs.
   a. Actual costing bases unit costs on actual costs incurred for direct materials, direct labor, and manufacturing overhead.
   b. Normal costing bases unit costs on actual costs incurred for direct materials and direct labor and an estimate of manufacturing overhead.
   c. Estimated overhead costs are the product of the actual activity base multiplied by the predetermined overhead rate.
      (1) At the end of the accounting period, the company adjusts the manufacturing overhead account as necessary to make the estimated overhead equal the actual overhead.

4. Job-order costing yields the unit cost of a particular job or batch of output.
   a. Job-order costing is most effective when a company produces a variety of products (or services) that incur different costs during production.
   b. Companies that use job-order costing track job costs with job cost sheets.

DEFINE

TERMS and CONCEPTS DEFINED in this CHAPTER

activity base (M58)
actual costing (M58)
job cost sheet (M61)
job-order costing (M61)
market share (M57)

normal costing (M58)
predetermined overhead rate (M58)
unit cost (M55)
unit profit margin (M57)

SELF-STUDY PROBLEM SOLUTIONS

SSP3-1 Managers need unit cost information for various decision-making purposes, including pricing products, deciding whether to drop a product, and allocating production and marketing resources. Unit cost information is also used for valuing inventory, preparing financial statements, and determining net income. Both the accuracy of unit cost information and what managers choose to include in unit cost can greatly affect the decisions that are made.

SSP3-2 Under the actual costing system, work-in-process inventory would contain the following costs: raw materials ($100,000), direct labor ($40,000), and actual overhead ($60,000) for a total of $200,000. Under the normal costing system, the account would contain: raw material ($100,000), direct labor ($40,000), and applied overhead ($67,500) for a total of $207,500. Thus, the difference between the two approaches would be $7,500.

Note: To assign overhead under the normal costing system, it is necessary to calculate the predetermined overhead rate. For Russell Lumber the rate would be $750,000 expected annual overhead costs ÷ $50,000 expected annual machine hours = $15 per machine hour. Therefore, for March, the amount of overhead applied would be $15 × 4,500 actual machine hours for the month = $67,500.

The difference of $7,500 is the overapplied overhead. More overhead was assigned to work-in-process inventory than was actually incurred. This means manufacturing overhead contains a positive balance of $7,500 and must be reduced to zero. Cost of goods sold is decreased by that amount also.

SSP3-3 The cost of job 2B38 includes total direct materials, direct labor, and manufacturing overhead that has been applied as follows:

Direct materials (10 pounds × $11.65)		$116.50
Direct labor:		
Cutting and forming (3 × $9.75)	$29.25	
Lathe and mill (4 × $11.50)	46.00	
Finishing (1 × $10.00)	10.00	
Total labor		85.25
Overhead applied (8 labor hours × $25.00)		200.00
Total costs for job 2B38		$401.75

The average cost per gear is $80.35 = $401.75 ÷ 5 gears produced.

Thinking Beyond the Question

How do we assign overhead costs to our products?

In this chapter Erin and Seth were introduced to overhead allocation. We discussed using a predetermined overhead rate to assign overhead costs to products using allocation bases such as direct labor hours, machine hours, and direct labor costs. To accurately assign overhead costs to products, allocation bases should capture the manner in which products consume resources. Do allocation bases such as the number of labor hours or the number of machine hours explain how products consume all types of overhead costs?

QUESTIONS

Q3-1
Obj. 1
Gloves to Go manufactures one product, a low-priced, no-frills winter glove. The company has been offering this product for 15 years, and has recently experienced a large decline in market share. Describe the likely importance of unit cost information to this company, and explain your reasoning.

Q3-2
Obj. 1
Explain the importance of unit costs at various stages of a product's life cycle.

Q3-3
Obj. 2
Rene Manzor plans to use a recent inheritance to buy a small factory that produces travel bags. Rene has done a great deal of reading about managing a business and realizes that she must establish a costing system to accumulate the costs of producing the bags. In her reading, she learned about two methods of accumulating product costs, actual and normal. Rene has no experience in accounting and is confused about the difference between the two methods. How would you explain the difference in cost accumulation between actual costing and normal costing?

Q3-4
Obj. 2
Hoy Heating and Air Conditioning Company repairs heating and cooling equipment. Each time a service technician completes a job, a time sheet is turned in and the job cost is computed. The company calculates the cost of each job by adding the cost of any materials used on the job, the labor cost of the service technician, and an overhead charge to cover administrative and support expenses. Hoy uses an estimated cost of support expenses in its calculation. Why do you think the company uses predetermined rates rather than actual costs in computing the costs of each service call?

Q3-5
Obj. 2
Assume fuel oil represents a significant overhead cost for a manufacturing company. Because of unexpected price increases in the cost per barrel, the company underapplied its overhead cost for the year. How might management have adapted to the change in prices to prevent a large amount of underapplied overhead?

Q3-6
Obj. 3
The accounting system of Gardner and Associates, a manufacturer of kitchen utensils and accessories, has an account called "Over- or Underapplied Overhead." How would you explain this account to management? How will Gardner's accountant adjust the over- or underapplied overhead account before preparing the company's financial statements?

Q3-7
Obj. 3
Engineers at Rose Company recently designed a new badminton racket for the company's sporting goods line. The technical drawings were sent to the production department, and the first lot of 1,000 rackets has been manufactured. Management at Rose is anxious to see the cost sheet for this job. What information does the job cost sheet contain that would generate such management interest?

Q3-8
Obj. 3
Danny Fitchen is the warehouse clerk for Big Chairs Limited. A production apprentice has asked Danny for a batch of raw materials, but he refuses to release the goods without the appropriate paperwork. What form is needed as supporting documentation for materials used in production? What are the essential parts of that form?

Q3-9
Obj. 3
Assume a service organization, such as an accounting firm, uses job-order costing to keep track of work performed for clients. Of the three types of product (service) costs—direct materials, direct labor, and overhead—which would be the most important for a service firm?

Q3-10
Obj. 3
Job-order costing also is used by service organizations. Why might a walk-in medical clinic use job-order costing to understand the cost of treating their patients?

EXERCISES

If your instructor is using Personal Trainer® in this course, you may complete your assignments online.

E3-1   Write a short definition for each of the terms listed in the *Terms and Concepts Defined in this Chapter* section.

E3-2   Rollo Enterprises recorded the following activity in work-in-process inventory for September:

Objs. 1, 2

Direct labor	$15,000
Direct materials	10,000
Factory supervisor's salary, September	3,000
Indirect materials	7,000
Factory utilities	500

1,000 units were started and completed during the month.

  a. Compute the amount of manufacturing overhead incurred for the month.
  b. Assume all costs are actual. Using actual costing, calculate the cost of one unit.

E3-3   The M & S Company uses normal costing. The following information pertains to a recent pro-
Objs. 1, 2   duction period:

Estimated manufacturing overhead	$70,000
Actual manufacturing overhead	$82,000
Machine hours	14,000
Actual machine hours	14,500
Estimated direct labor hours	2,000
Actual direct labor hours	2,300

  a. Determine the predetermined overhead rate if the company uses machine hours as the activity base.
  b. Determine the predetermined overhead rate if the company uses direct labor hours as the activity base.
  c. If machine hours is used as the activity base, how much manufacturing overhead would be applied for the period?

E3-4   DuraPlastics Inc. recorded the following activity in work-in-process inventory during July:
Objs. 1, 2

Direct labor (300 hours)	$3,000
Direct materials	5,000
Manufacturing overhead applied	2,400

DuraPlastics uses normal costing. The activity base used to apply manufacturing overhead is direct labor hours.

  a. What was the predetermined overhead rate used by DuraPlastics?
  b. Assume 800 units were produced during July. What was the cost of one unit?

E3-5   Montclair Products prepared the following estimates for 2005:
Objs. 1, 2

Manufacturing overhead	$400,000
Direct labor cost	500,000

Actual information recorded at the end of the year is as follows:

Manufacturing overhead	$420,000
Direct labor cost	$475,000
Direct materials cost	$220,000
Units produced	5,000

  a. Assume Montclair uses actual costing. What was the cost of one unit produced during 2005? For parts (b) and (c), assume instead that Montclair uses normal costing, with direct labor dollars as the activity base.
  b. What was the predetermined overhead rate used by Montclair in 2005?
  c. Was manufacturing overhead over- or underapplied for the year, and by how much?

E3-6
Objs. 1, 2

Harold Gordon operates a manufacturing company that uses a job-order costing system. The following activity was recorded in work-in-process inventory for August:

Direct materials	$ 150,000
Direct labor	80,000
Manufacturing overhead applied	120,000
Completed production	(322,000)

Harold charges overhead to work-in-process on the basis of direct labor dollars. There were no jobs in process as of August 1. At the end of August, only one job was still in process (Job 75). This job had incurred labor charges of $6,000 during the month.

  a. Compute the predetermined overhead rate that Gordon used in August.
  b. Compute the amount of manufacturing overhead and direct materials costs that were incurred in Job 75.

E3-7
Obj. 2

Tortolla Company is a manufacturing firm that uses a job-order costing system. The company uses machine hours to apply overhead to work-in-process. On January 1, Tortolla's management estimated that it would incur $700,000 in manufacturing overhead costs and 56,000 machine hours over the coming year.

  a. Compute the company's predetermined overhead rate for the year.
  b. Assume that the company uses only 54,000 machine hours over the year and incurs the following manufacturing costs:

Maintenance	$ 56,000
Depreciation	206,000
Indirect materials	76,000
Utilities	164,000
Insurance	94,000
Indirect labor	+ 64,000

Compute the amount of overhead that was applied to production and the amount of over- or underapplied overhead for the period.

E3-8
Obj. 2

Tom Brooks, production manager for Clarion Manufacturing, was told that product overhead costs were too high, and the amount of overhead applied to inventory is less than the actual costs incurred over the last few months. Tom responds that he doesn't understand what "applied" means when dealing with inventory costs. Explain to Tom what is meant by the statement overhead is *applied* to units of product. Must the actual amount of overhead costs incurred always equal the amount of overhead applied to inventory?

E3-9
Objs. 2, 3

Trackers Inc. is a manufacturer of various specially designed radar devices. During May, Trackers completed Job 66 and began work on Job 67. Partial information concerning the two jobs is as follows:

Job 66		Job 67	
Direct labor (30 hours)	$600	Direct labor (10 hours)	$200
Direct materials	$900	Direct materials	$450
Manufacturing overhead	??	Manufacturing overhead	??

Total manufacturing overhead applied to both jobs was $1,400. Trackers uses normal costing and assigns manufacturing overhead using direct labor hours as the activity base.

  a. What was the predetermined overhead rate used by Trackers?
  b. What was the total cost of Job 66?
  c. What are the costs incurred to date for Job 67?

E3-10
Objs. 2, 3

Small Company produces custom manufacturing equipment. The company uses job-order costing in conjunction with normal costing. Information pertaining to a recently completed job is as follows:

Job 423

Direct labor	$2,500
Direct materials	$750
Machine hours	60
Units produced	100

(Continued)

Small Company applies manufacturing overhead using machine hours as the activity base. The predetermined overhead rate is $5 per machine hour.

    a. What was the total cost of job 423?
    b. What was the cost of one unit for job 423?

E3-11
Obj. 3

Basic Closet Company manufactures stand-alone cedar-lined wardrobe closets. Basic received an order for ten specially designed wardrobes to be delivered in eight weeks. The order was assigned job number 293. During production of the wardrobes, the following activities took place:

1. Requisitioned $2,500 of wood and $500 of hardware. *direct material*
2. Time sheets revealed direct labor costs of $1,450 and indirect labor costs of $345.
3. Overhead was assigned using a predetermined overhead rate of 130% of direct labor costs.
4. Completed units were shipped to the customer. The selling price was 140% of cost.

    a. Calculate the manufacturing cost of one wardrobe.
    b. Calculate the selling price of each wardrobe.
    c. Describe how Basic traces material, manufacturing overhead, and labor costs to job 293.

PROBLEMS

If your instructor is using Personal Trainer® in this course, you may complete your assignments online.

P3-1
Objs. 1, 2

Unit Cost Using Actual and Normal Costing

Rocky Mountain Outfitters manufactures cowboy boots. Information related to a recent production period is as follows:

Estimated manufacturing overhead, 2004	$240,000
Estimated machine hours, 2004	12,000
Direct labor cost, September	$8,000
Direct materials cost, September	$5,000
Supervisor's salary, September	$3,000
Factory rent, September	$1,800
Factory utilities, September	$800
Indirect materials cost, September	$2,000
Machine hours worked, September	400

During September, 500 pairs of boots were produced.

Required

A. Using actual costing, what is the unit cost of one pair of boots produced during September?
B. Using normal costing, with machine hours as the activity base, what is the unit cost of one pair of boots produced during September?
C. If normal costing is used, was manufacturing overhead over- or underapplied during September? By how much?
D. What might have caused the amount of overhead applied to be different from the actual amount?
E. Why would managers at Rocky Mountain choose to use normal costing rather than actual costing?

P3-2
Objs. 1, 2

Unit Cost Using Actual and Normal Costing

Triple Play Sports manufactures baseball gloves. Information related to a recent production period is as follows:

Estimated manufacturing overhead, 2004	$100,000
Estimated machine hours, 2004	4,000
Direct labor cost, October	$5,000
Direct materials cost, October	$5,000
Supervisor's salary, October	$4,000
Factory rent, October	$1,000
Factory utilities, October	$1,000
Indirect materials cost, October	$1,400
Machine hours worked, October	300

During October, 2,000 gloves were produced.

Required

A. Using actual costing, what is the unit cost of one glove produced during October?
B. Using normal costing, with machine hours as the activity base, what is the unit cost of one glove produced during October?
C. If normal costing is used, was manufacturing overhead over- or underapplied during September? By how much?
D. What might have caused the amount of overhead applied to be different from the actual amount?
E. Why would managers at Triple Play Sports choose to use normal costing rather than actual costing?

P3-3
Objs. 2, 3

Applying Overhead Using a Job-Order Costing System

TCC Inc. has prepared the following estimates for the current year:

Direct labor hours	80,000
Direct labor cost	$1,000,000
Machine hours	60,000
Manufacturing overhead	$600,000

Required

A. Compute the predetermined overhead rate based on (1) direct labor hours, (2) direct labor cost, and (3) machine hours.
B. Assume the following jobs were worked during the year:

Job	Labor Hours	Labor Dollars	Machine Hours
123	18,000	$204,000	9,500
124	8,500	132,000	4,800
125	5,100	86,000	5,200

Compute the amount of overhead that would have been applied to each of these jobs using the various overhead rates you computed in part (A).
C. Explain why the amount of overhead applied to each job varies with the activity base.

P3-4
Objs. 2, 3

Job-Order Costing Using Multiple Predetermined Overhead Rates

Granger Shirt Assembly Company runs a printing operation that produces customized T-shirts. These shirts usually are manufactured with either hand-created embroidery, individual holograms, or customized beaded accessories. Most often the shirts are produced in a small run to satisfy the needs of an individual rock performer, who uses the shirts as a promotional item when his or her band is on tour. Granger currently uses job-order costing in conjunction with normal costing to measure and assign unit costs.

The following information is provided regarding the company's two production departments:

	Layout Department	Printing Department
Estimated MOH cost for the year	$180,000	$450,000
Activity base for department	Direct labor hours	Machine hours
Budgeted activity for the year	10,000 DL hours	9,000 machine hours

Three jobs were started during a recent period and two were completed, job 101 and job 102:

	Job 101	Job 102
Materials cost	$10,200	$24,000
Direct labor cost	$24,500	$22,000
Labor hours, layout department	1,130	220
Machine hours, printing department	30	190

The selling price for each job includes a markup on cost of 50%.

(Continued)

Required

A. Calculate the predetermined overhead rate for the layout and printing departments.
B. Why would Granger use two different predetermined overhead rates?
C. What is the total cost of job 101?
D. What is the total selling price of job 102?
E. Granger also started, but did not complete, job 103 during this period. At the end of the period, the balance in the work-in-process account was $17,600, all of which related to job 103. Four hundred labor hours costing $8,000 were worked in the layout department. No work was performed in the printing department. How much in materials costs had been incurred to date for job 103 at the end of this period?

P3-5   ## Job-Order Costing Using Multiple Predetermined Overhead Rates

Objs. 2, 3   Pike Skateboard Company makes specialized skateboards. Pike seeks to be the leader in designs for skateboards and produces designs in lot sizes of 1,000 units. Pike sells the full batch of skateboards to its marketing subsidiary. Pike uses job-order costing in conjunction with normal costing to measure and assign unit costs.

The following information is provided regarding the company's two production departments:

	Design Department	Assembly Department
Estimated overhead cost for the year	$100,000	$300,000
Activity base for department	Direct labor hours	Machine hours
Budgeted activity for the year	10,000 DL hours	5,000 machine hours

Three jobs were started during a recent period and two were completed, job 201 and job 202:

	Job 201	Job 202
Materials cost	$16,000	$24,000
Direct labor cost	$5,000	$12,000
Labor hours, design department	120	240
Machine hours, assembly department	100	120

Pike sells the skateboards to its marketing subsidiary at a markup on cost of 30%.

Required

A. What is the predetermined overhead rate for the design department? For the assembly department?
B. Why would Pike use two different predetermined overhead rates?
C. What is the total cost of job 201?
D. What is the total selling price of job 202?
E. Pike also started, but did not complete, job 203 during this period. At the end of the period, the balance in the work-in-process account was $6,000, which all related to job 203. One hundred labor hours costing $4,000 were worked in the design department. No work was performed in the assembly department. How much in materials costs had been incurred to date for job 203 at the end of this period?

P3-6   ## Allocating Overhead Costs

Objs. 2, 3   Art's Custom Cabinetry manufactures and installs custom cabinetry built to customer specifications. The prices of cabinets depend on the quality of the lumber selected by the customers and the complexity of designs.

The company is owned and operated by Art Bruce. Five years ago, he started the company in his garage. Over the five years, Art invested heavily in special equipment. Art assigns job numbers by customer name. The only job still in process at the end of 2004 was for Clara Cummins. That job had been charged with direct materials of $750, direct labor of $1,000, and overhead of $250.

Art is the sole employee of his company. He works an average of 2,800 hours a year and pays himself $20 an hour. Art bids on all jobs in his spare time and feels his overhead rate has kept him from obtaining some of the jobs he has bid on.

A summary of activity for January is as follows:

Job	Direct Materials	Direct Labor Cost	Direct Labor Hours
Clara Cummins	$ 600	$ 800	40
John Ryan	1,200	1,000	50
Kyle Smith	750	700	35
Ken Woods	950	600	30

The Kyle Smith job was completed during January and billed at cost plus 10%. All other jobs are still in process at the end of the month.

Required

A. Assume the overhead allocation rate for 2005 is $5 per labor hour. Calculate the total costs for each of the jobs Art worked on during January.
B. Calculate the balance of the company's work-in-process inventory account as of January 31, 2005. Which jobs are reflected in that balance?
C. Calculate the cost of goods sold in January 2005.
D. Calculate the unit profit margin that the company earned from jobs completed in January.
E. If the primary overhead cost was an electric bill from running Art's machines, is an overhead allocation based on direct labor a good allocation method or should another allocation method be used? Explain.

P3-7
Objs. 2, 3

Allocating Overhead Costs

Handywoman Holly builds log cabins based on customer specifications. The only job still in process on January 1, 2005, was job 100. That job had been charged with direct materials of $40,000, direct labor of $30,000, and overhead of $5,000.

A summary of activity for 2005 is as follows:

Job	Direct Materials	Direct Labor Cost	Direct Labor Hours
100	$20,000	$22,500	450
200	50,000	40,000	800
300	10,000	10,000	200

Job 100 was completed during 2005. The other jobs are still in process at the end of the year. Overhead costs were $10,000 for 2005.

Required

A. Calculate the overhead rate based on direct labor hours.
B. Calculate the total costs for each of the jobs Holly worked on during 2005.
C. Calculate the balance of the company's work-in-process inventory account as of December 31, 2005.
D. Assume the only overhead cost is speculation work that Holly does to try to land new customers. The cost of speculation work is the same regardless of the size of the cabin to be built. Based on this information, do you feel overhead should be based on direct labor hours or is there be a better allocation method? Explain.

P3-8
Objs. 2, 3

The law firm of Dewey, Louie, and Howe has six lawyers and ten support people. The firm uses a job-order costing system to accumulate costs by client. There are two departments, research and litigation. The firm uses a different predetermined overhead rate for each department. At the beginning of the year, the partners made the following estimates:

	Department	
	Research	Litigation
Planned attorney hours	2,500	11,600
Number of clients	1,000	230
Legal supplies	$12,000	$4,600
Direct attorney cost	$132,000	$696,000
Department overhead	$70,000	$406,000

(Continued)

The costs to clients are separated into three components: supplies, attorney costs, and overhead. Both departments base overhead on the number of attorney hours charged. Supplies are charged on a per-client basis. Clients are billed all costs plus 20%.

Case DR9312 was opened on January 3 and closed June 17. During that period, the following costs and time were recorded:

Attorney hours, research	55
Attorney hours, litigation	175
Attorney cost	$13,800

Required

A. Compute the rate each department should use to assign overhead costs.
B. Compute the amount per client that each department should use to allocate supply costs.
C. Using the rates computed in requirements (A) and (B), compute the total cost of case DR9312, including overhead, supply charges, and attorney fees.
D. Calculate the billing for case DR9312.

P3-9 **Applying Overhead in a Service Organization**

Objs. 2, 3

PPGV provides auditing services. PPGV developed the following estimates for the current year:

Direct labor hours	70,000
Direct labor cost	$2,800,000
Overhead	$1,500,000

Required

A. Compute the predetermined overhead rate based on (1) direct labor hours and (2) direct labor cost.
B. Assume the following jobs were worked during the year:

Job	Labor Hours	Labor Dollars
100	40,000	$1,520,000
200	20,000	$820,000
300	10,000	$460,000

Compute the amount of overhead that would have been applied to each of these jobs using the various overhead rates you computed in part (A).
C. Explain why the amount of overhead applied to each job varies with the activity base.
D. The reason some jobs have a higher billing rate is because more senior people are working on the job. Assume the primary overhead cost is secretarial assistance. If the senior-level people require more secretarial work than their subordinates, which of these two overhead rates better reflects this situation? Explain.

P3-10 **Ethics and Overhead Allocation**

Objs. 2, 3

Cape Horn Yacht Company produces custom sailboats. A potential client has selected a design that is estimated to cost the company $300,000 to manufacture. To establish the selling price, the company typically adds a 40% markup to its manufacturing cost. Therefore, the selling price for the boat will be $420,000. Cape Horn pays a sales commission of 10% of the selling price. Hal, one of the sales representatives, is eager to close a deal with a potential customer. Unfortunately, the client is not willing to spend more than $385,000.

The cost estimate of the yacht is as follows:

Materials	$105,000
Labor	75,000
Manufacturing overhead ($75,000 × $1.60)	120,000
	$300,000

Cape Horn uses a predetermined overhead rate of $1.60 per dollar of direct labor cost.

Assume you are the company's accountant. Hal is looking for ways to reduce costs in order to make the deal. He argues the predetermined overhead rate is just an estimate; actual costs may be less. If you would simply reduce the predetermined overhead rate, the company could get the order. Otherwise, the sale (and commission) will be lost. He also reminds you of the generous bonus that awaits everyone in the company if certain sales targets are met. At year-end, you could simply close the underapplied overhead to cost of goods sold. Your report to management would state that overhead costs were higher than expected.

Required

A. Is this situation considered an ethical issue? Why or why not?

B. How would you respond to Hal's argument for reducing the predetermined overhead rate?

P3-11

Excel in Action

SPREADSHEET

Music Makers uses a job-order system for its production process. Orders are received for specific CDs, and costs are tracked for each order. Job A310 was completed in April. Costs associated with the job included 2,500 blank CDs at a cost of $0.75 per CD, 2,500 plastic containers at $0.10 per container, 2,500 printed inserts at $0.08 per insert, and 2,500 feet of cellophane at $0.02 per foot. Labor costs included copying (20 hours at $12 per hour) and packaging (45 hours at $8 per hour). Manufacturing overhead is applied at the rate of $30.092 per direct labor hour.

Required Use a spreadsheet to prepare a job cost sheet for job A310. The format should be as follows:

	A	B	C
1	Job Cost Sheet		
2	Order Number	A310	
3		Unit	Total
4	Number of CDs		
5	Material Costs:		
6	Blank CDs		
7	Containers		
8	Inserts		
9	Cellophane		
10	Total Materials		
11	Labor Hours:		
12	Copying		
13	Packaging		
14	Labor Costs:		
15	Copying		
16	Packaging		
17	Total Labor		
18	Overhead:		
19	Rate		
20	Total Cost		
21	Average Unit Cost		

Column B should identify unit amounts (number of CDs, unit costs, and labor hours). Column C should provide job costs for each material, labor, and overhead category. Subtotals should be provided for materials, labor, and overhead. These amounts should be computed by using cell references to compute the amounts and the SUM function to compute subtotals and total cost. Shaded cells will contain no data. Use the Format, Cells command, or the Fill Color button to shade cells. Use underlines, alignment, and bold type as indicated in the format provided.

Format cells to properly indicate the type of data entered in the cells. Quantities should be whole numbers, with commas as needed. Dollar amounts should provide for cents and

(Continued)

commas as needed. Average unit cost should provide three decimal places. Use the Comma Style and Increase or Decrease Decimal buttons to format cells.

Once completed, the spreadsheet should be useful for computing other job cost amounts. For example, suppose job A310 had included 5,000 units rather than 2,500. By changing the number of CDs in cell B4, the costs for the job should be recomputed automatically. Use absolute cell referencing for the number of CDs ($B$4) so that copying formulas from one cell (C6 for example) to another (C7 for example) does not alter the reference to the number of CDs. A major advantage of spreadsheets is that, once designed, they permit reuse and recomputation with minimal data entry.

P3-12 Multiple-Choice Overview of the Chapter

1. Overapplied overhead would result if:
   a. the plant was operated at less than full capacity.
   b. factory overhead costs incurred were less than estimated overhead costs.
   c. factory overhead costs incurred were less than the overhead costs charged to production.
   d. factory overhead costs incurred were greater than the overhead costs charged to production.

2. Scott Corporation uses labor hours as the basis for allocating manufacturing overhead costs to production. At the beginning of last year, Scott estimated total manufacturing costs at $300,000 and total labor hours at 75,000 hours. Actual results for the period were total manufacturing overhead costs of $290,000 and total labor hours of 75,000 hours. As a result of this outcome, Scott would have:
   a. applied more overhead to work-in-process inventory than the actual amount of overhead costs for the year.
   b. applied less overhead to work-in-process inventory than the actual amount of overhead cost for the year.
   c. applied an amount of overhead to work-in-process inventory that was equal to the actual amount of overhead.
   d. found it necessary to recalculate the predetermined rate.

3. Melrose Company uses a job-order costing system. The company recorded the following data for July:

	July 1	Added During July	
	Work-in-Process	Direct	Direct
Job Number	Inventory	Materials	Labor
475	$1,500	$ 500	$ 300
476	1,000	700	900
477	900	1,000	1,500
478	700	1,200	2,000

   Melrose charges overhead to production on the basis of 80% of direct materials cost. Jobs 475, 477, and 478 were completed during July. The balance of Melrose's work-in-process inventory account on July 31 was:
   a. $7,280.
   b. $2,600.
   c. $3,160.
   d. $3,320.

4. Last year, Rembrandt Company incurred $250,000 in actual manufacturing overhead costs. The manufacturing overhead account showed that overhead was overapplied in the amount of $12,000 for the year. If the predetermined overhead rate was $8 per direct labor hour, how many direct labor hours were worked during the year?
   a. 31,250
   b. 30,250
   c. 32,750
   d. 29,750

5. Birk Inc. uses a job-order costing system. The following information appeared in Birk's work-in-process inventory for April:

Balance, April 1	$ 4,000
Direct materials added	24,000
Direct labor added	16,800
Factory overhead applied	13,440
Transferred to finished goods	(48,000)

Birk applies overhead to production at a predetermined rate of 80% of direct labor costs. Work-in-process on April 30 includes direct labor costs of $2,000. The amount of direct materials in the ending work-in-process inventory for April was:
   a. $3,000.
   b. $5,200.
   c. $9,600.
   d. $6,640.

6. During May, Roy Company produced 6,000 units of product X in job 344. The costs charged to job 344 were as follows:

Direct materials	$10,000
Direct labor	20,000

At the beginning of the year, management estimated the following costs would be incurred to produce 120,000 units for the year:

Factory overhead	$168,000
Selling expenses	84,000

Roy applies overhead to work-in-process on a per-unit basis. The cost to produce one unit of product X in job 344 was:
   a. $6.40.
   b. $5.10.
   c. $3.80.
   d. $3.50.

7. A job cost sheet contains which of the following information?
   a. Materials requisition number
   b. Employee labor rate
   c. Job number
   d. All of the above are correct.

8. The product life cycle consists of each of the following phases except the:
   a. growth phase.
   b. harvest and divest phase.
   c. first-quarter phase.
   d. hold phase.

9. In the growth phase, after a product has been introduced, the producer normally is interested in building:
   a. market share.
   b. greater levels of profit.
   c. a cash balance at the bank.
   d. a better cost accounting system.

10. Traditional overhead allocation bases include all of the following except:
   a. machine hours.
   b. direct labor hours.
   c. direct labor dollars.
   d. electricity costs.

CASES

C3-1   Unit Costing Policy

Objs. 1, 2, 3

Knight Manufacturing produces three different products: A, B, and C. Knight applies overhead to the products on the basis of direct labor dollars. The company has collected the following information about its overhead and labor costs:

Manufacturing overhead:	
Machine setup	$ 53,000
Depreciation	400,000
Receiving and handling	200,000
Factory operations	650,000
Packing and shipping	400,000
Total	$1,703,000
Total direct labor	$ 225,000

Predetermined overhead rate 757% of direct labor dollars ($1,703,000 ÷ $225,000)

Knight can produce:

Product A—2 units per hour
Product B—3 units per hour
Product C—4 units per hour

The costs of direct materials and direct labor are charged to each product under a job-order costing system. The average cost per unit based on the first of several production runs is as follows:

	Product		
	A	**B**	**C**
Direct materials	$ 25.00	$ 35.00	$ 15.00
Direct labor*	10.00	6.67	5.00
Overhead applied	75.70	50.49	37.85
Total per-unit cost	$110.70	$ 92.16	$ 57.85
Current selling price	$163.00	$125.00	$102.00

The average labor rate is $20 per labor hour.

The company manufactures each product in different batch sizes. Product A is manufactured in lot sizes of 10,000 units per run, product B in lots of 5,000 units per run, and product C in lots of 1,000 units per run. The average shipment size is 2,000 units of product A, 500 units of product B, and 100 units of product C. Over the past year, the company has sold 22,000 units of product A, 15,000 units of product B, and 32,000 units of product C.

In recent months, management at Knight has been puzzled by the company's sales and profit figures. The sales of product A have declined significantly since a competitor of that product reduced its selling price below Knight's current cost of manufacturing that product. In addition, Knight has increased its selling price of product C three times over the past year without losing any sales. Even though more product C is being sold, and it has the largest gross margin of the three products, overall profits have been falling.

Required

A. What problems do you see with the current unit costing methods Knight is using?
B. What reasons can you suggest for the market reactions to the pricing of products A and C?
C. What changes would you suggest to management about its current costing policies?

C3-2 Allocation of Overhead Costs

Objs. 1, 2, 3

(This case is a variation of P3-6.) Art's Custom Cabinetry manufactures and installs custom cabinetry built to customer specifications. The prices of cabinets depend on the quality of the lumber selected by the customers and the complexity of designs.

The company is owned and operated by Art Bruce. Five years ago, he started the company in his garage. Over the five years, Art invested heavily in special equipment. The annual depreciation on that equipment is $1,200. He also has moved operations to a building he rents for $4,800 per year. During 2004, Art incurred the following costs: utilities, $1,500; repairs and maintenance, $600; shop supplies, $2,100; paint and varnish, $800; insurance and taxes, $3,000. All of these costs are considered to be production costs and are assigned to jobs as overhead expense. These costs are expected to stay the same in 2005.

Art assigns job numbers by customer name. The only job still in process at the end of 2004 was Clara Cummins. That job had been charged with direct materials of $600, direct labor of $1,000, and overhead of $400, using an overhead allocation rate of 25% of direct costs (direct materials plus direct labor).

Art is the sole employee of his company. He works an average of 2,800 hours a year and pays himself $20 an hour. Art bids on all jobs in his spare time and feels his overhead rate has kept him from obtaining some of the jobs he has bid on.

A summary of activity for January is as follows:

Job	Direct Materials	Direct Labor Cost	Direct Labor Hours
Clara Cummins	$ 600	$ 800	40
John Ryan	1,200	1,000	50
Kyle Smith	750	700	35
Ken Woods	950	600	30

The Kyle Smith job was completed during January and billed at cost plus 10%. All other jobs are still in process at the end of the month.

Required

A. Comment on the overhead base used by Art's Custom Cabinetry. What changes would you recommend, if any, for the company?

B. Select a base for 2005, and calculate the predetermined overhead rate that should be used in the coming year.

C. Using your predetermined overhead rate [part (B)], calculate the total costs for each of the jobs Art worked on during January.

D. Calculate the balance of the company's work-in-process inventory as of January 31, 2005. Which jobs are reflected in that balance?

E. Calculate the cost of goods sold in January 2005.

F. Calculate the unit profit margin that the company earned from jobs completed in January.

PRODUCING GOODS AND SERVICES: CONTINUOUS PROCESSING

How do we account for products manufactured in a continuous process?

Erin and Seth now understand the importance of unit costs and realize they need monthly reports to show the costs of manufacturing each type of product. Erin and Seth use two different manufacturing processes in their furniture company. Because they believe their futon will be very popular with several customers, they are making it on a continuous basis. Other products are manufactured when they are ordered. Frequently a job requires specific modifications to meet customer needs. Seth is particularly concerned about matching the costing procedure to the type of manufacturing process.

FOOD FOR THOUGHT

If you were advising Seth and Erin, what would be your recommendation for associating costs with the furniture they are producing? Does manufacturing a product continuously versus building it to order make a difference in how product costs are collected and reported? Let's join Erin, Seth, and Roberta again as they discuss the situation.

Erin: We've been trying to decide how to assign manufacturing costs to our products. We're not sure if we can use the same approach for all of our products. Seth and I have been discussing this question and think we need two different costing methods. We should use job-order costing to assign manufacturing costs to our made-to-order products. If we divide the month's total overhead costs by the month's total for direct labor hours, we'll have an average we can apply for each labor hour. Then, we can assign overhead to each order by multiplying the overhead average by the number of labor hours worked on a particular job. Next, we will use job cost cards to record materials and labor costs for our batches of unique products. However, we need a different system to account for our futons that are produced continuously.

Seth: I agree. We are producing futons all the time and shipping them when orders are received. A futon may sit in the warehouse for three or four months before it is sold and shipped. How would we know how much cost to assign to a futon under these circumstances?

Roberta: An accounting system for a continuous process should track the costs of materials, labor, and overhead over a period. For example, each month the system should produce an average unit cost by dividing the manufacturing cost by the number of units produced during the period. Using two different product costing procedures should provide greater accuracy in product costs. You have to decide if the benefits of greater cost accuracy derived from using two procedures are worth the effort required to get the information.

Erin: I think I'm beginning to understand the differences between the two costing methods. Using job-order costing, we track costs to a specific job. In the continuous process situation, since there is no job, we have to assign some sort of average cost to the units produced. An average cost should work fine for the futons, because they are identical. How do we set up this type of costing system?

OBJECTIVES

Once you have completed this chapter, you should be able to:

1 Distinguish between job-order and process costing and describe when each method should be used.

2 Explain the concept of equivalent units.

3 Prepare and evaluate a departmental production report.

ASSIGNING UNIT COSTS

OBJECTIVE 1

Distinguish between job-order and process costing and describe when each method should be used.

Cost accounting systems are designed to provide product cost information to decision makers. These systems capture important characteristics of a company's underlying manufacturing process. To develop unit costs, a company must determine how to measure costs and assign them to individual units. Two methods, job-order costing and process costing, traditionally have been used to assign unit costs. Each method is suited to a specific type of manufacturing or service environment. Companies that build ships; provide legal, medical, or accounting services; manufacture airplanes; and repair automobiles would likely use job-order costing to assign unit costs to their products or services. Those products or services share certain characteristics:

- The units of a particular job are easy to identify because they are unique.
- Much of the cost of producing the product or service can be traced directly to a particular job.

Suppose **Boeing**, an aircraft manufacturer, builds a jumbo jet and a small commuter plane in the same plant. Obviously, the physical characteristics and costs of producing a jumbo jet are very different from the characteristics and costs of producing a small plane. If the company assigns manufacturing costs by simply dividing its total costs for the period by the number of planes it has produced, it will assign too little cost to the jumbo jet and too much to the commuter plane. The company has to know the cost of producing each type of plane. Thus, a company such as Boeing would use job cost sheets, as illustrated in the previous chapter, to accumulate costs for each type of airplane.

In contrast, process costing is best suited for production situations with the following characteristics:

- The products are alike.
- The processes used to manufacture those products flow from one into another.
- The costs of producing the products cannot be traced easily to individual units.

Process costing **totals the costs of all units produced in a given accounting period and divides by the units produced.** Thus, unit costs are calculated as follows:

Unit cost for the period = Cost of production for the period ÷ Units produced in the period

Consider a petroleum processing company, such as **Shell Oil**, where gasoline is produced in a continuous flow. The oil flows through a series of processes that transform it into gasoline. Once produced and stored, it is impossible to distinguish one gallon of gasoline from another, much less to identify when that particular gallon was produced. A refinery cannot trace the cost of manufacturing gasoline to individual gallons. In this case, an average cost is sufficiently accurate because the physical characteristics and costs of producing each unit of product are very much the same.

Batch processing **combines elements of individual-job and continuous-flow processing.** When Shell Oil produces a batch of Shell Regular gasoline followed by a batch of Shell Plus gasoline on the same production line, it is using batch processing. When products are produced in batches, the decision to use job-order costing or process costing often depends on the answers to the following questions:

- How much accuracy in the unit cost calculation does management require?
- How accurate is process costing compared to job-order costing?
- How difficult and costly is tracing costs to individual batches using a job-order system?

When products are processed in batches, the choice of a cost-assignment method involves weighing the need for accurate information against the cost of developing that information. The need for accuracy depends on the type of business and how the information is going to be used. The cost of developing accurate information is a function of the production process. Job-order costing generally is more accurate than process costing. However, a job-order system can be more costly and more difficult to implement in many manufacturing situations.

Exhibit 1 compares the two traditional methods for assigning costs to units of products. Job-order costing is more effective when jobs are manufactured separately rather than in continuous processes. In addition, job-order costing performs well when the units of each product vary in characteristics and costs. Process costing works best when production is continuous and when the units of each product are similar in characteristics and cost.

Exhibit 1
Job-Order and Process
Costing: Choosing a
Cost-Assignment
Method

	Job-Order Costing	Process Costing
Manufacturing Context	Products are manufactured in separate and distinct jobs.	Products are manufactured in a continuous process.
Computation of Unit Costs	Costs are traced to each job. The total cost of a job is divided by the number of units produced in the job to determine the unit cost.	Costs are accumulated for all units produced during a period. To determine the unit cost, total cost is divided by the number of units produced during the period.
Accuracy	Job-order costing tends to be more accurate because costs are traced directly to a particular job.	Process costing usually is less accurate because the unit cost is the average of all units produced during the period.

1 | **SELF-STUDY PROBLEM**   Which method, job-order costing or process costing, would be most appropriate for each of the following organizations? Briefly justify your answer.

WebTUTOR Advantage

a. A paint manufacturer
b. A glue manufacturer
c. An aircraft manufacturer
d. A home building company
e. An accounting firm
f. A hospital
g. A tire manufacturer
h. A manufacturer of specialty factory equipment
i. An interior decorator
j. A film studio
k. A brewery

The solution to Self-Study Problem 1 appears at the end of the chapter.

PROCESS COSTING

OBJECTIVE 2

Explain the concept of equivalent units.

The objective of process costing, like that of job-order costing, is to determine a unit cost for each finished product. Products manufactured in a process environment usually pass through a series of steps. In each step materials, labor, and overhead costs are added to the product. Processes usually are carried out in specific departments or process centers. When units of a product are completed, they are transferred as finished goods to a warehouse until they are shipped to customers. This section uses Syntex Fabrics to illustrate cost accumulation in a continuous manufacturing environment.

Syntex Fabrics: The Manufacturing Process and Cost Flows

Syntex Fabrics is an example of a manufacturing company that uses a process costing system. As shown in Exhibit 2, the manufacturing processes at Syntex Fabrics require three departments, A, B, and C. In the first process, fiber production (known as spinning), liquid synthetic resin is placed into a machine. At the top of the machine, fibers emerge from spinnerets (discs resembling a showerhead). Each hole in the spinneret produces a continuous strand of fiber. These fibers are wound onto spools for use in the weaving process. Exhibit 2 illustrates that direct materials, direct labor, and manufacturing overhead costs are added by Department A during the fiber production process.

Exhibit 2 Tracing Costs Through Syntex Fabric's Process Costing System

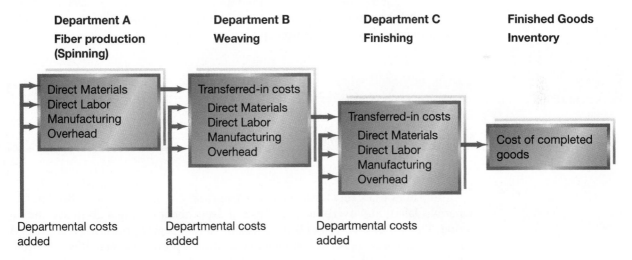

The second process, known as weaving, uses fiber transferred in from Department A to manufacture cloth on large high-tech looms. Various materials and supplies are used in preparing the loom (the machine used to weave fibers into cloth). First, fibers are wound side-by-side onto the loom in a process called warping. After the warping process, the loom contains fibers that are parallel and run the length of the loom. These fibers are called the warp. Fabric is created when weft fibers are woven over and under the warp fibers across the width of the loom. As shown in Exhibit 2, the weaving department adds direct materials, direct labor, and manufacturing overhead costs to convert the fiber into fabric.

When the weaving process is complete, the fabric is transferred to the third process, known as finishing, where various waterproofing and flame retarding coatings are applied. As shown in Exhibit 2, fabric costs are transferred in from the weaving department. The finishing department also adds direct materials, direct labor, and manufacturing overhead costs to the product during the conversion process. After the finishing process, the completed roll of fabric is transferred to finished goods inventory.

When the completed goods are sold, their accumulated costs are transferred from finished goods inventory to cost of goods sold.

Equivalent Units

In process costing systems, manufacturing costs are accumulated by department and are applied to equivalent units of production. *Equivalent units* **are the number of units that would have been produced during a period if all of the department's efforts had resulted in completed units.** For example, two units that are each one-half complete would be treated as one complete unit for purposes of assigning costs (2 units $\times \frac{1}{2}$ complete = 1 equivalent unit). Equivalent units are computed separately for each process center. The need to compute equivalent units arises because all of a department's efforts do not result in fully completed units during a period. Thus, process costing is complicated by work-in-process (WIP) inventory at the end of an accounting period. WIP for a particular department is made up of those units that are partially completed in that department.

Exhibit 3 illustrates how to calculate equivalent units for a department that transferred 65,000 units to another department. Though the units transferred out are not 100 percent complete, they are complete to the extent possible by the transferring department. Thus, units transferred out always are multiplied by 100 percent to calculate equivalent units. Remaining in the ending WIP inventory are 20,000 units that are 40 percent complete. As Exhibit 3 illustrates, these units are multiplied by the percentage of completion to determine the equivalent units remaining in ending WIP inventory. The total equivalent units produced by a department within an accounting period is calculated by adding the equivalent units transferred out to the equivalent units remaining in WIP inventory. Exhibit 3 reports 73,000 total equivalent units produced by the department during an accounting period.

Exhibit 3
Equivalent Unit
Calculation

Equivalent units transferred out	65,000	(65,000 × 100%)
Equivalent units remaining in ending WIP inventory	8,000	(20,000 × 40%)
Total equivalent units	73,000	

Companies track cost flows using *departmental production reports* **that describe materials, labor, and overhead used by each department during a given accounting period. The** *initial department* **is the department that begins producing a product. A** *subsequent department* **is a department that continues production activities on a product.** Using our Syntex example in Exhibit 2, fiber production is the initial department and the weaving and finishing processes are subsequent departments. The production cost follows the physical flow of the product as it moves from the initial department to subsequent departments. *Transferred-in costs* **are costs that have been transferred from a prior department in the production process to a subsequent department.**

To use process costing, a company must have a system keeping track of units produced, accumulating costs incurred during the period, and applying those costs to the units produced. The departmental production report summarizes all activities that affect the department's WIP inventory during a given period. Exhibit 4 presents an overview of a departmental production report that would be prepared for a continuous processor, such as Syntex. We later provide a numerical example to illustrate the details of a departmental production report. For now, let's look at the big picture.

The box at the left of Exhibit 4, the quantity schedule, provides a structure to guide you through the entire process of preparing a departmental production report. The quantity schedule reports the physical flow of units through the department. Thus, some companies refer to it as a physical flow schedule. The unit cost calculation associates dollar amounts (in the costs box) with the units to account for in the quantity schedule. The equivalent units calculation also is based on the quantity schedule. After the costs and equivalent units have been calculated, we simply divide costs by equivalent units to determine the cost per equivalent unit. Finally, in the cost reconciliation portion of the production report, we associate the cost per equivalent unit with the number of equivalent units produced during a period. As a result, the total costs in the cost reconciliation section equal the total costs to account for (in the costs box of the unit cost calculation).

Exhibit 4 Departmental Production Report—An Overview

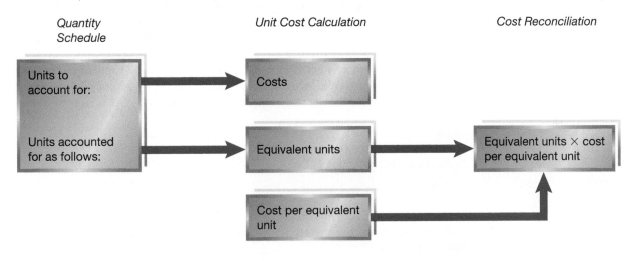

2   **SELF-STUDY PROBLEM**   Halyard Company uses two departments, braiding and finishing, to produce its primary product, $\frac{1}{2}$ inch diameter rope. During June, the braiding department transferred 30,000 yards of braided rope to the finishing department. The ending WIP inventory in the braiding department consisted of 800 yards of rope that were 30% complete.

WebTUTOR Advantage

Required Calculate the equivalent units that would be used to determine a cost per equivalent unit in the braiding department.

The solution to Self-Study Problem 2 appears at the end of the chapter.

PREPARING A DEPARTMENTAL PRODUCTION REPORT

OBJECTIVE 3

Prepare and evaluate a departmental production report.

Recall that Syntex Fabrics requires three departments, fiber production (or spinning), weaving, and finishing, to produce a completed roll of fabric. Accountants prepare departmental production reports for each department at the end of every month. We use the spinning department to illustrate the steps involved in producing a departmental production report for a continuous process manufacturer. The output from the department is measured in yards. The fiber is a high-tech material used in manufacturing fabric intended for rigorous outdoor applications. The high manufacturing cost per yard reflects the technical nature of the product. The objective is to determine the cost per yard and to assign material and conversion costs transferred to the weaving department and to the yards of unfinished product remaining in the department.

Assume the spinning department had 20,000 yards of partially completed fiber as WIP inventory on October 1, 2004. Material and conversion costs associated with the beginning inventory were $320 and $420, respectively. *Conversion costs* **are the direct**

labor and manufacturing overhead costs required to convert raw materials into finished goods. During the month the department began working on an additional 120,000 yards of fiber. Costs of materials and conversion added during the month were $3,050 and $4,500, respectively. The spinning department transferred 110,000 yards of fiber to the weaving department during October. The remaining 30,000 yards of WIP inventory at October 31, 2004, were 50 percent complete as for materials and 40 percent complete for conversion.

Step 1: Account for the Physical Flow of Units. The first step in developing a production report is to account for the physical flow of units worked on during the month. As shown in Exhibit 4, this portion of the production report is known as the quantity schedule. The spinning department at Syntex Fabrics had 20,000 yards of WIP inventory on October 1. They began working on an additional 120,000 yards during the month. Thus, the spinning department had 140,000 yards of fiber to account for (20,000 + 120,000 = 140,000). The department completed and transferred to the weaving department 110,000 yards of fiber. Thus, 30,000 yards of partially spun fiber remain in the department's ending WIP inventory (140,000 − 110,000 = 30,000). Using this information, we complete the quantity schedule as follows:

Units to account for:	Units
Work-in-process, October 1	20,000
Units started in production in October	+120,000
Total	140,000

Units accounted for as follows:	
Units completed and transferred out in October	110,000
Work-in-process, October 31	+ 30,000
Total	140,000

Step 2: Account for the Department's Production Costs. In this step, the company adds the costs of beginning WIP inventory and the costs added during the month. Often, labor and overhead are added together and are accounted for as a single conversion cost in process-costing systems. Notice the "Units to account for" section of the quantity schedule is included to illustrate where to assign the materials and conversion costs. For example, the beginning inventory consisted of 20,000 partially complete units. These units contained materials and conversion costs of $320 and $420, respectively. In addition, 120,000 yards were started during the month. The materials and conversion costs associated with these yards are $3,050 and $4,500, respectively. Thus, the total cost associated with the spinning department during the month of October is $8,290 ($320 + $420 + $3,050 + $4,500).

			Costs	
	Units	Materials	Conversion	Total
Work-in-process, October 1	20,000	$ 320	$ 420	$ 740
Costs added during October in the spinning department	120,000	3,050	4,500	7,550
Total for October	140,000	$3,370	$4,920	$8,290

Step 3: Calculate the Equivalent Units of Production. In this step, the company converts the physical units of production into equivalent units. Using the quantity schedule as a guide, we calculate the equivalent units associated with the units completed and transferred to the weaving department. In addition we calculate the equivalent units associated with the fiber remaining in ending WIP inventory. The percentage of completion associated with products transferred out is always 100 percent. These units are complete to the extent possible by the spinning department. For further processing, these units are transferred to the weaving department. Thus, if 110,000 yards

are transferred out, 110,000 equivalent units of materials and 110,000 equivalent units of conversion are transferred to the weaving department.

Unlike the number of units transferred out, we must adjust the ending inventory for the percentage of completion. For example, the ending WIP inventory consists of 30,000 yards that are 50 percent complete for materials and 40 percent complete for conversion costs. In other words, the department has added only one-half of the materials necessary to complete the 30,000 yards of fiber. They have added only 40 percent of the conversion costs (labor and overhead) necessary to complete the 30,000 yards of fiber. Therefore, the department has 15,000 equivalent units of materials (30,000 whole units × .50) and 12,000 equivalent units with respect to conversion (30,000 whole units × .40). During the month, the division produced a total of 125,000 equivalent units of materials (110,000 + 15,000 = 125,000) and 122,000 equivalent units of conversion (110,000 + 12,000 = 122,000). The equivalent unit calculation is shown as follows:

	Units	Materials	Conversion
Units completed and transferred out in October (100% complete)	110,000	110,000	110,000
Work-in-process, October 31:			
30,000 units × 50% complete for materials	30,000	15,000	
30,000 units × 40% complete for conversion			12,000
Equivalent units of production for October	140,000	125,000	122,000

Step 4: Calculate the Cost of Equivalent Units. The fourth step in developing the production report is to divide total costs (from step 2) by equivalent units (from step 3) to obtain the cost per equivalent unit. Total material costs of $3,370 are divided by 125,000 equivalent units of materials. The result is a material cost of $0.026960 per equivalent unit. Likewise, total conversion costs of $4,920 are divided by 122,000 equivalent units of conversion. The result is a conversion cost of $0.040328 per equivalent unit of conversion. The total unit product cost of $0.0673 is obtained by adding the equivalent unit cost for materials and conversion.

	Units	Costs		
		Materials	Conversion	Total
Work-in-process, October 1	20,000	$ 320	$ 420	$ 740
Costs added during October in the spinning department	120,000	3,050	4,500	7,550
Total costs for October	140,000	$3,370	$4,920	$8,290

	Units	Materials	Conversion
(100% complete)	110,000	110,000	110,000
Work-in-process, October 31:			
30,000 units × 50% complete for materials	30,000	15,000	
30,000 units × 40% complete for conversion			12,000
Equivalent units of production for October	140,000	125,000	122,000
		$\dfrac{\$3,370}{125,000}$	$\dfrac{\$4,920}{122,000}$
	$\$0.026960$ +	$\$0.040328$ =	$\$0.067288$

Step 4 indicates the spinning department incurred $0.027 in material cost and $0.040 in conversion cost for each yard of completed fiber. The cost of a yard of spun fiber transferred to the weaving department is $0.067 ($0.027 + $0.040).

Step 5: Assign Costs to Inventory. In the final step of the departmental production report, the company assigns production costs for the period to the units that are transferred out. These costs move into the WIP inventory of the weaving department. The costs transferred out equal the number of units transferred out multiplied by the total cost per equivalent unit. The costs assigned to WIP inventory equal the number of equivalent units in WIP multiplied by the cost per unit. Costs are assigned to units transferred out to the weaving department and to ending WIP inventory as follows:

	Units		
Costs transferred to the weaving department:			
(110,000 units × $0.067288)	110,000		$7,402
Costs assigned to work-in-process inventory:			
Materials (30,000 units × 50% × $0.026960)	30,000	404	
Conversion (30,000 units × 40% × $0.040328)		484	
Costs assigned to work-in-process inventory			888
Total costs assigned to units in October	140,000		$8,290

Notice that the total costs assigned to units in October ($8,290) equal the total costs to be accounted for in step 2.

Exhibit 5 combines steps 1–5 into a completed production report using the layout shown in Exhibit 4.

Exhibit 5 Completed Departmental Production Report for the Spinning Department at Syntex Fabrics

Units to account for:	Units	Materials	Conversion	Total	
Work-in-process, October 1	20,000	$ 320	$ 420	$ 740	
Units started during October	120,000	3,050	4,500	7,550	
Total	140,000	$3,370	$4,920	$8,290	
Units accounted for as follows:					
Units transferred out in October	110,000	110,000	110,000	Transferred out 110,000 × $0.067288 = $7,402	
Work-in-process, October 31	30,000	15,000	12,000	Ending WIP 15,000 × $0.026960 = 404	
Total	140,000	125,000	122,000	12,000 × $0.040328 = 484	
				$8,290	
Cost per unit		$3,370	$4,920		
		125,000	122,000		
		$0.026960 + $0.040328 = $0.067288			

Managers use cost information provided by the departmental production report in a variety of ways. For example, they can evaluate whether material, labor, and manufacturing overhead costs are consistent with expectations, based on prior periods. Most companies that use process costing systems are continuous manufacturers. Thus, managers should expect production levels and unit costs to remain stable unless the company experiences a manufacturing problem or a price increase for resources required in production. Companies also use output from a process costing system to help them value work-in-process and finished goods inventory. As we have seen, these values are reported in a company's published financial statements.

Case In Point

http://ingram.
swlearning.com

Learn more about the
Dow Chemical Company.

Cost Information and Decision-Making in a Continuous Process Industry

Understanding production costs, such as materials and conversion, are important to continuous processors. **Dow Chemical** recently was able to raise prices without losing volume. The company beat analysts' earnings forecasts by aggressively controlling operating costs and increasing prices. Management believes price increases were possible because of increased demand, and lower supply of their products.

Source: Chemical Week. New York, July 2–9, 2003. Vol. 165, Issue 24, page 49.

3 SELF-STUDY PROBLEM

WebTUTOR Advantage

Fizz Pop produces one product (a soft drink) that flows through two departments, mixing and bottling. Costs in WIP inventory on March 1 included $4,000 of materials and $2,500 of conversion costs. Costs added during March included $50,000 of materials and $35,000 of conversion costs.

A production report for the mixing department for March showed the following information:

	Units	Percentage Complete	
		Materials	Conversion
Units to account for:			
Work-in-process, March 1	50,000		
Units started in production in March	600,000		
Total units in production in March	650,000		
Units accounted for as follows:			
Units completed and transferred out in March	570,000		
Work-in-process, March 31	80,000	100%	50%
Total units accounted for	650,000		

Required Compute the total and unit costs for March. Also compute the amount of cost transferred to the bottling department during March and the amount of WIP on March 31 for the mixing department.

The solution to Self-Study Problem 3 appears at the end of the chapter.

REVIEW

SUMMARY of IMPORTANT CONCEPTS

1. Most companies use either process costing or job-order costing to assign costs to units of products.
   a. Each method is more effective in certain processing environments.

2. Equivalent units are used to determine unit costs for materials and conversion.

3. Process costing yields an average cost for each unit produced during a particular period.
   a. The departmental production report summarizes costs and units that flow through a department each period.
   b. A production report consists of three sections as follows:
      1. Quantity schedule
      2. Unit cost calculation
      3. Cost reconciliation
   c. As units of product move from one department to the next, the production costs of those products are transferred from department to department.

DEFINE

TERMS and CONCEPTS DEFINED in this CHAPTER

batch processing (M79)
conversion costs (M83)
departmental production report (M82)
equivalent units (M82)

initial department (M82)
process costing (M79)
subsequent department (M82)
transferred-in costs (M82)

SELF-STUDY PROBLEM SOLUTIONS

SSP4-1 Job-order costing is used in situations where many different products, jobs, or batches are produced each period. Process costing is used in situations where a homogeneous product is produced on a continuous basis.

	Process Costing	Job-Order Costing
a. A paint manufacturer	x	
b. A glue manufacturer	x	
c. An aircraft manufacturer		x
d. A home building company		x
e. An accounting firm		x
f. A hospital		x
g. A tire manufacturer	x	
h. A manufacturer of specialty factory equipment		x
i. An interior decorator		x
j. A film studio		x
k. A brewery	x	

SSP4-2

Yards transferred out	30,000	(30,000 × 100%)
Ending WIP	240	(800 × 30%)
Equivalent units	30,240	

SSP4-3

	Materials	Conversion	Total
Cost to account for:			
Work-in-process, March 1	$ 4,000	$ 2,500	$ 6,500
Costs added during March in mixing department	50,000	35,000	85,000
Total costs for March	$54,000	$37,500	$91,500

Equivalent units:

	Materials	Conversion
Units completed and transferred out in March	570,000	570,000
Work-in-process, March 31:		
80,000 units × 100% complete	80,000	
80,000 units × 50% complete		40,000
Equivalent units of production in March	650,000	610,000

Cost per equivalent unit:
Materials $54,000 ÷ 650,000 equivalent units = $0.083077 per equivalent unit
Conversion $37,500 ÷ 610,000 equivalent units = $0.061475 per equivalent unit

Total $0.144552 per equivalent unit

Costs assigned to inventory:		
Costs assigned to units transferred out 570,000 units × $0.144552		$82,395
Costs assigned to work-in-process inventory:		
Materials	80,000 units × 100% × $0.083077 =	6,646
Conversion	80,000 units × 50% × $0.061475 =	2,459
Costs assigned to work-in-process inventory		9,105
Total costs assigned to units in March ($82,395 + $9,105)		$91,500

Thinking Beyond the Question

How do we account for products manufactured in a continuous process?

Reflect back on Erin and Seth's discussion of batch versus continuous process costing. Earlier in the chapter, you learned to account for partially completed units using the equivalent units concept because some units manufactured during a given period may not be completed during that same period. You learned how to develop equivalent units for materials and conversion and to compute costs per equivalent unit for each category of cost. What happens, however, when more than one type of labor or material is used in a given department? How would you suggest accounting for such situations?

QUESTIONS

Q4-1
Obj. 1
During a family gathering you announce that you are studying managerial accounting and fully understand product costing. Your brother says that he works for a company that assigns product costs using job-order costing. Your sister says that her company uses something called process costing to assign product costs. Uncle Nick asks you to explain the difference between job-order costing and process costing. What do you tell him?

Q4-2
Obj. 1
Clark Lights produces lightbulbs. The plant is new, and the process is highly automated. All production is completed in a single two-step department. First, a bulb casing is made and is passed to a second machine process where a filament is inserted. The company manufactures several different wattage bulbs, including 40, 75, and 100. Once the machinery is set up, the company will produce the same wattage bulb for up to four days before changing to another wattage bulb. The only difference in processing the different wattage bulbs is the size of the filament that is inserted in the second step. The cost difference of the different size filaments is insignificant. Clark produces approximately 5,000 bulbs of each wattage per month. Identify the costing procedure that would be most appropriate given the different style bulbs that are produced. Explain the reason for your answer. Would your answer change if the cost of the materials was considered significantly different? Explain why or why not.

Q4-3
Obj. 1
Which method, job order or process costing, would be the most appropriate for each of the following organizations? Under what circumstances would managers choose job order costing? Under what circumstances would managers choose process costing?

a. A bakery that produces a variety of goods	f. A law firm
b. A bank	g. A pharmaceutical firm
c. A gasoline refinery	h. A soft drink bottler
d. A printing shop	i. A jewelry repair shop
e. A cement manufacturer	j. A custom boat builder
	k. A fertilizer producer

Q4-4
Obj. 1
You work in consulting and have been hired to redesign Hoyt Industries' costing systems. Hoyt produces soft drinks. You have already decided to use normal costing to measure costs, but must decide what method to use to assign costs to units of products, job-order or process costing. What are the differences between the two approaches?

Q4-5
Obj. 1
Carter Lumber Company processes timber into finished lumber. For 20 years, Carter has calculated the cost of lumber using job-order costing. Each production run was treated as a separate job. Carter recently changed accounting procedures and now calculates product costs using process costing. Do you think making the change was a good idea? Why or why not?

Q4-6
Obj. 2
The equivalent unit calculation adjusts ending WIP for partially completed units. The purpose is to make the cost per equivalent unit more accurate. Can you think of a situation in which adjusting for equivalent units would be unnecessary? Explain.

Q4-7
Obj. 2
Pegasus Wire Harness Company produces an electrical-wire harness used in the automotive industry. Pegasus accounts for product costs using process costing. Managers of Pegasus focus on two elements of product costs for planning and control purposes. What are the two elements that are assigned costs in process costing? Why are the two elements treated separately?

Q4-8
Obj. 2
The equivalent unit calculation attaches material, labor, and overhead costs equally to each unit produced during an accounting period. Under what circumstances does this system produce reasonably accurate product costs? Explain.

Q4-9
Obj. 3
How might a manager use a departmental production report to understand and manage costs?

Q4-10
Obj. 3
Assume you are the manager of the third department in a three-department process. Your company uses process costing to determine its product costs. When a product passes through your department, it is taken to the finished goods inventory warehouse. At the same time, an accounting entry is prepared to reduce WIP inventory in your department and to increase finished goods inventory. How would you know the total value of goods to transfer? Where did these costs come from?

Q4-11
Obj. 3
Paula Locum is a department manager for Dempsey Lumber Mill. She supervises the kiln drying operations and is directly responsible for ten employees and three large kiln dryers. Each month, Paula prepares a production report for the drying operation and submits her report to accounting. What are the key elements of a departmental production report?

EXERCISES

If your instructor is using Personal Trainer® in this course, you may complete your assignments online.

E4-1
Write a short definition for each of the terms listed in the *Terms and Concepts Defined in this Chapter* section.

E4-2
Obj. 1
For each characteristic listed below, indicate whether the characteristic is more descriptive of a (a) job-order costing system or a (b) process costing system.

1. More detailed information is required for costing purposes.
2. Products are similar in cost and in required manufacturing activities.
3. Cost estimates are less accurate because of averaging.
4. Costs are accumulated for a given period of time.
5. Products usually vary in cost and required manufacturing activities.
6. Identical units pass through a series of different processes.
7. The total cost for the period is divided by the total units produced during the period.
8. Costs are accumulated by batch or job number.
9. Each unit of product receives a similar amount of manufacturing costs.
10. Units of different products may receive a different amount of manufacturing costs.

E4-3
Obj. 1
If you were the manager of each of the following firms or companies, which costing system would you recommend: (a) job-order costing or (b) process costing?

1. An oil refinery
2. A ship builder
3. A management consulting firm
4. A paper mill
5. A dairy
6. A construction firm
7. A manufacturer of fertilizer
8. An advertising company

E4-4
Obj. 2
Wise Foods Company produces a high-protein food product. The following information relates to the baking department's activities during the month of April:

Beginning work-in-process	600 units	
Units started into production	380 units	
Ending work-in-process	400 units	(100% complete as to material costs 75% complete as to conversion costs)

Prepare a physical flow schedule and a schedule of equivalent units.

E4-5 Medi-Syrup is a large cough syrup producer. The cough syrup passes through several stages
Obj. 2 during production. In department B, the following activity was recorded for October:

- Beginning work-in-process on October 1 was 40,000 gallons.
- 20,000 gallons were started into production in department B during October.
- 55,000 gallons were completed and transferred out to department C during the month.
- The gallons remaining in work-in-process in department B at the end of the month were 80% complete as to material costs and 60% complete as to conversion costs.

Prepare a physical flow schedule and a schedule of equivalent units for the department.

E4-6 Aladdin Company manufactures a product that passes through two processes. The following
Obj. 2 information was available for the first department for January:

1. Beginning WIP consisted of 6,000 units.
2. Ending WIP consisted of 4,400 units, 100% complete with respect to material costs and 25% complete with respect to conversion costs.
3. 10,000 units started into production in January.

a. Prepare a physical flow schedule for the department.
b. Calculate equivalent units for materials and conversion costs.

E4-7 Blue Line Company makes two kinds of ink and uses a process costing system. The company's
Obj. 2 WIP inventory for blue ink on November 1 consisted of 10,000 units. An additional 8,000
units were entered into production in November, and 3,000 units were completed and transferred to finished goods inventory. The 15,000 units in ending WIP inventory were 100% complete as to materials and 80% complete as to conversion costs. Cost information for November
for blue ink production is as follows:

Costs in beginning WIP:

Direct labor	$20,000
Direct materials	10,000
Manufacturing overhead	30,000

The following costs were added during the month:

Direct labor	$ 5,000
Direct materials	14,840
Manufacturing overhead	20,000

a. Prepare a schedule of equivalent units.
b. Compute the cost per equivalent unit for materials.
c. Compute the cost per equivalent unit for conversion.

E4-8 Holbert Company produces a product that passes through two departments, mixing and heat-
Obj. 3 ing. The following information relates to activities in the mixing department for June:
Beginning WIP, June 1, 100,000 pounds. Costs in beginning WIP inventory were as follows:

SPREADSHEET

Materials	$20,000
Labor	10,000
Overhead	30,000

Ending WIP, June 30, 50,000 pounds, 100% complete with respect to material costs and 40%
complete with respect to conversion costs.
Units completed and transferred out totaled 370,000 pounds. The following costs were
added during the month:

Materials	$211,000
Labor	100,000
Overhead	269,500

a. Prepare a physical flow schedule.
b. Prepare a schedule of equivalent units.
c. Compute the cost per equivalent unit.
d. Compute the cost of goods transferred out and the value of the ending WIP inventory.

E4-9

Obj. 3

A varnish manufacturer uses process costing. Information concerning a recent production period is as follows:

Units in beginning work-in-process	12,000
Units started into production	16,000
Units completed and transferred out	4,000
Units in ending work-in-process	24,000

The units in ending WIP were 100% complete as to direct materials and 80% complete as to conversion costs.

The following costs were incurred:

Direct materials, beginning work-in-process	$10,000
Direct materials, added during the period	14,920
Conversion costs, beginning work-in-process	2,032
Conversion costs, added during the period	4,000

a. Compute the cost of the units completed and transferred out.
b. Compute the cost of the units in ending WIP.

E4-10

Obj. 3

Company X produces organic fertilizer and uses process costing. At the end of 2004, 20,000 bags of fertilizer were completed. The total value of these completed units was $12,000, of which $8,000 constituted conversion costs.

a. What was the cost per equivalent unit for materials?
b. If 10,000 units remained in WIP at the end of the year (30% complete as to direct materials, 40% complete as to conversion costs), what was the total value of ending WIP?

E4-11

Obj. 3

Smith Inc. produces plastic pellets. The following information refers to production activity during March:

Beginning work-in-process	5,000 units
Started into production	4,000 units
Completed	3,000 units
Ending work-in-process	6,000 units (60% complete as to direct materials, 75% complete as to conversion costs)

The value of the completed units was $6,000, of which $4,500 was direct materials costs and $1,500 was conversion costs. What was the value of direct materials and the value of conversion costs in ending WIP?

PROBLEMS

If your instructor is using Personal Trainer® in this course, you may complete your assignments online.

P4-1

Obj. 2

Unit Costs under Process Costing

Perfect Bread Company makes bread in its midwestern plant. The production process is described as follows:

> Flour, milk, yeast, and salt are combined and mixed in a large vat. The resulting dough is transferred by conveyor to a machine that shapes the dough into loaves and places the loaves into pans. The dough is allowed to rise for several hours. Then the pans move slowly through a long oven, where they bake for 45 minutes. When the baked bread emerges from the oven, another machine removes the loaves from the pans. The bread cools for 10 minutes and then is fed through a slicing machine and wrapped.

Last week, Perfect produced 5,000 loaves of bread. The total cost of materials for the week, including ingredients and packaging, was $750. The costs of labor and overhead totaled $1,600. There were no beginning or ending inventories.

Required

A. Compute the unit cost of the 5,000 loaves produced during the week.
B. Perfect does not maintain WIP inventory. What implications does that fact have on the calculations the company must perform?

C. Suppose that Perfect uses the same machinery to produce rolls and buns but that processing those other products is significantly different in terms of cost. What implications would that have on the company's accounting procedures?

P4-2   Cost Calculation Using Process Costing

Obj. 3

SPREADSHEET

Chester Smith manufactures cheddar cheese. The manufacture of cheese requires one period of production and storage in huge vats and two periods of aging in a cellar. The company uses process costing and prepares departmental production reports in each of its two departments, production and aging. All units in beginning WIP are transferred out by the end of that period.

		% Complete at Beginning of Period	
	Units	Ingredients	Conversion
Beginning work-in-process for production	2,400	90%	60%
Cheese started into production	2,600	0%	0%

Costs in the beginning work in process totaled $230,000 for ingredients and $406,000 for conversion costs. Costs incurred during the period included $258,000 for ingredients and $492,000 for conversion costs. During the period, all the cheese in beginning WIP was completed and transferred to the first aging process. The ending WIP for the cheese will have the same percent completions as the beginning WIP.

Required
A. Compute the cost per equivalent unit for ingredients (round to two decimal places).
B. Compute the cost per equivalent unit for conversion costs (round to two decimal places).
C. Compute the value of the cheese completed and transferred to aging (round to nearest whole dollar).
D. Compute the value of the cheese in ending work in process (round to nearest whole dollar).
E. What is the importance of having these unit costs? How would Chester use this information?

P4-3   Process Costing

Obj. 3

Metallic Company produces steel. At the end of 2005, 10,000 tons of steel I-beams were completed. The total value of these completed I-beams was $20,000,000, of which $17,000,000 constituted conversion costs.

Required
A. What was the cost per equivalent unit for materials?
B. If 200 tons of steel remained in WIP at the end of the year (90% complete as to direct materials, 30% complete as to conversion costs), what was the total value of ending WIP?
C. Metallic determines that if it uses higher-quality inputs, it can reduce the conversion costs. The extra inputs would cost $20 per ton and the conversion costs would decrease by $150,000 per year. Assuming Metallic produces 10,000 tons of steel each year, should it switch to these higher-quality inputs?

P4-4   Job-Order and Process Costing

Objs. 1, 3

SPREADSHEET

Forever Green Co. manufactures artificial Christmas trees. In 2004, Forever Green only produced one type of tree, the Merry Green Tree. However, in 2005 Forever Green introduced a new, top-of-the-line product, the Green As Can Be Tree. The two products require different materials and are manufactured in separate batches. Overhead is allocated on the basis of machine hours. The information from 2005 is as follows:

	Total	Merry Green	Green As Can Be
Units produced	110,000	100,000	10,000
Materials cost	$4,800,000	$4,000,000	$800,000
Direct labor cost	$9,900,000	$9,000,000	$900,000
Machine hours	130,000	100,000	30,000
Overhead	$1,000,000		*(Continued)*

Required

A. For each product, what is the cost per unit using process costing?
B. For each product, what is the cost per unit using job-order costing?
C. Which costing method is more accurate for this example? Explain.
D. Assume Forever Green decides to use process costing to calculate unit cost. If Forever Green prices its trees at a 30% markup on cost, what would be the unit price for the trees? Is this a good pricing strategy or is one product being overcharged and the other being undercharged?

P4-5

Objs. 1, 3

Job-Order and Process Costing

SPREADSHEET

Call Me manufactures telephones. In 2004, Call Me introduced a stylish telephone with a clear plastic casing, allowing you to see the parts of the phone. The two products are manufactured in separate batches. Overhead is allocated on the basis of machine hours. The information from 2004 is as follows:

	Total	Easy Touch	Clear Phone
Units produced	110,000	80,000	30,000
Materials cost	$640,000	$400,000	$240,000
Direct labor cost	$110,000	$80,000	$30,000
Machine hours	140,000	80,000	60,000
Overhead	$500,000		

Required

A. For each product, what is the cost per unit using process costing?
B. For each product, what is the cost per unit using job-order costing?
C. Which costing method is more accurate for this example? Explain.
D. Assume Call Me decides to use process costing to calculate unit cost. If Call Me prices its phones at a 30% markup on cost, what would be the unit price for the phones? Is this a good pricing strategy or is one product being overcharged and the other being undercharged?

P4-6

Obj. 3

Elements of the Departmental Production Report

Bella Cucina processes olive oil. Information regarding production during October is as follows:

Beginning work-in-process	200 litres
Oil started into production	300 litres
Oil completed	400 litres

The oil in ending WIP was 100% complete as to direct materials and 50% complete as to conversion costs. Costs in beginning WIP totaled $500 for direct materials and $630 for conversion costs. Costs incurred during the month included $750 for direct materials and $900 for conversion costs.

Required

A. Compute the cost per equivalent unit for direct materials.
B. Compute the cost per equivalent unit for conversion costs.
C. Compute the value of the oil completed.
D. Compute the value of the oil in ending WIP.

P4-7

Obj. 3

Elements of the Departmental Production Report

Pet Products manufactures dry dog food. The following information pertains to the month of February:

Beginning work-in-process	5,000 pounds
Started into production	6,000 pounds
Completed	4,000 pounds
Ending work-in-process	7,000 pounds (60% complete as to materials, 40% complete as to conversion costs)

Costs in beginning work-in-process:

Direct materials	$10,000
Conversion costs	2,460

Costs incurred during February:

Direct materials	$5,990
Conversion costs	4,000

Pet Products uses a process costing system to value its inventories.

Required

A. Compute the cost per equivalent unit for materials.
B. Compute the cost per equivalent unit for conversion.
C. Compute the value of ending WIP.
D. Compute the value of the units completed.

P4-8

Excel in Action

SPREADSHEET

Assume Music Makers has begun to produce blank CDs for its use and for sale to outside customers. Because the CDs are produced in a continuous process and are identical, management at Music Makers uses process costing. The unit of measure for Music Makers is a box of CDs. Management has gathered the following information from the molding department for January:

Units (boxes) in beginning inventory	10,000
Units (boxes) started into production	40,000
Units (boxes) transferred out	35,000
Units (boxes) remaining in work-in-process inventory	15,000
Cost of beginning inventory:	
Materials	$60,000
Conversion	80,000
Costs added during the period:	
Materials	$240,000
Conversion	320,000
Ending inventory—percentage of completion:	
Materials	50%
Conversion	30%

Required Use a spreadsheet to prepare a production report for the molding department for the month of January. The format should be as follows:

	A	B	C	D	E	F	G	H
1	**Departmental Production Report**							
2								
3	Ending WIP percentage of completion - materials	0.5						
4	Ending WIP percentage of completion - conversion	0.3						
5								
6		Quantity		Materials	Conversion	Total		Cost
7		Schedule		cost	cost			Reconciliation
8	Beginning inventory	10,000		$60,000	$80,000			
9	Units started	40,000		240,000	320,000			
10	Total units to account for							
11								
12	Transferred out	35,000						
13	Ending work-in-process inventory	15,000						
14	Total units accounted for							
15								
16								
17	Cost per unit							
18								
19								
20								

Sheet1 / Sheet2 / Sheet3 /

(Continued)

The data provided have been entered into the spreadsheet. You should prepare formulas for the shaded cells. Remember to format cells containing dollar values using the **format, cell, currency** commands. Once completed, the spreadsheet can be used to compute costs for later accounting periods. For example, suppose Music Makers reported the following during February:

Units in beginning inventory	15,000
Units started into production	29,000
Units transferred out	39,000
Units remaining in work-in-process inventory	5,000

Assume all production costs remain unchanged from January.

Calculate the unit cost for February. Compare your January and February spreadsheets. What do you observe?

P4-9 Multiple-Choice Overview of the Chapter

1. In a process costing system, costs flow from finished goods to:
   a. work-in-process.
   b. raw materials inventory.
   c. cost of goods sold.
   d. None of the above is correct.

2. In a process costing system, costs flow to finished goods from:
   a. work-in-process.
   b. raw materials inventory.
   c. cost of goods sold.
   d. None of the above is correct.

3. In a process costing system, costs are accumulated by:
   a. department.
   b. individual job.
   c. both job and department.
   d. neither job nor department.

4. Which of the following characteristics applies to process costing but does not apply to job-order costing?
   a. The need for averaging
   b. The use of equivalent units of production
   c. Separate, identifiable jobs
   d. The use of predetermined overhead rates

5. Equivalent units are calculated as follows:
   a. Equivalent units transferred out − Equivalent units in beginning inventory
   b. Equivalent units transferred out + Equivalent units in beginning inventory
   c. Equivalent units transferred out − Equivalent units in ending inventory
   d. Equivalent units transferred out + Equivalent units in ending inventory

6. An artist creates original works on commission. She is likely to use:
   a. job-order costing.
   b. process costing.
   c. actual costing.
   d. normal costing.

7. If a company that uses process costing did not adjust for partially completed units in the equivalent unit calculation, the effect on the cost per equivalent unit:
   a. would be zero.
   b. would be overstatement.
   c. would be understatement.
   d. cannot be determined from the information provided.

8. In process costing, a transferred-in cost is:
    a. a cost transferred from an earlier department.
    b. a cost that has been transferred in from the vendor who has supplied the raw materials.
    c. the cost of the labor that has been added to the process during the month.
    d. the conversion costs that were included in the beginning work-in-process inventory.

9. Listed below are the steps to calculate costs per equivalent unit using a process costing system. The steps are not presented in their proper order. Select the answer that places the steps in the correct order.
    i. divide the total costs for the department by the equivalent units
    ii. account for the flow of physical units
    iii. multiply the cost per equivalent unit by the goods transferred out and the equivalent units in ending inventory
    iv. account for the department's production costs recorded in the work in process
    v. convert the physical units into equivalent units

    The correct order is:
    a. v, iv, i, iii, ii.
    b. i, ii, iii, iv, v.
    c. ii, iv, v, i, iii.
    d. v, ii, i, iv, iii.

10. Companies in the service sector can use:
    a. job-order costing only.
    b. process costing only.
    c. either job-order or process costing.
    d. neither job-order nor process costing.

CASE

C4-1

Obj. 1

Deciding on a Costing System

Lux Electronics is completing a new plant that will begin manufacturing circuit boards within six months. Joan Keyes has just been appointed plant controller and must decide what type of cost accounting system the plant will use. The plant will manufacture many different models of two basic types of circuit boards: made-for-inventory boards and made-to-order boards.

In discussions with marketing and production managers, Joan learns that all models of the made-for-inventory circuit boards are commodity products, similar in design and requiring nearly identical materials, labor, and time in production. The commodity boards are made in very large batches that require long production periods. It is expected that a typical batch of commodity boards will take over a week to manufacture and result in tens of thousands of boards. Batches of commodity boards will be produced on a continuous basis.

The various models of made-to-order boards, on the other hand, are differentiated products. Each model is custom designed, and different models require modifications to the production process and times to manufacture. Differentiated models also require very different materials and varying amounts of labor. Differentiated boards will be manufactured sporadically in small batches of only a few hundred boards.

The two basic types of boards will be made using separate production lines within the same plant facility. Manufacturing overhead will comprise about 60% of the total manufacturing cost. Direct labor, direct materials, most indirect materials, line supervision, equipment costs, and some electrical costs can be traced directly to one of the two lines. Other manufacturing costs, such as those associated with plant supervision, personnel department, cafeteria, and plant office, are common to both lines. Some indirect labor will be shared by both types of boards. Further, some plant overhead costs, such as the cost of heating and air conditioning the plant, are difficult to assign except on some basis such as the amount of square footage occupied by each line.

Lux management expects that the commodity products will compete mainly on cost with low profit margins and will be priced based upon established market prices. Company management is therefore very concerned that the costing system accurately reflect the cost of manufacturing for these products. If commodity product costs are not reasonably accurate, Lux may experience poor cost control and lose money on these products.

Conversely, the differentiated models generally will be priced at cost plus a percentage markup over cost. Company management is therefore concerned that inaccurate product costing will lead to low profit margins if the boards are priced too low or lost sales if the boards are priced too high.

While gathering information before deciding on a costing system, Joan recently sent an e-mail message to Lux's assistant vice president in charge of marketing the new circuit boards, Joe Bally, asking how accurate the unit costs of the boards need to be. Joan is troubled by Joe's response to her question: "I have always assumed that unit costs are accurate to the nearest penny. Why would that not be the case? That's the way you accountants report them."

Joan is eager to get off on the right foot with the other managers involved with the new plant's operations and those engaged in marketing the products it will make. She knows that an inaccurate costing system can lead to poor operating performance. She is concerned that the wrong decisions now will lead to serious problems later.

Required

A. What type of costing system, job-order or process, is most appropriate for the commodity products and why?
B. What type of costing system, job-order or process, is most appropriate for the differentiated products and why?
C. If you recommended different costing systems for the different types of products, what problems do you foresee in using two costing systems?
D. Should Joan use actual or normal costing to assign overhead costs to commodity products? To differentiated products? Is this decision affected by the decisions about job-order and process costing? Explain your answers.
E. What problem do you see with Joe's response to Joan's question about the need for accuracy in unit costs? How should Joan respond to Joe?

COST ALLOCATION & ACTIVITY-BASED MANAGEMENT

Cost Allocation: Why is it a problem?

As we discussed in Chapter M4, Erin and Seth have been concerned about selling enough products to cover their manufacturing, administrative, and selling expenses. Moreover, they are beginning to wonder whether their cost accounting system is giving them correct information about the profitability of each product in their line. Seth has observed that some of the most profitable products, according to the cost accounting system, are complex and difficult to make. These products require lengthy machine setup activities and time-consuming special handling during manufacturing. However, selling prices for these products are not significantly more than the less complex products in the line. Seth is puzzled because his intuition tells him greater complexity must mean higher costs. Also, he has noticed products manufactured in large quantities are reported to be more costly to produce than those made in small quantities. Once again, his observation is counter-intuitive. He believes high-volume products must cost less on a per-unit basis than products manufactured in small batches.

Both Erin and Seth agree that material and labor costs are being properly traced to their products. They have established effective accounting procedures that accurately identify the quantity and cost of each material used in the production of a piece of furniture. Also, they have added electronic card readers on each production machine to record the name of the operator, wage rate, number of hours worked, and product produced. Thus, Erin and Seth believe labor is recorded and accurately traced to each product. However, they are not convinced manufacturing overhead is accurately traced to their products. Currently, overhead is attached to products using labor hours as an activity base. As a result, products requiring greater amounts of labor time receive more overhead costs than those requiring lesser amounts of labor time.

FOOD FOR THOUGHT

If you are an advisor to Erin and Seth, how might you help them understand overhead costs? Are there activity drivers that may more accurately connect overhead costs to products? What kinds of activities would you look for in their manufacturing process to help identify better activity drivers? After Seth and Erin discussed his observations, the following conversation took place between Seth, Erin, and their financial advisor, Roberta.

Roberta: I think you are right about the cost system misallocating overhead costs to products. The overhead allocation base that you currently use, labor hours, is a volume-based activity driver. Volume-based activity drivers typically assign more overhead costs to high-volume products and fewer overhead costs to low-volume products.

Seth: Maybe that's our problem. I can't imagine why high-volume products would be more costly to produce. That's like expecting to pay more at Kmart or Wal-Mart because they buy products in high volume.

Erin: I agree. We should see some per-unit savings as a result of producing in large batches. For example, if we spend $150 to make a machine changeover, shouldn't we spread that cost over the number of units produced following the machine changeover?

Roberta: *Yes, of course. Using your example, if you make one product following a $150 machine changeover, the changeover overhead cost per unit is $150. However, if you make ten products, the changeover overhead cost is only $15 per unit. That is called "economies of scale." Your existing cost system doesn't allocate costs in this way.*

Seth: *Ok, that partially explains why some of our product costs don't make sense. At least we can understand why the high- and low-volume product costs may be wrong. But what about the complexity issue?*

Roberta: *We will have to examine your production processes to look for better allocation bases for certain types of overhead. I'm confident that we can design a better cost-allocation system.*

Erin: *Let's do it soon. I believe our cost system may be responsible for our losing a bid to produce furniture for a new children's hospital. If the cost system overstates the cost of high-volume products, we probably overbid the contract. Our main competitor bid lower and won the contract.*

Seth: *That's true. Incorrect product costs can cause problems for us in many ways. What if we set our prices too low for our low-volume, complex products? We may make lots of sales, but these sales may be unprofitable.*

Erin: *We could actually lose money on each sale because our cost system incorrectly allocates overhead costs!*

OBJECTIVES

Once you have completed this chapter, you should be able to:

1 Explain the importance of overhead and how overhead traditionally has been applied to products and services.

2 Identify problems with traditional methods of allocating overhead costs.

3 Describe an activity hierarchy for classifying overhead costs.

4 Explain how activity-based costing works.

5 Explain how service organizations use cost information for decision making.

THE REASONS FOR COST ALLOCATION

OBJECTIVE 1

Explain the importance of overhead and how overhead traditionally has been applied to products and services.

Cost allocation is the process of assigning indirect costs to a product or service. Allocations are necessary because different products or services often share common resources. Companies cannot trace the work of a plant supervisor to a specific product, but the supervisor's work adds to the value of each product the plant manufactures. Hospitals cannot trace the work of a nursing supervisor to a specific patient, but the supervisor's efforts add to the value of the service each patient receives. Thus, companies must allocate the cost of this work. The accuracy of the allocation, and ultimately the usefulness of cost information in decision making, is a function of the allocation method an organization uses.

Recall that costs can be classified according to a number of criteria such as fixed or variable, product or period, and direct or indirect. Direct costs—the costs of direct materials and direct labor—are easy to trace to a specific product. Materials requisition forms, as discussed in Chapter M3, document the type and amount of materials used in production. Direct labor costs are traced to products using time sheets to record the hours workers spend on each job. On the other hand, indirect costs—the costs of materials handling, supervisors' salaries, and depreciation of factory equipment—usually cannot be traced to a particular product or product line. Instead, indirect costs are allocated to products. Allocating overhead costs accurately is especially important in a company that produces multiple products. Without accurate cost information, managers cannot make good decisions about their product mix. For example, managers cannot determine whether to promote or eliminate product A if they cannot distinguish the costs of product A from those of products B and C. When overhead costs increase as a percentage of a company's total manufacturing costs, accurate cost allocation becomes even more important. In this chapter we illustrate overhead allocation using Adventure Trails' sleeping bag manufacturing process.

Adventure Trails: Product Mix and Manufacturing Process

Adventure Trails produces a variety of outdoor products at numerous manufacturing sites. The company makes all of its sleeping bags at one manufacturing location. Because the plant produces only sleeping bags, all materials, labor, and overhead costs incurred in the plant are associated with the sleeping bag product line. The company's products are sold to a variety of retail stores. These stores add a markup and sell the sleeping bags to three different customer groups. A high-volume consumer product, targeted to a broad consumer market, is sold through large discount stores. These bags are the least expensive of Adventure Trails' product line and are designed for light-duty use, such as weekend camping trips or summer camps. The selling price of the high-volume consumer bag is $70. The second product is a medium-volume, three-season bag that sells for $100. This bag can be used in the spring, summer, and fall in moderate climates. The medium-volume bag is constructed from heavier materials than the high-volume consumer bag. This bag typically is sold through specialty outdoor shops to consumers who are more demanding of their outdoor gear. This bag is rugged enough to be used for prolonged outings.

The third bag produced by Adventure Trails is manufactured in very low volume. The selling price of $200 is twice the price of the medium-volume bag and over three times the price of the high-volume bag. This low-volume specialty bag is popular with serious climbers and backpackers who are likely to encounter severe weather conditions. Exhibit 1 summarizes the annual production volume of each type of sleeping bag.

Exhibit 1

Adventure Trails: Annual Production Volume

Product	Annual Production Volume
High-volume consumer bag	12,000
Medium-volume bag	6,000
Low-volume specialty bag	500
Total	18,500

The company uses automated cutting and sewing equipment. As a result, the machine time to cut and sew the material is equal across the three products. Material costs differ because the high- and medium-volume products consume less insulation and demand lower-cost, less technical fabrics. The high-volume and medium-volume bags require the same amount of labor; however, the complexity of the low-volume bag requires more inspection and attention to detail. The low-volume bag represents less than 3 percent of the units produced, but consumes 15 percent of the inspection activities.

Volume-Based Allocation: The Traditional Method

Management accounting techniques for calculating the cost of goods and services have been around a long time. In this section we briefly explore traditional techniques for allocating overhead costs and describe the changes that have taken place in manufacturing since those techniques first were introduced. In a later section, we examine today's business environment, an environment that has forced managers to find new ways to attach overhead costs to products and services.

Background

Many changes have taken place in manufacturing processes and in the information needs of managers since the early days of the industrial revolution in the United States.[1]

---

[1] See H. Thomas Johnson and Robert S. Kaplan, *Relevance Lost* (Boston: Harvard Business School Press), 1991.

Yet methods for allocating costs remain surprisingly similar to those used by early industrialists.

Before the industrial revolution, manufacturing was dominated by cottage industries. Skilled artisans worked in their homes on specialized tasks. Farmers produced wool or cotton. Spinners produced yarn from the wool or cotton provided by farmers and usually were paid according to the pounds of yarn they delivered. Weavers produced cloth from yarn; they usually were paid by the yards of cloth they produced. Finally, tailors were paid a certain amount for each garment they sewed from the cloth the weavers supplied. To obtain a woolen shirt, for example, a merchant would buy wool from a farmer, yarn from a spinner, cloth from a weaver, and the finished product from a tailor. The cost of each shirt was easy to calculate because each transaction was driven by market prices. The unit product cost was simply the sum of the various components purchased at market prices. Exhibit 2 shows how a merchant might have accumulated costs in pre-industrial times.

Exhibit 2

A Pre-Industrial Cost
Summary: 150 Woolen
Shirts

Paid to Tom Farmer for wool	$ 200
Paid to Harriet Spinner to spin wool into yarn	800
Paid to Cynthia Weaver to weave yarn into fabric	600
Paid to Chris Taylor to sew shirts from fabric	500
Total costs	$2,100
Total shirts produced	150
Cost per shirt ($2,100 ÷ 150)	$14

The industrial revolution brought raw materials, equipment, spinners, weavers, and tailors together in one facility. When factory owners hired craftspeople to work for them, they could not use external market prices to determine the cost of delivering a product. They needed a new source of information. Radical changes in manufacturing practices created new challenges for those who managed textile, steel, and transportation companies.

In the past, engineers (rather than accountants) developed management control techniques in response to changing production methods and competition. They needed to know how much material and labor should be consumed during the production process. As a result, engineers developed standards for material and labor consumption. This information enabled managers to determine whether manufacturing processes were working at peak efficiency. Through bar coding technology and electronic scanning devices, direct material costs (and other information) can be traced from a supplier to a final product. In many factories production workers electronically log on to equipment and identify the product on which they are working. The system records the time spent by an operator on a particular job. Accounting databases also store information, such as hourly wage rates, that are used to determine direct labor costs for products manufactured by a machine operator. However, allocating indirect costs—overhead costs that are not directly related to products or processes—can be troublesome. The problem has been made larger with the growing importance of overhead costs.

At one time, manufacturing overhead was a relatively small part of total manufacturing costs. Direct materials and direct labor costs dominated the costs of production. As a result, a simple process for attaching overhead costs to inventory was developed. That process used activity bases, such as direct labor hours, direct labor costs, or machine hours, to apply overhead costs to products. We considered these allocation bases in our discussion of predetermined overhead rates in Chapter M3.

Today, cost structures have changed. Overhead has become the dominant cost in many manufacturing and service industries. Advances in technology have led to the dramatic growth of support functions, while the number of employees directly involved in production has decreased. Consider what happens when automated equipment replaces skilled machinists. The machinists' wages, a direct labor cost, are replaced with wages of technical support engineers, an overhead cost. As a result of automation, companies incur higher indirect costs for support activities as well as more depreciation on expensive production equipment. Unfortunately, traditional allocation bases often do not yield accurate product costs for individual products in a product line. Traditional cost allocation systems can misallocate costs by attaching too much overhead to some products and not enough overhead to others. Misallocation can create problems for managers who make pricing and product mix decisions. Later in this chapter we consider how inaccurate cost information may mislead decision makers.

Volume-Based Allocation

Suppose Adventure Trails' marketing manager needs cost information to make a pricing decision for a large order of sleeping bags. The accounting department has been asked to prepare a product cost report that identifies overhead, materials, and labor costs for each of the three sleeping bags. Overhead is calculated using a predetermined overhead rate, or burden rate, as discussed in Chapter M3 of this text. The company uses machine hours as its activity base; the estimated machine hours for the year is 9,250. Total manufacturing overhead is estimated at $231,250 for the coming year. The predetermined overhead rate is calculated at $25 per machine hour as follows:

$$\text{Predetermined overhead rate} = \text{Estimated overhead costs} \div \text{Estimated machine hours}$$
$$= \$231,250 \div 9,250$$
$$= \$25 \text{ per machine hour}$$

The company uses automated cutting and sewing equipment. As a result, the machine time required to cut and sew the materials for a sleeping bag is equal across the three products. Each bag requires 0.50 hour of machine time. Using the overhead rate of $25.00 per machine hour, Exhibit 3 illustrates the overhead cost applied to each product. Observe the overhead is $12.50 per product, regardless of sales volume or product characteristics.

Exhibit 3
Overhead Cost per Unit

Product	Machine Hours	×	Predetermined Overhead Rate	=	Unit Overhead Cost
High-volume bag	0.50		$25.00		$12.50
Medium-volume bag	0.50		25.00		12.50
Low-volume bag	0.50		25.00		12.50

Exhibit 4 identifies the materials, labor, overhead, and total cost per sleeping bag. The high-volume, medium-volume, and low-volume bags require materials costing $30.00, $55.00, and $130.00, respectively. Material costs for the three bags are not equal because of differences in the amount of insulation, as well as differences in the quality of the materials. The high-volume and medium-volume bags require the same amount of labor, $20.00 per bag. The complexity of the low-volume specialty bag requires more labor. As shown in Exhibit 4, the labor cost of the high-volume specialty bag is $30.00. The overhead costs calculated in Exhibit 3 are added to the materials and labor costs in Exhibit 4. The resulting costs for the high-volume, medium-volume, and low-volume bags are $62.50, $87.50, and $172.50, respectively. The volume-based cost allocation system allocated equal amounts of overhead to the products because all three products required the same amount of machine time. If some types of overhead costs are not caused by machine hours, the accounting system may inaccurately allocate overhead to products. Inaccurate product costs can result in poor management decisions.

Exhibit 4
Unit Manufacturing
Costs

Product	Unit Materials Cost	+	Unit Labor Cost	+	Unit Overhead Cost	=	Total Unit Cost
High-volume bag	$ 30.00		$20.00		$12.50		$ 62.50
Medium-volume bag	55.00		20.00		12.50		87.50
Low-volume bag	130.00		30.00		12.50		172.50

Strategic Implications

Managers use product cost information to help them make strategic decisions. For example, a strategic decision at Adventure Trails may involve deciding to shift the product mix away from the high-volume consumer sleeping bag to the low-volume specialty bag. Exhibit 5 lists the selling price, manufacturing cost, and profit margin for each sleeping bag in Adventure Trails' product line. Using cost information, managers observe the profit margins vary widely across the product mix. The high-volume consumer bag has a profit margin of $7.50 per unit, while the low-volume specialty bag has a profit margin of $27.50 per bag. Each specialty bag produces roughly four times the profit margin of a consumer-grade bag ($7.50 versus $27.50). The accounting system is indicating the most profitable product (per unit) is the specialty bag.

Exhibit 5
Adventure Trails—
Profitability by Product
Line Using Volume-
Based Costing

Product	Selling Price	−	Manufacturing Cost	=	Profit Margin
High-volume bag	$ 70.00		$ 62.50		$ 7.50
Medium-volume bag	100.00		87.50		12.50
Low-volume bag	200.00		172.50		27.50

How might cost and profitability information influence decision makers? Based on the profit margins reported in Exhibit 5, managers may plan to add more low-volume, specialty products to the product line, while de-emphasizing the high-volume consumer market. The decision would be based in large part on the method Adventure Trails uses to allocate its manufacturing overhead costs. Does the traditional method of cost allocation give Adventure Trails' managers the information they need to make good decisions about the company's marketing strategy? Are they using accurate information to determine the company's product mix and to set sales policies? We answer these questions in the next section.

1 | **SELF-STUDY PROBLEM**   Troy Company is a small manufacturer of high-quality home gardening tools. Each tool in Troy's line is the product of years of ergonomic research and development.

WebTUTOR Advantage

Troy's marketing manager is thinking about changing the selling price of certain products and has asked the company's accountant for a summary of production costs. Information that was gathered from accounting and production records during the past six months is as follows:

Depreciation on plant assets	$50,000
Energy for plant operations	$20,000
Indirect labor costs	$60,000
Manufacturing supplies	$12,000
Direct labor hours worked	10,000

(handwritten: 130,000 ÷ 10,000 = 13,000)

Product A consumes $7 in direct materials and requires one-half hour of direct labor. Direct labor is paid at a rate of $10 per hour.

Required

A. Using the number of direct labor hours as an allocation base, calculate Troy's predetermined overhead rate.

B. Prepare a summary of the manufacturing costs for one unit of product A.

The solution to Self-Study Problem 1 appears at the end of the chapter.

THE PROBLEMS WITH VOLUME-BASED ALLOCATION

OBJECTIVE 2

Identify problems with traditional methods of allocating overhead costs.

The previous section addressed the traditional, volume-based method for allocating overhead costs to products and services. As shown in Exhibit 4, the volume-based system produces questionable results by allocating overhead costs equally to all three products. The bags are different in many ways; therefore, we may conclude they consume manufacturing resources differently. Overhead costs may be inaccurately allocated to the products because the accounting system does not recognize economies of scale or use accurate allocation bases.

Economies of Scale

Most manufacturing companies could produce hundreds if not thousands of different products by offering many variations of a basic product. For example, an automobile maker that produces an SUV and a sports sedan offers two basic products. What if each vehicle could be manufactured with a V-6 or V-8 engine? What if the company also offered each customer a choice of leather or cloth interior, and left-hand or right-hand steering (for U.S. and British markets)? Suddenly, our two-product company offers 24 unique products. Some of these products will be sold in large quantities, while others will be sold in very small quantities. Most manufacturers limit the number of different products they produce because they want to benefit from economies of scale. *Economies of scale* **are the savings a company realizes in unit costs by spreading fixed overhead costs over a larger number of units.** Making 100 units of the same product is less costly than making 100 different products. A company that is able to produce a product at a lower cost than its competitors has a distinct advantage in the market.

Look again at Exhibit 1. Adventure Trails manufactures 12,000 high-volume consumer sleeping bags per year and just 500 low-volume specialty bags. The company clearly can achieve economies of scale when producing consumer bags that it cannot achieve when producing specialty bags. Cost associated with machine setup activity is a good example. Let's assume setup costs are $800 to prepare the cutting and sewing machines for each new production run. Assume the company produces 4,000 consumer-grade sleeping bags at a time. The company incurs a unit setup cost of $0.20 per bag ($800 ÷ 4,000 bags per batch). Even if Adventure Trails produced all 500 specialty bags in a single batch, the unit cost of the machine setup would be $1.60 ($800 ÷ 500 bags per batch), a cost of eight times that of the consumer bags.

One of the problems with the traditional method of allocating overhead costs is that it does not take into account economies of scale. Recall that all overhead costs (including machine setup costs) are divided by an activity base, such as machine hours.

The predetermined overhead rate spreads all overhead to products without regard for economies of scale. The savings Adventure Trails realizes from its high-volume products are not reflected in the unit cost of overhead. Instead, all of the company's products, high-volume, medium-volume, and low-volume, are allocated the same overhead cost per unit.

Accurate Allocation Bases

A second problem with traditional cost allocation is the allocation base, the activity used to determine the predetermined overhead rate. Think about activities that cause manufacturing overhead in Adventure Trails' sleeping bag plant. When raw materials are received, workers unload, inspect, move, and store them. During the manufacturing process, workers move work-in-process to various production areas and prepare machines to make different products. Quality control inspectors draw samples and test the products to ensure products meet specifications. Supervisors assist production workers with any problems that arise during a production run. The supervisors, quality engineers, materials handlers, and machine setup operators are paid wages, consume supplies, and use assets that depreciate. Each of these costs is classified as manufacturing overhead.

Now think about the way Adventure Trails allocates its overhead costs. The company uses machine hours as its activity base. How do machine hours relate to the costs of receiving materials, moving work-in-process, and performing quality inspections? Does the number of machine hours explain those costs? Does the use of machine hours produce those costs? No, they do not.

Critics of the volume-based allocation method argue that it distorts unit overhead costs. Remember, volume-based cost allocation systems assume manufacturing overhead costs vary in proportion to an allocation base. Examples of traditional allocation bases include direct labor hours, machine hours, or direct labor dollars. If product A uses 10 machine hours and product B uses five machine hours, product A is allocated twice as much overhead as product B. Managers who want to cut overhead costs in their departments are given little guidance by a cost accounting system that assumes all overhead costs result from machine hours, direct labor hours, or direct labor dollars. Adventure Trails' managers cannot reduce the number of machine hours and expect overhead costs in the receiving department to go down. Those costs simply are not affected by machine hours.

To understand the shortcomings of volume-based allocation, consider the manufacturing environment that was in place when the accounting system was designed. Overhead costs were a much smaller percentage of total costs in years past. Thus, managers were not as concerned with precise allocations. In addition, accounting systems were developed to help companies put a value on inventory in their published financial statements. External auditors were concerned that the value of total inventory on the balance sheet was correct. They did not care if the cost per unit of one product was overstated while the cost of another was understated. Today's information needs are dramatically different, however. Accountants are developing better ways of allocating overhead to products.

A HIERARCHY OF OVERHEAD ACTIVITIES

OBJECTIVE 3

Describe an activity hierarchy for classifying overhead costs.

Recognizing that overhead costs are not always related to volume, Robin Cooper, a management accounting professor, developed a hierarchy of overhead costs. **The *overhead hierarchy* is a framework that explains how overhead costs change with various activities.** Exhibit 6 illustrates the hierarchy consisting of four categories: unit level, batch level, product level, and facility level.

Exhibit 6

Cooper's Hierarchy: Allocating Costs by Activity

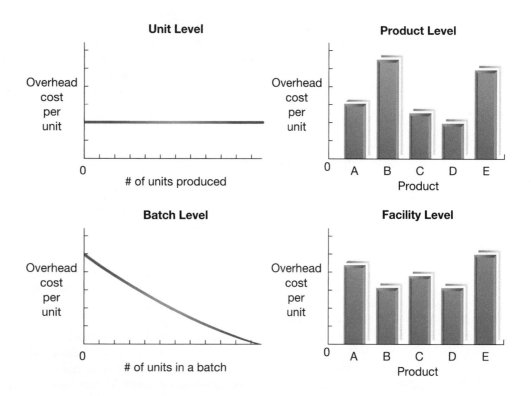

Unit-Level Costs

Unit-level costs behave like variable costs. Remember that variable costs change in total with the number of units produced but do not vary per unit with changes in volume. For example, the costs of manufacturing supplies and utilities are a function of production volume. Traditional allocation bases, such as machine hours, direct labor hours, and direct labor dollars, are appropriate for allocating unit-level costs. Suppose the cost of electricity to run a machine is $20 per hour. If the machine produces 100 units in one hour, the cost per unit is $0.20 ($20 ÷ 100 units). If the machine runs for 10 hours, the total cost of electricity is $200 ($20 × 10 hours), but the cost per unit is still $0.20 [$200 ÷ (100 units per hour × 10 hours)]. Traditional volume-based allocation systems attach overhead to products as if all costs were unit level. Some costs are allocated appropriately using machine hours or direct labor hours, but other costs are not. The overhead hierarchy offers managers three additional kinds of allocation bases.

Batch-Level Costs

Batch-level activities address one of the volume-related problems of traditional cost-allocation systems. By using a single activity base to allocate overhead costs, volume-based systems ignore economies of scale. They assume the cost of setting up a machine is the same per unit whether 10 units or 10,000 units are manufactured following the setup. Certain activities, such as raw materials handling and machine setups, are associated with each batch of production without regard to the number of units in a batch. To measure the overhead costs of a product accurately, batch-level costs must be allocated to specific production runs as follows:

Batch-level cost per unit = Total activity cost ÷ Units in the batch

If a machine setup costs $500 and the company produces 10 units in the batch, the setup cost per unit is $50 ($500 ÷ 10 units). If the company produces 1,000 units in the batch, the setup cost per unit is just $0.50 ($500 ÷ 1,000 units).

The batch-level cost per unit decreases as the number of units in the batch increases. Conversely, the batch-level cost per unit increases as the number of units in the batch decreases. Think of batch-level activities as a fixed cost. A batch-level cost is not influenced by the number of units produced following the batch-level activity. Batch-level overhead allocations capture economies of scale. Products manufactured in large batches typically benefit from an activity-based costing system, because the cost per unit will be lower. Products manufactured in small batches typically are allocated more overhead per unit.

Product-Level Costs

Product-level costs relate to a specific family of products. For example, suppose a company that manufactures brake systems for automobiles and trucks sells their products through automotive parts stores. The company also has a contract to provide brake systems for government vehicles. The governmental contract requires quality control tests on one unit out of each 50 produced to ensure the system complies with engineering specifications. The quality control test destroys the product. Assume the company has numerous quality control procedures in place to ensure the safety of its products. However, tests conducted on government products are significantly more rigorous than those performed on products sold through automotive stores. The cost of more rigorous quality testing should be allocated only to the governmental product family.

Another example is a design change for a product that currently is in production. Usually a design change affects newer product lines. Newer products often are redesigned to make them easier to assemble. Mature products typically have been in production for a long period of time. As a result, the manufacturing process is stable and does not require many engineering change orders. The cost system should not attach the cost of an engineering design change to well-established products that do not need modification. To do so may lead a marketing manager to over-price a mature product and under-price a new one because overhead costs were erroneously assigned.

Facility-Level Costs

Facility-level overhead costs include all overhead activities that are not unit level, batch level, or product level. Accurately allocating facility-level costs is difficult. Unfortunately, not all costs can be associated directly with a product. For example, the salary of a security guard does not relate directly to a specific unit, batch, or family of products. Therefore, facility-level costs tend to be allocated arbitrarily. Cost drivers of facility-level costs include the percentage of value-added, or the percentage of time a product remains in the manufacturing plant. The logic behind both of these measures is that products remaining in process longer, or requiring more value-added activities, probably consume greater levels of indirect manufacturing overhead costs.

---

2 SELF-STUDY PROBLEM

WebTUTOR Advantage

Highlands Machining Company produces bicycle gears from high-quality stainless steel. Assume you are an assistant department manager helping to develop a new cost-allocation system. Because you understand the weaknesses of the traditional volume-based method, you have been asked to classify some of the company's costs using Cooper's hierarchy. You have been given a list of four types of costs:

- Lighting costs for the production areas
- Raw materials movement costs: the wages and supplies consumed in moving raw materials from inventory storage to a production area (Materials are moved each time a different production order begins.)
- The costs of cooling the metal-cutting equipment (Metal-cutting equipment requires constant cooling during the production process. The cooling costs include

the costs of liquid coolant, pumps and hoses, and the energy to power the cooling system.)
- Research and development expenses incurred to develop a new product

Required Classify each cost as a unit-level, batch-level, product-level, or facility-level cost, and explain your classifications.

The solution to Self-Study Problem 2 appears at the end of the chapter.

Case In Point

http://ingram. swlearning.com

Learn more about ABC

Many larger firms use enterprise-wide accounting software, such as SAP. These software packages integrate and account for all key activities throughout a company. For example, when goods are received, workers at the loading dock enter various information such as product identification, cost, and quantity received. The accounting system automatically updates the inventory and accounts payable accounts. Since 1997, activity-based costing has been an important component of SAP. Costs and driver information are recorded in the software package and are used to calculate the cost of activities, products, and services. In addition, SAP helps managers predict future costs using activity-based budgeting.

Source: Osheroff, M. "The 123s of ABC in SAP," *Strategic Finance*, November 2002.

ACTIVITY-BASED COSTING

OBJECTIVE 4

Explain how activity-based costing works.

Activity-based costing (ABC) **allocates overhead costs to a product using activities required to produce the product.** The allocation bases are known as cost drivers. These cost drivers should relate to activities performed while manufacturing a good or providing a service. For example, machine hours do not drive the costs of moving materials from a loading dock into storage or from storage to a production area. The number of movements does. So a company might choose the number of material movements as a basis for attaching the costs of moving materials to products. The number of direct labor hours does not drive the costs of admitting patients to a hospital, but the number of admissions does. Thus, admitting costs could be allocated to patients by an allocation base such as the number of admissions.

Exhibit 7 illustrates the conceptual design of an ABC system. In an ABC system, cost allocation involves two stages. In the first stage, overhead costs such as depreciation, indirect salaries, and utilities are allocated to activity pools according to the type of activity carried out in each pool. *Activity pools* **are collections of costs that relate to an activity.** Exhibit 7 illustrates four kinds of activity pools, volume-based, setup, handling and inspection, and general overhead. Let's use the machine setup pool as an example to understand how costs flow through an ABC system. A pool for machine setups would include the cost of supplies, indirect labor, energy, and depreciation of equipment used in setup activities. A common method of allocating costs to a pool is in proportion to time or effort. Suppose 60 percent of an engineer's time is spent supervising machine setups and 40 percent is spent supervising material movements. The engineer's salary and benefits would be allocated in those proportions to a setup pool and a materials movement pool. Supplies, energy, and depreciation costs would be assigned to pools in a similar manner. They are pro-rated to cost pools based on an activity's proportionate consumption of a cost.

In the second stage, costs are allocated from activity pools to a cost object, such as a good or service. For example, all costs in the setup pool would be divided by the number of setups to determine the cost per setup. Alternatively, if setups vary in complexity, the allocation base could be the number of setup hours. In that case, output from the setup pool would be expressed in terms of a setup cost per hour. In Exhibit 7, setup costs are allocated to Adventure Trails' three products using the number of setups as an activity base. Notice the direct materials and direct labor costs are traced directly to products that consume the resources.

Exhibit 7 Conceptual Design of an ABC System

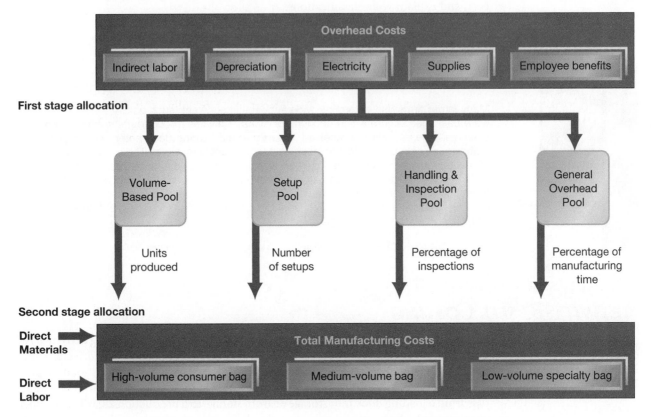

Using Exhibit 7 as a guide, we calculate activity-based costs for Adventure Trails' three products. Exhibit 8 classifies Adventure Trails' total overhead costs into pools using Cooper's hierarchy and identifies activity bases used to attach the costs to products. Assume the company used a variety of surveys and interviews to determine the proportion of costs that should be allocated in the first stage to each activity pool. Exhibit 8 presents the results of the first-stage allocation process. Total overhead costs of $231,250 have not changed from the amount used to calculate the predetermined overhead rate in our earlier example of $25 per machine hour. Exhibit 8 simply classifies the $231,250 of overhead into pools to gain a better understanding of the activities that cause overhead. Instead of using one predetermined overhead rate based on machine hours, Adventure Trails is using four allocation bases: units produced, number of setups, percentage of inspections by product line, and percentage of manufacturing time. Each base is the denominator in an overhead rate calculation. We also add direct materials and direct labor as before, to complete the product cost calculation.

Exhibit 8 Adventure Trails' Overhead Classified by Cooper's Hierarchy

	Overhead Costs	Activity Bases
Unit level	$ 90,000	Units produced
Batch level (setups)	8,800	Number of setups
Product level (handling and inspection)	60,000	Percentage of inspections by product line
Facility level	72,450	Percentage of manufacturing time
Total overhead costs	$231,250	

Before we can assign overhead to products, we need additional process information. Exhibit 9 reports Adventure Trails' batch sizes, number of setups, cost per setup, percentage of handling and inspections, handling and inspection costs, and percentage of manufacturing time. These values are used to calculate the activity-based cost of producing the three sleeping bags. For example, the high-volume bag is produced in batches of 4,000 units. During the year, the high-volume bag is produced three times (number of setups = 3). Observe that Adventure Trails makes three batches of the high-volume and medium-volume bag and five batches of the low-volume bag per year. This production schedule helps match production with demand to minimize inventory carrying costs. The cost to prepare the machines for each batch or production run is $800. Notice the setup cost does not vary in total with the batch size. Management estimates the high-volume bag consumes 60 percent of the handling and inspection activities. Thus, the cost of handling and inspection for this product line is $36,000 ($60,000 × .60). Finally, the high-volume bag consumes 50 percent of the manufacturing time.

Exhibit 9 Adventure Trails: Machine Hours, Batches, and Handling and Inspection by Product

Product	Batch Size	Number of Setups	Cost per Setup	Percentage of Handling & Inspections	Handling and Inspection Costs	Percentage of Manufacturing Time
High-volume bag	4,000	3	$800	60%	$36,000	50%
Medium-volume bag	2,000	3	800	25%	15,000	40%
Low-volume bag	100	5	800	15%	9,000	10%
Total						

Exhibit 10 illustrates how to calculate the unit cost of each product using activity-based costing. The first two columns report the materials and labor costs that were given in Exhibit 4. Traditional and ABC unit costs for materials and labor costs are the same. However, the ABC calculation uses four overhead allocation bases, rather than one. Exhibit 10 illustrates the amount of unit-level, batch-level, product-level, and facility-level costs allocated to each product.

Notice the unit-level cost is equal across the three product lines. Unit-level costs are calculated by dividing the total unit-level costs of $90,000 (shown in Exhibit 8) by the total units produced (shown in Exhibit 1). Unit-level costs shown in Exhibit 10 are calculated as follows:

Unit-level costs = Unit level costs ÷ Total units produced
= $90,000 (Exhibit 8) ÷ 18,500 units (Exhibit 1)
= $4.86

Next, batch-level costs are calculated by dividing the setup cost of $800 by the number of units manufactured in a batch. Notice the batch size varies across the three products. The high-volume, medium-volume, and low-volume products are manufactured in batches of 4,000, 2,000, and 100 units, respectively (see Exhibit 9). Batch-level costs shown in Exhibit 10 are calculated as follows:

Batch-level costs
High-volume bag = Setup costs ÷ Batch size
= $800 ÷ 4,000
= $0.20

Medium-volume bag = Setup costs ÷ Batch size
= $800 ÷ 2,000
= $0.40

Exhibit 10 Adventure Trails: Activity-Based Cost by Product*

| Product | Unit Materials Cost | Unit Labor Costs | Overhead | | | | Total |
			Unit Level	Batch Level	Product Level	Facility Level	
High-volume bag	$ 30.00	$20.00	$4.86	$0.20	$ 3.00	$ 3.02	$ 61.08
Medium-volume bag	55.00	20.00	4.86	0.40	2.50	4.83	87.59
Low-volume bag	130.00	30.00	4.86	8.00	18.00	14.49	205.35

*A slight rounding error would occur if unit-, batch-, product-, and facility-level overhead was added for each product and multiplied by the units produced.

Total overhead from Exhibit 8	$231,250	
Total overhead assigned using ABC (see calculation below)	231,175	
Difference due to rounding	$ 75	

| Product | Units Produced Annually (Exhibit 1) | | Overhead Costs per Unit | | | | | | | | Total Overhead Assigned Using ABC |
			Unit		Batch		Product		Facility		
High-volume bag	12,000	×	($4.86	+	$0.20	+	$3.00	+	$3.02)	=	$132,960
Medium-volume bag	6,000	×	($4.86	+	$0.40	+	$2.50	+	$4.83)	=	75,540
Low-volume bag	500	×	($4.86	+	$8.00	+	$18.00	+	$14.49)	=	22,675
											$231,175

$$\text{Low-volume bag} = \text{Setup costs} \div \text{Batch size}$$
$$= \$800 \div 100$$
$$= \$8.00$$

Product-level costs are allocated according to the amount of resources each type of product consumes. For example in Exhibit 9, production engineers estimate the high-volume bag demands 60 percent of the handling and inspecting activities. The medium-volume and low-volume bags demand 25 percent and 15 percent, respectively. The ABC system allocates resources to products according to the activities demanded by them. Product-level costs shown in Exhibit 10 are calculated as follows:

Product-level costs

$$\text{High-volume bag} = (\text{Inspection \& handling costs} \times \text{Percentage of inspections by product line}) \div \text{Units produced}$$
$$= (\$60,000 \times .60) \div 12,000$$
$$= \$36,000 \div 12,000$$
$$= \$3.00$$

$$\text{Medium-volume bag} = (\text{Inspection \& handling costs} \times \text{Percentage of inspections by product line}) \div \text{Units produced}$$
$$= (\$60,000 \times .25) \div 6,000$$
$$= \$2.50$$

$$\text{Low-volume bag} = (\text{Inspection \& handling costs} \times \text{Percentage of inspections by product line}) \div \text{Units produced}$$
$$= (\$60,000 \times .15) \div 500$$
$$= \$18.00$$

Facility-level costs are allocated to products according to the percentage of manufacturing time consumed by each type of product. Managers recognize that facility-level cost allocation is less precise than the other levels of overhead activity. However, they believe products consume resources according to the length of time they remain in the manufacturing process. Thus, the accounting system allocates facility-level overhead to products as a percentage of manufacturing time. Exhibit 9 reports management's estimates of the percentage of manufacturing time by product. Facility-level costs shown in Exhibit 10 are calculated as follows:

Facility-level costs

High-volume bag = (Facility-level costs × Percentage of manufacturing time) ÷
     Units produced
     = ($72,450 × .50) ÷ 12,000
     = $36,225 ÷ 12,000
     = $3.02

Medium-volume bag = (Facility-level costs × Percentage of manufacturing time) ÷
      Units produced
      = ($72,450 × .40) ÷ 6,000
      = $28,980 ÷ 6,000
      = $4.83

Low-volume bag = (Facility-level costs × Percentage of manufacturing time) ÷ Units
     produced
     = ($72,450 × .10) ÷ 500
     = $7,245 ÷ 500
     = $14.49

Exhibit 10 reports the total cost of producing the high-volume, medium-volume, and low-volume bag is $61.08, $87.59, and $205.35, respectively. How do the ABC values compare with those calculated using the traditional volume-based system? Exhibit 11 compares Adventure Trails' unit product costs using traditional volume-based allocation with those of activity-based costing. The exhibit suggests the volume-based method overstated the unit costs of the high-volume consumer sleeping bags and understated the unit costs of the low-volume specialty sleeping bags. The ABC system produced unit costs that were 2.3 percent less than traditional costs for the high-volume products. The low-volume product costs using the ABC system were 19 percent greater than those reported by the traditional system. The cost of medium-volume sleeping bags remains unchanged.

Exhibit 11 Volume-Based Costs per Unit versus Activity-Based Costs per Unit

Allocation Method	High-Volume Bag	Medium-Volume Bag	Low-Volume Bag
Volume-based (Exhibit 5)	$62.50	$87.50	$172.50
ABC (Exhibit 10)	61.08	87.59	205.35
Percentage change (ABC − volume-based) ÷ volume-based	−2.3%	0%	+19%

Why do the two allocation methods yield different unit costs? More specifically, why does the ABC method yield different unit costs for the high- and low-volume products? The unit-level overhead costs listed in Exhibit 10 do not explain the differences in unit product costs among the three products. The unit-level costs ($90,000) are divided by the total number of units produced (18,500). The resulting unit cost is $4.86 per bag, regardless of the type.

The batch-level costs explain much of the difference in unit costs across Adventure Trails' product line. Remember that batch-level costs address economies of scale. Here production volume makes a difference. Each batch of products requires a machine setup costing $800. The batch-level costs of consumer sleeping bags is $0.20 per product (setup cost ÷ batch size = $800 ÷ 4,000 = $0.20), while the batch-level costs of the specialty bags are $8.00 per unit (setup cost ÷ batch size = $800 ÷ 100 = $8.00). By not recognizing economies of scale, traditional allocation penalizes high-volume products and subsidizes low-volume products.

The product-level costs also help explain some of the variation in unit costs across the three types of sleeping bags. The exhibit also reports the profit margin using a traditional volume-based allocation method (from Exhibit 5). The ABC system tells managers that the specialty bags use far more handling and inspection resources than the other bags. Handling and inspections add to the unit costs of the specialty bags. Customers who purchase these bags depend on an extremely high level of quality. Thus, we are not surprised that the low-volume bags consume so many handling and inspection activities. What about the facility-level costs? Adventure Trails assigned them as a percentage of total manufacturing time. Thus, products that remain in process longer are allocated more overhead costs.

Exhibit 12 reports the selling price, activity-based manufacturing cost, and profit margin for each sleeping bag. What are the implications of our findings for Adventure Trails' management? First, specialty bags are not as profitable as the company's managers had thought. In fact, the company is losing money on them. The traditional volume-based system produced costs resulting in cross-subsidy. **Accountants use the term** *product cross-subsidy* **to describe a situation in which one product subsidizes (supports) the reported costs of another.** The high-volume consumer bags are subsidizing the low-volume specialty bags. Although Adventure Trails can sell the specialty bags for a higher price, the cost of producing those bags in low volume is extremely high. A long-run strategy of adding other specialty bags to the company's product line could be disastrous.

Of course, a company's long-run strategies for marketing and production are based on more than manufacturing costs. A company may choose to offer a full line of products because retailers would rather order from one manufacturer than from six. Also, a company may wish to establish its reputation as an expert, full-line producer. A well-designed system for allocating costs to activities and products cannot answer all of management's questions. It can give the basic information managers need to chart the future course of their company.

Exhibit 12 Adventure Trails—Profitability by Product Line Using Activity-Based Costing and Traditional Volume-Based Allocations

Product	Selling Price	−	ABC Manufacturing Cost	=	ABC Profit Margin	Traditional Profit Margin
High-volume bag	$ 70.00		$ 61.08		$ 8.92	$ 7.50
Medium-volume bag	100.00		87.59		12.41	12.50
Low-volume bag	200.00		205.35		(5.35)	27.50

COST ALLOCATION AND DECISION MAKING IN THE SERVICE SECTOR

OBJECTIVE 5

Explain how service organizations use cost information for decision making.

This chapter used the term *cost object* to refer to the product of a manufacturing process. ABC allows us to define cost objects very broadly. Services offered by organizations also may be classified as cost objects. ABC is used by service organizations to understand the cost of its core and noncore activities. **The primary activities a service organization carries out are its** *core activities*; **its supporting activities are called noncore activities.**

The core activity of a public school is education, teaching students subjects such as math, chemistry, biology, history, a foreign language, and English. To carry out that primary activity, schools rely on a host of noncore activities. For example, most school districts offer bus transportation to students. What are the costs of providing that supporting service? How do the people who manage school districts use that cost information?

Some school districts outsource their transportation services. In other words, they contract with a company that provides bus services for the district. For those districts the direct costs of transportation are defined in their contract with the bus company. For districts that provide their own transportation services, the direct costs of those services include the costs of buses, tires, fuel, drivers' wages and benefits, repairs, maintenance, and insurance. In both cases, there are the indirect costs of the administrators who set busing policy and develop the bus routes. A school district could have several different activity pools that capture the costs of delivering transportation services.

How do school districts use activity-based costing in their decision making? For some, that information is a basis for the decision to outsource transportation services. By focusing on their core activity (education) and reducing noncore activities (such as busing), some districts have reduced the costs of supporting activities and applied the savings to core areas.

Case In Point

http://ingram.
swlearning.com

Learn more about the
electric utility industry.

Customers who demand specialized services, greater supply choice, and lower costs are transforming the once-regulated electric utility industry into a competitive industry. The regulated electric utility industry provides consumers with a package of services, including the generation, transmission, and distribution of energy and a host of energy management services (metering, billing, dunning, and energy services). However, with the advent of competition, individual consumers will decide whether they want to purchase a package of services from a single vendor or whether they want to purchase different services from a variety of vendors. Compounding the situation, new organizations will enter markets where monopolies once dominated. When the transition to competition is complete, consumers will be able to shop around for energy services.

The electric utility industry's transition to competition has managerial accounting implications because questions persist about what parts of the energy services processes actually generate value. After the transition is complete, old cost accounting models for the electric utility industry may not be relevant. Under the old system, profitability is only measured on the corporate level. Public service commissions limit public utilities' revenues to prevent these organizations from taking advantage of their customers. However, in the competitive environment, managers must consider what is happening within individual departments because companies will provide services beyond the traditional package. This is where the value-added problem comes into play. One tool that has been proposed to combat the problem is activity-based costing. Under the new system, revenue will be generated four ways—electricity sales to individual customers, buying from and selling to other utility networks, selling and delivering other synergistic products and services to customers through the network distribution channel, and leasing capacity to other companies that can use this distribution channel (leasing space on electric poles to telephone companies so the telephone companies may hang their wires). Electric utilities may use activity-based costing to control overhead, to determine the cost of utility services, to compare revenues and costs for probability analysis, and to prepare strategic plans for the future in each profit center.

Source: Johnson, Scott. "The ABCs of the Electric Utility Industry," *Management Accounting* (November 1998): 25–28.

3 SELF-STUDY PROBLEM

WebTUTOR Advantage

Athena Company produces high-quality hand tools for wood-working. The company is conducting an ABC study. You are a manager at Athena, and you have been given the following information:

Costs and Activity Rates by Overhead Category

	Unit Level	Batch Level	Product Level	Facility Level
Estimated cost	$50,000	$20,000	$10,000	$20,000
Estimated activity	500 machine hours	80 materials movements	25 engineering drawings	(applied as a percentage of unit-, batch-, and product-level costs)

You have been asked to calculate the overhead costs associated with products A and B. The units produced of and the resources consumed by products A and B are as follows:

	Units Produced	Machine Hours	Materials Movements	Engineering Drawings
Product A	40	40	1	0
Product B	10	10	2	2

Required

A. Calculate the:
  1. cost per machine hour.
  2. cost per materials movement.
  3. cost per engineering drawing.
  4. predetermined overhead rate for facility-level costs.
B. Determine the total overhead costs and the unit overhead cost of products A and B.
C. Explain why the overhead costs of the two products are different.

The solution to Self-Study Problem 3 appears at the end of the chapter.

REVIEW

SUMMARY of IMPORTANT CONCEPTS

1. The volume-based method of allocating costs to products was developed at a time when overhead costs were a relatively small portion of product costs.
   a. The method uses a single activity base and a single predetermined overhead rate to allocate overhead costs to products.
   b. Throughout a period, overhead is allocated to products by multiplying the actual amount of the activity base used (machine hours, for example) by the predetermined overhead rate.
   c. Today, overhead costs make up the largest portion of a company's product costs.

2. With the growing importance of overhead costs has come a need for greater accuracy in the allocation of those costs.
   a. The traditional method ignores volume diversity; it makes no allowance for economies of scale.
   b. By limiting a company to a single activity base, the traditional method of cost allocation distorts costs.

3. Cooper's hierarchy of costs is based on allocation by activity rather than volume.
   a. Unit-level costs are like variable costs; they are constant per unit but change in total with the number of units produced.
   b. Batch-level costs are like fixed costs; they vary per unit but are constant in total. These costs recognize economies of scale.
   c. Product-level costs are incurred in manufacturing a product or product family.

d. Facility-level costs are not related to a particular unit or batch or family of products; they are necessary to sustain a company's overall operations.

4. Activity-based costing allocates overhead costs on the basis of the activities that are necessary to produce a product.
   a. In the first stage of the allocation process, a company assigns overhead costs to activity pools and chooses an activity base (a cost driver) for each pool.
   b. In the second stage, costs are assigned to a cost object, such as a good or service.

5. Activity-based costing gives managers of manufacturing and service companies the accurate cost information they need to make planning decisions.

DEFINE

TERMS and CONCEPTS DEFINED in this CHAPTER

activity pool   (M109)
activity-based costing   (M109)
core activities   (M114)

economies of scale   (M105)
overhead hierarchy   (M106)
product cross-subsidy   (M114)

SELF-STUDY PROBLEM SOLUTIONS

SSP5-1   A.   Troy's predetermined overhead rate is $14.20 per direct labor hour:

Predetermined overhead rate = Estimated overhead costs × Estimated direct labor hours
= ($50,000 + $20,000 + $60,000 + $12,000) ÷ 10,000
= $142,000 ÷ 10,000
= $14.20 per direct labor hour

B.   The unit cost of product A is $19.10:

Direct material costs per unit	$ 7.00
Direct labor costs per unit	5.00
Manufacturing overhead costs per unit	
($14.20 × 1/2 hour)	7.10
Total cost per unit	$19.10

SSP5-2   Lighting costs for the production areas are a facility-level cost. The lighting costs are not associated with any specific unit, batch, or family of products; they are related indirectly to all of the company's products.

Raw materials movement costs are a batch-level cost because raw materials are moved each time a new batch of product is placed into production.

The costs of cooling metal-cutting equipment are a unit-level cost. Those costs are a function of the number of hours the equipment is operating. When the equipment is idle, the cooling system also is idle.

The research and development expenses incurred to develop a product are a product-level cost. Those expenses can be associated with one product or product family. Although GAAP require that research and development costs be expensed in the period in which they are incurred, internal decision makers often treat those costs as overhead.

SSP5-3   A.
1. The cost per machine hour is $100 ($50,000 ÷ 500 hours).
2. The cost per materials movement is $250 ($20,000 ÷ 80 moves).
3. The cost per engineering drawing is $400 ($10,000 ÷ 25 drawings).
4. The facility-level predetermined overhead rate is .25 [$20,000 ÷ (50,000 + $20,000 + $10,000)].

B.

	Product A	Product B
Machine hours:		
40 hours × $100 per hour	$4,000	
10 hours × $100 per hour		$1,000
Movements:		
1 movement × $250	250	
2 movements × $250		500
Engineering drawings:		
0 drawings × $400	-0-	
2 drawings × $400		800
Subtotal (cost to date)	$4,250	$2,300
Facility-level cost subtotal × .25	1,063	575
Total overhead costs	$5,313	$2,875
Units produced	40	10
Overhead cost per unit	$133	$288

Economies of scale are evident in the lower cost per unit for product A, which is produced in a quantity four times that of product B. Also, product A was produced in one large batch versus two small batches of product B (one movement versus two). In addition, product A does not consume engineering services. Product A might be a mature product whose manufacturing process is stable and requires little attention.

Thinking Beyond the Question

Cost Allocation: Why is it a problem?

In the chapter opening scenario, you learned that Erin and Seth's cost accounting system allocates costs using direct labor hours as an activity driver, or allocation base. The owners believe costs allocated to some products are too high, while costs allocated to other products are too low. Why might the activity hierarchy developed by Robin Cooper help Erin and Seth more accurately allocate costs to their products? How does the activity hierarchy differ from traditional cost system design?

QUESTIONS

Q5-1
Obj. 2

Last month when his father, Nathan, retired, Norm Gregory became president of his family's manufacturing business. The company produces camping and mountain-climbing equipment that is sold in specialty shops throughout the country. At a retirement party, Nathan told his son, "I started this business 40 years ago producing a single model of tent. Now we make five models of tents and hundreds of other items! Our plant has been updated with the most modern equipment and manufacturing technologies." How do you think the company's expanded product line and technological advances have affected its allocation of manufacturing overhead?

Q5-2
Obj. 2

Quantro Enterprises has invested heavily in automated equipment over the past 10 years. In that time Quantro has installed materials handling systems and automated flexible manufacturing systems. All of these changes have allowed Quantro to reduce its labor costs by more than 35% while increasing production by 150%. Quantro has been applying overhead to products based on direct labor hours. What impact do the changes in Quantro's manufacturing process have on its application of its overhead? What impact on overhead assignment is created by economies of scale? Explain your answers.

Q5-3
Objs. 2, 3
Denver Materials Company operates a recycling center that separates metals and then sells them to steel mills. The company uses large machinery to sort, move, and crush the metals. Denver's business throughout the year is uneven, in large part because the collection of recyclable materials varies greatly from month to month. In some months, the plant is slow. In others, supervisors have to authorize overtime to work the mountains of materials that the company receives. Management charges overhead costs to each job based on total machine hours for each batch processed. Explain how changes in volume and activity can distort the cost of each batch.

Q5-4
Objs. 2, 3
T-Bar Industries, Inc., manufactures radios and compact disc players. For years T-Bar's production process has been labor-intensive; its primary production cost has been the wages of many direct laborers who assemble components along its production lines. Management at T-Bar is considering an investment in new technology that will automate 80% of the production process. The new machinery and the computer systems to operate it cost hundreds of thousands of dollars. T-Bar historically has allocated manufacturing overhead on the basis of direct labor hours. What change in cost structure should T-Bar expect if the company decides to invest in the new technology? What problems will that change in cost structure create? Explain your answer.

Q5-5
Obj. 3
Leslie Dunn is the controller of Demarco Company. Demarco produces six separate product lines in a single plant. Each line has a product manager who is accountable for the production costs of that line. Leslie is preparing for a meeting with the product managers to discuss the facility-level costs that will be allocated to each product line over the next year. She knows that the product managers are going to argue over these costs and the method of allocation to their product lines. Why would facility-level charges be a source of disagreement among the managers?

Q5-6
Obj. 4
Minor Medical Company is a manufacturer of blood pressure monitors, catheters, surgical instruments, and other medical products. In each of the past five years, Minor has added approximately 10 new products. Although its product line has become more diversified and its manufacturing processes more complex, Minor continues to apply overhead costs using a single activity base—direct labor hours. Explain why activity-based costing would benefit this company.

Q5-7
Obj. 4
Alice Glidden is the chief financial officer of Brown Ribbon Industries, Inc., a manufacturer of gift wraps, ribbons, and party supplies. A local certified management accountant has suggested that Alice implement an ABC system. The accountant told Alice that activity-based costing would not "overload" high-volume products with overhead costs. What did the accountant mean?

Q5-8
Objs. 1, 5
Jose Glass had a car accident last month and spent a night in the hospital. The bill came yesterday, and when he looked it over he noted that he had been charged $7 for a single aspirin. Believing it was a clerical error, Jose called the hospital and was told that the charge was correct. The person he spoke to in the billing department said that part of the charge was "overhead allocation" that included purchasing, handling, and other support-related costs. How does overhead allocation affect the cost of aspirin?

Q5-9
Objs. 2, 5
The law firm of Menard and Baker specializes in civil litigation. The overhead costs of operating the office are charged to clients as an administrative surcharge. The surcharge is based on attorneys' hours. The managing partner of the firm, Cynthia Menard, has noticed that clients who require extensive legal service often complain about the administrative surcharge. After reviewing costs and time sheets, Cynthia has determined that administrative costs usually are not a function of attorneys' hours, but of the time incurred by administrative personnel. How does volume affect the allocation of administrative costs? What changes should the firm consider? Why?

Q5-10
Objs. 4, 5
Apply the concepts of activity-based costing to an airline flight in which each passenger is a "unit of product." Give examples of unit-, batch-, product-, and facility-level costs.

EXERCISES   *If your instructor is using Personal Trainer® in this course, you may complete your assignments online.*

E5-1   Write a short definition of the terms listed in the *Terms and Concepts Defined in this Chapter* section.

E5-2   Average production costs representing three industries are as follows:

Obj. 1

	Paper	**Chemicals**	**Computer Manufacturing**
Raw materials	$ 5,000,000	$ 9,240,000	$1,440,000
Labor	5,000,000	1,760,000	560,000
Overhead	10,000,000	11,000,000	6,000,000
Total	$20,000,000	$22,000,000	$8,000,000

a. Calculate the material, labor, and overhead costs as a percentage of total production costs.
b. Explain how overhead costs differ from material and labor costs.
c. Explain why overhead costs might be significantly higher than labor and material costs in these industries.

E5-3   Traditional cost systems allocated overhead costs using a single allocation base, such as direct
Obj. 1   labor hours, direct labor costs, or machine hours. These simple allocation systems were appropriate because overhead costs typically did not represent a significant proportion of total manufacturing costs. Overhead costs were traced to a product as shown:

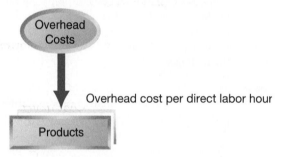

Assume the traditional method of overhead allocation is no longer relevant because of changes in manufacturing technology and support-related overhead costs. Significant activities and allocation bases are as follows:

Activity	**Allocation Base**
Quality control testing	Number of quality tests
Machine setup	Number of setups
Machine run time	Machine hours

Prepare a sketch to illustrate the application of overhead using relevant allocation bases. Then, explain why cost systems evolved in response to changes in manufacturing systems.

E5-4   Round Tire Company (RTC) uses a predetermined overhead rate to apply assembly overhead
Obj. 1   to products. Tire assembly is a labor-intensive process that requires one person to build a tire from a variety of components including inner liner, tread, and sidewall. Thus, the allocation base used by RTC is direct labor hours. During the month of June, RTC incurred overhead costs in the amount of $750,000 and worked 12,000 hours. Estimated assembly overhead for the year is $9,000,000 based on 120,000 labor hours. (*Hint:* Refer to Chapter M3 to review over- and underapplied overhead concepts.)

a. Calculate the predetermined overhead rate used by RTC.
b. Determine the amount of assembly overhead to be applied to production during June.
c. Is the overhead overapplied or underapplied? By how much?
d. What is the effect of the overapplied or underapplied overhead on the financial statements before they are adjusted?
e. Does the traditional allocation base, direct labor hours, make sense for RTC? Why or why not?

E5-5

Objs. 1, 2, 4

Auto Detail Company manufactures two basic types of products: vinyl and metallic adhesive-backed striping used by automobile manufacturers. The company traditionally has allocated manufacturing overhead to its product line using direct labor hours as a cost driver. More recently, the company has explored the use of two additional cost drivers as it evolves into an activity-based costing system. The following data summarize overhead application drivers and rates for the traditional and activity-based cost system.

Traditional: $175 per direct labor hour
Activity-based cost:
   $120 per direct labor hour
   $345 per machine changeover
   $100 per inspection

	Per Production Run	
	Vinyl Striping	**Metallic Striping**
Direct labor hours	10 hours	8 hours
Batch size	180 rolls	65 rolls
Number of inspections	0	3

   a. Calculate the overhead cost per roll to manufacture the vinyl striping and the metallic striping using the traditional method.
   b. Calculate the overhead cost per roll to manufacture the vinyl striping and the metallic striping using the activity-based cost method.
   c. Explain the cause or causes of the differences in cost for each product when using traditional and ABC methods.

E5-6

Objs. 1, 3, 4

Birmingham Cycle Manufacturing Company uses three activity pools to assign costs to products. Each activity pool has a unique cost driver, or activity base, used to apply overhead costs to products.

Activity	**Cost Driver**	**Estimated Overhead Costs**	**Estimated Activity Level**
Materials handling	Number of batches	$ 60,000	500 batches
Machine setup	Number of setups	150,000	300 setups
Machine operations	Machine hours	500,000	4,000 machine hours

Calculate the predetermined rate for each activity. Then, classify each activity as unit level, batch level, product level, or facility level.

E5-7

Objs. 1, 4

Second-stage activity drivers in an activity-based costing system allocate costs from activity pools to products. Cost system designers often make choices among a variety of potential drivers. Listed below are three cost pools and two potential allocation bases for each pool.

Activity Pool	**Driver #1**	**Driver #2**
Machine setup activities	Number of setups	Number of setup hours
Materials handling	Number of batches handled	Number of hours handling materials
Quality inspection	Number of inspections	Hours of quality inspection

Choosing the appropriate cost driver can make the difference between accurate and inaccurate product cost calculations.

   a. For each activity, specify the circumstances that would favor the use of cost driver #1. Explain your rationale.
   b. For each activity, specify the circumstances that would favor the use of cost driver #2. Explain your rationale.

E5-8

Objs. 1, 4

Taylor Sweets, Inc., produces a popular brand of chocolate candies. The company's manufacturing process is labor-intensive: Chocolate, sugar, and other ingredients are measured by hand, blended in a large mixer, and then heated. Next, the mixture is spread by hand into molds. When the mixture is cool, the candies are removed from the molds, placed in paper cups, and then boxed. All of these steps are done by hand.

(Continued)

Tim Gabet, Taylor's president, is considering a modernization project that would significantly increase the amount of candy the company can produce. Under his plan, the measuring and mold-filling procedures would be automated, and a single machine would remove the candies from the molds, wrap them individually, and box them.

Tim is excited about the possibility of increasing production volume but realizes that automation can be very expensive. If automation would increase Taylor's overhead cost more than $0.04 per unit, Tim knows he will have to reject the project. Taylor allocates overhead costs to production based on direct labor hours. Estimates of production volume and overhead costs under the current process and the automated process are as follows:

	Current Process	Automated Process
Production volume in units	50,000	450,000
Total overhead costs	$15,000	$162,000

a. Calculate the overhead cost per unit for the current process and the automated process.
b. Given Tim's target increase, should he go ahead with the automation project?
c. What is the minimum number of units (rounded to the nearest unit) that Taylor would have to produce at the expected level of overhead cost per unit to accept the project?
d. Suppose that Taylor allocates overhead on the basis of machine hours instead of direct labor hours. Would the project be accepted or rejected? Explain your answer.

E5-9
Objs. 2, 4

Complete the following sentences with the appropriate term(s) from the chapter.

1. To calculate a single plant-wide _Predetermined overhead rate_, a company does not have to separate indirect manufacturing costs into individual cost pools.
2. To calculate a burden rate, a company must estimate its indirect costs and a(n) _allocation base_.
3. _Facility-level activities_ are the costs that sustain a company's general manufacturing facilities. _(lighting, heat, electricity)_
4. Activity-based costing more accurately traces the costs of production by shifting overhead costs from _high volume_ goods or services to _low volume_ goods or services.
5. _Batch level_ costs are incurred each time a batch of goods is processed.
6. Cost _shifting_ is a problem when a company uses a single basis for allocating the costs of _overhead_.
7. Using activity-based costing, overhead costs that vary in direct proportion to the number of units produced would be _unit level_ costs.
8. Using activity-based costing, the costs of engineering a particular product line would be _product level_ costs.
9. The objective of activity-based costing is to associate as many costs as possible with specific _cost drivers_.
10. The savings a company realizes by spreading fixed manufacturing overhead costs over a large number of products is called _economies of scale_.

E5-10
Obj. 3

Classify the following activities as unit level, batch level, product level, or facility level according to the activity-based costing hierarchy developed by Cooper.

- Machine setups between batches of two different products
- Quality control inspections for specialty items
- Hours of machine run-time
- Plant security
- Refrigeration and special handling of certain inventory items in a pharmaceutical warehouse
- Hospital admissions (Assume admission costs do not vary according to length of stay.)
- Engineering costs for product redesign

E5-11
Obj. 4

Managers often make decisions about keeping or dropping a product after evaluating the profitability of each product in the product line. Bimini Products, Inc., recently completed an activity-based costing study. Management wishes to compare the results with the cost data produced by their traditional cost system. Product data are as follows:

SPREADSHEET

Product	Selling Price	Cost Traditional	Cost ABC
A	$100	$ 80	$ 65
B	150	120	140
C	130	80	90

Product A is produced in high volume using a stable process that does not require excessive support activities. Product B demands high levels of support activities and is produced in low volume. Product C is produced in moderate volume.

    a. For each product compute:
      1. Profit margin, traditional
      2. Profit margin, ABC
      3. Percentage change in profit margin as follows: (profit margin ABC − profit margin ÷ profit margin traditional)
    b. What kinds of product line decisions might your calculations support?

E5-12
Obj. 4
U-Build-It produces carpentry tools for homeowners. The company recently completed an activity-based costing study and is attempting to understand the results. The following table summarizes sales volume and overhead cost information for a sample of five products. In some cases, the activity-based costing study produced costs below the traditional product cost. In other instances, the activity-based cost study produced costs above the traditional product cost.

Product	Volume	Overhead Cost Traditional	Overhead Cost Activity-Based
A	Moderate	$100	$112
B	Moderate	75	75
C	High	87	73
D	Low	160	232
E	High	95	70

    a. Compute the percentage change for each product using the formula (activity-based cost − traditional cost) ÷ traditional cost.
    b. Sort the percentages calculated in requirement (a) from largest to smallest and prepare a bar graph summarizing the results.
    c. What relationship do you observe between volume and cost?
    d. How might you explain this relationship?

E5-13
Obj. 4
Good Earth Bakery traditionally has allocated manufacturing overhead to its product line using raw material weight as a cost driver. Assume the dough and other ingredients for one loaf weigh one pound. While evolving into an activity-based costing system, Good Earth explored the use of different cost drivers. The following data summarize overhead application drivers and rates for the traditional and activity-based cost systems.

Traditional: $0.95 per pound
Activity-based cost:
  $75 per oven hour
  $50 per blender setup (The blender is cleaned before each batch of product.)

	Whole Wheat Bread	Raisin Bread
Oven time	1/2 hour	3/4 hour
Batch size	100 loaves	50 loaves

    a. Calculate the overhead cost per loaf to manufacture whole wheat bread and raisin bread using the activity-based cost method.
    b. Identify the types of overhead cost pools (unit, batch, product, or facility) added by the Good Earth Bakery.
    c. Explain why the traditional and ABC methods produce different results.

E5-14
Obj. 4

Data from the accounting and production records of Hasgrow Company are as follows:

	Product 1	Product 2	Product 3
Units per batch	150	200	60
Direct materials per unit	$50	$75	$90
Direct labor per unit	$20	$15	$21
Number of setups	2	5	3
Machine hours per unit	0.10	0.15	0.20
Number of engineering change orders associated with each product	0	1	2

Activity Costs

Cost per setup	$300
Cost per machine hour	600
Cost per engineering change order	250

Managers wish to understand material, labor, and activity costs of each product to help guide their pricing decisions.

Compute the cost per unit of product 1, product 2, and product 3. Why do the costs differ across the three products?

E5-15
Obj. 4

Refer to the facts as shown in E5-14. The cost system designers at Hasgrow selected the number of setups as a cost driver to allocate setup costs to products. As an alternative, they could allocate setup costs to batches based on the number of setup hours for each changeover.

a. What assumption did the cost system designers make when they chose number of setups rather than number of setup hours to allocate machine setup costs?
b. Which alternative might result in easier (and perhaps less costly) data collection?

E5-16
Obj. 4

Gonzalez Manufacturing traced the following levels of activity to the products it manufactured during the first quarter of this year:

			Actual Level of Activity		
Activity Pool	**Cost per Activity**	**Product A**	**Product B**	**Product C**	**Product D**
Machine setups	$50/setup	500 setups	600	800	650
Inspection	$15/inspection	3,165 inspections	2,155	780	3,000
Receiving	$100/receipt	420 receipts	175	655	500
Factory	$20/machine hour	19,250 hours	14,300	21,500	15,950
Number of units		20,000	17,500	25,000	22,500

Determine the total overhead cost charged to each product for the quarter. In addition, calculate the overhead cost per unit.

E5-17
Obj. 5

America Outback is a rapidly growing service company that offers wilderness backpacking, canoeing, and rock-climbing expeditions at numerous locations across the United States. Management wants to gain a better understanding of overhead costs associated with various expeditions. The following is a brief overview of the company's activities and costs:

- The company provides all equipment, except personal items, for the expeditions. Overhead cost, which consists mainly of depreciation, varies according to the difficulty level of the expedition. More sophisticated and expensive gear is required for expeditions of greater difficulty.
- Each expedition requires one guide. However, enrollments vary by expedition to ensure a proper guide-to-participant ratio.
- Most of the expeditions are offered on National Park Service property. Thus, America Outback pays a park entrance fee for each participant.
- America Outback hires experienced naturalists as route planners who also schedule treks and order necessary provisions.

a. Identify the cost objects (products or services) associated with the operations of America Outback. Explain why you selected these services as cost objects.
b. Does a service company, such as America Outback, require materials, labor, and overhead to deliver its product? Explain.

E5-18
Obj. 3

Refer to the facts presented in E5-17.

a. Identify each cost as a unit-level, batch-level, product-level, or facility-level overhead cost.
b. Justify your answer.
c. How might America Outback use more accurate cost information in planning future expeditions?

....

PROBLEMS

If your instructor is using Personal Trainer® in this course, you may complete your assignments online.

P5-1
Obj. 1

The Ethics of Overhead Allocation

Justin owns a small factory that produces buttons for the garment industry. He wants to buy a new machine and has applied to a bank for financing. The loan officer has asked for operating statements for the past year. The company's net income has not been very good over that time, and inventory has grown substantially. Justin is concerned that the bank is not going to be as optimistic as he is about future sales and the company's ability to reduce its inventory.

Yesterday, Justin had the following conversation with Beth, the company's controller.

Justin: You know that I've applied for a bank loan and that the bank wants copies of our operating statements for the last twelve months.
Beth: I can have those ready for you in an hour.
Justin: I'd like you to make some changes before you prepare those statements, Beth.
Beth: What sort of changes?
Justin: I want you to increase our predetermined overhead rate by 30% and then recalculate the inventory figures and last year's income statement using the new rate. Also, move my salary and our office rent into the manufacturing overhead pool. I'll need those statements first thing in the morning.

Required

A. What effect would the change in predetermined overhead rate have on the company's inventory values?
B. What effect would the reclassification of Justin's salary and the office rent have on the company's product costs?
C. Do you agree with the changes Justin is asking for? What parts of the financial statements would reveal Justin's changes to the loan officer?

P5-2
Objs. 1, 2

Predetermined Overhead Rates Using Volume-Related Drivers

Mallory Chemical Corporation produces two products: A and B. The company's expected factory overhead costs for the coming year are as follows:

Overhead Category	Estimated Costs
Utilities	$ 300,000
Indirect materials	150,000
Indirect labor	50,000
Depreciation	100,000
Materials handling and storage	200,000
Repairs and maintenance	200,000
Supplies	180,000
Insurance	120,000
Other	50,000
Total	$1,350,000

[Handwritten notes: 1,350,00 ÷ 45,000 = $30/ direct labor; 1,350,000 ÷ 50,000 = $27/machine hour]

Its expected levels of production activity are as follows:

	Product A	Product B
Machine hours	35,000	15,000
Direct labor hours	20,000	25,000
Number of units produced	10,000	5,000
Direct materials used, in pounds	75,000	125,000

(Continued)

All labor costs $10 per hour; materials cost $1.80 per pound for product A and $2.40 per pound for product B.

Required

A. Calculate the predetermined overhead rate based on direct labor hours and based on machine hours.
B. Calculate the unit cost of each product if overhead is applied on the basis of direct labor hours.
C. Calculate the unit cost of each product if overhead is applied on the basis of machine hours.
D. Compare the unit costs you have just calculated. Why does the choice of an activity base affect unit cost? What implications would the selection of an activity base for allocating overhead have on managerial decisions? What factors should management consider in choosing an activity base for assigning costs?

P5-3   Overhead Allocation: Traditional Method

Obj. 2

Cast-Rite Company produces a variety of cast iron pipe products used by municipalities for water and sewer systems. Though many different product configurations are possible, products primarily differ on the basis of pipe diameter, length, and bell type (the type of fitting applied to the end of a pipe to enable it to be attached to other pipes).

The process begins when molten iron is poured into molds on the casting line. Casting machine setups are required between batches of different product types because casting molds must be changed between runs of pipes with different diameters. Following the casting process, all pipes are annealed (heated) in an oven to strengthen the pipe. Finally, some pipe products are lined on the inside with a thin concrete mixture.

Management is concerned that the traditional cost system, which assigns overhead using a predetermined rate based on a cost per ton, may not produce accurate results. Use the following information to prepare your responses to P5-3 and P5-4.

Product	Length	Diameter	Weight	Batch Size	Lined
A	10 ft.	12"	1,000 lbs.	50 units	yes
B	10 ft.	15"	1,200 lbs.	100 units	no
C	15 ft.	12"	1,500 lbs.	100 units	yes
D	15 ft.	15"	2,000 lbs.	150 units	yes
E	10 ft.	20"	2,300 lbs.	5 units	yes

The old cost system applied overhead at a rate of $407.68 per ton. Cast-Rite pays $200 per ton for scrap iron used in the melting process. Labor cost is insignificant and is included in the overhead rate.

Required

A. Using the traditional method of applying overhead, determine the cost for each product manufactured by Cast-Rite.
B. What can you learn about overhead consumption across the product classes?
C. What are the weaknesses of the traditional approach from a decision maker's perspective?

P5-4   Overhead Allocation: Traditional versus ABC

Obj. 4

Refer to the facts presented in P5-3. The activity-based costing study revealed the following revised cost estimates:

Predetermined overhead rate based on cost per ton	$300
Cost to change molds between batches of product	700
Cost to apply cement lining (per pipe)	100

Note: Total costs for traditional and ABC are the same ($191,875).

Required

A. For each product, calculate the activity-based cost of production.
B. Prepare a table with four headings as follows: Product, Traditional Cost, Activity-Based Cost, Percentage Change (defined as follows: [ABC cost − traditional cost] ÷ traditional cost). Complete the table using your calculations from P5-3 and part (A) of this problem.

C. What can you learn about overhead consumption across the product classes? Explain.

D. What types of decision alternatives might management consider in light of the new cost information?

P5-5 The Conceptual Design of an ABC System

Obj. 3

Auto-Plex produces windshields for a major international automobile manufacturer. The company is under increasing pressure to reduce costs. Thus, management authorized an activity-based costing study to help understand how various activities contribute to overhead costs. The following is an excerpt from the ABC study:

Cost Pool	Explanation
Glass melting oven	Silica (sand) is melted in a continuous flow, resulting in glass sheets used by all windshield types. The major cost is the natural gas consumed on an hourly basis.
Machine setup	Windshield molding machines must be reconfigured between runs of different products.
Special inspection	Radio antennas are molded into certain types of windshields. These specialty windshields require extra handling and inspection activities.
Supervision	Each shift employs three supervisors who support all manufacturing processes and products within the plant.

Required

A. Using Exhibit 7 as a model, construct a diagram of a two-stage cost allocation system for Auto-Plex.

B. Identify each activity pool in your model as unit level, batch level, product level, or facility level.

P5-6 The Two-Stage Allocation Process

Obj. 4

Refer to the information provided in P5-5. Assume the company employs six individuals who set up the equipment between runs of different products. Setup crew members devote approximately 90% of their time to physically changing machine specifications and molds to accommodate a different product. In addition, they spend approximately 10% of their time on special inspection activities. Crew salaries and related setup costs total $200,000 per year. Engineering studies indicate natural gas and other melting oven costs approximate $700,000 per year. The company employs two full-time quality control engineers, who each earn $65,000 annually. These engineers are responsible for special inspections (75% of their time) but also work with setup crews (25% of their time) to help minimize scrap rates. The company's three supervisors each earn $70,000 per year.

Required

A. Using your diagram from P5-5 as a guide, allocate the costs to each activity pool.

B. For each activity pool in your diagram, identify a reasonable cost allocation base (second-stage cost driver). Justify your answer.

P5-7 Multiple Cost Drivers: Calculating Predetermined Overhead Rates

Objs. 1, 4

Randall Foundry uses four activity pools to assign costs to its products. Each pool has its own cost driver, the activity base used to calculate and apply overhead costs. Last year Randall prepared the following estimates of overhead costs and activity levels for the first quarter of this year:

Activity Pool	Cost Driver	Estimated Overhead Costs	Estimated Activity Levels
Machine setups	Number of setups	$560,000	2,500 setups
Inspection	Number of inspections	$245,000	10,000 inspections
Receiving	Number of receiving reports	$21,300	1,200 receiving reports
Machine operations	Machine hours	$590,000	73,750 machine hours

(Continued)

Assume product A was produced in three 50-unit batches over the course of the first quarter. Additional information relevant to product A is as follows:

Number of inspections	9
Number of receiving reports	3
Number of machine hours	150

Required

A. Calculate the predetermined overhead rate for each activity pool.
B. Calculate the overhead cost per unit to produce product A.
C. Randall is planning to run smaller batch sizes in an effort to reduce its inventories. The flow of raw materials will not be affected by that decision. What concerns should management address before it actually implements the plan?

P5-8   Using the Activity Hierarchy to Classify Activities

Obj. 3

Dynamic Products, Inc., manufactures a wide variety of products in its plant in Macon, Georgia. Management has identified the following manufacturing and administrative activities:

1. Special equipment is used to add a protective finish to various products.
2. Purchase orders are issued to acquire raw materials.
3. Factory managers run training programs in quality control for new employees.
4. Machine setups are necessary for each batch of goods produced.
5. Janitors clean the offices and the plant floor each evening.
6. Warehouse personnel pull the stock needed for production and move the materials to the plant floor.
7. Receiving clerks inspect incoming materials and prepare receiving reports.
8. Quality control inspectors test each batch of goods before it is stored or shipped.
9. Payroll clerks process the factory workers' time cards and prepare weekly paychecks for distribution.
10. Engineers develop new-product specifications and redesign existing products as needed.

Required

A. Classify each of the activities listed as a unit-level, batch-level, product-level, or facility-level activity.
B. Identify a cost driver for each of the activities that could be used to apply costs to Dynamic's products.
C. For each activity, identify one or more traceable costs.
D. Explain how the hierarchy provides insights that affect decision making.

P5-9   The Conceptual Design of an ABC System—An Internet Company

Objs. 3, 5

Web-books.com is an Internet company that sells books on the World Wide Web. The president of the company authorized an activity-based costing study to understand the cost of various activities that are driving overhead at Web-books.com. Selected activities include:

- Web site maintenance—costs do not vary as a function of sales volume.
- Retrieving the order from the Web site and locating the product—costs vary as a function of order size (the number of books per order) because more time is required to fill larger orders.
- Specialty handling—unique packaging is required for oversized (large) products.
- Standard packaging—costs do not appear to vary by the number of books in the order, but are constant across all orders.

Required Using Exhibit 7 as a model, construct a diagram of a two-stage cost allocation system for Web-books.com. Identify each activity pool in your model as unit level, batch level, product level, or facility level.

P5-10   The Two-Stage Allocation Process

Objs. 4, 5

Refer to the information in P5-9. Assume the company employs three systems engineers at an annual salary of $75,000 each. The engineers devote 85% of their time to Web site maintenance and 15% to improving technical aspects of order retrieval. Eight people who pick orders consume supplies and equipment-related overhead costs of $20,000 each. Interviews during the activity-based costing design process indicated these employees devote 90% of their time to picking, but occasionally help with specialty handling requirements of large orders (10% of their time). Depreciation on equipment and tools for special handling activities total $70,000 per year. The packaging department employs four people who devote approximately 70% of their time to standard packaging activities and 30% to specialty handling. Each person consumes $15,000 annually in support-related overhead costs.

Information is presented in tabular form as follows:

Resource	Number	Resource Consumption	Activity Allocation
Systems engineers	3	$75,000 each	85% Web site maintenance
			15% order retrieval
Order pickers	8	$20,000 each	90% order retrieval
			10% specialty handling
Depreciation		$70,000	100% special handling
Packaging	4	$15,000	70% standard packaging
			30% specialty handling

Required

A. Using your diagram from P5-9 as a guide, determine the costs to be allocated in the first stage to each activity pool.
B. For each activity pool in your diagram, identify a reasonable cost allocation base (second-stage cost driver).
C. What factors might cost system designers consider when choosing among numerous potential cost drivers for cost-allocation purposes?

P5-11 Cost Allocation: Service Industry

Objs. 1, 4, 5

Franklin County Bank has a commercial loan department that makes loans to businesses that meet the bank's strict criteria. The department is staffed by eight loan officers. Each loan officer can grant loans up to a certain amount without the approval of the bank's lending committee. Loans that exceed that limit must be approved by the lending committee, which meets weekly.

The commercial loan department incurs significant costs administering and monitoring commercial loans. Among those costs are the wages of the credit analysts who review borrowers' financial statements; the wages of the administrative personnel who prepare loan packets; filing fees for security agreements; office rent; depreciation expense on office equipment, computers, and furniture; and fees for credit reports.

Anita Andrews, vice president of commercial loans, wants to allocate and collect administrative costs from borrowers in the form of a processing fee.

Required

A. What cost drivers could the bank use to allocate its overhead costs of processing commercial loans? What factors affect the choice of an activity base?
B. What estimates would be necessary to establish a processing fee if all costs are included?
C. How could activity-based costing be used to allocate overhead costs in the commercial loan department?

P5-12 Overhead Allocation: A Service Environment

Objs. 1, 4, 5

The East State Veterinary Clinic provides veterinary services for small domestic animals. Three certified veterinarians and four technical assistants work at the clinic. The clinic has three separate areas of operations: examinations, surgeries, and laboratory tests. The technical assistants help with exams and surgery and perform the majority of laboratory tests.

The clinic allocates administrative and operating overhead to the three service areas using a single rate based on the veterinarians' direct labor hours. Information about services and costs for the past fiscal quarter are as follows:

(Continued)

Veterinarians' Direct

Area of Operations	Labor Hours	Number of Patients
Examinations	1,200	800
Surgeries	200	60
Laboratory tests	100	600
Total	1,500	

Overhead Item	Cost
Maintenance and supplies, exam rooms	$ 8,500
Depreciation, surgical equipment	6,000
Surgical supplies	2,000
Depreciation, laboratory equipment	2,000
Laboratory supplies	4,000
Total	$22,500

Required

A. Calculate the clinic's predetermined overhead rate based on the activity in the most recent quarter, and use that rate to allocate costs to each service area.
B. How does the use of a single activity base and rate disproportionately allocate costs among the three service areas? Explain your answer.
C. Calculate separate overhead rates for each of the three service areas using the veterinarians' direct labor hours incurred in each area as the activity base. Why do the rates differ for each service area? Calculate the overhead cost (rounded to the nearest dollar) that would have been allocated to each area using the three separate rates.

P5-13 ABC—A Conceptual Design

Objs. 3, 4, 5

The Clearwater SCUBA Shop, owned and operated by Floyd Ridges, offers three types of services: retail sales, SCUBA instruction, and dive boat charters. As with many service organizations, the three elements of Floyd's business are not independent. Floyd earns revenue from SCUBA instruction and sales of gear to students. He uses the boat for open-water dives that are part of a student's SCUBA training. In addition, Floyd transports experienced divers to dive sites for a fee. After a student is certified, Floyd believes the dive boat generates additional equipment sales and dive charter revenue as newly certified divers acquire advanced skills and equipment.

Floyd wants to understand the costs associated with each business segment, retail sales, SCUBA instruction, and dive charters. Other than cost of goods sold for retail sales, he believes the dive boat is the single most expensive service he provides. Major costs include fuel, insurance, depreciation, dockage fees, interest costs, and wages for the mate who assists divers while on board. Floyd also carries extra liability insurance for higher risk certifications such as cave diving and wreck exploration.

Required

A. Identify the cost objects in Floyd Ridges' company.
B. What problems will Floyd experience as he undertakes the cost allocation?
C. The overhead costs associated with the dive charter operation may be classified according to a cost hierarchy. Using Clearwater's business description, identify an example of the following:

- Unit-level cost
- Batch-level cost
- Product-level cost
- Facility-level cost

P5-14 Excel in Action

Music Makers manufactures CDs for software and music companies. It classifies its products into two types: data CDs and music CDs. Because of the greater quality demands of music CDs, the manufacturing process requires greater quality control and longer manufacturing time for this product type. Music Makers produces 500,000 CDs per month. Eighty percent of the production is data CDs.

SPREADSHEET

Management of Music Makers has become concerned about the price it is charging for its products and the profitability of each product line. It sells its products for $2.40 per unit, regardless of product type. This price is higher than some of the company's competitors are charging for data disks, and Music Makers has begun to lose orders to these competitors. Because profits have been slipping a bit, management is worried. It has decided to analyze its production costs using activity-based costing.

For purposes of the analysis, the company has collected the following manufacturing overhead information. Unit-level costs include depreciation, $70,000; utilities, $51,000; and supplies and repairs, $8,500. Unit-level costs will be allocated on the basis of machine hours. The manufacturing process requires 100,000 machine hours per month. Data CDs require 60,000 hours, and music CDs require 40,000 hours. Batch-level costs include materials handling, $63,000; quality inspections, $41,000; and machine setups, $35,000. The company runs 50 batches per month. Half of the batches are for data CDs and half are for music CDs. Product-level costs include special quality inspections for music CDs of $25,000 per month. Facility-level costs include plant management costs of $30,000 per month and are attached to products using the number of units produced as an allocation base.

Required

A. Use Exhibit 10 in this chapter as an example and prepare a calculation of activity costs for Music Makers using a spreadsheet. Costs should be separated into unit, batch, product, and facility levels. Use cell references and formulas as appropriate to prepare the spreadsheet. The analysis should use the following format.

	A	B	C	D	E	F	G	H
1	Activity - Based Cost by Product							
2								
3		Units	Machine					
4	Product	Produced	Hours	Batches				
5								
6	Data							
7	Music							
8								
9					Overhead Costs			
10	Product	Materials	Labor	Unit	Batch	Product	Facility	Total
11	Data							
12	Music							
13								
14		Selling	Unit	Unit				
15		Price	Cost	Profit				
16	Data							
17	Music							

Direct materials cost is $0.92 per unit. Direct labor cost is $0.20 per unit.

B. Compare the unit production costs of each product with the unit selling price. What actions should Music Makers' management take as a result of this analysis? How would your analysis differ if total machine hours used in production had been 80,000 per month and 70,000 of these hours had been for data CDs?

P5-15   Multiple-Choice Overview of the Chapter

1. Overhead allocation based on volume alone:
   a. is a key element of activity-based costing.
   b. systematically overcosts high-volume products and undercosts low-volume products.
   c. systematically overcosts low-volume products and undercosts high-volume products.
   d. must be used to prepare external financial reports.

(Continued)

2. Using activity-based costing, overhead costs are accumulated in:
   a. a single, company-wide pool.
   b. departmental pools.
   c. pools created according to the number of cost drivers that can be identified.
   d. batches and allocated to products based on the costs of materials or labor.

3. First-stage allocations in an activity-based cost system:
   a. typically use percentages to allocate costs to activities.
   b. allocate fixed costs only.
   c. allocate variable costs only.
   d. are unnecessary because ABC requires a one-stage allocation process.

4. Activity-based costing would be least effective when:
   a. products differ substantially in volume and lot size.
   b. there is a close link between direct labor hours and overhead costs.
   c. managers use cost information to make pricing or other product decisions.
   d. the processes used to manufacture products differ substantially in terms of complexity.

5. All of the following are characteristic of activity-based costing except the:
   a. use of cost drivers as a basis for allocating costs.
   b. accumulation of costs by activities.
   c. failure to recognize economies of scale.
   d. use of volume as a possible cost driver.

6. The allocation of overhead costs:
   a. is used by service and manufacturing organizations to assign costs to products.
   b. is used only by manufacturing organizations.
   c. is used to assign the costs of direct materials and labor.
   d. must be based on sales or production volume.

7. The denominator used in calculating a predetermined overhead rate:
   a. should have a causal relationship to the costs being assigned.
   b. is not affected by varying levels of volume.
   c. should change monthly to allow for fluctuations in volume.
   d. is determined once volume and actual costs are known.

8. The level of activity that is most likely to use volume for the allocation of overhead is the:
   a. unit level.
   b. product level.
   c. batch level.
   d. facility level.

9. An example of a product-level cost is the cost:
   a. of setting up machines for different products.
   b. incurred to operate a break room.
   c. of a factory's payroll.
   d. incurred to operate a product-testing center.

10. An example of a batch-level cost is the cost:
    a. of setting up machines for different products.
    b. incurred to operate a break room.
    c. of a factory's payroll.
    d. incurred to operate a product-testing center.

CASES

C5-1   **Activity-Based Costing versus Traditional Cost Allocation**

Objs. 2, 4   C. Berry Manufacturing Company produces two guitar models. One is a standard acoustic guitar that sells for $600 and is constructed from medium-grade materials. The other model is a custom-made amplified guitar with pearl inlays and a body constructed from special woods. The custom guitar sells for $900. Both guitars require 10 hours of direct labor to produce, but the custom guitar is manufactured by more experienced workers who are paid at a higher rate.

Most of C. Berry's sales come from the standard guitar, but sales of the custom model have been growing. Following is the company's sales, production, and cost information for last year:

	Standard Guitar	Custom Guitar
Sales and production volume in units	900	100
Unit costs:		
Direct materials	$ 150	$375
Direct labor	180	240
Manufacturing overhead	135	135
Total unit costs	$ 465	$750
Manufacturing overhead costs:		
Building depreciation	$ 40,000	
Maintenance	15,000	
Purchasing	20,000	
Inspection	12,000	
Indirect materials	15,000	
Supervision	30,000	
Supplies	3,000	
Total manufacturing overhead costs	$135,000	

The company allocates overhead costs using the traditional method. Its activity base is direct labor hours. The predetermined overhead rate, based on 10,000 direct labor hours, is $13.50 ($135,000 ÷ 10,000 direct labor hours).

Nick Fessler, president of C. Berry, is concerned that the traditional cost-allocation system the company is using may not be generating accurate information and that the selling price of the custom guitar may not be covering its true cost.

Required

A. The cost-allocation system C. Berry has been using allocates 90% of overhead costs to the standard guitar because 90% of direct labor hours were spent on the standard model. How much overhead was allocated to each of the two models last year? Discuss why this might not be an accurate way to assign overhead costs to products.

B. How would the use of more than one cost pool improve C. Berry's cost allocation?

C. C. Berry's controller developed the following data:

Manufacturing Overhead Cost	Amount	Cost Driver	Standard Guitar	Custom Guitar
Building depreciation	$40,000	Square footage	3,000	1,000
Maintenance	15,000	Direct labor hours	9,000	1,000
Purchasing	20,000	Number of purchase orders	1,500	500
Inspection	12,000	Number of inspections	400	600
Indirect materials	15,000	Number of units	900	100
Supervision	30,000	Number of inspections	400	600
Supplies	3,000	Number of units	900	100

Use activity-based costing to allocate the costs of overhead per unit and in total to each model of guitar.

D. Calculate the cost of a custom guitar using activity-based costing. Why is the cost different from the cost calculated using the traditional allocation method? At the current selling price, is the company covering its true cost of production? Explain your answer.

C5-2 Forest Industries Paper Company: An ABC Costing Analysis*

Objs. 2, 4

Forest Industries Paper Company (FIPC) was a small, closely held paperboard manufacturer that produced a broad line of paperboard in large reels, termed parent rolls. These parent rolls were sold to converters who further processed them into containers used for a variety

*Case prepared by Dr. Thomas Albright for use in the Institute of Management Accountant's Regional Education Assistance Program (REAP) course in Strategic Cost Management. Used with permission.

of consumer products. The owners of FIPC had long pursued the strategy of producing a full range of products. While product diversity within a paperboard plant would not readily be apparent to the casual observer, subtle differences existed. For example, paperboard differs by basis weight (or thickness determined by caliper measurements) for a specified length of product.

FIPC produced 20 different grades of paperboard. Some were produced in large quantities requiring production runs of several days, while others were produced in smaller quantities requiring runs of only a few hours.

Pulp manufacturing begins with hardwood or softwood timber in the form of wood chips. The second step in the process is termed "digesting." Wood chips are cooked at 325 degrees Fahrenheit to break down the glue-like material bonding the wood fibers. Following the digesting process, brown fibers are washed and screened. A bleaching process is used to convert brown pulp into white pulp.

The paperboard manufacturing process begins by mixing pulp with water and chemicals in the first stage of a paper machine. The mixture is applied to a porous wire mesh; formation of paper actually occurs within this step. The wire mesh travels through a press that forces the pulp mixture against the wire to eliminate water within the mixture and to form the desired paper thickness. The material then proceeds to a drying section where it travels across numerous cylindrical dryers that are heated with steam. In the final section of the paper machine, long sections of paperboard are rolled up into parent rolls and are removed from the machine. The parent roll is further processed by FIPC's customers to make various types of paperboard containers.

Sometimes customers require additional processes to be performed on parent rolls. For example, food processors often require widths of 18 inches, rather than the standard width of a reel (approximately 12 feet). Thus, reels are loaded onto a rewinder slitter to produce eight reels 18 inches wide from one reel 12 feet wide. For convenience, Forest Industries had always combined labor and machine costs of the rewinder slitter with those of the paper machine for allocation purposes. Thus, all grades of paperboard shared in the costs of slitting even though most grades were not slit. Additionally, only a minor setup fee was charged to customers requesting slit parent rolls, as this was viewed as incidental customer service. Engineering studies suggest the slitting may be more expensive than previously thought.

Forest Industries traditionally applied overhead to production as a function of materials costs: thicker materials required more machine time to process as they demanded slower machine speeds and more energy to dry. Thus, unit-level drivers made sense for applying certain types of overhead to products. However, other important costs were incurred without respect to volume. For example, grade changes induce instabilities into the process that result in scrap until the process resumes stability. On average, production engineers estimate that approximately one-half reel is lost to scrap each time a grade change is made. Just as discrete-part manufacturers incur machine setup costs between production runs of two different products, scrap produced following grade changes is a predictable cost of production.

A sample representing significant categories of grades is presented in Exhibit A. The sample contains thin paperboard grades (caliper 0.013) as well as heavier grades (caliper 0.02). In addition, Exhibit A identifies whether a grade typically is slit. The sample is representative of the variation in batch quantities. As shown below, some grades are produced in small quantities, while the market demands significantly more production in other grades. Materials cost per reel includes pulp and chemical costs, while the selling price reflects recent market prices.

Exhibit A
Selected Product Grades with Production and Financial Data

Product	Caliper	Slit	Average Reels per Batch	Materials Cost per Reel	Selling Price per Reel
A	0.013	yes	50	$4,800	$12,600
B	0.014	no	2	5,200	13,500
C	0.015	yes	35	5,600	14,200
D	0.020	no	175	7,400	19,500

Total reels slit: 85 (50 + 35)
Total grade changes: 4 (grade A, grade B, grade C, grade D)

In the past, Forest Industries' accountants estimated that manufacturing overhead, including labor, energy, and depreciation on capital equipment, approximated 105% of material costs. Historically, product costs at Forest Industries were calculated by multiplying the overhead rate by direct material costs. However, brand managers had begun to suspect that some grades were subsidizing others with respect to costs. Two significant activities, grade changes and slitting, were identified to help reduce cross-subsidy and provide more accurate cost estimates. Exhibit B summarizes information obtained from the activity-based costing study.

Exhibit B

Activity Cost Pools and Activity Volumes

Total grade change costs	$47,000	Number of grade changes	4
Total slitting costs	$195,000	Number of reels	85
General overhead	0.911 × material costs per reel		

The capital-intensive structure of a paper company coupled with the cyclical nature of the industry makes accurate cost information an important strategic tool. Though current demand exceeds existing capacity, managers at Forest Industries know that a downturn is inevitable. They understood different pricing and production mix strategies are necessary when the economic environment changes. Gaining an understanding of the costs associated with grade changes and slitting is a first step that will enable managers to more effectively manage their business in good times and in bad.

Required

A. Compute the volume-based, traditional cost per reel for grades A–D identified in Exhibit A.
B. What is the total cost for Forest Industries to conduct a grade change?
C. What is the grade change cost for each reel? (*Hint:* The reel cost will differ because batch sizes are not equal.)
D. What is the cost to slit a reel of paperboard? (*Hint:* How many reels are slit? Do all reels require slitting services?)
E. Using the information in Exhibit B, calculate the amount of general overhead to be applied to each reel of paper.
F. Determine the activity-based cost for grades A–D.
G. Prepare a chart that illustrates the percentage change in costs between the volume-based system and the strategic activity-based cost system (ABC cost − volume-based system cost) ÷ volume-based system cost.
H. As a consultant to Forest Industries, what action would you recommend?

COMPUTERIZED MANUFACTURING SYSTEMS

How do we implement a computerized manufacturing system?

In previous chapters, we examined accounting systems for accumulating production costs. Job-order, process costing, and activity-based systems provide means for a company to track the flow of materials, labor, and overhead costs through the manufacturing process and to attach these costs to particular units of production. Managers use these systems to determine production costs and to monitor and evaluate the manufacturing process. The systems also are used to determine inventory costs and cost of goods sold for a particular fiscal period.

Like other components of a company's accounting system, the manufacturing systems used by most companies are computerized. Costs and physical data (number of units, production time, product identification) are maintained in databases. Data about purchases and use of materials, labor used in particular processes, and overhead are entered into the computer system by employees. The computer system accumulates these costs and attaches them to particular products or jobs.

This chapter describes the components and functions of computerized manufacturing systems. It provides an example of a simple computerized job-order system that could be used by a small business to accumulate job costs.

FOOD FOR THOUGHT

How does a computerized manufacturing system differ from a manual system? What issues must a company consider in using a computerized system? Erin and Seth discuss these questions with Roberta, their accountant.

Erin: *Recording transactions and preparing financial reports with our current accounting system is labor-intensive and a bit slow. It takes us several hours a week to record transactions and prepare reports. Sometimes we are several days or even weeks behind in updating our accounts.*

Seth: *At times, these delays are a major problem because we do not have accurate cost data for pricing our products. In some cases, we have sold products at prices below their costs, because our data are not timely. Should we be looking at a computerized accounting system?*

Roberta: *Yes, there are a number of good systems on the market that are not expensive and that will meet your needs.*

Seth: *How different are these systems from what we have been using? Will a computerized system be difficult for us to learn?*

OBJECTIVES

Once you have completed this chapter, you should be able to:

1 Identify the primary modules of a computerized manufacturing system.

2 Describe the components of a computerized information system used to process data in a manufacturing company.

3 Explain the use of relational databases to perform product cost functions.

COMPONENTS OF A COMPUTERIZED MANUFACTURING SYSTEM

OBJECTIVE 1

Identify the primary modules of a computerized manufacturing system.

Many of the mechanical functions of an accounting system, keeping track of cost data and updating account balances, and preparing schedules and reports from account data can be automated. Computers are capable of processing data through a series of steps to produce standard outputs such as reports. Consequently, certain accounting functions are automated in most companies.

Computerized accounting systems, even those for small companies like Young Designs, Inc., are composed of modules. Each module provides a mechanism for recording and reporting specific types of business activities. Common modules are those associated with the most common business activities: sales and customer relations, purchasing and inventory management, production, human resources, asset management, and financial management. A separate module is usually responsible for the general ledger and external financial reporting (GAAP-based financial statements) functions. Exhibit 1 illustrates an accounting system as a set of component modules.

Exhibit 1 Components of an Accounting Information System

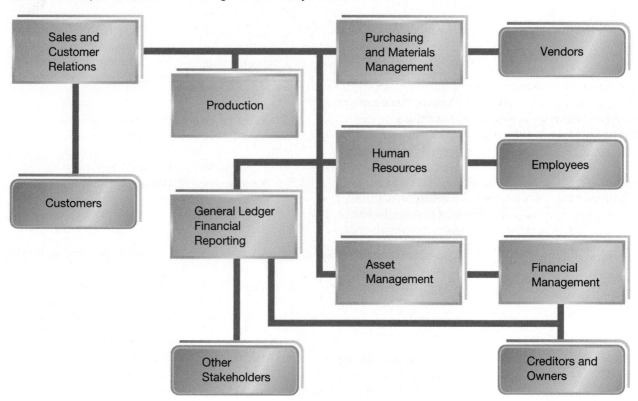

Each component in the information system has a particular role:

- The **sales module** receives sales order data from customers and maintains accounts receivable information.
- The **purchasing and materials management module** provides purchase order data to vendors. Vendors are those who supply specific products to a company. This module maintains accounts payable and inventory information. In a manufacturing company, this module is especially important for keeping track of the costs and use of raw materials.
- The **human resources module** maintains data about employees, hours worked, and wage rates. It is used for preparing payroll and payroll tax information.
- The **production module** tracks the flow of costs through the manufacturing process.
- The **asset management module** identifies long-term asset costs, their expected useful lives, and where these assets are located in a company.
- The **financial management module** keeps track of debt, when repayment is due, interest rates, and shareholder information. Also, it is used for managing a company's cash flows.
- The **general ledger/financial reporting module** provides information for use by external stakeholders, including shareholders and government regulators.

All of the modules are linked together in the system so they can interact with each other to share data. Some businesses use one software application that integrates all of these functions. **Systems that integrate most of the business information functions as a basis for management decisions are referred to as** *enterprise resource planning (ERP) systems.* Many large companies have implemented these systems from ERP developers such as **SAP, PeopleSoft,** and **Oracle.** Other companies may rely on software from different vendors for different components of their systems. Many smaller companies rely on software that handles most of the company's accounting functions. These systems lack the capabilities of larger systems but provide for most of the common accounting and financial reporting functions small businesses need. Thus, computerized accounting systems can be small basic systems such as QuickBooks, MAS, Peachtree, or Simply Accounting; middle-market systems such as Microsoft Business Solutions or ACCPAC; or large-scale systems such as SAP and Oracle Financials. Regardless of size, each of these systems is made up of component modules.

The modules available in SAP are described in the following sections. These modules are typical of those in other ERP systems. Most large manufacturing companies have implemented ERP systems, SAP being the most common for these companies. The primary modules, nearly all of which are linked to the manufacturing process, include:

- Financial accounting
- Controlling
- Asset management
- Project management
- Human resources
- Quality management
- Production planning
- Materials management
- Sales and distribution

These functions are integrated so that the work of one module overlaps with others in some cases.

The **financial accounting** module is designed for automated management and external reporting of general ledger, accounts receivable, accounts payable, and other accounts based on a user-defined chart of accounts. Key elements of the financial accounting module include:

Financial Accounting
Financial system for recording of transactions
General ledger for maintaining account balances and preparing financial statements

http://ingram.
swlearning.com

Learn more about these ERP developers and other computerized accounting systems.

Accounts payable for tracking amounts owed to vendors
Accounts receivable for tracking amounts owed by customers
Treasury for cash flow management
Consolidation for consolidation of a parent company's subsidiaries

The **controlling** module maintains and reports information about costs and revenues associated with specific functions or divisions of a company. Controlling is a tool for management decisions. Key elements of the controlling application module include:

Controlling
Cost center accounting for determining the costs of specific functions or divisions of a company
Internal order accounting for tracking the flow of costs among functions or departments within a company
Product costing analysis for determining and evaluating product costs
Profitability analysis for evaluating divisional and product profit performance
Activity-based costing for determining activity-based costs and allocation of overhead in the manufacturing process

The **asset management** module is designed for keeping track of property and equipment and similar long-term fixed assets. The asset management module includes:

Asset Management
Maintenance and repair for tracking costs and timing of these activities
Sale of assets for monitoring disposal decisions
Asset replacement for evaluating replacement decisions
Depreciation for determining and tracking asset depreciation for financial reporting, cost, and tax purposes
Investment management for making decisions about new acquisitions or replacements of property and equipment

The **project management** module supports the planning, control, and monitoring of long-term, highly complex projects with defined goals. It accelerates work and data flows and reduces routine tasks. The module includes:

Project Management
Funds and resource management to help project managers keep track of resources used in a project
Quality control to help with including quality issues in a project
Time management to assist in scheduling activities associated with a project

The **human resources** module is used for managing human resources and for maintaining employee and related financial data. The module includes a range of capabilities such as:

Human Resources
Recruitment for keeping track of job requirements and postings
Benefits for tracking employee benefits
Time management for determining and scheduling employee labor hours
Incentive wages for determining bonuses
Business trip management for maintaining reimbursement information and determining travel costs
Payroll for processing employee wages
Training and events management for coordination of training activities
Personnel development for tracking development activities for individual employees
Workforce planning for determining labor and labor cost requirements for various functions or divisions

The **quality management** application module is a quality control and information system supporting quality planning, inspection, and control for manufacturing, costing, and procurement. Primary elements of the module are:

Quality Management
Quality inspection for monitoring quality control
Quality planning for determining quality control requirements

The **production planning** module is used to plan and control the manufacturing activities of a company. The module includes:

Production Planning
Bills of material for identifying the materials that are used in each product
Master production scheduling for determining production schedules and the use of equipment and labor in the production process
Material requirements planning for coordinating the amount and availability of materials for scheduled production runs
Shop floor control for coordinating the flow of materials through production processes
Production orders for tracking order status and completion dates
Product costing and activity-based costing for determining the costs of units of production

The **materials management** module supports the procurement and inventory functions occurring in day-to-day business operations. This module includes:

Materials Management
Material procurement for purchasing materials and maintaining vendor data
Inventory management for determining inventory availability and costs
Reorder point processing facilitates determining when to reorder and placing orders
Invoice verification tracks orders and ensures company policies are followed in the ordering process
Material valuation provides for identifying quality or quantity problems with materials received
Vendor evaluation for monitoring vendor quality
External services procurement for facilitating the outsourcing of services
Warehouse management for maintaining data about the location of materials and for transferring materials into and out of the warehouse

The **sales and distribution** module helps to optimize all the tasks and activities carried out in sales, delivery, and billing. Key elements of the module include:

Sales and Distribution
Inquiry processing for responding to customer inquiries
Quotation processing for providing pricing information to customers
Sales order processing for recording and tracking sales orders
Delivery processing for recording and tracking delivery of goods to customers
Billing for submitting sales invoices to customers

For a large manufacturing company, these modules facilitate the financial, marketing, and production processes necessary for managing the company. A large-scale system of this type is complex but provides a mechanism for recording, maintaining, and reporting information for decisions throughout a company. The computer processes and infrastructure necessary to support the system are described in the next section.

A goal of modern information systems is to automate the supply chain (also referred to as the supply chain) to reduce delays in the production and delivery process and to reduce costs associated with data entry. The supply chain includes the entities and functions associated with procuring materials and labor, employing these materials and labor in the manufacturing process, and selling and distributing completed goods to customers. Exhibit 2 illustrates the supply chain and specific ERP modules that are important in the automation process.

The supply chain is automated when most of the functions occur without direct human intervention. The system identifies resource requirements and automatically

Exhibit 2 Automating the Value Chain

places orders with suppliers. Once goods are received, they are requisitioned and placed into production and tracked by the information system. Orders are received from customers and are processed by the system, which then schedules the production of goods to meet these orders. The goal is not the elimination of human interaction, which may still be needed for the physical movement and production of goods, but to reduce human involvement in support services associated with purchasing and order processing.

Case In Point

The Values of Manufacturing Systems

Profitable construction companies understand the cost of each job and use proper software for accounting and job costing. A purchasing component is a significant aspect of job costing software. For example, contractors who use such a system report improved control over purchasing activities and cost flow.

Source: Contractor's Business Management Report. New York, October 2002. Issue 10, page 3.

1   SELF-STUDY PROBLEM

Marco Co. constructs commercial buildings. Marco must keep accurate and timely information about its construction activities and costs.

Required Describe the modules of a computerized information system that Marco would need to keep track of its cost information and why they are important.

The solution to Self-Study Problem 1 appears at the end of the chapter.

DATA PROCESSING IN A COMPUTERIZED SYSTEM

OBJECTIVE 2

Describe the components of a computerized information system used to process data in a manufacturing company.

Each module of an information system receives data, stores the data, processes the data to create useful information, and reports that information to decision makers, as indicated in Exhibit 3.

Input into the system originates in business activities and can come from a variety of sources. It may originate as paper documents, such as **sales orders** prepared by or for customers or **sales receipts** indicating the sale of goods to customers. In computerized systems, data must be entered into the computer system. Data entry may be in the form of keystrokes entered by clerical personnel who transfer data from paper documents to computer files. Increasingly, data are entered directly into computer systems. For example, many retail stores use scanners to read bar code data from products. The bar codes are linked to the company's inventory data so that sales prices, costs, and inventory amounts can be recorded without keying data into the system.

Data associated with production processes can be entered by factory workers using computer terminals or scanning devices. Employees can enter identification codes

Exhibit 3 Data Processing in a Computerized Information System

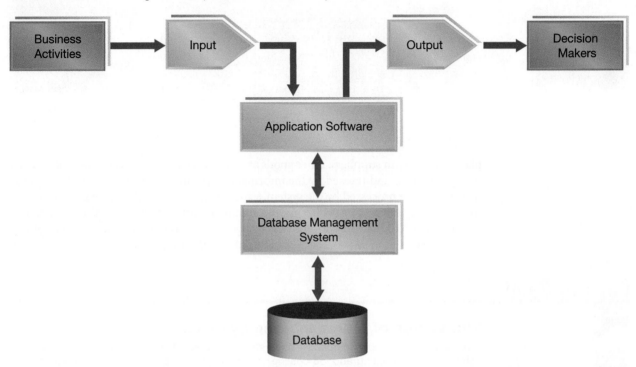

http://ingram.
swlearning.com
....
Visit the online shopping
sites of Amazon.com,
Southwest Airlines, and
Banana Republic.

at the beginning and end of a process that can be used to track the labor associated with that process. Tags attached to materials can be scanned to track their use in the production process.

Many companies provide web-based input systems that permit customers to place orders directly using the Internet. Companies such as **Amazon**, **Southwest Airlines**, and **Banana Republic** provide for online shopping, reservations, and sales. Data entered by customers updates company order and inventory files. Customers also can retrieve information about their orders from these systems.

The use of computer networks, like the Internet, to provide for customer sales is referred to as *E-business.* Some E-business systems provide a means for a company to receive sales orders from customers. These systems are referred to as business-to-customer (b2c) systems. Other systems permit companies to order goods from vendors and to track order information. These systems are referred to as business-to-business (b2b) systems. In either system, most of the customer data entry is prepared by the customer. These data become a basis for recording sales, accounts receivable, materials purchased, accounts payable, cost of goods sold, and related transactions. Thus, many routine transactions can be recorded and processed automatically without the seller or buyer having to take special steps to record these transactions.

Application software **includes the computer programs that permit data to be recorded and processed.** If a customer enters an order using a web browser, application software is needed to collect that data, to record it in the company's files, and to process the data to ensure that the appropriate actions occur. For example, a customer order must be recorded, shipping must be notified of the order so the goods can be shipped, a bill may need to be prepared and sent to the customer, and sales and accounts receivable accounts need to be updated. Application software automates these functions.

Databases often are used to store data that can be accessed by various components of a system. Data are transferred by application software to databases. **A** *database* **is a set of computerized files where company data are stored in a form that facilitates retrieval and updating of the data. A** *database management system* **controls database functions to ensure data are recorded properly and can be accessed only by those authorized to record, update, or retrieve the data.**

Many internal controls are built into computerized information systems. These controls are important for protecting data and for helping to prevent errors. Controls, such as passwords, are needed to make sure data are not accessed or modified by unauthorized personnel. Controls built into database management systems prevent more than one user from updating a particular record at the same time and make sure that all appropriate parts of a database are updated when a transaction is recorded.

Other controls require management action. For example, databases must be backed up on a regular basis so data will not be lost if a computer system fails or is destroyed. A company also must have a plan in case its computer system is destroyed because of natural disaster, sabotage, or terrorism. Failure to provide backup systems can result in a company being unable to do business if its primary system is unusable.

Output from information systems often is in the form of reports. These reports may contain prescribed information and may be prepared automatically by a system. They may be paper reports or electronic documents that are sent to users. Many output reports can be modified and retrieved as needed by the user. For example, production managers need information about outstanding orders and the status of existing orders.

Regardless of which of the modules in a company's accounting system is involved, data flow through the system from inputs to outputs. The processes that take place in association with these data flows depend on the module. Data flows are initiated by business activities but also stimulate these activities. For example, a request for materials results from a need for materials to be used in a production process. However, data about the request also result in a company ordering materials from vendors.

Computerized systems rely on networks for processing data. *Computer networks* **include the cables that connect the clients and servers and the hardware and software needed to make the networks function properly.** Exhibit 4 illustrates a computer network. Input devices, such as scanners, and client workstations provide a basis for data input and for users to access information from the computer system. A **client** is a computer or other network device that uses software that requests services from other software. The services are provided by server software that resides on other computers, referred to as **servers**.

Exhibit 4

An Illustration of a
Computer Network

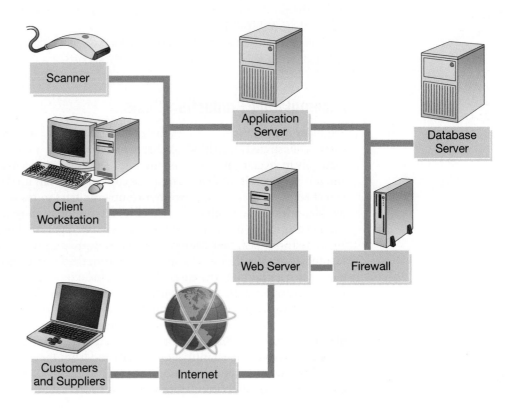

Application software usually resides on one or more **application servers** on the network. Application servers are connected to **database servers** where data are stored and managed. Companies engaged in E-business or which permit their employees to connect to their network from locations outside of the business, such as customer businesses, often use web servers to provide the software needed to interact across the Internet. The Internet provides a network so that almost any computer can connect to a company to do business.

Automating a company's supply chain and production process involves network connections among a company, its suppliers, and customers. Application software at the manufacturer identifies when materials are needed and places orders with suppliers with which the company partners. Arrangements with the suppliers provide for access by the manufacturer's computer system with the suppliers' systems so that purchase orders can be processed on a real-time basis. Orders placed by the manufacturer are filled by suppliers who ship goods to the manufacturer and submit bills to the manufacturer through its computer system. Bills can be processed by the manufacturer and funds can be transferred to suppliers.

Once materials are received by the manufacturer they can be transferred to production automatically as called for in production schedules or as requested by factory employees. Many companies now use just-in-time systems that move materials directly from receiving into production with a need for storing the materials in a warehouse. The fewer movements and less handling associated with the materials reduces production costs. Materials are tagged with computer-readable tags so that they can be tracked through the production process. Thus, at any time, the manufacturing company can determine the physical location, quantity, and cost of materials in production.

Customers can place orders with a manufacturer using the manufacturer's computer system. The orders can be placed directly through a web interface, for example, that provides access to the manufacturer's product price list. Because of the efficiencies of automated systems, a manufacturer may not produce goods until orders are received, thereby eliminating costs of maintaining finished goods inventories. Orders from customers pull the production process. The order is recorded by the manufacturer's production scheduling system, which notifies the materials management system to order materials. As soon as they are completed, goods are delivered to the customer. Streamlining the production process and eliminating unnecessary operations and costs is a major objective of ERP systems.

The next section examines various processes in a company's production system associated with the accumulation of production costs.

Accumulating Production Costs

Production costs include direct materials, direct labor, and manufacturing overhead costs as illustrated in Exhibit 5. Direct materials costs are derived from a company's materials management system or module. That module records the costs of materials and provides a basis for determining the costs of materials used in a production process. Direct labor costs are derived from a company's human resources module. That module identifies the amounts paid to various types of employees. Some manufacturing overhead costs are derived from the asset management module, which tracks the costs associated with facilities, equipment, and tools used in the production process. Other manufacturing overhead costs are derived from the financial accounting or other modules, which accumulate the costs of utilities, insurance, supplies, and similar items that are associated with the manufacturing process. Indirect labor costs included in manufacturing overhead are derived from the human resources module.

The cost data from the materials management, human resources, and other modules in Exhibit 5 are inputs to the production system. In the production system, these costs are linked to the quantity of materials and labor used in a particular job or period.

The difference between a job-order and a process costing system is largely in the cost object used for accumulating the costs. In the case of a job-order system, the cost

Exhibit 5 Accumulating Production Costs in Job-Order or Process Systems

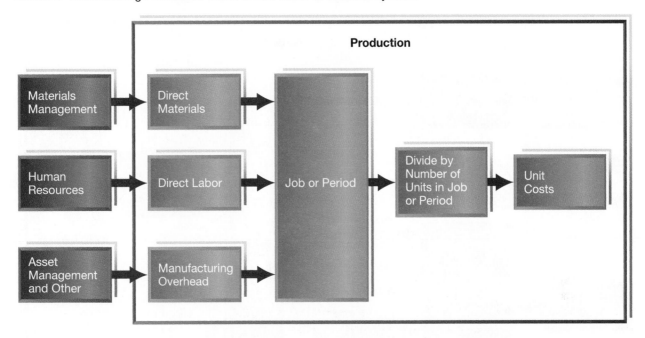

object is a job. Materials, labor, and overhead costs are accumulated for each job. In a process costing system, the costs are accumulated for a fiscal period for each product that is produced during that period. These costs are then assigned to each unit of product that results from the job or the period to determine unit costs. In a traditional system, manufacturing overhead costs are assigned to the production process using a predetermined allocation rate and basis, such as labor hours or labor costs.

In an activity-based costing system, manufacturing overhead costs are first grouped based on the types of costs, such as batch-, product-, or facility-level costs, as illustrated in Exhibit 6. These costs are allocated to each job or production process based on the drivers that are associated with each level of cost. Otherwise, the accumulation of costs is similar between traditional and activity-based costing systems.

The key to understanding any production system is to understand that the objective is to determine the cost of each unit produced. That cost is determined from the cost of materials that were used in producing those units (cost per item times the number of each item used), the cost of labor used in producing those items (labor rate for each type of employee times the amount of time each employee worked), and the amount of overhead allocated to those units. The total cost associated with the units produced is then divided by the number of units produced to determine the unit cost.

Automating a production cost system involves linking the modules that identify and track materials labor and overhead costs so that these costs can be accumulated throughout the production process. The next section of this chapter examines database management systems that are used to identify and track production costs and provides a simple example of a job-order cost system.

2 ┃ *SELF-STUDY PROBLEM*   Suppose you want to automate a production system so that materials and labor costs can be determined and tracked based on inputs within the production system.

Required Describe a computerized system for this purpose.

The solution to Self-Study Problem 2 appears at the end of the chapter.

Exhibit 6 Accumulating Production Costs in an Activity-Based Costing System

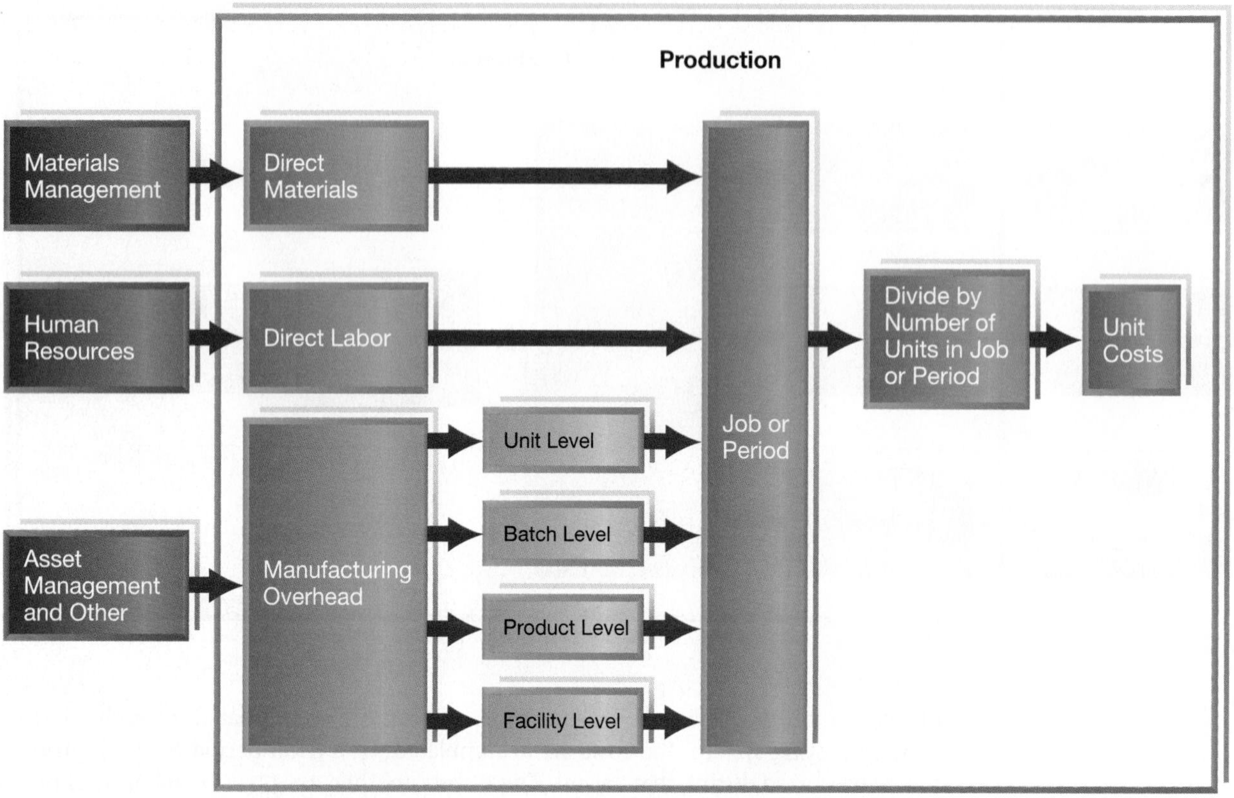

DATABASE SYSTEMS AND PRODUCT COSTS

OBJECTIVE 3

Explain the use of relational databases to perform product cost functions.

This chapter uses the example of Kwiki Oil Company to describe a computerized job-order system. Kwiki Oil is a small company that provides motor oil changes for passenger cars and light trucks. Most of the company's business is drive-in. The driver pulls into a bay where the oil and oil filter are replaced. The company's goal is to complete the process in 15 minutes or less. Three employees work on each vehicle, though two of the three often are working on more than one vehicle at the same time. Kwiki Oil's production system tracks the materials and labor that are used in each vehicle, as a basis for determining the cost of each job. After examining the components of a database, we will describe a simple job-order system for Kwiki Oil.

Most computerized accounting, including ERP, systems are constructed as relational databases. **A *relational database* is a set of related files that are linked together so that the files can be updated and information can be retrieved from the files efficiently.**

A relational database stores data in tables. **A *table* is a file that contains data represented as rows and columns.** Each column identifies a particular attribute of the entity or process described in the table. Each attribute is referred to as a **field** in the table. A vendor table would include vendor name and address attributes, for example. Each row in the table contains a record of data for a particular entity. Rows in a vendor table would contain data for each vendor. Separate tables are used for specific types of entities (vendors and products) and processes (purchase orders and production). Each table contains one or more **primary keys** that uniquely identify the entities or processes recorded in the rows of the table. These primary keys are used to connect the tables into relationships. The primary key in one table connects to the primary key or a **foreign key** in another table. A foreign key is a field that is a primary key in a different table. For example, Part_Number might be a primary key in a materials table. The same field might be a foreign key in a vendor table that identifies which parts are ordered from that vendor.

Exhibit 7 illustrates the tables and relationships in a database. The boxes represent tables, identified by their captions at the top. Fields stored in each table are listed in the boxes. Fields in bold are primary keys. Lines connect the keys that form the relationships in the database.

Exhibit 7
Tables in a Relational Database

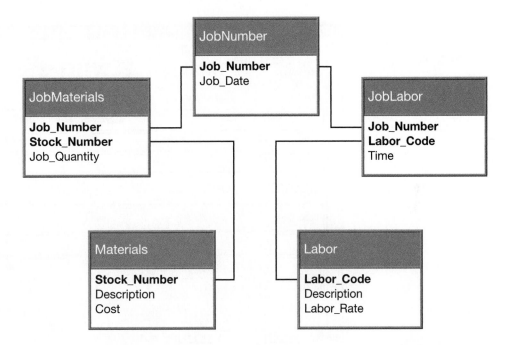

The relationships permit a change to a field that is in more than one table to affect each table containing that field. For example, when a job number is entered into the system, the Job_Number field is updated in the JobNumber, JobMaterials, and JobLabor tables. The relationships also permit a user to obtain data from more than one table. For instance, a particular job number can be used to obtain data from the JobMaterials and JobLabor tables because these tables are linked to the job number.

Thus, a relational database is a network of information objects that permits data to be stored and retrieved efficiently. Knowing the relationships in the database, a user can retrieve any combination of fields to serve a particular decision need.

Individual tables in the database store data about a particular entity or activity. Exhibit 8 provides an example of a simple table. The top row identifies the attributes stored in the table. The remaining rows are records. The first column of each record identifies the stock number that uniquely identifies that record. Records are listed sequentially by the stock number, which is the primary key for the table. Other fields identify other attributes associated with each stock number, such as the description and unit cost of each stock item.

Exhibit 8
An Example of a Table in a Database

Stock_Number	Description	Cost
F150	oil filter	$6.43
F160	oil filter	$7.20
F170	oil filter	$8.35
L235	5-30 weight	$0.92
L236	10-30 weight	$0.98
L245	5-30 weight premium	$1.15
L246	10-30 weight premium	$1.21

Data are entered into a database using **forms**. Forms are computer templates for entering data. Exhibit 9 provides an illustration of a simple form. The form provides input areas where data are keyed into the system. Form fields are linked to attributes in tables in the database. Thus, when a new job number is entered in the form in Exhibit 9, data are added to the JobNumber table and related tables in the company's database.

Exhibit 9

An Example of a Form for Data Entry

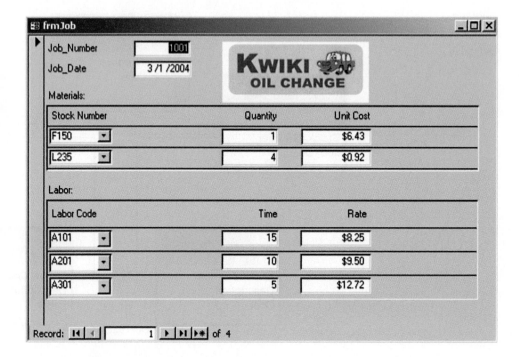

As noted earlier, much of the data needed by a computerized system may be entered automatically through scanning devices. Customers enter data in forms when they place orders using web-based systems. Much of the data needed in database systems are entered by a company's employees who are responsible for various data entry functions.

Each module of a computerized accounting system consists of tables and forms that collect and store data needed for the activities associated with that module. Individual tables often are part of more than one module. For example, an inventory table may be accessed by the sales module to determine product availability and price. It may be accessed by the production module to update it for finished goods.

The following section illustrates a database accounting system that is typical of a computerized production system, though it uses simple examples with limited transactions and examines only a small part of a total manufacturing system. The illustration is designed to help you see how accounting data are processed in actual systems from data entry to storage and reporting.

An Illustration of an Accounting System

This section illustrates various components of a computerized manufacturing system. The illustration examines the job cost module of Kwiki Oil Co.'s system. Example transactions are provided for March 2004 to illustrate production activities: creating a job number, accumulating direct materials and direct labor costs, allocating manufacturing overhead costs, and creating a job cost report.

The software used in this module is a Microsoft® Access database, which can be found on the CD that accompanies this text or downloaded from http://ingram.swlearning.com. Directions for use of the software are provided as part of the description that follows.

http://ingram. swlearning.com

Download database file (also available on the student CD).

To use the database, you must have a computer with a Microsoft® Windows® operating system and Access 2000 or a more recent version.

Access is application software built around a database system. It is inadequate for large-scale accounting applications but is useful for illustrating database systems. Unlike most business systems, all of the software runs on a workstation. Though it can be configured to run on a network with separate client and server components, it is easier to use and to understand when it is operated from a single computer.

Copying and Opening the Database

We highly recommend copying the database to another disk or your hard drive before using it. To copy the database, first insert the CD into your CD-ROM drive, open Windows® Explorer and select your CD-ROM drive where the database is located. Click on KwikiOil.mdb and drag it to a folder on your other disk or hard drive. Release the mouse button, and the database will be copied. It is a good idea to make several copies of the database under different names (KwikiOil1.mdb, KwikiOil2.mdb, and so on). If the database is modified or accidentally corrupted, you still have an unmodified version for use.

Use one of the following options to open the database.

Option 1. Open Access by clicking Start, Programs, Microsoft Access. Once Access has opened, click File, Open. Double-click KwikiOil.mdb in the folder to which it was copied.
Option 2. Open Windows Explorer. Select the folder in which the database was copied. Double-click on KwikiOil.mdb.

Database files can become large when they are modified through use. It is a good idea to compact the database periodically. To compact the database, open it in Access, click Tools, Database Utilities, Compact and Repair Database. The database will be compacted automatically. Compacting removes unused space in the database. Running a database from a 3.5″ disk requires frequent compacting.

Database Contents

A database consists of objects. Once the KwikiOil.mdb database has been opened, these objects appear in various categories: tables, queries, forms, reports, pages, macros, and modules. **Tables** contain the data stored in the system. **Queries** are short programs that permit a user to obtain data from one or more tables. **Forms** provide a means for entering or reading data stored in the database. **Reports** provide summary information intended primarily to be printed. Macros are sequences of steps a user performs to complete a particular task. A macro runs a task without the user having to enter each keystroke separately. **Pages** provide a means of creating web documents for accessing a database. **Modules** are computer programs (written in Visual Basic) to provide higher level functions in the database. The Kwiki Oil Co. database contains no macros or modules.

Tables. Tables are the key to understanding a database. Tables contain the data in the database. Other objects manipulate these data by adding new data, modifying existing data, deleting data, or retrieving data.

Begin by examining the tblJobNumber table. Click on the Tables tab in the Database window. Double-click on tblJobNumber or click on tblJobNumber and then click the Open button. Columns in the table identify categories (also known as fields or attributes) of data. The Job_Number is a code that uniquely identifies each job. Numbers are listed consecutively so that any missing jobs are easy to identify. Job_Date identifies the date that the job was completed and provides a basis for determining when revenues and costs associated with the job should be recognized. Close the table by clicking the X box in the upper right corner of the table window. Do not click the X box in the Access window (top right of screen) or you will close the Access program. If you close Access by mistake, reopen it and the KwikiOil.mdb database.

Next examine the tblMaterials table. This table identifies materials that Kwiki Oil uses in its jobs. The Stock_Number uniquely identifies each item. Description provides a narrative explanation for each item, and Cost identifies the unit cost for each item. The example assumes that each item has a specific cost.

The tblMaterials table is an example of a master file. Master files contain data that are relatively stable and that may be updated periodically. The tblJobNumber table is an example of a transaction file. Transaction files are updated each time a new transaction, such as a job, is recorded.

Other tables in the database include the tblLabor table that identifies the types of employees who work on jobs and the hourly rate earned by each type of employee. The tblJobMaterials table links data about materials with each job. It describes the materials that were used in a job and the quantity of those materials for each job. The tblJobLabor table links data about labor with each job. It identifies the employees who worked on each job and the time each employee spent on each job. Time is measured in minutes in this table.

You can examine the relationships among all the tables in the database by clicking on the Relationships button ⇒ in the top row of buttons in the database window. The relationship diagram that appears contains the tables and identifies the fields in each table. Lines in the diagram link the primary and foreign keys. Close the Relationship window by clicking on the bottom X in the upper right corner of the screen.

Entering Transactions. Job cost data would be entered by the supervisor in charge of each job. To enter a transaction, click on the Forms tab of the Database window. Then open the frmJob form. Notice that the form identifies the Job Number and Date. It also identifies materials and labor that were used in each job. You can click on the Record selector arrow ▶ at the bottom of the form window to view completed jobs.

To enter a new job, click on the New Record selector arrow ▶* at the bottom of the form window. Two sets of arrows appear near the bottom of the form. Use the bottom set of arrows to move among the jobs. Enter a new Job Number, 1006. You may wish to press the Caps Lock key when entering transaction data. Press the Tab key to go to the Job_Date box. Type 03/06/2004 in the box. Click on the Stock Number selector arrow ▾ to see a list of materials. Click on F150. The unit cost of the material appears in the Cost box. Enter 1 for the Quantity. In the next row, click on the selector arrow and select L245. Enter 5 for the Quantity.

Repeat the process to enter the labor used in the job. In the first row under labor code, select A101 from the drop-down box and enter 13 for Time. On the next row select A201 and enter 7; then select A301 on the third row and enter 4. To save the order, you can click the New Record selector arrow ▶* at the bottom of the form or close the form window.

To view the data entered for the order, open the tblJobNumber, tblJobMaterials, and tblJobLabor tables, scroll to the last row, and observe the new data.

Job Cost Reports. You can view a job cost report, including the one just entered, by selecting the Reports tab on the Database window and double-clicking on rptJob. A report appears listing the orders that have been entered in the database. To see the entire report you may need to enlarge the window and the zoom control on the menu bar. Jobs are listed in the report by Job Number. Each job appears on a separate page. The job you just entered is listed on the last page of the report. Use the page selection arrow at the bottom of the report to view page 6. A copy of the report can be printed if a printer is available. Close the report when you have finished examining it.

Determining production costs for Kwiki Oil is straightforward. Each job represents a unit of product. Costs are accumulated for each unit based on the quantity of each type of material used in the job times the cost of each type of material, the quantity of each type of employee that worked on the job times the wage rate paid that type of employee, and an allocation of manufacturing overhead based on a rate per hour times the total number of labor hours associated with the job.

The job cost report identifies the materials, labor, and manufacturing overhead costs applied to each job. Manufacturing overhead is applied on the basis of total labor hours at a rate of $9.00 per labor hour.

Some of the data in the Kwiki Oil Co. Job Cost reports are derived from queries. Queries obtain data from tables, manipulate these data to produce new data items, and store them temporarily. Click on the Queries tab to view the queries. Double-click on qryMaterials and view the data that appear in the query. The query is used to compute the total cost for each item of materials used on a job. The qryLabor query is used to compute the labor cost for each job.

---

3 SELF-STUDY PROBLEM

The description of Kwiki Oil Company's job-order system refers to tables, forms, queries, and reports that are used in the system.

Required Describe the purpose of tables, forms, queries, and reports and how each of these is related to the others.

The solution to Self-Study Problem 3 appears at the end of the chapter.

REVIEW

SUMMARY of IMPORTANT CONCEPTS

1. Most manufacturing companies use computerized accounting systems. Typically, these systems are part of larger information systems that integrate various management functions throughout an organization.

2. Computerized information systems are separated into modules. Common modules include sales, purchasing and materials management, human resources, production, asset management, financial management, and general ledger/financial reporting.

3. Enterprise resource planning (ERP) systems integrate the various management functions into a comprehensive information system.

4. ERP systems, like SAP, include many functions such as financial accounting, controlling, asset management, project management, human resources, quality management, production planning, materials management, and sales and distribution.

5. A goal of many companies is to automate their supply chain so that interaction with customers and vendors can be handled by the computer system with little human intervention.

6. Computer systems receive, store, and process data to create useful information that can be reported to decision makers.

7. E-business uses computer networks to provide customer sales.

8. Application software is part of a computer system that includes computer programs that permit data to be recorded and processed.

9. Data are stored in databases, and database management systems control the database functions to ensure accuracy and security of data.

10. Client-server networks provide for interaction by users through client workstations to application and database servers that process and store data.

11. The production module obtains input from the materials, human resources, asset management, and other modules. The production module accumulates production costs

and allocates these to individual units based on the number of units produced during a period or job.

12. Computerized information systems use relational databases, which store data in related tables. Forms are used to enter data in tables, and queries are used to retrieve and manipulate data for preparing reports.

DEFINE

TERMS and CONCEPTS DEFINED in this CHAPTER

application software   (M142)
computer network   (M143)
database   (M142)
database management system   (M142)
E-business   (M142)

enterprise resource planning (ERP) systems
   (M138)
relational database   (M146)
table   (M146)

SELF-STUDY PROBLEM SOLUTIONS

SSP6-1   Materials, labor, and overhead costs are important for a construction company. The company must determine the materials required for each construction project and track the use of those materials at each project. It must determine the amount of time employees spend on each project. Asset costs associated with the use of construction equipment also are important. The company must determine which types of equipment are used on each project and how much time the equipment is used. Consequently, materials management, human resources, asset management, and production are all essential. If the company borrows money to finance its projects during the construction process, the financial management module also may be important.

SSP6-2   Input data for the system would require computer-readable identifiers for materials and employees. Tags that could be scanned would be attached to materials. The tags would identify the item; the system could then link the item code back to a database that recorded the cost of the item and when and where the item was used. Electronic cards or badges could be issued to employees. These would be scanned at the beginning and end of a production process. The cards would identify the employee and permit the system to determine the amount of time an employee spent on a particular process or job. These data could be used by a database to determine labor costs for a period or job. The scanning devices would provide the clients for the network, which would connect to application servers that processed the data and database servers that maintained the data.

SSP6-3   Tables are used to store data in a relational database. Some of the data may be relatively fixed and provide information for other tables or processes. Some of the data changes in response to events or transactions associated with operations of the business, such as a production process or sale. Forms are used primarily to provide a means of entering data into a system. The data entered are stored in and used to update tables. Thus, the items in a form must be linked directly to fields in tables. Queries provide a means for obtaining data from various tables and summarizing these data (by summing, computing new variables, etc.) to provide a basis for preparing reports. Reports summarize data from the system in a format useful for decision makers.

Thinking Beyond the Question

How do we implement a computerized manufacturing system?

Computerized manufacturing systems are used by most manufacturing companies to facilitate the collection, reporting, and analysis of manufacturing cost information. What are some of the risks associated with using these systems?

QUESTIONS

Q6-1
Obj. 1
Why are integrated business systems more efficient than using individual systems for different functions in a business?

Q6-2
Obj. 1
How would the human resources module for a manufacturing company differ from that for a retail or service company?

Q6-3
Obj. 1
Irmo Co.'s asset management module lists each piece of equipment the company has purchased, when it was purchased, its cost, its expected life, and its location in the company. Why would the company want this information?

Q6-4
Obj. 1
Kreel Co.'s financial management module lists each loan the company has outstanding, when the money was borrowed, the amount borrowed, the interest rate, the dates payments were made, and the amounts of these payments. Why is this information important to the company?

Q6-5
Obj. 1
What purposes does a manufacturing company's purchasing module serve? What accounts and types of transactions will be associated with this module?

Q6-6
Obj. 1
What purposes does a manufacturing company's human resources module serve? What accounts and types of transactions will be associated with this module?

Q6-7
Obj. 1
Street Inc.'s purchasing module lists each vendor's name, address, the materials purchased from the vendor, and when purchases were made. What uses might the company make of this information?

Q6-8
Obj. 1
Why would the sales module of **Dell Computer Corporation** differ from the sales module of **Wal-Mart**? What transactions would Dell record as part of its sales process that would differ from those of Wal-Mart?

Q6-9
Obj. 1
Why is it important for the accounting department of a manufacturing company to receive data from human resources? What internal control function is served by this process?

Q6-10
Obj. 1
Why is it important for the accounting department of a manufacturing company to receive data from purchasing and receiving? What internal control function is served by this process?

Q6-11
Obj. 2
What is a computer network? Why are they used by businesses to maintain accounting systems?

Q6-12
Obj. 2
What is the purpose of a database management system?

Q6-13
Obj. 3
Suppose a company sells to customers through the web. Customers are required to pay for their orders with credit cards at the time of the order. What primary activities would be required of the sales module to process and account for these orders?

EXERCISES

If your instructor is using Personal Trainer® in this course, you may complete your assignments online.

E6-1
Write a short definition for each of the terms listed in the *Terms and Concepts Defined in this Chapter* section.

E6-2
Objs. 1, 2
Complete each sentence with the appropriate term.

1. Systems that integrate most of the business information functions are referred to as _____.

2. The use of computer networks, like the Internet, to provide for customer sales is referred to as _____.

3. _____ includes the computer programs that permit data to be recorded and processed.

4. A _____ is a set of computerized files where company data are stored in a form that facilitates retrieval and updating of the data.

5. A _____ controls database functions to ensure data are recorded properly and can be accessed only by those authorized to record, update, or retrieve the data.

6. The interaction of a company and its suppliers and customers is known as the company's _____.

7. A _____ is a set of related files that are linked together so that the files can be updated and information can be retrieved from the files efficiently.

E6-3
Objs. 1, 2

Match each term with the appropriate definition.

a. application software
b. database management system
c. database
d. E-business

e. enterprise resource planning (ERP) systems
f. relational database
g. supply chain

1. a set of computerized files where company data are stored in a form that facilitates retrieval and updating of the data
2. a set of related files that are linked together so that the files can be updated and information can be retrieved from the files efficiently
3. controls database functions to ensure data are recorded properly and can be accessed only by those authorized to record, update, or retrieve the data
4. includes the computer programs that permit data to be recorded and processed
5. systems that integrate most of the business information functions
6. the interaction of a company and its suppliers and customers
7. the use of computer networks, like the Internet, to provide for customer sales

E6-4
Obj. 1

Complete each sentence with the appropriate term for a component in the information system.

1. The _____ receives sales order data from customers and maintains accounts receivable information.
2. The _____ provides purchase order data to vendors. Vendors are those who supply specific products to a company. This module maintains accounts payable and inventory information.
3. The _____ maintains data about employees, hours worked, and wage rates. It is used for preparing payroll and payroll tax information.
4. The _____ tracks the flow of costs through the manufacturing process.
5. The _____ identifies long-term asset costs, their expected useful lives, and where these assets are located in a company.
6. The _____ keeps track of debt, when repayment is due, interest rates, and shareholder information. It is also used for managing a company's cash flows.
7. The _____ provides information for use by external stakeholders, including shareholders and government regulators.

E6-5
Obj. 1

Dell Computer Corporation is a large, well-known manufacturer of computers for home and business. Assume you logged onto its web site, ordered a computer system, and paid for it by credit card. Describe the business activities that would occur at Dell, including linkages from the sales order system to other modules of the company's information system, in handling your order.

E6-6
Obj. 1

Great Plains Manufacturing Co.'s receiving department received an order of raw materials. How will information about the order affect the various modules of the company's information system?

E6-7
Obj. 1

For each of the functions listed below, identify the module of an ERP system that would provide that function from the following list.

a. financial accounting
b. controlling
c. asset management
d. project systems
e. human resources

f. quality management
g. production planning
h. materials management
i. sales and distribution

1. cash flow management
2. coordination of employee training
3. coordination of the flow of materials through the production process

4. determining and evaluating product costs
5. determining and tracking asset depreciation
6. determining costs of specific functions or divisions of a company
7. determining employee hours
8. determining production schedules
9. determining quality control requirements
10. evaluating asset replacement decisions
11. identifying materials used in each product
12. maintaining account balances and preparing financial reports
13. monitoring vendor quality
14. planning for long-term projects
15. processing employee wages
16. purchasing materials
17. recording sales orders
18. responding to customer inquiries
19. tracking amounts owed to vendors
20. warehouse management

E6-8
Obj. 1
What does it mean to automate a company's supply chain? What are the advantages of automating the supply chain for a manufacturing company?

E6-9
Obj. 2
What is a computer network? Why are they used by businesses to maintain accounting systems?

E6-10
Obj. 2
What is the purpose of a database management system?

E6-11
Obj. 2
Computer networks in many organizations include client applications, business management programs and databases on servers, and connections among the computers running these programs. For each of the following activities, identify the portions of the computer system that would be affected. Explain how the portions are affected.

1. Access to company data is requested
2. Records are updated
3. Data are transferred between a client and a server
4. New data for processing are entered
5. Data that are being used by another user are required
6. Data to print a report are obtained

E6-12
Obj. 3
Modern accounting information systems often are maintained as relational databases. What is a relational database, and what are the advantages of these database systems? Identify the parts of a relational database and explain the purpose of each part.

E6-13
Obj. 3
Howard Co. manufactures household goods and maintains its accounting system using a relational database. In order to prepare information about purchase transactions, the company uses the following tables in its database. The fields that appear in each table are in brackets following the table.

- vendors [vendor ID, name, address, phone number]
- purchase orders [purchase order number, vendor ID, order date, product ID, order quantity]
- materials [product ID, product name, quantity on hand, unit cost]
- purchase invoice [purchase invoice number, purchase order number, invoice date]
- cash payments [purchase invoice number, cash payments amount, payment date]

A purchase order is prepared when materials are ordered from a vendor. A purchase invoice is recorded from billing information supplied by the vendor.

For each of the following events, identify the tables that would be needed to record the event.

1. Placed an order with Jones Co. for materials on November 3.
2. Received the materials from Jones Co. on November 16.
3. Received a bill from Jones Co. for the purchase order on November 28.
4. Sent a check to Jones Co. for the purchase on December 5.

E6-14 Refer to the information provided in E6-13.
Obj. 3

1. If a manager for Howard Co. wanted to query the company's database to obtain information about orders during November, which tables would be used to obtain the information? Explain why.
2. If a manager wanted to query the database to obtain information about amounts owed to vendors at the end of November, which tables would be used to obtain the information? Explain why.

PROBLEMS

If your instructor is using Personal Trainer® in this course, you may complete your assignments online.

P6-1 Modules in an ERP System
Obj. 1

The chapter describes the primary modules available in SAP, a producer of ERP systems.

Required Explain the functions provided by each of the following modules and why they are important for a manufacturing company: (a) financial accounting, (b) controlling, (c) materials management, and (d) production planning.

P6-2 Interaction with System Modules
Obj. 1

ERP systems provide for a variety of functions associated with planning, operating, and evaluating production activities.

Required In what ways would you be likely to interact with an ERP system in a manufacturing system if you were (a) a shop employee, (b) a manufacturing division supervisor, (c) a sales representative, (d) a cost accountant?

P6-3 Cost Systems
Obj. 1

Job-order, process, and activity-based costing systems are similar with respect to the accumulation of production costs.

Required Describe the similarities and differences in these cost systems. Why are different cost accumulation systems needed by different companies? What are the primary inputs and outputs of each of these cost accumulation systems?

P6-4 Computer Networks
Obj. 2

You have just been hired as a human resources manager for a large manufacturing company. Your supervisor shows you to your desk, which contains a workstation. She explains that the workstation is part of a network connecting all of the company's manufacturing operations through a client-server system. All of the company's data are maintained in databases on servers and are accessed through a database management system. To obtain employee information, you must log on to the network and use the company's human resources program on your workstation to retrieve data from the database.

Required What is the supervisor talking about? Explain the function of each part of the company's computer network. Why do most companies use computer networks for their accounting systems?

P6-5 Controlling Networks
Obj. 2

Dora Company uses a client-server network for its accounting system. The company's database servers are kept at a central computer center. Users of the system access the company's database through workstations on their desks. Data are updated continuously throughout the day based on sales, production, billing, and other transactions that are recorded by users. Dora is a large company and its network connects offices in several states.

Required Identify four threats to the accounting system and accounting data that exist in Dora's network system that should be managed through internal controls. Identify an internal control that would be useful for dealing with each threat.

P6-6 **Database Management Systems**

Obj. 2

Open an Access database like the Kwiki Oil Co. database described in this chapter. Examine the Tools menu in the database window.

Required What database management functions are provided by the Tools menu options? Based on your examination, what are some of the primary purposes of a database management system?

P6-7 **Network Components**

Obj. 2

DVC Co. has decided to automate its supply chain. It has developed a web site so that customers can identify products and order them online. It has signed agreements with vendors that permit it to place orders through the Internet for materials.

Required Describe a network configuration that DVC could use to support its E-business activities. What is the purpose of each network component?

P6-8 **Purpose of Relational Databases**

Obj. 3

Newbury Company produces industrial machinery. Materials are purchased from vendors throughout North America, primarily using Internet connections. Purchases are made on credit and materials are placed into production when received. Newbury uses a relational database for its information system.

Required Explain the purpose of a relational database and why it is useful to a company. Describe the parts of a relational database and identify specific examples of how these parts would be used by Newbury to place vendor orders.

P6-9 **Tables and Forms in Relational Databases**

Obj. 3

Exhibit 8 in this chapter provides an example of a table that might appear in a company's relational database. Exhibit 9 provides an example of a form.

Required Using these exhibits as examples, explain the purpose of tables and forms in a relational database. Be specific about what the rows and columns in a table represent and how individual entities are identified in tables. Explain how forms are related to tables.

P6-10 **Web Interfaces to Relational Databases**

Obj. 3

Connect to http://www.dell.com on a web browser.

Required Identify the data items that are collected and processed by Dell's web interface as part of selecting and placing an order for a computer. Which components of Dell's database system are likely to be directly affected by a customer's interaction with the system if (a) the customer is browsing for information about Dell computers, (b) the customer places an order for a computer?

P6-11 **Tables in Relational Databases**

Obj. 3

You have been assigned the responsibility of developing a purchasing module for a manufacturing company.

Required Identify the tables that you think would be necessary as part of a relational database that will store data for the module. Identify the fields that will be important in each table and the primary and foreign keys that will link the tables together.

P6-12 **Fields in a Relational Database**

Obj. 3

Linden Co. uses over 100 different types of nuts, bolts, and screws in its manufacturing process. Each type has an identification number and is described by its type, size, and material composition.

Required Linden Co. is developing a database system for its materials inventory. What fields would be important to include in the database for the inventory items? Why would these fields be important?

P6-13   Relational Database Design

Obj. 3

Niven Co. manufactures ornamental flamingoes. The flamingoes are sold to wholesalers who then sell the goods to retailers. The flamingoes come in a variety of colors, sizes, and materials. Niven produces its products once an order is received. Each order is treated as a job and the company tracks costs using a job-order system.

Required Design a relational database system that Niven might use for tracking the costs of its orders. Identify the tables, fields, primary, and foreign keys that would be part of the database.

P6-14   Diagramming a Relational Database

Obj. 3

Plaxa Co. developed a design for its material ordering system that consisted of three tables. Tables and associated fields are listed below. The primary keys for each table are underlined.

> Materials Table [Product ID, Description, Quantity Available]
> Vendor Table [Vendor ID, Name, Address, City, State, Zip, Email]
> Purchase Order Table [Vendor ID, Materials ID, Order Date, Quantity Ordered, Cost]

Required Provide a relational diagram for the order system like that illustrated in Exhibit 7.

P6-15   Multiple-Choice Overview of the Chapter

1. All of the following are advantages of a computerized accounting system EXCEPT:
   a. many accounting cycle steps are performed by the computer.
   b. it is easier to control than a manual system.
   c. it is faster than a manual system.
   d. fewer opportunities for error exist than in a manual system.
2. The following are parts of a computer network EXCEPT:
   a. transmitters.
   b. clients.
   c. servers.
   d. databases.
3. A field that is a primary key in a different table is called a:
   a. query key.
   b. foreign key.
   c. domestic key.
   d. validation key.
4. An information system that integrates most of the business information functions of a company is known as an:
   a. enterprise resource planning system.
   b. enterprise manufacturing relations system.
   c. enterprise resource module system.
   d. enterprise business planning system.
5. The part of a computer system that controls access to data and ensures reliability of processing in the system is the:
   a. relational database.
   b. application software.
   c. database management system.
   d. control module.
6. The part of a client-server system that requests services from the system is the:
   a. database server.
   b. application server.
   c. web server.
   d. client.

7. The Internet is an example of a:
   a. client.
   b. network.
   c. server.
   d. database.
8. The module in an accounting system that is most concerned with vendors is the:
   a. sales module.
   b. purchases module.
   c. human resources module.
   d. financial management module.
9. The field in a table that uniquely identifies records in the table is the:
   a. primary key.
   b. foreign key.
   c. relation key.
   d. access key.
10. The part of a relational database system that permits users to define the information needed as output from the system is a:
    a. form.
    b. table.
    c. query.
    d. report.

CASE

http://ingram.
swlearning.com

Download database file
(also available on the
student CD).

C6-1

Obj. 3

Working with a Relational Database System

Kwiki Oil Co. completed job number 1007 on March 8, 2004. The job required an F150 oil filter and six quarts of L245 oil. Labor time for the job was as follows: staff 1–10 minutes, staff 2–5 minutes, supervisor–2 minutes.

This case is based on the information provided in the Kwiki Oil Co. example in the chapter.

Required Use Kwiki Oil Co.'s database to record the job. Begin with the job form. Follow the example in the chapter for processing the job order. Once the job has been recorded, print the job cost report for this job.

ANALYZING COST BEHAVIOR

How much do we need to sell to make a profit?

Erin and Seth are staring rather dejectedly at the first quarter's financial report. The company is not yet close to making a profit, and they are concerned about how long the company can continue to operate at a loss. During the last month of the quarter, however, sales began to increase.

FOOD FOR THOUGHT

Seth and Erin are most concerned about not losing any more money. If you were running Young Designs, Inc., what would be the first step you would take to make the business profitable? Erin and Seth are meeting right now to discuss this question.

Erin: *I think the business is improving overall. Sales are growing. I think we'll eventually be ok if we can hang on long enough and keep paying the bills until we make a profit.*

Seth: *How much cash do we need?*

Erin: *That depends on how long it takes before we stop losing money—that is, how long before we break even. We need to know the minimum amount of sales needed so we are no longer operating at a loss. Then, we can determine what level of sales is required to reach the profit we want.*

Seth: *I agree. I think we can use our present sales growth rate to calculate when we will reach the breakeven level.*

Erin: *Yesterday, I talked with Roberta about our struggle to stop losing money. She told me cost-volume-profit, or CVP, analysis would help us calculate our sales breakeven point. Basically, she said that CVP analysis involves understanding how costs behave.*

Seth: *Huh, seems like our costs have been misbehaving. What's this cost behavior stuff?*

Erin: *Remember when we talked about some costs being variable and some being fixed?*

Seth: *Yes, we found out certain costs, like raw materials and direct labor, vary with the amount of products we produce. But, certain other costs, like the lease on our building, don't.*

Erin: *Evidently, part of our problem is our sales aren't high enough to cover our fixed costs.*

Seth: *We could just raise our prices, but that might make us more expensive than our competition. Then, we'll have fewer sales.*

Erin: *I agree. Roberta said our breakeven is the point where total sales equal total costs. What we have to do is figure out what our total variable and total fixed costs are, and then we will know the minimum amount of sales revenue we must have.*

Seth: *Ok, that's easy enough. It also sounds like we can use CVP analysis to determine how many units we need to sell to reach a certain level of profitability.*

Erin: *CVP can certainly be used to determine the amount of sales necessary to reach a certain target profit. In a breakeven calculation, the target profit is zero because the company's revenues equal its costs. In a target profit calculation, we would simply use the breakeven equation of total revenues = variable costs + fixed costs and add profits to the equation so that it becomes total revenues = variable costs + fixed costs + profits.*

Seth: *I understand. Since we know revenues, which are calculated as price times the number of units sold, the variable costs, which are calculated as unit variable cost times units sold, the fixed costs, and the target profit, we can solve for the number of units required.*

OBJECTIVES

Once you have completed this chapter, you should be able to:

1 Describe how costs respond to changes in activity.

2 Explain what contribution margins and breakeven points are and how the contribution margin is reflected in a variable-costing income statement.

3 Use CVP analysis to determine the breakeven point in sales and the sales volume necessary to earn a target profit.

4 Calculate unit product costs using variable and absorption costing.

5 Explain why costs are important for decision making in service companies.

COST BEHAVIOR

OBJECTIVE 1

Describe how costs respond to changes in activity.

This section considers the details of how managers explain changes in costs in regard to changes in activity. Direct materials, direct labor, and manufacturing overhead are categories of product costs. In this section we look at the behavior of those costs. First, consider how costs respond to changes in activity levels.

Black & Blue Manufacturing: The Product and Manufacturing Process

Black & Blue Manufacturing Company is a small company that manufactures skateboards. The boards are produced from composite fiberglass. Synthetic materials are prepared and poured into molds. The boards are finished and wheel assemblies are added. After inspection, the boards are shipped to retail sporting goods and specialty shops. Though the company produces several models based on the grade of materials used, the manufacturing process is the same for each model.

Cost Behavior in Relation to Changes in Activity Levels

Managers often make decisions about pricing, production levels, product mix, and external purchases after considering cost information. Later in this chapter, we examine the types of decisions managers commonly face. First, it is important to understand which costs are relevant to certain types of decisions. Often, whether a cost is relevant depends on how costs change (or do not change) when volume changes. The following paragraphs explore the impact of volume on manufacturing costs and identify examples of costs that typically are classified as variable, fixed, semivariable, and step-pattern.

Variable Costs. *Variable costs* **are costs that change in total with volume but remain fixed on a per-unit basis.** For example, the cost of materials Black & Blue uses in its manufacturing process is a variable cost because the total cost of materials varies in relation to the number of products manufactured. The cost of materials for each XR100 board produced is $20. If a single board is produced, the total cost of materials is $20. However, if 100 boards are manufactured, the total cost of materials would be $2,000.

Variable costs go up as the level of activity (volume) rises. Exhibit 1 illustrates that behavior pattern. Managers can predict the total cost of a direct material at any level of production by multiplying the cost per unit times the number of units produced:

Exhibit 1
Behavior Pattern:
Variable Costs

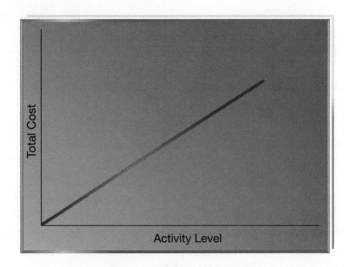

Cost per unit	× Number of units produced	= Total variable cost
$20	× 1 unit produced	= $20
$20	× 3 units produced	= $60
$20	× 100 units produced	= $2,000

Fixed Costs. *Fixed costs* **are costs that do not change in total with volume but vary on a per-unit basis.** Generally, depreciation is a fixed cost. A company's *total* depreciation cost does not change whether it produces 2,500 units or 5,000 units in a year, as illustrated in Exhibit 2. However, the cost *per unit* does vary with output because fixed depreciation costs are spread over a greater or lesser number of units.

Exhibit 2
Behavior Pattern:
Fixed Costs

Suppose, for example, that a company has $50,000 in depreciation expense this year. The total cost is fixed, but the cost per unit depends on the number of units produced:

Total fixed cost	÷ Number of units produced	= Cost per unit
$50,000	÷ 2,500 units produced	= $20
$50,000	÷ 5,000 units produced	= $10

Notice that fixed costs per unit fall as the number of units produced rises.

Semivariable or Mixed Costs. *Semivariable* or *mixed costs* **are a combination of variable and fixed costs.** For example, total electricity consumption at Black & Blue changes with production levels as the number of machine hours varies. Machinery consumes most of the electrical energy used in the plant. However, even if production falls to zero, electricity would be used for lighting and heating or cooling of plant facilities. Exhibit 3 shows how mixed costs react to changes in the amount of output. The key point: Total cost is a function of both variable and fixed costs; costs vary with output but cannot drop to zero as long as a company is in business.

Exhibit 3
Behavior Pattern:
Semivariable Costs

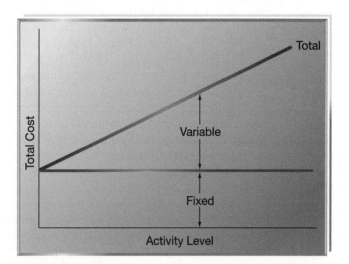

Step-Pattern Costs. *Step-pattern costs* **are costs that increase or decrease in total over a wide range of activity levels. However, these costs remain fixed over a narrow range of activity levels.** The relationship between variable costs and volume is linear as shown in Exhibit 1. Every unit produced increases total costs by the same amount. Step-pattern costs also vary with respect to volume but not in a linear pattern, as illustrated in Exhibit 4.

Exhibit 4
Behavior Pattern:
Step-Pattern Costs

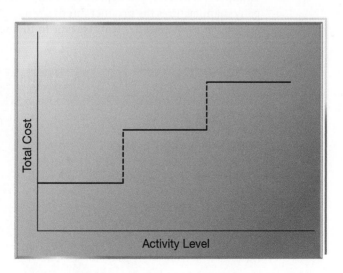

For example, assume that one quality control engineer can inspect up to 1,000 units a month. If Black & Blue increases its production to 1,500 units, it must hire another quality control engineer. The company cannot hire a portion of a quality control engineer;

it has to hire the entire person. If production levels increase to more than 2,000 units a month, the company is going to have to hire a third quality control engineer. Quality inspection costs move in a step pattern with respect to volume.

Cost Behavior and Decisions: A Make-or-Buy Example

A manager who must decide between manufacturing a component or buying that component from an outside source (outsourcing) is facing a make-or-buy decision. Typically managers evaluate many factors, including costs, before choosing to make or buy a component. Your understanding of cost behavior will enable you to analyze these situations and make informed recommendations to management.

Currently, Black & Blue is buying from an outside supplier the wheels it uses on its XR100 skateboards. Recall from Chapter M2, suppliers are part of a value chain that extends from raw material production to the sales and service of a product. The company's management is considering reconfiguring the value chain by outsourcing and would like to know which costs are relevant to its decision. *Relevant costs* **are costs that change under two or more decision alternatives.** For example, plant depreciation costs are not relevant to a make-or-buy decision because depreciation costs are fixed and will not change regardless of the decision. However, wheels and other materials used to produce the boards are relevant because these costs differ between the two decision alternatives of make or buy.

Let's evaluate the costs of outsourcing and manufacturing the wheels. Assume the wheels cost $8.00 per board. The $8.00 unit cost is relevant to the make-or-buy decision because if Black & Blue manufactures the wheels internally, it does not incur the $8.00 outsourcing cost. If the company purchases the product externally, it incurs the $8.00 cost. As shown in Exhibit 5, the total cost of making one unit is $8.70. At first glance, we may conclude outsourcing is the better option because $8.00 is less than $8.70. However, applying our understanding of cost behavior, we may reach a different conclusion. Included in the total cost calculation are both variable and fixed costs. However, the relevant cost calculation includes only variable costs totaling $7.75. The fixed costs of depreciation and supervision are not relevant to the make-or-buy decision because these costs do not change between the two decision alternatives. If the product is purchased externally, the materials, direct labor, electricity, and supplies costs disappear. However, the depreciation and supervision costs remain whether the company manufactures the product internally or purchases it externally. Thus, depreciation and supervision costs are not relevant to the outsourcing decision.

Exhibit 5
Make-or-Buy
Cost Analysis

	Total Cost to Make	Total Relevant Cost to Make	Outsourced Cost
Outsource cost			$8.00
Cost to make			
Direct materials (variable)	$5.45	$5.45	
Direct labor (variable)	2.00	2.00	
Manufacturing overhead:			
Electricity (variable)	0.25	0.25	
Supplies (variable)	0.05	0.05	
Depreciation costs (fixed)	0.70	0.00	
Supervision costs (fixed)	0.25	0.00	
Total cost per unit	$8.70	$7.75	$8.00

Our cost analysis suggests Black & Blue should make the wheels internally and save $0.25 ($8.00 − $7.75) per unit. However, cost is not the only factor managers consider when analyzing a make-or-buy decision. By manufacturing the wheels internally, the company controls both quality and product availability. Availability is especially important if a labor dispute or other event interrupts production at a supplier's facility. When a company outsources a product, it depends upon suppliers to meet delivery schedules. Outsourcing can bring other complications, as well. Sometimes external firms make low bids in an attempt to attract customers. Management must be careful when deciding to discontinue production of a component in favor of outsourcing, especially if they eliminate their ability to produce it later. Cost savings that initially appear attractive may disappear just as quickly if suppliers later increase prices.

Other Behavior Considerations: Management Policies and Time

Not all costs are inherently variable or fixed. Workers in an assembly department, for example, could be paid by the piece: the higher the level of production, the larger their paychecks. Here the terms of the contract tie the workers' wages to output; wages are a variable cost. On the other hand, if the company contracts with the same workers to pay them a fixed amount every week, whatever their output, their wages are fixed. You should be careful when you classify costs by behavior because costs that appear variable may in fact be fixed. For example, assume a factory worker is being paid on an hourly basis. Are these wages variable or fixed? Most people would say that the wages are variable because the total wage costs vary according to the number of hours worked. Suppose you have one more bit of information: workers in this factory are never told to go home, even during times when the factory is producing below expected volume. In other words, each employee works 40 hours a week. In this case, management's policy has changed what is traditionally a variable cost—the wages of hourly employees—into a fixed cost. Here the total hours worked do not vary with the level of production.

Another important factor in understanding the effect of volume on costs is time. For example, the cost of raw materials generally is thought to be variable; however, if raw materials have been purchased and are available in the warehouse, one could argue that their costs are fixed. In the short run, raw material costs do not vary because the materials have been paid for and are available. There are times when fixed costs respond more like variable costs. Depreciation on plant assets generally is considered a fixed cost. However, in the long run, as assets are acquired or sold in response to changes in demand, plant depreciation behaves like a variable cost. Thus, general patterns of cost behavior exist; however, most costs can be affected by management actions.

---

1 **SELF-STUDY PROBLEM**   Atta Baby Company produces infant seats for use in automobiles. During a recent fiscal period, the company incurred the following costs:

WebTUTOR Advantage

Metal for frames	$40,000
Foam filler	25,000
Plastic seat covering	15,000
Manufacturing wages	23,000
Inspector salaries	7,000
Administrative salaries	12,000
Depreciation	4,000
Utilities	1,600

The company produced and sold 3,190 seats at $50 per seat. Each inspector can inspect up to 2,000 seats during a period. Half of the utilities costs are associated with manufacturing and vary with production. Manufacturing employees are paid for hours worked.

Required

A. Classify each cost as variable, fixed, semivariable, or step.
B. For variable costs, including the variable portion of semivariable costs, calculate the unit cost of each seat produced and sold. Round unit costs to the nearest cent.
C. If the company had produced and sold 3,500 seats, what would you expect the total costs to have been? How much profit would the company have earned?

The solution to Self-Study Problem 1 appears at the end of the chapter.

CONTRIBUTION MARGIN AND THE VARIABLE-COSTING INCOME STATEMENT

OBJECTIVE 2

Explain what contribution margins and breakeven points are and how the contribution margin is reflected in a variable-costing income statement.

An organization has to assign costs to price its products and evaluate its performance. Managers have a choice. They can assign costs using either absorption or variable costing. *Absorption costing* **assigns costs by function, separating the costs of manufacturing products from the costs of selling, administration, and other nonmanufacturing activities.** Absorption costing is also called the *full-cost method.* That's because absorption costing assigns the full costs of manufacturing to product costs. It makes no distinction between variable and fixed manufacturing costs.

Variable costing **assigns costs by their behavior, separating them into variable and fixed components.** Key to this costing method is the *contribution margin,* **the difference between sales revenue and variable costs over an accounting period.** (In fact, variable costing is sometimes called the *contribution-margin method.*) It is the contribution margin that covers a company's fixed costs and defines its profits.

A traditional income statement lists expenses by function: the cost of goods sold, selling, and administration. The format does not distinguish between variable and fixed costs. In the administrative expenses category, for example, both variable and fixed administrative costs are reported as one amount. The traditional income statement provides information about revenues and expenses for investors and other external decision makers. It does not always give a company's management the information it needs to make planning and control decisions, however.

LEARNING NOTE

The term *costs* in cost behavior decisions refers to the costs of resources that have been consumed in producing goods sold during a period. Therefore, the terms costs and expenses are used interchangeably.

Managers need information in a format that can help them make decisions. **The** *variable-costing income statement* **is a managerial decision-making tool that measures net income by subtracting variable expenses from sales and then subtracting fixed expenses from the difference.** The difference between sales revenue and variable expenses for a period is the contribution margin. The contribution margin "contributes" to covering fixed expenses. What remains after fixed expenses have been covered is net income for the period. If the contribution margin is too small to cover all fixed expenses, the company reports a net loss. The order in which the contribution margin is applied is very important: first to cover fixed expenses, and then to provide profits.

Exhibit 6 shows a variable-costing income statement for Black & Blue Company. Notice that the amounts are listed both in total and per unit. In their analysis of profitability, managers can look at both overall performance and the per-unit effect of variable expenses.

Black & Blue generates a contribution margin of $10.40 per skateboard: Each skateboard the company sells contributes $10.40 toward covering fixed expenses. If the company sells enough skateboards to generate a $6,000 contribution margin, it can then cover all of its fixed expenses and break even for the month. **The** *breakeven point* **is that level of sales at which all variable and fixed expenses are covered, but no profit is generated.** Once sales reach the breakeven point, each additional unit sold contributes a profit equal to the contribution margin of that unit. As more units are sold, net income continues to go up by the contribution margin of each additional unit sold.

Exhibit 6

Black & Blue Company:
A Variable-Costing
Income Statement

Black & Blue Company
Variable-Costing Income Statement
For the Month Ended August 31, 2005

	Total	Per Unit
Sales revenue (1,000 skateboards)	$26,000	$26.00
Less variable expenses	15,600	15.60
Contribution margin	$10,400	$10.40
Less fixed expenses	6,000	
Net income	$ 4,400	

In addition to being expressed in total or on a per-unit basis, the contribution margin can be expressed as a percentage of sales as shown in Exhibit 7.

Exhibit 7

Black & Blue Company:
Contribution Margin as a
Percentage of Sales

	Total	Per Unit	Percentage
Sales (1,000 skateboards)	$26,000	$26.00	100%
Less variable expenses	15,600	15.60	60%
Contribution margin	$10,400	$10.40	40%
Less fixed expenses	6,000		
Net income	$ 4,400		

The ratio (expressed as a percentage) of contribution margin to total sales is called the *contribution margin ratio* **or the profit volume ratio:**

Contribution margin ratio = Contribution margin ÷ Sales
40% = $10,400 ÷ $26,000

When fixed costs stay the same, a company can use the contribution margin ratio to determine the effect on net income of a change in total sales. For example, suppose that Black & Blue plans to increase its sales next month by $10,000. That means it plans to increase the total contribution margin by $4,000 ($10,000 increase in sales × 40% contribution margin ratio). If the company's fixed costs do not change, Black & Blue can expect its net income to go up by $4,000.

The contribution margin ratio can also help managers allocate limited resources. Products that have a higher contribution margin ratio are more profitable to a company, and so a company is more likely to focus its advertising and production resources on those products.

COST-VOLUME-PROFIT ANALYSIS

OBJECTIVE 3

Use CVP analysis to
determine the breakeven
point in sales and the
sales volume necessary to
earn a target profit.

The variable-costing concept can be extended to help managers plan and make decisions about sales and profits. *Cost-volume-profit (CVP) analysis* **is the use of the relationships among costs, volume, and profits to make managerial decisions.** A change in any one of those components affects the others. As Exhibit 8 shows, an understanding of the relationships among product prices, activity levels, variable costs, and fixed costs can help managers develop marketing strategies, set pricing policies, and make resource decisions. Once costs have been separated into variable and fixed components, CVP analysis can be used to determine a company's breakeven point, to determine the sales volume necessary to earn a target profit, to measure the effect on net income of a

Exhibit 8

Cost-Volume-Profit
Analysis and
Managerial Decision
Making

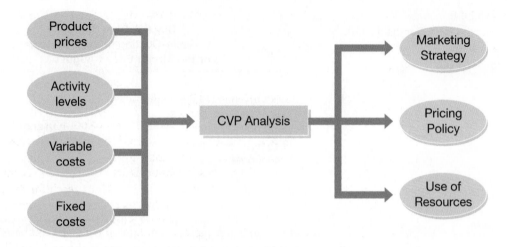

change in expenses, and to determine the most profitable mix of products in a multiple-product environment. CVP analysis also helps managers evaluate sales options and a company's level of operating risk.

CVP analysis makes certain assumptions about costs and activities. If those assumptions are violated, the analysis can be flawed. One assumption, for example, is that fixed costs remain constant over the range of production. If fixed costs change, the analysis is not valid. A company can provide only a certain volume of production and sales without adding workers or plant assets, which translates into higher fixed costs. If the existing machinery at Black & Blue is capable of producing just 60 skateboards a day, the company cannot produce 70 boards a day without additional equipment. That additional equipment would increase maintenance and depreciation expenses, which are part of the fixed cost of production.

CVP analysis is complicated by mixed (semivariable) costs. Remember that mixed costs have both fixed and variable components. A salesperson's compensation, for example, is a mixed cost if it is made up of a base salary plus a bonus that increases with sales.

Whenever possible, mixed costs should be separated into their variable and fixed components. For example, some equipment is depreciated on the basis of units of production. That is a variable expense. Other equipment is depreciated on a straight-line basis. That is a fixed expense. By keeping records of depreciation for individual pieces of equipment, a company can separate its depreciation expense into variable and fixed components.

Of course it is difficult to separate mixed costs because the costs are intermingled in the accounting records. For instance, a company may use a single account to record the costs of generating reports on a computer. The cost of reports that are produced weekly and sent to all departments in the company would be fixed. The cost of reports that are produced only at the request of a department would be variable. Although the company could separate the costs, it may choose not to if the additional accuracy does not justify the cost of keeping two accounts.

CVP analysis also is complicated by the fact that the cost of materials for a unit of product may not remain constant. For example, as a company produces more units, it buys more materials. As it buys more materials, volume discounts can lower the cost per unit of those materials. Another example is a shortage of materials in the market, which would push the price of those materials up. CVP analysis assumes that the cost of materials remains constant for each unit of a partic-

LEARNING NOTE

Remember our discussion in an earlier chapter about costs and the need for accurate information. Generally the more accurate the accounting information, the more costly it is to produce.

ular product. It is important, then, for managers using CVP analysis to talk with purchasing managers to be sure that variable costs per unit and fixed costs will not change over the period being considered.

Breakeven-Point Analysis

Breakeven-point analysis is one of the most common uses of CVP analysis. **Breakeven-point analysis** is a technique used to find the volume of sales—in units or dollars—at which a company just covers its total costs. Erin and Seth's situation at the beginning of the chapter underscores the importance of breakeven-point analysis. They need to know what sales level Young Designs, Inc., must reach for the company to cease being unprofitable. Breakeven-point analysis is a simple calculation that often has profound implications. Two ways to calculate the breakeven point are the equation method and the unit-contribution method.

The Equation Method. The equation method builds on the relationship among sales, total costs, and profits. In its simplest form,

Sales − Total costs = Profits

The next step is to separate the variable and fixed components of total costs:

Sales − (Variable costs + Fixed costs) = Profits

At the breakeven point, profits are zero. That means the equation can be rewritten as:

Sales = Variable costs + Fixed costs

Remember that we're looking for the volume of sales at which a company covers its total costs. Fixed costs are a given: we assume that however many units a company sells, its fixed costs remain constant. Our focus is on two terms: sales and variable costs. For the sales term we can substitute the selling price per unit multiplied by the number of units sold; for the variable-costs term, we can substitute the variable cost per unit multiplied by the number of units sold:

Sales   = Variable costs + Fixed costs
Selling price per unit × Units sold = (Variable cost per unit × Units sold) + Fixed costs

How does it work? Black & Blue sells its skateboards for $26.00 apiece, each skateboard has variable costs of $15.40, and the company has fixed costs each month of $6,000 (see Exhibit 6). How many skateboards does the company have to sell each month to break even?

Breakeven sales   = Variable costs + Fixed costs
Selling price per unit × Units sold = (Variable cost per unit × Units sold) + Fixed costs
$26.00 × Units sold   = ($15.60 × Units sold) + $6,000
($26.00 − $15.60) × Units sold = $6,000
$10.40 × Units sold   = $6,000
Units sold   = 577

Black & Blue's breakeven point is 577 units a month. If it sells 577 skateboards a month, the company can cover its fixed costs.

The Unit-Contribution Method. The unit-contribution method also can be used to determine the number of units a company must sell to break even. The method is based on the idea that each unit sold contributes toward covering fixed expenses. To determine the number of units that must be sold to break even, then, we divide fixed costs by the contribution margin per unit:

Breakeven units = Fixed costs ÷ Unit contribution margin

According to Exhibit 6, Black & Blue generates a $10.40 contribution margin on each skateboard it sells. On that basis, the company has to sell 577 skateboards a month to break even:

Breakeven units = Fixed costs ÷ Unit contribution margin
                = $6,000 ÷ $10.40
                = 577 skateboards

The unit-contribution method also can be used to determine the breakeven point in sales dollars—the amount of sales in dollars at which a company covers its fixed costs:

Breakeven sales dollars = Fixed costs ÷ Contribution margin ratio

Black & Blue's contribution margin ratio is 40% (Exhibit 7). So the company must sell $15,000 in skateboards each month to break even:

Breakeven sales dollars = Fixed costs ÷ Contribution margin ratio
                        = $6,000 ÷ 40%
                        = $15,000

Target-Profit Analysis

CVP analysis also can be used to determine the sales (in units or dollars) necessary to earn a target profit. **A** *target profit* **is the profit that a company wants to make over a given period.** The Food for Thought section in the beginning chapter scenario provides an intuitive feel for how this type of situation can arise in the business world. As Erin explained to Seth, the basic breakeven-point equation can be modified to permit a target profit calculation. As Erin indicated, breakeven-point analysis is the same thing as target-profit analysis with the target profit set at zero.

Suppose that Black & Blue wants to earn a profit of $2,000 a month. How many skateboards would it have to sell? One way to answer that question is to rework the breakeven-point equation, inserting target profit:

Target profit = (Selling price per unit × Units sold) −
                (Variable cost per unit × Units sold) − Fixed costs
$2,000   = ($26.00 × Units sold) − ($15.60 × Units sold) − $6,000
$8,000   = $10.40 × Units sold
Units sold   = 770 skateboards

Black & Blue can earn its target profit by selling 770 skateboards a month.

We can get the same answer using a variation of the unit-contribution method:

Units sold = (Target profit + Fixed costs) ÷ Contribution margin
           = ($2,000 + $6,000) ÷ $10.40
           = $8,000 ÷ $10.40
           = 770 skateboards

Profit-Sensitivity Analysis

CVP analysis also answers questions about how profits would change if the selling price, the units sold, or costs change. Black & Blue is selling 1,000 skateboards for $26.00

apiece at a variable cost per skateboard of $15.60. Suppose that the company's management is thinking about lowering the selling price to $24.00, a change that should increase sales by 20 percent, and cutting the variable cost per unit to $15.00. Do the changes make sense in terms of the company's profits?

To gauge the impact of the changes on profits, we can use the equation we used to determine the number of units the company would have to sell to earn its target profit. Here, though, we substitute profit for target profit:

Profit = (Selling price per unit × Units sold − (Variable cost per unit × Units sold) −
      Fixed costs
    = ($24.00 × 1,200)* − ($15.00 × 1,200) − $6,000
    = $28,800 − $18,000 − $6,000
    = $4,800

*1,200 units = 1,000 units × 1.20

At the new selling price, the new sales volume, and the new variable cost per unit, Black & Blue's profit would go up $400 ($4,800 − $4,400) (see Exhibit 6).

Cost Behavior and Operating Risk

Cost behavior affects operating risk. *Operating risk* **is the risk that a drop in sales volume will cause a company to earn an unsatisfactory profit.** Operating risk increases as the percentage of a company's fixed costs to total costs increases. As the percentage of fixed costs to total costs increases, reductions in sales result in smaller and smaller reductions in total costs. For example, major commercial airlines have enormous fixed costs associated with owning or leasing aircraft. If an airline's fixed costs to total costs percentage is 80 percent, then a drop in sales of $1.00 will result in a reduction in total cost of only $0.20 [(100% − 80% = 20%) × $1.00]. This is because only 20 percent of the total costs vary with sales volume.

When a company's operating risk becomes too high, managers frequently take steps to reduce this risk. This often means reducing discretionary fixed costs. *Discretionary fixed costs* **are fixed costs that can be eliminated in the relatively short term.** An example of a discretionary fixed cost is an advertising contract that is renewable each month. If a company does not wish to incur this cost next month it can simply choose not to renew the contract. In contrast, *committed fixed costs* **are costs that cannot be eliminated in the relatively short term.** An example of a committed fixed cost is a long-term lease on a warehouse. Even if the company does not need the warehouse space, it is still obligated to make lease payments.

Once committed fixed costs are incurred, it may be years before these costs can be eliminated. Well-managed companies often take great care before committing to large, nondiscretionary fixed costs. One way in which companies do this is by requiring that large expenditures for property, plant, and equipment be thoroughly evaluated through a formal approval process before a purchase is approved. Such evaluations are intended to identify the expected benefits, costs, and risks associated with the expenditures.

---

2 SELF-STUDY PROBLEM

WebTUTOR Advantage

Calhoun Carpets is considering a new line of carpeting for boats. The carpet would cost $3.00 a yard to make and would sell for $10.00 a yard. Calhoun would have to build a new plant and buy new equipment—at an annual cost of $4.2 million—to produce the new line.

Required

A. How many yards of carpet would Calhoun have to sell annually to break even? What would the company's breakeven point in sales dollars be?

B. How many yards would the company have to sell to make a target profit of $700,000 on the line? What is the sales dollars equivalent of that number of yards?

The solution to Self-Study Problem 2 appears at the end of the chapter.

VARIABLE AND ABSORPTION COSTING: A COMPARISON

OBJECTIVE 4

Calculate unit product costs using variable and absorption costing.

GAAP require companies to use absorption costing to develop their financial statements for external reporting. Under absorption costing, both variable and fixed production costs are recognized as the cost of goods sold. The Internal Revenue Service (IRS) also requires the use of that method to determine federal tax liability. However, a company can choose the costing method it uses for internal purposes—to set the selling price of products and to evaluate performance. Some companies use absorption costing for both external reporting and internal decision making. Other companies set up two accounting systems, using absorption costing for external reports and variable costing for internal reports.

The choice of costing method affects both the unit product cost—a measure sometimes used to determine a product's selling price—and a company's net income—a performance measure.

Unit Product Cost

A key measure in the pricing decision is the unit cost of the finished product—the unit product cost. That cost determines the value of finished goods inventory and, eventually, the cost of goods sold.

Remember that variable costing classifies costs by their behavior: variable or fixed. In calculating the unit product cost, variable costing uses only those costs that vary directly with production: the costs of direct materials, direct labor, and variable manufacturing overhead. Fixed manufacturing overhead costs are treated like period expenses. Like selling and administrative costs, those costs are expensed in the period in which they are incurred. The variable unit product cost never includes fixed costs.

Absorption costing, on the other hand, classifies costs by their function: manufacturing or nonmanufacturing. The unit product cost calculation using the absorption-costing method includes all the costs of manufacturing—variable and fixed. By definition, then, the variable unit product cost is always smaller than the absorption unit product cost because it does not include fixed production costs.

The Variable-Costing Calculation. The variable unit product cost is a measurement that helps managers make decisions about cost-volume-profit relationships. For example, as you have just seen in the discussion of CVP analysis, the variable unit cost of a product is key to breakeven-point analysis, target-profit analysis, and profit-sensitivity analysis.

Exhibit 9 shows how variable costing is used to calculate unit costs. Observe that unit cost includes only variable costs. Fixed costs are never part of the calculation. The unit variable cost is a *product cost*. Only the costs of direct materials, direct labor, and manufacturing overhead are part of its calculation. Selling and administrative expenses—whether they are variable or fixed—are treated as period expenses. Like fixed manufacturing overhead, they are recorded as expenses in the period in which they are incurred. The variable unit product cost times the number of units produced is recorded in finished goods inventory and then charged to cost of goods sold when the units are sold.

The Absorption-Costing Calculation. Absorption costing includes *all* production costs in the unit-cost calculations, whether those costs are variable or fixed. So the unit-

Exhibit 9

Calculating the Variable Product Cost per Unit

Number of units produced in the period	10,000
Variable costs per unit:	
Direct materials	$5
Direct labor	3
Variable manufacturing overhead	2
Variable selling and administrative expenses	2
Fixed costs per period:	
Fixed manufacturing overhead	$50,000
Fixed selling and administrative expenses	35,000
The variable unit product cost calculation:	
Direct materials cost per unit	$ 5
Direct labor cost per unit	3
Variable manufacturing overhead cost per unit	2
Total variable cost per unit	$10

cost calculation allocates fixed manufacturing overhead to each unit of product in addition to variable production costs. The cost of each unit in finished goods inventory and cost of goods sold include both variable and fixed components.

Exhibit 10 shows how costs are classified under variable and absorption costing. **Notice that the only difference between the two methods is in the way each treats the costs of fixed manufacturing overhead.**

Exhibit 10

Variable and Absorption Costing: Classifying Costs

Costs	Variable Costing	Absorption Costing
Direct materials	Product cost	Product cost
Direct labor	Product cost	Product cost
Variable manufacturing overhead	Product cost	Product cost
Fixed manufacturing overhead	**Period expense**	**Product cost**
Variable selling & administrative expenses	Period expense	Period expense
Fixed selling & administrative expenses	Period expense	Period expense

Let's calculate a unit product cost using absorption costing from the information in Exhibit 9. The unit product cost for the period would be $15:

Direct materials cost per unit	$ 5
Direct labor cost per unit	3
Variable manufacturing overhead cost per unit	2
Fixed manufacturing overhead cost per unit*	5
Total cost per unit	$15

$50,000 ÷ 10,000 units. See Exhibit 9.

Performance Evaluation: Net Income

Income calculated using variable costing differs from income calculated using absorption costing. Absorption-costing income is affected by changes in the ending inventory of finished goods. Variable-costing income is not affected by these changes.

Exhibit 11 compares income statements for Black & Blue Company for January using the variable- and absorption-costing methods.

Exhibit 11

Black & Blue Company: Income Statements for January

Absorption Costing	
Sales (8,000 units × $25)	$200,000
Cost of goods sold (8,000 units × $10) + $40,000	120,000
Gross margin	$ 80,000
Less administrative expenses ($35,000 fixed + $20,000 variable)	55,000
Net income	$ 25,000
Variable Costing	
Sales (8,000 units × $25)	$200,000
Cost of goods sold (8,000 units × $10)	80,000
Gross margin	$120,000
Less administrative expenses ($35,000 fixed + $20,000 variable)	55,000
Less fixed manufacturing overhead costs	50,000
Net income	$ 15,000

The following data were used to prepare the statements:

Direct materials cost per unit	$5
Direct labor cost per unit	$3
Variable manufacturing overhead cost per unit	$2
Total variable unit cost	$10
Fixed manufacturing overhead cost	$40,000
Unit selling price	$25
Units sold	8,000
Beginning finished goods inventory in units	0
Ending finished goods inventory in units	2,000
Fixed administrative expenses	$35,000
Variable administrative expenses	$20,000

Exhibit 11 reveals a $10,000 ($25,000 − $15,000) difference in income between the two costing methods. This $10,000 difference is a function of the way the costs of fixed manufacturing overhead are treated. Using the absorption-costing method, fixed overhead costs are carried as an asset in finished goods inventory until the units are sold. Black & Blue produced 10,000 units (2,000 units in inventory + 8,000 units sold) in January; it sold just 8,000 units. The company assigned each of the 2,000 units in ending inventory $5 of fixed manufacturing overhead costs. That means $10,000 (2,000 × $5) of fixed manufacturing overhead costs remained in inventory until the units were sold.

Under the variable-costing method, fixed manufacturing overhead is a period expense. The entire cost of fixed manufacturing overhead, $40,000, was deducted as an expense in the January period in which the costs were incurred. Again, using variable costing, all fixed overhead costs are recognized as expenses each period; no fixed overhead costs are recorded in inventory.

The differences in net income between the absorption- and variable-costing methods had to do with the level of finished goods. When the number of units in ending inventory *increases* from that of the *previous period*, net income reported under the absorption-costing method is *higher* than net income reported under the variable-costing method. When inventory *decreases*, however, net income reported under the absorption-costing method is *lower* than net income reported under the variable-costing method.

If manufacturing costs are constant (i.e., inventory levels do not change from the beginning to the end of a period) and production equals sales, variable costing and absorption costing produce the same net income. But production costs, inventory levels, and sales in a manufacturing company usually vary over time. That means that the methods should produce different income numbers from period to period. That difference can lead to important differences in managers' decisions, a subject considered in the next section.

Arguments For and Against Variable Costing

Many accountants argue that variable costing is more accurate than absorption costing because it treats fixed overhead as a period expense. They insist that it is theoretically wrong to inventory fixed costs because most fixed costs are incurred whether or not any products are produced during a period. Another argument for variable costing is the usefulness of variable-cost information in certain types of analyses, like breakeven-point analysis and target-profit analysis. Variable costing clarifies the cost-volume-profit relationship.

If decision makers think of each sale independently from all other sales, any sale that covers its variable costs is good because it increases the company's contribution margin. But there are two difficulties with that logic. First, in the long run a company must cover its fixed costs and make a profit or it cannot survive. If an airline's average ticket price doesn't cover the fixed costs of buying airplanes, the company is not going to be able to pay for its assets. Second, often one sale is not independent of other sales. Airline customers who have flown on discount tickets that just cover variable costs are more likely to shop for low-priced tickets in the future. This makes it important for the airline to sell full-priced tickets. This also makes it difficult for the airline to cover its fixed expenses and make the profit it needs to stay in business.

Despite the contribution fallacy, variable costing and the contribution method can be helpful when managers understand how they should be used. For instance, it may be fine to price above variable cost but below absorption cost in selling a one-time order in a market in which a company normally does not do business. It can be very dangerous, however, to set prices this way in markets in which the company routinely does business. Variable costing also is useful in profit-sensitivity analysis (to determine the effect on profits as sales go up or down) and breakeven-point analysis (to measure operating risk). The key to its usefulness is remembering that variable costing can lead to decisions that seem good in the short run but create serious problems in the long run.

MEASURING COSTS FOR DECISION MAKING IN SERVICE COMPANIES

OBJECTIVE 5

Explain why costs are important for decision making in service companies.

Cost information is as important for service companies as it is for manufacturers. A bank, for example, has to know how much it costs to execute a particular transaction or provide a particular service in order to price that transaction or service. The cost of a car loan is more than the amount being borrowed. The loan application has to be printed and processed, the amount has to be updated each month, and a bad-debt assessment and the bank's target profit have to be included in the pricing.

The process of measuring costs in service organizations is often more complex than in manufacturing organizations. Two factors are at work here. First, services do not have the tangible, physical nature of products. It is much easier to trace the costs of materials and labor to a physical object than it is to trace costs to a particular service and the transactions that make up that service. Second, services often require many transactions that are carried out by a number of departments. The same employees may work on many different services. Again, this makes it difficult to determine the cost associated with a particular transaction and to trace the cost of that transaction to a particular service.

The following Case in Point demonstrates two important aspects of using costs to make decisions in service organizations: (1) the difficulty of tracing costs to services and (2) the way in which costing decisions can influence pricing, marketing, and operations.

Case in Point

http://ingram.
swlearning.com

Find out about online
services offered by
some banks and sav-
ings and loans.

First National Bank, a bank, and **Home Federal Savings**, a savings and loan (S&L) association, were considering how to price a new service, a checking account that pays interest. In the past, the bank had offered checking accounts, but they did not pay interest. Based on cost estimates, the bank set a minimum balance of $2,200 for interest-paying accounts. The S&L set its minimum balance at $800. Why were the amounts so different?

In its estimates, the bank included all indirect costs of doing business. For example, it developed a charge for heating the building used by the customer service representatives who, in addition to their other duties, would handle customers' inquiries about their accounts. Citing the difficulty of accurately estimating certain indirect costs, the S&L's management chose to ignore any indirect costs that it could not estimate easily. The result was that the bank's estimate of the account costs was much higher than the S&L's.

The bank subsequently lost a great deal of its checking account business, but it continued to be very profitable. The S&L got many new accounts but was less profitable.

Which institution made the best pricing decision? It is difficult to say. The bank may have included costs that it should not have included. The S&L may have excluded too many costs. The process of measuring costs to make decisions in service companies is not an easy one.

---

3 SELF-STUDY PROBLEM

WebTUTOR Advantage

Kokomo Manufacturing Company produces a single product, model airplanes. A list of selected cost and operating data for last year follows:

Beginning finished goods inventory in units	0
Units produced during the year	15,000
Units sold during the year	13,500
Ending finished goods inventory in units	1,500
Selling price per unit	$60
Manufacturing costs:	
Variable costs per unit:	
Direct materials	$20
Direct labor	12
Variable manufacturing overhead	8
Fixed manufacturing overhead	$60,000
Selling and administrative expenses:	
Variable costs per unit sold	$5
Fixed expenses	$50,000

Required

A. Assuming that Kokomo uses absorption costing, compute the inventory cost per unit, and prepare an income statement for the year using a *traditional format*.

B. Assuming that the company uses variable costing, compute the product cost per unit, and prepare an income statement for the year showing the *contribution margin*.

C. Explain the difference between the variable-costing and absorption-costing net income figures.

D. Assuming that Kokomo had finished goods in inventory at the beginning of the year, what would have happened to the company's net income if the number of units sold during the period had been greater than the number of units produced? Explain your answer.

The solution to Self-Study Problem 3 appears at the end of the chapter.

REVIEW   *SUMMARY of IMPORTANT CONCEPTS*

1. Manufacturing costs may be classified according to their behavior with respect to changes in production volume as follows:
   a. Variable costs change in total with volume but are fixed per unit.
   b. Fixed costs do not change in total with volume but vary per unit.
   c. Semivariable or mixed costs combine variable and fixed costs.
   d. Step-pattern costs are fixed over a small range but vary over a wide range of activities.

2. Companies can use two different methods to assign product cost.
   a. The variable-costing method classifies costs by behavior, breaking costs down into variable and fixed components.
   b. The absorption-costing method classifies costs by function, manufacturing and non-manufacturing.

3. Key to variable costing is contribution margin, the difference between sales and variable expenses over a period. Profit is the contribution margin less fixed expenses.

4. The variable-costing method helps managers understand the relationship among costs, volume, and profits, an understanding that is basic to breakeven-point analysis, target-profit analysis, and profit-sensitivity analysis.

5. Operating risk increases as the percentage of fixed costs to total costs rises.

6. Both variable and absorption costing can be used to calculate unit product cost, an important element in a company's pricing decisions.
   a. Using variable costing, only those production costs that vary with volume are included in the unit product cost calculation.
   b. Using absorption costing, all product costs—fixed and variable—are part of the unit product cost calculation.
   c. The difference in the value of finished goods inventory between variable and absorption costing is a function of the way the methods treat fixed overhead costs.
      (1) Variable-costing expenses all fixed costs in the period in which they are incurred.
      (2) Absorption costing holds fixed overhead costs in inventory until the products are sold.

7. The way in which the methods treat inventory also has an impact on the net income figure each produces—a factor in the evaluation of managerial performance.

8. Variable costing is a managerial tool.
   a. Its proponents insist that it is more accurate than absorption costing and that it is critical to managerial decisions about costs, volume, and profits.
   b. Its critics argue that it is a tactical decision-making tool, useful only for making short-run decisions.

9. Absorption costing must be used for financial reporting. Some companies also use absorption costing for internal decision making.
   a. Absorption costing can be more effective than variable costing for strategic decision making.
   b. One limitation of the method is that it can create an incentive for overproduction.

10. Service organizations, like manufacturing companies, rely on variable or absorption costing to make managerial decisions, particularly decisions about pricing.

DEFINE   *TERMS and CONCEPTS DEFINED in this CHAPTER*

absorption costing   (M166)   committed fixed costs   (M171)
breakeven point   (M166)   contribution margin   (M166)

contribution margin ratio   (M167)
cost-volume-profit (CVP) analysis   (M167)
discretionary fixed costs   (M171)
fixed costs   (M162)
mixed costs   (M163)
operating risk   (M171)
relevant costs   (M164)

semivariable costs   (M163)
step-pattern costs   (M163)
target profit   (M170)
variable costing   (M166)
variable-costing income statement   (M166)
variable costs   (M161)

SELF-STUDY PROBLEM SOLUTIONS

SSP7-1   A. Materials and manufacturing wages are variable; administrative salaries and depreciation are fixed; utilities are semivariable; inspector salaries are step.

B.

	Total	Unit	
Metal for frames	$ 40,000	$12.54	
Foam filler	25,000	7.84	
Plastic seat covering	15,000	4.70	
Manufacturing wages	23,000	7.21	
Inspector salaries	7,000		
Administrative salaries	12,000		
Depreciation	4,000		
Utilities	1,600	0.25	($800 ÷ 3,190)
Total	$127,600	$32.54	

C.

Variable costs: 3,500 units × $32.54 =	$113,890
Inspector salaries	7,000
Administrative salaries	12,000
Depreciation	4,000
Fixed utilities	800
Total costs	$137,690
Revenues (3,500 × $50)	$175,000
Total costs	137,690
Net income	$ 37,310

SSP7-2   A. Calhoun would have to sell 600,000 yards to break even:

$$\text{Unit contribution margin} = \$10 - \$3$$
$$= \$7 \text{ per yard}$$
$$\text{Breakeven units} = \$4,200,000 \div \$7$$
$$= 600,000 \text{ yards}$$

The company's breakeven point in sales dollars would be $6 million (600,000 units sold × $10).

B. Calhoun would have to sell 700,000 yards of the carpet to earn a target profit of $700,000:

$$(\$700,000 + \$4,200,000) \div \$7 = 700,000 \text{ yards}$$

In sales dollars, sales of 700,000 yards equal $7 million (700,000 yards × $10).

SSP7-3   A. Using absorption costing, both fixed and variable manufacturing costs are included in the unit product cost. The unit product cost is $44:

Direct materials costs per unit	$20
Direct labor costs per unit	12
Variable manufacturing overhead costs per unit	8
Fixed manufacturing overhead costs per unit	
($60,000 ÷ 15,000 units)	4
Total cost per unit	$44

The absorption-costing income statement looks like this:

Sales revenue (13,500 × $60)	$810,000
Less cost of goods sold (13,500 × $44)	594,000
Gross margin	$216,000
Less selling and administrative expenses*	117,500
Net income	$ 98,500

*Variable selling and administrative	
expenses (13,500 units sold × $5)	$ 67,500
Fixed selling and administrative expenses	50,000
Total selling and administrative expenses	$117,500

B. Using variable costing, only variable product costs are included in the unit cost. The
unit product cost is $40:

Direct materials	$20
Direct labor	12
Variable manufacturing overhead	8
Total cost per unit	$40

The income statement looks like this:

Sales revenue (13,500 × $60)		$810,000
Less variable expenses:		
Variable cost of goods sold (13,500 × $40)	$540,000	
Variable selling and administrative		
expenses (13,500 × $5)	67,500	
Total variable expenses		607,500
Contribution margin		$202,500
Less fixed expenses:		
Fixed manufacturing overhead	$ 60,000	
Fixed selling and administrative expenses	50,000	
Total fixed expenses		110,000
Net income		$ 92,500

C. Kokomo's absorption-costing net income ($98,500) is $6,000 more than the variable-
costing net income ($92,500). That difference equals the fixed overhead costs of the units
that remained in finished goods inventory at the end of the year under the absorption-
costing method:

1,500 units in finished goods inventory × $4 fixed manufacturing overhead costs per
unit = $6,000

D. If Kokomo had sold more units than it produced during the year, the absorption-costing
net income would have been less than the variable-costing net income. Using absorption costing, a company's selling more units than it has produced has the effect of releasing fixed overhead costs that were deferred in previous periods.

Thinking Beyond the Question

How much do we need to sell to make a profit?

In Chapter M2, you learned how fixed costs remain fixed only within a relevant range. If sales and production are not in that relevant range, fixed costs do not stay constant. In the real world, the variable cost of making one unit may also change if sales and production vary a great deal. For example, if production exceeds the amount that can be produced within the normal work week, a higher-cost overtime wage is likely to be required. A certain amount of "normal" overtime may be assumed in the unit variable cost, but unusual amounts of overtime for extended periods will alter temporarily the unit variable cost and the company's breakeven point.

Think about Erin and Seth's dilemma at the beginning of the chapter. They want to determine the level of sales required to break even or to make a target profit. Suppose Young Designs, Inc.'s, sales and production temporarily exceed certain levels, and the unit variable cost changes substantially because of increased overtime costs. How can Erin and Seth deal with such changes within the context of breakeven analysis? Does this issue have any similarities to step fixed costs? Does the existence of multiple breakeven points invalidate breakeven analysis?

QUESTIONS

Q7-1
Obj. 1
You decide to study for an upcoming accounting exam with a friend. Your friend says that fixed costs are considered fixed because they remain constant, or "fixed," for each unit produced. Do you agree? Explain your answer.

Q7-2
Obj. 1
Pagoda Company manufactures metal picture-framing materials. Part of the manufacturing process is the coating and painting of the metal with finishes. Management of Pagoda believes the painting process is a variable cost that is incurred evenly for each unit that passes through the painting operation. An analysis of several recent production runs revealed, however, that costs differ on a per-unit basis when the run sizes differ. Is the cost of painting a variable cost? What explanation could you provide for the cost behavior of the painting operation?

Q7-3
Obj. 1
Explain the importance of cost behavior as it relates to various levels of production activity. Why is information about cost behavior important to managers? Identify some decisions that managers make that require information about cost behavior.

Q7-4
Obj. 2
Jane Pratt is the president of Capital Products, Inc. Capital manufactures adjustable baseball caps embroidered with the logos of college teams. The company is planning to produce a special hat with the logo of a university that recently won the national football championship. The hats will be sold throughout the country over the next three months. After meeting with the managers of sales, production, and purchasing, Jane has determined that the special hat will have a positive contribution margin of $1.50. Capital currently is earning a profit for the year. What does the contribution margin represent? Why is it important to Jane?

Q7-5
Obj. 2
Ampco Industries, Inc., produces audio and video circuit boards. Ampco sold 12,500 circuit boards last month, which was its breakeven point in sales units. Explain what the breakeven point is.

Q7-6
Obj. 2
Enterprises produces and sells a specialty soft drink called PowerPunch. The contribution margin ratio for PowerPunch is 40%. What percentage of total sales is used to cover variable costs? Will these percentages change with a rise or fall in sales volume? What does PowerPunch's contribution margin in dollars equal at the breakeven point?

Q7-7
Obj. 3
Snow Manufacturing Company produces a snowshoe that is sold in many parts of the upper Midwest. The company's production manager has decided to change the materials used in the production process, a change that should produce a savings in direct materials costs of $12

per pair of snowshoes. The sales manager has decided to pass the savings on to the customer by reducing the selling price of the snowshoes $12 a pair. What effect will these changes have on Snow's breakeven point in units?

Q7-8
Obj. 3
An automobile manufacturer is considering buying new robotic welders for its frame assembly operations that will replace existing manual welding. This change is expected to result in lower overall costs and higher quality. Explain the impact of this decision in terms of operating risk.

Q7-9
Obj. 4
Hendee Productions Company does personal and commercial videotaping. Hendee accumulates the cost of each video production on a per-job basis using the variable-costing method. Pete Conrad, the owner of the company, recently noticed that selling and administrative expenses are not included in the costs of production. Pete is considering a switch to absorption costing. Would selling and administrative expenses be treated differently under absorption costing? Explain your answer.

Q7-10
Obj. 4
Sam Merchant was recently hired as a cost accountant by Dolls and Such Manufacturing. The company's management desires more useful information. The controller asked Sam to review the company's inventory records and to convert the carrying value of each item in inventory from an absorption-costing value to a variable-costing value. What differences does Sam have to consider in making his calculations? Why might the controller have chosen to convert to variable costing?

Q7-11
Obj. 4
Over the past year, Darren, Inc., has seen its finished goods inventory go up significantly. Darren prepares financial statements for its stockholders using absorption costing. The company prepares another set of financial statements for its managers using variable costing. Which of the two statements is going to show a greater net income for the year? Why?

Q7-12
Obj. 4
Juanita Perez is the president of Allgood Manufacturing, Inc. Allgood manufactures electric power tools. The company uses the absorption-costing method. Over the past year, sales increased significantly at Allgood, reducing the company's inventories 60% from the beginning of the year. When she looked at the year's sales figures, Juanita was surprised that net income was lower than anticipated. What factors might have been at work here?

Q7-13
Obj. 4
Suppose that the number of units in a company's ending inventory equals the number of units in its beginning inventory and that its fixed costs have not changed from the previous year. Which costing method—variable or absorption costing—would yield a higher net income?

Q7-14
Obj. 4
Coyote Battery Company manufactures rechargeable nickel cadmium batteries. The company uses the variable-costing method to accumulate inventory costs. At the end of its fiscal year, Coyote has to prepare its financial statements and tax returns. Can Coyote use its inventory values for financial-reporting and tax purposes? Explain your answer.

Q7-15
Obj. 4
Jan and Fran Hook are hairdressers with over 40 years of experience between them. Recently they decided to combine their savings and buy a factory to produce men's hairpieces. Jan has assumed responsibility for administration, including the development of accounting procedures. Fran does not understand why the inventory value of a hairpiece should include plant and supervisory costs. How should Jan explain the process of placing a value on inventory to Fran?

Q7-16
Obj. 4
Absorption costing defers certain costs. Which costs are deferred? Where? When are these costs expensed? How does variable costing treat these costs?

Q7-17
Obj. 4
Randy Lightfoot is vice president of operations for MultiCo, Inc. He is responsible for the operations of the company's two manufacturing plants, one in Atlanta and one in St. Louis. Each plant has a manager who oversees the daily operations. During a recent review of operations for the year, prepared using absorption costing, Randy noted that the Atlanta plant reported net income and that the balance in finished goods inventory had grown significantly over the year. The St. Louis plant showed no net income, but its inventory fell over the year. According to MultiCo's policy, the Atlanta plant manager will receive a bonus this year based on the income generated at the plant; the St. Louis manager will not receive a bonus. Comment on Randy's observation. What conflicts are created when a company determines its managers' bonuses based on net income alone?

Q7-18
Obj. 4
Ruth Peevey is president of Tuffee Tools Company. Tuffee manufactures a wide variety of hand tools and sells them throughout the South. Ruth just completed a review of next year's budget and plans, which project an operating loss. Knowing that Tuffee's stockholders and

the bank that is financing the company will not be happy with an operating loss, Ruth has asked the company's controller to recalculate next year's predetermined overhead rate to include 50% of all budgeted administrative costs. What problems does this create for the controller? Should the controller make the changes?

EXERCISES

If your instructor is using Personal Trainer® in this course, you may complete your assignments online.

E7-1 Write a short definition of each of the terms listed in the *Terms and Concepts Defined in this Chapter* section.

E7-2 Use (a) variable costs, (b) fixed costs, (c) semivariable costs, and (d) step-pattern costs to classify
Obj. 1 each of the following costs based on its cost behavior. Provide a brief explanation of your answer.

a. Direct materials
b. Direct labor
c. Depreciation
d. Salary of production supervisor
e. Telephone expense
f. Machine repairs
g. Factory janitor wages
h. Property taxes
i. Sales commissions
j. Material handling

E7-3 The data for costs A, B, and C are as follows. Determine the cost behavior (variable, fixed, or semi-
Obj. 1 variable) of Cost A, Cost B, and Cost C. Prepare a graph depicting the cost behavior of each of the three costs, using total cost as the vertical axis and production volume as the horizontal axis.

	Number of Units Produced	Unit Cost	Total Cost
Cost A	1	?	$ 15
	10	?	150
	100	?	1,500
	1,000	?	15,000
Cost B	1	$6,000	?
	10	600	?
	100	60	?
	1,000	6	?
Cost C	1	?	$ 4,025
	10	?	4,250
	100	?	6,500
	1,000	?	29,000

E7-4 Sheldon Nast, an entry-level cost accountant, was asked by his supervisor to analyze mainte-
Obj. 1 nance costs. Sheldon produced the following plot of maintenance costs by production level:

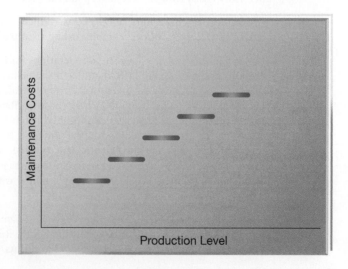

He immediately recognized how costs vary with production levels and remembered how to plot a line through data points to describe its slope. Convinced he had discovered a linear relationship that describes cost at any level of production, Sheldon produced the following graph to demonstrate his point at the next managers' meeting:

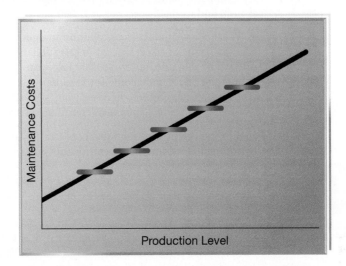

a. Do maintenance costs increase in a linear fashion as production levels increase? Why or why not?

b. What effect, if any, would cutting production by 10% have on maintenance department costs? Explain your answer.

E7-5

Obj. 2

Taylor, Inc., produces a child's wall clock that chimes the tune "Three Blind Mice" every hour. The contribution margin for this clock is $8, and the breakeven point is 8,000 units. How much profit will Taylor make if it sells 11,000 clocks? What are the company's total fixed costs?

E7-6

Obj. 2

The following partial information is from Brown Bag, Inc.'s income statement for 2006, prepared using variable costing:

Sales revenue	___
Less variable costs	___
Contribution margin	___
Less fixed costs	$30,000
Net income	$10,000

Brown Bag's contribution margin ratio is 40%. What percentage of Brown Bag's revenue is used to cover variable costs? What were variable costs at this sales volume? What was sales revenue in 2006?

E7-7

Obj. 2

Double R Company's most recent income statement, prepared on a contribution-margin basis, is as follows:

SPREADSHEET

	Total	Per Unit
Sales	$500,000	$25
Less variable costs	360,000	18
Contribution margin	$140,000	$ 7
Less fixed costs	110,000	
Net income	$ 30,000	

Prepare a new income statement under each of the following independent conditions:

a. Sales volume increases 20%.

b. The selling price drops $4 per unit, and sales volume increases 30%.

c. The selling price increases $2, fixed costs increase $10,000, and sales volume decreases 5%.

(Continued)

d. The selling price increases 20%, variable costs increase $2 per unit, and fixed costs increase 20%.

e. Variable costs increase $2 per unit, and fixed costs decrease by $40,000.

E7-8
Objs. 2, 3

Joey Company manufactures a product that sells for $27 per unit. Its variable costs are $15 per unit, and its fixed costs are $132,000 per year.

a. What is the product's contribution margin ratio?
b. What is the breakeven point in sales dollars?
c. Assume that sales go up $60,000 next year. If fixed costs do not change, how does the increase affect net income (or net loss)?
d. If Joey spends $30,000 on advertising, sales should go up $60,000. If the increased sales do not change the company's contribution margin ratio, should Joey buy the advertising?

E7-9
Objs. 2, 3

SPREADSHEET

Penquin Industries, Inc., manufactures a variety of plastic food containers and serving dishes. The company's income statement for this year in a variable-costing format is as follows:

Sales revenue	$960,000
Less variable production costs	192,000
Less variable selling expenses	96,000
Contribution margin	$672,000
Less fixed manufacturing overhead	300,000
Less fixed selling expenses	139,000
Net income	$233,000

Penquin's management believes that it can increase prices by an average of 6% next year without affecting the number of products sold. Advertising costs are expected to go up next year by $9,000; administrative expenses by $30,000. Production costs are not expected to change.

a. Calculate Penquin's breakeven point in sales dollars for this year.
b. Use the estimates for next year to prepare a variable-costing income statement for that year.
c. Using the forecasted changes, calculate Penquin's breakeven point in sales dollars for next year.

E7-10
Objs. 2, 3

SPREADSHEET

JLC Enterprises is a rapidly growing gardening supply company. Information for the year just ended is as follows:

Sales revenue	$300,000
Units sold	20,000
Unit contribution margin	$10
Total fixed costs	$120,000

What is JLC's breakeven point in dollars?

E7-11
Objs. 2, 3, 5

Green Acres is a lawn care service. Rachel Webb, the owner of the service, is trying to increase her number of regular customers. She has developed several proposals and is trying to decide which one to choose. Following is an income statement for the current year prepared using variable costing:

Green Acres Income Statement			
		Total	Per Job
Revenue		$80,000	$40.00
Less variable costs:			
Variable product costs	$15,000		7.50
Variable selling and administrative expenses	20,000	35,000	10.00
Contribution margin		$45,000	$22.50
Less fixed costs:			
Fixed product costs	$10,000		
Fixed selling and administrative expenses	6,000	16,000	
Net income		$29,000	

Prepare a new income statement under each of the following independent conditions:

a. Rachel increases her fixed advertising budget by $2,000 and sales increase by 10%.
b. Rachel reduces the selling price by $5 per job, and volume increases 50%.
c. Rachel reduces the selling price $3 per job, reduces fixed costs 8%, and volume increases to 2,500 jobs.

E7-12
Obj. 3

Carbon Industries, Inc., is considering buying new equipment to use in the manufacture of its product. The new machines, which would increase production capacity, would also require annual fixed costs of $480,000. Carbon expects variable costs to go down with more efficient use of materials and fewer direct labor hours. Those savings would be offset in part by higher variable manufacturing overhead costs related to machine maintenance. The net effect of the changes would be a 20% reduction overall in Carbon's variable manufacturing costs. Total sales are not expected to change in 2005. If the company does not buy the new machines, it expects the following next year:

Sales revenue	$8,000,000
Variable costs	70% of sales
Fixed costs	$1,600,000

If Carbon does buy the new equipment, what will be the net income next year?

E7-13
Obj. 3

Home Company never advertises. The Ad group, an advertising agency that has been trying to win Home over, claims that an aggressive advertising campaign would increase Home's sales by 22%. A summary of Home's sales and costs for the year just ended is as follows:

Units sold	150,000
Selling price per unit	$50
Variable manufacturing costs per unit	$10
Fixed costs:	
Manufacturing overhead	$800,000
Selling and administrative expenses	$700,000

Using this information, determine how much Home could pay for advertising and earn a target profit of $300,000.

E7-14
Obj. 3

Stillman, Inc., manufactures light bulb filaments and other miscellaneous parts for electronic equipment. Stillman has the opportunity to fill a large special order for a new customer. The special order would require Stillman to incur extra production costs. Selected cost information regarding the part is as follows:

Number of parts ordered	3,000
Revenue from special order	$25,000
Additional production costs for special order	$5,000
Contribution margin ratio	30%

Calculate the difference in profit or loss that would result if Stillman accepts the special order versus rejecting it.

E7-15
Obj. 3

SPREADSHEET

Matt Ledesma has recently been hired as vice president for marketing by Glencoe, Inc. Matt is convinced that Glencoe should launch a major new promotion that includes a tie-in with a movie. For every one of Glencoe's products sold, the customer would be given two free tickets to the movie. Glencoe's most recent income statement, based on sales of 100,000 units, is as follows:

Sales revenue	$300,000
Less variable costs	120,000
Contribution margin	$180,000
Less fixed costs	70,000
Net income	$110,000

(Continued)

Matt has conducted some market research and concluded that the promotion would increase sales by 15,000 units. The movie tickets would cost Glencoe $0.50 each. What would net income be if Glencoe does the promotion? What would net income be if one ticket instead of two is given away with each purchase?

E7-16
Obj. 3

Carol's Creations produces and markets a unique product. The president of the company has set a target profit of $50,025 for the coming year. Cost information for the company is as follows:

SPREADSHEET

Selling price per unit	$ 125
Variable product cost per unit	36
Variable selling and administrative expense per unit	14
Fixed manufacturing overhead per year	43,975
Fixed selling and administrative expense per year	56,000

a. Calculate the breakeven point in units.
b. Calculate the number of units Carol's Creations will need to sell to achieve the target profit of $50,025.

E7-17
Obj. 3

Atwater Enterprises sold 5,000 units of product A during July. It reported the following sales and cost information for the month:

Sales revenue	$400,000
Less variable costs	240,000
Less fixed costs	120,000
Net income	$ 40,000

Suppose Atwater increases the selling price of product A by 10%. How many units would it have to sell to continue generating a monthly income of $40,000?

E7-18
Obj. 3

In planning its operations for next year, Petrie, Inc. estimated sales of $6,000,000 and the following costs:

	Costs and Expenses	
	Variable	Fixed
Direct materials	$1,600,000	
Direct labor	1,400,000	
Factory overhead	600,000	$ 900,000
Selling expenses	240,000	360,000
Administrative expenses	60,000	140,000
Total	$3,900,000	$1,400,000

Calculate Petrie's breakeven point in sales dollars.

E7-19
Obj. 3

The following CVP graph shows the relationships in one company among costs, volume, and profits:

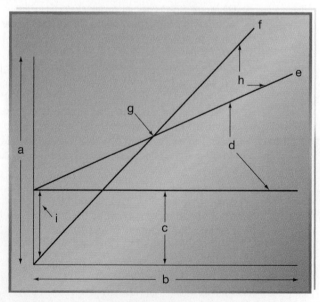

a. Label each of the lettered elements on the graph.
b. List the lettered elements in the graph that would be affected by each of the following actions and the nature of the effect. Treat each case independently. Ignore the effect on element h.
(1) The selling price per unit goes down from $50 to $45.
(2) Variable costs per unit go up from $18 to $23.
(3) Fixed costs fall $3,000.
(4) Sales volume goes up 1,500 units.
(5) The company sells a piece of production equipment, increasing labor hours and reducing fixed costs.
(6) Both variable costs and the selling price go up 10%.
(7) The company incurs advertising costs in the amount of $25,000 a year. Sales increase as a result.

E7-20
Obj. 4
Yellow Jacket Company manufactures one product, an organic bath soap. Information concerning production during the past year is as follows:

Units produced and sold	25,000
Direct labor cost	$40,000
Direct materials cost	$10,000
Factory supervisor's salary	$15,000
Other fixed manufacturing overhead	$5,000
Indirect materials (varies with production)	$1,300
Other variable manufacturing overhead	$1,200
Variable selling expenses	$1,000
Fixed selling and administrative expenses	$40,000

a. What is unit product cost using absorption costing?
b. What is unit product cost using variable costing?
c. What is the total unit variable cost?

E7-21
Obj. 4
Azure Company went into business two years ago. Information concerning production, costs, sales, and inventory levels for the last two years is as follows:

	2005	2004
Sales revenue	$1,200,000	$1,000,000
Sales in units	22,000	15,000
Production in units	20,000	20,000
Variable product cost per unit	$30	$30
Fixed manufacturing overhead	$10,000	$10,000
Fixed selling and administrative expenses	$30,000	$30,000
Variable selling and administrative expenses (per unit sold)	$5	$5

a. Calculate unit product cost using absorption costing.
b. Calculate unit product cost using variable costing.
c. Which costing method, variable or absorption, will report a higher net income for 2004?
d. Which costing method, variable or absorption, will report a higher net income for 2005?

E7-22
Obj. 4
Proto, Inc., manufactures a single product. The company's production results, sales, costs, and inventory levels last year is as follows:

Total production in units	96,600
Total sales in units	82,200
Fixed selling and administrative costs	$113,880
Selling price per unit	$12
Variable-costing net income	$11,880
Absorption-costing net income	$17,640

Calculate the total fixed manufacturing overhead costs and the fixed manufacturing overhead cost per unit. Prepare an income statement using the absorption-costing method.

E7-23
Obj. 4

During 2005, C & R Industries, Inc., produced 10,000 units and sold 8,000 units of its product. It began 2005 with no units in its finished goods inventory. The ending balance in finished goods inventory was $18,000 using absorption costing and $6,000 using variable costing. What was the total fixed manufacturing overhead cost for 2005? What was the difference in net income for the year if variable costing is used rather than absorption costing?

E7-24
Objs. 4, 5

Hill County Bank, a small, locally owned institution, is reexamining the way it prices its services. The bank's managers are concerned that some of their customers are less profitable than was believed, and are trying to decide what to include in the cost of various services. Cost estimates related to these services are as follows:

	Transaction	
	Withdrawal, Teller	**Withdrawal, ATM**
Direct labor per transaction	$0.75	—
Other variable costs per transaction	$0.25	$0.80
Average # transactions per month	10,000	15,000

Building utilities, depreciation expense on equipment (including the ATM machine), and other fixed costs total $5,000 per month.

  a. What is the cost of a withdrawal using a teller if both fixed and variable costs are included? (Allocate the fixed costs to all transactions.)

  b. What is the cost of an ATM withdrawal if both fixed and variable costs are included? (Allocate the fixed costs to all transactions.)

  c. Monthly depreciation expense on the ATM machine totals $750. What is the cost of an ATM withdrawal if that is the only fixed cost included in your calculations?

PROBLEMS

If your instructor is using Personal Trainer® in this course, you may complete your assignments online.

P7-1
Obj. 1

Cost Behavior

Tim Ricker lives in Atlanta. He is a toolmaker for Georgia Industries, a manufacturer of heavy equipment such as backhoes, graders, and earthmoving equipment. Tim makes specialty tools and jigs that are used on different machines in the plant. His annual salary is $35,000. Ann Thompson also works for Georgia Industries. She is an independent sales representative who lives in El Paso, Texas. She is paid a straight salary of $25,000 but also earns a 5% commission on sales. Ann is responsible for accounts in the west Texas area, works out of an office in her home, and is reimbursed by Georgia Industries for her travel expenses. The company provides Ann with a leased vehicle and a gasoline credit card.

Required

  A. Classify Tim and Ann's income as fixed, variable, or semivariable expenses.

  B. Classify Ann's travel expenses as fixed, variable, or semivariable. What considerations are important in arriving at your answer?

P7-2
Objs. 1–4

Cost Behavior and Employee Motivation

Refer to the facts presented in P7-1.

Required

  A. For financial reporting purposes, are Tim and Ann's salaries and expenses considered a product cost or a period expense?

  B. As illustrated in the problem, top management at Georgia Industries has established different compensation systems for manufacturing and sales employees. These managers made their decisions, based on an understanding of cost behavior, to help reduce risks and to motivate certain types of behavior. Would you classify Ann's salary as fixed, variable, or mixed? Why?

  C. What type of behavior are managers at Georgia Industries attempting to motivate?

  D. Does this type of compensation package reduce risk for Georgia Industries? Explain.

  E. Describe various types of analyses the partners might conduct using monthly financial information.

P7-3 **Cost Behavior**

Obj. 1

A company's cost structure may contain numerous different cost behavior patterns. Below are descriptions of several different costs; match these to the appropriate graphs. On each graph, the vertical axis represents cost and the horizontal axis represents level of activity or volume.

Required Identify, by letter, the graph that illustrates each of the following cost behavior patterns. Graphs may be used more than once.

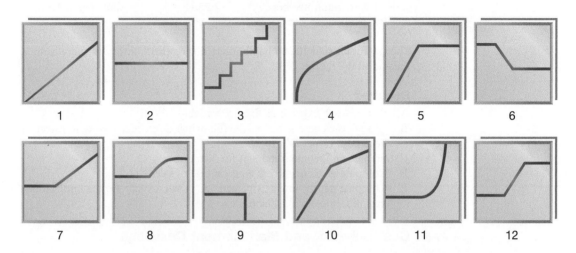

A. Cost of raw materials, where the cost decreases by 6 cents per unit for each of the first 150 units purchased, after which it remains constant at $2.75 per unit.

B. City water bill, which is computed as follows:

First 750,000 gallons or less $1,000 flat fee
Next 15,000 gallons $0.002 per gallon used
Next 15,000 gallons $0.005 per gallon used
Next 15,000 gallons $0.008 per gallon used
Etc. Etc.

C. Rent on a factory building donated by the city, where the agreement provides for a fixed-fee payment, unless 250,000 labor hours are worked, in which case no rent needs to be paid.

D. Cost of raw materials used.

E. Electricity bill—a flat fixed charge of $250 plus a variable cost after 150,000 kilowatt-hours are used.

F. Salaries of maintenance workers if one maintenance worker is needed for every 1,000 hours or less of machine time.

G. Depreciation of equipment using the straight-line method.

H. Rent on a factory building donated by the county, where the agreement provides for a monthly rental of $100,000 less $1 for each labor hour worked in excess of 200,000 hours. However, a minimum rental payment of $20,000 must be made each month.

I. Rent on a machine that is billed at $1,000 for up to 500 hours of machine time. After 500 hours of machine time, an additional charge of $1 per hour is paid up to a maximum charge of $2,500 per period.

(Material from the Uniform CPA Examination Questions and Unofficial Answers, Copyright © by the American Institute of Certified Public Accountants, Inc., is reprinted [or adapted] with permission.)

P7-4 **Cost Behavior and the Income Statement**

Objs. 1–4

Lauren Stephens owns William's Restaurant, which sells hamburgers for carry out or drive through only. Each hamburger sells for $2. Lauren employs several part-time employees and a full-time manager. She leases the building and hires a cleaning company to provide services on a weekly basis. The manager, who is paid a monthly salary, carries out all administrative functions such as hiring, scheduling, and counting cash.

(Continued)

The following expenses were incurred in November.

Ground meat	$1,500	Manager's salary	$2,100
Lettuce	350	Utilities	600
Tomatoes	400	Depreciation, grill	350
Buns	400	Depreciation, signs	100
Condiments	70	Advertising	75
Part-time labor, cooks	2,500	Rent	800
Part-time labor, servers	2,250	Cleaning service	300
Wrapping paper and bags	30		

The restaurant sold 10,000 hamburgers during the month, and there is no WIP inventory at the end of the month.

Required

A. Identify each expense as fixed or variable.
B. Classify each cost as one of the following: direct materials cost, direct labor cost, overhead cost, or period expense.
C. Prepare an income statement for November.
D. Compute gross margin as a percentage of sales.
E. Compute net income as a percentage of sales. What are the implications of your findings in terms of risk? Elaborate.

P7-5   ## Cost Behavior and Management Decisions

Objs. 1, 3

Shiny Company produces a line of cleaning products for both industrial and household use. While most of the company's products are processed independently, a few are related, such as Glow and Satin Silver Polish.

Glow is an abrasive cleaner used in industrial applications. It costs $1.60 per pound to produce and sells for $2.40 per pound. A small portion of Glow each year is combined with other ingredients to form Satin Silver Polish. Satin sells for $5.00 per jar.

Each jar of Satin uses $1/4$ pound of Glow. The other costs of ingredients and labor required for further processing are as follows:

Additional ingredients	$1.00
Additional direct labor	1.48
Total added cost	$2.48

The additional overhead costs required each month for further processing are:

Variable overhead	50% of additional labor costs
Fixed overhead	$3,000, related mainly to depreciation (none of the fixed costs are avoidable)

Advertising costs for Satin total $5,000 per month; the variable selling costs related to Satin are 10% of sales.

Because of a recent drop in demand for silver polish, the management of Shiny is thinking about stopping production of Satin. The sales manager believes it would be more profitable to just sell Glow.

Required

A. What is the additional revenue less the additional processing costs, per jar (contribution margin), from further processing Glow into Satin?
B. Assume that marketing projections indicate the company can sell 5,000 jars of Satin each month. What advice would you give to Shiny management? Support your advice with a calculation.

P7-6   ## Contribution Margin Ratio

Objs. 2, 3

Skyler Industries, Inc., produces and sells swimwear. The following information is for a recent period:

Production	10,000 units
Sales	7,000 units
Unit selling price	$50
Variable product costs	$80,000
Variable selling and administrative	$2 per unit sold
Fixed manufacturing overhead	$51,000
Fixed selling and administrative	$70,000

Required

A. What is the unit contribution margin? What are some actions Skyler could take to increase the unit contribution margin?
B. What is the contribution margin ratio? What does this mean?
C. Use the contribution margin ratio to calculate sales dollars at the breakeven point.

P7-7

Objs. 2, 3

SPREADSHEET

Contribution Margin and Breakeven Point

Elizabeth McClary recently began a small snowboard company called Pure Powder. She and her staff have assembled cost information regarding the snowboards.

Variable unit costs (per snowboard):	
Direct materials	$ 25
Direct labor	20
Variable manufacturing overhead	7
Variable selling and administrative	3
Fixed costs (for the period):	
Fixed manufacturing overhead	24,300
Fixed selling and administrative	40,075

The snowboards sell for $180.

Required

A. What is the unit contribution margin per snowboard?
B. What is the breakeven point in units?
C. Explain what the contribution margin is, and why it is useful information for Elizabeth.

P7-8

Objs. 2, 3

SPREADSHEET

Breakeven Point

Small Fries is a company that processes gourmet potatoes into little french fries. Each package has a contribution margin of $2.50. Small Fries has total fixed costs of $40,000 each period. The selling price of one package is $5. Sales for the most recent period totaled $90,000.

Required What is the company's breakeven point in units? In dollars?

P7-9

Objs. 2, 3

SPREADSHEET

Breakeven Point, Cost Structure, and Target Sales

Plainfield Bakers, Inc., manufactures and sells a popular line of fat-free cookies under the name Aunt May's Cookies. The process Plainfield uses to manufacture the cookies is labor-intensive; it relies heavily on direct labor. Last year Plainfield sold 300,000 dozen cookies at $2.50 per dozen. Variable costs at this level of production totaled $1.50 per dozen, and fixed costs for the year totaled $150,000.

Required

A. Prepare a contribution-margin income statement for last year.
B. Calculate the company's contribution-margin ratio and breakeven point in sales units for last year.
C. Plainfield's direct labor rate is going to go up $0.40 a dozen next year. Assuming that the selling price stays at $2.50 a dozen, calculate next year's contribution margin and breakeven point in sales units.
D. Plainfield's management is thinking about automating the production process, a change that would reduce variable costs by $0.60 a dozen but would raise fixed costs by

(Continued)

$150,000 a year. If the company undertakes the automation project, how would its contribution margin and breakeven point in sales units be affected?

E. Assuming that Plainfield does go ahead with the automation project [see requirement (D)], how many dozen cookies would the company have to sell at $2.50 a dozen to earn the same income it earned last year?

F. What are some of the nonfinancial aspects of the automation decision that Plainfield's management should consider when deciding whether to embark on the automation project or not?

P7-10 Graphing the Cost-Volume-Profit Relationship

Objs. 2, 3 Two CVP graphs and cost information for two unrelated companies, each of which manufactures a single product, follow:

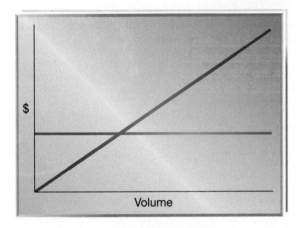

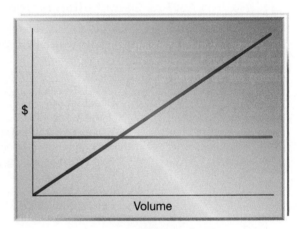

Company A
Fixed costs = $400,000
Sales = $150 per unit
Contribution margin = $20 per unit

Company B
Fixed costs = $400,000
Sales = $150 per unit
Contribution margin = $40 per unit

Required

A. Complete each graph by adding a total-cost line and the breakeven point, and by labeling each of the CVP graph lines.
B. Calculate the variable unit product cost for each company.
C. Calculate the breakeven point in sales units for each company.
D. Why are the companies' breakeven points different when both sell their products for the same price? How is that difference reflected in the CVP graphs in requirement (A)?

P7-11 Ethics and CVP Analysis

Obj. 3 Nathan Dechter is the controller of Specialty Candies, Inc., a manufacturer of candies and confections. The company's executive planning committee has asked Nathan to prepare an analysis of two alternatives the committee is considering. The first alternative is labor-intensive. Nathan's analysis revealed the following:

Sales revenue (projected at 6,000,000 units)	$1,800,000
Less variable costs	1,000,000
Contribution margin	$ 800,000
Less fixed costs	600,000
Net income	$ 200,000

The second alternative would automate the factory, increasing fixed costs and reducing variable costs:

Sales revenue (projected at 6,000,000 units)	$1,800,000
Less variable costs	800,000
Contribution margin	$1,000,000
Less fixed costs	800,000
Net income	$ 200,000

Before sharing his analysis with the executive planning committee, Nathan thought about the probable outcome of the committee's decision making. He knows that if the committee decides to automate the plant, many of his friends in the production department will lose their jobs. Although both alternatives yield net income of $200,000 at the projected level of sales, Nathan is afraid that management will opt for automation. Nathan could recalculate depreciation using a method that would increase fixed costs in the short run, which would encourage management to reject the automation alternative.

Required

A. Is there an argument that Nathan could make to support the labor-intensive alternative without manipulating the financial data? (*Hint:* Calculate the breakeven point for each alternative.)
B. Do you think Nathan should alter the fixed costs of the automation alternative? Would this be ethical? Would the manipulation be justified if it helps a number of employees keep their jobs? Why or why not?

P7-12   ## Contribution Margin and Purchase Decisions

Obj. 3   Douglas Cabinet Company manufactures a single model of bathroom cabinet. The company's contribution margin ratio is 45%. Douglas is considering an advertising campaign that would cost $8,000 but is expected to increase sales by $22,000.

Required

A. What dollar amount of the additional revenue will go to cover variable costs?
B. Should Douglas buy the advertising? Explain your answer.
C. If Douglas's contribution margin ratio is 30% instead of 45%, should it still buy the advertising? Explain your answer.

P7-13   ## Variable Costing and Production Variations

Objs. 2, 4   Jerry Sanchez is president of Heatco, Inc., a manufacturer of a single product. He is comparing this year's income statement with last year's and is wondering why net income is different for the same level of sales. "Our costs have not changed at all, yet look at our income. What did we do right this year?" The statements, both prepared using absorption costing, look like this:

	This Year	Last Year
Sales revenue (40,000 units each year)	$800,000	$800,000
Less cost of goods sold	400,000	460,000
Gross margin	$400,000	$340,000
Less selling and administrative expenses	300,000	300,000
Net income	$100,000	$ 40,000

Last year, the first year of operations, the company produced 40,000 units and sold them all. This year, the company increased production to maintain a margin of safety in its finished goods inventory. Fixed costs are applied to products on the basis of the number of units produced each year. Here is a summary of Heatco's production results, variable production costs, and fixed manufacturing overhead cost for both years:

	This Year	Last Year
Production in units	50,000	40,000
Production costs:		
Variable cost per unit	$4	$4
Fixed manufacturing overhead	$300,000	$300,000

(Continued)

Required

A. Calculate the unit product cost under variable costing and absorption costing.
B. Prepare an income statement for each year using variable costing.
C. Compare the net income figures in the variable-costing income statement [requirement (B)] and the absorption-costing income statement for each of the years. Explain any differences.
D. Why did Heatco earn more this year than last year using absorption costing, even though the company sold the same number of units?

P7-14 **Absorption and Variable Costing**

Obj. 4

SPREADSHEET

Joan Tyler started a small manufacturing company, JT Enterprises, at the beginning of 2005. Joan has prepared the following income statement for the first quarter of operations.

JT Enterprises Income Statement For the Quarter Ended March 31, 2005		
Sales revenue (25,000 units)		$1,200,000
Less variable costs:		
Variable cost of goods sold	$540,000	
Variable selling and administrative expenses	260,000	800,000
Contribution margin		$ 400,000
Less fixed costs:		
Fixed manufacturing overhead	$300,000	
Fixed selling and administrative expenses	150,000	450,000
Net loss		$ (50,000)

The variable cost of goods sold includes the costs of direct materials, direct labor, and variable manufacturing overhead. The company began the quarter with no inventory; it manufactured 30,000 units over the period. Variable selling and administrative expenses are based on units sold.

Required

A. Calculate the unit product cost using absorption costing.
B. Rework the income statement using absorption costing.
C. Does the net loss figure change using absorption costing? If yes, explain why.
D. During the second quarter of operations, JT again manufactured 30,000 units but sold 35,000 units. Prepare income statements for the second quarter using both the variable- and absorption-costing methods.
E. Explain the difference in net income (or loss) in the second quarter between the two statements prepared in requirement (D).

P7-15 **Absorption- versus Variable-Costing Income**

Obj. 4

A company that makes cameras uses both variable and absorption costing. The following information pertains to the year just ended:

Units produced	1,000
Units sold	750
Selling price per unit	$375
Variable product costs per unit	$100
Variable selling expense per unit	$20
Fixed manufacturing overhead for the year	$70,000
Fixed administrative expense for the year	$70,000

Required

A. Prepare an income statement using absorption costing.
B. Prepare an income statement using variable costing.
C. Assume that at the beginning of the year, the balance in the finished goods inventory was $0. What is the value of the finished goods inventory at the end of the year using absorption costing? What is the value using variable costing?
D. What causes the difference in net income between the two costing methods?

P7-16 **Using Variable Costing and Full Costing in Pricing Decisions**

Obj. 4

Beat You to the Punch is a young company specializing in computer game software. The company is facing stiff competition from larger, well-established companies. These companies are lowering their prices considerably in an effort to force Beat You out of the market. Managers at Beat You are trying to decide how much they can lower their price in order to remain competitive. Cost information for Beat You from a recent period is as follows:

Production	300 units
Variable product costs	$7 per unit
Variable selling expenses	$3 per unit sold
Fixed manufacturing overhead	$600
Fixed selling and administrative expenses	$20,000

Required

A. If Beat You's managers make their pricing decision based on variable cost and would like a minimum markup of 20%, what should the selling price be?
B. What are some arguments for and against using variable cost alone as the basis for making a pricing decision?
C. If Beat You bases its pricing decision on full cost, and still would like a 20% markup, what would be the selling price?
D. What are some arguments for and against using full cost as the basis for making a pricing decision?

P7-17 **Choosing a Costing Method**

Obj. 4

SPREADSHEET

Cedar Products is a company that produces wooden novelties. The controller has been asked by the president to review the company's costing methods. Currently, the company uses absorption costing for internal as well as external purposes, but they are considering using variable costing for internal reporting and decision making. Information related to a recent production period is as follows:

Units produced	6,000
Units sold	4,000
Direct labor	$6 per unit
Direct materials	$5 per unit
Variable manufacturing overhead	$4 per unit
Fixed manufacturing overhead	$36,000
Variable selling and administrative	$1.50 per unit sold
Fixed selling and administrative	$40,000

Required

A. Calculate the unit product cost using absorption costing.
B. Calculate the unit product cost using variable costing.
C. Cedar's president does not see any need to spend the extra time and money to develop a second costing system. The controller is in favor of doing so. What might the controller tell the president when trying to convince him to agree to use variable costing?

P7-18 **Absorption- and Variable-Costing Income Statements**

Obj. 4

MT Designs, Inc., manufactures a motorcycle accessory. The company was very successful in 2006 and demand for their product was much higher than anticipated. Use the following production and sales information to answer the questions.

(Continued)

Production	5,000 units
Sales	9,000 units
Selling price	$220
Direct materials used, 2004	$125,000
Direct labor cost, 2004	$200,000
Variable manufacturing overhead, 2004	$25,000
Fixed manufacturing overhead, 2004	$60,000
Variable selling expenses	$90,000
Fixed administrative and selling expenses	$130,000

Note: Assume all fixed costs and all variable unit costs remained the same from the previous year.

Required

A. Prepare an income statement using variable costing.
B. Prepare an income statement using absorption costing.
C. Explain why net income is higher using variable costing than absorption costing.
D. Suppose that MT Designs was facing an extended slump in demand for its product, and that the production manager is evaluated based on net income. What would be a possible drawback to using absorption costing in this instance?

P7-19   **Using Variable Costing to Make Business Decisions**

Objs. 3, 5

John Chang is president of Clean Machines, a new car washing service that makes house calls. John has decided that his goal for the coming year is to earn a profit of $40,000. Clean Machines reported the following sales and cost information for the year just ended:

Sales revenue	$60,000
Less all variable costs	20,000
Less all fixed costs	40,000
Net income	$ 0

Clean Machines performed 500 car washes during the year.

Required

A. How many car washes will Clean Machines need to do in order to earn John's target profit of $40,000?
B. If John thinks that that number of car washes is an unrealistically high goal, what else could he do to achieve his target profit?
C. John is considering raising the price of a car wash to $130. However, he anticipates that if he raises the price, demand will fall and he will perform 450 car washes. What will his net income be if this occurs? What do you think John should do?

P7-20   **Using Variable Costing to Make Pricing Decisions**

Objs. 3, 5

Letitia Green owns a small, independent off-Broadway theater. Her theater is about to begin performing a new play titled "Franklin County Blues." Letitia has invested her own funds to get the play off the ground, and wants to know how many tickets need to be sold before the theater breaks even. Information about the play follows:

Variable costs	$1,000 per performance
Fixed costs	$50,000 for the entire run of the play
Letitia's investment in the play	$60,000
Ticket price	$40
Theater capacity	300 seats

Required

A. How many performances must be put on before the theater breaks even? (Assume that each performance will be sold out.)
B. Letitia believes that the arts should be accessible to everyone, so she has decided to change the price structure for the play. If she offers 50 tickets at a reduced rate of $10

per ticket, and the other 250 tickets at $42 per ticket, how many performances would be necessary to break even?

C. Suppose instead that, based on past experience, Letitia anticipates there will only be enough demand for eight performances of the play. Although the play would not break even, what other factors might cause Letitia to go ahead with the production?

P7-21

Obj. 5

Variable and Absorption Costing in the Service Sector

PS Consultants specializes in computer systems design and programming. Most of the company's employees have a background in both computers and management. PS's average job takes three to four months to complete. The price PS quotes for consulting services is based on the expected number of consultant hours and an estimate of out-of-pocket expenses. When a job is finished, PS bases its charges on the actual number of hours and costs incurred on the job. The firm usually does not collect its fee until a consulting job is completed.

Currently PS records all of the firm's expenses in the periods in which they are incurred. Those expenses include the hourly wages of consultants and programmers as well as indirect costs—employee benefit packages, travel expenses, and other out-of-pocket expenses. Fixed overhead costs for administering the office, rent, advertising, depreciation on computer equipment, and software license fees also are expensed each period.

Leslie Rinauro is the firm's managing partner. She is concerned because the company's income fluctuates significantly from month to month. In the months when several jobs are billed, the firm shows respectable profits. In other months, the firm shows large losses, even though all of the consultants and programmers are busy. Leslie wants to use a costing method that will better reflect PS's income and smooth out the month-to-month profit fluctuations.

Required

A. How could PS better match the costs of its services with the income it generates?
B. How does the deferral of costs relate to PS's client services?
C. How do the concepts of variable and absorption costing affect PS?

P7-22

SPREADSHEET

Excel in Action

Music Makers expects to produce and sell 500,000 CDs each month. The sales price per unit is $2.45. Variable costs per unit are $1.20. Total fixed costs per month are $540,000. The company's target profit is $75,000 per month.

Required Use a spreadsheet to prepare a profit analysis for Music Makers. Use the following format.

	A	B	C
1		Unit	Total
2	**Profit Analysis**		
3	Units		
4	Sales price		
5	Variable costs		
6	Fixed costs		
7	Total costs		
8	Profit		
9	**Breakeven Analysis**		
10	Unit contribution margin		
11	Contribution margin ratio		
12	Breakeven		
13	**Target Profit Analysis**		
14	Target profit		
15	Units required		

(Continued)

Volume, unit cost, and ratio amounts should appear in column B. Total dollar amounts should appear in column C. Data will not appear in the shaded cells. Amounts in cells C4, C5, C7, C8, B10, B11, B12, C12, and B15 should be calculated using formulas and references to other cells. Cell B12 should report the breakeven point in units. Cell C12 should report the breakeven point in dollars. Appropriate formatting should be used throughout.

The spreadsheet should be designed so that a change in any of Music Makers' price or cost data can be entered and numbers in the spreadsheet will be recalculated automatically. What is the breakeven point if variable costs increase to $1.22 per unit? How many units must be sold to generate a target profit of $75,000 if the variable unit cost is $1.22? What is the breakeven point if fixed costs increase to $560,000?

P7-23 Multiple-Choice Overview of the Chapter

1. The breakeven point is that point where:
   a. total sales revenue equals total variable and fixed expenses.
   b. total contribution margin equals total fixed expenses.
   c. Both a and b are correct.
   d. Neither a nor b is correct.

2. Garth Company sells a single product that generates a positive contribution margin. If the selling price per unit and the variable cost per unit both increase 10% and fixed costs do not change, the:

	Unit Contribution Margin	Contribution Margin Ratio	Breakeven in Units
a.	increases	increases	decreases
b.	no change	no change	no change
c.	no change	increases	no change
d.	increases	no change	decreases

3. Honeybee Company's contribution margin ratio is 60%; the company's breakeven point in sales is $150,000. If the company wants to earn net income of $60,000 over the period, its sales would have to be:
   a. $200,000.   c. $250,000.
   b. $350,000.   d. $210,000.

4. Carlton Company sells its product for $40 per unit. The company's variable costs are $22 per unit; its fixed costs are $82,800 a year. Carlton's breakeven point is:
   a. $184,000.   c. $150,545.
   b. 3,764 units.   d. 2,070 units.

5. Fixed manufacturing overhead costs are allocated to each unit of product using:
   a. the absorption-costing method only.
   b. the variable-costing method only.
   c. both the absorption- and variable-costing methods.
   d. neither the absorption- nor the variable-costing method.

6. Last year Clarence Company sold 3,600 units at a price of $50 per unit. The company's variable cost per unit was $15; its fixed costs for the year were $40,530. If the company wants a profit of $40,000 next year, all other factors remaining constant, it will have to sell:
   a. 1,158 units.   c. 2,300 units.
   b. 1,958 units.   d. 800 units.

7. When production exceeds sales, absorption-costing net income generally:
   a. is less than variable-costing net income.
   b. is more than variable-costing net income.
   c. equals variable-costing net income.
   d. is higher or lower than variable-costing net income because no generalization can be made.

8. Last year, Bone Company produced 10,000 units of product X and incurred the following costs:

Direct materials costs	$10,000
Direct labor costs	14,000
Variable manufacturing overhead costs	5,000
Variable selling and general expenses	3,000
Fixed manufacturing overhead costs	9,000
Fixed selling and general expenses	4,000
Total	$45,000

Under absorption costing, any unsold units of product X would be carried in Finished Goods Inventory at a unit cost of:

a. $4.50.   c. $3.80.

b. $4.20.   d. $2.90.

9. Selling and administrative expenses are:
   a. a product cost under variable costing.
   b. a product cost under absorption costing.
   c. part of fixed manufacturing overhead under variable costing.
   d. a period expense under both variable and absorption costing.

10. Last year Smith Company had net income of $125,000 using variable costing and $105,000 using absorption costing. The company's variable production costs were $20 per unit; its total fixed overhead was $176,000. The company produced 11,000 units. Production levels and fixed costs have not changed in three years. During the year, Smith's finished goods inventory:
    a. increased by 1,000 units.   c. decreased by 1,000 units.
    b. increased by 1,250 units.   d. decreased by 1,250 units.

CASES

C7-1
Objs. 1, 2

Relevant Costs for Decision Making: Keep or Drop a Product Line

John Randazzo is the owner of a successful machine shop that produces automotive brake components for national auto parts chains. These auto stores sell "after-market" parts to replace those made by original equipment manufacturers such as **General Motors**, **Ford**, and **Toyota**. A great deal of volume diversity exists across the products manufactured by Randazzo's shop. For example, Randazzo may produce 80,000 brake components per year for vehicles such as the Chevrolet Lumina, Ford Taurus, or Toyota Corolla; however, he may produce only 5,000 for the Corvette market. Selling prices vary greatly across the product line as a result of market supply and demand.

The machine shop is highly automated and uses the most current computer-numerically controlled (CNC) equipment. By changing cutting tools and entering different measurements into the system, a variety of products can be manufactured. Thus, machine costs are not traceable to a single product line, but are common to all products. Alternatively, many production costs are variable and can be traced to individual products. For example, energy, material, and supply costs differ among the products.

Randazzo's cost accountant recently completed a study that associated cost and revenue data with each product listed in the company's catalog. Exhibit A identifies sales volume, selling prices per unit, and variable costs for a sample of ten products representing the mix manufactured by Randazzo. In addition to the variable costs identified in Exhibit A, the accountant estimated $600,000 of fixed costs would be associated with the production of these ten products.

Exhibit A

Product	A	B	C	D	E	F	G	H	I	J
Sales volume in units (× 1,000)	50	80	10	20	70	25	5	12	11	15
Selling price per unit	$12	$15	$2	$10	$15	$10	$2	$5	$5	$8
Variable cost	$10	$11	$3	$8	$10	$8	$4	$4	$5	$6

(Continued)

The study produced startling results; two of the ten products in the sample had variable costs exceeding their selling prices. Upon analyzing the cost report, Randazzo's marketing vice president immediately defended the current strategy of manufacturing a full product line. She argued that even though some products had costs in excess of their selling prices, Randazzo should consider the big picture. Many of their customers were controlling costs by reducing the number of vendors from which they purchased merchandise. She argued that if Randazzo no longer produced product G (Corvette brake components), retail chains would likely turn to Randazzo's competitors for other products as well.

Randazzo knew that dropping products from the line would necessitate lay-offs of some salaried and hourly employees. In the short run, lost production volume could not be made up by increases in production of other products. Over the years, he had worked hard to achieve a culture of trust and cooperation within the company and the community. He wondered about the options available to him.

Required

A. What financial and nonfinancial considerations are relevant to the management team's decision to keep or drop a product line?
B. Assume $70,000 of the $600,000 in fixed costs can be saved if products C and G are dropped. What is the total benefit to the company of dropping the two products?
C. Do you agree with the marketing vice president's concern about carrying a full product line?
D. As a consultant to Randazzo, what would you recommend to:
   1. ensure each product in the line is profitable, or
   2. ensure the entire line is profitable?

C7-2   Absorption versus Variable Costing—Effects on Income

Obj. 4

Rachel Yablonka assumed the responsibilities as executive manager of the Chair Division, Office Furniture and Fixtures, Inc. (OFF), on January 1, 2005, taking the place of her recently promoted predecessor. Rachel's own performance evaluation is directly tied to the division's annual net operating profit determined under absorption costing, and her quarterly bonus is determined as a percentage of net operating income.

Rachel immediately began taking measures designed to reduce costs during future periods. Part of her cost-reduction efforts involved examining better ways to deal with inventory. After a careful review of the division's sales and production over the past quarter, Rachel concluded that inventory had been accumulating faster than sales. The division makes to order and does not normally carry any excess inventory. She decided that the buildup of excess inventory might be contributing to low profits. Rachel knows that excess inventory can lead to higher costs of material-handling, warehousing, insurance, and auditing as well as keeping capital tied up when it could be more useful elsewhere. Further investigation disclosed that the excess inventory was being stored off site in newly rented warehouse facilities because of inadequate storage space in the division's own warehouses.

Rachel immediately set out to eliminate the excess inventory by slowing down the rate of production during the first quarter of 2005. However, she was very disappointed when she saw the first quarter 2005 results. Instead of profits improving, the division experienced a net operating loss even though sales were flat and there was some reduction in warehousing and material handling costs. Quarterly performance data for the two quarters are as follows:

	Fourth Quarter 2004	First Quarter 2005
Units of beginning inventory	0	50,000
Units sold	200,000	200,000
Units produced	250,000	150,000
Average selling price per unit	$500	$500
Unit cost of production:		
Direct labor cost per unit produced	$ 50	$ 50
Direct material cost per unit produced	200	200
Variable overhead cost per unit produced	30	25
Fixed overhead assigned to each unit produced	70	115
Total unit cost	$350	$390

	2004	2005
Revenue	$100,000,000	$100,000,000
Cost of goods sold	70,000,000	76,000,000
Gross margin	$ 30,000,000	$ 24,000,000
Selling and administrative expenses	25,000,000	25,000,000
Operating income	$ 5,000,000	$ (1,000,000)

Required

A. Why was the division's income significantly lower in first quarter 2005 than in fourth quarter 2004?

B. Why do you think the inventory buildup occurred at the end of the previous manager's term?

C. If you were Rachel, how would you handle this situation? Should you keep inventory levels low or high?

D. If you were the CEO of OFF, Inc., would you change Rachel's performance measurements? Explain why or why not?

C7-3 Effects of Cost-Plus Pricing—Beyond Absorption and Variable
Obj. 4 **Costing**

The Dobson Specialty Valve Division of American Industrial Group, Inc. (AIG) develops and manufactures complex valves and fittings for commercial uses. AIG has long operated other divisions engaged in making products such as furniture, metal doors, and windows. Dobson has just been acquired by AIG from another company, and AIG's management is considering what management accounting system to use for Dobson's cost-plus product pricing. A group of senior AIG officials recently held a meeting to discuss the issue.

Karen Sanchez (vice president and chief financial officer): AIG has always used variable costing when it was necessary to price our products on a cost-plus basis, but I have been reading that variable costing does not always work well for this purpose. Some consultants claim that using variable costing to cost products leads managers to overlook fixed costs and price products too low. These consultants say that absorption costing results in better recovery of fixed costs in product because it includes fixed costs in the cost of manufacturing.

John Warren (vice president, marketing): Although the consultants may be correct in some situations, I disagree in the case of Dobson. Dobson manufactures many small lots of specialty valves that require individual design and special handling. This means that direct labor and raw materials represent almost 70% of Dobson's manufacturing costs. After deducting variable overhead, fixed costs represent less than 20% of total manufacturing costs. There is little fixed manufacturing cost to recover. Further, only a small amount of our selling costs are fixed. We sell mostly through independent sales representatives who are paid on a 5% commission basis.

Susan Sabbagh (vice president, production): Given that Dobson's after-tax profit margins are in the 5%–6% range and our goal is to raise that to 8%, I would think that a 20% fixed manufacturing cost percentage is still very significant. If we do not recover our fixed costs on each job and make a profit, it will be difficult to increase our profit margins to the desired levels.

Sanchez: I am looking at a product cost and margin sheet for valve #2032 that was specially developed for one particular customer only. We do not know if this valve will ever be manufactured again. The job cost sheet only includes manufacturing costs. It does not include the costs of research and development (R&D) for the valve. The price is based upon a 30% markup over manufacturing costs. As you may remember from your financial accounting classes, generally accepted accounting principles require that R&D costs be expensed in the period in which they are incurred. R&D costs may not be inventoried. Therefore, R&D costs are not normally included in product costs, and neither our variable manufacturing-cost system nor the proposed absorption-cost system captures R&D costs. It seems to me that the cost of manufacturing the valve under either system is inadequate for product pricing because neither manufacturing cost captures the cost of R&D.

Product Unit Cost and Gross Margin—Job 99-1-2032

Direct labor	240 hours at $16.00 per hour	$ 3,840.00
Direct materials	50 units at $125.00 per unit	6,250.00
Manufacturing overhead	240 DL hours at $9.00 per hour	2,160.00
Total product manufacturing cost		$12,250.00
Unit cost	$12,250.00 ÷ 50 units	245.00
Cost-plus price per unit	$245.00 + (30% × $245.00)	318.50
Total sales value of order	$318.50 × 50 units	15,925.00
Gross margin	$15,925.00 − $12,250.00	3,675.00

Warren: We have not discussed that concern before, but you are correct. We have assumed that R&D costs are a small percentage of the total cost of a product because we expect to sell a large quantity of the product through many orders. In a situation where we incur significant R&D to develop a particular valve that we are unsure will sell in large quantities, we likely will lose money on the valve if we do not make provision for recovering R&D costs in our pricing.

Sabbagh: I believe that I understand everything that has been said, and yet I am more confused than ever. This discussion began with a debate about whether to use variable or absorption manufacturing costs to price products, and now we seem to have concluded that neither is adequate. Is there another type of costing that I have not heard about that would solve this problem? And why have we not discussed this problem before with respect to our other divisions? It seems to me that Karen is saying that every product should cover its fair share of all costs, but is it possible to accurately determine that fair share?

Required

A. Assess the arguments made by the various participants in the meeting. Are these arguments correct? Explain.

B. Why do you think that the problem of including R&D costs in product pricing has not been discussed before by AIG's senior management?

C. Suppose AIG estimates that it took approximately 50 hours of engineering design time to develop valve #2032 at $50.00 per hour and general administrative costs are allocated at $1,000 per job. How should AIG have priced the job to make the desired profit percentage on a full absorption-cost basis? Based upon this price, how well does the practice of using a 30% markup above gross margin appear to work in the case of job #99-1-2032?

D. What potential benefits and problems do you see for AIG if it attempts to assign a fair share of all costs to each product?

Cost Evaluation and Performance Measurement

THE BUDGETING PROCESS PLANNING BUSINESS ACTIVITIES

Why should budgets be carefully constructed?

Erin and Seth are comparing their actual financial performance of Young Designs, Inc., to the budgeted performance. The two sets of numbers are very different. It looks like the costs for last month are much greater than expected. They are meeting with Roberta later today, and they plan to ask her to explain why Young Designs' actual financial performance varied from budgeted performance and what they can do with the budget to better understand how well costs are being controlled.

FOOD FOR THOUGHT

What would you do to design a budget that considers differences between expected and actual sales? How would this budget help Erin and Seth better understand how well different types of costs are being controlled? How could this concept be extended to help managers anticipate different financial outcomes for different levels of sales? Now, let's join Erin and Seth in their meeting with Roberta.

Erin: *Last month we produced and sold more futons than we projected. Our raw material costs per unit were higher than expected because we got hit with unexpected price increases from our suppliers. Apparently there is a lumber shortage right now.*

Seth: *Selling more than we expected is a good thing, but unexpected raw material price increases are not. Overall, we ended up missing our profit goal by a fairly large margin. I guess that means the higher raw material prices more than offset the gains we got from selling more units.*

Erin: *That may not be the only reason. We also had higher than expected labor costs because we had to pay overtime for higher than expected production. In addition, our overhead costs exceeded projections.*

Seth: *So, Roberta, how do we go about sorting out all these revenues and costs to get a better understanding of what actually happened? We need to know how well we are controlling each type of manufacturing and selling cost. It seems to me that we need to produce a budget that shows what our costs should have been for the amount we actually sold.*

Roberta: *In budgeting, predicting the levels of sales is often the most important but most difficult task. This is because the level of sales drives much of the company's costs. For example, raw material, direct labor, variable overhead, and variable selling costs all vary with the level of sales.*

Seth: *If sales are that important yet that hard to predict accurately, won't we frequently have budgets that do not reflect reality?*

Roberta: *What you need is a flexible budget, which shows what you would have budgeted for costs and profits if you had known the actual amounts you would sell.*

Seth: *In other words, a flexible budget is a budget created after the fact to show what our costs should have been given actual levels of sales activity. I would suppose that this flexible budget concept uses the notion that some costs vary with production while other costs are fixed.*

Roberta: *Correct. This will allow you to better understand how well different costs were controlled. By comparing the flexible budget to the actual costs and profits, you will be able to see which costs are higher or lower than they should have been given the actual sales.*

Erin: *Will this work if we have more than one product with different costs?*

Roberta: *Certainly. In situations where there is more than one product, you simply develop the flexible budget to calculate the costs for each different product and then sum the results to get total revenues and expenses.*

Seth: *What about manufacturing overhead? Will this help us to better understand how much overhead was expensed and why?*

Roberta: *Yes, flexible budgets typically break down manufacturing overhead into its fixed and variable components. You will be able to compare how much variable overhead is expensed because of the actual level of sales versus the original budgeted sales.*

Erin: *I don't see why we couldn't use this same concept of flexible budgeting to assist us in another way. When we are preparing the budget, we could forecast what our company's financial performance would be for different levels of sales. This would help us establish a range of possible financial outcomes.*

Roberta: *That's called sensitivity analysis. Companies often use sensitivity analysis in flexible budgeting to develop best-case, worst-case, and most-likely-case scenarios. Since variations in sales can sometimes be difficult to predict, developing these scenarios helps management see how good or bad the financial results for a given period are likely to be.*

OBJECTIVES

Once you have completed this chapter, you should be able to:

1 Explain how budgets provide information to help managers prepare a pro forma (predicted) income statement and balance sheet.

2 Prepare the budgets and schedules that make up the master budget.

3 Prepare reports that describe the timing of cash receipts and payments during a fiscal period.

4 Describe the elements of a successful budgeting culture.

5 Explain the role of budgets in service organizations.

SIERRA CANOE: BUDGETING AND THE MANUFACTURING PROCESS

In this chapter, we consider elements of the master budget using Sierra Canoe Co. Before accounting for a product, managers should understand the processes and components that are necessary to manufacture it. Exhibit 1 illustrates the key parts of Sierra Canoe Co.'s product. The company produces canoes from plastic polymers and various accessories purchased from suppliers. The company also incurs direct labor costs during the manufacturing process. Workers operate machines that mold polymers to form the hull of the canoe. In addition, they attach various components, such as the seats, decks, and gunwales. Other manufacturing costs include overhead in the form of electricity, small tools, and supplies consumed during the manufacturing process. Sierra Canoe Co. also employs workers who perform sales and administrative duties.

Exhibit 1
Canoe Diagram

Demand for canoes varies throughout the year. Because Sierra Canoe Co. sells most of its products through retail stores in North America, the most active sales period occurs from April through August. The least active sales period occurs during the winter months of the first quarter of the year. Because sales vary in a predictable manner, management believes a budget can help them understand the timing of cash receipts and cash payments. If cash receipts are not sufficient to cover cash payments during the winter months, the company will need a short-term loan. During the summer months when cash receipts are expected to exceed cash payments, the company will repay the loan. Thus, managers at Sierra Canoe Co. are interested in determining the timing and amount of future cash inflows and outflows. In addition, they wish to understand the expected future financial position of the company.

TRANSACTION AND BUDGET SYSTEMS COMPARED

OBJECTIVE 1

Explain how budgets provide information to help managers prepare a pro forma (predicted) income statement and balance sheet.

As explained when you studied financial accounting, businesses enter the results of actual transactions into the accounting system to measure income for a fiscal period, such as a month, quarter, or year. Actual transactions, such as inventory purchases, wage payments, and sales, are recorded in the accounting system. These transactions are summarized, and account balances are calculated. Then, financial statements are prepared from the account balances. Using financial statement information, managers, lenders, and owners evaluate actual performance for an accounting period.

A *budget* **is a detailed plan describing the use of financial and operating resources over a specific period.** A company's budget system differs from its transaction system. Rather than collecting data from actual events, the budget system is based on *forecasts* from various departments within an organization. Preparing company-wide budgets requires coordination among the sales, production, and purchasing functions. For example, sales managers provide sales forecasts to production managers, who estimate the number of units necessary to ensure an adequate supply of products for sale. Using estimates provided by production managers, purchasing managers forecast the type, amount, and cost of resources to satisfy production requirements. Also, sales forecasts help managers estimate selling and administrative expenses. The budget process helps managers understand whether short-term loans will be needed during the forecast period, as materials and other manufacturing resources are purchased to meet production demands. Exhibit 2 illustrates differences between a transaction system and a budget system.

Exhibit 2

The Transaction System and Budget System Compared

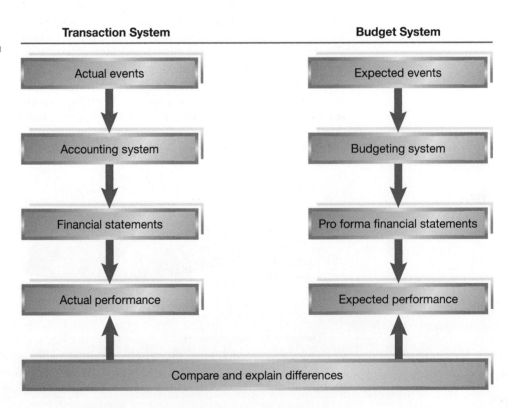

Pro forma, or predicted, financial statements are prepared by combining information from various budgets. The purpose of a pro forma balance sheet is to predict the financial position of the company. The purpose of the pro forma income statement is to predict revenues, expenses, and earnings. As shown in Exhibit 2, the transaction system produces financial statements based on *actual performance*; the budget system produces financial statements based on *expected performance*. Management can compare actual performance with expected performance to explain why differences may have occurred and to correct problems that create these differences.

Pro forma financial statements are produced at the end of the budgeting process. However, our discussion of the various budgets begins with a familiar set of financial statements, the pro forma income statement and balance sheet. The remainder of the chapter illustrates how account balances in these financial statements were determined using the budgeting process. The format of pro forma financial statements is the same as that of financial statements. The only difference is that pro forma financial statements report estimated, rather than actual, account balances. Exhibit 3, panel A, illustrates a pro forma income statement for Sierra Canoe Co. for the first quarter of 2005, ending on March 31. Panel B illustrates a balance sheet at December 31, 2004, and a pro forma balance sheet at March 31, 2005.

Exhibit 3

Panel A—The Pro Forma Income Statement

Sierra Canoe Co.
Pro Forma Income Statement
For the Quarter Ended March 31, 2005

Panel A

Sales	$336,000
Cost of goods sold	247,800
Gross margin	$ 88,200
Selling and administrative expenses	68,400
Net income	$ 19,800

Exhibit 3

Panel B—The Balance Sheet and Pro Forma Balance Sheet

Sierra Canoe Co.
Balance Sheet and Pro Forma Balance Sheet
At December 31, 2004 and March 31, 2005

Panel B

	Balance Sheet 12/31/2004	Pro Forma Balance Sheet 3/31/2005
Assets		
Cash	$ 50,000	$ 71,428
Accounts receivable	21,600	52,800
Inventory		
Raw materials	1,296	5,508
Finished goods	2,950	14,750
Property, plant, and equipment	350,000	350,000
Total assets	$425,846	$494,486
Liabilities and Equity		
Accounts payable	$ 33,491	$ 82,331
Contributed capital	300,000	300,000
Retained earnings	92,355	112,155*
Total liabilities and equity	$425,846	$494,486

*Beginning retained earnings	$ 92,355
Net income	19,800
Ending retained earnings	$112,155

THE MASTER BUDGET

OBJECTIVE 2

Prepare the budgets and schedules that make up the master budget.

Chapter M2 contrasted product expenses, such as materials, labor, and manufacturing overhead, with period expenses, such as selling and administrative expenses. Recall that materials, labor, and manufacturing overhead become part of inventory for a manufacturing company and are not expensed until the products are sold. Period expenses have an effect on the income statement in the period in which they are incurred. **A** *master budget* **is a collection of related budgets that includes the sales, production, purchasing, labor, overhead, selling and administrative, and cash budgets.** The master budget of a manufacturing company, such as Sierra Canoe Co., includes both product and period expenses. Managers want to understand the amount of resources to be consumed (both product and period) and when the resources are expected to be consumed. Exhibit 4 illustrates an overview of the budgeting process that results in a master budget. Exhibit 5 identifies the people at various levels of an organization who are responsible for information needed in the budgeting process. We consider the individual budgets that make up the master budget in this chapter.

The budgeting process for Sierra Canoe Co. begins with an estimate of expected unit sales for the coming year. As Exhibit 5 illustrates, the chief executive officer (CEO) works

Exhibit 4   Master Budget

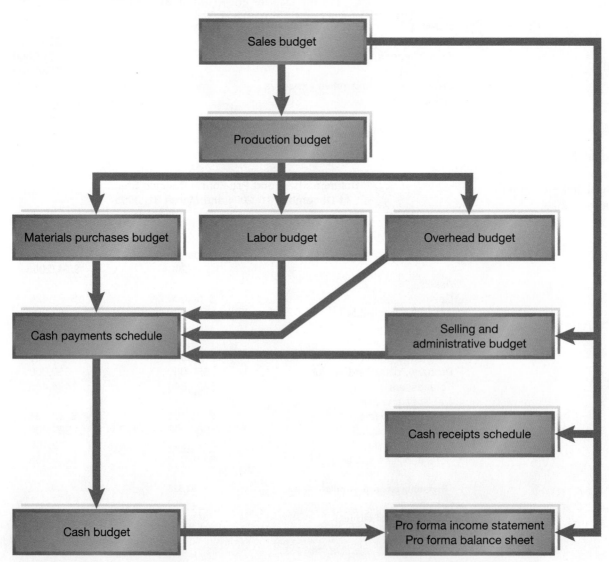

with the vice presidents (VP) of finance, marketing, manufacturing, and human resources (HR) to devise a sales forecast that results in a sales budget. The team agrees on a sales target after considering a variety of resource issues. As shown in Exhibit 4, production will be scheduled to meet expected sales demand. If sufficient units are not produced to meet sales demand, the company will lose sales. If production exceeds sales demand, the company will incur additional inventory expenses associated with damage, insurance, handling, and storage. Therefore, the sales budget drives the production budget.

After sales and production estimates are complete, the purchasing department prepares a materials purchases budget. As Exhibit 5 illustrates, the production manager

Exhibit 5 The Organizational Chart and the Budgeting Process

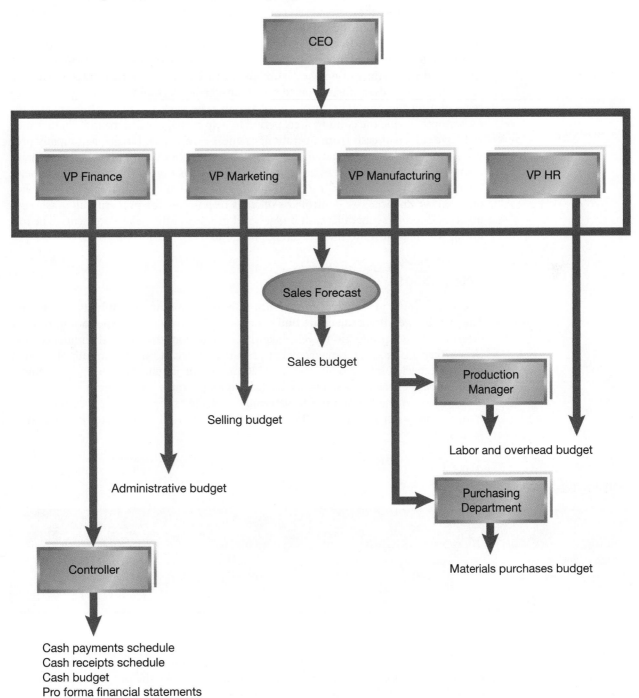

works with the VP of human resources to develop a labor and overhead budget. Purchase budgets permit managers to estimate the amount of raw materials, labor, and overhead necessary to meet production requirements. The costs that result from production activities appear as finished goods inventory on a company's balance sheet until the product is sold. When the product is sold, these costs appear as cost of goods sold on the income statement.

In addition to forecasting product expenses, managers at Sierra Canoe Co. must forecast period expenses associated with selling and administrative activities. As shown in Exhibit 4, the sales budget (or forecast) affects selling and administrative expenses. Selling and administrative expenses are an example of a semivariable expense, as discussed in Chapter M2. Therefore, they have a fixed component that is unaffected by sales volume and a variable component that changes with the number of products sold. As Exhibit 5 illustrates, the administrative expense budget is prepared at the vice president level, because these managers collectively understand the amount of administrative activity throughout the company.

Using information from the materials, labor, overhead, and selling and administrative budgets, accountants prepare a cash payments schedule. The cash payments schedule identifies the timing of cash outlays for various purchases during the year. The sales budget provides information to help managers understand the timing of cash receipts during the year. The cash budget summarizes cash receipts and payments for each month during the coming fiscal period to help managers understand whether they will have sufficient cash from operations to meet cash needs. Finally, a company prepares pro forma financial statements at the end of the budgeting process. These statements help managers understand what the financial position of the company will be, if forecasts are correct. The controller is an accountant that typically reports to the vice president of finance. The controller's office is responsible for preparing the cash payments and receipts schedule, cash budget, and pro forma financial statements. The following sections illustrate the budgeting process at Sierra Canoe Co.

Sales Budget

The *sales budget* **projects revenues from sales of a company's products or services.** The sales budget drives the entire budgeting process because sales expectations directly determine future production levels. Likewise, production levels directly influence purchases. Sierra Canoe Co.'s management prepared a forecast for each month of the first quarter. Expected sales are 50, 150, and 220 canoes for January, February, and March. Each canoe is expected to sell for $800. Exhibit 6 illustrates how the unit sales forecast is multiplied by the selling price to determine budgeted sales revenues. December sales information is not included in the quarter total, but will be used later in the budget process.

Exhibit 6 Sales Budget

	Actual	Expected			
	December	January	February	March	Quarter
Unit sales	90	50	150	220	420
Selling price per unit	$ 800	$ 800	$ 800	$ 800	$ 800
Sales revenue	$72,000	$40,000	$120,000	$176,000	$336,000

Exhibit 6 indicates expected revenues of $336,000 for the first quarter. Refer to the pro forma income statement in Exhibit 3, panel A. Note the pro forma sales account balance equals the quarterly sales amount calculated in Exhibit 6.

Case in Point

Forecasting "Sales" for a Bank

To a bank, loans to customers are like sales to manufacturers or retailers. Banks often use sophisticated forecasting models to project demand for loans. Some of the factors banks may consider in forecasting loans are economic growth, changes in interest rates, trends in consumer spending, and competition from other banks. A bank may develop a sales forecasting model that contains these and other variables. The expected value of each of these variables is inserted into the model to arrive at an estimate of future loan demand.

Production Budget

The *production budget* **identifies the amount of a product that must be produced to meet a company's needs for sales and inventory.** Using the unit sales forecast from Exhibit 6, management prepares the production budget shown in Exhibit 7. The number of units to be produced is based on expected sales, desired ending finished goods inventory, and beginning finished goods inventory. Sierra Canoe's management keeps a finished goods inventory of 10 percent of the following month's expected sales to ensure they do not run out of inventory for sale. The unit sales forecast is added to desired ending finished goods inventory to determine total inventory requirements. Next, beginning finished goods inventory is subtracted from total inventory requirements to determine the number of units to be produced.

Exhibit 7 Production Budget

	Actual	Expected				
	December	January	February	March	Quarter	April
Unit sales	90	50	150	220	420	250
Desired ending finished goods	5	15	22	25	25	30
Total units required	95	65	172	245	445	280
Beginning finished goods	9	5	15	22	5	25
Units to produce	86	60	157	223	440	255

For example, the sales forecast for January is 50 units. The desired ending inventory of 15 units is calculated by multiplying 10 percent times February sales of 150 units. Thus, Sierra Canoe Co.'s total inventory needs at the end of January are 65 (50 + 15) units. The company began the month with 5 units in inventory. Therefore, only 60 (65 − 5) units must be produced in January. Having calculated the number of canoes to be manufactured, the production manager will send the information to the purchasing manager. December information is included in Exhibit 7 because December's finished goods inventory balance, 5 units, becomes the beginning finished goods inventory balance for January. Likewise, April inventory information is included to permit us to determine desired ending finished goods inventory of 25 units for March (10% × 250). However, only January, February, and March are included in the quarterly total.

Materials Purchases Budget

The materials purchases budget links directly to the production budget. After production demands are known, the purchasing manager can determine how much material to acquire. In a similar fashion, the production manager can estimate labor and overhead requirements.

The canoe produced by Sierra Canoe Co. requires two types of raw materials:

- polymer (for use in molding the canoe), and
- an accessory package consisting of seats, gunwale, thwart, and decking.

Because of an imbalance in supply and demand, the company's polymer orders frequently are delayed. Therefore, management maintains an ending polymer inventory of 20 percent of the following month's production requirements to help prevent stockouts. However, no inventory of accessory packages is kept at the factory because Sierra Canoe Co. has agreements with reliable suppliers to deliver these materials daily as they are needed.

The *materials purchases budget* **identifies the amount of materials that will be required to support a company's total production needs.** Exhibit 8 illustrates the materials purchases budget for polymer. Each canoe requires 12 gallons. Thus, total polymer requirements are computed by multiplying total production (from Exhibit 7) times 12. Desired ending polymer inventory is added to production requirements to calculate total needs. Finally, beginning polymer inventory is subtracted from total requirements to calculate gallons to be purchased. The number of gallons to be purchased is converted into a dollar value by multiplying the purchase quantity by the cost per gallon.

Exhibit 8 Materials Purchases Budget for Polymer*

	Actual	Expected				
	December	January	February	March	Quarter	April
Production units	86	60	157	223	440	255
Gallons of polymer per unit	× 12	× 12	× 12	× 12	× 12	× 12
Total gallons required for production	1,032	720	1,884	2,676	5,280	3,060
Plus: Desired polymer ending inventory	144	377	535	612	612	1,215
Total requirements in gallons	1,176	1,097	2,419	3,288	5,892	4,275
Less: Beginning polymer inventory	206	144	377	535	144	612
Total gallons to be purchased	970	953	2,042	2,753	5,748	3,663
Cost per gallon	× $9	× $9	× $9	× $9	× $9	× $9
Total polymer purchases	$8,730	$8,577	$18,378	$24,777	$51,732	$32,967

*Amounts in this exhibit are rounded to whole units and whole dollar values.

For example, from the production budget we know Sierra Canoe Co. plans to manufacture 60 canoes during January. Each canoe consumes 12 gallons of polymer. Thus, to meet production demand, 720 (12 × 60) gallons are required. In addition, the company desires to maintain an ending inventory of polymer equal to 20 percent of the next month's production needs. For January, the desired ending inventory of polymer is 377 gallons (1,884 × .20 = 377). The purchasing manager needs 1,097 (720 + 377) gallons to meet production and inventory requirements; however, 144 gallons already are in beginning inventory. As a result, the purchasing manager must purchase 953 gallons (1,097 − 144) at $9 per gallon. Exhibit 8 indicates total polymer purchases of $8,577 (953 × $9) for January. Purchases for each month may be calculated in an identical manner.

The materials purchases budget provides information to help estimate the value of the ending raw materials inventory account shown on the pro forma balance sheet. For example, Sierra Canoe Co. wants to have 612 gallons of polymer on hand at the end of the quarter. Each gallon costs $9. Thus, the value of the ending raw materials inventory as shown in the pro forma balance sheet in Exhibit 3, panel B, is $5,508 (612 × $9 = $5,508).

In addition to polymer, Sierra Canoe Co. purchases an accessory package for $50. The budget for purchases of the accessory package is greatly simplified because Sierra Canoe Co. does not maintain an inventory of this item. By partnering with reliable suppliers who make daily deliveries, Sierra Canoe Company minimizes handling and storage costs. Using production values from Exhibit 7, purchase quantities for the accessory package are calculated in Exhibit 9. Purchase quantities are converted to dollar values by multiplying by the cost per package. For example, the production manager plans to manufacture 60 canoes in January. Therefore, 60 accessory packages at $50 each must be purchased to meet production requirements. The cost of polymer and accessory kits is placed on the balance sheet as inventory until the canoe that contains the materials is sold. Thus, accountants refer to materials, labor, and overhead as costs until a product is sold, and as an expense after the product is sold.

Exhibit 9 Materials Purchases Budget for Accessory Packages

	Actual	Expected			
	December	January	February	March	Quarter
Total production (units)	86	60	157	223	440
Component packages per unit	× 1	× 1	× 1	× 1	× 1
Total packages required	86	60	157	223	440
Cost per component package	× $50	× $50	× $50	× $50	× $50
Total component packages	$4,300	$3,000	$7,850	$11,150	$22,000

1 SELF-STUDY PROBLEM

WebTUTOR Advantage

A retail organization may prepare a merchandise purchases budget similar to the production budget illustrated in Exhibit 7. Assume a retail company that sells outdoor equipment expects to sell backpacks as shown in the following table. The company wants to keep a backpack inventory equal to 50 percent of the following month's expected sales volume. The backpacks cost the company $45 each.

	Actual	Expected				
	December	January	February	March	Quarter	April
Unit sales	16	10	6	20		30
Plus: Desired ending finished goods inventory	——	——	——	——	15	30
Total units required						60
Less: Beginning finished goods inventory	8	——	——	——	——	15
Total units purchased						
Cost per unit	$45	$45	$45	$45	$45	$45
Cost of purchases	═══	═══	═══	═══	═══	═══

Required Complete the inventory purchases table.

The solution to Self-Study Problem 1 appears at the end of the chapter.

Labor Budget

The *labor budget* **identifies labor resources required to meet production needs.** Labor costs, as shown in Exhibit 10, are based on production quantities from Exhibit 7. Industrial engineers have determined each canoe requires 6 hours of direct labor at an average rate of $22 per hour. Thus, the number of canoes to be produced is multiplied by the required number of labor hours per unit to determine total labor hours. Total labor expense is calculated by multiplying the labor rate per hour times the total hours required. For example, the production budget indicates 60 canoes will be manufactured in January. Each canoe requires 6 hours of labor; therefore, 360 hours (60 × 6) of labor are required for the month. Since each hour of labor costs $22, the total labor budget for January is $7,920 (360 hours × $22).

Exhibit 10 Labor Budget

	Actual	Expected			
	December	January	February	March	Quarter
Total production (units)	86	60	157	223	440
Hours per unit	× 6	× 6	× 6	× 6	× 6
Total hours required	516	360	942	1,338	2,640
Labor rate per hour	× $22	× $22	× $22	× $22	× $22
Total labor cost	$11,352	$7,920	$20,724	$29,436	$58,080

Overhead Budget

The *overhead budget* **provides a schedule of all costs of production other than materials and labor.** Manufacturing overhead costs are not as easily associated with specific products as are direct materials and direct labor. Manufacturing overhead costs usually are associated with activities that support a production process but often are not directly related to any specific product. Thus, overhead costs are classified as indirect manufacturing costs. Overhead costs typically are estimated using production forecasts, as shown in Exhibit 7. Sierra Canoe Co. associates overhead with products using a rate of $50 per direct labor hour. Recall that industrial engineers have determined each canoe requires 6 hours of direct labor. The number of units produced is multiplied by labor hours per unit to calculate total labor hours required. Total budgeted overhead costs are calculated by multiplying the overhead rate times the total hours required. For example, overhead cost for January is calculated in Exhibit 11 by multiplying total production of 60 canoes by 6 hours, the time required to assemble each canoe. Based on January production levels, 360 (60 × 6) hours of labor are required. Overhead is added to the product at a rate of $50 per labor hour; therefore, total budgeted overhead costs for January are $18,000 (360 × $50).

Exhibit 11 Overhead Budget

	Actual	Expected			
	December	January	February	March	Quarter
Total production (units)	86	60	157	223	440
Hours per unit	× 6	× 6	× 6	× 6	× 6
Total hours required	516	360	942	1,338	2,640
Overhead rate per hour	× $50	× $50	× $50	× $50	× $50
Total overhead costs	$25,800	$18,000	$47,100	$66,900	$132,000

Having completed the materials, labor, and overhead budgets, management may calculate an expected product cost. For example, by adding polymer, accessory package, labor, and overhead expenses we may determine a product cost of $590 as shown in Exhibit 12. Notice that overhead is a large portion of Sierra Canoe Co.'s total manufacturing cost. This is not uncommon for manufacturing companies. As we have seen in earlier chapters, companies design cost systems to help them understand, and reduce, overhead costs.

Exhibit 12
Canoe Cost Calculation

Materials:			
Polymer	($9 × 12 gallons)	$108	(Exhibit 8)
Accessory kit		50	(Exhibit 9)
Labor	(6 hours × $22 per hour)	132	(Exhibit 10)
Overhead	(6 hours × $50 per hour)	300	(Exhibit 11)
Total unit cost		$590	

Total product cost is used to determine cost of goods sold on the pro forma income statement. We may calculate cost of goods sold of $247,800, as shown in the income statement in Exhibit 3, panel A, by multiplying $590 times the number of units expected to be sold, as reported in the sales budget ($590 × 420 = $247,800). Likewise, we determine ending inventory by multiplying $590 times the desired number of finished canoes shown in the production budget (25). Thus, the desired finished goods inventory on the pro forma balance sheet in Exhibit 3, panel B, is $14,750 (25 units × $590).

Our pro forma income statement and balance sheet in Exhibit 3 are prepared using accrual concepts. As illustrated, pro forma cost of goods sold is calculated using the expected number of units sold, while the desired ending inventory of finished canoes is appropriately included on the balance sheet as a current asset. Unlike product costs that are expensed when goods are sold, selling and administrative expenses are reported on the income statement of the period in which they are incurred. The next section illustrates the budgeting process for selling and administrative expenses.

Selling and Administrative Budget

The *selling and administrative budget* **contains expenses related to selling a company's products and administering the business.** Exhibit 13 illustrates the selling and administrative budget. As Chapter M4 discussed, management can predict net income at various sales levels by understanding how expenses respond to changes in sales volume. The selling and administrative budget shown in Exhibit 13 uses a similar approach to forecast expenses.

Exhibit 13 Selling and Administrative Budget

	Actual December	January	February	March	Quarter
Total sales	$72,000	$40,000	$120,000	$176,000	$336,000
Variable expense per sales dollar	× 0.15	× 0.15	× 0.15	× 0.15	× 0.15
Total variable expense	$10,800	$ 6,000	$ 18,000	$ 26,400	$ 50,400
Fixed expense per month	6,000	6,000	6,000	6,000	18,000
Total selling and administrative expense	$16,800	$12,000	$ 24,000	$ 32,400	$ 68,400

Management at Sierra Canoe Co. estimates variable selling expenses are 15 percent of sales, while fixed selling expenses are $6,000 per month. Sales commissions are an example of a variable selling expense, while advertising and administrative salaries are examples of fixed selling expenses. Advertising expenses will not change if sales volume increases or decreases; however, sales commissions vary according to sales levels. Total selling and administrative expenses for January are calculated in two steps. Using sales volume from the sales budget shown in Exhibit 6, the variable expense is calculated at 15 percent of total sales ($40,000 × .15 = $6,000). Next, fixed selling expenses are added to variable selling expenses to determine the budgeted selling and administrative expense for January ($6,000 + $6,000 = $12,000).

The pro forma income statement shown in Exhibit 3, panel A, reports selling and administrative expense of $68,400 based on total quarterly selling and administrative expenses calculated in the selling and administrative budget.

2 SELF-STUDY PROBLEM

WebTUTOR Advantage

Assume the managers for the retail company introduced in Self-Study Problem 1 want to predict administrative expenses for the company during the months of January, February, and March. They believe fixed administrative expenses will be $20,000 per month. In addition, variable selling expenses are expected to be 20 percent of sales.

Required Prepare a selling and administrative budget for January, February, and March, assuming forecast sales are $30,000, $45,000, and $50,000, respectively.

The solution to Self-Study Problem 2 appears at the end of the chapter.

CASH BUDGET

OBJECTIVE 3

Prepare reports that describe the timing of cash receipts and payments during a fiscal period.

The *cash budget* summarizes expected cash collections and payments during an accounting period. For example, Exhibit 14 illustrates the cash budget for Sierra Canoe Co. during the first quarter of an accounting period. Expected cash collections are added to the beginning cash balance. Next, expected cash payments are subtracted to determine whether a cash excess or deficit exists. The amounts shown in Exhibit 14 are based on cash collection and payment schedules that are explained in later sections. Because the cash budget often is prepared for a twelve-month period, management can understand how cash balances vary throughout the year. If a cash shortage is expected in certain months, management can make arrangements to borrow necessary cash. The cash budget also provides information to lenders who want to know when short-term loans will be repaid. For example, assume Sierra Canoe's management wants to maintain at least $50,000 in cash at the end of each month. The cash budget indicates borrowing will be necessary in January. Also, the budget indicates sufficient cash will be available to repay the loan in March.

Exhibit 14 Cash Budget

	December	January	February	March	Quarter
Beginning cash balance		$50,000	$50,360	$ 62,586	$ 50,000
Plus: Cash collections		49,600	96,000	159,200	304,800
Less: Cash disbursements		58,240	83,774	141,358	283,372
Cash excess or deficit		41,360	62,586	80,428	71,428
Plus: Bank loans		9,000	0	0	9,000
Less: Bank repayments		0	0	9,000	(9,000)
Ending balance	$50,000	$50,360	$62,586	$ 71,428	$ 71,428

A cash budget can help managers make short-term and long-term cash management decisions. For example, managers may choose to invest excess cash in securities that earn a higher rate of return than typically is paid on business checking accounts. Also, if the cash budget permits, management may invest excess cash in long-term investments to enable them to pay off debt or to purchase equipment in the future.

The cash budget is used to determine the ending cash balance reported in the pro forma balance sheet. For example, the cash budget indicates an ending balance of $71,428. The same value is reported on the balance sheet shown in Exhibit 3, panel B. Thus, the cash budget is necessary to estimate the ending cash balance on the pro forma balance sheet. So far, we have assumed the cash collections and disbursements are given. The information about expected cash flows comes from two different schedules, the schedule of cash collections and the schedule of cash payments. Next, we consider these schedules.

Schedule of Cash Collections

The accrual basis can be used for determining value created during an accounting period. When you studied financial accounting, you considered how revenue is recorded when earned, not necessarily when cash is collected. As the budgeting process illustrates, cash collections often differ from revenues in the short run. A *schedule of cash collections* **identifies the timing of cash inflows from sales.** For example, assume Sierra Canoe Co. typically collects cash from sales in the following pattern:

- 70 percent in the month of sale
- 30 percent in the month following the sale

The schedule of cash collections is based on the sales budget and the company's historical experience with collecting cash from credit sales. Monthly cash receipts for Sierra Canoe Co. are affected by sales from the current month and from the previous month. Exhibit 15 describes the two-month collection pattern based on Sierra Canoe's collection experience. January cash collections are expected to be $49,600 (December sales of $72,000 × .30 = $21,600 plus January sales of $40,000 × .70 = 28,000). Cash collections for each month in the quarter may be calculated in an identical manner. As shown in Exhibit 15, Sierra Canoe Co. expects to collect $49,600, $96,000, and $159,200 in January, February, and March. Refer to the cash budget shown in Exhibit 14. Notice the monthly cash collections from Exhibit 15 also appear in the second row of Exhibit 14.

Exhibit 15 Schedule of Cash Collections for January, February, March, and Quarter*

	December	January	February	March	Quarter
December collections for December sales	$50,400				
January collections for December sales		$21,600			$ 21,600
January collections for January sales		28,000			28,000
February collections for January sales			$12,000		12,000
February collections for February sales			84,000		84,000
March collections for February sales				$ 36,000	36,000
March collections for March sales				123,200	123,200
		$49,600	$96,000	$159,200	$304,800

*See Exhibit 6 (Sales Budget). Each month's total collection is the sum of (prior month sales × 30%) + (current month sales × 70%).

The schedule of cash collections also is used to estimate ending accounts receivable. Notice Exhibit 3, panel B, reports an ending accounts receivable balance of $52,800 on the pro forma balance sheet. Consequently, Sierra Canoe Co. must have $52,800 of accounts receivable on March 31, the end of the quarter. From the sales budget we know March sales were estimated to be $176,000. March collections from March sales are expected to be $123,200 ($176,000 × .70). The remaining accounts receivable balance of $52,800 ($176,000 − $123,200) should be collected in April.

Schedule of Cash Payments

The *schedule of cash payments* **identifies the timing and amount of cash outflows related to production and administrative activities.** A schedule of cash payments is useful to help managers understand the timing of cash outlays resulting from purchases. For example, assume Sierra Canoe Co.'s cash payments typically occur in the following pattern:

- 50 percent in the month of purchase
- 50 percent in the month following a purchase

Before determining the timing of cash outflows for purchases, we must determine total purchases for materials, labor, overhead, and selling and administrative expenses by month by summing information from the purchases budgets as follows:

	December	January	February	March	Source
Materials:					
Polymer	$ 8,730	$ 8,577	$ 18,378	$ 24,777	Exhibit 8
Accessory packages	4,300	3,000	7,850	11,150	Exhibit 9
Labor	11,352	7,920	20,724	29,436	Exhibit 10
Overhead	25,800	18,000	47,100	66,900	Exhibit 11
Selling and administrative	16,800	12,000	24,000	32,400	Exhibit 13
	$66,982	$49,497	$118,052	$164,663	

Exhibit 16 identifies cash payments during January, February, and March. For example, January cash payments include the remaining 50 percent from December pur-

Exhibit 16 Schedule of Cash Payments*

	December	January	February	March	Quarter
December disbursements for December purchases	$33,491				
January disbursements for December purchases		$33,491			$ 33,491
January disbursements for January purchases		24,749			24,749
February disbursements for January purchases			$24,748		24,748
February disbursements for February purchases			59,026		59,026
March disbursements for February purchases				$ 59,026	59,026
March disbursements for March purchases				82,332	82,332
		$58,240	$83,774	$141,358	$283,372

*Each month's total payment is the sum of (prior month total purchases × 50%) + (current month total purchases × 50%).
Note: Amounts are rounded up to the nearest whole dollar.

chases ($66,982 $\times$ .50 = $33,491) plus 50 percent of the January purchases ($49,497 $\times$ .50 = $24,749). Therefore, January cash payments equal $58,240 ($33,491 + $24,749). Cash payments for each month are calculated in the same manner. The monthly disbursement totals are transferred to the cash budget.

The cash payment schedule provides accounts payable information to help prepare the pro forma balance sheet. For example, the amount remaining unpaid from March purchases totals $82,331 ($164,663 − $82,332 = $82,331). Recall that Sierra Canoe Co. pays 50 percent in the month of purchase and 50 percent in the first month following the purchase. Thus, the accounts payable balance at the end of March is $82,331 and appears in Exhibit 3, panel B, as the accounts payable balance in the pro forma balance sheet.

DEVELOPING A SOUND BUDGETING CULTURE

OBJECTIVE 4

Describe the elements of a successful budgeting culture.

The budgeting methods adopted by a company will greatly influence how successful the budgeting process will be. The culture of a business is the way people in the business think and behave. A sound budget culture relies on establishing a process that encourages participation by key employees in the development of budgets. Key employees are those charged with making critical decisions about sales, production, and expenditures. Key employees include top managers and others who are held accountable for critical decisions. Companies can undertake a variety of activities to develop a sound budget culture. These activities include directing attention to the budget, educating participants in the budget process, ensuring availability of information necessary to develop the budget, evaluating actual versus budgeted results, and motivating management to be active in the budget process.

Preparation of the master budget requires the involvement of managers throughout an organization. Each department or manager who participates in the planning process should understand the goals of the budget and the methods used to develop it. Therefore, a company should educate managers about the goals and procedures of the budgeting process.

To create an accurate budget, a thorough understanding of an organization's cost structure is required. Managers must understand expenses that affect their particular department or function. In addition, managers must understand the accounting methods a company uses in measuring expenses and accumulating data in their areas of responsibility. Responsibility accounting assigns responsibility for the performance of a company's departments to department managers. It requires that each manager's performance be evaluated on the basis of expenses or revenues that are directly under the manager's control. Responsibility accounting reports are produced periodically for the purpose of evaluating a department manager's effectiveness in generating revenues or controlling expenses.

Coordination is needed to bring together the various components of the master budget. In many organizations, a standing budget committee is responsible for the coordination of the master budget. This committee generally consists of the president and vice presidents in charge of various departments, such as sales, production, and finance. One role of the budget committee is to resolve disputes or misunderstandings among those involved in budget preparation.

Generally, the most successful budget processes are those that permit managers to participate in developing the budgets. Participative budgeting (or bottom-up budgeting) is a process that allows individuals at various levels of a company to participate in determining the company's goals and the plans for achieving those goals. It signals that senior managers value employee judgment and also results in a greater degree of employee acceptance of the budget. Senior managers often are not in a position to know the details of day-to-day operations as well as employees involved in these operations. Therefore, participation by employees can result in more accurate and achievable budgets. Further, employees who are involved in the development of a budget are more likely to work toward achieving budget goals.

Budget Revisions

As we illustrated earlier in this chapter, budgets forecast future costs of materials, labor, overhead, and selling and administrative activities. However, these forecasts are not always accurate. Substantial differences between a company's actual costs and those assumed in developing the budget can make the budget less useful. For example, a large increase in materials costs can cause the materials budget to be grossly understated. Evaluating managers responsible for materials purchases against such a budget would be unrealistic. Consequently, companies may find it necessary to revise the original budget if there are unforeseen changes.

Inaccurate forecasts raise two concerns. First, when is a forecast sufficiently inaccurate to justify a change in the budget? If budgets are changed frequently because of minor differences in expenses, they will lose meaning. Second, is the difference between the forecast and the actual amounts due to a bad forecast or to the failure of managers to control costs? If managers are allowed to escape responsibility too easily, the budget will lose its value. In deciding whether to permit a budget revision, senior management must weigh these concerns against the concern that the budget is inaccurate.

Behavioral Concerns in Budgeting

http://ingram.
swlearning.com

Find out more about
the Hawthorne
Research.

During the 1920s, a series of studies were conducted at the Hawthorne plant of the **Western Electric Company** to determine whether various elements of the physical environment in the plant affected employee efficiency and output. The experimenters varied employee work environments and measured resulting employee performance. At first, the researchers believed that increasing the levels of light had a positive effect on productivity. They later discovered that productivity increased whenever the researchers measured employees' work, regardless of the change in environment. The Hawthorne studies provide evidence that observing and measuring human behavior can alter behavior. Budgets provide benchmarks for measuring performance. By observing and measuring performance, companies hope to improve efficiency and effectiveness.

Participation in the Budget Process

Different leadership styles can lead to different types of budgeting processes. Budgets can be described as either top-down or bottom-up. Top-down budgets are established by management and then provided to lower levels of management. Bottom-up budgets involve all levels of an organization working to achieve the organization's goals.

For a bottom-up budget, the department managers usually submit proposed budgets and then negotiate with senior managers to create a master budget. This budget is used to evaluate the department's performance. There is two-way communication in bottom-up budgeting. In a bottom-up, participative budget setting, the chief executive officer might direct the vice president of sales to solicit information on sales goals for the coming year from the regional sales offices or departments. After reviewing the goals submitted by the regional sales offices and negotiating any desired changes, the vice president of sales would present a consolidated sales budget for the company to the chief executive. If the chief executive accepts the proposed budget, no further action is required. If the chief executive does not accept the budget, the vice president of sales renegotiates the regional sales budgets with the regional sales offices until an acceptable budget is reached.

Resources are necessary to meet objectives, but resources usually are limited. In many companies, departments compete with each other for a greater share of available resources. Sound planning requires decisions about the allocation of limited resources. Middle and lower-level managers tend to accept these decisions more readily if they have an active role in planning and setting budget goals. Participative budgeting encourages the acceptance of resource allocation decisions by creating a budget culture in which employees have a voice in decisions.

Case in Point

Bottom-Up Budgeting

The **National Bank of Georgia** conducted an annual budgeting process that included loan and deposit goals for each of its branches. Top management established budget targets for the entire bank and for the branch division as a whole. Branch managers participated in this process by developing budgets for their branches and submitting these budgets to Branch Administration. Branch administrators reviewed the budgets and compared them to the targets set for the division. If the branch budgets were not as aggressive as the targets set by top management, branch administrators negotiated with individual branch managers in an attempt to get them to increase their budget targets so that the sum of the individual branches' goals was equal to the division's goal.

Slack in Budgets

When budgets are prepared, departmental managers have incentives to build slack into budgets to make performance goals easier to achieve. *Budgetary slack* **is the difference between a less demanding budget value and a value managers believe they realistically can achieve.** The process of building slack into budgets is called padding. Budgets that have little or no slack are referred to as tight budgets. Managers perform best when faced with moderately difficult, but achievable, goals. Not all factors that affect department performance are under the control of departmental managers. While managers have little control over external variables, such as the general economy, they should understand the effect those variables will have on their department's performance. Examples of external factors that should be considered in the budgeting process include economic forecasts related to a particular product, market conditions that affect a particular industry, and interest rates.

Because external factors affect performance, department performance may not reflect managers' efforts. Budgetary slack reduces the risk that factors beyond the control of managers will cause them to fail to meet their budget goals. On the other hand, if budgets contain too much slack, department managers can perform at a less than optimal level. Senior managers and department managers must work together to create budgets that lead to satisfactory performance.

Budgets and Undesirable Behavior

Senior managers also should be aware that budget goals sometimes can cause lower-level managers to make decisions that are not in the best interest of the company as a whole. For example, suppose a plant's maintenance expenses are high relative to the budget. Further assume the plant manager expects to be promoted if plant performance targets are met. The plant manager may be tempted to defer needed maintenance in the hope of meeting budget targets and winning the promotion. The downside of such a decision, however, will be higher maintenance expenses in the future. Delaying maintenance leads to abnormal wear of a plant's equipment.

Managers need to be aware of the behavioral effects of the budgeting process. With proper planning, managers can reduce those problems. For example, some slack can be included in the budget to reduce incentives for undesirable behavior. Companies also can attempt to detect behavior problems. As an example, a company can monitor unusual decreases in maintenance expenses prior to the end of a budget period to make sure a department is not foregoing necessary maintenance activities.

BUDGETING IN SERVICE COMPANIES

OBJECTIVE 5

Explain the role of budgets in service organizations.

Service companies use budgets similarly to manufacturing companies. The preparation of budgets in service companies, however, can differ from budget preparation in manufacturing companies because service companies do not manufacture goods. Although service companies do not have to develop production and raw materials budgets, some aspects of budgeting can be more difficult in service organizations because it is often harder to trace costs to a particular service than to manufactured goods. In service companies, workers may be involved in the delivery of several different types of services during the same time period. In manufacturing companies, workers usually manufacture only one type of product at a time. When workers are involved with several different types of services at the same time, it is much more difficult to determine how much time (and therefore labor cost) is associated with providing one particular service. This makes it more difficult to develop budgets based on the expected amounts of services to be provided.

Consider checking account services, one of many services provided by banks. One of the costs bank management must budget for is the cost of the labor directly involved in providing checking accounts. This includes the work of tellers, new account personnel, and customer service personnel. These same personnel, however, help to provide many other types of services in addition to checking accounts, often at the same time they are dealing with checking accounts. For example, a teller may process a checking transaction, a loan payment, and a savings deposit for a given customer. How much of the cost of the teller's idle time should be assigned to each type of transaction? Although these cost allocation difficulties may be present in a manufacturing company to some extent, they are present to a greater extent in banks. The result is that banks are less able to accurately budget for the costs of providing for particular services than are manufacturing companies.

Although some aspects of service companies make budgeting more difficult than in manufacturing companies, other aspects potentially make budgeting easier and more useful. For example, some service companies, such as banks and automobile rental companies, operate many offices in different locations. The similarity of these separate offices provides a basis for analyzing budgets and evaluating performance that is not present in many manufacturing companies. The information for each unit can be compared with company-wide averages. This makes determination of good and bad performers easier than with manufacturing companies.

---

3 **SELF-STUDY PROBLEM**   Assume a company's management has forecast sales of $30,000, $37,000, $40,000, and $62,000, for June, July, August, and September, respectively. They estimate that 80 percent of their sales are collected the month of sale and 20 percent are collected in the month following the sale.

WebTUTOR Advantage

The company typically pays for 60 percent of its inventory purchases in the month of purchase. The remaining 40 percent is paid in the month following purchase. Assume purchases for June, July, August, and September are $15,000, $20,000, $22,000, and $30,000, respectively.

Required

A. Prepare a schedule of cash receipts for July, August, and September.
B. Prepare a schedule of cash payments for July, August, and September.

The solution to Self-Study Problem 3 appears at the end of the chapter.

REVIEW

SUMMARY of IMPORTANT CONCEPTS

1. The transaction system records actual events. The budget system records expected events.
   a. Pro forma, or predicted, financial statements are prepared by combining information from various budgets.
   b. The transaction system produces financial statements based on actual performance, while the budget system produces financial statements based on predicted performance.

2. A master budget has the following components:
   a. The sales budget shows the quantity and price of goods expected to be sold during the coming period.
   b. The production budget shows the type and quantity of products expected to be produced.
   c. The direct materials budget reflects the amount of raw materials expected to be purchased and used in production.
   d. The direct labor budget indicates the expected labor requirements for production.
   e. The manufacturing overhead budget reflects anticipated overhead costs.
   f. The selling and administrative expense budget shows anticipated costs.
   g. The cash budget shows expected cash receipts and disbursements.
   h. The pro forma income statement indicates the expected net income for the period.
   i. The pro forma balance sheet indicates anticipated levels of assets, liabilities, and owners' equity.

3. The cash budget summarizes expected cash collections and payments during an accounting period.
   a. A schedule of cash collections identifies the timing and amount of expected cash receipts.
   b. A schedule of cash payments identifies the timing and amount of cash outflows.

4. The budgeting culture influences the success of a company's budgeting efforts.
   a. Budget revisions may become necessary if assumptions made during the budgeting process later are found to be incorrect.
   b. Studies have shown that the process of observing and measuring behavior can influence behavior.
   c. Participation in the budgeting process often leads to budget acceptance.
   d. Budgetary slack is padding built into a budget in case cost and revenue targets are not met.
   e. Strict use of budgets can cause undesirable behavior as managers make short-term decisions that may have negative long-term effects.

5. Budgeting in service companies differs in some respects from budgeting in manufacturing companies.
   a. Workers in service companies often perform more than one type of service at the same time, making budgeting the cost of individual services more difficult.
   b. Service companies often operate many branches, providing a basis for analyzing budgets and evaluating performance that is not present in many manufacturing companies.

DEFINE

TERMS and CONCEPTS DEFINED in this CHAPTER

budget   (M206)
budgetary slack   (M221)
cash budget   (M216)
labor budget   (M214)
master budget   (M208)
materials purchases budget   (M212)

overhead budget   (M214)
production budget   (M211)
sales budget   (M210)
schedule of cash collections   (M217)
schedule of cash payments   (M218)
selling and administrative budget   (M215)

SELF-STUDY PROBLEM SOLUTIONS

SSP8-1

	Actual	Expected				
	December	January	February	March	Quarter	April
Unit sales	16	10	6	20	36	30
Plus: Desired ending finished goods inventory	5	3	10	15	15	30
Total units required	21	13	16	35	51	60
Less: Beginning finished goods inventory	8	5	3	10	5	15
Total units purchased	13	8	13	25	46	45
Cost per unit	$ 45	$ 45	$ 45	$ 45	$ 45	$ 45
Cost of purchases	$585	$360	$585	$1,125	$2,070	$2,025

SSP8-2

	January	February	March
Sales	$30,000	$45,000	$50,000
Variable expenses*	$ 6,000	$ 9,000	$10,000
Fixed expenses	20,000	20,000	20,000
Total expenses	$26,000	$29,000	$30,000

Variable expenses are .20 × sales.

SSP8-3   A.

	July	August	September
From June sales (.2 × 30,000)	$ 6,000		
From July sales (.8 × 37,000)	29,600		
From July sales (.2 × 37,000)		$ 7,400	
From August sales (.8 × 40,000)		32,000	
From August sales (.2 × 40,000)			$ 8,000
From September sales (.8 × 62,000)			49,600
Total	$35,600	$39,400	$57,600

B.

	July	August	September
From June purchases (.4 × 15,000)	$ 6,000		
From July purchases (.6 × 20,000)	12,000		
From July purchases (.4 × 20,000)		$ 8,000	
From August purchases (.6 × 22,000)		13,200	
From August purchases (.4 × 22,000)			$ 8,800
From September purchases (.6 × 30,000)			18,000
Total	$18,000	$21,200	$26,800

Thinking Beyond the Question

Why should budgets be carefully constructed?

Think about the chapter opening scenario. Suppose Erin and Seth want to develop a sound budgeting culture with Young Designs, Inc. Based upon what you learned in this chapter about the ways in which budgets can affect human behavior, would you suggest that Erin and Seth share their best-case/worst-case/most-likely-case sensitivity analysis with their sales and production managers and also with their lower-level employees? What advantages and disadvantages do you foresee in sharing this information?

QUESTIONS

Q8-1
Obj. 1
Why do managers compare expected results and actual results at the end of a fiscal period, after their actions can no longer influence results for that period?

Q8-2
Obj. 2
Why is communication among marketing and production managers necessary when developing a master budget?

Q8-3
Obj. 2
Why is the production budget necessary for estimating labor costs?

Q8-4
Obj. 2
Why is it important to the budgeting process to have an accurate sales forecast?

Q8-5
Obj. 2
Paul Reynolds recently was hired as a salesman for The Rocky Company, which sells gardening tools and potting soil through retail outlets. Paul has been asked to attend a meeting next week to discuss the preparation of the master budget for the coming year. Paul has asked you to explain what is meant by a master budget so that he can prepare for the meeting. What will you tell Paul?

Q8-6
Obj. 2
Markle Company is a merchandising firm that operates 26 stores. Marvle Industries is a manufacturer that operates a single plant. Both firms prepare detailed master budgets each year. How will the master budgets of the two firms differ?

Q8-10
Obj. 3
If management prepares a pro forma income statement that suggests the company will be profitable, why is a cash budget necessary?

Q8-11
Obj. 4
Why is an understanding of an organization's cost structure necessary for successfully preparing a master budget?

Q8-12   Why is employee participation important when developing a budget?
Obj. 4

Q8-13   Leroy Smith is the production manager of Alum Company. In addition to his salary, Leroy
Obj. 4   receives bonus compensation based solely on his ability to meet the budgeted production of
units. Comment on Leroy's bonus arrangement. What weaknesses might exist in this arrangement?

Q8-14   Discuss the implications associated with a budgetary approach in which budgetary data are
Obj. 4   imposed on managers from above. Contrast such an approach with one in which budgetary
data are self-imposed in a participative manner.

Q8-15   Rona Abraham is the purchasing manager for Flextech Incorporated, a manufacturer of fur-
Obj. 4   niture and bedding. Rona knows that as part of her bonus compensation, she must meet the
material purchasing budget that was established at the beginning of the year. In an effort to
meet this budget, Rona has been purchasing lower-grade materials at reduced costs and is
proud of her ability to spend less than the budgeted amounts on materials. What implications
do Rona's actions have for Flextech as a whole?

Q8-16   Lester Arbuckle is owner of Sheetco, a manufacturer of snow shovels. Lester and his managers
Obj. 4   do no budgeting or planning for Sheetco. Sheetco management does not anticipate problems
that arise, and as a result the company has slow production, missed shipment deadlines, and
lost sales. Discuss the reasons why Lester should wish to engage in budgeting and planning.

Q8-17   Service firms do not manufacture products; therefore, budgeting is not important to service
Obj. 5   firms. Do you agree? Explain your answer.

EXERCISES

*If your instructor is using Personal Trainer® in this course, you may complete your assignments
online.*

E8-1   Write a short definition of each of the terms listed in the *Terms and Concepts Defined in this
Chapter* section.

E8-2   Match the following budgets with their definitions.
Obj. 2

    a. sales budget
    b. production budget
    c. direct materials budget
    d. direct labor budget
    e. manufacturing overhead budget
    f. selling and administrative budget
    g. cash budget
    h. pro forma budgeted income statement
    i. pro forma budgeted balance sheet

    1. identifies the labor resources required to meet production needs
    2. identifies the amount of materials that will be required to support a company's total
production needs
    3. a schedule of revenues and expenses prepared from information developed in the bud-
get process
    4. identifies the expected amount of assets, liabilities, and owners' equity at the end of the
budget process
    5. contains a list of anticipated expenses for the period for activities other than manufac-
turing
    6. identifies the amount of a product that must be manufactured to meet a company's
needs for sales and inventory
    7. provides a schedule of all costs of production other than direct materials and direct labor
    8. describes cash requirements for the budget period
    9. projects revenues from sales of a company's products or services

E8-3   Hoop Action manufactures basketballs, which it sells for $50 each. Cash collections from sales
Obj. 2   are expected to be 80% in the quarter of the sale and 20% in the following quarter. The un-
collected portion of sales at January 1 was $40,000. The sales forecast for the next year is:

Expected Sales in Units

Quarter 1	2,000
Quarter 2	3,000
Quarter 3	5,000
Quarter 4	5,000

Create a sales budget and a schedule of cash collections.

E8-4
Obj. 2

Spooks Company makes a popular Halloween mask. Peak sales are in October of each year. The company's partial sales budget, in units, for 2004 is as follows:

August	September	October	November
15,000	35,000	50,000	10,000

The company has an inventory policy in which the end-of-month inventory must equal 10% of the following month's sales. The inventory as of July 31 was 1,500 units.

Prepare a production budget for the three months ended October 31, 2004. In your budget, show the number of units to be produced each month and for the quarter in total.

E8-5
Obj. 2

Razor Sharp produces a hedge trimmer used for lawn care. The company's sales budget for April through July is as follows:

April	May	June	July
300,000	350,000	250,000	150,000

The company has an inventory policy in which the end-of-month inventory must equal 5% of the following month's sales. The inventory as of March 31 was 15,000 units.

Prepare a production budget for April, May, and June. In your budget, show the number of units to be produced each month and for the quarter in total.

E8-6
Obj. 2

Young Company produces a dietary product called Veggy Bars. Each six-ounce Veggy Bar contains five ounces of mixed vegetables, which Young purchases for $.05 an ounce. Budgeted sales of vegetable bars for the first four months of 2004 is as follows:

	Units
January	100,000
February	120,000
March	110,000
April	100,000

Young has an inventory policy that requires the ending inventory of Veggy Bars to be 10% of the following month's sales.

Prepare a production budget for t'
in total. Calculate the amount ⁿᶠ

	Units
January	10,000
February	12,000
March	8,000
April	10,000

(Continued)

Chugalot has an inventory policy that ending inventory of mugs should be 10% of the following month's sales.

Prepare a purchasing budget for the first quarter of 2004 by month and for the quarter in total. Show the amount of materials required in unit and in dollar amounts.

E8-9
Obj. 2
Refer to the data in E8-8. Each mug requires .05 direct labor hour. The average labor rate is $20 per hour.

Prepare a direct labor budget for the first quarter of 2004, showing the number of hours needed and the total labor cost required by month and for the quarter in total.

E8-10
Obj. 2
Office Supply 4U manufactures staplers. The activity base used to allocate overhead is direct labor hours. The variable overhead rate is estimated at $1.50 per direct labor hour for 2004. The fixed overhead is budgeted at $20,000 per quarter, of which $5,000 represents depreciation. The budgeted direct labor hours are as follows:

Quarter	Direct Labor Hours
1	9,500
2	10,500
3	11,500
4	11,000

Prepare a manufacturing overhead budget for 2004, showing the total budgeted manufacturing overhead and the cash disbursements for manufacturing overhead by quarter and for the year in total. (*Hint:* Is there a periodic cash flow associated with depreciation?)

E8-11
Obj. 2
A+ Company manufactures study guides for students. A+ sells its study guides through door-to-door sales. Its salespeople receive a $20 commission per book sold. Fixed annual selling and administrative expenses for 2004 are estimated as follows:

Insurance	$ 200,000
Executive salaries	1,000,000
Property taxes	30,000
Depreciation	30,000

The sales for 2004 are estimated as follows:

Quarter	Unit Sales
1	5,000
2	10,000
3	20,000
4	7,000

Prepare a selling and administrative budget for 2004, showing the total budgeted selling and administrative expenses by quarter and for the year in total.

E8-12
Obj. 2
Tough Terrain Company manufactures professional quality lawn mowers. Tough Terrain incurs variable selling expenses of $15 per lawn mower. Other annual selling and administrative expenses for 2004 are estimated as follows:

Advertising	$200,000
Insurance	100,000
Executive salaries	500,000
Property taxes	20,000
Depreciation	10,000

The sales for 2004 are estimated as follows:

Quarter	Unit Sales
1	5,000
2	30,000
3	20,000
4	2,000

Prepare a selling and administrative budget for 2004, showing the total budgeted selling and administrative expenses and the cash disbursements for selling and administrative expenses by quarter and for the year in total. (*Hint:* Is there a periodic cash flow associated with depreciation?)

E8-13
Objs. 2, 3

On April 30, Sterling Enterprises had an inventory of 38,000 units of finished goods, and it had accounts receivable totaling $85,000. Sales, in units, have been budgeted as follows for the next four months:

May	60,000
June	75,000
July	90,000
August	81,000

Sterling has a policy that 40% of the following month's sales should be maintained in ending inventory. Each unit sells for $2. All sales are on account. The budgeted cash collections anticipate that one-third of sales will be collected in the month of sale and the remainder in the following month.

a. Prepare a production budget for the months of May, June, and July.
b. Prepare a schedule of cash collections for the months of May, June, and July.

E8-14
Obj. 3

Elm Company makes a product that has peak sales in September of each year. Excerpts from the annual sales budget are as follows:

	May	June	July	August	September
Budgeted sales	$450,000	$500,000	$500,000	$600,000	$750,000

The company is in the process of preparing a cash budget for the third quarter (July, August, and September) and must determine the cash collections by month. Collections on sales are expected to be as follows:

70% in the month of sale
20% in the month following the month of sale
8% in the second month following the month of sale
2% uncollectible

What are the expected cash collections for each month of the third quarter? (*Hint:* When calculating cash inflows, ignore the amount that is uncollectible.)

E8-15
Obj. 3

Beany-Toys Company makes small toys that it sells to retailers. Following are excerpts from the annual sales budget:

	August	September	October	November	December
Budgeted sales	$1,000,000	$800,000	$1,000,000	$2,500,000	$3,000,000

The company is in the

What are the expected cash collections for each month of the fourth quarter? (*Hint:* When calculating cash inflows, ignore the amount that is uncollectible.)

E8-16
Obj. 3

Cross Blade manufactures pocket knifes. The activity base used to allocate overhead is machine hours. The variable overhead rate is estimated at $4 per machine hour for 2004. The fixed overhead is budgeted at $80,000 per quarter. The budgeted machine hours are as follows:

(Continued)

Quarter	Machine Hours
1	5,000
2	4,000
3	4,500
4	5,000

Prepare a manufacturing overhead budget for 2004, showing the total budgeted manufacturing overhead by quarter and for the year in total.

PROBLEMS

If your instructor is using Personal Trainer® in this course, you may complete your assignments online.

P8-1   Pro Forma Income Statement

Obj. 1

Say Cheese Company manufactures picture frames that sell for $25 per frame. Say Cheese does not maintain an inventory; all items produced are sold during the period. Thus, all production costs appear on the income statement. The company has fixed manufacturing overhead of $30,000 per year. The company's fixed selling and administrative expense is $40,000 per year. Other expenses are as follows:

	Cost per Unit
Direct materials	$5.00
Direct labor	2.00
Variable manufacturing overhead	3.00
Variable selling and administrative expense	2.00

Say Cheese would like to estimate its net income if sales for 2004 are expected to be 8,000 units.

Required

A. Create a pro forma income statement using Exhibit 3 as a guide.
B. Discuss the uses for a pro forma income statement.

P8-2   Pro Forma Income Statement

Obj. 1

Technology Team manufactures laptops that sell for $2,200 each. Assume Technology Team does not maintain an inventory; all items produced are sold during the period. Thus, all production costs appear on the income statement. The company has fixed manufacturing overhead of $4,000,000 per year. The company's fixed selling and administrative expense is $3,000,000 per year. Other expenses are as follows:

	Cost per Unit
Direct materials	$1,200
Direct labor	150
Variable manufacturing overhead	50
Variable selling and administrative expense	30

Management at Technology Team believe sales for 2005 will be 10,000 units.

Required

A. Create a pro forma income statement using Exhibit 3 as a guide.
B. Discuss how a pro forma income statement helps managers make better decisions.

P8-3   Cash Budget

Objs. 1, 3

Kim Incorporated is preparing its master budget for 2004. Shown at the top of the next page are expected cash inflows and outflows resulting from the sales, purchases, and administrative budgets. In addition to these cash flows, assume the company expects to pay $10,000 in income taxes each quarter. Also, assume Kim expects to pay a $20,000 dividend in the fourth quarter. The beginning cash balance is $160,000.

SPREADSHEET

			Quarter		
	1	2	3	4	Year
Cash Collections from Sales Budget					
Total cash collections	$120,000	$140,000	$230,000	$250,000	$740,000
Cash Disbursements from Direct Materials Budget					
Total cash disbursements	$ 60,000	$ 70,000	$115,000	$125,000	$350,000
Direct Labor Disbursements					
Total direct labor disbursements	$ 16,000	$ 24,000	$ 40,000	$ 40,000	$120,000
Manufacturing Overhead Disbursements					
Cash disbursements for manufacturing overhead	$ 31,000	$ 39,000	$ 55,000	$ 55,000	$180,000
Selling and Administrative Disbursements					
Cash expenditures for selling and administrative expenses	$ 29,000	$ 31,000	$ 35,000	$ 35,000	$130,000

Required

A. Create a cash budget for 2004.
B. Assume that Kim has $1,000,000 of debt outstanding as of January 1, 2004. Given the cash budget should Kim borrow additional funds or repay any of the debt during 2004? Why or why not?
C. Why is it important to create a cash budget?

P8-4

Obj. 2

Purchasing Budget, Strategic Considerations

Noise Hollow launched a new stereo in January. The budget for the stereo is as follows:

	January	February
Unit sales	1,000	1,500
Add: Desired ending inventory	300	400
Subtotal	1,300	1,900
Less: Beginning inventory	0	300
Total production	1,300	1,600
Units of materials per finished good	10	10
Required units of materials	13,000	16,000
Cost of materials per unit	× $5	× $5
Total purchasing costs	$65,000	$80,000

Actual units of materials required per finished good were 12 units in January and 11 units in February. Actual cost of materials was $6 per unit in January and $5.50 per unit in February.

Required

A. Show what the budget would have looked like with the actual material requirements and costs.
B. What strategic considerations shou̶l̶d̶ ̶...

and bonuses are paid to key employees, including Bob, based on meeting budgeted results. For the past two years, Bob has received a very small bonus and has been chided by Yvonne for poor planning. Specifically, Yvonne has pointed out that the purchasing department has not maintained adequate levels of raw material inventory and is always in a rush to obtain materials, resulting in increased shipping and handling charges. Further, Regal must often pay

(Continued)

premium amounts for immediate shipment of materials. In her most recent evaluation, Yvonne stated to Bob, "The sales department and production department are doing an excellent job. They consistently exceed their budgets by 10% or more. I just don't understand why you can't meet your numbers. Perhaps it is time for some changes around here."

After getting chided by Yvonne, Bob went back and looked at his budget. He knew he had ordered the amount required by the budget. The budget for January and February is as follows:

	January	February
Unit sales	300,000	350,000
Add: Desired ending inventory	35,000	25,000
Subtotal	335,000	375,000
Less: Beginning inventory	30,000	35,000
Budgeted production	305,000	340,000
Pounds of raw materials per unit	1.1	1.1
Required pounds of raw materials	335,500	374,000
Add: Desired ending inventory of raw materials	37,400	27,500
Less: Beginning inventory of raw materials	33,550	37,400
Total raw material needs (pounds)	339,350	364,100

Required

A. If sales levels were 10% higher than budgeted, how many pounds of raw materials would Bob need to rush order each month so he can meet demand and the required ending inventory as shown in the budget?
B. Why does it appear that the purchasing department is having trouble meeting its budget?
C. Is it appropriate to blame Bob for all of the purchasing problems?
D. If Yvonne does "make some changes," what changes would you suggest she consider?

P8-6 Budgeting Culture and Behavior

Objs. 2, 4

Sue is the purchasing manager for Paper Goods Incorporated. Sue's budget for January and February was as follows:

	January	February
Finished goods to produce (units)	10,000	11,000
Add: Desired ending inventory	1,100	1,100
Subtotal	11,100	12,100
Less: Beginning inventory	1,000	1,100
Total	10,100	11,000
Pounds of raw materials per unit	2.0	2.0
Required pounds of raw materials	20,200	22,000
Add: Desired ending inventory of raw materials	2,200	2,200
Less: Beginning inventory of raw materials	2,020	2,200
Total raw material needs (pounds)	20,380	22,000

At the end of February, Sue's boss asked her, "Why are you ordering so many materials? The inventory stockroom is overflowing with materials." Puzzled, Sue checked her order amounts and saw that she had ordered the exact amount as stated by the budget. Sue then spoke to the production manager who explained that the plant had been running at only 90% capacity for the past two months due to lower demand.

Required

A. If sales and production levels were 10% lower than budgeted, how many pounds of raw materials are on hand at the end of February?
B. What is the problem with this system, and how would you suggest it be improved?

P8-7 Labor Requirement Planning, Service Provider

Objs. 2, 5

Ceco Grass Care is a small lawn maintenance service that provides a variety of landscape services. A large part of Ceco's sales are generated through lawn maintenance. Jeff Roberts manages Ceco. Jeff has reviewed the job order log for the next 12 weeks (three months ending July 26, 2005), and the log is full. Ceco recently acquired several commercial property accounts and has plenty of work planned. A summary of accounts shows that Ceco now has 11 commercial properties and 45 residential properties to maintain on a routine basis.

Each property is scheduled for maintenance every two weeks. The commercial accounts require 16 worker-hours to service, and the residential accounts require four worker-hours.

Ceco currently has a cutting crew of three, each of whom is paid $8.50 an hour.

Required

A. Prepare a direct labor budget for Ceco covering the next three months.

B. Does the budget raise any concerns for Ceco? Explain your answer.

P8-8 Sales Budget, Strategic Considerations

Obj. 3

SPREADSHEET

A new high-tech product was launched in July. This is the first product of its type in the marketplace. The budget for this product is as follows:

	July	August
Expected sales in units	2,000	3,000
Selling price per unit	$ 50	$ 50
Total sales	$100,000	$150,000

However, the actual sales were not quite as high as was anticipated. The actual sales were:

	July	August
Actual sales in units	1,000	2,500
Selling price per unit	$ 50	$ 50
Total sales	$50,000	$125,000

Mary, the vice president of finance, spoke harshly to John, the product manager, for not meeting the budgeted amounts. She threatened to discontinue the product if John did not meet budgeted sales for September. Mary also wants to know how much cash would have been collected if the budgeted sales had been achieved.

Required

A. Create a schedule of cash collections for the budgeted sales for July and August. Assume that 80% of sales are collected in the month of sale and the remaining 20% of sales are collected the following month.

B. What strategic considerations should Mary take into account? Explain.

P8-9 Budgeted Production and Cash Collections

Obj. 3

On August 31, Blake & Sons had an inventory of 50 units of finished goods, and it had accounts receivable totaling $75,000. Sales, in units, have been budgeted as follows for the next four months:

September	300
October	400
November	450
December	500

Blake has a policy that 20% of the following month's sales should be maintained in ending inventory. Each unit sells for $500. All sales are on account. The budgeted cash collections anticipate that one half of sales will be collected in the month of sale and the other half in the following month.

Required

A. Prepare a production budget for the months of September, October, and November.

B. Prepare a schedule of budgeted cash collections from sales for the months of September, October, and November.

(Continued)

C. Actual sales values (which drive the entire budgeting process) are not known with certainty. Are the various budgets and schedules meaningful since they are based on management's estimate of sales in the coming year? Can you identify other examples of accounting estimates?

P8-10   **Budgeting and Behavioral Implications**

Obj. 4

An effective budget converts the goals and objectives of management into specific performance targets. The master budget serves as a blueprint that reflects management's plans for the budgeted period. Moreover, the master budget serves as a basis for control in that performance can be evaluated by comparing actual results to budgeted or planned results.

Given the importance of budgeting within a company, the creation of an effective budget is essential for the successful operation of the company. There are several methods of generating budget information that can be employed, all of which require extensive contact with people at various operating levels within the company. The way in which people see their involvement with the budget process is important to the successful use of the budget as a management tool.

In the budget-setting process, budget A was put together by lower management, including sales representatives, purchasing managers, and factory supervisors. Budget B was put together by senior management.

	A	B
Unit sales	10,000	15,000
Dollar sales	$2,000,000	$3,000,000
Less variable expenses:		
Direct materials	$1,100,000	$1,500,000
Direct labor	220,000	300,000
Variable overhead	110,000	150,000
Variable selling and administrative expense	88,000	120,000
Total variable expenses	$1,518,000	$2,070,000
Contribution margin	$ 482,000	$ 930,000
Less fixed expenses:		
Manufacturing overhead	$ 350,000	$ 300,000
Selling and administrative	200,000	200,000
Taxes and interest	10,000	10,000
Total fixed expenses	$ 560,000	$ 510,000
Net income (loss)	$ (78,000)	$ 420,000

Required

A. Calculate the cost per unit for the variable costs.
B. Why do you think budget A has high costs and low sales forecasts?
C. Why do you think budget B has low costs and high sales forecasts? What are the behavioral implications of this top-down approach?
D. How should the two groups participate to come to a consensus on the budget? What are the advantages of this approach?

P8-11   **Budgeting and Behavioral Implications**

Obj. 4

Crunch Numbers is a manufacturer of calculators. In the budget-setting process, budget A was put together by lower and middle management. Budget B was put together by senior management.

	A	B
Unit sales	20,000	30,000
Dollar sales	$600,000	$900,000
Less variable expenses:		
Direct materials	$260,000	$360,000
Direct labor	40,000	60,000
Variable overhead	60,000	75,000
Variable selling and administrative expense	60,000	60,000
Total variable expenses	$420,000	$555,000
Contribution margin	$180,000	$345,000

Less fixed expenses:		
Manufacturing overhead	$ 60,000	$ 50,000
Selling and administrative	100,000	80,000
Taxes and interest	10,000	10,000
Total fixed expenses	$170,000	$140,000
Net income (loss)	$ 10,000	$205,000

Required

A. Calculate the cost per unit for the variable costs.
B. Why do you think budget A has high costs and low sales forecasts?
C. Why do you think budget B has low costs and high sales forecasts? What are the behavioral implications of this top-down approach?
D. How should the two groups participate to come to a consensus on the budget? What are the advantages of this approach?

P8-12 ## Excel in Action

SPREADSHEET

Music Makers expects to sell 500,000 CDs per month, including 350,000 data CDs and 150,000 music CDs. The selling price per unit is $2.30 for data CDs and $3.10 for music CDs. The desired level of ending inventory of raw materials is 5,000 units for blank CDs, containers, and cellophane wrap. Wrap is measured in feet, and each unit requires one foot of wrap. Paper inserts are obtained as needed, and the desired ending inventory is zero for these materials. At the beginning of May, Music Makers has 9,500 blank CDs, 2,500 containers, and 20,000 feet of cellophane in stock. The cost per unit of raw materials is $0.72 for CDs, $0.12 for containers, $0.07 for inserts, and $0.01 per foot of cellophane. Direct labor hours to produce each CD is 0.023 for copying and 0.015 for packaging. Direct labor cost is $12 per hour for copying and $8 per hour for packaging.

Required Use the data provided to prepare a (A) sales budget, (B) direct materials budget, and (C) direct labor budget for Music Makers for May. Use the following format. Use cell references and formulas where possible.

	A	B	C	D	E	F
1	Monthly Sales Budget					
2		Data	Music	Total		
3	Expected sales in units					
4	Selling price per unit					
5	Total sales					
6						
7	Direct Materials Budget					
8		CDs	Containers	Inserts	Cellophane	Total
9	Expected sales					
10	Desired ending inventory					
11	Total needs					
12	Beginning inventory					
13	Units to purchase					
14	Cost per unit					
15	Cost of materials					
20	Direct labor hour per unit					
21	Total hours					
22	Direct labor cost per hour					
23	Total direct labor cost					

(Continued)

Use appropriate formatting for numbers.

If expected sales were 400,000 data CDs and 100,000 music CDs, what would be the effect on the budgets?

P8-13   **Multiple-Choice Overview of the Chapter**

1. Which of the following represents the correct order in which the budget documents for a manufacturing company would be prepared?
   a. Sales budget, cash budget, direct materials budget, direct labor budget
   b. Production budget, sales budget, direct materials budget, direct labor budget
   c. Sales budget, cash budget, production budget, direct materials budget
   d. Sales budget, production budget, direct labor budget, cash budget, pro forma financial statements

2. Which of the following is *not* included as one of the four major sections of the cash budget?
   a. The receipts section
   b. The financing section
   c. The selling and administrative expense section
   d. The cash excess or deficiency section

3. A major advantage of budgeting is that it:
   a. eliminates major uncertainties associated with the business environment.
   b. ensures that management's objectives will be met.
   c. requires managers to give priority to the planning process.
   d. eliminates the need for stringent controls.

4. Which of the following is *not* correct with respect to the manufacturing overhead budget?
   a. The manufacturing overhead budget includes selling and administrative expenses.
   b. Manufacturing overhead can be broken down by cost behavior.
   c. The manufacturing overhead budget should include all costs of production other than direct materials and direct labor.
   d. The budgeted variable cost of manufacturing overhead is dependent on the number of units to be produced, as shown in the production budget.

5. Budgeted production needs are computed by:
   a. adding budgeted sales to the desired ending inventory and deducting the beginning inventory.
   b. adding budgeted sales to beginning inventory and deducting the desired ending inventory.
   c. adding budgeted sales to the desired ending inventory.
   d. deducting beginning inventory from budgeted sales.

6. Which of the following is *not* true with respect to a participative budgeting process?
   a. Participative budgeting requires less managerial involvement.
   b. Participative budgeting motivates managers by involving them in the budget process.
   c. Participative budgeting requires greater coordination between departments and disciplines.
   d. Participative budgeting relies on a bottom-up approach.

7. The materials purchases budget is prepared using which format?
   a. Beginning inventory + units to be produced − ending inventory
   b. Raw material required for production + desired ending raw materials inventory − beginning raw materials inventory
   c. Ending inventory + beginning inventory − units to be produced
   d. None of the above is correct.

8. The cash budget is comprised of all the following except:
   a. cash receipts.
   b. cash disbursements.
   c. accrued sales revenue.
   d. proceeds from loans and loan repayments.

9. A collection of related operating budgets is known as a:
   a. pro forma financial statement.
   b. flexible budget.
   c. static budget.
   d. master budget.

10. Budgeting in service companies:
    a. can be more difficult than in manufacturing companies because of complexities involved in tracing costs to a particular service.
    b. typically does not involve materials purchases.
    c. can help managers understand the cost of providing services.
    d. All of the above are correct.

CASES

C8-1

Objs. 2, 3

The Master Budget

Columbo Company manufactures a single model trench coat sold throughout the United States. Projected sales in units for the first five months of 2005 are as follows:

January	35,000
February	20,000
March	15,000
April	8,000
May	6,000

The following information relates to Columbo's production and inventory policies and balances:

1. Finished goods inventory is maintained at 80% of the following month's sales. Finished goods inventory at January 1, 2005, was 28,000 units.
2. Two materials are required for each trench coat manufactured, as follows:

Direct Materials	Yards per Unit	Cost per Yard
Polyester	5	$8
Lining material	3	2

Raw materials inventory is maintained at 10% of the following month's production needs. Inventory at January 1, 2005, was 51,000 yards of polyester and 30,600 yards of lining.

3. Direct labor used per unit is two hours. The average rate for labor is $9.50 per hour.
4. Overhead each month is estimated by adding the fixed cost component to the variable cost component. Direct labor hours is used as the basis for variable costs. A summary of expected overhead costs is as follows:

	Fixed Cost Component	Variable Cost Component
Factory supplies		$1.00
Utilities		0.75
Shop maintenance	$ 3,000	0.50
Supervision	4,000	
Depreciation	60,000	
Taxes	5,000	
Other	10,000	2.00
Total	$82,000	$4.25

(Continued)

5. Selling, general, and administrative expenses are also calculated by summing the fixed cost component and the variable cost component. The variable cost component is based on the number of units sold. Cost estimates are as follows:

	Fixed Cost Component	Variable Cost Component
Salaries	$18,000	
Commissions		$3.00
Depreciation	22,000	
Shipping		0.75
Other	10,000	1.50
Total	$50,000	$5.25

6. Each trench coat sells for $85.
7. All purchases are made in cash. All sales are on account. Collection of accounts receivable is planned as follows: 90% in the month of sale; 10% in the month following the month of sale. The accounts receivable balance at January 1, 2005, is $145,000, all of which is collectible. The cash balance at January 1, 2005, is $202,000.

Required

A. Prepare the following portions of the operating master budget, by month, for the first quarter of 2005:
   1. Sales budget
   2. Production budget
   3. Materials purchases budget
   4. Labor budget
   5. Overhead budget
   6. Selling and administrative budget
   7. Cash budget
B. Suppose Columbo's management believes that unseasonably warm weather in March and April could cause its sales in units to differ from the original projections as follows:

January	35,000
February	20,000
March	10,000
April	6,000
May	6,000

Explain how these fluctuations in sales will affect the other portions of the master budget developed in the previous requirements. What are the implications for the importance of forecasting sales accurately?

C8-2   Budgeting in a Service Company

Obj. 5

Juanita Testor owns and operates a hair salon under the name Clips n' Curls. There are currently seven hair stylists, including Juanita. In addition to hair styling, Clips n' Curls sells nail care, facials, skin and hair care products, fashion jewelry, and tanning bed time.

A full-time receptionist is employed to arrange appointments and perform other clerical duties, such as counter sales and record keeping. The receptionist is paid $1,500 a month.

Juanita has eight styling bays, each equipped with a sink, cabinet, and vacuum system. Each stylist provides his or her own instruments. Each stylist, including Juanita, "rents" a bay at a cost of $400 per month. Charges for all client services are billed and collected by the receptionist, who accumulates totals for each stylist. Collections for services are paid to the stylists on a weekly basis after deducting bay rent and cost of supplies. Any supplies used by the stylists must be purchased through the shop at Juanita's cost.

Nail care and facials are offered on a limited basis three days a week by a single individual, who receives 50% of collected billings as compensation. The tanning bed is owned by the shop. All income received from the bed goes to the shop. Variable shop costs are incurred based on the number of stylists. Based on a two-year study, Juanita has assembled the following information on monthly activity and costs to operate Clips n' Curls:

Average monthly billings per stylist	$4,000
Average product sales	600
Average gross margin on product sales	55%
Average gross nail and facial billings	$1,000
Average gross tanning bed billings	450
Fixed operating costs:	
Shop rent	500
Depreciation	400
Advertising	150
Other	100
Variable operating costs:	
Maintenance, utilities, and other	1,400*

Note: Variable operating costs are incurred as follows: 50% by stylists, 30% by tanning, nail care, and facials, 15% by product display, and 5% administrative.

Required

A. Assume that Juanita can hire an additional stylist who can generate the same average amount of business as the other stylists. Assume also that the additional stylist would have no impact on administrative expenses. What would be the change in average monthly shop income if Juanita hires the stylist to fill the remaining open bay? (*Hint:* Compare the change in revenues with the change in costs related to the incremental increase of one stylist.)

B. What is the average total monthly income of the shop given the number of stylists currently employed?

C. Juanita is considering a change in the bay rent agreement. Instead of charging a fixed amount per month, she is thinking of charging a stylist 12% of the stylist's billings. Would Juanita be better off with this new fee arrangement? Explain your answer.

M9

COST VARIANCES AND QUALITY MANAGEMENT

How are budgets used to evaluate performance?

Chapter M8 illustrated how Seth and Erin might use the budget process to plan future costs and expenses. Budgets also are useful to help managers understand performance at the end of an accounting period. For example, the accounting software that Erin and Seth use automatically compares expected, or budgeted, performance with actual performance. The difference is termed a variance. Seth and Erin must understand how to interpret variance reports and make process improvements based on their interpretations. One year has elapsed since they started their furniture business in a garage. They have been successful in producing and selling their line of juvenile furniture. However, actual financial results differ from expectations.

FOOD FOR THOUGHT

Put yourself in the role of Erin and Seth. You just received a report indicating the actual costs of materials, labor, and overhead are greater than the predicted, or budgeted, amount. As a result, actual income as reported by the income statement is less than budgeted net income. How could this difference have occurred? What would you do to correct the problem? Let's join Erin and Seth as they consider the use of variance information.

Seth: Wow, look at these figures! In some cases we really missed the mark when we budgeted our manufacturing costs. Our materials, labor, and overhead variances are all unfavorable.

Erin: So what does that mean?

Seth: An unfavorable cost variance means that all our actual costs for materials, labor, and overhead were larger than the budgeted amount. On the other hand, when an actual cost is less than the budgeted amount, the variance is favorable.

Erin: Okay, so now we know our actual cost of materials was greater than the budgeted cost of materials. What caused the difference, and how do we fix it? Did we spend more for materials than we planned?

Seth: That's certainly a possibility. However, the report shows a favorable materials price variance. That means our actual materials cost was less than the budget called for.

Erin: Have lumber prices changed since we prepared the budget?

Seth: Actually, I was able to get a better price on lumber by purchasing it in larger quantities. So our lumber prices were lower than we budgeted.

Erin: But this makes no sense. Paying less for materials should cause a favorable variance, yet you said our materials variance was unfavorable.

Seth: The price variance is only part of the total materials variance.

Erin: The other part must be the quantity of materials used. I'd be willing to bet we used more lumber than we should have.

Seth: I think that's the answer. The report says our materials quantity variance is unfavorable. In fact, we have a huge unfavorable quantity variance as compared to the small favorable price variance. Thus, our overall materials variance is unfavorable.

Erin: *How do we explain the unfavorable quantity variance, and how do we keep it from happening again?*

Seth: *You are asking the right questions, Erin. I need to go back and look at the production records to see if I can find a reason for using so much material. We could have had a machine problem that resulted in too much scrap or waste material. Sometimes the machine cutting tools become dull or damaged and ruin a piece of lumber.*

Erin: *Is it possible that we had an inexperienced craftsman making some of the furniture?*

Seth: *There could be lots of possibilities. Variance analysis can help us understand where problems may have occurred so we can make changes to prevent the same problems in the future. We also need to look at the labor and overhead variances in a similar manner to see why our budgeted costs differed from actual costs in these accounts.*

Erin: *I agree. If we can find where we are creating waste and inefficiency, we can improve our profitability.*

OBJECTIVES

Once you have completed this chapter, you should be able to:

1 Calculate and evaluate cost variances for direct materials and direct labor.

2 Explain how variance analysis can enhance managerial decision making.

3 Identify four types of quality costs and explain how managers use these costs to improve performance.

4 Describe how variability can affect production costs.

5 Explain how statistical process control provides useful information to managers of both production and administrative functions.

6 Explain the application of performance evaluation methods in service organizations.

METALART: PERFORMANCE EVALUATION AND THE MANUFACTURING PROCESS

Successful companies provide a return to investors by producing sales revenues in excess of costs. Thus, managers always are mindful of their customers' needs for quality, innovation, and reasonable prices. Control systems are used to ensure key processes are functioning as intended. Furthermore, compensation often is linked to outcomes as indicated by these control systems. As this chapter illustrates, a variety of techniques may be used to manage costs and to improve profitability. Thus, managers may use outcomes from these techniques as a *scorecard* to evaluate their success in achieving targets from internal operations.

The examples in this chapter are based on the experience of MetalArt, a company that prints graphic designs on flat metal sheets. The sheets are processed by other companies to make containers for ground coffee sold in grocery stores. Exhibit 1 illustrates the manufacturing process at MetalArt. Four interrelated processes (coil shearing, coating, printing, and wrapping and shipping) are required to produce MetalArt's product line. The following section briefly explains the activities taking place within each process.

Coil Shearing

The manufacturing process begins with coils of steel and ends with printed metal sheets that will be cut and welded into coffee cans by MetalArt's customers. Large rolls of steel (weighing approximately 20,000 pounds and called *coils*) are loaded onto a spindle that permits the coil to rotate as it is unwound for processing. Next, the steel passes through a pinhole detector, an optical scanning device that identifies light passing through the steel sheet. This step ensures that the finished can will be airtight and provide a perfect seal.

Exhibit 1 The Manufacturing Process at MetalArt

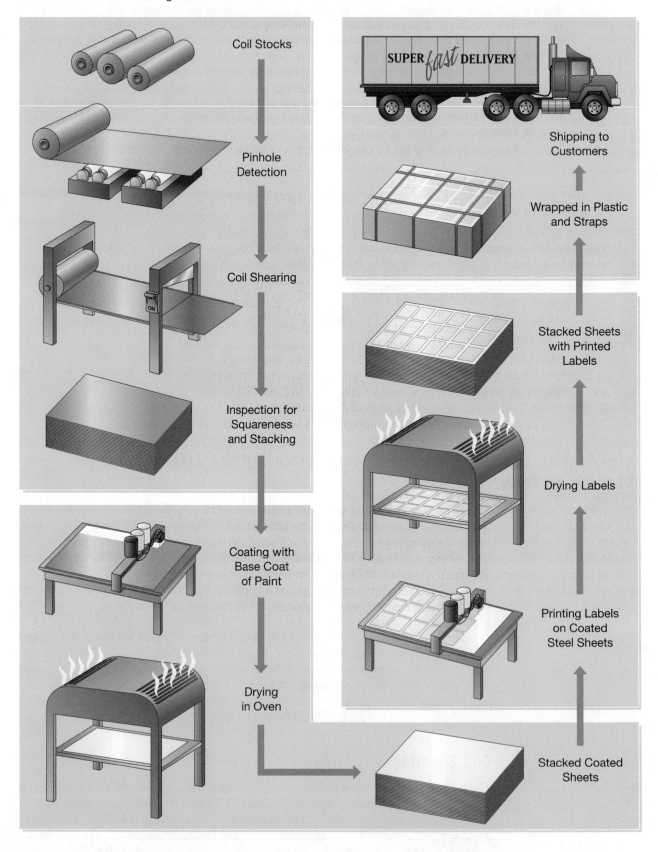

Coil Stocks

Pinhole Detection

Coil Shearing

Inspection for Squareness and Stacking

Coating with Base Coat of Paint

Drying in Oven

Stacked Coated Sheets

Printing Labels on Coated Steel Sheets

Drying Labels

Stacked Sheets with Printed Labels

Wrapped in Plastic and Straps

Shipping to Customers

SUPER *fast* DELIVERY

As a coil unwinds, the steel is sheared (cut) into sheets approximately three feet square. The steel sheets are randomly tested for squareness and must fall within specification limits to be passed on to the next stage of production. Those sheets that meet the quality standards are stacked in preparation for coating.

Coating

Coating is the first step in the printing process. A coat of white paint is applied to the metal sheet to provide a base to which colored ink will adhere. Following the base coat application, the sheet advances into an oven for drying. Since 18 or more cans are cut from one sheet of steel, the base coat is applied in rectangular patterns with strips of bare steel separating the rectangles. This frame of bare metal, called the *weld margin* (Exhibit 2), is very important. When the individual rectangles are cut from the sheet and welded to form the cylindrical can body, paint in the weld margin would cause major damage to the welding machine and disrupt the assembly process. Thus, a computer equipped with optical scanning devices monitors the coating of each sheet. A red flashing signal from the computer's control system lets the machine operator know when the coating process is beginning to produce weld margins that are too narrow. At the end of the coating step, the sheets are stacked and placed in a work-in-process area on the plant floor.

Exhibit 2 Sheet of Can Bodies

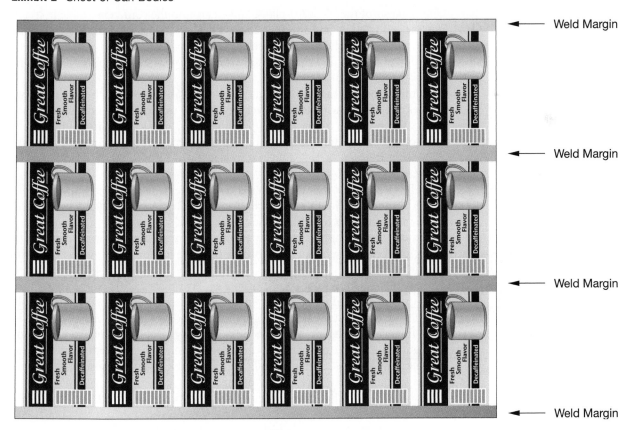

Printing

Printing is the next step in the process. The printing machines are capable of applying up to three colors to the sheets before they pass through a dryer that promotes rapid drying of the paint. The image that appears on the final product is printed using a process similar to silk screening. Three colors (such as red, blue, and yellow) are applied one after the other. Exhibit 2 illustrates a typical sheet of can bodies after coating and printing. At the end of the printing step, the sheets are stacked on platforms called *pallets* to await wrapping.

Wrapping and Shipping

Pallets of finished printed sheets are covered with plastic and bound with metal straps for shipping. Wrapping is a manual operation that requires two workers. After wrapping, pallets are loaded directly into trucks and delivered to customers. Finished goods inventory is not allowed to accumulate for more than a few hours.

MetalArt: Cost and Quality Management

This section documents the events occurring at MetalArt over a two-year period. The company found that its product quality was lower than that of its competitors. In addition, production costs were soaring out of control. MetalArt's managers discovered various cost management techniques to improve quality and reduce production costs.

We begin our discussion with the following events.

MetalArt—March 2005

Pat Allan, manager of the MetalArt plant, looked around the conference table in hopes that someone at the managers' meeting could explain why production costs had gone through the roof during the past few weeks. "I just don't understand. After all of our efforts to control costs, things have gotten worse. Corporate isn't going to be happy with our profitability figures."

Mary Smith, the production manager, replied, "Pat, remember the problems we had last week with bad raw materials? Everyone knows that rusty steel causes all kinds of headaches when we run it through the printing line. I suspect our profitability problems somehow are related to that. Also, I'm sure that some defective prints left the plant and that we'll hear about it from our customers. But we can't inspect everything; we don't have the resources."

"Mary, I don't think 'off-grade' material could have had *that* much impact on our bottom line," replied Lee Jones, the purchasing manager. "Anyway, by my estimates, I saved thousands of dollars by finding good steel prices."

Mary said, "Lee, we appreciate your efforts to control raw materials costs, but I scheduled a lot of overtime because our production line had to slow down to deal with off-grade raw material."

"I'm hearing two important issues," said Pat. "We have to find a way to *measure* the impact of material and labor cost overruns, and also to *prevent* production problems and their related costs before they get out of hand. It's clear to me that our disappointing financial results are linked to our operating problems. Let's get busy and put some controls in place that will help us improve operations and reduce costs. First, let's calculate cost variances for materials and labor. I'll evaluate those reports on a weekly basis to make sure we are staying on track."

"That's okay for you, Pat, but I need on-line, real-time tools to let me know when our process is out of control," said Mary. "I can't wait a week to find out that I need to look for a solution to a manufacturing problem. I think statistical process control methods would help us determine quickly when something has gone wrong."

"I agree," said Pat. "In addition, I think we should install a system for accounting for the costs of quality. I don't think we should rely on inspections to ensure that few defective units leave the plant. We can improve our processes so that they are reliable. In addition, we can illustrate to everyone from the shop floor worker to plant management how their actions affect our bottom line. We have good people, and I'm sure we can turn this plant around. Let's go to work!"

MetalArt—2007

Like other companies, MetalArt is constantly reviewing its operations, looking for ways to cut costs and improve quality. The employees have risen to the challenge and have managed to cut costs by 40 percent over the last two years while maintaining product quality. These improvements are due largely to employee suggestions and implementation efforts.

At each stage of production, the machine operator is assisted by software that signals when production quality slips out of control. With newer machines, data go directly from the machine to the computer. However, for older machines, the operator must enter the machine readings manually into the computer. The data are analyzed by a computerized statistical model that checks relevant variables to determine if production is within quality control limits. In addition, workers at all stages select samples from work in process, visually inspect printing quality, and reject products that do not meet very tight guidelines.

VARIANCE ANALYSIS FOR DIRECT MATERIALS AND DIRECT LABOR

OBJECTIVE 1

Calculate and evaluate cost variances for direct materials and direct labor.

As you learned from the discussion in the opening scenario to this chapter, Seth and Erin are interested in learning the cause of their unfavorable variances. Unlike the managers at MetalArt, Seth and Erin had established a standard cost system. Their job is to interpret the output. Let's learn how to set up a standard cost system from the managers at MetalArt.

The managers' meeting at MetalArt revealed an absence of controls. Pat Allen suggested the team must find a way to measure the cost of material and labor overruns and to implement systems that help prevent excessive costs. This section considers variance analysis as a tool for determining whether managers are using resources efficiently. We consider the environment in which the technique developed and its relevance to modern manufacturing companies. MetalArt is used to illustrate variance calculation and analysis.

MetalArt—April 2005

The first task undertaken by Pat Allan and the management team was to establish a standard cost reporting system that would allow *actual* material and labor costs to be compared with *standard* material and labor costs. *Standard costs* **represent the cost of the material and labor that should have been used to achieve actual production levels.** Accountants have used variance analysis for many years to evaluate how actual costs and quantities compare with predetermined standards.

In the later part of the nineteenth century and early part of the twentieth century, engineer-managers embraced a manufacturing philosophy known as scientific management. Frederick Taylor, who generally is regarded as the father of scientific management, believed that for every process there was one best way of doing it. He identified standards for labor efficiency and material usage. Then he compared these standards with actual operating performance. Typically, *standards* **are based on engineering studies to determine the amount of a resource (such as labor hours or pounds of material) necessary to manufacture a product.** Thus, standards tell us how much of a resource we should use or how much we should pay for materials and labor, given the number of units actually produced. Today, managers use variance analysis, which evolved from scientific management, to evaluate performance and to help them identify solutions to production problems. In addition, managers of service organizations use variance analysis. For example, hospitals use it to monitor the amount of nursing labor and hospital supplies used in treating patients. Retail organizations often analyze sales performance by comparing actual costs at a certain sales level with standard (or expected) costs. Examples may include travel and entertainment expenses, sales commissions, and other administrative support costs.

Direct Materials and Direct Labor Variances

We will calculate and interpret cost variances for the direct materials and direct labor used by MetalArt. At the most basic level, a variance is simply the difference between an actual cost and a standard cost. Using the diagram in Exhibit 3, total *actual* costs are compared with total *standard* costs to determine a total variance. Whether direct labor or direct materials is analyzed, the format is the same.

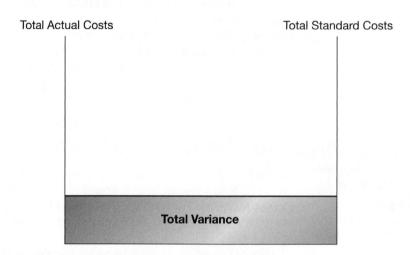

Exhibit 3
Total Variance Diagram

As shown in Exhibit 4, the total variance may be divided into two parts, a *price* component and a *quantity* component, by adding a middle prong to the total variance diagram. The reason for dividing a variance into its component parts is to determine whether a variance resulted from:

- *costs* of resources consumed that differed from standards,
- *physical amounts* of resources consumed that differed from standards, or
- a combination of *both costs and physical amounts* that differed from standards.

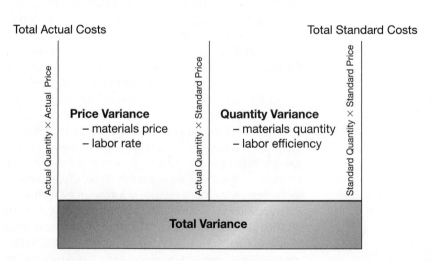

Exhibit 4
Variances Divided into Price and Quantity Components

Accountants typically use the terms material *price* and *quantity* and labor *rate* and *efficiency* to describe the price and quantity components of each variance.

MetalArt's experience illustrates how to calculate and interpret variances. Under the direction of Pat Allan, a team consisting of an engineer, an accountant, a personnel manager, and a purchasing manager prepared the information in Exhibit 5. They wanted to understand why manufacturing costs went through the roof during the second week of March 2005, as discussed in the weekly managers' meeting.

Exhibit 5

Production Information and Cost Information— Second Week of March 2005

Materials (Steel)		
Actual usage	× Actual price per pound	= Actual cost
500,000 pounds	× $0.25	= $125,000
Standard usage	× Standard price per pound	= Expected cost
460,000 pounds	× $0.30	= $138,000
Labor		
Actual usage	× Actual rate per hour	= Actual cost
5,300 hours	× $29	= $153,700
Standard usage	× Standard rate per hour	= Expected cost
4,600 hours	× $24	= $110,400

Materials (Steel). As shown in Exhibit 5, production records indicate that the actual quantity of steel purchased and used in the second week of March 2005 was 500,000 pounds. However, according to engineering standards, only 460,000 pounds should have been used during this period to make 6,000,000 finished coffee cans. Engineers designed coffee containers to precise specifications for length, width, thickness, and weight. Therefore, by multiplying the actual number of coffee cans manufactured times the standard weight per can, MetalArt's accountants determined the amount of steel that *should* have been used in production. In addition to physical standards for steel consumption, MetalArt established raw materials cost standards to evaluate the effectiveness of the purchasing department. Recall that MetalArt's purchasing manager, Lee Jones, had found a "good deal" on steel coils and had paid only $0.25 per pound, although the standard price was $0.30 per pound.

Labor. MetalArt employs many factory workers, each of whom is scheduled to work 40 hours per week; however, some are willing to work overtime when necessary to achieve production targets. In our opening discussion, Mary Smith indicated that extra labor time was needed because the manufacturing process had to operate at slower speeds as a result of inferior raw materials. As shown in Exhibit 5, the total number of hours worked during the second week of March was 5,300, at an actual cost of $29 per hour. By contrast, only 4,600 hours should have been worked during the period, at a rate of $24 per hour, to achieve the actual production level. Engineers developed time standards for producing a printed image for a coffee container. By multiplying the number of containers actually produced by the standard time per container, MetalArt's accountants determined the number of labor hours that *should* have been worked. Standard labor rates also were provided by MetalArt's personnel department. Recall that overtime wages, which are higher, were paid, causing the actual average hourly wage ($29) to exceed the standard hourly wage ($24).

The differences between actual and standard costs and usage for both materials and labor have been identified. In addition to calculating the amount of a variance, accountants also classify variances as favorable or unfavorable. **A** *favorable variance* **results when the actual price (or quantity) is less than the standard price (or quantity) for materials or labor.** On the other hand, an *unfavorable variance* **results when the actual price (or quantity) exceeds the standard.** Because variances may be interrelated, you must be careful when interpreting favorable and unfavorable variances. The term *favorable* does not always imply that something good has happened.

Calculation and Interpretation of Materials and Labor Variances

Recall that Erin and Seth are attempting to make sense of their standard cost report. This section outlines how to calculate materials and labor variances and provides more insight into how the standard cost reports are used for decision making. The managers at MetalArt face similar challenges. Pat Allan called another managers' meeting in May 2005 to review the work of the standard cost team.

Total Materials Variance. The plant controller began the discussion after passing copies of the variance report to each member of the team. "Refer to Exhibit 4, where the left-hand side is defined as *actual* cost. We multiplied the actual quantity of steel purchased by the actual price per pound to determine the total actual cost of our steel purchases. The right-hand side identifies the total *standard* cost allowed for actual production. We multiplied the standard quantity of steel allowed for actual production by the standard price to determine the standard cost. Thus, the total materials variance represents the difference between actual cost and standard cost, calculated as shown here."

Total materials variance = (Actual quantity × Actual price) − (Standard quantity × Standard price)

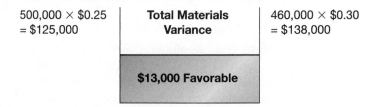

| 500,000 × $0.25
= $125,000 | **Total Materials
Variance** | 460,000 × $0.30
= $138,000 |

$13,000 Favorable

Pat examined the total materials variance and commented, "The plant's cost problems do not seem to be related to materials after all. A $13,000 favorable materials variance actually means that total material costs were *less* than the standards allowed."

However, Mary was quick to point out that a total variance does not tell the entire story. "Let's look beyond the total materials variance to the price and quantity elements and see what we find."

Materials Price Variance. "We divided the total variance for materials into price and quantity elements by adding a middle prong to the total variance diagram," explained the controller.

The middle prong shown in Exhibit 4 is defined as an actual quantity multiplied by a standard price. Thus, the price variance equation compares an *actual price* with a *standard price* to determine the *price variance per unit*.

MetalArt's controller continued, "We multiplied the number of pounds of purchased steel by the cost per pound (on the left side) and multiplied the actual number of pounds of purchased steel by the standard price (on the middle prong). The materials price variance is determined by subtracting the value found on the middle prong from that on the left side."

Materials price variance = (Actual quantity × Actual price) − (Actual quantity × Standard price)

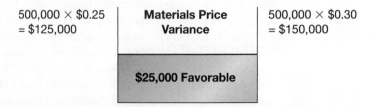

| 500,000 × $0.25
= $125,000 | **Materials Price
Variance** | 500,000 × $0.30
= $150,000 |

$25,000 Favorable

The purchasing manager, Lee Jones, smiled when the discussion turned to the materials price variance; he actually paid $0.05 ($0.30 − $0.25) per pound less than standard rates for steel purchases. Since 500,000 pounds were purchased, the result was a favorable price variance of $25,000 (500,000 × $0.05). Next, the discussion focused on the materials quantity variance.

Materials Quantity Variance. The plant controller continued, "As you know, we produced approximately 6,000,000 cans. Standards suggest that we should have used 460,000 pounds of steel. Thus, we multiplied the standard quantity of steel allowed for actual production by the standard cost per pound to arrive at the value found on the right side of the diagram. The materials quantity variance calculation compares the value on the middle prong with that on the right side."

Materials quantity variance = (Actual quantity × Standard price) − (Standard quantity × Standard price)

500,000 × $0.30 = $150,000	Materials Quantity Variance	460,000 × $0.30 = $138,000
	$12,000 Unfavorable	

"Unfortunately, the materials quantity variance of $12,000 is unfavorable. The difference between the actual quantity of materials used (500,000 pounds) and the standard quantity allowed for actual production (460,000 pounds) represents excess consumption of 40,000 pounds of material at a standard cost of $0.30 per pound," the controller explained. "Our calculations indicate that the total materials variance of $13,000 (favorable) can be divided into a $25,000 favorable price variance and a $12,000 unfavorable quantity variance ($25,000 favorable − $12,000 unfavorable = $13,000 favorable). As Mary suggested, off-grade materials affect the amount of steel required for production. The steel coils were blemished by small rust spots that did not affect the strength of the steel. Unfortunately, the blemishes were visible through the printed image, resulting in 40,000 pounds of scrap (500,000 actual pounds of steel − 460,000 standard pounds of steel)."

LEARNING NOTE

When the quantity of material purchased differs from the quantity actually used in production, the materials price variance is calculated using the actual quantity purchased, and the materials quantity variance is calculated using the actual quantity used in production. Thus, the purchasing agent is evaluated based on the amount purchased, whereas the production manager is evaluated based on the amount used. If more materials are purchased than are used, the difference is not a variance; it simply increases the value of the raw materials inventory.

Jones leaned back in his chair. "So what's the problem? Even though we used $12,000 more materials than our standards allow, I saved $25,000 by finding good steel prices. The net effect is still positive."

Mary turned the page to the labor variance report. "Lee, look at the next report. Poor-quality materials affect our process in other ways. I think a clearer picture will emerge after we consider labor variances."

Total Labor Variance. The controller continued, "The total labor variance is calculated in the same way as the total materials variance. Referring to Exhibit 4, the difference between actual labor costs and standard labor costs allowed for actual production (6,000,000 cans) is calculated as shown here."

Total labor variance = (Actual hours × Actual rate) − (Standard hours × Standard rate)

5,300 × $29 = $153,700	Total Labor Variance	4,600 × $24 = $110,400
	$43,300 Unfavorable	

"Look at how our labor costs were affected," said Mary.

"Wow, the $43,300 unfavorable labor variance wiped out my favorable materials variance. What caused the variance to be so large?" asked Lee.

Labor Rate Variance. The controller explained, "Lee, the labor variance is made up of two elements, the labor rate variance and the labor efficiency variance. Exhibit 5 identifies the actual and standard hourly labor rates as $29 and $24, respectively. We actually paid $5 per hour ($29 − $24) more than the standards allowed because we had to pay overtime. Since 5,300 hours actually were worked during the second week of March, an unfavorable labor rate variance of $26,500 (5,300 × $5) resulted. Many employees were asked to work overtime (at higher hourly wage rates) to achieve a production level of 460,000 pounds of printed steel. We computed the labor rate variance as shown here."

Labor rate variance = (Actual hours × Actual rate) − (Actual hours × Standard rate)

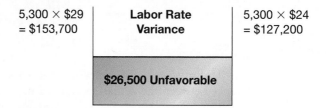

5,300 × $29
= $153,700

Labor Rate Variance

5,300 × $24
= $127,200

$26,500 Unfavorable

Labor Efficiency Variance. Mary said, "I not only paid higher hourly wages because of overtime, but also scheduled more hours trying to get materials to run properly. Our efficiency is really poor. Look at the labor efficiency report."

The controller explained, "We calculated the labor efficiency variance by subtracting the value found on the right side from the value on the middle prong."

Labor efficiency variance = (Actual hours × Standard rate) − (Standard hours × Standard rate)

5,300 × $24
= $127,200

Labor Efficiency Variance

4,600 × $24
= $110,400

$16,800 Unfavorable

"Only 4,600 hours were allowed by engineering standards to produce 6,000,000 cans. Our actual labor time was 5,300 hours. Thus, an excess of 700 hours (5,300 − 4,600) at a standard rate of $24 per hour caused an unfavorable labor efficiency variance of $16,800 (700 × $24). Our calculations indicate that the unfavorable labor variance of $43,300 is made up of an unfavorable rate variance of $26,500 and an unfavorable efficiency variance of $16,800 ($26,500 + $16,800 = $43,300)."

LEARNING NOTE

In a standard cost system, costs flow through the inventory accounts (Raw Materials Inventory, Work-in-Process Inventory, and Finished Goods Inventory) at standard values. Thus, the balance sheet reflects these standard costs. However, since actual costs of materials, labor, and overhead seldom equal standard costs, variances are created. At the end of an accounting cycle, these variances typically are closed out to cost of goods sold on the income statement. Thus, the cost of goods sold calculation on the income statement reflects actual (rather than standard) costs.

The team began to understand the financial impact of materials and labor variances. In addition, the relationship between purchasing and production decisions became apparent. Pat commented that perhaps management was to blame for the problem. In closing the meeting, Pat stated, "It appears that we are motivating managers to achieve local performance objectives without considering how their actions affect the organization as a whole."

"So, I'm not such a bad guy after all," quipped Lee.

"No, just a bit misdirected," teased Pat.

LIMITATIONS OF TRADITIONAL VARIANCE ANALYSIS

The MetalArt example illustrates a potential problem associated with using price variances to motivate behavior. Because he was focusing only on meeting price standards, Lee Jones cut corners on quality. In addition, purchasing managers may be encouraged to purchase inventory in quantities far greater than reasonable needs in order to receive volume purchase discounts. Unfortunately, costs saved on an initial purchase may be offset by inventory carrying charges, damage, and obsolescence.

In saving the company $25,000 in material costs, Lee Jones contributed to unfavorable variances totaling $55,300. Managers may add up the variances to determine whether a change (such as buying less expensive materials or using a different mix of labor) results in a favorable or an unfavorable net variance. In MetalArt's case, the unfavorable net variance may be calculated as follows:

Materials price variance		$25,000 favorable
Materials quantity variance	$12,000 unfavorable	
Labor rate variance	26,500 unfavorable	
Labor efficiency variance	16,800 unfavorable	55,300 unfavorable
Net variance		$30,300 unfavorable

While the MetalArt example suggests that poor raw material quality significantly contributes to the unfavorable labor efficiency variance, other factors also can hurt labor efficiency. For example, workers may simply make mistakes. In addition, poor training or problems with scheduling may affect workers' abilities to perform as desired.

The tendency in many organizations is to point the finger at plant managers when production-related variances occur. However, managers in marketing divisions can contribute to variances as well. For example, when a manufacturing facility gears up for a certain level of production in response to a sales forecast made by the marketing manager, it often takes on additional labor and equipment. If actual sales do not meet expectations, the factory cannot immediately eliminate the unnecessary resources. The lag in the response time will result in some workers being temporarily idle, creating an unfavorable labor efficiency variance. Alternatively, if sales exceed the forecast, unexpected overtime costs will be incurred, thereby affecting the labor rate variance. Thus, proper planning is an important element of cost control.

LEARNING NOTE

While variance analysis helps managers identify sources of inefficiency, some managers believe that the use of standards does not promote continuous improvement. For example, workers may focus merely on meeting the standards rather than finding better ways to manage existing processes.

In addition to materials and labor variances, some companies calculate variable and fixed overhead variances. Variable overhead variances are calculated in the same way as variances for labor and materials. In other words, variable overhead rate and efficiency variances may be calculated using the diagrams discussed earlier in this chapter. Many accountants, including the authors of this text, do not believe that overhead variances are especially useful; however, alternative methods for evaluating overhead are described in an earlier chapter. Also, recall that we have considered cost behavior with respect to volume; some costs change with activity levels, whereas others remain fixed. Fixed overhead can be analyzed in terms of two variances, budget and volume.

The fixed overhead budget variance is simply the difference between actual spending for fixed overhead and planned spending for fixed overhead. Alternatively, the fixed overhead volume variance is a measure of plant use. Managers who produce at higher levels have more units over which to spread fixed costs, making the fixed cost per unit smaller and creating more favorable variances. Thus, managers are encouraged to manufacture products in large quantities even if there is no market for them.

Many accountants argue that managers should focus instead on process improvements and product quality. The remainder of this chapter considers methods for evaluating processes and improving product quality. Both statistical process control charts and Taguchi's quality loss function were developed by statisticians and engineers for use in understanding factory operations. We also consider how accountants and managers can use engineering methods to improve administrative, as well as production, processes.

1 SELF-STUDY PROBLEM

WebTUTOR Advantage

Greasy Grimes is a chain of automotive repair shops owned by entrepreneur Terrel Grimes. Grimes established the company during the 1960s to compete with local garages and the service departments of new car dealerships. In addition to performing basic oil change and lubrication services, Greasy Grimes' mechanics do major and minor repairs on engine, transmission, and brake systems.

The company is unionized and has three labor classes, with the following wage rates:

	Hourly Rate
Apprentice mechanic	$25
Journeyman mechanic	30
Master mechanic	40

Each shop has a manager who prepares cost estimates for customers and assigns jobs to mechanics. Labor estimates are prepared using a book that identifies the number of standard labor hours required to perform various repairs.

Grimes is reviewing a monthly report that summarizes the transmission service activities of shop 222. The shop recently had a change in management, and Grimes is anxious to evaluate the new manager's ability to use labor effectively. Relevant data are as follows:

Shop 222 July Transmission Services Standard Labor Class: Apprentice			
Actual Hours	**Actual Rate**	**Standard Hours**	**Standard Rate**
500	$30	800	$25

Required Calculate the labor rate and labor efficiency variances for shop 222 during July and interpret your results.

The solution to Self-Study Problem 1 appears at the end of the chapter.

QUALITY COST CONCEPTS[1]

OBJECTIVE 3

Identify four types of quality costs and explain how managers use these costs to improve performance.

Quality costs **are costs incurred because poor quality can or does exist in a particular product, function, or business.**[2] Quality refers to conformance to design specifications. Thus, quality costs are costs incurred to ensure that quality standards are met or because quality standards are not met. These costs of conformance often are divided into three categories: prevention, appraisal, and failure.

Prevention costs are costs incurred to prevent the production of poor-quality units (in manufacturing organizations) or poor-quality services (in service organizations). MetalArt uses statistical process control to monitor production and to make necessary

[1] This section draws heavily from the following article: Albright, T. L., and H. P. Roth. 1992. The Measurement of Quality Costs: An Alternative Paradigm, *Accounting Horizons* (June): 15–27.
[2] The definitions in this section are based on Morse, Wayne J., Harold P. Roth, and Kay M. Poston. *Measuring, Planning, and Controlling Quality Costs* (Montvale, N.J.: National Association of Accountants, 1987).

changes if a process slips out of control. Thus, the cost of implementing statistical process control techniques to prevent paint from being applied in the wrong place is an example of prevention costs.

Appraisal costs are costs incurred to identify poor-quality products (or services) before a customer receives the goods or services. The cost of inspections within the MetalArt plant is classified as an appraisal cost. A goal of world-class organizations is to design a production process that is in a state of control and exhibits little random variation. A good process that is in control produces high-quality products, making less inspection necessary. Therefore, a company usually benefits by investing in prevention, rather than appraisal, activities.

Failure costs are costs incurred because poor quality exists. Failure costs may be divided into two categories: internal failure costs and external failure costs. If a defective product or service is discovered before it is delivered to the customer, the cost is considered an internal failure cost. However, if a customer discovers a defective product or service, the cost is considered an external failure cost. For example, if paint is applied outside of the proper location during printing and subsequently damages welding equipment when a customer manufactures a can, MetalArt has incurred an external failure cost. Some failure costs are easy to quantify; however, customer ill will associated with discovering a defective product or service is difficult to measure. When W. Edwards Deming, a famous industrial statistician, said that the costs of poor quality are unknown and unknowable, he referred to the inability to determine the cost of unhappy customers.

Firms that measure quality costs wish to track the level of internal failure, external failure, appraisal, and prevention costs over time. Typically, a firm that embraces a quality program invests additional resources in prevention and appraisal activities to reduce failure costs. Over time, as processes become more reliable, failure costs decline. Of course, the objective is not merely to substitute one type of quality cost for another. Managers wish to see a decline in total quality costs as investments in improved processes produce results.

Exhibit 6 illustrates MetalArt's experience in managing quality costs. At first, failure costs were high. Then management implemented appraisal and prevention measures. Over time, the quality of production at MetalArt improved, and total quality costs began to decline. Finally, total quality costs reached a level far below their initial amounts.

Exhibit 6
Quality Cost Mix

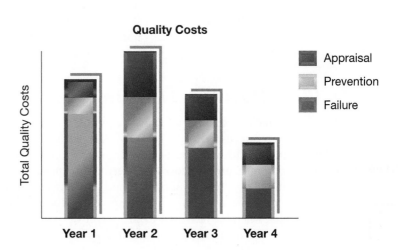

In attempting to use a quality cost system that classifies a product as defective or nondefective, several problems may be encountered. One of these problems is determining the amount of failure costs. Many failure costs, such as the costs of rework and warranty repairs, are available from accounting records, but others must be estimated. Costs such as lost customer goodwill, which occur because an organization produces poor-quality products, are not recorded by an accounting system. Thus, they often are referred to as hidden quality costs.

The traditional view of quality (defective versus nondefective) usually defines defective products as products with some characteristic that does not fall within the specification limits. By this definition, all units that fall within the specification limits are good, and all units outside the specification limits are defective. The problem with this view is all units within the specification limits are considered to be equally good, regardless of whether they fall near the target value or near the upper or lower specification limit.

Case in Point

http://ingram.
swlearning.com

Learn more about the
Malcolm Baldrige
Award.

Malcolm Baldrige Award for Quality

Recent recipients of the Malcolm Baldrige National Quality Award include **Motorola, Inc.** in the manufacturing category, **Branch-Smith Printing Division** in the small business category, and **SMM Health Care** in the health care division. Applicants for the Baldrige award are evaluated in seven categories: leadership, strategic planning, customer and market focus, information and analysis, human resources focus, process management, and business results.

Branch-Smith Printing's management team has developed a strong culture that emphasizes quality. For example, management frequently evaluates the company's action plans and quality improvement teams. Management also reviews all suggestions for improvement including customer complaints and supplier and internal reports concerning substandard products and processes. The review ensures timely communication, involvement, and accountability across all levels within the organization.

Quality and excellence are the foundations of the Baldrige award. At the awards ceremony, Commerce Secretary Don Evans stated, "For America to have a strong economy, we need sound businesses with ethical, responsible leaders. Great authority is vested in the men and women who run our public corporations, and with such power comes responsibility. Corporate leaders aren't simply stewards of their individual companies. They are stewards of American capitalism itself."

Source: Quality Troy: February 2003. Vol 42, Iss. 2, p. 12.

Many quality experts believe that units that fall within specification limits are not all equally desirable. Even if a unit is within limits, higher costs may result as a unit's deviation from expected value increases. The Taguchi loss function, considered in the next section, attempts to measure these costs of variability.

TAGUCHI S QUALITY LOSS FUNCTION

OBJECTIVE 4

Describe how variability
can affect production
costs.

http://ingram.
swlearning.com

Learn more about
Taguchi's quality loss
function.

Genichi Taguchi is a Japanese engineer who recognized the relationship between variation and cost. He developed a model, termed the quality loss function (QLF), to explain in financial terms the engineering concept of variability. In theory, **the *quality loss function* measures the loss to society from a product that does not perform satisfactorily.** In the quality loss function model, costs increase dramatically as actual product characteristics deviate from a target (expected) value. The loss function is quadratic, which means that when the deviation from a target value doubles, the loss increases by four times.

Taguchi justifies the quality loss function on the basis of experience:

> This is a simple approximation, to be sure, not a law of nature. . . . But the tremendous value of QLF, apart from its bow to common sense, is that it translates the engineer's notion of deviation from targets into a *simple cost estimate* managers can use.[3] (Emphasis added.)

[3] Taguchi, Genichi, and Don Clausing. 1990. Robust Quality, *Harvard Business Review* (January–February): 68.

The quality loss function estimates the loss that results from producing products that vary from a target value, regardless of whether they fall inside or outside the specification limits. This differs from the traditional view of losses from poor quality, which is illustrated in Exhibit 7. The traditional view suggests that no failure costs or losses are incurred if actual product measurements fall within the specification limits. However, total loss in the form of scrap, rework, or warranty replacement occurs if the product's actual dimensions are outside the specification limits.

Exhibit 7
Traditional Cost
Function

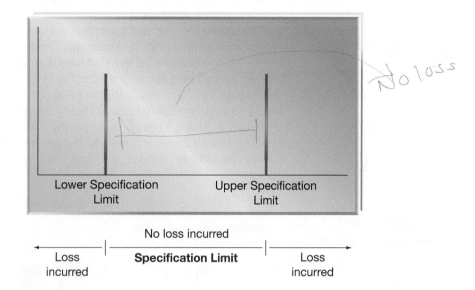

As an alternative to the traditional view, the quality loss function shown in Exhibit 8 shows a loss due to variability whenever a product deviates from a target value, even if the actual value falls within the specification limits. The loss is shown by the U-shaped curve that touches the horizontal axis at the target value. Thus, the quality loss function suggests that hidden quality costs exist any time a product varies from a target value. Once again, we use MetalArt to illustrate how a company may use the information from the quality loss function to make better decisions.

Exhibit 8
Taguchi Cost Function

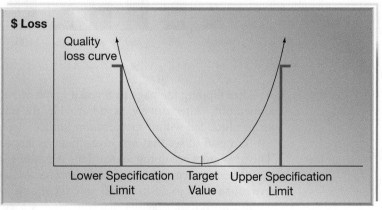

METALART   DECEMBER 2006

Pat Allan, plant manager of MetalArt, called another managers' meeting to address the cost of variability and the intense competition from KolorKan. The team has made a great deal of progress since its original meeting to discuss production problems and related costs. MetalArt has installed a quality cost system and added extra inspectors to the process. However, the team knows that prevention costs in the form of statistical process control soon will allow them to shift resources away from inspections as processes improve.

Pat said, "As you know, KolorKan has made production changes to reduce variability in color density during the printing process.[4] Our market studies suggest that as color densities vary from target values, customers become dissatisfied."

"I could have told you that," interjected Mary. "Remember what happened when we shipped the load of containers with images that varied from dark pink to dark red?"

"I certainly do. We had to replace the cans, and I don't think we've been able to get any more orders from that customer," responded Pat.

"We have reason to believe that KolorKan's products follow a normal distribution with an average near the target value," said Pat, while wrestling to assemble an easel. Producing a flip chart containing the graphic shown in Exhibit 9, Pat continued, "However, a normal distribution means that some of their products actually fall outside the specification limits. Though these products did not conform to specifications, they were shipped to customers anyway because the plant did not strive for zero defects through inspections. Instead, the focus was on achieving output consistent with a target value."

Exhibit 9

Normal Distribution of KolorKan

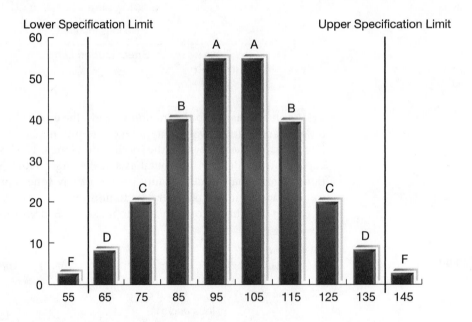

After flipping the page to reveal a graph identical to that shown in Exhibit 10, Pat pointed out, "Alternatively, as indicated by the uniform distribution shown here, all of our products fell within specification limits."

"I'm glad to see that our investment in inspection costs is paying off," said Mary. "The inspectors are doing a great job. We didn't ship a single out-of-spec order."

"While it's true that inspections prevented some embarrassing deliveries, we still have much work to do to reduce our variability," responded Pat. "The uniform distribution shown here suggests that our process is equally likely to produce a product at the target value, the upper specification limit, or the lower specification limit."

[4] The MetalArt example is based on Taguchi and Clausing's article describing the experience of Sony Corporation. Taguchi, Genichi, and Don Clausing. 1990. Robust Quality, *Harvard Business Review* (January–February): 65–75.

Exhibit 10
Rectangular Distribution of MetalArt

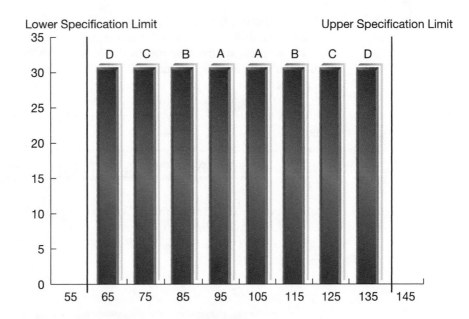

"Pat, what are you driving at?" Mary asked. "Who cares about normal and uniform distributions? Our quality is good; we didn't ship any defective units."

Pat replied, "Assume that we want to assign letter grades to MetalArt and KolorKan; an A represents achieving target specifications, while an F represents exceeding specification limits. We may say that KolorKan produced many more As than we did, even if they did get an F now and then. Most of KolorKan's production was in the A and B range. We earned an equal number of As, Bs, Cs, and Ds. We also made some out-of-specification prints, but we didn't ship our Fs; they were inspected out of the process. KolorKan shipped everything it printed without bothering to inspect anything."

Pat continued to flip pages on the chart. "I think we may have discovered a hidden source of costs. If the Taguchi model is right, our quality costs are approximately *double* KolorKan's. I have made some estimates based on the cost of production and the way in which our customers respond to product variation. Let me summarize the Taguchi model in terms of how it affects us.

"First of all, let's review the elements of the model," said Pat, pointing to the easel containing the following equation and definitions:

Quality loss $= K(y - T)^2$

y = actual value of a quality measurement

T = target value of a quality measurement

K = dollar value of loss associated with deviation from target. The value is based on estimates of the cost of rework, scrap, and customer ill will.

"In other words, the loss function simply takes the difference between a target specification and an actual measurement $(y - T)$ and squares the difference. Therefore, the larger the distance from the target value to the actual measurement, the greater the loss. Squaring the difference makes the cost increase dramatically!"

Lee responded, "So that means that as our products deviate more from a target value, our costs increase dramatically. The farther away they are, the greater the cost."

"Exactly. I've made some estimates of the cost of deviation; let's assume it's $5 and our target value for color density is 100. Assuming that our actual measure for color density is 95, our loss is $125." Pat turned the flip chart to reveal the following calculations:

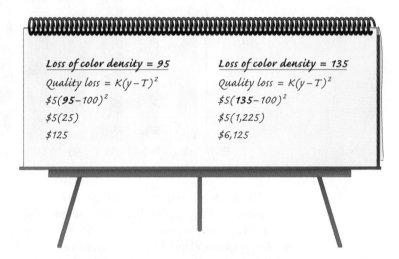

Loss of color density = 95	Loss of color density = 135
Quality loss = $K(y-T)^2$	Quality loss = $K(y-T)^2$
$5(95-100)^2$	$5(135-100)^2$
$5(25)	$5(1,225)
$125	$6,125

"By contrast," continued Pat, "if our actual measure for color density is 135, our loss is $6,125! The losses become large very quickly if we have many deliveries that are too far from the target specification."

Pat continued, "I have made some assumptions about KolorKan's process. If most of their production is close to the target value, as I have illustrated in Exhibit 11, their total quality costs approximate $359,000. On the other hand, our quality costs are approximately $651,000, because of variability in our process. We are equally likely to produce a unit at the upper specification limit, the lower specification limit, or the target."

Lee interjected, "Let me get this straight. Although we produced 248 units, the same number as KolorKan, our quality costs are approximately double theirs because our units are spread evenly between color densities of 65 and 135. On the other hand, KolorKan had most of their products clustered around the target value of 100."

After a few moments, Mary spoke. "I think I see the big picture. The manner in which we conduct our operations affects the income statement because costs and expenses reduce net income. Customer ill will also can affect net income through reduced sales. First, we used variance analysis, a tool that helps Pat and other upper-level managers compare actual performance with a standard. Statistical process control charts provide too much detail for the needs of upper management."

"That's right," responded Pat. "However, statistical process control tools help shop floor workers maintain control over their processes, thereby reducing operating costs."

"After we improve our processes and can maintain them in statistical control, we can work to reduce the common causes of variability. You have shown us that variability has a cost," Lee added. "All of our efforts are interrelated and ultimately affect profitability."

2 SELF-STUDY PROBLEM   Terrel Grimes wishes to implement a quality cost program at each Greasy Grimes service center. His goal is to reduce total quality costs by 30% over the next five years, but he does not fully understand how quality costs are classified.

Required Provide examples of each type of quality cost (internal failure, external failure, appraisal, and prevention) that Grimes may expect to incur at his service centers.

The solution to Self-Study Problem 2 appears at the end of the chapter.

Exhibit 11
Unit and Total Costs:
The Taguchi Quality
Loss Function

(From Exhibit 9) KolorKan			
Observed Value	Number of Units	Total Cost	Cost per Unit
55	1	$ 10,125	10,125
65	9	55,125	6,125
75	20	62,500	3,125
85	40	45,000	1,125
95	54	6,750	125
105	54	6,750	125
115	40	45,000	1,125
125	20	62,500	3,125
135	9	55,125	6,125
145	1	10,125	10,125
Total	248	$359,000	

(From Exhibit 10) MetalArt			
Observed Value	Number of Units	Total Cost	Cost per Unit
55	0	0	0
65	31	189,875	6,125
75	31	96,875	3,125
85	31	34,875	1,125
95	31	3,875	125
105	31	3,875	125
115	31	34,875	1,125
125	31	96,875	3,125
135	31	189,875	6,125
145	0	0	0
Total	248	$651,000	

STATISTICAL PROCESS CONTROL[5]

OBJECTIVE 5

Explain how statistical process control provides useful information to managers of both production and administrative functions.

As businesses seek to improve the quality of products and processes, methods for monitoring and evaluating performance have become increasingly important. One such tool that has become popular is the statistical process control (SPC) chart. Statistical process control charts can be applied to many different types of situations. When maintained continuously, they provide an early warning signal that a quality problem may exist. For example, control charts may be used to (a) identify errors or unpredictable processes and determine basic causes, (b) provide a warning of an unexpected change within a

[5] The authors relied on the following articles in preparing the section on statistical process control:
Albright, T. L., and H. P. Roth. 1993. Controlling Quality on a Multidimensional Level, *Journal of Cost Management* (Spring): 29–37.
Walter, R., M. Higgins, and H. Roth. 1990. Applications of Control Charts, *The CPA Journal* (April): 90–93, 95.
Duarte, J. 1991. Statistical Process Control in Marketing and Finance, *CMA Magazine* (May): 20–23.

process, (c) evaluate service or product consistency over time, and (d) decrease process variability and associated inspection costs.

Control charts measure two types of variation, special cause and common cause. A *special cause variation* **has an identifiable source, such as faulty equipment or processes. Alternatively, a** *common cause variation* **is the result of randomness inherent in a process.** Statistical control results when special causes of variation have been eliminated. Once a process is in a state of statistical control, the process is considered stable and predictable. A process in a state of statistical control is not necessarily a good process; rather, it is a *predictable* process. Once a process is in control, managers can focus their attention on making improvements that reduce common cause variation.

Though companies use many different types of statistical process control charts, the charts have common elements. In general, a control chart is a graph that shows measurements for a characteristic of interest. The characteristic may be a quantitative variable such as weight, length, or thickness of material, or it may be a qualitative attribute such as whether or not a product is defective.

Statistical process control charts typically include (a) a center line, representing the expected value of a characteristic, (b) a line above and another below the expected value, indicating the limits within which a characteristic is considered to be in control, (c) a horizontal axis, indicating the time order of observations of the characteristic, and (d) a vertical axis, measuring the values of the observations. A control chart used to monitor the printing line at MetalArt serves as an example to illustrate the elements and uses of control charts.

As described at the beginning of this chapter, the printing line sprays paint onto steel sheets to produce a finished image. Paint is applied to the surface of metal sheets through sprayer nozzles. If the sprayer nozzles become clogged, printing quality is affected because the images do not receive the correct amount of paint. Thus, MetalArt maintains on-line control charts to monitor paint flow coming from the nozzles. Exhibit 12 is an example of a control chart used by MetalArt.

Exhibit 12

Example of a Statistical Process Control Chart

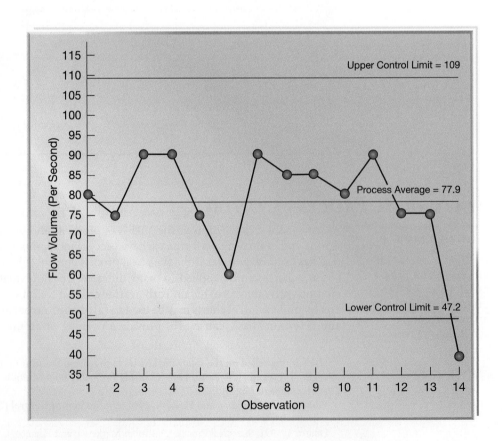

The vertical axis measures the flow volume per second through the sprayer nozzle. Values can range from zero, indicating no paint flow, to 120, indicating the maximum possible flow. The horizontal axis represents individual flow measurements taken throughout the day. Points on the chart represent flow values (y axis) for individual observations (x axis). A horizontal center line, or process average (expected value), is drawn through the center of the points. The process average (77.9) is the sum of the individual measurements divided by the total number of measurements [(80 + 75 + 90 + 90 + 75 + 60 + 90 + 85 + 85 + 80 + 90 + 75 + 75 + 40) ÷ 14 = 77.9].

In addition to the center line, the MetalArt control chart has an upper and a lower control limit, placed at 109 and 47.2, respectively. The area between the upper and lower control limits represents the band of normal variability for the printing process. **Control charts are designed to signal when a process is out of control.** At observation number 14, which exceeds the lower control limit, the sprayer process is no longer in statistical control. The chart informs the machine operator that an unusual situation has occurred so that the operator can take corrective action.

Thus, statistical process control charts are used to identify measurements of a characteristic that deviate from the process average and to discover changes in the measurement. If points on a control chart are randomly scattered around the center line and fall within the upper and lower control limits, the process is considered to be in statistical control. An out-of-control condition is indicated if points fall above or below the control limits. By analyzing conditions existing at the time an out-of-control signal occurs, a manager may discover the cause of the problem.

Control charts are appropriate for measuring and evaluating many different types of processes. Generally, they can be used in any repetitive situation in which a quantitative variable or qualitative attribute is measurable. However, statistical process control charts also can be used in other areas, including accounting, finance, and marketing. For example, MetalArt's accounting department prepares payroll checks and payments for inventory purchases. Internal auditors typically verify that proper internal control procedures, such as authorization of bills and approval to make payments, are used in preparing payroll checks and payments to suppliers. To do this, they can collect samples of paid invoices or canceled payroll checks and record the percentage of cases with proper authorization and approval on a control chart. An out-of-control signal would suggest that an unusually large percentage of cases did not conform to proper procedures. By investigating samples in which control limits are exceeded, auditors may trace the cause of errors. For example, a new employee may not be familiar with company policies. Employee training should keep this problem from occurring in the future. Thus, control charts may be used to identify and correct administrative problems, as well as problems within the manufacturing process.

Other examples of using control charts in an administrative capacity include monitoring (a) the number of invoices processed during each month, (b) the average age of accounts receivable, (c) the time required to prepare monthly financial statements, and (d) sales returns per salesperson. Thus, managers in many different areas can use statistical process control analysis to help them evaluate the quality of their activities.

When first implementing statistical process control methods, managers should use charts where they expect to find trouble. In addition, they should use charts in those areas where financial benefits from improving a process and reducing special causes of variability are most likely. Managers are more likely to support continued use of statistical process control methods if they are able to see positive, tangible financial results. Unfortunately, SPC does not measure variation in financial terms. Recently, Six Sigma techniques have evolved to fill this need.

Six Sigma is a management philosophy that is becoming popular with manufacturing and service organizations. The approach is based on statistical methods that help identify and reduce process variation. Proponents argue Six Sigma begins where statistical process control methods end. Like SPC, one goal of Six Sigma is to reduce process variation. However, Six Sigma is a management philosophy that attempts to link reduced variation to improved customer satisfaction and, ultimately, improved financial performance.

The term *Six Sigma* means that organizations should aspire to processes that virtually are error free. For example, six standard deviations (six sigma) from a process average represents only one misspelled word in all the books found in a small library. Put another way, if one product were produced each second for a century, only six products would be defective.[6] Clearly, these examples represent very low error rates. The Six Sigma approach enables management to financially justify process changes that help the company meet these high standards.

Case in Point

http://ingram.
swlearning.com
....
Find out more about
Six Sigma.

Six Sigma

Six Sigma requires rigorous analysis of business processes in order to achieve a low error, or defect, rate of 3.4 per million. A defect is defined as anything that does not meet customer expectations. In the banking industry a defect could be a loan application review that exceeds the promised 48 hours, a telephone inquiry that is not answered, or the bank's failure to pay property taxes held in escrow for a customer.

Industry experts estimate that 80 of the top 100 banks have implemented (or plan to implement) Six Sigma programs. **Bank of America Corporation** used Six Sigma techniques to develop a loan application process that requires 80 percent less paperwork than other banks require. Some have predicted that in a few years every bank will have an Internet-based, fully automated loan application process. Engineering-based Six Sigma techniques will be useful to make the transition from human-based to Internet-based lending.

Source: 2003. Six Sigma: Some Home Lenders See a Natural Fit, *American Banker* (February 12).

PERFORMANCE EVALUATION FOR SERVICE ORGANIZATIONS

OBJECTIVE 6

Explain the application of performance evaluation methods in service organizations.

Service organizations such as CPA firms, law firms, hospitals, cable TV companies, and telecommunications companies face performance issues similar to those encountered by manufacturing organizations. Though these organizations do not manufacture a tangible product, managers can nonetheless evaluate the effectiveness of service delivery processes. For example, both CPA firms and hospitals often develop labor standards, or estimates of the time required to perform certain activities. A new staff accountant in a CPA firm is expected to prepare a client's payroll tax return in a certain (standard) amount of time. Additionally, hospitals often use critical paths to estimate the amount of services required for each type of medical procedure. Physicians whose use of services deviates significantly from a critical path may be asked to justify such deviations. Thus, as in manufacturing organizations, the efficiency of labor may be monitored. Service organizations often seek to improve customer satisfaction by making the experience pleasurable. For example, minimizing the time it takes to receive the service may result in satisfied customers. Therefore, managers often monitor customer satisfaction in order to improve the company's service quality.

Statistical process control charts originally were developed for use in manufacturing organizations. However, these charts commonly are used within service organizations to determine if a service process is "in control." For example, some hospitals maintain control charts to determine if the time from admission to the beginning of hydration (adding fluid) for a leukemia patient meets expectations. Another example would be plotting the variable cost of each appendectomy surgery to determine if certain physicians significantly exceed the average cost.

[6] Breyfogle, F. W., J. Cupello, and B. Meadows. 2001. *Managing Six Sigma* (New York, NY: John Wiley and Sons, Inc.).

Many service organizations use quality cost systems that attempt to measure the cost of external failure. For example, many companies measure the amount of time a customer spends "on hold" before receiving assistance from a company representative. Additionally, many firms measure the number of customers who hang up while waiting to receive assistance. Costs or lost revenues associated with customers who "drop off" the line are seen as external failure costs. Thus, many processes in service organizations can be monitored in the same way as manufacturing processes.

3 SELF-STUDY PROBLEM

WebTUTOR Advantage

Corporate managers at Greasy Grimes began collecting data from each service center to analyze material price and quantity variances. Some managers are concerned that too much is being paid for materials and too many materials are being used in conducting repairs.

Managers collected quantity data from the past 12 months to use as a comparison with the variance figures for July of the current year:

12-Month Material Quantity Variance Data

Jul.	$1,000 F	Jan.	$350 F
Aug.	1,000 U	Feb.	400 F
Sep.	500 F	Mar.	250 F
Oct.	750 F	Apr.	300 U
Nov.	800 U	May	250 U
Dec.	750 U	Jun.	150 F

July Material Price and Quantity Data

Actual price	$200
Actual quantity	25
Standard price	$190
Standard quantity	23

Required

A. Construct a statistical process control chart for material quantity variances. In calculating the process average, treat favorable variances as positive values and unfavorable variances as negative values.
   1. Calculate the process average for the 12 months listed.
   2. Place the upper control limit at $+\$1,875$.
   3. Place the lower control limit at $-\$1,825$.
   4. Plot the material quantity variances for the past 12 months.

B. Calculate the material price and quantity variances for July of this year and add the quantity variance to your statistical process control chart.

C. Is the process in statistical control? Should managers investigate this July's material quantity variance for special causes? Explain.

The solution to Self-Study Problem 3 appears at the end of the chapter.

REVIEW

SUMMARY of IMPORTANT CONCEPTS

1. Companies may perform variance analysis of direct materials, direct labor, and overhead.
   a. A variance is defined as the difference between total actual costs and total standard costs allowed for actual production.
   b. Variances may be divided into a price (rate) component and a quantity (efficiency) component.
   c. Variances are defined as favorable if actual prices or quantities used are less than standard prices or quantities. However, because variances often are interrelated, *favorable* variances are not always good.

2. Quality costs:
   a. Quality costs are classified as internal failure, external failure, appraisal, and prevention.

b. External failure costs are the most expensive type of quality costs, though their amount can never be known with certainty. External failure costs include customer ill will as well as replacement and warranty costs.

3. Taguchi quality loss function:
   a. The Taguchi quality loss function is important because it associates costs with the engineering concept of variability.
   b. Customer dissatisfaction (and costs) occurs when product characteristics deviate from a target value, even if the characteristics are within specification limits.

4. Statistical process control:
   a. Statistical process control charts separate special cause variation from random variation in manufacturing or administrative processes.
   b. Statistical process control charts have a center line (representing a process average) and upper and lower control limits.

5. Service organizations:
   a. Service organizations generally can establish standards for measuring the efficiency and effectiveness of their delivery process.
   b. Many processes in service organizations can be evaluated with statistical process control charts.
   c. Quality costs are not limited to companies that manufacture tangible products. Service organizations also incur quality costs in delivering services to customers.

DEFINE

TERMS and CONCEPTS DEFINED in this CHAPTER

common cause variation (M260)	special cause variation (M260)
favorable variance (M247)	standard costs (M245)
quality costs (M252)	standards (M245)
quality loss function (M254)	unfavorable variance (M247)

SELF-STUDY PROBLEM SOLUTIONS

SSP9-1   Labor rate variance
= (Actual hours × Actual rate) − (Actual hours × Standard rate)
= (500 × $30) − (500 × $25)
= 500 × ($30 − $25)
= $2,500 unfavorable

Labor efficiency variance = (Standard rate × Actual hours) −
(Standard rate × Standard hours)
= ($25 × 500) − ($25 × 800)
= $25 × (500 − 800)
= $7,500 favorable

Total variance
= $5,000 favorable ($7,500 favorable − $2,500 unfavorable)

The new manager appears to have changed the mix of labor for services. Typically, an apprentice mechanic, receiving the lowest wage rate, performs the transmission services. The new manager assigned higher-paid journeyman mechanics to these jobs and created an unfavorable labor rate variance. However, the experienced journeyman mechanics were more efficient in performing the service, as indicated by the favorable labor efficiency variance. In fact, the higher labor rate was more than offset by greater efficiencies. The shift in mix resulted in a net $5,000 favorable labor variance. The new manager has found a way to improve the efficiency of transmission service at Greasy Grimes.

SSP9-2   *Internal Failure.* Costs resulting from repairs that have been performed incorrectly but are found before an automobile is returned to the customer are classified as internal failure. The costs of dealing with loose bolts or oil pan drain plugs that later could cause mechanical failure are examples.

External Failure. Costs resulting from repairs that were performed incorrectly and are discovered by the customer are classified as external failure costs. Examples include the cost of replacement parts, labor, customer ill will, and lost revenue (time spent reworking a repair is not available for other revenue-generating repairs). External failure costs also include the costs of lawsuits resulting from damages suffered by customers whose vehicles were damaged because of poor workmanship.

Appraisal. Appraisal costs generally relate to inspection costs. For example, the time spent by a mechanic on a test drive to ensure that repairs were made properly is an appraisal cost.

Prevention. Prevention costs can include training or technical workshops for mechanics. In addition, resources invested to identify reliable suppliers of high-quality parts are classified as prevention costs.

SSP9-3   A. In summing the favorable and unfavorable variances for the 12 months, the average is calculated as follows:

$$(1{,}000 - 1{,}000 + 500 + 750 - 800 - 750 + 350 + 400 + 250 - 300 - 250 + 150) \div 12 = 25$$

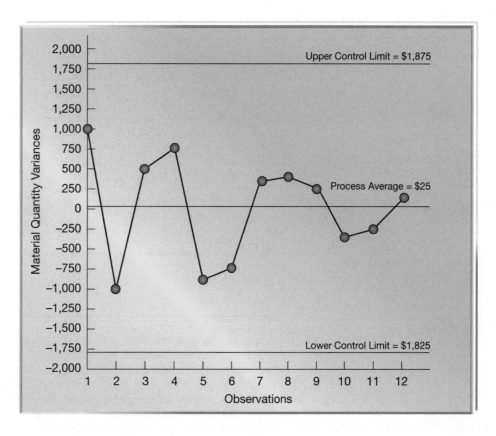

B.

Price variance   = (Actual quantity × Actual price) − (Actual quantity × Standard price)

 = (25   × $200)   −   (25   × $190)

 = 25   ×   ($200   − $190)

 = $250 U

Quantity variance = (Standard price × Actual quantity) − (Standard price × Standard quantity)

 = ($190   ×   25)   −   ($190   ×   23)

 = $190   ×   (25   −   23)

 = $380 U

The revised statistical process control chart appears in part (C).

C. The material quantity variances are in a state of statistical control. Though the July variance deviates from the process average, it is within the control limits. The variation seems to be random and normal. Managers should not attempt to find a special cause for the variation during the month of July.

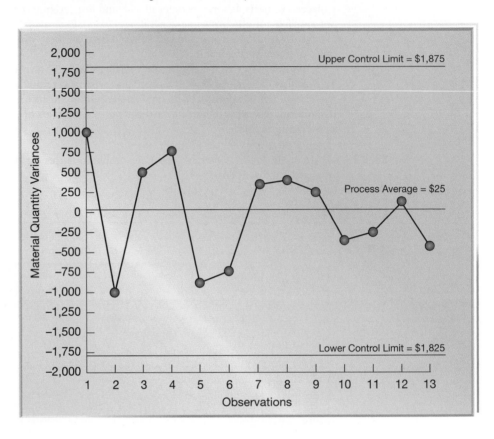

Thinking Beyond the Question

How are budgets used to evaluate performance?

At the beginning of this chapter, Erin and Seth were discussing their variance report. They were concerned because materials, labor, and overhead variances all were unfavorable. To determine why the budgeted and actual numbers differed, they examined the price and quantity variances. Seth and Erin will continue to grow their business and employ managers who will make purchasing and production decisions. Variance analysis also can be used to assess performance of individual managers. Typically, who is responsible for materials price and quantity variances? Explain your reasoning.

QUESTIONS

Q9-1
Obj. 1
Managers are held accountable for variances that occur in the areas under their control. Variances may arise in a manufacturing environment and in administrative functions as well. In general, what is meant by the term *variance*?

Q9-2
Obj. 1
Doall Company is establishing production standards for the coming year. Matt Mellon, the production manager, argues that the standards need to be relaxed. "Last year's standards were

based on ideal performance and did not reflect the practical realities of what could be achieved," he said. In establishing standards, what is the difference between practical and ideal standards?

Q9-3
Obj. 1
Keene, Inc., separates material variances into price and quantity components for purposes of management control and analysis. Why are variances generally separated into price and quantity components? What effect, if any, can the price variance have on the quantity variance?

Q9-4
Obj. 1
The cost records of Prichter Company reveal that as the unfavorable material price variance increased, the unfavorable material usage variance decreased. What might this suggest?

Q9-5
Obj. 1
Cadet Industries utilizes a standard cost system. When Cadet purchases raw materials, the materials are recorded at standard cost. Is this treatment by Cadet proper in a standard cost accounting system? Why or why not? What is the appropriate time to recognize material price and usage variances? Why?

Q9-6
Obj. 2
In a manufacturing environment, who would most likely be responsible for the materials price variance? The labor efficiency variance?

Q9-7
Obj. 2
In addition to material and labor variances, a company that utilizes standard cost accounting can compute fixed overhead variances. What are the two components of fixed overhead variance? What do the fixed overhead variances measure?

Q9-8
Obj. 2
Tim Winker Manufactured Housing, Inc., produces prefabricated modular housing. The company manufactures four styles of homes and uses a standard cost accounting system. The company uses a single account for capturing material variances and another account for recording labor variances. During a review of the general ledger for the past operating period, Tim Winker, the president, noted that the material variances were favorable and the labor variances were unfavorable. In general, what do these variances indicate regarding production costs for the period? What further information would management find useful in analyzing production costs and variances for the period?

Q9-9
Obj. 3
Electro Industries wants to analyze the costs associated with quality conformance in its manufacture of electronic capacitors and transistors, which are sold primarily to manufacturers of cellular telephones. What four broad categories of conformance costs should Electro use? What are the differences between these cost groups?

Q9-10
Obj. 3
Rayco Products manufactures audio speakers that are used in many applications. At the beginning of the current year, Rayco developed detailed operating budgets for all aspects of the company. Rayco now is considering purchasing new test equipment for the inspection department to use in checking the acoustical quality of speakers. This purchase was not considered during the preparation of operating budgets for the current year. If the equipment is acquired, depreciation will begin to be recognized immediately, using straight-line depreciation over an estimated useful life of five years; the result will be a monthly charge of $2,200. What effect would the equipment purchase have on quality costs and on meeting the company's current year budget?

Q9-11
Obj. 5
A machine operator cuts metal rods into six-inch lengths, measures output periodically, and records the measurements on a statistical process control chart. Over an eight-hour shift, the operator notes that the measurements vary greatly but are always within the acceptable limits of plus or minus 0.005 inch. Are these variations most likely examples of common cause or special cause variations? Explain your answer.

Q9-12
Obj. 5
Nathan Stuart is employed in the accounting department of a local manufacturer. During a recent management staff meeting, Nathan suggested that statistical control charts be established at key production steps to help increase quality and minimize defects. What is a statistical control chart? How is it used?

Using Minitab and Excel

For Statistical Process Control Charts

SPREADSHEET

What is Minitab?

Minitab for Windows is a package that permits a variety of analyses including basic statistics, regression, analysis of variance, and statistical control charts. Many college and university computer centers have a site license that permits students to use the package. Data are entered into a spreadsheet format similar to Microsoft Excel. Drop-down menus permit the user to specify the type of analysis. Certain problems and exercises in this chapter may be solved using the control chart menu.

Using Microsoft Excel to draw the statistical process control charts.

- Open Microsoft Excel and enter the data points in column A.
- Highlight column A and click on the Chart Wizard.
- A drop-down menu titled Step 1 of 4—Chart Type will appear. Click on Line. Click on Next>.
- A drop-down menu titled Step 2 of 4—Chart Source Data will appear. Click on Next>.
- A drop-down menu titled Step 3 of 4—Chart Options will appear. Select the Gridlines tab. Remove any check marks in boxes under Value (Y) axis.
- Click on Legend tab. Remove check mark in box before Show Legend.
- Click on Next>.
- A drop-down menu titled Step 4 of 4—Chart Location will appear. Click "as a new sheet." Click on Finish.

At this point you have a line graph. The last step is to draw the horizontal lines representing upper and lower control limits and the process average.
Using the drawing toolbar, select this button.

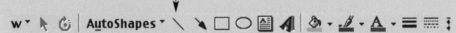

- Click on the left side of your line graph and drag the cursor to the right to create a horizontal line. Next press Copy one time and press Paste two times to make two more horizontal lines.

You now have a line graph containing your data points and three horizontal lines. Move the cursor to one of your horizontal lines. To create the upper control limit line, click on the horizontal line and drag it to the appropriate position. In the same manner, click and drag a second horizontal line to the appropriate position to represent the process average. Finally, click and drag the remaining horizontal line to the appropriate position for the lower control limit.

EXERCISES

If your instructor is using Personal Trainer® in this course, you may complete your assignments online.

E9-1 Write a short definition of each of the terms listed in the *Terms and Concepts Defined in this Chapter* section.

E9-2 Multiflow Products manufactures a single product, for which the following standards have
Obj. 1 been developed:

	Standard Quantity or Hours	Standard Price or Rate	Standard Cost
Direct materials	5 feet	$3 per foot	$15
Direct labor	? hours	? per hour	?

During October, the company purchased 15,200 feet of direct materials at a cost of $47,880, all of which was used in the production of 3,000 units.

A total of 5,400 hours was spent on production during the month. The actual cost of direct labor was $61,560. The following labor variances have been computed:

Total labor variance $1,185 Unfavorable
Labor rate variance $540 Favorable

a. For direct materials, compute (1) the actual cost paid for materials per foot, (2) the materials price variance, and (3) the materials usage variance.
b. For direct labor, compute (1) the standard labor rate per hour, (2) the standard hours allowed for the output of 3,000 units, and (3) the standard hours allowed per unit of product.
c. What is the value of direct materials and direct labor that has been applied to the work-in-process inventory account during the month, in total and on a per-unit basis?

E9-3
Obj. 1

World Wide Products has developed the following standards for one of its products:

Direct materials   25 pounds at $4 per pound
Direct labor   8 hours at $10 per hour

The following activity was recorded for the production of 12,000 units during the month of August:

Materials purchased   355,000 pounds at $4.15 a pound
Materials used   305,000 pounds
Direct labor   95,400 hours at $10.75 an hour

a. Compute the materials price variance.
b. Compute the materials usage variance.
c. Compute the labor rate variance.
d. Compute the labor efficiency variance.

E9-4
Objs. 1, 2

A nationally known blue jeans manufacturer purchases denim material and cuts it into a variety of components and sizes. Following the machine-intensive cutting operation, the parts are flown to another location for assembly. The following data summarize the assembly operations:

Standard hours allowed per pair	0.30	Actual hours worked	4,500
Standard wage rate per hour	$7.00	Actual labor rate per hour	$6.50
Actual pairs assembled	16,000		

Calculate the labor rate variance and the labor efficiency variance. Determine whether each variance is favorable or unfavorable. How might managers use variance information such as this to support decisions about changing a manufacturing process?

E9-5
Objs. 1, 2

Tawanda's Bakery uses variances to help control production-related costs. The following data summarize the production activity for June:

Standard resource consumption per 50-loaf batch
Materials   60 lbs. at $2.00 per pound
Labor   3 hours at $16.00 per hour

Actual resource consumption during June
Materials   1,100 lbs. at $2.10 per pound
Labor   80 hours at $15.00 per hour

During the month, Tawanda produced 20 batches.
Calculate each of the following and determine whether the variance is favorable or unfavorable:

a. materials price variance   c. labor rate variance
b. materials quantity variance   d. labor efficiency variance

At what level within an organization is variance analysis useful to support decision making? Explain.

E9-6   Metalworks, Inc., produces castings for various applications in the plumbing industry. Be-
Objs. 1, 2   cause the industry is mature, standardized products with known materials and labor requirements are the primary revenue generators for the company. The following information has
been assembled for the month of January:

	Standard resource consumption per batch of Faucet Value No. 337
Materials	500 lbs. at $2.50 per pound
Labor	40 hours at $11.00 per hour

	Actual resource consumption
Materials	530 lbs. at $2.10 per pound
Labor	45 hours at $14.00 per hour

Calculate each of the following for Faucet Value No. 337 and determine whether the variance
is favorable or unfavorable:

a. materials price variance   c. labor rate variance
b. materials quantity variance   d. labor efficiency variance

How might management determine whether a variance is significant and worthy of investigation? Explain.

E9-7   Sunclear Glass Company is a producer of architectural glass products sold through national
Objs. 1, 2   retail outlets. Glass production begins with sand and other chemicals that are placed into a
gas-fired melting chamber. The river of molten glass flows from the melting chamber through
equipment that cools the glass sheet and defines its width and thickness. As the solid ribbon
of glass emerges from the machine, it is cut into a variety of dimensions, packaged, and sold.
The following data summarize the production activities for Sunclear Glass Company. (*Hint:*
Remember to be consistent in your use of tons and pounds.)

Actual raw materials consumed:
200 tons at $0.07 per pound

Standard raw materials allowed for actual production:
198 tons at $0.05 per pound

Calculate the materials price variance and the materials quantity variance. Determine whether
each variance is favorable or unfavorable. Is variance analysis a meaningful exercise in an industry such as this? Explain. What are typical causes of price and quantity variances?

E9-8   Refer to the process description in E9-7. The following information was pulled from the com-
Obj. 3   pany's records:

- A container of glass was broken as the result of a forklift accident at the end of the production line.
- Customers returned 25% of a shipment to the company because the glass contained im-
purities.
- The melting oven crew members attended a national glass manufacturers' conference to
learn about new manufacturing technologies and methods.
- The company implemented a three-step raw materials inspection program to verify raw
material quality and purity.
- Managers at all levels were trained in statistical process control methods.

Classify each event as internal failure, external failure, prevention, or appraisal. Support your
answers.

E9-9   Companies that implement quality cost systems typically use four cost categories.
Obj. 3   Classify the following costs as internal failure, external failure, prevention, or appraisal:

- Scrap
- Warranty claims
- First-part inspection of a new production run
- Quality control education

- Unexpected machine downtime for repairs
- Litigation defense costs associated with product recalls
- Vendor certification
- Manufacturing process redesign

E9-10   Cable-Op, Inc., is a manufacturer of fiber-optic cable used in the communications industry.
Obj. 3   Management is considering implementing a cost of quality program to monitor progress in achieving targets. The following information has been accumulated for a four-year period:

Category	2004	2005	2006	2007
Internal failure	300,000	300,000	350,000	400,000
External failure	500,000	450,000	525,000	545,000
Prevention	60,000	72,000	70,000	65,000
Appraisal	80,000	105,000	110,000	110,000

Prepare a bar graph for each year that includes the four categories of quality costs. What trends do you observe? What types of managerial decisions may result from reviewing your cost of quality graph?

E9-11   Edwards Deming, a pioneer in the area of statistical quality control, stated, "The cost of poor
Obj. 3   quality is unknown and unknowable." The quality categories—internal failure, external failure, prevention, and appraisal—are used to categorize costs from the general ledger for use by management.

    a. Identify the category of quality cost to which Deming most likely refers. Justify your answer.
    b. Which of the four quality cost categories is most controllable by management in the short run? Explain.

E9-12   The following quality cost graph identifies the levels of four quality cost categories over a three-
Obj. 3   year period. External and internal failure costs have increased each year, while investments in prevention and appraisal activities have remained constant. Assume management wishes to reduce total quality costs in the long run.

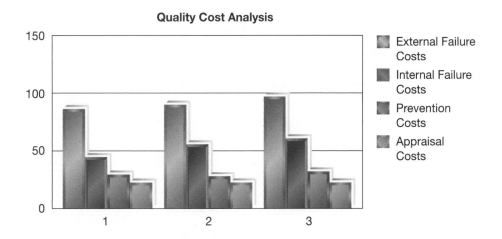

Discuss various management decisions that could be made to better manage quality costs in the organization. What kinds of quality costs are controllable by management in the short run? Are other kinds of quality costs controllable by management in the long run? Explain your answers.

E9-13   **Sony Corporation** conducted a survey to determine customer satisfaction levels with their
Obj. 4   television sets. Interestingly, after matching the survey satisfaction data with production records, Sony discovered the customers who purchased televisions manufactured in Plant 1

(Continued)

were more satisfied than customers whose sets were produced in Plant 2. Upon further investigation, Sony discovered the following distributions for a critical component in the television picture tube:

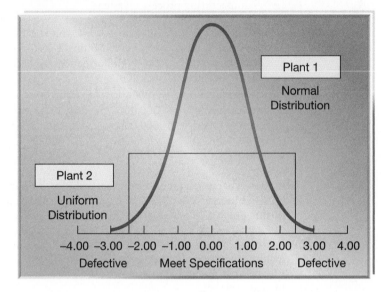

a. Which plant has more process variation?
b. Plant 2 did not ship any "defective" products because each television set was inspected. Plant 1 shipped a small number of "defective" products because products were not inspected. Why were customers whose sets were manufactured in Plant 1 generally happier with their purchases?

E9-14   In Exhibits 9 and 10 in this chapter, Pat Allan related the concept of variation to letter grades
Obj. 4   that could be assigned for plant performance.

a. Explain how the lessons Sony learned in E9-13 relate to the Taguchi loss function.
b. If you were assigning letter grades (A, B, C, D, and F) to the Sony factories illustrated in E9-13, how might you distribute the grades? (Assume each factory made 1,000 television sets.) You may make reasonable assumptions about how to divide the television sets so your distributions resemble those shown in Exhibit 9 in the text.

E9-15   The Taguchi loss function is represented as a U-shaped function. At the target specification,
Obj. 4   the quality loss is zero. As actual measurements move up or down from the target, quality losses occur at an increasing rate.
Taguchi also describes two variations of the U-shaped function as follows:

a. More is better.
b. Less is better.

The "more is better" function describes quality losses as a critical quality characteristic declines from a target. For example, weld strength is an example of a "more is better" function. This function is illustrated as follows:

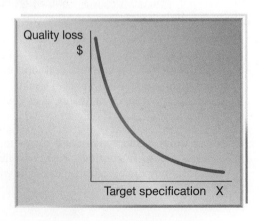

Using your understanding of the Taguchi loss function, prepare a sketch of the "less is better" loss function. Identify three examples of quality costs that might be described by the "less is better" loss function.

E9-16
Obj. 4

Traditionally, a product was considered acceptable if actual product characteristics fell within the upper and lower specification limits as determined by design engineers. This method of evaluating product conformance to specifications is known as the "goalpost" approach to quality. In the game of football, whether the ball is centered between the uprights or marginally passes inside either upright, a point after touchdown or field goal is considered good. Taguchi believed this concept is not applicable to product quality and developed the Taguchi loss function to explain the cost of variation from a target specification.

    a. Prepare a sketch of the traditional loss function and label each component.
    b. Prepare a sketch of the Taguchi loss function and label each component.
    c. Explain the reasoning that Taguchi used to support the loss function.
    d. List three examples of how the Taguchi loss function may apply to an industrial or service industry setting.

E9-17
Obj. 5

Travel-Tow, Inc., is a producer of small utility trailers. The company partners with suppliers to help reduce inventory carrying costs. Raw material deliveries are made every two hours. Materials are brought directly to the production line for immediate use. The following statistical process control chart captures variation in raw material delivery times.

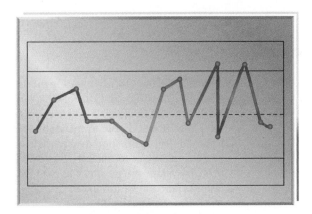

    a. Label the following elements on the control chart:
       1. Upper control limit
       2. Lower control limit
       3. Process average
    b. Is the process subject to common cause variation? Explain.
    c. Is the process subject to special cause variation? Explain.
    d. What might be an example of special cause variation in this manufacturing setting?

E9-18
Obj. 5

SPREADSHEET

Felicidad, Inc., uses statistical process control charts to determine whether material quantity variances are the result of special or common cause variation. The following variances represent the results of analyses over the previous 16 weeks. The week number is in parentheses. U and F indicate unfavorable and favorable.

(1) 520 F	(4) 325 F	(7) 200 U	(10) 115 F	(13) 1,500 U	(15) 125 F
(2) 550 F	(5) 127 U	(8) 200 U	(11) 150 U	(14) 225 U	(16) 130 F
(3) 250 U	(6) 525 U	(9) 150 F	(12) 530 F		

    a. Prepare a statistical process control chart to determine whether any of the material quantity variances might represent unusual circumstances worthy of investigation. (Treat favorable variances as positive numbers and unfavorable variances as negative numbers.) To solve the problem using Minitab, use the following instructions: Open Minitab. Enter variances for weeks 1–6 in column C1. Click on Stat. Click on Control Charts. Click on Individuals. Enter C1 into Variable field. Click OK.

(Continued)

Note: If you choose to manually solve the problem (or to use Excel), upper and lower control limits should be placed on your graph at *Y*-axis values 1,296 and −1,388, respectively. Refer to Exhibit 12 in the chapter for an illustration of control limit and process average placement. You may manually calculate the process average or use the average function within Excel.

b. Refer to the control chart that you prepared in part (a). In general, what may be potential causes of unfavorable material quantity variances?

c. How does statistical process control assist managers in making decisions about cost accounting information?

E9-19
Objs. 5, 6

SPREADSHEET

As part of a continuous quality improvement initiative, an accounting department quality team at Dexmar Pharmaceuticals was evaluating the quality of payroll services provided to employees. The team decided to use the percentage of payroll checks containing errors as a measure of payroll quality. Errors could be in the form of incorrect withholding for FICA, health insurance, or charitable contributions. Errors also may include the incorrect calculation of overtime pay, or use of an incorrect hourly wage rate. The following table illustrates the percentage of weekly payroll checks without errors for a six-month period:

1 0.98	8 0.99	15 0.95	22 0.98
2 0.99	9 0.80	16 0.97	23 0.98
3 0.95	10 0.85	17 1.00	24 0.96
4 0.96	11 0.90	18 0.99	25 0.96
5 0.99	12 0.97	19 0.96	26 0.94
6 0.98	13 0.97	20 0.98	
7 0.97	14 0.98	21 0.95	

a. Prepare a control chart using the data presented. To solve the problem using Minitab, use the following instructions: Open Minitab. Enter observations 1–26 in column C1. Click on Stat. Click on Control Charts. Click on Individuals. Enter C1 into Variable field. Click OK.

   Note: If you choose to manually solve the problem (or to use Excel), upper and lower control limits should be placed on your graph at *Y*-axis values 1.036 and 0.879, respectively. Refer to Exhibit 12 in the chapter for an illustration of control limit and process average placement. You may manually calculate the process average or use the average function within Excel.

b. Is the process in control?

c. Which types of variation are present? Explain.

E9-20
Objs. 5, 6

Refer to the information provided in E9-19. Control charts are designed to signal when an out-of-control event has occurred. However, the chart does not indicate the reason for the out-of-control event. Individuals must serve as detectives to investigate possible reasons for special cause variation.

a. Identify the *types* of questions you would ask in attempting to understand the cause of the lower percentages in periods 9 and 10. (For example, was there turnover in payroll staff during these periods?)

b. Though control charting techniques originally were developed to monitor manufacturing processes, their use has expanded beyond the manufacturing floor. Identify other examples of how control charts could be used to monitor the quality of administrative (or service-related) processes.

PROBLEMS

If your instructor is using Personal Trainer® in this course, you may complete your assignments online.

P9-1
Obj. 1

Establishing Material and Labor Standards, Multiple Departments

TCC Industries produces specialty tires in a variety of sizes and tread designs for use on trailers and farm equipment. TCC is planning to implement a standard cost accounting system. Valerie Siewert, the controller, has accumulated the following information on the standard cost of a particular bias tractor tire.

Each tire requires 15 pounds of carbon black, the basic tire component, which is added in the mixing department. Other materials, such as zinc and sulfur, which are added in the molding department, are required in such small quantities that they are treated as indirect materials and included as part of overhead. Each tire requires 15 minutes of processing time to mold and cure. An additional 45 minutes of time is required to mix the ingredients in the mixing department.

The standard cost for carbon black is $3.50 a pound. The standard cost of direct labor in the mixing department is $10.00 per labor hour, while the standard cost of direct labor in the molding department is $11.00 per hour.

Required

A. Develop the standard cost of materials and labor for the tractor tire. The standard cost should identify the standard quantity, the standard rate, and the total standard cost per unit.
B. Identify the advantages of implementing a standard cost system.
C. Explain the role each of the following people would have in developing the standard costs:
   1. Purchasing manager
   2. Mixing department supervisor
   3. Molding department supervisor
   4. Cost accountant
   5. Product engineer
D. Assume that a batch of tires has been completed and the following actual amounts were used to produce the batch:
   1. Actual output: 4,500 tires
   2. Actual carbon black utilized: 68,000 pounds
   3. Carbon black purchased: 75,000 pounds at a cost of $258,000
   4. Direct labor in mixing department: 3,220 hours at a cost of $31,073
   5. Direct labor in molding department: 1,075 hours at a cost of $12,384

Compute the materials price variance and the material usage variance. Also, compute the labor rate variance and labor efficiency variance for each department.

P9-2 Performance Evaluation and Variance Analysis

Obj. 2

Timber Industries manufactures unfinished furniture, which it sells through retail outlets. Timber produces many different styles of bookcases, tables, chairs, desks, and dressers that customers finish themselves with stain or paint. Timber utilizes a standard cost system and performs variance analysis. The company recently increased production to meet anticipated demand from several new retail outlets that opened in new sales territories. To accommodate the expected increase in sales demand, the production department hired five new employees from a local community college program. These new employees were immediately assigned to various production processes, such as milling, lathe, and assembly.

To meet the anticipated production needs, the purchasing department had to seek additional sources of lumber. The company ordered large quantities of high-grade oak, maple, and pine. The purchasing department insisted on obtaining high-quality materials, since poor-quality materials result in excess scrap, rework, and defects during the manufacturing process. Some of the new suppliers delivered materials that were warped or had too many knots or blemishes. Instead of returning the materials, the purchasing department negotiated "quality" credits from the suppliers. The poorer-quality wood then was sorted, remilled by Timber, and used in places where lower-quality material was acceptable, such as drawer bottoms and sides.

Several of the new retail outlets did not reach the sales volume that was originally expected. The sales department insists that with time, the new stores will gain recognition and their sales will increase. To deal with the increase in finished goods inventory, the sales department negotiated with a discount department chain to sell a limited line of Timber products in markets that did not compete directly with company-owned retail outlets.

Material and labor variances for Timber Industries were as follows:

Material price variance	Favorable
Material usage variance	Unfavorable
Direct labor rate variance	Favorable
Direct labor efficiency variance	Unfavorable

(Continued)

Required

A. Based on the facts stated, identify contributing factors for the variances noted.
B. Discuss how Timber Industries could use variance analysis to analyze the performance measures of the purchasing, production, and sales departments.

P9-3   ## Changes in Costs, Effects on Variances

Objs. 1, 2

Tempro, Inc., uses a standard cost accounting system. Variances for the year ended December 31, 2005, were as follows:

Material price variance	Unfavorable
Material usage variance	Favorable
Labor rate variance	Favorable
Labor efficiency variance	Unfavorable

Managers at Tempro are considering the following changes in operations for the year ending December 31, 2006.

1. An across-the-board pay increase of 5% will be given to all personnel.
2. The purchasing department will be allowed to purchase lower grades of materials.
3. Several key production workers will be transferred into managerial positions. These workers will be replaced either by new hires or by production personnel who will be transferred from another department.
4. Additional inspectors will be hired to ensure quality production. The cost of these inspectors will be considered administrative and general expense.

Required Assuming that product standards are not changed from the previous year, what impact, if any, would you expect each of the changes to have on the company's variances? Consider each decision separately, and identify the variance that would be affected by the decision and whether the change would increase or decrease the prior-year variance. Explain your answers.

P9-4   ## Establishing Labor Standards

Objs. 1, 2

Greenbriar Company is considering the addition of a new machine in its mold injection plant. Greenbriar already has five such machines that are operating three shifts a day. The company uses a standard cost accounting system. The number of pieces that currently are being produced on the existing machines is 300 per worker-hour. The vendor of the new equipment has stated that its studies indicate that the new machinery should be able to produce 400 pieces per worker-hour. Greenbriar engineers agree that under ideal conditions, the equipment should be able to generate 400 pieces an hour, and they support that rate as a labor standard. Production managers point out that the new machine is identical to the machines currently in use, and that the current production rate is only 300 pieces per worker-hour. Accordingly, production managers advocate the use of 300 pieces as the labor rate standard. The accounting staff believes that the most appropriate standard labor rate would be 350 pieces per labor hour.

Required

A. What arguments are most likely to be offered by engineering, production, and accounting to support their respective proposed standards?
B. Which alternative do you support? Consider the motivational aspects of establishing a standard and explain the reasons for your choice.

P9-5   ## Establishing a Standard Cost Accounting System

Objs. 1, 2

Tasha Smith is the president of Modern Machinery, Inc., which manufactures flexible manufacturing systems used in a wide variety of production processes. To remain competitive, Modern is continually improving product performance by increasing the sophistication of electronic controls, diversifying product offerings, and enhancing the quality of existing products. Many of Modern's customers dictate specific performance expectations and system designs. Modern employs a large engineering staff that coordinates system requirements with the designed components. Each manufactured system requires extensive design work and often results in over a hundred individual component drawings. Each drawing is developed in the engineering department and contains detailed manufacturing specifications. The use of computer-assisted design (CAD) allows Modern to provide system designs in an efficient manner, and has reduced design time. Since each system is manufactured to meet specific requirements, very few parts are interchangeable between systems.

Tasha is considering implementation of a standard cost accounting system. Her objective is to identify both rate and usage variances related to material and labor that are in excess of allowable standards. Tasha will require the engineering department to develop a standard cost sheet with each CAD design. The standard cost sheet will identify the amount of materials that should be used. For components already in use, the standard will assume the cost rates for materials that existed at the beginning of the year. For standards for new components, material costs will be taken from supplier catalogs. Standards for labor will be developed jointly by product and process engineers.

Tasha has determined that material price variances will be the responsibility of the purchasing department. Material usage and labor efficiency variances will be the responsibility of shop supervisors in each of four manufacturing areas (Mill Shop, CNC Manufacturing, Electrical Shop, and Assembly). The labor rate variance will be the responsibility of the human resource department.

Required Prepare a memo to Tasha Smith giving your advice concerning her plans. Specifically comment on the purpose of a standard cost system, the cost-benefit element of implementing such a system, and the inherent weaknesses in Tasha's proposed implementation plans.

P9-6 Quality Cost Analysis

Obj. 3

Management at Precise Manufacturing would like to analyze quality costs associated with the manufacturing process. In Year 1, Precise implemented a statistical process control system. In Year 2, further steps were taken in an effort to improve quality and focus on customer satisfaction. These included the addition of inspectors, expansion of statistical process control to additional processing steps, and further development of products through quality engineering. The benefits of the quality focus at Precise are apparent, as warranty costs and customer returns have declined since quality programs were implemented. However, total quality costs continue to be significant, and management is concerned that the quality focus has not reduced total costs, but has simply shifted costs from one area to another. Accordingly, management would like to analyze quality costs for the past two years. Precise had sales of $18,000,000 in both Year 2 and Year 1, and incurred the following costs related to quality control during those years:

	Year 2	Year 1
Inspection	$ 61,000	$ 30,000
Quality engineering	57,000	12,000
Quality training programs	26,000	39,000
Customer allowances	22,000	104,000
Scrap, net	25,000	8,000
Product testing	92,000	42,000
Rework	130,000	68,000
Statistical process control	50,000	34,000
Downtime due to defects	25,000	18,000
Warranty repairs	75,000	189,000
Field service	45,000	143,000
Testing supplies	15,000	16,000

Required

A. Categorize the costs and compute the total costs of conformance for each year by category.

B. Evaluate the distribution of quality costs at Precise. Discuss the distribution of quality costs and any trends in cost distribution. What effect does the distribution of quality costs have on total quality at Precise? Explain your answer.

C. What future trends should Precise expect if the current focus of quality programs continues? Explain your answer.

P9-7   **Quality Loss Function Analysis**

Obj. 4

Journal Paper Manufacturing produces newsprint paper for use in newspaper publishing. The thickness of the paper can vary slightly during the manufacturing process. If the paper is too thin, it will not hold up under the printing process and will tear, while paper that is too thick can result in printing press malfunction. As the paper is manufactured, it is rolled onto spools for shipping to newspaper publishers. Each spool is weighed after the manufacturing process is complete. The target value for a spool is exactly one ton (2,000 pounds). Management at Journal has determined that each pound deviation from the target value will increase quality costs by $0.50. The following production figures reflect production for the most recent month:

Spool Number	Total Gross Product Weight (in pounds)
1	2,119.20
2	1,924.62
3	1,907.32
4	2,141.91
5	1,974.43
6	2,030.21
7	2,053.92
8	2,142.12
9	1,936.90
10	1,899.97
11	1,997.87
12	2,112.25
13	1,943.40
14	2,071.75

Required

A. Calculate the total quality loss cost for Journal Paper Manufacturing, using the quality loss function.
B. What do your calculations suggest about the manufacturing process? What do your calculations suggest must be done by Journal? Explain your answer.

P9-8   **The Taguchi Loss Function: Plot Preparation and Interpretation**

Obj. 4

SPREADSHEET

Taguchi explained the basis for his loss function by providing an example from the nursery industry in Japan. Greenhouses typically are covered with plastic sheeting that permits the correct amount of sunlight to penetrate. If manufacturers of plastic sheeting deviate from target specifications, quality losses occur. For example, if the material is too thick, insufficient light will penetrate. If the material is too thin, it lacks sufficient strength to withstand inclement weather and will tear.

Assume the target specification is 50 microns (a micron is 1/1000 of a millimeter) and the dollar value of loss associated with variation is $200 [(k) = $200].

Required

A. Calculate the quality losses at the following points:
    1. 30 microns
    2. 40 microns
    3. 50 microns
    4. 60 microns
    5. 70 microns
B. Prepare a plot of the quality losses calculated in requirement (A).
C. Explain the results of your calculations and plot.
D. How might management use information from your plot to support decisions about quality improvement?

P9-9   **Statistical Process Control Charting**

Obj. 5

Power Source, Inc., produces electrical control harnesses used in the production of battery-powered carts and cars for children. These harnesses are sold to a toy manufacturer who re-

SPREADSHEET

quires close tolerances related to cable length. Power Source has implemented a statistical process control system to monitor harness production and performs statistical control charting related to cable length.

During a recent four-hour morning shift, the operator on the cable assembly line performed a cable measurement every 20 minutes and recorded the observation on a SPC control chart. The observed measurements were as follows:

Measurement		Measurement	
1	30.75 inches	7	33.50 inches
2	32.25 inches	8	31.95 inches
3	31.67 inches	9	32.00 inches
4	33.25 inches	10	31.08 inches
5	30.45 inches	11	30.99 inches
6	32.80 inches	12	32.15 inches

Required

A. Prepare a statistical process control chart to evaluate whether the process is in control. To solve the problem using Minitab, use the following instructions: Open Minitab. Enter observations 1–12 in column C1. Click on Stat. Click on Control Charts. Click on Individuals. Enter C1 into Variable field. Click OK.

    Note: If you choose to solve the problem manually (or to use Excel), upper and lower control limits should be placed on your graph at *Y*-axis values 35.11 and 29.69, respectively. Refer to Exhibit 12 in this chapter for an illustration of control limit and process average placement. You may manually calculate the process average or use the average function within Excel.

B. Do any of the observed measurements indicate that an out-of-control condition exists? Which measurement(s)? What steps should be taken to remedy this situation?

P9-10   Control Chart Preparation

Obj. 5

SPREADSHEET

Tuscaloosa Brickworks uses variance analysis to track materials price and quantity variances. Managers recognize that normal fluctuations occur, but want to investigate the cause of significant favorable or unfavorable variances. To help them assess whether a variance is significant, managers use statistical process control charts. Materials price variance data are presented for 25 periods as follows:

(1) 420 F	(6) 555 F	(10) 135 F	(14) 325 U	(18) 235 F	(22) 155 F
(2) 570 F	(7) 1,050 U	(11) 170 U	(15) 325 F	(19) 550 F	(23) 200 F
(3) 350 U	(8) 250 U	(12) 550 F	(16) 230 F	(20) 350 F	(24) 140 F
(4) 355 F	(9) 155 U	(13) 1,600 U	(17) 525 U	(21) 375 U	(25) 200 U
(5) 125 F					

Required

A. Prepare a statistical process control chart to evaluate whether materials price variances are in a state of statistical control. Use positive values for favorable variances and negative values for unfavorable variances. To solve the problem using Minitab, use the following instructions: Open Minitab. Enter observations 1–25 in column C1. Click on Stat. Click on Control Charts. Click on Individuals. Enter C1 into Variable field. Click OK.

    Note: If you choose to solve the problem manually (or to use Excel), upper and lower control limits should be placed on your graph at *Y*-axis values 1,564 and −1,572, respectively. Refer to Exhibit 12 in this chapter for an illustration of control limit and process average placement. You may manually calculate the process average or use the average function within Excel.

B. Which, if any, observations should management investigate?

C. Is the process subject to common and special cause variation? Explain.

D. Typically, who is responsible for a significant materials price variance? Explain.

P9-11, P9-12, & P9-13   These three problems are based on one business situation. The three-problem series links quality costs, the Taguchi loss function, and statistical process control.

P9-11   Quality Costs and Management Decisions

Obj. 3

AutoSafe, Inc., produces windshields for major international automobile manufacturers. To produce a shatter-proof windshield, a sheet of plastic-like material is sandwiched between two sheets of glass. The completed product must conform to a number of engineering specifications. For example, a completed windshield must not vary significantly from an established target thickness. Products that are too thick or too thin will not fit properly in the vehicle for which they are intended. Quality costs include extra installation time to make a poorly manufactured windshield fit properly; in a worst case scenario, the windshield may leak.

Management is interested in tracking internal failure, external failure, prevention, and appraisal costs.

Required

A. Machine operators indicate that a critical part in the assembly machine is subject to random failure. New tooling costing $250,000 is required to prevent future problems from occurring. How would the company classify capital expense associated with the process improvement initiative?

B. Assume management decided to invest in new tooling and quality training. As a result, total quality costs increased when compared to the prior year. How would you defend these decisions against critics who complained that total quality costs are increasing?

P9-12   The Taguchi Loss Function and Quality Costs

Obj. 4

SPREADSHEET

Refer to P9-11 for a description of AutoSafe's manufacturing process. Managers at AutoSafe collected twenty data points representing a batch of windshield XXR531. These data follow. The target thickness specification for product XXR531 is 2.5 millimeters. Management has estimated the cost of variability, or (k), in the Taguchi loss function at $12,000.

1	2.60	6	2.60	11	2.65	16	2.50
2	2.55	7	2.55	12	2.65	17	2.55
3	2.40	8	2.55	13	2.50	18	3.10
4	2.40	9	2.60	14	2.55	19	2.45
5	2.50	10	2.55	15	2.45	20	2.60

Required

A. Calculate the quality losses associated with process variability.
B. Will these losses appear in the accounting general ledger? Explain.
C. What types of costs are included in the Taguchi loss function?
D. Does the Taguchi function describe failure, prevention, or appraisal cost? Explain.

P9-13   Control Chart Preparation and Interpretation

Obj. 5

SPREADSHEET

As part of AutoSafe's quality program, control charts are prepared on a regular basis to evaluate whether the process is in a state of statistical control. Using process data shown in P9-12, complete the following requirements.

Required

A. Prepare a control chart for the AutoSafe glass windshield production process. To solve the problem using Minitab, use the following instructions: Open Minitab. Enter observations 1–20 in column C1. Click on Stat. Click on Control Charts. Click on Individuals. Enter C1 into Variable field. Click OK.

   Note: If you choose to solve the problem manually (or to use Excel), upper and lower control limits should be placed on your graph at *Y*-axis values 2.90 and 2.23, respectively. Refer to Exhibit 12 in this chapter for an illustration of control limit and process average placement. You may manually calculate the process average or use the average function within Excel.

B. Determine whether the process is in a state of statistical control. Explain your answer.

P9-14   Variance Analysis, Service Environment

Objs. 1, 6

Todd Judd separated from his wife, Stella, and filed for divorce. As part of the divorce, Todd realized that he would have to engage in a legal battle with Stella since the couple owned several parcels of property and had considerable investments, including a business Todd had acquired from his father. Todd spoke with several attorneys, explained his case, and asked each for an estimate of the cost to represent him in the proceedings. Perry Schmidt, a practicing attorney, provided Todd with the following estimate of costs if he were to represent Todd:

Item	Hours	Billing Rate	Total Cost
Attorney hours, planning and court time	150	$185 per hour	$27,750
Admin. and clerical support	60	75 per hour	4,500
Witness fees	n/a	n/a	1,500
Court costs	n/a	n/a	500
Total			$34,250

Todd hired Perry based on the estimate. In the course of the trial several unforeseen issues arose, continuances were granted, and the proceedings dragged on for 18 months. At the end of the trial, Perry provided Todd with a bill totaling $42,840. The following billing details were also provided:

Item	Hours	Total Cost
Attorney hours, planning and court time	187	$34,595
Admin. and clerical support	52	3,640
Witness fees	n/a	2,750
Deposition fees		1,255
Court costs	n/a	600
Total		$42,840

Perry offered the following explanations for the difference between the estimated and final billings.

1. Continuances and unforeseen issues resulted in the extra attorney hours.
2. Deposition fees were not anticipated in the original quote.
3. Although the number of filings was exactly as anticipated, Perry was not aware that the court had increased its filing fees, resulting in an extra $100.

Required

A. Calculate the average rate per hour that Todd was billed for attorney time and clerical assistance.
B. Based on the original budget estimate, was the labor efficiency variance for attorney time favorable or unfavorable?
C. Is the court filing fee variance related to volume? Explain your answer.
D. Calculate the labor rate, efficiency, and total variances associated with clerical support.

P9-15   Excel in Action

SPREADSHEET

Music Makers normally produces 500,000 CDs each month. Standard quantities and prices per unit of direct materials are as follows:

	Quantity	Price
Blank CDs	1	$0.75
Containers	1	0.11
Printed inserts	1	0.05
Cellophane	1	0.02

Standard labor hours per unit and rates per hour are:

	Hours	Rate
Copying	0.00667	$13.00
Packaging	0.01500	7.50

(Continued)

Production during June was higher than normal at 560,000 units. To meet the higher demand, Music Makers purchased a higher than normal amount of materials. Luckily the company's purchasing department found a manufacturer willing to provide some surplus CDs and containers at a discount. Actual quantities of direct materials used and prices per unit for June were as follows:

	Quantity	Price
Blank CDs	565,430	$0.71
Containers	562,109	0.09
Printed inserts	560,139	0.05
Cellophane	561,240	0.02

Because of the higher than normal production, Music Makers' labor hours and rates were higher than normal. The company paid extra overtime to complete the additional units. Actual labor hours and rates per hour were as follows:

	Hours	Rate
Copying	3,820	$12.25
Packaging	8,300	8.15

Required

A. Use the data provided to prepare an analysis of direct materials and direct labor variances for Music Makers for June. Column headings for material variances should include: Units Produced, Standard Quantity per Unit, Standard Price per Unit, Actual Quantity, Actual Price per Unit, Actual Quantity × Actual Price, Actual Quantity × Standard Price, and Standard Quantity × Standard Price. Rows should provide data for each type of direct material. Quantity × Price columns should be totaled and the differences should be calculated to determine the total price and quantity variances. A positive number should be a favorable variance, and a negative number should be an unfavorable variance.

Below the direct material variance calculations, repeat the same process for direct labor variances. Column headings should be: Units Produced, Standard Hours per Unit, Standard Rate per Hour, Actual Hours, Actual Rate per Hour, Actual Hours × Actual Rate, Actual Hours × Standard Rate, and Standard Hours × Standard Rate. Separate rows should be provided for copying and packaging labor. Hours × Rate columns should be totaled and used to determine rate and efficiency variances.

B. Use cell references and formulas where possible. Use appropriate formatting throughout. Evaluate Music Makers' direct materials and direct labor variances. What were the likely causes of the variances? Were the decisions to produce the extra CDs and purchase the blank CDs and containers at a discount good decisions?

C. Suppose Music Makers had paid $0.73 for CDs and $0.13 for containers used in June. What would the price and quantity variances have been? Suppose the company's actual labor hours had been 3,700 for copying and 8,300 for packaging. What would the rate and efficiency variances have been?

P9-16 Multiple-Choice Overview of the Chapter

1. A favorable material price variance coupled with an unfavorable material usage variance would most likely be the result of:
   a. labor efficiency problems.
   b. machine efficiency problems.
   c. the purchase and use of higher than standard quality materials.
   d. the purchase and use of lower than standard quality materials.

2. Standards preferably should be set so that:
   a. no allowance is made for machine breakdowns or other work interruptions.
   b. they are based on practical levels that can be achieved rather than on ideal levels.
   c. they reflect a level that can be achieved only by the most skilled and efficient employee working at peak effort 100% of the time.
   d. they can be used for motivational purposes rather than in forecasting cash flows and in planning inventory.

3. Inspection of products would be a(n):
   a. prevention cost.
   b. appraisal cost.
   c. internal failure cost.
   d. external failure cost.

4. Which of the following is NOT true with respect to statistical process control?
   a. It places the monitoring of quality at a workstation.
   b. It eliminates the need for a final inspection of goods.
   c. It is considered a prevention cost.
   d. It requires the charting of observed measurements.

Questions 5 through 8 are based on the following information.

Jackson Industries employs a standard cost system in which direct materials inventory is carried at standard cost. Jackson has established the following standards for the costs of one unit of product:

	Standard Quantity	Standard Price or Rate
Direct materials	5 pounds	$3.60 per pound
Direct labor	1.25 hours	$12.00 per hour

During May, Jackson purchased 125,000 pounds of direct material at a total cost of $475,000. The total factory direct labor wages for May were $327,600. Jackson manufactured 22,000 units of product during May, using 108,000 pounds of direct material and 28,000 direct labor hours.

5. The price variance for the direct material acquired by Jackson Industries during May is:
   a. $21,600 favorable.
   b. $25,000 unfavorable.
   c. $28,000 favorable.
   d. $21,600 unfavorable.

6. The direct material quantity (usage) variance for May is:
   a. $7,200 unfavorable.
   b. $7,600 favorable.
   c. $5,850 unfavorable.
   d. $7,200 favorable.

7. The direct labor rate variance for May is:
   a. $8,400 favorable.
   b. $7,200 unfavorable.
   c. $8,400 unfavorable.
   d. $6,000 favorable.

8. The direct labor efficiency variance for May is:
   a. $5,850 favorable.
   b. $7,200 favorable.
   c. $6,000 unfavorable.
   d. $5,850 unfavorable.

9. For the month of January 2006, Crabapple's records disclosed the following data related to direct labor:

Actual direct labor costs	$10,000
Labor rate variance	$1,000 Favorable
Labor efficiency variance	($1,500) Unfavorable

For the month of January, actual direct labor hours totaled 2,000. What was Crabapple's standard direct labor rate per hour?
   a. $5.50
   b. $5.00
   c. $4.75
   d. $4.50

(Continued)

10. Quality costs:
   a. relate only to the manufacturing process.
   b. should focus on appraisal activities.
   c. are minimized by having well-trained inspectors.
   d. cut across departmental lines and are often not reported to management.

CASES

C9-1   ### Establishing Standards, Variance Analysis

Objs. 1, 2

Stellhorn Snacks produces high-quality potato chips. The manufacturing process is highly automated, yet requires labor to handle, inspect, and sort potatoes and chips. Stellhorn has accumulated product costs using process costing in the past and is considering adopting a standard cost accounting system.

At the beginning of the manufacturing process, potatoes are scrubbed and cleaned in an automatic washer. The potatoes then are placed automatically on a conveyor that feeds them into an automatic peeling machine. After the potatoes are peeled, they are inspected manually to remove blemishes and to cut out eyes. After inspection, they are placed on another conveyor that feeds them into an automatic slicing machine. The slicer feeds the chips into vats, which are loaded manually into deep fryers and monitored closely by production personnel. After cooking, the chips are drained and placed on another conveyor for final inspection and seasoning. At this point, unacceptable chips are sorted from good production, and the good chips are fed into an automatic bagger. The bagging process is highly automated, requiring one operator to load the empty bags for filling, and another person to remove the bags once they have been sealed and place them in cartons for final shipment.

Stellhorn expects to purchase potatoes of acceptable grade and quality for $0.08 a pound. Based on historical records, Stellhorn has determined that it can produce 152 ounces of chips for every 10 pounds of potatoes placed into production. Each bag of chips produced contains 19 ounces of chips. Other direct materials include bags and boxes, which amount to $0.14 per bag of chips. All other materials, such as oil and seasoning, are treated as indirect costs.

Stellhorn operates under a union contract and has three distinct classes, or categories, of employees. The established classes and the agreed-upon hourly rates for direct laborers are as follows:

Handlers	$ 8.00 an hour
Machine operators	10.50 an hour
Inspectors	12.00 an hour

For the coming year, Stellhorn expects to produce six million bags of chips. For this level of production, the company has determined that it will require 10,800 hours of handler time, 12,000 hours of machine operator time, and 14,800 hours of inspection.

Variable overhead is applied on the basis of direct labor hours and historically has averaged 110% of labor dollars. The budgeted fixed overhead for the coming year is $1,350,000, and also is applied based on direct labor hours.

Required
A. Discuss the benefits Stellhorn would realize by adopting a standard cost accounting system.
B. Using the following format, develop a standard cost sheet for material, labor, and overhead for each bag of potato chips.

Cost Category   Standard Quantity   Standard Cost or Rate   Total Standard Cost

For requirements (C) and (D), assume that Stellhorn produced 6,200,000 bags of chips and incurred the following costs and levels of activity:

Materials: 7,800,000 pounds of potatoes purchased and used, at a cost of $608,400.

Labor:

Handlers	12,480 hours, at an actual cost of $89,280	
Machine operators	13,650 hours, at an actual cost of $130,200	
Inspectors	15,475 hours, at an actual cost of $185,700	

C. Calculate the material price and usage variances for potatoes.

D. Calculate the labor rate variance and labor efficiency variance for each labor category.

C9-2 Performance Measurement

Obj. 3

Petro-Flo Corporation designs and manufactures fluid transfer components found in engine and transmission systems of expensive, heavy equipment. These systems often are contained in earth-moving equipment used under harsh conditions ranging from Middle Eastern oil fields to Canadian real estate development projects. Because of protection granted by patented designs and the company's uncompromising dedication to service, Petro-Flo has enjoyed a dominant position within the industry. If a Petro-Flo fuel system malfunctions, regardless of where the equipment is in use, an engineer will be assigned to assist the customer. Sometimes the engineer can ship a replacement part by express air. However, occasionally he or she must travel to the job site to personally assess the cause of the problem and to make recommendations for repairing the system.

The business environment is changing as a result of innovations introduced by Petro-Flo's competitors. Therefore, cost management and quality control have received greater attention in recent years. In 2005, top management believed some managers had grown complacent as a result of previous successes in a very different business climate. As within many companies, the production, marketing, and service departments traditionally had functioned independently. In order to call attention to quality costs, management established a program to identify and manage quality expenditures as well as to serve as a basis for performance evaluation. Excerpts from the company's general ledger appear in Exhibit A.

Exhibit A Quality Cost Data (in thousands)

General Ledger Account	2004	2005	2006	2007
Sales	$2,000,000	$2,300,000	$2,500,000	$2,700,000
First-part inspection costs	30,000	35,000	40,000	50,000
Scrap/rework	70,000	60,000	50,000	45,000
Warranty claims	20,000	20,000	19,000	17,000
Product liability litigation	30,000	30,000	20,000	10,000
Vendor certification programs	0	20,000	30,000	20,000
Travel associated with field repairs	40,000	40,000	35,000	15,000
Quality training/education programs	5,000	20,000	15,000	10,000
R & D for better processes	20,000	40,000	40,000	20,000

After three years of using quality cost as a performance measurement criterion, some managers disagreed with the emphasis placed on identifying quality spending. These managers argued their main focus should be on nonfinancial variables such as scrap rates, machine downtime, on-time delivery, and the number of field breakdowns. They believed statistical process control charts provided immediately useful detailed process information for making quality improvements. These managers argued that after four years of tracking quality costs, total quality spending is not significantly lower than in 2004, one year prior to the introduction of the quality program.

Consider the following guidelines when preparing your analysis of the case.

Required

A. Discuss the purposes of a quality cost system as envisioned by management (such as cultural change and attention-getting).

(Continued)

B. Classify the costs in Exhibit A according to the following categories: internal failure, external failure, prevention, and appraisal.

C. Analyze the trends in quality spending. Prepare a stacked bar graph to analyze total quality costs. Prepare another graph to identify trends in spending by each type of cost category. (*Hint:* You may wish to prepare graphs in absolute dollars and percentage of sales.)

D. Consider the appropriate use of quality measures such as SPC charts and other nonfinancial measures of performance. Do these measures complement financial measures of quality?

E. How frequently should a company capture financial and nonfinancial measures?

MANAGING MULTI-DIVISIONAL ORGANIZATIONS

How do we set up meaningful performance measures?

Erin and Seth are continuing to grow their manufacturing business. They have learned about product costing and cost behavior. They also have become very adept at accurately budgeting their revenues and costs. As discussed in Chapter M9, they are beginning to understand how to use variance analysis as a type of performance measure for process improvement. They now have numerous employees with marketing, accounting, or production responsibilities. Seth and Erin share financial information throughout their organization hoping everyone will use the information to make the company more efficient, effective, and profitable. However, Erin and Seth realize their employees do not understand much of the information they are sharing. Also, the employees don't seem to understand how to use the information to make decisions that are consistent with the mission of the company. Erin and Seth would like to develop financial and nonfinancial performance measures that will help guide the actions of everyone.

FOOD FOR THOUGHT

Put yourself in the position of Erin and Seth. How would you design your performance measurement system so that it is understandable by everyone throughout the company? The system should promote decisions and behavior that are consistent with the company's strategy. Let's see what Erin and Seth are considering as they plan their system design.

Erin: *I have been considering launching a project to develop a better method of evaluating and rewarding performance.*

Seth: *What's wrong with our bonus plan based on earnings? After all, the purpose of our company is to make money. If everyone does his or her job well, we should be profitable. Our bonus system shares some of the profits with our employees.*

Erin: *I agree that financial performance is the bottom line, but basing rewards on financial performance alone seems very short-sighted. We could do an excellent job on things that really matter, but because of events beyond our control, our earnings could be disappointing. Also, I believe nonfinancial measures may provide more guidance for decision making.*

Seth: *I'm not sure that I follow you.*

Erin: *Ok. What if I ask one of our marketing managers to improve net income? Or, what if I ask the production manager to improve earnings this month? What actions should he or she take?*

Seth: *So, how would other measures help?*

Erin: *If we partially based the marketing manager's performance evaluation on the number of new customers signed up during the month, she would develop a plan to increase our customer base. Likewise, if the production manager's bonus is affected by the percentage of on-time deliveries, he would be more interested in making sure delivery dates are not missed.*

Seth: *I see your point. By establishing a variety of financial and nonfinancial performance measures, everyone would be made aware of important factors that ultimately affect net income. Also, these measures can be used to communicate competitive strategy throughout the company.*

Erin: *Right. For example, we have built our business around the principle of developing innovative, high-quality products, delivered on time, at a reasonable price. We could build performance measures into our system that encourage actions consistent with our strategy.*

Seth: *I can think of a few measures, such as defect rate, number of new product innovations, and percentage of on-time deliveries, that are consistent with our strategy.*

Erin: *We will need to involve everyone in the process of developing appropriate measures. Buy-in is important in order for people to support what we are trying to accomplish.*

Seth: *I agree. We also need to tailor the performance measures to specific areas of responsibility. It makes no sense to evaluate a production manager on the number of new customers or to evaluate a marketing manager on the number of defective products produced.*

Erin: *The key will be to develop a **small** number of measures that capture various aspects of our competitive strategy. If we can identify a few processes that we must do well and focus on these, I believe profits will follow.*

OBJECTIVES

Once you have completed this chapter, you should be able to:

1 Explain problems associated with managers acting on behalf of owners.

2 Identify various organizational levels within a company and explain how performance at each level may be evaluated.

3 Explain the historical context in which return on investment (ROI) was developed.

4 Calculate ROI and economic value added. Explain how they can motivate behavior that is consistent or inconsistent with the strategic objectives of an organization.

5 Discuss the four elements of the balanced scorecard approach to evaluating performance.

6 Explain how a manager who acts in the best interests of a division may harm the company as a whole.

7 Discuss various transfer pricing methods that have been developed to influence managerial behavior.

8 Explain how the performance of managers can be evaluated in decentralized service organizations.

AMERICAN PAPER COMPANY: THE MANUFACTURING PROCESS

This chapter uses American Paper Company to illustrate the concepts of responsibility centers, performance evaluation, and transfer pricing. American Paper is organized into two divisions, Pulp and Paper. Each division is responsible for producing and selling its products. Though most of the output from the Pulp Division is sold to external customers worldwide, some of it is sold to the Paper Division to be used as raw material.

As shown in Exhibit 1, pulp manufacturing begins with timber in the form of logs or wood chips. If raw materials are received in the form of logs, the first step in the process is debarking. A rotating debarking drum tumbles the logs to remove the bark. After the debarking, chippers cut the logs into one-inch cubes.

The second step in the process is "digesting." Wood chips are cooked to break down the glue-like material bonding the wood fibers. Chemicals used in the digestor are reclaimed and used in future pulp production. Following the digesting process, brown fibers, which are used in manufacturing so-called natural-colored coffee filters and paper towels, are washed and screened. A bleaching process may be used to convert natural-colored brown pulp into white pulp, which is used to manufacture products such as writing and printing paper. As a final step, the pulp mixture is dried, cut into sheets, and packaged for shipment.

The Paper Division of American Paper manufactures large rolls of paper. These rolls are sold to companies that convert the paper into writing, printing, and computer

Exhibit 1 The Pulp Manufacturing Process

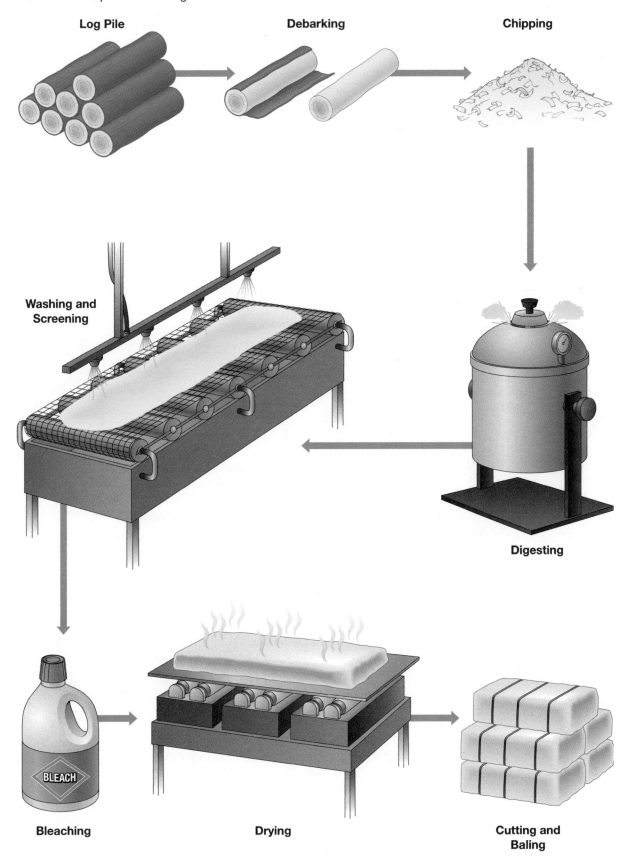

Log Pile

Debarking

Chipping

Washing and Screening

Digesting

Bleaching

Drying

Cutting and Baling

paper. As shown in Exhibit 2, the paper manufacturing process begins with the mixing of pulp with water and chemicals in the first stage of a paper machine. The mixture is spread out on a porous wire mesh; the actual formation of paper begins in this step. The wire mesh travels through a press that forces the pulp mixture against the wire to remove water from the mixture and make the paper the desired thickness. The material then proceeds to a drying section, where it travels across numerous cylindrical dryers that are heated with steam. In the final section of the paper machine, long sections of paper are rolled up into "parent rolls" and removed from the machine. The parent rolls are processed further by American Paper's customers to make various types of printing paper.

Exhibit 2 The Paper Manufacturing Process

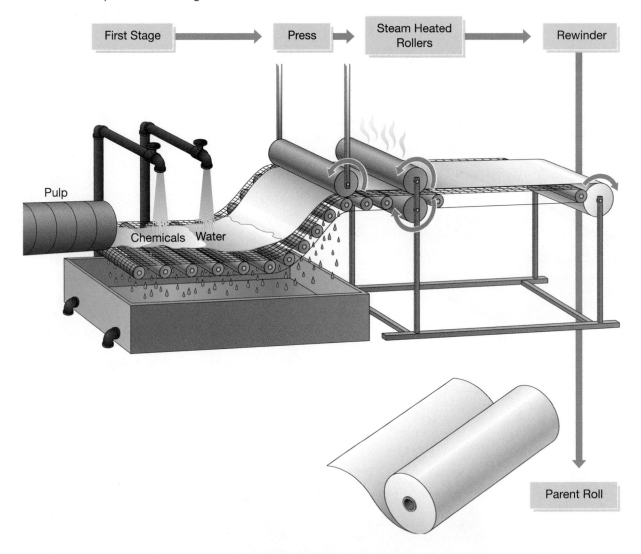

A paper plant requires a large amount of expensive production equipment—a new pulp mill can cost $750 million. In addition to the initial investment in equipment, these mills consume resources in the form of pulp, water, and chemicals. Some mills purchase electricity to power their operations, while others use heat produced by the chemical recovery process to generate electric power. The capital and organizational structures of a company, as well as its operating costs, are directly related to decisions managers face in a decentralized environment. The remainder of this chapter considers the related topics of responsibility accounting, performance measurement, and transfer pricing.

THEORETICAL FRAMEWORK FOR BEHAVIOR WITHIN ORGANIZATIONS

OBJECTIVE 1

Explain problems associated with managers acting on behalf of owners.

Seth and Erin are beginning to share decision-making authority with others in their company. This chapter illustrates some of the issues involving the sharing, or transferring, of authority to professional managers. Throughout this text you are learning how managers use accounting information to make marketing and operations decisions. In most large companies, professional managers make these decisions, thereby acting as agents for the owners (shareholders). *Agents* **are hired by owners and are expected to manage the company in a way consistent with the owners' interests.** Thus, a major consideration when designing a performance evaluation system is to build incentives for managers to act according to the owners' wishes.

Economic theory assumes the objective of a company is to maximize stockholder wealth. However, the theory does not assume managers will always behave in a way consistent with this objective. Thus, compensation packages often are constructed to give the managers incentives to maximize company value. For example, compensation arrangements often include bonuses when certain income targets are met. In a decentralized organization, divisional managers have authority to make many types of decisions, but are held accountable for the results of their decisions. Next, this chapter addresses various types of responsibility areas within decentralized organizations, and how managers of these areas may be evaluated.

MANAGEMENT OF DECENTRALIZED ORGANIZATIONS

OBJECTIVE 2

Identify various organizational levels within a company and explain how performance at each level may be evaluated.

Exhibit 3 presents the organizational chart of American Paper. Each division manager reports to a corporate-level vice president. Operations managers, who report to the division managers, are responsible for supervising the activities of the manufacturing and marketing functions.

Managers typically are evaluated on the basis of variables over which they have control. Thus, managers at different levels within an organization are evaluated by different criteria. For example, some managers can control costs but not revenues. Other managers may be responsible for controlling costs, earning revenues, and making decisions about acquiring additional plant assets. Thus, divisions within an organization often are categorized according to the types of responsibilities placed on managers. For example, the organizational structure of American Paper consists of four levels or types of responsibility centers:

- Cost centers
- Revenue centers
- Profit centers
- Investment centers

A *cost center* **is a division of an organization that consumes resources while performing its responsibilities, yet has no direct involvement in generating sales or acquiring property.** Thus, managers of cost centers are evaluated on their ability to control costs. For example, manufacturing plant managers can influence materials, labor, and overhead costs, but they cannot set selling prices for products, manage marketing campaigns, or acquire equipment without approval from divisional or corporate-level management. Thus, to evaluate the performance of a manufacturing plant manager on profitability would not be consistent with the objective of evaluating managers on activities over which they have control. Additionally, cost center managers often are evaluated on their ability to meet quality standards and delivery schedules. The two manufacturing plants identified in Exhibit 3 are examples of cost centers.

A *revenue center* **is a division of an organization that has responsibility for generating sales.** Thus, managers of revenue centers often are responsible for meeting sales quotas and managing distribution channels. However, these managers do not control most of the costs that affect net income. Therefore, revenue center managers should be

Exhibit 3 American Paper Company—Organizational Chart

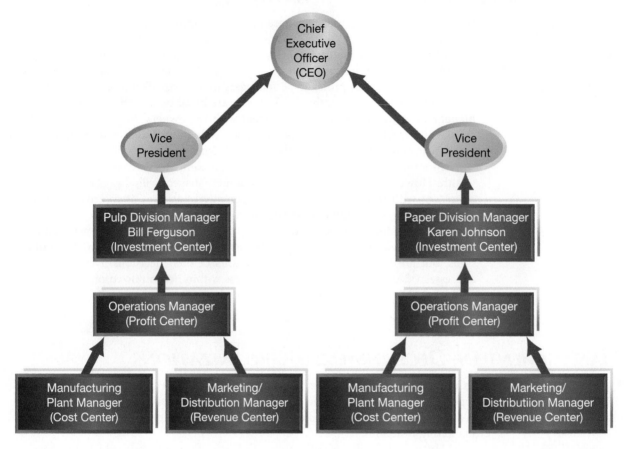

evaluated using sales, rather than income, as a performance criterion. In addition, revenue center managers may be responsible for managing inventory and may be evaluated using inventory measures. The Marketing and Distribution functions shown in Exhibit 3 are examples of revenue centers.

A *profit center* **is a division of an organization that is responsible for both generating sales and controlling costs and expenses.** Profit center managers typically have the responsibility for setting prices for products, determining product mix, and monitoring production activities. Thus, profit center managers are responsible for costs, sales volume, and profitability. As shown in Exhibit 3, American Paper has two operations managers whose departments function as profit centers. Since profitability is determined by the difference between sales revenue and costs, operations managers who are evaluated on profitability must have control over both variables.

An *investment center* **is a level within an organization that has the strategic responsibility for generating profits and managing assets.** In the American Paper example, division managers are considered investment center managers. Typically, performance measures such as return on assets (ROA) or a similar measure, return on investment (ROI), are used to evaluate investment center managers because they have control over costs, revenues, and assets. Investment center managers are evaluated using these measures because profit, or operating income, tells only part of the story about their effectiveness as managers. Typically, measures such as ROI or ROA are appropriate only if managers can determine the level of assets used by their area of responsibility. In this example, division managers can acquire and dispose of equipment. Thus, it is appropriate to evaluate division managers using ROA or ROI as a performance criterion. In addition, investment center managers are responsible for the strategic direction of the company. Thus, they are responsible for improving market share and successfully introducing new products.

Exhibit 4 summarizes responsibility centers often found within decentralized organizations and gives examples of relevant performance measures.

Exhibit 4

Performance Measures by Type of Responsibility Center

	Performance Measures
Cost centers	Manufacturing cost (materials, labor, overhead)
	Quality (defect rate)
	Percentage of on-time deliveries
Revenue centers	Sales volume in units
	Inventory turnover
	Sales revenue
Profit centers	Manufacturing costs
	Distribution costs
	Sales volume
	Profitability
Investment centers	ROI
	Market share
	Successful new product introductions

Benefits of Decentralization

A decentralized organization permits local managers, such as bank branch managers who are located far from corporate offices, to make certain decisions without approval from a central administrator. Localized decision making has many benefits for an organization. For example, local managers should be in touch with the economy and business conditions in their geographical areas; therefore, they often are in a better position to make informed judgments than their supervisors, who may be located hundreds of miles away.

The decentralized structure offers other benefits as well. Lower and middle managers are given the opportunity to develop and exercise their skills in preparation for greater responsibilities. Thus, a decentralized structure provides a training ground for future top-level managers. In addition, lower and middle managers' job satisfaction should be enhanced because they are allowed to have control over their areas of responsibility and should experience pride of ownership.

1 **SELF-STUDY PROBLEM** Assume you are the plant manager for a medium-sized company that manufactures a variety of types of telephones. The phones are produced by assembling an array of components, including electronic circuit boards that are purchased from another division within the company. Every Friday morning your corporate headquarters faxes you a production schedule indicating the type and amount of products to be produced during the following week. Thus, a major aspect of your job is meeting production schedules as efficiently as possible. Selling prices are set by senior-level management.

The following income statement and supporting schedule reflect sales, product costs, and expenses for your plant during the last twelve months. As you prepare for your annual performance evaluation, you recall a conversation from last year in which upper management set a net income target for products manufactured in your plant. However, you believe that certain costs on the income statement are beyond your control. Also, you wonder why net income is used to evaluate your performance at the plant level.

Required

A. In preparation for your meeting, identify the costs over which you have control.
B. Should your plant be evaluated as a cost center, revenue center, profit center, or investment center? Explain.

Income Statement

Sales	$100,000,000	
Cost of goods sold	75,000,000	
Gross margin		$25,000,000
Selling and administrative expenses:		
Depreciation on corporate aircraft	$ 1,000,000	
Sales commissions and other sales expenses	10,000,000	
Other direct plant-related expenses	13,000,000	
Total expenses		24,000,000
Net income		$ 1,000,000

Cost of Goods Sold Schedule

Beginning finished goods inventory	$ 5,000,000
Cost of goods manufactured	77,000,000*
Total	$82,000,000
Ending finished goods inventory	(7,000,000)
Cost of goods sold	$75,000,000

*Cost of goods manufactured includes materials, labor, and overhead costs. Overhead includes allocated corporate-level costs, such as quality assurance and computer time used for production scheduling.

The solution to Self-Study Problem 1 appears at the end of the chapter.

PERFORMANCE EVALUATION USING ROI

OBJECTIVE 3

Explain the historical context in which return on investment (ROI) was developed.

http://ingram.
swlearning.com

Find out about the DuPont Company today.

Recall that return on assets (ROA) is a ratio used to understand financial performance. This chapter considers a similar measure, return on investment (ROI), commonly used by internal managers to evaluate performance. The measures are used for different purposes. In this section, ROI is calculated and divided into its two components. In addition, the strengths of using ROI as a performance indicator to motivate managers are evaluated, and some criticisms of using ROI as the sole measurement of performance are considered.

Johnson and Kaplan[1] trace the roots of return on investment (ROI) to the **Du Pont Powder Company**. Three cousins purchased the assets of **E.I. du Pont de Nemours and Company** in exchange for corporate bonds and created the Du Pont Powder Company in 1903. The bond interest rate was based on the earnings of the old company. The new owners had to use the company's resources wisely in order to generate sufficient earnings to pay the bond interest and produce a profit. The cousins developed ROI for the purpose of assessing the performance of various departments and for making resource allocation decisions. They could not afford to invest assets in projects that earned less than the interest rate they were paying on the bonds issued to acquire their assets.

Of what benefit is ROI? Why don't managers simply compare the net incomes from their various operations to determine which is the most and least profitable? Net income tells only part of the story; other factors also must be considered. For example, assume that you are a senior manager in a corporation that has two divisions. Both division managers report directly to you. During the past year, both managers reported $500,000 in net income. Do you evaluate them equally? How would your answer change if you assume that one division employed assets of $2,500,000 while the other division

[1]   Johnson, H. Thomas, and Robert S. Kaplan. 1991. *Relevance Lost* (Boston: Harvard Business School Press).

employed assets of $5,000,000? A different picture now emerges; the smaller division (in terms of assets employed) produced the same net income as the larger division. This suggests that the smaller division is managed more efficiently than the larger division.

Recall that ROA can be divided into two components, profit margin and asset turnover. Profit margin is determined by dividing net income (adjusted for interest expense) by operating revenues (sales). Asset turnover is computed by dividing operating revenues (sales) by average total assets. From an external perspective, such analysis provides useful information about a company as a whole. For example, we can determine whether a company uses a high margin, low turnover strategy, in which the profit on each sale is high and the amount of sales compared to assets is low (as is the case with a phone company like **Southwestern Bell**), or a low margin, high turnover strategy, in which the profit on each sale is low and the amount of sales compared to assets is high (as is the case with a discount store like **Wal-Mart**). *Return on investment (ROI)* **is calculated by dividing operating income by operating assets.** Like ROA, ROI can be divided into two components, *margin* and *turnover*. As illustrated in Exhibit 5, *margin* **for ROI is operating income expressed as a percentage of sales.** For example, a 6 percent margin suggests that 6 cents of operating income are earned for every dollar of sales. *Turnover* **for ROI is sales divided by average operating assets employed.** A turnover value of 1.07 indicates that $1.07 of sales were generated for each dollar of operating assets used. Thus, as shown in Exhibit 5, ROI for the Pulp Division is margin times turnover ($0.064 = 0.06 \times 1.07$).

OBJECTIVE 4

Calculate ROI and economic value added. Explain how they can motivate behavior that is consistent or inconsistent with the strategic objectives of an organization.

Exhibit 5

ROI Data and Calculations for the Pulp and Paper Divisions

	Pulp	Paper
Average operating assets	$750,000,000	$200,000,000
Sales	800,000,000	275,000,000
Cost of goods sold	640,000,000	206,000,000
Operating expenses	112,000,000	58,000,000
Operating income	48,000,000	11,000,000

Pulp Division				
Margin	×	Turnover	=	ROI
$\dfrac{\text{Operating income}}{\text{Sales}}$	×	$\dfrac{\text{Sales}}{\text{Average operating assets}}$	=	ROI
$\dfrac{\$48,000,000}{\$800,000,000}$	×	$\dfrac{\$800,000,000}{\$750,000,000}$	=	ROI
0.06	×	1.07	=	0.064

Paper Division				
Margin	×	Turnover	=	ROI
$\dfrac{\text{Operating income}}{\text{Sales}}$	×	$\dfrac{\text{Sales}}{\text{Average operating assets}}$	=	ROI
$\dfrac{\$11,000,000}{\$275,000,000}$	×	$\dfrac{\$275,000,000}{\$200,000,000}$	=	ROI
0.04	×	1.38	=	0.055

Managers typically use *operating income* as the numerator of the margin calculation and *average operating assets* as the denominator of the turnover calculation. Operating income, rather than net income, is used because operating income is not affected by nonoperating revenues and expenses (such as interest and taxes). **Recall that** *operating income* is sales − (**cost of goods sold** + other operating expenses). *Operating assets* **are those assets controlled by the division; they include investments in cash, accounts receivable, inventory, and plant assets used in production.** Excluded from operating assets are assets such as land held for investment or long-term investments in marketable equity securities. While ROI and ROA are similar in their approach to measuring margin and turnover, ROI uses assets, revenues, and expenses that are more directly related to the daily operations of an investment center.

In the following paragraphs, information about American Paper Company is used to illustrate the calculation of margin, turnover, and ROI. In addition, the types of decisions managers make to improve ROI for their areas of responsibility are considered. From the organizational chart, note that the managers of the Pulp and Paper Divisions are Bill Ferguson and Karen Johnson, respectively. These division managers compete with each other; their salary levels, bonuses, and opportunities for promotion are related to their performance. Exhibit 5 presents information that permits us to evaluate the performance of each division using ROI.

Discussion of Results

The Pulp Division has a higher ROI than the Paper Division. An ROI of 0.064 means that for every dollar of assets, the Pulp Division earns almost six and a half cents. In contrast, the Paper Division earns only five and a half cents from every dollar of assets. How could Karen Johnson, manager of the Paper Division (who is embarrassed by her performance relative to the Pulp Division), improve her division's margin, turnover, and ROI?

Margin. To improve an investment center's margin, a manager must increase the size of operating income relative to sales. In other words, Johnson needs to earn more operating income from each dollar of sales. Since operating income is determined by subtracting cost of goods sold and operating expenses from sales, managers usually focus on cost control to improve the *margin* element of ROI. Of course, another alternative is to raise selling prices. However, managers typically are reluctant to raise prices because of competitive pressures. Margin may be expressed as follows:

$$\text{Margin} = \frac{\text{Operating income}}{\text{Sales}} = \frac{\text{Sales} - (\text{Cost of goods sold} + \text{Operating expenses})}{\text{Sales}}$$

Let's assume that Johnson decides to reduce costs in the next period to improve the division's margin. She predicts that she can achieve a cost savings of $2,750,000 by reducing production overhead costs (which become part of cost of goods sold) by $2,000,000 and reducing operating expenses by $750,000. Specifically, Johnson plans to change administrative procedures to eliminate costs associated with activities such as purchasing and payroll. She understands that if non-value-added work can be eliminated, the associated costs also will disappear. Most of the savings will be realized by reducing the size of support departments and eliminating unnecessary job classifications.

In addition, Johnson plans to realize savings from redesigning the product mix and manufacturing process. For example, analysts within the plant currently are examining the product mix to eliminate product types (termed "grades") that are manufactured in small batches, or that require special handling or expensive finishing operations. Exhibit 6 provides examples of the product and volume diversity within Johnson's plant. The process of changing the paper machine from the production of one grade to another results in scrap, and so Johnson expects to reduce the plant's scrap rate by making fewer grade changes. The number of grade changes can be reduced by eliminating products that are manufactured in small quantities. This should result in significant scrap reductions and cost savings. Eliminating some of the product line will not affect the plant's overall output. The remaining grades will simply be produced in larger quantities. Currently, demand for paper exceeds supply. Thus, Johnson is confident sales revenues will not decline. Additionally, she plans to redirect the quality control engineers' efforts to pulp inspection. If only top-quality raw materials are allowed into production, scrap rates and related costs should further decline.

Exhibit 6 Product and Volume Diversity within the Paper Plant

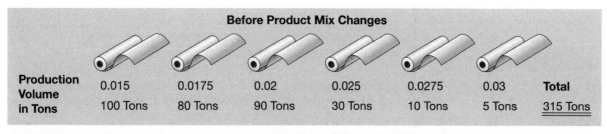

Before Product Mix Changes

Production Volume in Tons	0.015	0.0175	0.02	0.025	0.0275	0.03	Total
	100 Tons	80 Tons	90 Tons	30 Tons	10 Tons	5 Tons	315 Tons

After Product Mix Changes

Production Volume in Tons	0.015	0.0175	0.02	Total
	120 Tons	100 Tons	95 Tons	315 Tons

As illustrated in Exhibit 5, the Paper Division's cost of goods sold and operating expenses are $206,000,000 and $58,000,000, respectively. Let's evaluate the Paper Division's margin under the proposed cost-cutting program as follows:

$$\text{Margin} = \frac{\text{Operating income}}{\text{Sales}} = \frac{\text{Sales} - (\text{Cost of goods sold} + \text{Operating expenses})}{\text{Sales}}$$

$$0.05 = \frac{\$13,750,000}{\$275,000,000} = \frac{\$275,000,000 - (\$206,000,000 - \$2,000,000 + \$58,000,000 - \$750,000)}{\$275,000,000}$$

$$= 0.05$$

This calculation indicates that the Paper Division's margin should improve from 0.04 to 0.05 after establishing the cost-cutting program. Therefore, if Johnson's predictions are correct, the cost-cutting program will improve the division's ROI from 0.055 to 0.069, as follows:

	Margin	×	Turnover	=	ROI
Paper Division ROI before cost-cutting program	0.04	×	1.38	=	0.055
Paper Division ROI after cost-cutting program	0.05	×	1.38	=	0.069

In addition to cost-cutting strategies, managers also can improve ROI by effectively managing assets under their control. The next section addresses turnover decisions.

Turnover. Sales are divided by operating assets to calculate turnover. Because larger turnover values are preferred to smaller values, managers are motivated to keep asset levels low while maintaining or increasing sales levels. Let's use the information from Exhibit 5 to illustrate the concept of turnover and to consider the types of decisions managers may make in an attempt to improve turnover within their area of responsibility.

Assume that Johnson has identified assets in the form of inventory, accounts receivable, and equipment totaling $25,000,000 that can be eliminated. For example, she plans to aggressively pursue collections of accounts receivable. She plans to permanently reduce the level of accounts receivable and submit excess cash to the corporate offices. In addition, by reducing the level of raw materials, finished goods, and supplies inventory, Johnson can reduce the asset base of her plant. She may do this by employing just-in-time inventory techniques. Modifying the product line and manufacturing process may make certain types of equipment unnecessary. Thus, further decreases in the asset base will be possible. How would these reductions affect the Paper Division's turnover ratio? After removing $25,000,000 from the asset base, turnover is calculated as follows:

$$\text{Turnover} = \frac{\text{Sales}}{\text{Operating assets}} = \frac{\$275,000,000}{\$200,000,000 - \$25,000,000} = 1.57$$

This calculation indicates that eliminating $25,000,000 from the asset base improves turnover from 1.38 (before reducing the asset level) to 1.57 (after reducing the asset level).

How does improving the turnover ratio affect the Paper Division's ROI? First, let's look at the improvement in ROI attributable only to improved turnover. Then we calculate the predicted ROI if both margin and turnover ratio are improved.

	Margin	×	Turnover	=	ROI
Paper Division ROI—improved turnover only	0.04	×	1.57	=	0.063

If Johnson improved only turnover, without undertaking a cost-cutting campaign, her division's ROI would improve from 0.055 to 0.063.

However, by improving both margin and turnover, Johnson can report an ROI of 0.079, as follows:

	Margin	×	Turnover	=	ROI
Paper Division ROI—improved margin and turnover	0.05	×	1.57	=	0.079

This analysis shows that Johnson can improve ROI *in the short run* by increasing margin, turnover, or both margin and turnover simultaneously. In a competitive environment, managers make decisions to improve the measures that are used to evaluate their performance. Unfortunately, a focus on short-term performance may have disastrous long-term consequences.

Criticisms of Using ROI to Evaluate Performance

Earlier, this chapter discussed managers' roles as agents and the objective of selecting performance measures that align the interests of agents with those of owners. How can using ROI as a performance indicator achieve this objective? What does it communicate to managers? Using ROI instructs managers to earn the greatest net income possible, while minimizing assets employed. Thus, managers are motivated to increase the numerator and to reduce the denominator of the ROI calculation. The discussion of margin identified strategies to increase the income component (numerator) of the ROI calculation, while the discussion of turnover considered methods to reduce the average operating asset level (denominator) of the ROI calculation.

Some accountants argue that focusing on ROI promotes short-sighted decision making that can harm a company in the long run. The following discussion gives examples of decisions that improve ROI in the short run but may have negative long-term effects. The first set of examples involves decisions affecting the margin component of ROI. Since managers are encouraged to reduce operating costs and administrative expenses, they may be encouraged to sacrifice "investments" necessary for future growth. Such investments include research and development (R&D) expenses.

Generally accepted accounting principles (GAAP) require companies to expense R&D in the period incurred, even though most companies view R&D as an investment to benefit future periods. By cutting R&D expenses, managers may realize an immediate improvement in operating income. However, the long-term consequences of a reduced R&D budget may include less competitive products, which are likely to lead to lost market share and lower profitability.

Managers also may capture short-term savings by reducing maintenance expenditures for manufacturing equipment. Typically, maintenance costs, such as lubricants, spare parts, and salaries of maintenance crews, are treated as overhead cost items. Therefore, trimming maintenance costs may improve a division's operating income in the short run. However, a reduced maintenance program may result in very large equipment repair or replacement costs in the future.

Finally, since using ROI encourages reduced asset levels, some managers may be reluctant to make the investments in plant assets necessary to ensure superior quality and reliable product delivery. Therefore, while ROI has many positive attributes as a performance measure, if used improperly it may encourage managers to make short-term decisions that negatively affect long-term performance.

Exhibit 7 summarizes some of the criticisms of using ROI as the only measure of performance.

Economic Value Added Compared to ROI

Chapter M1 briefly introduced the concept of economic value added,[2] a new term for a traditional concept, residual income. Companies must provide an adequate return to

Exhibit 7
Criticisms of Using ROI as the Only Measure of Performance

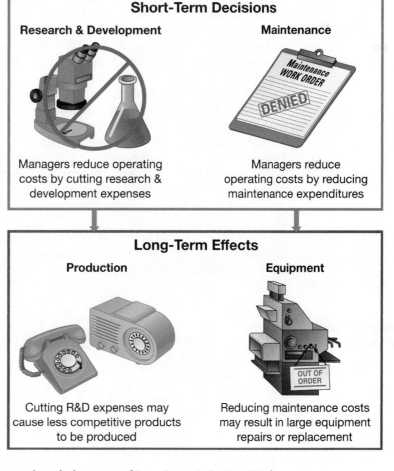

ROI Downside

Short-Term Decisions

Research & Development

Managers reduce operating costs by cutting research & development expenses

Maintenance

Managers reduce operating costs by reducing maintenance expenditures

Long-Term Effects

Production

Cutting R&D expenses may cause less competitive products to be produced

Equipment

Reducing maintenance costs may result in large equipment repairs or replacement

---

[2] EVA is a trademarked measure of Stern Stuart & Co., New York.

encourage investors to help finance the company's activities. This return represents a cost to the company. The first step in calculating economic value added involves producing an income statement. After calculating operating income, the cost of investors' capital is deducted. The result is economic value added. Examples of organizations that have adopted economic value added concepts include **Best Buy**, **California Public Employees Retirement System**, **Coca-Cola**, **Quaker Oats**, and **Bank of America**.[3]

To illustrate residual value concepts, we use the Western Division of Crimson Company. Crimson Company is a multi-divisional company with offices located across the North American continent. Assume Crimson Company's investors require a 20 percent return on their invested capital. The division manager of the Western Division employs invested capital of $1,000,000. As shown in Exhibit 8, Western Division management produced an economic value added of $50,000. Thus, they produced revenues in excess of all operating and capital costs.

Exhibit 8

Residual Income Calculation for the Western Division

Sales	$2,000,000
Cost of goods sold	1,300,000
Gross profit	$ 700,000
General selling and administrative costs	450,000
Operating income	$ 250,000
Cost of capital (0.20 × $1,000,000)	200,000
Economic value added	$ 50,000

Using financial information presented in Exhibit 8 we can calculate ROI for the Western Division. Earlier in this chapter we used average operating assets as the denominator for the ROI calculation. For purposes of comparison, we assume invested capital was used to acquire operating assets. Thus, in our example, operating assets and invested capital are the same. ROI for the Western Division is calculated as follows: Operating income ÷ average operating assets ($250,000 ÷ $1,000,000 = 0.25). The Western Division produced an ROI of 0.25 and an economic value added of $50,000. Which measure should corporate managers use to assess a division manager's performance?

Both ROI and economic value added have strengths and weaknesses. ROI permits managers to compare performance across large and small divisions. Using ROI as a performance measure, operating income is divided by asset size to capture a manager's efficiency in using assets to produce operating income. Alternatively, economic value added is not as useful in comparing divisions of different sizes because economic value added is not divided by assets employed. However, using ROI as a performance measure also may discourage managers from making investments that are good for the company.

Using the Western Division as an example, assume the manager could make an investment in a new product line. Also, assume the investment is expected to produce the financial results shown in Exhibit 9.

Exhibit 9

The Western Division Forecast for a New Product Line

Sales	$600,000
Cost of goods sold	450,000
Gross profit	$150,000
General selling and administrative costs	95,000
Operating income	$ 55,000
Cost of capital (0.20 × $250,000)	50,000
Economic value added	$ 5,000

---

[3] Lucey, Brian, and Louise Turner. 1999. Out with the Old, In with the New? *Accountancy Ireland* (December): 14–15.

Management believes an investment of $250,000 will produce an operating income of $55,000. If forecasts are correct, the new investment will generate an ROI of 22 percent ($55,000 ÷ $250,000). If management is rewarded based on ROI, they will not invest in the new line. Why? Currently the Western Division is earning an ROI of 25 percent. The new investment will earn only 22 percent. Thus, the new investment will reduce the division's ROI.

If division management were evaluated using economic value added, rather than ROI, would they invest in the new product line? Yes, because the investment produces a *positive* economic value added. The new investment is expected to generate revenues sufficient to satisfy all operating and capital costs. The company would be better off with the investment than without it. Thus, in this case, economic value added would motivate management to make the correct investment decision, while ROI would not.

How do managers design performance measurement systems that encourage behavior consistent with the long-term objectives of an organization? The next section considers an evaluation method that permits performance criteria to be linked to a company's strategy. Both financial and nonfinancial performance criteria are used in the approach termed the balanced scorecard.

THE BALANCED SCORECARD APPROACH

OBJECTIVE 5

Discuss the four elements of the balanced scorecard approach to evaluating performance.

http://ingram.
swlearning.com

Learn more about the
balanced scorecard.

Recall that Seth and Erin were discussing the use of both financial and nonfinancial measures in their new performance measurement system. They want a few carefully selected measures to help guide managers in their decision making. This section considers the balanced scorecard as a method for providing structure to the design of a performance measurement system.

People use information continuously to evaluate their environment and to help them make appropriate decisions. For example, if you drove a car to class today, you probably monitored your speed, checked the rear-view and side-view mirrors to evaluate the position of other vehicles relative to yours, glanced at the gasoline gauge, and so forth. However, while the rear-view mirror is certainly an important piece of safety equipment, driving your car using only the rear-view mirror would produce disastrous results. People must view and react to many different types of performance measures at the same time.

Some accountants have argued that ignoring important nonfinancial performance measures while focusing exclusively on financial measures can spell disaster for organizations. Therefore, managers need a short list of key indicators that signal current as well as future performance. A "balanced scorecard" approach has been used by some companies to bring together many different aspects of their corporate *strategy* in one report. **The** *balanced scorecard* **has key performance criteria in four categories: financial, customer satisfaction, internal business processes, and learning and growth.** Thus, operating performance measures are developed that are consistent with an organization's strategic goals. In addition, the balanced scorecard prevents managers from improving only one aspect of performance while simultaneously allowing other important aspects of performance to decline.

The balanced scorecard approach to performance evaluation is based on linking a company's strategic goals with specific, concrete measures designed to motivate behavior consistent with factors that will help the organization achieve success in the long run. The approach views a financial measure, such as ROI, as an important indicator, but not the only measure at which managers must excel. Thus, the approach represents a broader, more balanced view of an organization's success in achieving its long-term strategic goals.

Financial performance measures motivate managers to consider how the company looks in the eyes of the shareholders. Typically, managers are evaluated using criteria such as profitability, ROI, market share, and cash flow. Thus, managers are encouraged to make decisions that increase revenues, contain costs, or both.

In line with the objectives of total quality management (TQM), the balanced score-card contains a category of indicators that encourage managers to consider how their company looks in the eyes of customers. Customer satisfaction performance measures may include the percentage of on-time deliveries and customer response time for service or other assistance. When customer satisfaction is included as a key performance indicator, managers are encouraged to make decisions consistent with customers' needs.

Managers who are evaluated by internal business criteria ask themselves, "At what must we excel?" Thus, the link to customer satisfaction is made explicit. Managers are encouraged to improve processes internally to ensure customer satisfaction. Internal business indicators include measures that promote manufacturing excellence, such as cycle time, scrap rate, and lead time from placing an order until delivery. Managers are encouraged to improve internal processes that add value for customers. Once again, the balanced scorecard emphasizes long-term investments and continuous improvement, rather than short-term savings from cost reductions.

The learning and growth category requires management to consider the question, "What is necessary to meet the ambitious goals of the financial, customer, and internal-business perspectives?" Common objectives for the learning and growth category include improving employee skills through training, providing adequate resources to employees who strive to meet difficult targets, empowering employees to make decisions, and motivating employees with meaningful rewards when goals are met. Companies that have found a strategic payoff from implementing balanced scorecard concepts include **Whirlpool Europe**, **Lands' End Direct Merchants**, and **Bass Brewers**.[4]

Exhibit 10 illustrates the relationships among the various components of the balanced scorecard, using the Paper Division of American Paper Company as an example.

Exhibit 10

Performance Measures Using the Balanced Scorecard Approach for the Paper Division of American Paper Company

Perspective	Actual	Desired
Financial		
ROI	0.055	0.08
Customer		
On-time deliveries	80%	85%
Response time to inquiries	2 days	3 hours
Internal Business Processes		
Cycle time	6 weeks	5 weeks
Scrap rate	5%	2%
Manufacturing lead time	10 hours	8 hours
Learning and Growth		
Percentage of employees with specialized training or skills	8%	25%

Using American Paper Company as an example, how would Johnson's decision to restructure the division and reduce costs affect other important factors identified by a balanced scorecard approach? Certainly reducing the scrap rate (and presumably improving the quality of products delivered to customers) would be viewed favorably from the customer perspective. Additionally, reducing the number of different products would result in faster cycle and delivery times. However, her strategy to pursue collections of accounts receivable aggressively may have an adverse effect on customer relations (though in the short run cash flow would be improved).[5] Finally, using ROI as a

---

[4] Anonymous. 1999. Building and Implementing a Balanced Scorecard. Management Services; Enfield (February): Vol. 43.

[5] Customers who wish to purchase all of their paper from one supplier may be disappointed to learn that Johnson no longer produces a full line of products. These customers may take all of their business elsewhere.

measure does not encourage Johnson to invest resources in seeking opportunities to develop new products. In a mature industry such as pulp and paper, innovation may result in long-term financial rewards.

This section has considered how to evaluate performance in decentralized organizations and how to motivate behavior to achieve long-term success. The next section examines how transfer pricing policies can affect decisions made by divisional managers. Often, financially based performance measures encourage managers to optimize divisional earnings, yet harm the overall organization. Thus, transfer pricing and performance measurement issues are of key importance to managers in decentralized organizations.

Case in Point

http://ingram.
swlearning.com

Learn more about
Southwest Airlines.

Balanced Scorecard

Southwest Airlines Co. has developed a variety of balanced scorecards for use throughout the organization. Historically, accountants have understood terms such as "profit and loss," while operations personnel understood terms such as "fast ground turnaround." The company hopes the balanced scorecard will associate rapidly preparing an airplane for its next flight with profitability. Southwest plans to continue collecting hundreds of detailed operational measures; however, the balanced scorecard will be used to display a few of the most important ones. The company wants management to focus on key measurements that impact financial performance.

Source: 2003. Balanced Scorecard. *Computerworld* (February 17).

---

2 SELF-STUDY PROBLEM

WebTUTOR Advantage

Refer to the financial information presented in Self-Study Problem 1. In addition to the financial statement data, your records indicate that the division employed operating assets valued at $20,000,000.

Required

A. Calculate the division's operating profit margin and describe various ways a manager may improve his or her performance with respect to operating profit margin.
B. Calculate the division's turnover and describe various ways a manager may improve his or her performance with respect to turnover.
C. Calculate the division's ROI.
D. What are some of the criticisms of using ROI as the sole performance measure?
E. Identify other measures that may promote organizational success in the long run.

The solution to Self-Study Problem 2 appears at the end of the chapter.

TRANSFER PRICING

OBJECTIVE 6

Explain how a manager who acts in the best interests of a division may harm the company as a whole.

Transfer pricing **involves setting appropriate selling prices for goods or services when both buyer and seller are within the same company.** Thus, transfer pricing decisions typically arise within multi-divisional organizations. In a decentralized business, managers are free to make many decisions locally. Some of the decisions managers make relate to the acquisition of materials, labor, and overhead to be used in production. When a corporation has many divisions, situations often occur in which one division buys products from another division. Because internal transfer prices affect revenues (for the selling division) and costs (for the buying division), transfer pricing policies affect a division's ROI. Thus, divisional managers are very interested in the price at which goods are transferred internally.

The classical transfer pricing problem involves setting a transfer pricing policy that encourages managers to act in the best interests of the overall organization. Naturally, when *divisional* managers are evaluated by a measure such as ROI, they take actions that produce the highest possible *divisional* ROI. To maximize ROI, what options are available to a manager? Since ROI boils down to operating income ÷ operating assets, the manager has an incentive to increase income or reduce assets (or some combination of the two). For purposes of our discussion, let's focus on the management of operating income. If you are Bill Ferguson, manager of the Pulp Division, you wish to receive the highest possible price for pulp sold to the Paper Division. On the other hand, if you are Karen Johnson, manager of the Paper Division, you maximize ROI by paying the lowest possible price for raw materials (assuming quality is not affected adversely). As a result of divisional competition and performance evaluations exclusively based on ROI, the following scenario is unfolding within American Paper Company.

The Scenario

Karen Johnson, manager of the Paper Division, was unhappy with her division's performance in comparison to that of the Pulp Division (refer to Exhibit 5). Her division purchased all of its raw materials from the Pulp Division at a transfer price of $400 per ton. However, Karen wondered if she could outsource (buy pulp from an outside supplier) at a cost below that quoted by her sister division. Since the divisions were decentralized and had a *market-based* transfer pricing policy, she was free to purchase raw materials from any source. A *market-based transfer pricing policy* **requires buyers and sellers to transfer goods based on externally verifiable market prices.** Thus, bids from outside vendors often are used to establish a market price to serve as a basis for transferring goods.

Karen knew that market prices for pulp had been falling because of worldwide oversupply. Thus, she requested a bid from Southland Pulp Company to determine if the transfer price charged by her sister division was competitive. This morning, a bid of $350 per ton arrived by fax from Southland. The bid specified that to qualify for the reduced price of $350 per ton, the Paper Division must purchase one-half of its annual demand from Southland. Karen quickly made a few computations to determine the potential impact on her division's ROI.

She understood that her division's cost of goods sold ($206,000,000, as shown in Exhibit 5) represented pulp costs as well as other manufacturing costs incurred by her division to convert pulp into paper. She estimated that one-half of the cost of goods sold value, $103,000,000 ($206,000,000 ÷ 2 = $103,000,000), represented pulp costs. The remaining portion of the cost of goods sold value represented labor, electricity, water, chemicals, and overhead costs for depreciation and supervision. Thus, "If our annual pulp cost is $103,000,000 at an average of $400 per ton, we must have used 257,500 ($103,000,000 ÷ $400) tons last year," Karen reasoned. "Southland wants one-half of our volume, or 128,750 tons."

"Wow," Karen said under her breath. "Bill isn't going to like losing the sale of almost 130,000 tons, especially in this slow market."

Karen continued to work with the bid. "Let's see, what's the bottom-line savings if I agree to this deal? Okay, at a savings of $50 per ton ($400 from Bill versus $350 from Southland), that works out to be a total savings of $6,437,500 ($50 per ton × 128,750 tons to be purchased). What does that do for my ROI?" Karen said to herself as she continued to enter values into her calculator.

"Our operating income was $11,000,000, to which we can add an expected savings of $6,437,500. That results in an estimated operating income of $17,437,500. Now, if I divide by operating assets of $200,000,000, I have a predicted ROI of 0.087."

Karen reclined at her desk. The prospects for outsourcing one-half of her pulp requirements looked promising. Assuming that her sales and other expenses remained at a constant level, she could improve the division's ROI from 0.055 to 0.087, a whopping

60 percent improvement $[0.58 = (0.087 - 0.055) \div 0.055]$! Karen did not look forward to announcing her intentions to Bill Ferguson, manager of the Pulp Division.

Bill had been in a bad mood recently because of soft market conditions and a union contract that required a 40-hour work week for each of his three shifts. Because of sluggish demand, each shift required only 30 hours per week in production time. The remaining 10 hours were spent maintaining equipment and making general repairs. Therefore, Bill was watching sales volume fall while most of the division's manufacturing costs continued unchanged. Karen was certain that her decision to outsource one-half of the Paper Division's pulp requirements would send shock waves throughout the corporation.

Karen was correct. Her company subscribed to a "hands-off" policy with regard to letting divisional managers make their own decisions. However, Karen contacted Deborah Truth, a vice president at the corporate office, and revealed her intention of acquiring one-half of her pulp requirements from an external supplier. Karen's phone rang, and Deborah was on the other end of the line requesting a meeting with both divisional managers as soon as possible to discuss their transfer pricing problem.

A few days later, Karen made her way from the airport to the corporate offices. Because her flight had arrived before Bill's, she had a few minutes to review her notes before the meeting. Deborah was the next to enter the conference room, and finally Bill arrived. Following greetings and casual chatter, Deborah began the meeting by referring to the analysis Karen had faxed after receiving the bid from Southland.

"You must admit," Karen began, "a $50 savings per ton can have a dramatic effect on my division's profitability. That represents a 13 percent price reduction. Do you realize how difficult it would be to reduce operating costs by that amount and still maintain the same level of quality?"

Bill could hardly contain himself any longer. "Karen, let's talk about quality. The first time you ship a load of unbleached paper that contains strands of chlorinated fibers, there will be trouble." Bill was referring to "twilight pulp" that is temporarily produced between production runs of bleached and unbleached pulp. This "twilight" mixture is produced until the system cleans out all the chlorine from the pulp mill. Bill's mill has stringent quality control measures to prevent the shipment of mixed, or twilight, pulp.

Karen understood Bill's point. Customers who are environmentally sensitive will not tolerate bleached fibers mixed with environmentally friendly "unbleached" fibers. She certainly had no complaints about the quality she was receiving from Bill.

"And what about reliable delivery?" Bill continued. "In a continuous-process manufacturing environment, such as pulp and paper, you know very well what happens if production interruptions occur. You can't just turn your paper machines on and off like a saw. Remember the studies that show how scrap costs are associated with paper machine downtime? If you start messing around with your process and making late shipments yourself, you'll soon see that 13 percent cost savings evaporate into thin air."

Karen knew that Bill was right. A paper process is complex. Any production interruption introduces instabilities into the process, with undesirable consequences. However, Karen also knew that Bill was suggesting that Southland's quality was poor and their delivery times were unreliable. Admittedly, Karen had never had a problem with quality or on-time delivery from Bill's division.

Bill was on a roll, and he continued his assault against Southland. "Furthermore, I'll bet Southland will give you one contract at that price and later will raise their bid. I think they are bidding below market price so that they can get their foot in the door."

OBJECTIVE 7

Discuss various transfer pricing methods that have been developed to influence managerial behavior.

Deborah considered all that had taken place. She knew why Bill was fighting to keep Karen's business. Since Bill had idle capacity (the division could produce more pulp than the market currently required), his production costs per unit were increasing. "Let's try to remember we are all on the same team here," Deborah began. "Bill has made some good points regarding quality, delivery reliability, and cost. We need to work together to make sure that American Paper Company doesn't suffer as a result of decisions that improve divisional performance." Deborah walked to the board at the head of the conference table and wrote the following outline:

TRANSFER PRICING METHODS

A. Market-based   B. Cost-based   C. Negotiated
                    Variable cost
                    Fully absorbed

"What do you two remember from your college accounting course about different ways to set up transfer pricing policies?" Deborah asked.

"Not much," admitted Bill. "I memorized some formulas, but beyond that . . ."

"Then, let's reason through these methods and consider the pros and cons of each. Maybe we can find a mutually agreeable solution to our transfer pricing problems," continued Deborah.

"Market-based. That's our existing policy," volunteered Karen. "The market determines the value at which transfers take place. As a buyer, I'm in favor of a market-based approach because it keeps guys like Bill honest."

Karen continued, "I operate a division that sells paper to the outside market at competitive prices. If my costs are too high, I can't compete. Therefore, using a market-based policy throughout the company seems to be a control that forces our internal divisions to be competitive with those outside our company. I'll buy from Bill if he meets the external price. I'd like to keep the business within the company."

Bill walked to the board and scribbled the following numbers:

Variable cost per ton $110
Fixed cost per ton   250
Total cost per ton $360

"Karen," he said, "I recently completed a major capital expansion at my plant. As a result, I estimate that next year my cost structure will look like this. As you can see, if I sell at $350 a ton, I won't even cover my costs. My variable costs include items such as timber, chemicals, water, and electricity; however, the majority of my costs are fixed. These fixed costs include depreciation on my plant equipment and most labor costs. Unfortunately, those costs will be incurred whether the machines are making pulp or not."

Karen looked at the figures. She now understood why Bill was fighting so hard to convince her to reject the Southland bid. If Bill's production volume declined further, the cost of each ton would become larger because his fixed costs would be spread over fewer tons. To cover his higher unit costs, he would have to raise prices. However, raising prices would cause further declines in volume, which in turn would raise his unit costs—definitely not a happy scenario.

Deborah interjected, "Bill, you have moved the discussion to the topic of cost-based transfer pricing policies. Leave your numbers on the board. Some accountants advocate using a cost-based approach," she added. "However, two distinct versions of cost definition emerge, variable and fully absorbed. Variable-cost transfer prices include only variable manufacturing costs, while fully absorbed transfer prices include both variable and fixed manufacturing costs."

Karen spoke quickly, "As a buyer, I'd be in favor of a cost-based approach if cost is defined as variable cost."

Bill retorted, "Sure you would. Your profits would look great because you would leave me holding the bag for all the fixed costs of your raw materials production. I could not pass those along to you. How could you expect me to show a profit under those circumstances?"

Deborah intervened. "Most companies do not use a variable-cost transfer policy for that reason. The buyer's profitability is overstated, and the seller's profitability is understated."

Bill added, "What about using a full-cost approach, one that includes both variable and fixed costs? Admittedly, I would not earn a profit, but at least I could recover my costs. Since sales to Karen represent only a portion of my total sales volume, a breakeven situation would not hurt my division's profitability too badly."

Karen squirmed in her seat. "Bill, remember our discussion about market-based policies. I really don't want to have my profitability affected by your decisions. If your costs increase, a full-cost transfer price permits you simply to pass them along to me. I find that unacceptable."

Deborah interjected, "Perhaps there is room for compromise. The third method for determining transfer prices is through negotiation. Perhaps we can put aside our divisional interests momentarily and look at the problem from the corporate point of view." Deborah returned to the board and wrote the following equation:

Transfer price = Variable cost + Opportunity cost

"Bill, is this the equation you memorized for your accounting class?" asked Deborah.

"I think so. Somehow it looks familiar," responded Bill.

"Karen, what is the most you would be willing to pay per ton?" Deborah asked.

"I can't see why I should pay more than Southland's bid of $350, all other things being equal," responded Karen.

Deborah wrote $350 on the board with the word "Ceiling" beside it. Next, she turned to Bill. "What is the lowest price you would be willing to accept?"

"Deborah, I've already told you. I need $400 per ton to cover my costs and make a decent profit," responded Bill.

"Let's step back a moment. What is American Paper Company's cost to make a ton of pulp?" asked Deborah.

"Look at the board. It's $360 per ton," responded Bill.

"But, what is our direct out-of-pocket cost?" continued Deborah.

"Are you talking about my variable cost of $110 per ton?" asked Bill.

"Exactly," said Deborah. "You have already told us that your fixed costs are incurred whether you make pulp or not. Thus, let's use your variable cost as a floor, below which you would never consider selling the product." Deborah completed the board, which now looked like this:

Transfer price = Variable cost + Opportunity cost
Ceiling $350
Floor $110

Deborah began the discussion. "Bill, if you could sell every ton you could produce at $400, would you be willing to negotiate with Karen for a lower price?"

"Of course not. Why should I? If I can sell everything I can make at $400 per ton, why should I take less?"

"Let's put your answer into our formula," responded Deborah. "In other words, your 'opportunity cost' of taking a ton off the market and selling it to Karen is the difference between the selling price of $400 and your variable costs of $110, as follows:"

selling price	*$400*
variable cost	*110*
Contribution margin (opportunity cost)	*$290*

"If we add your variable cost to the opportunity cost, our transfer price formula gives us a value of $400, or the original selling price."

$$\text{Transfer price} = \text{Variable cost} + \text{Opportunity cost}$$
$$\$400 \qquad\qquad = 110 \qquad\qquad + 290$$

"That makes sense," replied Bill. " Since I can sell all I can make at $400 per ton, the formula says that if Karen wants some of my tons, she will have to pay $400 for them. Otherwise, I'll sell them to other customers."

"Exactly," responded Deborah.

"But, Bill, aren't you forgetting something?" interjected Karen. "You have excess capacity—you can't sell everything you make. Thus, you are not forgoing profits by selling me a ton of product because you cannot sell that product to someone else. Your opportunity cost is zero when you have excess capacity. According to Deborah's model, if your opportunity cost is zero, the transfer price should be $110, your variable cost. When you have idle capacity, the opportunity cost becomes zero because external sales are not forgone."

Karen walked to the board and plugged new numbers into the equation as follows:

$$\text{Transfer price} = \text{Variable cost} + \text{Opportunity cost}$$
$$\$110 \qquad\qquad = 110 \qquad\qquad + 0$$

"Karen, you seem to be suggesting that I sell to you at variable cost. We already dismissed that plan when we discussed cost-based transfer policies."

Deborah once again broke into the conversation. "What do these calculations suggest? From a company-wide viewpoint, what can we learn from our model?"

Bill spoke first. "Since I have excess capacity, the model says that the company is better off if I sell to Karen at a price that at least covers my variable costs. Since my fixed costs are incurred whether I produce or not, they are not relevant to the decision. From the company's perspective, the variable cost to produce pulp is $110; if we purchase it from Southland, the variable cost to the company is $350. Thus, the company would lose $240 per ton."

Karen responded, "So that's what the floor and ceiling represent. The floor represents the minimum acceptable transfer price to the seller, and the ceiling represents the maximum acceptable transfer price to the buyer."

"Exactly," said Deborah.

Bill spoke after a few moments of thought. "Deborah, you've certainly given us a lot to think about. But somehow, I can't help but believe that the problem is not with the transfer pricing policy, but rather with our performance evaluation policies. Everything is tied to divisional profitability and ROI. Who knows how many times decisions are made that may affect corporate profitability in the long run, but in the short run make managers look good on paper."

Deborah agreed. "That sounds like a problem for another day. Think about what we discussed and let me know what you decide. I appreciate the time you took from your busy schedules to meet with me today. Have a safe flight home."

As Karen and Bill left the room, they both knew that corporate management would not permit them to optimize divisional performance at the expense of the overall organization. American Paper was decentralized; however, corporate management had sent a strong signal regarding the outsourcing decision. Both Karen and Bill knew that the transfers would take place internally; however, they had a great deal of work still to do to negotiate a transfer price acceptable to both of them.

Transfer Pricing Summary

Given the preceding exchanges, how can we summarize the key issues with regard to transfer pricing? The exclusive use of financially based performance measures such as ROI and profitability may encourage managers to make decisions that benefit their divisions, but at the same time harm the overall organization. The use of market-based transfer prices helps managers assess their efficiency with respect to external companies producing similar products. Market-based transfer pricing policies rely on external market prices for identical (or comparable) goods or services to establish transfer prices. Cost-based transfer prices are easy to calculate and apply; however, their use can cause problems because inefficiencies may be passed along to subsequent departments. *Cost-based transfer pricing policies* **use either full cost or variable cost as a basis for determining a transfer price.** *Negotiated transfer pricing policies* **permit managers to consider factors such as cost and external market prices when negotiating a mutually acceptable transfer price between two business units.**

Capacity issues should affect decisions concerning appropriate transfer prices. If a division has excess capacity, a transfer price between the variable cost of the selling division and the outside market price may be negotiated. Theoretically, if a company has excess capacity (thus, zero opportunity cost), it would be worse off if it purchased goods from an external supplier at a purchase price that exceeded the internal variable cost. Exhibit 11 summarizes the key points of each of the major transfer pricing methods.

LEARNING NOTE

When divisions sell goods exclusively to other divisions within a company, market-based and negotiated transfer pricing policies generally are not used. If a division does not sell to external customers, the division should be evaluated as a cost center, rather than as a profit center, and transfers should take place at standard costs. The division managers' performance would be based on their ability to control costs when compared to standards.

Case in Point

Transfer Pricing and the IRS

Transfer pricing problems can occur within multi-divisional corporations if divisions buy and sell among themselves. The problems become even more complex if divisions are located in different states or countries. Typically, managers prefer to transfer costs from divisions in states (or countries) having low tax rates into divisions in states (or countries) having higher tax rates. Such a strategy reduces a company's tax payments because subtracting higher costs from revenues results in lower taxable income. Because of adverse tax consequences, tax authorities work diligently to ensure corporations transfer costs appropriately.

Prior to the May 2002 merger of **Compaq Computer Corporation** with **Hewlett-Packard Corporation**, the IRS challenged Compaq's transfer pricing policies in tax court. The IRS believed Compaq was transferring printed circuit assemblies from its Singapore division at inflated prices. As a result, the IRS believed Compaq's cost of goods sold was too high and its taxable income was too low. Fortunately, Compaq also had purchased printed circuit assemblies from external suppliers at prices comparable to the company's internal transfer price. Thus, Compaq could show the transfer price was not overstated, based on market conditions. The IRS lost the case.

Source: Lowell, Cym H. 1999. Compaq: A Rare Taxpayer Victory in a Transfer Pricing Case. *Journal of International Taxation.* Warren Gorham Lamont (October): 10–43.

MANAGEMENT OF DECENTRALIZED SERVICE ORGANIZATIONS

OBJECTIVE 8

Explain how the performance of managers can be evaluated in decentralized service organizations.

In this chapter, a manufacturing company was used to demonstrate issues facing decentralized organizations. However, managers of service organizations face many of the same issues. For example, banks often have branch offices in various locations. Rather than referring all loan applications to a centralized loan committee, branch managers are given authority to make certain types of lending decisions. Thus, a decentralized structure often permits faster processing of loan applications. In addition, local managers

Exhibit 11
Transfer Pricing
Methods

Cost-based
Strengths: Cost-based transfer pricing methods are easy to apply because standard (or actual) product costs generally are available from the accounting system.
Weaknesses: Cost-based transfer pricing methods do not encourage and reward efficiency. Often, costs are transferred from one department to the next without concern for the price at which the final product will sell.

Market-based
Strengths: Market-based transfer pricing methods force departmental managers to be as cost-efficient as the best competitor.
Weaknesses: Market-based transfer pricing methods require time and effort because external bids must be acquired and evaluated.

Negotiated
Strengths: Negotiated transfer pricing methods encourage dialogue among division managers. Such conversations may promote transfers internally when they are in the best interest of the overall company. For example, when excess capacity exists, the opportunity cost is zero. Thus, the company will be better off if an internal transfer is made.
Weaknesses: Negotiated transfer pricing methods take management time and can result in stronger negotiators acquiring better deals. Thus, performance may be affected by negotiating skills rather than by a manager's ability to control costs.

may better understand the risks associated with granting loans if they are familiar with the local economy.

Decentralized service organizations can be made up of cost centers, profit centers, revenue centers, and investment centers. For example, branch banks often are evaluated as profit centers. The performance of bank branch managers is evaluated using a number of criteria. For instance, they are responsible for generating profits by charging more interest on money loaned to their customers than they pay to depositors. In addition, they are responsible for increasing the amounts of deposits and loans at their branch. Thus, two common performance measures within the banking industry are (1) yield (a measure of loan profitability) and (2) loan growth (the rate by which a manager increases the dollar value of loans outstanding). Analogies in manufacturing organizations include ROI and sales growth. While this example illustrates financial measures of performance, service organizations also may use a balanced scorecard approach to evaluate performance. In addition to performance evaluation issues, managers in service industries face other challenges often associated with manufacturing companies.

LEARNING NOTE

Both service and manufacturing companies make special pricing decisions to attract customers who would otherwise buy goods or services from competitors. When negotiating special pricing arrangements, a manager must understand which costs are relevant and which costs are not relevant. Costs that change between alternatives typically are considered relevant to special pricing decisions. For example, pricing that covers variable costs of materials, labor, overhead, and special handling expenses will benefit the company in the short run. However, many academics warn against the long-term consequences of continuously basing prices on variable rather than full (variable + fixed) costs. Though special sales may appear profitable in the short term, all costs of production must be recovered in the long term if the company is to survive.

In a manufacturing organization, transfers between divisions occur when one division buys goods from another division. Transfer pricing is a major issue in banking also. For example, to meet legal requirements aimed at protecting depositors and other interested parties, banks must maintain a certain ratio of loans to deposits. A loan-to-deposit ratio of 65 percent means that a bank has loaned 65 cents for every dollar it holds in deposits. Assume that an aggressive branch manager has exceeded the maximum loan-to-deposit ratio, while another branch manager (within the same banking corporation) has not. Corporate management would transfer funds from the branch with excess funds to the branch exceeding the limit. The funds transfer would involve "interest charges" to the borrowing bank and "interest revenues" to the lending bank. The interest rate selected for the transfer is similar to the transfer price in a manufacturing organization. Many options exist for determining the interest charge, or transfer price. For example, the interest charge could be based on the corporation's average cost of funds, or perhaps on the highest rate paid on deposits. Thus, like manufacturing organizations, banks transfer goods and services among divisions and must determine an acceptable price for the transaction.

This chapter has shown that manufacturing and service organizations may use a decentralized organizational structure. The banking example illustrates the way service organizations face many of the same challenges as manufacturing organizations face. Managers of service organizations must find ways to be responsive to a changing environment, evaluate performance using a variety of indicators, and determine the cost of resources transferred among divisions.

3 SELF-STUDY PROBLEM

WebTUTOR Advantage

Refer to the financial data presented in Self-Study Problem 1. The financial statements represent the operations of your division during the past 12 months. Assume that you are a divisional manager who purchases raw materials from other divisions within the company. Your company has a market-based transfer pricing policy. Thus, managers commonly seek transfer prices consistent with bids submitted by outside companies.

Before entering into price negotiations to purchase raw materials from the manager of Division B, you wish to understand Division B's cost structure and other factors that may affect the negotiations.

Required Respond to the following questions.

A. You estimate that 25% of the materials used by your division was purchased from Division B. Assuming that your division's total cost of materials was $40,000,000, what was the cost of materials purchased from Division B?

B. If the selling division (Division B) typically earns a 20% gross margin [(sales − cost of goods sold) ÷ sales], what was Division B's cost of goods sold?

C. You recall from past meetings that Division B is very capital intensive (they use expensive equipment, whose costs are fixed in the short run). Their variable costs are 30% of total manufacturing costs, while fixed costs make up the remaining 70%. Using the transfer pricing equation, transfer price = variable cost + opportunity cost, calculate the minimum acceptable transfer price (from the seller's perspective). Assume that Division B is operating at full capacity.

D. Should the manager of Division B consider negotiating a lower transfer price if the division is not operating at capacity? Explain.

The solution to Self-Study Problem 3 appears at the end of the chapter.

REVIEW

SUMMARY of IMPORTANT CONCEPTS

1. Managers use accounting information to make marketing and operation decisions.
   a. Managers (agents) are hired by owners to make decisions consistent with the owners' interests.
   b. Compensation packages are designed to encourage managers to maximize company value.

2. A responsibility center is defined as any business unit or segment over which managers have control and managerial authority.
   a. Cost center managers are evaluated on their ability to control costs.
   b. Revenue center managers are responsible for generating sales or revenues.
   c. Profit center managers are responsible for both costs and revenues.
   d. Investment center managers are held accountable for costs, revenues, profits, and efficient asset use.

3. Managerial performance is often evaluated using ROI and economic value added.
   a. Return on investment (ROI) is made up of two elements, margin and turnover.
   b. Margin is defined as operating income ÷ sales.
   c. Turnover is defined as sales ÷ operating assets.
   d. The use of ROI for performance evaluation encourages managers to maximize operating income while at the same time minimizing the level of assets employed.
   e. Economic value added is calculated by subtracting the cost of invested capital from operating income.
   f. Economic value added motivates managers to invest in projects that produce a return above the cost of invested capital.

4. Performance evaluation using the balanced scorecard includes four sets of measures:
   a. Financial: How do we look to shareholders?
   b. Customer satisfaction: How do customers see us?
   c. Learning and growth: How may we continue to improve and create value?
   d. Internal business: At what must we excel?

5. A number of transfer pricing issues can arise in organizations.
   a. Transfer pricing issues typically occur in decentralized organizations.
   b. Financially based evaluation programs often encourage managers to act in the best interests of their own division, rather than the best interests of the company as a whole.
   c. Typically, three methods are used for determining transfer prices among business units:
      (1) Cost-based transfer pricing policies use either full cost or variable cost as a basis for determining transfer prices.
      (2) Market-based transfer pricing policies rely on external market prices for identical (or comparable) goods or services to establish transfer prices.
      (3) Negotiated transfer pricing policies permit managers to consider factors such as cost and external market prices when negotiating a mutually acceptable transfer price between two business units.

6. Many of the same issues arise in service organizations.
   a. Service organizations often are decentralized and face many of the same challenges as manufacturing companies.
   b. Managers of decentralized service organizations must develop financial (and nonfinancial) measures with which to evaluate performance.
   c. Transfer pricing policies are important to decentralized service organizations because services are transferred among divisions.

DEFINE

TERMS and CONCEPTS DEFINED in this CHAPTER

agents (M291)	operating assets (M296)
balanced scorecard (M301)	operating income (M296)
cost center (M291)	profit center (M292)
cost-based transfer pricing policy (M309)	return on investment (ROI) (M295)
investment center (M292)	revenue center (M291)
margin (M295)	transfer pricing (M303)
market-based transfer pricing policy (M304)	turnover (M295)
negotiated transfer pricing policy (M309)	

SELF-STUDY PROBLEM SOLUTIONS

SSP10-1   A. A plant manager typically is responsible for controlling materials, labor, and overhead costs within the plant. These costs are included in the cost of goods manufactured as shown on the cost of goods sold schedule. Some of the overhead costs appear to be allocated from the corporate level and are not directly controllable by you, such as the cost of corporate computer time used for production scheduling. The income statement also includes corporate cost allocations over which a plant manager has no control, such as depreciation on corporate aircraft (used by the senior-level executives). Finally, as plant manager, you have no control over sales commissions and expenses.

B. The scenario presented suggests that the plant manager determines neither product mix nor selling prices. Thus, to evaluate the plant manager on his or her ability to generate income is not consistent with the principles of performance evaluation. This manager should be evaluated on his or her ability to manage costs, meet production schedules, and achieve quality specifications. Thus, the plant in our example should be evaluated as a cost center rather than a profit center.

Senior-level managers may evaluate a plant's ability to contribute to corporate income. An analysis based on income is appropriate at higher levels because higher-level managers make product mix and pricing decisions. However, the plant manager in our example is not responsible for decisions such as these.

SSP10-2   A. Margin = Operating income ÷ Sales

$$= \$1,000,000 \div \$100,000,000$$
$$= 0.01$$

Managers may consider ways to reduce direct materials, direct labor, manufacturing overhead, and other general or administrative costs. Such actions would increase operating income, assuming no changes in sales volume.

Another approach involves raising prices to generate more operating income per sales dollar. Managers must be careful when raising prices because both sales volume and operating income could decline, resulting in a lower profit margin.

B. Turnover = Sales ÷ Operating assets

$$= \$100,000,000 \div \$20,000,000$$
$$= 5$$

Turnover motivates managers to create lean organizations by producing greater sales volume while simultaneously employing fewer operating assets. Thus, turnover can be improved by

1. increasing sales while maintaining the same level of operating assets,
2. reducing operating assets while maintaining the same level of sales, or
3. increasing sales and reducing the level of operating assets.

Strategies to reduce assets may include (1) collecting on accounts receivable and submitting excess cash to corporate management, (2) reducing inventory levels, and (3) eliminating unnecessary equipment that creates excess capacity.

C. Margin × Turnover = ROI

$$0.01 \times 5 = 0.05$$

D. Focusing exclusively on financial measures of performance may encourage managers to sacrifice long-term success for short-term gains. For example, managers may cut back on research and development expenditures, quality programs, and preventive maintenance in order to improve short-term performance.

E. The balanced scorecard identifies four classes of performance measures: financial, customer, learning and growth, and internal business. Financial measures may include ROI or market share. Customer measures may include percentage of on-time deliveries or external failure rate (percentage of products delivered that are defective). Innovation and learning measures may include such things as the number of technological innovations. Internal business measures may include such things as scrap rates.

SSP10-3   A. $40,000,000 cost of materials × 0.25 = $10,000,000.

B. First, let's establish the relationship among sales, cost of goods sold, and gross margin as follows:

Sales − Cost of goods sold = Gross margin
Gross margin = 0.20 × $10,000,000 = $2,000,000

Selling price	$10,000,000	100%
(less) Gross margin	(2,000,000)	20%*
Cost of goods sold	$ 8,000,000	80%

$$* \frac{\$10,000,000 - \$8,000,000}{\$10,000,000} = 20\%$$

Therefore, it cost Division B $8,000,000 to produce the goods it sold to your division.

C.

Variable cost 0.3 × $8,000,000 = $2,400,000
Fixed cost   0.7 × $8,000,000 = 5,600,000
    Total cost $8,000,000

Opportunity cost = Sales   − Variable cost
$7,600,000   = $10,000,000 − $2,400,000

Transfer price   = Variable cost + Opportunity cost
$10,000,000   = $2,400,000   + $7,600,000

Thus, the manager of Division B would have no incentive to reduce the selling price from $10,000,000 because all units could be sold to external buyers at a price of $10,000,000. Therefore, negotiations could be difficult.

D. Theoretically, the manager of Division B should be willing to make price concessions if the division has idle capacity. The transfer pricing formula suggests that if excess capacity exists, managers may consider prices that are sufficient to cover the variable costs of production as follows:

Transfer price = Variable cost + Opportunity cost
$2,400,000   = $2,400,000   + 0

When a division has idle capacity, the opportunity cost becomes zero because external sales are not forgone.

Thinking Beyond the Question

How do we set up meaningful performance measures?

Seth and Erin understand the importance of communicating goals and objectives throughout their organization. Also, they believe relevant, verifiable performance measures should be used to motivate decisions consistent with these goals and objectives. Why should they consider using both financial and nonfinancial measures as part of a balanced scorecard?

QUESTIONS

Q10-1
Obj. 1
Heather Stone is a production manager for Bohemia Company. Her father, Alex, is a shareholder of the company but does not work for Bohemia. Which of the Stones would be considered an agent for Bohemia? What role does an agent play in an organization?

Q10-2
Obj. 2
Tenco Company manufactures high-quality playground equipment. There are several plants within Tenco. Plant A produces plastic slides and swings that are used in manufacturing at Plant B. What type of responsibility center is Plant A? Explain your answer.

Q10-3
Obj. 2
Assume that the performance of the plant manager at Tenco's Plant A, discussed in Q10-2, is being evaluated by the vice president of operations at Tenco's headquarters. What performance objectives are most likely to be used to evaluate the manager's performance?

Q10-4
Obj. 2
Granite Industries is a multi-divisional corporation in which each division operates autonomously. Division A is considered an investment center of Granite. Given this, would you expect the divisional manager of Division A to be able to make decisions regarding the acquisition of new machinery and equipment necessary to conduct divisional business? Explain your answer.

Q10-5
Obj. 2
Logistics, Inc., is a decentralized company with branch operations in 15 of the largest metropolitan areas of the United States. Each division is operated as a separate profit center, and there is a corporate vice president in charge at each location. The company has a decentralized decision-making philosophy by which the vice president at each location is empowered to make the necessary decisions to operate the profit center. What benefits would be realized from the decentralized decision-making philosophy at Logistics? What sort of localized decisions would the profit center managers be expected to make?

Q10-6
Obj. 2
Leslie Greenwood is a plant manager for Ambrose Manufacturing. Leslie's plant is operated and evaluated as a profit center. Leslie has reviewed the plant's sales and costs for the last 12 months in preparation for her annual review. She has noticed that while margins and the cost of goods manufactured have improved over the last year, overall profitability has declined as a result of increased corporate cost allocations. The corporate controller has told Leslie that the cost allocations relate mainly to insurance, interest, and data processing costs, which have increased significantly over the prior-year levels. What arguments should Leslie be prepared to make when her performance is evaluated?

Q10-7
Obj. 3
Assume that two different companies, Company A and Company B, have earned net income of $10 million and $1 million, respectively, over the same fiscal period. Would it be fair to say that Company A earned a higher ROI than Company B?

Q10-8
Obj. 4
The manager of Zelta Corporation's southeast region, Art McCormick, must improve the investment center's margin in order to achieve the performance goals established for his segment of the company. A 5% increase in sales price would achieve the desired margin. After meeting with the sales and marketing staff, however, Art is sure that an increase in sales price would result in a loss of sales and that target income would not be achieved, even though margins would increase. If sales prices cannot be increased, how can Art attain the desired margins?

Q10-9
Obj. 4
Elmer Woods is a plant manager for Lima Corporation, a producer of paints and solvents. Elmer's performance evaluation, and his bonus compensation, is based in part on his plant's turnover ratio. Elmer wants to increase the turnover ratio in order to maximize his bonus. What are the two elements of turnover, and how would they need to change in order to increase Elmer's turnover ratio?

Q10-10
Objs. 4, 5
The board of directors at Mays Company calculates the company president's performance based strictly on the turnover ratio. The denominator for the calculation is cash, accounts receivables, inventory, and fixed assets. The company has been engaged in a plant revitalization project over the past two years and has added or upgraded many of the fixed assets. How will these changes in fixed assets affect the president's performance evaluation assuming sales do not increase? Do you agree with the method the board uses to evaluate the president? Why or why not?

Q10-11
Obj. 6
Lana Martinez is a divisional manager with Power Source, Inc. Over the last several years, Lana has trimmed equipment maintenance costs in an effort to improve her division's operating income and improve financial performance measures. What effect, if any, will such a move have on the long-term profitability of the division?

Q10-12
Obj. 7
For establishing transfer prices between divisions of a company, what alternative is there to using current market prices or a cost-based formula? What are the strengths and weaknesses of such an approach?

EXERCISES   *If your instructor is using Personal Trainer® in this course, you may complete your assignments online.*

E10-1
Write a short definition of each of the terms listed in the *Terms and Concepts Defined in this Chapter* section.

E10-2
Obj. 1
Listed below are a number of actions that could be taken by managers within the context of an owner/agent relationship. For each decision, determine whether an agent's actions are

(Continued)

consistent with the best interests of owners who hired them. For each situation in which managers appear to act in their own interests, identify the economic benefits received.

- Currently, the company cannot produce enough goods to meet demand. Managers acquire additional assets to expand production.
- The marketing vice president authorized funds to remodel marketing department office space. He justified the lavish furnishings as a necessary investment to ensure the company projects a successful image.
- Managers hired additional research scientists to ensure the company's products remain technologically competitive in the future.
- Soon after the new vice president of finance arrived, she implemented plans to improve the company's visibility in the financial community. As such, the new vice president often was seen at the country club shooting 18 holes with community bankers.
- The production manager will receive a bonus if the quality and quantity of products manufactured during the quarter exceed targets by a certain percentage. The production manager understands the production processes better than higher-level managers and sets the targets at easily attainable levels.

E10-3
Obj. 2

The organizational structure of a decentralized organization often contains four levels, as follows:

Organizational level
Cost center
Revenue center
Profit center
Investment center

Match the correct definition below with the appropriate organizational level.

Definition
- A level within an organization that has the strategic responsibility for generating profits and managing assets
- A level of an organization that has responsibility for generating sales
- A level of an organization that consumes resources while performing its responsibilities yet has no direct involvement in generating sales or acquiring property
- A level of an organization that is responsible for both generating sales and controlling costs and expenses

E10-4
Obj. 2

Following are a variety of performance measures used to evaluate responsibility centers in decentralized organizations. For each performance measure, identify the organizational level for which the measure would be appropriate. Explain your reasoning.

- Manufacturing costs
- ROI
- Quality
- Profitability
- Percentage of on-time deliveries
- Successful new product introductions
- Market share
- Inventory turnover

E10-5
Obj. 2

The following are independent situations.

1. LonnMark, Inc., operates a *satellite plant* that produces components for many of the company's products. The plant is operated by a plant manager, who coordinates scheduling and material acquisition with the company's home office. The plant manager also is directly responsible for a labor force consisting of 350 employees. This manager controls overhead but may not add any equipment without home office approval.
2. A nationally known soft drink company acquires a *coal mining company*. The decision to acquire the mining operation is strategic and is based on anticipated growth in the industry. The mining operation is run by a local management group independent of soft drink management.

3. Black and Runyan, Inc., of Chicago, owns a grain elevator and storage facility in rural Iowa. The *grain facility* is run by Dave Bailey. Dave and 22 other grain facility operators report to the senior vice president of operations, located in Chicago. Dave has day-to-day control in running the Iowa facility and routinely buys and sells grain.

4. Sandra Falls is the California senior account representative for a national copier manufacturer. Sandra has overall responsibility for the 12 *showrooms* located in the state. Each showroom employs approximately six sales representatives. Sandra's representatives sell copiers, but maintenance on the copiers is provided by certified subcontractors who are coordinated through the national headquarters.

Categorize each of the organizations listed in italics as either a cost center, profit center, revenue center, or investment center. Briefly justify your answers.

E10-6
Obj. 3

In 1903, the du Pont cousins acquired the assets of **E.I. Du Pont de Nemours and Company** in exchange for bonds. In the language of today, the cousins conducted a leveraged buyout of the company. Explain why a measurement such as ROI was needed to help ensure financial survival of the new company. If the bond interest rate was 4%, explain how ROI might be used by the du Ponts to evaluate financial performance on existing assets and to consider additional investment opportunities.

E10-7
Obj. 4

LaKeesha Roberts is a successful division manager for Textron Industries. Her division's ROI currently is 22%. Roberts is evaluating a plant expansion opportunity that is expected to produce an annual income of $500,000 and require an investment of $3,000,000. The corporation's cost of capital is 12%.

a. If Roberts' performance is based on ROI, will she be inclined to make the investment? Explain.
b. Calculate the residual income for the proposed investment.
c. If Roberts' performance is based on residual income, will she be inclined to make the investment? Explain.
d. Would corporate management encourage Roberts to make the investment? Explain

E10-8
Obj. 4

The following information for the past two years relates to a division of Wheel Company:

	2006	2007
Sales	$31,000,000	$39,000,000
Net operating income	2,700,000	2,900,000
Average operating assets	55,000,000	55,000,000

a. Compute the return on investment for both years. .049, .053
b. Compute the margin and turnover ratio for each year.
c. Explain why the return on investment increased from 2006 to 2007 despite a lower margin in 2007.

E10-9
Obj. 4

	Company 1	Company 2	Company 3	Company 4
Sales revenue	$10,000	$20,000	$148,000	?
Expenses	7,000	13,000?	126,000	?
Net income	3,000	7,000	22,000?	?
Average assets	20,000	25,000	65,000	$120,000
Margin	?	40%	?	7%
Turnover	?	0.8	?	2
ROI	?	?	?	?

Calculate the missing information for each of the four companies. Treat each company independently.

E10-10
Obj. 5

One attribute of the balanced scorecard approach lies in performance measure diversity. For each scorecard category, identify appropriate performance measures from the following list:

(Continued)

Scorecard category	Performance measures
Financial	ROI
Internal business processes	Lead time
Learning and growth	On-time delivery
Customer satisfaction	Cash flow
	Manufacturing lead time
	Sales dollars per square feet of retail space
	Percentage of sales from new products

E10-11
Objs. 4, 5

ROI is computed by multiplying a margin times turnover as follows:

$$\frac{\text{Operating income}}{\text{Sales}} \times \frac{\text{Sales}}{\text{Operating assets}}$$

The ROI measure is intended to motivate managers to make their divisions lean, efficient, and profitable. However, the exclusive use of ROI may motivate short-sighted decision making.

a. Provide two examples of how the margin component of ROI may be managed for short-term benefit with long-run consequences.
b. Provide two examples of how the turnover component of ROI may be managed for short-term benefit with long-run consequences.
c. How does the balanced scorecard approach reduce the incentive for managers to focus on activities that result in short-term benefits and long-term consequences?

E10-12
Obj. 5

Following are a variety of performance measures that could be used with the balanced score-card approach. Classify each measure as financial, internal business processes, customer satisfaction, or learning and growth. Justify your answer.

Customer loyalty	Defect rate
Net income	Material yield
Cycle time	Percentage of employees that participate in
Sales growth	annual training seminars
Employee retention and satisfaction	Market share

E10-13
Obj. 6

Tide Company has two divisions, Division A and Division B. Division A currently sells components to Division B for $10 per unit. The cost of Division A to produce a component follows:

Variable cost per unit	$5
Fixed cost per unit	$2 (based on 100,000 units)

Division A typically sells 40,000 components to Division B and 40,000 components to external customers. The manager of Division B is considering buying components from an outside supplier that submitted a bid of $8.

a. Calculate the cost savings to Division B if the manager decides to purchase the component externally.
b. Assume Division A cannot replace lost sales in the short run if Division B purchases components externally. How does the fixed cost per unit change?
c. From the perspective of the corporation as a whole, should Division B purchase the components externally? Explain.
d. What other factors should Division B's management consider in its decision of whether to buy from an outside source?

E10-14
Obj. 6

Java-Time Coffee Company is organized into two divisions. Division A roasts, blends, and packages gourmet coffees for sale to specialty shops and coffee bars. Division B designs and produces packaging materials for Division A as well as for external customers. The cost of producing a pound of Java-Time specialty coffee is $3.50, including the transfer price of $0.50 for the packaging materials. The cost to Division B to design and produce packaging materials is $0.35.

The manager of Division A has acquired a bid from an external producer that would reduce the cost of packaging materials by 20%. The reduced purchase price would significantly improve Division A's ROI.

What is motivating the manager of Division A to buy packaging materials from an outside supplier? Why might corporate-level managers at Java-Time Coffee Company encourage the manager of Division A to continue purchasing the packaging materials from Division B? Explain.

E10-15
Obj. 7

SportCo, Inc., is a multi-divisional company that produces and sells athletic equipment. Division 1 produces components for a variety of products, while Division 2 assembles the components and packages the finished product. Both divisions are free to buy and sell internally or externally. For a particular soccer ball, the cost structure within Division 1 and market price are as follows:

Variable cost	$ 4
Fixed cost	2
Market price	10

a. Assuming Division 1 *is not* operating at capacity, calculate the minimum acceptable transfer price.
b. Assuming Division 1 *is* operating at capacity, calculate the transfer price.
c. Explain why capacity is a factor in the transfer pricing decision.

E10-16
Obj. 7

For each transfer pricing method identified, match the appropriate strength and weakness.

Transfer pricing method
a. Cost-based
b. Market-based
c. Negotiated

Strength or weakness
1. Easy to apply
2. Takes management time to help settle disputes
3. Requires time and effort because external bids must be obtained and evaluated
4. Performance may be affected by negotiating skills rather than by a manager's ability to control costs
5. Does not encourage and reward efficiency
6. Forces managers to be as cost-efficient as the best competitor
7. Encourages dialogue among division managers

E10-17
Obj. 7

Tandem Manufacturing transfers a product between two plants. The product has variable costs of $65 per unit and fixed overhead costs of $25 per unit. This product can be purchased from an outside source with acceptable levels of quality and quantity at $83 per unit. Assuming Tandem has excess production capacity for this product, what would be the acceptable ceiling and floor transfer pricing amounts for the product?

E10-18
Obj. 7

The Frame Division of Reliable Computers manufactures storage housings for personal and midsize computers, which it sells externally to computer manufacturers. The division is operating at full capacity. One of the most popular housings has variable costs of $34 and is sold to outside customers at $52 per unit. These housings also are needed by the Component Division of Reliable, which produces a line of small business computers. The Frame Division can sell all of its production to outside customers at $52 or can transfer a significant amount of its production to the Component Division. At what cost should the Frame Division transfer production? Why?

E10-19
Obj. 7

Transfer pricing terminology includes the concepts of floor and ceiling, representing the seller's minimum acceptable price and buyer's maximum acceptable price, respectively. The following data are presented from transfer pricing negotiations among managers at Douglas Company:

Ceiling	$550
Floor	315

(Continued)

a. What is the market price of the product?
b. What is the variable cost of the product?
c. Calculate the contribution margin.
d. Calculate the opportunity cost if the selling division is not at capacity.
e. Calculate the opportunity cost if the selling division is at capacity.

E10-20
Obj. 8

Decentralized service organizations may be classified into a variety of responsibility centers including cost centers, profit centers, and investment centers. Following are a variety of responsibility centers from a national public accounting firm.

1. Managers and partners within the firm have the responsibility of managing the audit engagement and signing the audit opinion that is presented with a client's annual report. In addition, they are responsible for practice development activities, including bidding for audits and expanding professional services.
2. Lower-level accountants and their supervisers have the primary responsibility for conducting the work (audit tests) associated with the annual audit.
3. Managing partners at regional offices make decisions about expanding the firm by opening offices in new cities or by acquiring smaller firms.

Classify each responsibility center as a cost center, profit center, or investment center as appropriate. Justify your answer. How do you think the components of ROI would differ between a public accounting firm and a steel manufacturing company? Explain.

E10-21
Obj. 8

Soldwell Bankers operates a national chain of realty offices. While some activities are conducted centrally, others are conducted on a decentralized basis. The following activities were conducted by Soldwell during December. Identify the activities that would be performed most efficiently on a centralized basis. Then, identify the activities that would be performed most efficiently on a decentralized basis. Explain your reasoning.

- A client, currently located in San Jose, California, is relocating to Atlanta, Georgia. Managers at Soldwell contacted the office manager in Atlanta and managed the client introduction.
- After discussions with a realtor, the client received neighborhood locator sheets with photographs and price listings.
- The client was taken on a real estate tour to view property.
- Realtors were present at the closing when all legal documents completing the real estate purchase were signed.
- A public accounting firm was hired to conduct the annual audit.
- Soldwell managers contracted with a national advertising agency to develop a television advertising campaign.
- The Atlanta office hired 20 new realtors.
- Soldwell modified its commission policy on a national basis.

PROBLEMS

If your instructor is using Personal Trainer® in this course, you may complete your assignments online.

P10-1
Obj. 1

Compensation Strategies in the Owner/Agent Relationship

As discussed in this chapter, managers are hired as agents to make decisions in the best interests of the owners. Often, employment contracts are put into place to help align the goals of managers and owners. For example, **Nike, Inc.** has implemented a variety of conditions within its executive compensation package. Below is an excerpt from DEF 14 A 1999 - 09 - 22 (the proxy statement) that Nike, Inc. filed with the Securities and Exchange Commission.

(1) The Compensation Plan Subcommittee established a series of performance targets based on fiscal 2000 and 2001 revenues and earnings per share corresponding to award payouts ranging from 10% to 150% of the target awards. Participants would have been entitled to a payout at the highest percentage level at which both performance targets are met, subject to the Committee's discretion to reduce or eliminate any award based on Company or individual performance. Under the terms of the awards, on August 15, 2000 and 2001 the Company would issue in the name of each participant a number of shares of Class B Stock with a value equal to the award payout based on the closing price of the Class B Stock on that date on the

New York Stock Exchange. The shares would be restricted for three years thereafter and subject to forfeiture to the Company if the participant ceases to be an employee of the Company for any reason during such three-year period.

Required Identify the types of incentive packages used by Nike stockholders to align the goals of management with theirs.

P10-2
Objs. 2, 4

Organizational Structure and Performance Evaluation

Timberline Corporation is a multi-divisional manufacturing company. Each of the two division managers has responsibility for sales, costs, and profitability. Division 1 has three manufacturing plants, while Division 2 has four plants that produce a variety of products as requested by the divisional marketing department. The divisional marketing department is responsible for setting prices, determining product mix, managing advertising, and meeting income projections. The division manager is responsible for coordinating production and marketing activities across the various levels within the division. Sales and operating data for each division are as follows:

	Division 1	Division 2
Sales	$10,000,000	$6,000,000
Cost of goods sold	6,000,000	4,200,000
Gross margin	$ 4,000,000	$1,800,000
Operating expenses	3,500,000	1,000,000
Operating income	$ 500,000	$ 800,000
Average assets	$ 8,000,000	$7,000,000

Required

A. Construct an organization chart that illustrates the various levels of responsibility within Timberline.
B. Classify each level according to the responsibility centers identified in this chapter.
C. Identify appropriate performance measures for each level of responsibility. Justify your answer.
D. Calculate ROI for the two divisions. Evaluate the results of your calculation.

P10-3
Obj. 2

Responsibility Centers and Relevant Costs for Performance Evaluation

Darius Taylor, manager of the Industrial Products Division, was preparing for his annual performance evaluation. Though Darius has been successful in generating sales growth and controlling manufacturing costs, he has not achieved his income target for the year. Financial information for his division is as follows:

Industrial Products Division **Statement of Income** **For the Year Ended 2006**		
Sales	$18,500,000	
Cost of goods sold	10,000,000	
Gross margin		$8,500,000
General selling and administrative expenses:		
Advertising	$ 450,000	
Salaries	1,000,000	
Depreciation	2,000,000	
Insurance	600,000	
Other	900,000	
Total		4,950,000
Net income		$3,550,000

(Continued)

Industrial Products Division
Statement of Income
For the Year Ended 2007

Sales	$21,500,000	
Cost of goods sold	10,965,000	
Gross margin		$10,535,000
General selling and administrative expenses:		
Advertising	$ 760,000	
Salaries	1,900,000	
Allocation of corporate administrative overhead	1,500,000	
Depreciation	2,700,000	
Insurance	600,000	
Other	800,000	
Total		8,260,000
Net income		$ 2,275,000

Required

A. What type of responsibility center does Darius manage?
B. Identify the appropriate measures for the type of responsibility center identified in requirement (A). Explain your reasoning.
C. Prepare a revised income statement that more accurately reflects Darius' division performance. If you were Darius, what points would you make during your performance evaluation? Explain.

P10-4 **The Use of ROI and Its Effect on Management Decision Making**

Obj. 4

As discussed in this chapter, the use of ROI by managers can create incentives for managers to make short-term decisions that have negative effects on long-term performance. However, ROI, if used properly, can also encourage managers to utilize assets effectively to produce higher returns for investors.

Required

A. Write the ROI formula, breaking it down into its components as follows:

Margin: Operating income ÷ Sales
Turnover: Sales ÷ Average operating assets

For the numerator and denominator of each component, identify actions that may improve ROI in the short term but may harm the company in the long run.
B. Explain why managers often are under pressure to make short-term decisions that may have adverse long-term consequences.

P10-5 **Enhancing Return on Investments: Ethical Considerations**

Obj. 4

Carter Consumer Products has three operating divisions, which are appropriately treated as investment centers. Each of the investment centers is run by a divisional manager. The managers are evaluated on the basis of ROI performance. Those managers with the best ROI figures are most likely to be promoted to higher-level corporate positions. Edwin Jones is one of the divisional managers for Carter. He is an ambitious person who desperately wants a promotion to headquarters. The investment center for which Edwin is responsible manufactures a line of patio furniture. This investment center has two plants, which employ over 500 workers. Operating results for each of the plants and for the division in total for the most recent year are as follows:

	Total	Plant A	Plant B
Revenues	$180,000	$120,000	$60,000
Expenses	$150,000	$100,000	$50,000
Net income	$25,000	$15,000	$10,000
Average operating assets	$170,000	$110,000	$60,000

Carter's cost of capital is 11%. Sales, marketing, and production managers who work for Edwin have proposed adding production capabilities for the manufacture of picnic table umbrellas. They have compiled figures that show that the estimated cost of the assets needed to produce an umbrella line is $120,000. They further estimate that the umbrella line would increase net income by $15,000 a year. After careful consideration, Edwin rejected the idea and added, "This is no time to add to our production facilities. In fact, I've been thinking of closing Plant B and moving its production to Plant A."

Required

A. What is the most likely reason why Edwin turned down the proposal to produce umbrellas?

B. Would the company as a whole be better off by producing the umbrellas? Explain your answer. Using the economic value added (residual income) approach, provide computations to support your reasoning.

C. Why do you believe Edwin has suggested closing Plant B? How does ROI as a performance measure adversely affect the company in total?

P10-6 Segment Reporting and Analysis

Obj. 4

The following is Tennis Today's financial statement for the year ending December 31, 2006, in total and by division:

	Total	Division A	Division B
Assets:			
Cash	$ 46,000	$ 10,000	$ 36,000
Accounts receivable	89,000	37,000	52,000
Inventory	198,000	72,000	126,000
Fixed assets	1,850,000	900,000	950,000
Total	$2,183,000	$1,019,000	$1,164,000
Liabilities:			
Accounts payable	$ 65,000	$ 28,000	$ 37,000
Bank debt	1,620,000	800,000	820,000
Total	$1,685,000	$ 828,000	$ 857,000
Stockholders' equity	498,000		
Total liabilities and equity	$2,183,000		
Revenues	$1,500,000	$ 500,000	$1,000,000
Expenses	1,150,000	300,000	850,000
Net income	$ 350,000	$ 200,000	$ 150,000

Required

A. If the stockholders own shares of the company in total, and not in the individual divisions, how can the divisional managers' performance be evaluated in terms of building stockholder wealth?

B. From an ROI perspective, which of the two divisions has shown better performance? (Assume that ending assets reflect average operating assets for the year.)

P10-7 Scorecard Development: The Customer Perspective

Obj. 5

An internationally known electric guitar manufacturer produces its legendary instruments from a variety of purchased components. Suppliers are held accountable for strict quality standards. To ensure proper sound quality, meeting engineering tolerances is crucial. In addition, the guitar company does not carry a large parts inventory. Therefore, suppliers make small deliveries multiple times each week. A late or defective shipment would result in a major disruption of the production line.

Assume you are a manager for the company that supplies electrical pickups used in producing the instruments. Recently you have been assigned to design a balanced scorecard for your company. Currently, you and a group of team members are working on the customer aspect of the scorecard.

(Continued)

Required Using your knowledge of the balanced scorecard, develop performance indicators for the customer perspective. Consider the appropriate number of measures as well as the types of measures the company should include. Justify your answer.

P10-8   Balanced Scorecard Approach to Performance Evaluation

Obj. 5

Carol Rolfson is a divisional manager for Klinger Products. Carol operates a division that manufactures clocks and timepieces that are distributed through retail stores. Over the past year, Carol's division recorded the highest net income in the division's history. Internal records indicate that customer returns have declined significantly as a result of the division's improved quality. Many of the improvements were generated as a result of a vigorous program of enhanced technology in which most of the division's equipment was replaced or updated over the last 18 months.

Carol has noticed a change in morale as a result of the plant improvements. Employees have become more interested in their work and have suggested additional improvements to the production process. One of the suggestions led to a new product that has shown strong sales potential. The improved processes have also resulted in lower scrap rates and more timely shipments.

As a divisional manager, Carol is eligible for an annual bonus under Klinger's executive compensation plan. She has been notified, however, that her bonus for the year will be significantly less than in prior years. The executive compensation plan calculates a manager's effectiveness based solely on return on investment. The president of Klinger pointed out to Carol that while her division's income has improved, the addition of all the new equipment overshadowed the higher earnings.

Required

A. What weaknesses do you see in Klinger's executive bonus plan?
B. How does the company's current compensation plan differ from a balanced scorecard approach to bonus compensation?
C. If the company utilized a balanced scorecard approach, what do you believe would be the impact on Carol's bonus compensation? Explain your answer.

P10-9   Performance Evaluations

Objs. 2, 5

The Promotion and Advertising Department at Jefferson Corporation coordinates point of purchase promotions for its distributors. Employees of this department are graphic arts or marketing majors who develop campaign materials and conduct market research. The department does not collect any revenue for these services. The department manager is evaluated based on the department's ability to operate within its budget. For the last several years, the manager has had to curtail many promotional programs a month before year-end in order to stay within budget.

Sales personnel, marketing representatives, and customers frequently complain when these services are terminated. Dan Beck, the department manager, told a colleague, "I hate taking all this heat every year. But I just can't afford to blow the budget." He also noted that "soon the new budget will be out, and I can give everyone what they want!"

Required

A. What type of responsibility center is the Promotion and Advertising Department?
B. How is the department currently being evaluated? What are the important elements on which the department should be evaluated?
C. What appear to be the reasons for the department's budget problems? What implications does this have for the company?

P10-10   Outsourcing Decisions: Relevant Factors

Obj. 6

Salvo Corporation produces cast metal parts used in the plumbing industry. The company is organized into two divisions, mining and casting. Managers of the two divisions are evaluated based on divisional ROI.

The Mining Division sells ore to the Casting Division as well as to external customers. Currently, the Mining Division has excessive inventory and has reduced production because of weak demand for its product.

In an effort to reduce material costs, the manager of the Casting Division obtained bids from external suppliers to provide the ore. Some external bids were below the prices charged by the Mining Division at Salvo, making purchasing from external sources appear attractive.

Required

A. Identify the relevant facts for the outsourcing decision.
B. Explain why purchasing the ore from an outside company may not be the best decision for Salvo.
C. How would capacity and market conditions affect the outsourcing decision?

P10-11

Objs. 6, 7

Transfer Pricing, Idle Capacity

At its Video Division, Crew Enterprises manufactures computer monitors. These can be sold internally to the EDD Division of Crew or externally to independent customers. Sales and costs of the most popular monitor are as follows:

Per unit selling price	$134.00
Per unit variable cost	$103.00
Per unit fixed costs*	$28.00
Full production capacity	11,000 units per month
Current level of production	8,500 units per month

*Based on full production capacity

The Video Division of Crew plans to sell a maximum of 96,000 of these monitors to outside customers in the coming year. The EDD Division of Crew plans to buy 20,000 identical monitors from an outside supplier at a price of $134. The manager of the Video Division has offered to supply these 20,000 monitors to the EDD Division at a price of $130.

Required

A. What is the minimum transfer price for the monitor that the Video Division should be willing to accept on an internal transfer? What is the maximum price the EDD Division should be willing to pay for these monitors on an internal transfer?
B. Suppose the managers of the EDD Division learn of the idle capacity at the Video Division and make an offer of $122 for these monitors. Would you expect the Video Division to accept? What would be the effect on net income for the Video Division of accepting this offer?
C. What would be the effect on net income for Crew as a whole if the transfer price of $122 were accepted?

P10-12

Objs. 6, 7

Transfer Pricing, Full Capacity

The USA Company's Box Division produces cardboard boxes used for packaging microwavable fast foods. The Consumer Products Division produces a variety of fast-food entrees that are packaged in boxes. In the past the Consumer Products Division has purchased its boxes from the Box Division for $0.15 each. The Box Division currently is producing at capacity and sells 6,000,000 of these boxes each year at a price of $0.15. The Consumer Products Division has offered to buy 500,000 boxes per year from the Box Division at an internal transfer price of $0.13 per box. The Box Division's cost to produce each box consists of $0.09 of variable costs and $0.04 of fixed costs.

Required

A. What is the minimum transfer price that would be acceptable to the Box Division?
B. Assume that by selling the boxes internally, the Box Division would avoid $0.03 of variable costs. Should the internal transfer be accepted at $0.13 per box? Explain.

P10-13

Objs. 5, 8

Service Organizations versus Manufacturing Companies: The Financial Perspective

Decentralized service organizations face many of the same problems as those faced by manufacturing companies. Service organization managers are responsible for profitable, efficient operations that result in sufficient returns for investors. The financial perspective of the balanced scorecard asks the question, "How do we look to shareholders?" Measures such as ROI, cash flow, and profitability may be used as financial performance measures.

(Continued)

http://ingram.
swlearning.com

Required Go to the Internet site for this text; select the text and Student Resources. Select SEC under the hotlinks for this chapter. From this site you will be able to access the SEC's database. Search for the financial statements (Form 10k) for **H&R Block, Inc.** and for **General Mills.** Use your knowledge of financial performance measures to compare the results of H&R Block, Inc. (a service company) and General Mills (a manufacturing company). Include in your analysis a calculation of ROI for each company. Also compare the margin and turnover components. Are your results consistent with your expectations? Why or why not?

P10-14

Objs. 6, 8

Transfer Pricing in a Service Environment

Waldo and Company, LLP, is a partnership that provides public accounting services. Waldo has three offices located in New Orleans, Baton Rouge, and Lafayette. Each of the offices employs approximately 30 professional accountants who are hired by and work solely for the office to which they are assigned. The offices are run independently, and there is a managing partner in charge of each office. Bonuses are paid to each managing partner based on criteria that include the number of staff hours worked and total billings for the respective office.

The Lafayette office was recently hired by a large petroleum company to conduct an audit. This engagement will require more accounting personnel than are currently available in the Lafayette office. Nancy Bloom, managing partner of the Lafayette office, has asked the other offices to "lend" her some professional staff to assist on this engagement. The other offices want to help, but are concerned that "lending" their personnel will reduce the number of staff hours worked in their own offices, thereby reducing their billings and resulting bonuses.

Required Why does this situation reflect a transfer pricing problem for the firm? How should the firm handle the interoffice transfer of personnel from a pricing standpoint? If there are professional staff available in the New Orleans and Baton Rouge offices who are not servicing clients, would the interoffice transfer price be affected?

P10-15

Excel in Action

SPREADSHEET

As part of an effort to increase sales and profit margin, Music Makers' management is adopting a transfer pricing plan. The copying and packaging departments have been placed under divisional managers. As an incentive to cut costs, each division is expected to earn a gross margin of 10% on its divisional costs. The copying division will sell its output to the packaging division, and the packaging division will sell its output to the corporation. The company expects to produce and sell 535,000 units per month, and the maximum it is willing to pay to the packaging division for the units is $1,075,000.

Variable manufacturing costs per unit in the copying division include $0.70 for materials, $0.09 for labor, and $0.04689 for overhead. Fixed costs in the copying division are $268,000 per month. Variable manufacturing costs per unit in the packaging division include $0.20 for materials, $0.11 for labor, and $0.04 for overhead. Fixed costs in the packaging division are $76,000 per month.

Required Use a spreadsheet to determine the total costs for each division and the sales price each division will need to charge to earn a 10% gross margin. The sales price can be calculated as total cost ÷ (1 − profit margin).

Provide data for the copying division in column B and the packaging division in column C. Captions should appear in column A. Enter headings in row 1, the number of units to produce in row 2, and gross profit margin in row 3. In row 4, enter a heading "Variable Costs per Unit." Then, enter variable unit costs for materials, labor, and overhead in rows 5 through 7. Calculate total unit variable costs in row 8. Calculate total variable costs in row 9. Enter fixed costs in row 10. Calculate total manufacturing costs in row 11. Calculate the price including required margin in row 12. In the following rows, calculate the total price of the products transferred from the packaging division to the corporation and the amount under (over) the maximum transfer price of $1,075,000. Use cell references and formulas where possible. Use appropriate formatting throughout.

If you were manager of the copying division, what price would you want for the units sold to the packaging division? If you were manager of the packaging division, what price would you want to pay for the goods purchased from the copying division?

How would your answers change if the gross margin expected of each division were 8%?

P10-16 Multiple-Choice Overview of the Chapter

1. Which of the following responsibility centers would appropriately be evaluated in terms of the margin and turnover together?
   a. Cost center
   b. Profit center
   c. Investment center
   d. Revenue center

2. Which of the following is true regarding return on investment?
   a. An increase in sales would affect the margin but not the turnover.
   b. Return on investment is applied only to profit centers.
   c. An increase in assets will decrease the return on investment when sales remain constant.
   d. Plant and equipment are the only assets used to calculate the return on investment.

3. A company establishing transfer prices for products between divisions should:
   a. transfer products at prices that would be paid by outside customers.
   b. utilize transfer prices that will result in the highest income to the transferring division.
   c. allow negotiated prices that result in the greatest benefit to the corporation as a whole.
   d. require the transferee division to accept price quotes without negotiation.

4. A principal expectation for agents is that:
   a. agents will operate the company in a way consistent with the owners' interests.
   b. agents may not act on behalf of owners in important business matters.
   c. agents must always operate a company in order to maximize shareholder wealth.
   d. agents' compensation should not include incentives, as this can create conflicts of interest.

5. A decentralized organization:
   a. permits managers to make decisions based on local economic situations.
   b. allows middle managers to develop skills in preparation for greater responsibilities.
   c. is characterized by multiple divisions or operating segments.
   d. includes all of the above.

6. When used as an internal tool for evaluating managerial performance, ROI is:
   a. calculated by dividing operating assets by net income.
   b. calculated by dividing sales revenue by operating assets.
   c. calculated by dividing operating income by operating assets.
   d. not meaningful since it is subject to manipulation by division managers.

7. The turnover ratio:
   a. is considered to improve when the ratio decreases.
   b. demonstrates the effectiveness of asset management.
   c. encourages managers to increase the asset base.
   d. cannot increase unless the company's margin also increases.

8. The balanced scorecard approach to performance evaluation includes:
   a. financial performance measures.
   b. customer satisfaction measures.
   c. internal business criteria.
   d. All of the above are correct.

9. The transfer pricing policy that requires managers to transfer goods based on external price conditions is referred to as:
   a. negotiated transfer pricing.
   b. a market-based transfer policy.
   c. a cost-plus transfer policy.
   d. None of the above is correct.

10. When a division is operating at less than full capacity:
   a. the company as a whole would be better off utilizing a market-based transfer pricing policy.
   b. internal transfers generally should be made at a price that equals the variable cost of production.
   c. the turnover ratio will increase.
   d. fixed costs are being fully recovered.

CASES

C10-1   The Balanced Scorecard at Golden Grain Foods

Obj. 5

Golden Grain Foods produces consumer food products including cereals, dessert mixes, microwave popcorn, snack foods, and mixes that enhance and simplify meal preparation. During the previous year, reported sales grew at a rate of 8% to reach $6 billion. Earnings after taxes grew at a rate of 10% to $522 million. Every one of Golden Grain Foods' domestic operating divisions posted earnings gains of at least 10%, and combined international earnings grew at an even stronger rate.

The double-digit earnings growth was driven by unit volume gains. Worldwide unit volume increased 9%, with good performance from established businesses and strong contributions from the cereal and snack brands. In addition, productivity improvements helped lower the cost per case of manufactured products. In spite of double-digit earnings growth, the stock price grew just 6% while the S&P index grew 29%. The growth differential reflects concern among investors about the market for ready-to-eat cereal in the United States Investors also are concerned that recent sales growth of lower-priced bagged cereals and store brands will inhibit sales of premium quality brands such as those produced by Golden Grain Foods.

Management is optimistic about the future of cereal products because of favorable demographic trends and cereal's fit with today's emerging health and nutrition recommendations. Golden Grain Foods will use product improvement, health news and brand-building marketing, effective trade merchandising programs, and good new products to drive cereal growth.

The company's financial goals are to achieve 12% average annual growth in earnings per share, to generate a minimum 25% return on invested capital, to exhibit financial strength that merits an "A" bond rating, and to pay out between 50% and 60% of earnings as dividends. Three factors will be key to achieving 12% earnings per share growth as follows:

- Strong unit volume
- Improved productivity
- Profit contributions from international operations

Actions have been taken to stimulate more and better innovation throughout the company by sharpening the focus and increasing the level of resources committed to new products and business development. In addition, management has consolidated the supply chains for flour milling, foodservice, and packaged foods business. These changes will create productivity opportunities.

The company plans to keep leading brands vital with a steady diet of product improvements, innovation, and consumer-focused marketing. Plans include meaningful improvement on several key products, such as cake mixes and frosting. New products are critical to the company's long-term growth. In recent years, an average 27% of volume has come from products five years old or less.

Innovation will be focused on consumer needs. When it comes to snacks, consumers crave variety. New variations of microwave popcorn and new fruit snack products drove volume and share growth in the past. Consumers want mix products that make popular foods a snap to prepare. In addition, consumers are asking for nutritious foods to eat on the go. Strong levels of innovation have been key to increasing dollar market share for yogurt brands to nearly 27%. The company used a steady stream of indulgent new flavor varieties to drive growth in the core yogurt lines.

To meet its long-term goals, the company is after really big ideas—everything from new packaging concepts to new health benefits to new food technologies. Consistent with key strategic objectives, employee teams have been empowered to design and develop new and creative ways to use information and manufacturing technology. Additionally, procedures are in place to supply information to key users within the company. Management has recently taken actions to accelerate the flow of their innovation pipeline. Operating divisions now focus at least 25% of total resources on new products and new business ideas.

In addition to innovations in production, Golden Grain Foods is exploring new distribution channels. The company is targeting a broader penetration of products in vending machines and other foodservice outlets. New retail outlets include convenience stores, membership clubs, drug stores, and mass merchandisers.

Management has been finding ways to buy smarter, manufacture more efficiently, and distribute products at a lower cost. Strong productivity and improved operating leverage combined to lower average cost an additional 5%. Golden Grain Foods seeks to deliver ongoing productivity gains with innovative thinking and breakthrough performance. For example, the company borrowed techniques from racing pit crews to achieve a 30% reduction in the time it takes to change a cereal line from one product to another. The results are significant cost savings and an important increase in manufacturing capacity. In addition, managers are working to more closely integrate the flour milling, foodservice, and packaged foods supply chains. Across all functions, Golden Grain Foods is exploring outsourcing and other strategies to increase efficiency and reduce administrative expense.

Assume corporate managers at Golden Grain Foods want to develop a set of performance indicators to help align decision making with the company's strategic plans. These measures should encourage key activities within the four elements of the balanced scorecard, financial, internal, customer, and innovation and learning.

Required

A. In what businesses does Golden Grain Foods operate?
B. Discuss the financial performance of the company.
C. What are the primary concerns and opportunities identified by management?
D. Prepare a balanced scorecard for Golden Grain Foods. You may wish to classify key activities or initiatives cited in the case as financial, internal business processes, learning and growth, or customer satisfaction. Having identified key initiatives, develop a performance measure that could be used to evaluate progress in that particular activity or initiative.

C10-2 Transfer Pricing

Objs. 6, 7

Cameo Products has two divisions: Office Products and Furniture. Divisional managers are encouraged to maximize ROI at their respective divisions. Managers are free to decide whether goods will be transferred internally and to determine the prices at which transfers will occur.

The Furniture Division would like to purchase a particular chair manufactured in the Office Products Division and sell it with a computer desk the division recently has designed. The Furniture Division can purchase a similar chair from an outside supplier for $45. The Office Products Division currently is producing this chair at full capacity and sells it to outside customers at $45. The manager of the Furniture Division is hoping to receive a price concession if the chair is bought internally. The fully absorbed cost to produce the chair is $40 ($32 represents variable costs). If the chair is sold internally, $3 of variable selling expenses can be avoided.

The managers of the two divisions met to discuss the possible transaction. After some discussion and negotiation, it was decided that the Furniture Division would purchase the chair at the current outside selling price for the next six months. At the end of six months, negotiations can be reopened by either party if desired.

Required

A. Based on current information, what is the highest price that the Furniture Division should be willing to pay for the chair? What is the lowest price that the Office Products Division should be willing to accept?
B. Assume that the outside sales price of the chair increases to $47. How would this affect the internal transfer price of the chair?
C. Assume that because of soft market conditions, demand for the chair has decreased significantly, creating excess idle capacity within the Office Products Division. How would this change affect the internal transfer price of the chair?
D. Why is it in the best interest of the company as a whole to allow the division managers to negotiate internal transfer prices instead of using a fixed, nonnegotiable formula for establishing transfer prices?

IMPROVING OPERATIONAL PERFORMANCE

How can managerial accounting help beat emerging competition?

Young Designs, Inc., is confronted by competition from a foreign furniture producer that has a cost advantage because of lower labor rates. Because of this, Seth and Erin are considering ways to meet this competition by adding value to make their products more competitive. Their strategy is to provide innovative, high-quality products to their customers. Thus, they are focusing on product differentiation rather than on cost leadership. However, cost control is becoming increasingly important as competitors introduce products at significantly lower prices.

One of the challenges Seth and Erin face is that of converting their company into a lean enterprise. Lean enterprises are characterized by efficient operations that rely on minimal levels of raw materials, work-in-process, and finished goods inventory. Also, lean enterprises make efficient use of their assets.

FOOD FOR THOUGHT

Imagine yourself managing Young Designs, Inc. If your strategy is to sell differentiated products that command higher prices, how do you ensure your products provide value to customers? How do you offer significantly better quality and more features desired by customers to justify a higher price? In addition, how do you organize your production area to improve efficiency and reduce costs? Let's listen as Erin and Seth discuss ways of becoming a lean enterprise.

Erin: I have been in touch with a number of our customers during the past few weeks. It seems we now have competition from an overseas furniture producer. Our customers tell me their products are quite a bit less expensive than ours.

Seth: How do their products compare with ours in terms of innovation and quality? Also, can the competition meet our reliable delivery record?

Erin: I'm sure our products are better; however, the cost differential is rather dramatic. I've been thinking that we should consider changing some of our processes in the production area. Maybe we can find a way to remove inefficiency and cost. While we currently do a good job with on-time delivery, I believe we have room for improvement.

Seth: There is no doubt that we have grown comfortable with our processes. We have far too much invested in inventory. Although the excess helps provide a margin of safety, we still need to become a lean producer.

Erin: I'm not sure that I follow you.

Seth: Right now, if we make a mistake in production, we simply go to the storage area and get more materials. We don't think about how to improve the process to prevent the mistake from occurring again. I order inventory in quantities large enough to last a month or so. That's a lot of material to count, move, store, and insure against loss. Thus, the excess inventory is very costly to maintain.

Also, I sometimes believe we do not efficiently route products through the factory. I often walk through the production area and find batches of parts that should have been completed weeks ago. Some machines *are churning away, while others seem to sit idle for days at a time. We need to figure out which machines are crucial to our production processes and make sure we don't lose valuable time on those machines.*

Erin: *In other words, if we become a lean producer, we will reduce our costs and increase the number of products we are able to complete in a given time period. Our efficiencies should translate into lower prices for our customers. Also, we should be able to offer better service when a customer places an order.*

Seth: *That's right. If we can provide rapid, reliable delivery to our customers, they may reduce their investment in inventory. Again, we may be able to deliver cost savings to our customers. By working smarter, we can compete with companies that have lower labor costs or other cost advantages.*

OBJECTIVES

Once you have completed this chapter, you should be able to:

1 Explain the difference between strategic and operational decisions and how accounting information supports these decisions.

2 Explain the philosophy of total quality management (TQM) and how a modern cost management system can be used to support the philosophy.

3 Describe the just-in-time (JIT) manufacturing philosophy and evaluate its

strengths and weaknesses from financial and operating perspectives.

4 Explain how a traditional "process-oriented" plant layout differs from a "product-oriented" plant layout, and describe the financial consequences of each layout.

5 Identify the primary components of the theory of constraints.

6 Explain how new manufacturing environment concepts apply to service organizations.

THE NEW COMPETITIVE ENVIRONMENT

OBJECTIVE 1

Explain the difference between strategic and operational decisions and how accounting information supports these decisions.

In the opening scenario, Seth and Erin decided they must convert their company to a lean enterprise. The following pages address in more detail the concept of lean organizations and how they evolved.

The Japanese automobile industry generally is given credit for developing the concept of a lean enterprise.[1] The lean enterprise was born out of necessity. The Japanese automobile industry did not have a great deal of manufacturing equipment during the 1950s and 1960s. Thus, manufacturers were forced to produce automobiles in small quantities, using far less equipment than their competitors around the world. **Toyota** found ways to reduce setup time on metal presses from days to minutes. Small-batch production became economically possible as a result of efficient metal press setup times. Unfortunately, small-batch production created other problems that had to be resolved.

Because small-batch production results in lower inventory levels, extra components to replace a defective batch often were not available. Thus, lean production systems, while very efficient, demand strict attention to quality control. As a result, programs such as zero defects and total quality management (TQM) were developed to help minimize defects that could disrupt an entire production system. In summary, systems such as total quality management and just-in-time were developed in response to international competition. These concepts have been implemented by manufacturers around the world.

Modern management accounting systems should provide relevant information to support managers who make decisions in a rapidly changing competitive environment. For example, accounting systems should capture the economic results of small-batch production in highly automated processes, such as those found at Toyota. Management accounting systems also provide information to support customer-oriented TQM

[1] Cooper, Robin, 1995. *When Lean Enterprises Collide* (Boston: Harvard Business School Press).

programs. Because management accountants help design innovative performance measurement systems, they must have a solid understanding of manufacturing processes and the dynamics that drive these processes. This chapter considers many recent manufacturing innovations used by organizations throughout the world.

TUFF CUT: THE COMPETITIVE ENVIRONMENT AND MANUFACTURING PROCESS

Examples in this chapter are based on the experiences of Tuff Cut, a company that manufactures rotary mowers used for industrial and agricultural purposes. Its rotary mowers are towed behind tractors to clear brush from rough, wide terrain. Tuff Cut has produced mowers in the United States for the past 40 years and has enjoyed consistent growth and loyal customers because of its high-quality product line. Customers include agricultural companies; individual landowners; and city, county, and state governments.

In recent years, some of Tuff Cut's market share has been eroded by competing products manufactured in the United States and abroad. Thus, managers at Tuff Cut are looking for ways to become more competitive in terms of price, quality, and delivery. As part of their effort, corporate officers are considering strategic changes in the way they manage their organization. **Strategic decisions** include decisions about the types of products a company should manufacture (such as commercial, agricultural, or residential) and how these products should be distributed (through wholesale distributors or company-owned retail outlets). In addition, questions concerning whether to enter new markets, such as China, Europe, Japan, and South America, are strategic issues. **Operational decisions** focus on day-to-day activities of the organization, but are linked directly to strategic objectives. For example, if receiving a product very soon after placing an order is important to Japanese customers, improving machine setup times to reduce cycle time is an operational activity that can be carried out at the factory floor level in support of strategic objectives. **Cycle time** is the total minutes, hours, or days a product remains in a manufacturing system. Cycle time includes producing, moving, and waiting time.

Tuff Cut has embraced a "customer-focused" philosophy that places many operating decisions in the hands of teams of employees, rather than in the hands of management. To help reduce costs, improve competitiveness, and understand their position in the industry, Tuff Cut's managers evaluated the suppliers and manufacturing processes within the industry and used the information to assist in making strategic decisions. In addition, Tuff Cut made operational changes on the factory floor, such as maintaining very low inventory levels and strengthening relationships with suppliers. Finally, plant managers evaluated the flow of resources through their manufacturing facilities to identify bottlenecks and increase each plant's output. This chapter evaluates the changes implemented by Tuff Cut and explores the manufacturing philosophies supporting these changes. First, let's begin with a description of the manufacturing process.

As shown in Exhibit 1, Tuff Cut's manufacturing process involves fabricating (cutting metal to desired specifications), welding, painting, and assembling steel sheets and components to conform to engineering specifications. Sheets of steel are removed by an overhead crane from the steel stores area, located on the factory floor, and delivered to the fabrication area. In the fabrication area, steel is cut and pressed to the required shape. These cut shapes go to the welding area, where individual pieces of steel are welded together to make the mower body. Following the welding process, the mower body is painted and sent to the assembly area, where workers attach wheels, gear boxes, and various other components. Following assembly, finished units are transported to the loading dock for shipment to dealers.

Exhibit 1 The Manufacturing Process at Tuff Cut

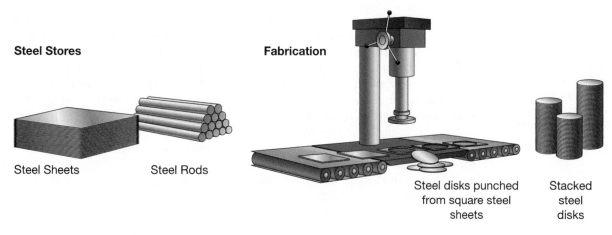

Steel Stores

Steel Sheets   Steel Rods

Fabrication

Steel disks punched from square steel sheets

Stacked steel disks

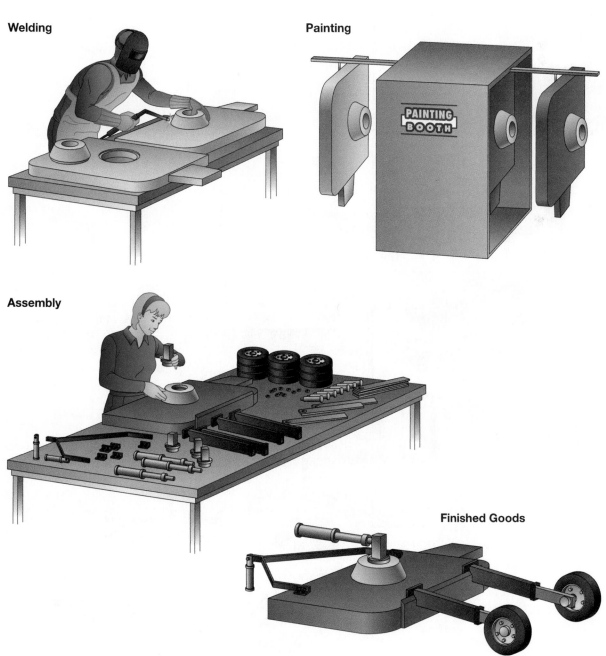

Welding

Painting

PAINTING BOOTH

Assembly

Finished Goods

TUFF CUT: TOTAL QUALITY MANAGEMENT

Total quality management (TQM) **is a management system that seeks continual improvement by asking everyone in an organization to understand, meet, and exceed the needs of customers.** A key question underlying all business activities should be, "Who are the customers, and what are their needs?" For example, total quality management as embraced by a university would include opening additional sections of classes to accommodate large student enrollments. Also, in response to long lines in university bookstores, managers may open additional cash registers to speed the check-out process at the beginning of each term.

Though total quality management is a continually evolving concept, the primary focus is on delivering value to a customer. As shown in Exhibit 2, every activity within an organization should contribute ultimately to the strategic objective of satisfying customers. Thus, the cascading set of TQM tasks shown in the exhibit links strategic objectives with operational activities. In the following paragraphs, Tuff Cut is used to illustrate examples of each task identified in Exhibit 2.

Exhibit 2 Elements of TQM

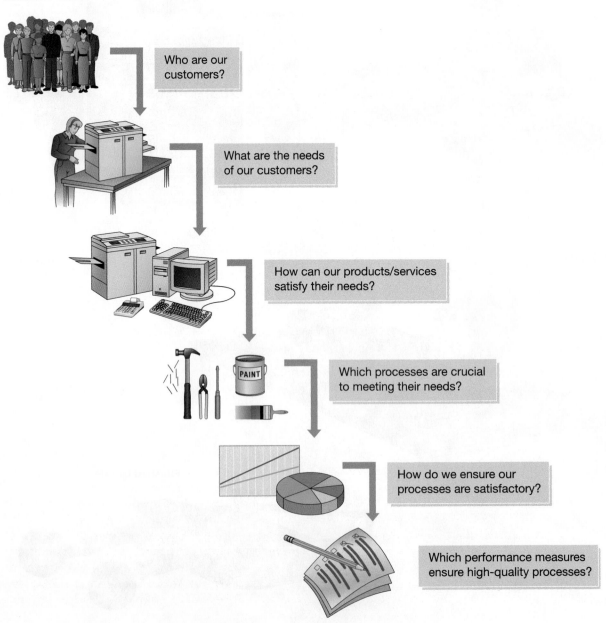

Who are our customers?

What are the needs of our customers?

How can our products/services satisfy their needs?

Which processes are crucial to meeting their needs?

How do we ensure our processes are satisfactory?

Which performance measures ensure high-quality processes?

http://ingram.
swlearning.com

Learn more about TQM.

- *Identify the customers.* At first glance, we may be tempted to say that dealers and retail buyers are Tuff Cut's only customers. However, closer examination reveals additional customers internal, as well as external, to the company. For example, welders are customers of the fabrication process, and painters are customers of the welding process. Each operation produces output that is used by later processes.
- *Identify customer needs.* Having identified its customers, Tuff Cut prepared a list of customer needs. For example, *internal customers* demand rugged, high-quality raw materials consistent with engineering specifications. *External customers* require dependable delivery times and sturdy products capable of withstanding the abuse associated with mowing rough terrain.
- *Identify product (or service) features.* For Tuff Cut customers, important *product* features include strong welds and sturdy gear boxes. Important *service* features include rapid delivery of spare parts and availability of repair services in the event of a mechanical breakdown.
- *Identify process (production or delivery) features.* Customers have identified rugged, high-quality products as essential. To meet this need, strong welds and sturdy components are required. Therefore, the next logical step is to design processes that result in strong welds and sturdy components. Tuff Cut evaluated various welding technologies, including robotic and manual, to ensure that these processes were consistent with the demands of the market.
- *Establish controls.* Having identified key quality processes, management put controls in place to ensure that processes are performed at the appropriate quality level. Often, entire processes are redesigned to meet process requirements for quality.
- *Assess performance against goals from the perspective of both internal and external customers.* Tuff Cut must continuously improve production processes and service functions critical to ensuring that customers are satisfied. Managers assess performance on a number of quality criteria by comparing actual performance with predetermined targets (or benchmarks).

Case in Point

http://ingram.
swlearning.com

Learn more about maquiladoras and manufacturing in Mexico.

Customer-Focused Quality Programs

Maquiladoras (pronounced ma kee' a dor as) are manufacturing plants established in Mexico by foreign companies. The goods produced by maquiladoras are for export only. A major factor in the success of these plants has been the fact that they meet the requirements for international quality certification. Thus, the maquiladoras are creating a quality culture based on the concepts shown in Exhibit 2 in this chapter. These concepts are being used successfully by Mexico's manufacturing companies to change the country's image from a relatively inexpensive source of labor to that of a global manufacturing power.

Source: Aly, Nael, and Danies Schloss. 2003. Assessing Quality Management Systems of Mexico's Maquiladoras, *The TQM Magazine.*

To support TQM activities managers also set benchmarks by comparing their products (or services) against the best on the market. Managers in world-class companies understand their competitors' products, manufacturing processes, and manufacturing costs. Often a competitor's product is purchased and disassembled to understand the types of materials and assembly processes used. Such information is useful during the design phase of a new product. However, when a product is in the production phase, managers look for opportunities to improve quality and to reduce costs. These activities often are termed "Kaizen," or continuous process improvement. Thus, competitive benchmarking and continuous process improvement are consistent with the TQM philosophy. These techniques help managers deliver higher quality products (or services) to their customers at a lower cost.

The remainder of this chapter explores two topics that are consistent with the objectives of total quality management. Just-in-time (JIT) inventory management and the theory of constraints have received much attention from business leaders in recent years. The operations of Tuff Cut are used to demonstrate these concepts. The purpose is to illustrate how real-world companies implement change in order to remain competitive in a dynamic environment.

1 SELF-STUDY PROBLEM

WebTUTOR Advantage

To illustrate the concepts in this chapter, all the self-study problems use the production process of Autobrake. Autobrake produces aftermarket (replacement) brake cylinders used by automobile repair companies. Autobrake purchases steel bar stock from wholesale distributors and manufactures and assembles components for brake cylinders at its plant. The purchasing manager seeks the lowest steel prices (consistent with strict quality standards) from a large number of vendors. Orders for raw materials must often be delivered very rapidly because of poor communication between the production floor and the purchasing department. The company has been growing at a rapid pace because of its reputation for high-quality products. Thus, Autobrake is in the position of having more orders than it currently can process. As a result, it maintains a production backlog of approximately 12 weeks.

The manufacturing process consists of five steps. First, steel bar stock is placed into automatic turning equipment (lathes) (step 1). Clamps secure each end of the bar stock, which spins rapidly while a cutting tool cuts the external dimensions to meet engineering specifications. The process requires two turning operations, first stage and second stage. The operations are similar; however, second-stage turning further refines the shape of the component. Studies conducted by the industrial engineering department suggest that average processing times for first-stage and second-stage turning are five and four minutes per component, respectively. Both turning operations require machine setups between runs of different brake systems. These setups are lengthy and require highly skilled machine operators.

Following second-stage turning, a milling operation takes place (step 2). The component is held in place while a cutting tool removes metal according to specifications. Engineering studies have determined that the milling operation requires approximately seven minutes for each component. The milling machines are old and subject to unexpected breakdowns. Because Autobrake does not maintain large amounts of work-in-process inventory, a machine failure often causes other machines to be idle from lack of input.

After milling, a component is ground to meet final specifications (step 3). The grinding operation requires approximately three minutes per component and is the last process before the cylinders are assembled.

Assembly of various components is a manual operation (step 4). The average assembly time per cylinder is six minutes. Following assembly, each cylinder is carefully packaged in an individual paperboard box that bears the name and logo of Autobrake (step 5). Autobrake gets its packaging materials from a company that buys rolls of paper stock from paper mills and produces custom-printed boxes. Management is considering automating the packaging line to reduce labor costs. Automated equipment would reduce the packaging time of 15 seconds to 8 seconds.

Autobrake contracts with trucking lines to transport its products to wholesalers, who then sell the brake cylinders to various retail stores. However, a major retailer of auto parts has contacted Autobrake to explore the possibilities of buying cylinders directly from the factory, without going through a wholesaler. In addition, the retailer wishes to buy cylinders in bulk containers rather than in individual packages.

Required

A. Draw a diagram that represents the five-step process Autobrake uses. Include processing times.
B. Discuss how Autobrake might apply TQM principles to improve its competitiveness.

The solution to Self-Study Problem 1 appears at the end of the chapter.

PRINCIPLES OF JUST-IN-TIME MANUFACTURING

OBJECTIVE 3

Describe the just-in-time (JIT) manufacturing philosophy and evaluate its strengths and weaknesses from financial and operating perspectives.

http://ingram.
swlearning.com

Learn more about JIT.

Erin and Seth discussed the costs of making infrequent, large raw material purchases. These costs included handling, storing, and insuring. They also discussed providing better service to their customers by improving delivery time, which in turn would minimize the finished goods inventory costs. Minimizing inventory levels is a condition of just-in-time (JIT) manufacturing systems, which have become popular in recent years. *Just-in-time manufacturing* **is a production system that pulls products through the manufacturing process on the basis of market demand.** Inventory levels are minimized (parts are delivered "just-in-time"), thereby improving asset turnover and reducing manufacturing costs. The concepts underlying just-in-time are not new; Japanese manufacturing companies have benefited from lean, integrated manufacturing systems for many years. A just-in-time manufacturing system typically has a number of related elements. For example, inventory is pulled through the system based on market demand. Companies using just-in-time have small inventories of raw materials and finished goods; therefore, high-quality raw materials are critical to success. Poor-quality raw materials can stop a production line. Because high-quality materials are extremely important, companies usually establish close business relationships with a small number of high-quality, certified suppliers. Engineers work to minimize machine changeover (setup) times to permit manufacturing products in small batches. Short manufacturing cycle times result from small-batch production. Thus, just-in-time manufacturing is an important element of time-based competition. High-quality materials, rapid setup times, small-batch production, and minimal inventory levels are all important elements of just-in-time systems.

Just-in-time principles require inventory to be pulled through the plant based on market demand. For example, the last operation in a process acts as a trigger, signaling earlier (upstream) work centers to begin production. The pull system is in contrast to traditional "push" systems, which determine production levels from forecasted demand.

The push system is illustrated in Exhibit 3, panel A. Production is started in Department 1 based on market forecasts of customer demand. The goods produced are placed in inventory until they are needed. The alternative, the pull (or just-in-time) system, is illustrated in panel B of the exhibit. When a customer places an order, a signal is sent to the assembly department to begin production. The assembly department removes components from work-in-process and assembles them, and the product is delivered to the customer. When components are removed from work-in-process, a signal to process additional components is sent to the painting department. Thus, the painting department takes cut components from work-in-process, paints them, and places the painted components into work-in-process. By removing cut components from work-in-process, the painting department sends a signal to the sawing department to cut more materials. Therefore, the sawing department places an order for materials from an outside vendor. The materials are cut and put into work-in-process. In summary, a just-in-time system pulls products through the factory at the rate of customer demand. Information flows from right to left, as indicated by the blue arrows in Exhibit 3 (B). Materials flow from left to right, as shown by the red arrows in the exhibit. A key component of the pull system is low work-in-process inventory and rapid product movement.

To move products through a plant quickly, a company looks for ways to reduce machine setup (or changeover) times. By making setup times short enough, a company can produce units in small batches. Small-batch production results in low inventory levels because products move through the process in small quantities, rather than in large blocks. The company enjoys fast cycle times. Cycle time is considered in the following section.

Just-in-time principles require small amounts of all types of inventory, even raw materials inventory. Therefore, a good relationship with vendors is extremely important. Vendors must make many deliveries of small amounts of high-quality raw materials, rather than making weekly or monthly deliveries of large quantities. Because only small amounts are delivered at a time, quality must be high, or the production line will stop because of lack of raw material. To achieve the objectives of just-in-time, **nonfinancial performance measures** are used to evaluate critical factors such as cycle time,

Exhibit 3 Push System (A) of Production Compared to Pull System (B)

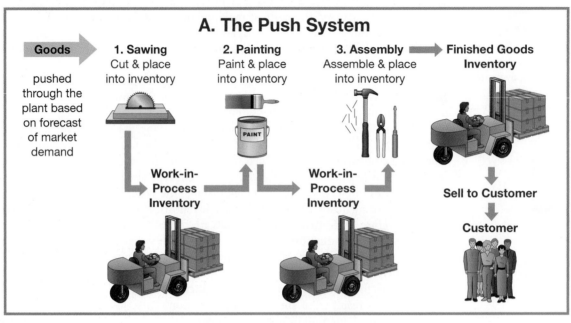

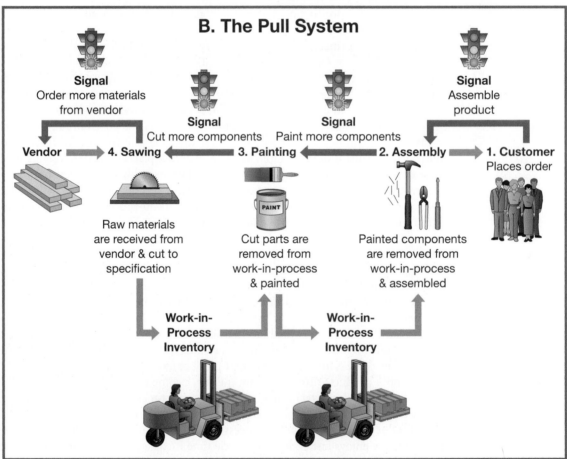

production rate, and throughput. The following section considers measures that are consistent with the philosophies of just-in-time and total quality management.

Nonfinancial Performance Measures

In today's manufacturing environment, employees often are asked to participate in cross-functional teams made up of individuals with various types of professional expertise. For example, teams may consist of accountants, industrial engineers, production managers, purchasing managers, and finance managers. Often, teams are responsible for improving processes, reducing manufacturing costs, and developing key nonfinancial performance indicators. Performance is no longer measured only in financial terms, such as net income or return on investment. While better financial performance is the ultimate goal, financial measures often do not provide guidance to managers who want to improve manufacturing performance. Thus, measurements such as *cycle time*, *throughput*, and *bottleneck management* have been added to the list of performance criteria.

To illustrate these concepts, Exhibit 4 contains processing times for various work centers within the Tuff Cut plant. For example, the fabrication area has the capacity to produce 20 units per hour, while the welding, painting, and assembly areas are capable of processing 10, 30, and 25 units per hour, respectively. From these data, we can determine several key performance indicators for the Tuff Cut plant. The following sections consider the concepts of cycle time, production rate, and throughput.

Cycle Time. *Cycle time* **is defined as the total time required to move a unit from raw materials inventory to finished goods inventory.** Cycle time is the sum of processing time, moving time, and waiting time. Exhibit 4 indicates that the **processing time** required to produce one rotary mower is:

	Processing Time (minutes)
Fabrication	3.0
Welding	6.0
Painting	2.0
Assembly	2.4
Total	13.4

Each rotary mower requires 13.4 minutes of total processing time from beginning (fabrication) to end (assembly). **Processing time is the number of minutes in which value is added to raw materials.** Does this mean that Tuff Cut can produce a unit from start to finish in 13.4 minutes? Probably not. Processing time is only one part of cycle time; the other part is **wait time, the time a unit spends waiting to be processed.** For example, assume that each work center has six hours of work-in-process inventory waiting to be processed. Six hours of work-in-process inventory represent the production of less than one shift. Most manufacturers have far more work-in-process inventory. Thus, 24 hours of wait time (6 hours before the fabrication area + 6 hours before the welding area + 6 hours before the painting area + 6 hours before the assembly area = 24 hours) are built into Tuff Cut's manufacturing process. Therefore, the cycle time for completing one mower is calculated as follows:

Wait time (24 hours × 60 minutes)	1,440.0 minutes
Processing time	13.4 minutes
Cycle time	1,453.4 minutes

Wait time makes up the major portion of the cycle time required to move a unit of product through the plant. Imagine a four-step class registration process at your university that requires a six-hour wait at each step to accomplish a task requiring only a

Exhibit 4 Workcenter Processing Times within the Tuff Cut Plant

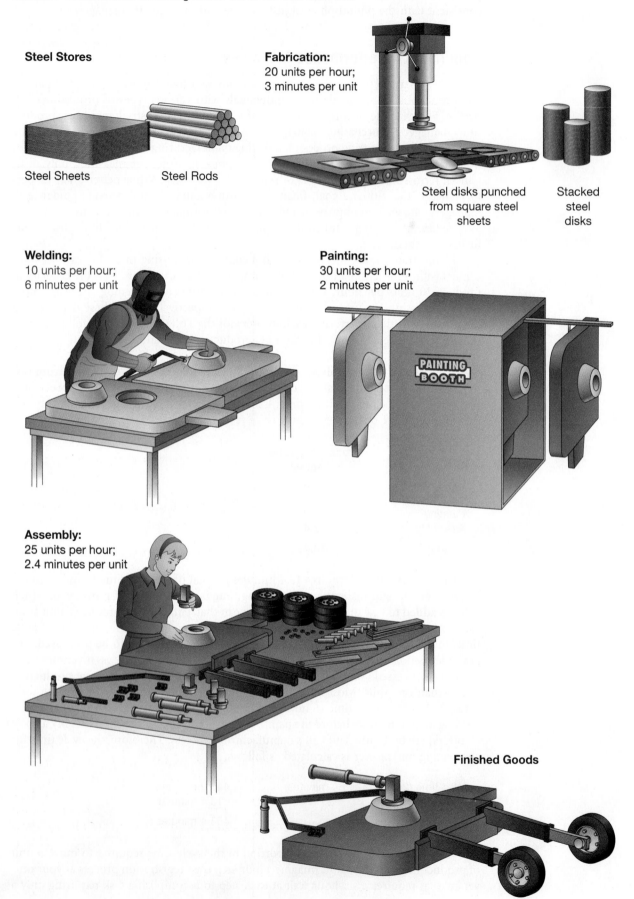

Steel Stores

Steel Sheets   Steel Rods

Fabrication:
20 units per hour;
3 minutes per unit

Steel disks punched
from square steel
sheets

Stacked
steel
disks

Welding:
10 units per hour;
6 minutes per unit

Painting:
30 units per hour;
2 minutes per unit

PAINTING BOOTH

Assembly:
25 units per hour;
2.4 minutes per unit

Finished Goods

few minutes. You probably would say that the university registration process is inefficient. The same is true with a manufacturing process.

Why would Tuff Cut keep six hours of inventory at each work center? The answer involves process reliability. For example, without such inventory, if a work center becomes idle because of a mechanical breakdown, all later (downstream) work centers must stop processing because of lack of input. Therefore, inventory is viewed as insurance against unreliable equipment. Unfortunately, the insurance is not free. Just-in-time manufacturing practices require reducing the level of inventory to reduce carrying costs and to improve cycle time.

So, why are cycle time and work-in-process levels important? What is the downside of having high work-in-process levels and long cycle times? Maintaining high inventory levels is expensive because of the potential for damage or obsolescence as well as the cost of storage. Also, managers often are evaluated using return on assets[2] as a performance criterion. High inventory levels make the asset base larger and reduce a company's return. There are other considerations as well. A company that has low levels of work-in-process inventory can move an order through the process in much less time than a company whose inventory levels require many hours of waiting time. Thus, fast-cycle companies may enjoy a strategic advantage in the marketplace by being able to deliver goods faster than their competition.

In addition to cycle time, production rate often is used as a nonfinancial performance measure. The next section considers production rate in connection with the Tuff Cut plant.

Production Rate. *Production rate* **is the number of units a manufacturing system is capable of producing in a given time period.** For example, if a manufacturing system can produce 10 products every hour (or 10 units/60 minutes), a new product would be completed every six minutes (10 units/60 minutes = 1 unit/6 minutes). For Tuff Cut, which manufacturing center (fabrication, welding, painting, or assembly) drives the production rate? The slowest process in the chain, the welding area, drives the production rate for the entire system. Since welders need six minutes to process a unit, it does not matter that the fabrication department can process one unit every three minutes, or that the painting department can process one unit every two minutes. The welders take the longest time to process a unit, and the system as a whole cannot move faster than the slowest process will permit. **Processes that work at slow production rates and restrict the flow of goods or services are termed** *bottlenecks.* Just as the small-diameter opening in a bottle restricts the flow of liquid, a production bottleneck restricts the output of a process.

The fabrication area can process units twice as fast as the welding area; however, processing at a rate faster than ten units per hour merely results in excess work-in-process inventory accumulating in front of the welding area. The painting and assembly areas also process faster than the welding area. Unfortunately, their output is held down by the welding area's inability to provide parts fast enough for them to achieve their potential. Thus, the production rate of the entire plant is determined by the slowest manufacturing center, the welding process.

This section has evaluated cycle time and production rate as performance indicators. Another important measure of a manufacturing facility is throughput, which is discussed in the following section.

Throughput. *Throughput* **represents the number of units completed by a process.** Marketing managers are interested in both cycle time and throughput. Cycle time affects a salesperson's ability to deliver goods to customers quickly, and throughput affects the number of units available for sale. Of course, throughput is related to production rate. For example, to calculate the number of units Tuff Cut can produce in one eight-hour shift, multiply the available production time by the production rate.

---

[2] Recall that Return on assets = Asset turnover × Profit margin

$$= \frac{\text{Sales}}{\text{Average assets}} \times \frac{\text{Earnings}}{\text{Sales}}$$

Thus, by multiplying available production time by production rate, throughput can be determined as follows:

8 hours per shift × 60 minutes per hour =		480 available minutes per shift
Production rate	=	1/6 (or 1 unit every 6 minutes)
Throughput	= 480 × 1/6 =	80 units per eight-hour shift

Therefore, Tuff Cut has the ability to produce 80 units per eight-hour shift. During periods when demand for rotary mowers is high, managers must ensure that throughput is maximized to avoid lost sales.

PRODUCT-ORIENTED VERSUS PROCESS-ORIENTED PLANT LAYOUT

OBJECTIVE 4

Explain how a traditional "process-oriented" plant layout differs from a "product-oriented" plant layout, and describe the financial consequences of each layout.

Some organizations have explored various approaches to plant organization in an attempt to improve operations and reduce manufacturing costs. Innovative plant layouts have been developed that can support minimal inventory levels, fast setup times, high-quality products, and responsive cycle times. Traditionally, designs for manufacturing facilities were *process-oriented*. Each area of the plant was designed to carry out a certain type of process, and work-in-process inventory was transported between processes. For example, as illustrated in Exhibit 5, the steel storage area at Tuff Cut was located in the northwest corner of the plant. Materials were transported to the fabrication area in large batches by forklift. Following fabrication, the pieces were transported to the welding area to await processing. Following the welding operation, extensive handling and transportation was needed to move units to the painting process and back to final assembly. Clearly, Tuff Cut organized its factory by grouping similar processes together, an example of a process-oriented plant layout. *Process-oriented plant layouts* **typically are arranged according to machine function, with machines that perform similar functions placed together.**

Exhibit 5 Traditional "Process-Oriented" Plant Layout

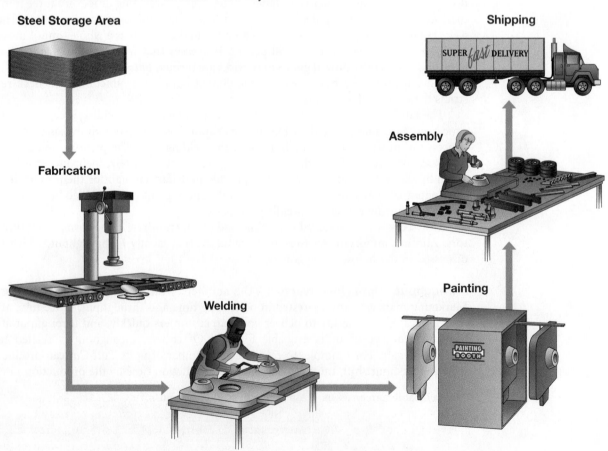

What are some of the cost considerations in a traditional process-oriented plant? First of all, to make efficient use of assets and the people who move parts from one workstation to another, a process-oriented plant typically produces in large batches. Therefore, work-in-process levels are high and lead times are long.

As an alternative, many companies are reorganizing their plants. As illustrated in Exhibit 6, **a** *product-oriented plant layout* **is based on manufacturing cells that meet the production requirements of products or product families (products that have similar characteristics).**

Exhibit 6 Cellular "Product-Oriented" Plant Layout

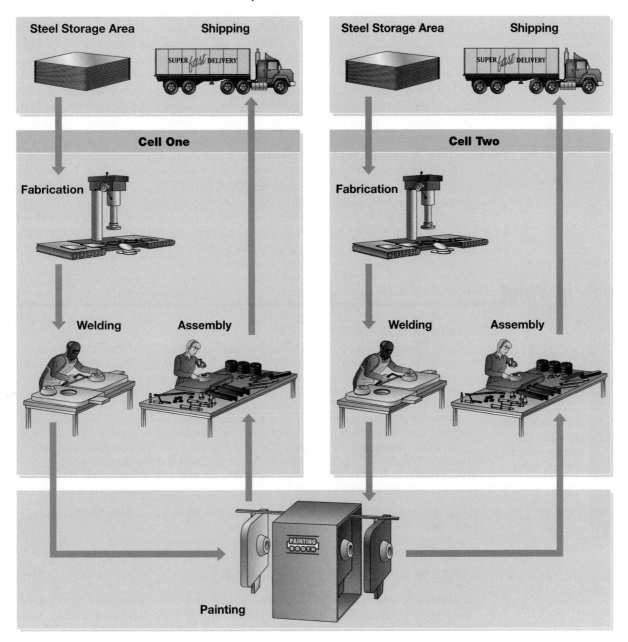

Because of rapid changes in product characteristics, manufacturing systems are developed to be flexible. Rather than buying a machine that serves only one function, such as drilling, cutting, or welding, companies are investing in flexible machinery that can perform a number of functions. Typically, flexible manufacturing systems are characterized by their ability to change rapidly from one type of process to another. For example, automatic tool changers may remove a drill bit that makes $\frac{1}{2}$-inch-diameter holes and replace it with a drill bit that makes $\frac{1}{4}$-inch-diameter holes. In addition, many flexible systems contain automatic error detection in the form of statistical process control software. Finally, most flexible systems have the ability to increase or decrease the rate of output.[3]

A *manufacturing cell* **is a group of related machines, typically arranged in the shape of a U.** Raw materials enter one prong of the U, and finished goods exit from the other prong. Exhibit 6 illustrates how Tuff Cut might reorganize its plant floor to achieve a product-oriented layout. The industrial engineers designed work cells by placing equipment in two cells based on the manufacturing requirements of their product line. The painting process presented a few problems because the paint line cannot be divided. Thus, the design linked both cells to the painting area.

As indicated by the arrows in Exhibit 6, raw materials enter the cell and are processed, and completed products leave the cell. Because machines within the cell are close to one another, extensive handling and transportation of work-in-process inventory is not required. Work cells are arranged according to the needs of product families and are consistent with the concepts of just-in-time manufacturing. Because batch sizes are small, work-in-process levels are lower than those of process-oriented plants. Cycle times also are much shorter because units do not sit for long periods of time waiting for processing. Plants that use a cellular design often have many cells, each dedicated to a product or product family.

Cellular manufacturing requires few arbitrary overhead allocations because costs associated with each cell tend to be direct. Thus, identifying the resources used by each product or product family usually is easier with a plant layout based on manufacturing cells. In addition, since batch sizes are small, waste and scrap costs should be minimal. For example, if a machine operator makes an error in setting the width of a cut for a small batch, only a few units are affected.

Case in Point

http://ingram.
swlearning.com

Find out about the winners of the Shingo Prize for excellence in lean manufacturing.

Lean Manufacturing

Medalist LaserFab is an Oshkosh, Wisconsin-based company that makes sheet metal parts such as fenders and steps for Oshkosh Truck Corporation. The company is doing more with less. Its goal is to reduce waste, inventory levels, and production stoppages. We "bring the raw material in, cut it, and get it out," according to John Mazur, president of Medalist LaserFab.

Ariens Company, a member of the same consortium as Medalist LaserFab, also practices lean manufacturing. Using manufacturing cells as described in this chapter, the company reported the following: "The process builds on the company's decision to assemble machinery in pods that did away with labyrinthine assembly lines that used to snake through the plant." As a result, the company reports reduced lead time, reduced costs, and increased cash flow.

Source: 2003. Manufacturers in Appleton, Wisconsin Area Learn to Think Like Service Suppliers, *Knight Ridder Tribune Business News* (April 30).

Financial Benefits Resulting from JIT

Managers who make operational changes consistent with just-in-time management principles expect these changes to improve profitability. As discussed in this section, just-in-time principles help managers increase revenues as well as reduce operating costs. For example, companies maintain minimal levels of raw materials, work-in-process, and finished goods inventories when products are pulled through the factory at the rate demanded by customers. Reduced inventory levels result in lower carrying costs, which

[3] For more information on flexible manufacturing systems, see Black, J. T. 1991. *The Design of the Factory with a Future* (New York: McGraw-Hill, Inc.).

include costs of financing, obsolescence, and damage. Fast setup times contribute to short manufacturing cycle times. Often, responsive factories gain a competitive advantage that translates into increased sales. This section considers the financial effects of reduced inventory levels, improved manufacturing cycle times, and increased throughput.

Selected financial information for Tuff Cut follows. The company currently has sales of $93 million annually while employing assets of $139.5 million. The controller estimates that variable manufacturing costs are 40 percent of sales. In addition, fixed manufacturing expenses and fixed administrative expenses are $28 million and $11 million, respectively. Thus, Tuff Cut's return on assets currently is 12 percent.

Annual sales		$93,000,000
Variable manufacturing expenses, 40% of sales		
(0.40 × $93,000,000)	$37,200,000	
Fixed manufacturing costs	28,000,000	
Fixed general and administrative costs	11,000,000	76,200,000
Operating income		$16,800,000

Return on assets before process changes:

$$\underset{\text{Profit Margin}}{(\text{Operating income}^4 \div \text{Sales})} \times \underset{\text{Asset Turnover}}{(\text{Sales} \div \text{Assets}^5)} = \text{Return on assets}$$

$$(\$16,800,000 \div \$93,000,000) \times (\$93,000,000 \div \$139,500,000) = \text{Return on assets}$$

$$0.18 \times 0.67 = 0.12$$

Let's consider how implementing just-in-time can improve Tuff Cut's return on assets. First, assume that demand for Tuff Cut's products exceeds supply and that improvements in throughput will result in a 10 percent increase in sales. Further, assume that reductions in raw materials, work-in-process, and finished goods inventories will result in a 1 percent decrease in assets. In addition, variable manufacturing costs will be reduced from 40 percent of sales to 38.5 percent of sales because inventory carrying costs and scrap rates will decrease. Product and process reengineering efforts often reduce fixed manufacturing costs. In this case, Tuff Cut's fixed manufacturing costs will decrease from $28 million to $27 million because of reductions in materials handling activities and the elimination of unnecessary manufacturing equipment. Finally, fixed administrative costs will be reduced from $11 million to $10 million because of changes in administrative support functions. For example, fixed administrative costs can be reduced by restructuring processes and reducing the amount of indirect labor and equipment. The following calculations summarize our assumptions:

Annual sales ($93,000,000 × 1.1)		$102,300,000
Variable manufacturing expenses,		
38.5% of sales (0.385 × $102,300,000)	$39,385,500	
Fixed manufacturing costs	27,000,000	
Fixed general and administrative costs	10,000,000	76,385,500
Operating income		$ 25,914,500

Assets following a 1% decrease = $139,500,000 × 0.99 = $138,105,000

Return on assets after process changes:

$$\underset{\text{Profit Margin}}{(\text{Operating income} \div \text{Sales})} \times \underset{\text{Asset Turnover}}{(\text{Sales} \div \text{Assets})} = \text{Return on assets}$$

$$(\$25,914,500 \div \$102,300,000) \times (\$102,300,000 \div \$138,105,000) = \text{Return on assets}$$

$$0.25 \times 0.74 = 0.19$$

---

[4] Operating income is equivalent to earnings.
[5] The asset information given here is assumed to be equal to average costs.

These calculations suggest that Tuff Cut's return on assets will improve from 12 to 19 percent as a result of implementing just-in-time principles. Our example illustrates the potential financial effects of changes in manufacturing strategy. Companies that have successfully implemented just-in-time see it as a strategy for long-run continuous improvement. Thus, just-in-time is not a "magic pill" that suddenly will improve a company's profitability. However, as our example illustrates, just-in-time includes sound operating principles that affect a company's revenues and costs.

Drawbacks to the Just-in-Time Manufacturing Philosophy

Just-in-time manufacturing is a system with many positive attributes; however, it has its disadvantages. In the economic recovery of the early 1990s, many companies reduced inventories to record low levels. Unfortunately, some companies experienced difficulties because of these low levels. Assume that you are the general manager of two plants, a manufacturing plant and an assembly plant. The manufacturing plant provides components to the assembly plant. Unexpectedly, the union at the manufacturing plant goes on strike. In the past, negotiations were lengthy and difficult, but at that time, the assembly plant had six months of components in inventory. Now, consistent with the just-in-time philosophy, the assembly plant has three days of inventory. How do you think just-in-time will affect your ability to bargain effectively? The union at the manufacturing plant has successfully closed two plants instead of one.

In a just-in-time environment, cost savings from reducing inventories can be offset by increased delivery costs imposed by suppliers who are now making daily (or even hourly) deliveries. In addition, management must explain to workers why they are being asked to increase the number of batches and machine setups. Finally, in an economy experiencing rapid growth, managers may increase inventory to levels *inconsistent* with just-in-time because they fear that they will run out of inventory at a time when customers are ready to purchase goods.

On balance, just-in-time principles have helped many manufacturers improve operations and reduce waste. In addition, by reducing work-in-process inventory levels, bottlenecks become apparent. As we discussed earlier in this section, bottlenecks in a production process affect production rates, and thus the number of units processed through the system (throughput). Understanding how to manage bottleneck resources is important for improving operating performance. The following section addresses the issue of managing bottlenecks.

Case in Point

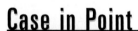

http://ingram.
swlearning.com

Learn more about
NUMMI.

JIT

New United Motor Manufacturing, Inc. (NUMMI) is a joint venture between **General Motors Corporation** and **Toyota Motor Corporation**. Using a JIT system, NUMMI produces trucks and automobiles in its Fremont, California, plant. The company shut down its truck line for five days and its car line for two days as a result of a West Coast dock strike. The strike caused parts and supplies necessary for production to remain loaded on ships docked in the harbor. The port dispute is one of many examples of challenges that can disrupt production in a JIT manufacturing environment. Other events that could challenge JIT producers include terrorist attacks that would close borders, economic crises overseas, and weather disasters.

NUMMI responded to the port crisis by temporarily using very costly air transportation. The company has used trucks when flooding disrupted rail transportation. Will the company abandon its JIT program as a result of these "wildcard" events? According to Michael Damer of NUMMI, "Is it really reasonable to build up a couple of months inventory in the event this happens again? We don't have facilities for that inventory, and we don't want them."

Source: 2002. *Industry Week* (December).

2 SELF-STUDY PROBLEM Refer to the information presented in Self-Study Problem 1.

Required

A. Calculate the following for the manufacturing process at Autobrake:
   1. Production rate
   2. Total processing time
   3. Throughput
B. Why would you expect cycle time to be different from the total processing time calculated in part (A2) above?
C. Assume that management at Autobrake is considering redesigning the plant layout from a process-oriented layout to a product-oriented layout by establishing work cells. Discuss the benefits of a product-oriented plant layout.

The solution to Self-Study Problem 2 appears at the end of the chapter.

THE THEORY OF CONSTRAINTS

OBJECTIVE 5

Identify the primary components of the theory of constraints.

Recall that Seth discussed the importance of efficiently routing products through the manufacturing process. As part of his discussion, he mentioned the importance of using resources wisely. This section considers the theory of constraints, a system that encourages managers to identify bottlenecks and manage them efficiently.

As indicated in the previous section, the welding area of the Tuff Cut factory was found to be a bottleneck. In this area, steel sheets are assembled to form the mower housing. As part of the strategic objective of reducing cycle time and increasing throughput, management began reducing the level of work-in-process inventory. In doing so, they observed some troubling outcomes. Certain machines were forced to become idle, which resulted in a *decrease*, rather than an increase, in throughput.

While touring the plant in search of answers to the decline in productivity, managers noticed several things that suggested the presence of a bottleneck. First, in the welding area, managers observed large stacks of work-in-process inventory sitting in front of the welding machines waiting to be processed. Though work-in-process inventories in most areas of the plant contained output from only a few hours of production, the work-in-process inventory in the welding area contained output from several days of production. Second, after observing the welding operation over a number of days, managers noticed that the welders never were idle, except during scheduled breaks. In contrast, they noticed that the downstream painting process often was forced to shut down temporarily because workers had no materials to paint. From observing the manufacturing process, management reasoned that the welding area must be a production bottleneck, or constraint.

Bottleneck processes exist in almost every manufacturing plant. They result when the processing speed of a machine or production area is less than that of other machines or production areas in the plant. Bottlenecks never can be eliminated entirely, because as the processing capability of one machine or production area is increased, a *different* machine or production area often becomes a bottleneck. Thus, in the spirit of continuous process improvement, managers continually adjust processes to improve throughput and reduce operating costs.

Steps to Improve Performance

This section explores various steps management can take to improve throughput consistent with the theory of constraints.[6] **The** *theory of constraints (TOC)* **states that by**

---

[6] The principles of the theory of constraints were developed and discussed in Goldratt, Eliyahn M., and Jeff Cox. 1992. *The Goal* (Great Barrington: North River Press).

identifying a constraint, such as a bottleneck, that exists in the processing of a good or service and taking corrective steps, the process will be improved. The five steps recommended for process improvement are as follows:

- Step 1: Attack a bottleneck by **identifying** the system's constraints.
- Step 2: Decide how to make the **best use** of the constraint.
- Step 3: **Subordinate** all other decisions to those made in step 2.
- Step 4: **Improve the performance** of the constraint.
- Step 5: If a constraint has been broken (the old bottleneck is gone) but a different bottleneck has been created, **go back to step 1 and start over.**

Implementation of the Theory of Constraints

Let's assume that managers at Tuff Cut have correctly identified the welding area as a bottleneck. Thus, the second step involves deciding how to make the best use of the welding area. For example, because a minute of lost time on a bottleneck results in a minute of lost production for the entire plant, the bottleneck resource must never be allowed to remain idle during lunchtime and breaks. If automated equipment is used, workers simply make certain the raw material supply bins are filled with parts before they leave the work area for a break. Alternatively, workers may be encouraged to have flexible break times and lunchtimes to ensure that the bottleneck is not idle.

Another way to reduce the effect of the bottleneck is to inspect materials before they are processed at the bottleneck. For example, if scrap rates are a problem in the manufacturing process, inspection centers can be located before the bottleneck. Thus, the bottleneck does not waste valuable processing time on parts that will be unusable.

Step 3 suggests that all other decisions should be subordinated to those made in step 2. In other words, the entire plant should be scheduled and managed by considering the bottleneck. For example, components that require processing on a bottleneck resource should receive highest priority at nonbottleneck work centers. Thus, all work centers should schedule production orders to ensure that the bottleneck resource is never idle.

The fourth step requires managers to improve the performance of the bottleneck. What are some strategies Tuff Cut can use to improve performance on the bottleneck in the welding area? They can minimize downtime on the bottleneck by making machine setups less time-consuming. One method of reducing setup time is to convert on-line setup time to off-line setup time. Production machinery often has removable parts, such as saw blades, grippers, and drill bits, called machine tools. Complex tool changes can be made more quickly if two or more sets of tools are used. While a machine is actively producing with one set of tools, a machinist prepares the settings of a second set of tools at a workbench. Changeovers become rapid because one set of tools is simply replaced by a second set that already has been prepared. Thus, productive time is gained by reducing downtime associated with setup activities.

Extra capacity can be created for the bottleneck resource in several ways. Purchasing additional machinery can reduce the effects of a bottleneck by providing more processing capability. If management decides that capital for additional equipment is not available, some components could be purchased from external sources, thereby increasing the output of the entire plant. Additionally, more workers can be hired. At Tuff Cut, management acquired a new machine to operate along with existing equipment. The new machine provided the capacity needed to increase throughput, while decreasing inventory. Let's assume that the new equipment was more efficient and increased the number of units processed from 10 per hour to 25 per hour. How will the investment affect throughput?

Exhibit 7 illustrates the relationships among Tuff Cut's processing centers after adding the new equipment. What is the production rate under the new arrangement? Just as before, the bottleneck controls the rate of product flow through the plant. Do we have the same bottleneck as before?

Exhibit 7 Revised Workcenter Processing Times within the Tuff Cut Plant

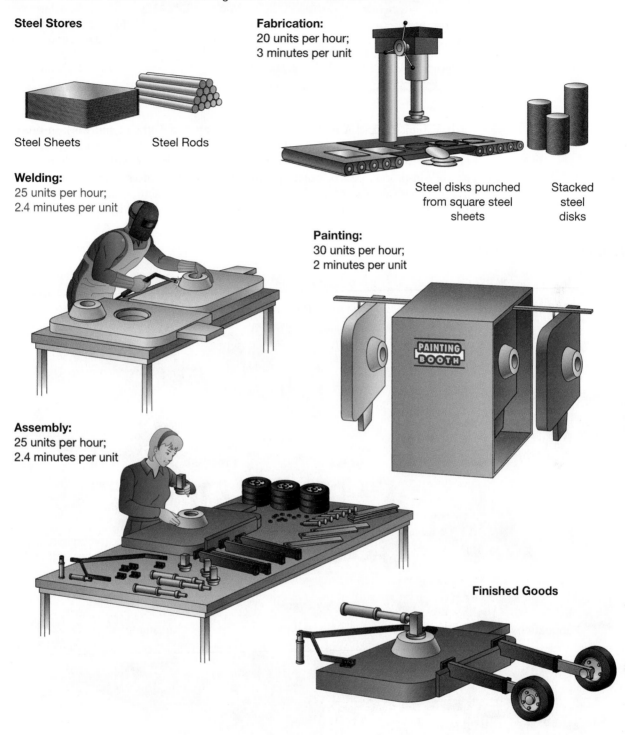

Steel Stores

Steel Sheets   Steel Rods

Fabrication:
20 units per hour;
3 minutes per unit

Steel disks punched
from square steel
sheets

Stacked
steel
disks

Welding:
25 units per hour;
2.4 minutes per unit

Painting:
30 units per hour;
2 minutes per unit

Assembly:
25 units per hour;
2.4 minutes per unit

Finished Goods

Exhibit 8 indicates that with the capacity of the welding department increased to 25 units per hour, the fabrication department, with a productive capacity of 20 units per hour, now becomes the process bottleneck. Thus, the production rate has changed from one completed unit every six minutes (10 units per hour = 6 minutes per unit) to one completed unit every three minutes (20 units per hour = 3 minutes per unit). The theoretical throughput per eight-hour shift is calculated by multiplying the number of minutes in an eight-hour shift (60 minutes × 8 hours = 480 minutes) by the production rate. As the following calculations illustrate, improving the process capability of the bottleneck resource dramatically increases the throughput from 80 units per shift to 160 units per shift.

Exhibit 8
Throughput Comparison,
Old System versus New
System

	Before new CNC welder	After new CNC welder
Bottleneck	Welding area	Fabrication area
Production rate	6 minutes per unit	3 minutes per unit
Throughput per 8-hour shift	480 × 1/6 = 80	480 × 1/3 = 160

In Exhibit 9, panel A represents the four processes of Tuff Cut and work-in-process levels between each process. Under the old system, large amounts of inventory piled up in front of the welding area because it was the bottleneck, or slowest work center in the plant. The work-in-process areas before the painting and assembly processes were empty because these processes were faster than the welding process. Thus, painting and assembly workers had idle time between completing a unit and receiving another one from the welding area.

Exhibit 9 Bottleneck Identification

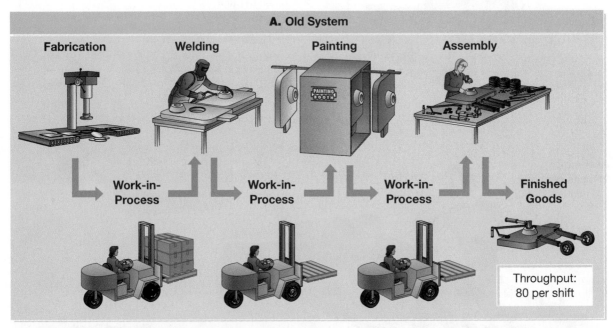

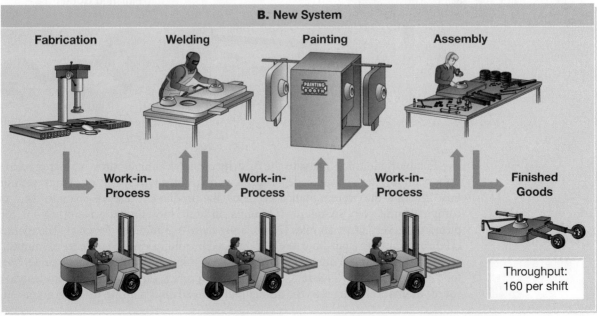

The new system is presented in Exhibit 9, panel B. Now, the fabrication department is the bottleneck, or slowest work center, in the plant. What is the difference in work-in-process levels between panel A and panel B? In panel B, since all processes are faster than the first one in the sequence, no work-in-process inventory accumulates between work centers. In other words, the welding, painting, and assembly work centers can complete a unit of product before the fabricating department places another unit into work-in-process.

In the spirit of continuous process improvement, the fifth step requires management to start over with step 1. As indicated by Exhibit 8, the improvements have shifted the bottleneck operation from the welding area to the fabrication area. Therefore, managers must look for ways to reduce the new constraint, the fabrication area.

If managers increase the processing capacity of nonbottleneck resources, will throughput increase? What if the managers of Tuff Cut learn of robots that can double the speed of the *assembly* process? Thinking every modern manufacturing plant needs advanced technology to survive, they redesign the assembly process and install robots. Press conferences are held in the community to advertise how the company has modernized the plant and how modernization will carry the company forward into the twenty-first century. The plant managers eagerly await the productivity reports in the month following the installation. What result do you predict? Assume the same information presented in Exhibit 7 except that the assembly department now produces at 50 units per hour. Where is the bottleneck? What is the production rate? What is the throughput? Of course, the fabrication area remains the bottleneck, the production rate continues to be the rate of the slowest production area, and throughput does not increase at all. What has happened? Managers invested in faster machines in an area that already had excess capacity. In other words, the bottleneck (the fabrication area) already restricted the rate at which the assembly area could produce. Adding speed to a nonbottleneck resource does nothing for throughput. However, it increases costs and investment, thus reducing operating income and return on assets.

Just-in-Time and Theory of Constraints Similarities and Differences

This chapter used the operations of Tuff Cut to illustrate the concepts of just-in-time inventory management and the theory of constraints. Just-in-time emphasizes external relationships in an attempt to improve operations and profitability. An example includes developing stronger relationships with fewer suppliers. Also, just-in-time emphasizes fast-cycle, low-inventory manufacturing practices. Performance measures consistent with just-in-time include cycle time, setup time, and work-in-process inventory levels.

The theory of constraints also emphasizes the external environment by considering market demand when determining production levels. Both just-in-time and the theory of constraints have the objective of reducing work-in-process inventory levels; however, the theory of constraints emphasizes placing small amounts of inventory in front of constraints to ensure that they are never idle. Both just-in-time and the theory of constraints emphasize the importance of reducing lead times. Thus, just-in-time and the theory of constraints embrace the concepts of total quality management with respect to satisfying customer needs.

Though the approaches discussed in this chapter have different characteristics, a pattern emerges. To compete in the global economy, companies are learning that identifying and serving customer needs is crucial. In addition, inventory management and cost control are major elements of most companies' competitive strategies.

SERVICE ORGANIZATIONS IN A GLOBAL BUSINESS ENVIRONMENT

OBJECTIVE 6

Explain how new manufacturing environment concepts apply to service organizations.

The concepts illustrated in this chapter also are directly applicable to companies that deliver services, rather than tangible products, to their customers. For example, an insurance company specializing in automobile coverage can apply TQM principles in its quest to meet the needs of policyholders. Assume that Fender Bender Insurance Company knows that customers want their insurance claims processed quickly in the event of an automobile accident. Fender Bender may analyze activities in its claims processing department to discover ways to reduce cycle time.

Assume that a study conducted by Fender Bender showed that the average policyholder waits three weeks (15 working days) after submitting a claim before receiving a check. Further studies showed that it takes four hours to process an average claim. Thus, value-added time represents a very small portion of total cycle time. Why does a claim remain in work-in-process so long? Perhaps a bottleneck exists.

For Fender Bender, the number of claims processed is equivalent to throughput for a manufacturing company. Thus, to improve throughput, bottleneck activities must be identified and improved. The check preparation function is an example of a bottleneck within Fender Bender. After cost estimates are received from three separate repair facilities and an insurance adjuster gives final approval, the final step is check preparation. Fender Bender's checks are computer-generated; however, an office employee must enter the amount and the payee into the computer. Fender Bender discovered that the employee responsible for entering check data sometimes waited three or four days between processing batches of checks. Rather than preparing checks several times per day, the employee allowed claim forms to accumulate for processing in one large batch. Thus, work-in-process levels and cycle time increased, resulting in slower claims service and dissatisfied policyholders.

The check-processing activity is only one potential bottleneck, but it illustrates the concepts of a customer-focused total quality management philosophy, bottlenecks, throughput, and cycle time within a *service* organization. Understanding administrative processes permits managers in various service industries to deliver value to their customers. Other examples of customer-oriented services include one-day mortgage loan approval offered by certain mortgage lenders, fast checkout procedures offered by major hotel chains, and rapid car rental and drop-off services provided by leading car rental agencies.

---

3 SELF-STUDY PROBLEM

Autobrake wishes to identify bottlenecks in the production process.

Required

A. How would you identify potential bottlenecks by observing a manufacturing process?
B. If the bottleneck in Autobrake's process is idle for one hour, what is the effect on plant throughput?
C. How would an hour of lost time on a nonbottleneck machine affect throughput?
D. Identify some ways to ensure that production time on the bottleneck process is not wasted.

The solution to Self-Study Problem 3 appears at the end of the chapter.

REVIEW

SUMMARY of IMPORTANT CONCEPTS

1. Managers use accounting information to help them make strategic and operational decisions.
   a. Strategic decisions are major, high-level decisions that affect the overall direction of an organization.
   b. Operational decisions focus on the day-to-day operations of the company.

2. Total quality management includes the following activities:
   a. Identify customers.
   b. Identify customer needs.
   c. Identify product (good or service) features.
   d. Identify process (production or delivery) features.
   e. Establish controls and conduct operations.
   f. Assess performance against goals from both internal and external customer perspectives.

3. Just-in-time (JIT) has the following key elements:
   a. High-quality input and output are required.
   b. Inventory levels are reduced.
   c. Production rates become faster.
   d. Suppliers become partners, rather than adversaries.
   e. Machine changeover (setup) times must be short.
   f. Production batch sizes are small.
   g. Inventory is pulled through a plant based on market demand.

4. Manufacturing plants typically are organized as process-oriented or product-oriented facilities.
   a. Process-oriented facilities typically group equipment by function; all welders, painters, or grinders are located together in one part of the facility.
   b. Product-oriented facilities arrange equipment according to the needs of products or product families; a production area may contain a welder, grinder, and painter to accommodate the needs of a particular product.

5. The theory of constraints has the following key steps:
   a. Identify the process constraint (the bottleneck).
   b. Decide how to make the most efficient use of the constraint.
   c. Subordinate all other decisions to those identified as making efficient use of the constraint.
   d. Improve the processing capability of the constraint.

6. The concepts of total quality management, just-in-time, and the theory of constraints can be applied to service organizations.
   a. All organizations use processes to deliver their goods or services to customers.
   b. TQM principles apply to service organizations as well as to manufacturing companies.
   c. Processes within service organizations can contain bottlenecks that affect lead time and throughput.

DEFINE

TERMS and CONCEPTS DEFINED in this CHAPTER

bottlenecks (M341)
cycle time (M339)
just-in-time manufacturing (M337)
manufacturing cell (M344)
process-oriented plant layout (M342)

production rate (M341)
product-oriented plant layout (M343)
theory of constraints (TOC) (M347)
throughput (M341)
total quality management (TQM) (M334)

SELF-STUDY PROBLEM SOLUTIONS

SSP11-1   A.

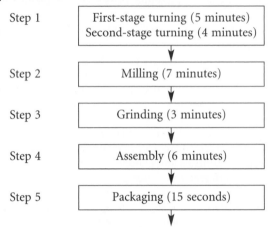

Step 1 — First-stage turning (5 minutes) / Second-stage turning (4 minutes)

Step 2 — Milling (7 minutes)

Step 3 — Grinding (3 minutes)

Step 4 — Assembly (6 minutes)

Step 5 — Packaging (15 seconds)

Within the plant, raw material goes through five operations: turning (first and second stage), milling, grinding, assembly, and packaging. Following packaging, cylinders are shipped to wholesalers, who sell and ship to retailers.

B. Using TQM principles, there are several clues for improvement in the process description. For example, Autobrake orders raw materials from many vendors, using the lowest cost as a criteria. In addition, communication between the plant floor and the purchasing department often is very poor. Perhaps Autobrake could reduce the costs of acquiring raw materials by working closely with a few selected vendors. Understanding suppliers' cost drivers may also help Autobrake reduce acquisition costs. For example, production needs could be forecast well in advance and provided to vendors, who then might pass along savings resulting from better communication between the two companies. Delivery costs often can be reduced by careful planning.

The process description also suggests that setup times between batches of different products are very lengthy. Since the process appears to be capacity-constrained (Autobrake has a backlog of orders), an hour used to set up equipment cannot be used to make brake cylinders. Therefore, if a faster method of performing machine setups can be developed, nonproductive setup time can be converted into productive manufacturing time.

The scenario at the close of the problem suggests that Autobrake has the opportunity to sell directly to a large retailer and to eliminate packaging costs. Packaging includes raw materials (in the form of paperboard boxes) and also labor and overhead costs associated with handling.

Thus, by identifying key process features and establishing controls to ensure that Autobrake meets or exceeds demands placed on these processes, Autobrake's quality may be improved and costs may be reduced. The end result is a satisfied customer who receives a quality product at a competitive price.

SSP11-2   A. 1. Production rate is defined as the number of units a manufacturing system is capable of producing in a given time period. The production process consists of the following steps and associated manufacturing times:

First-stage turning	5 minutes	
Second-stage turning	4 minutes	
Milling	**7 minutes**	**(Milling is the bottleneck)**
Grinding	3 minutes	
Assembly	6 minutes	
Packaging	$\frac{1}{4}$ minute (15 seconds)	

To determine the production rate, identify the slowest process because it determines the rate of flow through the plant. In the Autobrake facility, the milling department requires seven minutes to process a component; thus, we would expect to see a component available for shipment every seven minutes.

2. Total processing time is determined by adding the time required to process a unit at each step in the process, as follows: $5 + 4 + 7 + 3 + 6 + \frac{1}{4} = 25\frac{1}{4}$ minutes.

3. Plant throughput (assuming no breakdowns) is calculated by multiplying 60 minutes by the production rate (60 minutes per hour $\times \frac{1}{7} = 8.6$) Thus, the plant would produce approximately nine cylinders per hour.

B. Total processing time should be shorter than cycle time. Cycle time is the sum of processing time, moving time, and waiting time. The cycle time required to move a unit of product from the raw materials inventory to the finished goods storage area is the sum of all processing and waiting times. Waiting and moving times are considered non-value-added activities. Alternatively, processing time is value-added time, in which materials are converted from their original form.

C. Traditionally, plants were organized according to the machine functions, and products were transported through the plant to carry out various manufacturing steps. These process-oriented plants consume many resources in moving and handling materials. Alternatively, work cells typically are U-shaped and consist of machines dedicated to a product or product family. Machines are arranged according to product requirements. Work-in-process inventory levels usually are small, and cycle times usually are short. In addition, materials moving and handling is reduced greatly as a result of locating machines close together. From a cost management perspective, production costs are associated more easily with products and product families because many costs can be traced directly to cells and then to products manufactured within the cells.

SSP11-3　A. Since bottlenecks produce at a slower rate than other machines in the plant, stacks of work-in-process inventory usually are piled up in front of the bottleneck to await processing. Other clues include a machine or work center that constantly is active. In other words, bottleneck resources do not have slack time because they are attempting to catch up with faster processes that continue to add work to their "to do" list.

B. An hour of lost time on a bottleneck resource translates into an hour of lost production for the entire plant. In Self-Study Problem 2, the production rate of the plant was found to be approximately nine units per hour. Therefore, an hour of lost time on the bottleneck resource results in a loss of nine units.

C. An hour of lost time on a nonbottleneck resource may have no impact on throughput. Since the rate of flow through the plant is determined by the processing speed of the bottleneck, other machines have faster processing speeds and can "make up for lost time."

D. Inspection points can be placed in front of the bottleneck, so that valuable time is not spent processing defective units. Also, workers can be asked to cooperate with respect to lunch and break periods, to permit constant operation of the bottleneck resource. Setup times can be reduced by either devising ways to perform setups faster or developing part or all of the setup "off-line" while the machine is engaged in production. This technique is referred to as converting on-line setup time to off-line setup time.

Thinking Beyond the Question

How can managerial accounting help beat emerging competition?

Erin and Seth have determined they must make better use of bottleneck resources within their production area. Seth has observed that some machines occasionally are idle during lunch breaks. He has attempted to explain the importance of minimizing downtime on these key resources. However, some of the production workers do not understand why bottleneck resources impact production levels differently from nonbottleneck resources. If Seth and Erin want to maximize the number of units produced, what are some strategies to ensure production time on a constraint is maximized?

QUESTIONS

Q11-1
Obj. 1
NCCB produces pool tables and billiard supplies. The company is considering changes in the billiard ball production process that would reduce operating costs but would not affect any physical aspects of the product. It also is considering an expansion of operations whereby it would begin manufacturing pinball machines, a product it has not produced in the past. Which of these plans represents an operating decision? Which represents a strategic decision? What is the difference between operating and strategic decision making?

Q11-2
Obj. 2
Madrid Manufacturing Company produces roller skates designed for use in indoor skating rinks. Over the past five years, Madrid has seen sales decline significantly. The company has not added any new products or changed manufacturing processes in the past 20 years. Some changes have been made in materials, but the basic product has not changed. The company produces standard roller skates with four polyurethane wheels and leather uppers. How could elements of TQM assist Madrid in improving performance and meeting customer needs?

Q11-3
Obj. 2
Quick Drain Plumbing has six full-time plumbers who perform residential and commercial plumbing services. Based on a review of service records over the last several months, it was noted that, on average, plumbers must return to the shop to obtain parts or equipment on one out of every three service calls. How could TQM philosophies improve the performance of the plumbers? Explain your answer.

Q11-4
Obj. 3
Many manufacturing companies experience inventory losses. These losses often result from excess inventory that must be handled, stored, and accounted for, during which time it risks being damaged, being lost, or becoming obsolete. Explain a key cause of excess inventory in an organization.

Q11-5
Obj. 3
Dexter Pharmaceuticals manufactures a variety of over-the-counter pain relievers. Each employee in the production area of Dexter has been trained on a single piece of equipment, which they operate during eight-hour shifts. How would implementation of a JIT philosophy at Dexter affect the workforce?

Q11-6
Obj. 3
Mitchell Gabriel is the plant manager for Carry-All Company. Carry-All produces a soft shell book bag/attaché that is popular with students and young business professionals. During production, the bag passes through a number of steps, such as cutting, sewing, assembly, and finishing. Mitchell wants to increase the number of products being packaged for shipment each day. What advice would you give Mitchell to help increase throughput?

Q11-7
Obj. 3
Leeza Vicaro is a divisional manager for Liddon Industries. Leeza is responsible for the production at three of Liddon's plants. Production at Plant 1 provides components to Plant 2, which in turn provides components to Plant 3. In the second and third plants, component parts from the previous plant are added to raw materials during the production process. Leeza is considering the implementation of JIT manufacturing at all three plants. What are some drawbacks of adopting the JIT system that Leeza should consider?

Q11-8
Objs. 2, 3
Tom Mast is a lathe operator for a company that manufactures precision metal products. The lathe is the first step in the manufacturing process. Jobs begin at the lathe based on customer orders that call for specific numbers of pieces to be shipped. When an order is started, Tom generates the number of pieces ordered, plus a 10% cushion. According to Tom, "This overrun is necessary to allow for errors and scrap in subsequent manufacturing steps." Since production begins based on customer demand, is the company using a JIT system? How could principles of TQM and JIT help the company?

Q11-9
Objs. 2, 3
Brayton Manufacturing has been utilizing JIT concepts in its single manufacturing plant for the past year. One of the key elements in Brayton's production process is the ability of any worker to completely stop the entire production line if he or she detects quality problems. Why is it essential for employees to have such control in a TQM production environment? Explain your answer.

Q11-10
Obj. 4
Alverez Manufacturing produces five different types of battery-operated hand tools. There are four production departments at Alverez, each of which performs similar functions on the various products. A great amount of time is spent in each department changing tools and setting

up machinery to work on the different products. How could a product-oriented plant layout assist Alverez in reducing cost and improving production? Explain your answer.

Q11-11
Obj. 4

Traditionally, companies have designed their plant floors so that similar machines are grouped together. Such a process-oriented layout results in all drill presses in one place, all lathes in one place, and so forth. How does the traditional plant layout add cost to the manufacturing environment? How would this layout change with the implementation of a product-oriented manufacturing system? Explain your answer.

Q11-12
Obj. 5

Step 4 in Goldratt's theory of constraints (TOC) involves improving performance on a constraint. Identify two examples of how managers may improve performance on a constrained resource. Explain.

Q11-13
Objs. 2, 6

Why is a commitment to continuous improvement necessary for the successful implementation of a total quality production process? Is the commitment to continuous improvement isolated to the manufacturing process? Explain your answer.

EXERCISES

If your instructor is using Personal Trainer® in this course, you may complete your assignments online.

E11-1

Write a short definition of each of the terms listed in the *Terms and Concepts Defined in this Chapter* section.

E11-2
Obj. 1

Five types of decisions follow. Classify each decision as strategic or operational. Justify your answer.

a. A steel company's managers implement a policy of charging extra handling fees for orders of less than a full truckload. The policy is intended to encourage customers to buy in larger quantities, which will improve the efficiency of the production process.
b. A South American producer of breakfast beverages decides to build a production and distribution facility in the People's Republic of China to service an expanding market.
c. A plant manager decides to use a third shift to increase production, rather than to ask employees to work overtime.
d. An automobile manufacturing company decides to build a new assembly plant. Rather than producing all of the components necessary to make a vehicle, the company decides to buy most of the components from suppliers. This plan permits the company to reduce investment costs for manufacturing equipment.
e. Management for Telxx Communication decides to accept a special order for one of its products at a reduced price because Telxx currently has excess capacity.

E11-3
Obj. 1

Five types of decisions follow. Classify each decision as strategic or operational. Justify your answer.

a. The head nurse for Riverview City Hospital revised the nursing schedule for July 5–11 because of changes in the hospital's patient load.
b. A company that previously sold its products using a door-to-door sales force began exclusively marketing its products through retail stores.
c. A major state university accepts applications for admission only through its Internet web site. Previously, all applications were received by mail.
d. An automobile company reduces the number of suppliers and forms new, long-term alliances with suppliers of key components.
e. A manufacturing company hires an additional quality control engineer to ensure only high-quality products are shipped to customers.

E11-4
Obj. 1

Managerial decisions may be classified as either operational or strategic. Five business decisions follow. Classify each decision as operational or strategic and justify your answer.

a. A manufacturing firm decides to pursue a low-cost strategy by reducing the number of products offered and increasing production volume of the remaining products.
b. A division manager of a retailing organization decides to increase spending for advertising in advance of the holiday season.

(Continued)

c. A company decides to sell certain divisions that provide components used in the manufacture of a key product. In the future, the components will be acquired from high-quality suppliers.

d. An engineering design team decides to change the specifications for purchased materials.

e. A company attempts to differentiate its product line from competitors by introducing high-cost, high-quality features.

E11-5
Obj. 2
The Northport YMCA operates an indoor pool that permits year-round swimming. The YMCA offers a variety of member services such as youth and adult swimming lessons, lap swimming, and unstructured open recreational swimming. The aquatics director wishes to implement TQM at the facility and has prepared a list of questions to help achieve her objective. Using your knowledge of recreational facilities, such as the Northport YMCA, provide examples of answers for each of the following TQM questions.

- Who are our customers?
- What are the needs of our customers?
- How can our services satisfy their needs?
- Which processes are crucial to meeting their needs?
- How do we ensure our processes are satisfactory?
- Which performance measures ensure high-quality processes?

E11-6
Obj. 2
As discussed in Exhibit 2 of the chapter, six elements comprise the TQM philosophy. Match the correct description to each of the following TQM elements:

TQM Element
1. Who are our customers?
2. What are the needs of our customers?
3. How can our products or services satisfy their needs?
4. Which processes are crucial to meeting their needs?
5. How do we ensure our processes are satisfactory?
6. Which performance measures ensure high-quality processes?

TQM Description
a. Visual inspection, statistical process control charts
b. Wholesalers, retailers, patients, downstream processes
c. Scrap rate percentage, on-time delivery percentage, number of new product introductions, cost per unit
d. Welding, gold-plating, corrosion-proofing zinc bath
e. Efficient, cost-effective products capable of operating in extreme climatic conditions
f. Corrosion-resistant materials used in all products subject to adverse operating conditions

E11-7
Obj. 2
The elements of TQM follow. Explain the logic supporting the ordering of the TQM elements.

- Who are our customers?
- What are the needs of our customers?
- How can our products or services satisfy their needs?
- Which processes are crucial to meeting their needs?
- How do we ensure our processes are satisfactory?
- Which performance measures ensure high-quality processes?

E11-8
Obj. 3
Three nonfinancial performance measures and definitions follow. Match the appropriate definition to each nonfinancial performance measure. Why is gaining an understanding of these measures important?

Nonfinancial performance measures
1. Cycle time
2. Production rate
3. Throughput

Definition
a. The number of units completed by a process in a given period of time
b. The number of units completed by a process
c. Total time required to move a unit from raw materials inventory to finished goods inventory

E11-9
Obj. 3
The manufacturing process at SteelCo. Office Products consists of cutting, assembly, and finishing. Each product requires five minutes for cutting, seven minutes for assembly, and four minutes for finishing. Determine the production rate using the information provided. Explain how production rate affects throughput.

E11-10
Obj. 3
City Surgical Center specializes in outpatient surgery. Typically, each patient requires 12 minutes for admitting and completing insurance documentation, 19 minutes of surgical preparation, 25 minutes of surgery, and two hours of recovery time. During recovery, nurses continually monitor a patient's status by checking vital signs such as blood pressure and temperature. Typically, a 35-minute wait occurs between the admitting process and the surgical preparation process. Calculate the total cycle time for a typical patient at City Surgical Center. How much of the total cycle time would be considered processing time? Explain.

E11-11
Obj. 4
Following are characteristics of product-oriented plant designs. Explain why each characteristic is associated with product-oriented plant layouts.

    a. Minimal transportation (materials handling) cost
    b. Small batch sizes
    c. Short cycle times
    d. Few arbitrary allocations
    e. Minimal setup costs

E11-12
Obj. 4
Point Co. produces artificial stone materials used by landscapers. Investment in fixed assets totals $1,400,000. Sales and expense information is as follows:

Sales	$1,000,000
Variable manufacturing and administrative costs	600,000
Fixed manufacturing and administrative costs	300,000
Operating income	$ 100,000

Management at Point Co. believes variable costs could be reduced from 60% of sales to 53% of sales by using a product-oriented layout, rather than a process-oriented layout. To reconfigure the plant would require additional fixed costs of $25,000 annually, but total assets would remain constant. Assume the change also would help the company increase sales by 6%.

    a. Calculate the company's return on assets (NI/Assets) prior to converting to the product-oriented layout.
    b. Calculate the company's return on assets (NI/Assets) after converting to the product-oriented layout.
    c. Give examples of the types of costs the company might save as a result of reconfiguring the plant.

E11-13
Obj. 5
Arizona Jewelry Company makes individual pieces of sterling and turquoise jewelry in a multistep process as follows:

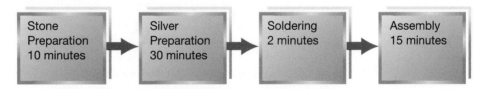

    a. Identify the bottleneck process at Arizona Jewelry Company and explain your reasoning.
    b. If the silver preparation process breaks down for one hour and requires unscheduled maintenance, how much production would the company lose?
    c. If the soldering process breaks down for one hour and requires unscheduled maintenance, how much production would the company lose?
    d. Why is your answer to part (c) different from your answer for part (b)?

E11-14
Obj. 5
A manufacturing process consists of four steps as follows:

Materials Movement	12 minutes
Cutting	28 minutes
Assembly	120 minutes
Packaging	5 minutes

(Continued)

     a. Identify the bottleneck process. Explain your answer.

     b. Calculate the throughput that would result from an eight-hour manufacturing period.

E11-15
Obj. 5
Mary Wells sat in her office after a long walk through the manufacturing plant. She has been under a great deal of pressure from corporate to reduce the backlog of late orders. She knew the key to improving throughput was constraint management; however, the company has not managed the constraint very well. In fact, the bottleneck was idle as she toured the plant. The operators were taking their lunch break but failed to load the automated machine prior to leaving. Mary decided to call a meeting with production managers in the afternoon to discuss techniques for bottleneck management.

     a. Explain how managers may identify bottleneck processes.

     b. Why does an hour of lost production on a bottleneck affect throughput, but an hour of lost production on a nonbottleneck process does not?

     c. What kinds of decisions might managers make concerning the efficient use of a bottleneck?

E11-16
Obj. 5
The theory of constraints often is used to improve process performance by wisely managing bottlenecks or constraints. The proper ordering of the five steps recommended to improve process performance has been scrambled in the following list. Arrange the five steps of process improvement in the proper order. Provide an example of how performance on a constraint may be improved.

- Decide how to make the best use of the constraint.
- Attack a bottleneck by identifying the systems constraints.
- If a constraint has been broken but a different bottleneck has been created, start over at step 1.
- Subordinate all other decisions to those made in step 2.
- Improve performance on the constraint.

E11-17
Obj. 5
Deb Samson is the owner of a company that produces glass products, such as shower doors, table tops, and specialty windows for recreational vehicles. The process involves cutting glass into the proper shape, smoothing the edges, heat treating, and packaging. The cutting process is automated and very rapid; two minutes are required to cut a piece of glass to the proper dimensions. The smoothing, heat treating, and packaging processes require eight minutes, ten minutes, and three minutes, respectively. A simple diagram of the process is as follows:

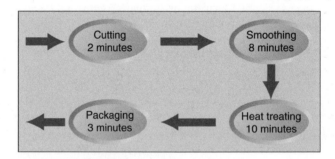

     a. Identify the bottleneck or process constraint.

     b. Explain how you identified the bottleneck.

     c. Calculate the throughput for an eight-hour shift.

E11-18
Obj. 5
Use the information presented in E11-17.

     Using the theory of constraints, Deb Samson invested in technology to improve the processing speed of the bottleneck from 10 minutes per unit to 7 minutes.

     a. Identify the bottleneck after the investment in technology.

     b. Calculate the throughput after investing in technology to improve the bottleneck.

     c. Explain why throughput changed.

E11-19
Obj. 6
A large regional financial consulting firm currently is making a number of important strategic and operational decisions as a result of rapid growth during the past three years. Examples of recent decisions follow. For each decision, determine whether it is considered operating or strategic. Explain your reasoning.

a. Two years ago the company bought a smaller firm that specialized in estate tax planning. Prior to the acquisition, the parent company had limited experience in this area.

b. Partners voted to upgrade the firm's telephone system.

c. The firm implemented a "rapid response" policy to ensure high-profile clients are contacted by a partner within one hour of receiving a request for services.

d. Partners have become concerned about the turnover rate among entry-level consultants. Many talented people leave the firm within two years, citing excessive travel and time away from family as reasons. The firm is exploring ways to make its work assignment policies less burdensome for their consultants.

E11-20
Obj. 6

A national automobile insurance company uses a multistep process to evaluate automobile damage and to settle damage claims for their policyholders. When a policyholder notifies the company that an accident has occurred, a claims adjuster is assigned to the case. He or she evaluates the damage and prepares a claims report. Multiple repair facility estimates are compared with the claims report prepared by the adjuster and repairs are authorized. This is the most time-consuming step in the claims process. When the repairs are complete, the repair facility is paid by check. The company typically completes 5,000 claims per week. Most claims are paid within 10 days from the time a claims adjuster initially evaluates the damage.

a. Identify throughput for the insurance company.

b. What is the cycle time associated with a typical claim?

c. What is the bottleneck process?

d. Are the concepts of throughput, cycle time, and bottlenecks relevant to both service and manufacturing firms? Explain.

E11-21
Obj. 6

Jiffy Lunch is a service organization that prepares and delivers meals to elderly people. As a service project, a university sorority provides most of the delivery services. Each of the 20 volunteer drivers typically delivers five meals. The kitchen facility is small but can potentially produce 120 meals per day. Currently, demand for services exceeds the number of meals Jiffy Lunch can provide.

a. Which process appears to be the constraint or bottleneck?

b. Using your understanding of constraint management, how might Jiffy Lunch increase the number of lunches served?

c. Under what circumstances would the kitchen facility become the constraint or bottleneck?

d. Assume the kitchen facility becomes the bottleneck. Identify examples of ways to improve the performance.

PROBLEMS

If your instructor is using Personal Trainer® in this course, you may complete your assignments online.

P11-1
Obj. 1

Operational versus Strategic Decisions

Gulf Coast Shipping Co. (GCSC) is interested in developing a new type of market for transportation services. They wish to develop a high-speed vessel to compete with slow-moving freight ships that offer low-cost transportation and with rapid-delivery cargo planes that offer high-cost transportation. Managers at GCSC believe a middle market exists that would enable the company to gain business from slower freight ships as well as from more expensive cargo planes. The proposed high-speed vessel would be faster than freight ships but slower than cargo planes.

The company has been experimenting with a number of hull forms and propulsion systems that would make the venture economically feasible. For example, multihull and single-hull designs have been considered. Additionally, engineers must determine whether the vessel should be constructed of steel, aluminum, or some kind of composite material. Possible propulsion systems include water-jet and propeller.

Required Using the information provided, respond to the following questions.

A. Identify the major strategic issue facing managers at GCSC.

B. What are some examples of operational decisions the managers must make? Explain.

C. How do strategic decisions differ from operational decisions?

P11-2
Obj. 2

TQM Principles Applied to a University Setting

Professor Smith was discussing TQM with his accounting class. A student asked how TQM principles might be applied to a university setting. Smith replied, "There seems to be a great deal of confusion among many academics about the application of TQM principles to the classroom. Students are not customers; they are work in process. The customers of a university are the companies that hire our students upon graduation."

Required

A. Respond to Professor Smith's comment.
B. Identify three more customers of a university. Indicate if they are internal or external.
C. Using the concepts presented in Exhibit 2 in this chapter, explain the types of decisions university administrators may face when implementing TQM principles.

P11-3
Obj. 3

JIT: Supplier Relationships

Sung Yu Chen is a purchasing manager for Hilbert Construction, a builder of custom homes. Hilbert is implementing JIT philosophies and has informed Sung Yu that new purchasing procedures need to be developed. For the past 10 years, to obtain the lowest possible cost on building materials, Hilbert has requested quotes from many different suppliers.

Building materials usually are stored in the company's inventory area, where employees select the materials needed for the day, load the materials, and take them to the job site. Materials received in the inventory area are inspected by the shop supervisor. Sometimes the inspection occurs days after receipt. After inspection, poor-quality materials are separated and returned to the supplier.

Under the new plan, the inventory area would be eliminated and suppliers would deliver materials directly to job sites. The delivery of materials must be made as construction progresses, with no buildup or excess inventory held at any site.

Required

A. What changes in supplier relationships will result from the implementation of JIT philosophies?
B. How will the implementation of JIT affect internal and external communications?
C. Under the new plan, how would the inspection process change?

P11-4
Obj. 3

Measuring Cycle Time and Throughput

Clean Products, Inc., manufactures a dust-free computer enclosure that is designed to be used on plant floors and in other harsh environments. The steps required to manufacture the all-steel enclosure and the amount of time each step takes on a per-unit basis are as follows:

Department	Processing Time per Unit
Forming	8 minutes
Milling	11 minutes
Grinding	9 minutes
Assembly	32 minutes
Finishing	25 minutes

Required

A. Calculate the production rate for a completed enclosure.
B. Assume that the company has a total of 384 minutes per day available in each department. Calculate the total daily throughput of completed enclosures.
C. Assume that the company currently has a manufacturing cycle time of 123 minutes per enclosure. Calculate the total process time and total wait time for an enclosure. What does the wait time reveal about the manufacturing process?
D. Which of the departments represents a manufacturing bottleneck? If all departments are operating at maximum output, what effect does the bottleneck have on inventory levels and unit output? Explain your answer.

P11-5 Just-In-Time Objectives

Obj. 3

Apex Technologies produces automotive filters that are used by original equipment manufacturers of automobiles and light trucks. The company also markets a line of replacement filters that are sold through retail distributors.

Apex operates a single plant that manufactures over 100 different filters. The first manufacturing department is metal fabrication. This department stamps out casings and housings that are needed by other departments later in the production process. The metal fabrication department has implemented a JIT system with respect to raw material purchases. No other departments at Apex have yet implemented a JIT system.

Juan Spanoza is the production manager of the metal fabrication department. Although work-in-process inventories have declined significantly since the implementation of JIT, Juan is frustrated at the amount of time that he now spends coordinating with suppliers and with other departments in order to meet production demands. With no buildup of inventory in his department, Juan must now tend to problems immediately, since failure to do so could halt the department's production.

Other managers at Apex have observed Juan's problems and are reluctant to implement JIT in their areas. The plant manager, Chris O'Connor, has scheduled a meeting to discuss further JIT implementation plans for the plant with department supervisors.

Required

A. What are the objectives of a JIT system that Chris should communicate to the department supervisors?
B. What are some actions that Apex could take to ease the transition to a JIT system?
C. In order to successfully implement the JIT system, what arrangements must the company make with vendors? How will these arrangements be formalized?

P11-6 JIT, Ethical Considerations

Objs. 2, 3

McMahon Food Services is a provider of vending machine meals, snacks, and sandwiches. The company operates under a JIT philosophy. Each morning, food is received at the company's commissary, where meals are prepared and packaged. Company route drivers load trucks and deliver the food to vending machines throughout a large metropolitan area.

On a daily basis, the company relies on suppliers providing fresh food materials that are free of contamination, mold, and foreign objects. The only materials that McMahon stockpiles are cases of soda, which are purchased on a weekly basis and are stored in the company's warehouse.

Management at McMahon has received a notice from a food supplier indicating that a delivery of coffee may have been contaminated with a nontoxic cleaning solution used in the supplier's packaging machine. The notice indicated that the cleaning solution posed no risk to health, but would cause a significant foul taste in the coffee.

Managers at McMahon do not wish to recall the coffee from vending machines. They believe that the cost of retrieving the coffee is not warranted, since there is no foreseeable health risk involved. In support of this position, they also note that federal law allows food to contain small traces of foreign substances, provided there is no risk to consumers.

Required

A. What does the coffee contamination suggest about supplier responsibilities and a company's selection of supply sources under a TQM system?
B. In measuring the quality of the product, what ethical considerations should McMahon consider?
C. Comment on the measurement of quality in this situation. Who measures quality, and what implications do those measurements have for McMahon?

P11-7 Process-Oriented versus Product-Oriented Plant Layout

Obj. 4

Gearworks, Inc., manufactures parts for industrial machinery. The manufacturing process requires a variety of machines that grind, heat treat, and polish steel into various shapes. Three different product lines are produced using a traditional process-oriented plant layout as follows:

(Continued)

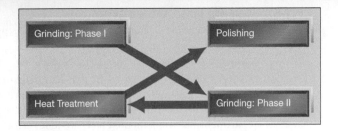

Required

A. Discuss the differences in traditional process-oriented plant layouts and cellular product-oriented plant layouts.

B. Draw a revised plant layout for Gearworks, assuming management wishes to redesign the plant layout to use three manufacturing cells.

C. Why are product-oriented plant layouts more efficient than process-oriented plant layouts? Explain.

D. What types of savings would managers expect to realize by redesigning the plant layout from process-oriented to product-oriented?

P11-8   **A Product-Oriented versus Process-Oriented Plant Layout**

Obj. 4

Millworks, Inc., is a manufacturer of defense systems used by the military. Typically, Millworks produces three types of components in four different work centers. Though the components are part of the same defense system, they differ in size and complexity. Presently, the company uses a process-oriented facility to manufacture the components. The company has had problems with growing levels of work-in-process inventory. In addition, materials handling costs have become excessively high. As a result of these problems, management is considering reconfiguring the plant as a product-oriented facility. The process includes cutting, milling, assembly, and testing.

Required

A. Draw a diagram of Millworks' existing production processes. Assume the production facility has a square floorplan. Each process requires one-fourth of the floorspace. The first process begins in the top left corner. Products move clockwise around the facility, exiting at the bottom left corner of the building.

B. Draw a diagram that represents how Millworks might rearrange its processes consistent with cellular manufacturing concepts.

C. Explain how your two drawings differ. What are the benefits of a product-oriented plant layout?

P11-9   **Push vs. Pull Inventory Systems**

Objs. 2, 3, 4

Lamar Manufacturing produces radio alarm clocks. The company offers three clock models with various features. Each clock is assembled in a single plant that is laid out in a functional format. Each worker has been highly trained to perform a particular function in the manufacturing process.

In Department 1, circuit boards are combined with electrical components and attached to a "base." When a batch is completed, the base units are forwarded to Department 3, where they are shelved in work-in-process bins until needed.

In Department 2, speakers are attached to the radio cabinet, and buttons and knobs are attached. Each batch of cabinets is then forwarded to Department 3, where the units are also stored until needed in production.

Department 3 is the finishing department. In this area, the radio cabinets are attached to the base unit and the clock is packaged. The work-in-process area of Department 3 is always full. If a completed batch from an earlier department is found to be defective, Department 3 workers will automatically stop work on that particular model and work on another while the error is corrected.

Completed units are stored in the company's finished goods warehouse. On average, clocks are stored in the warehouse for 45 days before shipment.

Required

A. Is the company operating a push or a pull system of inventory management? Explain your answer.

B. What changes would be necessary to adapt the plant layout to a product-oriented facility? What benefits would the company realize from such changes?

C. Assume that the company implements total quality management by arranging the plant into a product-oriented facility and is successful in reducing work-in-process and finished goods inventories. What further actions should the company take to achieve total quality?

P11-10 Continuous Improvements, Behavioral Implications

Objs. 2, 4

Franklin Berm & Company is a manufacturer of sporting goods. The company employs over 700 workers who are organized under a labor union contract. Management at Franklin plans to implement total quality management and to reorganize the company's operations into a product-oriented layout. The company's plans include the restructuring of production so teams of 15 employees will work on specific product lines. The company wants to eliminate several layers of factory supervisors and place responsibility for production quality on the team leaders.

The company's plan will result in fewer job classifications by reducing the number of employee job descriptions and pay rates. The new job classifications will require broader employee knowledge and ability. In order for an employee to receive a raise under the plan, the employee will be required to learn additional skills and advance to a new job level. Compensation also will be tied to the quality of employee output.

Union leaders have reviewed the plan and are concerned that the restructuring is an attempt to eliminate jobs and to limit employee pay. They argue the plan will discriminate against slow learners and will require workers to dilute their technical skills by spreading their time among more activities. They are concerned that quality will not improve without new machinery and equipment, and that failure to achieve improved quality will be blamed on the workers.

Required

A. Why might the labor union constrain the successful implementation of quality-oriented programs?

B. What ethical obligations does management have toward workers implementing quality programs?

C. What role do employees have in implementing quality programs and continuous improvement?

P11-11 Plant Layout and Work-in-Process

Objs. 3, 4

Brown and Pickens manufactures a variety of battery-operated hand tools, including a cordless screwdriver, drill, and hand saw. The company produces these items in a plant organized in a process-oriented layout in two separate buildings. Batteries are outsourced to a dependable, high-quality supplier who makes deliveries to Brown and Pickens on a daily basis.

The main components of the tools are a motor, gears, and a casing. The company winds motors in one area of the plant, using coil-winding machines. The casings are manufactured in another area of the plant, using an injection molding machine. The gears are milled in the machine shop, using computer-controlled milling machines. All of the component parts are moved to the assembly area, where they are combined to form a finished product. Setup time on these machines is significant. To change any of these machines from one product to another takes over an hour.

The manufactured motors are moved to the assembly area by forklift every other day. The casings are produced in large batches and stored in a warehouse adjacent to the assembly area. The gears are manufactured in a separate building, across the street, and are held in that building until needed by assembly. The assembly area maintains just enough gears to meet production needs for a single day. Gears are delivered to the assembly department in small batches as needed to keep production flowing.

(Continued)

Required

A. How would having a manufacturing cell for each of the products differ from the current plant layout? What changes would this create in the product flow? How would work-in-process inventory be affected?

B. How could changes in the plant layout improve material handling and storage practices at Brown and Pickens? What effect would a change in plant layout have on the value of work-in-process? Explain your answer.

C. The gears are delivered in small batches just as needed by production. Would you consider this proper use of JIT? Why or why not?

P11-12   Performance Evaluation, Constraints

Obj. 5

Corsair Window Company manufactures custom-insulated windows and screens for residential and commercial uses. Each window is manufactured to specific building measurements. Corsair utilizes a JIT approach to manufacturing and plans each production run so that it can be shipped as soon as it is completed. Shipping dates are very important to Corsair, as most sales contracts contain a monetary penalty for late delivery.

All windows pass through a finishing station. At this station, hardware is installed, screens are attached, and an inspection is performed to ensure the windows meet specifications. The company has only one finishing station in its plant. Managers have long talked about adding a second finishing station. However, a second station is not warranted because the amount of processing time is so small. On average, a window is in the finishing station for 15 minutes, which is the least amount of time a window spends in any single process.

Recently, a large shipment of windows was not delivered on time, and the company incurred a significant penalty. After review of the manufacturing logs for these windows, it was determined that the shipment was late because all 48 windows in the order were delivered to the finishing station on the afternoon the windows were to be shipped. In addition, several of the windows had to be returned to other stations in the plant for minor rework and adjustments.

Required

A. How does the finishing station impose a constraint on production?

B. How does the finishing station constraint affect the utilization of other workstations and the amount of work in process in the other areas of production?

C. Should the inspection process be placed ahead of the finishing station? Where should the inspection process occur? Explain your answer.

P11-13   Bottlenecks, Value-Added Activities, and Process Improvement in a Service Organization

Obj. 6

Second Mortgage Lenders (SML) was established in 1985 for the purpose of writing home equity loans, often referred to as second mortgages. For example, if a homeowner's property has a market value of $250,000 with a mortgage balance of $180,000, the homeowner would have $70,000 in equity ($250,000 − $180,000). Second Mortgage Lenders would lend a homeowner up to 85% of the equity value for home improvements, college costs, or other personal needs.

The process of writing second mortgages involves an interview, credit history evaluation, financial analysis, property appraisal, loan committee meeting, and closing. At the interview, an SML loan officer would initially screen potential clients and provide a loan application packet. Upon receipt of the loan application, the loan officer would conduct a credit check and analyze the financial information provided by the applicant. Variables such as annual salary and employment history are considered. Next, a real estate appraiser is hired to estimate the property value. Following the appraisal, the loan committee meets to make a decision after considering all of the inputs. If the loan is approved, a meeting is scheduled to sign papers that close the loan agreement.

A typical loan package requires approximately two weeks from the initial interview until closing. SML wants to be more responsive to its customers by providing more rapid loan decisions. The following times are estimates based on past transactions.

Activity	Time Required
Interview	20 minutes
Credit history evaluation	$\frac{1}{2}$ hour
Financial analysis	$1\frac{1}{2}$ hours
Property appraisal	5 business days*
Loan committee meeting	10 minutes
Closing	35 minutes

*The actual appraisal requires approximately 4 hours.

Required

A. Why does SML want to reduce the time required to approve (or reject) a loan application?
B. Where is the bottleneck process?
C. What is the value-added time required to produce and to close a mortgage?
D. What is the non-value-added time associated with the loan process?
E. What recommendations would you make to SML?

P11-14

Objs. 2, 6

TQM in a Service Environment

Olympic Insurance provides home and auto coverage to policyholders in six states. Olympic has agents in many cities, but has a central office in Atlanta, Georgia. This office issues policies and settles all claims.

If policyholders wish to file a claim, they contact their local agent. The agent gathers information, prepares a report on the damage, and submits the claim to the home office for processing. Managers at Olympic have determined that three weeks are required from the filing of the agent's report to the issuance of a check. Many customers have complained about the three-week delay, and Olympic would like to speed up the processing time.

Managers have determined that the delay in issuing checks occurs in the accounting department. The average claim is held in the accounting department for more than one week before it is processed and a check is prepared. Accounting personnel insist that weekly check runs are adequate to settle claims in a timely manner. The main reason for delays, they say, is incomplete files submitted by the claims processors that must be sent back to the processors for further work.

Required

A. How could Olympic utilize total quality management techniques to improve claims processing?
B. What does the information related to the accounting department suggest about processing time and product quality?

P11-15

SPREADSHEET

Excel in Action

Music Makers currently has the capacity to produce 500,000 CDs per month. It produces 400,000 data CDs and sells these for $2.50 per unit. It produces 100,000 music CDs and sells these for $3.10 per unit. Demand for the company's products is sufficient that it could sell more CDs if it could produce more.

CDs are produced in two departments. The copying department includes six work cells, one for each of six copying machines. Each cell can produce 150 units per hour and is capable of operating 600 hours per month under normal conditions. The packaging department includes 12 work cells. Each cell can produce $66\frac{2}{3}$ units per hour and is capable of operating 625 hours per month under normal conditions.

The company is considering the acquisition of new packaging equipment. The equipment would permit each cell to produce 75 units per hour. Each cell would operate only 600 hours per month because of the need for extra maintenance of the equipment. The equipment would require an additional investment in assets of $1,200,000 and would result in additional fixed manufacturing costs of $18,000 per month. Variable manufacturing costs would be reduced from 50% of sales dollars to 49%. The company could sell all the additional units it produced. Half of this additional production would be for data CDs and half for music CDs. The CDs could be sold at current sales prices.

(Continued)

Current fixed manufacturing costs are $326,000 per month, and current fixed general and administrative costs are $210,000 per month. The general and administrative costs would not be affected by the purchase. The company's current investment in assets is $6,550,000.

Required Determine the current production capacity of Music Makers' copying and packaging departments using a spreadsheet. What would the capacity be if the equipment is purchased? Calculate the company's sales, variable costs, fixed costs, and profits for the current and revised options. Also calculate the company's annual profit margin, asset turnover, and return on assets for each option. Annual asset turnover and return on assets is 12 times the monthly amount. Should Music Makers invest in the equipment?

Your analysis should use cell references and formulas where possible. Use appropriate formatting throughout.

Suppose the equipment required an investment of $1,600,000 and resulted in an increase in fixed manufacturing costs of $24,000 per month. Should Music Makers invest in the equipment?

P11-16 Multiple-Choice Overview of the Chapter

1. A key concept of the JIT inventory system is to:
   a. utilize work-in-process as a cushion for production when material deliveries are late or a department is unable to operate.
   b. purchase raw materials from many suppliers.
   c. keep large stocks of raw materials in order to maintain a high rate of productivity.
   d. keep inventories to minimum levels, or eliminate them entirely, through careful planning.

2. The flow of goods through a JIT system is based on:
   a. a department completing a batch of units as quickly as possible so that the units can be pushed to the next department.
   b. processing goods in large batches rather than less economical small batches.
   c. maintaining a stockpile of raw materials in anticipation of errors in production.
   d. meeting customer demand by pulling inventory through production, with no buildup of inventory at any point in the production process.

3. A successful JIT system is based upon which of the following concepts?
   a. A large number of suppliers ensures frequent deliveries of small lots.
   b. Suppliers offering the lowest prices should always be accepted.
   c. Long-term contracts with suppliers should be avoided.
   d. Suppliers make frequent deliveries, thus avoiding the buildup of material inventories on hand.

4. The plant layout under the JIT concept emphasizes a:
   a. functional approach, in which machines performing the same function are grouped together.
   b. product approach, in which all machines needed in the production of a particular product are grouped together.
   c. facilities approach, in which all machines of a similar nature are located in one plant building.
   d. contractual approach, in which the processing of certain subassemblies is performed by a small number of independent machine shops under contract to the manufacturing company.

5. The term *throughput* means:
   a. the length of time required to turn materials into products.
   b. the total volume of production.
   c. the time involved to prepare a machine for the production of a different item.
   d. production of goods without the accumulation of raw materials or work-in-process inventories.

6. A cluster of two or more related machines at a single workstation is referred to as a(n):
   a. manufacturing cell.
   b. activity center.
   c. functional layout.
   d. bottleneck.

7. Which of the following statements regarding total quality management is *not* correct?
   a. Inspection of finished goods is performed by quality control inspectors.
   b. Total quality demands that suppliers provide prompt delivery of goods that are free of defects.
   c. Defective components can halt the entire manufacturing process.
   d. The inspection function for incoming goods is shifted from the company to its suppliers.

8. Production rate refers to the:
   a. total amount of time to move a unit from raw materials inventory to finished goods.
   b. number of units completed by a process in a given period of time.
   c. number of minutes that pass between units completed.
   d. amount of time needed to prepare a machine for its next operation.

9. Under a total quality management system:
   a. understanding customer needs is critical.
   b. once a popular product has been perfected, a company can be assured that customers will continue to buy it.
   c. the primary focus is on accumulating quality accounting information.
   d. always having a lot of inventory available is critical.

10. Under JIT, the plant floor is:
    a. laid out in a functional format, with similar types of machines grouped together.
    b. laid out in a product-oriented flow.
    c. laid out in a single line through which all products must pass.
    d. usually cluttered with excessive work-in-process.

CASES

C11-1
Objs. 3, 5

Reducing Process Time

Many companies have made shortening the production rate of various processes their primary goal. Most of these companies have reviewed costs and eliminated as much product cost as feasible. Now the focus is on speed. The commitment to speed affects every phase of a company's business. Administration, sales, engineering, and production are all expected to complete tasks faster and more efficiently than ever before. Improved computer technologies have allowed companies to organize, synthesize, and analyze information, giving firms that can operate faster a competitive advantage.

Required

A. Explain how faster processes can be applied in areas such as engineering and administration. How can reduced process times in these areas help a company be more competitive?
B. Explain why improved quality is essential to a company that is able to work faster and reduce process times.
C. Teamwork is essential to any successful effort to reduce process time and speed up processes. Do you agree? Why or why not?
D. What are potential problems that may arise from the increased speed of processes?

C11-2
Obj. 5

Bottleneck Identification and Management at Perma-Clear Glass Company

Perma-Clear Glass Company was founded in 1980 by Rob Samson and enjoyed rapid growth as demand for new construction materials exceeded supply. The company became efficient at
(Continued)

converting large sheets of glass into various smaller dimensions demanded by residential and commercial builders. In recent years, Perma-Clear diversified its product line to include specialty glass items, such as tempered glass tabletops and shower doors. More recently, large vertically integrated competitors have captured market share from Perma-Clear because these companies efficiently produce standard products in very large volumes.

In response to shrinking profit margins on standard high-volume architectural products, the marketing department at Perma-Clear identified a low-volume, high-margin niche in the sports/recreational vehicle industry. Because builders of specialty boats, custom vans, and travel trailers often require small orders of tempered glass cut in unusual shapes, these glass products command a market premium. Managers at Perma-Clear believe they can obtain a significant portion of this market because their competitors are not equipped to make small-volume, complex glass shapes efficiently.

Managers at Perma-Clear are analyzing the potential impact on existing production processes using a computer-based factory simulation package. They wonder whether the introduction of a new product line may adversely affect existing manufacturing processes. Specifically, they are concerned that introducing many small-batch production orders may reduce the plant's total throughput in units and profitability.

The production process for the standard architectural product consists of four steps: cutting, shape edging, tempering, and packaging. The cutting process utilizes a computer numerically-controlled cutting machine to produce various sizes and shapes from a large piece of glass. Following cutting, the glass pieces advance to the shape-edging area where workers fasten each piece onto a jig and grind the edges to meet engineering specifications. Following the shape-edging process, the piece is tempered. In the tempering process, glass passes through a heated oven for a specified period of time. Heat from the tempering process causes irreversible structural changes in the glass. If broken, a sheet of tempered glass should shatter harmlessly into many tiny pieces. Following the tempering process, individual orders are carefully packaged and attached to pallets for shipping.

Management has asked the industrial engineering department to compile relevant information about the process. A summary of the report is shown in Exhibit A. The report identified several key characteristics of the production process. Changeover times in the cutting area are rapid because of computer numerically-controlled equipment. Data from the shape-edging area present a different story. Long setups in the shape-edging area are required as jigs are changed between batches. Tempering setup requires adjusting the temperature controls and loading the racks for processing. The packaging area requires very little setup time, and the process is fast and reliable. An engineer noted that a major problem associated with packaging is the time required to bundle orders consisting of many different items.

Exhibit A
Processing Time and
Setup Time by Process

	Cutting	Shape Edging	Tempering	Packaging
Processing time (average per unit)	3 minutes	6 minutes	4 minutes	2 minutes
Setup time (average per batch)	2 minutes	10 minutes	3 minutes	1 minute

Managers are unsure how introducing a new product into the mix will affect existing processes. They would like the simulation model to help management identify the process constraint and to understand how the new marketing strategy will impact day-to-day operations at Perma-Clear.

Required

A. Discuss the competitive environment of Perma-Clear. What are its competitive strengths?
B. What is the nature of the new proposal?
C. Prepare a sketch of the manufacturing process at Perma-Clear. Include processing times in your sketch.

D. Where is the bottleneck located? Explain.
E. Using the information presented in Exhibit A, determine the number of products that can be produced in an eight-hour shift.
F. Can throughput increase if the cutting area is given increased capacity? Explain.
G. What do you think will happen to production volume (throughput) as a result of introducing a variety of new small-volume products? Why?
H. Are there additional factors that management should consider before adding new items to the product line?

M12

CAPITAL INVESTMENT DECISIONS

How can managerial accounting help in choosing new manufacturing facilities?

Erin and Seth are debating whether to invest in new, largely automated, equipment for sealing and varnishing furniture parts. Young Designs, Inc., has been sealing and varnishing manually. At present, employees place furniture parts on racks and spray them by hand. After that, the racks are moved into a drying room and then into parts inventory until used in production.

Seth believes production volume will increase enough during the next year to justify investing in an automated system. Under the new system, furniture parts will travel on a conveyer belt. The parts will be dipped into a tank containing sealant and varnish, then continue along the conveyer belt through an automatic dryer, and move directly into the parts inventory.

FOOD FOR THOUGHT

What is the primary risk Erin and Seth face in making this decision? What type of financial model do you think would be appropriate for making this type of decision? Suppose the new system would reduce manufacturing throughput time by two-thirds. Based upon what you have learned about manufacturing so far, how might this influence the decision? Let's listen as Seth, Erin, and Roberta discuss the issues regarding the new manufacturing process.

Seth: *The new system will save a great deal on our cost of labor by cutting total labor hours by 20 percent.*

Erin: *That assumes we are operating at practical capacity. Currently, we are operating well below capacity.*

Seth: *Agreed. But over the last six months our sales have been increasing steadily. Based on that, we will be close to capacity by the beginning of next year. It will take that long to purchase and install the new system.*

Erin: *Even so, our fixed costs will go up. We will have to pay more for maintenance in addition to the purchase and installation costs. We will also have a one-time training cost to teach our finishers how to use the system. Plus, we will have depreciation cost to consider. Will the lower operating cost of the new system really justify the cost of the investment?*

Seth: *That depends upon the volume we expect to produce, and how certain we are that we can achieve that volume. Also, Roberta tells me depreciation is not a cost. It is an expensing of a cost that has already been incurred—the cost of purchasing and installing the new system. If we count both depreciation and the cost of the investment in our analysis, we will be double counting.*

Erin: *What about the cost of the varnish?*

Seth: *The cost of the varnish is the same using either the manual or automated system. I don't think it's relevant. We should consider only those costs that differ if we use one system or the other.*

Erin: *Well, it sounds to me like we need to put all the relevant data into a model that will help us decide if we should make the investment.*

Roberta: *I agree. You should be concerned about the risks of making such an investment. Consider fixed costs, breakeven point, and operating risk. If you make this investment, your operating risk will increase.*

Seth: *So if we believe making the investment has the potential to reduce labor costs, we have to be willing to accept the risk that our breakeven point will increase.*

Erin: *Even if we are willing to accept the higher operating risk, how do we determine if this investment will pay for itself?*

Roberta: *Well, one way is to compare the value of the expected cash inflows from the investment to the value of the expected cash outflows. Since these inflows and outflows are likely to occur at different times, you need to adjust the value of the flows to a common point in time. This method is called discounted cash flow.*

Seth: *I can see that money has a time value. Certainly, money received sooner is more valuable than money received later. But, I'm a little concerned that we haven't considered all the benefits of making this investment. For example, I've read that decreasing the amount of time products spend in the manufacturing process—throughput time—can reduce the overall cost of manufacturing. The new system we're considering will reduce throughput time. How do we try to capture this benefit?*

Roberta: *We will need to identify benefits from the faster throughput, such as lower inventory levels, and attempt to quantify these benefits so that they can be included in the financial model.*

Erin: *Let's get some of this information together. Once we look it over, we can talk further about this investment.*

OBJECTIVES

Once you have completed this chapter, you should be able to:

1 Identify factors that affect capital investment decisions and explain why these decisions are important to companies.

2 Calculate net present value, internal rate of return, payback, and accounting rate of return.

3 Describe the effect of the new manufacturing environment on capital investment decisions.

4 Identify factors that are important for strategic capital investment decisions.

5 Describe the factors affecting capital investment decisions in service organizations.

FACTORS AFFECTING CAPITAL INVESTMENT DECISIONS

OBJECTIVE 1

Identify factors that affect capital investment decisions and explain why these decisions are important to companies.

When a company makes a decision to invest in long-term assets such as plant and equipment, it is making a *capital investment decision.* These decisions often involve large outlays of cash for long periods. **The process of making these decisions is known as** *capital budgeting.*

Capital investment decisions can be classified in various ways. One way is to view these decisions as either operational or strategic. *Operational capital investment decisions* **are those that affect only a part of a company's operations, have easily predictable lives, and represent relatively small capital outlays for a business.** An example is the purchase of several new personal computers to track operating data on a production line of a printer manufacturer. *Strategic capital investment decisions* **affect all or a considerable part of a company's operations, have uncertain lives, and require large investments.** A new computer-assisted, robotic production facility to manufacture transmissions is an example. Another example of a strategic capital investment decision is Young Designs, Inc.'s, decision regarding the automated varnishing system. Although this might be considered an operational capital investment decision for a large manufacturer, Erin and Seth would likely consider it a strategic decision because Young Designs is a small manufacturer, and the risks are likely to be considerable. The risks associated with strategic capital investment decisions are different from and considerably greater than those associated with operational capital investment decisions.

Capital investments affect a company's profits and cash flows as well as its assets. For example, Exhibit 1 illustrates that the purchase of new equipment, such as a computer, results in:

- A payment of cash for the equipment
- A payment of wages for employees
- Additional interest on money borrowed to finance the purchase
- Additional depreciation expense
- Additional revenues from the sale of goods or services

Exhibit 1

Financial Effects of Capital Investment Decisions

Activity	Cash Flow	Assets	Profits
Increased sales	+ Cash		+ Revenue
Purchase equipment	– Cash	Equipment	– Depreciation expense
Labor costs	– Cash		– Wages expense
Interest costs	– Cash		– Interest expense

Risk

Exhibit 2 depicts several factors that affect the risk associated with capital investment decisions. The outcomes of most investment decisions are uncertain. In addition to the effect of a decision on expected cash flows, risk is an important factor in determining the value of an investment. Erin and Seth are concerned about a particular type of risk—operating risk, which is the risk associated with a company becoming unprofitable because it cannot cover its fixed costs. In the following discussion we will learn that there are many other types of risk that are present in capital investment decisions.

Exhibit 2

Factors Affecting the Risk of Capital Investments

Factors that *Increase* Risk

1. Large investment size relative to the company's total investment (assets)
2. Long-term recovery of the cost of the investment
3. Management inexperience with similar investments
4. Difficulty in reversing the investment decision
5. High uncertainty about whether the asset will perform as expected

Factors that *Decrease* Risk

1. Large potential for recovery of investment through resale of the investment asset
2. Recovery of the investment in a short time period
3. Management experience with similar investments

A company is at greater risk if an investment fails when the investment is large relative to the company's size. For instance, a company that invests all of its investment funds in one large project is accepting greater risk than a similar company that invests its funds in five different projects. In addition, the longer it takes to recover the cost of an investment, the greater the risk of the investment because the opportunity for the investment to fail is greater. When the expected performance of the asset is uncertain, prior experience with similar investments can help reduce risk.

Companies typically invest large amounts of money in capital investments. Usually, a company cannot recover the amount it has invested if a project is unsuccessful. For example, consider the construction of a new bank branch. The bank must acquire land and have a building designed, constructed, and landscaped. Specialized construction is necessary, such as installation of a vault. A sign with the bank's logo must be erected, and drive-in windows must be installed. If the branch is unprofitable, other banks may be unwilling to purchase it for an amount close to its original cost. A non-bank purchaser would not need or pay for the specialized assets. As a result, banks are careful in making decisions about construction of branches so that they can avoid losses from unsuccessful investments.

Another factor that increases the risk associated with capital investments is uncertainty about performance, such as that associated with new technology. In general, the newer the technology, the greater the uncertainty about its performance. In addition, there is the risk that competitors will develop newer technology that will make a company's existing technology out of date and result in the loss of business. Often, it takes time to make new technology work correctly.

Case in Point

http://ingram.
swlearning.com
....
Visit Intel's home page
to learn more about the
company.

A Concern About Accuracy

Intel experienced a problem with the accuracy of calculations made by its Pentium® processor, which **IBM** and other companies installed in their personal computers. New versions of the processor corrected this problem. However, the problem was an embarrassment to the company and required the costly replacement of many processors.

Generally, the greater the amount of the original investment that can be recaptured through the sale of the assets, the lower the risk. In the case of a branch bank, it is unlikely that a significant portion of the initial cost could be recovered unless the branch were sold to another bank. Likewise, the greater the value of the asset at the end of its service to a company, the smaller the portion of the investment that must be recovered in cash flows during its service to the company. For example, suppose computers purchased by a software development company can be sold at the end of their service lives for 50 percent of their cost. In this case, only half of the investment in the computers will have to be recovered during their operation at the software company. The rest will be recovered by their sale.

Finally, the more experience management has with a particular type of investment, the less likely the company is to develop problems. For example, if a company's usual business is making corrugated cardboard boxes for packaging, purchase of equipment to improve the efficiency of the business is less risky than purchase of equipment to enter a new line of business, such as making specialty gift boxes. The new line will require management to gain experience with a new manufacturing process and new markets.

Competing for Capital Investment Funds

Large capital investment decisions often involve company politics. Different divisions of companies compete for investment funds. Capital investment projects usually must meet a minimum rate of return on investment requirement before a company will commit funds. Often managers have a strong interest in having their projects funded. This means they are more likely to make favorable assumptions about the projects. However, since some of these projects actually will deliver lower rates of return than were estimated, key decision makers in companies tend to be very careful when they evaluate projects. They try to determine if assumptions are realistic.

Capital investment decisions often involve cash outflows over more than one period. Therefore, these projects must be monitored over time. Monitoring helps ensure that projects are developing satisfactorily and that continued investment is justified. Companies often use a milestone approach to monitoring.

Milestones, **which are major decision points,** are established at the beginning of a capital investment project. At each milestone, the project is reevaluated and a continue or discontinue decision is made. These decisions may be difficult because investments often do not produce positive returns for some time after an initial investment is made. The absence of positive returns during the developmental stage of projects increases investment risk. (Recall that the longer it takes to recover the cost of the investment, the higher the investment risk.)

Consider the decision by **General Electric** to produce a new model of refrigerator. This new model requires additional plant space, equipment, and tools. Considerable cost will be incurred before production can begin. If the model is unsuccessful, much of this cost will not be recovered. However, General Electric may be better off accepting its losses rather than continuing to invest in the product in an effort to make it successful. *Sunk costs* **are costs associated with decisions that have already been made.** For example, the costs of designing and making specific tools that are useful only in producing the new model of refrigerator are sunk costs. Sunk costs are not relevant for future decisions because future decisions cannot alter these costs.

Monitoring the progress of investment projects can be difficult, as can evaluation of the managers responsible for the projects. To develop forecasts about the amount and timing of returns on these projects, assumptions are necessary. It is frequently difficult to forecast the amount of time it will take to develop and market a new product. For example, Food and Drug Administration approval is required for new pharmaceutical products. In developing a new pharmaceutical product, there is often a long approval process during which the product is tested. In the meantime, the life span of the patent on the product is passing. This means that the pharmaceutical company will have fewer years in which it can market the product exclusively before its patent expires and generic brands begin to erode its sales. If delays occur, they may not be the fault of project managers. It is difficult to assess performance accurately because of uncertainty about what the performance should be.

TRADITIONAL APPROACHES TO CAPITAL INVESTMENT DECISIONS

OBJECTIVE 2

Calculate net present value, internal rate of return, payback, and accounting rate of return.

As discussed in the previous section, capital investments often involve long-term cash outlays. Consequently, the time value of money is an important consideration in making capital investment decisions. There are several tools that can assist managers in deciding whether or not to make a capital investment and in choosing between competing projects. Traditional tools can be divided into discounting and nondiscounting methods. *Discounting methods* **are those that rely on the time value of money.** *Nondiscounting methods* **ignore the time value of money.** Each method has advantages and disadvantages. Nondiscounting methods are less reliable than discounting methods, though some companies use them because they are easier to use. Roberta recommended that Erin and Seth use discounted cash flow analysis, which compares the expected cash inflows and outflows resulting from a capital investment. She said this method considers how the value of cash flows is affected based on *when* cash flows are received.

An important point to remember about the application of discounting methods to capital investment decisions is that they can be misleading when used improperly. This section describes how these methods are used in making capital investment decisions. Subsequent sections will discuss some of their shortcomings, especially in the new manufacturing environment. Also, it is important to keep in mind that these methods require long-term revenue and cost estimates, which often are uncertain. The most difficult task in using these methods is developing reasonable forecasts of revenues and costs.

Net Present Value

Recall that an important attribute of money is that it can be invested to earn interest. A dollar today is not worth the same as a dollar a year from now. **The translation of** future dollars into current dollars is known as *discounting.* The *net present value (NPV)* of an investment is the difference between the present value of expected cash inflows and the present value of expected cash outflows from the investment.

The net present value compares the present value of expected cash inflows and cash outflows associated with a project as shown in the following equation:

$$NPV = \sum \frac{C}{1 + R^t} - I$$

where NPV = net present value
I = amount invested at the beginning of the project
C = net cash inflow expected in period *t*
R = required rate of return
t = time period
Σ = summation for all periods

Thus, the net present value of an investment is the difference between the present value of expected future cash flows and the amount invested. Exhibit 3 illustrates an example. Assume that Stockdale Company has an opportunity to invest $60,000 in new equipment. Management expects the company to receive cash inflows of approximately $25,000 per year from sales of goods produced from the equipment. The equipment is expected to have a useful life of three years. In considering the investment, Stockdale's managers determine that the company has $30,000 available in an investment account that earns 8 percent interest per year. It would have to borrow the remaining $30,000 at 12 percent per year. Should Stockdale invest in the equipment?

Exhibit 3

An Illustration of Net Present Value

	Time			
Present		**Year 1**	**Year 2**	**Year 3**
Expected future cash flows		$25,000	$25,000	$25,000
Discounted to present value at 10%				
$22,727 ← $25,000 ÷ 1.10^1				
20,661 ← $25,000 ÷ 1.10^2				
18,783 ← $25,000 ÷ 1.10^3				
$62,171				
Less:				
Amount invested	60,000			
Net present value	$ 2,171			

To answer this question, consider the rate of return Stockdale will require. If the company uses the $30,000 from its investments, it will forgo the 8 percent interest on the invested funds for the coming year, or $2,400 (0.08 × $30,000). The $2,400 of lost interest is an opportunity cost that should be considered in the decision. *Opportunity costs* **are the costs associated with not taking a particular course of action.** Also, the cost to borrow $30,000 is $3,600 (0.12 × $30,000) for the next year. Thus, to break even on the investment, Stockdale will need to recover the $60,000 invested and earn an additional $6,000 ($2,400 + $3,600) per year. Any amount earned over $6,000 will increase company value and make the investment desirable. The $6,000 represents Stockdale's *cost of capital,* **which is the cost of funds that can be used to finance a project.** The rate of return necessary to earn $6,000 is considered Stockdale's *required rate of return.* **This rate sometimes is referred to as a** *hurdle rate* **because it is the rate that must be earned before an investment is made.** It is also known as the **discount rate** because it is the rate used to discount (reduce) future cash flows to their present value. In this case, Stockdale requires a 10 percent rate of return ($6,000 ÷ $60,000 = 10%).

Using the discount rate of 10 percent, we can compute the present value of the cash flows expected from the investment at the end of each of the three years.

$$PV = \frac{\$25,000}{(1.10)^1} + \frac{\$25,000}{(1.10)^2} + \frac{\$25,000}{(1.10)^3}$$
$$= \$22,727 + \$20,661 + \$18,783$$
$$= \$62,171$$

Alternatively, we can use the interest factor for an annuity from Table 4 (inside back cover) for three periods at 10 percent: $\$25,000 \times 2.48685 = \$62,171$. Recall that an annuity results when the same amount is received each period over the life of an investment. The net present value, then, is the difference between the present value of the expected net cash inflows and the amount invested.

$$NPV = \sum \frac{C}{1 + R^t} - I$$
$$= \$62,171 - \$60,000$$
$$= \$2,171$$

A positive net present value indicates that the initial investment has been recovered and a return greater than the initial investment and cost of capital has been received. Thus, if the net present value is zero or greater than zero, the investment is expected to earn an acceptable return. If the net present value is less than zero, the investment should be rejected because it will earn less than the required rate of return.

To use net present value analysis, an organization must identify an appropriate discount rate. Usually, the discount rate is the company's average cost of capital, the average cost of all sources of financing available to a company, such as bank loans and expected returns to stockholders. Generally, managers should select those projects that promise the highest net present value.

In calculating the present value of cash flows, it is important to include all relevant cash flows. For example, if a capital investment is in property or equipment that has an expected disposal value, that value should be included. Suppose Stockdale invested in equipment that it expects to sell at the end of year 3 for $5,000. The net cash inflow in year 3 would be $30,000 ($25,000 of annual cash flows plus the $5,000 disposal value of the equipment).

If additional cash outflows were required each year as a result of the purchase of the equipment, those cash outflows also should be considered. For example, assume the equipment purchased by Stockdale would require additional insurance costs of $1,000 per year. The net cash flow each year would be $24,000 ($25,000 from sales minus $1,000 of additional insurance).

Also, observe that cash flows should be used in determining the net present value of a capital investment. Revenues and expenses are relevant only if they are consistent with cash flows. Depreciation, for example, is not relevant for a capital investment decision. The cost associated with the purchase of property and equipment occurs at the time the purchase is made. Depreciation is a noncash expense and is not relevant to the determination of net present value.

A cost savings is treated the same as a cash inflow. If the acquisition of equipment by Stockdale reduces annual operating costs (lower labor costs, for example) by $2,000 per year, those cost reductions can be treated as additional cash inflows because the company's cash flow increases by $2,000 per year.

---

1 **SELF-STUDY PROBLEM**

WebTUTOR Advantage

The management of Joyful Car, Inc., is considering replacing the company's current semiautomated car washing equipment with a fully-automated system that would eliminate all labor except that required to clean car interiors. Though the new system will reduce labor costs, it represents a substantial capital investment for the small company. Management has developed the following data regarding the investment:

Cost of the new system	$100,000
Sales value of the old system	$ 40,000
Sales value of the new system at the end of its five-year life	0
Required rate of return	10%
Net decrease in annual operating costs	$ 15,000

Assume that Joyful has the cash to pay for the new equipment, and ignore any tax effects.

Required Evaluate the investment using the NPV method. Assess the factors that increase or reduce the risk associated with the capital investment decision in this case. Explain whether you consider the investment to be an operational or a strategic decision for the company, and why.

The solution to Self-Study Problem 1 appears at the end of the chapter.

Internal Rate of Return

Another discounting method that sometimes is used in addition to or instead of net present value is the internal rate of return. **The** *internal rate of return (IRR)* **is the interest rate that results in the present value of cash outflows being equal to the present value of cash inflows from an investment.** In other words, it is the interest rate that results in a net present value of zero. The following equation can be used to determine a project's IRR:

$$PV = \sum \frac{C}{1 + R^t}$$

where PV = present value of the project
C = cash inflow to be received in period t
R = required rate of return
t = time period
Σ = summation for all periods

Let's consider Stockdale Company's investment decision using the internal rate of return method. Recall that an investment of $60,000 is estimated to return $25,000 each year for three years. The cost to Stockdale of the $60,000 it will invest is $6,000, or 10 percent, which is the hurdle rate.

Using the internal rate of return method, the investment would be accepted if its internal rate of return is greater than 10 percent. The internal rate of return is the interest rate that equates $25,000 each year for three years with $60,000 today. The IRR would be calculated as follows:

$$PV = \sum \frac{C}{1 + R^t}$$

$$\$60,000 = \frac{\$25,000}{(1 + R)^1} + \frac{\$25,000}{(1 + R)^2} + \frac{\$25,000}{(1 + R)^3}$$

We can find R by trial and error, or we can approximate the value using Table 4 from the back of the book. Table 4 provides an interest factor that associates the present value of an annuity with expected future cash flows:

$$PV = C \times IF$$

where PV = present value
C = expected cash flow each period
IF = interest factor

Therefore,

$$PV = C \times IF$$
$$\$60,000 = \$25,000 \times IF$$
$$\$60,000 \div \$25,000 = IF$$
$$2.4 = IF$$

Look at the third row of Table 4. (The investment is for three years.) Note that an interest factor of 2.4 is the approximate value in the 12 percent column.

Thus, the internal rate of return is 12 percent. Because the internal rate of return is greater than the required rate of return of 10 percent, the investment should be accepted. The internal rate of return is higher than the cost of capital; thus, accepting the investment would add value to the company.

The internal rate of return for a multiyear project where the net cash inflows are not the same each year is the interest rate that will make the present value of the cash flows equal to the initial cash investment. Consider a project with an initial investment of $15,403 that is estimated to return cash flows of $4,000, $4,000, $5,000, and $8,000 for years 1 through 4 of the project, respectively. Again, the interest rate that will make the cash flows from operations equal to the initial cash outlay can be found by trial and error. Exhibit 4 calculates the present value of cash flows from operations using a discount rate of 10 percent and the interest factor from Table 3 (inside back cover). (Table 4 cannot be used because the expected net cash inflows are not the same amount each year.)

Exhibit 4

Present Value Calculation

Year	Expected Cash Flow		Interest Factor for 10% from Table 3		Present Value
1	$4,000	×	0.90909	=	$ 3,636
2	4,000	×	0.82645	=	3,306
3	5,000	×	0.75131	=	3,757
4	8,000	×	0.68301	=	5,464
					$16,163

The present value of the project is $16,163. This amount is greater than the initial investment of $15,403; therefore, 10 percent is *not* the IRR. A different interest rate must be tried. Should a higher or a lower rate be used? **The higher the interest rate, the lower the present value.** Since $16,163 is greater than $15,403, a higher interest rate must be used so that a lower present value is obtained. The present value using a rate of 12 percent is shown in Exhibit 5.

At 12 percent the present value of future cash flows from operations is exactly equal to the initial investment.

Exhibit 5

Present Value Calculation

Year	Expected Cash Flow		Interest Factor for 12% from Table 3		Present Value
1	$4,000	×	0.89286	=	$ 3,571
2	4,000	×	0.79719	=	3,189
3	5,000	×	0.71178	=	3,559
4	8,000	×	0.63552	=	5,084
					$15,403

Since the interest rate that makes the cash flow from operations equal the initial investment is 12 percent, this is the IRR for the investment. A trial-and-error procedure must be used to determine the IRR when the cash flows from operations are not the same each year. Computer programs, such as Excel®, contain functions that simplify the calculation. Even these programs begin with an estimated rate of return and use trial and error to find the internal rate of return.

Although the internal rate of return is easily understood by managers, a major disadvantage is that it does not differentiate between two projects that have identical rates of return but that differ in some other important way. For example, consider a $100 investment and a $100,000 investment, both of which have a 15 percent rate of return. Using the IRR method, both investments would be equally desirable, since they have identical returns. However, these investments are not equal because of the substantial difference in the cash outlays required.

Another disadvantage of the IRR method is that it assumes cash flows from operations can be reinvested at the internal rate of return. For example, if a project is expected to have an IRR of 20 percent, it is assumed that each time a cash flow from operations is received, the company will be able to reinvest the cash and earn 20 percent over the remaining life of the investment. This assumption is not always true and is a weakness of the IRR method. If the reinvested cash flow earns only a 15 percent return, the overall return on the investment will be less than 20 percent.

Using Excel to Calculate NPV and IRR

Exhibit 6 illustrates how Excel can be used to determine NPV and IRR using the values shown in Exhibit 5. The NPV or IRR functions can be selected by clicking the insert function button or command and selecting NPV or IRR from the financial category. The cash flows are entered in the spreadsheet.

The NPV calculation in panel A includes the cash flows for each year from Exhibit 5. For example, the initial investment ($15,403) represents a negative cash flow and is entered into cell A1. The annual cash inflows for the following four years are entered into cells A2 through A5. The NPV function is entered in cell A6. The rate of return is entered as .12 and the values are referenced as cells A1:A5. The function returns a value of 0.22317, which is $0.22 or approximately 0, indicating that the NPV of the investment is $0.

In panel B, the IRR function is entered in cell A6. The values field in the dialog box refers to the values in A1 to A5 and an IRR guess is entered into the guess field. The value of the guess is not particularly important, but Excel will take longer to calculate the answer when the guess is not close the final answer. Excel reports the IRR as 12 percent.

Payback Period

An approach to capital investment decision making that does not involve discounting is based on the payback period. The *payback period* **is the time required to recover an original investment from expected future cash flows.** For example, if the original investment is $60,000 and the estimated cash inflows are $25,000 per year, then the payback period is 2.4 years ($60,000 ÷ $25,000 per year). When the future cash flows for each period are expected to be equal, the payback period can be computed as follows:

Payback period = Original investment ÷ Periodic cash inflow

If the periodic cash inflows are not the same, the payback period is computed by adding each cash inflow until the sum equals the invested amount. Management decides on a time period in which the invested amount is to be recovered. A project that does not pay back its original investment within this period is rejected. There are shortcomings to such an approach, however. Consider the following cash flows for two projects, each requiring an initial investment of $100,000.

Exhibit 6

Using Excel to Solve an
NPV or IRR Problem

Panel A

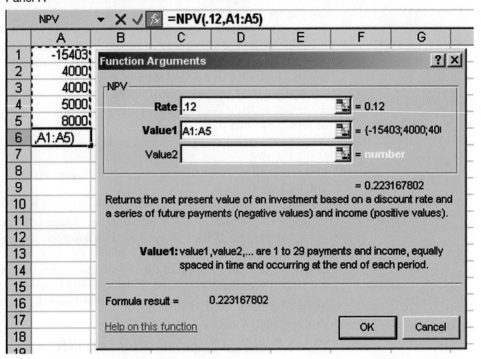

Panel B

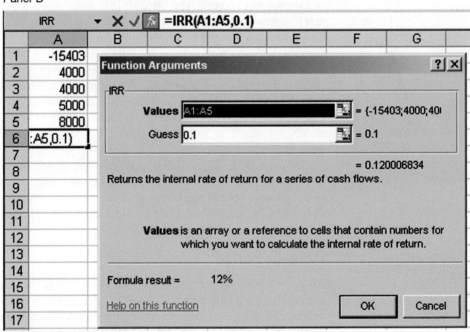

	Investment A	Investment B
Year 1	$20,000	$90,000
Year 2	80,000	10,000
Year 3	5,000	10,000

Both investments have payback periods of two years ($20,000 + $80,000 = $100,000, and $90,000 + $10,000 = $100,000). Thus, if a manager uses the payback period method, both would be equally desirable. In reality, however, B should be preferred over A. Project B returns $90,000 in the first year, compared to $20,000 for project A. The extra $70,000 can be invested in other projects during year 2. In addition, project B continues to return greater cash flows after year 2. Accordingly, the payback method ignores total profitability and the time value of money.

Many companies use the payback period as one of several criteria when making investment decisions. In addition, managers may use the payback method to choose among projects when other attributes, such as NPV, are similar.

Accounting Rate of Return

The accounting rate of return is another commonly used decision-making method that does not require discounting. The *accounting rate of return (ARR)* **is the average accounting income a project generates per period divided by the amount of the investment in the project.** ARR differs from discounting methods in that it uses income rather than cash flows to measure return. ARR is computed as follows:

Accounting rate of return = Average income ÷ Investment

The average income of a project is obtained by adding the net income for each period of the project and dividing by the number of periods over which the project will produce income. To illustrate the computation of accounting rate of return, assume that an investment requires an initial outlay of $100,000. The life of the investment is five years, and it is expected to produce net income as follows:

Year	Net Income
1	$10,000
2	10,000
3	20,000
4	15,000
5	25,000
Total	$80,000

The average net income is $16,000 ($80,000 ÷ 5), and the accounting rate of return is 16 percent ($16,000 ÷ $100,000).

Unlike the payback method, the accounting rate of return considers a project's profitability. Like the payback method, the accounting rate of return ignores the time value of money. Failure to consider the time value of money may lead a manager to select a project that does not maximize company value. However, future cash flows are not always easy to determine. Many investments involve combinations of resources such as plant assets, working capital, and labor, making cash flow from a project difficult to estimate. ARR, therefore, may be used instead of cash flows to approximate the return on investment.

Other Considerations

In addition to the considerations discussed in the prior section, there are other considerations that affect the use of discounting models. Three of these considerations are (1) the service lives and residual values of investments, (2) the effects of income taxes on cash flows, and (3) the risk associated with capital investment decisions.

The trade-in or *residual value* **of an investment refers to its market value at the end of its useful life or service life to a company.** *Service life* **refers to the period during which an investment is expected to be used.** A residual value must be estimated in order to make net present value and internal rate of return calculations. Failing to include the residual value understates the cash flows from an investment and could lead to rejection of an acceptable investment. Residual values can be difficult to estimate for an investment in equipment that has an uncertain life.

Sometimes managers overestimate the service lives of assets such as computers because they fail to consider the rate of change of technology. When new technology becomes available (for example, new computer technology), management must decide whether to continue to operate with old assets or to purchase new assets sooner than expected.

Recall that depreciation is a noncash expense. However, depreciation reduces a corporation's taxable income because it is a tax-deductible expense. This reduction in taxes is cash that the company will not have to pay out. Therefore, although depreciation itself does not affect cash flows, its effect on taxes does. As a result, it is important to include the income tax benefits of depreciation when calculating the net present value or internal rate of return of capital investment projects. The following example illustrates how service life, residual values, and depreciation can affect investment decisions.

Merchants' Bank is considering an investment in a new computer system to replace the old computer that is used to process deposits, loans, and other customer transactions. The bank uses the net present value method in its analysis of investment decisions.

The new system, including workstations, a network, and software, will cost $450,000 and will have an estimated useful life of five years. The expected residual value at the end of five years is $50,000. Straight-line depreciation is used for accounting and tax purposes. The old computer system, which has been depreciated to its residual value, can be sold for $20,000. The bank's income tax rate is 35 percent, and its required rate of return is 10 percent. Bank managers believe that the bank can save $100,000 net of any income tax effects each year if the new system is purchased. Should the bank invest in the new computer system?

Exhibit 7 provides an analysis of the investment to answer this question. The analysis involves a series of steps. In step 1, the amount to be invested ($430,000) is determined. In step 2, the amount of depreciation ($80,000 per year) and the effect of depreciation on taxes (savings of $28,000 per year) are calculated. In step 3, the expected cash flows associated with the investment each year are identified. Step 4 involves calculating the present value of the expected cash flows ($516,267). Finally, in step 5, the net present value of the investment ($86,267) is determined.

Because the net present value of $86,267 is greater than zero, the bank should invest in the new computer. In this analysis, the effect of tax savings is important. It adds $106,142 to the present value of the investment (step 4). Without these savings, the present value would be $410,125 ($516,267 − $106,142), and the investment would be unacceptable. Thus, it is important to consider all of the financial consequences of an investment in making a capital budgeting decision.

When managers are unsure about the accuracy of assumptions used in making investment decisions, they often test the sensitivity of their decisions to these assumptions. For example, suppose the managers of Merchants' Bank are unsure about the cost savings they expect from investing in the new computer system. They believe that the savings are most likely to be $100,000 per year, but that they could be as low as $75,000 per year. What effect would the lower level of savings have on the decision? The present value of an annuity of $75,000 per year for five years at 10 percent is $284,309 ($75,000 × 3.79079). Therefore, the total present value of expected cash flows (step 4) would be $421,497 ($284,309 + $106,142 + $31,046), and the net present value (step 5) would be −$8,503 ($421,497 − $430,000). At the lower cost savings, the project would be rejected. The managers now must decide whether they believe the lower cost savings are likely to occur or whether they are confident that the higher savings are likely. Net present value analysis, like other decision tools, does not make decisions for managers. It provides them with information to help them with their decisions.

Exhibit 7

Net Present Value
Analysis of Computer
Purchase

Step 1: Amount of Investment

Cost of new computer	$450,000
Less: Sale price of old computer	20,000
Amount to be invested	$430,000

Step 2: Tax Savings per Year

Cost of computer	$450,000
Less: Residual value	50,000
Amount to depreciate	$400,000
Expected life	÷ 5
Depreciation per year	$ 80,000
Income tax rate	× 0.35
Tax savings per year	$ 28,000

Step 3: Expected Future Cash Flows

Year	Cost Savings*	Tax Savings	Residual Value
1	$100,000	$28,000	
2	100,000	28,000	
3	100,000	28,000	
4	100,000	28,000	
5	100,000	28,000	$50,000

Step 4: Computation of Present Value of Expected Future Cash Flows

Present value of annuity of $100,000 per year for 5 years at 10%:	
$100,000 × 3.79079 (interest factor from Table 4) =	$379,079
Present value of annuity of $28,000 per year for 5 years at 10%:	
$28,000 × 3.79079 =	106,142
Present value of single amount of $50,000 at the end of 5 years at 10%:	
$50,000 × 0.62092 (interest factor from Table 3) =	31,046
Total present value of expected future cash flows	$516,267

Step 5: Computation of Net Present Value of Investment

Total present value	$516,267
Amount to be invested	430,000
Net present value	$ 86,267

*Assume this cost savings is net of any tax effect due to an increase in income from the capital investment.

THE NEW MANUFACTURING ENVIRONMENT

OBJECTIVE 3

Describe the effect of the
new manufacturing
environment on capital
investment decisions.

The new manufacturing environment has changed the way capital investment decisions are viewed. Before the new manufacturing environment, many companies relied heavily on methods such as net present value to justify capital investments. Traditional capital investment analysis focused mainly on the immediate direct benefits, such as labor savings, reduced waste, lower inventories, and improved capacity. Less tangible benefits such as improved quality often were not considered. In the 1980s, foreign companies that produced high-quality products began to compete with U.S. companies. This competition increased the pressure on U.S. companies to improve the quality of their products, which, in turn, increased the need to consider quality improvements when making capital investments.

Increased automation is a major feature of many production processes in the new manufacturing environment. Automation has become a priority for many companies as they replace older equipment. Much of the older U.S. equipment is not computer-controlled, in contrast to that used in countries like Japan.

Another example of the association between the new manufacturing environment and capital investment decisions surfaced in the chapter opening scenario. Many companies embrace the notion of reducing throughput time as a means of reducing costs. Reduction of throughput time can be one objective of reorganizing plant layout and automating production processes.

Automation and Modern Manufacturing

The objective of automation often is not only to increase capacity but also to produce high-quality goods in a consistent, rapid, and economical manner. Used effectively, automation can improve a company's ability to deliver high-quality products, to create value for customers. Automation can help eliminate variation from production standards due to human error. The new manufacturing environment requires a fresh look at the ways capital investment decisions are made. The costs of quality and efficiency are important to many capital investment decisions. These costs are especially relevant when companies automate their production processes.

Frequently, automation is part of a plan to redesign the value chain. Redesigning the value chain can involve many activities, from changing a company's production process to eliminating activities such as inventory storage, material handling, and excessive rework.

In the new manufacturing environment, capital investments involving automation can be classified into four categories, as illustrated in Exhibit 8.

1. *Stand-alone tools*, such as robots used to weld steel, are commonly controlled by computers. Stand-alone tools are the most common form of automation. They can improve quality, speed, or capacity. The amount invested is relatively small compared to that needed for other types of automation. Also, the payback period is relatively short.
2. *Cells of machines* consist of multiple pieces of isolated equipment grouped closely together. An example of a cell is a computer-controlled machine for materials handling grouped with computer-controlled molding equipment to manufacture automobile body parts. These machines have a short setup time and can be quickly changed from the manufacture of one part to another. The amount of the investment often is much higher and the payback period much longer than for stand-alone tools.
3. *Linked islands* consist of cells of machines connected through computerized information networks. Islands give a company the ability to respond rapidly to developing markets by creating new, custom-designed products. Investments are large, and payback periods are long. Also, if one component of an island fails, the entire island is likely to fail.
4. *Computer-integrated manufacturing* links an entire manufacturing process through an extensive information network. For example, **Monsanto Plastics Division** manufactures plastics for use in automobiles, computers, and other products. In its old manufacturing process, changing from one type of plastic to another took hours. The division installed a computer-integrated manufacturing system that permits much faster changeover times, improved quality, and less waste.

Automated production can give a company a powerful competitive advantage in the global marketplace because it allows improved product innovation and quality, shorter delivery time, efficient production scheduling, and lower cost. Computer-integrated manufacturing can involve what are sometimes referred to as "greenfield factories" because virtually the entire factory is redesigned. This type of capital investment has been referred to as a "you bet your company" decision because of the high level of risk involved. Failure of the strategy often means failure of the company.

These capital investment categories in the new manufacturing environment involve different levels of decisions, ranging from lower-level, operational decisions for stand-alone tools to very costly strategic decisions for computer-integrated manufacturing.

Exhibit 8
Categories of
Automation

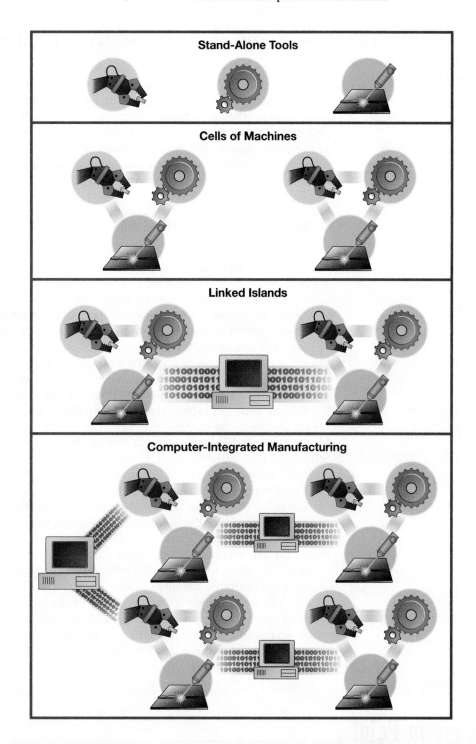

The new manufacturing environment has changed the way many companies make capital investment decisions:

- Investments are becoming more significant. Automation can be large in scope and affect an entire company.
- Equipment is more complex and expensive than the equipment that was the focus of traditional investment decisions.
- The cash flows required to justify capital investments are received over a longer period of time.

In short, capital investment decisions have become longer-term and riskier. The next section examines how managers make capital investment decisions in this new strategic environment.

MAKING STRATEGIC CAPITAL INVESTMENT DECISIONS

Managers making capital investment decisions in the new manufacturing environment do not rely solely on traditional methods, such as net present value. This section highlights problems in making capital investment decisions and provides guidance on how these decisions should be made in the new manufacturing environment to avoid such problems. These problems have led some companies to underestimate the value of strategic investments that would improve their ability to compete in the new manufacturing environment. In some cases these investments are necessary for the survival of companies in intensely competitive markets.

Problems in Making Decisions

What are these problems? First, residual values often are critical to investment decisions. Estimating residual values can require managers to forecast technological, economic, operational, strategic, and market developments over several years. Residual values are especially difficult to estimate because they come at the end of the investment's expected service life. For example, a company may have difficulty estimating the residual value of a computer system in five years because the value depends on new systems introduced by manufacturers during the five-year period. Managers sometimes ignore the residual value of an asset because of uncertainty about its value. However, because strategic decisions usually involve high residual values, the failure to include estimates of residual values in discounting models biases decisions against strategic investments.

Second, because strategic investments in the new manufacturing environment often are long term, the discount rate has a major effect on capital investment decisions. Many companies use discount rates that are higher than their current cost of capital. Setting discount rates too high biases decisions against strategic investments by decreasing the present value of the future cash flows.

Third, managers often fail to include the opportunity costs associated with not making a strategic investment. In the new manufacturing environment, these opportunity costs usually consist of the loss of future potential sales as a result of inferior quality, slower and less reliable delivery, and the inability to respond rapidly to customer demands for new products. These typical customer concerns in the new manufacturing environment often require strategic investments. Unfortunately, difficulty in estimating these opportunity costs often leads managers to omit them from their discounting models. Yet, consideration of the opportunity costs of not investing can be critical, not only to a single investment decision but also to the future of a company or a division.

As an example of a case in which opportunity costs are important, consider the following Case in Point, the World Transmission Project at the **Allison Transmission Division of General Motors.**

Case in Point

Opportunity Costs

Allison Transmission is a world leader in making transmissions for heavy trucks. Allison has long been a very successful division of General Motors Corporation, with a reputation for consistently generating good cash flows.

During the 1980s, existing technology for making heavy transmissions was becoming obsolete. Further, foreign competitors threatened to build state-of-the-art facilities to manufacture a new generation of transmissions if Allison chose not to take this step. At the same time, General Motors was experiencing a financial downturn that made Allison's positive cash flows important to the company.

The facility that Allison needed if it was to continue to dominate the truck transmission market required an investment of over $500 million in robotics and built-in quality controls such as cameras that detected incorrectly assembled parts. Production scheduling and operations would be governed by a computer system that would integrate virtually all aspects of manufacturing.

Allison drew up plans for the new plant, called the World Transmission (WT) Project. It would take years to build the facility, to develop a new generation of transmissions, to train the workforce that would operate the new equipment, and to establish the products in the marketplace. Consequently, it would be some time before the new facility would begin to show positive cash flows. This presented a dilemma for General Motors. If Allison did not go forward with the WT Project, one of several foreign competitors probably would build a similar plant, and Allison would lose its edge in the market. If Allison built the plant, it would no longer produce positive cash flows for some time to come. After some delay, the project was approved. The opportunity cost of not modernizing the production process was too high not to make the investment.

Avoiding Problems

How should managers avoid the pitfalls associated with making capital investments in the new manufacturing environment? First, in applying traditional techniques for making capital investments, managers need to be careful in estimating residual values and discount rates. Second, managers need to include the opportunity costs of not investing in their strategic decisions. Third, managers should recognize the uncertainty of cash flows in many strategic investment situations.

Moving Baseline Concept

Traditional capital investment techniques compare the expected results of new investments with the company's current operating results. This comparison assumes that the company's current operating results will continue indefinitely and will not be hurt by the decision not to make an investment. If this assumption is wrong, the company will experience an opportunity cost by not investing in assets that will allow it to maintain its market share.

One method that addresses this issue is the *moving baseline concept.* **Instead of assuming that current operating cash flows will continue indefinitely, this concept assumes that if the investment is not made the cash flows will decrease because of the competition's superior quality.** For example, assume that Sandy States Insurance Company is considering upgrading its automated customer service system to lower costs and improve service. The lower costs will result in an improved net cash flow from operations of $75 million each year as shown in the table in Exhibit 9. The system will cost $450 million to purchase at the present time, but it will permit Sandy States to recover $525 million in three years when part of the present customer service facility is sold. After seven years, Sandy States expects to build an entirely new facility, with the selling price offsetting any residual value of the remaining old facility. New investments in software and hardware upgrades costing $50 million each year are expected in years 5–7.

If Sandy States does not switch to the new system it will likely begin to lose some business each year as a result of customer dissatisfaction. These losses are expected to accumulate to $435 million by the end of year 7 as the old system becomes increasingly obsolete, leading to greater and greater dissatisfaction. Including the losses due to customer dissatisfaction is what is meant by the moving baseline approach. Management has two choices: to assume that the current cash flows will continue or to assume that cash flows will decrease if the investment is not made.

Exhibit 9 compares the cash flows with the moving baseline (line a) to those without the moving baseline (line b). The moving baseline approach (line a) includes the benefits of improved customer service from investing in the new system, both in terms of reaching breakeven point sooner (c versus d) and in terms of total cash flows over the life of the investment. Including the cash flows that are preserved by the improved customer service could make the difference between Sandy States investing and not investing.

Exhibit 9

Comparison of
Cumulative Cash Flows
With and Without
Moving Baseline

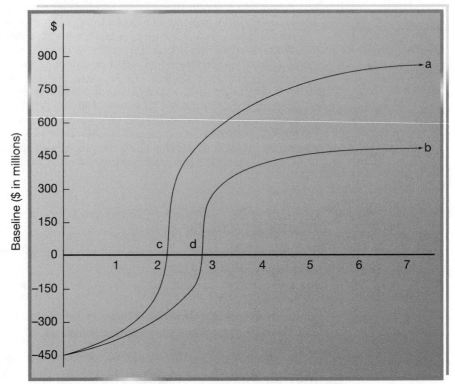

a = investment cash flows including the moving baseline
b = investment cash flows not including the moving baseline

Year	0	1	2	3	4	5	6	7
Investment cash in(out) flows	$(450)	$ 0	$ 0	$525	$ 0	$ (50)	$ (50)	$ (50)
Annual improvement in net cash flow from operations		75	75	75	75	75	75	75
Cumulative cash flow without moving baseline (line b)	$(450)	$(375)	$(300)	$300	$375	$400	$425	$450
Cumulative loss of business avoided with new system		25	300	350	375	400	425	435
Cumulative cash flow with moving baseline (line a)	$(450)	$(350)	$ 0	$650	$750	$800	$850	$885

Uncertain and Hidden Costs

Strategic investments often involve uncertain costs that are difficult to measure but that are extremely important to the decision. An example is a decision by a company to develop a new product line for unfamiliar markets. For example, **Pennzoil** made the mistake of underestimating warranty costs when it decided to invest in quick-change oil facilities. The failure of employees to remove and properly reinsert plugs in oil pans led to engine failures and unexpectedly high warranty costs. The company's lack of experience in the automobile maintenance business resulted in its failure to include adequate warranty costs in its investment decision.

The problems associated with strategic capital investments are not limited to manufacturing companies. Service companies can face similar decisions that have far-reaching consequences. Furthermore, marketing assumptions often are critical to the success of a strategic capital investment project, regardless of whether a company is a manufacturing or service business. Self-Study Problem 2 provides examples of two banks that made strategic capital investment decisions. In both cases, subjective marketing considerations were instrumental in the banks' decisions to fund the project. In analyzing this problem, keep the following points in mind:

- Capital investment decisions sometimes are made for reasons other than return on investment. For example, management may believe that being in a particular market improves the company's image. Image may be important to a company's marketing strategy. If return on investment is much lower than expected, however, any marketing advantage may be more than offset by the cost of the investment.
- Where uncertainty about future cash flows is high because of uncertainty about revenues and costs, managers should consider a range of possible outcomes resulting from the capital investment.
- In situations where cash flows are uncertain, managers should be careful that their assumptions regarding factors that could affect future cash flows are realistic.

2 SELF-STUDY PROBLEM

In the middle 1970s, the **National Bank of Georgia** (NBG) seized an opportunity to establish a branch in a major office complex that was being built in downtown Atlanta. The facility represented a new concept in urban office space for the city. It was to contain its own shops, restaurants, and branch banks. Workers in the office space could work, shop, eat, and bank without ever leaving the complex. Some were touting this approach as the wave of the future. The complex attracted a great deal of attention, and branch banks located in it were expected to be high-profile signals of the banks' presence in the downtown Atlanta market. At the time, NBG was the fifth largest bank in the city. NBG's management was trying to make a major push to become larger and more visible. Although the lease expenses and costs of improvements would be very high, the new office complex seemed to afford the type of opportunity the bank wanted.

At about the same time NBG was considering its branching decision, **Home Federal Savings** of Rome, Georgia, was considering a strategic branching decision of its own. Rome was a small city of approximately 40,000 people. Home Federal was a small, independent S&L that was totally oriented toward making home loans and accepting savings deposits from individuals. It had long had a conservative banking philosophy. Despite its retail orientation, it operated from only one downtown location, unlike most of its competitors, which long ago had embraced branch banking. Home Federal's management, however, had come to the conclusion that the city's growth was headed in a westerly direction and that it had to establish a branch on that side of town or lose customers who considered the drive into town too inconvenient. Home Federal had the opportunity to acquire and remodel a vacant facility that had been used as a fast-food restaurant at a cost that, although significant, was considerably lower than the cost of building a new branch. The facility is in a highly visible location. Home Federal's logo would be seen by thousands of motorists driving by each week.

Both banks elected to make the capital investments in branching. NBG's investment failed. The branch was closed within two years because the new office concept failed to generate enough customers. Leasing of office space in the complex was slower than expected, and far fewer customers than expected used the shops and restaurants. Conversely, Home Federal's branch was a great success. The branch was profitable within months after opening and continued to show good growth and profitability thereafter.

Required What factors could account for the difference between these two strategic investment decisions? Why are marketing assumptions often critical to the success or failure of strategic capital investment decisions?

The solution to Self-Study Problem 2 appears at the end of the chapter.

RESPONDING TO BAD CAPITAL INVESTMENT DECISIONS

Capital investment projects sometimes are funded in stages. Decisions are made at each stage about whether to continue to fund a project. Once it becomes apparent that the project has failed, these decisions pose serious difficulties because a decision to continue can be very costly. This problem occurs in a bank when a loan officer continues to lend money to a failing customer to delay recognizing a loss. Managers should know that there is a tendency to continue funding failed projects and be able to recognize the causes of this tendency.

Costs of a project that cannot be recovered are sunk costs. Decision makers should ignore these costs when deciding whether to invest additional money in a project. Unfortunately, they often fall into a sunk cost trap, as shown in Exhibit 10.

Exhibit 10   The Escalation Cycle

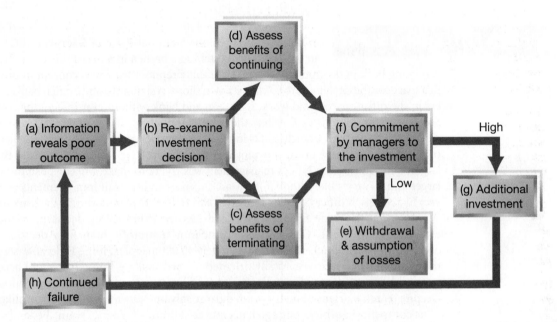

Adapted from Staw, Barry M. and Jerry Ross. 1987. Behavior in Escalation Situations: Antecedents, Prototypes, and Solutions, *Research in Organizational Behavior*: 39–78.

When decision makers become aware that an investment is failing (a), they reexamine the investment (b) and weigh the benefits of terminating the investment (c) against the benefits of continuing (d). If the estimated costs of terminating the project are less than the benefits, decision makers should withdraw from the project and accept the losses associated with withdrawal (e). However, if their commitment to the project is high (f), decision makers may continue to fund it (g) even though it is failing (h).

For example, suppose that a bank loaned money to a remanufacturer of automobile parts to buy raw materials for inventory production. Because of bad management practices, the remanufacturer used these funds to make inventory it could not sell. The remanufacturer then asked the bank for more money to buy raw materials to manufacture more inventory. The bank, fearing that the remanufacturer would fail if it did not loan the funds, made the second loan. The remanufacturer repeated its first mistake and ultimately failed. The bank lost considerably more money than it would have lost if it had recognized its first mistake and not loaned the additional funds. The bank focused on the sunk cost of the first loan and loaned additional money instead of cutting its losses.

In this cycle, information about a project's performance causes a reexamination of the project. If managers are committed to a project, they often fund the project until additional information is received.

Why do they do this? The reasons can be divided into four categories:

- *Project determinants:* These are objective features of a project. For instance, large sunk costs that cannot be recovered if the project is discontinued or the fact that there are no competing projects that provide higher returns are both features that may contribute to the decision to continue.
- *Psychological determinants:* These are forces that can introduce error into managers' estimates of the gains and losses. Such forces influence the decision to continue or discontinue a project and can lead to greater investment. Examples: (1) Managers may have made the earlier decision to invest in the project and may feel a strong desire to continue investing because of their earlier decision. (2) Decision makers may believe withdrawing from the project will mean a loss of money already sunk instead of viewing the withdrawal as saving money not yet spent.
- *Social determinants:* These are pressures within the organizational environment. The need to save face, the desire to beat a competitor, the support of others for a project, and attitudes such as "never quit no matter what" encourage increased investment.
- *Structural determinants:* These are features of the organization itself. For example, the absence of appropriate project controls and a desperate need for a company to show progress can lead to continuing a project.

To avoid these problems, a company periodically may replace some members of the project management team with new members to bring fresh insights and to prevent too much personal identification with the project. Also, initial investment decisions can be separated from later investment decisions by requiring rejustification of a project with every funding decision. Companies can reduce the threat of failure for decision makers by acknowledging that well-managed projects are sometimes unsuccessful. For example, many banks encourage aggressive lending by loan officers. Loan officers who never generate loan losses are not sufficiently aggressive.

Identifying the opportunity costs associated with continuing to invest in failing projects may help managers make termination decisions. Also, it may be helpful to identify the potential costs of terminating a project before initial funding of the project, so that these costs will be more obvious from the beginning. Some risk of failure is associated with any project, and some failures must be expected. Managers should learn to evaluate and accept some failures.

CAPITAL INVESTMENT DECISIONS IN SERVICE COMPANIES

OBJECTIVE 5

Describe the factors affecting capital investment decisions in service organizations.

Like manufacturing companies, service companies must make capital investment decisions. A service company must invest in those fixed assets that are necessary if it is to provide a service to its customers. This may mean investment in long-term construction projects such as railroad tracks, telephone lines, and even telecommunication satellites.

When making capital investment decisions, managers in service companies must take the same factors into consideration as managers in manufacturing companies. In addition, service companies such as railroads, telecommunication companies, and power companies often are government-regulated. Regulators frequently set the rates that service companies can charge their customers. They become concerned if they believe that the customers are being charged too much or are not being given good service. Regulators monitor regulated service companies' capital investments to determine whether they will lead to requests for higher rates and how they will affect customer service.

Remember that investment capital usually is scarce, so managers must put it to the best possible use. Managers in regulated service companies sometimes must choose between capital investments that will provide better service to different sets of customers. In such cases, regulators may exert pressure on the company to limit capital investment of one type in order to be sure that enough capital is invested in other services. This may be true even if the investment that the regulators limit has the potential to provide greater cash flows.

3 SELF-STUDY PROBLEM

Refer to the Case in Point involving General Motors' decision to fund the Allison Transmission "World Transmission Project." GM originally expected to spend approximately $500 million on the WT Project. After the project had been underway for several years, it became obvious that cost overruns would result in the project costing in excess of $600 million. By the time the overruns became known, GM already had spent over $250 million on the project. Further, Allison experienced some production problems with the new transmissions. The division's cash flows were negative.

Required Assume you are part of GM management. What factors would you consider in deciding whether to invest the additional $100 million to complete the WT Project? Discuss the factors in terms of the four categories of reasons for continuing to fund unsuccessful investments. What alternative(s) to abandoning the project might GM consider?

The solution to Self-Study Problem 3 appears at the end of the chapter.

REVIEW

SUMMARY of INFORMATION CONCEPTS

1. Capital investment decisions are important decisions about acquiring long-term assets.
   a. Operational decisions are those decisions that affect the day-to-day operations of the company and the short-run outcomes of those operations.
   b. Strategic decisions are those decisions that affect the major directions the company is taking and the long-run outcome of those directions.

2. Capital investment decisions often involve large outlays of cash for long periods of time.
   a. Several factors affect the risk associated with capital investments.
   b. Capital investment decisions can be difficult to reverse without large losses.
   c. Capital investment decisions often are political because different divisions compete for funds.

3. Traditional approaches to justifying capital investments are of two types, discounting and nondiscounting.
   a. Discounting methods take into account the time value of money.
      1. The net present value method compares the net present value of expected cash inflows and outflows associated with the investment.
      2. The internal rate of return method involves determining the interest rate that results in the present values of cash inflows and outflows being equal.
   b. Nondiscounting methods do not consider the time value of money.
      1. The payback period method involves determining the amount of time required to recover the initial investment.
      2. The accounting rate of return method uses the average accounting income a project generates per period divided by the amount of the investment.

4. Several additional factors should enter into capital investment decisions.
   a. The service life is the period during which an investment is expected to be used.
   b. Residual value is the market value of an investment at the end of its useful life.
   c. The income tax effects of depreciation on cash flows must be considered, because although depreciation is a noncash expense, it is tax-deductible.
   d. When there is uncertainty about future cash flows, managers should test the sensitivity of their decision to their assumptions.

5. The new manufacturing environment has changed capital investment decision making for many companies.
   a. Capital investment decisions have become more strategic.
   b. The costs of capital investments are increasing, and the payback periods are becoming longer.

6. Making sound strategic capital investment decisions requires managers to avoid several pitfalls.
   a. Managers should carefully consider salvage values and use appropriate discount rates.
   b. Managers should consider in their decisions the opportunity cost of not making a capital investment.

7. Managers often are reluctant to terminate a failing project.
   a. Reasons for this reluctance can be divided into project, psychological, social, and structural determinants.
   b. Managers can reduce this reluctance by being aware of the problem and taking steps to prevent it.

DEFINE

TERMS and CONCEPTS DEFINED in this CHAPTER

accounting rate of return (ARR)   (M383)
capital budgeting   (M373)
capital investment decision   (M373)
cost of capital   (M377)
discounting   (M377)
discounting methods   (M376)
hurdle rate   (M377)
internal rate of return (IRR)   (M379)
milestones   (M376)
moving baseline concept   (M389)
net present value (NPV)   (M377)

nondiscounting methods   (M376)
operational capital investment
   decision   (M373)
opportunity costs   (M377)
payback period   (M381)
required rate of return   (M377)
residual value   (M383)
service life   (M383)
strategic capital investment
   decision   (M373)
sunk costs   (M376)

SELF-STUDY PROBLEM SOLUTIONS

SSP12-1   Evaluation using net present value method:

Year Cash Flow	0 Present Value	
Purchase of new system	$(100,000)	
Net decrease in operating costs	56,862	$15,000 × 3.79079 from Table 4.
Sales value of old equipment	40,000	
Net present value	$ (3,138)	

In this case, the net present value analysis indicates that the new investment should be rejected because the net present value is negative.

Joyful Car is already in the car washing business, so this is an investment in a business in which management has experience. This tends to reduce the risk. On the other hand, this would seem to be a large investment for a small company, increasing the risk. It is likely that part of the $100,000 total investment cost is installation cost for the new system, which probably would not be recaptured if the system had to be sold before the end of its useful life. This also increases the risk. Overall, this would appear to be a strategic investment for Joyful Car. Even though a car washing system may not seem like a major investment for many companies, it is for Joyful Car.

SSP12-2   The difference in the outcomes of the two branching decisions can be explained by the fact that Home Federal appears to have been much more careful to reduce its risk than NBG. Home Federal kept its costs down by buying a building at a reduced cost and renovating it. Home Federal also appears to have a better understanding of its market. While NBG was inexperienced in dealing with the marketing environment of its new branch, Home Federal's management had observed the population movement in the area of its new branch for some time and was confident that the trade would support the branch.

Capital investment decisions often depend greatly on marketing assumptions. NBG's branch was inside a large office complex and not visible from the street. People driving by might not be aware of its existence. NBG gambled on a new concept in self-contained office space and hoped that the stores and restaurants would bring in enough outside clientele to support the branch. This did not happen—at least not in time to save the branch. In contrast, Home Federal's branch was in a visible location seen by many potential customers. NBG took a significant risk and lost, partly encouraged by the hope that being in a prestigious location would enhance its image. Home Federal took the safe road and was successful.

SSP12-3   GM should reconsider the costs and benefits of the WT Project. Among the factors to be reconsidered probably would be (1) the future stream of cash inflows and outflows based on revised marketing and production forecasts, (2) the likelihood of resolving the production difficulties with the new transmissions, and (3) any costs associated with abandoning the project, such as contract cancellation costs.

The WT Project falls into the category of computer-integrated manufacturing in terms of the level of automation. Virtually the entire manufacturing operation is controlled by computers.

It is difficult to determine at this point whether the WT Project is an escalation situation. After several years and over $500 million invested in the WT Project, it is unlikely that GM would abandon the project for several reasons. Some of these, categorized in terms of Staw and Ross's four determinants of escalation, are:

Project determinant: There is the possibility that the setback in the WT Project is only temporary and that it still might succeed in the long run.

Psychological determinant: There is a very large sunk cost in the WT Project that GM management would be reluctant to write off.

Social determinant: GM might naturally be reluctant to admit to a high-profile mistake such as the failure of a project like the WT Project.

Structural determinant: GM is in a battle with foreign competitors in many of its markets. Maintaining its position as the leading manufacturer of high-quality transmissions for heavy equipment could be important to GM's image.

GM did continue to fund the WT Project. However, it attempted to sell Allison Transmission to other corporations in the hope of eliminating the negative cash flows associated with the WT Project.

Thinking Beyond the Question

How can managerial accounting help in choosing new manufacturing facilities?

Currently, Young Designs, Inc., has been unable to sell to certain retailers that demand exceptionally high-quality finishes on their products. Suppose that by purchasing the new system discussed in the chapter opening scenario, the overall quality of the finish on the company's products is improved to such an extent that it would permit the company to enter the high-quality markets. If the company does not invest in the new system, it will continue to be excluded from the high-quality market. How would you analyze this cost of *not* investing in the new system? How should this cost affect the investment decision? What difficulties do you foresee in being able to forecast this cost?

QUESTIONS

Q12-1
Obj. 1
Managers at Precision Products are considering a change in the method used to apply paint to the company's products. The new method represents the newest technology. Instead of traditional "wet" painting, it uses electromagnetics to make powdered paint adhere to product surfaces. Precision's major competitors already have adopted the new paint method. The new method would require replacement of the paint booths currently being used, resulting in a $250,000 capital expenditure. Nearly all of Precision's products require painting. The new paint method is expected to improve the paint quality, reduce the product rejects, and enhance customer satisfaction. Is the decision to change painting methods an operational or strategic capital investment decision? Explain your answer.

Q12-2
Obj. 1
A local manufacturing company is planning to purchase a new computer software system that will affect the entire company. The new system will allow the receptionist to log all incoming calls and messages on the company's electronic mail system so that users will have immediate notice of incoming calls. The cost of the new system will be $20,000, and it is estimated that the investment will have a useful service life of five years. Would this investment be considered operational or strategic? Explain your answer.

Q12-3
Obj. 1
Tim and Tom are brothers who split a large inheritance. Tim used all of his money to buy a company that manufactures a single product used in high-tech industries. Tom used his money to lease two small retail stores in a nearby mall, one that sells candles and another that sells yogurt. He also purchased inventory and equipment to start the businesses. Assuming that neither of the brothers has any experience in his new endeavor, which of the brothers has the greater investment risk, and why?

Q12-4
Obj. 1
Caltron Enterprises operates a multimillion-dollar plant and is considering an expansion of its facilities to support a new product line. Should the cost of the company's existing plant and equipment affect the expansion decision? Explain your answer.

Q12-5
Obj. 1
Classify each of the following capital investment decisions as either operational or strategic. Briefly justify your answers.

1. A bank decides to build a new branch in the same town where it has 15 other branches. The new branch will cost $200,000 and will have an estimated service life of 25 years with a $150,000 residual value.
2. A bank decides to add automatic teller machines (ATMs) in the lobby of each of its 15 branches. The bank has never offered ATMs to customers in the past. The machines will have an estimated service life of 15 years with no residual value.
3. A company automates an entire production process that had not previously been automated. The automation includes computer-controlled equipment linked together in work cells. The machines will improve quality and increase the number of products offered, and they are expected to head off entry into the market by a major competitor. The machines will have an estimated useful life of nine years with a residual value of $350,000.
4. A company updates several pieces of factory equipment with new models. The new models have increased safety features and can operate faster than the older models. The new machines also have new features that will allow workers to perform tasks that the old machines could not perform. The estimated service life of the new machines is 10 years, and they will have a residual value of $75,000.

Q12-6
Obj. 2
Assume that a friend has asked to borrow $100 from you. You agree, as long as your friend pays you 6% annual interest to provide for the time value of money. Your friend wants to know what is meant by "time value of money." How would you explain this concept?

Q12-7
Obj. 2
Erin Brady won a $500 prize in a raffle. The winning ticket states, "Prizes are payable in six months from contest date, or may be discounted at 10% for immediate payment." Erin has asked you what is meant by the term "discounted." What will you tell her?

Q12-8
Obj. 2
Douglas Wright has calculated the net present value of a proposed project investment and has obtained a negative amount. Assuming that Douglas calculated the net present value properly, what does the negative amount indicate about this investment?

Q12-9
Obj. 2
Julie Russo attended a company meeting to discuss a potential investment in new machinery. The company uses the payback method to analyze potential investments. After reviewing the figures, Julie commented, "These figures are not reliable. They have not been discounted." Do you agree with Julie? Why or why not?

Q12-10
Obj. 2
Bill Rubble, president of Melinco Company, reviewed a proposal for a project investment that was submitted by the vice president of production. Bill attached a note to the proposal that said, "Please recalculate this proposal—adjust the rate of return by 2% to compensate for the higher risk involved." Should the vice president increase or decrease the rate of return when recalculating the proposal?

Q12-11
Obj. 2
Samuel Sanchez is a project manager for Johnson Industries. Samuel wants to analyze a potential investment. He seeks a method that considers the project's profitability but is not affected by the time value of money. What method would you suggest Samuel utilize?

Q12-12
Obj. 2
Capital budgeting models such as NPV, internal rate of return, payback, and accounting rate of return make managing easier, because future projects can be approved immediately if target values are obtained. Do you agree or disagree? Why?

Q12-13
Obj. 2
Paul Bruce, controller of Chief Industries, performs investment analysis for all of the company's capital projects. Paul has complained that investment analysis is difficult because there are so many estimates that must be made. What are some of the variables that typically must be estimated in a capital budgeting decision?

Q12-14
Obj. 2
Assume that the internal rate of return on a particular capital investment project has been calculated and is exactly equal to the target rate a company has established for such projects. If tax rates are expected to increase in the future, would the investment become more or less desirable from an internal rate of return standpoint?

Q12-15
Obj. 2
Woodcrest, Inc., a textile manufacturer, is considering purchasing a new type of technology that is advertised to improve the efficiency and lower the cost of its cloth dyeing process. What factors should be considered in making the decision to acquire this equipment?

Q12-16
Obj. 3
Auto Parts, Inc., uses traditional manufacturing assembly lines to manufacture starters and alternators. Much of Auto Parts' equipment is wearing out, and company management is considering what type of production facilities to invest in. Several factors have been changing in the industry. Over the past two decades the number of different automobile models has increased substantially. Because of this, customers are demanding many more models of alternators and starters but in smaller quantities. Labor costs have increased substantially. Customers are much less willing to accept problems with quality and frequently desire just-in-time deliveries. How should these changes affect management's decisions regarding investment in the new capital equipment?

Q12-17
Obj. 3
Tanguchi Equipment Company manufactures cabs and chassis for fire trucks, ambulances, and other emergency vehicles. Parts manufactured by Tanguchi require precision and quality. The company employs a highly trained workforce that produces most parts by hand and has maintained a moderate level of production quality. How would quality affect capital decisions at Tanguchi?

Q12-18
Obj. 3
Newhart Company is planning a major capital investment program to automate its production processes, which are currently labor-intensive. What impact on its cost structure should the company expect from its factory automation program?

Q12-19
Obj. 4
Everyday Plastics Corporation wants to invest in new machinery that will allow the company to be more responsive to changes in customer demand. The company has an excellent credit rating and can borrow funds at the prevailing prime interest rate. To be on the "safe" side, however, the company has analyzed the potential investment using a discount rate that is 3% above the prevailing prime interest rate. Why would the company want to increase the discount rate to be on the safe side, and what is the likely effect of using a rate higher than the available borrowing rate on the company's analysis of the investment decision?

Q12-20
Obj. 4
In an effort to convince the president of Utah Instruments to expand the company's product lines, Lynnette Peters, vice president of marketing, inflated potential future sales figures on a proposed product. Lynnette believed that without the inflated marketing estimates, the new

product would not be pursued. If the new product is undertaken, extensive capital investment will be required. How could improper or poor estimates of market conditions adversely affect a capital investment decision?

Q12-21
Objs. 2, 4

Chambers Industries manufactures copper tubing used in many mechanical applications. The company believes that it must invest in a new facility if it is to remain competitive with foreign manufacturers. A preliminary analysis of the proposed investment indicates that property, plant, and equipment costing more than $50 million will be needed to bring the facility into operation. The residual value of the investment would be $1.5 million at the end of 15 years. Failure to commit to the new investment will cause the company to realize an estimated $250,000 a year in lost income. What are the relevant costs that Chambers should include in its capital investment decision, and why?

Q12-22
Objs. 2, 4

Westco, Inc., is considering a capital investment project. Explain how each of the following situations would affect the capital investment decision Westco is considering. Explain whether each situation would make the project more or less likely to be accepted. Consider each situation independently.

1. The net present value of the proposed investment is zero.
2. The estimated service life used to evaluate the investment was 10 years, when in reality the actual service life is 12 years. The investment was analyzed using the accounting rate of return model.
3. The company desires a 12% return on the investment but inadvertently used a 14% factor in its analysis. The company utilizes the net present value method of investment analysis.
4. In its original internal rate of return analysis of the investment Westco failed to consider the income tax effects of depreciation on the investment. The net present value model was used in the analysis.
5. The residual value of the project under consideration was estimated at $30,000, when in reality the actual residual value of the project is $20,000. The company utilized the net present value method of investment analysis.

Q12-23
Obj. 4

Allen Hardaway is president of Fly High Shoes. Allen recently approved the purchase of several acres of land near the company factory to build a retail shoe outlet. Allen's plan to sell shoes directly to the public at the factory store was met with immediate disapproval by several of Fly High's largest customers, who have threatened to take their business to a competitor if the factory outlet is opened. "Never mind them," said Allen. "This project is a great idea. Besides, we already bought the land and paid an architect for store plans. We can't stop now!" Do you think Allen is throwing good money after bad if he pursues the factory outlet investment? What advice would you give Allen?

Q12-24
Obj. 4

JetPak, Inc., delivers overnight business letters internationally and very recently began building a new capital investment in an airport distribution center in Cincinnati. The project has been touted as the most significant investment decision in JetPak's history. Indianapolis had been considered as an alternate site, but Bob Smith, project manager, argued strongly in favor of Cincinnati on the basis of better airport facilities. Smith stated that the better facilities would allow JetPak's planes to arrive and depart much more efficiently with less time lost to airport delays. Smith is evaluated on the cost of building the facility compared to its budgeted cost and previously announced that he would ". . . bring the project in on time and under budgeted cost." Just after ground was broken on the new facility, a major airline announced that it would begin using Cincinnati as a regional hub. This decision is expected to increase the traffic at the airport by 30%. Further, the Indianapolis Airport just announced that it intends to build two new runways to expedite arrivals and departures. Despite these changes and a buyer that wants to purchase the land on which the Cincinnati facility is being built, Smith is adamantly opposed to reconsidering the location decision. Can you explain Smith's opposition?

Q12-25
Obj. 5

Home First Bank must invest in a new computer system to handle banking transactions. Management has considered buying from one of two vendors. National Computers, Inc., offers higher-priced equipment that has a higher residual value and a lower-priced contract service. American Computers, Inc., offers lower-priced equipment with a lower residual value and a more expensive contract service package. Both systems have the same expected useful life, and both have an established record of performing satisfactorily. It has been determined that there is no impact on customer service or operating costs other than service regardless of which vendor is chosen. Home First Bank's president, Jane Greene, has asked her chief financial officer, John Warren, how the decision should be made. Assume you are the CFO. How would you respond?

Q12-26
Obj. 5
Central European Telephone Service (CETS) wants to expand its cellular operations in a developing country. The country currently has a penetration rate of cable telephone service to only one in forty households. CETS would prefer to spend its funds available for capital investment on expanding cellular service since the company believes that cellular is more profitable than cable given the way rates have been set by the country's government. The government is opposing this approach, insisting that CETS raise the cable penetration rate to one in twenty before further expanding cellular service. Can you think of possible reasons why CETS and the government are taking these positions?

EXERCISES

If your instructor is using Personal Trainer® in this course, you may complete your assignments online.

E12-1
Write a short definition of each of the terms listed in the *Terms and Concepts Defined in this Chapter* section.

E12-2
Obj. 2
Audrey buys a new tanning bed for her salon. The tanning bed costs $6,000. The tanning bed generates cash flows of $2,500 the first year, $3,500 the second year, and $5,000 the third year. What is the payback period?

E12-3
Obj. 2
Alison Mayer, owner of a sports complex, is considering adding a climbing wall. The climbing wall costs $30,000. Alison estimates the climbing wall will generate cash flows of $8,000 the first year, $10,000 the second year, and $12,000 the third year. What is the payback period?

E12-4
Obj. 2
Shannon bought an ice cream truck for $20,000. Her net income was $3,500 the first year, $5,000 the second year, and $6,500 the third year of business. Calculate the accounting rate of return.

E12-5
Obj. 2
Stephanie bought a stereo system for her DJ service for $4,000. Her net income was $500 the first year, $900 the second year, and $1,000 the third year of business. Calculate the accounting rate of return.

E12-6
Obj. 2
Gerrish Corporation bought a new machine for $50,000. The net income from this machine is $8,000 in year 1 and $10,000 in year 2. In order to obtain an accounting rate of return of 20%, what would Gerrish have to make in the third and final year of this machine's life?

E12-7
Obj. 2
Kelly Sloan, purchasing manager at an Internet service provider, bought a new server for $4,000. The net income from this machine is $700 in year 1 and $900 in year 2. In order to obtain an accounting rate of return of 25%, what will they have to make in the third and final year of this machine's life?

E12-8
Obj. 2
Amy Sims runs an advertisement firm. She estimates that a $7,000 high-resolution printer will result in increased cash inflows of $2,000 in year 1, $4,000 in year 2, and $4,500 in year 3. Amy's cost of capital is 10%. Calculate the net present value. What is the internal rate of return at this price?

E12-9
Obj. 2
Ryan, owner of a furniture business, currently leases a small building for $20,000 per year. He is considering leasing a large store for his furniture business. He estimates the new store will result in increased net cash inflows (inflows − outflows) of $10,000 in year 1, $12,000 in year 2, and $13,500 in year 3. Ryan's cost of capital is 8%. Calculate the net present value.

E12-10
Obj. 2
Bill, owner of a video arcade, is considering buying a new game. The game would cost $5,000. He estimates the new game will result in increased cash inflows of $2,000 in year 1, $2,000 in year 2, and $2,000 in year 3. Calculate the internal rate of return.

E12-11
Obj. 2
Mike Gallager, owner of a bowling alley, is considering buying a new pool table. The pool table would cost $3,000. He estimates the pool table will result in increased cash inflows of $750 per year for five years. Calculate the internal rate of return.

E12-12
Obj. 2
Geory, general manager at a water park, installed a new waterslide with an estimated useful life of 10 years. The waterslide will generate cash inflows of $10,000 each year over the next 10 years. The waterslide has no salvage value at the end of 10 years, and the company's discount rate is 12%. Geory calculates the NPV of the investment to be $20,000. What is the cost of the waterslide? Assuming the waterslide costs $50,000, what is the payback period?

E12-13
Obj. 2
Henry, manager of a widget factory, bought a new machine with an estimated useful life of five years. The machine will generate cash inflows of $12,000 each year over the next five years. The machine has no salvage value at the end of five years, and the company's discount rate is 10%. Henry calculates the NPV of the investment to be $10,000. What is the cost of the machine? What is the payback period?

E12-14
Obj. 2
Briggs Corporation, a lawn mowing service, bought a new commercial lawn mower. The mower costs $12,000 and is expected to have a service life of five years. At the end of five years, the lawn mower can be sold for $2,000. Briggs has a 30% tax rate. What is the annual depreciation expense? What is the annual tax savings from depreciation?

E12-15
Obj. 2
Fix-It-Yourself, a rental equipment store, bought a jackhammer. The jackhammer costs $8,000 and is expected to have a service life of six years. At the end of six years, the jackhammer can be sold for $2,000. Fix-It-Yourself has a 30% tax rate. What is the annual depreciation expense? What is the annual tax savings from depreciation?

E12-16
Obj. 2
Matt invested $100,000 to open Steakhouse. He withdrew $10,000 at the end of each year for three years. At the end of the third year, Matt sold the restaurant for $120,000 cash. His discount rate is 15%. What is the net present value of Matt's investment? What is the internal rate of return on this business?

E12-17
Obj. 2
Elizabeth Ann invested $80,000 to start a business at the beginning of 2004. She withdrew $5,000 at the end of each year for three years. At the end of the third year, Elizabeth sold the business for $100,000 cash. Her discount rate is 10%. What is the net present value of Elizabeth's business investment? What is the internal rate of return on this business?

E12-18
Obj. 2
The Wild Side Bowling Alley is planning to invest in pinball machines and pool tables for use by its patrons. The equipment will cost $3,896 to acquire and will have an estimated service life of seven years with a $100 residual value. Based on estimates by the owner, the tables and games will generate approximately $800 a year of cash inflow after all expenses have been met. Compute the internal rate of return promised by the table and games. Assume that the owner will not invest in the equipment unless it has a 12% internal rate of return. Compute the amount of annual cash inflows that would be required on the initial investment to obtain this rate of return.

E12-19
Obj. 2
John's Arcade is planning on purchasing a virtual reality simulator for $210,000. The simulator's estimated service life is seven years with a residual value of $25,000. The simulator is expected to bring in $40,000 per year after expenses. Compute the internal rate of return on the simulator. If John wanted to get a 13% internal rate of return, what would the annual cash flows need to be in order generate this rate of return?

E12-20
Obj. 2
Alice owns a tow truck company. She is considering buying a new tow truck for $55,000. The service life of the truck is five years. At the end of the five years, Alice estimates she can sell the truck for $5,000. She estimates her revenues from the truck will be $15,000 per year. The tax rate of the company is 30% and its discount rate is 10%. What is the depreciation expense for the truck? How much tax will Alice owe each year? (*Hint:* Include savings from depreciation.) What will the annual cash flows be for the truck? What is the NPV of the truck?

E12-21
Obj. 2
Jim owns an ice cream store. He is considering buying a new waffle cone machine for $600. The service life of the machine is five years. At the end of the five years, Jim estimates he can sell the machine for $100. He estimates his net contribution from the machine will be $300 per year. The tax rate of the company is 20% and its discount rate is 10%. What is the depreciation expense for the machine? How much tax will Jim owe each year? (*Hint:* Include savings from depreciation.) What will the annual cash flows be for the machine? What is the NPV of the machine?

PROBLEMS

If your instructor is using Personal Trainer® in this course, you may complete your assignments online.

P12-1   ### Calculating Accounting Rate of Return

Obj. 2

A machine was purchased for $10,000. The net income from the machine is as follows:

Year 1	$3,000
Year 2	2,000
Year 3	1,000

Required

A. Calculate the accounting rate of return.
B. What are the drawbacks to using the accounting rate of return as a method of selecting projects?

P12-2   ### Payback versus NPV

Obj. 2

The cash flows from two capital expenditure projects follow. The discount rate is 10%.

	Project A	Project B
Initial cost	$(10,000)	$(10,000)
Year 1	6,000	2,000
Year 2	5,000	4,000
Year 3	1,000	8,000
Year 4	0	16,000

Required

A. What are the payback periods for both projects?
B. What is the NPV for both projects?
C. What are the drawbacks from using payback as a method for selecting projects?

P12-3   ### Internal Rate of Return versus NPV

Obj. 2

John is considering two capital expenditure projects; however, he has only enough money to do one project. The cash flows follow and the discount rate is 12%.

	Project A	Project B
Initial cost	$(50,000)	$(100,000)
Year 1	30,000	55,000
Year 2	30,000	55,000
Year 3	30,000	55,000

Required

A. What is the internal rate of return for each project?
B. What is the NPV for each project?
C. Which project should John choose?
D. What are the drawbacks to using internal rate of return?

P12-4   ### Accounting Rate of Return and Payback

Obj. 2

Mark Brown has an opportunity to invest in a bicycle franchise shop under a nationally recognized brand name. Mark has assembled the following information and estimates relating to this opportunity:

1. Rent on an operating facility would total $4,000 per month.
2. Estimated sales income would total $800,000 per year, and the variable cost of goods sold would be 70% of sales revenue.
3. Costs to operate the shop would include $87,000 per year for salaries and benefits, $4,000 per year for insurance, $15,000 per year for utilities, and $10,000 per year for office expenses.

4. Display racks, repair equipment, and other fixed assets would cost $270,000 and have an estimated service life of 15 years, with no salvage value at the end of the service life. Mark would use the straight-line depreciation method.
5. Mark must pay a commission of 5% of sales to the bicycle supplier.

If Mark does not invest in the bicycle shop, he could invest his funds in long-term bonds that would pay 8% annual interest.

Required

A. Determine the net annual income that Mark would realize from the franchise, ignoring income taxes. (Use the contribution approach format income statement.)
B. Compute the accounting rate of return that would be obtained by the franchise. Based on the accounting rate of return, would Mark be better off financially by investing in the franchise or the long-term securities?
C. Compute the payback period on the franchise. If Mark wants a payback period of five years or less, should he invest in the franchise? (Ignore income taxes.)

P12-5 **Accounting Rate of Return and Payback**

Obj. 2

Billy Boehm has a chance to invest in a company that manufactures televisions. Billy obtained the following information for his investment analysis:

1. Rent on the manufacturing facility is $5,000 per month.
2. Estimated sales income would be $1,000,000 per year, and the variable cost of goods sold would be 65% of sales revenue.
3. Costs to operate the facility would include $150,000 per year for salaries and benefits, $10,000 per year for insurance, $12,000 per year for utilities, and $8,000 per year for office expenses.
4. Storage racks, repair equipment, and other fixed assets would cost $400,000 and have an estimated service life of 20 years, with no salvage value at the end of the service life.

If Billy does not invest in the television manufacturer, he could invest in bonds that would pay a 10% interest rate.

Required

A. Determine the net annual income that Billy would realize from the company, ignoring income taxes. (Use the contribution approach format income statement.)
B. Compute the accounting rate of return that would be obtained by Billy. Based on the accounting rate of return, would Billy be better off financially by investing in the bonds?
C. Compute the payback period on the company. If Billy wants a payback period of six years or less, should he invest in the franchise?

P12-6 **Payback, Internal Rate of Return**

Obj. 2

A piece of labor-saving equipment is available to Armtech Company that could be used to reduce costs at one of its plants. Relevant data related to this particular equipment are as follows:

Purchase price of equipment	$432,000
Net annual cash savings provided by the new equipment	$90,000
Estimated service life of equipment	12 years
Required rate of return	14%

Required

A. Compute the payback period for the new equipment. If the company requires a payback period of four years or less, would you recommend purchase of the equipment? Explain your answer.
B. Compute the internal rate of return on the equipment. Use straight-line depreciation based on the equipment's estimated service life. Would you recommend that the equipment be purchased? Explain your answer.

P12-7 **Payback, Internal Rate of Return**

Obj. 2

Automation of the shipping department at Computer Mart would save labor costs. Details about the automation equipment are as follows:

Purchase price of automation equipment	$1,200,000
Net annual cash savings provided by the new equipment	$200,000
Estimated service life of equipment	10 years
Required rate of return	12%

Required

A. Compute the payback period for the automation equipment. If Computer Mart requires a payback of five years or less, would you recommend purchase of the equipment? Explain your answer.
B. Compute the internal rate of return on the equipment. Use straight-line depreciation based on the equipment's estimated service life. Would you recommend that the equipment be purchased? Explain your answer.

P12-8 **Basic Net Present Value Analysis**

Obj. 2

Community Drycleaning would like to purchase a new machine for cleaning large quilts and comforters. The current cleaning operation on quilts and comforters is done by hand. The new machine would cost $12,500. The estimated service life is 12 years, at which time it is estimated that the machine could be sold for $500.

The company estimates that it would cost $700 per year to operate the machine. The current cost of manual cleaning is $3,000 per year. In addition to reducing costs, the new machine would increase the drycleaner's ability to clean quilts and comforters by 600 per year. The company realizes a net contribution margin after tax effects of $1.50 per quilt or comforter. A 10% rate of return is required on all investments. Community expects its tax rate to be 30%.

Required

A. What are the annual net cash inflows that would be realized from the new machine?
B. Compute the net present value of the investment (round to the nearest dollar). Use straight-line depreciation based on the machine's estimated service life. Would you recommend that the machine be purchased? Explain your answer.

P12-9 **Basic Net Present Value Analysis**

Obj. 2

Ice Cream Galore, a manufacturer of gourmet ice cream, is considering purchasing a new, energy-efficient machine that will mix ice cream for a cost of $110,000. The estimated service life is 15 years, at which time the machine could be sold for $5,000. Ice Cream Galore expects the machine will cost $5,000 per year to operate. The current machine costs $10,000 per year to operate. The new machine will also be able to handle chunkier mixes, of which the company estimates they can sell 10,000 gallons per year. The company's contribution margin is $2 per gallon. A 12% rate of return is required on all investments, and the company's tax rate is 30%.

Required

A. What are the annual net cash inflows that would be realized from the new machine?
B. Compute the net present value of the investment. Use straight-line depreciation based on the machine's estimated service life. Would you recommend that the machine be purchased? Explain your answer.

P12-10 **Analysis of Investment Decision**

Obj. 2

John bought stock valued at $10,000. He received a cash dividend of $300 in year 1, $350 in year 2, and $400 in year 3. The cash dividends were not reinvested. At the end of year 3, John sold the stock for $12,000. If John didn't invest in stock, he would have invested in bonds that had an 8% return.

Required

A. What was the rate of return on John's stock?
B. Assuming the stock and bonds had equal risk, did John make the right decision to invest in the stock?

P12-11

Objs. 2, 3

Net Present Value and Automation Decision

Tony Setimi, president of Solidex Machinery, is considering the purchase of an automated stamping machine. In reviewing the figures prepared by the production department, Tony has noted that the machine would cost $500,000 plus another $80,000 for controls and programming. In addition, the production department estimates that the machine would cost $3,000 a month to maintain. Further, the production department estimates that repairs totaling $45,000 would be required at the end of seven years.

Tony gave the figures to Becky Roberts, the controller, and asked her to analyze the situation and be prepared to offer her opinion in the morning. Becky determined that the new machine would replace six workers and save $108,000 a year in labor costs. She also determined that $6,500 a year in scrap costs could be avoided and that the current equipment being replaced could be sold for $12,000. She then calculated depreciation on the new machine, assuming it would last 12 years and have a residual value of $20,000. She noted that the company's current cost of capital is 11%.

Required

A. Compute the net annual cost savings that would be realized from the new machine. (Ignore income taxes.)
B. Using the data from requirement (A) and information from the problem, compute the new machine's net present value. (Ignore income taxes.)
C. Assume that there are intangible benefits such as reduced setup time, improved quality, and greater flexibility of production. What annual dollar value would the company have to assign to these intangible factors in order to make the new machine an acceptable investment?

P12-12

Objs. 2, 3

Net Present Value and Automation Decision

A local printing company is trying to decide if it should install an automated job sorter. The details of the sorter are as follows:

Original cost	$53,000
Maintenance costs per month	$1,000
Labor expense savings	$20,000 per year
Depreciable life	10 years
Residual value	$3,000
Cost of capital	11%

Required

A. Compute the net annual cost savings that would be realized from the sorter. (Ignore income taxes.)
B. Compute the net present value of the sorter.
C. Assume that there are intangible benefits such as improved quality and efficiency. What annual dollar value would the printing company have to assign to these intangible factors in order to make the new machine an acceptable investment?

P12-13

Objs. 2, 4

Strategic Capital Investment Decisions

Feldman Cages manufactures cages for pets. Joe, the VP of operations at Feldman Cages, is considering a major capital investment decision. It would cost $2,000,000 to put new, highly automated machines in the factory. The equipment would last about 20 years and would have no salvage value at the end of that period. The equipment will replace eight workers, saving Feldman $200,000 per year in direct labor. Operating and maintenance costs on the machines are expected to cost $100,000 per year. The automated equipment is expected to improve quality. Feldman's main competitors are installing similar equipment. If Feldman installs the

(Continued)

equipment, its revenues are expected to remain steady. If Feldman chooses not to install the equipment, its contribution margin is expected to fall by $200,000 per year as a result of lower quality compared to its competitors. Feldman's discount rate is 10% and its tax rate is 30%.

Required

A. How much is Feldman expected to save each year if it installs the equipment (including tax effects)?
B. How much will Feldman lose each year if it does not install the equipment (including tax effects)?
C. Describe the moving baseline concept and how you would apply it to this problem.
D. Should Feldman purchase the new machines?

P12-14   ## Strategic Capital Investment Decisions

Objs. 2, 4

Smith Electronics manufactures portable CD players. Lillian Perez, the VP of operations at Smith Electronics, is considering a major capital investment decision. It would cost $2,500,000 to put new, highly automated machines in the factory. The equipment would last about 15 years and would have no salvage value at the end of that period. The equipment will replace 10 workers, saving Smith $300,000 per year in direct labor. Operating and maintenance costs on the machines are expected to cost $100,000 per year. The automated equipment is expected to improve quality. Smith's main competitors are installing similar equipment. If Smith installs the equipment, its revenues are expected to remain steady. If Smith chooses not to install the equipment, its contribution margin is expected to fall by $200,000 per year as a result of lower quality compared to its competitors. Smith's discount rate is 10% and its tax rate is 30%.

Required

A. How much is Smith expected to save each year if it installs the equipment (including tax effects)?
B. How much will Smith lose each year if it does not install the equipment (including tax effects)?
C. Explain how you would analyze this problem in order to determine if Smith should purchase the new machines.
D. Should Smith purchase the new machines?
E. Assume that programming and maintenance costs turn out to be much higher than Lillian's estimates. However, despite the fact that the automation equipment increased costs, Lillian still wants to continue with the project. Explain why Lillian might not want to scrap the equipment.

P12-15   ## Ethics and Investment Decisions

Objs. 2, 4

Ally Kat is the manager of the continuing education division of Rayford Enterprises, a large financial services firm. The division provides seminars and workshops for Rayford employees to keep them up to date with current economic events that affect their responsibilities in servicing customers and marketing products. Ally attended a trade show recently, where she saw the latest technology in computer learning systems. She wants to acquire this technology for her division and has prepared the following information:

Initial cost of hardware and software	$400,000
Cost to maintain system	$130,000 annually
Expected useful life of system	5 years
Residual value at end of five years	$50,000
Reduction in training costs	$30,000 annually
Increase in sales from improved services	$200,000 annually
Required rate of return	10%

You are responsible for approving the request. In researching the request, you collect the following additional information. The expected useful life of this type of system has historically been closer to three years than to five. Ally argues that she will use the system for five years regardless of future changes in technology. The required rate of return for other projects approved in the last year has been 12%. Ally argues that 10% is adequate because borrowing costs have decreased in the past year. The residual value estimated by Ally is based on the residual value of other equipment used in the continuing education division. The estimated reduction in training costs and increases in sales are based on estimates provided by the vendor of the learning system.

Required

A. Do you see any ethical problems with Ally's request?
B. Prepare a NPV analysis of the request using the data provided by Ally.
C. Provide a comparative NPV analysis using data that you believe are appropriate.
D. Explain how you would respond to Ally's request.

P12-16 Net Present Value Decisions in the Service Industry

Objs. 2, 5

A phone company with a discount rate of 8% is considering two investments.

	Residential Service	Commercial Service
Initial cost	$(50,000)	$(100,000)
Year 1	20,000	50,000
Year 2	20,000	50,000
Year 3	20,000	50,000

Required

A. Calculate the NPV for both services.
B. If the phone company can provide only one service currently, which project should it choose?
C. If this is a regulated service industry, explain why the phone company may have to invest in the residential service.

P12-17 Excel in Action

SPREADSHEET

As an additional cost savings measure, Music Makers is considering the purchase of a computerized office management system. The system would cost $98,000. It would have an expected life of 48 months and would be depreciated for tax purposes using the sum-of-the-years-digits' method. The company's tax rate is 30%. The company expects to save $2,500 per month from the system in addition to the tax savings. It requires at least a 12% return on investment (annual interest rate) for the project.

Required Use a spreadsheet to prepare a net present value and internal rate of return analysis for Music Makers. Use the format provided below as an example. Enter the data or use formulas to calculate data in column B, rows 1 through 7. Use references to these data to prepare the analysis beginning in row 10. Computations for month 0 (the date of the investment) and month 1 (the date the first cost savings are incurred) are provided as examples.

	A	B	C	D	E	F
1	Annual interest rate					
2	Monthly interest rate					
3	Investment					
4	Life (months)					
5	Tax rate					
6	Cost savings					
7	Internal rate of return					
8						
9	Month	Depreciation	Tax Savings	Cost Savings	Net Cash Flow	Present Value
10	0				(98,000.00)	(98,000.00)
11	1	4,000.00	1,200.00	2,500.00	3,700.00	3,663.37

(Continued)

In the Month column, enter each month for the computation, from 0 to 48. If you enter data in A10 and A11, you can select these two cells and drag them downward to automatically enter the remaining months (12 to 48). To calculate depreciation in column B, use the function button f_x and select Financial, SYD for sum-of-the-years-digits. In the pop-up box, enter references to the Cost ($B$3), Salvage (0), Life ($B$4), and Period (Per) (A11). Use absolute references for those cells that will not change in the calculation. Tax savings are the amount of depreciation each month times the tax rate. Cost savings are $2,500 per month. Net cash flow is the sum of tax savings and cost savings. Present value is calculated from the formula $PV = C/(1 + R)^t$, where C is the net cash flow for the month from column E, R is the monthly interest rate ($B$2), and t is the month from column A. The net cash flow in month 0 is the amount of the investment and is negative because it is a cash outflow. Once data are entered in row 11, you can select the cells in the row and drag them down to copy the formulas for the remaining months.

To calculate the net present value of the investment, sum the data in column F. Evaluate whether Music Makers should make the investment based on its net present value.

To calculate the internal rate of return in cell A7, select the cell, then click on the function button and select Financial, IRR. In the pop-up box, enter the Values by selecting the net cash flow cells (E10:E58). You can leave the Guess box empty or enter an estimate of the IRR (0.12, for example). The function uses this guess as a starting point to estimate the internal rate of return. Evaluate whether Music Makers should make the investment based on its internal rate of return.

Suppose Music Makers' annual required return is 25%. Would the investment still be justified? Recompute the net present value.

P12-18   **Multiple-Choice Overview of the Chapter**

1. In which of the following situations would it be appropriate to accept a project under the net present value method?
   I. Net present value is positive.
   II. Net present value is zero.
   III. Net present value is negative.
   a. Only I.
   b. Only II.
   c. Both I and II.
   d. Both II and III.

2. An investment for which the net present value is $300 would result in which of the following conclusions?
   a. The net present value is too small, so the project should be rejected.
   b. The investment project promises more than the required rate of return.
   c. The net present value method is not suitable for evaluating this project.
   d. The investment project should be accepted only if the net present value is zero.

3. Which of the following statements regarding investments in automated equipment is correct?
   a. The cost of automating a process is always minor compared to other alternatives.
   b. The total cost to automate a process consists of outlays for machinery and equipment.
   c. The benefits of automation are always tangible, direct, and easy to quantify.
   d. A decision to automate often results from a commitment to quality and customer satisfaction.

4. When a company considers an investment in automated equipment, it should:
   a. focus primarily on ways to reduce direct labor cost.
   b. select only automation projects with positive net present values.
   c. consider both the tangible and intangible benefits of automation.
   d. automate the entire process rather than take a piecemeal approach to automation.

5. Wilson Company purchased a machine with an estimated useful life of seven years. The machine will generate cash inflows of $8,000 each year over the next seven years. If the machine has no salvage value at the end of seven years and the company's discount rate is 10%, what is the purchase price of the machine if the net present value of the investment is $12,000? (Round to the nearest dollar.)
   a. $38,947
   b. $26,947
   c. $12,000
   d. $50,947

6. Elizabeth Rankin invested $60,000 to start a business at the beginning of 2005. She withdrew $10,000 at the end of each year for the next five years. At the end of the fifth year, Elizabeth sold the business for $100,000 cash. At a 12% discount rate, what is the net present value of Elizabeth's business investment? (Round to the nearest dollar.)
   a. $60,000
   b. $36,048
   c. $56,743
   d. $32,791

7. Anthony operates a part-time auto repair service. He estimates that a new diagnostic computer system will result in increased cash inflows of $1,200 in year 1, $2,300 in year 2, and $3,500 in 3. If Anthony's cost of capital is 10%, then the most he would be willing to pay for the new computer system would be (rounded to the nearest dollar):
   a. $4,599.
   b. $5,502.
   c. $5,621.
   d. $5,107.

8. The moving baseline concept is based on the assumption that:
   a. current cash flows can continue indefinitely into the future.
   b. customer dissatisfaction can be avoided with increased quality.
   c. a competitor will adversely affect a company's cash flows if an investment is not made.
   d. investment in new equipment is an opportunity cost.

9. A manager who fails to terminate a failing capital investment project:
   a. is probably unaware that the investment is failing.
   b. may do so because sunk costs are not being ignored.
   c. may be reacting to pressures within the organizational environment.
   d. All of the above are correct.

10. Which of the following items must be estimated when a capital investment decision is made?
    a. Service life of investment
    b. Residual value of investment
    c. Both a and b are correct.
    d. Neither a nor b is correct.

(Continued)

CASES

C12-1 Capital Investment Decision, Discounting and Nondiscounting
Obj. 2 **Methods of Analysis**

Leroy Mandel is investigating the possibility of starting a hardware business. Leroy would sell home products, supplies, and maintenance materials. He has determined that the initial cost of the store would be $400,000 to acquire a suitable lease, obtain store fixtures, and fund working capital requirements. To obtain the needed funds, Leroy intends to sell $300,000 of stock and borrow $100,000 from a bank. The stock would pay annual dividends of 8%, and the bank loan will carry interest of 16%.

Leroy also has estimated that the store will generate an annual cash inflow of $50,000. For purposes of analysis, Leroy expects to operate the business for 20 years and then retire. Leroy does not want to invest unless he can fully recover his investment within nine years. There will be no residual value at the end of the 20 years, as the lease will expire, the inventory will be sold through normal operations, and store fixtures will be scrapped.

Required
A. Compute Leroy's cost of capital.
B. Calculate the payback period.
C. Assuming that depreciation is $10,000 per year, compute the accounting rate of return. (Ignore income taxes.)
D. Compute the net present value of the investment.
E. Compute the internal rate of return of the investment.
F. If you were Leroy, would you invest in the store? Why or why not?

C12-2 Investment Analysis, NPV, Payback, Uncertainty
Objs. 2, 4

Perfect Chef Company is constantly developing and marketing new cooking accessories. Based on past experience in forecasting cash flows for a new product, Perfect Chef has been able to predict cash flows within 10% of actual results. The longer the estimated life of a particular product, the greater the uncertainty surrounding future cash flows. The company currently is evaluating a project that is expected to have a five-year service life.

Accordingly, in performing net present value analysis of new product offerings, the company computes three different net present value figures: most likely, optimistic, and pessimistic. On a five-year project, the pessimistic computation assumes that the cash flows are overstated by 10% in the first three years of the project and by 50% in the last two years. The optimistic computation assumes that the estimates are understated by 10% in the first three years and 50% during the last two years. The most likely computations use the estimates without adjustment.

Perfect Chef is developing a new pressure cooker. To produce the pressure cooker, $625,000 must be invested in special equipment. The following are estimated net annual cash inflows that have been developed to analyze the potential product:

Year	Projected Net Annual Cash Inflows
1	$200,000
2	250,000
3	200,000
4	150,000
5	100,000

The company's cost of capital is 8%.

Required

A. Prepare a schedule of cash flows for five years based on the three methods described.
B. Compute the net present value for each of the three methods.
C. Compute the payback period for each of the three methods.
D. Based on your calculations in requirements (B) and (C), would you advise Perfect Chef to produce the cooker? Explain your answer.
E. Explain why Perfect Chef might not want to invest in a product that has a payback period greater than three years.

A CLOSER LOOK AT SERVICE ORGANIZATIONS

What's different about a service business?

Erin and Seth are considering whether to expand their business to include interior design consulting. Currently, they sell their furniture directly to retail stores. The retail stores then market the juvenile furniture to consumers. After purchasing a product or products, consumers may be referred to Erin and Seth's agency for assistance in creating innovative juvenile spaces within their homes. Thus, no conflict of interest exists, as Erin and Seth would not make recommendations about furniture purchases. The consulting business will produce additional sources of revenue. However, Erin and Seth are unsure about how to set prices for their services and how to determine the cost of providing the service.

FOOD FOR THOUGHT

Assume you are advising Seth and Erin. Do service companies, such as law firms, accounting firms, architecture firms, and hospitals, face different cost accounting problems than do manufacturing companies? What are the primary differences between service companies and manufacturing companies? Let's listen to Seth and Erin's discussion about expanding their business.

Seth: *Erin, I think your idea to expand our company to include interior design consulting is a good one. It will help ensure that our customers get the maximum benefit from their purchases. Also, it helps us to establish a direct relationship with the end user of our products.*

Erin: *There's no doubt that the new service will provide a strategically important advantage to our business. However, I'm still not sure how we go about attaching costs to each consulting engagement and determing the appropriate amount to charge for each service. Unlike our furniture business, each consulting engagement will be different. Some engagements will be simple, while others will be lengthy and complex; no two will be the same!*

Seth: *I see your point. It seems to me our consultants must record the time they spend on each engagement, just as accountants and attorneys do. We will bill clients as a function of time.*

Erin: *I understand how professional time would be used to calculate the labor cost of a consulting engagement. But, there must be other costs as well.*

Seth: *Our consultants will use supplies, but I doubt the cost will be significant. Consulting supplies used will be on a much smaller scale than materials used in furniture production. Overhead costs, however, will be more important to understand.*

Erin: *I've been thinking about how to allocate overhead costs from various departments. The consulting business will use indirect resources that must be considered when determining the total cost of a job. For example, our accounting department will provide services to the consulting business; however, we cannot bill our customers directly for these accounting activities. Also, you and I will provide our time to help the manager of the consulting company establish and run the business. We need to make sure the job cost includes these indirect support costs.*

Seth: *We can think of our accounting, human resources, and systems support departments as service departments that assist the revenue-producing departments, such as furniture production or interior design* *consulting. The costs incurred in these departments may be seen as indirect costs. The cost of making furniture or providing consulting services must include both direct and indirect costs.*

Erin: *The prices we charge for our products and services must be sufficient to cover both direct and indirect costs if our company is to be profitable. Also, we need to develop methods to accurately trace indirect costs to revenue-producing departments. Otherwise, our product costs will be distorted and not representative of resources consumed.*

OBJECTIVES

Once you have completed this chapter, you should be able to:

1 Explain how costs are classified within service organizations.

2 Allocate support department costs to revenue-producing departments.

3 Calculate costs of providing various services to customers and discuss how service costs may be used to make better decisions.

4 Describe various strategies used by service organizations to improve quality and reduce costs.

STONEBROOK MEDICAL CENTER: BACKGROUND AND ENVIRONMENT

A major insurer asked us to bid on performing all of its open-heart surgeries in the southeast United States. We prepared a bid by pulling cost information from our old cost system on all open-heart surgery patients we had treated. We did not get the contract, and we had no idea whether to be disappointed or relieved. From talks with third-party payers and major employers, we believed that we would be bidding for portions of business, like open-heart surgeries, on a regular basis. We realized that we needed a much better understanding of our costs if we were to be able to compete effectively.
—Jay Williams, Administrative Leader, Stonebrook Medical Center

Stonebrook Medical Center is a for-profit medical facility that offers a wide range of health-care services, including extended outpatient surgery, labor and delivery, psychiatry, and heart surgery. In addition, Stonebrook has initiated a number of programs to promote knowledge and wellness in the community. These programs include health and fitness courses, a cancer program, and a diabetes program.

The health-care industry currently is receiving more and more attention by the media, government, and public as a result of increasing health-care costs. In order to survive, providers must cope with constantly changing conditions. They must deliver high-quality health-care services in a time of intense competition.

The market for health-care services includes both patients and insurance companies. Thus, medical facilities are expected to deliver high-quality health-care services, while controlling health-care costs. Stonebrook and many other medical facilities are taking steps to improve their cost-reporting systems. In addition, hospitals are redesigning health-care delivery processes to reduce costs and improve quality.

Jay Williams, an administrative leader at Stonebrook Medical Center, selected a group of individuals with diverse professional backgrounds to serve on a committee to improve the clinical and financial outcomes at Stonebrook. The team consisted of Beth Rogers, the cost accounting manager; Linda Reynolds, a specialty nurse; and Tim Harris, a clinical case manager. Linda and Tim were asked to join the team because they have clinical and managerial experience. Beth and Jay brought accounting and business systems knowledge to the group.

Jay and his team had to find ways to improve the health-care delivery processes within the hospital. In addition, because of pressure from insurance companies, they had to reduce costs and at the same time improve the quality of care delivered to patients at Stonebrook. The health-care environment is changing rapidly because of managed-care systems. Employers often contract with insurance companies to provide health-care coverage for their employees at a fixed annual rate per employee. The insurance companies then contract with health-care providers, such as Stonebrook, to provide care at predetermined rates. Thus, hospitals that offer lower costs while providing quality care are more successful in securing contracts with managed-care systems. As a result, hospital cost systems have become increasingly important to managers as they attempt to understand the cost of providing services such as open-heart surgery and cancer treatment.

As indicated by Jay's quote at the beginning of this section, Stonebrook is facing a rapidly changing environment. The existing cost management system is inadequate for the decisions that managers must make. Of growing concern is the unexplained variation in physicians' practice patterns. As administrators attempt to control costs and modify physicians' behavior, accurate information on resource use by physicians would prove very useful. It is difficult to improve processes without accurate cost data.

An analysis of the effectiveness of care also would permit decisions about the types of clinical procedures Stonebrook and member physicians performed. Evaluating the effectiveness of a medical procedure involves clinical understanding. Thus, to be adequate for decision making in tomorrow's health-care environment, an information system must include the ability to gather and distribute information about the results of clinical procedures.

Other decisions that administrators face include cost versus value of care. For example, new medical technologies are developing continually. The decision to make investments in new technology is a complex process that compares existing clinical results with those promised by the new technology. Often, cost information can be a key factor in decisions about purchasing new technology.

Cost management systems for hospital use are evolving. Until recently, many hospitals used a facility-wide cost-to-charge ratio to estimate the cost of a medical procedure. This ratio is similar in principle to manufacturers using a facility-wide predetermined overhead rate to apply overhead to products. Thus, total annual facility-wide costs were divided by total annual facility-wide charges (billings) to determine a facility-wide cost-to-charge ratio. To estimate the cost of a procedure, the charge (amount billed) was multiplied by the facility-wide cost-to-charge ratio. For example, assume the following costs and charges for Stonebrook:

Cost and Revenue Data for 12 Months Ending December 31, 2005

Revenue Center	Total Costs	Total Charges
Radiology	$ 7,000,000	$ 7,000,000
Psychiatric care	5,000,000	6,000,000
Intensive care	9,000,000	9,200,000
Chemotherapy	5,000,000	7,000,000
Coronary care	7,200,000	7,400,000
Nursing/surgical	8,000,000	9,000,000
Emergency room	6,300,000	6,800,000
Operating room	26,000,000	45,800,000
Labor and delivery	9,000,000	11,200,000
Laboratory	5,000,000	15,000,000
Diabetes center	500,000	600,000
Total	$88,000,000	$125,000,000

The facility-wide cost-to-charge ratio is calculated as follows:

$$\frac{\text{Total costs}}{\text{Total charges}} = \frac{\$88,000,000}{\$125,000,000} = 0.704$$

If Stonebrook charged $5,000 for an appendectomy procedure, the estimated cost would be $3,520 ($5,000 $\times$ 0.704). Also, if charges for an open-heart surgery were

$30,000, the estimated cost would be $21,120 ($30,000 × 0.704). The system was adequate for determining the average cost of all procedures; however, it was not useful in helping managers determine the cost of a specific procedure. Unfortunately, many hospitals continue to use the cost-to-charge ratio to estimate costs. However, better cost management systems are becoming a necessity for survival as hospitals submit bids to insurance companies to acquire managed-care contracts.

MODERN COST MANAGEMENT SYSTEMS FOR SERVICE ORGANIZATIONS

OBJECTIVE 1

Explain how costs are classified within service organizations.

As you read earlier, Seth and Erin know they must allocate indirect costs to their new service business. They understand the consulting company will incur direct and indirect costs. This chapter uses Stonebrook Medical Center to illustrate the mechanics of indirect cost allocation to revenue-producing departments.

Jay and Beth sat at a table and sketched the structure of a cost system that would accurately trace costs to revenue-producing departments. Their sketch is reproduced in Exhibit 1. The system had to be one that could be understood easily because cost management systems for health-care decisions must be accessible by everyone in the organization. They began by classifying departments as either support departments or revenue-producing departments.

Exhibit 1 Conceptual Design of the Stonebrook Medical Center Cost Accounting System

Support Departments

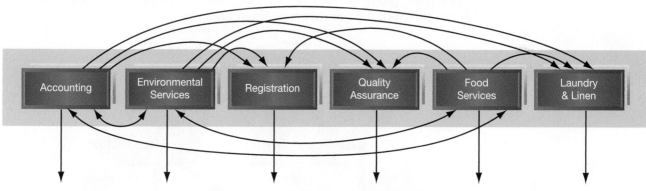

Allocations per Simultaneous Algebraic Equations

Revenue-Producing Departments

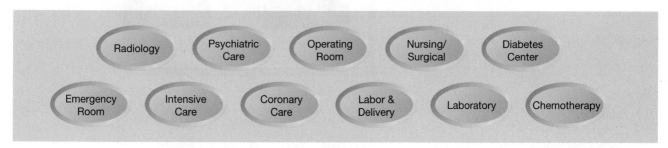

Revenue-producing departments at Stonebrook include the operating room, psychiatric care, radiology, the diabetes center, and coronary care. Each revenue-producing department incurred direct costs, such as supplies and salaries. Departments such as accounting, environmental services (janitorial and maintenance), registration, and quality assurance support the revenue-producing departments. Jay and Beth reasoned that the total cost of providing operating room services should include direct operating room costs plus part of the support department costs. Thus, allocations were necessary to transfer support department costs to revenue-producing departments.

In addition to providing services to revenue-producing departments, support departments often provide services to other support departments. For example, the environmental services department cleans the accounting department offices. Likewise, the accounting department provides payroll functions for the environmental services department. **A** *reciprocal service arrangement* **exists when support departments exchange services.** Health-care cost systems commonly use either a step-down or a simultaneous algebraic equation method to allocate costs among support departments. Simultaneous equations for real organizations are too complex to be solved manually. However, the following simple example illustrates key principles found in complex computer-based cost systems.

Step-Down and Simultaneous Algebraic Equation Methods for Allocating Reciprocal Support Costs

OBJECTIVE 2

Allocate support
department costs to
revenue-producing
departments.

For illustration purposes, assume that Stonebrook has only two support departments, accounting and environmental services. In addition, assume that Stonebrook has only two revenue-producing departments, operating room and psychiatric care. A study conducted by the accounting department revealed that its efforts were distributed among the other three departments as follows: environmental services, 5 percent; operating room, 45 percent; and psychiatric care, 50 percent. A manager of the environmental services department estimated that the department's efforts and resources were consumed as follows: accounting, 10 percent; operating room, 60 percent; and psychiatric care, 30 percent. Exhibit 2 illustrates the relationships among the support departments and revenue-producing departments. Direct costs (before allocations have been performed) for each department are shown in Exhibit 3.

Exhibit 2
Reciprocal Service
Relationships
(Chart of %)

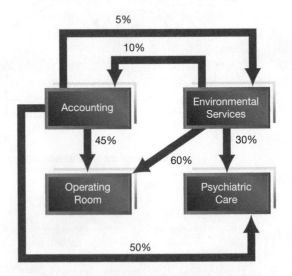

Exhibit 3
Departmental Direct
Costs Prior to Allocation

Accounting	$ 100,000
Environmental services	300,000
Operating room	1,600,000
Psychiatric care	1,000,000
Total	$3,000,000

This section considers two methods for allocating service department costs to revenue-producing departments: step-down and simultaneous algebraic equations. Allocations of service department costs using the step-down method recognize reciprocal relationships to only a limited extent because cost allocations flow in only one direction. Once costs are transferred out of a department, they do not flow back into it. Typically, departments that provide the most resources to other departments are allocated first. Using Stonebrook as an example, the step-down method first allocates the costs of environmental services to accounting, operating room, and psychiatric services. Next, the accounting department's costs (beginning costs and those transferred from environmental services) are allocated to the operating room and psychiatric care departments. Exhibit 4 illustrates the cost flows using the step-down method.

Exhibit 4

Graph of Cost Flows
Using Step-Down
Method

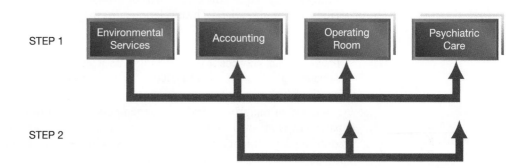

As indicated earlier, environmental services department costs were allocated as follows: accounting, 10 percent; operating room, 60 percent; and psychiatric care, 30 percent. Thus, to allocate the costs of the environmental services department, $300,000 is multiplied by the service percentages ($300,000 × 0.10 = $30,000; $300,000 × 0.60 = $180,000; $300,000 × 0.30 = $90,000).

After the costs of environmental services are allocated, the next step is to allocate the accounting department's costs. Although the accounting department provides resources to environmental services, the step-down method does not permit costs to be allocated into a department whose costs already have been allocated. Thus, the accounting department costs are allocated to the operating room and psychiatric care. From Exhibit 2 we know that the operating room and psychiatric care departments consume 45 and 50 percent of the accounting department's services, respectively. As a result, the allocation base is 95 percent (45% + 50%) rather than 100 percent. Thus, the operating room receives $61,579 ($130,000 × 0.45 ÷ 0.95), and the psychiatric services department receives $68,421 ($130,000 × 0.50 ÷ 0.95) from the accounting department. Exhibit 5 summarizes the allocation process for the step-down method.

Exhibit 5 Cost Allocation from Service to Revenue-Producing Departments, Step-Down Method

	Environmental Services	Accounting	Operating Room	Psychiatric Care	Total
Beginning	$ 300,000	$ 100,000	$1,600,000	$1,000,000	$3,000,000
Environmental services distribution	(300,000)	30,000	180,000	90,000	
Accounting distribution		(130,000)	61,579	68,421	
Ending	$ 0	$ 0	$1,841,579	$1,158,421	$3,000,000

The step-down method was commonly used in health-care organizations before sophisticated computer packages became generally available. This method recognizes reciprocal transfers among service departments to only a limited degree because costs flow in only one direction. The primary advantage of the step-down method is the ease of calculation. Also, because simultaneous equations or matrix algebra is not required, users of information easily understand how costs are allocated. However, the team at Stonebrook decided to use a computerized system to perform allocations based on simultaneous algebraic equations. Before the system could crunch the numbers, mathematical models of departmental relationships had to be constructed. The group asked Jay to develop these mathematical relationships.

Jay began to define the relationships among departments in mathematical terms. For example, the cost of providing environmental services equals $300,000 plus 5 percent of the costs incurred by the accounting department. The cost of providing accounting services equals the direct costs of $100,000 plus 10 percent of the cost incurred by environmental services. These relationships may be expressed mathematically as follows:

Environmental services = $300,000 + (0.05 × accounting)
Accounting   = $100,000 + (0.10 × environmental services)

Because of reciprocal service arrangements, the cost of the environmental services department is affected by the cost of the accounting department, and the cost of the accounting department is affected by the cost of the environmental services department. Thus, simultaneous equations are used to arrive at a solution. First, solve the equation for the environmental services department as follows:

Step 1. *Define the mathematical relationship.*

Environmental services = $300,000 + (0.05 × accounting)

Step 2. *Substitute the mathematical definition of accounting.*

Environmental services = $300,000 + 0.05 [$100,000 + (0.10 × environmental services)]

Step 3. *Distribute 0.05 across both terms in parentheses.*

Environmental services = $300,000 + $5,000 + (0.005 × environmental services)

Step 4. *Subtract 0.005 × environmental services from each side of the equation.*

Environmental services − (0.005 × environmental services) = $300,000 + $5,000

Step 5. *Combine terms.*

0.995 × environmental services = $305,000

Step 6. *Divide each side of the equation by 0.995.*

Environmental services = $306,533

Therefore, the cost of operating the environmental services department is $306,533 after considering costs allocated from the accounting department. Next, solve the accounting equation by substituting $306,533 for the environmental services term in the equation.

Step 1. *Define the mathematical relationship.*

Accounting = $100,000 + (0.10 × environmental services)

Step 2. *Substitute the value from the previous step 6 into the accounting equation.*

Accounting = $100,000 + (0.10 × $306,533)

Step 3. *Multiply terms within parentheses.*

Accounting = $100,000 + $30,653

Step 4. *Combine terms.*

Accounting = $130,653

The simultaneous equations produce values for environmental services and accounting that are allocated among each of the four departments according to the percentages identified in Exhibit 2. This method commonly is used by hospitals to allocate the costs of service departments to other service departments and finally to revenue-producing departments. Though a computer routine performs the complex algebraic calculations, managers should understand the underlying concepts.

Having determined service department costs, Jay prepared the allocation schedule shown in Exhibit 6. He prepared a column for each department and placed the direct costs from Exhibit 3 into the columns to represent beginning balances before allocations. He noted the total cost of $3,000,000.

Exhibit 6 Cost Allocation from Service to Revenue-Producing Departments

	Accounting	Environmental Services	Operating Room	Psychiatric Care	Total
Beginning	$100,000	$300,000	$1,600,000	$1,000,000	$3,000,000
Accounting distribution	(130,653)	6,533	58,794	65,326	
Environmental services distribution	30,653	(306,533)	183,920	91,960	
Ending	$ 0	$ 0	$1,842,714	$1,157,286	$3,000,000

Jay began by allocating the accounting department's costs. In step 4 above, the algebraic solution stated that $130,653 was incurred by the accounting department. Thus, Jay subtracted $130,653 from the accounting department to distribute among environmental services, operating room, and psychiatric care using the percentages from Exhibit 2 ($130,653 × 0.05 = $6,533; $130,653 × 0.45 = $58,794; $130,653 × 0.50 = $65,326).

Next Jay subtracted $306,533 (from step 6 above) from the environmental services column to distribute among accounting, operating room, and psychiatric services using the percentages identified in Exhibit 2 ($306,533 × 0.10 = $30,653; $306,533 × 0.60 = $183,920; $306,533 × 0.30 = $91,960).

As shown in Exhibit 6, after the service department costs are distributed, both the accounting and the environmental services columns contain zero balances, while the revenue-producing departments, operating room and psychiatric care, contain all the costs from the service departments. Notice also that the total costs before and after allocation equal $3,000,000.

Managers use cost reports containing allocations to make various kinds of decisions. An objective of support department cost allocation is to understand the revenue-producing departments' total cost of providing services. To make pricing decisions, managers must understand how total resource consumption rates vary across revenue-producing departments. For example, in a hospital, the operating room and the psychiatric department consume support department resources differently because each has its unique function. Thus, the cost system must trace support department costs to revenue-producing departments accurately to allow managers to understand the cost of providing different types of services. When reciprocal service arrangements occur among service departments, cost allocation among these departments is necessary to determine each service department's total cost.

To improve processes and reduce costs, managers must understand cost drivers, the activities that cause costs. Choosing appropriate cost drivers, or allocation bases, helps managers understand the sources of costs and where to look for clues as to how to reduce costs. For example, managers may look at the allocated cost of lab services and consider whether the value of the services received equals the cost. If costs are thought to be excessive, consumption patterns may change, or a manager may decide to purchase these services from an independent laboratory. Finally, accurate allocations are necessary to reduce cross-subsidy among services provided. The cost-to-charge ratio averages many types of costs across various services. As a result, some services are reported at a cost greater than the actual, while other services are reported at a cost less than the actual. This is known as *cross-subsidy*. Eliminating cross-subsidy is important because managers using costs based on averages may make poor pricing decisions.

1 SELF-STUDY PROBLEM

WebTUTOR Advantage

Liberty School is a private institution offering preschool and kindergarten classes. All teachers are experts in the field of early childhood education. To support the primary function of classroom instruction, Liberty maintains a personnel department and an administrative department. The manager of the administrative department estimates that her department provides services to other departments as follows:

Personnel	15%
Preschool instruction	50
Kindergarten instruction	35
	100%

The manager of the personnel department estimates that his department provides services to other departments as follows:

Administrative	30%
Preschool instruction	45
Kindergarten instruction	25
	100%

The departmental direct costs are as follows:

Administrative	$100,000
Personnel	75,000
Preschool instruction	300,000
Kindergarten instruction	500,000
Total	$975,000

Required

A. Discuss the circumstances that create reciprocal relationships among service departments.
B. Draw a chart of the relationships among the four departments.
C. Allocate the service department costs to revenue-producing departments using the step-down method.
D. Set up the equations to mathematically explain the costs of providing administrative and personnel services.

E. Determine the costs of maintaining the administrative and personnel departments using simultaneous algebraic equations.

F. Allocate the costs from the administrative and personnel departments to the preschool and kindergarten departments.

The solution to Self-Study Problem 1 appears at the end of the chapter.

Cost Management Systems for Service Companies

Erin and Seth discussed the importance of understanding the cost of each consulting engagement in their new consulting business. Unlike their furniture business, each consulting engagement will require different amounts of resources. Managers of all types of service organizations, like their counterparts in manufacturing, need to understand the cost of providing goods or services to their customers. They must understand how costs change with activity levels if they are to determine appropriate prices for their services. Additionally, managers may use cost accounting information to help them identify expensive, inefficient processes that are candidates for improvement. Finally, having accurate cost information may permit managers to compare the cost of their services with those of competitors. The cost structure of most service organizations presents interesting challenges for managers. This section illustrates the design and use of a cost system in a service environment.

A Health-Care Cost Report for an Appendectomy Procedure. A cost system for attaching costs to services may use a two-stage process. In the first stage, support department costs are allocated to revenue-producing departments. In the second stage, costs are attached to a specific product, service, or customer.

Jay and Beth continued to work on their drawing of a new cost system for Stonebrook. Their final objective was to design a cost system that would attach costs to each patient based on resources consumed while treating the patient. Thus far, their model allocated costs among support departments and to revenue-producing departments. These support-related costs were added to the direct costs of the revenue-producing department, as illustrated in Exhibit 6. Their next step was to ensure that costs from revenue-producing departments were allocated to the patient, based on the resources consumed. Exhibit 7 illustrates the model designed by Jay and Beth.

Exhibit 7 extends the model shown in Exhibit 1 by adding allocations from revenue-producing departments to patients. As in manufacturing cost systems, a variety of allocation bases are used to attach costs to patient procedures. For example, from discussions with the clinical members of their team, Jay and Beth knew that some costs are incurred as a function of hours, whereas others are incurred at a daily rate. Finally, other costs should be applied to procedures using the actual cost, such as supplies.

Jay and Beth pulled data on a patient who recently received care at Stonebrook. Their cost analysis is shown in Exhibit 8. The patient was admitted to the emergency room for an appendectomy procedure. Jay and Beth identified departments and the description of services provided. Linda Reynolds, the specialty nurse, said that patients could receive various levels of nursing attention. Thus, when designing the system, Jay and Beth allocated nursing costs to patients based on a daily rate at various acuity levels. **Acuity levels** identify the amount of care required; higher acuity levels indicate sicker patients. The patient in their report required one day at acuity level 1 and two days at acuity level 2.

Jay and Beth used an hourly charge to allocate costs from the operating room. As shown in Exhibit 8, the patient spent one hour in the operating room. In the cost model, operating room supplies and central stores supplies are assigned to the patient using the items' actual costs. For example, five sutures costing $24 each were required for the appendectomy procedure.

Food services and laundry/linen costs were attached to the patient using a daily rate because costs of meals and laundry service typically do not vary significantly by the type

Exhibit 7 Design of the Cost Allocation System

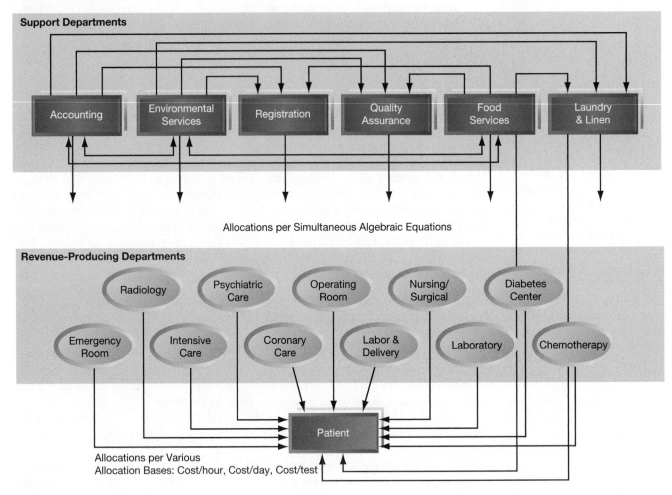

Exhibit 8 Appendectomy Cost Report

Department Description	Product Description	Cost	Quantity	Total Cost
Nursing—surgical	Acuity level 1—daily rate	$313.00	1	$ 313.00
	Acuity level 2—daily rate	369.00	2	738.00
Operating room (OR)	Major surgery—1 hour	449.00	1	449.00
Operating room supplies	Sutures	24.00	5	120.00
	Basic surgical pack	23.00	1	23.00
	Additional OR supplies	251.50	1	251.50
Food services	Daily hospital service	42.00	3	126.00
Laundry/linen	Daily hospital service	15.00	3	45.00
Emergency room (ER)	ER visit level II—intensive	222.00	1	222.00
				$2,287.50

of patient or procedure. Finally, emergency room costs of $222 were associated with the patient.

By way of comparison, Jay calculated the cost of the appendectomy procedure using the cost-to-charge ratio and compared the result with that found using his new cost system. Pulling data on the appendectomy patient, he found that the charge was $8,100. Thus, using the facility-wide cost-to-charge ratio of 0.704, Jay calculated the cost as follows: $8,100 × 0.704 = $5,702. The cost-to-charge ratio had greatly overestimated the cost of this patient's appendectomy procedure. How could Stonebrook possibly use information based on the cost-to-charge ratio to submit bids? No wonder it had been unsuccessful in winning bids for procedures. Using this case as an example, Stonebrook would have overestimated its costs by $3,414 ($5,702 − $2,288). Jay then had a frightening thought. If Stonebrook overestimated its costs (and bids), the worst that would happen was that another hospital would win the contract. What if the cost-to-charge ratio caused Stonebrook to underestimate its costs, thereby winning long-term contracts for procedures whose actual costs exceeded contract revenue!

Clinical Decisions Using Cost Information. The cost system designed by Jay and Beth as shown in Exhibit 7 is far superior to systems that estimate costs using a facility-wide cost-to-charge ratio. Like managers of manufacturing companies, managers of healthcare facilities can use cost reports to understand the way in which clinical procedures consume resources. Opportunities for both cost control and quality improvement may be identified by careful analysis. For example, physicians can make decisions about the cost/benefit relationship of laboratory tests. They may reduce the number of unnecessary lab tests performed by specifying only required tests, rather than ordering an entire list of tests. Physicians may order lab tests every other day, rather than daily, if this is consistent with proper clinical practice. Where appropriate, physicians also may consider early discharge. In addition, carefully selecting the level of care may have a positive impact on costs. In the appendectomy example, the patient received two days of care at acuity level 2 and one day at acuity level 1. The physician can evaluate whether the additional clinical attention at acuity level 2 ($369 per day) rather than acuity level 1 ($313 per day) is necessary. Thus, better cost systems assist managers in making various types of operational decisions.

Case in Point

Cost Systems: Differences between Manufacturing and Nonmanufacturing Firms

A survey published by the Cost Management Group of the Institute of Management Accountants found differences in cost system design between manufacturing and non-manufacturing firms. For example, approximately 78 percent of manufacturing firms responding to the survey use a standard costing system (as discussed in Chapter M9). Thus, these companies routinely compute materials and labor variances. Alternatively, only 34 percent of non-manufacturing firms use standard costing systems. Managers indicated that standard costs are difficult to develop in service organizations because of unique services offered to clients.

Source: Krumwiede, Kip R. 2000. Results of 1999 Cost Management Survey: The Use of Standard Costing and Other Costing Practices, *Cost Management Update* (December/January).

The next section considers various ways service organizations may evaluate processes to reduce waste. While many factors are important to the delivery of healthcare services, the cost system may highlight areas for improvement. However, many decisions and clinical assessments must be made by those who have medical, rather than financial, knowledge. Once again, a team approach to cost management is an effective management tool.

2 SELF-STUDY PROBLEM

WebTUTOR Advantage

Paradise Air is a small airline company located in the Florida Keys. The company provides transportation services to various Caribbean islands. Because Paradise Air competes directly with major carriers, controlling costs and setting appropriate fares are vital to the company's survival. Thus, management is preparing an analysis to assist it in understanding the cost of providing various services to customers. Five categories of costs have been identified:

1. Ticketing
2. Fuel, wages, maintenance, and operating expenses
3. First-class on-board services
4. Coach-class on-board services
5. Baggage handling

Managers at Paradise predicted the following costs and activity levels for the next month:

Ticketing	$10,000
Passengers	1,500 coach-class
	500 first-class
Fuel, wages, maintenance, operating expenses	$1.50 per passenger mile*
Baggage handling	$9,000
Number of baggage transfers	3,000
First-class in-flight service	$25,000
Coach-class in-flight service	$15,000

*Assume that management at Paradise had conducted a long-term study and determined the cost to be $1.50 per passenger mile. Therefore, to determine the fuel, wages, maintenance, and operating expenses cost of each ticket, $1.50 was multiplied by the number of miles traveled.

Ticketing costs are assigned using a cost per passenger basis. Fuel, wages, maintenance, and other operating expenses are assigned using cost per mile as a basis. Baggage handling costs are assigned using the number of times baggage is transferred. Finally, costs of in-flight services, including food, beverages, and other amenities, were estimated for each class of service.

Required

A. Describe the "product" delivered by Paradise Air.
B. Calculate the cost of providing first-class service to a passenger who requires two baggage transfers and travels 200 miles.

The solution to Self-Study Problem 2 appears at the end of the chapter.

PERFORMANCE MEASUREMENT AND COST MANAGEMENT STRATEGIES IN THE SERVICE ENVIRONMENT

OBJECTIVE 4

Describe various strategies used by service organizations to improve quality and reduce costs.

Jay and the team understood that developing a new management information system was only part of the plan to improve quality and reduce costs at Stonebrook. He and Beth had relied heavily on various clinical experts when designing the new cost system. Once again, a team orientation would be required to make the organizational changes that were necessary if Stonebrook was to become competitive in a managed-care environment.

In reaction to changes in the reimbursement policies of health-care payers, many health-care providers are making strategic changes in the way they deliver services. Though this chapter uses a health-care organization as an example, the same principles apply to other service (and manufacturing) organizations. Three strategies for improving the health-care delivery process are illustrated.

The team had gathered to consider the next step in restructuring the clinical-care delivery system at Stonebrook. *Operations restructuring* **involves a complete evaluation of the relationships among multiple processes and is conducted to improve the quality and efficiency of services provided to customers.** After months of design and implementation effort by Jay and Beth, the new cost system was in place. Armed with better cost information, the team considered the next step in the restructuring process.

While the cost system was under development, the clinical team members, Linda and Tim, had pursued another aspect of the restructuring effort.

Linda began, "As you know, the purpose of our restructuring effort is to improve efficiency and reduce the costs of our clinical delivery process. The result should be increased customer satisfaction and improved patient outcomes."

"We used the blood specimen procurement system as a trial process," continued Tim. "It was a very complex system, consisting of over 100 steps and requiring 10 employees. Everyone from the patients to the clinicians was dissatisfied with it."

"We studied the process and made recommendations for changes," Linda went on. "The new system is far less inconvenient for patients because the number of steps has been drastically reduced. Clinical staff members also appreciate the efficiency."

"The new process is less costly, too," added Beth.

"That's right. Beth helped clinicians see their processes from a financial perspective. She was a great help as clinicians struggled to let go of old ways of providing care," Tim said.

"Operations restructuring is the first strategy for becoming more competitive," said Linda. "Our new blood procurement system is an example. We think two other strategies are crucial to successfully changing the way we deliver care. The first is outcomes data dissemination, and the second is critical path utilization. Outcomes data dissemination involves communicating financial and clinical data to physicians and others who make clinical and resource decisions at Stonebrook."

Tim added, "Critical path utilization standardizes treatment routines for various medical procedures."

Outcomes Data Dissemination

The Stonebrook team decided that a key component of successfully improving clinical and financial outcomes involved communicating and acting on relevant data. *Outcomes data dissemination* **is the practice of sharing process and outcomes information with those who make resource decisions.** As with manufacturing processes, the people involved in the delivery of services must understand key process variables. Thus, Linda and Tim collected cost and outcomes data to help physicians improve their practice patterns so that they resulted in better outcomes and lower costs. An example of Linda and Tim's data is shown in Exhibit 9, which summarizes the cost per case for six physicians (A through F).

Exhibit 9
Outcomes Data
Dissemination: Cost
per Case

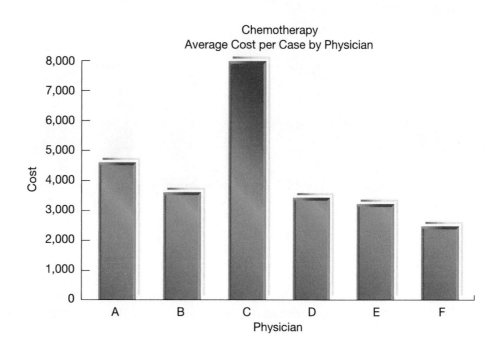

Linda pointed out that Physician C appears to have a high cost per case relative to other physicians in the group. In addition, Exhibit 10 suggests that Physician C's patients remain in the hospital longer than the patients of other physicians. At first, the team thought that Physician C's patients were sicker than those of other physicians. However, Exhibit 11 identifies AWAS (average weighted admission severity) scores for each physician. An AWAS score is a measure of patients' clinical conditions at the time of admission to the hospital; higher scores indicate sicker patients. Physician C's average patient AWAS score is lower than those of almost all of the other physicians in the group. Thus, upon admission to the hospital, Physician C's chemotherapy patients are not as sick as other chemotherapy patients in the sample, but they stay longer and have a higher average cost per case.

Exhibit 10

Outcomes Data
Dissemination: LOS Data

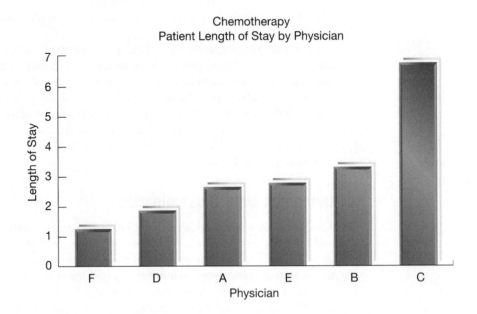

Exhibit 11

Outcomes Data
Dissemination: AWAS

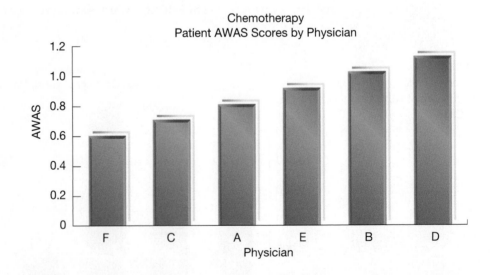

"Physician C contacted us for assistance," noted Tim. "He was interested in reducing his cost per case in order to be attractive to a managed-care company."

"We looked at his practice patterns. Using the new cost system, we made clinical recommendations for reducing waste. We also estimated the resulting cost savings," continued Linda. "For example, Physician C typically asks for a full list of lab work on all admissions. We recommended ordering lab work only for specific tests."

"In addition, most of the electrocardiograms and chest x-rays could be eliminated or completed on an outpatient basis. Full labwork would be completed only on selective groups as needed," said Tim.

Jay and his team borrowed numerous techniques traditionally used by manufacturing organizations. For example, they viewed each service as a process. To determine whether these processes were in a state of statistical control, the team used SPC (statistical process control) charts. One such process, called hydration, involves administering fluids to chemotherapy patients prior to treatment. As shown in Exhibit 12, the elapsed time from admission to the beginning of hydration for chemotherapy patients is plotted to determine if the process is in a state of statistical control. The average time from admission to the beginning of hydration is 89 minutes. However, significant variation in time exists among patients. As indicated by the point above the upper control limit, the chemotherapy administration process is not in a state of statistical control. Using their clinical expertise, Tim and Linda evaluated the process to discover underlying causes of variability and to make recommendations for improvement. They understood that reducing waiting time is important for patient satisfaction and continuous process improvement.

Exhibit 12   Statistical Process Control Chart for Hydration Data

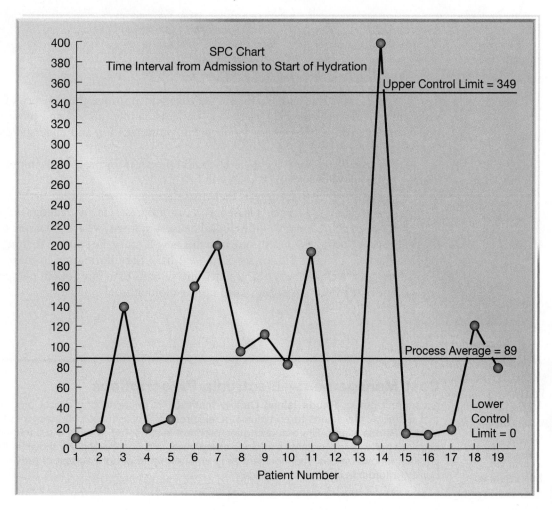

Critical Path Utilization

Before further improvements could be made in delivering clinical care to patients, the team found it necessary to develop standard treatment protocols. Thus, they developed critical paths for various clinical procedures. **A *critical path* outlines the steps needed to complete a process.** In the case of a health-care organization, this could be the sequence of tests, treatments, and medication provided to patients. The quantity and type of all procedures, tests, and labwork needed by patients were specified by the critical path. Cost data were evaluated to choose procedures that presented opportunities for cost and quality improvement.

This text has illustrated manufacturing processes that use concepts similar to a critical path. For example, as described in an earlier chapter, Tuff Cut's products were manufactured according to a "critical path" consisting of cutting, welding, painting, and assembly. Exhibit 13 illustrates a critical path for chemotherapy treatment.

Exhibit 13 Critical Path Chemotherapy Treatment

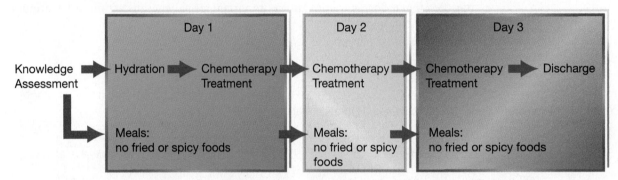

"The use of critical paths helps standardize and improve the delivery of care," said Linda. "Critical paths help everyone—patients, family, nurses, and physicians—understand the order and sequencing of care. Communication and understanding are improved."

"At the same time, adopting the best clinical practices for procedures improves the average quality of care," added Jay.

"We have evidence that suggests that costs decline, as well," added Beth.

Jay said, "We should be very pleased with our progress. Having redesigned the cost system and restructured many of the clinical delivery systems, we are preparing to meet the challenges of providing health care into this new century. I'm certain that next time we are asked to submit a bid for services, we'll have the information to make an informed analysis. We have better clinical delivery systems than most of our competitors, and we understand our costs. Let's keep up the momentum."

Case in Point

http://ingram.
swlearning.com

....

Learn more about
Rhode Island Quality
Institute.

Cost Management—Electronic Prescriptions

A nonprofit group, **Rhode Island Quality Institute**, is implementing a pilot program that will allow physicians to communicate electronically with most pharmacies in the state of Rhode Island. The e-subscription program is expected to reduce subscription costs for patients, physicians, insurance companies, and pharmacies. As shown in this chapter, innovative cost management programs are an important aspect of providing quality, affordable health-care services.

Source: 2003. *The Wall Street Journal* (February 25).

3 SELF-STUDY PROBLEM   Refer to Self-Study Problem 2 for an introduction to Paradise Air.

Required

A. Discuss various strategies Paradise Air can use to improve quality and reduce the cost of performing maintenance services on aircraft. Use the techniques discussed in connection with Stonebrook to direct your answer.

B. Identify appropriate team members to analyze costs and recommend improvements in maintenance service.

The solution to Self-Study Problem 3 appears at the end of the chapter.

REVIEW   *SUMMARY of IMPORTANT CONCEPTS*

1. Service organizations deliver intangible products (or services) to their customers.
   a. Though their products are intangible, service organizations have processes for delivering their services.
   b. Service companies may use tools developed by manufacturing companies to help them evaluate and improve processes.

2. Support department costs must be allocated to revenue-producing departments for a full understanding of the cost of delivering services.
   a. Reciprocal service arrangements exist among support departments when support departments provide (and consume) services of other support departments.
   b. The step-down and simultaneous algebraic equation methods are commonly used to allocate support department costs to revenue-producing departments.

3. Service companies need high-quality cost management systems to understand the cost of providing services to their customers.

4. Like manufacturing companies, service companies monitor their operations and seek ways to improve their processes to promote efficiency and improve quality.
   a. Operations restructuring involves evaluating the relationships among multiple processes.
   b. Outcomes data dissemination is used to communicate important financial and operating information to decision makers.
   c. Critical paths are used to standardize the processes for cost reduction and quality enhancement.

DEFINE   *TERMS and CONCEPTS DEFINED in this CHAPTER*

critical path   (M428)
operations restructuring   (M424)

outcomes data dissemination   (M425)
reciprocal service arrangement   (M416)

SELF-STUDY PROBLEM SOLUTIONS

SSP13-1   A. Reciprocal service arrangements occur when support departments provide services to other support departments, as well as to revenue-producing departments. To recognize properly the cost of maintaining a support department, all costs must be recognized, including those provided by other support departments.

B.

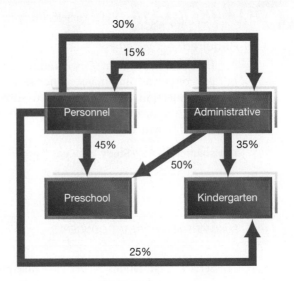

C.

	Administrative	Personnel	Preschool Instruction	Kindergarten Instruction	Total
Beginning	$100,000	$75,000	$300,000	$500,000	$975,000
Administrative	(100,000)	15,000*	50,000	35,000	
Personnel		(90,000)	57,857†	32,143	
Ending	$ 0	$ 0	$407,857	$567,143	$975,000

*$100,000 × 0.15 = $15,000
†($90,000 × 0.45) ÷ (0.45 + 0.25) = $57,857

D. Personnel   = $75,000 + (0.15 × administrative)
    Administrative = $100,000 + (0.30 × personnel)

E. Step 1. Personnel = $75,000 + (0.15 × administrative)
    Step 2. Personnel = $75,000 + {0.15 × [$100,000 + (0.30 × personnel)]}
    Step 3. Personnel = $75,000 + $15,000 + (0.045 × personnel)
    Step 4. Personnel − (0.045 × personnel) = $75,000 + $15,000
    Step 5. 0.955 × personnel = $90,000
    Step 6. Personnel = $94,241
    Step 1. Administrative = $100,000 + (0.30 × personnel)
    Step 2. Administrative = $100,000 + (0.30 × $94,241)
    Step 3. Administrative = $100,000 + $28,272
    Step 4. Administrative = $128,272

F.

	Administrative	Personnel	Preschool Instruction	Kindergarten Instruction	Total
Beginning	$100,000	$75,000	$300,000	$500,000	$975,000
Administrative	(128,272)	19,241	64,136	44,895	
Personnel	28,272	(94,241)	42,408	23,561	
Ending	$ 0	$ 0	$406,544	$568,456	$975,000

SSP13-2   A. The product delivered by Paradise Air is airline transportation. In addition to safe and timely travel, the company must provide dependable baggage handling and high-quality in-flight cabin service.

B.

Ticketing cost: $10,000 ÷ 2,000 passengers	$ 5
Fuel, wages, maintenance, operating expenses:	
$1.50 × 200 miles	300
Baggage handling: $9,000 ÷ 3,000 transfers = $3 per transfer;	
$3 × 2 transfers	6
First-class cabin service: $25,000 ÷ 500 first-class passengers	50
Total cost	$361

SSP13-3　A. Maintenance is one of the many processes required to provide airline services to customers. Using the Stonebrook techniques of outcomes data dissemination and critical path utilization, one may consider the following:

Outcomes data dissemination—Information regarding costs for routine maintenance may be distributed to the aircraft mechanics.
Critical path utilization—The team may develop a critical path for performing maintenance services. As with a critical path in a hospital, aircraft maintenance may be specified according to the number of hours of operation and other variables. Various tests and preventive maintenance may be routinely performed according to a schedule.

B. Teams consisting of mechanics, cost accountants, and managers should be formed to analyze processes. Presumably, mechanics have the necessary technical skills to recommend improvement in maintenance processes. Managers may add insights about forecasting passenger demand and FAA regulations. Accountants may assist with analyzing and interpreting financial information.

Thinking Beyond the Question

What's different about a service business?

Seth and Erin are considering expanding their company to provide consulting services. As a result, they face new challenges because service organizations differ from manufacturing companies. As they consider the opportunity, they realize a variety of costing and performance measurement issues will emerge. What are some of the primary differences in service and manufacturing organizations?

QUESTIONS

Q13-1
Obj. 1
Big Al's Car Care provides auto repairs such as tune-ups, brake work, and engine overhauls on all models of cars. Over 60% of the revenue generated by Big Al's is from the sale of parts. Would you consider Big Al's a service organization? Explain your answer.

Q13-2
Obj. 1
Nickles Consulting Services is a nonprofit organization that provides free legal assistance to clients who meet certain income criteria. The company's funding is obtained by means of fund-raising activities conducted by the board of directors. The directors are not compensated for their time, but Nickles does reimburse them for any out-of-pocket expenses that they incur in conducting company activities. Would the board of directors be classified as a cost center? Why or why not?

Q13-3
Obj. 2
Estella Rodriquez is a staff accountant for Baylor Software. Baylor has two separate departments, programming and consultation. The programming department provides services for

(Continued)

small manufacturing companies that are not large enough to employ their own programmers. The consultation department designs special software that is marketed under the Baylor logo. The president of Baylor has asked Estella to prepare an allocation of the company's in-house computer costs, dividing the costs of operating the company's large mainframe computer between the two departments. What is meant by cost allocation, and how can cost allocation be used by managers?

Q13-4
Obj. 2
What information must be known or estimated in order to allocate support department costs to revenue-producing departments?

Q13-5
Obj. 2
Trans Comm Airline flies domestic routes among several large regional airports. What information would management need in order to allocate the costs of services such as baggage handling, ticketing, and customer service among revenue-producing departments?

Q13-6
Obj. 2
Would you consider the step-down method of cost allocation to be more accurate than the simultaneous algebraic equation method of allocating service costs? Why or why not? What are the limitations or weaknesses of the step-down method?

Q13-7
Obj. 3
Service industries do not deliver a product to their customers; therefore, product costing concerns are limited to manufacturing organizations. Do you agree or disagree? Explain your answer.

Q13-8
Obj. 4
Southern Technical College is an accredited university that grants two- and four-year degrees. The registration process at Southern requires students to stand in long lines to obtain forms for the courses they desire, then take the forms to a service window where they are processed. Could operations restructuring assist Southern in improving the quality or efficiency of the service provided to customers? Explain your answer.

Q13-9
Obj. 4
A-1 Appliance Repair provides in-home service for major brands of household appliances. The company has six trucks staffed by service technicians, which it dispatches based on phone orders. Mark Maddox, owner of A-1, has noted a wide range of charges from his different technicians for similar repair work. He is worried that certain technicians may be performing excess repairs, or that others may be failing to identify problems that should be considered. How could A-1 use data dissemination to improve its service process?

EXERCISES

If your instructor is using Personal Trainer® in this course, you may complete your assignments online.

E13-1
Write a short definition of each of the terms listed in the *Terms and Concepts Defined in this Chapter* section.

E13-2
Obj. 1
Complete the following statements:

a. A _____ exists when support departments exchange services.
b. The _____ or _____ method could be used to allocate costs from service departments to revenue-producing departments.
c. Examples of _____ departments in a hospital include accounting, food services, and registration.
d. Examples of _____ departments in a hospital include the operating room, radiology, intensive care, and coronary care.
e. Service department costs must be _____ to revenue-producing departments to understand the full cost of providing products or services to customers.

E13-3
Obj. 1
Support department costs are allocated to revenue-producing departments. Often a reciprocal relationship exists among the support departments.

a. Prepare a sketch to illustrate how costs would flow among three support departments and two revenue-producing departments if a reciprocal support department relationship exists. Base your sketch on Exhibit 1 in this chapter.
b. Using your chart, describe how costs flow among the departments. Include a brief explanation of how allocation percentages are determined.

E13-4

Obj. 1

Following are various departments that may be found in an organization. Classify each department as a support or revenue-producing department. Explain.

Cafeteria (in a manufacturing organization)   Painting
Welding   Quality control
Tax department (in a CPA firm)   Accounting (in a manufacturing organization)
Assembly   Labor and delivery (in a hospital)
Personnel   Cafeteria (in a food services chain)

E13-5

Obj. 1

Sandy Lodges Hospital historically has used a facility-wide cost-to-charge ratio to determine the cost of various procedures. Cost and revenue data for a 12-month period are as follows:

Revenue Center	Costs	Charges
Nursing	$ 600,000	$ 750,000
Coronary care	1,500,000	2,300,000
Radiology	750,000	1,500,000
Laboratory	300,000	800,000
Emergency room	500,000	950,000

a. Calculate the facility-wide cost-to-charge ratio for Sandy Lodges Hospital.
b. Using the cost-to-charge ratio from part (a), calculate the cost of an emergency room visit that resulted in a charge of $7,500.
c. Why is the cost-to-charge ratio inadequate for making cost-based decisions in a hospital setting?

E13-6

Obj. 2

Assume Rockton Bank has two revenue-producing departments: mortgage lending and small business lending. To support the activities of these departments, Rockton uses three departments: financial research, account management, and personnel. The company uses the step-down method for allocating support department costs to revenue-producing departments.

Prepare a sketch to illustrate the cost flows among the five departments at Rockton. Assume support department costs are allocated in the same order as listed above. Identify potential allocation bases Rockton's management could use to allocate support department costs to revenue-producing departments.

E13-7

Obj. 2

Phillip Technologies has two support departments, A and B, that provide services to producing departments, C and D. Direct costs for service departments A and B are $250,000 and $300,000, respectively. The cost accountant estimates the proportion of services provided by the support departments as follows:

Service Department A	Service Department B
25% to Department B	40% to Department A
40% to Department C	35% to Department C
35% to Department D	25% to Department D

a. Draw a sketch of the reciprocal relationships among the various departments. Indicate the percentage of services provided by each support department to other departments.
b. Prepare the algebraic equation that describes the cost of operating each service department. (You do not have to solve the equation.)

E13-8

Obj. 2

Samson Enterprises uses the step-down method to allocate service department costs to revenue-producing departments. The support departments, personnel and janitorial, allocate their costs based on the number of employees and departmental square footage, respectively. Relevant data are presented as follows:

			Revenue Producing	
	Personnel	Janitorial	Department 1	Department 2
Employees	7	10	20	25
Square feet	3,000	1,000	10,000	15,000
Direct costs	$400,000	$500,000	$1,500,000	$2,000,000

Allocate the personnel and janitorial costs to the revenue-producing departments using the step-down method. Explain how service department allocation bases are selected.

E13-9 The algebraic method for allocating service department costs recognizes reciprocity among
Obj. 2 various departments. In the real world, computer programs solve complex allocations when
a company must allocate costs among many (more than two) departments. However, the same
logic is applied for simple models having only two service departments.

Assume a company has two service departments, 1 and 2, and two revenue-producing
departments, A and B. The direct costs of operating Service Department 1 and Service Department 2 are $500,000 and $600,000, respectively.

Allocation percentages are as follows:

Service Department 1	Service Department 2
35% to Department 2	40% to Department 1
30% to Department A	40% to Department A
35% to Department B	20% to Department B

a. Prepare the algebraic equations that express the cost of operating each service department.
b. Solving the equations you prepared in part (a), determine the total cost to be allocated
to other departments within the company.
c. Explain why simultaneous algebraic equations are necessary to fully capture the reciprocal agreements among departments.

E13-10 The following illustration shows reciprocal service relationships expressed in percentages of
Obj. 2 effort provided.

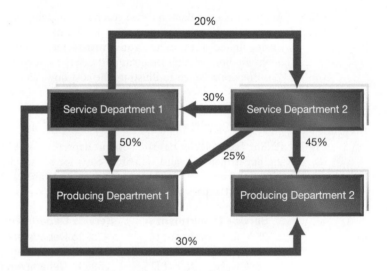

a. Explain the relationships shown in the illustration.
b. Express the reciprocal service relationships in mathematical terms. Assume Service Department 1 has direct costs of $250,000 and Service Department 2 has direct costs of
$400,000.

E13-11 Mary Taylor fell and broke her clavicle while on a university-sponsored weekend rock-climbing
Obj. 2 expedition. Mary was transported to the emergency room at a local hospital where she received services from emergency room physicians, the laboratory technicians, and radiologists.
When she received her bill for services, Mary was surprised by the large amount of charges.
The accounts receivable clerk explained how indirect charges in the form of overhead from
support departments such as accounting, food services, and education are included in the cost
of delivering emergency room, laboratory, and radiology services.

Assuming the hospital uses algebraic equations to allocate service department costs, prepare a sketch to illustrate how costs would flow among the departments and to a patient. Identify reasonable cost drivers (or allocation bases) that may be used to attach emergency room,
laboratory, and radiology costs to a patient. Defend your choices.

E13-12 Bill Watts awoke with intense pain in his side. After a 911 call, he was transported to the emer-
Obj. 3 gency room at Lodi Community Hospital, where he underwent surgery for a ruptured ap-

pendix. The surgical procedure required 30 minutes. His hospital stay lasted three days, one of which was classified as acuity level 2.

The following information has been retrieved from Lodi Community Hospital's cost information system:

Nursing:

Acuity level 1	$350 per day
Acuity level 2	$400 per day
Food services	$65 per day
Operating room	$450 per half hour
Laundry	$35 per day
Emergency room admission	$250 per admission
Emergency medical transportation	$300

Calculate the cost incurred by Lodi Community Hospital to care for Bill. Assume Lodi Community Hospital invoices clients on a cost-plus basis. If the markup percentage is 20%, what is the amount of Bill's invoice?

E13-13
Obj. 3

Jack Turner was reviewing his hospital bill upon returning to his home following a five-day stay in Stockton Community Hospital. He required two hours of surgery upon admission to the hospital's intensive care facility. He was classified as an acuity level 1 patient for two days and an acuity level 2 patient for three days. The hospital incurred a cost of $600 for surgical supplies associated with Jack's visit.

The following information has been retrieved from Stockton Community Hospital's cost information system. Calculate the cost incurred by the hospital to provide Jack's care.

Nursing:

Acuity level 1	$325 per day
Acuity level 2	$400 per day
Food services	$75 per day
Laundry	$20 per day
Emergency room admission	$200 per admission
Operating room	$550 per half hour

E13-14
Obj. 3

Glendale City Hospital uses a facility-wide cost-to-charge ratio to estimate the cost of providing a variety of medical services. The hospital has the following departments and associated financial information:

	Costs	Charges
Emergency	$2,000,000	$3,750,000
Labor and delivery	3,000,000	4,000,000
Laboratory	750,000	900,000
Cardiology	4,000,000	6,000,000
Radiology	1,000,000	1,500,000

a. Calculate the facility-wide cost-to-charge ratio for Glendale City Hospital.
b. Assume a cardiology patient is charged $75,000 for a procedure. Using the cost-to-charge ratio, calculate the cost to Glendale of performing the procedure.
c. Assume a family is charged $10,000 for the normal delivery of an infant. Using the cost-to-charge ratio, calculate the cost to Glendale of delivering the infant.
d. Compare your answers from parts (b) and (c). What is your impression of the cost-to-charge ratio as a tool to help hospitals understand costs?

E13-15
Obj. 3

Zippy Shipping Lines transports high-value freight across the Gulf of Mexico from New Orleans, Louisiana, to Miami, Florida. The company competes directly with trucking lines and air carriers. Service companies often use multiple activity drivers based on hours, days, voyages, and so on, in determining the cost of providing services to clients.

A cost summary to deliver a load of cargo for a client is as follows:

(Continued)

Service	Cost	Quantity	Total Cost
Freight handling—loading	$300 per hour	10 hours	
Fuel	$0.33 per gallon	_____	$50,000
Crew costs	_____	1.5 days	$ 3,000
Freight handling—unloading	_____	12 hours	$ 4,200
Total			

a. Calculate the *total* cost of freight handling—loading.
b. Calculate the quantity of fuel consumed per *voyage*.
c. Calculate the crew cost per *day*.
d. Calculate the freight handling—unloading cost per *hour*.
e. Calculate the total cost of delivering the load of cargo.
f. Explain why a variety of rates were necessary to calculate the cost of providing shipping services.

E13-16 Complete the following definitions.

Obj. 4

a. _____ involves a complete evaluation of the relationships among multiple processes and is conducted to improve the quality and efficiency of services provided to customers.
b. _____ is the practice of sharing process and outcomes information with those who make resource decisions.
c. A _____ outlines steps needed to complete a process.
d. The strategy used by a hospital when changing the procedures for acquiring and analyzing blood samples is referred to as _____.
e. Standard treatment protocols are identified in a _____.

E13-17 Operations restructuring, outcomes data dissemination, and critical path are three strategies used by service (as well as manufacturing) organizations to improve efficiency and to reduce costs. Listed below are a variety of characteristics. Match each characteristic with the appropriate strategy.

Obj. 4

Strategy
Operations restructuring
Outcomes data dissemination
Critical path

Characteristic
a. This strategy may involve the use of statistical process control charts to determine whether a process is in a state of statistical control.
b. The purpose of this strategy is to improve efficiency and to reduce the costs of delivering products or services to customers.
c. In the case of a hospital, this could be the sequence of tests, treatments, and medication provided to patients.
d. This strategy involves sharing process and outcomes information with those who make resource decisions.
e. Team members would conduct a complete evaluation of the relationships among multiple processes to improve the quality and efficiency of services provided.
f. The use of this strategy helps standardize and improve the delivery of care.

E13-18 Minneapolis Physician Partners (MPP) is considering adding laboratory equipment to permit restructure of the clinical process of gathering and analyzing blood samples. Currently the process is as follows:

Obj. 4

- Physician orders blood test.
- Nurse informs office staff to schedule appointment with patient.
- Office staff telephones patient to schedule appointment.
- Laboratory assistant gathers specimen.
- Laboratory assistant collects a batch of 10 blood specimens before contacting medical courier.
- Courier transports batch of specimens to laboratory across town.
- Lab conducts lab tests requiring 20 minutes and contacts courier.

- Courier returns batch of specimens to MPP after tests are complete.
- Laboratory assistant receives test results, places reports into patients' files, and notifies nurse that reports have returned from lab.
- Nurse gives patient reports to physician for analysis and informs office staff to schedule appointment with patient.
- Office staff telephones patient to schedule appointment.
- Physician meets with patient to discuss report and treatments, if necessary.

Using your understanding of operations restructuring, explain how MPP could simplify the process by purchasing equipment to process blood samples. Explain why operations restructuring may result in more efficient, cost-effective care. Might operations restructuring also benefit the patient? Explain your reasoning.

E13-19
Obj. 4

Dr. Walston is an accounting professor in a major state university. As part of the reaccreditation process, the college is systematically evaluating the quality and rigor of teaching within the various departments. A committee that Dr. Walston chairs is reviewing instructional data, including course grade distributions, course syllabi, student teaching evaluation scores and comments, and peer evaluation reports, for each professor in the college. Dr. Walston's committee will prepare a variety of charts and tables that summarize information by faculty member and department and will distribute the information to each faculty member for consideration. The anonymity of the faculty member and department is ensured. All parties will be identified as faculty A, B, or C, and department A, B, or C.

Using the terms in this chapter, what strategy is the college using to improve operations? How might this strategy be used in a university setting to improve teaching effectiveness? Explain your answer.

PROBLEMS

If your instructor is using Personal Trainer® in this course, you may complete your assignments online.

P13-1
Obj. 1

Cost Allocation and Performance Evaluation

William Davidson, departmental manager for an engineering consulting firm, recently attended a meeting to discuss a proposal for a new firm-wide cost accounting system. The proposal would change the method of allocating support department costs to producing departments. Management wants to better understand how resources are consumed across all departments. Currently, the step-down method is used; however, the proposed accounting system will require the company to redefine support department relationships to better capture reciprocal service arrangements.

William manages a revenue-producing department and is very interested in how costs flow into his department, as his bonuses are based on ROI. However, he sees the project as little more than a smoke-and-mirrors exercise—all form and no substance. "I can't see how a different allocation process will change the way in which I acquire services from internal departments such as information technology, accounting, personnel, and others. Will the new system really lead to better decision making, or are we simply rearranging the same accounting numbers?"

Required

A. Explain how the algebraic method of support department cost allocation might do a better job than the step-down method of capturing reciprocal service arrangements.
B. Do you agree, or disagree, with William? Explain.
C. Are allocated costs irrelevant to the decision-making process of departmental managers? Explain.

P13-2
Obj. 2

Service Departments in a Manufacturing Environment

Omega Manufacturing Company has two production divisions, industrial products and consumer electronics, and three service departments, administration, personnel, and maintenance. Budgeted costs for each service department are as follows:

(Continued)

Administration	$600,000
Personnel	280,000
Maintenance	320,000

Management has decided that administration and personnel service costs should be directly allocated based on the number of employees in each revenue-producing department, and maintenance should be directly allocated based on the dollar amount of assets employed in each revenue-producing department. The number of employees and dollar value of assets employed by each revenue-producing department are as follows:

	Number of Employees	Dollar Value of Assets Employed
Industrial products	225	$4,000,000
Consumer electronics	275	6,000,000

Required

A. Calculate the amount of service costs that should be allocated based on number of employees.
B. Determine the allocation percentages based on both number of employees and dollar value of assets employed.
C. Calculate the amount of service costs that would be allocated to industrial products and consumer electronics using the direct method.

P13-3 **Service Department Cost Allocation**

Obj. 2

First State Bank has two revenue-producing departments, demand deposits and loans. The bank also has three service areas, administration, personnel, and accounting. The direct costs per month and the interdepartmental service relationships are reflected below. The bank allocates costs in the following order:

1. Administration
2. Personnel
3. Accounting

Department	Direct Costs	Administration	Personnel	Accounting	Deposits	Loans
Administration	$40,000		10	10	30	50
Personnel	60,000	10		20	40	30
Accounting	60,000	10	10		40	40
Demand deposits	50,000					
Loans	80,000					

Column group header: **Percent of Service Used By** (spans Administration, Personnel, Accounting, Deposits, Loans)

Required

A. Compute the total cost for each revenue-producing department using the step-down method.
B. Define the algebraic equations reflecting the reciprocal service cost functions for the personnel, administration, and accounting departments.

P13-4 **Service Department Cost Allocation**

Obj. 2

Med Alert is a 24-hour walk-in medical service provider that has two revenue-producing departments, laboratory and patient care. It also has two service departments, administration and custodial services. Service costs for the most recent year of operation were as follows:

Service costs:	
Administration	$ 340,000
Custodial services	100,000
Laboratory	250,000
Patient care	739,000
Total costs	$1,429,000

Med Alert utilizes two different allocation bases, labor hours worked and service space occupied, in assigning service department costs. Information on these allocation bases for the most recent year was as follows:

Labor hours worked:
Administration	12,000
Custodial services	6,000
Laboratory	18,000
Patient care	30,000

Service space occupied (square feet):
Administration	10,000
Custodial services	0
Laboratory	5,000
Patient care	45,000

Administration costs are allocated to revenue-producing departments based on labor hours. Custodial services costs are allocated based on service space occupied.

Required

A. Assume that Med Alert currently allocates costs to the revenue-producing departments individually and without regard to any reciprocal service arrangements. Determine the service costs that would be allocated to the revenue-producing departments using this approach.
B. Compute the costs of the revenue-producing departments using the step-down method to allocate service costs. Allocate administration costs first.
C. Which method of allocation provides a more accurate indication of service costs in the revenue-producing departments?

P13-5 ## Budgeted versus Actual Allocation Costs

Obj. 2

Dempsey Manufacturing operates a cafeteria for the benefit of all employees. The cost of operating the cafeteria is allocated to the operating departments on the basis of number of employees in the respective departments. Budgeted and actual data for operating the cafeteria during the previous month are shown as follows:

	Budgeted	**Actual**
Cafeteria services	$60 per employee	$72 per employee

The budgeted and actual number of employees in each operating department during the previous month are as follows:

	Departments			
	Receiving	Assembly	Machining	Administration
Budgeted number of employees	12	240	175	44
Actual number of employees	11	243	173	43

Required

A. For purposes of allocating cafeteria service costs, should budgeted or actual cost be used? Explain your answer.
B. Determine the amount of cafeteria service costs that should be allocated to each of the four operating departments.
C. How should cafeteria service costs be treated when evaluating the costs of each of the four operating departments for purposes of comparing actual to planned performance?
D. How should cafeteria service costs be treated by receiving and administration if these service department costs are also allocated to assembly and machining?

P13-6   Cost Allocation, Simultaneous Algebraic Equation Method

Obj. 2

SPREADSHEET

Rivercity Mortgage Company provides mortgage servicing for financial institutions. As a mortgage servicer, Rivercity collects mortgage payments from homeowners on behalf of banks and other mortgage lenders. The bank, or lender, pays Rivercity half of 1% of all funds collected as a fee for performing this service. The department that generates these revenues is called the mortgage service center.

Rivercity also coordinates escrow accounting, collecting funds from mortgagees that are used to pay real estate owners' taxes and insurance. Twice a year, Rivercity sends a report to each homeowner explaining the amount of escrow funds that have been collected and disbursed. Each time Rivercity processes an escrow analysis, it charges the lending bank a flat rate of $2.50. This revenue is generated by the escrow analysis department.

Rivercity maintains two departments that support mortgage servicing and escrow analysis: financial administration and computer services. The financial administration department provides accounting and auditing services for each department (mortgage servicing, escrow analysis, and computer services). Computer services provides the necessary computer hardware and programming for each department (mortgage servicing, escrow analysis, and financial administration). The computer services department also supports the financial administration department.

It is estimated that computer services dedicates approximately 70% of its efforts to support mortgage servicing, 20% to support escrow analysis, and 10% to support financial administration. The financial administration department has determined that approximately 60% of its efforts support mortgage servicing, 25% support escrow analysis, and 15% support computer services.

The direct costs to operate each department for the most recent year, prior to any cost allocation, were as follows:

Mortgage servicing	$360,000
Escrow analysis	284,000
Financial administration	235,000
Computer services	315,000

Required

A. Calculate the cost of mortgage servicing and escrow analysis using simultaneous algebraic equations.
B. How might managers of Rivercity Mortgage Company use the results of cost allocation to help make operating decisions?
C. Assume the mortgage servicing and escrow analysis departments had revenues of $800,000 and $475,000, respectively. Calculate costs as a percentage of revenues. What is your assessment?

P13-7   Service Activities

Obj. 3

Public Airlines provides low-cost commuter flight service between 10 cities in the northwest United States. During a recent stop in Seattle, the plane for Flight 107 had 4,000 pounds of passenger baggage and 2,000 pounds of commercial freight unloaded. Similar amounts of baggage and freight then were loaded onto the plane in preparation for the next leg of its flight. During this stopover, airline custodial personnel boarded the plane to clean the lavatories, seat pockets, and floors. The airline catering crew performed an inventory of drinks and restocked the refreshments. The catering crew loaded in-flight meals into the plane's galley. Laundry personnel exchanged soiled pillows, blankets, and first class linens with clean supplies. While all this activity was occurring, ground crew mechanics were busy inspecting and refueling the plane. Ticket agents issued seat assignments, and flight attendants checked passengers onto the aircraft.

Required

A. Why must management at Public understand all of the activities that occur on a plane during layover? What impact do these activities have on the cost of the flight?
B. How will the cost of these activities be recovered by Public? What can Public do in order to reduce some of the cost associated with providing these activities?

C. Airlines such as Public desire to minimize the amount of time it takes to prepare an aircraft for service. Why do you believe it is important for an airline to decrease a plane's "turnaround" time?

P13-8   Costing and Pricing Service Activities

Obj. 3

Ace Auto Repair Shop provides service repairs for most domestic car models. Ace charges customers based on the time and materials that are used for service repairs. At the beginning of each year, the shop calculates a standard labor rate that is based on estimated costs plus a per hour markup. The markup is based on the competitive environment that management must assess each year. For the coming year, management believes that a $5 per labor hour markup would be acceptable based on current market conditions. Any parts that are used during service repairs are billed to the customer at cost plus 15%. The 15% markup is expected to cover the cost of ordering parts, providing a parts manager, and other carrying costs. Estimated operating costs for the coming year are as follows:

Mechanic wages	$320,000
Employee benefits	36,000
Supervision	40,000
Supplies	2,400
Utilities	42,000
Property taxes	9,200
Depreciation	88,400
Environmental	12,000
Total	$550,000

Management estimates that there will be 25,000 mechanic hours charged during the coming year.

Required

A. Calculate the billing rate that should be used during the coming year.
B. Assume a customer service job results in the following: Labor time = 4 hours; Parts (at cost) = $200. Calculate the total cost for this particular service job.

P13-9   Product Costing in a Service Environment

Obj. 3

SPREADSHEET

Linus Railway operates a freight line connecting the southeast United States with ports located in Texas, New York, New Jersey, and South Carolina. Cost accounting data are used to help management understand the activities required for transporting a specific freight car. Linus Railway uses three factors to capture service costs:

- Costs per ton-mile
- Number of switches (number of times a freight car is connected to a different locomotive)
- Hazardous substance classification

Railroad engineers have long used cost per ton-mile as a cost estimate for moving a ton of freight over a one-mile distance. Freight cars often must be switched from one locomotive to another, just as airline passengers often change planes to reach their final destinations. Thus, the number of switches often is used to capture the costs of delivering a specific freight car to its final destination. Finally, if a freight car contains a hazardous substance, additional handling and equipment are required. These costs are attached to the shipments demanding the extra services.

Estimated costs based on ton-miles	$12,000,000
Estimated ton-miles	100,000,000
Estimated switching costs	$1,500,000
Estimated number of switches	60,000
Estimated hazardous substance costs	$200,000
Estimated hazardous substance shipments	5,000

(Continued)

Assume a client wishes to transport a three-ton container for 3,000 miles (9,000 ton-miles). The scheduler at Linus has determined the shipment will require three switches. In addition, the freight car will contain material considered hazardous.

Required

A. Calculate the cost to Linus for providing the transportation service.
B. How does the cost accounting system for a service company, such as Linus, compare to those of manufacturing companies? Explain.
C. In addition to pricing decisions, how might managers at Linus Railway use cost information? Explain.

P13-10   Cost Driver Selection and Policy Implications

Obj. 3

Use the cost information presented in Exhibit 8 of this chapter to assist you in preparing your responses to this problem.

Various stakeholder groups are interested in the cost and quality of health care. As evidenced by the national debate over health-care reform, patients, hospitals, physicians, employers, traditional insurance companies, pharmaceutical companies, and health maintenance organizations often have goals and objectives that seem incompatible. Though cost accounting information is one source of input for decision makers, many factors, including clinical and political, affect decisions made by health-care providers.

Required

A. Evaluating Exhibit 8, identify a key cost driver that a physician may control as a result of his or her orders. This particular driver affects nursing, food services, and laundry/linen costs.
B. Though pharmaceutical costs are not included in Exhibit 8, many health maintenance organizations encourage patients to request generic, rather than name brand, medications. What are the ethical issues associated with hospital length of stay and medication decisions?
C. In your opinion, should legislators and others who make health-care decisions consider cost when determining the amount and availability of care? Why or why not?

P13-11   Service Provider, Ethical Dilemma

Obj. 4

Ted Macintosh is a computer programmer for Warsaw Products. The computer programming department at Warsaw provides service support to every other department within the company, including other service departments such as accounting and human resources. The gossip at Warsaw is that upper management is considering the elimination of the programming department and outsourcing of programming requirements to a third-party consulting firm. According to the rumors that Ted has heard, the main reason for this possible change is the high cost of maintaining an in-house programming staff.

In response to these rumors, Ted has begun making unauthorized changes to many programs in an effort to "hide" certain programming costs and to make special-use programs too difficult for third parties to understand. Ted hopes that his actions will keep the programming staff from being eliminated.

Required

A. Many services that are provided within an organization can be obtained from outside sources. What are some of the main concerns management should consider before outsourcing a particular service?
B. If the programming staff at Warsaw is eliminated, would the allocation of service costs to other departments be eliminated as well? Explain your answer.
C. What are some arguments for and against Ted's actions? What is the ethical dilemma raised here?

P13-12   Cost and Quality Control

Obj. 4

Medic Delivery provides transportation services between doctors' offices and a hospital laboratory. The company owns three small cars and a minivan. Each morning the company runs specific routes to the offices of various physicians and collects lab specimens that are then delivered to the hospital for testing. Upon reaching the laboratory, the driver collects the previous day's examination results, if any, and delivers the results back to the physician offices in the afternoon. Every route covers over 100 miles each morning and afternoon. The drivers take the company vehicles home at night and begin their respective routes directly from home.

When a driver picks up either a lab specimen or test result, he or she records the pickup in a log book. Physicians are charged a fixed fee for each lab specimen or exam result that is handled by Medic personnel. If a physician has no specimens to be transported, or lab results to be delivered, there is no charge for the day.

Required

A. What data do the managers at Medic need to properly operate and control the business? How would this information improve quality or reduce operating costs?
B. How could the route drivers assist in improving the company's service and profitability?

P13-13 **Operations Restructuring in Service Organizations**

Obj. 4

A major airline is interested in restructuring its service operations to become more efficient, competitive, and customer-oriented. Management has identified the following areas to investigate:

- Ticketing
- On-board meal services

The ticketing process traditionally has been very labor intensive, requiring many customer representatives to individually assist customers in selecting flight schedules and then to issue tickets. Likewise, on-board meal services have been very labor intensive and expensive. On many routes, additional flight attendants were needed to help serve meals.

Two ideas have been suggested to help the company restructure its ticketing and on-board meal services operations:

1. The use of Internet web sites for flight selection and ticket processing
2. Using external suppliers to provide bag lunches that customers can select when boarding a flight

Required

A. Discuss the inefficiencies of traditional customer service representatives for ticketing and the problems associated with serving hot meals aboard aircraft.
B. How will Internet sites and self-serve lunches provided by suppliers help the airline reduce costs and improve service? Explain.

P13-14 **Outcomes Data Dissemination and Decision Making**

Obj. 4

Wild Bill's Muffler Shop employs mechanics to replace automobile muffler and exhaust systems for customers. The exhaust systems of certain vehicles are more complex than others and require more time to replace. Bill currently employs four mechanics. Their names have been disguised in this problem for confidentiality reasons.

Bill has been working on a program to improve the efficiency of his repair process. He would like to identify the best mechanics and help the others learn a few "tricks of the trade" from them.

Following are performance data collected by Bill:

SPREADSHEET

	Average Labor Cost	Average Parts Cost	Average Repair Difficulty
Tom	$80	$155	33
June	65	135	30
Sam	90	180	25
Kate	78	165	40

Required

A. Prepare three bar graphs similar to Exhibits 9, 10, and 11 in this chapter. Assume larger numbers in the average repair difficulty column indicate more difficult repairs.

(Continued)

B. Evaluate your graphs.

C. What decisions might Bill make as a result of your analysis?

P13-15   Excel in Action

SPREADSHEET

James Academy is a private school providing K-12 education. The academy operates three divisions: Lower, Middle, and Upper Schools. Two additional divisions provide support to these operating divisions: Administration and Human Resources. Direct cost data for each division are provided in the following partial spreadsheet. The percentage of costs that should be allocated from each support division to each of the other divisions also is reported in the spreadsheet.

	A	B	C	D	E	F	G
1	Cost and Allocation Data						
2		Administration	Human Resources	Lower School	Middle School	Upper School	Total
3	Direct Costs	560,000.00	325,000.00	1,300,000.00	1,200,000.00	1,486,500.00	4,871,500.00
4	Administration %		10%	30%	30%	30%	
5	Human Resources %	20%		20%	25%	35%	

Required Use the data provided to determine the total cost of each of the school divisions after allocation of support costs. Accomplish this task as follows: (1) Copy the data into a spreadsheet. (2) Use the simultaneous equations method to determine the costs of the support divisions that need to be allocated to the operating divisions. You will need to make these calculations and enter them in the spreadsheet. (3) Below the data and calculations you have entered, prepare a cost allocation schedule similar to Exhibit 6 in this chapter. Use cell references and formulas where possible. Use appropriate formatting throughout.

P13-16   Multiple-Choice Overview of the Chapter

1. Service department costs must be allocated to revenue-producing departments in order to:
   a. determine the proper value of services provided.
   b. assist in determining the profitability of services provided.
   c. provide managers with information to assist in planning and control.
   d. do all of the above.

2. The use of statistical process control in a service industry:
   a. is not possible, since services do not result in the fixed, measurable activities on which statistical process control is based.
   b. is impractical, since the outcome of services cannot be measured on a control chart.
   c. can be an effective management tool.
   d. will not reveal common cause exceptions.

3. Which of the following reflects a similarity between manufacturing and service companies in the use of accounting information?
   a. Both manufacturing companies and service companies use accounting information to value inventories.
   b. Both manufacturing companies and service companies can utilize just-in-time theories to control inventory purchases.
   c. Both manufacturing companies and service companies utilize processes that require accounting information to analyze and control.
   d. There are no similarities between manufacturing and service companies.

4. The allocation of service department costs to revenue-producing departments is necessary:
   a. only in service organizations.
   b. to accurately reflect the total cost of providing a particular product or service.
   c. unless reciprocal service relationships exist.
   d. only in manufacturing organizations.

5. The basic difference between a service department and an operating department is that:
   a. operating departments can have no reciprocal relationships with other departments.
   b. service departments have no identifiable customers.
   c. operating departments generate revenues, whereas service departments do not.
   d. service departments are not essential to the organization's product or service.

6. Which of the following would *not* be considered a service organization?
   a. A mortuary
   b. An airline company
   c. An advertising agency
   d. All of the above are service organizations.

7. In order for services to be delivered in a more efficient and cost-effective manner:
   a. service managers must receive information regarding process outcomes.
   b. interrelated services must be evaluated in order to improve quality.
   c. the critical service path must be identified by service providers.
   d. All of the above are true.

CASES

C13-1
Obj. 2

Service Cost Allocation, Multiple Departments and Bases

Majestic Manufacturing Company has three service departments: maintenance, cafeteria, and material handling. The company also has two operating departments: fabrication and assembly. The service departments provide services to each other as well as to the operating departments. The bases for service department cost allocation are as follows:

Department	Allocation Base
Maintenance	Square footage occupied
Cafeteria	Number of employees
Material handling	Direct labor hours

Service costs are assigned using the step-down method in the following department order:

1. Maintenance
2. Cafeteria
3. Material handling

The following costs were incurred during the most recent quarter of operations:

Maintenance	$130,000
Cafeteria	74,000
Material handling	42,000

The following operating data relate to the most recent quarter of operations:

Department	Number of Employees	Square Footage of Space Occupied	Direct Labor Hours
Maintenance	6	3,000	
Cafeteria	9	4,000	
Material handling	30	1,000	
Fabrication	190	8,000	300,000
Assembly	250	13,000	500,000

In addition to the above, the fabrication department incurred $1,240,000 of manufacturing overhead, and the assembly department incurred $1,536,000 of manufacturing overhead during the most recent quarter.

(Continued)

Required

A. Determine the amounts that should be used as a basis for allocating service costs to each of the operating departments, assuming the step-down method is used.

B. Prepare a cost allocation schedule for the most recent quarter using the step-down method.

C. Determine the total costs of operating the fabrication and assembly departments for the most recent quarter.

D. Which operating department consumes more indirect resources?

E. How would you respond to complaints from the assembly department manager who believes his/her department received a disproportionate share of indirect overhead cost?

C13-2   **Strategic Planning and Cost Management in a Competitive**
Obj. 4   **Environment: Brookwood Medical Center**

C. Everett Koop, former Surgeon General of the United States, said:

> The goal of healthcare reform should be a healthy society. People must take charge of their own health, should choose lifestyles so that they won't get sick, and should use the healthcare system less often. Healthcare providers must remember that the ethical imperative for healthcare reform is most important and must not focus only on cutting costs. In addition, we should all remember that it is healthcare, not healthcure. Caring is cheap and always ethical; curing costs billions of dollars and isn't always necessary or ethical.

Brookwood Medical Center (BMC) opened in March 1973 with 288 beds and immediately began its expansion program. BMC continued to grow during the 1980s by adding a heart catheterization laboratory, a detoxification unit (for both drug and alcohol abuse), intensive care units, additional surgical facilities, and an on-site motel. BMC also modernized its original hospital facilities through an extensive renovation program.

By the mid-1990s, BMC offered a wide range of health-care services including extended outpatient surgery and ancillary services, nuclear medicine, advanced radiological technology, CT scan, labor and delivery, neurosurgery, and heart surgery. BMC also initiated a wide range of service programs to promote knowledge and wellness in the community. These programs included health and fitness courses, a cancer program, a diabetes program, and medical education programs.

Technology was exerting upward pressure on health delivery costs, while payers, such as health maintenance organizations (HMOs) and preferred provider organizations (PPOs), simultaneously made demands for cost containment and reduction. Hospitals not associated with a university or governmental organization must generate revenues sufficient to cover costs in the long run. Hospitals unable to contain costs faced decreasing profitability, and ultimately, financial failure. Thus, Brookwood Medical Center executives designed a program to help develop a cost-effective, coordinated health-care delivery system that was designed for growth.

In a capitated environment, hospitals charge an annual fee per person for medical care and accept the risk that the costs of care will exceed a predetermined contract rate. Success in a capitated environment requires an increased level of cost sophistication and actuarial skills on the part of the provider. Employer coalitions require capitated contracts that provide complete coverage for their employees' families at a cost that is competitive with plans offered by other insurers. Under capitation, a provider assumes all risk of providing health-care services. Administrators at BMC are considering possible consequences of capitation for highly unprofitable procedures.

Three conditions were causing trouble for health-care providers and were making it necessary to consider economic-based decisions. The conditions are as follows:

1. Fixed fee per service
2. Competition leading to lower fees
3. Technology leading to higher costs

Fixed fee reimbursement policies were limiting the abilities of hospitals to pass along costs to payers. In addition, excess capacity resulted in competition among providers to secure contracts with HMOs and PPOs. The result often led to a decline in revenue per service. Finally, improvements in medical technology led to increased costs as providers acquired newer, modern equipment. Thus, hospitals found themselves in the middle of a big squeeze; revenues were declining while costs were increasing. Potential reactions by providers include implementing wellness programs and health-care rationing.

Capitation, soon to be a reality at BMC, required changes in the delivery of health-care services. The focus of health care changed from treatment to early detection and prevention. In order to survive in a capitated environment, BMC had to assume responsibility for the long-term health of its patients. Before capitation, hospital revenues increased as patient volumes increased; however, under capitation, hospital profitability increased only if capitated patient volumes decreased. Thus, it was necessary for BMC to help its patients take charge of their own health, choose healthy lifestyles, and use the health-care system less often. If BMC could find effective methods of caring for its patients before disease or complications developed, it could increase profitability by avoiding the need to provide high-cost cures and treatments.

The Diabetes Project: BMC's Outcome Management (OM) division compiled clinical and financial outcomes data for specific patient groups. This information was used to design, implement, and improve health-care processes. With the move to capitation, the OM division identified specific Diagnostic Related Groups (DRGs) that would benefit from early hospital intervention. One such group included patients admitted under Diagnostic Related Group (DRG) 294, Diabetes Out of Control. This patient group was targeted for a clinical study at BMC to determine if early intervention and patient education would improve clinical and financial outcomes. An interdisciplinary team, the Diabetes Quality Improvement Team (DQIT), was formed to review existing literature relating to clinical outcomes and compliance behaviors, to study BMC outcomes data, and to develop an intervention program for improving outcomes for BMC's diabetic patients.

Clinical Factors: Diabetes is a progressive and chronic illness with the potential for severe complications. The DQIT found that patients admitted under DRG 294 had high readmission rates and high costs per case. The DQIT found the incidence of strokes twice as common in diabetic populations compared to the general population. In addition, coronary artery disease was more severe in the diabetic patient and is responsible for as many as 60% of the deaths in diabetics. The team concluded that both illness and mortality rates were much higher for the diabetic patient than for the general patient population. However, the team also found evidence that negative outcomes can be altered by early and consistent patient education, support, and intervention. Thus, both physician and community groups supported the establishment of a diabetes education program. In addition, BMC could realize significant gains in profitability under capitation if the program was a success because of the high volume of diabetics treated.

Compliance Behaviors: The next step for the DQIT was to determine how to intervene in the treatment of diabetic patients. Team members found that research on diabetic compliance was inconclusive. However, the studies suggest that diabetic patients who receive education about diabetes and self-care tasks will be more likely to take better care of themselves and to experience positive clinical outcomes.

BMC's Intervention Program: The DQIT developed an intervention program to improve clinical outcomes of patients admitted to BMC with diabetes. DQIT members attempted to increase patient compliance and outcomes by providing patient education, social support, and increased medical support. First, diabetic patients were identified and recruited into the program. Next, patients took a pretest to measure their knowledge of diabetes and self-care processes. Team members found that patients had extremely low levels of knowledge about their disease before the education process despite the length of time since their original diagnosis as diabetics. In fact, the long-term diabetics suffered worse outcomes and consumed more resources than those who had been recently diagnosed. Diabetic patients received extensive education and were instructed about appropriate self-care tasks. BMC set up an outpatient support team so patients would have a source of support and information after hospital discharge. Patients were encouraged to take advantage of BMC's outpatient support team and to comply with physician recommendations regarding future care.

The DQIT measured changes associated with the diabetes intervention program by collecting data from patients at discharge, and at three months, six months, and 12 months postdischarge. The team obtained measures of clinical variables to evaluate the effects of the training program. Selected information appears in Exhibit A.

(Continued)

Outcome: Patients who participated in the Diabetes Outcomes Project have achieved enhanced quality of both care and life, decreased physical consequences of the debilitating disease, and improved self-care abilities. The diabetic patients in the study were not the only group to benefit. External payors experienced financial benefits from the decreased costs per case and the maintenance of stable lengths of stay. Although the diabetes project temporarily reduced BMC's revenue stream, the project has shown that appropriate intervention and proper education of patient populations can positively affect its bottom line when the hospital moves to a capitated environment.

Exhibit A

Compliance Behavior Percentages at Discharge, Three Months, and Six Months Following Discharge

	Compliance Percentages		
	At Discharge	Three Months	Six Months
Compliance Behavior			
Blood glucose monitoring	78	88	92
Calories	29	84	83
Follow doctor's advice	90	100	92
Blood pressure monitoring	90	100	100
Weight control	33	74	85

Required

A. Discuss the competitive environment and financial pressures facing BMC.
B. How is BMC responding to the new competitive environment?
C. Using the outcomes dissemination techniques discussed in the chapter, prepare informative graphs based on the data provided in Exhibit A.
D. What conclusions can you draw from your analysis of the data?
E. Do preventive measures, such as the diabetes intervention program, make sense (both clinically and financially) in a capitated environment? Explain.

APPENDIX A

Coca-Cola Annual Report: Letter to Shareholders

Dear *fellow share owners,*

Time and again throughout our long history, we have demonstrated that when our brands, our people and our bottling partners are working together and performing at their best, The Coca-Cola Company is unbeatable.

This year, we focused intently on strengthening the connections—the trusting relationships—that are the heart of that formula for success. We have more to do, including securing your trust that we will deliver the long-term value you expect and deserve. Nevertheless, given the scope and severity of the business challenges we—like every company—faced this year, our results reflect the momentum we are beginning to see:

- *worldwide volume increased by 4 percent with strong international growth of 5 percent and clear signs that our North American business is growing solidly and predictably;*

- *earnings per share grew by 82 percent, as we delivered on our commitment to create volume growth while aggressively managing costs;*
- *return on common equity grew from 23 percent in 2000 to 38 percent this year;*
- *return on capital increased from 16 percent in 2000 to 27 percent in 2001; and*
- *as we managed our business more effectively, we generated free cash flow of $3.1 billion, up from $2.8 billion in 2000, a clear indication of our underlying financial strength.*

Importantly, we began to see consistency and stability in our results over the course of the year, demonstrating that the work we have done to improve the efficiency and productivity of our operations is taking hold. At the same time, we made considerable progress against our strategy.

THE COCA-COLA COMPANY

OUR BRANDS: ACCELERATING CARBONATED
SOFT-DRINK GROWTH...

In 2001, we grew our carbonated soft-drink business by
nearly 250 million unit cases and generated record
volumes. Because carbonated soft drinks are the largest
growth segment within the nonalcoholic ready-to-drink
beverage category measured by volume, we know that
accelerating this pace is crucial to our future success.

Our performance this year was led by the steady
progress we made with Coca-Cola. Through innovative
marketing programs, we deepened the already strong
connections between consumers and the world's most
popular brand, reminding them of why they trust us to
deliver refreshment anytime, anywhere—from New York
to Shanghai.

In 2002, we expect that growing momentum from
our marketing programs for Coca-Cola, as well as
successful new product launches such as diet Coke with
lemon, will generate additional growth opportunities for
the cola category and for our brands in particular.

This year, we also energized many of our other
carbonated brands. For example, Fanta, the third-largest
carbonated soft drink brand in the world outside
North America, became a truly global brand when we
reintroduced it in an array of fruit flavors to key regions
in the United States.

...AND SELECTIVELY BROADENING OUR FAMILY
OF BEVERAGE BRANDS

Even as we grew our carbonated soft-drink business to
ensure long-term growth, we profitably expanded our
family of beverage brands. This year, by satisfying
consumer tastes and preferences, we had the fastest-
growing juice, sports drink and water brands in the
United States. We transformed our juice and juice-based
beverage business into a true growth driver, building a
global business that is the largest in the world, with nearly
one billion unit cases sold annually.

With brands such as Minute Maid, Hi-C,
Simply Orange and Disney juices and juice drinks in the
United States, Qoo in Asia, Kapo in Latin America and
Bibo in Africa, The Minute Maid Company has a firm

footing for growth worldwide. With the acquisition of
Odwalla, Inc. and its refrigerated distribution system, it
is also developing profitable alternative routes to market.

This year, we relaunched our global sports-drink
business, investing in new products, packaging, position-
ing and marketing. The results speak for themselves: Our
global sports drinks, led by POWERADE and Aquarius,
grew by 13 percent in 2001, nearly double the growth
rate of the worldwide sports-drink category. Revitalized
in the United States, we introduced POWERADE in
nearly every major Western European market, including
Great Britain, Germany and Spain, as well as in Mexico
and Latin America.

This year, The Coca-Cola Company also successfully energized a major piece of our beverage strategy—
water. By the end of 2001, our bottled water volume
exceeded 570 million unit cases, making it our second
biggest contributor to our growth after carbonated soft
drinks. Three of our water brands, Dasani, Ciel and
Bonaqua each achieved sales of over 100 million unit
cases for the year.

Our commitment to devote resources to water only
in markets where we expect profitable growth paid
dividends. We successfully applied our approach to
brands in several key markets, including Ciel in Mexico,
Mori No Mizudayori in Japan, Bonaqua in Russia and
Kinley in India. Backed by our strong network of
bottling partners throughout the United States, Dasani
became the nation's fastest-growing water brand.

In 2001, we also made good progress in coffees and
teas. Beverage Partners Worldwide, our renewed and
strengthened marketing partnership with Nestlé S.A.,
began operations this year. This partnership combines
Nestlé's knowledge in life science, research and development with our expertise in brand-building and distribution.

At the same time, we grew GEORGIA coffee
in Japan by 3 percent through award-winning marketing
in a category that was flat for the year. Also in Japan—
where The Coca-Cola Company is the leader in the
total tea category, the second-largest category in the
nonalcoholic ready-to-drink segment—we launched
Marocha Green Tea. With sales of 46 million unit cases

VOLUME GROWTH IN 2001 WAS DRIVEN BY CARBONATED
SOFT DRINKS AND BY SELECTIVELY
BROADENING OUR FAMILY OF BEVERAGE BRANDS.

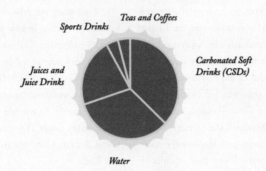

WORLDWIDE INCREMENTAL UNIT CASE GROWTH IN 2001

for the year, Marocha Green Tea was the fastest-growing product in the fastest-growing category: green tea. The popularity of Marocha was also recognized by the industry with a leading trade journal naming Marocha the most popular new food and beverage product of the year.

OUR PEOPLE: INNOVATING IN ALL WE DO

Throughout The Coca-Cola Company, our people devised new, creative ways to forge bonds with our consumers. Fresh ideas are required in every corner of the business, and this year we had them in abundance. In addition to those initiatives mentioned throughout this Annual Report, in North America, Katherine Skinner and Rohan Oza put together a team of talented young managers that transformed POWERADE into our newest global brand. In Mexico, our largest Latin American market, Verónica de la Mora, Nemesio Díez, Sandra Osorio and their team worked with almost all of our bottling partners there on the introduction of Senzao, a guaraná-flavored beverage. With over 17 million unit cases sold in its first 10 months, Senzao was our most successful new product in Mexico this year. In Eurasia, the entire Turkuaz brand team worked together to launch Turkey's first purified water brand. Thanks to their efforts, Turkuaz has enjoyed great initial success.

OUR BOTTLING PARTNERS: GROWING TOGETHER

The financial health and success of our bottling partners is a critical component of The Coca-Cola Company's ability to build and deliver leading brands. In 2001, we worked with our bottlers to turn good intentions into reality by improving the system economics, and a number of key bottlers made significant strides in enhancing their financial health.

Our results in 2001 reflect this steadily improving and mutually constructive relationship between the Company and our bottling partners. Working with our largest partner, Coca-Cola Enterprises Inc., we agreed upon a joint strategic program to continue realizing shared opportunities for growth, with closer coordination of operations including customer relationships, logistics and production.

In other important markets we worked together with bottlers to optimize distribution capabilities and ownership structures. In the Philippines, the Company, together with San Miguel Corporation, purchased Coca-Cola Bottlers Philippines, Inc. from Coca-Cola Amatil Limited. With the subsequent purchase of a majority interest in Cosmos Bottling Corporation, we are able to offer our consumers the broadest range of category-leading brands.

THE COCA-COLA COMPANY

In Russia, The Coca-Cola Company created a single bottling franchise and successfully completed its sale to Coca-Cola HBC S.A. With this transaction, we have established a platform for significant growth of the business, capitalizing on the efficiencies of a single bottler system appropriate to the market. Russia achieved 25 percent volume growth in 2001, including an 18 percent increase in unit case sales of Coca-Cola.

A TRUSTED CORPORATE CITIZEN

Our commitment to corporate social responsibility is integral to the way we do business. Through our actions, we strive to earn the world's continued trust in our Company and our brands. This month we will publish "Keeping Our Promise," reflecting the value we place on citizenship throughout our system.

There can be no better evidence of how we view our responsibility to our communities than the direct response of The Coca-Cola Company to the catastrophe of September 11. Our actions demonstrated the heritage of The Coca-Cola Company as one rooted in relationships—a company our communities can count on for support in the worst of times as well as in the best. Thousands of our people, working tirelessly with their peers at several of our bottling partners, rose to deliver whatever was needed most. We will demonstrate our support once again as we hold our upcoming Annual Meeting of Share Owners in New York City.

As I said at the outset, your Company is unbeatable when our system is operating at its peak, that is, when our people and our partners are working in close cooperation to innovate, create and deliver the world's greatest brands. That combination infuses all the elements of the strategy that we are implementing to deliver value to our share owners in the year to come, and well into the future:

- *accelerate carbonated soft-drink growth, led by Coca-Cola;*
- *selectively broaden our family of beverage brands to drive profitable growth;*
- *grow system profitability and capability together with our bottling partners;*
- *serve customers with creativity and consistency to generate growth across all channels;*
- *direct investments to highest potential areas across markets; and*
- *drive efficiency and cost-effectiveness everywhere.*

The examples outlined in the following pages demonstrate how we are working to optimize the powerful combination of these fundamental and enduring attributes—our brands and our people working in tandem with our bottling partners.

There is still much to accomplish. We are mindful that we must continually challenge ourselves to perform better and embrace change as an ever-present factor in the life of any competitive endeavor. I want to thank all the people of The Coca-Cola Company for the hard work necessary to deliver long-term value to the share owners of this great enterprise. In doing so, we will fulfill the Promise of The Coca-Cola Company—that we exist to benefit and refresh everyone who is touched by our business.

Douglas N. Daft
CHAIRMAN, BOARD OF DIRECTORS, AND
CHIEF EXECUTIVE OFFICER

APPENDIX B

General Mills, Inc.
2002 Annual Report

ANNUAL REPORT 2002

GENERAL MILLS

FINANCIAL HIGHLIGHTS

In Millions, Except per Share Data; Fiscal Year Ended	May 26, 2002	May 27, 2001	Change
Net Sales	$7,949	$5,450	46%
Earnings Before Interest, Taxes and Unusual Items (EBIT)	1,273	1,169	9
Earnings Before Interest, Taxes, Depreciation, Amortization and Unusual Items	1,569	1,392	13
Net Earnings Before Unusual Items and Accounting Change	581	643	(10)
Net Earnings	458	665	(31)
Earnings per Share:			
Diluted, before unusual items, accounting change and goodwill amortization	1.70	2.28	(25)
Basic	1.38	2.34	(41)
Diluted	1.34	2.28	(41)
Average Common Shares Outstanding:			
Basic	331	284	17
Diluted	342	292	17
Dividends per Share	$ 1.10	$ 1.10	–
Cash Flow from Operations	$ 916	$ 740	24

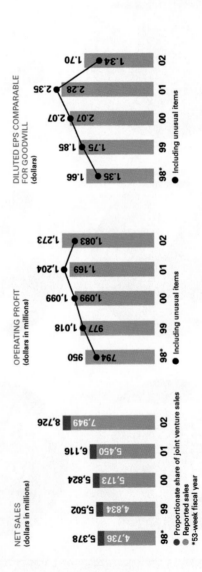

NET SALES
(dollars in millions)

98* 5,378 / 4,736
99 5,502 / 4,834
00 5,824 / 5,173
01 6,116 / 5,450
02 8,726 / 7,949

● Proportionate share of joint venture sales
● Reported sales
*53-week fiscal year

OPERATING PROFIT
(dollars in millions)

98* 950 / 794
99 1,018 / 977
00 1,099 / 1,099
01 1,204 / 1,169
02 1,273 / 1,083

● Including unusual items

DILUTED EPS COMPARABLE
FOR GOODWILL
(dollars)

98* 1.66 / 1.35
99 1.85 / 1.75
00 2.07 / 2.07
01 2.35 / 2.28
02 1.70 / 1.34

● Including unusual items

See Note Three to the consolidated financial statements for information about unusual items.
1998 and 1999 unusual expenses relate to restructuring charges (including our share of joint ventures' unusual items in EPS).

TO OUR SHAREHOLDERS:

For General Mills, fiscal 2002 was a year of significant change. On Oct. 31, 2001, we completed our long-anticipated acquisition of Pillsbury. Overnight our annualized revenues nearly doubled, our workforce more than doubled, and our portfolio of leading brands expanded to include the *Pillsbury Doughboy*, *Progresso*, *Totino's*, *Green Giant*, *Old El Paso*, and more. Over the next seven months, we rapidly integrated work teams and activities. By year-end, much of the hard work to create one sales force, one supply chain organization and one unified marketing plan for our businesses was completed. As a result, we entered 2003 more confident than ever that the combination of General Mills and Pillsbury creates a powerful consumer foods company with excellent prospects for delivering superior long-term growth and returns.

But while integration progress met or exceeded our objectives, our unit volume and earnings performance during the integration period did not. We expected our pace of unit volume growth to slow in the second half of the fiscal year, given the company-wide focus on integration activities and the initial challenge our salespeople faced getting up to speed on product lines that were new to them. But the disruption was greater than we had anticipated. Our domestic retail shipments were down 3 percent in the second half on a comparable basis (as if we had owned Pillsbury in the prior year, too). This volume performance limited our operating profit growth in fiscal 2002 and, after factoring in higher interest expense and increased shares outstanding as a result of the acquisition, our diluted earnings per share declined significantly to $1.70 before unusual items.

The interruption in our growth momentum restrained price appreciation by General Mills shares in fiscal 2002. Our stock price rose 7 percent for the year, and total return to share-holders including dividends of $1.10 per share was 9.5 percent. This trailed the S&P Food Products group's return but it out-paced the S&P 500 index, which declined 14 percent for the

year, and the Nasdaq index, which fell 26 percent. In the first quarter of fiscal 2003, our stock price has followed the overall market down. We can't change broad market sentiment, but history shows that if we deliver superior financial performance our stock price will reflect it over time. For the most recent five-year period, total return to General Mills shareholders compounded at an annual rate of 10 percent, exceeding performance by our industry peer group and the broader market indices.

LOOKING AHEAD

We expect the new General Mills to deliver strong growth in fiscal 2003. Our business plan calls for comparable unit volume growth of approximately 4 percent worldwide. We also expect to realize $350 million in cost savings next year from the Pillsbury acquisition. Meeting these unit volume and cost synergy objectives should enable us to achieve strong profit growth. Our target is diluted earnings per share of approximately $2.60 before unusual items in fiscal 2003 – roughly 50 percent growth from our 2002 results.

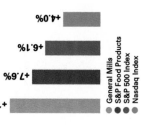

TOTAL SHAREHOLDER RETURN
MAY 1997–MAY 2002
(compound growth rate,
price appreciation plus dividends)

+10.1%
+7.6%
+6.1%
+4.0%

● General Mills
● S&P Food Products
● S&P 500 Index
● Nasdaq Index

The strategies that will drive our growth in 2003 – and beyond – are the same ones that have guided General Mills in the past:

THE FIRST KEY IS PRODUCT INNOVATION

Whether it's product improvements, new flavor varieties, or entirely new lines, innovation drives unit volume growth and market share gains for our businesses. As you can see from the table below, our major retail categories are growing, because they are on trend with consumers. And our brands hold strong share positions in these attractive markets. We think our expanded portfolio provides terrific opportunities for product and marketing innovation.

OUR SECOND GROWTH STRATEGY IS CHANNEL EXPANSION

Today's consumers are picking up groceries in lots of new places, from general merchandise chains to convenience stores. In addition, sales for food eaten away from home are expected to grow faster than at-home food sales over the long term. Our Bakeries and Foodservice business is focused on expanding sales of our products with foodservice distributors and operators, bakeries, convenience stores and vending companies. Adding Pillsbury quadrupled the size of this business for General Mills, and we are already generating new volume by selling General Mills product lines to established Pillsbury customers and vice versa.

INTERNATIONAL EXPANSION IS A THIRD KEY STRATEGY

Adding Pillsbury doubles the size of our business in Canada, and gives us established operations in fast-growing markets across Europe, Latin America and Asia. Pillsbury also created several joint ventures in Asia to market *Häagen-Dazs* ice cream. These businesses, plus our Cereal Partners Worldwide joint venture with Nestlé and our Snack Ventures Europe joint venture with PepsiCo, are expected to generate strong earnings growth in fiscal 2003 and beyond.

OUR FINAL KEY STRATEGY IS MARGIN EXPANSION

The immediate opportunity we see is for significant cost synergies from combining General Mills and Pillsbury. As mentioned earlier, we expect to capture $350 million of cost savings in 2003. In fact, we've already completed actions – such as combining media purchases or eliminating overlapping administrative jobs – that generate 75 percent of this cost target. By fiscal 2004, we expect our merger cost synergies to reach $475 million. And beyond these synergies, we expect our larger supply chain to create opportunities for ongoing productivity savings as we leverage our increased scale.

As this report goes to press in early August, our new fiscal year is off to a good start. We have a high level of product innovation planned across our U.S. Retail, Foodservice and International businesses. You'll see a number of these products pictured on the pages that follow. We plan to support our product news with strong levels of brand-building marketing. With the distractions of integration largely behind us, the focus will be on driving our business plans with our usual high level of execution. General Mills people – now more than 29,000 strong – are committed to doing just that.

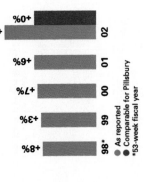

WORLDWIDE UNIT VOLUME GROWTH (cases)

98* +8%	99 +3%	00 +7%	01 +6%	02 +49%	+0%

● As reported
● Comparable for Pillsbury
*53-week fiscal year

Leading Market Positions

Dollars in Millions, Fiscal 2002	Category Size	Category Dollar Growth	Our Dollar Share	Rank
Ready-to-eat Cereals	$7,570	2%	32%	2
Refrigerated Yogurt	2,570	12	37	1
Frozen Vegetables/Meal Starters*	2,450	0	20	2
Refrigerated Dough	1,570	3	72	1
Ready-to-serve Soup	1,480	9	26	2
Dessert Mixes	1,450	2	39	1
Frozen Breakfast Foods	880	3	31	2
Frozen Baked Goods	820	21	18	1
Frozen Hot Snacks	820	12	22	1
Microwave Popcorn	800	9	21	2
Dinner Mixes*	650	23	58	1
Fruit Snacks	550	9	65	1
Mexican Dinner Kits/Shells	280	8	51	1

Source: ACNielsen, plus Wal-Mart projections
Excludes Wal-Mart

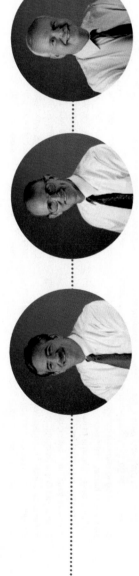

Left to right:
Steve Sanger
Steve Demeritt
Ray Viault

ACQUISITION SYNERGY TARGETS
(dollars in millions)

02	03	04
25	350	475

OUR COMMITMENT TO SHAREHOLDERS

In closing, let us say a few words about corporate responsibility and our commitment to shareholders. Ultimately, our business purpose is to create value for our shareholders, and we work hard to do that in concrete ways. By improving our existing brands and developing strong new products, so that our sales increase. By finding profitable new business opportunities. By taking costs out of our manufacturing and distribution process, so that our margins improve. By making our marketing spending more efficient. We look for ways to reduce our financing costs and lower our tax rate on a sustainable basis, too. But our success is driven by superior product quality, effective selling, innovative marketing and top-notch execution. So that's what we'll continue to focus on.

Our compensation programs strongly link pay and performance. Cash incentive payments vary depending on company and business-unit results, so total compensation is above the peer-group average when our performance is above average,

and below average when our performance drops. We firmly believe stock ownership aligns employee and shareholder interests, so our stock option program includes grants to all employees, not just senior management. Options are issued at the market price on the date granted, and we don't reprice them. For a complete description of our compensation practices, please refer to pages 25 to 31 of your 2002 proxy statement.

We are guided by a strong, independent board of directors, who all stand for re-election by shareholders every year. Each of our working board committees is composed solely of independent directors. A full discussion of General Mills' corporate governance practices can be found on pages 13 and 14 of your 2002 proxy statement, or on our Web site at www.generalmills.com.

This annual report and our proxy statement describe to the best of our ability your company's recent performance, financial condition, business practices and future prospects. We stand behind these reports to you, as we always have.

Sincerely,

STEPHEN W. SANGER
Chairman of the Board and
Chief Executive Officer

STEPHEN R. DEMERITT
Vice Chairman

RAYMOND G. VIAULT
Vice Chairman

August 8, 2002

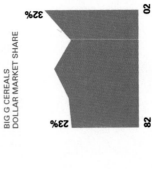

TIME TO EAT!

At General Mills, we're excited about the expanded opportunities we have to grow. Our portfolio includes more great-tasting food products than ever before, for consumers to enjoy at home or on the go, in markets around the world. We're focused on innovating to improve our established brands and develop new food choices that meet consumers' needs whenever – and wherever – it's time to eat.

Let's start with breakfast. Our Big G cereal division is bringing news to its best-selling brands. For example, sales for 60-year-old *Cheerios* continue to grow on news that it can help lower cholesterol. In January, we improved *Honey Nut Cheerios* so that it offers this same heart-healthy benefit and sales increased 5 percent in fiscal 2002.

Running late? We've made cereal nutrition portable with *Chex Morning Mix* and Big G Milk 'n Cereal Bars. This spring we added new flavor varieties to both of these grab-and-go breakfast options.

In June 2002, we introduced four new, certified organic cereals as part of our *Cascadian Farm* line, a leading brand in natural and organic food stores. You can increase the nutritional benefit of these cereals by pouring on soymilk from 8th Continent, our joint venture with DuPont.

Our cereal brands are growing in markets outside the United States, too. In Canada, our cereal volume grew 7 percent last year, and we now hold a 22 percent share of category sales. Cereal Partners Worldwide (CPW), our joint venture

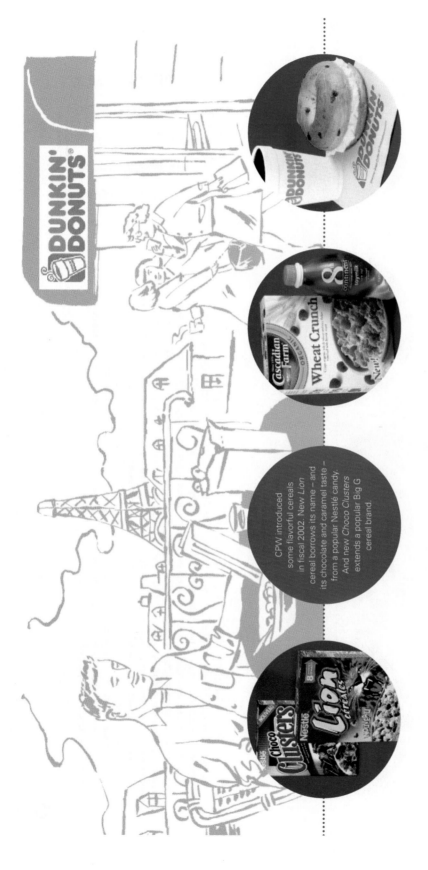

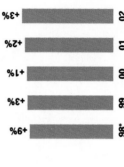

CPW introduced some flavorful cereals in fiscal 2002. New *Lion* cereal borrows its name – and its chocolate and caramel taste – from a popular Nestlé candy. And new *Choco Clusters* extends a popular Big G cereal brand.

with Nestlé, achieved 9 percent volume growth in fiscal 2002, and our 50 percent share of this venture's net sales increased to $410 million. CPW will continue to build market shares for its established cereal brands and introduce new products that appeal to consumers around the world.

Just like cereal, baked goods are a popular breakfast choice the world over. In the United States, *Pillsbury* leads the refrigerated dough market with 72 percent of category sales, thanks to delicious, easy-to-prepare products such as our *Grands!* line of sweet rolls. In fiscal 2002, we made these rolls taste even better and saw an 8 percent increase in retail sales. We are currently adding new *Grands!* Orange Sweet Rolls. And this

summer we introduced two new kid-friendly flavors of *Toaster Strudel*, a quick freezer-to-the-toaster breakfast option.

In international markets, we sell convenient dough products under the *Pillsbury* name or using local brands. For example, *Pillsbury* chocolate croissants are a popular breakfast treat in Greece. And in Germany, we market breakfast rolls under the local *Knack & Back* brand.

Consumers who eat breakfast away from home can find General Mills products in a variety of outlets, from cinnamon rolls at a Cinnabon store to a bowl of *Lucky Charms* cereal in a college cafeteria. And we are a key supplier to Dunkin' Donuts for their growing bagel business.

U.S. REFRIGERATED DOUGH CATEGORY DOLLAR SALES

98*	99	00	01	02
+6%	+3%	+1%	+2%	+3%

Source: ACNielsen, plus Wal-Mart projections
*53-week fiscal year

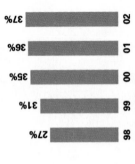

WANT TO GRAB SOME LUNCH?

Where do you eat lunch? At school, at your desk, or on the go? General Mills has lots of options for your midday meal.

Progresso soup is a great choice for a fast and nutritious lunch. The health and convenience of ready-to-serve soup drove category dollar sales up 9 percent in fiscal 2002. The *Progresso* line offers consumers a variety of delicious, adult-oriented flavors, and we'll continue to add new ones, like Grilled Chicken Italiano.

Our line of *Bowl Appétit!* microwavable entrées posted double-digit growth in U.S. sales for fiscal 2002. In January, we launched *Bowl Appétit!* in Canada, where it has been an early

hit with consumers. We will continue to expand this line in both the United States and Canada with new flavors coming soon.

Yoplait yogurt makes a great light lunch. New *Yoplait Whips!* was introduced nationally in January 2002 and continues to gain dollar share. To meet consumers' demand for variety, we're adding several great new flavors such as Crème Caramel *Yoplait* Custard yogurt and Boston Cream Pie *Colombo* Light yogurt. Sales for our *Yoplait* and *Colombo* brands grew 15 percent in fiscal 2002, and our dollar share of the $2 billion U.S. refrigerated yogurt category grew by more than a point to 37 percent.

6

Yogurt is a popular food choice the world over. But in the United States, per capita consumption is still well below rates in many other countries. We see great growth opportunities ahead for our U.S. yogurt brands, including new *Yoplait Whips!* and *Nouriche.*

Nouriche is the newest introduction from *Yoplait.* This yogurt drink is packed with 20 vitamins and minerals, along with protein and fiber, giving it all the nourishment of a meal. *Nouriche* comes in four flavors and is currently available in the western third of the United States.

Many of our brands make great additions to lunch away from home. If you pack a lunch, you can use a variety of our Bakeries and Foodservice products. Our mixes are used to create *Pillsbury* and *Country Hearth* fresh breads. And we provide customized mixes to wholesale bakeries that sell sweet treats under the *Hostess,® Dolly Madison,® Little Debbie,® Entenmann's®* and *Tastykake®* names.

Yoplait yogurt is a favorite menu choice in school cafeterias. *Go-GURT,* our kid-friendly yogurt in a tube, is now available at McDonald's. And *Fruit by the Foot* snacks were recently added to meals for kids at KFC.

In addition, our Bakeries and Foodservice division provides dough products to several popular quick-service restaurants where you might grab lunch. For example, we provide Subway® Sandwich restaurants across the United States and Canada with dough for their breads and rolls. Lunch is one of the fastest-growing meal occasions in quick-service restaurants. Sales for lunch in these outlets have been growing at an average rate of 6 percent over the past five years.

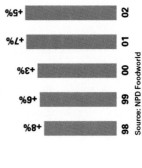

LUNCH DOLLAR SALES GROWTH
IN QUICK-SERVICE RESTAURANTS

98	99	00	01	02
+8%	+6%	+3%	+7%	+5%

Source: NPD Foodworld

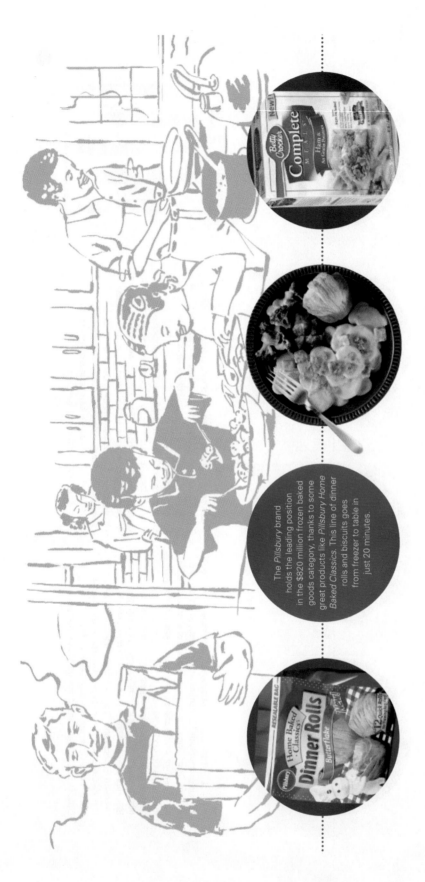

The *Pillsbury* brand holds the leading position in the $820 million frozen baked goods category, thanks to some great products like *Pillsbury Home Baked Classics*. This line of dinner rolls and biscuits goes from freezer to table in just 20 minutes.

WHAT'S FOR DINNER?

At dinnertime, you can count on General Mills products for a delicious, convenient meal. *Hamburger Helper* dinner mixes have been a family favorite for 30 years, and this line holds a 58 percent share of dinner mix category sales. This fall, we will introduce an even more convenient option – *Betty Crocker Complete Meals*. This new line has everything you need for a hearty meal, including the meat, all in one box.

Mexican food is growing in popularity with families around the world. In the United States, *Old El Paso* is the No. 1 brand in the Mexican dinner kit category, where sales are growing at an 8 percent rate. In addition, *Old El Paso* dinner kits are sold

in nearly 80 countries from Sweden to Australia. Volume for these dinner kits grew an average of 15 percent over the past fiscal year in our top six markets around the world.

Green Giant is another popular global brand, with a presence in nearly 90 countries. *Green Giant* is the leading brand of canned corn in France, Spain and the United Kingdom, all markets in which it is considered a delicacy. It also is the leading canned corn as far away as Taiwan. In the United States, our convenient frozen vegetables with sauce in large, resealable bags helped *Green Giant* grow its frozen vegetable sales 6 percent in fiscal 2002. We're expanding this line with new varieties.

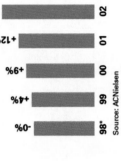

U.S. DINNER MIX CATEGORY
DOLLAR SALES GROWTH

	-0%	+4%	+9%	+12%	+23%
	98*	99	00	01	02

Source: ACNielsen
*53-week fiscal year

We've made it convenient to add fresh-baked dinner rolls to your meal, too. The *Pillsbury Home Baked Classics* line of frozen dough products offers the taste and aroma of fresh-baked bread in 20 minutes. And the resealable bag allows you to make as many or as few biscuits as you need. In September, we will add new Butterflake Dinner Rolls and Flaky Layers Biscuits to this popular line.

No dinner is complete without dessert. *Betty Crocker* holds the leading position in the dessert mix category, and she is full of great ideas for quick, easy-to-prepare treats. For example, her mixes in pouches give consumers homemade cakes

or cookies fresh from the oven in 30 minutes or less. Sales for these pouch mixes continue to grow, and we have introduced new flavors such as Rainbow Chocolate Candy cookies.

Eating out for dinner? Our Bakeries and Foodservice division provides restaurant and cafeteria operators with high-quality ingredients, and quick and easy preparation. For example, we supply Red Lobster with mixes for its irresistible Cheddar Bay Biscuits, and we make brownies for McDonald's new Brownie Sundae. We also sell baking mixes and frozen baked goods to foodservice operators, like ARAMARK and Sodexho, who manage a variety of foodservice outlets.

OLD EL PASO DINNER KITS
2002 RETAIL UNIT VOLUME
*Includes Wal-Mart projections

United States*	+6%
United Kingdom*	+9%
Australia	+5%
Canada	+19%
France	+74%
Sweden	+11%

Source: ACNielsen

9

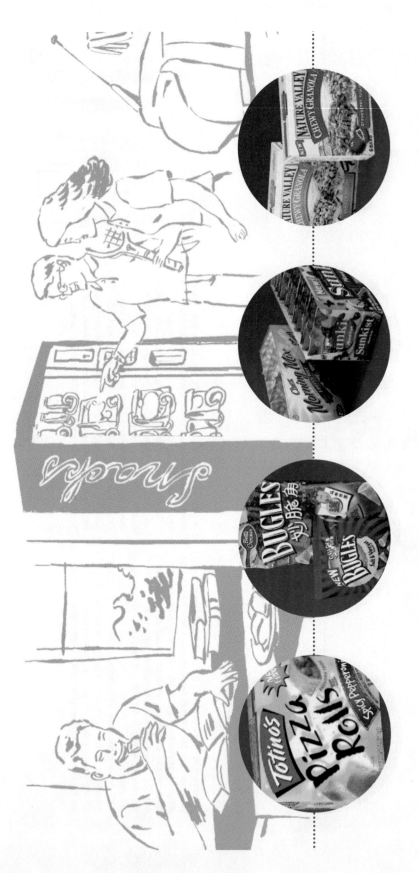

NATURE VALLEY GRANOLA BARS
DOLLAR SALES GROWTH

+48%	02
+34%	01
+14%	00
+23%	99
–9%	98*

Source: ACNielsen
*53-week fiscal year

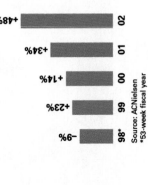

A BIG SELECTION OF SNACKS

General Mills feeds consumers' cravings anytime with a variety of snack options. Our *Nature Valley* Granola Bars had their fourth straight year of double-digit unit volume growth thanks to new flavors on our line of crunchy granola bars and new products like Chewy Trail Mix bars. This summer, we added *Nature Valley* chewy granola bars dipped in a vanilla or strawberry yogurt coating. *Totino's Pizza Rolls* are a savory snack favorite, especially with teens. Sales for *Pizza Rolls* grew 7 percent this past fiscal year, and we're building on that momentum by introducing two new flavors – Spicy Pepperoni and Cheesy Taco.

For a sweet snack, try *Pillsbury* ready-to-bake cookies. Sales for these cookies more than doubled in fiscal 2002 thanks to the introduction of some great new flavors. Now we have made this entire line more convenient with resealable bags. And we're introducing a new line of *Big Deluxe Classics* cookies. These convenient, larger-sized cookies are available in four delicious flavors popular with adults and kids.

Consumers look for snacks wherever they are when hunger hits. Sales of our snacks in convenience stores and vending machines grew 12 percent last year. Our Bakeries and Foodservice division is expanding the snack options available in these channels with *Chex Morning Mix* and new *Sunkist®* fruit snacks. And we are expanding our presence in these channels by bringing *Pillsbury* brands into these outlets.

10

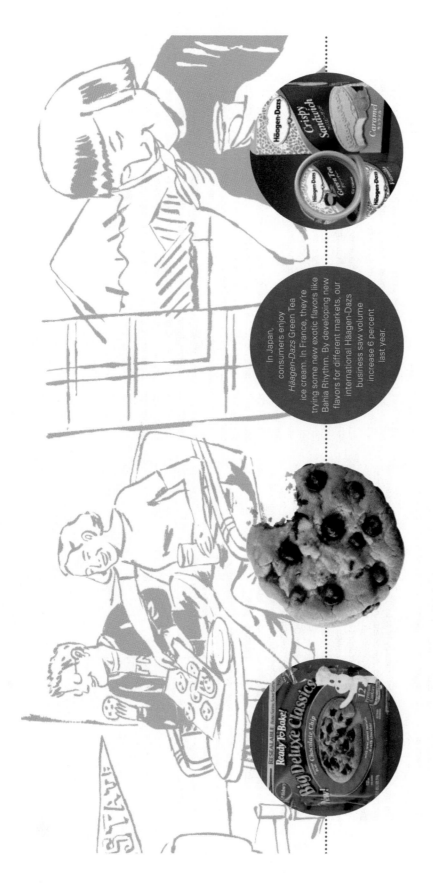

Salty snacks are popular around the world. In October 2001, we expanded distribution of *Bugles* corn snacks, including a unique Salt & Vinegar flavor, across the United Kingdom, and they have become a top-selling snack there. In China, we are introducing two new flavors of *Bugles* corn snacks made especially for that market. In addition, Snack Ventures Europe, our joint venture with PepsiCo, posted 4 percent volume growth this past fiscal year in its markets across continental Europe.

Ice cream is another global food favorite. We market *Häagen-Dazs* superpremium ice cream in nearly 80 countries outside the United States and Canada through grocery stores and retail shops that have become popular gathering places

for consumers. *Häagen-Dazs* is known for unique international flavors, such as Dulce de Leche, a caramel variety popular in several markets.

We participate in several joint ventures to manufacture and sell *Häagen-Dazs* ice cream in Asia. In Japan, our new crispy ice cream sandwich received rave reviews, so we have introduced a new cappuccino flavor. In total, our Häagen-Dazs joint ventures posted double-digit volume growth in fiscal 2002.

This report shows you just a portion of the product news and innovation we have planned for fiscal 2003. We are excited by the opportunities we see to build our business by offering foods that meet the needs of consumers around the world, at any time of day.

In Japan, consumers enjoy *Häagen-Dazs* Green Tea ice cream. In France, they're trying some new exotic flavors like Bahia Rhythm. By developing new flavors for different markets, our international Häagen-Dazs business saw volume increase 6 percent last year.

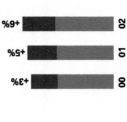

HÄAGEN-DAZS ICE CREAM
INTERNATIONAL UNIT VOLUME GROWTH

+3% 00
+5% 01
+9% 02

● Joint Ventures
● Consolidated Sales

MANAGEMENT'S DISCUSSION AND ANALYSIS

General Mills is a global consumer foods company. We compete in markets around the world by developing differentiated food products that consumers recognize as superior to alternative offerings. We market our value-added products under unique brand names, and build the equity of those brands with strong consumer-directed advertising and innovative merchandising. We believe this brand-building strategy is the key to winning and sustaining market share leadership. With the addition of the Pillsbury businesses, we have expanded our portfolio of leading consumer brands. We believe that this portfolio will generate superior financial returns for our shareholders over the long term.

Our financial performance is determined by how well we execute the key elements of our business model. These business drivers are: unit volume growth, which is the single most critical element; productivity initiatives, to mitigate the effects of cost inflation; efficient utilization of capital; and prudent management of risk. This section of the annual report discusses our critical accounting policies, the results of our operations, our liquidity and financial condition, and our risk management practices.

CRITICAL ACCOUNTING POLICIES For a complete description of our significant accounting policies, please see Note One on page 24 of this report. Our critical accounting policies are those that have meaningful impact on the reporting of our financial condition and results, and that require significant management judgment and estimates. These policies include our accounting for (a) trade and consumer promotion activities; (b) asset impairments; and (c) income taxes.

The amount and timing of expense recognition for trade and consumer promotion activities involve management judgment related to estimated participation and performance levels. The vast majority of year-end liabilities associated with these activities are resolved within the following fiscal year and therefore do not require highly uncertain long-term estimates.

Evaluating the impairment of long-lived assets, including goodwill, involves management judgment in estimating the fair values and future cash flows related to these assets. Although the predictability of long-term cash flows may be somewhat uncertain, our evaluations indicate fair values of assets significantly in excess of stated book values. Therefore, we believe the risk of unrecognized impairment is low.

Income tax expense involves management judgment as to the ultimate resolution of any tax issues. Historically, our assessments of the ultimate resolution of tax issues have been reasonably accurate. The current open issues are not dissimilar from historical items.

NEW ACCOUNTING RULES ADOPTED In fiscal 2002, we adopted four new accounting policies, all required by new accounting standards. Each of these new rules is discussed in more detail in Note One (N) to the consolidated financial statements.

At the beginning of the year, we adopted Statement of Financial Accounting Standards (SFAS) No. 133, "Accounting for Derivative Instruments and Hedging Activities," which requires all derivatives to be recorded at fair value on the balance sheet and establishes new accounting rules for hedging. The cumulative effect of adopting this accounting change was a $3 million after-tax charge to earnings and a $158 million after-tax charge to Accumulated Other Comprehensive Income, recorded in the first quarter of fiscal 2002.

SFAS No. 141, "Business Combinations," requires all business combinations to be accounted for using the purchase method. The Pillsbury transaction was accounted for as a purchase. Under SFAS No. 142, "Goodwill and Other Intangible Assets," the amortization of goodwill is eliminated and goodwill is tested for impairment. We completed our assessment of goodwill in the second quarter of 2002 and found no impairment.

In the fourth quarter of 2002, we adopted Emerging Issues Task Force (EITF) Issue 01-09, which resulted in the reclassification of certain coupon and trade promotion expenses from selling, general and administrative expenses to a reduction of net sales. All sales and selling, general and administrative expenses throughout this report and our consolidated financial statements reflect the adoption of Issue 01-09.

RESULTS OF OPERATIONS – 2002 VS. 2001 The acquisition of The Pillsbury Company, on Oct. 31, 2001, significantly affected fiscal 2002 comparisons for our results of operations. Annual net sales rose 46 percent, to $7.95 billion, including seven months of Pillsbury results. Worldwide unit volume for fiscal 2002 was 49 percent above last year's. However, on a comparable basis, as if General Mills had owned Pillsbury for all of fiscal 2001 and 2002, worldwide unit volume grew only slightly. This performance, caused by the initial disruption of combining General Mills' and Pillsbury's organizations, was significantly below General Mills' historical trends and reduced our earnings in fiscal 2002.

The Pillsbury acquisition also materially altered our business structure. Our Bakeries and Foodservice and International business segments, which now represent larger portions of our sales and earnings, have lower gross margins than General Mills' historical margin. These businesses also are generally supported with lower marketing spending as a percent of sales.

Cost of goods sold as a percent of sales rose from 52 percent in fiscal 2001 to 60 percent in 2002. The increase was due to our new business structure, along with weak unit volume trends that greatly reduced operating leverage.

Selling, general and administrative costs declined as a percent of sales, from 26 percent in fiscal 2001 to 24 percent in fiscal 2002. This reflects lower marketing spending levels in Bakeries and Foodservice and International, and the benefit of administrative cost synergies achieved in the second half of the year.

Earnings before interest, taxes and unusual items (EBIT) grew 9 percent to $1.27 billion. Earnings after tax declined 10 percent before unusual items, reflecting the impact of additional interest expense associated with the Pillsbury acquisition. Average diluted shares outstanding were 342 million in 2002, up 17 percent from 292 million in fiscal 2001 due to the additional shares issued to Diageo. Diluted earnings per share excluding unusual items and the effect of adopting SFAS No. 133 discussed earlier were $1.70, 25 percent lower than the $2.28 earned in 2001 (comparable for the elimination of goodwill amortization).

Our fiscal 2002 net results included unusual items expense of $190 million pretax, $120 million after tax, or 35 cents per diluted share. After unusual items and the accounting change, our net diluted EPS was $1.34 compared to $2.28 in fiscal 2001. These unusual expenses primarily were related to Pillsbury transaction and integration costs, and costs for reconfiguring General Mills' cereal manufacturing necessitated

13

FISCAL 2002
OPERATING PROFIT
BY SEGMENT
(before unusual items)

3%
12%
85%

● U.S. Retail
● Bakeries and Foodservice
● International

by the sale of our Toledo, Ohio, plant as required to obtain regulatory clearance for the acquisition of Pillsbury. Other fiscal 2002 unusual items included expenses related to our decision in fiscal 2001 to exit the *Squeezit* beverage business, flour mill restructuring/closing charges and expenses net of insurance recovery associated with a flash flood in July 2001 at our Cincinnati, Ohio, cereal plant. These expenses were partially offset by insurance settlement proceeds related to a 1994 oats handling incident. We anticipate additional unusual expense related to Pillsbury transaction and integration activities in fiscal 2003. Our current estimate of this unusual expense is approximately $100 million pretax.

U.S. RETAIL SEGMENT Our U.S. Retail segment includes Big G cereals, Meals, Pillsbury USA, Baking Products, Snacks, Yoplait-Colombo and Small Planet Foods. Net sales for these operations totaled $6.14 billion in fiscal 2002, compared to $4.79 billion in fiscal 2001. Operating profits before unusual items totaled $1.07 billion, up 1 percent from the prior year. Comparable unit volume was 1 percent below the prior year, primarily due to the disruption caused by our sales force integration, as well as a reduced level of new products and promotional activity during the integration period. Volume gains in Yoplait-Colombo, Snacks and Pillsbury USA were more than offset by declines in Big G cereals, Meals and Baking Products.

BAKERIES AND FOODSERVICE SEGMENT Our Bakeries and Foodservice business includes sales to wholesale and retail bakeries, foodservice distributors, convenience stores, vending and foodservice operators. Net sales for our Bakeries and Foodservice operations reached $1.03 billion in fiscal 2002 compared to $397 million in fiscal 2001, and operating profits before unusual items rose 60 percent to $146 million, reflecting the incremental contribution from Pillsbury's operations and good growth in General Mills' foodservice business. Comparable unit volume was essentially unchanged, reflecting overall weak foodservice industry trends and lower results for our in-store retail bakery segment.

INTERNATIONAL SEGMENT Our International operations include our business in Canada, as well as our consolidated operations in Europe, Asia and Latin America. With the addition of Pillsbury's international businesses, net sales for our International operations totaled $778 million in fiscal 2002 compared to $263 million in 2001. Operating profits before unusual items grew to $45 million, more than double last year's $17 million total. Comparable unit volume rose 4 percent for the year, driven by good growth in Canada, Europe and Asia.

CORPORATE ITEMS Interest expense roughly doubled in fiscal 2002 to $416 million, as we incurred additional debt related to our Pillsbury acquisition and our repurchase of 55 million shares from Diageo. We have entered into interest rate swap contracts to lock in our interest rate on floating-rate debt. These contracts total a net $3.5 billion in notional amount and convert floating-rate debt to an average fixed rate of approximately 6 percent with maturities averaging three years. Taking into account the effect of these interest rate swaps, the average interest rate on our total debt is approximately 6½ percent. For fiscal 2003, we estimate our interest expense will be approximately $600 million. Our effective tax rate in fiscal 2002 was 36 percent. We expect our tax rate for fiscal 2003 to be a maximum of 35½ percent, and we may be able to reduce it further during the year.

JOINT VENTURE EARNINGS
(after tax, dollars in millions)

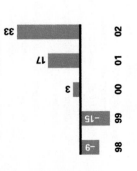

JOINT VENTURES General Mills' proportionate share of joint venture net sales grew to $777 million, compared to $666 million in fiscal 2001. Total after-tax earnings from joint venture operations reached $33 million in fiscal 2002, compared with $17 million reported a year earlier. Profits for Cereal Partners Worldwide (CPW), our joint venture with Nestlé, and Snack Ventures Europe (SVE), our joint venture with PepsiCo, together grew to $31 million. In addition, Häagen-Dazs joint ventures established by Pillsbury in Asia contributed profits for the six months included in our results. These profit gains were partially offset by introductory marketing expense of 8th Continent, the Company's soymilk joint venture with DuPont.

FISCAL 2001 RESULTS VS. 2000 In fiscal 2001, net sales grew 5 percent to $5.45 billion. Operating profits grew 6 percent to $1.17 billion before an unusual gain from a partial insurance settlement related to a 1994 oats handling incident. Earnings after tax excluding unusual items grew 5 percent to $643 million. Excluding unusual items, diluted earnings per share comparable for goodwill grew 10 percent to $2.28, up from $2.07 in fiscal 2000. Net earnings after tax were $665 million in fiscal 2001 compared to $614 million in fiscal 2000. Net earnings per diluted share comparable for goodwill were $2.35 compared to $2.07 in fiscal 2000. Net earnings per diluted share as reported were $2.28 vs. $2.00 in fiscal 2000.

Total U.S. Retail unit volume grew 4 percent in fiscal 2001, led by gains in Big G cereals, Yoplait-Colombo and Snacks. Net sales grew 5 percent to $4.79 billion. Operating profits grew 4 percent to $1.06 billion. Foodservice results in 2001 included 9 percent unit volume growth. Net sales and operating profit each grew 12 percent, to $397 million and $91 million, respectively. International unit volume grew 10 percent with gains across our business. Net sales were up 2 percent to $263 million and operating profit was essentially flat at $17 million.

Fiscal 2000 earnings before unusual items grew 8 percent to $614 million. Diluted earnings per share before unusual items and comparable for goodwill grew 12 percent to $2.07 from $1.85. Net earnings after tax grew to $614 million compared to $535 million for fiscal 1999. Net earnings per diluted share comparable for goodwill grew to $2.07 from $1.75. Net earnings per diluted share as reported increased to $2.00 from $1.70 in fiscal 1999. Net sales grew 7 percent to reach $5.2 billion.

It is our view that changes in the general rate of inflation have not had a significant effect on profitability over the three most recent years. We attempt to minimize the effects of inflation through appropriate planning and operating practices. Our market risk management practices are discussed later in this section.

CASH FLOWS Sources and uses of cash in the past three years are shown in the following table. Over the most recent three-year period, General Mills' operations have generated $2.4 billion in cash. In 2002, cash flow from operations totaled $916 million. That was up from the previous year due to higher operating earnings before depreciation, amortization and unusual items, as well as decreased use of working capital, partially offset by components of our earnings which did not generate operating cash flows: pension income and joint venture earnings.

CASH FLOW FROM OPERATIONS
(dollars in millions)

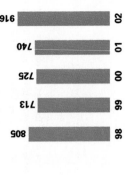

Cash Sources (Uses)

In Millions, Fiscal Year	2002	2001	2000
From continuing operations	$ 916	$ 740	$ 725
From discontinued operations	(3)	(3)	(3)
Fixed assets, net	(485)	(306)	(262)
Investments in businesses, intangibles and affiliates, net	(3,688)	(96)	(295)
Change in marketable securities	24	(28)	(6)
Proceeds from disposition of businesses	939	–	–
Other investments, net	(61)	(30)	(1)
Increase in outstanding debt, net	5,746	183	956
Proceeds from minority investors	150	–	–
Common stock issued	139	107	76
Treasury stock purchases	(2,436)	(226)	(820)
Dividends paid	(358)	(312)	(329)
Other	28	10	(20)
Increase in Cash and Cash Equivalents	$ 911	$ 39	$ 21

In fiscal 2002, capital investment for fixed assets grew to $540 million, including seven months of Pillsbury fixed asset spending. We expect capital expenditures to increase in fiscal 2003, to approximately $750 million. Regular capital investment will grow as we support a full year of Pillsbury-related fixed asset spending. We also plan to add capacity for fast-growing businesses such as *Yoplait* yogurt. In addition, we have two acquisition-related projects requiring capital expenditures in 2003. We have construction costs to expand our headquarters so that we can consolidate at one location. We also are integrating Pillsbury into General Mills' information systems.

In order to obtain regulatory clearance for the acquisition of Pillsbury, we arranged to divest certain businesses as described more fully in Note Two on page 26 of this report. In addition, Nestlé USA exercised its right, triggered by the change of ownership of Pillsbury, to purchase our stake in a joint venture. Net cash proceeds from these dispositions of $939 million were used to reduce our debt level.

Dividends in 2002 totaled $1.10 per share, a payout of 65 percent of diluted earnings per share before unusual items. We intend to maintain the prevailing $1.10 annual dividend rate per share in fiscal 2003. We currently estimate that average diluted shares outstanding in fiscal 2003 will increase to 382 million.

Cash used for share repurchases in 2002 totaled $2.44 billion. Of that, $2.32 billion was used to repurchase 55 million shares from Diageo at a price of $42.14 per share. The company repurchased an additional 3.2 million shares on the open market at an average price of approximately $28, net of put and call option premiums. We do not expect to repurchase any significant number of shares in fiscal 2003.

FINANCIAL CONDITION

Our balance sheet changed significantly with the acquisition of Pillsbury. As shown in the table below, our adjusted debt plus minority interest grew to over $9 billion, and our stockholders' equity grew to $3.6 billion due to the net 79 million shares issued to Diageo. The market value of General Mills stockholders' equity increased as well, due to price appreciation and the increase in shares outstanding. As of May 26, 2002, our equity market capitalization was $16.6 billion, based on a price of $45.10 per share with 367 million basic shares outstanding. Our total market capitalization, including debt, minority interest and equity capital, is shown in the chart at right.

TOTAL CAPITALIZATION
(at fiscal year-end, dollars in billions)

Fiscal Year	Adjusted debt plus minority interest	Market value of equity	Total
02	9.1	16.6	25.7
01	3.6	12.0	15.6
00	3.5	11.7	15.2

● Market value of equity
● Adjusted debt plus minority interest

Capital Structure

In Millions	May 26, 2002	May 27, 2001
Notes payable	$ 3,600	$ 858
Current portion of long-term debt	248	349
Long-term debt	5,591	2,221
Deferred income taxes – tax leases	71	74
Total debt	9,510	3,502
Debt adjustments:		
Leases – debt equivalent	423	266
Certain cash and cash equivalents	(894)	–
Marketable investments, at cost	(135)	(143)
Adjusted debt	8,904	3,625
Minority interest	153	–
Adjusted debt plus minority interest	9,057	3,625
Stockholders' equity	3,576	52
Total Capital	$12,633	$3,677

On Oct. 31, 2001, when we acquired Pillsbury, the associated debt we took on was primarily short term. In February 2002, we issued $3.5 billion in five- and 10-year bonds, replacing a portion of that short-term debt. As discussed earlier, we have entered into interest rate swap contracts to lock in our interest rate on our floating-rate debt. Combined, nearly 90 percent of our debt is now fixed rate. We consider our leases and deferred income taxes related to tax leases as part of our debt structure, and both are fixed-rate obligations. The next table, when reviewed in conjunction with the capital structure table, shows the composition of our debt structure including the impact of using derivative instruments.

Debt Structure

In Millions	May 26, 2002		May 27, 2001	
Floating-rate	$ 602	7%	$1,974	55%
Fixed-rate	7,961	88%	1,311	36%
Leases – debt equivalent	423	4%	266	7%
Deferred income taxes – tax leases	71	1%	74	2%
Adjusted Debt plus Minority Interest	$9,057	100%	$3,625	100%

At the end of fiscal 2002, approximately half of our debt was long term, 41 percent was short term (excluding the impact of reclassification from our long-term credit facility), and the balance was leases and tax-benefit leases. We plan to refinance the majority of our short-term debt with long-term debt in fiscal 2003.

Commercial paper is a continuing source of short-term financing. We can issue commercial paper in the United States and Canada, as well as in Europe through a program established in fiscal 1999. The table below details the fee-paid credit lines we had available as of May 26, 2002. We have $4 billion in committed credit lines available to us, $2.1 billion as part of our core facilities and $1.9 billion as part of a bridge facility we set up at the time of the acquisition. Additionally, we have $45 million in uncommitted credit lines available.

Committed Credit Facilities

	Amount	Expiration
Core Facilities	$1.05 billion	January 2003
	$1.05 billion	January 2006
Bridge Facility	$1.90 billion	October 2002
Total Credit Lines	$4.00 billion	

We believe that two important measures of financial strength are the ratios of fixed charge coverage and cash flow to debt. With the increased debt associated with our acquisition, our fixed charge coverage in fiscal 2002 was 2.9 times before unusual items, and cash flow to debt was 10 percent. We do not expect to pay down any significant amount of debt in 2003. However, given the cash generating nature of our business, we expect that stronger cash flow over the following years will allow us to reduce our debt and significantly strengthen our ratios. Our goal is to return to a mid single-A rating for our long-term debt, and to the top tier short-term rating, where we were prior to our announcement of the Pillsbury acquisition.

Currently, Standard and Poor's Corporation has ratings of "BBB+" on our publicly held long-term debt and "A-2" on our commercial paper. Moody's Investors Services, Inc. has ratings of "Baa1" for our long-term debt and "P-2" for our commercial paper. Fitch Ratings, Inc. rates our long-term debt "BBB+" and our commercial paper "F-2." Dominion Bond Rating Service in Canada currently rates General Mills as "A-low."

In fiscal 2002, we established a minority interest structure, which provides some attractive opportunities for us to refinance some of our short-term debt. In May, we sold a minority interest in a subsidiary to a third-party investor for $150 million. This subsidiary holds some of our manufacturing assets and trademarks. All assets, liabilities and results of operations of the subsidiary are reflected in our financial statements, and the third party's investment is reflected as minority interest on our balance sheet. We did not have any preferred distribution obligations to the third-party investor in fiscal 2002. We may sell additional minority interests, as this structure may provide favorable financing terms, as they can be viewed more positively by the rating agencies and generate tax efficiencies. Subsequent to fiscal year end, we sold a minority interest in another subsidiary for $150 million. For more information on these minority interests, refer to Note Nine on page 32 of this report.

CONTRACTUAL OBLIGATIONS AND COMMERCIAL COMMITMENTS

Long-term Financial Obligations

In Millions, Payments Due by Period	Total	Less Than 1 Year	1–3 Years	4–5 Years	After 5 Years
Long-term debt, including current maturities	$5,839	$248	$329	$1,590	$3,672
Operating leases	287	59	79	53	96
Total	$6,126	$307	$408	$1,643	$3,768

Our other commercial commitments as of May 26, 2002, include:

- Guarantees of approximately $212 million of debt and other obligations of unconsolidated affiliates, primarily CPW and SVE.

- Commitments for the purchase of goods, services and equipment to be used in the production of our products for approximately $500 million with terms up to three years. These commitments do not exceed projected requirements over the related terms and are in the normal course of business.

We are contingently liable for the payment of up to $395 million to Diageo, depending on the General Mills stock price during the 20-day period preceding April 30, 2003.

EURO CONVERSION Twelve of the 15 member countries of the European Economic and Monetary Union adopted the euro as a common legal currency in January 2002. General Mills' operating subsidiaries affected have addressed the systems and business issues raised by the euro currency conversion. These issues included, among others (1) the need to adapt computer and other business systems and equipment to accommodate euro-denominated transactions; and (2) the competitive impact of cross-border price transparency. The euro conversion has not had material impact on General Mills' operations or financial results.

MARKET RISK MANAGEMENT

MARKET RISK MANAGEMENT Our Company is exposed to market risk stemming from changes in interest rates, foreign exchange rates and commodity prices. Changes in these factors could cause fluctuations in our earnings and cash flows. In the normal course of business, we actively manage our exposure to these market risks by entering into various hedging transactions, authorized under company policies that place clear controls on these activities. The counterparties in these transactions are highly rated financial institutions. Our hedging transactions include (but are not limited to) the use of a variety of derivative financial instruments. We use derivatives only where there is an underlying exposure; we do not use them for trading or speculative purposes. Additional information regarding our use of financial instruments is included in Note Seven to the consolidated financial statements.

Interest rates – We manage our debt structure and our interest rate risk through the use of fixed- and floating-rate debt, and through the use of derivatives. We use interest rate swaps to hedge our exposure to interest rate changes, and also to lower our financing costs. Generally under these swaps, we agree with a counterparty to exchange the difference between fixed-rate and floating-rate interest amounts based on an agreed notional principal amount. Our primary exposure is to U.S. interest rates.

Foreign currency rates – Foreign currency fluctuations can affect our net investments and earnings denominated in foreign currencies. We primarily use foreign currency forward contracts and option contracts to selectively hedge our cash flow exposure to changes in exchange rates. These contracts function as hedges, since they change in value inversely to the change created in the underlying exposure as foreign exchange rates fluctuate. Our primary exchange rate exposure is with the Canadian dollar, the euro, the Japanese yen and the British pound against the U.S. dollar.

Commodities – Certain ingredients used in our products are exposed to commodity price changes. We manage this risk through an integrated set of financial instruments, including purchase orders, noncancelable contracts, futures contracts, futures options and swaps. Our primary commodity price exposures are to cereal grains, sugar, vegetables, fruits, other agricultural products, vegetable oils, packaging materials and energy costs.

Value at risk – These estimates are intended to measure the maximum potential fair value General Mills could lose in one day from adverse changes in market interest rates, foreign exchange rates or commodity prices, under normal market conditions. A Monte Carlo (VAR) methodology was used to quantify the market risk for our exposures. The models assumed normal market conditions and used a 95 percent confidence level.

The VAR calculation used historical interest rates, foreign exchange rates and commodity prices from the past year to estimate the potential volatility and correlation of

these rates in the future. The market data were drawn from the RiskMetrics™ data set. The calculations are not intended to represent actual losses in fair value that we expect to incur. Further, since the hedging instrument (the derivative) inversely correlates with the underlying exposure, we would expect that any loss or gain in the fair value of our derivatives would be generally offset by an increase or decrease in the fair value of the underlying exposures. The positions included in the calculations were: debt; investments; interest rate swaps; foreign exchange forwards and options; and commodity swaps, futures and options. The calculations do not include the underlying foreign exchange and commodities-related positions that are hedged by these market-risk-sensitive instruments.

The table below presents the estimated maximum potential one-day loss in fair value for our interest rate, foreign currency and commodity market-risk-sensitive instruments outstanding on May 26, 2002. The amounts were calculated using the VAR methodology described earlier.

In Millions	At May 26, 2002	Average during 2002	At May 27, 2001
			Fair Value Impact
Interest rate instruments	$39	$36	$28
Foreign currency instruments	1	1	1
Commodity instruments	1	1	1

FORWARD-LOOKING STATEMENTS Throughout this report to shareholders, we discuss some of our expectations regarding the Company's future performance. All of these forward-looking statements are based on our current expectations and assumptions. Such statements are subject to certain risk and uncertainties that could cause actual results to differ.

In particular, our predictions about future volume and earnings could be affected by difficulties resulting from the Pillsbury acquisition, such as integration problems; failure to achieve synergies; unanticipated liabilities; inexperience in new business lines; and changes in the competitive environment. Our future results also could be affected by a variety of additional factors such as: competitive dynamics in the U.S. ready-to-eat cereal market, including pricing and promotional spending levels by competitors; the impact of competitive products and pricing; product development; actions of competitors other than as described above; acquisitions or disposals of business assets; changes in capital structure; changes in laws and regulations, including changes in accounting standards; customer demand; effectiveness of advertising and marketing spending or programs; consumer perception of health-related issues; and economic conditions including currency rate fluctuations. The Company undertakes no obligation to publicly revise any forward-looking statements to reflect future events or circumstances.

SIX-YEAR FINANCIAL SUMMARY

In Millions, Except per Share Data	May 26, 2002	May 27, 2001	May 28, 2000	May 30, 1999	May 31, 1998	May 25, 1997
FINANCIAL RESULTS						
Earnings per share – basic	$ 1.38	$ 2.34	$ 2.05	$ 1.74	$ 1.33	$ 1.41
Earnings per share – diluted	1.34	2.28	2.00	1.70	1.30	1.38
Dividends per share	1.10	1.10	1.10	1.08	1.06	1.02
Return on average total capital	9.1%	23.6%	24.4%	23.7%	20.0%	23.3%
Net sales	7,949	5,450	5,173	4,834	4,736	4,398
Costs and expenses:						
Cost of sales	4,767	2,841	2,698	2,593	2,538	2,475
Selling, general and administrative	1,909	1,440	1,376	1,223	1,248	1,064
Interest, net	416	206	152	119	117	101
Unusual expenses (income)	190	(35)	–	41	156	48
Earnings before taxes and earnings (losses) of joint ventures	667	998	947	858	677	710
Income taxes	239	350	336	308	246	259
Earnings (losses) of joint ventures	33	17	3	(15)	(9)	(6)
Earnings before accounting changes	461	665	614	535	422	445
Accounting changes	(3)	–	–	–	–	–
Earnings including accounting changes	458	665	614	535	422	445
Earnings before interest, taxes and unusual items	1,273	1,169	1,099	1,018	950	859
Earnings before interest, taxes and unusual items as a % of sales	16.0%	21.4%	21.2%	21.1%	20.1%	19.5%
Earnings before interest, taxes, depreciation, amortization and unusual items	1,569	1,392	1,308	1,212	1,145	1,042
Earnings as a % of sales	5.8%	12.2%	11.9%	11.1%	8.9%	10.1%
Average common shares:						
Basic	331	284	299	306	316	316
Diluted	342	292	307	315	325	323
FINANCIAL POSITION						
Total assets	16,540	5,091	4,574	4,141	3,861	3,902
Land, buildings and equipment, net	2,764	1,501	1,405	1,295	1,186	1,279
Working capital at year-end	(2,310)	(801)	(1,339)	(598)	(408)	(281)
Long-term debt, excluding current portion	5,591	2,221	1,760	1,702	1,640	1,530
Stockholders' equity	3,576	52	(289)	164	190	495
OTHER STATISTICS						
Total dividends	358	312	329	331	336	321
Purchases of land, buildings and equipment	506	307	268	281	184	163
Research and development	131	83	77	70	66	61
Advertising media expenditures	489	358	361	348	366	306
Wages, salaries and employee benefits	1,105	666	644	636	608	564
Number of employees (actual)	29,859	11,001	11,077	10,664	10,228	10,200
Common stock price:						
High for year	52.86	46.35	43.94	42.34	39.13	34.38
Low for year	41.61	31.38	29.38	29.59	30.00	26.00
Year-end	45.10	42.20	41.00	40.19	34.13	32.13

All share and per share data have been adjusted for the two-for-one stock split in November 1999.
All sales-related and selling, general and administrative information prior to fiscal 2002 has been restated for the adoption of EITF Issue 01-09.

REPORT OF MANAGEMENT RESPONSIBILITIES

The management of General Mills, Inc. is responsible for the fairness and accuracy of the consolidated financial statements. The statements have been prepared in accordance with accounting principles that are generally accepted in the United States, using management's best estimates and judgments where appropriate. The financial information throughout this report is consistent with our consolidated financial statements.

Management has established a system of internal controls that provides reasonable assurance that assets are adequately safeguarded and transactions are recorded accurately in all material respects, in accordance with management's authorization. We maintain a strong audit program that independently evaluates the adequacy and effectiveness of internal controls. Our internal controls provide for appropriate separation of duties and responsibilities, and there are documented policies regarding use of Company assets and proper financial reporting. These formally stated and regularly communicated policies demand highly ethical conduct from all employees.

The Audit Committee of the Board of Directors meets regularly with management, internal auditors and independent auditors to review internal control, auditing and financial reporting matters. The independent auditors, internal auditors and employees have full and free access to the Audit Committee at any time.

We believe these consolidated financial statements do not misstate or omit any material facts. Our formal certification to the Securities and Exchange Commission is being made with the filing of our 10-K.

The independent auditors, KPMG LLP, were retained to audit our consolidated financial statements. Their report follows.

S. W. Sanger

S. W. SANGER
Chairman of the Board and
Chief Executive Officer

J. A. Lawrence

J. A. LAWRENCE
Executive Vice President,
Chief Financial Officer

August 8, 2002

INDEPENDENT AUDITORS' REPORT

The Stockholders and the Board of Directors of General Mills, Inc.:

We have audited the accompanying consolidated balance sheets of General Mills, Inc. and subsidiaries as of May 26, 2002 and May 27, 2001, and the related consolidated statements of earnings, stockholders' equity and cash flows for each of the fiscal years in the three-year period ended May 26, 2002. These consolidated financial statements are the responsibility of the Company's management. Our responsibility is to express an opinion on these consolidated financial statements based on our audits.

We conducted our audits in accordance with auditing standards generally accepted in the United States of America. Those standards require that we plan and perform the audit to obtain reasonable assurance about whether the financial statements are free of material misstatement. An audit includes examining, on a test basis, evidence supporting the amounts and disclosures in the financial statements. An audit also includes assessing the accounting principles used and significant estimates made by management, as well as evaluating the overall financial statement presentation. We believe that our audits provide a reasonable basis for our opinion.

In our opinion, the consolidated financial statements referred to above present fairly, in all material respects, the financial position of General Mills, Inc. and subsidiaries as of May 26, 2002 and May 27, 2001, and the results of their operations and their cash flows for each of the fiscal years in the three-year period ended May 26, 2002 in conformity with accounting principles generally accepted in the United States of America.

KPMG LLP

Minneapolis, Minnesota
June 24, 2002

CONSOLIDATED STATEMENTS OF EARNINGS

In Millions, Except per Share Data, Fiscal Year Ended	May 26, 2002	May 27, 2001	May 28, 2000
Net Sales	$7,949	$5,450	$5,173
Costs and Expenses:			
Cost of sales	4,767	2,841	2,698
Selling, general and administrative	1,909	1,440	1,376
Interest, net	416	206	152
Unusual items – expense (income)	190	(35)	–
Total Costs and Expenses	7,282	4,452	4,226
Earnings before Taxes and Earnings from Joint Ventures	667	998	947
Income Taxes	239	350	336
Earnings from Joint Ventures	33	17	3
Earnings before Cumulative Effect of Change in Accounting Principle	461	665	614
Cumulative Effect of Change in Accounting Principle	(3)	–	–
Net Earnings	$ 458	$ 665	$ 614
Earnings per Share – Basic:			
Earnings before cumulative effect of change in accounting principle	$ 1.39	$ 2.34	$ 2.05
Cumulative effect of change in accounting principle	(.01)	–	–
Net Earnings per Share – Basic	$ 1.38	$ 2.34	$ 2.05
Average Number of Common Shares	331	284	299
Earnings per Share – Diluted:			
Earnings before cumulative effect of change in accounting principle	$ 1.35	$ 2.28	$ 2.00
Cumulative effect of change in accounting principle	(.01)	–	–
Net Earnings per Share – Diluted	$ 1.34	$ 2.28	$ 2.00
Average Number of Common Shares – Assuming Dilution	342	292	307

See accompanying notes to consolidated financial statements.

CONSOLIDATED BALANCE SHEETS

In Millions	May 26, 2002	May 27, 2001
ASSETS		
Current Assets:		
Cash and cash equivalents	$ 975	$ 64
Receivables, less allowance for doubtful accounts of $21 in 2002 and $6 in 2001	1,010	664
Inventories	1,055	519
Prepaid expenses and other current assets	156	99
Deferred income taxes	241	62
Total Current Assets	3,437	1,408
Land, Buildings and Equipment at cost, net	2,764	1,501
Goodwill	8,473	804
Other Intangible Assets	90	66
Other Assets	1,776	1,312
Total Assets	$16,540	$ 5,091
LIABILITIES AND EQUITY		
Current Liabilities:		
Accounts payable	$ 1,217	$ 619
Current portion of long-term debt	248	349
Notes payable	3,600	858
Other current liabilities	682	383
Total Current Liabilities	5,747	2,209
Long-term Debt	5,591	2,221
Deferred Income Taxes	336	349
Deferred Income Taxes – Tax Leases	71	74
Other Liabilities	1,066	186
Total Liabilities	12,811	5,039
Minority Interest	153	–
Stockholders' Equity:		
Cumulative preference stock, none issued	–	–
Common stock, 502 shares issued in 2002 and 408 shares issued in 2001	5,733	745
Retained earnings	2,568	2,468
Less common stock in treasury, at cost, 135 shares in 2002 and 123 shares in 2001	(4,292)	(3,014)
Unearned compensation	(57)	(54)
Accumulated other comprehensive income	(376)	(93)
Total Stockholders' Equity	3,576	52
Total Liabilities and Equity	$16,540	$ 5,091

See accompanying notes to consolidated financial statements.

CONSOLIDATED STATEMENTS OF CASH FLOWS

In Millions, Fiscal Year Ended	May 26, 2002	May 27, 2001	May 28, 2000
Cash Flows – Operating Activities:			
Net earnings	$ 458	$ 665	$ 614
Adjustments to reconcile net earnings to cash flow:			
Depreciation and amortization	296	223	209
Deferred income taxes	93	49	44
Changes in current assets and liabilities, excluding effects from businesses acquired	37	(73)	(126)
Tax benefit on exercised options	46	33	34
Cumulative effect of change in accounting principle	3	–	–
Unusual items expense (income)	190	(35)	–
Other, net	(207)	(122)	(50)
Cash provided by continuing operations	916	740	725
Cash used by discontinued operations	(3)	(3)	(3)
Net Cash Provided by Operating Activities	913	737	722
Cash Flows – Investment Activities:			
Purchases of land, buildings and equipment	(506)	(307)	(268)
Investments in businesses, intangibles and affiliates, net of investment returns and dividends	(3,688)	(96)	(295)
Purchases of marketable securities	(46)	(98)	(18)
Proceeds from sale of marketable securities	70	70	12
Proceeds from disposal of land, buildings and equipment	21	1	6
Proceeds from disposition of businesses	939	–	–
Other, net	(61)	(30)	(1)
Net Cash Used by Investment Activities	(3,271)	(460)	(564)
Cash Flows – Financing Activities:			
Change in notes payable	2,688	295	566
Issuance of long-term debt	3,485	296	501
Payment of long-term debt	(427)	(408)	(111)
Proceeds from minority investors	150	–	–
Common stock issued	139	107	76
Purchases of common stock for treasury	(2,436)	(226)	(820)
Dividends paid	(358)	(312)	(329)
Other, net	28	10	(20)
Net Cash Provided (Used) by Financing Activities	3,269	(238)	(137)
Increase in Cash and Cash Equivalents	911	39	21
Cash and Cash Equivalents – Beginning of Year	64	25	4
Cash and Cash Equivalents – End of Year	$ 975	$ 64	$ 25
Cash Flows from Changes in Current Assets and Liabilities, Excluding Effects from Businesses Acquired:			
Receivables	$ 265	$ (94)	$ 11
Inventories	(12)	(9)	(51)
Prepaid expenses and other current assets	12	(17)	(5)
Accounts payable	(90)	7	(50)
Other current liabilities	(138)	40	(31)
Changes in Current Assets and Liabilities	$ 37	$ (73)	$(126)

See accompanying notes to consolidated financial statements.

CONSOLIDATED STATEMENTS OF STOCKHOLDERS' EQUITY

$.10 Par Value Common Stock
(One Billion Shares Authorized)

In Millions, Except per Share Data	Issued Shares	Amount	Treasury Shares	Amount	Retained Earnings	Unearned Compensation	Accumulated Other Comprehensive Income	Total
BALANCE AT MAY 30, 1999	408	$ 658	(104)	$(2,195)	$1,828	$(69)	$ (57)	$ 165
Comprehensive Income:								
Net earnings					614			614
Other comprehensive income, net of tax:								
Unrealized losses on securities							(8)	(8)
Foreign currency translation							(22)	(22)
Minimum pension liability adjustment							1	1
Other comprehensive income							(29)	(29)
Total comprehensive income								585
Cash dividends declared ($1.10 per share), net of income taxes of $1					(328)			(328)
Stock compensation plans (includes income tax benefits of $39)		25	4	101				126
Shares purchased			(23)	(848)				(848)
Put and call option premiums/settlements, net		(2)	–	7				5
Unearned compensation related to restricted stock awards						(13)		(13)
Earned compensation and other						19		19
BALANCE AT MAY 28, 2000	408	$ 681	(123)	$(2,935)	$2,114	$(63)	$(86)	$(289)
Comprehensive Income:								
Net earnings					665			665
Other comprehensive income, net of tax:								
Unrealized losses on securities							5	5
Foreign currency translation							(7)	(7)
Minimum pension liability adjustment							(5)	(5)
Other comprehensive income							(7)	(7)
Total comprehensive income								658
Cash dividends declared ($1.10 per share), net of income taxes of $1					(311)			(311)
Stock compensation plans (includes income tax benefits of $38)		34	5	124				158
Shares purchased			(5)	(198)				(198)
Put and call option premiums/settlements, net		30	–	(5)				25
Unearned compensation related to restricted stock awards						(13)		(13)
Earned compensation and other						22		22
BALANCE AT MAY 27, 2001	408	$ 745	(123)	$(3,014)	$2,468	$(54)	$(93)	$ 52
Comprehensive Income:								
Net earnings					458			458
Other comprehensive income, net of tax:								
Cumulative effect of adopting SFAS No. 133							(158)	(158)
Unrealized losses on hedge derivatives							(114)	(114)
Unrealized losses on securities							(11)	(11)
Foreign currency translation							(4)	(4)
Minimum pension liability adjustment							4	4
Other comprehensive income							(283)	(283)
Total comprehensive income								175
Cash dividends declared ($1.10 per share), net of income taxes of $1					(358)			(358)
Shares issued for acquisition	94	4,902	40	992				5,894
Shares repurchased from Diageo			(55)	(2,318)				(2,318)
Stock compensation plans (includes income tax benefits of $53)		46	6	176				222
Shares purchased			(3)	(119)				(119)
Put and call option premiums/settlements, net		40	–	(9)				31
Unearned compensation related to restricted stock awards						(29)		(29)
Earned compensation and other						26		26
BALANCE AT MAY 26, 2002	502	$5,733	(135)	$(4,292)	$2,568	$(57)	$(376)	$3,576

See accompanying notes to consolidated financial statements.

NOTES TO CONSOLIDATED FINANCIAL STATEMENTS

1. SUMMARY OF SIGNIFICANT ACCOUNTING POLICIES

Preparing our consolidated financial statements in conformity with generally accepted U.S. accounting principles requires us to make estimates and assumptions that affect reported amounts of assets, liabilities, disclosures of contingent assets and liabilities at the date of the financial statements, and the reported amounts of revenues and expenses during the reporting period. Actual results could differ from our estimates. Certain prior years' amounts have been reclassified to conform with the current year presentation.

(A) PRINCIPLES OF CONSOLIDATION – Our consolidated financial statements include parent company operations and majority-owned subsidiaries as well as General Mills' investment in and share of net earnings or losses of 20- to 50-percent-owned companies, which are recorded on an equity basis.

Our fiscal year ends on the last Sunday in May. Years 2002, 2001 and 2000 each consisted of 52 weeks. Our wholly owned international operations, with the exception of Canada and our export operations, are reported for the 12 calendar months ending April 30. The results of the acquired Pillsbury operations are reflected in our financial results from Nov. 1, 2001.

(B) LAND, BUILDINGS, EQUIPMENT AND DEPRECIATION – Buildings and equipment are depreciated over estimated useful lives, primarily using the straight-line method. Buildings are usually depreciated over 40 to 50 years, and equipment is depreciated over three to 15 years. Depreciation charges for 2002, 2001 and 2000 were $283 million, $194 million, and $183 million, respectively. Accelerated depreciation methods generally are used for income tax purposes. When an item is sold or retired, the accounts are relieved of its cost and related accumulated depreciation; the resulting gains and losses, if any, are recognized.

(C) INVENTORIES – Inventories are valued at the lower of cost or market. We generally use the LIFO method of valuing inventory because we believe that it is a better match with current revenues. However, FIFO is used for most foreign operations, where LIFO is not recognized for income tax purposes and the operations often lack the staff to handle LIFO complexities accurately.

(D) INTANGIBLE ASSETS – Goodwill represents the difference between the purchase prices of acquired companies and the related fair values of net assets acquired and accounted for by the purchase method of accounting. On May 28, 2001, we adopted Statement of Financial Accounting Standards (SFAS) No. 142, "Goodwill and Intangible Assets." This Statement eliminates the amortization of goodwill and instead requires that goodwill be tested annually for impairment. See Note One (N) for the effects of this adoption. The costs of patents, copyrights and other amortizable intangible assets are amortized evenly over their estimated useful lives.

(E) RECOVERABILITY OF LONG-LIVED ASSETS – We review long-lived assets, including identifiable intangibles and goodwill, for impairment when events or changes in circumstances indicate that the carrying amount of an asset may not be recoverable. An asset is deemed impaired and written down to its fair value if estimated future cash flows are less than its carrying amount.

(F) FOREIGN CURRENCY TRANSLATION – For most of our foreign operations, local currencies are considered the functional currency. Assets and liabilities are translated using exchange rates in effect at the balance sheet date. Results of operations are translated using the average exchange rates prevailing throughout the period. Translation effects are classified within Accumulated Other Comprehensive Income in Stockholders' Equity.

(G) FINANCIAL INSTRUMENTS – See Note One (N) for a description of our adoption of SFAS No. 133, "Accounting for Derivative Instruments and Hedging Activities." See Note Seven for a description of our accounting policies related to financial instruments.

(H) REVENUE RECOGNITION – We recognize sales upon shipment to our customers.

(I) RESEARCH AND DEVELOPMENT – All expenditures for research and development are charged against earnings in the year incurred. The charges for 2002, 2001 and 2000 were $131 million, $83 million, and $77 million, respectively.

(J) ADVERTISING COSTS – Advertising expenses (including production and communication costs) for 2002, 2001 and 2000 were $489 million, $358 million and $361 million, respectively. Prepaid advertising costs (including syndication properties) of $36 million and $34 million were reported as assets at May 26, 2002, and May 27, 2001, respectively. We expense the production costs of advertising the first time that the advertising takes place.

(K) STOCK-BASED COMPENSATION – We use the intrinsic value method for measuring the cost of compensation paid in Company common stock. This method defines our cost as the excess of the stock's market value at the time of the grant over the amount that the employee is required to pay. Our stock option plans require that the employee's payment (i.e., exercise price) be the market value as of the grant date.

(L) EARNINGS PER SHARE – Basic Earnings per Share (EPS) is computed by dividing net earnings by the weighted average number of common shares outstanding. Diluted EPS includes the effect of all dilutive potential common shares (primarily related to outstanding in-the-money stock options).

(M) CASH AND CASH EQUIVALENTS – We consider all investments purchased with an original maturity of three months or less to be cash equivalents. Cash and cash equivalents totaling $77 million are designated as collateral for certain derivative liabilities.

(N) ACCOUNTING RULES ADOPTED – On the first day of fiscal 2002, we adopted three new accounting rules. SFAS No. 133, "Accounting for Derivative Instruments and Hedging Activities," requires all derivatives to be recorded at fair value on the balance sheet and establishes new accounting rules for hedging. We recorded the cumulative effect of adopting this accounting change, as follows:

In Millions, Except per Share Data	Included in Earnings	Included in Accumulated Other Comprehensive Income
Pretax	$ (5)	$(251)
Income tax effects	2	93
Total	$ (3)	$(158)
Per Diluted Share Net Earnings Effect	$(.01)	

This cumulative effect was primarily associated with the impact of lower interest rates on the fair-value calculation for delayed-starting interest rate swaps we entered into in anticipation of our Pillsbury acquisition and other financing requirements. Refer to Note Seven and Note Ten for more information.

We also adopted SFAS No. 141, "Business Combinations," which requires use of the purchase method of accounting for all business combinations initiated after June 30, 2001.

The third Statement we adopted at the start of the year was SFAS No. 142, "Goodwill and Intangible Assets." This Statement eliminates the amortization of goodwill and instead requires that goodwill be tested annually for impairment. Goodwill amortization expense in fiscal 2001 totaled $23 million pretax, $22 million after tax. Transitional impairment tests of our goodwill did not require adjustment to any of our goodwill carrying values.

The following table adjusts earnings and earnings per share for the adoption of SFAS No. 142.

In Millions, Except per Share Data, Fiscal Year Ended	May 26, 2002	May 27, 2001	May 28, 2000
Reported Net Earnings:	$ 458	$ 665	$ 614
Addback goodwill amortization	–	22	21
Adjusted Net Earnings	$ 458	$ 687	$ 635
Basic Earnings per Share:			
Reported EPS – basic	$1.38	$2.34	$2.05
Addback goodwill amortization	–	.08	.07
Adjusted Basic EPS	$1.38	$2.42	$2.12
Diluted Earnings per Share:			
Reported EPS – diluted	$1.34	$2.28	$2.00
Addback goodwill amortization	–	.07	.07
Adjusted Diluted EPS	$1.34	$2.35	$2.07

The Financial Accounting Standard Board's (FASB's) Emerging Issues Task Force (EITF) Issue 01-09, "Accounting for Consideration Given by a Vendor to a Customer or a Reseller of the Vendor's Products," requires recording certain coupon and trade promotion expenses as reductions of revenues and was effective for us in our fourth quarter 2002. Since adopting this requirement resulted only in the reclassification of certain expenses from selling, general and administrative expense to a reduction of net sales, it did not affect our financial position or net earnings. The impact was a reduction of net sales, and a corresponding reduction in selling, general and administrative expense, of $2,246 million, $1,628 million and $1,527 million in 2002, 2001 and 2000, respectively.

(O) NEW ACCOUNTING RULES – In August 2001, the FASB issued SFAS No. 144, "Accounting for the Impairment or Disposal of Long-Lived Assets." SFAS No. 144 requires that a single accounting model be used for long-lived assets to be disposed of by sale, and broadens the presentation of discontinued operations to include more disposal transactions. SFAS No. 144 is effective for us with the beginning of fiscal 2003. We do not expect the adoption of SFAS No. 144 to have a material impact on the Company's financial statements.

2. ACQUISITIONS

On Oct. 31, 2001, we acquired the worldwide Pillsbury operations from Diageo plc (Diageo). Pillsbury, based in Minneapolis, Minn., has built a portfolio of leading food brands, such as *Pillsbury* refrigerated dough, *Green Giant, Old El Paso, Progresso* and *Totino's.* Pillsbury had sales of $6.1 billion (before EITF Issue 01-09 reclassification) in its fiscal year ended June 30, 2001, including businesses subsequently divested. We believe the addition of Pillsbury's businesses will enhance our future growth and generate significant cost synergies.

The transaction was accounted for as a purchase. Under terms of the agreement between General Mills and Diageo, we acquired Pillsbury in a stock and cash transaction. Consideration to Diageo included 134 million General Mills common shares. Under a stockholders' agreement, Diageo had a put option to sell directly to us 55 million shares of General Mills common stock at a price of $42.14 per share, which Diageo exercised on Nov. 1, 2001. Therefore, those 55 million shares were valued at a total of $2,318 million. The 79 million shares of General Mills common stock retained by Diageo were valued at $3,576 million based on the three-day average trading price prior to the closing of $45.27 per share. Therefore, the total stock consideration was $5,894 million. The cash paid to Diageo and assumed debt of Pillsbury totaled $3,830 million. As a result, the total acquisition consideration (exclusive of direct acquisition costs) was approximately $9,724 million.

Under terms of the agreement, Diageo holds contingent value rights that may require payment to Diageo on April 30, 2003, of up to $395 million, depending on the General Mills stock price and the number of General Mills shares that Diageo continues to hold on that date. If the General Mills stock price averages less than $49 per share for the 20 trading days prior to that date, Diageo will receive an amount per share equal to the difference between $49 and the General Mills stock trading price, up to a maximum of $5 per share.

The stockholders' agreement between General Mills and Diageo includes a standstill provision, under which Diageo is precluded from buying additional shares in General Mills for a 20-year period following the close of the transaction, or for three years following the date on which Diageo owns less than 5 percent of General Mills' outstanding shares, whichever is earlier. The agreement also generally requires pass-through voting by Diageo, so its shares will be voted in the same proportion as the other General Mills shares are voted. So long as Diageo owns at least 50 percent of the 134 million shares it originally received in this transaction, Diageo may designate two individuals to the General Mills Board of Directors.

The excess of the purchase price over the estimated fair value of the net assets purchased was approximately $8 billion. The allocation of the purchase price is based on preliminary estimates, subject to revisions when appraisals and integration plans have been finalized. Revisions to the allocation, which may be significant, will be reported as changes to various assets and liabilities, including goodwill, other intangible assets, and deferred income taxes. As of May 26, 2002, the goodwill balance includes all of the excess purchase price of the Pillsbury acquisition, as the valuation of specific intangible assets has not yet been completed. We expect the valuation to result in a significant value for nonamortizable brands. We do not anticipate significant amounts to be allocated to amortizable intangible assets and, therefore, the amount of intangibles amortization is not expected to be material to the results of operations in future periods.

In order to obtain regulatory clearance for the acquisition of Pillsbury, we arranged to divest certain businesses. On Nov. 13, 2001, International Multifoods Corporation (IMC) purchased the Pillsbury dessert and specialty products businesses as well as certain General Mills brands and the General Mills Toledo production facilities for $316 million. After-tax cash proceeds from this transaction were used to reduce General Mills debt. Under the agreement with IMC, General Mills expects to spend approximately $70 million for the purchase and installation of certain production assets at the Toledo plant, of which $47 million has been expended through May 26, 2002.

As part of the transaction, IMC received an exclusive royalty-free license to use the *Doughboy* trademark and *Pillsbury* brand in the desserts and baking mix categories.

The licenses are renewable without cost in 20-year increments at IMC's discretion. Since the sale of the assets to IMC was integral to the Pillsbury acquisition, and because the assets sold were adjusted to fair market value as part of the purchase of Pillsbury, there was no gain or loss recorded on the sale in the Company's consolidated statement of earnings.

Pillsbury had a 50 percent equity interest in Ice Cream Partners USA LLC (ICP), a joint venture Pillsbury formed with Nestlé USA during fiscal 2000 for the manufacture, marketing and distribution of *Häagen-Dazs* and Nestlé ice cream products in the United States. On Dec. 26, 2001, Nestlé USA exercised its right, triggered by the change of ownership of Pillsbury, to buy the 50 percent stake of ICP that it did not already own. Nestlé paid us $641 million for our 50 percent of the joint venture and a long-term, paid-in-full license for the *Häagen-Dazs* brand in the United States. Net proceeds from this transaction also were used to reduce our debt level.

We are reconfiguring our cereal production as a result of selling our Toledo, Ohio, plant to IMC. We also incurred a number of one-time costs associated with the acquisition of Pillsbury, and the associated divestiture of certain businesses and assets to IMC. (See Note Three.)

In February 2002, we decided to close two Pillsbury facilities in order to utilize the operating capacity of the newly combined companies more fully. We closed the Geneva, Ill., plant, which produced frozen breakfast products; and the Anthony, Texas, production facility, which produced various Mexican food products. Our exit liabilities connected to these plant closures amount to $22 million and have been included in the purchase price allocation of Pillsbury. Approximately 370 employees were affected by these two plant closures.

We continue to evaluate plans to consolidate manufacturing, warehouse and distribution activities into fewer locations. The closure of additional Pillsbury facilities could result in additional severance and other exit liabilities, which would increase the excess purchase price. These amounts will be recorded on our consolidated balance sheet as adjustments to the excess purchase price when plans have been finalized and announced. The integration of Pillsbury into General Mills' operations also may result in the restructuring of certain General Mills activities. These actions could result in additional unusual charges, which will be recorded as expense in our consolidated statements of earnings in the period during which plans are finalized.

Actual results of acquired business operations are included in the consolidated statement of earnings for the period from Nov. 1, 2001 through May 26, 2002. The following unaudited pro forma information presents a summary of our consolidated results of operations and the acquired Pillsbury operations as if the acquisition had occurred on May 29, 2000.

In Millions, Except per Share Data, Fiscal Year Ended	May 26, 2002	May 27, 2001
Net sales	$9,936	$10,089
Earnings before cumulative effect of change in accounting principle	495	849
Net earnings	492	849
Earnings per Share – Basic		
EPS before cumulative effect of change in accounting principle	1.36	2.34
Net EPS – Basic	1.35	2.34
Earnings per Share – Diluted		
EPS before cumulative effect of change in accounting principle	1.32	2.29
Net EPS – Diluted	1.31	2.29

These unaudited pro forma results have been prepared for comparative purposes only and include certain adjustments, such as increased interest expense on acquisition debt. They do not reflect the effect of synergies that would have been expected to result from the integration of the Pillsbury businesses. The pro forma information does not purport to be indicative of the results of operations that actually would have resulted had the combination occurred on May 29, 2000, or of future results of the consolidated entities.

On Jan. 13, 2000, we acquired Small Planet Foods of Sedro-Woolley, Wash. Small Planet Foods is a leading producer of branded organic food products marketed under the *Cascadian Farm* and *Muir Glen* trademarks. On Aug. 12, 1999, we acquired Gardetto's Bakery, Inc. of Milwaukee, Wis. *Gardetto's* is a leading national brand of baked snack mixes and flavored pretzels. On June 30, 1999, we acquired certain grain elevators and related assets from Koch Agriculture Company. The aggregate purchase price of these acquisitions, which were accounted for using the purchase method, was approximately $227 million, and associated goodwill was $153 million. The results of the acquired businesses have been included in the consolidated financial statements since their respective acquisition dates. Our fiscal 2000 financial results would not have been materially different if we had made these acquisitions at the beginning of the fiscal year.

Through fiscal 2001, the goodwill associated with the acquisitions made in fiscal 2000 was amortized over 40 years on a straight-line basis. As described in Note One (N), we adopted SFAS No. 142, which eliminated goodwill amortization at the beginning of fiscal 2002.

3. UNUSUAL ITEMS

In fiscal 2002, we recorded unusual items totaling $190 million pretax expense, $120 million after tax ($.35 per diluted share), consisting of $91 million pretax of Pillsbury transaction and integration costs; $87 million pretax of cereal reconfiguration charges; a $30 million pretax charge for a special contribution to the General Mills Foundation to increase its post-acquisition net assets to a level consistent with the guidelines of the Foundation; $9 million pretax of

two flour mill and *Squeezit* beverage restructuring/closing charges; and $3 million, net of insurance recovery, associated with a flash flood at our Cincinnati, Ohio, cereal plant. These expenses were partially offset by insurance settlement proceeds of $30 million pretax stemming from a 1994 oats handling incident.

In 2001, we reached a partial settlement with a group of global insurance companies that participated in the reinsurance of a property policy covering the oats handling incident. We recorded this partial settlement, totaling $55 million pretax income net of associated costs, in the fourth quarter of 2001. We also expensed certain transaction costs associated with our pending acquisition of Pillsbury totaling $8 million pretax. Finally, in the fourth quarter of 2001, we made the decision to exit the *Squeezit* beverage business. The charge associated with this action, primarily noncash write-downs associated with asset disposals, totaled $12 million pretax. At May 26, 2002, there was no remaining reserve balance related to the exit of the *Squeezit* beverage business. The net of these unusual items totaled income of $35 million pretax, $22 million after tax ($.08 per diluted share).

Analysis of our restructuring and integration reserve activity is as follows:

In Millions	Severance	Supply Chain Asset Write-off	Other	Total	Transaction/ Integration	Other	Total
Reserve balance at May 30, 1999	$ 3	$ 14	$ 14	$ 31	$ –	$ 13	$ 44
1998 Amounts utilized	–	–	(9)	(9)	–	(2)	(11)
1999 Amounts utilized	(2)	(14)	–	(16)	–	(7)	(23)
Reserve balance at May 28, 2000	1	–	5	6	–	4	10
2001 Charges	–	–	–	–	–	12	12
1998 Amounts utilized	–	–	–	–	–	(2)	(2)
1999 Amounts utilized	–	–	(2)	(2)	–	(1)	(3)
2001 Amounts utilized	–	–	–	–	–	(8)	(8)
Reserve balance at May 27, 2001	1	–	3	4	–	5	9
2002 Charges	26	58	12	96	90	4	190
1998 Amounts utilized	–	(2)	(1)	(3)	–	–	(3)
1999 Amounts utilized	–	–	(1)	(1)	–	–	(1)
2001 Amounts utilized	–	–	–	–	–	(4)	(4)
2002 Amounts utilized	(3)	(6)	(12)	(20)	(51)	(4)	(75)
Reserve balance at May 26, 2002	$ 24	$ 51	$ 1	$ 76	$ 39	$ 1	$ 116

4. INVESTMENTS IN JOINT VENTURES

We have a 50 percent equity interest in Cereal Partners Worldwide (CPW), a joint venture with Nestlé that manufactures and markets ready-to-eat cereals outside the United States and Canada. We have a 40.5 percent equity interest in Snack Ventures Europe (SVE), our joint venture with PepsiCo that manufactures and markets snack foods in continental Europe. We have a 50 percent equity interest in 8th Continent, LLC, a domestic joint venture formed in 2001 with DuPont to develop and market soy foods and beverages. As a result of the Pillsbury acquisition, we have 50 percent interests in the following joint ventures for the manufacture, distribution and marketing of *Häagen-Dazs* frozen ice cream products and novelties: Häagen-Dazs Japan K.K., Häagen-Dazs Korea Company Limited, Häagen-Dazs Taiwan Limited, Häagen-Dazs Distributors (Thailand) Company Limited, and Häagen-Dazs Marketing & Distribution (Philippines) Inc. We also have a 50 percent interest in Seretram, a joint venture with Co-op de Pau for the production of *Green Giant* canned corn in France.

The joint ventures are reflected in our financial statements on an equity accounting basis. We record our share of the earnings or losses of these joint ventures. (The table that follows reflects the joint ventures on a 100 percent basis.) We also receive royalty income from certain of these joint ventures, incur various expenses (primarily research and development) and record the tax impact of certain of the joint venture operations that are structured as partnerships.

Our cumulative investment in these joint ventures (including our share of earnings and losses) was $326 million, $218 million and $198 million at the end of 2002, 2001 and 2000, respectively. We made aggregate investments in the joint ventures of $38 million, $25 million and $29 million (net of a $6 million loan repayment) in 2002, 2001 and 2000, respectively. We received aggregate dividends from the joint ventures of $17 million, $3 million and $5 million in 2002, 2001 and 2000, respectively.

Summary combined financial information for the joint ventures on a 100 percent basis follows. Since we record our share of CPW results on a two-month lag, CPW information is included as of and for the 12 months ended March 31. The Häagen-Dazs and Seretram joint ventures are reported as of and for the six months ended April 30, 2002. The SVE and 8th Continent information is consistent with our May year-end.

Combined Financial Information – Joint Ventures – 100% Basis

In Millions, Fiscal Year	2002	2001	2000
Net Sales	$1,693	$1,468	$1,429
Gross Profit	755	664	619
Earnings (losses) before Taxes	94	61	(4)
Earnings (losses) after Taxes	78	48	(22)

In Millions	May 26, 2002	May 27, 2001
Current Assets	$587	$476
Noncurrent Assets	712	614
Current Liabilities	630	585
Noncurrent Liabilities	9	2

Our proportionate share of joint venture sales was $777 million, $666 million and $652 million for 2002, 2001 and 2000, respectively.

5. BALANCE SHEET INFORMATION

The components of certain balance sheet accounts are as follows:

In Millions	May 26, 2002	May 27, 2001
Land, Buildings and Equipment:		
Land	$54	$25
Buildings	1,151	636
Equipment	2,916	2,226
Construction in progress	497	292
Total land, buildings and equipment	4,618	3,179
Less accumulated depreciation	(1,854)	(1,678)
Net land, buildings and equipment	$2,764	$1,501
Goodwill:		
Total goodwill	$8,559	$892
Less accumulated amortization	(86)	(88)
Goodwill	$8,473	$804
Intangible Assets:		
Intangible assets, primarily capitalized software	$129	$93
Less accumulated amortization	(39)	(27)
Intangible assets	$90	$66
Other Assets:		
Prepaid pension	$1,001	$677
Marketable securities, at market	160	187
Investments in and advances to affiliates	320	214
Miscellaneous	295	234
Total other assets	$1,776	$1,312

The changes in the carrying amount of goodwill for the fiscal year ended May 26, 2002, are as follows:

In Millions	U.S. Retail	Bakeries and Foodservice	International	Corporate	Pillsbury Unallocated Excess Purchase Price	Total
Balance at May 27, 2001	$745	$59	$ —	$ —	$ —	$ 804
Pillsbury transaction	—	—	—	—	7,669	7,669
Balance at May 26, 2002	$745	$59	$ —	$ —	$7,669	$8,473

The Pillsbury acquisition valuation and purchase price allocation has not yet been completed. (See Note Two.) Therefore, all the excess purchase price is currently accounted for in goodwill. When the purchase price allocation is completed, the amount allocated to goodwill will change and the remaining goodwill will be allocated to our operating segments.

Intangible asset amortization expense was $13 million, $6 million and $5 million for fiscal 2002, 2001 and 2000, respectively. Excluding amortization for intangible assets acquired as part of the Pillsbury acquisition, estimated amortization expense for the next five fiscal years (in millions) is as follows: $15 in 2003, $12 in 2004, $11 in 2005, $9 in 2006 and $8 in 2007.

As of May 26, 2002, a comparison of cost and market values of our marketable securities (which are debt and equity securities) was as follows:

In Millions	Cost	Market Value	Gross Gain	Gross Loss
Held to maturity:				
Debt securities	$ 3	$ 3	$ –	$ –
Equity securities	2	2	–	–
Total	$ 5	$ 5	$ –	$ –
Available for sale:				
Debt securities	$130	$155	$ 25	$ –
Equity securities	–	–	–	–
Total	$130	$155	$ 25	$ –

Realized gains from sales of marketable securities were $15 million, $4 million and $3 million in 2002, 2001 and 2000, respectively. The aggregate unrealized gains and losses on available-for-sale securities, net of tax effects, are classified in Accumulated Other Comprehensive Income within Stockholders' Equity.

Scheduled maturities of our marketable securities are as follows:

	Held to maturity		Available for sale	
In Millions	Cost	Market Value	Cost	Market Value
Under one year (current)	$ –	$ –	$ –	$ –
From 1 to 3 years	–	–	45	52
From 4 to 7 years	–	–	5	5
Over 7 years	3	3	80	98
Equity securities	2	2	–	–
Totals	$ 5	$ 5	$130	$155

6. INVENTORIES

The components of inventories are as follows:

In Millions	May 26, 2002	May 27, 2001
Raw materials, work in process and supplies	$ 234	$129
Finished goods	753	326
Grain	99	94
Reserve for LIFO valuation method	(31)	(30)
Total inventories	$1,055	$519

At May 26, 2002, and May 27, 2001, respectively, inventories of $720 million and $282 million were valued at LIFO. LIFO accounting had negligible impact on 2002, 2001 and 2000 earnings. Results of operations were not materially affected by a liquidation of LIFO inventory. The difference between replacement cost and the stated LIFO inventory value is not materially different from the reserve for LIFO valuation method.

7. FINANCIAL INSTRUMENTS AND RISK MANAGEMENT

The carrying amounts and fair values of our financial instruments (based on market quotes and interest rates at the balance sheet dates) were as follows:

	May 26, 2002		May 27, 2001	
In Millions	Carrying Amount	Fair Value	Carrying Amount	Fair Value
Assets:				
Cash and cash equivalents	$ 975	$ 975	$ 64	$ 64
Receivables	1,010	1,010	664	664
Marketable securities	160	160	187	187
Liabilities:				
Accounts payable	1,217	1,217	619	619
Debt	9,439	9,507	3,428	3,500
Derivatives relating to:				
Debt	(435)	(435)	–	(250)
Commodities	9	9	–	–
Foreign currencies	(6)	(6)	–	4

The Company is exposed to certain market risks as a part of its ongoing business operations and uses derivative financial and commodity instruments, where appropriate, to manage these risks. Derivatives are financial instruments whose value is derived from one or more underlying financial instruments. Examples of underlying instruments are currencies, equities, commodities and interest rates. In general, instruments used as hedges must be effective at reducing the risk associated with the exposure being hedged, and must be designated as a hedge at the inception of the contract.

With the adoption of SFAS No. 133, "Accounting for Derivative Instruments and Hedging Activities," as of May 28, 2001, we record the fair value of all outstanding derivatives in receivables or other liabilities. Gains and losses related to the ineffective portion of any hedge are recorded in various costs and expenses, depending on the nature of the derivative.

Each derivative transaction we enter into is designated at inception as a hedge of risks associated with specific assets, liabilities or future commitments, and is monitored to determine if it remains an effective hedge. Effectiveness is based on changes in the derivative's market value or cash flows being highly correlated with changes in market value or cash flows of the underlying hedged item. We do not enter into or hold derivatives for trading or speculative purposes.

We use derivative instruments to reduce financial risk in three areas: interest rates, foreign currency and commodities. The notional amounts of derivatives do not represent actual amounts exchanged by the parties and, thus, are not a measure of the Company's exposure through its use of derivatives. We enter into interest rate swap, foreign exchange, and commodity swap agreements with a diversified group of highly rated counterparties. We enter into commodity futures transactions through various regulated exchanges. These transactions may expose the Company to credit risk to the extent that the instruments have a positive fair value, but we have not experienced any material losses nor do we anticipate any losses. The Company does not have a significant concentration of risk with any single party or group of parties in any of its financial instruments.

Qualifying derivatives are reported as part of hedge arrangements as follows:

CASH FLOW HEDGES – Gains and losses on these instruments are recorded in Other Comprehensive Income until the underlying transaction is recorded in earnings. When the hedged item is realized, gains or losses are reclassified from Accumulated Other Comprehensive Income to the Consolidated Statements of Earnings on the same line item as the underlying transaction risk.

FOREIGN EXCHANGE TRANSACTION RISK – The Company is exposed to fluctuations in foreign currency cash flows related primarily to third-party purchases, intercompany product shipments, and intercompany loans. Forward contracts of generally less than 12 months duration are used to hedge some of these risks. Effectiveness is assessed based on changes in forward rates.

INTEREST RATE RISK – The Company is exposed to interest rate volatility with regard to existing variable-rate debt and planned future issuances of fixed-rate debt. The Company uses interest rate swaps, including forward-starting swaps, to reduce interest rate volatility, and to achieve a desired proportion of variable vs. fixed-rate debt, based on current and projected market conditions.

Variable-to-fixed interest rate swaps are accounted for as cash flow hedges, with effectiveness assessed based on either the hypothetical derivative method or changes in the present value of interest payments on the underlying debt.

PRICE RISK – The Company is exposed to price fluctuations primarily as a result of anticipated purchases of ingredient and packaging materials. The Company uses a combination of long cash positions with suppliers, exchange-traded futures and option contracts and over-the-counter hedging mechanisms to reduce price fluctuations in a desired percentage of forecasted purchases over a period of generally less than one year. Commodity contracts are accounted for as cash flow hedges, with effectiveness assessed based on changes in futures prices.

We use a grain merchandising operation to provide us efficient access to and more informed knowledge of various commodities markets. This operation uses futures and options to hedge its net inventory position to minimize market exposure. As of May 26, 2002, our grain merchandising operation had futures and options contracts that essentially hedged its net inventory position. None of the contracts extended beyond May 2003. All futures contracts and futures options are exchange-based instruments with ready liquidity and determinable market values. Neither results of operations nor

the year-end positions from our grain merchandising operation were material to the Company's overall results.

Unrealized losses from cash flow hedges recorded in Accumulated Other Comprehensive Income as of May 26, 2002, totaled $432 million pretax, primarily related to interest rate swaps we entered into in contemplation of future borrowings and other financing requirements (primarily related to the Pillsbury acquisition), which are being reclassified into interest expense over the life of the interest rate hedge. (See Note Eight regarding swaps settled or neutralized.) Other insignificant amounts related to foreign currency and commodity price cash flow hedges will be reclassified, as appropriate, into earnings during the next 12 months.

FAIR VALUE HEDGES – Fair value hedges involve recognized assets, liabilities or firm commitments as the hedged risks.

FOREIGN EXCHANGE TRANSLATION RISK – The Company is exposed to fluctuations in the value of foreign currency investments in subsidiaries and cash flows related primarily to repatriation of these investments. Forward contracts, generally less than 12 months duration, are used to hedge some of these risks. Effectiveness is assessed based on changes in forward rates. Effective gains and losses on these instruments are recorded as a foreign currency translation adjustment in Other Comprehensive Income.

The Company enters into foreign currency forward contracts to reduce volatility in the translation of foreign currency earnings to U.S. dollars. Gains and losses on these instruments are recorded in selling, general and administrative expense, generally reducing the exposure to translation volatility during a full-year period.

Our net balance sheet exposure consists of the net investment in foreign operations, translated using the exchange rates in effect at the balance sheet date. The components of our net balance sheet exposure by geographic region are as follows:

In Millions	May 26, 2002	May 27, 2001
Europe	$363	$181
North/South America	248	37
Asia/Other	101	16
Net Balance Sheet Exposure	$712	$234

INTEREST RATE RISK – The Company currently uses interest rate swaps to reduce funding costs associated with certain debt issues and to achieve a desired proportion of variable vs. fixed-rate debt, based on current and projected market conditions.

Fixed-to-variable interest rate swaps are accounted for as fair value hedges with effectiveness assessed based on changes in the fair value of the underlying debt, using incremental borrowing rates currently available on loans with similar terms and maturities. Effective gains and losses on these derivatives and the underlying hedged items are recorded as interest expense.

The following table indicates the types of swaps used to hedge various assets and liabilities, and their weighted average interest rates. Average variable rates are based on rates as of the end of the reporting period. The swap contracts mature during time periods ranging from 2003 to 2014.

In Millions	May 26, 2002		May 27, 2001	
	Asset	Liability	Asset	Liability
Pay floating swaps – notional amount	–	$2,692	–	$ 340
Average receive rate	–	5.4%	–	7.1%
Average pay rate	–	1.8%	–	4.0%
Pay fixed swaps – notional amount	–	$6,814	–	$5,766
Average receive rate	–	1.8%	–	4.1%
Average pay rate	–	6.4%	–	6.6%

The interest rate differential on interest rate swaps used to hedge existing assets and liabilities is recognized as an adjustment of interest expense or income over the term of the agreement.

8. DEBT

NOTES PAYABLE – The components of notes payable and their respective weighted average interest rates at the end of the periods are as follows:

In Millions	May 26, 2002		May 27, 2001	
	Notes Payable	Weighted Average Interest Rate	Notes Payable	Weighted Average Interest Rate
U.S. commercial paper	$ 3,288	2.1%	$ 733	4.4%
Canadian commercial paper	34	2.3	27	4.6
Euro commercial paper	809	2.2	768	4.9
Financial institutions	519	2.1	330	4.4
Amounts reclassified to long-term debt	(1,050)	–	(1,000)	–
Total Notes Payable	$ 3,600		$ 858	

See Note Seven for a description of related interest-rate derivative instruments.

To ensure availability of funds, we maintain bank credit lines sufficient to cover our outstanding short-term borrowings. As of May 26, 2002, we had $4.0 billion in committed lines and $45 million in uncommitted lines.

We have revolving credit agreements expiring in January 2006 covering the fee-paid credit lines that provide us with the ability to refinance short-term borrowings on a long-term basis; accordingly, a portion of our notes payable has been reclassified to long-term debt. The revolving credit agreements provide for borrowings of up to $1.05 billion.

LONG-TERM DEBT – During fiscal 2002, General Mills filed a Registration Statement with the Securities and Exchange Commission covering the sale of up to $8.0 billion in debt securities. In February 2002, we issued $3.5 billion of notes: $2.0 billion of 6 percent notes due 2012 with an effective interest rate of 7.75 percent; and $1.5 billion of 5⅛ percent notes due 2007 with an effective interest rate of 5.90 percent. Interest is payable semiannually on Feb. 15 and Aug. 15, beginning Aug. 15, 2002. Proceeds from the notes were used to repay short-term debt incurred in connection with the Pillsbury acquisition. Following the February offering, $4.5 billion remains available under the Registration Statement for future use.

In anticipation of the Pillsbury acquisition and other financing needs, we entered into interest rate swap contracts during fiscal 2001 and fiscal 2002 totaling $7.1 billion to attempt to lock in our interest rate on associated debt. In connection with the February notes offering, we closed out $3.5 billion of these swaps. A portion was settled for cash, and the remainder was neutralized with offsetting swaps. These swaps had been designated as cash flow hedges. Therefore, the mark-to-market value for these swaps has been recorded in Other Comprehensive Income. The amount currently recorded in Accumulated Other Comprehensive Income ($242 million pretax) will be reclassified to interest expense over the lives of the swap contracts (primarily five to 10 years).

In Millions	May 26, 2002	May 27, 2001
6% notes due 2012	$2,000	$ –
5⅛% notes due 2007	1,500	–
Medium-term notes, 4.8% to 9.1%, due 2003 to 2078	922	1,274
7.0% notes due Sept. 15, 2004	150	157
Zero coupon notes, yield 11.1%, $261 due Aug. 15, 2013	78	70
Zero coupon notes, yield 11.7%, $54 due Aug. 15, 2004	42	38
8.2% ESOP loan guaranty, due through June 30, 2007	21	30
Notes payable, reclassified	1,050	1,000
Other	76	1
	5,839	2,570
Less amounts due within one year	(248)	(349)
Total Long-term Debt	$5,591	$2,221

See Note Seven for a description of related interest-rate derivative instruments.

In 2001, we issued $284 million of debt under our medium-term note program with maturities up to two years and interest rates varying from 7.0 to 7.4 percent.

The Company has guaranteed the debt of the Employee Stock Ownership Plan; therefore, the loan is reflected on our consolidated balance sheets as long-term debt with a related offset in Unearned Compensation in Stockholders' Equity.

The sinking fund and principal payments due on long-term debt are (in millions) $248, $104, $225, $54 and $1,536 in 2003, 2004, 2005, 2006 and 2007, respectively. The 2005 and 2006 amounts are exclusive of $12 million and $5 million, respectively, of interest yet to be accreted on zero coupon notes. The notes payable that are reclassified under our revolving credit agreement are not included in these principal payments.

Our marketable securities (see Note Five) include zero coupon U.S. Treasury and other top-rated securities. These investments are intended to provide funds for the payment of principal and interest for the zero coupon notes due Aug. 15, 2004, and Aug. 15, 2013.

9. MINORITY INTEREST

In April 2002, the Company and certain of its wholly owned subsidiaries contributed assets with an aggregate fair market value of approximately $4 billion to another subsidiary (GMC), a limited liability company. GMC is a separate and distinct legal entity from the Company and its subsidiaries, and has separate assets, liabilities, businesses and operations. The contributed assets consist primarily of manufacturing assets and intellectual property associated with the production and retail sale of Big G ready-to-eat cereals, Progresso soups and Old El Paso products. In exchange for the contribution of these assets, GMC issued the managing membership interest and Class A and Class B preferred membership interests to wholly owned subsidiaries of the Company. The managing member directs the business activities and operations of GMC and has fiduciary responsibilities to GMC and its members. Other than rights to vote on certain matters, holders of the Class A and Class B interests have no right to direct the management of GMC.

In May 2002, GMC sold approximately 30 percent of the Class A interests to an unrelated third-party investor in exchange for $150 million. The Class A interests receive quarterly preferred distributions at a floating rate equal to the three-month LIBOR plus 90 basis points. The GMC limited liability company agreement requires that the rate of the preferred distributions for the Class A interests be reset by agreement between the third-party investors and GMC every five years, beginning in May 2007. If GMC and the investors fail to mutually agree on a new rate of preferred distributions, GMC must

remarket the securities. Upon a failed remarketing, the rate over LIBOR will be increased by 75 basis points (up to a maximum total of 300 basis points following a scheduled reset date). In the event of four consecutive failed remarketings, the third-party investors can force a liquidation and winding up of GMC.

GMC has a scheduled duration of 20 years. However, GMC, through the managing member, may elect to redeem all of the Class A interests held by third-party investors at any time for an amount equal to the investors' capital accounts, plus an optional retirement premium if such retirement occurs prior to June 2007. Under certain circumstances, GMC also may be dissolved and liquidated earlier. Events requiring liquidation include, without limitation, the bankruptcy of GMC or its subsidiaries, failure to deliver the preferred quarterly return, failure to comply with portfolio requirements, breaches of certain covenants, and four consecutive failed attempts to remarket the Class A interests. In the event of a liquidation of GMC, the third-party investors that hold the Class A interests would be entitled to repayment from the proceeds of liquidation prior to the subsidiaries of the Company that are members of GMC. The managing member may avoid liquidation in most circumstances by exercising an option to purchase the preferred interests. An election to redeem the preferred membership interests could impact the Company's liquidity by requiring the Company to refinance the redemption price or liquidate a portion of GMC assets.

Currently, all of the Class B interests are held by a subsidiary of the Company. The Company may offer the Class B interests and the remaining, unsold Class A interests to third-party investors on terms and conditions to be determined.

For financial reporting purposes, the assets, liabilities, results of operations, and cash flows of GMC are included in the Company's consolidated financial statements. The third-party investor's Class A interest in GMC is reflected as a minority interest on the consolidated balance sheet of the Company.

Subsequent to fiscal year end, General Mills Capital, Inc. (GM Capital), a wholly owned subsidiary, sold $150 million of its Series A preferred stock to an unrelated third-party investor. GM Capital regularly enters into transactions with the Company to purchase receivables. These receivables are included in the consolidated balance sheet and the $150 million purchase price for the Series A preferred stock will be reflected as additional minority interest on the balance sheet. The proceeds from the issuance of the preferred stock were used to pay down commercial paper.

10. STOCKHOLDERS' EQUITY

Cumulative preference stock of 5 million shares, without par value, is authorized but unissued.

We have a shareholder rights plan that entitles each outstanding share of common stock to one right. Each right entitles the holder to purchase one two-hundredths of a share of cumulative preference stock (or, in certain circumstances, common stock or other securities), exercisable upon the occurrence of certain events. The rights are not transferable apart from the common stock until a person or group has acquired 20 percent or more, or makes a tender offer for 20 percent or more, of the common stock. Then each right will entitle the holder (other than the acquirer) to receive, upon exercise, common stock of either the Company or the acquiring company having a market value equal to two times the exercise price of the right. The initial exercise price is $120 per right. The rights are redeemable by the Board of Directors at any time prior to the acquisition of 20 percent or more of the outstanding common stock. The shareholder rights plan has been specifically amended so that the Pillsbury transaction described in Note Two does not trigger the exercisability of the rights. The rights expire on Feb. 1, 2006. At May 26, 2002, there were 367 million rights issued and outstanding.

The Board of Directors has authorized the repurchase, from time to time, of common stock for our treasury, provided that the number of treasury shares shall not exceed 170 million.

Through private transactions in fiscal 2002 and 2001 that were a part of our stock repurchase program, we issued put options and purchased call options related to our common stock. In 2002 and 2001, we issued put options for 7 million and 17 million shares for $17 million and $36 million in premiums paid to the Company, respectively. As of May 26, 2002, put options for 10 million shares remained outstanding at exercise prices ranging from $37.00 to $47.00 per share with exercise dates from June 14, 2002, to May 20, 2003. In 2002 and 2001, we purchased call options for 4 million and 8 million shares for $16 million and $34 million in premiums paid by the Company, respectively. As of May 26, 2002, call options for 9 million shares remained outstanding at exercise prices ranging from $34.00 to $54.84 per share with exercise dates from June 17, 2002, to Nov. 20, 2003.

The following table provides details of Other Comprehensive Income:

In Millions	Pretax Change	Tax (Expense) Benefit	Other Comprehensive Income
Fiscal year ended May 28, 2000			
Foreign currency translation	$ (25)	$ 3	$ (22)
Minimum pension liability	1	–	1
Other fair value changes:			
Securities	(13)	5	(8)
Other Comprehensive Income	$ (37)	$ 8	$ (29)
Fiscal year ended May 27, 2001			
Foreign currency translation	$ (8)	$ 1	$ (7)
Minimum pension liability	(8)	3	(5)
Other fair value changes:			
Securities	8	(3)	5
Other Comprehensive Income	$ (8)	$ 1	$ (7)
Fiscal year ended May 26, 2002			
Foreign currency translation	$ (4)	$ –	$ (4)
Minimum pension liability	7	(3)	4
Other fair value changes:			
Securities	(3)	1	(2)
Hedge derivatives	(343)	127	(216)
Reclassification to earnings:			
Securities	(15)	6	(9)
Hedge derivatives	163	(61)	102
Cumulative effect of adopting SFAS No. 133	(251)	93	(158)
Other Comprehensive Income	**$(446)**	**$163**	**$(283)**

Except for reclassification to earnings, changes in Other Comprehensive Income are primarily noncash items.

Accumulated Other Comprehensive Income balances were as follows:

In Millions	May 26, 2002	May 27, 2001
Foreign currency translation adjustments	$(113)	$(109)
Unrealized gain (loss) from:		
Securities	16	27
Hedge derivatives	(272)	–
Pension plan minimum liability	(7)	(11)
Accumulated Other Comprehensive Income	$(376)	$ (93)

11. STOCK PLANS

The Company uses broad-based stock plans to help ensure alignment with stock-holders' interests. A total of 8,984,631 shares are available for grant under the 1998 senior management plan through Oct. 1, 2005, the 1998 employee plan (which has no specified duration) and the 2001 director plan through Sept. 30, 2006. Shares available for grant are reduced by shares issued, net of shares surrendered to the Company in stock-for-stock exercises. Options may be priced only at 100 percent of the fair market value at the date of grant. No options now outstanding have been re-priced since the original date of grant. Options now outstanding include some granted under the 1988, 1990, 1993 and 1995 option plans, under which no further rights may be granted. All options expire within 10 years and one month after the date of grant. The stock plans provide for full vesting of options upon completion of specified service periods, or in the event there is a change of control.

Stock subject to a restricted period and a purchase price, if any (as determined by the Compensation Committee of the Board of Directors), may be granted to key employees under the 1998 employee plan. Restricted stock, up to 50 percent of the value of an individual's cash incentive award, may be granted through the Executive Incentive Plan. Certain restricted stock awards require the employee to deposit personally owned shares (on a one-for-one basis) with the Company during the restricted period. The 2001 director plan allows each nonemployee director to annually receive 1,000 restricted stock units convertible to common stock at a date of the director's choosing following his or her one-year term. In 2002, 2001 and 2000, grants of 691,115, 353,500 and 330,229 shares of restricted stock or units were made to employees and directors with weighted average values at grant of $46.93, $37.61 and $38.49 per share, respectively. On May 26, 2002, a total of 1,634,158 restricted shares and units were outstanding under all plans.

The 1988 plan permitted the granting of performance units corresponding to stock options granted. The value of performance units was determined by return on equity and growth in earnings per share measured against preset goals over three-year performance periods. For seven years after a performance period, holders may elect to receive the value of performance units (with interest) as an alternative to exercising corresponding stock options. On May 26, 2002, there were 48,614 options outstanding with corresponding performance unit accounts. The value of these options exceeded the value of the performance unit accounts.

The following table contains information on stock option activity. Approximately 33 percent of the options outstanding at May 26, 2002, were granted under the Salary Replacement Option and Deposit Stock Option Plans, both of which have been discontinued.

	Options Exercisable (Thousands)	Weighted Average Exercise Price per Share	Options Outstanding (Thousands)	Weighted Average Exercise Price per Share
Balance at May 30, 1999	24,232	$25.05	53,076	$28.17
Granted			11,445	37.49
Exercised			(5,679)	21.82
Expired			(552)	33.42
Balance at May 28, 2000	25,412	26.40	58,290	30.57
Granted			11,600	38.07
Exercised			(5,651)	24.60
Expired			(741)	35.98
Balance at May 27, 2001	27,724	27.79	63,498	32.40
Granted			14,567	48.17
Exercised			(6,569)	27.64
Expired			(421)	39.44
Balance at May 26, 2002	30,149	$29.18	71,075	$36.03

The following table provides information regarding options exercisable and outstanding as of May 26, 2002:

Range of Exercise Price per Share	Options Exercisable (Thousands)	Weighted Average Exercise Price per Share	Options Outstanding (Thousands)	Weighted Average Exercise Price per Share	Weighted Average Remaining Contractual Life (Years)
Under $25	4,976	$22.61	4,982	$22.61	2.26
$25–$30	12,392	26.46	12,401	26.47	2.53
$30–$35	9,822	32.24	19,836	33.28	6.65
$35–$40	173	36.96	8,464	37.43	6.25
Over $40	2,786	41.77	25,392	45.02	8.91
	30,149	$29.18	71,075	$36.03	6.38

Stock-based compensation expense related to restricted stock for 2002, 2001 and 2000 was $16 million, $11 million and $9 million, respectively, using the intrinsic value-based method of accounting for stock-based compensation plans. Effective with 1997, we adopted the disclosure requirements of SFAS No. 123, "Accounting for Stock-Based Compensation." SFAS No. 123 allows either a fair value-based method or an intrinsic value-based method of accounting for such compensation plans. Had compensation expense for our stock option plan grants been determined using the fair value-based method, net earnings, basic earnings per share and diluted earnings per share would have been approximately $384 million, $1.16 and $1.13, respectively, for 2002; $621 million, $2.19 and $2.15, respectively, for 2001; and, $575 million, $1.92 and $1.89, respectively, for 2000. The weighted average fair values at grant date of the options granted in 2002, 2001 and 2000 were estimated as $11.77, $8.78 and

$8.89, respectively, using the Black-Scholes option-pricing model with the following weighted average assumptions:

	2002	2001	2000
Risk-free interest rate	5.1%	5.6%	6.3%
Expected life	7 years	7 years	7 years
Expected volatility	20%	20%	18%
Expected dividend growth rate	8%	8%	8%

The Black-Scholes model requires the input of highly subjective assumptions and may not provide a reliable measure of fair value.

12. EARNINGS PER SHARE

Basic and diluted earnings per share (EPS) were calculated using the following:

In Millions, Fiscal Year	2002	2001	2000
Net earnings	$458	$665	$614
Average number of common shares – basic EPS	331	284	299
Incremental share effect from:			
Stock options	11	8	8
Restricted stock, stock rights and puts	–	–	–
Average number of common shares – diluted EPS	342	292	307

The diluted EPS calculation does not include 4 million, 8 million and 9 million average anti-dilutive stock options, nor does it include 13 million, 15 million and 8 million average anti-dilutive put options in 2002, 2001 and 2000, respectively.

13. INTEREST EXPENSE

The components of net interest expense are as follows:

In Millions, Fiscal Year	2002	2001	2000
Interest expense	$445	$223	$168
Capitalized interest	(3)	(2)	(2)
Interest income	(26)	(15)	(14)
Interest, net	$416	$206	$152

During 2002, 2001 and 2000, we paid interest (net of amount capitalized) of $346 million, $215 million and $167 million, respectively.

14. RETIREMENT AND OTHER POSTRETIREMENT BENEFIT PLANS

We have defined-benefit retirement plans covering most employees. Benefits for salaried employees are based on length of service and final average compensation. The hourly plans include various monthly amounts for each year of credited service. Our funding policy is consistent with the requirements of federal law. Our principal retirement plan covering salaried employees has a provision that any excess pension assets would vest in plan participants if the plan is terminated within five years of a change in control.

We sponsor plans that provide health-care benefits to the majority of our retirees. The salaried health-care benefit plan is contributory, with retiree contributions based on years of service. We fund related trusts for certain employees and retirees on an annual basis.

Trust assets related to the above plans consist principally of listed equity securities, corporate obligations and U.S. government securities.

Reconciliation of the funded status of the plans and the amounts included in the balance sheet are as follows:

In Millions	Pension Plans 2002	Pension Plans 2001	Postretirement Benefit Plans 2002	Postretirement Benefit Plans 2001
Fair Value of Plan Assets				
Beginning fair value	$1,606	$1,578	$ 237	$230
Actual return on assets	(2)	83	(10)	(2)
Acquisition	1,167	–	–	–
Company contributions	7	11	29	28
Plan participant contributions	–	–	5	2
Benefits paid from plan assets	(107)	(66)	(28)	(21)
Ending Fair Value	$2,671	$1,606	$ 233	$237
Projected Benefit Obligation				
Beginning obligations	$1,077	$ 958	$ 286	$231
Service cost	34	18	11	6
Interest cost	122	79	33	21
Plan amendment	21	1	(13)	–
Curtailment	5	–	2	–
Plan participant contributions	–	–	5	2
Actuarial loss (gain)	(15)	87	72	42
Acquisition	963	–	248	–
Actual benefits paid	(107)	(66)	(33)	(16)
Ending Obligations	$2,100	$1,077	$ 611	$286
Funded Status of Plans	$ 571	$ 529	$(378)	$ (49)
Unrecognized actuarial loss	334	106	154	59
Unrecognized prior service costs (credits)	49	36	(17)	(5)
Unrecognized transition asset	(3)	(18)	–	–
Net Amount Recognized	$ 951	$ 653	$(241)	$ 5
Amounts Recognized on Balance Sheets				
Prepaid asset	$1,001	$ 677	$ 82	$ 75
Accrued liability	(62)	(44)	(323)	(70)
Intangible asset	–	1	–	–
Minimum liability adjustment in equity	12	19	–	–
Net Amount Recognized	$ 951	$ 653	$(241)	$ 5

Plans with obligations in excess of plan assets:

In Millions	Pension Plans		Postretirement Benefit Plans	
	2002	2001	2002	2001
Accumulated benefit obligation	$71	$44	$466	$166
Plan assets at fair value	9	–	45	41

Assumptions as of year-end are:

	Pension Plans		Postretirement Benefit Plans	
	2002	2001	2002	2001
Discount rate	7.50%	7.75%	7.50%	7.75%
Rate of return on plan assets	10.4	10.4	10.0	10.0
Salary increases	4.4	4.4	–	–
Annual increase in cost of benefits	–	–	8.3	6.6

The annual increase in cost of postretirement benefits is assumed to decrease gradually in future years, reaching an ultimate rate of 5.2 percent in the year 2007.

Components of net benefit (income) or expense each year are as follows:

In Millions	Pension Plans			Postretirement Benefit Plans		
	2002	2001	2000	2002	2001	2000
Service cost	$ 34	$ 18	$ 20	$ 11	$ 6	$ 6
Interest cost	122	79	69	33	21	17
Expected return on plan assets	(241)	(159)	(142)	(23)	(23)	(22)
Amortization of transition asset	(15)	(15)	(14)	–	–	–
Amortization of (gains) losses	2	2	1	3	1	1
Amortization of prior service costs (credits)	8	6	6	(1)	(2)	(2)
Settlement or curtailment losses	5	–	–	2	–	–
Net (income) expense	$ (85)	$ (69)	$ (60)	$ 25	$ 3	$ –

Assumed trend rates for health-care costs have an important effect on the amounts reported for the postretirement benefit plans. If the health-care cost trend rate increased by 1 percentage point in each future year, the aggregate of the service and interest cost components of postretirement expense would increase for 2002 by $5 million, and the postretirement accumulated benefit obligation as of May 26, 2002, would increase by $51 million. If the health-care cost trend rate decreased by 1 percentage point in each future year, the aggregate of the service and interest cost components of postretirement expense would decrease for 2002 by $4 million, and the postretirement accumulated benefit obligation as of May 26, 2002, would decrease by $44 million.

The General Mills Savings Plan is a defined contribution plan that covers our salaried and nonunion employees. It had net assets of $1,666 million at May 26, 2002, and $1,071 million at May 27, 2001. This plan is a 401(k) savings plan that includes a number of investment funds and an Employee Stock Ownership Plan (ESOP). The ESOP's only assets are Company common stock and temporary cash balances. Company expense recognized in 2002, 2001 and 2000 was $9 million, $8 million and $8 million, respectively. The ESOP's share of this expense was $3 million, $7 million and $7 million, respectively. The ESOP's expense is calculated by the "shares allocated" method.

The ESOP uses Company common stock to convey benefits to employees and, through increased stock ownership, to further align employee interests with those of shareholders. The Company matches a percentage of employee contributions to the ESOP with a base match plus a variable year-end match that depends on annual results. Employees receive the Company match in the form of common stock.

The ESOP originally purchased Company common stock principally with funds borrowed from third parties (and guaranteed by the Company). The ESOP shares are included in net shares outstanding for the purposes of calculating earnings per share. The ESOP's third-party debt is described in Note Eight.

The Company treats cash dividends paid to the ESOP the same as other dividends. Dividends received on leveraged shares (i.e., all shares originally purchased with the debt proceeds) are used for debt service, while dividends received on unleveraged shares are passed through to participants.

The Company's cash contribution to the ESOP is calculated so as to pay off enough debt to release sufficient shares to make the Company match. The ESOP uses the Company's cash contributions to the plan, plus the dividends received on the ESOP's leveraged shares, to make principal and interest payments on the ESOP's debt. As loan payments are made, shares become unencumbered by debt and are committed to be allocated. The ESOP allocates shares to individual employee accounts on the basis of the match of employee payroll savings (contributions), plus reinvested dividends received on previously allocated shares. In 2002, 2001 and 2000, the ESOP incurred interest expense of $2 million, $3 million and $4 million, respectively. The ESOP used dividends of $8 million, $7 million and $9 million, along with Company contributions of $3 million, $6 million and $6 million to make interest and principal payments in the respective years.

The number of shares of Company common stock in the ESOP is summarized as follows:

Number of Shares, in Thousands	May 26, 2002	May 27, 2001
Unreleased shares	1,170	1,652
Committed to be allocated	15	24
Allocated to participants	5,500	5,680
Total shares	6,685	7,356

15. PROFIT-SHARING PLAN

The Executive Incentive Plan provides incentives to key employees who have the greatest potential to contribute to current earnings and successful future operations. These awards are approved by the Compensation Committee of the Board of Directors, which consists solely of independent, outside directors. Awards are based on performance against pre-established goals approved by the Committee. Profit-sharing expense was $11 million, $12 million and $10 million in 2002, 2001 and 2000, respectively.

16. INCOME TAXES

The components of earnings before income taxes and earnings of joint ventures and the corresponding income taxes thereon are as follows:

In Millions, Fiscal Year	2002	2001	2000
Earnings before income taxes:			
U.S.	$653	$991	$919
Foreign	14	7	28
Total earnings before income taxes	$667	$998	$947
Income taxes:			
Current:			
Federal	$127	$283	$280
State and local	8	20	14
Foreign	11	(2)	(2)
Total current	146	301	292
Deferred:			
Federal	84	42	44
State and local	15	5	(5)
Foreign	(6)	2	5
Total deferred	93	49	44
Total Income Taxes	$239	$350	$336

During 2002, 2001 and 2000, we paid income taxes of $196 million, $231 million and $284 million, respectively.

In fiscal 1982 and 1983 we purchased certain income tax items from other companies through tax lease transactions. Total current income taxes charged to earnings reflect the amounts attributable to operations and have not been materially affected by these tax leases. Actual current taxes payable relating to 2002, 2001 and 2000 operations were increased by approximately $3 million, $16 million and $22 million, respectively, due to the current effect of tax leases. These tax payments do not affect taxes for statement of earnings purposes since they repay tax benefits realized in prior years. The repayment liability is classified as Deferred Income Taxes – Tax Leases.

The following table reconciles the U.S. statutory income tax rate with the effective income tax rate:

Fiscal Year	2002	2001	2000
U.S. statutory rate	35.0%	35.0%	35.0%
State and local income taxes, net of federal tax benefits	2.3	1.6	1.3
Other, net	(1.5)	(1.6)	(.8)
Effective Income Tax Rate	35.8%	35.0%	35.5%

The tax effects of temporary differences that give rise to deferred tax assets and liabilities are as follows:

In Millions	May 26, 2002	May 27, 2001
Accrued liabilities	$106	$ 65
Unusual charges	104	9
Compensation and employee benefits	111	73
Unrealized hedge losses	163	–
Tax credit carryforwards	51	8
Other	23	14
Gross deferred tax assets	558	169
Depreciation	281	134
Prepaid pension asset	289	255
Intangible assets	22	10
Other	51	54
Gross deferred tax liabilities	643	453
Valuation allowance	10	3
Net Deferred Tax Liability	$ 95	$287

We have not recognized a deferred tax liability for unremitted earnings of $87 million from our foreign operations because we do not expect those earnings to become taxable to us in the foreseeable future and because a determination of the potential liability is not practicable. If a portion were to be remitted, we believe income tax credits would substantially offset any resulting tax liability.

17. LEASES AND OTHER COMMITMENTS

An analysis of rent expense by property leased follows:

In Millions, Fiscal Year	2002	2001	2000
Warehouse space	$26	$25	$24
Equipment	23	11	8
Other	19	7	7
Total Rent Expense	$68	$43	$39

Some leases require payment of property taxes, insurance and maintenance costs in addition to the rent payments. Contingent and escalation rent in excess of minimum rent payments and sublease income netted in rent expense were insignificant.

Noncancelable future lease commitments (in millions) are: $59 in 2003, $44 in 2004, $35 in 2005, $31 in 2006, $22 in 2007 and $96 after 2007, with a cumulative total of $287. These future lease commitments will be partially offset by future sublease receipts of $46 million.

We are contingently liable under guarantees and comfort letters for $212 million. The guarantees and comfort letters are principally issued to support borrowing arrangements, primarily for our joint ventures. We remain the guarantor on certain leases and other obligations of Darden Restaurants, Inc. (Darden), an entity we spun off as of May 28, 1995. However, Darden has indemnified us against any related loss.

The Company is involved in various claims, including environmental matters, arising in the ordinary course of business. In the opinion of management, the ultimate disposition of these matters, either individually or in aggregate, will not have a material adverse effect on the Company's financial position or results of operations.

18. BUSINESS SEGMENT AND GEOGRAPHIC INFORMATION

We operate exclusively in the consumer foods industry, with multiple operating segments organized generally by product categories.

Following the acquisition of Pillsbury, we restructured our management organization. Consistent with our new organization and SFAS No. 131, "Disclosures about Segments of an Enterprise and Related Information," we have aggregated our operating segments into three reportable segments: 1) U.S. Retail; 2) Bakeries and Foodservice; and 3) International. U.S. Retail consists of cereals, meals, refrigerated and frozen dough products, baking products, snacks, yogurt and other. Our Bakeries and Foodservice segment consists of products marketed to bakeries and offered to the commercial and noncommercial foodservice sectors throughout the United States and Canada. The International segment includes our retail business outside the United States and our foodservice business outside of the United States and Canada.

During 2002, there was one individual customer that generated 12 percent of our net sales. There were no individual customers that generated more than 10 percent of our net sales during 2001 and 2000.

Management reviews operating results to evaluate segment performance. Operating profit for the reportable segments excludes general corporate expenses. Interest expense and income taxes are centrally managed at the corporate level and, therefore, are not allocated to segments since they are excluded from the measure of segment profitability reviewed by the Company's management. Under our supply chain organization, our manufacturing, warehouse, distribution and sales activities are substantially integrated across our operations in order to maximize efficiency and productivity. As a result, fixed assets, capital expenditures for long-lived assets, and depreciation and amortization expenses are not maintained nor available by operating segment.

The measurement of operating segment results is generally consistent with the presentation of the consolidated statements of earnings. Intercompany transactions between reportable operating segments were not material in the periods presented.

In Millions, Fiscal Year	2002	2001	2000
Net Sales:			
U.S. Retail	$6,143	$4,790	$4,560
Bakeries and Foodservice	1,028	397	355
International	778	263	258
Total	7,949	5,450	5,173
Operating Profit Before Unusual Items:			
U.S. Retail	$1,066	$1,057	$1,013
Bakeries and Foodservice	146	91	81
International	45	17	18
Unallocated Corporate Items	16	4	(13)
Total	1,273	1,169	1,099
Operating Profit Including Unusual Items:			
U.S. Retail	$ 999	$1,100	$1,013
Bakeries and Foodservice	144	91	81
International	45	17	18
Unallocated Corporate Items	(105)	(4)	(13)
Total	1,083	1,204	1,099
Interest, net	416	206	152
Income Taxes	239	350	336
Earnings from Joint Ventures	33	17	3
Earnings before cumulative effect of change in accounting principle	461	665	614
Cumulative effect of change in accounting principle	(3)	—	—
Net Earnings	$ 458	$ 665	$ 614

The following table provides net sales information for our primary product categories:

In Millions, Fiscal Year	2002	2001	2000
Product Categories:			
U.S. Retail:			
Big G Cereals	$1,866	$1,963	$1,986
Meals	1,161	580	555
Pillsbury USA	793	—	—
Baking Products	786	824	804
Snacks	722	711	630
Yogurt/Health Ventures/Other	815	712	585
Total U.S. Retail	6,143	4,790	4,560
Bakeries and Foodservice	1,028	397	355
International:			
Canada	283	177	178
Rest of World	495	86	80
Total International	778	263	258
Consolidated Total	$7,949	$5,450	$5,173

The following table provides earnings information for our joint venture activities by operating segment:

In Millions, Fiscal Year	2002	2001	2000
Earnings (Loss) After Tax:			
U.S. Retail	$ (6)	$ –	$ –
International	39	17	3
Total	$33	$17	$ 3

The following table provides financial information by geographic area:

In Millions, Fiscal Year	2002	2001	2000
Net sales:			
U.S.	$7,139	$5,187	$4,915
Non-U.S.	810	263	258
Consolidated Total	$7,949	$5,450	$5,173
Long-lived assets:			
U.S.	$2,549	$1,488	$1,395
Non-U.S.	215	13	10
Consolidated Total	$2,764	$1,501	$1,405

19. QUARTERLY DATA (UNAUDITED)

Summarized quarterly data for 2002 and 2001 follows:

In Millions, Except per Share and Market Price Amounts	First Quarter		Second Quarter		Third Quarter		Fourth Quarter	
	2002	2001	2002	2001	2002	2001	2002	2001
Net sales	$1,404	$1,306	$1,842	$1,500	$2,379	$1,323	$2,324	$1,321
Gross profit	683	653	802	747	881	615	816	594
Earnings before cumulative effect of change in accounting principle	191	159	130	203	83	157	57	146
Net earnings	188	159	130	203	83	157	57	146
Earnings per share before cumulative effect of change in accounting principle:								
Basic	.67	.56	.43	.72	.23	.55	.16	.51
Diluted	.65	.55	.41	.70	.22	.54	.15	.50
Net earnings per share:								
Basic	.66	.56	.43	.72	.23	.55	.16	.51
Diluted	.64	.55	.41	.70	.22	.54	.15	.50
Dividends per share	.275	.275	.275	.275	.275	.275	.275	.275
Market price of common stock:								
High	45.36	41.75	51.16	43.44	52.86	45.40	50.39	46.35
Low	42.05	32.13	42.50	31.38	43.22	38.75	41.61	37.26

See Note Three for a description of unusual items. In fiscal 2002, the net earnings impact was $9 million income, $68 million expense, $24 million expense, and $37 million expense in quarters one, two, three, and four, respectively. The net impact per diluted share in fiscal 2002 was $.03 income, $.22 expense, $.06 expense and $.10 expense in quarters one, two, three, and four, respectively. In fiscal 2001, the net earnings impact was under $1 million expense, $1 million expense, and $1 million expense in quarters one, two and three, respectively. There was no impact to diluted EPS in these quarters. The net earnings impact in the fourth quarter of 2001 was $24 million income ($.08 per diluted share).

SENIOR MANAGEMENT

Y. MARC BELTON
Senior Vice President,
Yoplait-Colombo, Canada and New Business

PETER J. CAPELL
Senior Vice President;
President, Snacks Unlimited

RANDY G. DARCY
Senior Vice President, Supply Chain Operations

RORY A. DELANEY
Senior Vice President,
Strategic Technology Development

STEPHEN R. DEMERITT
Vice Chairman

IAN R. FRIENDLY
Senior Vice President;
President, Big G Cereals

DAVID P. HOMER
Vice President;
President, Baking Products

JAMES A. LAWRENCE
Executive Vice President,
Chief Financial Officer

JOHN T. MACHUZICK
Senior Vice President,
Convenient Food Solutions,
Bakeries and Foodservice

SIRI S. MARSHALL
Senior Vice President,
Corporate Affairs;
General Counsel and Secretary

CHRISTOPHER D. O'LEARY
Senior Vice President;
President, Meals

S. PAUL OLIVER
Senior Vice President;
President, Bakeries and Foodservice

MICHAEL A. PEEL
Senior Vice President,
Human Resources and Corporate Services

KENDALL J. POWELL
Senior Vice President;
Chief Executive Officer,
Cereal Partners Worldwide

LUCIO RIZZI
Senior Vice President;
President, International

PETER B. ROBINSON
Senior Vice President;
President, Pillsbury USA

JEFFREY J. ROTSCH
Senior Vice President,
Sales and Channel Development

STEPHEN W. SANGER
Chairman of the Board and
Chief Executive Officer

CHRISTINA L. SHEA
Senior Vice President;
President, General Mills Foundation

CHRISTI L. STRAUSS
Vice President;
President, General Mills Canada

DANNY L. STRICKLAND
Senior Vice President,
Innovation, Technology and Quality

AUSTIN P. SULLIVAN JR.
Senior Vice President,
Corporate Relations

KENNETH L. THOME
Senior Vice President,
Financial Operations

DAVID B. VANBENSCHOTEN
Vice President, Treasurer

RAYMOND G. VIAULT
Vice Chairman

ROBERT F. WALDRON
Vice President;
President, Yoplait-Colombo

40

SHAREHOLDER INFORMATION

GENERAL MILLS WORLD HEADQUARTERS

Number One General Mills Boulevard
Minneapolis, MN 55426-1348
Phone: (763) 764-7600

INTERNET: www.generalmills.com

MARKETS

New York Stock Exchange
Trading Symbol: GIS

TRANSFER AGENT, REGISTRAR, DIVIDEND PAYMENTS AND DIVIDEND REINVESTMENT PLAN

Wells Fargo Bank Minnesota, N.A.
161 North Concord Exchange
P.O. Box 64854
St. Paul, MN 55164-0854
Phone: (800) 670-4763 or (651) 450-4084
E-mail: stocktransfer@WellsFargo.com
Account access via Web site:
www.shareowneronline.com

INDEPENDENT AUDITOR

KPMG LLP
4200 Wells Fargo Center
90 South 7th Street
Minneapolis, MN 55402-3900
Phone: (612) 305-5000

INVESTOR INQUIRIES

Contact the Investor Relations department at (800) 245-5703 or (763) 764-3202. Quarterly earnings reports, corporate news and company information are available on our Web site: www.generalmills.com.

The General Mills Corporate Secretary's Department may be reached at (800) 245-5703, option 1.

NOTICE OF ANNUAL MEETING

The annual meeting of General Mills shareholders will be held at 11 a.m., Central Daylight Time, Monday, Sept. 23, 2002, at the Children's Theatre Company, 2400 Third Avenue South, Minneapolis, Minnesota.

FORM 10-K REPORT

We believe that the financial statements in this annual report include all the significant financial data contained in the Form 10-K annual report filed with the Securities and Exchange Commission. The Form 10-K is available on our Web site, or shareholders may request a free copy by writing to:

Corporate Secretary
General Mills, Inc.
P.O. Box 1113
Minneapolis, MN 55440-1113

CORPORATE CITIZENSHIP REPORT

General Mills' 2002 Corporate Citizenship Report details the company's many community service and philanthropic activities. To receive a copy, write to:

General Mills Community Action
P.O. Box 1113
Minneapolis, MN 55440-1113

A NEW CORPORATE LOGO

With the acquisition of Pillsbury, we updated our corporate logo to represent the new General Mills. The familiar "G" remains, but it's now a dark blue with a dotted line base – both borrowed from the Pillsbury logo. The General Mills name is featured in a new, more contemporary way.

GENERAL MILLS

GENERAL MILLS
P.O. Box 1113 • Minneapolis, MN 55440-1113

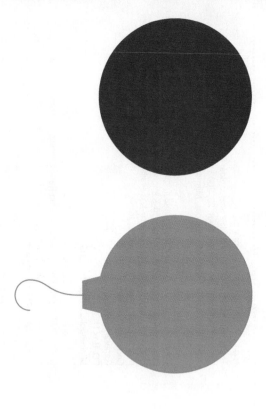

HOLIDAY GIFT BOXES

General Mills Gift Boxes are a part of many shareholders' December holiday traditions. To request an order form, please call us toll free at (866) 314-2078 or write, including your name, street address, city, state, zip code and phone number (including area code) to:

2002 Holiday Gift Box Offer
General Mills, Inc.
P.O. Box 6631
Stacy, MN 55078-6631

Please contact us after September 1, 2002.

APPENDIX C

Sources of Information about Companies and Industries

Many college and public libraries offer print and electronic resources that provide information about companies and industries. The following listing describes some of the resources you may find useful. The listing is not comprehensive. Check with your librarian for other resources that may be available in your library.

Industry Classification

- The *North American Industry Classification System* (NAICS) categorizes companies using an industry classification code. Companies with the same classification code produce similar products. Other reference materials often use NAICS codes to identify companies and industries. You can find the NAICS codes on the Web at http://www.census.gov/epcd/www/naics.html.
- The *Standard Industrial Classification Manual* provides an earlier system for classifying companies and industries. Some reference materials still use Standard Industrial Classification (SIC) codes to organize information. You can find SIC codes on the Web at http://www.osha.gov/oshstats/sicser.html.

Business Periodicals

- *Business Week* provides general coverage of a wide variety of business issues, including individual companies and industries. Some articles are available on the Web at http://www.businessweek.com/.
- *Fortune* provides descriptive articles on many companies and industries. Special issues provide rankings of companies by sales, both overall and within industries. Some articles are available on the Web at http://www.fortune.com/.
- *Forbes* provides descriptive articles on many companies and industries. Special issues provide summary information for large companies. Some articles are available on the Web at http://www.forbes.com/.
- *The Wall Street Journal* provides daily coverage of major events related to specific companies and industries as well as the overall economy. Some articles are available on the Web at http://www.wsj.com/.

Company Profiles

- *Hoover's Handbook of American Business* gives profiles of companies, including overview, history, financial data, products and brands, and major competitors. Even more company profiles are available at *Hoover's Online* at http://www.hoovers.com/.
- *Standard & Poor's Corporation Records* provides a brief profile and financial information on public companies. *Standard & Poor's Stock Reports* also provides a brief profile but includes more information about the company's stock. Information

from both sources is also included in the electronic database from Standard & Poor's called *NetAdvantage.*

- *Mergent* (formerly *Moody's*) *Industrial Manual* provides profiles of companies, including history, subsidiaries, financial information, and a description of the company's long-term debt and equity offerings. Other manuals cover other industries, such as transportation and public utilities. This information is also available in Mergent's electronic database called *FIS Online.*
- *Thomson Research* (formerly *Global Access*) is an electronic database that contains extensive information on companies such as financial information, stock data, and so on.
- *Factiva.com* (formerly *Dow Jones Interactive*) provides several ways to research a company. Look at company filings, review stock price history, or search for articles about the company in the Publications Library.
- *Value Line Investment Survey* provides analysis and commentary on major industries and companies.
- *EDGAR* offers free access to public company filings with the Securities and Exchange Commission. Visit EDGAR on the Web at http://www.sec.gov/edgar.shtml.
- A company's annual report to the shareholders often contains useful information about its products and markets in addition to their financial statements. Many companies now post their annual report on their Web site. Use your favorite search engine (e.g., Google at http://www.google.com/) to search for the company's home page. Look for an "Information for Investors" or "Investor Relations" section to find the company's annual report.
- *International Directory of Company Histories* is a large multi-volume set that gives extensive background information on the history of individual companies.

Industry Profiles

- *Standard & Poor's Industry Surveys* provides detailed analysis of over 50 major industries. This information is also contained in the electronic database from Standard & Poor's called *NetAdvantage.*
- *Encyclopedia of American Industries* gives profiles of industries arranged by SIC code. Almost every code has a profile, so information can be quite specific.
- *U.S. Industry & Trade Outlook* (formerly *U.S. Industrial Outlook*) contains information on major industries in the United States, along with forecasts of future prospects.
- *Manufacturing & Distribution USA* gathers industry statistics from the U.S. Census Bureau and other sources and organizes them by SIC code.
- *Marketresearch.com* contains market research reports on individual industries and types of products.

Articles in Magazines and Newspapers

There are numerous databases that allow the user to search for articles on a given topic, company, or industry. Even general-subject databases usually contain a large number of articles on business topics. Here are a few examples of databases that are particularly useful for the business researcher:

- *ABI/INFORM* is a database covering over a thousand business-related magazines and journals. Search for articles about a topic, a company, or an industry. Many articles are available full-text.
- *Business Source Elite* is another database that covers a huge number of business magazines and journals, with many offered full-text.
- *Lexis-Nexis Academic Universe* provides access to articles in thousands of magazines, journals, and newspapers. It also contains information from other types of sources such as radio and television programs.
- The Publications Library in *Factiva.com* contains the full-text of thousands of business magazines, trade journals, and news releases.

Government Information

The federal government gathers huge amounts of data about the economy, trade, and industry. Much of this information is now distributed freely on the Web. Here are a few examples:

- *Economic Indicators* includes the gross national product, consumer price indexes, unemployment rates, interest rates, and many more commonly used economic statistics. Find it on the Web at http://www.access.gpo.gov/congress/eibrowse/broecind.html.
- The Federal Reserve Banks gather economic data about their various regions and share the data through publications on their Web sites. A good example is *FRED®*, a database of economic information compiled by the Federal Reserve Bank of St. Louis on the Web at http://research.stlouisfed.org/fred/.
- *Survey of Current Business* provides more detailed economic data, as well as articles about foreign investment, personal income, and other economic topics.
- *The U.S. Census Bureau* gathers huge amounts of data and offers it to the public at their Web site at http://www.census.gov/. Note particularly the Economic Census, where you can find data on individual industries at the national, state, or local level.
- *Statistical Abstract of the United States* gathers into one place the most frequently requested statistics gathered by all the various departments and agencies of the federal government. Find it on the Web at http://www.census.gov/prod/www/statistical-abstract-us.html.

Industry Ratios

Industry averages for a variety of ratios and other accounting measures are available in *RMA* (formerly Robert Morris Associates) *Annual Statement Studies*, Dun & Bradstreet's *Industry Norms & Key Business Ratios*, and Leo Troy's *Almanac of Business and Industrial Financial Ratios*.

GLOSSARY

A

accelerated depreciation
A depreciation method that allocates a larger portion of the cost of a plant asset to expense early in the asset's life. (F11)

absorption costing
Costing method that assigns costs by function, separating the costs of manufacturing products from the costs of selling, administration, and other nonmanufacturing activities. (M7)

account
A record of increases and decreases in the dollar amount associated with a specific resource or activity. (F2)

accounting
An information system for the measurement and reporting of the transformation of resources into goods and services and the sale or transfer of these goods and services to customers. (F1)

accounting cycle
The process of recording, summarizing, and reporting accounting information. (F3)

accounting rate of return (ARR)
The average accounting income a project generates per period divided by the amount of the investment in the project. (M12)

accounts payable
A liability account that identifies an obligation to pay suppliers in the near future. (F3)

accounts receivable
An asset account that increases when goods are sold on credit. (F3)

accounts receivable turnover
The ratio of sales revenues (from the income statement) to accounts receivable (from the balance sheet); it measures a company's ability to convert revenues into cash. (F14)

accrual accounting
A form of accounting in which revenues are recognized when they are earned and expenses are recognized when they are incurred. (F3)

accrued expenses
Expenses recognized prior to the payment of cash. (F3)

accrued liabilities
Liabilities that record the obligation to make payments for expenses that have been incurred or for assets that have been acquired but for which payment has not been made. (F3)

accrued revenue
Revenue recognized prior to the receipt of cash. (F3)

accumulated depreciation
A contra-asset account used to identify the total amount of depreciation recorded for a company's assets. (F3)

activity base
A production activity (such as direct labor hours or machine hours) or a measure of the cost of production activity (direct labor cost, for example). (M3)

activity pools
Collections of costs that relate to an activity. (M5)

activity-based costing (ABC)
Costing method that allocates overhead costs to a product based on the cost of the activities that are required to produce the product. (M1, M5)

actual costing
Costing method that measures unit costs based on the actual costs of direct materials, direct labor, and overhead incurred in producing the units. (M3)

adjusting entry
A transaction recorded in the accounting system to ensure the correct account balances are reported for a particular fiscal period. (F3)

agents
People hired by owners who are expected to manage the company in a way consistent with the owners' interests. (M10)

amortization expense
The allocation of the cost of long-term intangible assets to the fiscal periods that benefit from their use. (F4)

annuity
A series of equal amounts received or paid over a specified number of equal time periods. (F8)

application software
Software that includes the computer programs that permit data to be recorded and processed. (F7, M8)

articulation
The relationship among financial statements in which the numbers on one statement explain numbers on other statements. (F4)

asset turnover
The ratio of revenues to total assets. (F12)

assets
Resources controlled by a business. (F2)

attestation
An auditor's affirmation of the fairness of financial statements and other information. (F6)

audit
A detailed, systematic investigation of a company's accounting records and procedures for the purpose of determining the reliability of financial reports. (F1, F6)

average collection period
The ratio of accounts receivable to average daily sales. (F14)

B

balance sheet
A financial statement that identifies a company's assets and claims to those assets by creditors and owners at a specific date. (F2)

balanced scorecard
An approach to evaluation that uses key performance criteria in four categories: financial, customer satisfaction, learning

and growth, and internal business processes. (M10)

batch processing
Process that combines elements of individual-job and continuous-flow processing. (M4)

book value
Total assets minus total liabilities. (F10)

bottlenecks
Processes that work at slow rates and restrict the flow of goods or services. (M11)

breakeven point
The level of sales at which all variable and fixed expenses are covered, but no profit is generated. (M7)

budget
A detailed plan describing the use of financial and operating resources over a specific period. (M8)

budgetary slack
The difference between a less demanding budget value and a value managers believe they realistically can achieve. (M8)

business activities
Events that occur when a business acquires, uses, or sells resources or claims to those resources. (F2)

business organization
Organizations that sell their goods and services to make a profit. (F1)

C

capital expenditures
Expenditures made to acquire new plant assets or to extend the life or enhance the value of existing plant assets. (F11)

capital budgeting
The process of making capital investment decisions. (M12)

capital investment decision
A decision to invest in long-term assets such as plant and equipment. (M12)

capital stock
See *common stock*. (F9)

capital structure
The relative amounts of debt and equity used by a company to finance its assets. (F10)

cash
The financial resources in the form of coins and currency, bank deposits, and short-term investments that can be converted easily into currency and that can be used to pay for resources and obligations of a company. (F2)

cash budget
A budget that describes cash requirements for the budget period. (M8)

charter
The legal right granted by a state that permits a corporation to exist. (F9)

closing entries
Transactions that reset the balances of each revenue and expense account to zero and transfer these balances to Retained Earnings. (F3)

commitment
A promise to engage in some future activity that will have an economic effect. (F9)

committed fixed costs
Costs that cannot be eliminated in the relatively short term. (M7)

common cause variation
A variation that is the result of randomness inherent in a process. (M9)

common stock
The stock that conveys primary ownership rights in a corporation (also called capital stock). (F4, F9)

comprehensive income
The change in a company's owners' equity during a period that is the result of all non-owner transactions and activities. (F4)

computer network
A network that includes the cables that connect the clients and servers and the hardware and software needed to make the networks function properly. (F7, M8)

consolidated financial statements
A report that includes the activities of the parent and its subsidiaries as though they were one company. (F4)

contingency
An existing condition that may result in an economic effect if a future event occurs. (F9)

contra account
An account that offsets another account. (F3)

contracts
Legal agreements for the exchange of resources and services. (F1)

contributed capital
An owners' equity account that identifies amounts contributed to a company by its owners; the direct investment made by stockholders in a corporation. (F2, F9)

contribution margin
The difference between sales revenue and variable costs over an accounting period. (M7)

contribution margin ratio
The ratio (expressed as a percentage) of contribution margin to total sales. (M7)

control accounts
Summary accounts that maintain totals for all subsidiary accounts of a particular type. (F7)

conversion costs
The costs required to convert materials into products. (M2) The direct labor and manufacturing overhead costs required to convert raw materials into finished goods. (M4)

core activities
The primary activities a service organization carries out. (M5)

corporation
A legal entity with the right to enter into contracts; the right to own, buy, and sell property; and the right to sell stock. (F1)

cost center
A division of an organization that consumes resources while performing its responsibilities, yet has no direct involvement in generating sales or acquiring property. (M10)

cost drivers
Activities that create costs. (M1)

cost leadership strategy
Companies that lead their competitors in selling high quantities of products by keeping the prices of these products low. (F14)

cost of capital
The cost of funds that can be used to finance a project. (M12)

cost of goods sold
An expense that identifies the cost to the company of the goods transferred to customers. (F2)

cost of services sold
The cost of material, labor, and other resources consumed directly in producing services sold during a period. (F4)

cost-based transfer pricing policy
A policy that uses either full cost or variable cost as a basis for determining a transfer price. (M10)

cost-volume-profit (CVP) analysis
The use of an understanding of the relationship among costs, volume, and profits to make managerial decisions. (M7)

creditor
A person or organization who loans financial resources to an organization. (F1)

credits
Decreases in elements on the left (assets) side of the accounting equation and in-

creases in elements on the right (liabilities and owners' equity) side. (F2)

critical path
The steps needed to complete a process. (M13)

cumulative effect of a change in accounting method
A gain or loss associated with changing accounting methods or adopting new accounting standards. (F13)

current assets
Cash or other resources that management expects to convert to cash or consume during the next fiscal year. (F4)

current liabilities
Those obligations that management expects to fulfill during the next fiscal year. (F4)

current ratio
Current assets divided by current liabilities. (F4, F10)

cycle time
The total time required to move a unit from raw materials inventory to finished goods inventory. (M11)

D

database
A set of computerized files in which company data are stored in a form that facilitates retrieval and updating of the data. (F7, M8)

database management system
A system that controals database functions to ensure data are recorded properly and can be accessed only by those authorized to record, update, or retrieve the data. (F7, M8)

date of declaration
Date on which a corporation's board of directors announces that a dividend will be paid. (F9)

date of payment
Date on which the dividends are mailed to those receiving dividends. (F9)

date of record
Date used to determine those owners who will receive the dividend. (F9)

day's sales in inventories
The ratio of inventory to average daily cost of goods sold. (F14)

debits
Increases in elements on the left (assets) side of the accounting equation and decreases in elements on the right (liabilities and owners' equity) side. (F2)

debt-to-assets ratio
Total debt divided by total assets. (F10)

debt-to-equity ratio
Total debt divided by total stockholders' equity. (F10)

deferred charges
The assets that result when a company prepays expenses that produce long-term benefits. (F3)

deferred expenses
Expenses recognized after the payment of cash. (F3)

deferred revenue
Revenue recognized after cash has been received. (F3)

departmental production reports
Reports that describe the materials, labor, and overhead used by each department during a given accounting period. (M4)

depletion
The process of allocating the cost of natural resources to expenses in the periods that benefit from their use. (F4, F11)

depreciation
The allocation of the cost of assets to the fiscal periods that benefit from the assets' use. (F3)

direct labor costs
The costs of workers who add value to a product through their direct involvement in the production process. (M2)

direct material costs
The costs of the significant raw materials from which a product is manufactured. (M2)

discontinued operations
Product lines or major parts of a company from which the company will no longer derive income because it has sold or closed the facilities that produced the product line or that included that part of the company. (F13)

discounting methods
Methods of evaluating capital investments that rely on the time value of money. (M12)

discounting
The translation of future dollars into current dollars. (M12)

discretionary fixed costs
Fixed costs that can be eliminated in the relatively short term. (M7)

discussion memorandum
A document that identifies accounting issues and alternative approaches to resolving the issues. (F6)

dividend payout ratio
Total dividends divided by net income. (F10)

dividends
Distributions of cash or stock by a corporation to its stockholders. (F4)

E

earnings per share
A measure of the earnings performance of each share of common stock during a fiscal period. (F4)

e-business
Using computer networks, such as the Internet, to make customer sales. (F7, M8)

economies of scale
The savings a company realizes in unit costs by spreading fixed overhead costs over a larger number of units. (M5)

effective business
An organization that is successful in providing goods and services demanded by customers. (F1)

efficient business
An organization that keeps the costs of resources consumed in providing goods and services low relative to the selling prices of these goods and services. (F1)

enterprise resource planning (ERP) systems
Systems that integrate most of the business information functions as a basis for management decisions. (F7, M8)

equivalent units
The number of units that would have been produced during a period if all of the department's efforts had resulted in completed units. (M4)

expense
The amount of resources consumed in the process of acquiring and selling goods and services. (F2)

exposure draft
A document that describes a proposed accounting standard. (F6)

extraordinary items
Gains or losses that are both unusual and infrequent for a particular company. (F13)

F

FASB conceptual framework
A set of objectives, principles, and definitions to guide the development of new accounting standards. (F6)

favorable variance
A variance that results when the actual price (or quantity) is less than the standard price (or quantity) for materials or labor. (M9)

financial accounting
The process of preparing, reporting, and interpreting accounting information that is provided to external decision makers. (F1)

Financial Accounting Standards Board (FASB)
The primary organization for setting accounting standards for businesses in the United States since 1973. (F6)

financial leverage (FL)
The use of debt to increase a company's return on equity; total assets divided by total stockholders' equity. (F10)

financial statements
Reports that summarize the results of a company's accounting transactions for a fiscal period. (F2)

financing activities
Events that occur when owners or creditors provide resources to a company or when a company transfers resources to owners or creditors. (F2)

finished goods inventory
The costs of products that have been completed in the manufacturing process and are available for sale to customers. (F13)

first-in, first-out (FIFO) method
Inventory method that assumes that the units of inventory acquired first are sold first. (F13)

fiscal period
Any time period for which a company wants to report its financial activities. (F2)

fixed asset turnover
The ratio of sales revenues to fixed assets (property and equipment). (F14)

fixed assets
Long-term, tangible resources (also called plant assets). (F4)

fixed costs
Costs that do not change in total with volume but vary on a per-unit basis. (M7)

future value
The value of an amount at a particular time in the future. (F8)

G

General Accounting Office (GAO)
The primary federal government agency that oversees accounting in the federal government. (F6)

general ledger
The primary ledger a company uses to record its account balances; contains records for each control account. (F3, F7)

generally accepted accounting principles (GAAP)
Standards developed by professional accounting organizations to identify appropriate accounting and reporting procedures. (F1)

generally accepted auditing standards (GAAS)
Procedures used in conducting an audit to help auditors form an opinion about the fairness of the audited statements. (F6)

going concern
An organization with an indefinite life that is sufficiently long that, over time, all currently incomplete transactions will be completed. (F6)

goodwill
The excess of the price paid for a company over the fair market value of the net assets (assets less liabilities) of the acquired company. (F4, F11)

Governmental Accounting Standards Board (GASB)
The organization that sets accounting standards for state and local governmental units. (F6)

governmental and nonprofit organizations
Organizations that provide goods or, more typically, services without the intent of making a profit. (F1)

gross profit
The difference between the selling price of goods or services sold to customers during a period and the cost of the goods or services sold. (F4)

gross profit margin
The ratio of gross profit (sales revenues minus cost of goods sold) to sales revenues; it measures efficiency in the production or purchase of goods for sale. (F14)

H

historical cost
The purchase or exchange price of an asset or liability at the time it is acquired or incurred. (F4)

hurdle rate
The rate that must be earned before an investment is made; also called required rate of return. (M12)

I

income statement
A financial statement that reports revenues and expenses for a fiscal period as a means of determining how well a com-

pany has performed in creating profit for its owners. (F2)

information
Facts, ideas, and concepts that help us understand the world. (F1)

initial departmentz
The department that begins producing a product. (M3)

intangible assets
Long-term legal rights resulting from the ownership of patents, copyrights, trademarks, and similar items. (F4)

interest
The cost of borrowing that is paid to creditors in addition to the repayment of principal. (F2)

internal controls
Procedures a company uses to protect its assets and ensure the accuracy of its accounting information. (F6)

internal rate of return (IRR)
The interest rate that results in the present value of cash outflows being equal to the present value of cash inflows from an investment. (M12)

International Accounting Standards Board (IASB)
The organization that recommends accounting standards that it believes are appropriate for a broad range of global activities involving companies in many nations. (F6)

inventory turnover
The ratio of cost of goods sold (from the income statement) to inventory (from the balance sheet); it measures the success of a company in converting its investment in inventory into sales. (F14)

investing activities
Activities involving the acquisition or disposal of long-term resources used by a business. (F2)

investing cash flow to total assets
Net investing cash flow divided by total assets. (F10)

investment center
A level within an organization that has the strategic responsibility for generating profits and managing assets. (M10)

J

journal
A chronological record of a company's transactions. (F3)

job cost sheet
A record used to identify each job and to accumulate the costs of manufacturing associated with that job. (M3)

job-order costing
A practice that assigns the cost associated with a particular job to the units produced in that job. (M3)

just-in-time (JIT)
A manufacturing philosophy that attempts to eliminate activities that do not add value by reducing inventory levels. (M2)

just-in-time manufacturing
A production system that pulls products through the manufacturing process on the basis of market demand. (M11)

L

last-in, first-out (LIFO) method
Inventory method that assumes that the last units of inventory acquired are the first sold. (F13)

labor budget
A budget that identifies labor resources required to meet production needs. (M8)

ledger
A file in which each of a company's accounts and the balances of those accounts are maintained. (F3)

liability
The claim of a creditor to a company's resources. (F2)

limited liability company (LLC)
A business organization that provides certain advantages of a partnership and a corporation in that it combines the tax treatment of a partnership with the limited liability of corporations. (F1)

limited liability partnership (LLP)
A partnership that restricts the personal liability of each partner for obligations created by the company. (F1)

liquid assets
Resources that can be converted to cash in a relatively short period. (F4)

long-term intangible assets
Assets that provide benefits to the company for more than one fiscal period. (F4)

long-term investments
Occur when a company lends money to or purchases stock issued by other organizations and does not intend to sell those investments in the coming fiscal year. (F4)

long-term liabilities
Obligations not classified as current liabilities. (F4)

lower of cost or market inventory
Situation where the inventories must be written down to the current market costs if current market costs are below the costs resulting from the use of an estimation method such as FIFO or LIFO. (F13)

M

management's discussion and analysis (MD&A)
A section on a corporate annual report that explains important events and changes in performance during the years presented in the financial statements. (F6)

management accountant
An accountant who produces managerial accounting information for a specific company. (M1)

managerial accounting (management accounting)
The process of preparing, reporting, and interpreting accounting information for use by an organization's internal decision makers. (F1, M1)

manufacturing cell
A group of related machines, typically arranged in the shape of a U. (M11)

manufacturing companies
Organizations that produce goods that they sell to consumers, to merchandising companies, or to other manufacturing companies. (F1)

manufacturing overhead costs
Usually produced by activities that support a process but often are not directly related to any specific product. (M2)

margin
For ROI, operating income expressed as a percentage of sales. (M10)

market share
That portion of sales a particular brand or company has of the total sales for all similar products. (M3)

market value
Total shares outstanding times the market value per share. (F10)

market
Any location or process that permits resources to be bought and sold. (F1)

market-based transfer pricing policy
A policy that requires buyers and sellers to transfer goods based on externally verifiable market prices. (M10)

market-to-book-value ratio
Market value of the entire company divided by the book value of the entire company. (F10)

mark-to-market accounting
Process of trading securities and available-for-sale securities being reported on the balance sheet at current market value. (F11)

master budget
A one-year financial plan for a company. (M1) A collection of related operating budgets covering sales, production, purchasing, labor, manufacturing overhead, administrative expenses, and financing activities. (M8)

matching principle
An accounting concept which requires companies to recognize the expenses used to generate revenue in the same accounting period in which the revenues are recognized. (F3)

materials purchases budget
A budget that identifies the amount of materials that will be required to support a company's total production needs. (M8)

merchandise inventory
An asset account that identifies the cost of goods a company has purchased that are available for sale to customers. (F2)

merchandising companies
Organizations that sell to consumers goods that are produced by other companies. (F1)

milestones
Major decision points. (M12)

mixed costs
A combination of variable and fixed costs. (M7)

moral hazard
The condition that exists when agents have superior information to principals and are able to make decisions that favor their own interests over those of the principals. (F1)

moving baseline concept
The assumption that if the investment is not made cash flows will decrease because of the competition's superior quality. (M12)

mutual agency
A legal right that permits a partner to enter into contracts and agreements that are binding on all members of a partnership. (F1)

N

net income
The amount of profit earned by a business during a fiscal period. (F2)

negotiated transfer pricing policies
Policies that permit managers to consider factors such as cost and external market prices when negotiating a mutually ac-

ceptable transfer price between two business units. (M10)

net income available for common stockholders
The amount earned by common stockholders. (F13)

net present value (NPV)
The difference between the present value of expected future cash inflows from the investment and the present value of expected cash outflows invested. (M12)

nondiscounting methods
Methods of evaluating capital investments that ignore the time value of money. (M12)

normal costing
Measures unit costs by adding the actual costs of direct materials and direct labor to an estimated overhead cost incurred in producing the units. (M3)

notes payable
A liability account used to identify amounts a company owes to creditors with whom a formal agreement, or note, has been signed. (F2)

O

operating activities
Activities necessary to acquire and sell goods and services. (F2)

operating assets
Those assets controlled by the division; they include investments in cash, accounts receivable, inventory, and plant assets used in production. (M10)

operating cash flow to total assets
Net operating cash flow divided by total assets. (F10)

operating expenditures
Expenditures to repair or maintain plant assets that do not extend the life or enhance the value of the assets. (F11)

operating expenses
Costs of resources consumed as part of operating activities during a fiscal period and that are not directly associated with specific goods or services. (F4)

operating income
Sales − (cost of goods sold + other operating expenses). (M10)

operating income
The excess of gross profit over operating expenses. (F4)

operating leverage
The use of fixed costs to increase net income as sales increase. (F12)

operating profit margin
The ratio of operating income (sales revenues minus operating expenses) to sales revenue. (F14)

operating risk
The risk that a drop in sales volume will cause a company not to break even. (M7)

operational capital investment decision
A capital investment decision that affects only part of a company's operations, has an easily predictable life, and represents a relatively small capital outlay for a business. (M12)

operational planning
Identifying objectives for day-to-day activities. (M1)

operations restructuring
A complete evaluation of the relationships among multiple processes, conducted to improve the quality and efficiency of services provided to customers. (M13)

opportunity costs
Costs associated with not taking a particular course of action. (M2, M12)

organization
A group of people who work together to develop, produce, and/or distribute goods or services. (F1)

outcomes data dissemination
The practice of sharing process and outcomes information with those who make resource decisions. (M13)

overhead budget
A budget that provides a schedule of all costs of production other than materials and labor. (M8)

overhead hierarchy
A framework that explains how overhead costs change with various activities. (M5)

owners' equity
A contribution by owners to a business, along with any profits that are kept in the business. (F2)

P

paid-in capital in excess of par value
The amount in excess of the stock's par value received by a corporation from the sale of its stock. (F9)

par value
The value assigned to each share of stock by a corporation in its corporate charter. (F9)

parent
The controlling corporation. (F4)

partnership
A business owned by two or more persons, with no legal identity distinct from that of the owners. (F1)

payback period
The time required to recover an initial investment from expected future cash flows. (M12)

periodic inventory system
Inventory system of recording cost of goods sold and updating inventory balances at the end of a fiscal period. (F13)

periodic measurement
The situation when the accounting system measures and reports the performance of an organization for particular fiscal periods so that decisions can be made using timely information. (F6)

perpetual inventory system
Inventory system of recording cost of goods sold and updating inventory balances at the time goods are sold. (F13)

plant assets
Long-term, tangible resources (also called fixed assets). (F4)

posting
The process of transferring transactions to specific accounts in a company's ledger. (F3)

predetermined overhead rate
An estimate of the amount of overhead that management believes should be assigned to a unit of product. (M3)

preemptive right
The right of stockholders to maintain the same percentage of ownership when new shares are issued. (F9)

preferred stock
Stock with a higher claim on dividends and assets than common stock. (F9)

prepaid expense
An asset account that identifies a resource that has been paid for but not used. (F3)

present value
The value of an amount on a particular date prior to the time the amount is paid or received. (F8)

principal
The amount a company borrows. (F2)

process costing
Costing method that totals the costs of all units produced in a given accounting period and divides by the total units produced to develop a unit cost. (M4)

process-oriented plant layout
A plant arranged according to machine function, with machines that perform similar functions placed together. (M11)

product cost-subsidy
Term used to describe a situation in which one product subsidizes (supports) the reported costs of another. (M5)

product differentiation strategy
Companies that compete by offering products with special features or qualities that customers are willing to buy. (F14)

production budget
A budget that identifies the amount of a product that must be produced to meet the company's needs for sales and inventory. (M8)

production rate
The number of units a manufacturing system is capable of producing in a given period of time. (M11)

product-oriented plant layout
A plant based on manufacturing cells that meet the production requirements of products or product families (products that have similar characteristics). (M11)

profit
The difference between the price a seller receives for goods or services and the total cost to the seller of all resources consumed in developing, producing, and selling those goods or services during a particular period. (F1)

profit center
A division of an organization that is responsible for both generating sales and controlling costs and expenses. (M10)

profit margin
The ratio of net income to sales (also called return on sales). (F12)

property and equipment
Long-term, tangible assets that are used in a company's operations. (F4)

proprietorship
A business owned by one person, with no legal identity distinct from that of the owner. (F1)

Q

quality costs
Costs incurred because poor quality can or does exist in a particular product, function, or business. (M9)

quality loss function
A measure of the loss to society from a product that does not perform satisfactorily. (M9)

R

raw materials inventory
The costs of component parts or ingredients that become part of the product being manufactured. (F13)

reciprocal service arrangement
An arrangement whereby support departments exchange services. (M13)

relational database
A set of related files that are linked together so that the files can be updated and information can be retrieved from the files efficiently. (F7, M8)

relevant costs
Costs that change under two or more decision alternatives. (M7)

required rate of return
The rate that must be earned before an investment is made (also called hurdle rate). (M12)

residual value
The market value of an investment at the end of its useful life or service life to a company. (M12)

retail companies
See *merchandising companies*. (F1)

retained earnings
A subcategory of owners' equity that are the accumulated profits of a business that have been reinvested in the business. (F2)

return on assets (ROA)
The ratio of net income to total assets; net income divided by total assets. (F2, F10)

return on equity (ROE)
Net income divided by stockholders' equity. (F10)

return on investment
The amount of profits earned by a business that could be paid to owners. (F1)

return on investment (ROI)
A performance indicator calculated by dividing operating income by operating assets. (M10)

return on sales
See *profit margin*. (F12)

revenue
The amount a company expects to receive when it sells goods or services. (F2)

revenue center
A division of an organization that has responsibility for generating sales. (M10)

risk
Uncertainty about an outcome. (F1)

S

sales budget
A budget that projects revenues from sales of a company's products or services. (M8)

sales revenue
Revenue that identifies the amount a company earns from selling its products. (F2)

schedule of cash collections
A schedule that identifies the timing of cash inflows from sales. (M8)

schedule of cash payments
A schedule that identifies the timing and amount of cash outflows related to production and administrative activities. (M8)

Securities Act of 1933
Legislation that required most corporations to file registration statements before selling stock to investors. (F6)

Securities and Exchange Commission (SEC)
A federal agency that was given responsibility for overseeing external financial reporting by publicly traded corporations. (F6)

Securities Exchange Act of 1934
Legislation that required corporations to provide annual financial reports to stockholders. (F6)

selling and administrative expense budget
A budget containing a list of anticipated expenses for the period for activities other than manufacturing. (M8)

semivariable costs
A combination of variable and fixed costs. (M7)

service companies
Organizations that sell services rather than goods. (F1)

service life
The period during which an investment is expected to be used. (M12)

shareholders
See *stockholders*. (F1)

special cause variation
A variation with an identifiable source, such as faulty equipment or processes. (M9)

stakeholders
Those who have an economic interest in an organization and those who are affected by its activities. (F1)

standard costs
The cost of the material and labor that should have been used to achieve actual production levels. (M9)

standards
A cost reporting system based on engineering studies to determine the amount of a resource (such as labor hours or pounds of material) necessary to manufacture a product. (M9)

statement of cash flows
A financial statement that reports events that affected a company's cash account during a fiscal period. (F2)

statement of stockholders' equity
A financial statement that reports changes in a corporation's owners' equity for a fiscal period. (F4)

Statements of Financial Accounting Standards
FASB standards that establish acceptable accounting procedures or financial report content. (F6)

step-pattern costs
Costs that increase or decrease in total over a wide range of activity levels. (M7)

stock
A certificate of ownership that represents an equal share in the ownership of a corporation. (F1)

stock dividends
Shares of stock distributed by a company to its current stockholders without charge to the stockholders. (F9)

stock rights
Authorization for existing stockholders to purchase new shares. (F9)

stock split
The issuance by a corporation of a multiple of the number of shares of stock outstanding before the split. (F9)

stockholders
Owners of a corporation. (F1)

straight-line depreciation
A depreciation method that allocates an equal amount of the cost of a plant asset to expense during each fiscal period of the asset's expected useful life. (F11)

strategic capital investment decision
A capital investment decision that affects all or a considerable part of a company's operations, has an uncertain life, and requires a large investment. (M12)

subsequent department
A department that continues production on a product. (M4)

subsidiaries
The companies owned or controlled by the parent corporation. (F4)

subsidiary accounts
Accounts that record financial data about individual items of importance to a company, such as transactions for individual customers, suppliers, or products. (F7)

sunk costs
Costs associated with decisions that have already been made. (M12)

supply-chain management
The interaction of a company and its suppliers. (F7)

T

table
A file that contains data represented as rows and columns. (F7, M8)

target profit
The profit that a company wants to make over a given period. (M7)

theory of constraints (TOC)
A theory that states that by identifying a constraint, such as a bottleneck, that exists in the processing of a good or service and taking corrective steps, the process will be improved. (M11)

throughput
The number of units completed by a process in a given period of time. (M11)

times interest earned
The ratio of operating income (income before interest and taxes) to interest expense. (F14)

total quality management (TQM)
A management philosophy that attempts to eliminate all waste, defects, and activities that do not add value to a company's products. (M1); A management system that seeks continual improvement by asking everyone in an organization to understand, meet, and exceed the needs of customers. (M11)

total revenue
The amount earned from selling goods and services. (F4)

transactions
Descriptions of business activities (or events) that are measured in dollar values and recorded in accounts. (F2)

transfer pricing
A decision involving setting appropriate selling prices for goods or services when both buyer and seller are within the same company. (M10)

transferred-in costs
Costs that have been transferred from an earlier department to a later department in the production process. (M4)

treasury stock
Stock repurchased by a company from its stockholders. (F9)

turnover
For ROI, sales divided by average operating assets employed. (M10)

U

unearned revenue
A liability account that results when a company receives cash from a customer for goods or services to be provided in the future. (F3)

unfavorable variance
A variance that results when the actual price (or quantity) exceeds the standard. (M9)

unit cost
The cost of producing one unit of a specific product. (M3)

unit profit margin
The difference between the selling price per unit of a product and the unit cost. (M3)

units-of-production depreciation
A depreciation method that produces a level amount of depreciation expense per unit of output (rather than per fiscal period). (F11)

V

value chain
The set of value-creating activities that extends from the production of raw materials to the sale and servicing of finished goods. (M2)

variable costing
Costing method that assigns costs by their behavior, separating them into variable and fixed components. (M7)

variable costs
Costs that change in total with volume but remain fixed on a per-unit basis. (M7)

variable-costing income statement
A managerial decision-making tool that measures net income by subtracting variable expenses from sales and then subtracting fixed expenses from the difference. (M7)

W

weighted-average method
Inventory method that uses the average cost of units of inventory available during a period as the cost of units sold. (F13)

working capital
The difference between current assets and current liabilities. (F4)

working capital ratio
The ratio of current assets to current liabilities. (F4)

work-in-process inventory
The costs of materials, labor, and overhead that have been applied to products that are in the process of being manufactured. (F13)

INDEX

TABLE 1
FUTURE VALUE OF SINGLE AMOUNT

Interest Rate

Period	0.01	0.02	0.03	0.04	0.05	0.06	0.07	0.08	0.09	0.10	0.11	0.12
1	1.01000	1.02000	1.03000	1.04000	1.05000	1.06000	1.07000	1.08000	1.09000	1.10000	1.11000	1.12000
2	1.02010	1.04040	1.06090	1.08160	1.10250	1.12360	1.14490	1.16640	1.18810	1.21000	1.23210	1.25440
3	1.03030	1.06121	1.09273	1.12486	1.15763	1.19102	1.22504	1.25971	1.29503	1.33100	1.36763	1.40493
4	1.04060	1.08243	1.12551	1.16986	1.21551	1.26248	1.31080	1.36049	1.41158	1.46410	1.51807	1.57352
5	1.05101	1.10408	1.15927	1.21665	1.27628	1.33823	1.40255	1.46933	1.53862	1.61051	1.68506	1.76234
6	1.06152	1.12616	1.19405	1.26532	1.34010	1.41852	1.50073	1.58687	1.67710	1.77156	1.87041	1.97382
7	1.07214	1.14869	1.22987	1.31593	1.40710	1.50363	1.60578	1.71382	1.82804	1.94872	2.07616	2.21068
8	1.08286	1.17166	1.26677	1.36857	1.47746	1.59385	1.71819	1.85093	1.99256	2.14359	2.30454	2.47596
9	1.09369	1.19509	1.30477	1.42331	1.55133	1.68948	1.83846	1.99900	2.17189	2.35795	2.55804	2.77308
10	1.10462	1.21899	1.34392	1.48024	1.62889	1.79085	1.96715	2.15892	2.36736	2.59374	2.83942	3.10585
11	1.11567	1.24337	1.38423	1.53945	1.71034	1.89830	2.10485	2.33164	2.58043	2.85312	3.15176	3.47855
12	1.12683	1.26824	1.42576	1.60103	1.79586	2.01220	2.25219	2.51817	2.81266	3.13843	3.49845	3.89598
13	1.13809	1.29361	1.46853	1.66507	1.88565	2.13293	2.40985	2.71962	3.06580	3.45227	3.88328	4.36349
14	1.14947	1.31948	1.51259	1.73168	1.97993	2.26090	2.57853	2.93719	3.34173	3.79750	4.31044	4.88711
15	1.16097	1.34587	1.55797	1.80094	2.07893	2.39656	2.75903	3.17217	3.64248	4.17725	4.78459	5.47357
16	1.17258	1.37279	1.60471	1.87298	2.18287	2.54035	2.95216	3.42594	3.97031	4.59497	5.31089	6.13039
17	1.18430	1.40024	1.65285	1.94790	2.29202	2.69277	3.15882	3.70002	4.32763	5.05447	5.89509	6.86604
18	1.19615	1.42825	1.70243	2.02582	2.40662	2.85434	3.37993	3.99602	4.71712	5.55992	6.54355	7.68997
19	1.20811	1.45681	1.75351	2.10685	2.52695	3.02560	3.61653	4.31570	5.14166	6.11591	7.26334	8.61276
20	1.22019	1.48595	1.80611	2.19112	2.65330	3.20714	3.86968	4.66096	5.60441	6.72750	8.06231	9.64629
21	1.23239	1.51567	1.86029	2.27877	2.78596	3.39956	4.14056	5.03383	6.10881	7.40025	8.94917	10.80385
22	1.24472	1.54598	1.91610	2.36992	2.92526	3.60354	4.43040	5.43654	6.65860	8.14027	9.93357	12.10031
23	1.25716	1.57690	1.97359	2.46472	3.07152	3.81975	4.74053	5.87146	7.25787	8.95430	11.02627	13.55235
24	1.26973	1.60844	2.03279	2.56330	3.22510	4.04893	5.07237	6.34118	7.91108	9.84973	12.23916	15.17863
25	1.28243	1.64061	2.09378	2.66584	3.38635	4.29187	5.42743	6.84848	8.62308	10.83471	13.58546	17.00006

TABLE 2
FUTURE VALUE OF ANNUITY (AMOUNTS PAID OR RECEIVED AT END OF PERIOD)

Interest Rate

Period	0.01	0.02	0.03	0.04	0.05	0.06	0.07	0.08	0.09	0.10	0.11	0.12
1	1.00000	1.00000	1.00000	1.00000	1.00000	1.00000	1.00000	1.00000	1.00000	1.00000	1.00000	1.00000
2	2.01000	2.02000	2.03000	2.04000	2.05000	2.06000	2.07000	2.08000	2.09000	2.10000	2.11000	2.12000
3	3.03010	3.06040	3.09090	3.12160	3.15250	3.18360	3.21490	3.24640	3.27810	3.31000	3.34210	3.37440
4	4.06040	4.12161	4.18363	4.24646	4.31013	4.37462	4.43994	4.50611	4.57313	4.64100	4.70973	4.77933
5	5.10101	5.20404	5.30914	5.41632	5.52563	5.63709	5.75074	5.86660	5.98471	6.10510	6.22780	6.35285
6	6.15202	6.30812	6.46841	6.63298	6.80191	6.97532	7.15329	7.33593	7.52333	7.71561	7.91286	8.11519
7	7.21354	7.43428	7.66246	7.89829	8.14201	8.39384	8.65402	8.92280	9.20043	9.48717	9.78327	10.08901
8	8.28567	8.58297	8.89234	9.21423	9.54911	9.89747	10.25980	10.63663	11.02847	11.43589	11.85943	12.29969
9	9.36853	9.75463	10.15911	10.58280	11.02656	11.49132	11.97799	12.48756	13.02104	13.57948	14.16397	14.77566
10	10.46221	10.94972	11.46388	12.00611	12.57789	13.18079	13.81645	14.48656	15.19293	15.93742	16.72201	17.54874
11	11.56683	12.16872	12.80780	13.48635	14.20679	14.97164	15.78360	16.64549	17.56029	18.53117	19.56143	20.65458
12	12.68250	13.41209	14.19203	15.02581	15.91713	16.86994	17.88845	18.97713	20.14072	21.38428	22.71319	24.13313
13	13.80933	14.68033	15.61779	16.62684	17.71298	18.88214	20.14064	21.49530	22.95338	24.52271	26.21164	28.02911
14	14.94742	15.97394	17.08632	18.29191	19.59863	21.01507	22.55049	24.21492	26.01919	27.97498	30.09492	32.39260
15	16.09690	17.29342	18.59891	20.02359	21.57856	23.27597	25.12902	27.15211	29.36092	31.77248	34.40536	37.27971
16	17.25786	18.63929	20.15688	21.82453	23.65749	25.67253	27.88805	30.32428	33.00340	35.94973	39.18995	42.75328
17	18.43044	20.01207	21.76159	23.69751	25.84037	28.21288	30.84022	33.75023	36.97370	40.54470	44.50084	48.88367
18	19.61475	21.41231	23.41444	25.64541	28.13238	30.90565	33.99903	37.45024	41.30134	45.59917	50.39594	55.74971
19	20.81090	22.84056	25.11687	27.67123	30.53900	33.75999	37.37896	41.44626	46.01846	51.15909	56.93949	63.43968
20	22.01900	24.29737	26.87037	29.77808	33.06595	36.78559	40.99549	45.76196	51.16012	57.27500	64.20283	72.05244
21	23.23919	25.78332	28.67649	31.96920	35.71925	39.99273	44.86518	50.42292	56.76453	64.00250	72.26514	81.69874
22	24.47159	27.29898	30.53678	34.24797	38.50521	43.39229	49.00574	55.45676	62.87334	71.40275	81.21431	92.50258
23	25.71630	28.84496	32.45288	36.61789	41.43048	46.99586	53.43614	60.89330	69.53194	79.54302	91.14788	104.60289
24	26.97346	30.42186	34.42647	39.08260	44.50200	50.81558	58.17667	66.76476	76.78981	88.49733	102.17415	118.15524
25	28.24320	32.03030	36.45926	41.64591	47.72710	54.86451	63.24904	73.10594	84.70090	98.34706	114.41331	133.33387

TABLE 3
PRESENT VALUE OF SINGLE AMOUNT

Interest Rate

Period	0.01	0.02	0.03	0.04	0.05	0.06	0.07	0.08	0.09	0.10	0.11	0.12
1	0.99010	0.98039	0.97087	0.96154	0.95238	0.94340	0.93458	0.92593	0.91743	0.90909	0.90090	0.89286
2	0.98030	0.96117	0.94260	0.92456	0.90703	0.89000	0.87344	0.85734	0.84168	0.82645	0.81162	0.79719
3	0.97059	0.94232	0.91514	0.88900	0.86384	0.83962	0.81630	0.79383	0.77218	0.75131	0.73119	0.71178
4	0.96098	0.92385	0.88849	0.85480	0.82270	0.79209	0.76290	0.73503	0.70843	0.68301	0.65873	0.63552
5	0.95147	0.90573	0.86261	0.82193	0.78353	0.74726	0.71299	0.68058	0.64993	0.62092	0.59345	0.56743
6	0.94205	0.88797	0.83748	0.79031	0.74622	0.70496	0.66634	0.63017	0.59627	0.56447	0.53464	0.50663
7	0.93272	0.87056	0.81309	0.75992	0.71068	0.66506	0.62275	0.58349	0.54703	0.51316	0.48166	0.45235
8	0.92348	0.85349	0.78941	0.73069	0.67684	0.62741	0.58201	0.54027	0.50187	0.46651	0.43393	0.40388
9	0.91434	0.83676	0.76642	0.70259	0.64461	0.59190	0.54393	0.50025	0.46043	0.42410	0.39092	0.36061
10	0.90529	0.82035	0.74409	0.67556	0.61391	0.55839	0.50835	0.46319	0.42241	0.38554	0.35218	0.32197
11	0.89632	0.80426	0.72242	0.64958	0.58468	0.52679	0.47509	0.42888	0.38753	0.35049	0.31728	0.28748
12	0.88745	0.78849	0.70138	0.62460	0.55684	0.49697	0.44401	0.39711	0.35553	0.31863	0.28584	0.25668
13	0.87866	0.77303	0.68095	0.60057	0.53032	0.46884	0.41496	0.36770	0.32618	0.28966	0.25751	0.22917
14	0.86996	0.75788	0.66112	0.57748	0.50507	0.44230	0.38782	0.34046	0.29925	0.26333	0.23199	0.20462
15	0.86135	0.74301	0.64186	0.55526	0.48102	0.41727	0.36245	0.31524	0.27454	0.23939	0.20900	0.18270
16	0.85282	0.72845	0.62317	0.53391	0.45811	0.39365	0.33873	0.29189	0.25187	0.21763	0.18829	0.16312
17	0.84438	0.71416	0.60502	0.51337	0.43630	0.37136	0.31657	0.27027	0.23107	0.19784	0.16963	0.14564
18	0.83602	0.70016	0.58739	0.49363	0.41552	0.35034	0.29586	0.25025	0.21199	0.17986	0.15282	0.13004
19	0.82774	0.68643	0.57029	0.47464	0.39573	0.33051	0.27651	0.23171	0.19449	0.16351	0.13768	0.11611
20	0.81954	0.67297	0.55368	0.45639	0.37689	0.31180	0.25842	0.21455	0.17843	0.14864	0.12403	0.10367
21	0.81143	0.65978	0.53755	0.43883	0.35894	0.29416	0.24151	0.19866	0.16370	0.13513	0.11174	0.09256
22	0.80340	0.64684	0.52189	0.42196	0.34185	0.27751	0.22571	0.18394	0.15018	0.12285	0.10067	0.08264
23	0.79544	0.63416	0.50669	0.40573	0.32557	0.26180	0.21095	0.17032	0.13778	0.11168	0.09069	0.07379
24	0.78757	0.62172	0.49193	0.39012	0.31007	0.24698	0.19715	0.15770	0.12640	0.10153	0.08170	0.06588
25	0.77977	0.60953	0.47761	0.37512	0.29530	0.23300	0.18425	0.14602	0.11597	0.09230	0.07361	0.05882